Praise for *Cultural Theory*

"This anthology is an extraordinarily useful toolbox for teaching cultural theory. But more than that, by organizing the texts around a series of core concepts, it not only provides students with an excellent introduction but also gives scholars a fresh perspective on the field."

Michael Hardt, Duke University

"Cultural theory has expanded its influence immensely over the past two decades. Now we have a comprehensive selection of the best and most influential writers in the field, ably compiled and introduced by expert editors."

Toby Miller, University of California, Riverside

"Although there is no end to the compiling of anthologies on critical and cultural theory, this collection is genuinely and usefully different: instead of providing a menu of theoretical approaches, thereby ratifying a take-it-or-leave-it eclecticism as the reader's default position, Szeman and Kaposy organize their material around the crucial and unavoidable topics that set the agenda for modern thinking about culture. The result is more than just a familiar tour of classic set-pieces: by showing how critical interventions regarding culture, power, ideology, space, time, and subjectivity engage conceptually with one another, the editors allow the reader to assess each author's contribution both on its own terms and as part of an ongoing series of debates. This is the way many professors teach the field, and it is welcome to have recourse to a single-volume anthology that obviates the need for course packs. The introductory chapters for each section are uniformly cogent and well written, and while there will always be quibbles over what's included and what's left out, the choices of material are judicious and at times refreshingly unexpected. *Cultural Theory: An Anthology* is set to become the standard classroom text in the field."

Nicholas Lawrence, University of Warwick

"The contested space of cultural theory has until now lacked a map of its key reference-points that takes us beyond the particular stories told of cultural studies. This anthology provides that map, bringing together an exciting and globally diverse range of seminal texts from political economy, spatial theory, sociology of power, cultural history, and work on subjectivity. With a useful glossary and lucid introductory comments, this anthology is essential reading for all students of culture, whatever their disciplinary background."

Nick Couldry, Goldsmiths, University of London

"This is an exciting and provocative collection whose structure emphasizes the political charge, as well as the intellectual drive, behind cultural theory. Its section introductions are clear and concise, and the texts selected are invaluable for students and teachers of culture."

Jonathan P. Eburne, Pennsylvania State University

D0760574

Cultural Theory

An Anthology

Edited by

Imre Szeman and Timothy Kaposy

A John Wiley & Sons, Ltd., Publication

Contents

Acknowledgments

Sarah Blacker and Nicholas Holm helped with the preparation of the manuscript and with numerous other tasks involved in bringing this book together; thanks to both of them for their excellent work. Justin Sully provided us with some superb last-minute help with editing and revisions.

The students in McMaster University's Cultural Studies and Critical Theory MA program in 2007–8 and 2008–9 served as energetic test subjects for the organization and structure of this book, even if they didn't know it at the time. Many thanks to all of them – they know who they are.

And finally: thanks to all of our old friends and colleagues at McMaster and our new ones at George Mason University and the University of Alberta, for their energy, insight, and passion for ideas.

This book was supported in part by funding from the Social Sciences and Humanities Research Council of Canada.

Introduction

_____

What _is_ cultural theory? This is the inevitable and appropriate question with which to begin an introduction to an anthology on the topic; and it is perhaps just as inevitable that we might want to defer a direct and simple answer, preferring a careful, detailed, and nuanced response. But let's set such scholarly caution aside, at least to begin with. Cultural theory consists of theories about culture – how it works, what it means (and what it doesn't), how our understanding of it has changed over time (and all the ways in which it hasn't), and how it relates to processes which are commonly thought to take place apart from culture. There are innumerable studies _of_ culture, which range from books of literary criticism to studies of cultural practices in different historical periods and countries, from sociological analyses of subcultures to anthropological accounts of the lives of tribal communities, and from explorations of the themes hidden in the latest hit television series to the significance of trends in popular self-help writing. Cultural theory, on the other hand, constitutes a step back from an immediate engagement with culture to a place of critical reflection where insights gained and lessons learned in the study of culture are consolidated into general frameworks and organizing principles for future analysis and investigation. It consists of the body of ideas and concepts which have helped, in the first instance, in the identification of appropriate objects of study: that is, with a sense of which sorts of activities and practices are properly understood to be "culture" (e.g., skateboarding, watching films and listening to music, notions of what constitute social success, etc.) and those which might not be (e.g., parliamentary politics, economic laws, sewage-management plans, design schemes for microprocessors). Cultural theory provides us with tools for analyzing these activities, practices, and artifacts, for understanding the ways in which they are connected to the broader forces and developments which comprise human societies, and for providing an assessment of the contribution they make to the societies to which they belong, e.g., why they exist and what purposes they serve with the overall framework of social life.

The immediate problem with such a definition of cultural theory is its immense scope. Many (if not all) of the academic fields of study grouped into the humanities and social sciences address culture, each doing so in its own unique way. Linguistics has developed important theories about the operation of language; the field of Classics has created classificatory schemes for Roman and Greek architecture and theories about the causes of the decline of the Roman Empire; and Art Historians have developed their own important and influential theories about various aspects of visual culture, including what sorts of objects qualify as art. When these fields and their particular cultural objects (i.e., language, architecture and civilization, art) are added to the areas of study already named above (anthropology, literary studies, sociology, media studies, etc.), it is legitimate to wonder whether this anthology has set itself an impossibly large task. But while there are many theories about various aspects of culture, what has come to be known as cultural theory (in the singular) has a smaller and more defined frame of reference. The aim of _Cultural Theory: An Anthology_ is to bring together the most important readings which have helped to shape and define the contemporary study of culture, specifically the area of scholarship to which cultural theory is most closely related: cultural studies.[1] While there are many existing anthologies of cultural studies available today, for the most part these assemble work done on various cultural artifacts and practices with the intent of showcasing the rich and complex work taking place under the aegis of this term around the world.[2] This anthology has a different goal: with an eye to its use by students and scholars working in many different areas of study, it brings together the theories and concepts which lie at the core of cultural studies – that is, those writings which have had a determinate impact on the direction and the shape of the field and which animate the study of culture today.

The book is organized around key areas of theoretical inquiry in contemporary cultural study: the status and significance of culture itself, power, ideology, space and scale, temporality, and subjectivity. It is more common in anthologies or introductory textbooks in cultural studies or cultural theory to frame the study of culture around distinct "approaches" (such as feminism, formalism, psychoanalysis, semiotics, structuralism, and post-structuralism) or schools of thought which often have a genesis in specific national locales (such as British cultural studies, the Frankfurt School, Russian Formalism, French feminism, or the Subaltern Studies group from India). One of the interventions made by this anthology is to focus attention back on the conceptual problematics around which cultural theory is produced. The theorists collected here don't confine their work to a school or a specific approach when they set out to understand an artifact, practice, situation, or problem. While the work of theorists such as Fredric Jameson, Judith Butler, and Ranajit Guha (for example) contribute to the fields of Marxism, psychoanalysis, and postcolonial studies respectively, to narrowly confine their work to these areas of study is to misrepresent not just their wider influence, but the questions and problems which drive their inquiries. In the examples of their work included in this book, these theorists investigate the politics and nature of culture (Jameson), the character of subjectivity (Butler), and the shape of history and temporality (Guha) – issues which thinkers working with different theoretical backgrounds and influences also address. By dividing the anthology into topics of study instead of schools of thought, we hope to mobilize and enable new uses of the powerful tools, provocative concepts, and productive insights generated by the essays we have selected.

While the theorists compiled in this volume have each made contributions vital to contemporary cultural studies, it will be clear immediately that many of the essays and excerpts included here are not always focused on culture per se – even in the expanded sense of culture that cultural studies has given us. Michel Foucault's theories of power, Carl Schmitt's reflections on sovereignty, and Gilles Deleuze's provocative description of "societies of control" may not speak directly to (say) the nature of contemporary media systems or the circulation of world literatures. Nevertheless these ideas have proven to be crucial for thinking about the forces and relations that shape contemporary culture and for describing the differences between present and past social formations. The changing conceptions of power, sovereignty, and social control mapped out in the section on "Power" are fundamental for work that renders visible dominant and emergent forms of political exclusion, such as the tightening controls placed on migration, the global expansion of slum dwellers, and the increasing restrictions on citizenship. In addition to being a repressive force currently fostering our own "states of exception," this section presents power as a normative force of assimilation: that is, power is located in the imperatives contained in self-help books and aspirations to accumulate wealth as much as in drone bombers and physical imprisonment. Medical diagnostics of the healthy body, the management of populations through precarious labor, and a pervasive culture of indebtedness all impel us to reckon with the vicissitudes of power – a reckoning which also limns their possible interconnection. The other sections of this anthology do similar work in framing the key ideas and theories behind some of central conceptual issues that have been taken up in cultural studies.

It might seem as if this anthology reproduces a questionable or dangerous divide between theory and practice, the abstract and the concrete – or in classroom terms, between "primary" and "secondary" texts. What differentiates these texts from others that might have been included is not the fact that they engage solely in theoretical or philosophical reflection and leave the work of on-the-ground ethnographic study, sociological number crunching, or focused close reading of literary texts to others. "Theory" does not name some artificial separation from "practice," such that the essays collected here are intended to provide the "form" into which might be placed all manner of specific cultural "content." Rather, theory is better understood as "the guiding compass of empirical investigation."[3] The impact and influence of the essays collected here is the result of the ways in which each follows its compass points unwaveringly to the ends of the problems they have set for themselves: in every one of these texts, theory emerges from an encounter with cultural and social phenomena, whether this is the situation of postcolonial nationalisms (in the case of Fanon), new urban youth culture (for Hebdige), the sensation of cultural inauthenticity felt in Brazil (Schwarz), or any of the other sites of investigation whose shape and character have demanded the creation of new theoretical pathways.

Cultural theory is animated by a progressive politics whose intent is to help bring about significant social change through a clearer and more comprehensive understanding of the complex character of social, political, and cultural structures and antagonisms. It is this politics which finds expression in one form or another (if to varying degrees) in all the essays in this volume. Michael Denning has described cultural studies as "a fundamental break with the notion of the humanities, with the assumption that the study of arts and letters is separate from the study of society, that the humanities are best represented by a canon of classics, and that the arts and letters are primarily reflections on the human."[4] "If the humanities are about humans," he writes, "cultural studies are about people."[5] What distinguishes "people" from the "human" (as we make clear in the section on "Subjectivity") is that while the latter falls back on ideas of apparently natural and unchallengeable ways of being, the former category is necessarily an invention of societies and individuals, shaped by divisions, antagonisms, and processes of inclusion and exclusion occurring at multiple levels. Cultural studies displaces the human from the center of culture and in doing so introduces two additional innovations to the study of culture. The first is to insist on the importance of economics and politics for understanding culture *and* on the significance of culture for making sense of economics and politics. To put this differently, history plays a central role in cultural theory: culture is malleable, ever changing, buffeted by all the forces making up social life, and not a space of immutable and transhistorical essences. What this means is, second, that cultural theory is of necessity relentlessly self-reflexive, challenging its own preconceptions and framing assumptions even as it identifies the gaps, elisions, and preconceptions of so many of the beliefs taken for fact about the world. If cultural studies is, as Denning puts it, "a new name for the humanities, or more accurately, the key slogan in the left's redefinition of the humanities,"[6] cultural theory is that part of the new humanities in which one can find both the conceptual resources for questioning existing modes of thought and those needed to construct the new ones we need for creating more equitable and just futures.

In a recent essay outlining the pre-eminent modes of critique since 1989, Göran Therborn describes social theory as "strung between two ambitious poles: on the one hand, providing a comprehensive explanatory framework for a set of social phenomena; and on the other, something 'making sense' of such phenomena … this is an ecumenical conception of 'theory' that applies both to explanation, the more wide-ranging the more important, and to *Sinnstiftung*, the constitution of meaning."[7] Replacing "social" with "cultural" brings us close to what we described as "cultural theory": an explanation of and accounting for cultural phenomena (socially, politically, structurally, historically, and so on) which also pays attention to the way in which such phenomena are endowed with meaning. This movement between poles is unavoidable in the study of culture. Cultural theory contends with the often perplexing nature of constitutive social, political, and cultural antagonisms; it does so through an attention to those practices, activities, and artifacts that we have understood to be "culture," but with an awareness of the shifts and deformations that this concept has undergone over the past century – developments which have made it increasingly difficult to meaningfully separate the levels of the social (cultural, economic, politics, etc.) from one another.

Cultural Theory: An Anthology is organized into six sections. Each section is prefaced by a short introduction which makes connections between the essays and relates them to the framing concept or problem; these sections are followed by a list of relevant texts which can be consulted for further information about the topic or author.

Notes

1 Of the major existing reference works in cultural theory, only Andrew Edgar and Peter Sedgwick (in the Introduction to their *Key Concepts* volume) feel the need to pause to point out the link between cultural theory and cultural studies; the remainder just assume it. See Peter Brooker, *A Concise Glossary of Cultural Theory* (London: Arnold, 1999); Andrew Edgar and Peter Sedgwick, *Cultural Theory: The Key Concepts* (New York: Routledge, 1999) and *Cultural Theory: The Key Thinkers* (New York: Routledge, 2002); and Philip Smith and Alexander Riley, *Cultural Theory: An Introduction*, 2nd edition (Oxford: Blackwell, 2009).

2 See, for example, Ackbar Abbas and John Nyuget Erni (eds.), *Internationalizing Cultural Studies: An Anthology* (Oxford: Wiley-Blackwell, 2004); Pepi Leistyna (ed.), *From Theory to Action* (Oxford: Wiley-Blackwell, 2004); and Michael Ryan (ed.), *Cultural Studies: An Anthology* (Oxford: Wiley-Blackwell, 2008). See also the reviews of such texts offered by Greg Noble, "How Do You Teach Cultural Studies? Or, the Uses of Textbooks," *Continuum* 23.2 (2009), 401–8; and Julian Murphet's review of Ryan's anthology in the same issue, pp. 416–22.

3 Göran Therborn, "After Dialectics: Radical Social Theory in a Post-Communist World," *New Left Review* 43 (2007), 79.

4 Michael Denning, *Culture in the Age of Three Worlds* (New York: Verso, 2004), 148.

5 Ibid., 151.

6 Ibid., 148.

7 Therborn, "After Dialectics: Radical Social Theory in a Post-Communist World," 79.

Part 1

Reforming Culture

Introduction

"Culture," Raymond Williams reminds us at the beginning of his entry in *Keywords*, "is one of the two or three most complicated words in the English language."[1] Yet it is also one of the most common concepts used in public discourse, a concept that despite its complexity is freely employed by everyone and used fearlessly in political debates, newspaper editorials, and coffee-shop banter. Culture is also a word that despite its significance (or perhaps, because of it) defies rigorous attempts at clarification or definition. An enormous fault line cuts the term into two: "culture" can be the name for a whole way of life, or can describe those specific arts and practices typically connected to social meaning making. The fact that the latter (for instance, writing, music, painting, and so on) are often seen as playing a key role in defining the former (French culture, Roma culture, hippie culture) adds to the confusions which exist when we try to consider either side of the dividing line on its own in an effort to simplify things. Everyone would agree that opera, jazz, and rock music are practices readily described as cultural. But what about singing (badly) with one's friends in the basement with the help of the video game *Garage Band?* And what size or shape do whole ways of life take? Do they have to come packaged in the form of nations (French) or in conjunction with ethnicities (Roma), or is it enough to point to the specific ways of life of hippies, b-boys, WASPs, DINKs and all the other subgroupings that have accumulated in a giant conceptual heap in recent years? It might seem to be especially important for a practice called "cultural theory" to be absolutely clear about the subject about which it generates theories. But in many respects, it is the uncertain terrain around the concept of culture which cultural theory mines for insights. It does so not in order to settle the question of what, finally, culture *is* – an impossible and ultimately unproductive aim, since any single definition would fail to capture all the uses of the term – but to better grasp the range and overlap of meanings in an effort to explain what culture *does*. Cultural theory deals with culture both as a form of life and as distinctive kinds of social practices, not in the hope of simplifying its complexity but to make sense of the social processes, forces, relations, and imaginaries which the concept folds together and pushes apart.

As a distinct sphere of human activity and critical inquiry, culture has long been associated with those values and norms absent from the hurly-burly of the economic life of capitalism. The latter is utilitarian, characterized by a means–ends rationality which ties it indelibly to the messy materiality of daily life. By contrast, culture has been imagined as a sphere of transcendence, an expression of the very best to which humanity can aspire, the locus of the good which makes the agony, injustice, and banality of everyday class society bearable; it is the soul of humanity which animates and gives meaning to the flesh and bones of the social body. By such measures, only certain practices have been deemed to be of significant quality or elevation to count as "Culture," especially when it comes to its study and analysis; working-class culture or popular cultural forms – long seen as more flesh and bones than soul – have generally been thought to lack the appropriate gravitas and timeless significance. If we spend our days engaged in the drudgery of those activities which pay the bills, culture is what we reward ourselves with in the evenings. But there's a difference between culture and Culture, between spending time on the couch in front of the television and taking in an exhibit at a museum. Only the latter represents the values, seriousness, and higher ends of our society; visiting a museum is more than just killing time, which is why we drag our children away from the flat screen to see paintings on the wall or to wander in sculpture gardens.

In the twentieth century, this view of culture, which has lingered despite the predominance of all manner of commodity culture – cultural objects, activities, and experiences made for sale, exchange, consumption, and profit – has drawn repeated criticism due to its exclusion of a huge range of cultural objects and practices which give shape to social experience. Cultural theorists insist on an understanding of culture that allows for the study of graffiti art as well as neoclassical poetry, and websites as well as Renaissance paintings. Within cultural theory, criticism has also been directed not just at the content of culture – those topics, issues, and genres which gate-keeping scholarly elites have decided are legitimate and permissible – but the ideological function of the very concept. The reason this section is named "reforming culture" (as opposed to just "culture") is to capture the intent of some of the most important and influential works of cultural theory in the twentieth century, which has been to reveal the myriad ways in which culture has been imbued with a politics which has shaped not just the study of culture but the very shape and structure of contemporary societies. Critics have argued that the constitution of culture as a category that captures the higher values of humanity has merely excused the strife and pain experienced by most people in everyday life. As Herbert Marcuse puts it in "The Affirmative Character of Culture," "Man does not live by bread alone; this truth is thoroughly falsified by the interpretation that spiritual nourishment is an adequate substitute for too little bread."[2] Finally, criticism has been directed at the use of culture in legitimating existing social divisions. Those in higher echelons of society have argued that they occupy their positions in part because they are appropriately "cultured," closer to the higher things in life whether through nature, breeding, or education; the "masses" might be satisfied with television or the internet, but the chosen few require paintings and sculpture to elevate and nourish the spirit. Against such claims and beliefs, cultural theory has sought to expose the manner in which control over access to cultural goods (through education, for example) and the power to define what counts as appropriate acculturation (through control over social and cultural institutions) has fundamentally structured the production and reproduction of the status quo.

Matthew Arnold's *Culture and Anarchy* (1869), which has been described as "culture's first sacred book,"[3] is a characteristic expression of the model of culture which has been seen by many theorists as in need of reform. Culture is viewed by Arnold as having important functions both internally and externally. Great works of culture – "the best that has been thought and known in the world," or "the study of perfection" – nourish the soul, permitting individuals to define and develop toward higher ends in line with Enlightenment ideals of growth and progress. This internal development has an external purpose as well. Beauty and harmony, "sweetness and light," are values which produce social order and keep anarchy at bay. The class bias of Arnold's views on what constitutes perfect forms of culture is obvious; he believes, for example, that ordinary popular literature tends to "teach down to the level of inferior masses."[4] Presumably, exposure to "higher" forms of serious literature would have the opposite effect: to elevate the masses and embody in them the values of their superiors, i.e., those who identify which forms of culture are higher to begin with! Arnold is reacting to a situation of social instability and uncertainty; he is alarmed by the waning of a moral order once guaranteed by religion and the emergence in its place of a soulless instrumentality connected to a capitalist market in which everything is for sale. His sense of culture as an arena of human possibility in a world otherwise structured by the empty utilitarianism of the bourgeois "Philistines" and aristocratic "Barbarians" alike has had a major influence on how we understand culture in the twentieth century. While he has become an exemplar of an elitist view of culture (the capital "C" idea of "Culture" we refer to in the opening paragraphs), Arnold's views on the impact of commercial culture on cultural experience and expression shares more with many critical twentieth-century positions than is often imagined.

Thorstein Veblen's *The Theory of the Leisure Class* (1899) paved the way for culture to be studied as a social phenomenon rather than imagined strictly as a practice of internal transformation and spiritual development.

"Conspicuous consumption" characterizes the behavior of the nouveau riche (Arnold's Philistines) who emerged as a class at the end of the nineteenth century. Veblen seeks to understand the social rules that govern consumption above the level of absolute necessity – a circumstance which became more and more common as the century progressed and large middle classes emerged for the first time. It is one thing to buy food or clothing when you are just trying to survive; quite another when you have the means to experiment with haute cuisine or enter the game of ever-changing clothing fashions. Veblen finds that consumption takes "conspicuous" forms because "the only practicable means of impressing one's pecuniary ability on these unsympathetic observers of one's everyday life is an unremitting demonstration of ability to pay."[5] Social display and class distinction through consumption becomes an increasingly important part of twentieth-century culture, and not just through the social semiotics of luxury goods of all kinds (houses, automobiles, clothing, etc.), but in terms of the types of cultural objects made use of and identified with by people across the class spectrum.

In an expansion of Veblen's ideas, sociologist Pierre Bourdieu explores the ways in which aesthetic distinctions and dispositions are connected to class in his groundbreaking book *Distinction: A Social Critique of the Judgment of Taste* (1979). Through both empirical studies and theoretical reflection, Bourdieu outlines the important role of aesthetic and cultural discrimination in the establishment and maintenance of class divisions. In both *Distinction* and "The Forms of Capital," he punctures the false divide that has been erected between culture and economics. Social hierarchies may be underwritten by divisions in economic capital (bluntly: how much money one has) but depend equally on the accumulation of "cultural capital" – one's cultural experience and education – and "social capital" – the networks of influence in which one is positioned – which function to justify class divisions and help to reproduce the status quo. As Bourdieu writes, "the transmission of cultural capital is no doubt the best hidden form of hereditary transmission of capital, and it therefore receives proportionately greater weight in the system of reproduction strategies, as the direct, visible forms of transmission tend to be more strongly censored and controlled."[6] Knowing how to behave in different circumstances and what is appropriate to like and dislike (everything from clothing and furniture to novels and films) plays a role in managing and maintaining class divisions, as does the status of the educational and social institutions in which one participates; presumably one learns the same mathematical equations at Northeastern University as at M.I.T., yet an engineering degree from the latter invariably earns you a higher social status and income than the former. The assessments of the social function of culture offered by both Bourdieu and Veblen raise serious questions with which scholars are still grappling. Far from being the innocent, soulful "other" of economics, both theorists show that culture has a deep impact on the dynamics and politics of social life, in no small part by the very fact of its supposed distance from it, a gap which helps shield culture from being experienced and understood as part of a far from innocent social calculus.

Members of the Frankfurt School have also influentially examined the politics of contemporary culture. Max Horkheimer and Theodor Adorno's well-known chapter from *Dialectic of Enlightenment*, "The Culture Industry," confirms Arnold's fears about the evolving impact of economics on contemporary society. For Horkheimer and Adorno, however, culture has itself been subject to forms of standardization that have rendered it inauthentic and left it far from being a space of resistance to commodification and instrumental reason (the use of human reason for strictly means–ends calculations). While culture seems to offer endless possibilities for novel and meaningful experiences, this apparent freedom and choice disguises the very real limits of contemporary life: "Something is provided for all so that none may escape."[7] There may be many kinds of films to see – from erudite art films to scream-filled horror movies – but the overall place and function of film in social life is the same: to give you something to do in the evenings so that you can return refreshed to the work the next day. "The Culture Industry" has become an important text for the development of theories of mass culture and is often taken as a key example of elitist dismissals of contemporary popular culture, despite the fact that Adorno's later comments about the fate of culture in the twentieth century indicate a more wholesale (high and low culture alike) condemnation of what culture has become.[8] Less commonly read but perhaps more powerful in its assessment of the politics of culture, Herbert Marcuse's "The Affirmative Character of Culture" analyzes the deception enacted by the category of culture in an historical and philosophical register. Marcuse sees the problems with culture emerging not from the industrialization of cultural industry, but from the social logic which lies at the root of its establishment as a distinct, modern category. For him, the imaginative possibilities contained within culture for individual self-development and social transformation is a fiction. "Affirmative culture," he writes, "uses the soul as a protest against reification, only to succumb to it in the end. The soul is sheltered as the only area of life that has not been drawn into the social labour process ... the freedom of the soul was used to excuse the poverty, martyrdom, and bondage of the body."[9] Once again, culture is shown to be other than it claims – not a negation of class society, but evidence of its concrete reality and its solid hold on our political and social imaginations.

The exploration of the ideological and political function of culture offered by these writers might seem to suggest that we should reject the category and concept entirely. But other critics have taught us to tread more cautiously. While being cognizant of the problem of affirmative culture described by Marcuse, Raymond Williams insists nevertheless on the importance of culture for understanding the full complexity of social life. "Culture Is Ordinary" offers a defense of culture that is in many ways the inverse of Horkheimer and Adorno's criticisms. "A desire to know what is best, and to do what is good, is the whole positive nature of man,"[10] Williams writes. Though this passage evokes Arnold's view of culture as "the best that has been thought and known," for Williams culture does not have more or less appropriate forms through which the best and good are articulated, nor is it the property of a single class for whom it serves to legitimate social and economic power. Its ordinariness means that culture – that is, socialization and social change, tradition and creativity, communal values and individual meanings – is a resource for all groups and classes. The worry that the masses are ignorant or duped by commodity culture is rejected outright by Williams: "there are no masses, but only ways of seeing people as masses."[11] This is not to say that culture is absent of politics or ideology, or that it isn't used in games of distinction and class legitimation described by the other theorists in this section. But in contrast to Bourdieu or Marcuse, for Williams culture can be the source of a counter-politics which works to undermine class divisions as well. Stuart Hall's description of "popular culture" as existing in a "continuing tension (relationship, influence, antagonism) to the *dominant* culture," a site "where the struggle for and against a culture of the powerful is engaged,"[12] echoes Williams's claims for the ordinariness of culture and for an understanding of the popular as something other than the debased commercial culture produced by the culture industry. Hall draws our attention not just to the continued existence of forms of cultural expression outside of the calculations of profit, but also to its potential to challenge those cultural games which divide us from each other and control access to social rights, privileges, and status. The idea that certain kinds of cultural activities might effectively undermine or subvert existing forms of power has fueled a great deal of scholarly research and debate in the field of cultural studies, especially in the 1990s as it developed and grew into an academic field in the United States.[13]

In light of these ongoing debates, the last essay we discuss in this section offers a model for how we might interpret culture at the present time. Fredric Jameson's "Reification and Utopia in Mass Culture" approaches the oppositions between low and high culture, popular and elite culture, mass commodity culture and modernism (often framed as the former's high art opposite) in a distinct way. He affirms neither high nor ordinary culture, and does not challenge the productivity of the category of culture in a general sense, but argues that critics need to examine "the social and aesthetic situation – the dilemma of form and of a public – shared and faced by both modernism and mass culture, but 'solved' in antithetical ways."[14] Fundamental to the discussions and debates about the social function of culture today is the "universal commodification of our object world" which has created a circumstance in which "everything in our consumer society has taken on an aesthetic dimension."[15] For Jameson, both mass culture and high culture (in his case modernism) are reactions to this historically original situation, each offering in its own way imaginary resolutions to the social contradictions they encounter. In his characteristically insightful way, Jameson draws our attention to the way in which contemporary culture participates in reification (draining the cultural objects we encounter of their social origins), but also highlights the manner in which it exhibits longings for genuine collectivities that might exist outside of the narrow scope of a life dominated by commodities. In doing so, he shows us how we can productively engage with culture today, analyzing and assessing its social function and the meanings it carries with it, while also remaining aware of the politics of the concept itself and its role in reinforcing social divisions.

The critique of culture as concept which has been used to disguise and legitimate differences in power has animated a great deal of work in cultural theory. So, too, has the view that culture is "the place where power is crystallized and submission bred,"[16] which is in large part why it has attracted special theoretical attention and analysis. At the same time, it is important to remember that, as Raymond Williams writes, "no mode of production and therefore no dominant social order and therefore no dominant culture ever in reality excludes or exhausts all human practice, human energy, and human intention."[17] The ongoing challenge for cultural theory is to take seriously both the limits and possibilities named by the category of culture in relation to the increasingly complex social and political terrain of contemporary life.

Notes

1   Raymond Williams, *Keywords: A Vocabulary of Culture and Society* (London: Taylor & Francis, 1976), 76.
2   Herbert Marcuse, "The Affirmative Character of Culture," in *Negations: Essays in Critical Theory*, trans. Jeremy Shapiro (London: Free Association Books, 1988), 109. Reproduced in this volume.
3   Fred Inglis, *Culture* (Cambridge: Polity, 2004), 24.
4   Matthew Arnold, *Culture and Anarchy* (Oxford: Oxford University Press, 2006), 7. Reproduced in this volume.
5   Thorstein Veblen, "Conspicuous Consumption," in *The Consumer Society Reader*, ed. Juliet Schor and Douglas Holt (New York: New Press, 2000), 197. Reproduced in this volume.
6   Pierre Bourdieu, "The Forms of Capital," in *Education, Culture, Economy, and Society*, ed. A. H. Halsey, Hugh Lauder, Phillip Brown, and Amy Stuart Wells (New York: Oxford University Press, 1997), 49. Reproduced in this volume.
7   Max Horkheimer and Theodor Adorno, *Dialectic of Enlightenment*, trans. John Cumming (New York: Continuum, 1973), 123. Reproduced in this volume.
8   See Theodor Adorno, "The Culture Industry Reconsidered," in *The Adorno Reader*, ed. Brian O'Connor (Oxford: Blackwell, 2000), 230–8.
9   Marcuse, "The Affirmative Character of Culture," 108–9.
10 Raymond Williams, "Culture Is Ordinary," in *Resources of Hope: Culture, Democracy, Socialism* (New York: Verso, 1989), 7. Reproduced in this volume.
11 Ibid., 11.
12 Stuart Hall, "Notes on Deconstructing 'the Popular'," in *People's History and Socialist Theory*, ed. Raphael Samuel (London: Routledge, 1981), 235 and 239 respectively. Reproduced in this volume.
13 See Stephen Duncombe (ed.), *The Cultural Resistance Reader* (New York: Verso, 2002) for an overview of these developments.
14 Fredric Jameson, "Reification and Utopia in Mass Culture," *Social Text* 1 (1979), 134. Reproduced in this volume.
15 Ibid., 132.
16 Terry Eagleton, "Introduction Part 1," in *Marxist Literary Theory: A Reader*, ed. Terry Eagleton and Drew Milne (New York: Blackwell, 1996), 7.
17 Raymond Williams, *Marxism and Literature* (Oxford: Oxford University Press, 1977), 125.

1

"Sweetness and Light" (1869)

Matthew Arnold

The disparagers of culture make its motive curiosity; sometimes, indeed, they make its motive mere exclusiveness and vanity. The culture which is supposed to plume itself on a smattering of Greek and Latin is a culture which is begotten by nothing so intellectual as curiosity; it is valued either out of sheer vanity and ignorance or else as an engine of social and class distinction, separating its holder, like a badge or title, from other people who have not got it. No serious man would call this *culture*, or attach any value to it, as culture, at all. To find the real ground for the very different estimate which serious people will set upon culture, we must find some motive for culture in the terms of which may lie a real ambiguity; and such a motive the word *curiosity* gives us.

I have before now pointed out that we English do not, like the foreigners, use this word in a good sense as well as in a bad sense. With us the word is always used in a somewhat disapproving sense. A liberal and intelligent eagerness about the things of the mind may be meant by a foreigner when he speaks of curiosity, but with us the word always conveys a certain notion of frivolous and unedifying activity [...].

But there is of culture another view, in which not solely the scientific passion, the sheer desire to see things as they are, natural and proper in an intelligent

being, appears as the ground of it. There is a view in which all the love of our neighbour, the impulses towards action, help, and beneficence, the desire for removing human error, clearing human confusion, and diminishing human misery, the noble aspiration to leave the world better and happier than we found it, – motives eminently such as are called social, – come in as part of the grounds of culture, and the main and pre-eminent part. Culture is then properly described not as having its origin in curiosity, but as having its origin in the love of perfection; it is *a study of perfection*. It moves by the force, not merely or primarily of the scientific passion for pure knowledge, but also of the moral and social passion for doing good. As, in the first view of it, we took for its worthy motto Montesquieu's words: "To render an intelligent being yet more intelligent!" so, in the second view of it, there is no better motto which it can have than these words of Bishop Wilson: "To make reason and the will of God prevail!"[1]

Only, whereas the passion for doing good is apt to be over-hasty in determining what reason and the will of God say, because its turn is for acting rather than thinking and it wants to be beginning to act; and whereas it is apt to take its own conceptions, which proceed from its own state of development and share in all the imperfections and immaturities of this, for a basis of action; what distinguishes culture is, that it is possessed by the scientific passion as well as by the passion of doing good; that it demands worthy notions of reason and the will of God, and does not readily suffer its own crude conceptions to substitute themselves for them. And knowing that no action or institution can

Matthew Arnold, "Sweetness and Light," pp. 58, 59–60, 61–4, 65, 66–7, 68–70, 71–2, 78–80 from *Culture and Anarchy and Other Writings*, ed. Stefan Collini. Cambridge: Cambridge University Press, 1993. Reprinted by permission of Cambridge University Press.

be salutary and stable which is not based on reason and the will of God, it is not so bent on acting and instituting, even with the great aim of diminishing human error and misery ever before its thoughts, but that it can remember that acting and instituting are of little use, unless we know how and what we ought to act and to institute.

[…]

The moment this view of culture is seized, the moment it is regarded not solely as the endeavour to see things as they are, to draw towards a knowledge of the universal order which seems to be intended and aimed at in the world, and which it is a man's happiness to go along with or his misery to go counter to, – to learn, in short, the will of God, – the moment, I say, culture is considered not merely as the endeavour to *see* and *learn* this, but as the endeavour, also, to make it *prevail*, the moral, social, and beneficent character of culture becomes manifest. The mere endeavour to see and learn the truth for our own personal satisfaction is indeed a commencement for making it prevail, a preparing the way for this, which always serves this, and is wrongly, therefore, stamped with blame absolutely in itself and not only in its caricature and degeneration. But perhaps it has got stamped with blame, and disparaged with the dubious title of curiosity, because in comparison with this wider endeavour of such great and plain utility it looks selfish, petty, and unprofitable.

And religion, the greatest and most important of the efforts by which the human race has manifested its impulse to perfect itself, – religion, that voice of the deepest human experience, – does not only enjoin and sanction the aim which is the great aim of culture, the aim of setting ourselves to ascertain what perfection is and to make it prevail; but also, in determining generally in what human perfection consists, religion comes to a conclusion identical with that which culture, – culture seeking the determination of this question through *all* the voices of human experience which have been heard upon it, of art, science, poetry, philosophy, history, as well as of religion, in order to give a greater fulness and certainty to its solution, – likewise reaches. Religion says: *The kingdom of God is within you*; and culture, in like manner, places human perfection in an *internal* condition, in the growth and predominance of our humanity proper, as distinguished

from our animality. It places it in the ever-increasing efficacy and in the general harmonious expansion of those gifts of thought and feeling, which make the peculiar dignity, wealth, and happiness of human nature. As I have said on a former occasion: "It is in making endless additions to itself, in the endless expansion of its powers, in endless growth in wisdom and beauty, that the spirit of the human race finds its ideal. To reach this ideal, culture is an indispensable aid, and that is the true value of culture."[2] Not a having and a resting, but a growing and a becoming, is the character of perfection as culture conceives it; and here, too, it coincides with religion.

And because men are all members of one great whole, and the sympathy which is in human nature will not allow one member to be indifferent to the rest or to have a perfect welfare independent of the rest, the expansion of our humanity, to suit the idea of perfection which culture forms, must be a *general* expansion. Perfection, as culture conceives it, is not possible while the individual remains isolated. The individual is required, under pain of being stunted and enfeebled in his own development if he disobeys, to carry others along with him in his march towards perfection, to be continually doing all he can to enlarge and increase the volume of the human stream sweeping thitherward. And here, once more, culture lays on us the same obligation as religion, which says, as Bishop Wilson has admirably put it, that "to promote the kingdom of God is to increase and hasten one's own happiness."

But, finally, perfection, – as culture from a thorough disinterested study of human nature and human experience learns to conceive it, – is a harmonious expansion of *all* the powers which make the beauty and worth of human nature, and is not consistent with the over-development of any one power at the expense of the rest. Here culture goes beyond religion, as religion is generally conceived by us.

If culture, then, is a study of perfection, and of harmonious perfection, general perfection, and perfection which consists in becoming something rather than in having something, in an inward condition of the mind and spirit, not in an outward set of circumstances, – it is clear that culture, instead of being the frivolous and useless thing which Mr. Bright, and Mr. Frederic Harrison, and many other Liberals are apt to call it, has a very important function to fulfil for mankind. And this function is particularly important in our modern world, of which the whole civilisation is, to a much greater degree than the civilisation of Greece and Rome, mechanical and external, and tends constantly to become more so. But above all in our own country has culture a weighty part to perform, because here that mechanical character, which civilisation tends to take everywhere, is shown in the most eminent degree. Indeed nearly all the characters of perfection, as culture teaches us to fix them, meet in this country with some powerful tendency which thwarts them and sets them at defiance. The idea of perfection as an *inward* condition of the mind and spirit is at variance with the mechanical and material civilisation in esteem with us, and nowhere, as I have said, so much in esteem as with us. The idea of perfection as a *general* expansion of the human family is at variance with our strong individualism, our hatred of all limits to the unrestrained swing of the individual's personality, our maxim of "every man for himself." Above all, the idea of perfection as a *harmonious* expansion of human nature is at variance with our want of flexibility, with our inaptitude for seeing more than one side of a thing, with our intense energetic absorption in the particular pursuit we happen to be following. So culture has a rough task to achieve in this country. Its preachers have, and are likely long to have, a hard time of it, and they will much oftener be regarded, for a great while to come, as elegant or spurious Jeremiahs than as friends and benefactors. That, however, will not prevent their doing in the end good service if they persevere. And, meanwhile, the mode of action they have to pursue, and the sort of habits they must fight against, ought to be made quite clear for every one to see, who may be willing to look at the matter attentively and dispassionately.

Faith in machinery is, I said, our besetting danger; often in machinery most absurdly disproportioned to the end which this machinery, if it is to do any good at all, is to serve; but always in machinery, as if it had a value in and for itself. What is freedom but machinery? what is population but machinery? what is coal but machinery? what are railroads but machinery? what is wealth but machinery? what are, even, religious organisations but machinery? Now almost every voice in England is accustomed to speak of these

things as if they were precious ends in themselves, and therefore had some of the characters of perfection indissolubly joined to them. I have before now noticed Mr. Roebuck's stock argument for proving the greatness and happiness of England as she is, and for quite stopping the mouths of all gainsayers. Mr. Roebuck is never weary of reiterating this argument of his, so I do not know why I should be weary of noticing it. "May not every man in England say what he likes?" – Mr. Roebuck perpetually asks; and that, he thinks, is quite sufficient, and when every man may say what he likes, our aspirations ought to be satisfied. But the aspirations of culture, which is the study of perfection, are not satisfied, unless what men say, when they may say what they like, is worth saying, – has good in it, and more good than bad. In the same way the *Times*, replying to some foreign strictures on the dress, looks, and behaviour of the English abroad, urges that the English ideal is that every one should be free to do and to look just as he likes. But culture indefatigably tries, not to make what each raw person may like the rule by which he fashions himself; but to draw ever nearer to a sense of what is indeed beautiful, graceful, and becoming, and to get the raw person to like that.

[…]

[…] The use of culture is that it helps us, by means of its spiritual standard of perfection, to regard wealth as but machinery, and not only to say as a matter of words that we regard wealth as but machinery, but really to perceive and feel that it is so. If it were not for this purging effect wrought upon our minds by culture, the whole world, the future as well as the present, would inevitably belong to the Philistines. The people who believe most that our greatness and welfare are proved by our being very rich, and who most give their lives and thoughts to becoming rich, are just the very people whom we call Philistines. Culture says: "Consider these people, then, their way of life, their habits, their manners, the very tones of their voice; look at them attentively; observe the literature they read, the things which give them pleasure, the words which come forth out of their mouths, the thoughts which make the furniture of their minds; would any amount of wealth be worth having with the condition that one was to become just like these people by having it?" And thus culture begets a dissatisfaction which is of the highest possible value in stemming the common tide of men's thoughts in a wealthy and industrial community, and which saves the future, as one may hope, from being vulgarised, even if it cannot save the present.

[…]

[…] The point of view of culture, keeping the mark of human perfection simply and broadly in view, and not assigning to this perfection, as religion or utilitarianism assigns to it, a special and limited character, this point of view, I say, of culture is best given by these words of Epictetus: – "It is a sign of ἀφυΐα," says he, – that is, of a nature not finely tempered, – "to give yourselves up to things which relate to the body; to make, for instance, a great fuss about exercise, a great fuss about eating, a great fuss about drinking, a great fuss about walking, a great fuss about riding. All these things ought to be done merely by the way: the formation of the spirit and character must be our real concern." This is admirable; and, indeed, the Greek word εὐφυΐα, a finely tempered nature, gives exactly the notion of perfection as culture brings us to conceive it: a harmonious perfection, a perfection in which the characters of beauty and intelligence are both present, which unites "the two noblest of things," – as Swift, who of one of the two, at any rate, had himself all too little, most happily calls them in his *Battle of the Books*, – "the two noblest of things, *sweetness and light*." The εὐφυής is the man who tends towards sweetness and light; the ἀφυής, on the other hand, is our Philistine. The immense spiritual significance of the Greeks is due to their having been inspired with this central and happy idea of the essential character of human perfection; and Mr. Bright's misconception of culture, as a smattering of Greek and Latin, comes itself, after all, from this wonderful significance of the Greeks having affected the very machinery of our education, and is in itself a kind of homage to it.

[…]

Nothing is more common than for people to confound the inward peace and satisfaction which follows the subduing of the obvious faults of our animality with what I may call absolute inward peace and satisfaction, – the peace and satisfaction which are reached as we draw near to complete spiritual perfection, and not merely to moral perfection, or rather to relative moral perfection. No people in the world have done more and struggled more to attain this relative moral perfection than our English race has. For no people in the world has the command to *resist the devil*, to *overcome the wicked one*, in the nearest and most obvious sense of those words, had such a pressing force and reality. And we have had our reward, not only in the great worldly prosperity which our obedience to this command has brought us, but also, and far more, in great inward peace and satisfaction. But to me few things are more pathetic than to see people, on the strength of the inward peace and satisfaction which their rudimentary efforts towards perfection have brought them, employ, concerning their incomplete perfection and the religious organisations within which they have found it, language which properly applies only to complete perfection, and is a far-off echo of the human soul's prophecy of it. Religion itself, I need hardly say, supplies them in abundance with this grand language. And very freely do they use it; yet it is really the severest possible criticism of such an incomplete perfection as alone we have yet reached through our religious organisations.

The impulse of the English race towards moral development and self-conquest has nowhere so powerfully manifested itself as in Puritanism. Nowhere has Puritanism found so adequate an expression as in the religious organisation of the Independents.[3] The modern Independents have a newspaper, the *Nonconformist*, written with great sincerity and ability. The motto, the standard, the profession of faith which this organ of theirs carries aloft, is: "The Dissidence of Dissent and the Protestantism of the Protestant religion." There is sweetness and light, and an ideal of complete harmonious human perfection! One need not go to culture and poetry to find language to judge it. Religion, with its instinct for perfection, supplies language to judge it, language, too, which is in our mouths every day. "Finally, be of one mind, united in feeling," says St. Peter. There is an ideal which judges the Puritan ideal: "The Dissidence of Dissent and the Protestantism of the Protestant religion!" And religious organisations like this are what people believe in, rest in, would give their lives for! Such, I say, is the wonderful virtue of even the beginnings of perfection, of having conquered even the plain faults of our animality, that the religious organisation which has helped us to do it can seem to us something precious, salutary, and to be propagated, even when it wears such a brand of imperfection on its forehead as this. And men have got such a habit of giving to the language of religion a special application, of making it a mere jargon, that for the condemnation which religion itself passes on the shortcomings of their religious organisations they have no ear; they are sure to cheat themselves and to explain this condemnation away. They can only be reached by the criticism which culture, like poetry, speaking a language not to be sophisticated, and resolutely testing these organisations by the ideal of a human perfection complete on all sides, applies to them.

But men of culture and poetry, it will be said, are again and again failing, and failing conspicuously, in the necessary first stage to a harmonious perfection, in the subduing of the great obvious faults of our animality, which it is the glory of these religious organisations to have helped us to subdue. True, they do often so fail. They have often been without the virtues as well as the faults of the Puritan; it has been one of their dangers that they so felt the Puritan's faults that they too much neglected the practice of his virtues. I will not, however, exculpate them at the Puritan's expense. They have often failed in morality, and morality is indispensable. And they have been punished for their failure, as the Puritan has been rewarded for his performance. They have been punished wherein they erred; but their ideal of beauty, of sweetness and light, and a human nature complete on all its sides, remains the true ideal of perfection still; just as the Puritan's ideal of perfection remains narrow and inadequate, although for what he did well he has been richly rewarded. Notwithstanding the mighty results of the Pilgrim Fathers' voyage, they and their standard of perfection are rightly judged when we figure to ourselves Shakspeare or Virgil, – souls in whom sweetness and light, and all that in human nature is most humane, were eminent, – accompanying them on their voyage, and think what intolerable company Shakspeare and Virgil would have found them! In the same way let us judge the religious organisations which we see all around us. Do not let us deny the good and the happiness which they have accomplished; but do not let us fail to see clearly that their idea of human perfection is narrow and inadequate, and that the Dissidence of Dissent and the Protestantism of the Protestant religion will never bring humanity to its true goal. As I said with regard to wealth: Let us look at the life of those who live in and for it, – so I say with regard to the religious organisations. Look at the life imaged in such a newspaper as the *Nonconformist*, – a life of jealousy of the Establishment, disputes, tea-meetings, openings of chapels, sermons; and then think of it as an ideal of a human life completing itself on all sides, and aspiring with all its organs after sweetness, light, and perfection!

[…]

Culture […] shows its single-minded love of perfection, its desire simply to make reason and the will of God prevail, its freedom from fanaticism, by its attitude towards all this machinery, even while it insists that it *is* machinery. Fanatics, seeing the mischief men do themselves by their blind belief in some machinery or other, – whether it is wealth and industrialism, or whether it is the cultivation of bodily strength and activity, or whether it is a political organisation, or whether it is a religious organisation, – oppose with might and main the tendency to this or that political and religious organisation, or to games and athletic exercises, or to wealth and industrialism, and try violently to stop it. But the flexibility which sweetness and light give, and which is one of the rewards of culture pursued in good faith, enables a man to see that a tendency may be necessary, and even, as a preparation for something in the future, salutary, and yet that the generations or individuals who obey this tendency are sacrificed to it, that they fall short of the hope of perfection by following it; and that its mischiefs are to be criticised, lest it should take too firm a hold and last after it has served its purpose.

[…]

The pursuit of perfection, then, is the pursuit of sweetness and light. He who works for sweetness and light, works to make reason and the will of God prevail. He who works for machinery, he who works for hatred, works only for confusion. Culture looks beyond machinery, culture hates hatred; culture has one great passion, the passion for sweetness and light. It has one even yet greater! – the passion for making them *prevail*. It is not satisfied till we *all* come to a perfect man; it knows that the sweetness and light of the few must be imperfect until the raw and unkindled masses of humanity are touched with sweetness and light. If I have not shrunk from saying that we must work for sweetness and light, so neither have I shrunk from saying that we must have a broad basis, must have sweetness and light for as many as possible. Again and again I have insisted how those are the happy moments of humanity, how those are the marking epochs of a people's life, how those are the flowering times for literature and art and all the creative power of genius, when there is a *national* glow of life and thought, when the whole of society is in the fullest measure permeated by thought, sensible to beauty, intelligent and alive. Only it must be *real* thought and *real* beauty; *real* sweetness and *real* light. Plenty of people will try to give the masses, as they call them, an intellectual food prepared and adapted in the way they think proper for the actual condition of the masses. The ordinary popular literature is an example of this way of working on the masses. Plenty of people will try to indoctrinate the masses with the set of ideas and judgments constituting the creed of their own profession or party. Our religious and political organisations give an example of this way of working on the masses. I condemn neither way; but culture works differently. It does not try to teach down to the level of inferior classes; it does not try to win them for this or that sect of its own, with ready-made judgments and watchwords. It seeks to do away with classes; to make the best that has been thought and known in the world current everywhere; to make all men live in an atmosphere of sweetness and light, where they may use ideas, as it uses them itself, freely, – nourished, and not bound by them.

This is the *social idea*; and the men of culture are the true apostles of equality. The great men of culture are those who have had a passion for diffusing, for making prevail, for carrying from one end of society to the other, the best knowledge, the best ideas of their time; who have laboured to divest knowledge of all that was harsh, uncouth, difficult, abstract, professional, exclusive; to humanise it, to make it efficient outside the clique of the cultivated and learned, yet still remaining the *best* knowledge and thought of the time, and a true

source, therefore, of sweetness and light. Such a man was Abelard in the Middle Ages, in spite of all his imperfections: and thence the boundless emotion and enthusiasm which Abelard excited. Such were Lessing and Herder in Germany, at the end of the last century; and their services to Germany were in this way inestimably precious. Generations will pass, and literary monuments will accumulate, and works far more perfect than the works of Lessing and Herder will be produced in Germany; and yet the names of these two men will fill a German with a reverence and enthusiasm such as the names of the most gifted masters will hardly awaken. And why? Because they *humanised* knowledge; because they broadened the basis of life and intelligence; because they worked powerfully to diffuse sweetness and light, to make reason and the will of God prevail. With Saint Augustine they said: "Let us not leave thee alone to make in the secret of thy knowledge, as thou didst before the creation of the firmament, the division of light from darkness; let the children of thy spirit, placed in their firmament, make their light shine upon the earth, mark the division of night and day, and announce the revolution of the times; for the old order is passed, and the new arises; the night is spent, the day is come forth; and thou shalt crown the year with thy blessing, when thou shalt send forth labourers into thy harvest sown by other hands than theirs; when thou shalt send forth new labourers to new seed-times, whereof the harvest shall be not yet."

Notes

1   Thomas Wilson (1663–1755), Bishop of Sodor and Man; Arnold quoted him very frequently, especially his *Maxims of Piety and of Christianity*, but he was so little known that Arnold was accused of having invented him.
2   Arnold is quoting from his *A French Eton* (1864).
3   The Independents, who insisted on the autonomy of each congregation, had played an important part in the Puritan opposition to Charles I; by the nineteenth century they were more generally known as Congregationalists.

2

"Conspicuous Consumption" (1899)

Thorstein Veblen

In what has been said of the evolution of the vicarious leisure class and its differentiation from the general body of the working classes, reference has been made to a further division of labour – that between the different servant classes. One portion of the servant class, chiefly those persons whose occupation is vicarious leisure, come to undertake a new, subsidiary range of duties – the vicarious consumption of goods. The most obvious form in which this consumption occurs is seen in the wearing of liveries and the occupation of spacious servants' quarters. Another, scarcely less obtrusive or less effective form of vicarious consumption, and a much more widely prevalent one, is the consumption of food, clothing, dwelling, and furniture by the lady and the rest of the domestic establishment.

But already at a point in economic evolution far antedating the emergence of the lady, specialised consumption of goods as an evidence of pecuniary strength had begun to work out in a more or less elaborate system. The beginning of a differentiation in consumption even antedates the appearance of anything that can fairly be called pecuniary strength. It is traceable back to the initial phase of predatory culture, and there is even a suggestion that an incipient differentiation in this respect lies back of the beginnings of the predatory life. This most primitive differentiation in the consumption of goods is like the later differentiation with which we are all so intimately

familiar, in that it is largely of a ceremonial character, but unlike the latter it does not rest on a difference in accumulated wealth. The utility of consumption as an evidence of wealth is to be classed as a derivative growth. It is an adaption to a new end, by a selective process, of a distinction previously existing and well established in men's habits of thought.

In the earlier phases of the predatory culture the only economic differentiation is a broad distinction between an honourable superior class made up of the able-bodied men on the one side, and a base inferior class of labouring women on the other. According to the ideal scheme of life in force at the time it is the office of the men to consume what the women produce. Such consumption as falls to the women is merely incidental to their work; it is a means to their continued labour, and not a consumption directed to their own comfort and fulness of life. Unproductive consumption of goods is honourable, primarily as a mark of prowess and a perquisite of human dignity; secondarily it becomes substantially honourable in itself, especially the consumption of the more desirable things. The consumption of choice articles of food, and frequently also of rare articles of adornment, becomes tabu to the women and children; and if there is a base (servile) class of men, the tabu holds also for them. With a further advance in culture this tabu may change into simple custom of a more or less rigorous character; but whatever be the theoretical basis of the distinction which is maintained, whether it be a tabu or a larger conventionality, the features of the conventional scheme of consumption do not change easily. When the quasi-peaceable stage of industry is reached,

Thorstein Veblen, "Conspicuous Consumption," pp. 187–98, 199–200, 202–4 from *The Consumer Society Reader*, ed. Juliet Schor and Douglas B. Holt. New York: The New Press, 2000.

with its fundamental institution of chattel slavery, the general principle, more or less rigorously applied, is that the base, industrious class should consume only what may be necessary to their subsistence. In the nature of things, luxuries and the comforts of life belong to the leisure class. Under the tabu, certain victuals, and more particularly certain beverages, are strictly reserved for the use of the superior class.

The ceremonial differentiation of the dietary is best seen in the use of intoxicating beverages and narcotics. If these articles of consumption are costly, they are felt to be noble and honorific. Therefore the base classes, primarily the women, practice an enforced continence with respect to these stimulants, except in countries where they are obtainable at a very low cost. From archaic times down through all the length of the patriarchal régime it has been the office of the women to prepare and administer these luxuries, and it has been the perquisite of the men of gentle birth and breeding to consume them. Drunkenness and the other pathological consequences of the free use of stimulants therefore tend in their turn to become honorific, as being a mark, at the second remove, of the superior status of those who are able to afford the indulgence. Infirmities induced by over-indulgence are among some peoples freely recognised as manly attributes. It has even happened that the name for certain diseased conditions of the body arising from such an origin has passed into everyday speech as a synonym for "noble" or "gentle." It is only at a relatively early stage of culture that the symptoms of expensive vice are conventionally accepted as marks of a superior status, and so tend to become virtues and command the deference of the community; but the reputability that attaches to certain expensive vices long retains so much of its force as to appreciably lessen the disapprobation visited upon the men of the wealthy or noble class for any excessive indulgence. The same invidious distinction adds force to the current disapproval of any indulgence of this kind on the part of women, minors, and inferiors. This invidious traditional distinction has not lost its force even among the more advanced peoples of to-day. Where the example set by the leisure class retains its imperative force in the regulation of the conventionalities, it is observable that the women still in great measure practise the same traditional continence with regard to stimulants.

This characterisation of the greater continence in the use of stimulants practised by the women of the reputable classes may seem an excessive refinement of logic at the expense of common sense. But facts within easy reach of any one who cares to know them go to say that the greater abstinence of women is in some part due to an imperative conventionality; and this conventionality is, in a general way, strongest where the patriarchal tradition – the tradition that the woman is a chattel – has retained its hold in greatest vigour. In a sense which has been greatly qualified in scope and rigour, but which has by no means lost its meaning even yet, this tradition says that the woman, being a chattel, should consume only what is necessary to her sustenance, – except so far as her further consumption contributes to the comfort or the good repute of her master. The consumption of luxuries, in the true sense, is a consumption directed to the comfort of the consumer himself, and is, therefore, a mark of the master. Any such consumption by others can take place only on a basis of sufferance. In communities where the popular habits of thought have been profoundly shaped by the patriarchal tradition we may accordingly look for survivals of the tabu on luxuries at least to the extent of a conventional deprecation of their use by the unfree and dependent class. This is more particularly true as regards certain luxuries, the use of which by the dependent class would detract sensibly from the comfort or pleasure of their masters, or which are held to be of doubtful legitimacy on other grounds. In the apprehension of the great conservative middle class of Western civilisation the use of these various stimulants is obnoxious to at least one, if not both, of these objections; and it is a fact too significant to be passed over that it is precisely among these middle classes of the Germanic culture, with their strong surviving sense of the patriarchal proprieties, that the women are to the greatest extent subject to a qualified tabu on narcotics and alcoholic beverages. With many qualifications – with more qualifications as the patriarchal tradition has gradually weakened – the general rule is felt to be right and binding that women should consume only for the benefit of their masters. The objection of course presents itself that expenditure on women's dress and household paraphernalia is an obvious exception to this rule; but it will appear in the sequel that this exception is much more obvious than substantial.

During the earlier stages of economic development, consumption of goods without stint, especially consumption of the better grades of goods, – ideally all consumption in excess of the subsistence minimum, – pertains normally to the leisure class. This restriction tends to disappear, at least formally, after the later peaceable stage has been reached, with private ownership of goods and an industrial system based on wage labour or on the petty household economy. But during the earlier quasi-peaceable stage, when so many of the traditions through which the institution of a leisure class has affected the economic life of later times were taking form and consistency, this principle has had the force of a conventional law. It has served as the norm to which consumption has tended to conform, and any appreciable departure from it is to be regarded as an aberrant form, sure to be eliminated sooner or later in the further course of development.

The quasi-peaceable gentleman of leisure, then, not only consumes of the staff of life beyond the minimum required for subsistence and physical efficiency, but his consumption also undergoes a specialisation as regards the quality of the goods consumed. He consumes freely and of the best, in food, drink, narcotics, shelter, services, ornaments, apparel, weapons and accoutrements, amusements, amulets, and idols or divinities. In the process of gradual amelioration which takes place in the articles of his consumption, the motive principle and the proximate aim of innovation is no doubt the higher efficiency of the improved and more elaborate products for personal comfort and well-being. But that does not remain the sole purpose of their consumption. The canon of reputability is at hand and seizes upon such innovations as are, according to its standard, fit to survive. Since the consumption of these more excellent goods is an evidence of wealth, it becomes honorific; and conversely, the failure to consume in due quantity and quality becomes a mark of inferiority and demerit.

This growth of punctilious discrimination as to qualitative excellence in eating, drinking, etc., presently affects not only the manner of life, but also the training and intellectual activity of the gentleman of leisure. He is no longer simply the successful, aggressive male, – the man of strength, resource, and intrepidity. In order to avoid stultification he must also cultivate his tastes, for it now becomes incumbent on him to discriminate with some nicety between the noble and the ignoble in consumable goods. He becomes a connoisseur in creditable viands of various degrees of merit, in manly beverages and trinkets, in seemly apparel and architecture, in weapons, games, dancers, and the narcotics. This cultivation of æsthetic faculty requires time and application, and the demands made upon the gentleman in this direction therefore tend to change his life of leisure into a more or less arduous application to the business of learning how to live a life of ostensible leisure in a becoming way. Closely related to the requirement that the gentleman must consume freely and of the right kind of goods, there is the requirement that he must know how to consume them in a seemly manner. His life of leisure must be conducted in due form. Hence arise good manners in the way pointed out in an earlier chapter. High-bred manners and ways of living are items of conformity to the norm of conspicuous leisure and conspicuous consumption.

Conspicuous consumption of valuable goods is a means of reputability to the gentleman of leisure. As wealth accumulates on his hands, his own unaided effort will not avail to sufficiently put his opulence in evidence by this method. The aid of friends and competitors is therefore brought in by resorting to the giving of valuable presents and expensive feasts and entertainments. Presents and feasts had probably another origin than that of naïve ostentation, but they acquired their utility for this purpose very early, and they have retained that character to the present; so that their utility in this respect has now long been the substantial ground on which these usages rest. Costly entertainments, such as the potlatch or the ball, are peculiarly adapted to serve this end. The competitor with whom the entertainer wishes to institute a comparison is, by this method, made to serve as a means to the end. He consumes vicariously for his host at the same time that he is witness to the consumption of that excess of good things which his host is unable to dispose of single-handed, and he is also made to witness his host's facility in etiquette.

In the giving of costly entertainments other motives, of more genial kind, are of course also present. The custom of festive gatherings probably originated in motives of conviviality and religion; these motives are also present in the later development, but they do not continue to be the sole motives. The latter-day leisure-class festivities and entertainments may continue in some slight degree to serve the religious need and in a higher degree the needs of recreation and conviviality, but they also serve an invidious purpose; and they serve it none the less effectually for having a colourable non-invidious ground in these more avowable motives. But the economic effect of these social amenities is not therefore lessened, either in the vicarious consumption of goods or in the exhibition of difficult and costly achievements in etiquette.

As wealth accumulates, the leisure class develops further in function and structure, and there arises a differentiation within the class. There is a more or less elaborate system of rank and grades. This differentiation is furthered by the inheritance of wealth and the consequent inheritance of gentility. With the inheritance of gentility goes the inheritance of obligatory leisure; and gentility of a sufficient potency to entail a life of leisure may be inherited without the complement of wealth required to maintain a dignified leisure. Gentle blood may be transmitted without goods enough to afford a reputably free consumption at one's case. Hence results a class of impecunious gentlemen of leisure, incidentally referred to already. These half-caste gentlemen of leisure fall into a system of hierarchical gradations. Those who stand near the higher and the highest grades of the wealthy leisure class, in point of birth, or in point of wealth, or both, outrank the remoter-born and the pecuniarily weaker. These lower grades, especially the impecunious, or marginal, gentlemen of leisure, affiliate themselves by a system of dependence or fealty to the great ones; by so doing they gain an increment of repute, or of the means with which to lead a life of leisure, from their patron. They become his courtiers or retainers, servants; and being fed and countenanced by their patron they are indices of his rank and vicarious consumers of his superfluous wealth. Many of these affiliated gentlemen of leisure are at the same time lesser men of substance in their own right; so that some of them are scarcely at all, others only partially, to be rated as vicarious consumers. So many of them, however, as make up the retainers and hangers-on of the patron may be classed as vicarious consumers without qualification. Many of these again, and also many of the other aristocracy of less degree, have in turn attached to their persons a more or less comprehensive group of vicarious consumers in the persons of their wives and children, their servants, retainers, etc.

Throughout this graduated scheme of vicarious leisure and vicarious consumption the rule holds that these offices must be performed in some such manner, or under some such circumstance or insignia, as shall point plainly to the master to whom this leisure or consumption pertains, and to whom therefore the resulting increment of good repute of right inures. The consumption and leisure executed by these persons for their master or patron represents an investment on his part with a view to an increase of good fame. As regards feasts and largesses this is obvious enough, and the imputation of repute to the host or patron here takes place immediately, on the ground of common notoriety. Where leisure and consumption is performed vicariously by henchmen and retainers, imputation of the resulting repute to the patron is effected by their residing near his person so that it may be plain to all men from what source they draw. As the group whose good esteem is to be secured in this way grows larger, more patent means are required to indicate the imputation of merit for the leisure performed, and to this end uniforms, badges, and liveries come into vogue. The wearing of uniforms or liveries implies a considerable degree of dependence, and may even be said to be a mark of servitude, real or ostensible. The wearers of uniforms and liveries may be roughly divided into two classes – the free and the servile, or the noble and the ignoble. The services performed by them are likewise divisible into noble and ignoble. Of course the distinction is not observed with strict consistency in practice; the less debasing of the base services and the less honorific of the noble functions are not infrequently merged in the same person. But the general distinction is not on that account to be overlooked. What may add some perplexity is the fact that this fundamental distinction between noble and ignoble, which rests on the nature of the ostensible service performed, is traversed by a secondary distinction into honorific and humiliating, resting on the rank of the person for whom the service is performed or whose livery is worn. So, those offices which are by right the proper employment of the leisure class are noble; such as government, fighting, hunting, the care of arms and accoutrements, and the like, – in short, those which may be classed as ostensibly predatory employments.

On the other hand, those employments which properly fall to the industrious class are ignoble; such as handicraft or other productive labour, menial services and the like. But a base service performed for a person of very high degree may become a very honorific office; as for instance the office of a Maid of Honour or of a Lady in Waiting to the Queen, or the King's Master of the Horse or his Keeper of the Hounds. The two offices last named suggest a principle of some general bearing. Whenever, as in these cases, the menial service in question has to do directly with the primary leisure employments of fighting and hunting, it easily acquires a reflected honorific character. In this way great honour may come to attach to an employment which in its own nature belongs to the baser sort.

In the later development of peaceable industry, the usage of employing an idle corps of uniformed men-at-arms gradually lapses. Vicarious consumption by dependents bearing the insignia of their patron or master narrows down to a corps of liveried menials. In a heightened degree, therefore, the livery comes to be a badge of servitude, or rather servility. Something of a honorific character always attached to the livery of the armed retainer, but this honorific character disappears when the livery becomes the exclusive badge of the menial. The livery becomes obnoxious to nearly all who are required to wear it. We are yet so little removed from a state of effective slavery as still to be fully sensitive to the sting of any imputation of servility. This antipathy asserts itself even in the case of the liveries or uniforms which some corporations prescribe as the distinctive dress of their employees. In this country the aversion even goes the length of discrediting – in a mild and uncertain way – those government employments, military and civil, which require the wearing of a livery or uniform.

With the disappearance of servitude, the number of vicarious consumers attached to any one gentleman tends, on the whole, to decrease. The like is of course true, and perhaps in a still higher degree, of the number of dependents who perform vicarious leisure for him. In a general way, though not wholly nor consistently, these two groups coincide. The dependent who was first delegated for these duties was the wife, or the chief wife; and, as would be expected, in the later development of the institution, when the number of persons by whom these duties are customarily performed gradually narrows, the wife remains the last. In the higher grades of society a large volume of both these kinds of service is required; and here the wife is of course still assisted in the work by a more or less numerous corps of menials. But as we descend the social scale, the point is presently reached where the duties of vicarious leisure and consumption devolve upon the wife alone. In the communities of the Western culture, this point is at present found among the lower middle class.

And here occurs a curious inversion. It is a fact of common observance that in this lower middle class there is no pretence of leisure on the part of the head of the household. Through force of circumstances it has fallen into disuse. But the middle-class wife still carries on the business of vicarious leisure, for the good name of the household and its master. In descending the social scale in any modern industrial community, the primary fact – the conspicuous leisure of the master of the household – disappears at a relatively high point. The head of the middle-class household has been reduced by economic circumstances to turn his hand to gaining a livelihood by occupations which often partake largely of the character of industry, as in the case of the ordinary business man of to-day. But the derivative fact – the vicarious leisure and consumption rendered by the wife, and the auxiliary vicarious performance of leisure by menials – remains in vogue as a conventionality which the demands of reputability will not suffer to be slighted. It is by no means an uncommon spectacle to find a man applying himself to work with the utmost assiduity, in order that his wife may in due form render for him that degree of vicarious leisure which the common sense of the time demands.

The leisure rendered by the wife in such cases is, of course, not a simple manifestation of idleness or indolence. It almost invariably occurs disguised under some form of work or household duties or social amenities, which prove on analysis to serve little or no ulterior end beyond showing that she does not and need not occupy herself with anything that is gainful or that is of substantial use. As has already been noticed under the head of manners, the greater part of the customary round of domestic cares to which the middle-class housewife gives her time and effort is of this character. Not that the results of her attention to household matters, of a decorative and mundificatory character, are not pleasing to the sense of men trained in middle-class proprieties; but the taste to which these effects of household adornment and tidiness appeal is a taste which has been formed under the selective guidance of a canon of propriety that demands just these evidences of wasted effort. The effects are pleasing to us chiefly because we have been taught to find them pleasing. There goes into these domestic duties much solicitude for a proper combination of form and colour, and for other ends that are to be classed as æsthetic in the proper sense of the term; and it is not denied that effects having some substantial æsthetic value are sometimes attained. Pretty much all that is here insisted on is that, as regards these amenities of life, the housewife's efforts are under the guidance of traditions that have been shaped by the law of conspicuously wasteful expenditure of time and substance. If beauty or comfort is achieved, – and it is a more or less fortuitous circumstance if they are, – they must be achieved by means and methods that commend themselves to the great economic law of wasted effort. The more reputable, "presentable" portion of middle-class household paraphernalia are, on the one hand, items of conspicuous consumption, and on the other hand, apparatus for putting in evidence the vicarious leisure rendered by the housewife.

The requirement of vicarious consumption at the hands of the wife continues in force even at a lower point in the pecuniary scale than the requirement of vicarious leisure. At a point below which little if any pretence of wasted effort, in ceremonial cleanness and the like, is observable, and where there is assuredly no conscious attempt at ostensible leisure, decency still requires the wife to consume some goods conspicuously for the reputability of the household and its head. So that, as the latter-day outcome of this evolution of an archaic institution, the wife, who was at the outset the drudge and chattel of the man, both in fact and in theory, – the producer of goods for him to consume, – has become the ceremonial consumer of goods which he produces. But she still quite unmistakably remains his chattel in theory; for the habitual rendering of vicarious leisure and consumption is the abiding mark of the unfree servant.

This vicarious consumption practised by the household of the middle and lower classes can not be counted as a direct expression of the leisure-class scheme of life, since the household of this pecuniary grade does not belong within the leisure class. It is rather that the leisure-class scheme of life here comes to an expression at the second remove. The leisure class stands at the head of the social structure in point of reputability; and its manner of life and its standards of worth therefore afford the norm of reputability for the community. The observance of these standards, in some degree of approximation, becomes incumbent upon all classes lower in the scale. In modern civilised communities the lines of demarcation between social classes have grown vague and transient, and wherever this happens the norm of reputability imposed by the upper class extends its coercive influence with but slight hindrance down through the social structure to the lowest strata. The result is that the members of each stratum accept as their ideal of decency the scheme of life in vogue in the next higher stratum, and bend their energies to live up to that ideal. On pain of forfeiting their good name and their self-respect in case of failure, they must conform to the accepted code, at least in appearance.

The basis on which good repute in any highly organised industrial community ultimately rests is pecuniary strength; and the means of showing pecuniary strength, and so of gaining or retaining a good name, are leisure and a conspicuous consumption of goods. Accordingly, both of these methods are in vogue as far down the scale as it remains possible; and in the lower strata in which the two methods are employed, both offices are in great part delegated to the wife and children of the household. Lower still, where any degree of leisure, even ostensible, has become impracticable for the wife, the conspicuous consumption of goods remains and is carried on by the wife and children. The man of the household also can do something in this direction, and, indeed, he commonly does; but with a still lower descent into the levels of indigence – along the margin of the slums – the man, and presently also the children, virtually cease to consume valuable goods for appearances, and the woman remains virtually the sole exponent of the household's pecuniary decency. No class of society, not even the most abjectly poor, foregoes all customary conspicuous consumption. The last items of this category of consumption are not given up except under stress of the direst necessity. Very much of squalor and discomfort will be endured before the last trinket or the last pretence of pecuniary decency is put away. There is no class and no country that has yielded so abjectly before the pressure of physical want as to deny themselves all gratification of this higher or spiritual need.

★ ★ ★

From the foregoing survey of the growth of conspicuous leisure and consumption, it appears that the utility of both alike for the purposes of reputability lies in the element of waste that is common to both. In the one case it is a waste of time and effort, in the other it is a waste of goods. Both are methods of demonstrating the possession of wealth, and the two are conventionally accepted as equivalents. The choice between them is a question of advertising expediency simply, except so far as it may be affected by other standards of propriety, springing from a different source. On grounds of expediency the preference may be given to the one or the other at different stages of the economic development. The question is, which of the two methods will most effectively reach the persons whose convictions it is desired to affect. Usage has answered this question in different ways under different circumstances.

So long as the community or social group is small enough and compact enough to be effectually reached by common notoriety alone, – that is to say, so long as the human environment to which the individual is required to adapt himself in respect of reputability is comprised within his sphere of personal acquaintance and neighborhood gossip, – so long the one method is about as effective as the other. Each will therefore serve about equally well during the earlier stages of social growth. But when the differentiation has gone farther and it becomes necessary to reach a wider human environment, consumption begins to hold over leisure as an ordinary means of decency. This is especially true during the later, peaceable economic stage. The means of communication and the mobility of the population now expose the individual to the observation of many persons who have no other means of judging of his reputability than the display of goods (and perhaps of breeding) which he is able to make while he is under their direct observation.

The modern organisation of industry works in the same direction also by another line. The exigencies of the modern industrial system frequently place individuals and households in juxtaposition between whom there is little contact in any other sense than that of juxtaposition. One's neighbours, mechanically speaking, often are socially not one's neighbours, or even acquaintances; and still their transient good opinion has a high degree of utility. The only practicable means of impressing one's pecuniary ability on these unsympathetic observers of one's everyday life is an unremitting demonstration of ability to pay. In the modern community there is also a more frequent attendance at large gatherings of people to whom one's everyday life is unknown; in such places as churches, theatres, ballrooms, hotels, parks, shops, and the like. In order to impress these transient observers, and to retain one's self-complacency under their observation, the signature of one's pecuniary strength should be written in characters which he who runs may read. It is evident, therefore, that the present trend of the development is in the direction of heightening the utility of conspicuous consumption as compared with leisure.

It is also noticeable that the serviceability of consumption as a means of repute, as well as the insistence on it as an element of decency, is at its best in those portions of the community where the human contact of the individual is widest and the mobility of the population is greatest. Conspicuous consumption claims a relatively larger portion of the income of the urban than of the rural population, and the claim is also more imperative. The result is that, in order to keep up a decent appearance, the former habitually live hand-to-mouth to a greater extent than the latter. So it comes, for instance, that the American farmer and his wife and daughters are notoriously less modish in their dress, as well as less urbane in their manners, than the city artisan's family with an equal income. It is not that the city population is by nature much more eager for the peculiar complacency that comes of a conspicuous consumption, nor has the rural population less regard for pecuniary decency. But the provocation to this line of evidence, as well as its transient effectiveness, are more decided in the city. This method is therefore more readily resorted to, and in the struggle to outdo one another the city population push their normal standard of conspicuous consumption to a higher point, with the result that a relatively greater expenditure in this direction is required to indicate a given degree of pecuniary decency in the city. The requirement of conformity to this higher conventional standard becomes mandatory. The standard of decency is higher, class for class, and this requirement of decent appearance must be lived up to on pain of losing caste.

Consumption becomes a larger element in the standard of living in the city than in the country. Among the country population its place is to some extent taken by savings and home comforts known through the medium of neighborhood gossip sufficiently to serve the like general purpose of pecuniary repute. These home comforts and the leisure indulged in – where the indulgence is found – are of course also in great part to be classed as items of conspicuous consumption; and much the same is to be said of the savings. The smaller amount of the savings laid by by the artisan class is no doubt due, in some measure, to the fact that in the case of the artisan the savings are a less effective means of advertisement, relative to the environment in which he is placed, than are the savings of the people living on farms and in the small villages. Among the latter, everybody's affairs, especially everybody's pecuniary status, are known to everybody else. Considered by itself simply – taken in the first degree – this added provocation to which the artisan and the urban labouring classes are exposed may not very seriously decrease the amount of savings; but in its cumulative action, through raising the standard of decent expenditure, its deterrent effect on the tendency to save cannot but be very great.

[…]

The early ascendency of leisure as a means of reputability is traceable to the archaic distinction between noble and ignoble employments. Leisure is honourable and becomes imperative partly because it shows exemption from ignoble labour. The archaic differentiation into noble and ignoble classes is based on an invidious distinction between employments as honorific or debasing; and this traditional distinction grows into an imperative canon of decency during the early quasi-peaceable stage. Its ascendency is furthered by the fact that leisure is still fully as effective an evidence of wealth as consumption. Indeed, so effective is it in the relatively small and stable human environment to which the individual is exposed at that cultural stage, that, with the aid of the archaic tradition which deprecates all productive labour, it gives rise to a large impecunious leisure class, and it even tends to limit the production of the community's industry to the subsistence minimum. This extreme inhibition of industry is avoided because slave labour, working under a compulsion more rigorous than that of reputability, is forced to turn out a product in excess of the subsistence minimum of the working class. The subsequent relative decline in the use of conspicuous leisure as a basis of repute is due partly to an increasing relative effectiveness of consumption as an evidence of wealth; but in part it is traceable to another force, alien, and in some degree antagonistic, to the usage of conspicuous waste.

[…]

Throughout the entire evolution of conspicuous expenditure, whether of goods or of services or human life, runs the obvious implication that in order to effectually mend the consumer's good fame it must be an expenditure of superfluities. In order to be reputable it must be wasteful. No merit would accrue from the consumption of the bare necessaries of life, except by comparison with the abjectly poor who fall short even of the subsistence minimum; and no standard of expenditure could result from such a comparison, except the most prosaic and unattractive level of decency. A standard of life would still be possible which should admit of invidious comparison in other respects than that of opulence; as, for instance, a comparison in various directions in the manifestation of moral, physical, intellectual, or æsthetic force. Comparison in all these directions is in vogue to-day; and the comparison made in these respects is commonly so inextricably bound up with the pecuniary comparison as to be scarcely distinguishable from the latter. This is especially true as regards the current rating of expressions of intellectual and æsthetic force or proficiency; so that we frequently interpret as æsthetic or intellectual a difference which in substance is pecuniary only.

The use of the term "waste" is in one respect an unfortunate one. As used in the speech of everyday life the word carries an undertone of deprecation. It is here used for want of a better term that will adequately describe the same range of motives and of phenomena, and it is not to be taken in an odious sense, as implying an illegitimate expenditure of human products or of human life. In the view of economic theory the expenditure in question is no more and no less legitimate than any other expenditure. It is here called "waste" because this expenditure does not serve human life or human well-being on the whole, not because it is waste or misdirection of effort or expenditure as viewed from the standpoint of the individual consumer who chooses it. If he chooses it, that disposes of the question of its relative utility to him, as compared with other forms of consumption that would not be deprecated on account of their wastefulness. Whatever form of expenditure the consumer chooses, or whatever end he seeks in making his choice, has utility to him by virtue of his preference. As seen from the point of view of the individual consumer, the question of wastefulness does not arise within the scope of economic theory proper. The use of the word "waste" as a technical term, therefore, implies no deprecation of the motives or of the ends sought by the consumer under this canon of conspicuous waste.

But it is, on other grounds, worth noting that the term "waste" in the language of everyday life implies deprecation of what is characterised as wasteful. This common-sense implication is itself an outcropping of the instinct of workmanship. The popular reprobation of waste goes to say that in order to be at peace with himself the common man must be able to see in any and all human effort and human enjoyment an enhancement of life and well-being on the whole. In order to meet with unqualified approval, any economic fact must approve itself under the test of impersonal usefulness – usefulness as seen from the point of view of the generically human. Relative or competitive advantage of one individual in comparison with another does not satisfy the economic conscience, and therefore competitive expenditure has not the approval of this conscience.

In strict accuracy nothing should be included under the head of conspicuous waste but such expenditure as is incurred on the ground of an invidious pecuniary comparison. But in order to bring any given item or element in under this head it is not necessary that it should be recognised as waste in this sense by the person incurring the expenditure. It frequently happens that an element of the standard of living which set out with being primarily wasteful, ends with becoming, in the apprehension of the consumer, a necessary of life; and it may in this way become as indispensable as any other item of the consumer's habitual expenditure. As items which sometimes fall under this head, and are therefore available as illustrations of the manner in which this principle applies, may be cited carpets and tapestries, silver table service, waiter's services, silk hats, starched linen, many articles of jewellery and of dress. The indispensability of these things after the habit and the convention have been formed, however, has little to say in the classification of expenditures as waste or not waste in the technical meaning of the word. The test to which all expenditure must be brought in an

attempt to decide that point is the question whether it serves directly to enhance human life on the whole – whether it furthers the life process taken impersonally. For this is the basis of award of the instinct of workmanship, and that instinct is the court of final appeal in any question of economic truth or adequacy. It is a question as to the award rendered by a dispassionate common sense. The question is, therefore, not whether, under the existing circumstances of individual habit and social custom, a given expenditure conduces to the particular consumer's gratification or peace of mind; but whether, aside from acquired tastes and from the canons of usage and conventional decency, its result is a net gain in comfort or in the fulness of life. Customary expenditure must be classed under the head of waste in so far as the custom on which it rests is traceable to the habit of making an invidious pecuniary comparison – in so far as it is conceived that it could not have become customary and prescriptive without the backing of this principle of pecuniary reputability or relative economic success.

It is obviously not necessary that a given object of expenditure should be exclusively wasteful in order to come in under the category of conspicuous waste. An article may be useful and wasteful both, aud its utility to the consumer may be made up of use and waste in the most varying proportions. Consumable goods, and even productive goods, generally show the two elements in combination, as constituents of their utility; although, in a general way, the element of waste tends to predominate in articles of consumption, while the contrary is true of articles designed for productive use. Even in articles which appear at first glance to serve for pure ostentation only, it is always possible to detect the presence of some, at least ostensible, useful purpose; and on the other hand, even in special machinery and tools contrived for some particular industrial process, as well as in the rudest appliances of human industry, the traces of conspicuous waste, or at least of the habit of ostentation, usually become evident on a close scrutiny. It would be hazardous to assert that a useful purpose is ever absent from the utility of any article or of any service, however obviously its prime purpose and chief element is conspicuous waste; and it would be only less hazardous to assert of any primarily useful product that the element of waste is in no way concerned in its value, immediately or remotely.

3

"The Affirmative Character of Culture" (1937)

Herbert Marcuse

The doctrine that all human knowledge is oriented toward practice belonged to the nucleus of ancient philosophy. It was Aristotle's view that the truths arrived at through knowledge should direct practice in daily life as in the arts and sciences. In their struggle for existence, men need the effort of knowledge, the search for truth, because what is good, beneficial, and right for them is not immediately evident. Artisan and merchant, captain and physician, general and statesman – each must have correct knowledge in his field in order to be capable of acting as the changing situation demands.

While Aristotle maintained the practical character of every instance of knowledge, he made a significant distinction between forms of knowledge. He ordered them, as it were, in a hierarchy of value whose nadir is functional acquaintance with the necessities of everyday life and whose zenith is philosophical knowledge. The latter has no purpose outside itself. Rather, it occurs only for its own sake and to afford men felicity. Within this hierarchy there is a fundamental break between the necessary and useful on the one hand and the "beautiful" on the other. "The whole of life is further divided into two parts, business and leisure, war and peace, and of actions some aim at what is necessary and useful, and some at what is beautiful [τὰ καλά]." Since this division is not itself questioned, and since, together with other regions of the "beautiful," "pure" theory congeals into an independent activity alongside and above other activities, philosophy's original demand disintegrates: the demand that practice be guided by known truths. Separating the useful and necessary from the beautiful and from enjoyment initiated a development that abandons the field to the materialism of bourgeois practice on the one hand and to the appeasement of happiness and the mind within the preserve of "culture" on the other.

One theme continually recurs in the reasons given for the relegation of the highest form of knowledge and of pleasure to pure, purposeless theory: the world of necessity, of everyday provision for life, is inconstant, insecure, unfree – not merely in fact, but in essence. Disposal over material goods is never entirely the work of human industry and wisdom, for it is subject to the rule of contingency. The individual who places his highest goal, happiness, in these goods makes himself the slave of men and things. He surrenders his freedom. Wealth and well-being do not come or persist due to his autonomous decision but rather through the changeable fortune of opaque circumstances. Man thus subjects his existence to a purpose situated outside him. Of itself, such an external purpose can vitiate and enslave men only if the material conditions of life are poorly ordered, that is, if their reproduction is regulated through the anarchy of opposing social interests. In this order the preservation of the common existence is incompatible with individual happiness and freedom. Insofar as philosophy is concerned with man's happiness – and the theory of classical antiquity held it to be the highest good – it cannot find it in the established material organization of life. That is why it must transcend this order's facticity.

Herbert Marcuse, "The Affirmative Character of Culture," pp. 88–117, 130–3 from *Negations: Essays in Critical Theory*. London: Free Association Books, 1988.

Along with metaphysics, epistemology, and ethics, this transcendence also affects psychology. Like the extrapsychic world, the human soul is divided into a lower and a higher region. The history of the soul transpires between the poles of sensuality and reason. The devaluation of sensuality results from the same motives as that of the material world: because sensuality is a realm of anarchy, of inconstancy, and of unfreedom. Sensual pleasure is not in itself bad. It is bad because, like man's lower activities, it is fulfilled in a bad order. The "lower parts of the soul" drive man to covet gain and possessions, purchase and sale. He is led to "admire and value nothing but wealth and its possessors." Accordingly the "appetitive" part of the soul, which is oriented toward sensual pleasure, is also termed by Plato the "money-loving" part, "because money is the principal means of satisfying desires of this kind."

All the ontological classifications of ancient idealism express the badness of a social reality in which knowledge of the truth about human existence is no longer incorporated into practice. The world of the true, the good, and the beautiful is in fact an "ideal" world insofar as it lies beyond the existing conditions of life, beyond a form of existence in which the majority of men either work as slaves or spend their life in commerce, with only a small group having the opportunity of being concerned with anything more than the provision and preservation of the necessary. When the reproduction of material life takes place under the rule of the commodity form and continually renews the poverty of class society, then the good, beautiful, and true are transcendent to this life. And if everything requisite to preserving and securing material life is produced in this form, then whatever lies beyond it is certainly "superfluous." What is of authentic import to man, the highest truths, the highest goods, and the highest joys, is separated in significance from the necessary by an abyss. They are a "luxury." Aristotle did not conceal this state of affairs. "First philosophy," which includes the highest good and the highest pleasure, is a function of the leisure of the few, for whom all necessities of life are already adequately taken care of. "Pure theory" is appropriated as the profession of an elite and cordoned off with iron chains from the majority of mankind. Aristotle did not assert that the good, the beautiful, and the true are

universally valid and obligatory values which should also permeate and transfigure "from above" the realm of necessity, of the material provision for life. Only when this claim is raised are we in the presence of the concept of culture that became central to bourgeois practice and its corresponding weltanschauung. The ancient theory of the higher value of truths above the realm of necessity includes as well the "higher" level of society. For these truths are supposed to have their abode in the ruling social strata, whose dominant status is in turn confirmed by the theory insofar as concern with the highest truths is supposed to be their profession.

In Aristotelian philosophy, ancient theory is precisely at the point where idealism retreats in the face of social contradictions and expresses them as ontological conditions. Platonic philosophy still contended with the social order of commercial Athens. Plato's idealism is interlaced with motifs of social criticism. What appears as facticity from the standpoint of the Ideas is the material world in which men and things encounter one another as commodities. The just order of the soul is destroyed by

> the passion for wealth which leaves a man not a moment of leisure to attend to anything beyond his personal fortunes. So long as a citizen's whole soul is wrapped up in these, he cannot give a thought to anything but the day's takings.

And the authentic, basic demand of idealism is that this material world be transformed and improved in accordance with the truths yielded by knowledge of the Ideas. Plato's answer to this demand is his program for a reorganization of society. This program reveals what Plato sees as the root of evil. He demands, for the ruling strata, the abolition of private property (even in women and children) and the prohibition of trade. This same program, however, tries to root the contradictions of class society in the depths of human nature, thereby perpetuating them. While the majority of the members of the state are engaged for their entire lives in the cheerless business of providing for the necessities of life, enjoyment of the true, the good, and the beautiful is reserved for a small elite. Although Aristotle still lets ethics terminate in politics, for him the reorganization of society no longer occupies a central role in philosophy. To the extent to which he is more "realistic" than Plato, his idealism is more resigned in the face of the historical tasks of mankind. The true philosopher is for him no longer essentially the true statesman. The distance between facticity and Idea has increased precisely because they are conceived of as in closer relationship. The purport of idealism, viz. realization of the Idea, dissipates. The history of idealism is also the history of its coming to terms with the established order.

Behind the ontological and epistemological separation of the realm of the senses and the realm of Ideas, of sensuousness and reason, of necessity and beauty, stands not only the rejection of a bad historical form of existence, but also its exoneration. The material world (i.e. the manifold forms of the respective "lower" member of this relation) is in itself mere matter, mere potentiality, akin more to Non-Being than to Being. It becomes real only insofar as it partakes of the "higher" world. In all these forms the material world remains bare matter or stuff for something outside it which alone gives it value. All and any truth, goodness, and beauty can accrue to it only "from above" by the grace of the Idea. All activity relating to the material provision of life remains in its essence untrue, bad, and ugly. Even with these characteristics, however, such activity is as necessary as matter is for the Idea. The misery of slave labor, the degradation of men and things to commodities, the joylessness and lowliness in which the totality of the material conditions of existence continuously reproduces itself, all these do not fall within the sphere of interest of idealist philosophy, for they are not yet the actual reality that constitutes the object of this philosophy. Due to its irrevocably material quality, material practice is exonerated from responsibility for the true, good, and beautiful, which is instead taken care of by the pursuit of theory. The ontological cleavage of ideal from material values tranquillizes idealism in all that regards the material processes of life. In idealism, a specific historical form of the division of labor and of social stratification takes on the eternal, metaphysical form of the relationship of necessity and beauty, of matter and Idea.

In the bourgeois epoch the theory of the relationship between necessity and beauty, labor and enjoyment, underwent decisive changes. First, the view that concern with the highest values is appropriated as a profession by particular social strata disappears. In its place emerges the thesis of the universality and universal validity of "culture." With good conscience, the theory of antiquity had expressed the fact that most men had to spend their lives providing for necessities while a small number devoted themselves to enjoyment and truth. Although the fact has not changed, the good conscience has disappeared. Free competition places individuals in the relation of buyers and sellers of labor power. The pure abstractness to which men are reduced in their social relations extends as well to intercourse with ideas. It is no longer supposed to be the case that some are born to and suited to labor and others to leisure, some to necessity and others to beauty. Just as each individual's relation to the market is immediate (without his personal qualities and needs being relevant except as commodities), so his relations to God, to beauty, to goodness, and to truth are relations of immediacy. As abstract beings, all men are supposed to participate equally in these values. As in material practice the product separates itself from the producers and becomes independent as the universal reified form of the "commodity," so in cultural practice a work and its content congeal into universally valid "values." By their very nature the truth of a philosophical judgment, the goodness of a moral action, and the beauty of a work of art should appeal to everyone, relate to everyone, be binding upon everyone. Without distinction of sex or birth, regardless of their position in the process of production, individuals must subordinate themselves to cultural values. They must absorb them into their lives and let their existence be permeated and transfigured by them. "Civilization" is animated and inspired by "culture."

This is not the place to discuss the various attempts to define culture. There is a concept of culture that can serve as an important instrument of social research because it expresses the implication of the mind in the historical process of society. It signifies the totality of social life in a given situation, insofar as both the areas of ideational reproduction (culture in the narrower sense, the "spiritual world") and of material reproduction ("civilization") form a historically distinguishable and comprehensible unity. There is, however, another fairly widespread usage of the concept of culture, in which the spiritual world is lifted out of its social context, making culture a (false) collective noun and attributing (false) universality to it. This second concept of culture (clearly seen in such expressions as "national culture," "Germanic culture," or "Roman culture") plays off the spiritual world against the material world by holding up culture as the realm of authentic values and self-contained ends in opposition to the world of social utility and means. Through the use of this concept, culture is distinguished from civilization and sociologically and valuationally removed from the social process. This concept itself has developed on the basis of a specific historical form of culture, which is termed "affirmative culture" in what follows. By affirmative culture is meant that culture of the bourgeois epoch which led in the course of its own development to the segregation from civilization of the mental and spiritual world as an independent realm of value that is also considered superior to civilization. Its decisive characteristic is the assertion of a universally obligatory, eternally better and more valuable world that must be unconditionally affirmed: a world essentially different from the factual world of the daily struggle for existence, yet realizable by every individual for himself "from within," without any transformation of the state of fact. It is only in this culture that cultural activities and objects gain that value which elevates them above the everyday sphere. Their reception becomes an act of celebration and exaltation.

Although the distinction between civilization and culture may have joined only recently the mental equipment of the social and cultural sciences, the state of affairs that it expresses has long been characteristic of the conduct of life and the weltanschauung of the bourgeois era. "Civilization and culture" is not simply a translation of the ancient relation of purposeful and purposeless, necessary and beautiful. As the purposeless and beautiful were internalized and, along with the qualities of binding universal validity and sublime beauty, made into the cultural values of the bourgeoisie, a realm of apparent unity and apparent freedom was constructed within culture in which the antagonistic relations of existence were supposed to be stabilized and pacified. Culture affirms and conceals the new conditions of social life.

In antiquity, the world of the beautiful beyond necessity was essentially a world of happiness and enjoyment. The ancient theory had never doubted that men's concern was ultimately their worldly gratification, their happiness. Ultimately, not immediately; for man's first concern is the struggle for the preservation and protection of mere existence. In view of the meager development of the productive forces in the ancient economy, it never occurred to philosophy that material practice could ever be fashioned in such a way that it would itself contain the space and time for happiness. Anxiety stands at the source of all idealistic doctrines that look for the highest felicity in ideational practice: anxiety about the uncertainty of all the conditions of life, about the contingency of loss, of dependence, and of poverty, but anxiety also about satiation, ennui, and envy of men and the gods. Nonetheless, anxiety about happiness, which drove philosophy to separate beauty and necessity, preserves the demand for happiness even within the separated sphere. Happiness becomes a preserve, in order for it to be able to be present at all. What man is to find in the philosophical knowledge of the true, the good, and the beautiful is ultimate pleasure, which has all the opposite characteristics of material facticity: permanence in change, purity amidst impurity, freedom amidst unfreedom.

The abstract individual who emerges as the subject of practice at the beginning of the bourgeois epoch also becomes the bearer of a new claim to happiness, merely on the basis of the new constellation of social forces. No longer acting as the representative or delegate of higher social bodies, each separate individual is supposed to take the provision of his needs and the fulfillment of his wants into his own hands and be in immediate relation to his "vocation," to his purpose and goals, without the social, ecclesiastical, and political mediations of feudalism. In this situation the individual was allotted more room for individual requirements and satisfactions: room which developing capitalist production began to fill with more and more objects of possible satisfaction in the form of commodities. To this extent, the bourgeois liberation of the individual made possible a new happiness.

But the universality of this happiness is immediately canceled, since the abstract equality of men realizes itself in capitalist production as concrete inequality. Only a small number of men dispose of the purchasing power required for the quantity of goods necessary in order to secure happiness. Equality does not extend to the conditions for attaining the means. For the strata of the rural and urban proletariat, on whom the bourgeoisie depended in their struggle against the feudal powers, abstract equality could have meaning only as real equality. For the bourgeoisie, when it came to power, abstract equality sufficed for the flourishing of real individual freedom and real individual happiness, since it already disposed of the material conditions that could bring about such satisfaction. Indeed, stopping at the stage of abstract freedom belonged to the conditions of bourgeois rule, which would have been endangered by a transition from abstract to concrete universality. On the other hand, the bourgeoisie could not give up the general character of its demand (that equality be extended to all men) without denouncing itself and openly proclaiming to the ruled strata that, for the majority, everything was still the same with regard to the improvement of the conditions of life. Such a concession became even less likely as growing social wealth made the real fulfillment of this general demand possible while there was in contrast the relatively increasing poverty of the poor in city and country. Thus the demand became a postulate, and its object a mere idea. The vocation of man, to whom general fulfillment is denied in the material world, is hypostatized as an ideal.

The rising bourgeois groups had based their demand for a new social freedom on the universality of human reason. Against the belief in the divinely instituted eternity of a restrictive order they maintained their belief in progress, in a better future. But reason and freedom did not extend beyond these groups' interest, which came into increasing opposition to the interest of the majority. To accusing questions the bourgeoisie gave a decisive answer: affirmative culture. The latter is fundamentally idealist. To the need of the isolated individual it responds with general humanity, to bodily misery with the beauty of the soul, to external bondage with internal freedom, to brutal egoism with the duty of the realm of virtue. Whereas during the period of the militant rise of the new society all of these ideas had a progressive character by pointing beyond the attained organization of existence, they entered increasingly into the service of the suppression of the discontented masses and of mere self-justifying exaltation, once bourgeois rule began to be stabilized. They

concealed the physical and psychic vitiation of the individual.

But bourgeois idealism is not merely ideology, for it expresses a correct objective content. It contains not only the justification of the established form of existence, but also the pain of its establishment: not only quiescence about what is, but also remembrance of what could be. By making suffering and sorrow into eternal, universal forces, great bourgeois art has continually shattered in the hearts of men the facile resignation of everyday life. By painting in the luminous colors of this world the beauty of men and things and trans-mundane happiness, it has planted real longing alongside poor consolation and false consecration in the soil of bourgeois life. This art raised pain and sorrow, desperation and loneliness, to the level of metaphysical powers and set individuals against one another and the gods in the nakedness of physical immediacy, beyond all social mediations. This exaggeration contains the higher truth that such a world cannot be changed piecemeal, but only through its destruction. Classical *yes!* bourgeois art put its ideal forms at such a distance from everyday occurrence that those whose suffering and hope reside in daily life could only rediscover themselves through a leap into a totally other world. In this way art nourished the belief that all previous history had been only the dark and tragic prehistory of a coming existence. And philosophy took this idea seriously enough to be concerned about its realization. Hegel's system is the last protest against the degradation of the idea: against playing officiously with the mind as though it were an object that really has nothing to do with human history. At least idealism maintained that the materialism of bourgeois practice is not the last word and that mankind must be led beyond it. Thus idealism belongs to a more progressive stage of development than later positivism, which in fighting metaphysical ideas eliminates not only their metaphysical character, but their content as well. It thus links itself inevitably to the status quo.

Culture is supposed to assume concern for the individual's claim to happiness. But the social antagonisms at the root of culture let it admit this claim only in an internalized and rationalized form. In a society that reproduces itself through economic competition, the mere demand for a happier social existence constitutes rebellion. For if men value the enjoyment of worldly happiness, then they certainly cannot value acquisitive activity, profit, and the authority of the economic powers that preserve the existence of this society. The claim to happiness has a dangerous ring in an order that for the majority means need, privation, and toil. The contradictions of such an order provide the impetus to the idealization of that claim. But the real gratification of individuals cannot be contained by an idealistic dynamic which either continually postpones gratification or transmutes it into striving for the unattained. It can only be realized *against* idealist culture, and only *against* this culture is it propagated as a general demand: the demand for a real transformation of the material conditions of existence, for a new life, for a new form of labor and of enjoyment. Thus it has remained active in the revolutionary groups that have fought the expanding new system of injustice since the waning of the Middle Ages. And while idealism surrenders the earth to bourgeois society and makes its ideas unreal by finding satisfaction in heaven and the soul, materialist philosophy takes seriously the concern for happiness and fights for its realization in history. In the philosophy of the Enlightenment, this connection becomes clear.

> False philosophy can, like theology, promise us an eternal happiness and, cradling us in beautiful chimeras, lead us there at the expense of our days or our pleasure. Quite different and wiser, true philosophy affords only a temporal happiness. It sows roses and flowers in our path and teaches us to pick them.

Idealist philosophy, too, admits the centrality of human happiness. But in its controversy with stoicism, the Enlightenment adopted precisely that form of the claim to happiness which is incompatible with idealism and with which affirmative culture cannot deal:

> And how we shall be anti-Stoics! These philosophers are strict, sad, and hard; we shall be tender, joyful, and agreeable. All soul, they abstract from their body; all body, we shall abstract from our soul. They show themselves inaccessible to pleasure and pain; we shall be proud to feel both the one and the other. Aiming at the sublime, they elevate themselves above all occurrences and believe themselves to be truly men only insofar as they cease to exist. Ourselves, we shall not control what governs us, although circumstances will not command our feelings.

By acknowledging their lordship and our bondage, we shall try to make them agreeable to us, in the conviction that it is here that the happiness of life resides. Finally, we shall believe ourselves that much happier, the more we feel nature, humanity, and all social virtues. We shall recognize none but these, nor any life other than this one.

★ ★ ★

In its idea of pure humanity, affirmative culture took up the historical demand for the general liberation of the individual. "If we consider mankind as we know it according to the laws which it embodies, we find nothing higher in man than humanity." This concept is meant to comprise everything that is directed toward "man's noble education to reason and freedom, to more refined senses and instincts, to the most delicate and the heartiest health, to the fulfillment and domination of the earth." All human laws and forms of government are to have the exclusive purpose of "enabling man, free from attack by others, to exercise his powers and acquire a more beautiful and freer enjoyment of life." The highest point which man can attain is a community of free and rational persons in which each has the same opportunity to unfold and fulfill all of his powers. The concept of the person, in which the struggle against repressive collectivities has remained active through the present, disregards social conflicts and conventions and addresses itself to all individuals. No one relieves the individual of the burden of his existence, but no one prescribes his rights and sphere of action – no one except the "law in his own breast."

> Nature intended that man generate entirely out of himself everything going beyond the mechanical organization of his animal existence, and that he partake of no other happiness or perfection than that which he provides for himself, free of instinct, by means of his own reason.

All wealth and all poverty derive from him and react back upon him. Each individual is immediate to himself: without worldly or heavenly mediations. And this immediacy also holds for his relations to others. The clearest representation of this idea of the person is to be found in classical literature since Shakespeare. In its dramas, individuals are so close to one another that between them there is nothing that is in principle ineffable or inexpressible. Verse makes possible what has already become impossible in prosaic reality. In poetry men can transcend all social isolation and distance and speak of the first and last things. They overcome the factual loneliness in the glow of great and beautiful words; they may even let loneliness appear in its metaphysical beauty. Criminal and saint, prince and servant, sage and fool, rich and poor join in discussion whose free flow is supposed to give rise to truth. The unity represented by art and the pure humanity of its persons are unreal; they are the counterimage of what occurs in social reality. The critical and revolutionary force of the ideal, which in its very unreality keeps alive the best desires of men amidst a bad reality, becomes clearest in those times when the satiated social strata have accomplished the betrayal of their own ideals. The ideal, to be sure, was conceived in such a fashion that its regressive and apologetic, rather than its progressive and critical, characteristics predominated. Its realization is supposed to be effected through the cultural education of individuals. Culture means not so much a better world as a nobler one: a world to be brought about not through the overthrow of the material order of life but through events in the individual's soul. Humanity becomes an inner state. Freedom, goodness, and beauty become spiritual qualities: understanding for everything human, knowledge about the greatness of all times, appreciation of everything difficult and sublime, respect for history in which all of this has become what it is. This inner state is to be the source of action that does not come into conflict with the given order. Culture belongs not to him who comprehends the truths of humanity as a battle cry, but to him in whom they have become a posture which leads to a mode of proper behavior: exhibiting harmony and reflectiveness even in daily routine. Culture should ennoble the given by permeating it, rather than putting something new in its place. It thus exalts the individual without freeing him from his factual debasement. Culture speaks of the dignity of "man" without concerning itself with a concretely more dignified status for men. The beauty of culture is above all an inner beauty and can only reach the external world from within. Its realm is essentially a realm of the *soul*.

That culture is a matter of spiritual (*seelisch*) values is constitutive of the affirmative concept of culture at least since Herder. Spiritual values belong to the definition of culture in contrast to mere civilization.

Alfred Weber was merely summing up a conceptual scheme with a long history when he wrote:

> Culture … is merely spiritual expression and spiritual will and thus the expression and will of an "essence" that lies behind all intellectual mastery of existence, of a "soul" that, in its striving for expression and in its willing, pays no regard to purposiveness and utility. … From this follows the concept of culture as the prevailing form in which the spiritual is expressed and released in the materially and spiritually given substance of existence.

The soul posited by this interpretation is other and more than the totality of psychic forces and mechanisms (such as might be the object of empirical psychology). Rather, this noncorporeal being of man is asserted as the real substance of the individual.

The character of the soul as substance has since Descartes been founded upon the uniqueness of the ego as *res cogitans*. While the entire world outside the ego becomes in principle one of measurable matter with calculable motion, the ego is the only dimension of reality to evade the materialistic rationality of the rising bourgeoisie. By coming into opposition to the corporeal world as a substance differing from it in essence, the ego is subjected to a remarkable division into two regions. The ego as the subject of thought (*mens*, mind) remains, in the independence of self-certainty, on this side of the being of matter – its a priori, as it were – while Descartes attempts to explain materialistically the ego as soul (*anima*), as the subject of "passions" (love and hate, joy and sorrow, shame, jealousy, regret, gratitude, and so forth). The passions of the soul are traced to blood circulation and its transformation in the brain. This reduction does not quite succeed. To be sure, all muscular movements and sense perceptions are thought to depend on the nerves, which "are like small filaments or small pipes that all come from the brain," but the nerves themselves contain "a certain very fine air or wind called animal spirits." Despite this immaterial residue, the tendency of the interpretation is clear: the ego is either mind (thought, *cogito me cogitare*) or, insofar as it is not merely thought (*cogitatio*), it is no longer authentically ego, but rather corporeal. In the latter case, the properties and activities ascribed to it belonged to *res extensa*. Yet they do not quite admit of being dissolved into matter. The soul remains an unmastered intermediate realm between the unshakable self-certainty of pure thought and the mathematical and physical certainty of material being. Already in the original project of rationalism there is no room in the system for what is later considered actually to compose the soul, viz. the individual's feelings, appetites, desires, and instincts. The position within rationalism of empirical psychology, i.e. of the discipline really dealing with the human soul, is characteristic, for it exists although reason is unable to legitimate it.

Kant polemized against the treatment of empirical psychology within rational metaphysics (by Baumgarten). Empirical psychology must be "completely banished from the domain of metaphysics; it is indeed already completely excluded by the very idea of the latter science." But, he goes on, "in conformity, however, with scholastic usage we must allow it some sort of a place (although as an episode only) in metaphysics, and this from economical motives, because it is not yet so rich as to be able to form a subject of study by itself, and yet is too important to be entirely excluded and forced to settle elsewhere. ... It is thus merely a stranger who is taken in for a short while until he finds a home of his own, in a complete anthropology." And in his metaphysics lectures of 1792–93 Kant expressed himself even more sceptically about this "stranger": "Is an empirical psychology possible as science? No – our knowledge of the soul is entirely too limited."

Rationalism's estrangement from the soul points to an important state of affairs. For in fact the soul does not enter into the social labor process. Concrete labor is reduced to abstract labor that makes possible the exchange of the products of labor as commodities. The idea of the soul seems to allude to those areas of life which cannot be managed by the abstract reason of bourgeois practice. It is as though the processing of matter is accomplished only by a part of the *res cogitans:* by technical reason. Beginning with the division of labor in manufacture and brought to completion in machine industry, "the intellectual [*geistigen*] potencies of the material process of production" come into opposition to the immediate producers as "the property of another and as a power that rules them." To the extent that thought is not immediately technical reason, it has freed itself since Descartes from conscious connection with social practice and tolerates the reification that it itself promotes. When in this practice

human relations appear as material relations, as the very laws of things, philosophy abandons the individual to this appearance by retreating and re-establishing itself at the level of the transcendental constitution of the world in pure subjectivity. Transcendental philosophy does not make contact with reification, for it investigates only the process of cognition of the immemorially (*je schon*) reified world.

The soul is not comprehended by the dichotomy of *res cogitans* and *res extensa*, for it cannot be understood merely as one or the other. Kant destroyed rational psychology without arriving at an empirical psychology. For Hegel, every single attribute of the soul is comprehended from the standpoint of mind (*Geist*), into which the soul passes over (*übergeht*); for mind reveals itself to be the soul's true content. The soul is essentially characterized by its "not yet being mind." Where Hegel treats psychology, i.e. the human soul, in his doctrine of subjective mind, the guiding principle is no longer soul but mind. Hegel deals with the soul principally as part of "anthropology," where it is still completely "bound to the attributes of nature." He examines planetary life on a general scale, natural racial distinctions, the ages of man, magic, somnambulism, various forms of psychopathic self-images, and – only for a few pages – the "real soul." For him the latter is nothing but the transition to the ego of consciousness, wherewith the anthropological doctrine of soul is already left behind, and the phenomenology of mind arrived at. The soul is thus allotted to physiological anthropology on the one hand and the philosophy of mind on the other. Even in the greatest system of bourgeois rationalism there is no place for the independence of the soul. The authentic objects of psychology, feelings, instincts, and will, are conceived only as forms of the existence of mind.

With its concept of the soul, however, affirmative culture means precisely what is not mind. Indeed, the concept of soul comes into ever sharper contradiction to the concept of mind. What is meant by soul "is forever inaccessible to the lucid mind, to the understanding, or to empirical, factual research. ... One could sooner dissect with a knife a theme by Beethoven or dissolve it with an acid than analyze the soul with the means of abstract thought." In the idea of the soul, the noncorporeal faculties, activities, and properties of man (according to the traditional classifications, reason, will, and appetite) are combined in an indivisible unity that manifestly endures through all of the individual's behavior and, indeed, constitutes his individuality.

The concept of the soul typical of affirmative culture was not developed by philosophy, and the examples from Descartes, Kant, and Hegel were intended only to illustrate philosophy's embarrassment with regard to the soul. This concept found its first positive expression in the literature of the Renaissance. Here the soul is in the first instance an unexplored part of the world to be discovered and enjoyed. To it are extended those demands with whose proclamation the new society accompanied the rational domination of the world by liberated man: freedom and the intrinsic worth of the individual. The riches of the soul, of the "inner life," were thus the correlate of the new-found riches of external life. Interest in the neglected "individual, incomparable, living states" of the soul belonged to the program of "living out one's life fully and entirely." Concern with the soul "reacts upon the increasing differentiation of individualities and augments man's consciousness of enjoying life with a natural development rooted in man's essence." Seen from the standpoint of the consummated affirmative culture of the eighteenth and nineteenth centuries, this spiritual demand appears as an unfulfilled promise. The idea of "natural development" remains, but it signifies primarily inner development. In the external world the soul cannot freely "live itself out." The organization of this world by the capitalist labor process has turned the development of the individual into economic competition and left the satisfaction of his needs to the commodity market. Affirmative culture uses the soul as a protest against reification, only to succumb to it in the end. The soul is sheltered as the only area of life that has not been drawn into the social labor process.

The word "soul" gives the higher man a feeling of his inner existence, separated from all that is real or has evolved, a very definite feeling of the most secret and genuine potentialities of his life, his destiny, his history. In the early stages of the languages of all cultures, the word "soul" is a sign that encompasses everything that is not world.

And in this − negative − quality it now becomes the only still immaculate guarantor of bourgeois ideals. The soul glorifies resignation. The ideal that man,

individual, irreplaceable man, beyond all natural and social distinctions, be the ultimate end; that truth, goodness, and justice hold between men; that all human weaknesses be expiated by humanity − this ideal can be represented, in a society determined by the economic law of value, only by the soul and as spiritual occurrence. All else is inhuman and discredited. The soul alone obviously has no exchange value. The value of the soul does not enter into the body in such a way as to congeal into an object and become a commodity. There can be a beautiful soul in an ugly body, a healthy one in a sick body, a noble one in a common body − and vice versa. There is a kernel of truth in the proposition that what happens to the body cannot affect the soul. But in the established order this truth has taken on a terrible form. The freedom of the soul was used to excuse the poverty, martyrdom, and bondage of the body. It served the ideological surrender of existence to the economy of capitalism. Correctly understood, however, spiritual freedom does not mean the participation of man in an eternal beyond where everything is righted when the individual can no longer benefit from it. Rather, it anticipates the higher truth that in this world a form of social existence is possible in which the economy does not preempt the entire life of individuals. Man does not live by bread alone; this truth is thoroughly falsified by the interpretation that spiritual nourishment is an adequate substitute for too little bread.

The soul appears to escape reification just as it does the law of value. As a matter of fact, it can almost be defined by the assertion that through its means all reified relations are dissolved into human relations and negated. The soul institutes an all-encompassing inner community of men that spans the centuries. "The first thought in the first human soul links up with the last thought in the last human soul." In the realm of culture spiritual education and spiritual greatness overcome the inequality and unfreedom of everyday competition, for men participate in culture as free and equal beings. He who looks to the soul sees through economic relations to men in themselves. Where the soul speaks, the contingent position and merit of men in the social process are transcended. Love breaks through barriers between rich and poor, high and lowly. Friendship keeps faith even with the outcast and despised, and truth raises its voice even before

Soul ⇒ empty, internal ideal.

the tyrant's throne. Despite all social obstacles and encroachments, the soul develops in the individual's interior. The most cramped surroundings are large enough to expand into an infinite environment for the soul. In its classical era, affirmative culture continually poetized the soul in such a manner.

The individual's soul is first set off from, and against, his body. Its adoption as the decisive area of life can have two meanings: the release of sensuality (as the irrelevant area of life) or, to the contrary, the subjection of sensuality to the domination of the soul. Affirmative culture unequivocally took the second course. Release of sensuality would be release of enjoyment, which presupposes the absence of guilty conscience and the real possibility of gratification. In bourgeois society, such a trend is increasingly opposed by the necessity of disciplining discontented masses. The internalization of enjoyment through spiritualization therefore becomes one of the decisive tasks of cultural education. By being incorporated into spiritual life, sensuality is to be harnessed and transfigured. From the coupling of sensuality and the soul proceeds the bourgeois idea of love.

The spiritualization of sensuality fuses matter with heaven and death with eternity. The weaker the belief in a heavenly beyond, the stronger the veneration of the spiritual beyond. The idea of love absorbs the longing for the permanence of worldly happiness, for the blessing of the unconditional, for the conquest of termination. In bourgeois poetry, lovers love in opposition to everyday inconstancy, to the demands of reality, to the subjugation of the individual, and to death. Death does not come from outside, but from love itself. The liberation of the individual was effected in a society based not on solidarity but on conflict of interests among individuals. The individual has the character of an independent, self-sufficient monad. His relation to the (human and non-human) world is either abstractly immediate (the individual constitutes the world immemorially in itself as knowing, feeling, and willing ego) or abstractly mediated (i.e. determined by the blind laws of the production of commodities and of the market). In neither case is the monadic isolation of the individual overcome. To do so would mean the establishment of real solidarity and presupposes the replacement of individualist society by a higher form of social existence.

The idea of love, however, requires that the individual overcome monadic isolation and find fulfillment through the surrender of individuality in the unconditional solidarity of two persons. In a society in which conflict of interest is the *principium individuationis*, this complete surrender can appear in pure form only in death. For only death eliminates all of the external conditions that destroy permanent solidarity and in the struggle with which individuals wear themselves out. It appears not as the cessation of existence in nothingness, but rather as the only possible consummation of love and thus as its deepest significance.

While in art love is elevated to tragedy, it threatens to become mere duty and habit in everyday bourgeois life. Love contains the individualistic principle of the new society: it demands exclusiveness. The latter appears in the requirement of unconditional fidelity which, originating in the soul, should also be obligatory for sensuality. But the spiritualization of sensuality demands of the latter what it cannot achieve: withdrawal from change and fluctuation and absorption into the unity and indivisibility of the person. Just at this point, inwardness and outwardness, potentiality and reality are supposed to be found in a pre-established harmony which the anarchic principle of society destroys everywhere. This contradiction makes exclusive fidelity untrue and vitiates sensuality, which finds an outlet in the furtive improprieties of the petit bourgeois.

Purely private relationships such as love and friendship are the only realm in which the dominion of the soul is supposed to be immediately confirmed in reality. Otherwise the soul has primarily the function of elevating men to the ideal without urging the latter's realization. The soul has a tranquilizing effect. Because it is exempted from reification, it suffers from it least, consequently meeting it with the least resistance. Since the soul's meaning and worth do not fall within historical reality, it can maintain itself unharmed in a bad reality. Spiritual joys are cheaper than bodily ones; they are less dangerous and are granted more willingly. An essential difference between the soul and the mind is that the former is not oriented toward critical knowledge of truth. The soul can understand what the mind must condemn. Conceptual knowledge attempts to distinguish the one from the other and resolves contradiction only on the basis of the "dispassionately proceeding necessity of the object," while the soul rapidly reconciles all "external" antitheses in some "internal" unity. If there is a Western, Germanic, Faustian soul, then a Western, Germanic, and Faustian culture belongs to it, and feudal, capitalist, and socialist societies are nothing but manifestations of such souls. Their firm antitheses dissolve into the beautiful and profound unity of culture. The reconciliatory nature of the soul manifests itself clearly where psychology is made the organon of the social and cultural sciences, without foundation in a theory of society that penetrates behind culture. The soul has a strong affinity with historicism. As early as Herder we find the idea that the soul, freed from rationalism, should be capable of universal empathy (*einfühlen*). He adjures the soul,

> Entire nature of the soul that rules all things, that models all other inclinations and psychic forces after itself and tinges even the most indifferent actions – in order to feel these, do not answer in words, but penetrate into the epoch, into the region of heaven, into all of history, feel yourself into everything. …

With its property of universal empathy the soul devalues the distinction between true and false, good and bad, or rational and irrational that can be made through the analysis of social reality with regard to the attainable potentialities of the organization of material existence. Every historical epoch, then, as Ranke stated, manifests but another facet of the same human spirit. Each one possesses its own meaning, "and its value rests not on what results from it, but on its very existence, on its own self." Soul has nothing to do with the correctness of what it expresses. It can do honor to a bad cause (as in Dostoevski's case). In the struggle for a better human future, profound and refined souls may stand aside or on the wrong side. The soul takes fright at the hard truth of theory, which points up the necessity of changing an impoverished form of existence. How can an external transformation determine the authentic, inner substance of man? Soul lets one be soft and compliant, submitting to the facts; for, after all, they do not really matter. In this way the soul was able to become a useful factor in the technique of mass domination when, in the epoch of authoritarian states, all available forces had to be mobilized against a real transformation of the social

existence. With the help of the soul, the bourgeoisie in advanced capitalist society buried its ideals of an earlier period. That soul is of the essence makes a good slogan when only power is of the essence.

But the Soul really is essential – as the unexpressed, unfulfilled life of the individual. The culture of souls absorbed in a false form those forces and wants which could find no place in everyday life. The cultural ideal assimilated men's longing for a happier life: for humanity, goodness, joy, truth, and solidarity. Only, in this ideal, they are all furnished with the affirmative accent of belonging to a higher, purer, nonprosaic world. They are either internalized as the duty of the individual soul (to achieve what is constantly betrayed in the external existence of the whole) or represented as objects of art (whereby their reality is relegated to a realm essentially different from that of everyday life). There is a good reason for the exemplification of the cultural ideal in art, for only in art has bourgeois society tolerated its own ideals and taken them seriously as a general demand. What counts as utopia, phantasy, and rebellion in the world of fact is allowed in art. There affirmative culture has displayed the forgotten truths over which "realism" triumphs in daily life. The medium of beauty decontaminates truth and sets it apart from the present. What occurs in art occurs with no obligation. When this beautiful world is not completely represented as something long past (the classic artistic portrayal of victorious humanity, Goethe's *Iphigenie*, is a "historical" drama), it is deprived of concrete relevance by the magic of beauty.

In the medium of beauty, men have been permitted to partake of happiness. But even beauty has been affirmed with good conscience only in the ideal of art, for it contains a dangerous violence that threatens the given form of existence. The immediate sensuousness of beauty immediately suggests sensual happiness. According to Hume the power to stimulate pleasure belongs to the essential character of beauty. Pleasure is not merely a by-product of beauty, but constitutes its very essence. And for Nietzsche beauty reawakens "aphrodisiac bliss." He polemizes against Kant's definition of the beautiful as the object of completely disinterested pleasure (*Wohlgefallen*) and opposes to it Stendhal's assertion that beauty is "une promesse de bonheur." Therein lies its danger in a society that must rationalize and regulate happiness. Beauty is fundamentally shameless. It displays what may not be promised openly and what is denied the majority. In the region of mere sensuality, separated from its connection with the ideal, beauty falls prey to the general devaluation of this sphere. Loosed from all spiritual and mental demands, beauty may be enjoyed in good conscience only in well delimited areas, with the awareness that it is only for a short period of relaxation or dissipation.

Bourgeois society has liberated individuals, but as persons who are to keep themselves in check. From the beginning, the prohibition of pleasure was a condition of freedom. A society split into classes can afford to make man into a means of pleasure only in the form of bondage and exploitation. Since in the new order the regulated classes rendered services not immediately, with their persons, but only mediated by the production of surplus value for the market, it was considered inhuman to exploit an underling's body as a source of pleasure, i.e., to use men directly as means (Kant). On the other hand, harnessing their bodies and intelligence for profit was considered a natural activation of freedom. Correspondingly, for the poor, hiring oneself out to work in a factory became a moral duty, while hiring out one's body as a means to pleasure was depravity and "prostitution." Also, in this society, poverty is a condition of profit and power, yet dependence takes place in the medium of abstract freedom. The sale of labor power is supposed to occur due to the poor man's own decision. He labors in the service of his employer, while he may keep for himself and cultivate as a sacred preserve the abstraction that is his person-in-itself, separated from its socially valuable functions. He is supposed to keep it pure. The prohibition against marketing the body not merely as an instrument of labor but as an instrument of pleasure as well is one of the chief social and psychological roots of bourgeois patriarchal ideology. Here reification has firm limits important to the system. Nonetheless, insofar as the body becomes a commodity as a manifestation or bearer of the sexual function, this occurs subject to general contempt. The taboo is violated. This holds not only for prostitution but for all production of pleasure that does not occur for reasons of "social hygiene" in the service of reproduction.

Those social strata, however, which are kept back in semi-medieval forms, pushed to the lowest margin of society, and thoroughly demoralized, provide, even in these circumstances, an anticipatory memory. When the body has completely become an object, a beautiful thing, it can foreshadow a new happiness. In suffering the most extreme reification man triumphs over reification. The artistry of the beautiful body, its effortless agility and relaxation, which can be displayed today only in the circus, vaudeville, and burlesque, herald the joy to which men will attain in being liberated from the ideal, once mankind, having become a true subject, succeeds in the mastery of matter. When all links to the affirmative ideal have been dissolved, when in the context of an existence marked by knowledge it becomes possible to have real enjoyment without any rationalization and without the least puritanical guilt feeling, when sensuality, in other words, is entirely released by the soul, then the first glimmer of a new culture emerges.

[…]

From the standpoint of the interest of the status quo, the real abolition of affirmative culture must appear utopian. For it goes beyond the social totality in which culture has been enmeshed. Insofar as in Western thought culture has meant affirmative culture, the abolition of its affirmative character will appear as the abolition of culture as such. To the extent that culture has transmuted fulfillable, but factually unfulfilled, longings and instincts, it will lose its object. The assertion that today culture has become unnecessary contains a dynamic, progressive element. It is only that culture's lack of object in the authoritarian state derives not from fulfillment but from the awareness that even keeping alive the desire for fulfillment is dangerous in the present situation. When culture gets to the point of having to sustain fulfillment itself and no longer merely desire, it will no longer be able to do so in contents that, as such, bear an affirmative character. "Gratitude" will then perhaps really be its essence, as Nietzsche asserted of all beautiful and great art. Beauty will find a new embodiment when it no longer is represented as real illusion but, instead, expresses reality and joy in reality. A foretaste of such potentialities can be had in experiencing the unassuming display of Greek statues or the music of Mozart or late Beethoven. Perhaps, however, beauty and its enjoyment will not even devolve upon art. Perhaps art as such will have no objects. For the common man it has been confined to museums for at least a century. The museum was the most suitable place for reproducing in the individual withdrawal from facticity and the consolation of being elevated to a more dignified world – an experience limited by temporal restriction to special occasions. This museum-like quality was also present in the ceremonious treatment of the classics, where dignity alone was enough to still all explosive elements. What a classic writer or thinker did or said did not have to be taken too seriously, for it belonged to another world and could not come into conflict with this one. The authoritarian state's polemic against the cultural (*museal*) establishment contains an element of correct knowledge. But when it opposes "grotesque forms of edification," it only wants to replace obsolete methods of affirmation with more modern ones.

Every attempt to sketch out the counterimage of affirmative culture comes up against the ineradicable cliché about the fools' paradise. It would be better to accept this cliché than the one about the transformation of the earth into a gigantic community center, which seems to be at the root of some theories of culture. There is talk of a "general diffusion of cultural values," of the "right of all members of the nation [*Volk*] to cultural benefits," of "raising the level of the nation's physical, spiritual, and ethical culture." But all this would be merely raising the ideology of a conflicted society to the conscious mode of life of another, making a new virtue out of its necessity. When Kautsky speaks of the "coming happiness," he means primarily "the gladdening effects of scientific work,"

and "sympathetic enjoyment in the areas of science and art, nature, sport, and games." "Everything hitherto created in the way of culture should be … put at the disposal of the masses," whose task is "to conquer this entire culture for themselves." This can mean nothing other than winning the masses to the social order that is affirmed by the "entire culture." Such views miss the main point: the abolition of this culture. It is not the primitive, materialistic element of the idea of fools' paradise that is false, but its perpetuation. As long as the world is mutable there will be enough conflict, sorrow, and suffering to destroy the idyllic picture. As long as there is a realm of necessity, there will be enough need. Even a nonaffirmative culture will be burdened with mutability and necessity: dancing on the volcano, laughter in sorrow, flirtation with death. As long as this is true, the reproduction of life will still involve the reproduction of culture: the molding of unfulfilled longings and the purification of unfulfilled instincts. In affirmative culture, renunciation is linked to the external vitiation of the individual, to his compliance with a bad order. The struggle against ephemerality does not liberate sensuality but devalues it and is, indeed, possible only on the basis of this devaluation. This unhappiness is not metaphysical. It is the product of an irrational social organization. By eliminating affirmative culture, the abolition of this social organization will not eliminate individuality, but realize it. And "if we are ever happy at all, we can do nothing other than promote culture."

4

"The Culture Industry: Enlightenment as Mass Deception" (1944)

Max Horkheimer and Theodor Adorno

The sociological theory that the loss of the support of objectively established religion, the dissolution of the last remnants of precapitalism, together with technological and social differentiation or specialization, have led to cultural chaos is disproved every day; for culture now impresses the same stamp on everything. Films, radio and magazines make up a system which is uniform as a whole and in every part. Even the aesthetic activities of political opposites are one in their enthusiastic obedience to the rhythm of the iron system. The decorative industrial management buildings and exhibition centers in authoritarian countries are much the same as anywhere else. The huge gleaming towers that shoot up everywhere are outward signs of the ingenious planning of international concerns, toward which the unleashed entrepreneurial system (whose monuments are a mass of gloomy houses and business premises in grimy, spiritless cities) was already hastening. Even now the older houses just outside the concrete city centers look like slums, and the new bungalows on the outskirts are at one with the flimsy structures of world fairs in their praise of technical progress and their built-in demand to be discarded after a short while like empty food cans. Yet the city housing projects designed to perpetuate the individual as a supposedly independent unit in a small hygienic dwelling make him all the more subservient to his adversary – the absolute power of capitalism. Because the inhabitants, as producers and as consumers, are drawn into the center in search of work and pleasure,

all the living units crystallize into well-organized complexes. The striking unity of microcosm and macrocosm presents men with a model of their culture: the false identity of the general and the particular. Under monopoly all mass culture is identical, and the lines of its artificial framework begin to show through. The people at the top are no longer so interested in concealing monopoly: as its violence becomes more open, so its power grows. Movies and radio need no longer pretend to be art. The truth that they are just business is made into an ideology in order to justify the rubbish they deliberately produce. They call themselves industries; and when their directors' incomes are published, any doubt about the social utility of the finished products is removed.

Interested parties explain the culture industry in technological terms. It is alleged that because millions participate in it, certain reproduction processes are necessary that inevitably require identical needs in innumerable places to be satisfied with identical goods. The technical contrast between the few production centers and the large number of widely dispersed consumption points is said to demand organization and planning by management. Furthermore, it is claimed that standards were based in the first place on consumers' needs, and for that reason were accepted with so little resistance. The result is the circle of manipulation and retroactive need in which the unity of the system grows ever stronger. No mention is made of the fact that the basis on which technology acquires power over society is the power of those whose economic hold over society is greatest. A technological rationale is the rationale of domination itself. It is the coercive nature of society alienated from itself. Automobiles,

Max Horkheimer and Theodor W. Adorno, "The Culture Industry," pp. 120–47 from *Dialectic of Enlightenment*. New York: Herder and Herder, 1972.

bombs, and movies keep the whole thing together until their leveling element shows its strength in the very wrong which it furthered. It has made the technology of the culture industry no more than the achievement of standardization and mass production, sacrificing whatever involved a distinction between the logic of the work and that of the social system. This is the result not of a law of movement in technology as such but of its function in today's economy. The need which might resist central control has already been suppressed by the control of the individual consciousness. The step from the telephone to the radio has clearly distinguished the roles. The former still allowed the subscriber to play the role of subject, and was liberal. The latter is democratic: it turns all participants into listeners and authoritatively subjects them to broadcast programs which are all exactly the same. No machinery of rejoinder has been devised, and private broadcasters are denied any freedom. They are confined to the apocryphal field of the "amateur," and also have to accept organization from above. But any trace of spontaneity from the public in official broadcasting is controlled and absorbed by talent scouts, studio competitions and official programs of every kind selected by professionals. Talented performers belong to the industry long before it displays them; otherwise they would not be so eager to fit in. The attitude of the public, which ostensibly and actually favors the system of the culture industry, is a part of the system and not an excuse for it. If one branch of art follows the same formula as one with a very different medium and content; if the dramatic intrigue of broadcast soap operas becomes no more than useful material for showing how to master technical problems at both ends of the scale of musical experience – real jazz or a cheap imitation; or if a movement from a Beethoven symphony is crudely "adapted" for a film sound-track in the same way as a Tolstoy novel is garbled in a film script: then the claim that this is done to satisfy the spontaneous wishes of the public is no more than hot air. We are closer to the facts if we explain these phenomena as inherent in the technical and personnel apparatus which, down to its last cog, itself forms part of the economic mechanism of selection. In addition there is the agreement – or at least the determination – of all executive authorities not to produce or sanction anything that in any way differs from their own rules, their own ideas about consumers, or above all themselves.

In our age the objective social tendency is incarnate in the hidden subjective purposes of company directors, the foremost among whom are in the most powerful sectors of industry – steel, petroleum, electricity, and chemicals. Culture monopolies are weak and dependent in comparison. They cannot afford to neglect their appeasement of the real holders of power if their sphere of activity in mass society (a sphere producing a specific type of commodity which anyhow is still too closely bound up with easygoing liberalism and Jewish intellectuals) is not to undergo a series of purges. The dependence of the most powerful broadcasting company on the electrical industry, or of the motion picture industry on the banks, is characteristic of the whole sphere, whose individual branches are themselves economically interwoven. All are in such close contact that the extreme concentration of mental forces allows demarcation lines between different firms and technical branches to be ignored. The ruthless unity in the culture industry is evidence of what will happen in politics. Marked differentiations such as those of A and B films, or of stories in magazines in different price ranges, depend not so much on subject matter as on classifying, organizing, and labeling consumers. Something is provided for all so that none may escape; the distinctions are emphasized and extended. The public is catered for with a hierarchical range of mass-produced products of varying quality, thus advancing the rule of complete quantification. Everybody must behave (as if spontaneously) in accordance with his previously determined and indexed level, and choose the category of mass product turned out for his type. Consumers appear as statistics on research organization charts, and are divided by income groups into red, green, and blue areas; the technique is that used for any type of propaganda.

How formalized the procedure is can be seen when the mechanically differentiated products prove to be all alike in the end. That the difference between the Chrysler range and General Motors products is basically illusory strikes every child with a keen interest in varieties. What connoisseurs discuss as good or bad points serve only to perpetuate the semblance of competition and range of choice. The same applies to the Warner Brothers and Metro Goldwyn Mayer productions. But even the differences between the more expensive and cheaper models put out by the same firm steadily diminish: for automobiles, there are such differences as the number of cylinders, cubic capacity, details of patented gadgets; and for films there are the number of stars, the extravagant use of technology, labor, and equipment, and the introduction of the latest psychological formulas. The universal criterion of merit is the amount of "conspicuous production," of blatant cash investment. The varying budgets in the culture industry do not bear the slightest relation to factual values, to the meaning of the products themselves. Even the technical media are relentlessly forced into uniformity. Television aims at a synthesis of radio and film, and is held up only because the interested parties have not yet reached agreement, but its consequences will be quite enormous and promise to intensify the impoverishment of aesthetic matter so drastically, that by tomorrow the thinly veiled identity of all industrial culture products can come triumphantly out into the open, derisively fulfilling the Wagnerian dream of the *Gesamtkunstwerk* – the fusion of all the arts in one work. The alliance of word, image, and music is all the more perfect than in *Tristan* because the sensuous elements which all approvingly reflect the surface of social reality are in principle embodied in the same technical process, the unity of which becomes its distinctive content. This process integrates all the elements of the production, from the novel (shaped with an eye to the film) to the last sound effect. It is the triumph of invested capital, whose title as absolute master is etched deep into the hearts of the dispossessed in the employment line; it is the meaningful content of every film, whatever plot the production team may have selected.

The man with leisure has to accept what the culture manufacturers offer him. Kant's formalism still expected a contribution from the individual, who was thought to relate the varied experiences of the senses to fundamental concepts; but industry robs the individual of his function. Its prime service to the customer is to do his schematizing for him. Kant said that there was a secret mechanism in the soul which prepared direct intuitions in such a way that they could be fitted into the system of pure reason. But today that secret has been deciphered. While the mechanism is to all appearances planned by those who serve up the data of experience, that is, by the culture industry, it is in fact forced upon the latter by the power of society, which remains irrational, however we may try to rationalize it; and this inescapable force

is processed by commercial agencies so that they give an artificial impression of being in command. There is nothing left for the consumer to classify. Producers have done it for him. Art for the masses has destroyed the dream but still conforms to the tenets of that dreaming idealism which critical idealism balked at. Everything derives from consciousness: for Malebranche and Berkeley, from the consciousness of God; in mass art, from the consciousness of the production team. Not only are the hit songs, stars, and soap operas cyclically recurrent and rigidly invariable types, but the specific content of the entertainment itself is derived from them and only appears to change. The details are interchangeable. The short interval sequence which was effective in a hit song, the hero's momentary fall from grace (which he accepts as good sport), the rough treatment which the beloved gets from the male star, the latter's rugged defiance of the spoilt heiress, are, like all the other details, ready-made clichés to be slotted in anywhere; they never do anything more than fulfill the purpose allotted them in the overall plan. Their whole *raison d'être* is to confirm it by being its constituent parts. As soon as the film begins, it is quite clear how it will end, and who will be rewarded, punished, or forgotten. In light music, once the trained ear has heard the first notes of the hit song, it can guess what is coming and feel flattered when it does come. The average length of the short story has to be rigidly adhered to. Even gags, effects, and jokes are calculated like the setting in which they are placed. They are the responsibility of special experts and their narrow range makes it easy for them to be apportioned in the office. The development of the culture industry has led to the predominance of the effect, the obvious touch, and the technical detail over the work itself – which once expressed an idea, but was liquidated together with the idea. When the detail won its freedom, it became rebellious and, in the period from Romanticism to Expressionism, asserted itself as free expression, as a vehicle of protest against the organization. In music the single harmonic effect obliterated the awareness of form as a whole; in painting the individual color was stressed at the expense of pictorial composition; and in the novel psychology became more important than structure. The totality of the culture industry has put an end to this. Though concerned exclusively with effects, it crushes their insubordination and makes them subserve the formula, which replaces the work. The same fate is inflicted on whole and parts alike. The whole inevitably bears no relation to the details – just like the career of a successful man into which everything is made to fit as an illustration or a proof, whereas it is nothing more than the sum of all those idiotic events. The so-called dominant idea is like a file which ensures order but not coherence. The whole and the parts are alike; there is no antithesis and no connection. Their prearranged harmony is a mockery of what had to be striven after in the great bourgeois works of art. In Germany the graveyard stillness of the dictatorship already hung over the gayest films of the democratic era.

The whole world is made to pass through the filter of the culture industry. The old experience of the movie-goer, who sees the world outside as an extension of the film he has just left (because the latter is intent upon reproducing the world of everyday perceptions), is now the producer's guideline. The more intensely and flawlessly his techniques duplicate empirical objects, the easier it is today for the illusion to prevail that the outside world is the straightforward continuation of that presented on the screen. This purpose has been furthered by mechanical reproduction since the lightning takeover by the sound film.

Real life is becoming indistinguishable from the movies. The sound film, far surpassing the theater of illusion, leaves no room for imagination or reflection on the part of the audience, who is unable to respond within the structure of the film, yet deviate from its precise detail without losing the thread of the story; hence the film forces its victims to equate it directly with reality. The stunting of the mass-media consumer's powers of imagination and spontaneity does not have to be traced back to any psychological mechanisms; he must ascribe the loss of those attributes to the objective nature of the products themselves, especially to the most characteristic of them, the sound film. They are so designed that quickness, powers of observation, and experience are undeniably needed to apprehend them at all; yet sustained thought is out of the question if the spectator is not to miss the relentless rush of facts. Even though the effort required for his response is semi-automatic, no scope is left for the imagination. Those who are so absorbed by the world of the movie – by its images, gestures, and words – that they are unable to supply what really makes it a world, do not have to dwell on particular points of its mechanics during a screening.

All the other films and products of the entertainment industry which they have seen have taught them what to expect; they react automatically. The might of industrial society is lodged in men's minds. The entertainments manufacturers know that their products will be consumed with alertness even when the customer is distraught, for each of them is a model of the huge economic machinery which has always sustained the masses, whether at work or at leisure – which is akin to work. From every sound film and every broadcast program the social effect can be inferred which is exclusive to none but is shared by all alike. The culture industry as a whole has molded men as a type unfailingly reproduced in every product. All the agents of this process, from the producer to the women's clubs, take good care that the simple reproduction of this mental state is not nuanced or extended in any way.

The art historians and guardians of culture who complain of the extinction in the West of a basic style-determining power are wrong. The stereotyped appropriation of everything, even the inchoate, for the purposes of mechanical reproduction surpasses the rigor and general currency of any "real style," in the sense in which cultural *cognoscenti* celebrate the organic pre-capitalist past. No Palestrina could be more of a purist in eliminating every unprepared and unresolved discord than the jazz arranger in suppressing any development which does not conform to the jargon. When jazzing up Mozart he changes him not only when he is too serious or too difficult but when he harmonizes the melody in a different way, perhaps more simply, than is customary now. No medieval builder can have scrutinized the subjects for church windows and sculptures more suspiciously than the studio hierarchy scrutinizes a work by Balzac or Hugo before finally approving it. No medieval theologian could have determined the degree of the torment to be suffered by the damned in accordance with the *ordo* of divine love more meticulously than the producers of shoddy epics calculate the torture to be undergone by the hero or the exact point to which the leading lady's hemline shall be raised. The explicit and implicit, exoteric and esoteric catalog of the forbidden and tolerated is so extensive that it not only defines the area of freedom but is all-powerful inside it. Everything down to the last detail is shaped accordingly. Like its counterpart, avant-garde art, the entertainment industry determines its own language, down to its very syntax and vocabulary, by the use of anathema. The constant pressure to produce new effects (which must conform to the old pattern) serves merely as another rule to increase the power of the conventions when any single effect threatens to slip through the net. Every detail is so firmly stamped with sameness that nothing can appear which is not marked at birth, or does not meet with approval at first sight. And the star performers, whether they produce or reproduce, use this jargon as freely and fluently and with as much gusto as if it were the very language which it silenced long ago. Such is the ideal of what is natural in this field of activity, and its influence becomes all the more powerful, the more technique is perfected and diminishes the tension between the finished product and everyday life. The paradox of this routine, which is essentially travesty, can be detected and is often predominant in everything that the culture industry turns out. A jazz musician who is playing a piece of serious music, one of Beethoven's simplest minuets, syncopates it involuntarily and will smile superciliously when asked to follow the normal divisions of the beat. This is the "nature" which, complicated by the ever-present and extravagant demands of the specific medium, constitutes the new style and is a "system of non-culture, to which one might even concede a certain 'unity of style' if it really made any sense to speak of stylized barbarity."[1]

The universal imposition of this stylized mode can even go beyond what is quasi-officially sanctioned or forbidden; today a hit song is more readily forgiven for not observing the 32 beats or the compass of the ninth than for containing even the most clandestine melodic or harmonic detail which does not conform to the idiom. Whenever Orson Welles offends against the tricks of the trade, he is forgiven because his departures from the norm are regarded as calculated mutations which serve all the more strongly to confirm the validity of the system. The constraint of the technically-conditioned idiom which stars and directors have to produce as "nature" so that the people can appropriate it, extends to such fine nuances that they almost attain the subtlety of the devices of an avant-garde work as against those of truth. The rare capacity minutely to fulfill the obligations of the natural idiom in all branches of the culture industry becomes the criterion of efficiency. What and how they say it must be measurable by everyday language, as in logical positivism. The producers are experts. The idiom demands an astounding productive power, which it absorbs and squanders. In a diabolical way it has overreached the culturally conservative distinction between genuine and artificial style. A style might be called artificial which is imposed from without on the refractory impulses of a form. But in the culture industry every element of the subject matter has its origin in the same apparatus as that jargon whose stamp it bears. The quarrels in which the artistic experts become involved with sponsor and censor about a lie going beyond the bounds of credibility are evidence not so much of an inner aesthetic tension as of a divergence of interests. The reputation of the specialist, in which a last remnant of objective independence sometimes finds refuge, conflicts with the business politics of the Church, or the concern which is manufacturing the cultural commodity. But the thing itself has been essentially objectified and made viable before the established authorities began to argue about it. Even before Zanuck acquired her, Saint Bernadette was regarded by her latter-day hagiographer as brilliant propaganda for all interested parties. That is what became of the emotions of the character. Hence the style of the culture industry, which no longer has to test itself against any refractory material, is also the negation of style. The reconciliation of the general and particular, of the rule and the specific demands of the subject matter, the achievement of which alone gives essential, meaningful content to style, is futile because there has ceased to be the slightest tension between opposite poles: these concordant extremes are dismally identical; the general can replace the particular, and vice versa.

Nevertheless, this caricature of style does not amount to something beyond the genuine style of the past. In the culture industry the notion of genuine style is seen to be the aesthetic equivalent of domination. Style considered as mere aesthetic regularity is a romantic dream of the past. The unity of style not only of the Christian Middle Ages but of the Renaissance expresses in each case the different structure of social power, and not the obscure experience of the oppressed in which the general was enclosed. The great artists were never those who embodied a wholly flawless and perfect style, but those who used style as a way of hardening themselves against the chaotic expression of suffering, as a negative truth. The style of their works gave what was expressed that force without which life flows away unheard. Those very art forms which are known as classical, such as Mozart's music, contain objective trends which represent something different to the style which they incarnate. As late as Schönberg and Picasso, the great artists have retained a mistrust of style, and at crucial points have subordinated it to the logic of the matter. What Dadaists and Expressionists called the untruth of style as such triumphs today in the sung jargon of a crooner, in the carefully contrived elegance of a film star, and even in the admirable expertise of a photograph of a peasant's squalid hut. Style represents a promise in every work of art. That which is expressed is subsumed through style into the dominant forms of generality, into the language of music, painting, or words, in the hope that it will be reconciled thus with the idea of true generality. This promise held out by the work of art that it will create truth by lending new shape to the conventional social forms is as necessary as it is hypocritical. It unconditionally posits the real forms of life as it is by suggesting that fulfillment lies in their aesthetic derivatives. To this extent the claim of art is always ideology too. However, only in this confrontation with tradition of which style is the record can art express suffering. That factor in a work of art which enables it to transcend reality certainly cannot be detached from style; but it does not consist of the harmony actually realized, of any doubtful unity of form and content, within and without, of individual and society; it is to be found in those features in which discrepancy appears: in the necessary failure of the passionate striving for identity. Instead of exposing itself to this failure in which the style of the great work of art has always achieved self-negation, the inferior work has always relied on its similarity with others – on a surrogate identity.

In the culture industry this imitation finally becomes absolute. Having ceased to be anything but style, it reveals the latter's secret: obedience to the social hierarchy. Today aesthetic barbarity completes what has threatened the creations of the spirit since they were gathered together as culture and neutralized. To speak of culture was always contrary to culture. Culture as a common denominator already contains in embryo that schematization and process of cataloging and

classification which bring culture within the sphere of administration. And it is precisely the industrialized, the consequent, subsumption which entirely accords with this notion of culture. By subordinating in the same way and to the same end all areas of intellectual creation, by occupying men's senses from the time they leave the factory in the evening to the time they clock in again the next morning with matter that bears the impress of the labor process they themselves have to sustain throughout the day, this subsumption mockingly satisfies the concept of a unified culture which the philosophers of personality contrasted with mass culture.

And so the culture industry, the most rigid of all styles, proves to be the goal of liberalism, which is reproached for its lack of style. Not only do its categories and contents derive from liberalism – domesticated naturalism as well as operetta and revue – but the modern culture monopolies form the economic area in which, together with the corresponding entrepreneurial types, for the time being some part of its sphere of operation survives, despite the process of disintegration elsewhere. It is still possible to make one's way in entertainment, if one is not too obstinate about one's own concerns, and proves appropriately pliable. Anyone who resists can only survive by fitting in. Once his particular brand of deviation from the norm has been noted by the industry, he belongs to it as does the land-reformer to capitalism. Realistic dissidence is the trademark of anyone who has a new idea in business. In the public voice of modern society accusations are seldom audible; if they are, the perceptive can already detect signs that the dissident will soon be reconciled. The more immeasurable the gap between chorus and leaders, the more certainly there is room at the top for everybody who demonstrates his superiority by well-planned originality. Hence, in the culture industry, too, the liberal tendency to give full scope to its able men survives. To do this for the efficient today is still the function of the market, which is otherwise proficiently controlled; as for the market's freedom, in the high period of art as elsewhere, it was freedom for the stupid to starve. Significantly, the system of the culture industry comes from the more liberal industrial nations, and all its characteristic media, such as movies, radio, jazz, and magazines, flourish there. Its progress, to be sure, had its origin in the general laws of capital.

Gaumont and Pathé, Ullstein and Hugenberg followed the international trend with some success; Europe's economic dependence on the United States after war and inflation was a contributory factor. The belief that the barbarity of the culture industry is a result of "cultural lag," of the fact that the American consciousness did not keep up with the growth of technology, is quite wrong. It was pre-Fascist Europe which did not keep up with the trend toward the culture monopoly. But it was this very lag which left intellect and creativity some degree of independence and enabled its last representatives to exist – however dismally. In Germany the failure of democratic control to permeate life had led to a paradoxical situation. Many things were exempt from the market mechanism which had invaded the Western countries. The German educational system, universities, theaters with artistic standards, great orchestras, and museums enjoyed protection. The political powers, state and municipalities, which had inherited such institutions from absolutism, had left them with a measure of the freedom from the forces of power which dominates the market, just as princes and feudal lords had done up to the nineteenth century. This strengthened art in this late phase against the verdict of supply and demand, and increased its resistance far beyond the actual degree of protection. In the market itself the tribute of a quality for which no use had been found was turned into purchasing power; in this way, respectable literary and music publishers could help authors who yielded little more in the way of profit than the respect of the connoisseur. But what completely fettered the artist was the pressure (and the accompanying drastic threats), always to fit into business life as an aesthetic expert. Formerly, like Kant and Hume, they signed their letters "Your most humble and obedient servant," and undermined the foundations of throne and altar. Today they address heads of government by their first names, yet in every artistic activity they are subject to their illiterate masters. The analysis Tocqueville offered a century ago has in the meantime proved wholly accurate. Under the private culture monopoly it is a fact that "tyranny leaves the body free and directs its attack at the soul. The ruler no longer says: You must think as I do or die. He says: You are free not to think as I do; your life, your property everything shall remain yours, but from this day on you are a stranger among us."[2] Not to conform means to be rendered powerless, economically and

therefore spiritually – to be "self-employed." When the outsider is excluded from the concern, he can only too easily be accused of incompetence. Whereas today in material production the mechanism of supply and demand is disintegrating, in the superstructure it still operates as a check in the rulers' favor. The consumers are the workers and employees, the farmers and lower middle class. Capitalist production so confines them, body and soul, that they fall helpless victims to what is offered them. As naturally as the ruled always took the morality imposed upon them more seriously than did the rulers themselves, the deceived masses are today captivated by the myth of success even more than the successful are. Immovably, they insist on the very ideology which enslaves them. The misplaced love of the common people for the wrong which is done them is a greater force than the cunning of the authorities. It is stronger even than the rigorism of the Hays Office, just as in certain great times in history it has inflamed greater forces that were turned against it, namely, the terror of the tribunals. It calls for Mickey Rooney in preference to the tragic Garbo, for Donald Duck instead of Betty Boop. The industry submits to the vote which it has itself inspired. What is a loss for the firm which cannot fully exploit a contract with a declining star is a legitimate expense for the system as a whole. By craftily sanctioning the demand for rubbish it inaugurates total harmony. The connoisseur and the expert are despised for their pretentious claim to know better than the others, even though culture is democratic and distributes its privileges to all. In view of the ideological truce, the conformism of the buyers and the effrontery of the producers who supply them prevail. The result is a constant reproduction of the same thing.

A constant sameness governs the relationship to the past as well. What is new about the phase of mass culture compared with the late liberal stage is the exclusion of the new. The machine rotates on the same spot. While determining consumption it excludes the untried as a risk. The movie-makers distrust any manuscript which is not reassuringly backed by a bestseller. Yet for this very reason there is never-ending talk of ideas, novelty, and surprise, of what is taken for granted but has never existed. Tempo and dynamics serve this trend. Nothing remains as of old; everything has to run incessantly, to keep moving. For only the universal triumph of the rhythm of mechanical production and reproduction promises that nothing changes, and nothing unsuitable will appear. Any additions to the well-proven culture inventory are too much of a speculation. The ossified forms – such as the sketch, short story, problem film, or hit song – are the standardized average of late liberal taste, dictated with threats from above. The people at the top in the culture agencies, who work in harmony as only one manager can with another, whether he comes from the rag trade or from college, have long since reorganized and rationalized the objective spirit. One might think that an omnipresent authority had sifted the material and drawn up an official catalog of cultural commodities to provide a smooth supply of available mass-produced lines. The ideas are written in the cultural firmament where they had already been numbered by Plato – and were indeed numbers, incapable of increase and immutable.

Amusement and all the elements of the culture industry existed long before the latter came into existence. Now they are taken over from above and brought up to date. The culture industry can pride itself on having energetically executed the previously clumsy transposition of art into the sphere of consumption, on making this a principle, on divesting amusement of its obtrusive naïvetés and improving the type of commodities. The more absolute it became, the more ruthless it was in forcing every outsider either into bankruptcy or into a syndicate, and became more refined and elevated – until it ended up as a synthesis of Beethoven and the Casino de Paris. It enjoys a double victory: the truth it extinguishes without it can reproduce at will as a lie within. "Light" art as such, distraction, is not a decadent form. Anyone who complains that it is a betrayal of the ideal of pure expression is under an illusion about society. The purity of bourgeois art, which hypostasized itself as a world of freedom in contrast to what was happening in the material world, was from the beginning bought with the exclusion of the lower classes – with whose cause, the real universality, art keeps faith precisely by its freedom from the ends of the false universality. Serious art has been withheld from those for whom the hardship and oppression of life make a mockery of seriousness, and who must be glad if they can use time not spent at the production line just to keep going. Light art has been the shadow of autonomous art. It is the social bad conscience of serious art. The truth

which the latter necessarily lacked because of its social premises gives the other the semblance of legitimacy. The division itself is the truth: it does at least express the negativity of the culture which the different spheres constitute. Least of all can the antithesis be reconciled by absorbing light into serious art, or vice versa. But that is what the culture industry attempts. The eccentricity of the circus, peepshow, and brothel is as embarrassing to it as that of Schönberg and Karl Kraus. And so the jazz musician Benny Goodman appears with the Budapest string quartet, more pedantic rhythmically than any philharmonic clarinettist, while the style of the Budapest players is as uniform and sugary as that of Guy Lombardo. But what is significant is not vulgarity, stupidity, and lack of polish. The culture industry did away with yesterday's rubbish by its own perfection, and by forbidding and domesticating the amateurish, although it constantly allows gross blunders without which the standard of the exalted style cannot be perceived. But what is new is that the irreconcilable elements of culture, art and distraction, are subordinated to one end and subsumed under one false formula: the totality of the culture industry. It consists of repetition. That its characteristic innovations are never anything more than improvements of mass reproduction is not external to the system. It is with good reason that the interest of innumerable consumers is directed to the technique, and not to the contents – which are stubbornly repeated, outworn, and by now half-discredited. The social power which the spectators worship shows itself more effectively in the omnipresence of the stereotype imposed by technical skill than in the stale ideologies for which the ephemeral contents stand in.

Nevertheless the culture industry remains the entertainment business. Its influence over the consumers is established by entertainment; that will ultimately be broken not by an outright decree, but by the hostility inherent in the principle of entertainment to what is greater than itself. Since all the trends of the culture industry are profoundly embedded in the public by the whole social process, they are encouraged by the survival of the market in this area. Demand has not yet been replaced by simple obedience. As is well known, the major reorganization of the film industry shortly before World War I, the material prerequisite of its expansion, was precisely its deliberate acceptance of the public's needs as recorded at the box-office – a procedure which was hardly thought necessary in the pioneering days of the screen. The same opinion is held today by the captains of the film industry, who take as their criterion the more or less phenomenal song hits but wisely never have recourse to the judgment of truth, the opposite criterion. Business is their ideology. It is quite correct that the power of the culture industry resides in its identification with a manufactured need, and not in simple contrast to it, even if this contrast were one of complete power and complete powerlessness. Amusement under late capitalism is the prolongation of work. It is sought after as an escape from the mechanized work process, and to recruit strength in order to be able to cope with it again. But at the same time mechanization has such power over a man's leisure and happiness, and so profoundly determines the manufacture of amusement goods, that his experiences are inevitably after-images of the work process itself. The ostensible content is merely a faded foreground; what sinks in is the automatic succession of standardized operations. What happens at work, in the factory, or in the office can only be escaped from by approximation to it in one's leisure time. All amusement suffers from this incurable malady. Pleasure hardens into boredom because, if it is to remain pleasure, it must not demand any effort and therefore moves rigorously in the worn grooves of association. No independent thinking must be expected from the audience: the product prescribes every reaction: not by its natural structure (which collapses under reflection), but by signals. Any logical connection calling for mental effort is painstakingly avoided. As far as possible, developments must follow from the immediately preceding situation and never from the idea of the whole. For the attentive movie-goer any individual scene will give him the whole thing. Even the set pattern itself still seems dangerous, offering some meaning – wretched as it might be – where only meaninglessness is acceptable. Often the plot is maliciously deprived of the development demanded by characters and matter according to the old pattern. Instead, the next step is what the script writer takes to be the most striking effect in the particular situation. Banal though elaborate surprise interrupts the story-line. The tendency mischievously to fall back on pure nonsense, which was a legitimate part of popular art, farce and clowning, right up to Chaplin and the Marx Brothers, is most obvious in the unpre-

tentious kinds. This tendency has completely asserted itself in the text of the novelty song, in the thriller movie, and in cartoons, although in films starring Greer Garson and Bette Davis the unity of the socio-psychological case study provides something approximating a claim to a consistent plot. The idea itself, together with the objects of comedy and terror, is massacred and fragmented. Novelty songs have always existed on a contempt for meaning which, as predecessors and successors of psychoanalysis, they reduce to the monotony of sexual symbolism. Today detective and adventure films no longer give the audience the opportunity to experience the resolution. In the non-ironic varieties of the genre, it has also to rest content with the simple horror of situations which have almost ceased to be linked in any way.

Cartoons were once exponents of fantasy as opposed to rationalism. They ensured that justice was done to the creatures and objects they electrified, by giving the maimed specimens a second life. All they do today is to confirm the victory of technological reason over truth. A few years ago they had a consistent plot which only broke up in the final moments in a crazy chase, and thus resembled the old slapstick comedy. Now, however, time relations have shifted. In the very first sequence a motive is stated so that in the course of the action destruction can get to work on it: with the audience in pursuit, the protagonist becomes the worthless object of general violence. The quantity of organized amusement changes into the quality of organized cruelty. The self-elected censors of the film industry (with whom it enjoys a close relationship) watch over the unfolding of the crime, which is as drawn-out as a hunt. Fun replaces the pleasure which the sight of an embrace would allegedly afford, and postpones satisfaction till the day of the pogrom. In so far as cartoons do any more than accustom the senses to the new tempo, they hammer into every brain the old lesson that continuous friction, the breaking down of all individual resistance, is the condition of life in this society. Donald Duck in the cartoons and the unfortunate in real life get their thrashing so that the audience can learn to take their own punishment.

The enjoyment of the violence suffered by the movie character turns into violence against the spectator, and distraction into exertion. Nothing that the experts have devised as a stimulant must escape the weary eye; no stupidity is allowed in the face of all the trickery; one has to follow everything and even display the smart responses shown and recommended in the film. This raises the question whether the culture industry fulfills the function of diverting minds which it boasts about so loudly. If most of the radio stations and movie theaters were closed down, the consumers would probably not lose so very much. To walk from the street into the movie theater is no longer to enter a world of dream; as soon as the very existence of these institutions no longer made it obligatory to use them, there would be no great urge to do so. Such closures would not be reactionary machine wrecking. The disappointment would be felt not so much by the enthusiasts as by the slow-witted, who are the ones who suffer for everything anyhow. In spite of the films which are intended to complete her integration, the housewife finds in the darkness of the movie theater a place of refuge where she can sit for a few hours with nobody watching, just as she used to look out of the window when there were still homes and rest in the evening. The unemployed in the great cities find coolness in summer and warmth in winter in these temperature-controlled locations. Otherwise, despite its size, this bloated pleasure apparatus adds no dignity to man's lives. The idea of "fully exploiting" available technical resources and the facilities for aesthetic mass consumption is part of the economic system which refuses to exploit resources to abolish hunger.

The culture industry perpetually cheats its consumers of what it perpetually promises. The promissory note which, with its plots and staging, it draws on pleasure is endlessly prolonged; the promise, which is actually all the spectacle consists of, is illusory: all it actually confirms is that the real point will never be reached, that the diner must be satisfied with the menu. In front of the appetite stimulated by all those brilliant names and images there is finally set no more than a commendation of the depressing everyday world it sought to escape. Of course works of art were not sexual exhibitions either. However, by representing deprivation as negative, they retracted, as it were, the prostitution of the impulse and rescued by mediation what was denied. The secret of aesthetic sublimation is its representation of fulfillment as a broken promise. The culture industry does not sublimate; it represses. By repeatedly exposing the objects of desire, breasts in a clinging sweater or the naked torso of the athletic hero, it only stimulates the unsublimated forepleasure which habitual deprivation has long since reduced to a masochistic semblance. There is no erotic situation which, while insinuating and exciting, does not fail to indicate unmistakably that things can never go that far. The Hays Office merely confirms the ritual of Tantalus that the culture industry has established anyway. Works of art are ascetic and unashamed; the culture industry is pornographic and prudish. Love is down-graded to romance. And, after the descent, much is permitted; even license as a marketable speciality has its quota bearing the trade description "daring." The mass production of the sexual automatically achieves its repression. Because of his ubiquity, the film star with whom one is meant to fall in love is from the outset a copy of himself. Every tenor voice comes to sound like a Caruso record, and the "natural" faces of Texas girls are like the successful models by whom Hollywood has typecast them. The mechanical reproduction of beauty, which reactionary cultural fanaticism wholeheartedly serves in its methodical idolization of individuality, leaves no room for that unconscious idolatry which was once essential to beauty. The triumph over beauty is celebrated by humor – the *Schadenfreude* that every successful deprivation calls forth. There is laughter because there is nothing to laugh at. Laughter, whether conciliatory or terrible, always occurs when some fear passes. It indicates liberation either from physical danger or from the grip of logic. Conciliatory laughter is heard as the echo of an escape from power; the wrong kind overcomes fear by capitulating to the forces which are to be feared. It is the echo of power as something inescapable. Fun is a medicinal bath. The pleasure industry never fails to prescribe it. It makes laughter the instrument of the fraud practised on happiness. Moments of happiness are without laughter; only operettas and films portray sex to the accompaniment of resounding laughter. But Baudelaire is as devoid of humour as Hölderlin. In the false society laughter is a disease which has attacked happiness and is drawing it into its worthless totality. To laugh at something is always to deride it, and the life which, according to Bergson, in laughter breaks through the barrier, is actually an invading barbaric life, self-assertion prepared to parade its liberation from any scruple when the social occasion arises. Such a laughing audience is a parody of humanity. Its members are monads, all dedicated to the pleasure of being ready for anything at the expense of everyone else. Their harmony is a caricature of solidarity. What is fiendish about this false laughter is that it is a compelling parody of the best, which is conciliatory. Delight is austere: *res severa verum gaudium*. The monastic theory that not asceticism but the sexual act denotes the renunciation of attainable bliss receives negative confirmation in the gravity of the lover who with foreboding commits his life to the fleeting moment. In the culture industry, jovial denial takes the place of the pain found in ecstasy and in asceticism. The supreme law is that they shall not satisfy their desires at any price; they must laugh and be content with laughter. In every product of the culture industry, the permanent denial imposed by civilization is once again unmistakably demonstrated and inflicted on its victims. To offer and to deprive them of something is one and the same. This is what happens in erotic films. Precisely because it must never take place, everything centers upon copulation. In films it is more strictly forbidden for an illegitimate relationship to be admitted without the parties being punished than for a millionaire's future son-in-law to be active in the labor movement. In contrast to the liberal era, industrialized as well as popular culture may wax indignant at capitalism, but it cannot renounce the threat of castration. This is fundamental. It outlasts the organized acceptance of the uniformed seen in the films which are produced to that end, and in reality. What is decisive today is no longer puritanism, although it still asserts itself in the form of women's organizations, but the necessity inherent in the system not to leave the customer alone, not for a moment to allow him any suspicion that resistance is possible. The principle dictates that he should be shown all his needs as capable of fulfillment, but that those needs should be so pre-determined that he feels himself to be the eternal consumer, the object of the culture industry. Not only does it make him believe that the deception it practices is satisfaction, but it goes further and implies that, whatever the state of affairs, he must put up with what is offered. The escape from everyday drudgery which the whole culture industry promises may be compared to the daughter's abduction in the cartoon: the father is holding the

ladder in the dark. The paradise offered by the culture industry is the same old drudgery. Both escape and elopement are pre-designed to lead back to the starting point. Pleasure promotes the resignation which it ought to help to forget.

Amusement, if released from every restraint, would not only be the antithesis of art but its extreme role. The Mark Twain absurdity with which the American culture industry flirts at times might be a corrective of art. The more seriously the latter regards the incompatibility with life, the more it resembles the seriousness of life, its antithesis; the more effort it devotes to developing wholly from its own formal law, the more effort it demands from the intelligence to neutralize its burden. In some revue films, and especially in the grotesque and the funnies, the possibility of this negation does glimmer for a few moments. But of course it cannot happen. Pure amusement in its consequence, relaxed self-surrender to all kinds of associations and happy nonsense, is cut short by the amusement on the market: instead, it is interrupted by a surrogate overall meaning which the culture industry insists on giving to its products, and yet misuses as a mere pretext for bringing in the stars. Biographies and other simple stories patch the fragments of nonsense into an idiotic plot. We do not have the cap and bells of the jester but the bunch of keys of capitalist reason, which even screens the pleasure of achieving success. Every kiss in the revue film has to contribute to the career of the boxer, or some hit song expert or other whose rise to fame is being glorified. The deception is not that the culture industry supplies amusement but that it ruins the fun by allowing business considerations to involve it in the ideological clichés of a culture in the process of self-liquidation. Ethics and taste cut short unrestrained amusement as "naïve" – naïveté is thought to be as bad as intellectualism – and even restrict technical possibilities. The culture industry is corrupt; not because it is a sinful Babylon but because it is a cathedral dedicated to elevated pleasure. On all levels, from Hemingway to Emil Ludwig, from Mrs. Miniver to the Lone Ranger, from Toscanini to Guy Lombardo, there is untruth in the intellectual content taken ready-made from art and science. The culture industry does retain a trace of something better in those features which bring it close to the circus, in the self-justifying and nonsensical skill of riders, acrobats and clowns, in the "defense and justification of physical as against intellectual art."[3] But the refuges of a mindless artistry which represents what is human as opposed to the social mechanism are being relentlessly hunted down by a schematic reason which compels everything to prove its significance and effect. The consequence is that the nonsensical at the bottom disappears as utterly as the sense in works of art at the top.

The fusion of culture and entertainment that is taking place today leads not only to a depravation of culture, but inevitably to an intellectualization of amusement. This is evident from the fact that only the copy appears: in the movie theater, the photograph; on the radio, the recording. In the age of liberal expansion, amusement lived on the unshaken belief in the future: things would remain as they were and even improve. Today this belief is once more intellectualized; it becomes so faint that it loses sight of any goal and is little more than a magic-lantern show for those with their backs to reality. It consists of the meaningful emphases which, parallel to life itself, the screen play puts on the smart fellow, the engineer, the capable girl, ruthlessness disguised as character, interest in sport, and finally automobiles and cigarettes, even where the entertainment is not put down to the advertising account of the immediate producers but to that of the system as a whole. Amusement itself becomes an ideal, taking the place of the higher things of which it completely deprives the masses by repeating them in a manner even more stereotyped than the slogans paid for by advertising interests. Inwardness, the subjectively restricted form of truth, was always more at the mercy of the outwardly powerful than they imagined. The culture industry turns it into an open lie. It has now become mere twaddle which is acceptable in religious bestsellers, psychological films, and women's serials as an embarrassingly agreeable garnish, so that genuine personal emotion in real life can be all the more reliably controlled. In this sense amusement carries out that purgation of the emotions which Aristotle once attributed to tragedy and Mortimer Adler now allows to movies. The culture industry reveals the truth about catharsis as it did about style.

The stronger the positions of the culture industry become, the more summarily it can deal with consumers' needs, producing them, controlling them, disciplining them, and even withdrawing amusement: no limits are set to cultural progress of this kind. But the tendency is immanent in the principle of amusement itself, which is enlightened in a bourgeois sense. If the need for amusement was in large measure the creation of industry, which used the subject as a means of recommending the work to the masses – the oleograph by the dainty morsel it depicted, or the cake mix by a picture of a cake – amusement always reveals the influence of business, the sales talk, the quack's spiel. But the original affinity of business and amusement is shown in the latter's specific significance: to defend society. To be pleased means to say Yes. It is possible only by insulation from the totality of the social process, by desensitization and, from the first, by senselessly sacrificing the inescapable claim of every work, however inane, within its limits to reflect the whole. Pleasure always means not to think about anything, to forget suffering even where it is shown. Basically it is helplessness. It is flight; not, as is asserted, flight from a wretched reality, but from the last remaining thought of resistance. The liberation which amusement promises is freedom from thought and from negation. The effrontery of the rhetorical question, "What do people want?" lies in the fact that it is addressed – as if to reflective individuals – to those very people who are deliberately to be deprived of this individuality. Even when the public does – exceptionally – rebel against the pleasure industry, all it can muster is that feeble resistance which that very industry has inculcated in it. Nevertheless, it has become increasingly difficult to keep people in this condition. The rate at which they are reduced to stupidity must not fall behind the rate at which their intelligence is increasing. In this age of statistics the masses are too sharp to identify themselves with the millionaire on the screen, and too slow-witted to ignore the law of the largest number. Ideology conceals itself in the calculation of probabilities. Not everyone will be lucky one day – but the person who draws the winning ticket, or rather the one who is marked out to do so by a higher power – usually by the pleasure industry itself, which is represented as unceasingly in search of talent. Those discovered by talent scouts and then publicized on a vast scale by the studio are ideal types of the new dependent average. Of course, the starlet is meant to symbolize the typist in such a way that the splendid evening dress seems meant for the actress as distinct from the real girl. The girls in the audience not only feel that they could be on the screen, but realize the great gulf separating them from it. Only one girl can draw the lucky ticket, only one man can win the prize, and if, mathematically, all have the same chance, yet this is so infinitesimal for each one that he or she will do best to write it off and rejoice in the other's success, which might just as well have been his or hers, and somehow never is. Whenever the culture industry still issues an invitation naïvely to identify, it is immediately withdrawn. No one can escape from himself any more. Once a member of the audience could see his own wedding in the one shown in the film. Now the lucky actors on the screen are copies of the same category as every member of the public, but such equality only demonstrates the insurmountable separation of the human elements. The perfect similarity is the absolute difference. The identity of the category forbids that of the individual cases. Ironically, man as a member of a species has been made a reality by the culture industry. Now any person signifies only those attributes by which he can replace everybody else: he is interchangeable, a copy. As an individual he is completely expendable and utterly insignificant, and this is just what he finds out when time deprives him of this similarity. This changes the inner structure of the religion of success – otherwise strictly maintained. Increasing emphasis is laid not on the path *per aspera ad astra* (which presupposes hardship and effort), but on winning a prize. The element of blind chance in the routine decision about which song deserves to be a hit and which extra a heroine is stressed by the ideology. Movies emphasize change. By stopping at nothing to ensure that all the characters are essentially alike, with the exception of the villain, and by excluding nonconforming faces (for example, those which, like Garbo's, do not look as if you could say "Hello sister!" to them), life is made easier for movie-goers at first. They are assured that they are all right as they are, that they could do just as well and that nothing beyond their powers will be asked of them. But at the same time they are given a hint that any effort would be useless because even bourgeois luck no longer has any connection with the calculable effect of their own work. They take the hint. Fundamentally they all recognize chance (by which one occasionally makes his fortune) as the other side of planning. Precisely because

the forces of society are so deployed in the direction of rationality that anyone might become an engineer or manager, it has ceased entirely to be a rational matter who the one will be in whom society will invest training or confidence for such functions. Chance and planning become one and the same thing, because, given men's equality, individual success and failure – right up to the top – lose any economic meaning. Chance itself is planned, not because it affects any particular individual but precisely because it is believed to play a vital part. It serves the planners as an alibi, and makes it seem that the complex of transactions and measures into which life has been transformed leaves scope for spontaneous and direct relations between man. This freedom is symbolized in the various media of the culture industry by the arbitrary selection of average individuals. In a magazine's detailed accounts of the modestly magnificent pleasure-trips it has arranged for the lucky person, preferably a stenotypist (who has probably won the competition because of her contacts with local bigwigs), the powerlessness of all is reflected. They are mere matter – so much so that those in control can take someone up into their heaven and throw him out again: his rights and his work count for nothing. Industry is interested in people merely as customers and employees, and has in fact reduced mankind as a whole and each of its elements to this all-embracing formula. According to the ruling aspect at the time, ideology emphasizes plan or chance, technology or life, civilization or nature. As employees, men are reminded of the rational organization and urged to fit in like sensible people. As customers, the freedom of choice, the charm of novelty, is demonstrated to them on the screen or in the press by means of the human and personal anecdote. In either case they remain objects.

[…]

Notes

1   Nietzsche, *Unzeitgemässe Betrachtungen, Werke*, vol. 1 (Leipzig, 1917), p. 187.
2   Alexis de Tocqueville, *De la Démocratie en Amérique*, vol. II (Paris, 1864), p. 151.
3   Frank Wedekind, *Gesammelte Werke*, vol. IX (Munich, 1921), p. 426.

5

"Culture Is Ordinary" (1958)

Raymond Williams

The bus stop was outside the cathedral. I had been looking at the Mappa Mundi, with its rivers out of Paradise, and at the chained library, where a party of clergymen had got in easily, but where I had waited an hour and cajoled a verger before I even saw the chains. Now, across the street, a cinema advertised the *Six-Five Special* and a cartoon version of *Gulliver's Travels*. The bus arrived, with a driver and a conductress deeply absorbed in each other. We went out of the city, over the old bridge, and on through the orchards and the green meadows and the fields red under the plough. Ahead were the Black Mountains, and we climbed among them, watching the steep fields end at the grey walls, beyond which the bracken and heather and whin had not yet been driven back. To the east, along the ridge, stood the line of grey Norman castles; to the west, the fortress wall of the mountains. Then, as we still climbed, the rock changed under us. Here, now, was limestone, and the line of the early iron workings along the scarp. The farming valleys, with their scattered white houses, fell away behind. Ahead of us were the narrower valleys: the steel-rolling mill, the gasworks, the grey terraces, the pitheads. The bus stopped, and the driver and conductress got out, still absorbed. They had done this journey so often, and seen all its stages. It is a journey, in fact, that in one form or another we have all made.

I was born and grew up halfway along that bus journey. Where I lived is still a farming valley, though

the road through it is being widened and straightened, to carry the heavy lorries to the north. Not far away, my grandfather, and so back through the generations, worked as a farm labourer until he was turned out of his cottage and, in his fifties, became a roadman. His sons went at thirteen or fourteen on to the farms, his daughters into service. My father, his third son, left the farm at fifteen to be a boy porter on the railway, and later became a signalman, working in a box in this valley until he died. I went up the road to the village school, where a curtain divided the two classes – Second to eight or nine, First to fourteen. At eleven I went to the local grammar school, and later to Cambridge.

Culture is ordinary: that is where we must start. To grow up in that country was to see the shape of a culture, and its modes of change. I could stand on the mountains and look north to the farms and the cathedral, or south to the smoke and the flare of the blast furnace making a second sunset. To grow up in that family was to see the shaping of minds: the learning of new skills, the shifting of relationships, the emergence of different language and ideas. My grandfather, a big hard labourer, wept while he spoke, finely and excitedly, at the parish meeting, of being turned out of his cottage. My father, not long before he died, spoke quietly and happily of when he had started a trade-union branch and a Labour Party group in the village, and, without bitterness, of the 'kept men' of the new politics. I speak a different idiom, but I think of these same things.

Culture is ordinary: that is the first fact. Every human society has its own shape, its own purposes, its

Raymond Williams, "Culture Is Ordinary," pp. 5–6, 14 from *Resources of Hope: Culture, Democracy, Socialism*, ed. Robin Gable. London: Verso, 1989.

own meanings. Every human society expresses these, in institutions, and in arts and learning. The making of a society is the finding of common meanings and directions, and its growth is an active debate and amendment under the pressures of experience, contact, and discovery, writing themselves into the land. The growing society is there, yet it is also made and remade in every individual mind. The making of a mind is, first, the slow learning of shapes, purposes, and meanings, so that work, observation and communication are possible. Then, second, but equal in importance, is the testing of these in experience, the making of new observations, comparisons, and meanings. A culture has two aspects: the known meanings and directions, which its members are trained to; the new observations and meanings, which are offered and tested. These are the ordinary processes of human societies and human minds, and we see through them the nature of a culture: that it is always both traditional and creative; that it is both the most ordinary common meanings and the finest individual meanings. We use the word culture in these two senses: to mean a whole way of life – the common meanings; to mean the arts and learning – the special processes of discovery and creative effort. Some writers reserve the word for one or other of these senses; I insist on both, and on the significance of their conjunction. The questions I ask about our culture are questions about our general and common purposes, yet also questions about deep personal meanings. Culture is ordinary, in every society and in every mind.

Now there are two senses of culture – two colours attached to it – that I know about but refuse to learn. The first I discovered at Cambridge, in a teashop. I was not, by the way, oppressed by Cambridge. I was not cast down by old buildings, for I had come from a country with twenty centuries of history written visibly into the earth: I liked walking through a Tudor court, but it did not make me feel raw. I was not amazed by the existence of a place of learning; I had always known the cathedral, and the bookcases I now sit to work at in Oxford are of the same design as those in the chained library. Nor was learning, in my family, some strange eccentricity; I was not, on a scholarship in Cambridge, a new kind of animal up a brand-new ladder. Learning was ordinary; we learned where we could. Always, from those scattered white

houses, it had made sense to go out and become a scholar or a poet or a teacher. Yet few of us could be spared from the immediate work: a price had been set on this kind of learning, and it was more, much more, than we could individually pay. Now, when we could pay in common, it was a good, ordinary life.

I was not oppressed by the university, but the teashop, acting as if it were one of the older and more respectable departments, was a different matter. Here was culture, not in any sense I knew, but in a special sense: the outward and emphatically visible sign of a special kind of people, cultivated people. They were not, the great majority of them, particularly learned; they practised few arts; but they had it, and they showed you they had it. They are still there, I suppose, still showing it, though even they must be hearing rude noises from outside, from a few scholars and writers they call – how comforting a label is! – angry young men. As a matter of fact there is no need to be rude. It is simply that if that is culture, we don't want it; we have seen other people living.

But of course it is not culture, and those of my colleagues who, hating the teashop, make culture, on its account, a dirty word, are mistaken. If the people in the teashop go on insisting that culture is their trivial differences of behaviour, their trivial variations of speech habit, we cannot stop them, but we can ignore them. They are not that important, to take culture from where it belongs.

Yet, probably also disliking the teashop, there were writers I read then, who went into the same category in my mind. When I now read a book such as Clive Bell's *Civilisation*. I experience not so much disagreement as stupor. What kind of life can it be, I wonder, to produce this extraordinary fussiness, this extraordinary decision to call certain things culture and then separate them, as with a park wall, from ordinary people and ordinary work? At home we met and made music, listened to it, recited and listened to poems, valued fine language. I have heard better music and better poems since; there is the world to draw on. But I know, from the most ordinary experience, that the interest is there, the capacity is there. Of course, farther along that bus journey, the old social organization in which these things had their place has been broken. People have been driven and concentrated into new kinds of work, new kinds of relationship;

work, by the way, which built the park walls, and the houses inside them, and which is now at last bringing, to the unanimous disgust of the teashop, clean and decent and furnished living to the people themselves. Culture is ordinary: through every change let us hold fast to that.

[…]

[…] When I got to Cambridge I encountered two serious influences which have left a very deep impression on my mind. The first was Marxism, the second the teaching of Leavis. Through all subsequent disagreement I retain my respect for both.

The Marxists said many things, but those that mattered were three. First, they said that a culture must be finally interpreted in relation to its underlying system of production. I have argued this theoretically elsewhere – it is a more difficult idea than it looks – but I still accept its emphasis. Everything I had seen, growing up in that border country, had led me towards such an emphasis: a culture is a whole way of life, and the arts are part of a social organization which economic change clearly radically affects. I did not have to be taught dissatisfaction with the existing economic system, but the subsequent questions about our culture were, in these terms, vague. It was said that it was a class-dominated culture, deliberately restricting a common inheritance to a small class, while leaving the masses ignorant. The fact of restriction I accepted – it is still very obvious that only the *deserving* poor get much educational opportunity, and I was in no mood, as I walked about Cambridge, to feel glad that I had been thought deserving; I was no better and no worse than the people I came from. On the other hand, just because of this, I got angry at my friends' talk about the ignorant masses: one kind of Communist has always talked like this, and has got his answer, at Poznan and Budapest, as the imperialists, making the same assumption, were answered in India, in Indo-China, in Africa. There is an English bourgeois culture, with its powerful educational, literary and social institutions, in close contact with the actual centres of power. To say that most working people are excluded from these is self-evident, though the doors, under sustained pressure, are slowly opening. But to go on to say that working people are excluded from English culture is nonsense; they have their own growing institutions, and much of the strictly bourgeois cul-

ture they would in any case not want. A great part of the English way of life, and of its arts and learning, is not bourgeois in any discoverable sense. There are institutions, and common meanings, which are in no sense the sole product of the commercial middle class; and there are art and learning, a common English inheritance, produced by many kinds of men, including many who hated the very class and system which now take pride in consuming it. The bourgeoisie has given us much, including a narrow but real system of morality; that is at least better than its court predecessors. The leisure which the bourgeoisie attained has given us much of cultural value. But this is not to say that contemporary culture is bourgeois culture: a mistake that everyone, from Conservatives to Marxists, seems to make. There is a distinct working-class way of life, which I for one value – not only because I was bred in it, for I now, in certain respects, live differently. I think this way of life, with its emphases of neighbourhood, mutual obligation, and common betterment, as expressed in the great working-class political and industrial institutions, is in fact the best basis for any future English society. As for the arts and learning, they are in a real sense a national inheritance, which is, or should be, available to everyone. So when the Marxists say that we live in a dying culture, and that the masses are ignorant, I have to ask them, as I asked them then, where on earth they have lived. A dying culture, and ignorant masses, are not what I have known and see.

What I had got from the Marxists then, so far, was a relationship between culture and production, and the observation that education was restricted. The other things I rejected, as I rejected also their third point, that since culture and production are related, the advocacy of a different system of production is in some way a cultural directive, indicating not only a way of life but new arts and learning. I did some writing while I was, for eighteen months, a member of the Communist Party, and I found out in trivial ways what other writers, here and in Europe, have found out more gravely: the practical consequences of this kind of theoretical error. In this respect, I saw the future, and it didn't work. The Marxist interpretation of culture can never be accepted while it retains, as it need not retain, this directive element, this insistence that if you honestly want socialism you must write, think, learn in certain prescribed ways. A culture is common meanings, the product of a whole people, and offered individual meanings, the product of a man's whole committed personal and social experience. It is stupid and arrogant to suppose that any of these meanings can in any way be prescribed; they are made by living, made and remade, in ways we cannot know in advance. To try to jump the future, to pretend that in some way you *are* the future, is strictly insane. Prediction is another matter, an offered meaning, but the only thing we can say about culture in an England that has socialized its means of production is that all the channels of expression and communication should be cleared and open, so that the whole actual life, that we cannot know in advance, that we can know only in part even while it is being lived, may be brought to consciousness and meaning.

Leavis has never liked Marxists, which is in one way a pity, for they know more than he does about modern English society, and about its immediate history. He, on the other hand, knows more than any Marxist I have met about the real relations between art and experience. We have all learned from him in this, and we have also learned his version of what is wrong with English culture. The diagnosis is radical, and is rapidly becoming orthodox. There was an old, mainly agricultural England, with a traditional culture of great value. This has been replaced by a modern, organized, industrial state, whose characteristic institutions deliberately cheapen our natural human responses, making art and literature into desperate survivors and witnesses, while a new mechanized vulgarity sweeps into the centres of power. The only defence is in education, which will at least keep certain things alive, and which will also, at least in a minority, develop ways of thinking and feeling which are competent to understand what is happening and to maintain the finest individual values. I need not add how widespread this diagnosis has become, though little enough acknowledgement is still made to Leavis himself. For my own part, I was deeply impressed by it: deeply enough for my ultimate rejection of it to be a personal crisis lasting several years.

For, obviously, it seemed to fit a good deal of my experience. It did not tell me that my father and grandfather were ignorant wage-slaves; it did not tell me that the smart, busy, commercial culture (which I had come to as a stranger, so much so that for years

I had violent headaches whenever I passed through London and saw underground advertisements and evening newspapers) was the thing I had to catch up with. I even made a fool of myself, or was made to think so, when after a lecture in which the usual point was made that 'neighbour' now does not mean what it did to Shakespeare, I said – imagine! – that to me it did. (When my father was dying, this year, one man came in and dug his garden; another loaded and delivered a lorry of sleepers for firewood; another came and chopped the sleepers into blocks; another – I don't know who, it was never said – left a sack of potatoes at the back door; a woman came in and took away a basket of washing.) But even this was explicable; I came from a bit of the old society, but my future was Surbiton (it took me years to find Surbiton, and have a good look at it, but it's served a good many as a symbol – without having lived there I couldn't say whether rightly). So there I was, and it all seemed to fit.

Yet not all. Once I got away, and thought about it, it didn't really fit properly. For one thing I knew this: at home we were glad of the Industrial Revolution, and of its consequent social and political changes. True, we lived in a very beautiful farming valley, and the valleys beyond the limestone we could all see were ugly. But there was one gift that was overriding, one gift which at any price we would take, the gift of power that is everything to men who have worked with their hands. It was slow in coming to us, in all its effects, but steam power, the petrol engine, electricity, these and their host of products in commodities and services, we took as quickly as we could get them, and were glad. I have seen all these things being used, and I have seen the things they replaced. I will not listen with patience to any acid listing of them – you know the sneer you can get into plumbing, baby Austins, aspirin, contraceptives, canned food. But I say to these Pharisees: dirty water, an earth bucket, a four-mile walk each way to work, headaches, broken women, hunger and monotony of diet. The working people, in town and country alike, will not listen (and I support them) to any account of our society which supposes that these things are not progress: not just mechanical, external progress either, but a real service of life. Moreover, in the new conditions, there was more real freedom to dispose of our lives, more real personal grasp where it mattered, more real say. Any account of our culture which explicitly or implicitly denies the value of an industrial society is really irrelevant: not in a million years would you make us give up this power.

So then the social basis of the case was unacceptable, but could one, trying to be a writer, a scholar, a teacher, ignore the indictment of the new cultural vulgarity? For the plumbing and the tractors and the medicines could one ignore the strip newspapers, the multiplying cheapjacks, the raucous triviality? As a matter of priorities, yes, if necessary; but was the cheapening of response really a consequence of the cheapening of power? It looks like it, I know, but is this really as much as one can say? I believe the central problem of our society, in the coming half-century, is the use of our new resources to make a good common culture; the means to a good, abundant economy we already understand. I think the good common culture can be made, but before we can be serious about this, we must rid ourselves of a legacy from our most useful critics – a legacy of two false equations, one false analogy, and one false proposition.

The false proposition is easily disposed of. It is a fact that the new power brought ugliness: the coal brought dirt, the factory brought over-crowding, communications brought a mess of wires. But the proposition that ugliness is a price we pay, or refuse to pay, for economic power need no longer be true. New sources of power, new methods of production, improved systems of transport and communication can, quite practically, make England clean and pleasant again, and with much more power, not less. Any new ugliness is the product of stupidity, indifference, or simply incoordination; these things will be easier to deal with than when power was necessarily noisy, dirty, and disfiguring.

The false equations are more difficult. One is the equation between popular education and the new commercial culture: the latter proceeding inevitably from the former. Let the masses in, it is said, and this is what you inevitably get. Now the question is obviously difficult, but I can't accept this equation, for two reasons. The first is a matter of faith: I don't believe that the ordinary people in fact resemble the normal description of the masses, low and trivial in taste and habit. I put it another way: that there are in fact no masses, but only ways of seeing people as masses. With the coming of industrialism, much of the old social organization broke down and it became a matter of

difficult personal experience that we were constantly seeing people we did not know, and it was tempting to mass them, as 'the others', in our minds. Again, people were physically massed, in the industrial towns, and a new class structure (the names of our social classes, and the word 'class' itself in this sense, date only from the Industrial Revolution) was practically imposed. The improvement in communications, in particular the development of new forms of multiple transmission of news and entertainment, created unbridgeable divisions between transmitter and audience, which again led to the audience being interpreted as an unknown mass. Masses became a new word for mob: the others, the unknown, the unwashed, the crowd beyond one. As a way of knowing other people, this formula is obviously ridiculous, but, in the new conditions, it seemed an effective formula – the only one possible. Certainly it was the formula that was used by those whose money gave them access to the new communication techniques; the lowness of taste and habit, which human beings assign very easily to other human beings, was assumed, as a bridge. The new culture was built on this formula, and if I reject the formula, if I insist that this lowness is not inherent in ordinary people, you can brush my insistence aside, but I shall go on holding to it. A different formula, I know from experience, gets a radically different response.

My second reason is historical: I deny, and can prove my denial, that popular education and commercial culture are cause and effect. I have shown elsewhere that the myth of 1870 – the Education Act which is said to have produced, as its children grew up, a new cheap and nasty press – is indeed myth. There was more than enough literacy, long before 1870, to support a cheap press, and in fact there were cheap and really bad newspapers selling in great quantities before the 1870 Act was heard of. The bad new commercial culture came out of the social chaos of industrialism, and out of the success, in this chaos, of the 'masses' formula, not out of popular education. Northcliffe did few worse things than start this myth, for while the connection between bad culture and the social chaos of industrialism is significant, the connection between it and popular education is vicious. The Northcliffe Revolution, by the way, was a radical change in the financial structure of the press, basing it on a new kind of revenue – the new mass advertising of the 1890s – rather than the making of a cheap popular press, in which he had been widely and successfully preceded. But I tire of making these points. Everyone prefers to believe Northcliffe. Yet does nobody, even a Royal Commission, read the most ordinarily accessible newspaper history? When people do read the history, the false equation between popular education and commercial culture will disappear for ever. Popular education came out of the other camp, and has had quite opposite effects.

The second false equation is this: that the observable badness of so much widely distributed popular culture is a true guide to the state of mind and feeling, the essential quality of living of its consumers. Too many good men have said this for me to treat it lightly, but I still, on evidence, can't accept it. It is easy to assemble, from print and cinema and television, a terrifying and fantastic congress of cheap feelings and moronic arguments. It is easy to go on from this and assume this deeply degrading version of the actual lives of our contemporaries. Yet do we find this confirmed, when we meet people? This is where 'masses' comes in again, of course: the people *we* meet aren't vulgar, but God, think of Bootle and Surbiton and Aston! I haven't lived in any of those places; have you? But a few weeks ago I was in a house with a commercial traveller, a lorry driver, a bricklayer, a shopgirl, a fitter, a signalman, a nylon operative, a domestic help (perhaps, dear, she is your very own treasure). I hate describing people like this, for in fact they were my family and family friends. Now they read, they watch, this work we are talking about; some of them quite critically, others with a good deal of pleasure. Very well, I read different things, watch different entertainments, and I am quite sure why they are better. But could I sit down in that house and make this equation we are offered? Not, you understand, that shame was stopping me; I've learned, thank you, how to behave. But talking to my family, to my friends, talking, as we were, about our own lives, about people, about feelings, could I in fact find this lack of quality we are discussing? I'll be honest – I looked; my training has done that for me. I can only say that I found as much natural fineness of feeling, as much quick discrimination, as much clear grasp of ideas within the range of experience as I have found anywhere. I don't altogether understand this, though I am not really surprised.

Clearly there is something in the psychology of print and image that none of us has yet quite grasped. For the equation looks sensible, yet when you test it, in experience – and there's nowhere else you can test it – it's wrong. I can understand the protection of critical and intelligent reading: my father, for instance, a satisfied reader of the *Daily Herald*, got simply from reading the company reports a clear idea, based on names, of the rapid development of combine and interlocking ownership in British industry, which I had had made easy for me in two or three academic essays; and he had gone on to set these facts against the opinions in a number of articles in the paper on industrial ownership. That I understand; that is simply intelligence, however partly trained. But there is still this other surprising fact: that people whose quality of personal living is high are apparently satisfied by a low quality of printed feeling and opinion. Many of them still live, it is true, in a surprisingly enclosed personal world, much more so than mine, and some of their personal observations are the finer for it. Perhaps this is enough to explain it, but in any case, I submit, we need a new equation, to fit the observable facts.

Now the false analogy, that we must also reject. This is known, in discussions of culture, as a 'kind of Gresham's Law'. Just as bad money will drive out good, so bad culture will drive out good, and this, it is said, has in fact been happening. If you can't see, straight away, the defect of the analogy, your answer, equally effective, will have to be historical. For in fact, of course, it has not been happening. There is more, much more bad culture about; it is easier, now, to distribute it, and there is more leisure to receive it. But test this in any field you like, and see if this has been accompanied by a shrinking consumption of things we can all agree to be good. The editions of good literature are very much larger than they were; the listeners to good music are much more numerous than they were; the number of people who look at good visual art is larger than it has ever been. If bad newspapers drive out good newspapers, by a kind of Gresham's Law, why is it that, allowing for the rise in population, *The Times* sells nearly three times as many copies as in the days of its virtual monopoly of the press, in 1850? It is the law I am questioning, not the seriousness of the facts as a whole. Instead of a kind of Gresham's Law, keeping people awake at nights with the now orthodox putropian nightmare, let us put it another way, to fit the actual facts: we live in an expanding culture, and all the elements in this culture are themselves expanding. If we start from this, we can then ask real questions: about relative rates of expansion; about the social and economic problems raised by these; about the social and economic answers. I am working now on a book to follow my *Culture and Society*, trying to interpret, historically and theoretically, the nature and conditions of an expanding culture of our kind. I could not have begun this work if I had not learned from the Marxists and from Leavis; I cannot complete it unless I radically amend some of the ideas which they and others have left us.

[...]

6

"Reification and Utopia in Mass Culture" (1979)

Fredric Jameson

The theory of mass culture – or mass audience culture, commercial culture, "popular" culture, the culture industry, as it is variously known – has always tended to define its object against so-called high culture without reflecting on the objective status of this opposition. As so often, positions in this field reduce themselves to two mirror-images, and are essentially staged in terms of value. Thus the familiar motif of *elitism* argues for the priority of mass culture on the grounds of the sheer numbers of people exposed to it; the pursuit of high or hermetic culture is then stigmatized as a status hobby of small groups of intellectuals. As its anti-intellectual thrust suggests, this essentially negative position has little theoretical content but clearly responds to a deeply rooted conviction in American radicalism and articulates a widely based sense that high culture is an establishment phenomenon, irredeemably tainted by its association with institutions, in particular with the university. The value invoked is therefore a social one: it would be preferable to deal with TV programs, *The Godfather*, or *Jaws*, rather than with Wallace Stevens or Henry James, because the former clearly speak a cultural language meaningful to far wider strata of the population than what is socially represented by intellectuals. Radicals are however also intellectuals, so that this position has suspicious overtones of the guilt trip; meanwhile it overlooks the anti-social and critical, negative (although generally not revolutionary) stance of much of the most important forms of modern art; finally,

Fredric Jameson, "Reification and Utopia in Mass Culture," pp. 130–2, 133–5, 138–48 from *Social Text* 1 (1979).

it offers no method for reading even those cultural objects it valorizes and has had little of interest to say about their content.

This position is then reversed in the theory of culture worked out by the Frankfurt School; as is appropriate for this exact antithesis of the radical position, the work of Adorno, Horkheimer, Marcuse, and others is an intensely theoretical one and provides a working methodology for the close analysis of precisely those products of the culture industry which it stigmatizes and which the radical view exalted. Briefly, this view can be characterized as the extension and application of Marxist theories of commodity reification to the works of mass culture. The theory of reification (here strongly overlaid with Max Weber's analysis of rationalization) describes the way in which, under capitalism, the older traditional forms of human activity are instrumentally reorganized and "taylorized," analytically fragmented and reconstructed according to various rational models of efficiency, and essentially restructured along the lines of a differentiation between means and ends. But this is a paradoxical idea; it cannot be properly appreciated until it is understood to what degree the means/ends split effectively brackets or suspends ends themselves, hence the strategic value of the Frankfurt School term "instrumentalization" which usefully foregrounds the organization of the means themselves over against any particular end or value which is assigned to their practice. In traditional activity, in other words, the value of the activity is immanent to it, and qualitatively distinct from other ends or values articulated in other forms of human work or play. Socially, this meant that various kinds of work in such communities were properly incomparable; in ancient Greece, for instance, the familiar Aristotelian schema of the four-fold causes at work in handicraft or *poeisis* (material, formal, efficient, and final) were applicable only to artisanal labor, and not to agriculture or war which had a quite different "natural" – which is to say super-natural or divine – basis. It is only with the universal commodification of labor power, which Marx's *Capital* designates as the fundamental precondition of capital-ism, that all forms of human labor can be separated out from their unique qualitative differentiation as distinct types of activity (mining as opposed to farm-ing, opera composition as distinct from textile manu-facture), and all universally ranged under the common denominator of the quantitative, that is, under the universal exchange value of money. At this point, then, the quality of the various forms of human activity, their unique and distinct "ends" or values, has effec-tively been bracketted or suspended by the market system, leaving all these activities free to be ruthlessly reorganized in efficiency terms, as sheer means or instrumentality.

The force of the application of this notion to works of art can be measured against the definition of art by traditional aesthetic philosophy (in particular by Kant) as a "finality without an end," that is, as a goal-oriented activity which nonetheless has no practical purpose or end in the "real world" of business or politics or concrete human praxis generally. This tra-ditional definition surely holds for all art that works as such: not for stories that fall flat or home movies or inept poetic scribblings, but rather for the successful works of mass and high culture alike. We suspend our real lives and our immediate practical preoccupations just as completely when we watch *The Godfather* as when we read *The Wings of the Dove* or hear a Beethoven sonata.

At this point, however, the concept of the com-modity introduces the possibility of structural and historical differentiation into what was conceived as the universal description of the aesthetic experience as such and in whatever form. The concept of the commodity cuts across the phenomenon of reification – described above in terms of activity or production – from a different angle, that of consumption. In a world in which everything, including labor power,

has become a commodity, ends remain no less undifferentiated than in the production schema – they are all rigorously quantified, and have become abstractly comparable through the medium of money, their respective price or wage – yet we can now phrase their instrumentalization, their reorganization along the means/ends split, in a new way by saying that by its transformation into a commodity a thing of what-ever type, has been reduced to a means for its own consumption. It no longer has any qualitative value in itself, but only insofar as it can be "used": the various forms of activity lose their immanent intrinsic satis-factions as activity and become means to an end. The objects of the commodity world of capitalism also shed their independent "being" and intrinsic qualities and come to be so many instruments of commodity satisfaction: the familiar example is that of tourism – the American tourist no longer lets the landscape "be in its being" as Heidegger would have said, but takes a snapshot of it, thereby graphically transforming space into its own material image. The concrete activity of looking at a landscape – including, no doubt, the dis-quieting bewilderment with the activity itself, the anxiety that must arise when human beings, confront-ing the non-human, wonder what they are doing there and what the point or purpose of such a con-frontation might be in the first place – is thus com-fortably replaced by the act of taking possession of it and converting it into a form of personal property. This is the meaning of the great scene in Godard's *Les Carabiniers*, when the new world conquerors exhibit their spoils: unlike Alexander, they merely own the images of everything, and triumphantly display their photos of the Coliseum, the pyramids, Wall Street, Angkor Wat, like so many dirty pictures. This is also the sense of Guy Debord's assertion, in an important book, *The Society of the Spectacle*, that the ultimate form of commodity reification in contemporary consumer society is precisely the image itself. With this universal commodification of our object world, the familiar accounts of the other-directedness of contemporary conspicuous consumption and of the sexualization of our objects and activities are also given: the new model car is essentially an image for other people to have of us, and we consume, less the thing itself, than its abstract idea, capable of the libidinal investments ingeniously arrayed for us by advertising.

It is clear that such an account of commodification has immediate relevance to aesthetics, if only because it implies that everything in consumer society has taken on an aesthetic dimension. The force of the Adorno–Horkheimer analysis of the culture industry, however, lies in its demonstration of the unexpected and imperceptible introduction of commodity structure into the very form and content of the work of art itself. Yet this is something like the ultimate squaring of the circle, the triumph of instrumentalization over that "finality without an end" which is art itself, the steady conquest and colonization of the ultimate realm of non-practicality, of sheer play and anti-use, by the logic of the world of means and ends. But how can the sheer materiality of a poetic sentence be "used" in that sense? And while it is clear how we can buy the idea of an automobile or smoke for the sheer libidinal image of actors, writers, and models with cigarettes in their hands, it is much less clear how a narrative could be "consumed" for the benefit of its own idea.

[…]

It will be clear, then, that I consider the Frankfurt School's analysis of the commodity structure of mass culture of the greatest interest: if, below, I propose a somewhat different way of looking at the same phenomena, it is not because I feel that their approach has been exhausted. On the contrary, we have scarcely begun to work out all the consequences of such descriptions, let alone to make an exhaustive inventory of variant models and of other features besides commodity reification in terms of which such artifacts might be analyzed.

What is unsatisfactory about the Frankfurt School position is not its negative and critical apparatus, but rather the positive value on which the latter depends, namely the valorization of traditional modernist high art as the locus of some genuinely critical and subversive, "autonomous" aesthetic production. Here Adorno's later work (as well as Marcuse's *The Aesthetic Dimension*) mark a retreat over the dialectically ambivalent assessment of a Schoenberg's achievement in *The Philosophy of Modern Music*: what has been omitted from the later judgments is precisely Adorno's fundamental discovery of the historicity, and in particular, the irreversible aging process, of the greatest modernist forms. But if this is so, then the great work of modern high culture – whether it be Schoenberg,

Beckett, or even Brecht himself – cannot serve as a fixed point or eternal standard against which to measure the "degraded" status of mass culture: indeed, fragmentary and as yet undeveloped tendencies in recent art production – hyper- or photo-realism in visual art, "new music" of the type of Lamonte Young, Terry Riley, or Phil Glass, post-modernist literary texts like those of Pynchon – suggest an increasing interpenetration of high and mass cultures.

For all these reasons, it seems to me that we must rethink the opposition high culture/mass culture in such a way that the emphasis on evaluation to which it has traditionally given rise, and which – however the binary system of value operates (mass culture is popular and thus more authentic than high culture, high culture is autonomous and therefore utterly incomparable to a degraded mass culture) – tends to function in some timeless realm of absolute aesthetic judgment, is replaced by a genuinely historical and dialectical approach to these phenomena. Such an approach demands that we read high and mass culture as objectively related and dialectically interdependent phenomena, as twin and inseparable forms of the fission of aesthetic production under late capitalism. From this perspective, the dilemma of the double standard of high and mass culture remains, but it has become – not the subjective problem of our own standards of judgment – but rather an objective contradiction which has its own social grounding. Indeed, this view of the emergence of mass culture obliges us historically to respecify the nature of the "high culture" to which it has conventionally been opposed: the older culture critics indeed tended loosely to raise comparative issues about the "popular culture" of the past. Thus, if you see Greek tragedy, Shakespeare, *Don Quijote*, still widely read romantic lyric of the type of Hugo, or best-selling realistic novels like those of Balzac or Dickens, as uniting a wide "popular" audience with high aesthetic quality, then you are fatally locked into such false problems as the relative value – weighed against Shakespeare or even Dickens – of such popular contemporary *auteurs* of high quality as Chaplin, John Ford, Hitchcock, or even Robert Frost, Andrew Wyeth, Simenon, or John O'Hara. The utter senselessness of this interesting subject of conversation becomes clear when it is understood that from a historical point of view the only form of "high culture" which can be said to constitute the dialectical opposite of mass culture is that high cultural production contemporaneous with the latter, which is to say that artistic production generally designated as *modernism*. The other term would then be Wallace Stevens, or Joyce, or Schoenberg, or Jackson Pollock, but surely not cultural artifacts such as the novels of Balzac or the plays of Molière which essentially precede the historical separation between high and mass culture.

But such specification clearly obliges us to rethink our definitions of mass culture as well: the commercial products of the latter can surely not without intellectual dishonesty be assimilated to so-called popular, let alone, folk art of the past, which reflected and were dependent for their production on quite different social realities, and were in fact the "organic" expression of so many distinct social communities or castes, such as the peasant village, the court, the medieval town, the polis, and even the classical bourgeoisie when it was still a unified social group with its own cultural specificity. The historically unique tendencial effect of late capitalism on all such groups has been to dissolve and to fragment or atomize them into agglomerations (*Gesellschaften*) of isolated and equivalent private individuals, by way of the corrosive action of universal commodification and the market system. Thus, the "popular" as such no longer exists, except under very specific and marginalized conditions (internal and external pockets of so-called underdevelopment within the capitalist world system). The commodity production of contemporary or industrial mass culture thus has nothing whatsoever to do, and nothing in common, with older forms of popular or folk art.

Thus understood, the dialectical opposition and profound structural interrelatedness of modernism and contemporary mass culture opens up a whole new field for cultural study, which promises to be more intelligible historically and socially than research or disciplines which have strategically conceived their mission as a specialization in this or that branch (e.g., in the university, English vs. Popular Culture departments or programs). Now the emphasis must lie squarely on the social and aesthetic situation – the dilemma of form and of a public – shared and faced by both modernism and mass culture, but "solved" in antithetical ways. Thus, in another place, I have suggested that modernism can also be most adequately understood in terms of that commodity production whose all-informing structural influence on mass culture we have described above; only for modernism, the omnipresence of the commodity form determines a reactive stance, so that modernism conceives its formal vocation to be the resistance to commodity form, *not* to be a commodity, to devise an aesthetic language incapable of offering commodity satisfaction, and resistant to instrumentalization. The difference between this position and the valorization of modernism by the Frankfurt School (or, later, by *Tel Quel*) lies in its designation of modernism as reactive, that is, as a symptom and a result of cultural crisis, rather than a new "solution" in its own right: not only is the commodity the prior form in terms of which alone modernism can be structurally grasped, but the very terms of its solution – the conception of the modernist text as the production and the protest of an isolated individual, and the logic of its sign systems as so many private languages ("styles") and private religions – are contradictory and make the social or collective realization of its aesthetic project (Mallarmé's ideal of *Le Livre* can be taken as the latter's fundamental formulation) an impossible one (a judgment which, it ought not to be necessary to add, is not a judgment of value about the "greatness" of the modernist texts).

[…]

The above reflections by no means raise, let alone address, all the most urgent issues which confront an approach to mass culture today. In particular, we have neglected a somewhat different judgment on mass culture, which also loosely derives from the Frankfurt School position on the subject, but whose adherents number "radicals" as well as "elitists" on the Left today. This is the conception of mass culture as sheer manipulation, sheer commercial brainwashing and empty distraction by the multinational corporations who obviously control every feature of the production and distribution of mass culture today. If this were the case, then it is clear that the study of mass culture would at best be assimilated to the anatomy of the techniques of ideological marketing and be subsumed under the analysis of advertising. Roland Barthes' seminal investigation of the latter, however, in his *Mythologies*, opened them up to the whole realm of the operations and functions of culture in everyday life; but since the sociologists of manipulation (with the exception, of course, of the Frankfurt School itself) have, almost by definition, no interest in the hermetic or "high" art production whose dialectical interdependency with mass culture we have argued above, the general effect of their position is to suppress considerations of culture altogether, save as a kind of sand-box affair on the most epiphenomenal level of the superstructure. The implication is thus to suggest that real social life – the only features of social life worth addressing or taking into consideration when political theory and strategy is at stake – are what the Marxian tradition designates as the political, the ideological, and the juridical levels of superstructural reality. Not only is this repression of the cultural moment determined by the university structure and by the ideologies of the various disciplines – thus, political science and sociology at best consign cultural issues to that ghettoizing rubric and marginalized "field of specialization" called the "sociology of culture" – it is also and in a more general way the unwitting perpetuation of the most fundamental ideological stance of American business society itself, for which "culture" – reduced to plays and poems and high-brow concerts – is par excellence the most trivial and non-serious activity in the "real life" of the rat race of daily existence. Yet even the vocation of the esthete (last sighted in the U.S. during the pre-political heyday of the 1950s) and of his successor, the university literature professor, had a socially symbolic content and expressed (generally unconsciously) the anxiety aroused by market competition and the repudiation of the primacy of business pursuits and business values: these are then, to be sure, as thoroughly repressed from academic formalism as culture is from the work of the sociologists of manipulation, a repression which goes a long way towards accounting for the resistance and defensiveness of contemporary literary study towards anything which smacks of the painful reintroduction of just that "real life" – the socio-economic, the historical context – which it was the function of the aesthetic vocation to deny or to mask out in the first place.

What we must ask the sociologists of manipulation, however, is whether they really inhabit the same world we do. Speaking for at least a few, I will say that culture, far from being an occasional matter of the reading of a monthly good book or a trip to the drive-in, seems to me the very element of consumer society itself; no society has ever been saturated with signs and messages like this one. If we follow Debord's argument about the omnipresence and the omnipotence of the image in consumer capitalism today, then if anything the priorities of the real become reversed, and everything is mediated by culture, to the point where even the political and the ideological "levels" have initially to be disentangled from their primary mode of representation which is cultural. Howard Jarvis, Carter, even Castro, the Red Brigade, Vorster, the Communist "penetration" of Africa, the war in Vietnam, strikes, inflation itself – all are images, all come before us with the immediacy of cultural representations of which one can be fairly certain that they are by a long shot not historical reality itself. If we want to go on believing in categories like social class, then we are going to have to dig for them in the insubstantial bottomless realm of cultural and collective fantasy. Even ideology has in our society lost its clarity as prejudice, false consciousness, readily identifiable opinion: our racism gets all mixed up with clean-cut black actors on TV and in commercials, our sexism has to make a detour through new stereotypes of the "women's libber" on the network series. After that, if one wants to stress the primacy of the political, so be it: until the omnipresence of culture in this society is even dimly sensed, realistic conceptions of the nature and function of political praxis today can scarcely be framed.

It is true that manipulation theory sometimes finds a special place in its scheme for those rare cultural objects which can be said to have overt political and social content: thus, 1960s protest songs, *The Salt of the Earth*, Clancey Segal's novels or Sol Yurick's, chicano murals, and the San Francisco Mime Troop. This is not the place to raise the complicated problem of political art today, except to say that our business as culture critics requires us to raise it and to rethink what are still essentially 1930s categories in some new and more satisfactory contemporary way. But the problem of political art – and we have nothing worth saying about it if we do not realize that it is a problem, rather than a choice or a readymade option – suggests an important qualification to the scheme outlined in the first part of the present essay. The implied presupposition of those earlier remarks was that authentic cultural creation is dependent for its existence on authentic collective life, on the vitality of the "organic" social group in whatever form (and such groups can range from the classical polis to the peasant village, from the commonality of the ghetto to the shared values of an embattled pre-revolutionary bourgeoisie). Capitalism systematically dissolves the fabric of all cohesive social groups without exception, including its own ruling class, and thereby problematizes aesthetic production and linguistic invention which have their source in group life. The result, discussed above, is the dialectical fission of older aesthetic expression into two modes, modernism and mass culture, equally dissociated from group praxis. Both of these modes have attained an admirable level of technical virtuosity but it is a day-dream to expect that either of these semiotic structures could be retransformed, by flat, miracle, or sheer talent, into what could be called, in its strong form, political art, or in a more general way, that living and authentic culture of which we have virtually lost the memory, so rare an experience it has become. This is to say that of the two most influential recent Left aesthetics – the Brecht–Benjamin position which hoped for the transformation of the nascent mass-cultural techniques and channels of communication of the 1930s into an openly political art, the *Tel Quel* position which reaffirms the "subversive" and revolutionary efficacy of language revolution and modernist and post-modernist formal innovation – we must reluctantly conclude that neither addresses the specific conditions of our own time.

The only authentic cultural production today has seemed to be that which can draw on the collective experience of marginal pockets of the social life of the world system: black literature and blues, British working-class rock, women's literature, gay literature, the *roman québécois*, the literature of the Third World; and this production is possible only to the degree to which these forms of collective life or collective solidarity have not yet been fully penetrated by the market and by the commodity system. This is not necessarily a negative prognosis, unless you believe in an increasingly windless and all-embracing total system, what shatters such a system – it has unquestionably been falling into place all around us since the development of industrial capitalism – is however very precisely collective praxis or, to pronounce its traditional and

unmentionable name, class struggle. Yet the relationship between class struggle and cultural production is not an immediate one; you do not reinvent an access onto political art and authentic cultural production by studding your individual artistic discourse with class and political signals. Rather, class struggle, and the slow and intermittent development of genuine class consciousness, are themselves the process whereby a new and organic group constitutes itself, whereby the collective breaks through the reified atomization (Sartre calls it the seriality) of capitalist social life. At that point, to say that the group exists and that it generates its own specific cultural life and expression, are one and the same. This is, if you like, the third term missing from my initial picture of the fate of the aesthetic and the cultural under capitalism; yet no useful purpose is served by speculation on the forms such a third and authentic type of cultural language might take in situations which do not yet exist. As for the artists, for them too "the owl of Minerva takes its flight at dusk," for them too, as with Lenin in April, the test of historical inevitability is always after the fact, and they cannot be told any more than the rest of us what is historically possible until after it has been tried. *then they?*

This said, we can now return to the question of mass culture and manipulation. Manipulation theory implies a psychology, but this is all very well and good: Brecht taught us that under the right circumstances you could remake anybody over into anything you liked (*Mann ist Mann*), only he insisted on the situation and the raw materials fully as much or more than on the techniques. Perhaps the key problem about the concept, or pseudo-concept, of manipulation can be dramatized by juxtaposing it to the Freudian notion of repression. The Freudian mechanism, indeed, comes into play only after its object – trauma, charged memory, guilty or threatening desire, anxiety – has in some way been aroused, and risks emerging into the subject's consciousness. Freudian repression is therefore determinate, it has specific content, and may even be said to be something like a "recognition" of that content which expresses itself in the form of denial, forgetfulness, slip, *mauvaise foi*, displacement, substitution, or whatever.

But of course the classical Freudian model of the work of art (as of the dream or the joke) was that of the symbolic fulfillment of the repressed wish, of a complex structure of indirection whereby desire could elude the repressive censor and achieve some measure of a to be sure purely symbolic satisfaction. A more recent "revision" of the Freudian model, however – Norman Holland's *The Dynamics of Literary Response* – proposes a scheme more useful for our present problem, which is to conceive how (commercial) works of art can possibly be said to "manipulate" their publics. For Holland, the psychic function of the work of art must be described in such a way that these two inconsistent and even incompatible features of aesthetic gratification – on the one hand, its wish-fulfilling function, but on the other the necessity that its symbolic structure protect the psyche against the frightening and potentially damaging eruption of powerful archaic desires and wish-material – be somehow harmonized and assigned their place as twin drives of a single structure. Hence Holland's suggestive conception of the vocation of the work of art to *manage* this raw material of the drives and the archaic wish or fantasy material. To rewrite the concept of a management of desire in social terms now allows us to think repression and wish-fulfillment together within the unity of a single mechanism, which gives and takes alike in a kind of psychic compromise or horse-trading, which strategically arouses fantasy content within careful symbolic containment structures which defuse it, gratifying intolerable, unrealizable, properly imperishable desires only to the degree to which they can again be laid to rest.

This model seems to me to permit a far more adequate account of the mechanisms of manipulation, diversion, degradation, which are undeniably at work in mass culture and in the media. In particular it allows us to grasp mass culture not as empty distraction or "mere" false consciousness, but rather as a transformational work on social and political anxieties and fantasies which must then have some effective presence in the mass cultural text in order subsequently to be "managed" or repressed. Indeed, the initial reflections of the present essay suggest that such a thesis ought to be extended to modernism as well, even though we will not here be able to develop this part of the argument further. I will therefore argue that both mass culture and modernism have as much content, in the loose sense of the word, is the older social realisms; but that this content is processed in a very different way than in the latter. Both modernism and mass culture

entertain relations of repression with the fundamental social anxieties and concerns, hopes and blind spots, ideological antinomies and fantasies of disaster, which are their raw material; only where modernism tends to handle this material by producing compensatory structures of various kinds, mass culture represses them by the narrative construction of imaginary resolutions and by the projection of an optical illusion of social harmony.

I will now demonstrate this proposition by a reading of three extremely successful […] commercial films: *Jaws* (now *Jaws I*), and the two parts of *The Godfather*. The readings I will propose are at least consistent with my earlier remarks about the volatilization of the primary text in mass culture by repetition, to the degree of which they are differential, "intertextually" comparative decodings of each of these filmic messages.

In the case of *Jaws*, however, the version or variant against which we will read the film is not the shoddy and disappointing sequel, but rather the bestselling novel from which the film – one of the most successful box office attractions in movie history – was adapted. We will see that the adaptation involved significant changes in the original narrative; our attention to such strategic alterations may indeed arouse some initial suspicion of the official or "manifest" content preserved in both these texts, and on which most of the discussion of *Jaws* has tended to focus. Thus critics from Gore Vidal and *Pravda* all the way to Stephen Heath have tended to emphasize the problem of the shark itself and what it "represents": such speculation ranges from the psychoanalytic to historic anxieties about the Other that menaces American society – whether it be the Communist conspiracy or the Third World – and even to internal fears about the unreality of daily life in American today, and in particular the haunting and unmentionable persistence of the organic – of birth, copulation, and death – which the cellophane society of consumer capitalism desperately recontains in hospitals and old age homes, and sanitizes by means of a whole strategy of linguistic euphemisms which enlarge the older, purely sexual ones: on this view, the Nantucket beaches "represent" consumer society itself, with its glossy and commodified images of gratification, and its scandalous and fragile, ever suppressed, sense of its own possible mortality. Now none of these readings can be said to be wrong or aberrant, but their very multiplicity suggests that the vocation of the symbol – the killer shark – lies less in any single message or meaning than in its very capacity to absorb and organize all of these quite distinct anxieties together. As a symbolic vehicle, then, the shark must be understood in terms of its essentially polysemous function rather than any particular content attributable to it by this or that spectator. Yet it is precisely this polysemousness which is profoundly ideological, insofar as it allows essentially social and historical anxieties to be folded back into apparently "natural" ones, to be both expressed and recontained in what looks like a conflict with other forms of biological existence.

Interpretive emphasis on the shark, indeed, tends to drive all these quite varied readings in the direction of myth criticism, where the shark is naturally enough taken to be the most recent embodiment of Leviathan, so that the struggle with it effortlessly folds back into one of the fundamental paradigms or archetypes of Professor Frye's storehouse of myth. To rewrite the film in these terms is thus to emphasize what I will shortly call its Utopian dimension, that is, its ritual celebration of the renewal of the social order and its salvation, not merely from divine wrath, but also from unworthy leadership.

But to put it this way is to begin to shift our attention from the shark itself to the emergence of the hero – or heroes – whose mythic task it is to rid the civilized world of the archetypal monster. This is, however, precisely the issue – the nature and the specification of the "mythic" hero – about which the discrepancies between the film and the novel have something instructive to tell us. For the novel involves an undisguised expression of class conflict in the tension between the island cop and the high-society oceanographer, who used to summer in Easthampton and ends up sleeping with Brody's wife: Hooper is indeed a much more important figure in the novel than in the film, while by the same token the novel assigns Quint a very minor role in comparison to his crucial presence in the film. Yet the most dramatic surprise the novel holds in store for viewers of the film will evidently be the discovery that in the book Hooper dies, a virtual suicide and a sacrifice to his somber and romantic fascination with death in the person of the shark. Now while it is unclear to me how the American reading public can have responded to the rather alien and exotic resonance of this element of the fantasy – the aristocratic obsession with death would seem to be a more European motif – the social overtones of the novel's resolution – the triumph of the islander and the yankee over the decadent playboy challenger – are surely unmistakable, as is the systematic elimination and suppression of all such class overtones from the film itself.

The latter therefore provides us with a striking illustration of a whole work of displacement by which the written narrative of an essentially class fantasy has been transformed, in the Hollywood product, into something quite different, which it now remains to characterize. Gone is the whole decadent and aristocratic brooding over death, along with the erotic rivalry in which class antagonisms were dramatized; the Hooper of the film is nothing but a technocratic whiz-kid, no tragic hero but instead a good-natured creature of grants and foundations and scientific know-how. But Brody has also undergone an important modification: he is no longer the small-town island boy married to a girl from a socially prominent summer family; rather, he has been transformed into a retired cop from New York City, relocating on Nantucket in an effort to flee the hassle of urban crime, race war, and ghettoization. The figure of Brody now therefore introduces overtones and connotations of law-and-order, rather than of yankee shrewdness, and functions as a TV-police show hero transposed into this apparently more sheltered but in reality equally contradictory milieu which is the great American summer vacation.

I will therefore suggest that in the film the socially resonant conflict between these two characters has for some reason that remains to be formulated been transformed into a vision of their ultimate partnership, and joint triumph over Leviathan. This is clearly the moment to come to Quint, whose enlarged role in the film thereby becomes strategic. The myth-critical option for reading this figure must at once be noted: it is indeed tempting to see Quint as the end term of the three-fold figure of the ages of man into which the team of shark-hunters is so obviously articulated, Hooper and Brody then standing as youth and maturity over against Quint's authority as an elder. But such a reading leaves the basic interpretive problem intact: what can be the allegorical meaning of a ritual in which the elder figure follows the intertextual paradigm of Melville's Ahab to destruction while the other two paddle back in triumph on the wreckage of his vessel? Or, to formulate it in a different way, why is the Ishmael survivor-figure split into the two survivors of the film (and credited with the triumphant destruction of the monster in the bargain)?

Quint's determinations in the film seem to be of two kinds: first, unlike the bureaucracies of law enforcement and science-&-technology (Brody and Hooper), but also in distinction to the corrupt island Mayor with his tourist investments and big business interests, Quint is defined as the locus of old-fashioned private enterprise, of the individual entrepreneurship not merely of small business, but also of local business – hence the insistence on his salty Down-East typicality. Meanwhile – but this feature is also a new addition to the very schematic treatment of the figure of Quint in the novel – he also strongly associates himself with a now distant American past by way of his otherwise gratuitous reminiscences about World War II and the campaign in the Pacific. We are thus authorized to read the death of Quint in the film as the two-fold symbolic destruction of an older America – the America of small business and individual private enterprise of a now outmoded kind, but also the America of the New Deal and the crusade against Nazism, the older America of the depression and the war and of the heyday of classical liberalism.

Now the content of the partnership between Hooper and Brody projected by the film may be specified socially and politically, as the allegory of an alliance between the forces of law-and-order and the new technocracy of the multinational corporations: an alliance which must be cemented, not merely by its fantasized triumph over the ill-defined menace of the shark itself, but above all by the indispensable precondition of the effacement of that more traditional image of an older America which must be eliminated from historical consciousness and social memory before the new power system takes its place. This operation may continue to be read in terms of mythic archetypes, if one likes, but then in that case it is a Utopian and ritual vision which is also a whole – very alarming – political and social program. It touches on

present-day social contradictions and anxieties only to use them for its new task of ideological resolution, symbolically urging us to bury the older populisms and to respond to an image of political partnership which projects a whole new strategy of legitimation; and it effectively displaces the class antagonisms between rich and poor which persist in consumer society (and in the novel from which the film was adapted) by substituting for them a new and spurious kind of fraternity in which the viewer rejoices without understanding that he or she is excluded from it.

Jaws is therefore an excellent example, not merely of ideological manipulation, but also of the way in which genuine social and historical content must be first be tapped and given some initial expression if it is subsequently to be the object of successful manipulation and containment. In my second reading, I want to give this new model of manipulation an even more decisive and paradoxical turn: I will now indeed argue that we cannot fully do justice to the ideological function of works like these unless we are willing to concede the presence within them of a more positive function as well: of what I will call, following the Frankfurt School, their Utopian or transcendent potential – that dimension of even the most degraded type of mass culture which remains implicitly, and no matter how faintly, negative and critical of the social order from which, as a product and a commodity, it springs. At this point in the argument, then, the hypothesis is that the works of mass culture cannot be ideological without at one and the same time being implicitly or explicitly Utopian as well: they cannot manipulate unless they offer some genuine shred of content as a fantasy bribe to the public about to be so manipulated. Even the "false consciousness" of so monstrous a phenomenon of Nazism was nourished by collective fantasies of a Utopian type, in "socialist" as well as in nationalist guises. Our proposition about the drawing power of the works of mass culture has implied that such works cannot manage anxieties about the social order unless they have first revived them and given them some rudimentary expression; we will now suggest that anxiety and hope are two faces of the same collective consciousness, so that the works of mass culture, even if their function lies in the legitimation of the existing order – or some worse one – cannot do their job without deflecting in the latter's service the deepest and most fundamental hopes and fantasies of the collectivity, to which they can therefore, no matter in how distorted a fashion, be found to have given voice.

We therefore need a method capable of doing justice to both the ideological and the Utopian or transcendent functions of mass culture simultaneously. Nothing less will do, as the suppression of either of these terms may testify: we have already commented on the sterility of the older kind of ideological analysis, which, ignoring the Utopian components of mass culture, ends up with the empty denunciation of the latter's manipulatory function and degraded status. But it is equally obvious that the complementary extreme – a method that would celebrate Utopian impulses in the absence of any conception or mention of the ideological vocation of mass culture – simply reproduces the litanies of myth criticism at its most academic and aestheticizing and impoverishes these texts of their semantic content at the same time that it abstracts them from their concrete social and historical situation.

The two parts of *The Godfather* have seemed to me to offer a virtual textbook illustration of these propositions; for one thing, recapitulating the whole generic tradition of the gangster film, it reinvents a certain "myth" of the Mafia in such a way as to allow us to see that ideology is not necessarily a matter of false consciousness, or of the incorrect or distorted representation of historical "fact," but can rather be quite consistent with a "realistic" faithfulness to the latter. To be sure, historical inaccuracy (as, e.g., when the 1950s are telescoped into the 1960s and 1970s in the narrative of Hoffa's career in *F.I.S.T.*) can often provide a suggestive lead towards ideological function: not because there is any scientific virtue in the facts themselves, but rather as a symptom of a resistance of the "logic of the content," of the substance of historicity in question, to the narrative and ideological paradigm into which it has been thereby forcibly assimilated.

The Godfather, however, obviously works in and is a permutation of a generic convention; one could write a history of the changing social and ideological functions of this convention, showing how analogous motifs are called upon in distinct historical situations to emit strategically distinct yet symboli-

cally intelligible messages. Thus the gangsters of the classical 1930s films (Robinson, Cagney, etc.) were dramatized as psychopaths, sick loners striking out against a society essentially made up of wholesome people (the archetypal democratic "common man" of New Deal populism). The post-war gangsters of the Bogart era remain loners in this sense but have unexpectedly become invested with tragic pathos in such a way as to express the confusion of veterans returning from World War II, struggling with the unsympathetic rigidity of institutions, and ultimately crushed by a petty and vindictive social order.

The Mafia material was drawn on and alluded to in these earlier versions of the gangster paradigm, but did not emerge as such until the late 1950s and the early 1960s: this very distinctive narrative content – a kind of saga or family material analogous to that of the medieval *chansons de geste*, with its recurrent episodes and legendary figures returning again and again in different perspectives and contexts – can at once be structurally differentiated from the older paradigms by its collective nature: in this, reflecting an evolution towards organizational themes and team narratives which studies like Will Wright's *Sixguns and Society* have shown to be significant developments in the other sub-genres of mass culture (the western, the caper film, etc.) during the 1960s.

Such an evolution, however, suggests a global transformation of post-war American social life and a global transformation of the potential logic of its narrative content without yet specifying the ideological function of the Mafia paradigm itself. Yet this is surely not very difficult to identify. When indeed we reflect on an organized conspiracy against the public, one which reaches into every corner of our daily lives and our political structures to exercise a wanton ecocidal and genocidal violence at the behest of distant decision-makers and in the name of an abstract conception of profit – surely it is not about the Mafia, but rather about American business itself that we are thinking, American capitalism in its most systematized and computerized, dehumanized, "multinational" and corporate form. What kind of crime, said Brecht, is the robbing of a bank, compared to the founding of a bank? Yet until recent years, American business has enjoyed a singular freedom from popular criticism and articulated collective resentment; since the depolitization of the New Deal, the McCarthy era and the beginning of the Cold War and of media or consumer society, it has known an inexplicable holiday from the kinds of populist antagonisms which have only recently (white collar crime, hostility to utility companies or to the medical profession) shown signs of reemerging. Such freedom from blame is all the more remarkable when we observe the increasing squalor that daily life in the U.S. owes to big business and to its unenviable position as the purest form of commodity and market capitalism functioning anywhere in the world today.

This is the context in which the ideological function of the myth of the Mafia can be understood, as the substitution of crime for big business, as the strategic displacement of all the rage generated by the American system onto this mirror-image of big business provided by the movie screen and the various TV series, it being understood that the fascination with the Mafia remains ideological even if in reality organized crime has exactly the importance and influence in American life which such representations attribute to it. The function of the Mafia narrative is indeed to encourage the conviction that the deterioration of daily life in the United States today is an ethical rather than an economic matter, connected, not with profit, but rather "merely" with dishonesty, and with some omnipresent moral corruption whose ultimate mythic source lies in the pure Evil of the Mafiosi themselves. For genuinely political insights into the economic realities of late capitalism, the myth of the Mafia strategically substitutes the vision of what is seen to be a criminal aberration from the norm, rather than the norm itself; indeed, the displacement of political and historical analysis by ethical judgments and considerations is generally the sign of an ideological maneuver and of the intent to mystify. Mafia movies thus project a "solution" to social contradictions – incorruptibility, honesty, crime fighting, and finally law-and-order itself – which is evidently a very different proposition from that diagnosis of the American misery whose prescription would be social revolution.

But if this is the ideological function of Mafia narratives like *The Godfather*, what can be said to be their transcendent or Utopian function? The latter is to be sought, it seems to me, in the fantasy message projected by the title of this film, that is, in the family

itself, seen as a figure of collectivity and as the object of a Utopian longing, if not a Utopian envy. A narrative synthesis like *The Godfather* is possible only at the conjuncture in which ethnic content – the reference to an alien collectivity – comes to fill the older gangster schemas and to inflect them powerfully in the direction of the social; the superposition on conspiracy of fantasy material related to ethnic groups then triggers the Utopian function of this transformed narrative paradigm. In the United States, indeed, ethnic groups are not only the object of prejudice, they are also the object of envy; and these two impulses are deeply intermingled and reinforce each other mutually. The dominant white middle-class groups – already given over to *anomie* and social fragmentation and atomization – find in the ethnic and racial groups which are the object of their social repression and status contempt at one and the same time the image of some older collective ghetto or ethnic neighborhood solidarity; they feel the envy and *ressentiment* of the *Gesellschaft* for the older *Gemeinschaft* which it is simultaneously exploiting and liquidating.

Thus, at a time when the disintegration of the dominant communities is persistently "explained" in the (profoundly ideological) terms of a deterioration of the family, the growth of permissiveness and the loss of authority of the father, the ethnic group can seem to project an image of social reintegration by way of the patriarchal and authoritarian family of the past. Thus the tightly knit bonds of the Mafia family (in both senses), the protective security of the (god-) father with his omnipresent authority, offers a contemporary pretext for a Utopian fantasy which can no longer express itself through such outmoded paradigms and stereotypes as the image of the now extinct American small town.

The drawing power of a mass cultural artifact like *The Godfather* may thus be measured by its twin capacity to perform an urgent ideological function at the same time that it provides the vehicle for the investment of a desperate Utopian fantasy. Yet the film is doubly interesting from our present point of view in the way in which its sequel – released from the restrictions of the bestselling fictional text on which Part I was based – tangibly betrays the momentum and the operation of an ideological and Utopian logic in something like a free or unbound state. *Godfather II,* indeed, offers a striking illustration of Pierre Macherey's thesis, in *Towards a Theory of Literary Production*, that the work of art does not so much *express* ideology as, by endowing the latter with aesthetic representation and figuration, it ends up enacting the latter's own virtual unmasking and self-criticism.

It is as though the unconscious ideological and Utopian impulses at work in *Godfather I* could in the sequel be observed to work themselves towards the light and towards thematic or reflexive foregrounding in their own right. The first film held the two dimensions of ideology and Utopia together within a single generic structure, whose conventions remained intact. With the second film, however, this structure falls as it were into history itself, which submits it to a patient deconstruction that will in the end leave its ideological content undisguised and its displacements visible to the naked eye. Thus the Mafia material, which in the first film served as a substitute for business, now slowly transforms itself into the overt thematics of business itself, just as "in reality" the need for the cover of legitimate investments ends up turning the Mafiosi into real businessmen. The climactic end moment of this historical development is then reached (in the film, but also in real history) when American business, and with it American imperialism, meet that supreme ultimate obstacle to their internal dynamism and structurally necessary expansion which is the Cuban Revolution.

Meanwhile, the Utopian strand of this filmic text, the material of the older patriarchal family, now slowly disengages itself from this first or ideological one, and, working its way back in time to its own historical origins, betrays its roots in the pre-capitalist social formation of a backward and feudal Sicily. Thus these two narrative impulses as it were reverse each other: the ideological myth of the Mafia ends up generating the authentically Utopian vision of revolutionary liberation; while the degraded Utopian content of the family paradigm ultimately unmasks itself as the survival of more archaic forms of repression and sexism and violence. Meanwhile, both of these narrative strands, freed to pursue their own inner logic to its limits, are thereby driven to the outer reaches and historical boundaries of capitalism itself, the one as it touches the pre-capitalist societies of the past, the other at the beginnings of the future and the dawn of socialism.

These two parts of *The Godfather* – the second so much more demonstrably political than the first – may serve to dramatize our second basic proposition in the present essay, namely the thesis that all contemporary works of art – whether those of high culture and modernism or of mass culture and commercial culture – have as their underlying impulse – albeit in what is often distorted and repressed, unconscious form – our deepest fantasies about the nature of social life, both as we live it now, and as we feel in our bones it ought rather to be lived. To reawaken, in the midst of a privatized and psychologizing society, obsessed with commodities and bombarded by the ideological slogans of big business, some sense of the ineradicable drive towards collectivity that can be detected, no matter how faintly and feebly, in the most degraded works of mass culture just as surely as in the classics of modernism – is surely an indispensable precondition for any meaningful Marxist intervention in contemporary culture.

7

"Notes on Deconstructing 'the Popular'" (1981)

Stuart Hall

First, I want to say something about periodisations in the study of popular culture. Difficult problems are posed here by periodisation – I don't offer it to you simply as a sort of gesture to the historians. Are the major breaks largely descriptive? Do they arise largely from within popular culture itself, or from factors which are outside of but impinge on it? With what other movements and periodisations is 'popular culture' most revealingly linked? Then I want to tell you some of the difficulties I have with the term 'popular'. I have almost as many problems with 'popular' as I have with 'culture'. When you put the two terms together, the difficulties can be pretty horrendous.

Throughout the long transition into agrarian capitalism and then in the formation and development of industrial capitalism, there is a more or less continuous struggle over the culture of working people, the labouring classes and the poor. This fact must be the starting point for any study, both of the basis for, and of the transformations of, popular culture. The changing balance and relations of social forces throughout that history reveal themselves, time and again, in struggles over the forms of the culture, traditions and ways of life of the popular classes. Capital had a stake in the culture of the popular classes because the constitution of a whole new social order around capital required a more or less continuous, if intermittent, process of re-education, in the broadest sense. And

Stuart Hall, "Notes on Deconstructing 'the Popular,'" pp. 227–39 from *People's History and Socialist Theory*, ed. R. Samuel. London: Routledge, 1981. Reproduced by permission of Taylor & Francis Books UK.

one of the principal sites of resistance to the forms through which this 'reformation' of the people was pursued lay in popular tradition. That is why popular culture is linked, for so long, to questions of tradition, of traditional forms of life – and why its 'traditionalism' has been so often misinterpreted as a product of a merely conservative impulse, backward looking and anachronistic. Struggle and resistance – but also, of course, appropriation and *ex*-propriation. Time and again, what we are really looking at is the active destruction of particular ways of life, and their transformation into something new. 'Cultural change' is a polite euphemism for the process by which some cultural forms and practices are driven out of the centre of popular life, actively marginalised. Rather than simply 'falling into disuse' through the Long March to modernisation, things are actively pushed aside, so that something else can take their place. The magistrate and the evangelical police have, or ought to have, a more 'honoured' place in the history of popular culture than they have usually been accorded. Even more important than ban and proscription is that subtle and slippery customer – 'reform' (with all the positive and unambiguous overtones it carries today). One way or another, 'the people' are frequently the object of 'reform': often, for their own good, of course – 'in their best interests'. We understand struggle and resistance, nowadays, rather better than we do reform and transformation. Yet 'transformations' are at the heart of the study of popular culture. I mean the active work on existing traditions and activities, their active re-working, so that they come out a different way: they appear to 'persist' – yet, from one period to another, they come to stand in a different relation to the ways working people live and the ways they define their relations to each other, to 'the others' and to their conditions of life. Transformation is the key to the long and protracted process of the 'moralisation' of the labouring classes, and the 'demoralisation' of the poor, and the 're-education' of the people. Popular culture is neither, in a 'pure' sense, the popular traditions of resistance to these processes; nor is it the forms which are superimposed on and over them. It is the ground on which the transformations are worked.

In the study of popular culture, we should always start here: with the double-stake in popular culture, the double movement of containment and resistance, which is always inevitably inside it.

The study of popular culture has tended to oscillate wildly between the two alternative poles of that dialectic – containment/resistance. We have had some striking and marvellous reversals. Think of the really major revolution in historical understanding which has followed as the history of 'polite society' and the Whig aristocracy in eighteenth-century England has been upturned by the addition of the history of the turbulent and ungovernable people. The popular traditions of the eighteenth-century labouring poor, the popular classes and the 'loose and disorderly sort' often, now, appear as virtually independent formations: tolerated in a state of permanently unstable equilibrium in relatively peaceful and prosperous times; subject to arbitrary excursions and expeditions in times of panic and crisis. Yet, though formally these were the cultures of the people 'outside the walls', beyond political society and the triangle of power, they were never, in fact, outside of the larger field of social forces and cultural relations. They not only constantly pressed on 'society'; they were linked and connected with it, by a multitude of traditions and practices. Lines of 'alliance' as well as lines of cleavage. From these cultural bases, often far removed from the dispositions of law, power and authority, 'the people' threatened constantly to erupt: and, when they did so, they break on to the stage of patronage and power with a threatening din and clamour – with fife and drum, cockade and effigy, proclamation and ritual – and, often, with a striking, popular, ritual discipline. Yet never quite overturning the delicate strands of paternalism, deference and terror within which they were constantly if insecurely constrained. In the following century, where the 'labouring' and the 'dangerous' classes lived without benefit of that fine distinction the reformers were so anxious to draw (this was a *cultural* distinction as well as a moral and economic one: and a great deal of legislation and regulation was devised to operate directly on it), some areas preserved for long periods a virtually impenetrable enclave character. It took virtually the whole length of the century before the representatives of 'law and order' – the new police – could acquire anything like a regular and customary foothold within them. Yet, at the same time, the penetration of the cultures of the labouring masses and the urban poor was deeper, more continuous – and more continuously 'educative' and reformatory – in that period than at any time since.

One of the main difficulties standing in the way of a proper periodisation of popular culture is the profound transformation in the culture of the popular classes which occurs between the 1880s and the 1920s. There are whole histories yet to be written about this period. But, although there are probably many things not right about its detail, I do think Gareth Stedman Jones's article on the 'Re-making of the English working class' in this period has drawn our attention to something fundamental and qualitatively different and important about it. It was a period of deep structural change. The more we look at it, the more convinced we become that somewhere in this period lies the matrix of factors and problems from which *our* history – and our peculiar dilemmas – arise. Everything changes – not just a shift in the relations of forces but a reconstitution of the terrain of political struggle itself. It isn't just by chance that so many of the characteristic forms of what we now think of as 'traditional' popular culture either emerge from or emerge in their distinctive modern form, in that period. What has been done for the 1790s and for the 1840s, and is being done for the eighteenth century, now radically needs to be done for the period of what we might call the 'social imperialist' crisis.

The general point made earlier is true, without qualification, for this period, so far as popular culture is concerned. There is no separate, autonomous, 'authentic' layer of working-class culture to be found. Much of the most immediate forms of popular recreation, for example, are saturated by popular imperialism. Could we expect otherwise? How could we explain, and what would we *do* with the idea of, the culture of a dominated class which, despite its complex interior formations and differentiations, stood in a very particular relation to a major restructuring of capital; which itself stood in a peculiar relation to the rest of the world; a people bound by the most complex ties to a changing set of material relations and conditions; who managed somehow to construct 'a culture' which remained untouched by the most powerful dominant ideology – popular imperialism? Especially when that ideology – belying its name – was directed as much at them as it was at Britain's changing position in a world capitalist expansion?

Think, in relation to the question of popular imperialism, of the history and relations between the people and one of the major means of cultural expression: the press. To go back to displacement and superimposition – we can see clearly how the liberal middle-class press of the mid-nineteenth century was constructed on the back of the active destruction and marginalisation of the indigenous radical and working-class press. But, on top of that process, something qualitatively new occurs towards the end of the nineteenth century and the beginning of the twentieth century in this area: the active, mass insertion of a developed and mature working-class audience into a new kind of *popular*, commercial press. This has had profound cultural consequences: though it isn't in any narrow sense exclusively a 'cultural' question at all. It required the whole reorganisation of the capital basis and structure of the cultural industry; a harnessing of new forms of technology and of labour processes; the establishment of new types of distribution, operating through the new cultural mass markets. But one of its effects was indeed a reconstituting of the cultural and political relations between the dominant and the dominated classes: a change intimately connected with that containment of popular democracy on which 'our democratic way of life' today, appears to be so securely based. Its results are all too palpably with us still, today: a popular press, the more strident and virulent as it gradually shrinks; organised by capital 'for' the working classes; with, nevertheless, deep and influential roots in the culture and language of the 'underdog', of 'Us': with the power to represent the class to itself in its most traditionalist form. This is a slice of the history of 'popular culture' well worth unravelling.

Of course, one could not begin to do so without talking about many things which don't usually figure in the discussion of 'culture' at all. They have to do with the reconstruction of capital and the rise of the collectivisms and the formation of a new kind of 'educative' state as much as with recreation, dance and popular song. As an area of serious historical work, the study of popular culture is like the study of labour history and its institutions. To declare an interest in it is to correct a major imbalance, to mark a significant oversight. But, in the end, it yields most when it is seen in relation to a more general, a wider history.

I select this period – the 1880s–1920s – because it is one of the real test cases for the revived interest in popular culture. Without in any way casting aspersions on the important historical work which has been done and remains to do on earlier periods, I do believe that many of the real difficulties (theoretical as well as empirical) will only be confronted when we begin to examine closely popular culture in a period which begins to resemble our own, which poses the same kind of interpretive problems as our own, and which is informed by our own sense of contemporary questions. I am dubious about that kind of interest in 'popular culture' which comes to a sudden and unexpected halt at roughly the same point as the decline of Chartism. It isn't by chance that very few of us are working in popular culture in the 1930s. I suspect there is something peculiarly awkward, especially for socialists, in the non-appearance of a militant, radical mature culture of the working class in the 1930s when – to tell you the truth – most of us would have expected it to appear. From the viewpoint of a purely 'heroic' or 'autonomous' popular culture, the 1930s is a pretty barren period. This 'barrenness' – like the earlier unexpected richness and diversity – cannot be explained from *within* popular culture alone.

We have now to begin to speak, not just about discontinuities and qualitative change, but about a very severe fracture, a deep rupture – especially in popular culture in the postwar period. Here it is not only a matter of a change in cultural relations between the classes, but of the changed relationship between the people and the concentration and expansion of the new cultural apparatuses themselves. But could one seriously now set out to write the history of popular culture without taking into account the monopolisation of the cultural industries, on the back of a profound technological revolution (it goes without saying that no 'profound technological revolution' is ever in any sense 'purely' technical)? To write a history of the culture of the popular classes exclusively from inside those classes, without understanding the ways in which they are constantly held in relation with the institutions of dominant cultural production, is not to live in the twentieth century. The point is clear about the twentieth century. I believe it holds good for the nineteenth and eighteenth centuries as well.

So much for 'some problems of periodisation'.

Next, I want to say something about 'popular'. The term can have a number of different meanings: not all of them useful. Take the most common-sense meaning: the things which are said to be 'popular' because masses of people listen to them, buy them, read them, consume them, and seem to enjoy them to the full. This is the 'market' or commercial definition of the term: the one which brings socialists out in spots. It is quite rightly associated with the manipulation and debasement of the culture of the people. In one sense, it is the direct opposite of the way I have been using the word earlier. I have, though, two reservations about entirely dispensing with this meaning, unsatisfactory as it is.

First, if it is true that, in the twentieth century, vast numbers of people *do* consume and even indeed enjoy the cultural products of our modern cultural industry, then it follows that very substantial numbers of working people must be included within the audiences for such products. Now, if the forms and relationships, on which participation in this sort of commercially provided 'culture' depend, are purely manipulative and debased, then the people who consume and enjoy them must either be themselves debased by these activities or else living in a permanent state of 'false consciousness'. They must be 'cultural dopes' who can't tell that what they are being fed is an up-dated form of the opium of the people. That judgment may make us feel right, decent and self-satisfied about our denunciations of the agents of mass manipulation and deception – the capitalist cultural industries: but I don't know that it is a view which can survive for long as an adequate account of cultural relationships; and even less as a socialist perspective on the culture and nature of the working class. Ultimately, the notion

of the people as a purely *passive*, outline force is a deeply unsocialist perspective.

Second, then: can we get around this problem without dropping the inevitable and necessary attention to the manipulative aspect of a great deal of commercial popular culture? There are a number of strategies for doing so, adopted by radical critics and theorists of popular culture, which, I think, are highly dubious. One is to counterpose to it another, whole, 'alternative' culture – the authentic 'popular culture'; and to suggest that the 'real' working class (whatever that is) isn't taken in by the commercial substitutes. This is a heroic alternative; but not a very convincing one. Basically what is wrong with it is that it neglects the absolutely essential relations of cultural power – of domination and subordination – which is an intrinsic feature of cultural relations. I want to assert on the contrary that there is *no* whole, authentic, autonomous 'popular culture' which lies outside the field of force of the relations of cultural power and domination. Second, it greatly underestimates the power of cultural implantation. This is a tricky point to make, for, as soon as it is made, one opens oneself to the charge that one is subscribing to the thesis of cultural incorporation. The study of popular culture keeps shifting between these two, quite unacceptable, poles: pure 'autonomy' or total incapsulation.

Actually, I don't think it is necessary or right to subscribe to either. Since ordinary people are not cultural dopes, they are perfectly capable of recognising the way the realities of working-class life are reorganised, reconstructed and reshaped by the way they are represented (i.e. re-presented) in, say, *Coronation Street*. The cultural industries do have the power constantly to rework and reshape what they represent; and, by repetition and selection, to impose and implant such definitions of ourselves as fit more easily the descriptions of the dominant or preferred culture. That is what the concentration of cultural power – the means of culture-making in the heads of the few – actually means. These definitions don't have the power to occupy our minds; they don't function on us as if we are blank screens. But they do occupy and rework the interior contradictions of feeling and perception in the dominated classes; they do find or clear a space of recognition in those who respond to them. Cultural domination has real effects – even if these are neither all-powerful nor all-inclusive. If we were to argue that these imposed forms have no influence, it would be tantamount to arguing that the culture of the people can exist as a separate enclave, outside the distribution of cultural power and the relations of cultural force. I do not believe that. Rather, I think there is a continuous and necessarily uneven and unequal struggle, by the dominant culture, constantly to disorganise and reorganise popular culture; to enclose and confine its definitions and forms within a more inclusive range of dominant forms. There are points of resistance; there are also moments of supersession. This is the dialectic of cultural struggle. In our times, it goes on continuously, in the complex lines of resistance and acceptance, refusal and capitualtion, which make the field of culture a sort of constant battlefield. A battlefield where no once-for-all victories are obtained but where there are always strategic positions to be won and lost.

This first definition, then, is not a useful one for our purposes; but it might force us to think more deeply about the complexity of cultural relations, about the reality of cultural power and about the nature of cultural implantation. If the forms of provided commercial popular culture are not purely manipulative, then it is because, alongside the false appeals the foreshortenings, the trivialisation and short circuits, there are also elements of recognition and identification, something approaching a recreation of recognisable experiences and attitudes, to which people are responding. The danger arises because we tend to think of cultural forms as whole and coherent: either wholly corrupt or wholly authentic. Whereas, they are deeply contradictory; they play on contradictions especially when they function in the domain of the 'popular'. The language of the *Daily Mirror* is neither a pure construction of Fleet Street 'newspeak' nor is it the language which its working-class readers actually speak. It is a highly complex species of linguistic *ventriloquism* in which the debased brutalism of popular journalism is skilfully combined and intricated with some elements of the directness and vivid particularity of working-class language. It cannot get by without preserving some element of its roots in a real vernacular – in 'the popular'. It wouldn't get very far unless it were capable of reshaping popular elements into a species of canned and neutralised demotic populism.

The second definition of 'popular' is easier to live with. This is the descriptive one. Popular culture is all those things that 'the people' do or have done. This is close to an 'anthropological' definition of the term: the culture, mores, customs and folkways of 'the people'. What defines their 'distinctive way of life'. I have two difficulties with this definition, too.

First, I am suspicious of it precisely because it is too descriptive. This is putting it mildly. Actually, it is based on an infinitely expanding inventory. Virtually *anything* which 'the people' have ever done can fall into the list. Pigeon-fancying and stamp-collecting, flying ducks on the wall and garden gnomes. The problem is how to distinguish this infinite list, in any but a descriptive way, from what popular culture is *not*.

But the second difficulty is more important – and relates to a point made earlier. We can't simply collect into one category all the things which 'the people' do, without observing that the real analytic distinction arises, not from the list itself – an inert category of things and activities – but from the key opposition: the people/not of the people. That is to say the structuring principle of 'the popular' in this sense is the tensions and oppositions between what belongs to the central domain of elite or dominant culture, and the culture of the 'periphery'. It is this opposition which constantly structures the domain of culture into the 'popular' and the 'non-popular'. But you cannot construct these oppositions in a purely descriptive way. For, from period to period, the *contents* of each category changes. Popular forms become enhanced in cultural value, go up the cultural escalator – and find themselves on the opposite side. Others things cease to have high cultural value, and are appropriated into the popular, becoming transformed in the process. The structuring principle does not consist of the contents of each category – which, I insist, will alter from one period to another. Rather it consists of the forces and relations which sustain the distinction, the difference: roughly, between what, at any time, counts as an elite cultural activity or form, and what does not. These categories remain, though the inventories change. What is more, a whole set of institutions and institutional processes are required to sustain each – and to continually mark the difference between them. The school and the education system is one such institution – distinguishing the valued part of the culture, the cultural heritage, the history to be transmitted, from the 'valueless' part. The literary and scholarly apparatus is another – marking-off certain kinds of valued knowledge from others. The important fact, then, is not a mere descriptive inventory – which may have the negative effect of freezing popular culture into some timeless descriptive mould – but the relations of power which are constantly punctuating and dividing the domain of culture into its preferred and its residual categories.

So I settle for a third definition of 'popular', though it is a rather uneasy one. This looks, in any particular period, at those forms and activities which have their roots in the social and material conditions of particular classes; which have been embodied in popular traditions and practices. In this sense, it retains what is valuable in the descriptive definition. But it goes on to insist that what is essential to the definition of popular culture is the relations which define 'popular culture' in a continuing tension (relationship, influence and antagonism) to the dominant culture. It is a conception of culture which is polarised around this cultural dialectic. It treats the domain of cultural forms and activities as a constantly changing field. Then it looks at the relations which constantly structure this field into dominant and subordinate formations. It looks at the *process* by which these relations of dominance and subordination are articulated. It treats them as a process; the process by means of which some things are actively preferred so that others can be dethroned. It has at its centre the changing and uneven relations of force which define the field of culture – that is, the question of cultural struggle and its many forms. Its main focus of attention is the relation between culture and questions of hegemony.

What we have to be concerned with, in this definition, is not the question of the 'authenticity' or organic wholeness of popular culture. Actually, it recognises that almost *all* cultural forms will be contradictory in this sense, composed of antagonistic and unstable elements. The meaning of a cultural form and its place or position in the cultural field is *not* inscribed inside its form. Nor is its position fixed once and forever. This year's radical symbol or slogan will be neutralised into next year's fashion; the year after, it will be the object of a profound cultural nostalgia. Today's rebel folksinger ends up, tomorrow, on the cover of *The Observer*

colour magazine. The meaning of a cultural symbol is given in part by the social field into which it is incorporated, the practices with which it articulates and is made to resonate. What matters is *not* the intrinsic or historically fixed objects of culture, but the state of play in cultural relations: to put it bluntly and in an over-simplified form – what counts is the class struggle in and over culture.

Almost every fixed inventory will betray us. Is the novel a 'bourgeois' form? The answer can only be historically provisional: when? which novels? for whom? under what conditions?

What that very great Marxist theoretician of language who used the name Volosinov, once said about the sign – the key element of all signifying practices – is true of cultural forms:

> Class does not coincide with the sign community, i.e. with … the totality of users of the same sets of signs for ideological communication. Thus various different classes will use one and the same language. As a result, differently oriented accents intersect in every ideological sign. Sign becomes an arena of class struggle. … By and large it is thanks to this intersecting of accents that a sign maintains its vitality and dynamism and the capacity for further development. A sign that has been withdrawn from the pressure of the social struggle – which so to speak crosses beyond the pale of the social struggle – inevitably loses force, degenerating into an allegory and becoming the object not of live social intelligibility but of philosophical comprehension. … The ruling class strives to impart a supraclass, eternal character to the ideological sign, to extinguish or drive inward the struggle between social value judgements which occurs in it, to make the sign unaccentual. In actual fact, each living ideological sign has two faces, like Janus. Any current curse word can become a word of praise, any current truth must inevitably sound to many people as the greatest lie. This inner dialectic quality of the sign comes out fully in the open only in times of social crisis or revolutionary change.[1]

Cultural struggle, of course, takes many forms: incorporation, distortion, resistance, negotiation, recuperation. Raymond Williams has done us a great deal of service by outlining some of these processes, with his distinction between emergent, residual and incorporated moments. We need to expand and develop this rudimentary schema. The important thing is to look at it dynamically: as an historical process.

Emergent forces reappear in ancient historical disguise; emergent forces, pointing to the future, lose their anticipatory power, and become merely backward looking; today's cultural breaks can be recuperated as a support to tomorrow's dominant system of values and meanings. The struggle continues: but it is almost never in the same place, over the same meaning or value. It seems to me that the cultural process – cultural power – in our society depends, in the first instance, on this drawing of the line, always in each period in a different place, as to what is to be incorporated into 'the great tradition' and what is not. Educational and cultural institutions, along with the many positive things they do, also help to discipline and police this boundary.

This should make us think again about that tricky term in popular culture, 'tradition'. Tradition is a vital element in culture; but it has little to do with the mere persistence of old forms. It has much more to do with the way elements have been linked together or articulated. These arrangements in a national-popular culture have no fixed or inscribed position, and certainly no meaning which is carried along, so to speak, in the stream of historical tradition, unchanged. Not only can the elements of 'tradition' be rearranged, so that they articulate with different practices and positions, and take on a new meaning and relevance. It is also often the case that cultural struggle arises in its sharpest form just at the point where different, opposed traditions meet, intersect. They seek to detach a cultural form from its implantation in one tradition, and to give it a new cultural resonance or accent. Traditions are not fixed forever: certainly not in any universal position in relation to a single class. Cultures, conceived not as separate 'ways of life' but as 'ways of struggle' constantly intersect: the pertinent cultural struggles arise at the points of intersection. Think of the ways in the eighteenth century, in which a certain language of legality, of constitutionalism and of 'rights' becomes a battleground, at the point of intersection between two divergent traditions between the 'tradition' of gentry 'majesty and terror' and the traditions of popular justice. Gramsci, providing a tentative answer to his own question as to how a new 'collective will' arises, and a national-popular culture is transformed, observed that

> What matters is the criticism to which such an ideological complex is subjected by the first representatives of the new historical phase. This criticism makes possible a process of differentiation and change in the relative weight that the elements of old ideologies used to possess. What was previously secondary and subordinate, even incidental, is now taken to be primary – becomes the nucleus of a new ideological and theoretical complex. The old collective will dissolves into its contradictory elements since the subordinate ones develop socially.

This is the terrain of national-popular culture and tradition as a battlefield.

This provides us with a warning against those self-enclosed approaches to popular culture which, valuing 'tradition' for its own sake, and treating it in an a-historical manner, analyse popular cultural forms as if they contained within themselves from their moment of origin, some fixed and unchanging meaning or value. The relationship between historical position and aesthetic value is an important and difficult question in popular culture. But the attempt to develop some universal popular aesthetic, founded on the moment of origin of cultural forms and practices, is almost certainly profoundly mistaken. What could be more eclectic and random than that assemblage of dead symbols and bric-a-brac, ransacked from yesterday's dressing-up box, in which, just now, many young people have chosen to adorn themselves? These symbols and bits and pieces are profoundly ambiguous. A thousand lost cultural causes could be summoned up through them. Every now and then, amongst the other trinkets, we find that sign which, above all other signs, ought to be fixed – solidified – in its cultural meaning and connotation forever: the swastika. And yet there it dangles, partly – but not entirely – cut loose from its profound cultural reference in twentieth-century history. What does it mean? What is it signifying? Its signification is rich, and richly ambiguous: certainly unstable. This terrifying sign may delimit a range of meanings but it carries no guarantee of a single meaning within itself. The streets are full of kids who are not 'fascist' because they may wear a swastika on a chain. On the other hand, perhaps they *could* be. … What this sign means will ultimately depend, in the politics of youth culture, less on the intrinsic cultural symbolism of the thing in itself, and more on the balance of forces between, say, the National Front and the Anti-Nazi League, between White Rock and the Two Tone Sound.

Not only is there no intrinsic guarantee within the cultural sign or form itself. There is no guarantee that, because at one time it was linked with a pertinent struggle, that it will always be the living expression of a class: so that every time you give it an airing it will 'speak the language of socialism'. If cultural expressions register for socialism, it is because they have been linked as the practices, the forms and organisation of a living struggle, which has succeeded in appropriating those symbols and giving them a socialist connotation. Culture is not already permanently inscribed with the conditions of a class before that struggle begins. The struggle consists in the success or failure to give 'the cultural' a socialist accent.

The term 'popular' has very complex relations to the term 'class'. We know this, but are often at pains to forget it. We speak of particular forms of working-class culture; but we use the more inclusive term, 'popular culture' to refer to the general field of enquiry. It's perfectly clear that what I've been saying would make little sense without reference to a class perspective and to class struggle. But it is also clear that there is no one-to-one relationship between a class and a particular cultural form or practice. The terms 'class' and 'popular' are deeply related but they are not absolutely interchangeable. The reason for that is obvious. There are no wholly separate 'cultures' paradigmatically attached, in a relation of historical fixity, to specific 'whole' classes – although there are clearly distinct and variable class-cultural formations. Class cultures tend to intersect and overlap in the same field of struggle. The term 'popular' indicates this somewhat displaced relationship of culture to classes. More accurately, it refers to that alliance of classes and forces which constitute the 'popular classes'. The culture of the oppressed the excluded classes: this is the area to which the term 'popular' refers us. And the opposite side to that – the side with the cultural power to decide what belongs and what does not – is, by definition, not another 'whole' class, but that other alliance of classes, strata and social forces which constitute what is not 'the people' and not the 'popular classes': the culture of the power-bloc.

The people versus the power-bloc: this, rather than 'class-against-class', is the central line of contradiction around which the terrain of culture is polarised. Popular culture, especially, is organised around the contradiction: the popular forces versus the power-bloc. This gives to the terrain of cultural struggle its own kind of specificity. But the term 'popular', and even more, the collective subject to which it must refer – 'the people' – is highly problematic. It is made problematic by, say, the ability of Mrs Thatcher to pronounce a sentence like, 'We have to limit the power of the trade unions because that is what the people want.' That suggests to me that, just as there is no fixed content to the category of 'popular culture', so there is no fixed subject to attach to it – 'the people'. 'The people' are not always back there, where they have always been, their culture untouched, their liberties and their instincts intact, still struggling on against the Norman yoke or whatever: as if, if only we can 'discover' them and bring them back on stage, they will always stand up in the right, appointed place and be counted. The capacity to *constitute* classes and individuals as a popular force – that is the nature of political and cultural struggle: to *make* the divided classes and the separated peoples – divided and separated by culture as much as by other factors – *into* a popular-democratic cultural force.

We can be certain that *other* forces also have a stake in defining 'the people' as something else: 'the people' who need to be disciplined more, ruled better, more effectively policed, whose way of life needs to be protected from 'alien cultures', and so on. There is some part of both those alternatives inside each of us. Sometimes we can be constituted as a force against the power-bloc: that is the historical opening in which it is possible to construct a culture which is genuinely popular. But, in our society, if we are not constituted like that, we will be constituted into its opposite: an effective populist force, saying 'Yes' to power. Popular culture is one of the sites where this struggle for and against a culture of the powerful is engaged: it is also the stake to be won or lost in that struggle. It is the arena of consent and resistance. It is partly where hegemony arises, and where it is secured. It is not a sphere where socialism, a socialist culture – already fully formed – might be simply 'expressed'. But it is one of the places where socialism might be constituted. That is why 'popular culture' matters. Otherwise, to tell you the truth, I don't give a damn about it.

Note

1   A. Volosinov, *Marxism and the Philosophy of Language* (New York, 1977).

Further Reading

Bailey, Peter, *Leisure and Class in Victorian England 1830–1885*, London, 1978.

Hall, Stuart and Whannel, A. D., *The Popular Arts*, London, 1964.

Johnson, Richard, 'Three problematics: elements of a theory of working-class culture' in *Working-Class Culture, Studies in History and Theory*, ed. by John Clarke, Charles Chrichter and Richard Johnson, London, 1979.

Malcolmson, R. W., *Popular Recreation in English Society, 1700–1850*, Cambridge, 1973.

Nowell-Smith, Geoffrey, 'Gramsci and the national-popular', *Screen Education*, Spring 1977.

Stedman Jones, Gareth, 'Working-Class culture and working class politics in London, 1870–1890', *Journal of Social History*, Summer 1974.

Thompson, E. P., 'Patrician society, plebeian culture', *Journal of Social History*, Summer 1974.

Williams, Raymond, 'Radical or popular' in *The Press We Deserve*, ed. by James Curran, London, 1970.

8

"The Forms of Capital" (1986)

Pierre Bourdieu

The social world is accumulated history, and if it is not to be reduced to a discontinuous series of instantaneous mechanical equilibria between agents who are treated as interchangeable particles, one must reintroduce into it the notion of capital and with it, accumulation and all its effects. Capital is accumulated labor (in its materialized form or its 'incorporated,' embodied form) which, when appropriated on a private, i.e., exclusive, basis by agents or groups of agents, enables them to appropriate social energy in the form of reified or living labor. It is a *vis insita*, a force inscribed in objective or subjective structures, but it is also a *lex insita*, the principle underlying the immanent regularities of the social world. It is what makes the games of society – not least, the economic game – something other than simple games of chance offering at every moment the possibility of a miracle. Roulette, which holds out the opportunity of winning a lot of money in a short space of time, and therefore of changing one's social status quasi-instantaneously, and in which the winning of the previous spin of the wheel can be staked and lost at every new spin, gives a fairly accurate image of this imaginary universe of perfect competition or perfect equality of opportunity, a world without inertia, without accumulation, without heredity or acquired properties, in which every moment is perfectly independent of the previous one, every soldier has a marshal's baton in his knapsack,

and every prize can be attained, instantaneously, by, everyone, so that at each moment anyone can become anything. Capital, which, in its objectified or embodied forms, takes time to accumulate and which, as a potential capacity to produce profits and to reproduce itself in identical or expanded form, contains a tendency to persist in its being, is a force inscribed in the objectivity of things so that everything is not equally possible or impossible.[1] And the structure of the distribution of the different types and subtypes of capital at a given moment in time represents the immanent structure of the social world, i.e., the set of constraints, inscribed in the very reality of that world, which govern its functioning in a durable way, determining the chances of success for practices.

It is in fact impossible to account for the structure and functioning of the social world unless one reintroduces capital in all its forms and not solely in the one form recognized by economic theory. Economic theory has allowed to be foisted upon it a definition of the economy of practices which is the historical invention of capitalism; and by reducing the universe of exchanges to mercantile exchange, which is objectively and subjectively oriented toward the maximization of profit, i.e., (economically) *self-interested*, it has implicitly defined the other forms of exchange as noneconomic, and therefore *disinterested*. In particular, it defines as disinterested those forms of exchange which ensure the *transubstantiation* whereby the most material types of capital – those which are economic in the restricted sense – can present themselves in the immaterial form of cultural capital or social capital and vice versa. Interest, in the restricted sense it is

Pierre Bourdieu, "The Forms of Capital," pp. 46–58 from *Handbook of Theory and Reasearch for the Sociology of Education*, ed. J. Richardson, trans. Richard Nice. New York: Greenwood, 1986. Reproduced by permission of ABC-CLIO, LLC.

given in economic theory, cannot be produced without producing its negative counterpart, disinterestedness. The class of practices whose explicit purpose is to maximize monetary profit cannot be defined as such without producing the purposeless finality of cultural or artistic practices and their products; the world of bourgeois man, with his double-entry accounting, cannot be invented without producing the pure, perfect universe of the artist and the intellectual and the gratuitous activities of art-for-art's sake and pure theory. In other words, the constitution of a science of mercantile relationships which, inasmuch as it takes for granted the very foundations of the order it claims to analyze – private property, profit, wage labor, etc. – is not even a science of the field of economic production, has prevented the constitution of a general science of the economy of practices, which would treat mercantile exchange as a particular case of exchange in all its forms.

It is remarkable that the practices and assets thus salvaged from the 'icy water of egotistical calculation' (and from science) are the virtual monopoly of the dominant class – as if economism had been able to reduce everything to economics only because the reduction on which that discipline is based protects from sacrilegious reduction everything which needs to be protected. If economics deals only with practices that have narrowly economic interest as their principle and only with goods that are directly and immediately convertible into money (which makes them quantifiable), then the universe of bourgeois production and exchange becomes an exception and can see itself and present itself as a realm of disinterestedness. As everyone knows, priceless things have their price, and the extreme difficulty of converting certain practices and certain objects into money is only due to the fact that this conversion is refused in the very intention that produces them, which is nothing other than the denial (*Verneinung*) of the economy. A general science of the economy of practices, capable of reappropriating the totality of the practices which, although objectively economic, are not and cannot be socially recognized as economic, and which can be performed only at the cost of a whole labor of dissimulation or, more precisely, *euphemization*, must endeavor to grasp capital and profit in all their forms and to establish the laws whereby the different types

of capital (or power, which amounts to the same thing) change into one another.[2]

Depending on the field in which it functions, and at the cost of the more or less expensive transformations which are the precondition for its efficacy in the field in question, capital can present itself in three fundamental guises: as *economic capital*, which is immediately and directly convertible into money and may be institutionalized in the form of property rights; as *cultural capital*, which is convertible, on certain conditions, into economic capital and may be institutionalized in the form of educational qualifications; and as *social capital*, made up of social obligations ('connections'), which is convertible, in certain conditions, into economic capital and may be institutionalized in the form of a title of nobility.[3]

Cultural Capital

Cultural capital can exist in three forms: in the *embodied* state, i.e., in the form of long-lasting dispositions of the mind and body; in the *objectified* state, in the form of cultural goods (pictures, books, dictionaries, instruments, machines, etc.), which are the trace or realization of theories or critiques of these theories, problematics, etc.; and in the *institutionalized* state, a form of objectification which must be set apart because, as will be seen in the case of educational qualifications, it confers entirely original properties on the cultural capital which it is presumed to guarantee.

The reader should not be misled by the somewhat peremptory air which the effort at axiomization may give to my argument.[4] The notion of cultural capital initially presented itself to me, in the course of research, as a theoretical hypothesis which made it possible to explain the unequal scholastic achievement of children originating from the different social classes by relating academic success, i.e., the specific profits which children from the different classes and class fractions can obtain in the academic market, to the distribution of cultural capital between the classes and class fractions. This starting point implies a break with the presuppositions inherent both in the commonsense view, which sees academic success or failure as an effect of natural aptitudes, and in human capital theories. Economists might seem to deserve credit for explicitly raising the question of the relationship between the rates of profit on educational investment and on economic investment (and its evolution). But their measurement of the yield from scholastic investment takes account only of *monetary* investments and profits, or those directly convertible into money, such as the costs of schooling and the cash equivalent of time devoted to study; they are unable to explain the different proportions of their resources which different agents or different social classes allocate to economic investment and cultural investment because they fail to take systematic account of the structure of the differential chances of profit which the various markets offer these agents or classes as a function of the volume and the composition of their assets (see esp. Becker 1964b). Furthermore, because they neglect to relate scholastic investment strategies to the whole set of educational strategies and to the system of reproduction strategies, they inevitably, by a necessary paradox, let slip the best hidden and socially most determinant educational investment, namely, the domestic transmission of cultural capital. Their studies of the relationship between academic ability and academic investment show that they are unaware that ability or talent is itself the product of an investment of time and cultural capital (Becker 1964a: 63–6). Not surprisingly, when endeavoring to evaluate the profits of scholastic investment, they can only consider the profitability of educational expenditure for society as a whole, the 'social rate of return,' or the 'social gain of education as measured by its effects on national productivity' (Becker 1964b: 121, 155). This typically functionalist definition of the functions of education ignores the contribution which the educational system makes to the reproduction of the social structure by sanctioning the hereditary transmission of cultural capital. From the very beginning, a definition of human capital, despite its humanistic connotations, does not move beyond economism and ignores, *inter alia*, the fact that the scholastic yield from educational action depends on the cultural capital previously invested by the family. Moreover, the economic and social yield of the educational qualification depends on the social capital, again inherited, which can be used to back it up.

The embodied state

Most of the properties of cultural capital can be deduced from the fact that, in its fundamental state, it is linked to the body and presupposes embodiment. The accumulation of cultural capital in the embodied state, i.e., in the form of what is called culture, cultivation, *Bildung*, presupposes a process of embodiment, incorporation, which, insofar as it implies a labor of inculcation and assimilation, costs time, time which must be invested personally by the investor. Like the acquisition of a muscular physique or a suntan, it cannot be done at second hand (so that all effects of delegation are ruled out).

The work of acquisition is work on oneself (self-improvement), an effort that presupposes a personal cost (*on paie de sa personne*, as we say in French), an investment, above all of time, but also of that socially constituted form of libido, *libido sciendi*, with all the privation, renunciation, and sacrifice that it may entail. It follows that the least inexact of all the measurements of cultural capital are those which take as their standard the length of acquisition – so long, of course, as this is not reduced to length of schooling and allowance is made for early domestic education by giving it a positive value (a gain in time, a head start) or a negative value (wasted time, and doubly so because more time must be spent correcting its effects), according to its distance from the demands of the scholastic market.[5]

This embodied capital, external wealth converted into an integral part of the person, into a habitus, cannot be transmitted instantaneously (unlike money, property rights, or even titles of nobility) by gift or bequest, purchase or exchange. It follows that the use or exploitation of cultural capital presents particular problems for the holders of economic or political capital, whether they be private patrons or, at the other extreme, entrepreneurs employing executives endowed with a specific cultural competence (not to mention the new state patrons). How can this capital, so closely linked to the person, be bought without buying the person and so losing the very effect of legitimation which presupposes the dissimulation of dependence? How can this capital be concentrated – as some undertakings demand – without concentrating the possessors of the capital, which can have all sorts of unwanted consequences?

Cultural capital can be acquired, to a varying extent, depending on the period, the society, and the social class, in the absence of any deliberate inculcation, and therefore quite unconsciously. It always remains marked by its earliest conditions of acquisition which, through the more or less visible marks they leave (such as the pronunciations characteristic of a class or region), help to determine its distinctive value. It cannot be accumulated beyond the appropriating capacities of an individual agent; it declines and dies with its bearer (with his biological capacity, his memory, etc.). Because it is thus linked in numerous ways to the person in his biological singularity and is subject to a hereditary transmission which is always heavily disguised, or even invisible, it defies the old, deep-rooted distinction the Greek jurists made between inherited properties (*ta patroa*) and acquired properties (*epikteta*), i.e., those which an individual adds to his heritage. It thus manages to combine the prestige of innate property with the merits of acquisition. Because the social conditions of its transmission and acquisition are more disguised than those of economic capital, it is predisposed to function as symbolic capital, i.e., to be unrecognized as capital and recognized as legitimate competence, as authority exerting an effect of (mis)-recognition, e.g., in the matrimonial market and in all the markets in which economic capital is not fully recognized, whether in matters of culture, with the great art collections or great cultural foundations, or in social welfare, with the economy of generosity and the gift. Furthermore, the specifically symbolic logic of distinction additionally secures material and symbolic profits for the possessors of a large cultural capital: any given cultural competence (e.g., being able to read in a world of illiterates) derives a scarcity value from its position in the distribution of cultural capital and yields profits of distinction for its owner. In other words, the share in profits which scarce cultural capital secures in class-divided societies is based, in the last analysis, on the fact that all agents do not have the economic and cultural means for prolonging their children's education beyond the minimum necessary for the reproduction of the labor-power least valorized at a given moment.[6]

Thus the capital, in the sense of the means of appropriating the product of accumulated labor in the objectified state which is held by a given agent, depends for its real efficacy on the form of the distribution of the means of appropriating the accumulated and objectively available resources; and the relationship of appropriation between an agent and the resources objectively available, and hence the profits they produce, is mediated by the relationship of (objective and/or subjective) competition between himself and the other possessors of capital competing for the same goods, in which scarcity – and through it social value – is generated. The structure of the field, i.e., the unequal distribution of capital, is the source of the specific effects of capital, i.e., the appropriation of profits and the power to impose the laws of functioning of the field most favourable to capital and its reproduction.

But the most powerful principle of the symbolic efficacy of cultural capital no doubt lies in the logic of its transmission. On the one hand, the process of appropriating objectified cultural capital and the time necessary for it to take place mainly depend on the cultural capital embodied in the whole family – through (among other things) the generalized Arrow effect and all forms of implicit transmission.[7] On the other hand, the initial accumulation of cultural capital, the precondition for the fast, easy accumulation of every kind of useful cultural capital, starts at the outset, without delay, without wasted time, only for the offspring of families endowed with strong cultural capital; in this case, the accumulation period covers the whole period of socialization. It follows that the transmission of cultural capital is no doubt the best hidden form of hereditary transmission of capital, and it therefore receives proportionately greater weight in the system of reproduction strategies, as the direct, visible forms of transmission tend to be more strongly censored and controlled.

It can immediately be seen that the link between economic and cultural capital is established through the mediation of the time needed for acquisition. Differences in the cultural capital possessed by the family imply differences first in the age at which the work of transmission and accumulation begins – the limiting case being full use of the time biologically available, with the maximum free time being harnessed to maximum cultural capital – and then in the capacity, thus defined, to satisfy the specifically cultural demands of a prolonged process of acquisition.

Furthermore, and in correlation with this, the length of time for which a given individual can prolong his acquisition process depends on the length of time for which his family can provide him with the free time, i.e., time free from economic necessity, which is the precondition for the initial accumulation (time which can be evaluated as a handicap to be made up).

The objectified state

Cultural capital, in the objectified state, has a number of properties which are defined only in the relationship with cultural capital in its embodied form. The cultural capital objectified in material objects and media, such as writings, paintings, monuments, instruments, etc., is transmissible in its materiality. A collection of paintings, for example, can be transmitted as well as economic capital (if not better, because the capital transfer is more disguised). But what is transmissible is legal ownership and not (or not necessarily) what constitutes the precondition for specific appropriation, namely, the possession of the means of 'consuming' a painting or using a machine, which, being nothing other than embodied capital, are subject to the same laws of transmission.[8]

Thus cultural goods can be appropriated both materially – which presupposes economic capital – and symbolically – which presupposes cultural capital. It follows that the owner of the means of production must find a way of appropriating either the embodied capital which is the precondition of specific appropriation or the services of the holders of this capital. To possess the machines, he only needs economic capital; to appropriate them and use them in accordance with their specific purpose (defined by the cultural capital, of scientific or technical type, incorporated in them), he must have access to embodied cultural capital, either in person or by proxy. This is no doubt the basis of the ambiguous status of cadres (executives and engineers). If it is emphasized that they are not the possessors (in the strictly economic sense) of the means of production which they use, and that they derive profit from their own cultural capital only by selling the services and products which it makes possible, then they will be classified among the dominated groups; if it is emphasized that they draw their profits from the use of a particular form of capital, then they will be classified among the dominant groups. Everything suggests that as the cultural capital incorporated in the means of production increases (and with it the period of embodiment needed to acquire the means of appropriating it), so the collective strength of the holders of cultural capital would tend to increase – if the holders of the dominant type of capital (economic capital) were not able to set the holders of cultural capital in competition with one another. (They are, moreover, inclined to competition by the very conditions in which they are selected and trained, in particular by the logic of scholastic and recruitment competitions.)

Cultural capital in its objectified state presents itself with all the appearances of an autonomous, coherent universe which, although the product of historical action, has its own laws, transcending individual wills, and which, as the example of language well illustrates, therefore remains irreducible to that which each agent, or even the aggregate of the agents, can appropriate (i.e., to the cultural capital embodied in each agent or even in the aggregate of the agents). However, it should not be forgotten that it exists as symbolically and materially active, effective capital only insofar as it is appropriated by agents and implemented and invested as a weapon and a stake in the struggles which go on in the fields of cultural production (the artistic field, the scientific field, etc.) and, beyond them, in the field of the social classes – struggles in which the agents wield strengths and obtain profits proportionate to their mastery of this objectified capital, and therefore to the extent of their embodied capital.[9]

The institutionalized state

The objectification of cultural capital in the form of academic qualifications is one way of neutralizing some of the properties it derives from the fact that, being embodied, it has the same biological limits as its bearer. This objectification is what makes the difference between the capital of the autodidact, which may be called into question at any time, or even the cultural capital of the courtier, which can yield only ill-defined profits, of fluctuating value, in the market of high-society exchanges, and the cultural capital academically sanctioned by legally guaranteed qualifications, formally independent of the person of their bearer. With the academic qualification, a certificate of cultural competence which confers on its holder a conventional, constant, legally guaranteed value with respect to culture, social alchemy produces a form of cultural capital which has a relative autonomy vis-à-vis its bearer and even vis-à-vis the cultural capital he effectively possesses at a given moment in time. It institutes cultural capital by collective magic, just as, according to Merleau-Ponty, the living institute their dead through the ritual of mourning. One has only to think of the *concours* (competitive recruitment examination) which, out of the continuum of infinitesimal differences between performances, produces sharp, absolute, lasting differences, such as that which separates the last successful candidate from the first unsuccessful one, and institutes an essential difference between the officially recognized, guaranteed competence and simple cultural capital, which is constantly required to prove itself. In this case, one sees clearly the performative magic of the power of instituting, the power to show forth and secure belief or, in a word, to impose recognition.

By conferring institutional recognition on the cultural capital possessed by any given agent, the academic qualification also makes it possible to compare qualification holders and even to exchange them (by substituting one for another in succession). Furthermore, it makes it possible to establish conversion rates between cultural capital and economic capital by guaranteeing the monetary value of a given academic capital.[10] This product of the conversion of economic capital into cultural capital establishes the value, in terms of cultural capital, of the holder of a given qualification relative to other qualification holders and, by the same token, the monetary value for which it can be exchanged on the labor market (academic investment has no meaning unless a minimum degree of reversibility of the conversion it implies is objectively guaranteed). Because the material and symbolic profits which the academic qualification guarantees also depend on its scarcity, the investments made (in time and effort) may turn out to be less profitable than was anticipated when they were made (there having been a *de facto* change in the conversion rate between academic capital and economic capital). The strategies for converting economic capital into cultural capital, which are among the short-term factors of the schooling explosion and the inflation of qualifications, are

governed by changes in the structure of the chances of profit offered by the different types of capital.

Social Capital

Social capital is the aggregate of the actual or potential resources which are linked to possession of a durable network of more or less institutionalized relationships of mutual acquaintance and recognition – or in other words, to membership in a group[11] – which provides each of its members with the backing of the collectivity-owned capital, a 'credential' which entitles them to credit, in the various senses of the word. These relationships may exist only in the practical state, in material and/or symbolic exchanges which help to maintain them. They may also be socially instituted and guaranteed by the application of a common name (the name of a family, a class, or a tribe or of a school, a party, etc.) and by a whole set of instituting acts designed simultaneously to form and inform those who undergo them; in this case, they are more or less really enacted and so maintained and reinforced, in exchanges. Being based on indissolubly material and symbolic exchanges, the establishment and maintenance of which presuppose reacknowledgment of proximity, they are also partially irreducible to objective relations of proximity in physical (geographical) space or even in economic and social space.[12]

The volume of the social capital possessed by a given agent thus depends on the size of the network of connections he can effectively mobilize and on the volume of the capital (economic, cultural or symbolic) possessed in his own right by each of those to whom he is connected.[13] This means that, although it is relatively irreducible to the economic and cultural capital possessed by a given agent, or even by the whole set of agents to whom he is connected, social capital is never completely independent of it because the exchanges instituting mutual acknowledgment presuppose the reacknowledgment of a minimum of objective homogeneity, and because it exerts a multiplier effect on the capital he possesses in his own right.

The profits which accrue from membership in a group are the basis of the solidarity which makes them possible.[14] This does not mean that they are consciously pursued as such, even in the case of groups like select clubs, which are deliberately organized in order to concentrate social capital and so to derive full benefit from the multiplier effect implied in concentration and to secure the profits of membership – material profits, such as all the types of services accruing from useful relationships, and symbolic profits, such as those derived from association with a rare, prestigious group.

The existence of a network of connections is not a natural given, or even a social given, constituted once and for all by an initial act of institution, represented, in the case of the family group, by the genealogical definition of kinship relations, which is the characteristic of a social formation. It is the product of an endless effort at institution, of which institution rites – often wrongly described as rites of passage – mark the essential moments and which is necessary in order to produce and reproduce lasting, useful relationships that can secure material or symbolic profits (see Bourdieu 1982). In other words, the network of relationships is the product of investment strategies, individual or collective, consciously or unconsciously aimed at establishing or reproducing social relationships that are directly usable in the short or long term, i.e., at transforming contingent relations, such as those of neighborhood, the workplace, or even kinship, into relationships that are at once necessary and elective, implying durable obligations subjectively felt (feelings of gratitude, respect, friendship, etc.) or institutionally guaranteed (rights). This is done through the alchemy of *consecration*, the symbolic constitution produced by social institution (institution as a relative – brother, sister, cousin, etc. – or as a knight, an heir, an elder, etc.) and endlessly reproduced in and through the exchange (of gifts, words, women, etc.) which it encourages and which presupposes and produces mutual knowledge and recognition. Exchange transforms the things exchanged into signs of recognition and, through the mutual recognition and the recognition of group membership which it implies, reproduces the group. By the same token, it reaffirms the limits of the group, i.e., the limits beyond which the constitutive exchange – trade, commensality, or marriage – cannot take place. Each member of the group is thus instituted as a custodian of the limits of the group: because the definition of the criteria of entry is at stake in each new entry, he can modify the

group by modifying the limits of legitimate exchange through some form of misalliance. It is quite logical that, in most societies, the preparation and conclusion of marriages should be the business of the whole group, and not of the agents directly concerned. Through the introduction of new members into a family, a clan, or a club, the whole definition of the group, i.e., its fines, its boundaries, and its identity, is put at stake, exposed to redefinition, alteration, adulteration. When, as in modern societies, families lose the monopoly of the establishment of exchanges which can lead to lasting relationships, whether socially sanctioned (like marriage) or not, they may continue to control these exchanges, while remaining within the logic of laissez-faire, through all the institutions which are designed to favor legitimate exchanges and exclude illegitimate ones by producing occasions (rallies, cruises, hunts, parties, receptions, etc.), places (smart neighborhoods, select schools, clubs, etc.), or practices (smart sports, parlor games, cultural ceremonies, etc.) which bring together, in a seemingly fortuitous way, individuals as homogeneous as possible in all the pertinent respects in terms of the existence and persistence of the group.

The reproduction of social capital presupposes an unceasing effort of sociability, a continuous series of exchanges in which recognition is endlessly affirmed and reaffirmed. This work, which implies expenditure of time and energy and so, directly or indirectly, of economic capital, is not profitable or even conceivable unless one invests in it a specific competence (knowledge of genealogical relationships and of real connections and skill at using them, etc.) and an acquired disposition to acquire and maintain this competence, which are themselves integral parts of this capital.[15] This is one of the factors which explain why the profitability of this labor of accumulating and maintaining social capital rises in proportion to the size of the capital. Because the social capital accruing from a relationship is that much greater to the extent that the person who is the object of it is richly endowed with capital (mainly social, but also cultural and even economic capital), the possessors of an inherited social capital, symbolized by a great name, are able to transform all circumstantial relationships into lasting connections. They are sought after for their social capital and, because they are well known, are worthy of being known ('I know him well'); they do not need to 'make the acquaintance' of all their 'acquaintances'; they are known to more people than they know, and their work of sociability, when it is exerted, is highly productive.

Every group has its more or less institutionalized forms of delegation which enable it to concentrate the totality of the social capital, which is the basis of the existence of the group (a family or a nation, of course, but also an association or a party), in the hands of a single agent or a small group of agents and to mandate this plenipotentiary, charged with *plena potestas agendi et loquendi*,[16] to represent the group, to speak and act in its name and so, with the aid of this collectively owned capital, to exercise a power incommensurate with the agent's personal contribution. Thus, at the most elementary degree of institutionalization the head of the family, the *pater familias*, the eldest, most senior member, is tacitly recognized as the only person entitled to speak on behalf of the family group in all official circumstances. But whereas in this case, diffuse delegation requires the great to step forward and defend the collective honor when the honor of the weakest members is threatened, the institutionalized delegation, which ensures the concentration of social capital, also has the effect of limiting the consequences of individual lapses by explicitly delimiting responsibilities and authorizing the recognized spokesmen to shield the group as a whole from discredit by expelling or excommunicating the embarrassing individuals.

If the internal competition for the monopoly of legitimate representation of the group is not to threaten the conservation and accumulation of the capital which is the basis of the group, the members of the group must regulate the conditions of access to the right to declare oneself a member of the group and, above all, to set oneself up as a representative (delegate, plenipotentiary, spokesman, etc.) of the whole group, thereby committing the social capital of the whole group. The title of nobility is the form *par excellence* of the institutionalized social capital which guarantees a particular form of social relationship in a lasting way. One of the paradoxes of delegation is that the mandated agent can exert on (and, up to a point, against) the group the power which the group enables him to concentrate. (This is perhaps especially true in the limiting cases in which the mandated agent creates the group which creates him but which only

exists through him.) The mechanisms of delegation and representation (in both the theatrical and the legal senses) which fall into place – that much more strongly, no doubt, when the group is large and its members weak – as one of the conditions for the concentration of social capital (among other reasons, because it enables numerous, varied, scattered agents to act as one man and to overcome the limitations of space and time) also contain the seeds of an embezzlement or misappropriation of the capital which they assemble.

This embezzlement is latent in the fact that a group as a whole can be represented, in the various meanings of the word, by a subgroup, clearly delimited and perfectly visible to all, known to all, and recognized by all, that of the *nobiles*, the 'people who are known', the paradigm of whom is the nobility, and who may speak on behalf of the whole group, represent the whole group, and exercise authority in the name of the whole group. The noble is the group personified. He bears the name of the group to which he gives his name (the metonymy which links the noble to his group is clearly seen when Shakespeare calls Cleopatra 'Egypt' or the King of France 'France,' just as Racine calls Pyrrhus 'Epirus'). It is by him, his name, the difference it proclaims, that the members of his group, the liegemen, and also the land and castles, are known and recognized. Similarly, phenomena such as the 'personality cult' or the identification of parties, trade unions, or movements with their leader are latent in the very logic of representation. Everything combines to cause the signifier to take the place of the signified, the spokesmen that of the group he is supposed to express, not least because his distinction, his 'outstandingness,' his visibility constitute the essential part, if not the essence, of this power, which, being entirely set within the logic of knowledge and acknowledgment, is fundamentally a symbolic power; but also because the representative, the sign, the emblem, may be, and create, the whole reality of groups which receive effective social existence only in and through representation.[17]

Conversions

The different types of capital can be derived from *economic capital*, but only at the cost of a more or less great effort of transformation, which is needed to produce the type of power effective in the field in question. For example, there are some goods and services to which economic capital gives immediate access, without secondary costs; others can be obtained only by virtue of a social capital of relationships (or social obligations) which cannot act instantaneously, at the appropriate moment, unless they have been established and maintained for a long time, as if for their own sake, and therefore outside their period of use, i.e., at the cost of an investment in sociability which is necessarily long-term because the time lag is one of the factors of the transmutation of a pure and simple debt into that recognition of nonspecific indebtedness which is called gratitude.[18] In contrast to the cynical but also economical transparency of economic exchange, in which equivalents change hands in the same instant, the essential ambiguity of social exchange, which presupposes misrecognition, in other words, a form of faith and of bad faith (in the sense of self-deception), presupposes a much more subtle economy of time.

So it has to be posited simultaneously that economic capital is at the root of all the other types of capital and that these transformed, disguised forms of economic capital, never entirely reducible to that definition, produce their most specific effects only to the extent that they conceal (not least from their possessors) the fact that economic capital is at their root, in other words – but only in the last analysis – at the root of their effects. The real logic of the functioning of capital, the conversions from one type to another, and the law of conservation which governs them cannot be understood unless two opposing but equally partial views are superseded: on the one hand, economism, which, on the grounds that every type of capital is reducible in the last analysis to economic capital, ignores what makes the specific efficacy of the other types of capital, and on the other hand, semiologism (nowadays represented by structuralism, symbolic interactionism, or ethnomethodology), which reduces social exchanges to phenomena of communication and ignores the brutal fact of universal reducibility to economics.[19]

In accordance with a principle which is the equivalent of the principle of the conservation of energy, profits in one area are necessarily paid for by costs in another (so that a concept like wastage has no meaning in a general science of the economy of practices). The

universal equivalent, the measure of all equivalences, is nothing other than labor-time (in the widest sense); and the conservation of social energy through all its conversions is verified if, in each case, one takes into account both the labor-time accumulated in the form of capital and the labor-time needed to transform it from one type into another.

It has been seen, for example, that the transformation of economic capital into social capital presupposes a specific labor, i.e., an apparently gratuitous expenditure of time, attention, care, concern, which, as is seen in the endeavor to personalize a gift, has the effect of transfiguring the purely monetary import of the exchange and, by the same token, the very meaning of the exchange. From a narrowly economic standpoint, this effort is bound to be seen as pure wastage, but in the terms of the logic of social exchanges, it is a solid investment, the profits of which will appear, in the long run, in monetary or other form. Similarly, if the best measure of cultural capital is undoubtedly the amount of time devoted to acquiring it, this is because the transformation of economic capital into cultural capital presupposes an expenditure of time that is made possible by possession of economic capital. More precisely, it is because the cultural capital that is effectively transmitted within the family itself depends not only on the quantity of cultural capital, itself accumulated by spending time, that the domestic group possess, but also on the usable time (particularly in the form of the mother's free time) available to it (by virtue of its economic capital, which enables it to purchase the time of others) to ensure the transmission of this capital and to delay entry into the labor market through prolonged schooling, a credit which pays off, if at all, only in the very long term.[20]

The convertibility of the different types of capital is the basis of the strategies aimed at ensuring the reproduction of capital (and the position occupied in social space) by means of the conversions least costly in terms of conversion work and of the losses inherent in the conversion itself (in a given state of the social power relations). The different types of capital can be distinguished according to their reproducibility or, more precisely, according to how easily they are transmitted, i.e., with more or less loss and with more or less concealment; the rate of loss and the degree and concealment tend to vary in inverse ratio. Everything which helps to disguise the economic aspect also tends to increase the risk of loss (particularly the inter-generational transfers). Thus the (apparent) incom-mensurability of the different types of capital introduces a high degree of uncertainty into all trans-actions between holders of different types. Similarly, the declared refusal of calculation and of guarantees which characterizes exchanges tending to produce a social capital in the form of a capital of obligations that are usable in the more or less long term (exchanges of gifts, services, visits, etc.) necessarily entails the risk of ingratitude, the refusal of that recognition of non-guaranteed debts which such exchanges aim to pro-duce. Similarly, too, the high degree of concealment of the transmission of cultural capital has the disad-vantage (in addition to its inherent risks of loss) that the academic qualification which is its institutioni-lized form is neither transmissible (like a title of nobil-ity) nor negotiable (like stocks and shares). More precisely, cultural capital, whose diffuse, continuous transmission within the family escapes observation and control (so that the educational system seems to award its honors solely to natural qualities) and which is increasingly tending to attain full efficacy at least on the labor market, only when validated by the educa-tional system, i.e., converted into a capital of qualifica-tions, is subject to a more disguised but more risky transmission than economic capital. As the educa-tional qualification, invested with the specific force of the official, becomes the condition for legitimate access to a growing number of positions, particularly the dominant ones, the educational system tends increasingly to dispossess the domestic group of the monopoly of the transmission of power and privileges – and, among other things, of the choice of its legitimate heirs from among children of different sex and birth rank.[21] And economic capital itself poses quite different problems of transmission, depending on the particular form it takes. Thus, according to Grassby (1970), the liquidity of commercial capital, which gives immediate economic power and favors transmission, also makes it more vulnerable than landed property (or even real estate) and does not favor the establishment of long-lasting dynasties.

Because the question of the arbitrariness of appro-priation arises most sharply in the process of transmission – particularly at the time of succession, a critical moment for all power – every reproduction strategy is at the same time a legitimation strategy aimed at con-secrating both an exclusive appropriation and its repro-duction. When the subversive critique which aims to weaken the dominant class through the principle of its perpetuation by bringing to light the arbitrariness of the entitlements transmitted and of their transmission (such as the critique which the Enlightenment *philos-ophes* directed, in the name of nature, against the arbi-trariness of birth) is incorporated in institutionalized mechanisms (for example, laws of inheritance) aimed at controlling the official, direct transmission of power and privileges, the holders of capital have an ever greater interest in resorting to reproduction strategies capable of ensuring better-disguised transmission, but at the cost of greater loss of capital, by exploiting the convertibility of the types of capital. Thus the more the official transmission of capital is prevented or hindered, the more the effects of the clandestine circulation of capital in the form of cultural capital become determi-nant in the reproduction of the social structure. As an instrument of reproduction capable of disguising its own function, the scope of the educational system tends to increase, and together with this increase is the unification of the market in social qualifications which gives rights to occupy rare positions.

Notes

1 This inertia, entailed by the tendency of the structures of capital to reproduce themselves in institutions or in dispositions adapted to the structures of which they are the product, is, of course, reinforced by a specifically political action of concerted conservation, i.e., of demo-bilization and depoliticization. The latter tends to keep the dominated agents in the state of a practical group, united only by the orchestration of their dispositions and condemned to function as an aggregate repeatedly performing discrete, individual acts (such as consumer or electoral choices).

2 This is true of all exchanges between members of differ-ent fractions of the dominant class, possessing different types of capital. These range from sales of expertise, treatment, or other services which take the form of gift exchange and dignify themselves with the most decorous names that can be found (honoraria, emoluments, etc.)

to matrimonial exchanges, the prime example of a transaction that can only take place insofar as it is not perceived or defined as such by the contracting parties. It is remarkable that the apparent extensions of economic theory beyond the limits constituting the discipline have left intact the asylum of the sacred, apart from a few sacrilegious incursions. Gary S. Becker, for example, who was one of the first to take explicit account of the types of capital that are usually ignored, never considers anything other than monetary costs and profits, forgetting the nonmonetary investments (*inter alia*, the affective ones) and the material and symbolic profits that education provides in a deferred, indirect way, such as the added value which the dispositions produced or reinforced by schooling (bodily or verbal manners, tastes, etc.) or the relationships established with fellow students can yield in the matrimonial market (Becker 1964a).

3   *Symbolic capital*, that is to say, capital – in whatever form – insofar as it is represented, i.e., apprehended symbolically, in a relationship of knowledge or, more precisely, of misrecognition and recognition, presupposes the intervention of the habitus, as a socially constituted cognitive capacity.

4   When talking about concepts for their own sake, as I do here, rather than using them in research, one always runs the risk of being both schematic and formal, i.e., theoretical in the most usual and most usually approved sense of the word.

5   This proposition implies no recognition of the value of scholastic verdicts; it merely registers the relationship which exists in reality between a certain cultural capital and the laws of the educational market. Dispositions that are given a negative value in the educational marker may receive very high value in other markets – not least, of course, in the relationships internal to the class.

6   In a relatively undifferentiated society, in which access to the means of appropriating the cultural heritage is very equally distributed, embodied culture does not function as cultural capital, i.e., as a means of acquiring exclusive advantages.

7   What I call the generalized Arrow effect, i.e., the fact that all cultural goods – paintings, monuments, machines, and any objects shaped by man, particularly all those which belong to the childhood environment – exert an educative effect by their mere existence, is no doubt one of the structural factors behind the 'schooling explosion,' in the sense that a growth in the quantity of cultural capital accumulated in the objectified state increases the educative effect automatically exerted by the environment. If one adds to this the fact that embodied cultural capital is constantly increasing, it can be seen that,

in each generation, the educational system can take more for granted. The fact that the same educational investment is increasingly productive is one of the structural factors of the inflation of qualifications (together with cyclical factors linked to effects of capital conversion).

8   The cultural object, as a living social institution, is, simultaneously, a socially instituted material object and a particular class of habitus, to which it is addressed. The material object – for example, a work of art in its materiality – may be separated by space (e.g., a Dogon statue) or by time (e.g., a Simone Martini painting) from the habitus for which it was intended. This leads to one of the most fundamental biases of art history. Understanding the effect (not to be confused with the function) which the work tended to produce – for example, the form of belief it tended to induce – and which is the true basis of the conscious or unconscious choice of the means used (technique, colors, etc.), and therefore of the form itself, is possible only if one at least raises the question of the habitus on which it 'operated.'

9   The dialectical relationship between objectified cultural capital – of which the form *par excellence* is writing – and embodied cultural capital has generally been reduced to an exalted description of the degradation of the spirit by the letter, the living by the inert, creation by routine, grace by heaviness.

10 This is particularly true in France, where in many occupations (particularly the civil service) there is a very strict relationship between qualification, rank, and remuneration (translator's note).

11 Here, too, the notion of cultural capital did not spring from pure theoretical work, still less from an analogical extension of economic concepts. It arose from the need to identify the principle of social effects which, although they can be seen clearly at the level of singular agents – where statistical inquiry inevitably operates – cannot be reduced to the set of properties individually possessed by a given agent. These effects, in which spontaneous sociology readily perceives the work of 'connections,' are particularly visible in all cases in which different individuals obtain very unequal profits from virtually equivalent (economic or cultural) capital, depending on the extent to which they can mobilize by proxy the capital of a group (a family, the alumni of an elite school, a select club, the aristocracy, etc.) that is more or less constituted as such and more or less rich in capital.

12 Neighborhood relationships may, of course, receive an elementary form of institutionalization, as in the

Bearn – or the Basque region – where neighbors, *lous besis* (a word which, in old texts, is applied to the legitimate inhabitants of the village, the rightful members of the assembly), are explicitly designated, in accordance with fairly codified rules, and are assigned functions which are differentiated according to their rank (there is a 'first neighbor,' a 'second neighbor,' and so on), particularly for the major social ceremonies (funerals, marriages, etc.). But even in this case, the relationships actually used by no means always coincide with the relationships socially instituted.

13 Manners (bearing, pronunciation, etc.) may be included in social capital insofar as, through the mode of acquisition they point to, they indicate initial membership of a more or less prestigious group.

14 National liberation movements or nationalist ideologies cannot be accounted for solely by reference to strictly economic profits, i.e., anticipation of the profits which may be derived from redistribution of a proportion of wealth to the advantage of the nationals (nationalization) and the recovery of highly paid jobs (see Breton 1964). To these specifically economic anticipated profits, which would only explain the nationalism of the privleged classes, must be added the very real and very immediate profits derived from membership (social capital) which are proportionately greater for those who are lower down the social hierarchy ('poor whites') or, more precisely, more threatened by economic and social decline.

15 There is every reason to suppose that socializing, or, more generally, relational, dispositions are very unequally distributed among the social classes and, within a given class, among fractions of different origin.

16 A 'full power to act and speak' (translator).

17 It goes without saying that social capital is so totally governed by the logic of knowledge and acknowledgment that it always functions as symbolic capital.

18 It should be made clear, to dispel a likely misunderstanding, that the investment in question here is not necessarily conceived as a calculated pursuit of gain, but that it has every likelihood of being experienced in terms of the logic of emotional investment, i.e., as an involvement which is both necessary and disinterested. This has not always been appreciated by historians, who (even when they are as alert to symbolic effects as E. P. Thompson) tend to conceive symbolic practices – powdered wigs and the whole paraphernalia of office – as explicit strategies of domination, intended to be seen (from below), and to interpret generous or charitable conduct as 'calculated acts of class appeasement.' This naively Machiavellian view

forgets that the most sincerely disinterested acts may be those best corresponding to objective interest. A number of fields, particularly those which most tend to deny interest and every sort of calculation, like the fields of cultural production, grant full recognition, and with it the consecration which guarantees success, only to those who distinguish themselves by the immediate conformity of their investments, a token of sincerity and attachment to the essential principles of the field. It would be thoroughly erroneous to describe the choices of the habitus which lead an artist, writer, of researcher toward his natural place (a subject, style, manner, etc.) in terms of rational strategy and cynical calculation. This is despite the fact that, for example, shifts from one genre, school, or speciality to another, quasi-religious conversions that are performed 'in all sincerity,' can be understood as capital conversions, the direction and moment of which (on which their success often depends) are determined by a 'sense of investment' which is the less likely to be seen as such the more skillful it is. Innocence is the privilege of these who move in their field of activity like fish in water.

19 To understand the attractiveness of this pair of antagonistic positions which serve as each other's alibi, one would need to analyze the unconscious profits and the profits of unconsciousness which they procure for intellectuals. While some find in economism a means of exempting themselves by excluding the cultural capital and all the specific profits which place them on the side of the dominant, others can abandon the detestable terrain of the economic, where everything reminds them that they can be evaluated, in the last analysis, in economic terms, for that of the symbolic. (The latter merely reproduce, in the realm of the symbolic, the strategy whereby intellectuals and artists endeavor to impose the recognition of their values, i.e., their value, by inverting the law of the market in which what one has or what one earns completely defines what one is worth and what one is – as is shown by the practice of banks which, with techniques such as the personalization of credit, tend to subordinate the granting of loans and the fixing of interest to a exhaustive inquiry into the borrower's present and future resources.)

20 Among the advantages procured by capital in all its types, the most precious is the increase in volume of useful time that is made possible through the various methods of appropriating other people's time (in the form of services). It may take the form either of increased spare time, secured by reducing the time

consumed in activities directly channeled toward producing the means of reproducing the existence of the domestic group, or of more intense use of the time so consumed, by recourse to other people's labor or to devices and methods which are available only to those who have spent time learning how to use them and which (like better transport or living close to the place of work) make it possible to save time. (This is in contrast to the cash savings of the poor, which are paid for in time – do-it-yourself, bargain hunting, etc.) None of this is true of mere economic capital; it is possession of cultural capital that makes it possible to derive greater profit not only from labor-time, by securing a higher yield from the same time, but also from spare time, and so to increase both economic and cultural capital.

21   It goes without saying that the dominant fractions, who tend to place ever greater emphasis on educational investment, within an overall strategy of asset diversification and of investments aimed at combining security with high yield, have all sorts of ways of evading scholastic verdicts. The direct transmission of economic capital remains one of the principal means of reproduction, and the effect of social capital ('a helping hand,' 'string-pulling,' the 'old boy network') tends to correct the effect of academic sanctions. Educational qualifications never function perfectly as currency. They are never entirely separable from their holders: their value rises in proportion to the value of their bearer, especially in the least rigid areas of the social structure.

References

Becker, G. S. (1964a), *A Theoretical and Empirical Analysis with Special Reference to Education* (New York: National Bureau of Economic Research).

Becker, G. S. (1964b), *Human Capital* (New York: Columbia University Press).

Bourdieu, P. (1982), 'Les rites d'institution', *Actes de la recherche en sciences sociales*, 43: 58–63.

Breton, A. (1962), 'The Economies of Nationalism', *Journal of Political Economy*, 72: 376–86.

Grassby, R. (1970), 'English Merchant Capitalism in the Late Seventeenth Century: The Composition of Business Fortunes', *Past and Present*, 46: 87–107.

Additional Readings

Arnold

Joseph Carroll. *The Cultural Theory of Matthew Arnold*. Berkeley: University of California Press, 1982.
Carroll argues that Arnold's contributions to cultural theory are more than just a body of criticism but instead constitute an overarching interpretative and empirical model of cultural analysis.

Jane Garnett. "Introduction" to Matthew Arnold, *Culture and Anarchy*. Oxford: Oxford University Press, 2006, vii–xxvii.
An introduction to the life and thought of Matthew Arnold which situates his work within the wider social forces and attitudes of his time. Garnett also suggests how Arnold might have perceived the purpose and relevance of *Culture and Anarchy*.

Veblen

Stjepan Mestrovic. *Thorstein Veblen on Cultural and Society*. London: Sage Publications, 2003.
A selection of essays that advocate for the continued relevance of Veblen's work while attempting to convey the original and critical nature of his sociological insights.

Michael Spindler. *Veblen and Modern America: Revolutionary Iconoclast*. Sterling, VA: Pluto Press, 2002.
Spindler sets Veblen's work within the intellectual and social context in which it was produced, outlines the main features of his thinking, and evaluates the ways in which Veblen's work is still relevant to an understanding of modern America.

Rick Tilman. *The Intellectual Legacy of Thorstein Veblen: Unresolved Issues*. Westport, CT: Greenwood Press, 1996.
A book that argues for an interpretation of Veblen as a singular thinker whose work defies classification or categorization. Tilman considers Veblen in light of multiple intellectual traditions such as Darwinism, Pragmatism, and the New Deal.

Andrew B. Trigg. "Veblen, Bourdieu, and Conspicuous Consumption." *Journal of Economic Issues* 35.1 (2001): 99–115.
Trigg defends Veblen's theory of conspicuous consumption as a viable method by which to understand contemporary society and draws parallels between the thought of Veblen and Pierre Bourdieu.

Marcuse

John Abromeit and William Mark Cobb, eds. *Herbert Marcuse: A Critical Reader*. New York: Routledge, 2004.
A collection of essays which provides a comprehensive reassessment of Marcuse's work with specific reference to the legacy of his thought, the growing relevance of his writings to ecological commentators, and his personal life.

Joel Pfister. "Complicity Critiques." *American Literary History* 3.12 (2000): 610–32.
A critical and sustained investigation of Marcuse's concept of "affirmative culture."

Charles Reitz. *Art, Alienation, and the Humanities: A Critical Engagement with Herbert Marcuse*. New York: State University of New York Press, 2000.
An investigation of Marcuse's writings which emphasizes the educational focus of his work through reference to a wide range of European philosophers and pedagogical theory.

Horkheimer and Adorno

Theodor Adorno. *The Culture Industry*. London: Routledge, 2002. See esp. chap. 3, "Culture Industry Reconsidered."
A collection of Adorno's essays which addresses the role of mass culture and media in contemporary society. In "Culture Industry Reconsidered," Adorno responds to criticisms of the Culture Industry thesis and attempts to clarify and expand upon the critical points of the argument.

Deborah Cook. *The Culture Industry Revisited*. New York: Rowman & Littlefield, 1996.
Cook provides an overview of Adorno's cultural theory and the debates and discussions that have arisen in response to his work on popular culture.

Fredric Jameson. *Late Marxism: Adorno, or, the Persistence of the Dialectic*. New York: Verso, 2006.
A reinterpretation of Adorno's work by one of the foremost scholars of contemporary Marxism. In addition to Adorno's contributions regarding popular culture, Jameson also addresses his work on aesthetic theory and dialectics.

Simon Jarvis. *Adorno: A Critical Introduction*. New York: Routledge, 1998.
A comprehensive and accessible account of Adorno's work, which re-examines his writings within the context of classical German philosophy.

Jeffrey T. Nealon and Caren Irr, eds. *Rethinking the Frankfurt School: Alternative Legacies of Cultural Critique*. Albany, NY: State University of New York Press, 2002.
A collection of essays which examines the ideas of the Frankfurt School in light of new developments in cultural theory and cultural studies. Includes Imre

Szeman's "The Limits of Culture: The Frankfurt School and/for Cultural Studies."

Robert W. Witkin. *Adorno on Popular Culture*. New York: Routledge, 2003.
Aimed at students, Witkin's book unpacks Adorno's work with reference to specific media forms, e.g., jazz, film, television.

Williams

Paul Jones. *Raymond Williams's Sociology of Culture*. New York: Palgrave MacMillan, 2004.
A detailed account of the sociological aspects of Williams's work on culture. Provides an overview of the central themes in his thought.

Gail Lewis. "Racializing Culture Is Ordinary." *Cultural Studies* 21.6 (2007): 866–86.
Lewis explores the ways in which Williams's proposition that "culture is ordinary" can be used to understand the ways in which everyday culture becomes racialized.

Christopher Prendergast, ed. *Cultural Materialism: On Raymond Williams*. Minneapolis: University of Minnesota Press, 1995.
This collection of essays is framed as a tribute to Williams and investigates the continued relevance of his theories of "cultural materialism" in light of various schools of thoughts and academic disciplines.

Jameson

Perry Anderson. *The Origins of Postmodernity*. London: Verso, 1998.
A sweeping account of the origins of the notions of postmodernity and postmodernism, with special attention paid to the foundational work of Fredric Jameson.

Ian Buchanan. *Fredric Jameson: Live Theory*. London: Continuum, 2007.
An invaluable and accessible introduction to the work of Jameson, organized according to the major themes and texts of his career.

Fredric Jameson. *Jameson on Jameson: Conversations on Cultural Marxism.* Edited by Ian Buchanan. Durham, NC: Duke University Press, 2007.
A collection of interviews with accomplished scholars ranging over two decades in which Jameson explains central concepts in his work.

Douglas Kellner and Sean Homer, eds. *Fredric Jameson: A Critical Reader.* London: Palgrave, 2004.
A collection of previously unpublished essays which covers the full scope of Jameson's work, including several works addressing his writings on popular culture and mass media.

Hall

Helen Davis. *Understanding Stuart Hall.* London: Sage, 2004.
Offers a cogent account of Hall's intellectual development throughout his long and distinguished career, while providing a critical account of his major contributions to the field of cultural studies.

Paul Gilroy, Lawrence Grossberg, and Angela McRobbie, eds. *Without Guarantees: In Honour of Stuart Hall.* London: Verso, 2000.
Produced upon the occasion of Hall's retirement, this collection of essays by leading academics takes up and expands upon a range of issues arising out of Hall's work.

Janice Peck. "Itinerary of a Thought: Stuart Hall, Cultural Studies, and the Unresolved Problem of the Relation of Culture to 'Not Culture'." *Cultural Critique* 48 (2001): 200–49.
Peck considers the ways in which "culture" is configured in the work of Hall, particularly with respect to the continuing influence of Marxism.

Chris Rojek. *Stuart Hall.* Cambridge: Polity, 2003.
A book-length analysis and introduction to the work of Stuart Hall which traces the development of his political and intellectual positions while arguing for an understanding of Hall as the leading figure in contemporary cultural studies.

Bourdieu

Pierre Bourdieu. *Distinction: A Social Critique of the Judgement of Taste.* Translated by Richard Nice. Cambridge, MA: Harvard University Press, 2000.
In *Distinction*, Bourdieu makes use of a wide range of empirical studies to argue that aesthetic judgments concerning "taste" function to reproduce social classes and structures of power and domination in society.

Nicholas Brown and Imre Szeman, eds. *Pierre Bourdieu: Fieldwork in Art, Literature, and Culture.* Lanham, MD: Rowman & Littlefield, 2000.
A series of essays which examine how Bourdieu's theories have been taken up in the North American context, particularly with respect to cultural production; includes several case studies.

Craig Calhoun, Edward LiPuma, and Moishe Postone, eds. *Pierre Bourdieu: Critical Perspectives.* Chicago: University of Chicago Press, 1992.
The contributors to this volume seek to appraise the usefulness and validity of Bourdieu's approach to culture from a variety of intellectual perspectives, such as linguistics, anthropology, and feminism.

Bridget Fowler. *Pierre Bourdieu and Cultural Theory: Critical Investigations.* London: Sage Publications, 1997.
Fowler outlines the central debates around Bourdieu's work with particular emphasis on the key terms of capital (particularly cultural capital) and habitus.

General

Roland Barthes. *Mythologies.* Translated by Annette Lavers. New York: Farrar, Strauss, & Giroux, 2000.
A classic work, collecting a series of short essays, in which Roland Barthes argues that culture functions through the creation of social value systems which he labels "myths."

Michael Denning. *The Cultural Front: The Laboring of American Culture in the Twentieth Century.* London: Verso, 1998.

A work of cultural history which addresses the role of politics in the formation of American popular culture.

Fred Inglis. *Culture*. Cambridge: Polity, 2004.
A short, engagingly opinionated overview of the development of the idea of culture from the late eighteenth century to the present.

Juliet B. Schor and Douglas B. Holt, eds. *The Consumer Society Reader*. New York: New Press, 2000.
An excellent collection which examines the impact of consumer society and commodity culture on the character of contemporary social experience.

Max Weber. *The Protestant Ethic and the Spirit of Capitalism*. Translated by Peter Baehr and Gordon Wells. New York: Penguin, 2002.
In this historical work of sociology, Max Weber argues that the ethical and cultural edicts of religion can shape the economic and material forces of society; in particular, that Protestantism gave rise to modern capitalism.

George Yúdice. *The Expediency of Culture*. Durham, NC: Duke University Press, 2003.
Yúdice argues that in the contemporary globalized world, culture has come to be seen as a resource to be invested, contested, and made use of for achieving various practical ends.

Part 2

Power

Introduction

The political has become one of the central themes animating recent investigations of culture. The relationship of culture to politics is no longer an issue only for those interested in the practices of artistic or literary avant-gardes who might explicitly envision their activities as having political outcomes, social movements which make use of culture in their political activities, or the variety of cultural policies enacted by states. This relationship is now an important one to understand for anyone wanting to make sense of the role and function of culture in contemporary society: the critical challenge to the autonomy of culture examined in the previous section has made an accounting of its political function unavoidable. The past several decades of academic work which has taken place under the umbrella of the field of "cultural studies" has done just this, highlighting many of the ways in which diverse cultural practices engage with and are produced by relations of politics and power. But it has been a more general tendency as well in fields of study including art history, film studies, literary studies, and music. Indeed, culture and politics have become so closely linked that there has been a reactionary attempt on the part of some critics to revive older discourses of beauty and edification, which they believe continue to form the correct and appropriate language through which to assess culture.[1] Yet to limit cultural criticism to culture alone and to exclude politics is itself wrapped up in political considerations. In some cases, the rejection of a link between culture and politics constitutes an attempt to reclaim the place of older theoretical and critical approaches which have fallen out of favor, such as strict formalisms or modes of cultural history limited to an idealist progression of one artistic genre to another. In others, there is an unexpressed or hidden desire to maintain class and social divisions whose borders are established in part by expertise and knowledge about what constitutes true beauty – one of the central elements of the politics of culture which Pierre Bourdieu has so thoroughly exposed in his work.

One critical tradition has not needed to be reminded of the link between politics and culture. From its origins (which lie in Georg Lukács's *History and Class Consciousness* [1923]), Marxist cultural criticism has always assumed that aesthetic and cultural phenomena have political and ideological content of necessity. Culture is produced in specific social and economic circumstances which cannot help but leave their traces in both form and content, if not always in obvious or easy-to-comprehend ways. An influential text in establishing a framework for understanding the relationship between politics and culture is Karl Marx's "Preface" to *A Contribution to a Critique of Political Economy* (1859). This short piece is one of the most widely read of Marx's writings, in part because it contains the clearest and most concise description of "historical materialism," Marx's theory of the development of history. It also contains an influential passage concerning the relationship between economic and material life – the engine of history and social change – and "social, political and intellectual life"; it is his account of this relationship which has proved to be provocative and frustrating in equal measure. "The totality of these relations of production constitutes the economic structure of society," Marx writes, "the real foundation, on which arises a legal and political superstructure and to which correspond definite forms of social consciousness … It is not the consciousness of men that determines their existence, but their existence that determines their consciousness."[2] The spaces and practices of consciousness are an outcome of the economic conditions of production; but this does not mean, as has often been assumed, that the relationship between economic "base" and sociocultural "superstructure" are related in a mechanical fashion, with the latter merely reflecting a more primary reality that exists at another level. As Fredric Jameson has pointed out, "*Uberbau* [superstructure] and *Basis* [base] … which so often suggest to people a house and its foundations, seem in fact to have been railroad terminology and to have designated the rolling stock and the rails respectively, something which suddenly jolts us into a rather different picture of ideology and its effects."[3] Even in Marx's original passage, we can see that the relationship is a complex one. It is in the "ideological forms" of the superstructure – "legal, political, religious, artistic or philosophic" – where the conflicts of politics and power embodied in the very structure of the economy become known and are fought out. The base/superstructure model reminds us that culture is the product of forces and relations of power, but also that changes in these forces and relations take place in and through culture, too.

Since politics takes place at levels and in spheres other than the one that has come to be narrowly understood as the political – that is, the internal and external actions and dynamics of nation-states, especially with respect to their legislative functions and the games of elections – it is "power" which has become the more common concept used in cultural theory to explore the shape taken by contemporary politics. Power is a fundamental force in human social life. It is through power that societies are ordered and organized, hierarchies built up and privileges meted out, and the status quo maintained – *or*, on the contrary, challenged, attacked, torn apart, and reimagined. Traditionally, power was thought to emanate from the body of the sovereign, whether literally in the case of kings, emperors, and dictators, or figuratively from parliaments, congresses, or other legislative bodies which have come to occupy their ruling position and function. Power is generally imagined as a top down affair exercised by those who possess it and have a right to it. And power has fields of study devoted to it: political philosophy concerns itself with the shape and legitimacy of power, and the balance between social order, governance, individual liberties, and freedom, while political science examines the actual practice and exercise of power, including the empirical challenges encountered in trying to manage populations and ensure the continuation of political regimes on into the future. Cultural theory takes up the question of power in different, if related ways.

The most obvious way in which power is exercised is through physical force: the police enforce laws through the threat of incarceration and the use of tear gas and truncheons; armies defend borders or eliminate enemies of the state with guns, tanks, and atomic weapons. But this isn't the only or even primary way in which power is exerted. Political power depends equally on the production and management of a population's consent to the existing shape and form of government. Governments who rule by force alone are unlikely to last long; the ability to exercise sovereign power requires careful attention to the "ideological forms" which Marx identifies above – that is, to all the spheres of meaning making in and through which social life is experienced. To put it bluntly: power involves the molding and shaping of cultural life as well as the sting of tear gas and the threat of incarceration, and it is to the complex processes involved in this shaping that cultural theory has focused its attention.

To be able to see culture as an important site of politics has required a transformation in how power is conceptualized. Without question, the most important thinker in reimagining our understanding of power and its role in shaping and defining individuals and societies has been Michel Foucault. The examples of Foucault's work included here point to just two of his influential contributions to contemporary theories of power. The first is his challenge to and redefinition of received ideas about sovereignty and power. In the section on "Method" from Volume 1 of *The History of Sexuality* (1976), one of the places in which he speaks directly and at length about his understanding of power, Foucault begins by describing power as other than a "mode of subjugation" or "a general system of domination exerted by one group over another"[4] which is anchored in the sovereignty of the state. Power is not something "acquired, seized or shared," and then organized for use within a headquarters that governs society as if standing outside of it. As Foucault writes, "power is not an institution, and not a structure; neither is it a certain strength we are endowed with; it is the name that one attributes to a complex strategic situation in a particular society."[5] The introduction of the idea of power as a network of strategies existing everywhere, as something which "comes from below" and includes resistance within it, has produced as many confusions as insights into its modern character. Foucault's insistence on the multiplicity of power and its exercise from innumerable points is intended (in part) to snap us out of a view of power which sees it as a force which we should want to cast off in order to achieve an impossible "pure" freedom in the absence of power. The multiplicity of power does not, however, mean that anyone and everyone has the "power" to create possibilities different than the ones which presently exist – a reading which takes up Foucault's redefinition of power within the terms of the older view that he is attempting to circumvent, in which it is precisely a thing that one possesses and uses as opposed to the name for a web of social strategies.

What makes Foucault's view of power so productive, especially in thinking about the politics of culture, is the way in which it draws attention to the range of systems – and the role played by knowledge and discourse within these systems – which shape societies and subjectivities in terms of norms and assumptions whose logic exceeds that of any given caste, class, or state. Power is imbued with aims and objectives; it produces hierarchies and is non-egalitarian. The role of the cultural theorist is to carefully draw out the character and implications of those discourses which create the social forms we live in and which define and shape us, just as Foucault did in his studies of the institutions and knowledges through which we have come to define madness, criminality, and sexuality.

Foucault's second contribution to our understanding of power is one whose implications continue to be assessed and debated within cultural theory. The long-standing association of power with sovereignty alone is not a category mistake or theoretical error, but constitutes a failure to understand changes in the dominant ways in which power is organized and exercised across time. In *Society Must Be Defended* (1975–6) and elsewhere, Foucault describes an epochal shift in hegemonic forms of power. In the classical theory of sovereignty, the sovereign was the one who had power over life and death. This is displaced in the seventeenth and eighteenth centuries by techniques of power organized around the control of individual bodies – a "whole system of sur- veillance, hierarchies, inspections, bookkeeping, and reports"[6] which he terms "disciplinary society." But a shift to yet another regime of power develops, one which begins in the second half of the eighteenth century and continues up to the present. This is a form of power which deals not with individual bodies but with collective phenomena with mass effects. If disciplinary society involves forms of power directed at man-as-body, "bio- politics" is concerned with "man-as-species," that is, with the management of the entire population as a politi- cal problem. Power in disciplinary society is exercised through institutions such as prisons, schools, hospitals, and factories. Biopolitics, on the other hand, uses forms of knowledge such as rates of birth and mortality, the status of public hygiene, and the like, "not to modify any given phenomenon as such, or to modify a given individual insofar as he is an individual, but, essentially, to intervene at the level at which these general phenom- ena are determined, to intervene at the level of their generality."[7] From sovereignty as the power to take life or let live we have moved to a mode of power organized around "the right to make live and to let die."[8]

Foucault's distinction between disciplinary society and a society of biopolitical power has been employed by a number of theorists intent on understanding the specific form of contemporary power. In *Empire* (2000), Michael Hardt and Antonio Negri use Foucault's distinction to describe the new forms of power which they see as characteristic of the "mixed sovereignty" of globalization. In the wake of disciplinary society arises "the society of control," a phrase coined originally by Gilles Deleuze in his own remapping of Foucault's ideas. Deleuze's view of "societies of control" and Foucault's discussion of biopolitics differ in important respects: Deleuze's description of a system which has moved from the enclosures of disciplinary society into the dis- persed, disembodied, and discontinuous space of marketing (which has supplanted production), and of subjects engulfed either in debt or poverty comes closer to our own global realities than the now-familiar census takers and actuaries who shape Foucault's biopolitical state. For Hardt and Negri, bio*power* is not a phase or stage of power (i.e., it is not the same as biopolitics) but names the nature of power in societies of control. In the excerpt from *Empire* included here, they attempt to relate biopower to the nature of contemporary production, highlighting the ways in which "economic production and political constitution tend increasingly to coincide."[9]

Globalization may be an era shaped profoundly by biopower. But the power exerted by sovereign states – especially with respect to waging war and securing borders – has hardly disappeared, and may itself be seen as taking novel forms requiring new theories. Hardt and Negri refer to the military actions of modern nation-states as resting on "a state of permanent exception."[10] Their work and that of Giorgio Agamben and Achille Mbembe has generated new interest in the ideas of political theorist Carl Schmitt.[11] Agamben's analysis of the processes by which subjects are reduced to "bare life" absent of the possibility or potentiality that properly characterizes human existence, and Mbembe's provocative theorization of what he calls "necropolitics" – "the generalized instrumentalization of human existence and the material destruction of human bodies and populations"[12] – both rely on Schmitt's treatment of the exception as the rule of sovereignty. "Sovereign is he who decides on the exception," begins Schmitt's *Political Theology* (1922). Schmitt argues that the exception – the situation in which the rule of law has to be suspended – is the fundamental, defining characteristic of sovereignty; the power to cancel out the law means that the sovereign's powers are absolute, since it is he who decides when and if an emergency exists. This defining gap at the center of political power is more than just a matter of interest to political philosophy. The permanent state of exception which many believe exists today means that states exert their power with seemingly little worry about laws and norms, as evidenced so prominently by the decision of the United States to invade Iraq in 2003 and to treat prisoners captured in the war of terrorism (in Guantánamo and elsewhere) outside of the tenets of the Geneva Convention.

The excerpt from Frantz Fanon's *The Wretched of the Earth* (1961) points to yet another form of power which continues to shape contemporary political reality and to be of interest to cultural theory. Fanon offers one of the most detailed and compelling assessments of the reasons for the bad nationalisms which have all too often shaped postcolonial politics. The vacuum left by the colonial bourgeoisie is filled by an indigenous bourgeoisie who occupy the structural place of the colonizers, but who are "a bourgeoisie in spirit only":[13] they lack the true economic power which animates this class in developed countries. Their attempt to maintain political power at all costs, in no small part because they wish to accumulate their country's economic wealth for themselves, produces the myriad conflicts and problems that have become associated with the politics of many postcolonial nations. For Fanon, a "real" bourgeoisie is a necessary and natural step in the development of nation into an equitable and genuinely democratic society (in line with Marxist ideas about politico-historical development). Its lack in the postcolony is a crisis which demands the immediate involvement of the masses in the management of the government. Fanon's description of the problems and possibilities of new nationalisms reminds us of what is at stake in the analysis of the forms taken by power in today's world – a world which remains deeply divided, and far from just and equal, either formally or materially.

Discussions and descriptions of the ways in which cultural phenomena have shaped and been articulated through power take many forms in contemporary theory. Taken together, the readings in this section trace out the broad field of concepts within which power and politics are studied in cultural theory today.

Notes

1 See, for example, James Elkins, *Pictures and Tears: People Who Have Cried in Front of Paintings* (New York: Routledge, 2001); Elaine Scarry, *On Beauty and Being Just* (Princeton, NJ: Princeton University Press, 1999); and Wendy Steiner, *Venus in Exile: The Rejection of Beauty in Twentieth-Century Art* (New York: Free Press, 2001).

2 Karl Marx, "Preface," in *A Contribution to a Critique of Political Economy* (Moscow: Progress Publishers, 1970), 20–1. Reproduced in this volume.

3 Fredric Jameson, *Late Marxism: Adorno; Or, The Persistence of the Dialectic* (London: Verso, 1990), 46.

4   Michel Foucault, *The History of Sexuality: Volume 1: An Introduction*, trans. Robert Hurley (New York: Vintage Books, 1987), 94. Reproduced in this volume.

5   Ibid., 95 and 94 respectively.

6   Michel Foucault, *"Society Must Be Defended": Lectures at the Collège de France, 1975–1976*, trans. David Macey (New York: Picador, 2003), 242. Reproduced in this volume.

7   Ibid., 246.

8   Ibid., 241.

9   Michael Hardt and Antonio Negri, *Empire* (Cambridge, MA: Harvard University Press, 2000), 41. Reproduced in this volume.

10 Ibid., 39.

11 See Giorgio Agamben, *Homo Sacer: Sovereign Power and Bare Life*, trans. Daniel Heller-Roazen (Stanford: Stanford University Press, 1998) and *State of Exception*, trans. David Attell (Chicago: University of Chicago Press, 2005); and Achille Mbembe, "Necropolitics," *Public Culture* 15.1 (2003), 11–40.

12 Mbembe, "Necropolitics," 14.

13 Frantz Fanon, *The Wretched of the Earth*, trans. Richard Philcox (New York: Grove, 2005), 122. Reproduced in this volume.

9

"Preface" to *A Contribution to a Critique of Political Economy* (1859)

Karl Marx

I examine the system of bourgeois economy in the following order: *capital, landed property, wage-labour, the State, foreign trade, world market*. The economic conditions of existence of the three great classes into which modern bourgeois society is divided are analysed under the first three headings; the interconnection of the other three headings is self-evident. The first part of the first book, dealing with Capital, comprises the following chapters: 1. The commodity; 2. Money or simple circulation; 3. Capital in general. The present part consists of the first two chapters. The entire material lies before me in the form of monographs, which were written not for publication but for self-clarification at widely separated periods; their remoulding into an integrated whole according to the plan I have indicated will depend upon circumstances.

A general introduction, which I had drafted, is omitted, since on further consideration it seems to me confusing to anticipate results which still have to be substantiated, and the reader who really wishes to follow me will have to decide to advance from the particular to the general. A few brief remarks regarding the course of my study of political economy may, however, be appropriate here.

Although I studied jurisprudence, I pursued it as a subject subordinated to philosophy and history. In the year 1842–3, as editor of the *Rheinische Zeitung*, I first found myself in the embarrassing position of having to discuss what is known as material interests. The

Karl Marx, "Preface," pp. 19–23 from *A Contribution to the Critique of Political Economy*. New York: International Publishers, 1970. Reprinted by permission of International Publishers.

deliberations of the Rhenish Landtag on forest thefts and the division of landed property; the official polemic started by Herr von Schaper, then Oberpräsident of the Rhine Province, against the *Rheinische Zeitung* about the condition of the Moselle peasantry, and finally the debates on free trade and protective tariffs caused me in the first instance to turn my attention to economic questions. On the other hand, at that time when good intentions. "to push forward" often took the place of factual knowledge, an echo of French socialism and communism, slightly tinged by philosophy, was noticeable in the *Rheinische Zeitung*. I objected to this dilettantism, but at the same time frankly admitted in a controversy with the *Allgemeine Augsburger Zeitung* that my previous studies did not allow me to express any opinion on the content of the French theories. When the publishers of the *Rheinische Zeitung* conceived the illusion that by a more compliant policy on the part of the paper it might be possible to secure the abrogation of the death sentence passed upon it, I eagerly grasped the opportunity to withdraw from the public stage to my study.

The first work which I undertook to dispel the doubts assailing me was a critical re-examination of the Hegelian philosophy of law; the introduction to this work being published in the *Deutsch-Französische Jahrbücher* issued in Paris in 1844. My inquiry led me to the conclusion that neither legal relations nor political forms could be comprehended whether by themselves or on the basis of a so-called general development of the human mind, but that on the contrary they originate in the material conditions of life, the totality of which Hegel, following the example of English and French thinkers of the eighteenth century, embraces within the term "civil society"; that the anatomy of this civil society, however, has to be sought in political economy. The study of this, which I began in Paris, I continued in Brussels, where I moved owing to an expulsion order issued by M. Guizot. The general conclusion at which I arrived and which, once reached, became the guiding principle of my studies can be summarised as follows. In the social production of their existence, men inevitably enter into definite relations, which are independent of their will, namely relations of production appropriate to a given stage in the development of their material forces of production. The totality of these relations of production constitutes the economic structure of society, the real foundation, on which arises a legal and political superstructure and to which correspond definite forms of social consciousness. The mode of production of material life conditions the general process of social, political and intellectual life. It is not the consciousness of men that determines their existence, but their social existence that determines their consciousness. At a certain stage of development, the material productive forces of society come into conflict with the existing relations of production or – this merely expresses the same thing in legal terms – with the property relations within the framework of which they have operated hitherto. From forms of development of the productive forces these relations turn into their fetters. Then begins an era of social revolution. The changes in the economic foundation lead sooner or later to the transformation of the whole immense superstructure. In studying such transformations it is always necessary to distinguish between the material transformation of the economic conditions of production, which can be determined with the precision of natural science, and the legal, political, religious, artistic or philosophic – in short, ideological forms in which men become conscious of this conflict and fight it out. Just as one does not judge an individual by what he thinks about himself, so one cannot judge such a period of transformation by its consciousness, but, on the contrary, this consciousness must be explained from the contradictions of material life, from the conflict existing between the social forces of production and the relations of production. No social order is ever destroyed before all the productive forces for which it is sufficient have been developed, and new superior relations of production never replace older ones before the material conditions for their existence have matured within the framework of the old society. Mankind thus inevitably sets itself only such tasks as it is able to solve, since closer examination will always show that the problem itself arises only when the material conditions for its solution are already present or at least in the course of formation. In broad outline, the Asiatic, ancient, feudal and modern bourgeois modes of production may be designated as epochs marking progress in the economic development of society. The bourgeois mode of production is the last antagonistic form of the social process of production – antagonistic not in the sense of individual antagonism but of an antagonism that emanates from the individuals' social conditions of existence – but the productive forces developing within bourgeois society create also the material conditions for a solution of this antagonism. The prehistory of human society accordingly closes with this social formation.

Frederick Engels, with whom I maintained a constant exchange of ideas by correspondence since the publication of his brilliant essay on the critique of economic categories (printed in the *Deutsch-Französische Jahrbücher*), arrived by another road (compare his *Lage der arbeitenden Klasse in England*[1]) at the same result as I, and when in the spring of 1845 he too came to live in Brussels, we decided to set forth together our conception as opposed to the ideological one of German philosophy, in fact to settle accounts with our former philosophical conscience. The intention was carried out in the form of a critique of post-Hegelian philosophy. The manuscript, two large octavo volumes, had long ago reached the publishers in Westphalia when we were informed that owing to changed circumstances it could not be printed. We abandoned the manuscript to the gnawing criticism of the mice all the more willingly since we had achieved our main purpose – self-clarification. Of the scattered works in which at that time we presented one or another aspect of our views to the public, I shall mention only the *Manifesto of the Communist Party*, jointly written by Engels and myself, and a *Discours sur le libre échange*, which I myself published. The salient points of our conception were first outlined in an academic, although polemical, form in my *Misère de la philosophie* ...,[2] this book which was aimed at Proudhon appeared in 1847. The publication of an essay on *Wage-Labour* written in German in which I combined the lectures I had held on this subject at the German Workers' Association in Brussels, was interrupted by the February Revolution and my forcible removal from Belgium in consequence.

The publication of the *Neue Rheinische Zeitung* in 1848 and 1849 and subsequent events cut short my economic studies, which I could only resume in London in 1850. The enormous amount of material relating to the history of political economy assembled in the British Museum, the fact that London is a convenient vantage point for the observation of bourgeois society, and finally the new stage of development which this society seemed to have entered with the discovery of gold in California and Australia, induced me to start again from the very beginning and to work carefully through the new material. These studies led partly of their own accord to apparently quite remote subjects on which I had to spend a certain amount of time. But it was in particular the imperative necessity of earning my living which reduced the time at my disposal. My collaboration, continued now for eight years, with the *New York Tribune*, the leading Anglo-American newspaper, necessitated an excessive fragmentation of my studies, for I wrote only exceptionally newspaper correspondence in the strict sense. Since a considerable part of my contributions consisted of articles dealing with important economic events in Britain and on the Continent,

I was compelled to become conversant with practical details which, strictly speaking, lie outside the sphere of political economy.

This sketch of the course of my studies in the domain of political economy is intended merely to show that my views – no matter how they may be judged and how little they conform to the interested prejudices of the ruling classes – are the outcome of conscientious research carried on over many years. At the entrance to science, as at the entrance to hell, the demand must be made:

> *Qui si convien lasciare ogni sospetto*
> *Ogni viltà convien che qui sia morta.*[3]

Karl Marx
London, January 1859

Notes

1 See Frederick Engels, "The Condition of the Working Class in England", *On Britain* (Moscow, 1962), pp. 3–338. – *Ed.*

2 See K. Marx, *The Poverty of Philosophy* (Moscow, 1962). – *Ed.*

3 Dante, *Divina Commedia*.

> Here must all distrust be left;
> All cowardice must here be dead.
>> (The English translation is taken from Dante, *The Divine Comedy*, Illustrated Modern Library, Inc., 1944, p. 22.) – *Ed.*

10

"Definition of Sovereignty" (1922)

Carl Schmitt

Sovereign is he who decides on the exception.[1]

Only this definition can do justice to a borderline concept. Contrary to the imprecise terminology that is found in popular literature, a borderline concept is not a vague concept, but one pertaining to the outermost sphere. This definition of sovereignty must therefore be associated with a borderline case and not with routine. It will soon become clear that the exception is to be understood to refer to a general concept in the theory of the state, and not merely to a construct applied to any emergency decree or state of siege.

The assertion that the exception is truly appropriate for the juristic definition of sovereignty has a systematic, legal-logical foundation. The decision on the exception is a decision in the true sense of the word. Because a general norm, as represented by an ordinary legal prescription, can never encompass a total exception, the decision that a real exception exists cannot therefore be entirely derived from this norm. When Robert von Mohl[2] said that the test of whether an emergency exists cannot be a juristic one, he assumed that a decision in the legal sense must be derived entirely from the content of a norm. But this is the question. In the general sense in which Mohl articulated his argument, his notion is only an expression of constitutional liberalism and fails to apprehend the independent meaning of the decision.

Carl Schmitt, "Definition of Sovereignty," pp. 5–15 from *Political Theology: Four Chapters on the Concept of Sovereignty*, trans. George Schwab. Cambridge, MA: MIT Press, 1986. Copyright © 1986 Massachusetts Institute of Technology, by permission of The MIT Press.

From a practical or a theoretical perspective, it really does not matter whether an abstract scheme advanced to define sovereignty (namely, that sovereignty is the highest power, not a derived power) is acceptable. About an abstract concept there will in general be no argument, least of all in the history of sovereignty. What is argued about is the concrete application, and that means who decides in a situation of conflict what constitutes the public interest or interest of the state, public safety and order, *le salut public*, and so on. The exception, which is not codified in the existing legal order, can at best be characterized as a case of extreme peril, a danger to the existence of the state, or the like. But it cannot be circumscribed factually and made to conform to a preformed law.

It is precisely the exception that makes relevant the subject of sovereignty, that is, the whole question of sovereignty. The precise details of an emergency cannot be anticipated, nor can one spell out what may take place in such a case, especially when it is truly a matter of an extreme emergency and of how it is to be eliminated. The precondition as well as the content of jurisdictional competence in such a case must necessarily be unlimited. From the liberal constitutional point of view, there would be no jurisdictional competence at all. The most guidance the constitution can provide is to indicate who can act in such a case. If such action is not subject to controls, if it is not hampered in some way by checks and balances, as is the case in a liberal constitution, then it is clear who the sovereign is. He decides whether there is an extreme emergency as well as what must be done to eliminate it. Although he stands outside the normally valid legal system, he nevertheless belongs to it, for it is he who must decide whether the constitution needs to be suspended in its entirety.[3] All tendencies of modern constitutional development point toward eliminating the sovereign in this sense. The ideas of Hugo Krabbe and Hans Kelsen [...] are in line with this development. But whether the extreme exception can be banished from the world is not a juristic question. Whether one has confidence and hope that it can be eliminated depends on philosophical, especially on philosophical-historical or metaphysical, convictions.

There exist a number of historical presentations that deal with the development of the concept of sovereignty, but they are like textbook compilations of abstract formulas from which definitions of sovereignty can be extracted. Nobody seems to have taken the trouble to scrutinize the often-repeated but completely empty phraseology used to denote the highest power by the famous authors of the concept of sovereignty. That this concept relates to the critical case, the exception, was long ago recognized by Jean Bodin. He stands at the beginning of the modern theory of the state because of his work "Of the True Marks of Sovereignty" (chapter 10 of the first book of the *Republic*) rather than because of his often-cited definition ("sovereignty is the absolute and perpetual power of a republic"). He discussed his concept in the context of many practical examples, and he always returned to the question: To what extent is the sovereign bound to laws, and to what extent is he responsible to the estates? To this last, all-important question he replied that commitments are binding because they rest on natural law; but in emergencies the tie to general natural principles ceases. In general, according to him, the prince is duty bound toward the estates or the people only to the extent of fulfilling his promise in the interest of the people; he is not so bound under conditions of urgent necessity. These are by no means new theses. The decisive point about Bodin's concept is that by referring to the emergency, he reduced his analysis of the relationships between prince and estates to a simple either/or.

This is what is truly impressive in his definition of sovereignty; by considering sovereignty to be indivisible, he finally settled the question of power in the state. His scholarly accomplishment and the basis for his success thus reside in his having incorporated the decision into the concept of sovereignty. Today there is hardly any mention of the concept of sovereignty that does not contain the usual quotation from Bodin. But nowhere does one find cited the core quote from that chapter of the *Republic*. Bodin asked if the commitments of the prince to the estates or the people dissolve his sovereignty. He answered by referring to the case in which it becomes necessary to violate such commitments, to change laws or to suspend them entirely according to the requirements of a situation, a time, and a people. If in such cases the prince had to consult a senate or the people before he could act, he would have to be prepared to let his subjects dispense with him. Bodin considered this an absurdity because, according to him, the estates were not masters over the laws; they in turn would have to permit their prince to dispense with them. Sovereignty would thus become a play between two parties: Sometimes the people and sometimes the prince would rule, and that would be contrary to all reason and all law. Because the authority to suspend valid law – be it in general or in a specific case – is so much the actual mark of sovereignty, Bodin wanted to derive from this authority all other characteristics (declaring war and making peace, appointing civil servants, right of pardon, final appeal, and so on).

In contrast to traditional presentations, I have shown in my study of dictatorship that even the seventeenth-century authors of natural law understood the question of sovereignty to mean the question of the decision on the exception.[4] This is particularly true of Samuel von Pufendorf. Everyone agrees that whenever antagonisms appear within a state, every party wants the general good – therein resides after all the *bellum omnium contra omnes*. But sovereignty (and thus the state itself) resides in deciding this controversy, that is, in determining definitively what constitutes public order and security, in determining when they are disturbed, and so on. Public order and security manifest themselves very differently in reality, depending on whether a militaristic bureaucracy, a self-governing body controlled by the spirit of commercialism, or a radical party organization decides when there is order and security and when it is threatened or disturbed. After all, every legal order is based on a decision, and also the concept of the legal order, which is applied as something self-evident, contains within it the contrast of the two distinct elements of the juristic – norm and decision. Like every other order, the legal order rests on a decision and not on a norm.

Whether God alone is sovereign, that is, the one who acts as his acknowledged representative on earth, or the emperor, or prince, or the people, meaning those who identify themselves directly with the people, the question is always aimed at the subject of sovereignty, at the application of the concept to a concrete situation. Ever since the sixteenth century, jurists who discuss the question of sovereignty have derived their ideas from a catalogue of determining, decisive features of sovereignty that can in essence be traced to the points made by Bodin. To possess those powers meant to be sovereign. In the murky legal conditions of the old German Reich the argument on public law ran as follows: Because one of the many indications of sovereignty was undoubtedly present, the other dubious indications also had to be present. The controversy always centered on the question, Who assumes authority concerning those matters for which there are no positive stipulations, for example, a capitulation? In other words, Who is responsible for that for which competence has not been anticipated?

In a more familiar vein it was asked, Who is supposed to have unlimited power? Hence the discussion about the exception, the *extremus necessitatis casus*. This is repeated with the same legal-logical structure in the discussions on the so-called monarchical principle. Here, too, it is always asked who is entitled to decide those actions for which the constitution makes no provision; that is, who is competent to act when the legal system fails to answer the question of competence. The controversy concerning whether the individual German states were sovereign according to the constitution of 1871 was a matter of minor political significance. Nevertheless, the thrust of that argument can easily be recognized once more. The pivotal point of Max Seydel's attempt to prove that the individual states were sovereign had less to do with the question whether the remaining rights of the individual states were or were not subsumable than with the assertion that the competence of the Reich was circumscribed by the constitution, which in principle meant limited, whereas the competence of the individual states was in principle unlimited.

According to article 48 of the German constitution of 1919, the exception is declared by the president of the Reich but is under the control of parliament, the Reichstag, which can at any time demand its suspension. This provision corresponds to the development and practice of the liberal constitutional state, which attempts to repress the question of sovereignty by a division and mutual control of competences. But only the arrangement of the precondition that governs the invocation of exceptional powers corresponds to the liberal constitutional tendency, not the content of article 48. Article 48 grants unlimited power. If applied without check, it would grant exceptional powers in the same way as article 14 of the [French] Charter of 1815, which made the monarch sovereign. If the individual states no longer have the power to declare the exception, as the prevailing opinion on article 48 contends, then they no longer enjoy the status of states. Article 48 is the actual reference point for answering the question whether the individual German states are states.

If measures undertaken in an exception could be circumscribed by mutual control, by imposing a time limit, or finally, as in the liberal constitutional procedure governing a state of siege, by enumerating extraordinary powers, the question of sovereignty would then be considered less significant but would certainly not be eliminated. A jurisprudence concerned with ordinary day-to-day questions has practically no interest in the concept of sovereignty. Only the recognizable is its normal concern; everything else is a "disturbance." Such a jurisprudence confronts the extreme case disconcertedly, for not every extraordinary measure, not every police emergency measure or emergency decree, is necessarily an exception. What characterizes an exception is principally unlimited authority, which means the suspension of the entire existing order. In such a situation it is clear that the state remains, whereas law recedes. Because the exception is different from anarchy and chaos, order in the juristic sense still prevails even if it is not of the ordinary kind.

The existence of the state is undoubted proof of its superiority over the validity of the legal norm. The decision frees itself from all normative ties and becomes in the true sense absolute. The state suspends the law in the exception on the basis of its right of self-preservation, as one would say. The two elements of the concept *legal order* are then dissolved into independent notions and thereby testify to their conceptual independence. Unlike the normal situation, when the autonomous moment of the decision recedes to a minimum, the norm is destroyed in the exception. The exception remains, nevertheless, accessible to jurisprudence because both elements, the norm as well as the decision, remain within the framework of the juristic.

It would be a distortion of the schematic disjunction between sociology and jurisprudence if one were to say that the exception has no juristic significance and is therefore "sociology." The exception is that which cannot be subsumed; it defies general codification, but it simultaneously reveals a specifically juristic element – the decision in absolute purity. The exception appears in its absolute form when a situation in which legal prescriptions can be valid must first be brought about. Every general norm demands a normal, everyday frame of life to which it can be factually applied and which is subjected to its regulations. The norm requires a homogeneous medium. This effective normal situation is not a mere "superficial presupposition" that a jurist can ignore; that situation belongs precisely to its immanent validity. There exists no norm that is applicable to chaos. For a legal order to make sense, a normal situation must exist, and he is sovereign who definitely decides whether this normal situation actually exists.

All law is "situational law." The sovereign produces and guarantees the situation in its totality. He has the monopoly over this last decision. Therein resides the essence of the state's sovereignty, which must be juristically defined correctly, not as the monopoly to coerce or to rule, but as the monopoly to decide. The exception reveals most clearly the essence of the state's authority. The decision parts here from the legal norm, and (to formulate it paradoxically) authority proves that to produce law it need not be based on law.

The exception was something incommensurable to John Locke's doctrine of the constitutional state and the rationalist eighteenth century. The vivid awareness of the meaning of the exception that was reflected in the doctrine of natural law of the seventeenth century was soon lost in the eighteenth century, when a relatively lasting order was established. Emergency law was no law at all for Kant. The contemporary theory of the state reveals the interesting spectacle of the two tendencies facing one another, the rationalist tendency, which ignores the emergency, and the natural law tendency, which is interested in the emergency and emanates from an essentially different set of ideas. That a neo-Kantian like Kelsen does not know what to do with the exception is obvious. But it should be of interest to the rationalist that the legal system itself can anticipate the exception and can "suspend itself." That a norm or an order or a point of reference "establishes itself" appears plausible to the exponents of this kind of juristic rationalism. But how the systematic unity and order can suspend itself in a concrete case is difficult to construe, and yet it remains a juristic problem as long as the exception is distinguishable from a juristic chaos, from any kind of anarchy. The tendency of liberal constitutionalism to regulate the exception as precisely as possible means, after all, the attempt to spell out in detail the case in which law suspends itself. From where does the law obtain this force, and how is it logically possible that a norm is valid except for one concrete case that it cannot factually determine in any definitive manner?

It would be consequent rationalism to say that the exception proves nothing and that only the normal can be the object of scientific interest. The exception confounds the unity and order of the rationalist scheme. One encounters not infrequently a similar argument in the positive theory of the state. To the question of how to proceed in the absence of a budget law, Gerhard Anschütz replied that this was not at all a legal question. "There is not only a gap in the law, that is, in the text of the constitution, but moreover in law as a whole, which can in no way be filled by juristic conceptual operations. Here is where public law stops."[5]

Precisely a philosophy of concrete life must not withdraw from the exception and the extreme case, but must be interested in it to the highest degree. The exception can be more important to it than the rule, not because of a romantic irony for the paradox, but because the seriousness of an insight goes deeper than the clear generalizations inferred from what ordinarily repeats itself. The exception is more interesting than the rule. The rule proves nothing; the exception proves everything: It confirms not only the rule but also its existence, which derives only from the exception. In the exception the power of real life breaks through the crust of a mechanism that has become torpid by repetition.

A Protestant theologian[6] who demonstrated the vital intensity possible in theological reflection in the nineteenth century stated: "The exception explains the general and itself. And if one wants to study the general correctly, one only needs to look around for a true exception. It reveals everything more clearly than does the general. Endless talk about the general becomes boring; there are exceptions. If they cannot be explained, then the general also cannot be explained. The difficulty is usually not noticed because the general is not thought about with passion but with a comfortable superficiality. The exception, on the other hand, thinks the general with intense passion."[7]

Notes

1 [Tr.] In the context of Schmitt's work, a state of exception includes any kind of severe economic or political disturbance that requires the application of extraordinary measures. Whereas an exception presupposes a constitutional order that provides guidelines on how to confront crises in order to reestablish order and stability, a state of emergency need not have an existing order as a reference point because *necessitas non habet legem*. See George Schwab, *The Challenge of the Exception* (Berlin, 1970), pp. 7, 42.

2 [Tr.] *Staatsrecht, Völkerrecht und Politik: Monographien*, vol. 2 (Tübingen, 1862), p. 626.

3 [Tr.] As already noted in the introduction, Schmitt, in his study of dictatorship (*Die Diktatur*), considered the powers of the president to be commissarial in nature, that is, to be understood in the context of article 48. In the case of an exception the president could thus suspend the constitution but not abrogate it – an act characteristic of a sovereign form of dictatorship.

4 [Tr.] *Die Diktatur.*

5 [Tr.] See Georg Meyer, *Lehrbuch des Deutschen Staatsrechts*, 7th edn, vol. 3, ed. G. Anschütz (Munich and Leipzig, 1919), p. 906.

6 [Tr.] The reference here is to Søren Kierkegaard.

7 [Tr.] The quote is from Kierkegaard's *Repetition*.

11

"The Trials and Tribulations of National Consciousness" (1961)

Frantz Fanon

History teaches us that the anticolonialist struggle is not automatically written from a nationalist perspective. Over a long period of time the colonized have devoted their energy to eliminating iniquities such as forced labor, corporal punishment, unequal wages, and the restriction of political rights. This fight for democracy against man's oppression gradually emerges from a universalist, neoliberal confusion to arrive, sometimes laboriously, at a demand for nationhood. But the unpreparedness of the elite, the lack of practical ties between them and the masses, their apathy and, yes, their cowardice at the crucial moment in the struggle, are the cause of tragic trials and tribulations.

Instead of being the coordinated crystallization of the people's innermost aspirations, instead of being the most tangible, immediate product of popular mobilization, national consciousness is nothing but a crude, empty, fragile shell. The cracks in it explain how easy it is for young independent countries to switch back from nation to ethnic group and from state to tribe – a regression which is so terribly detrimental and prejudicial to the development of the nation and national unity. As we shall see, such shortcomings and dangers derive historically from the incapacity of the national bourgeoisie in underdeveloped countries to rational-

ize popular praxis, in other words their incapacity to attribute it any reason.

The characteristic, virtually endemic weakness of the underdeveloped countries' national consciousness is not only the consequence of the colonized subject's mutilation by the colonial regime. It can also be attributed to the apathy of the national bourgeoisie, its mediocrity, and its deeply cosmopolitan mentality.

The national bourgeoisie, which takes over power at the end of the colonial regime, is an underdeveloped bourgeoisie. Its economic clout is practically zero, and in any case, no way commensurate with that of its metropolitan counterpart which it intends replacing. In its willful narcissism, the national bourgeoisie has lulled itself into thinking that it can supplant the metropolitan bourgeoisie to its own advantage. But independence, which literally forces it back against the wall, triggers catastrophic reactions and obliges it to send out distress signals in the direction of the former metropolis. The business elite and university graduates, who make up the most educated category of the new nation, are identifiable by their small numbers, their concentration in the capital, and their occupations as traders, landowners and professionals. This national bourgeoisie possesses neither industrialists nor financiers. The national bourgeoisie in the underdeveloped countries is not geared to production, invention, creation, or work. All its energy is channeled into intermediary activities. Networking and scheming seem to be its underlying vocation. The national bourgeoisie has the psychology of a businessman, not that of a captain of industry. And it should go without saying that the rapacity of the colonists and the embargo system installed by colonialism hardly left it any choice.

Under the colonial system a bourgeoisie that accumulates capital is in the realm of the impossible. To our thinking, therefore, the historical vocation of an authentic national bourgeoisie in an underdeveloped country is to repudiate its status as bourgeois and an instrument of capital and to become entirely subservient to the revolutionary capital which the people represent.

In an underdeveloped country, the imperative duty of an authentic national bourgeoisie is to betray the vocation to which it is destined, to learn from the people, and make available to them the intellectual and technical capital it culled from its time in colonial universities. We will see, unfortunately, that the national bourgeoisie often turns away from this heroic and positive path, which is both productive and just, and unabashedly opts for the antinational, and therefore abhorrent, path of a conventional bourgeoisie, a bourgeois bourgeoisie that is dismally, inanely, and cynically bourgeois.

We have seen that the objective of the nationalist parties from a certain period onward is geared strictly along national lines. They mobilize the people with the slogan of independence and anything else is left to the future. When these parties are questioned on their economic agenda for the nation or the regime they propose to establish they prove incapable of giving an answer because, in fact, they do not have a clue about the economy of their own country.

This economy has always developed outside their control. As for the present and potential resources of their country's soil and subsoil, their knowledge is purely academic and approximate. They can only talk about them in general and abstract terms. After independence, this underdeveloped bourgeoisie, reduced in number, lacking capital and rejecting the road to revolution, stagnates miserably. It cannot give free expression to its genius that was in the past hampered by colonial domination, or so it claims. The precariousness of its resources and the scarcity of managerial talent force it for years into an economy of cottage industries. In its inevitably highly limited perspective, the bourgeoisie's idea of a national economy is one based on what we can call local products. Grandiloquent speeches are made about local crafts. Unable to establish factories which would be more profitable for the country and for themselves, the bourgeoisie cloaks local artisanship in a chauvinistic tenderness which not only ties in with the new national dignity, but also ensures them substantial profits. This cult for local products, this incapacity to invent new outlets is likewise reflected in the entrenchment of the national bourgeoisie in the type of agricultural production typical of the colonial period.

Independence does not bring a change of direction. The same old groundnut harvest, cocoa harvest, and olive harvest. Likewise the traffic of commodities goes unchanged. No industry is established in the country. We continue to ship raw materials, we continue to grow produce for Europe and pass for specialists of unfinished products.

Yet the national bourgeoisie never stops calling for the nationalization of the economy and the commercial sector. In its thinking, to nationalize does not mean placing the entire economy at the service of the nation or satisfying all its requirements. To nationalize does not mean organizing the state on the basis of a new program of social relations. For the bourgeoisie, nationalization signifies very precisely the transfer into indigenous hands of privileges inherited from the colonial period.

Since the bourgeoisie has neither the material means nor adequate intellectual resources such as engineers and technicians, it limits its claims to the takeover of businesses and firms previously held by the colonists. The national bourgeoisie replaces the former European settlers as doctors, lawyers, tradesmen, agents, dealers, and shipping agents. For the dignity of the country and to safeguard its own interests, it considers it its duty to occupy all these positions. Henceforth it demands that every major foreign company must operate through them, if it wants to remain in the country or establish trade. The national bourgeoisie discovers its historical mission as intermediary. As we have seen, its vocation is not to transform the nation but prosaically serve as a conveyor belt for capitalism, forced to camouflage itself behind the mask of neocolonialism. The national bourgeoisie, with no misgivings and with great pride, revels in the role of agent in its dealings with the Western bourgeoisie. This lucrative role, this function as small-time racketeer, this narrow-mindedness and lack of ambition are symptomatic of the incapacity of the national bourgeoisie to fulfil its historic role as bourgeoisie. The dynamic, pioneering aspect, the inventive, discoverer-of-new-worlds aspect common to every national bourgeoisie is here lamentably absent. At the core of the national bourgeoisie of the colonial countries a hedonistic mentality prevails – because on a psychological level it identifies with the Western bourgeoisie from which it has slurped every lesson. It mimics the Western bourgeoisie in its negative and decadent aspects without having accomplished the initial phases of exploration and invention that are the assets of this Western bourgeoisie whatever the circumstances. In its early days the national bourgeoisie of the colonial countries identifies with the last stages of the Western bourgeoisie. Don't believe it is taking short cuts. In fact it starts at the end. It is already senile, having experienced neither the exuberance nor the brazen determination of youth and adolescence.

In its decadent aspect the national bourgeoisie gets considerable help from the Western bourgeoisies who happen to be tourists enamored of exoticism, hunting and casinos. The national bourgeoisie establishes holiday resorts and playgrounds for entertaining the Western bourgeoisie. This sector goes by the name of tourism and becomes a national industry for this very purpose. We only have to look at what has happened in Latin America if we want proof of the way the ex-colonized bourgeoisie can be transformed into "party" organizer. The casinos in Havana and Mexico City, the beaches of Rio, Copacabana, and Acapulco, the young Brazilian and Mexican girls, the thirteen-year-old mestizas, are the scars of this depravation of the national bourgeoisie. Because it is lacking in ideas, because it is inward-looking, cut off from the people, sapped by its congenital incapacity to evaluate issues on the basis of the nation as a whole, the national bourgeoisie assumes the role of manager for the companies of the West and turns its country virtually into a bordello for Europe.

Once again we need only to look at the pitiful spectacle of certain republics in Latin America. US businessmen, banking magnates and technocrats jet "down to the tropics," and for a week to ten days wallow in the sweet depravity of their private "reserves."

The behavior of the national landowners is practically the same as that of the urban bourgeoisie. As soon as independence is proclaimed the big farmers demand the nationalization of the agricultural holdings. Through a number of schemes they manage to lay hands on the farms once owned by the colonists, thereby reinforcing their control over the region. But they make no attempt to diversify, increase production or integrate it in a genuinely national economy.

In fact the landowners call on the authorities to increase a hundredfold the facilities and privileges now theirs but once reserved for the foreign colonists. The exploitation of farm workers is intensified and justified. Capitalizing on two or three slogans, these new colonists demand a colossal effort from these farm laborers – in the name of the national interest, of course. There is no modernization of agriculture, no development plan, no initiative, for initiatives imply a degree of risk, and would throw such milieus into a panic, and put to flight a wary, overcautious, landed bourgeoisie which is sinking deeper and deeper into the ruts established by colonialism. In such regions, initiatives are handled by the government. It is the government which approves them, encourages them and finances them. The landed bourgeoisie refuses to take the slightest risk. It is hostile to gambling and ventures. It has no intention of building upon sand. It demands solid investments and quick returns. The profits it pockets are enormous compared to the gross national product, and are not reinvested. Its only mentality is to hoard its savings. This bourgeoisie especially in the aftermath of independence, has no scruples depositing in foreign banks the profits it has made from the national resources. Major sums, however, are invested for the sake of prestige in cars, villas, and all those ostentatious goods described by economists as typical of an underdeveloped bourgeoisie.

We have said that the colonized bourgeoisie which attains power utilizes the aggressiveness of its class to grab the jobs previously held by foreigners. In the aftermath of independence, faced with the human consequences of colonialism, it wages a ruthless struggle against the lawyers, tradespeople, landowners, doctors, and high-ranking civil servants "who insult the national dignity." It frantically brandishes the notions of nationalization and Africanization of the managerial classes. In fact, its actions become increasingly tinged with racism. It bluntly confronts the government with the demand that it must have these jobs. And it does not tone down its virulence until it occupies every single one of them.

The urban proletariat, the unemployed masses, the small artisans, those commonly called small traders, side with this nationalist attitude; but, in all justice, they are merely modeling their attitude on that of their bourgeoisie. Whereas the national bourgeoisie competes with the Europeans, the artisans and small traders pick fights with Africans of other nationalities. In the Ivory Coast, outright race riots were directed against the Dahomeans[1] and Upper Voltans who controlled much of the business sector and were the target of hostile demonstrations by the Ivorians following independence. We have switched from nationalism to ultranationalism, chauvinism, and racism. There is a general call for these foreigners to leave, their shops are burned, their market booths torn down and some are lynched; consequently, the Ivorian government orders them to leave, thereby satisfying the demands of the nationals. In Senegal it was the anti-Sudanese[2] demonstrations that caused Mamadou Dia to state: "The people of Senegal owe their blind belief in the Federation of Mali to their affection for its leaders. Their deep attachment to Mali has no other basis but a repeated act of faith in the politics of these leaders. The issue of Senegalese territory was no less alive in their minds, especially as the Sudanese presence in Dakar was far too visible for the problem to be overlooked. This is the reason why, far from causing any regrets, the breakup of the Federation was greeted by the masses with relief and there was no support from any quarter in its favor."[3]

Whereas certain categories of Senegalese jump at the opportunity offered by their own leaders to get rid of the Sudanese, who are unwelcome elements in the business and administrative sectors, the Congolese, who watched in disbelief as the Belgians left en masse, decide to put pressure on the Senegalese established at Léopoldville and Elizabethville and in turn get them to leave.

As we can see, the mechanism is identical in both cases. Whereas the ambitions of the young nation's intellectuals and business bourgeoisie are thwarted by the

Europeans, for the majority of the urban population, competition stems mainly from Africans of other nations. In the Ivory Coast it is the Dahomeans; in Ghana, the inhabitants of Niger; and in Senegal, the Sudanese.

Whereas the demand for Africanization and Arabization of management by the bourgeoisie is not rooted in a genuine endeavor at nationalization, but merely corresponds to a transfer of power previously held by the foreigners, the masses make the very same demand at their own level but limit the notion of African or Arab to territorial limits. Between the vibrant calls for African unity and this mass behavior inspired by the managerial class, a number of attitudes emerge. There is a constant pendulum motion between African unity, which sinks deeper and deeper into oblivion, and a depressing return to the most heinous and virulent type of chauvinism.

"As for the Senegalese leaders who were the main theoreticians of African unification and who, on several occasions, sacrificed their local political organizations as well as their personal careers to this idea, they undeniably bear a great deal of responsibility, although admittedly in all good faith. Their mistake, our mistake, under the pretext of combating Balkanization, was not to take into consideration that pre-colonial factor of territoriality. Our mistake was not to give enough attention in our analyses to this factor, exacerbated by colonialism, but also a sociological fact which no theory on unity, however commendable or appealing, can eliminate. We let ourselves be tempted by the mirage whose configuration is the most satisfying for the mind, and taking our ideal for reality, we believed we only needed to condemn territoriality and its natural offshoot, micro nationalism, to get the better of them and ensure the success of our chimerical endeavor."[4]

From Senegalese chauvinism to Wolof tribalism, there is but one small step. And consequently, wherever the petty-mindedness of the national bourgeoisie and the haziness of its ideological positions have been incapable of enlightening the people as a whole or have been unable to put the people first, wherever this national bourgeoisie has proven to be incapable of expanding its vision of the world, there is a return to tribalism, and we watch with a raging heart as ethnic tensions triumph. Since the only slogan of the bourgeoisie is "Replace the foreigners," and they rush into every sector to take the law into their own hands and fill the vacancies, the petty traders such as taxi drivers, cake sellers, and shoe shiners follow suit and call for the expulsion of the Dahomeans or, taking tribalism to a new level, demand that the Fulani go back to their bush or back up their mountains.

The triumph of federalism in certain young independent nations must be interpreted along these lines. We know that colonial domination gave preferential treatment to certain regions. The colony's economy was not integrated into that of the nation as a whole. It is still organized along the lines dictated by the metropolis. Colonialism almost never exploits the entire country. It is content with extracting natural resources and exporting them to the metropolitan industries thereby enabling a specific sector to grow relatively wealthy, while the rest of the colony continues, or rather sinks, into underdevelopment and poverty.

In the aftermath of independence the nationals who live in the prosperous regions realize their good fortune and their gut reaction is to refuse to feed the rest of the nation. The regions rich in groundnuts, cocoa, and diamonds stand out against the empty panorama offered by the rest of the country. The nationals of these regions look upon the others with hatred detecting envy, greed, and murderous impulses. The old precolonial rivalries, the old intertribal hatreds resurface. The Balubas refuse to feed the Luluas. Katanga becomes a state on its own and Albert Kalondji crowns himself king of southern Kasai.

African unity, a vague term, but nevertheless one to which the men and women of Africa were passionately attached and whose operative function was to put incredible pressure on colonialism, reveals its true face and crumbles into regionalisms within the same national reality. Because it is obsessed with its immediate interests, because it cannot see further than the end of its nose, the national bourgeoisie proves incapable of achieving simple national unity and incapable of building the nation on a solid, constructive foundation. The national front that drove back colonialism falls apart and licks its wounds.

This ruthless struggle waged by the ethnic groups and tribes, and this virulent obsession with filling the vacancies left by the foreigners also engender religious rivalries. In the interior and the bush, the minor confraternities, the local religions, and *marabout* cults spring back to life and resort once more to the vicious circle of mutual denunciation. In the urban centers the authorities are confronted with a clash between the two major revealed religions: Islam and Catholicism.

Colonialism, which the birth of African unity had trembling on its foundations, is now back on its feet, and now undertakes to break this will to unify by taking advantage of every weak link in the movement. Colonialism will attempt to rally the African peoples by uncovering the existence of "spiritual" rivalries. In Senegal the magazine *Afrique Nouvelle* secretes its weekly dose of hatred against Islam and the Arabs. The Lebanese, who control most of the small businesses along the West Coast of Africa, are publicly vilified. The missionaries opportunely remind the masses that the great African empires were dismantled by the invasion of the Arabs long before the arrival of European colonialism. They even go so far as to say that the Arab occupation paved the way for European colonialism; references are made to Arab imperialism, and the cultural imperialism of Islam is denounced. Muslims are generally kept out of managerial positions. In other regions the reverse is true and it is the indigenous Christians who are the targets and treated as conscious enemies of national independence.

Colonialism shamelessly pulls all these strings, only too content to see the Africans, who were once in league against it, tear at each other's throats. The notion of another Saint Bartholomew's massacre takes shape in some people's minds, and colonialism snickers when it hears the magnificent speeches on African unity. Within the same nation, religion divides the people and sets the spiritual communities, fostered and encouraged by colonialism and its apparatus, at odds with each other. Totally unexpected events break out here and there. In predominantly Catholic or Protestant countries the Muslim minority redoubles its religious fervor. Muslim festivals are revived and Islam defends itself every inch of the way against the violent absolutism of the Catholic religion. Ministers are heard telling certain individuals that if they are not content, they should go and live in Cairo. In some cases American Protestantism transports its anti-Catholic prejudices onto African soil and uses religion to encourage tribal rivalries.

On the scale of the continent this religious tension can take the shape of the crudest form of racism. Africa is divided into a white region and a black region. The substitute names of sub-Saharan Africa and North Africa are unable to mask this latent racism. In some places you hear that White Africa has a thousand-year-old tradition of culture, that it is Mediterranean, an extension of Europe and is part of Greco-Roman civilization. Black Africa is looked upon as a wild, savage, uncivilized, and lifeless region. In other places, you hear day in and day out hateful remarks about veiled women, polygamy, and the Arabs' alleged contempt for the female sex. The aggressiveness of all these remarks recalls those so often attributed to the colonist. The national bourgeoisie of each of these two major regions, who have assimilated to the core the most despicable aspects of the colonial mentality, take over from the Europeans and lay the foundations for a racist philosophy that is terribly prejudicial to the future of Africa. Through its apathy and mimicry it encourages the growth and development of racism that was typical of the colonial period. It is hardly surprising then in a country which calls itself African to hear remarks that are nothing less than racist and to witness paternalistic behavior bitterly reminiscent of Paris, Brussels, or London.

In certain regions of Africa, bleating paternalism toward blacks and the obscene idea drawn from Western culture that the black race is impermeable to logic and science reign in all their nakedness. There are some places where black minorities are confined in semi slavery, which justifies the caution, even distrust, that the countries of Black Africa manifest toward the countries of White Africa. It is not unusual for a citizen of Black Africa walking in a city of White Africa to hear children call him "nigger" or to find the authorities speaking to him in pidgin.

Unfortunately, alas, it is all too likely that students from Black Africa enrolled in schools north of the Sahara will be asked by their schoolmates whether people live in houses in their home countries, whether they have electricity, and if their family practices cannibalism. Unfortunately, alas, it is all too likely that in certain regions north of the Sahara Africans from the south will encounter fellow countrymen who beg them to take them "anywhere there are blacks." Likewise, in certain newly independent states of Black Africa, members of parliament, even government ministers, solemnly declare that the danger lies not in a reoccupation of their country by a colonial power but a possible invasion by "Arab vandals from the north."

As we have seen, the inadequacies of the bourgeoisie are not restricted to economics. Achieving power in the name of a narrow-minded nationalism, in the name of the race, and in spite of its magnificently worded declarations totally void of content, irresponsibly wielding phrases straight out of Europe's treatises on ethics and political philosophy, the bourgeoisie proves itself incapable of implementing a program with even a minimum humanist content. When it is strong, when it organizes the world on the basis of its power, a bourgeoisie does not hesitate to maintain a pretense of universal democratic ideas. An economically sound bourgeoisie has to be faced with exceptional circumstances to force it to disregard its humanist ideology. Although fundamentally racist, the Western bourgeoisie generally manages to mask this racism by multiplying the nuances, thereby enabling it to maintain intact its discourse on human dignity in all its magnanimity.

Western bourgeoisie has erected enough barriers and safeguards for it to fear no real competition from those it exploits and despises. Western bourgeois racism toward the "nigger" and the "towelhead" is a racism of contempt – a racism that minimizes. But the bourgeois ideology that proclaims all men to be essentially equal, manages to remain consistent with itself by urging the subhuman to rise to the level of Western humanity that it embodies.

The racism of the young national bourgeoisie is a defensive racism, a racism based on fear. Basically it does not differ from common tribalism or even rivalry between clans or confraternities. It is easy to understand why perspicacious international observers never really took the lofty speeches on African unity very seriously. The flagrant flaws are so numerous that one clearly senses that all these contradictions must first be solved before unity can be achieved.

The peoples of Africa have recently discovered each other and, in the name of the continent, have decided to pressure the colonial regimes in a radical way.

The national bourgeoisies, however, who, in region after region, are in a hurry to stash away a tidy sum for themselves and establish a national system of exploitation, multiply the obstacles for achieving this "utopia." The national bourgeoisies, perfectly clear on their objectives, are determined to bar the way to this unity, this coordinated effort by 250 million people to triumph over stupidity, hunger, and inhumanity. This is why we must understand that African unity can only be achieved under pressure and through leadership by the people, i.e., with total disregard for the interests of the bourgeoisie.

[…]

The theoretical question, which has been posed for the last fifty years when addressing the history of the underdeveloped countries, i.e., whether the bourgeois phase can be effectively skipped, must be resolved through revolutionary action and not through reasoning. The bourgeois phase in the underdeveloped countries is only justified if the national bourgeoisie is sufficiently powerful, economically and technically, to build a bourgeois society, to create the conditions for developing a sizeable proletariat, to mechanize agriculture, and finally pave the way for a genuine national culture.

The bourgeoisie, which evolved in Europe, was able to elaborate an ideology while strengthening its own influence. This dynamic, educated, and secular bourgeoisie fully succeeded in its undertaking of capital accumulation and endowed the nation with a minimum of prosperity. In the underdeveloped countries we have seen that there was no genuine bourgeoisie but rather an acquisitive, voracious, and ambitious petty caste, dominated by a small-time racketeer mentality, content with the dividends paid out by the former colonial power. This short-sighted bourgeoisie lacks vision and inventiveness. It has learned by heart what it has read in the manuals of the West and subtly transforms itself not into a replica of Europe but rather its caricature.

★ ★ ★

The struggle against the bourgeoisie in the underdeveloped countries is far from being simply theoretical. It is not a question of deciphering the way history has judged and condemned it. The national bourgeoisie in the underdeveloped countries should not be combated because it threatens to curb the overall, harmonious development of the nation. It must be resolutely opposed because literally it serves no purpose. Mediocre in its winnings, in its achievements and its thinking, this bourgeoisie attempts to mask its mediocrity by ostentatious projects for individual prestige, chromium-plated American cars, vacations on the French Riviera and weekends in neon-lit nightclubs.

This bourgeoisie, which increasingly turns its back on the overall population, fails even to squeeze from the West such spectacular concessions as valuable investments in the country's economy or the installation of certain industries. Assembly plants, however, are on the increase, a tendency that confirms the neocolonialist model in which the national economy is struggling. In no way, therefore, can it be said that the national bourgeoisie slows the country's development, that it is wasting the nation's time or possibly leading it into a dead end. But the truth is that the bourgeois phase in the history of the underdeveloped countries is a useless phase. Once this caste has been eliminated, swallowed up by its own contradictions, it will be clear to everyone that no progress has been made since independence and that everything has to be started over again from scratch. This restructuring of the economy will not be based on the order set in place by the bourgeoisie during its reign, since this caste has done nothing else but prolong the heritage of the colonial economy, thinking, and institutions.

It is that much easier to neutralize this bourgeois class since, as we have seen, it is numerically, intellectually, and economically weak. In the colonized territories after independence the bourgeois caste draws its main strength from agreements signed with the former colonial power. The national bourgeoisie has an even greater chance of taking over from the colonialist oppressor since it has been given every opportunity to maintain its close links with the ex-colonial power. But deep-rooted contradictions shake the ranks of this bourgeoisie, giving the close observer an impression of instability. There is not yet a homogeneity of caste. Many intellectuals, for instance, condemn this regime based on domination by a select few. In the underdeveloped countries there are intellectuals, civil servants, and senior officials who sincerely feel the need for a planned economy, for outlawing profiteers and doing away with any form of mystification. Moreover, such men, to a certain degree, are in favor of maximum participation by the people in the management of public affairs.

In underdeveloped countries that acquire independence there is almost always a small number of upstanding intellectuals, without set political ideas, who instinctively distrust the race for jobs and handouts that is symptomatic of the aftermath of independence. The personal situation of these men (breadwinners for an extended family) or their life story (hardship and strict moral upbringing) explains their clear distrust for the smart alecks and profiteers. These men need to be used intelligently in the decisive struggle to steer the nation in a healthy direction. Barring the way to the national bourgeoisie is a sure way of avoiding the pitfalls of independence, the trials and tribulations of national unity, the decline of morals, the assault on the nation by corruption, an economic downturn and, in the short term, an antidemocratic regime relying on force and intimidation. But it also means choosing the only way to go forward.

The profoundly democratic and progressive elements of the young nation are reluctant and shy about making any decision due to the apparent resilience of the bourgeoisie. The colonial cities of the newly independent underdeveloped countries are teeming with the entire managerial class. For want of any serious analysis of the population as a whole, observers are inclined to believe in the existence of a powerful and perfectly organized bourgeoisie. In fact we now know that there is no bourgeoisie in the underdeveloped countries. What makes a bourgeoisie is not its attitude, taste, or manners. It is not even its aspirations. The bourgeoisie is above all the direct product of precise economic realities.

Economic reality in the colonies, however, is a foreign bourgeois reality. It is the metropolitan bourgeoisie, represented by its local counterparts, which is present in the colonial towns. Before independence the bourgeoisie in the colonies is a Western bourgeoisie, an authentic branch of the metropolitan bourgeoisie from which it draws its legitimacy, its strength and its stability. During the period of unrest preceding independence, indigenous intellectual and business elements within this imported bourgeoisie endeavor to identify themselves with it. Theirs is a wish to identify permanently with the bourgeois representatives from the metropolis.

This bourgeoisie, which has unreservedly and enthusiastically adopted the intellectual reflexes characteristic of the metropolis, which has alienated to perfection its own thought and grounded its consciousness in typically foreign notions, has difficulty swallowing the fact that it is lacking in the one thing that makes a bourgeoisie – money. The bourgeoisie of the underdeveloped countries is a bourgeoisie in spirit only. It has neither the economic power, nor the managerial dynamism, nor the scope of ideas to qualify it as a bourgeoisie. Consequently, it is in its early stages and remains a bourgeoisie of civil servants. Whatever confidence and strength it possesses will derive from the position it occupies in the new national administration. Given time and opportunity by the authorities, it will succeed in amassing a small fortune that will reinforce its domination. But it will still prove incapable of creating a genuine bourgeois society with all the economic and industrial consequences this supposes.

[…]

The duty of a leadership is to have the masses on their side. Any commitment, however, presupposes awareness and understanding of the mission to be accomplished, in short a rational analysis, no matter how embryonic. The people should not be mesmerized, swayed by emotion or confused. Only underdeveloped countries led by a revolutionary elite emanating from the people can today empower the masses to step onto the stage of history. But once again on the condition that we vigorously and decisively reject the formation of a national bourgeoisie, a caste of privileged individuals. To politicize the masses is to make the nation in its totality a reality for every citizen. To make the experience of the nation, the experience of every citizen. As President Sékou Touré so aptly reminded us in his address to the Second Congress of African Writers: "In the realm of thought, man can claim to be the brain of the world, but in reality, where every action affects spiritual and physical being, the world is still the brain of mankind for it is here that are concentrated the totalization of powers and elements of thought, the dynamic forces of development and improvement, and it is here too that energies are merged and the sum total of man's intellectual values is finally inscribed." Since individual experience is national, since it is a link in the national chain, it ceases to be individual, narrow and limited in scope, and can lead to the truth of the nation and the world. Just as every fighter clung to the nation during the period of armed struggle, so during the period of nation building every citizen must continue in his daily purpose to embrace the nation as a whole, to embody the constantly dialectical truth of the nation, and to will here and now the triumph of man in his totality. If the building of a bridge does not enrich the consciousness of those working on it, then don't build the bridge, and let the citizens continue to swim across the river or use a ferry. The bridge must not be pitchforked or foisted upon the social landscape by a deus ex machina, but, on the contrary, must be the product of the citizens' brains and muscles. And there is no doubt architects and engineers, foreigners for the most part, will probably be needed, but the local party leaders must see to it that the techniques seep into the desert of the citizen's brain so that the bridge in its entirety and in every detail can be integrated, redesigned, and reappropriated. The citizen must appropriate the bridge. Then, and only then, is everything possible.

A government that proclaims itself national must take responsibility for the entire nation, and in underdeveloped countries the youth represents one of the most important sectors. The consciousness of the younger generation must be elevated and enlightened. It is this younger generation that will compose the national army. If they have been adequately informed, if the National Youth Movement has done its work of integrating the youth into the nation then the mistakes that have compromised, even undermined, the future of the Latin American republics, will have been avoided. The army is never a school for war, but a school for civics, a school for politics. The soldier in a mature nation is not a mercenary but a citizen who defends the nation by the use of arms. This is why it is paramount that the soldier knows he is at the service of his country and not of an officer, however illustrious he may be. Military and civilian national service

must be used to raise the level of national consciousness, to detribalize and unify. In an underdeveloped country the mobilization of men and women should be undertaken as quickly as possible. The underdeveloped country must take precautions not to perpetuate feudal traditions that give priority to men over women. Women shall be given equal importance to men, not in the articles of the consitution, but in daily life, at the factory, in the schools, and in assemblies. If the countries of the West station their soldiers in barracks, this does not mean this is the best solution. We are not obliged to militarize recruits. National service can be civilian or military, and in any case every ablebodied citizen should be able to join his fighting unit at a moment's notice to defend the freedom of the nation and its civil liberties.

The major public works projects of national interest should be carried out by the recruits. This is a highly effective way of stimulating stagnant regions and getting the greatest number of citizens to learn of the country's realities. We should avoid transforming the army into an autonomous body that sooner or later, idle and aimless, will "go into politics" and threaten the authorities. By dint of haunting the corridors of power, armchair generals dream of pronunciamentos. The only way of avoiding this is to politicize the army, i.e., nationalize it. Likewise there is an urgent need to strengthen the militia. In the event of war, it is the entire nation which fights or works. There should be no professional soldiers, and the number of career officers should be kept to a minimum; first of all, because very often the officers are selected from university graduates who would be much more useful elsewhere − an engineer is a thousand times more indispensable to the nation than an officer − and secondly, because any hint of a caste consciousness should be eliminated. We have seen in the preceding pages how nationalism, that magnificent hymn which roused the masses against the oppressor, disintegrates in the aftermath of independence. Nationalism is not a political doctrine, it is not a program. If we really want to safeguard our countries from regression, paralysis, or collapse, we must rapidly switch from a national consciousness to a social and political consciousness. The nation can only come into being in a program elaborated by a revolutionary leadership and enthusiastically and lucidly appropriated by the masses. The national effort must be constantly situated in the general context of the underdeveloped countries. The front line against hunger and darkness, the front line against poverty and stunted consciousness, must be present in the minds and muscles of the men and women. The work of the masses, their determination to conquer the scourges that for centuries have excluded them from the history of the human mind, must be connected to the work and determination of all the underdeveloped peoples. There is a kind of collective endeavor, a common destiny among the underdeveloped masses. The peoples of the Third World are not interested in news about King Baudoin's wedding or the affairs of the Italian bourgeoisie. What we want to hear are case histories in Argentina or Burma about the fight against illiteracy or the dictatorial behavior of other leaders. This is the material that inspires us, educates us, and greatly increases our effectiveness. As we have seen, a government needs a program if it really wants to liberate the people politically and socially. Not only an economic program but also a policy on the distribution of wealth and social relations. In fact there must be a concept of man, a concept about the future of mankind. Which means that no sermon, no complicity with the former occupier can replace a program. The people, at first unenlightened and then increasingly lucid, will vehemently demand such a program. The Africans and the underdeveloped peoples, contrary to what is commonly believed, are quick to build a social and political consciousness. The danger is that very often they reach the stage of social consciousness before reaching the national phase. In this case the underdeveloped countries' violent calls for social justice are combined, paradoxically enough, with an often primitive tribalism. The underdeveloped peoples behave like a starving population – which means that the days of those who treat Africa as their playground are strictly numbered. In other words, their power cannot last forever.

A bourgeoisie that has only nationalism to feed the people fails in its mission and inevitably gets tangled up in a series of trials and tribulations. If nationalism is not explained, enriched, and deepened, if it does not very quickly turn into a social and political consciousness, into humanism, then it leads to a dead end. A bourgeois leadership of the underdeveloped countries confines the national consciousness to a sterile formalism. Only the massive commitment by men and women to judicious and productive tasks gives form and substance to this consciousness. It is then that flags and government buildings cease to be the symbols of the nation. The nation deserts the false glitter of the capital and takes refuge in the interior where it receives life and energy. The living expression of the nation is the collective consciousness in motion of the entire people. It is the enlightened and coherent praxis of the men and women. The collective forging of a destiny implies undertaking responsibility on a truly historical scale. Otherwise there is anarchy, repression, the emergence of tribalized parties and federalism, etc. If the national government wants to be national it must govern by the people and for the people, for the disinherited and by the disinherited. No leader, whatever his worth, can replace the will of the people, and the national government, before concerning itself with international prestige, must first restore dignity to all citizens, furnish their minds, fill their eyes with human things and develop a human landscape for the sake of its enlightened and sovereign inhabitants.

Notes

1 [Translator's note]: Present-day Beninese and Burkinabés.
2 [Translator's note]: Present-day Malian.
3 Mamadou Dia, *Nations africaines et solidarité mondiale*, P.U.F., p. 140.
4 Ibid.

12

"Society Must Be Defended, 17 March 1976" (1976)

Michel Foucault

It is time to end then, to try to pull together what I have been saying this year. I have been trying to raise the problem of war, seen as a grid for understanding historical processes. It seemed to me that war was regarded, initially and throughout practically the whole of the eighteenth century, as a war between races. It was that war between races that I wanted to try to reconstruct. And last time, I tried to show you how the very notion of war was eventually eliminated from historical analysis by the principle of national universality. I would now like to show you how, while the theme of race does not disappear, it does become part of something very different, namely State racism. So today I would like to tell you a little about State racism, or at least situate it for you.

It seems to me that one of the basic phenomena of the nineteenth century was what might be called power's hold over life. What I mean is the acquisition of power over man insofar as man is a living being, that the biological came under State control, that there was at least a certain tendency that leads to what might be termed State control of the biological. And I think that in order to understand what was going on, it helps if we refer to what used to be the classical theory of sovereignty, which ultimately provided us with the backdrop to – a picture of – all these analyses of war, races, and so on. You know that in the classical theory of sovereignty, the right of life

and death was one of sovereignty's basic attributes. Now the right of life and death is a strange right. Even at the theoretical level, it is a strange right. What does having the right of life and death actually mean? In one sense, to say that the sovereign has a right of life and death means that he can, basically, either have people put to death or let them live, or in any case that life and death are not natural or immediate phenomena which are primal or radical, and which fall outside the field of power. If we take the argument a little further, or to the point where it becomes paradoxical, it means that in terms of his relationship with the sovereign, the subject is, by rights, neither dead nor alive. From the point of view of life and death, the subject is neutral, and it is thanks to the sovereign that the subject has the right to be alive or, possibly, the right to be dead. In any case, the lives and deaths of subjects become rights only as a result of the will of the sovereign. That is, if you like, the theoretical paradox. And it is of course a theoretical paradox that must have as its corollary a sort of practical disequilibrium. What does the right of life and death actually mean? Obviously not that the sovereign can grant life in the same way that he can inflict death. The right of life and death is always exercised in an unbalanced way: the balance is always tipped in favor of death. Sovereign power's effect on life is exercised only when the sovereign can kill. The very essence of the right of life and death is actually the right to kill: it is at the moment when the sovereign can kill that he exercises his right over life. It is essentially the right of the sword. So there is no real symmetry in the right over life and death. It is not the right to put people to

Michel Foucault, "17 March 1976," pp. 239–58 from *Society Must Be Defended: Lectures at the Collège de France, 1975–76.* New York: Picador, 2003.

death or to grant them life. Nor is it the right to allow people to live or to leave them to die. It is the right to take life or let live. And this obviously introduces a startling dissymmetry.

And I think that one of the greatest transformations political right underwent in the nineteenth century was precisely that, I wouldn't say exactly that sovereignty's old right – to take life or let live – was replaced, but it came to be complemented by a new right which does not erase the old right but which does penetrate it, permeate it. This is the right, or rather precisely the opposite right. It is the power to "make" live and "let" die. The right of sovereignty was the right to take life or let live. And then this new right is established: the right to make live and to let die.

This transformation obviously did not occur all at once. We can trace it in the theory of right (but here, I will be extraordinarily rapid). The jurists of the seventeenth and especially the eighteenth century were, you see, already asking this question about the right of life and death. The jurists ask: When we enter into a contract, what are individuals doing at the level of the social contract, when they come together to constitute a sovereign, to delegate absolute power over them to a sovereign? They do so because they are forced to by some threat or by need. They therefore do so in order to protect their lives. It is in order to live that they constitute a sovereign. To the extent that this is the case, can life actually become one of the rights of the sovereign? Isn't life the foundation of the sovereign's right, and can the sovereign actually demand that his subjects grant him the right to exercise the power of life and death over them, or in other words, simply the power to kill them? Mustn't life remain outside the contract to the extent that it was the first, initial, and foundational reason for the contract itself? All this is a debate within political philosophy that we can leave on one side, but it clearly demonstrates how the problem of life began to be problematized in the field of political thought, of the analysis of political power. I would in fact like to trace the transformation not at the level of political theory, but rather at the level of the mechanisms, techniques, and technologies of power. And this brings us back to something familiar: in the seventeenth and eighteenth centuries, we saw the emergence of techniques of power that were essentially centered on the body, on the individual body. They included all devices that were used to ensure the spatial distribution of individual bodies (their separation, their alignment, their serialization, and their surveillance) and the organization, around those individuals, of a whole field of visibility. They were also techniques that could be used to take control over bodies. Attempts were made to increase their productive force through exercise, drill, and so on. They were also techniques for rationalizing and strictly economizing on a power that had to be used in the least costly way possible, thanks to a whole system of surveillance, hierarchies, inspections, bookkeeping, and reports – all the technology that can be described as the disciplinary technology of labor. It was established at the end of the seventeenth century, and in the course of the eighteenth.[1]

Now I think we see something new emerging in the second half of the eighteenth century: a new technology of power, but this time it is not disciplinary. This technology of power does not exclude the former, does not exclude disciplinary technology, but it does dovetail into it, integrate it, modify it to some extent, and above all, use it by sort of infiltrating it, embedding itself in existing disciplinary techniques. This new technique does not simply do away with the disciplinary technique, because it exists at a different level, on a different scale, and because it has a different bearing area, and makes use of very different instruments.

Unlike discipline, which is addressed to bodies, the new nondisciplinary power is applied not to man-as-body but to the living man, to man-as-living-being; ultimately, if you like, to man-as-species. To be more specific, I would say that discipline tries to rule a multiplicity of men to the extent that their multiplicity can and must be dissolved into individual bodies that can be kept under surveillance, trained, used, and, if need be, punished. And that the new technology that is being established is addressed to a multiplicity of men, not to the extent that they are nothing more than their individual bodies, but to the extent that they form, on the contrary, a global mass that is affected by overall processes characteristic of birth, death, production, illness, and so on. So after a first seizure of power over the body in an individualizing mode, we have a second seizure of power that is not individualizing but, if you like, massifying, that is directed not at man-as-body but at man-as-species. After the anatomo-politics of the human body established in the course of the eighteenth century, we have, at the end of that century, the emergence of something that is no longer an anatomo-politics of the human body, but what I would call a "biopolitics" of the human race.

What does this new technology of power, this biopolitics, this biopower that is beginning to establish itself, involve? I told you very briefly a moment ago; a set of processes such as the ratio of births to deaths, the rate of reproduction, the fertility of a population, and so on. It is these processes – the birth rate, the mortality rate, longevity, and so on – together with a whole series of related economic and political problems (which I will not come back to for the moment) which, in the second half of the eighteenth century, become biopolitics' first objects of knowledge and the targets it seeks to control. It is at any rate at this moment that the first demographers begin to measure these phenomena in statistical terms. They begin to observe the more or less spontaneous, more or less compulsory techniques that the population actually used to control the birth rate; in a word, if you like, to identify the phenomena of birth-control practices in the eighteenth century. We also see the beginnings of a natalist policy, plans to intervene in all phenomena relating to the birth rate. This biopolitics is not concerned with fertility alone. It also deals with the problem of morbidity, but not simply, as had previously been the case, at the level of the famous epidemics, the threat of which had haunted political powers ever since the early Middle Ages (these famous epidemics were temporary disasters that caused multiple deaths, times when everyone seemed to be in danger of imminent death). At the end of the eighteenth century, it was not epidemics that were the issue, but something else – what might broadly be called endemics, or in other words, the form, nature, extension, duration, and intensity of the illnesses prevalent in a population. These were illnesses that were difficult to eradicate and that were not regarded as epidemics that caused more frequent deaths, but as permanent factors which – and that is how they were dealt with – sapped the population's strength, shortened the working week, wasted energy, and cost money, both because

they led to a fall in production and because treating them was expensive. In a word, illness as phenomena affecting a population. Death was no longer something that suddenly swooped down on life – as in an epidemic. Death was now something permanent, something that slips into life, perpetually gnaws at it, diminishes it and weakens it.

These are the phenomena that begin to be taken into account at the end of the eighteenth century, and they result in the development of a medicine whose main function will now be public hygiene, with institutions to coordinate medical care, centralize information, and normalize knowledge. And which also takes the form of campaigns to teach hygiene and to medicalize the population. So, problems of reproduction, the birth rate, and the problem of the mortality rate too. Biopolitics' other field of intervention will be a set of phenomena some of which are universal, and some of which are accidental but which can never be completely eradicated, even if they are accidental. They have similar effects in that they incapacitate individuals, put them out of the circuit or neutralize them. This is the problem, and it will become very important in the early nineteenth century (the time of industrialization), of old age, of individuals who, because of their age, fall out of the field of capacity, of activity. The field of biopolitics also includes accidents, infirmities, and various anomalies. And it is in order to deal with these phenomena that this biopolitics will establish not only charitable institutions (which had been in existence for a very long time), but also much more subtle mechanisms that were much more economically rational than an indiscriminate charity which was at once widespread and patchy, and which was essentially under church control. We see the introduction of more subtle, more rational mechanisms: insurance, individual and collective savings, safety measures, and so on.[2]

Biopolitics' last domain is, finally – I am enumerating the main ones, or at least those that appeared in the late eighteenth and early nineteenth centuries; many others would appear later – control over relations between the human race, or human beings insofar as they are a species, insofar as they are living beings, and their environment, the milieu in which they live. This includes the direct effects of the geographical, climatic, or hydrographic environment: the

health

problem, for instance, of swamps, and of epidemics linked to the existence of swamps throughout the first half of the nineteenth century. And also the problem of the environment to the extent that it is not a natural environment, that it has been created by the population and therefore has effects on that population. This is, essentially, the urban problem. I am simply pointing out some of biopolitics' starting points, some of its practices, and the first of its domains of intervention, knowledge, and power: biopolitics will derive its knowledge from, and define its power's field of intervention in terms of, the birth rate, the mortality rate, various biological disabilities, and the effects of the environment.

In all this, a number of things are, I think, important. The first appears to be this: the appearance of a new element – I almost said a new character – of which both the theory of right and disciplinary practice knew nothing. The theory of right basically knew only the individual and society: the contracting individual and the social body constituted by the voluntary or implicit contract among individuals. Disciplines, for their part, dealt with individuals and their bodies in practical terms. What we are dealing with in this new technology of power is not exactly society (or at least not the social body, as defined by the jurists), nor is it the individual-as-body. It is a new body, a multiple body, a body with so many heads that, while they might not be infinite in number, cannot necessarily be counted. Biopolitics deals with the population, with the population as political problem, as a problem that is at once scientific and political, as a biological problem and as power's problem. And I think that biopolitics emerges at this time.

Second, the other important thing – quite aside from the appearance of the "population" element itself – is the nature of the phenomena that are taken into consideration. You can see that they are collective phenomena which have their economic and political effects, and that they become pertinent only at the mass level. They are phenomena that are aleatory and unpredictable when taken in themselves or individually, but which, at the collective level, display constants that are easy, or at least possible, to establish. And they are, finally, phenomena that occur over a period of time, which have to be studied over a certain period of time; they are serial phenomena. The phenomena

addressed by biopolitics are, essentially, aleatory events that occur within a population that exists over a period of time.

On this basis – and this is, I think, the third important point – this technology of power, this biopolitics, will introduce mechanisms with a certain number of functions that are very different from the functions of disciplinary mechanisms. The mechanisms introduced by biopolitics include forecasts, statistical estimates, and overall measures. And their purpose is not to modify any given phenomenon as such, or to modify a given individual insofar as he is an individual, but, essentially, to intervene at the level at which these general phenomena are determined, to intervene at the level of their generality. The mortality rate has to be modified or lowered; life expectancy has to be increased; the birth rate has to be stimulated. And most important of all, regulatory mechanisms must be established to establish an equilibrium, maintain an average, establish a sort of homeostasis, and compensate for variations within this general population and its aleatory field. In a word, security mechanisms have to be installed around the random element inherent in a population of living beings so as to optimize a state of life. Like disciplinary mechanisms, these mechanisms are designed to maximize and extract forces, but they work in very different ways. Unlike disciplines, they no longer train individuals by working at the level of the body itself. There is absolutely no question relating to an individual body, in the way that discipline does. It is therefore not a matter of taking the individual at the level of individuality but, on the contrary, of using overall mechanisms and acting in such a way as to achieve overall states of equilibration or regularity; it is, in a word, a matter of taking control of life and the biological processes of man-as-species and of ensuring that they are not disciplined, but regularized.[3]

Beneath that great absolute power, beneath the dramatic and somber absolute power that was the power of sovereignty, and which consisted in the power to take life, we now have the emergence, with this technology of biopower, of this technology of power over "the" population as such, over men insofar as they are living beings. It is continuous, scientific, and it is the power to make live. Sovereignty took life and let live. And now we have the emergence of a power that

I would call the power of regularization, and it, in contrast, consists in making live and letting die.

I think that we can see a concrete manifestation of this power in the famous gradual disqualification of death, which sociologists and historians have discussed so often. Everyone knows, thanks in particular to a certain number of recent studies, that the great public ritualization of death gradually began to disappear, or at least to fade away, in the late eighteenth century and that it is still doing so today. So much so that death – which has ceased to be one of those spectacular ceremonies in which individuals, the family, the group, and practically the whole of society took part – has become, in contrast, something to be hidden away. It has become the most private and shameful thing of all (and ultimately, it is now not so much sex as death that is the object of a taboo). Now I think that the reason why death had become something to be hidden away is not that anxiety has somehow been displaced or that repressive mechanisms have been modified. What once (and until the end of the eighteenth century) made death so spectacular and ritualized *it* so much was the fact that it was a manifestation of a transition from one power to another. Death was the moment when we made the transition from one power – that of the sovereign of this world – to another – that of the sovereign of the next world. We went from one court of law to another, from a civil or public right over life and death, to a right to either eternal life or eternal damnation. A transition from one power to another. Death also meant the transmission of the power of the dying, and that power was transmitted to those who survived him: last words, last recommendations, last wills and testaments, and so on. All these phenomena of power were ritualized.

Now that power is decreasingly the power of the right to take life, and increasingly the right to intervene to make live, or once power begins to intervene mainly at this level in order to improve life by eliminating accidents, the random element, and deficiencies, death becomes, insofar as it is the end of life, the term, the limit, or the end of power too. Death is outside the power relationship. Death is beyond the reach of power, and power has a grip on it only in general, overall, or statistical terms. Power has no control over death, but it can control mortality. And to that

extent, it is only natural that death should now be privatized, and should become the most private thing of all. In the right of sovereignty, death was the moment of the most obvious and most spectacular manifestation of the absolute power of the sovereign; death now becomes, in contrast, the moment when the individual escapes all power, falls back on himself and retreats, so to speak, into his own privacy. Power no longer recognizes death. Power literally ignores death.

To symbolize all this, let's take, if you will, the death of Franco, which is after all a very, very interesting event. It is very interesting because of the symbolic values it brings into play, because the man who died had, as you know, exercised the sovereign right of life and death with great savagery, was the bloodiest of all the dictators, wielded an absolute right of life and death for forty years, and at the moment when he himself was dying, he entered this sort of new field of power over life which consists not only in managing life, but in keeping individuals alive after they are dead. And thanks to a power that is not simply scientific prowess, but the actual exercise of the political biopower established in the eighteenth century, we have become so good at keeping people alive that we've succeeded in keeping them alive when, in biological terms, they should have been dead long ago. And so the man who had exercised the absolute power of life and death over hundreds of thousands of people fell under the influence of a power that managed life so well, that took so little heed of death, and he didn't even realize that he was dead and was being kept alive after his death. I think that this minor but joyous event symbolizes the clash between two systems of power: that of sovereignty over death, and that of the regularization of life.

I would now like to go back to comparing the regulatory technology of life and the disciplinary technology of the body I was telling you about a moment ago. From the eighteenth century onward (or at least the end of the eighteenth century onward) we have, then, two technologies of power which were established at different times and which were superimposed. One technique is disciplinary; it centers on the body, produces individualizing effects, and manipulates the body as a source of forces that have to be rendered both useful and docile. And we also have a second technology which is centered not upon the body but upon life: a technology which brings together the mass

life measurable after the production of death. - Iraq, Haiti, Pakistan.

effects characteristic of a population, which tries to control the series of random events that can occur in a living mass, a technology which tries to predict the probability of those events (by modifying it, if necessary), or at least to compensate for their effects. This is a technology which aims to establish a sort of homeostasis, not by training individuals, but by achieving an overall equilibrium that protects the security of the whole from internal dangers. So, a technology of drilling, as opposed to, as distinct from, a technology of security; a disciplinary technology, as distinct from a reassuring or regulatory technology. Both technologies are obviously technologies of the body, but one is a technology in which the body is individualized as an organism endowed with capacities, while the other is a technology in which bodies are replaced by general biological processes.

One might say this: It is as though power, which used to have sovereignty as its modality or organizing schema, found itself unable to govern the economic and political body of a society that was undergoing both a demographic explosion and industrialization. So much so that far too many things were escaping the old mechanism of the power of sovereignty, both at the top and at the bottom, both at the level of detail and at the mass level. A first adjustment was made to take care of the details. Discipline had meant adjusting power mechanisms to the individual body by using surveillance and training. That, of course, was the easier and more convenient thing to adjust. That is why it was the first to be introduced – as early as the seventeenth century, or the beginning of the eighteenth – at a local level, in intuitive, empirical, and fragmented forms, and in the restricted framework of institutions such as schools, hospitals, barracks, workshops, and so on. And then at the end of the eighteenth century, you have a second adjustment; the mechanisms are adjusted to phenomena of population, to the biological or biosociological processes characteristic of human masses. This adjustment was obviously much more difficult to make because it implied complex systems of coordination and centralization.

So we have two series: the body-organism-discipline-institutions series, and the population-biological processes-regulatory mechanisms-State. An organic institutional set, or the organism-discipline of the

institution, if you like, and, on the other hand, a biological and Statist set, or bioregulation by the State. I am not trying to introduce a complete dichotomy between State and institution, because disciplines in fact always tend to escape the institutional or local framework in which they are trapped. What is more, they easily take on a Statist dimension in apparatuses such as the police, for example, which is both a disciplinary apparatus and a State apparatus (which just goes to prove that discipline is not always institutional). In similar fashion, the great overall regulations that proliferated throughout the nineteenth century are, obviously enough, found at the State level, but they are also found at the sub-State level, in a whole series of sub-State institutions such as medical institutions, welfare funds, insurance, and so on. That is the first remark I would like to make.

What is more, the two sets of mechanisms – one disciplinary and the other regulatory – do not exist at the same level. Which means of course that they are not mutually exclusive and can be articulated with each other. To take one or two examples. Take, if you like, the example of the town or, more specifically, the rationally planned layout of the model town, the artificial town, the town of utopian reality that was not only dreamed of but actually built in the nineteenth century. What were working-class housing estates, as they existed in the nineteenth century? One can easily see how the very grid pattern, the very layout, of the estate articulated, in a sort of perpendicular way, the disciplinary mechanisms that controlled the body, or bodies, by localizing familes (one to a house) and individuals (one to a room). The layout, the fact that individuals were made visible, and the normalization of behavior meant that a sort of spontaneous policing or control was carried out by the spatial layout of the town itself. It is easy to identify a whole series of disciplinary mechanisms in the working-class estate. And then you have a whole series of mechanisms which are, by contrast, regulatory mechanisms, which apply to the population as such and which allow, which encourage patterns of saving related to housing, to the renting of accommodations and, in some cases, their purchase. Health-insurance systems, old-age pensions; rules on hygiene that guarantee the optimal longevity of the population; the pressures that the very organization of the town brings to bear on sexuality and therefore procreation; child care, education, et cetera, so you have [certain] disciplinary measures and [certain] regulatory mechanisms.

Take the very different – though it is not altogether that different – take a different axis, something like sexuality. Basically, why did sexuality become a field of vital strategic importance in the nineteenth century? I think that sexuality was important for a whole host of reasons, and for these reasons in particular. On the one hand, sexuality, being an eminently corporeal mode of behavior, is a matter for individualizing disciplinary controls that take the form of permanent surveillance (and the famous controls that were, from the late eighteenth to the twentieth century, placed both at home and at school on children who masturbated represent precisely this aspect of the disciplinary control of sexuality). But because it also has procreative effects, sexuality is also inscribed, takes effect, in broad biological processes that concern not the bodies of individuals but the element, the multiple unity of the population. Sexuality exists at the point where body and population meet. And so it is a matter for discipline, but also a matter for regularization.

It is, I think, the privileged position it occupies between organism and population, between the body and general phenomena, that explains the extreme emphasis placed upon sexuality in the nineteenth century. Hence too the medical idea that when it is undisciplined and irregular, sexuality also has effects at two levels. At the level of the body, of the undisciplined body that is immediately sanctioned by all the individual diseases that the sexual debauchee brings down upon himself. A child who masturbates too much will be a lifelong invalid: disciplinary sanction at the level of the body. But at the same time, debauched, perverted sexuality has effects at the level of the population, as anyone who has been sexually debauched is assumed to have a heredity. Their descendants also will be affected for generations, unto the seventh generation and unto the seventh of the seventh and so on. This is the theory of degeneracy:[4] given that it is the source of individual diseases and that it is the nucleus of degeneracy, sexuality represents the precise point where the disciplinary and the regulatory, the body and the population, are articulated. Given these conditions, you can understand how and why a technical knowledge such as medicine,

or rather the combination of medicine and hygiene, is in the nineteenth century, if not the most important element, an element of considerable importance because of the link it establishes between scientific knowledge of both biological and organic processes (or in other words, the population and the body), and, because, at the same time, medicine becomes a political intervention-technique with specific power-effects. Medicine is a power-knowledge that can be applied to both the body and the population, both the organism and biological processes, and it will therefore have both disciplinary effects and regulatory effects.

In more general terms still, we can say that there is one element that will circulate between the disciplinary and the regulatory, which will also be applied to body and population alike, which will make it possible to control both the disciplinary order of the body and the aleatory events that occur in the biological multiplicity. The element that circulates between the two is the norm. The norm is something that can be applied to both a body one wishes to discipline and a population one wishes to regularize. The normalizing society is therefore not, under these conditions, a sort of generalized disciplinary society whose disciplinary institutions have swarmed and finally taken over everything – that, I think, is no more than a first and inadequate interpretation of a normalizing society. The normalizing society is a society in which the norm of discipline and the norm of regulation intersect along an orthogonal articulation. To say that power took possession of life in the nineteenth century, or to say that power at least takes life under its care in the nineteenth century, is to say that it has, thanks to the play of technologies of discipline on the one hand and technologies of regulation on the other, succeeded in covering the whole surface that lies between the organic and the biological, between body and population.

We are, then, in a power that has taken control of both the body and life or that has, if you like, taken control of life in general – with the body as one pole and the population as the other. We can therefore immediately identify the paradoxes that appear at the points where the exercise of this biopower reaches its limits. The paradoxes become apparent if we look, on the one hand, at atomic power, which is not simply the power to kill, in accordance with the rights that are granted to any sovereign, millions and hundreds of millions of people (after all, that is traditional). The workings of contemporary political power are such that atomic power represents a paradox that is difficult, if not impossible, to get around. The power to manufacture and use the atom bomb represents the deployment of a sovereign power that kills, but it is also the power to kill life itself. So the power that is being exercised in this atomic power is exercised in such a way that it is capable of suppressing life itself. And, therefore, to suppress itself insofar as it is the power that guarantees life. Either it is sovereign and uses the atom bomb, and therefore cannot be power, biopower, or the power to guarantee life, as it has been ever since the nineteenth century. Or, at the opposite extreme, you no longer have a sovereign right that is in excess of biopower, but a biopower that is in excess of sovereign right. This excess of biopower appears when it becomes technologically and politically possible for man not only to manage life but to make it proliferate, to create living matter, to build the monster, and, ultimately, to build viruses that cannot be controlled and that are universally destructive. This formidable extension of biopower, unlike what I was just saying about atomic power, will put it beyond all human sovereignty.

You must excuse this long digression into biopower, but I think that it does provide us with a basic argument that will allow us to get back to the problem I was trying to raise.

If it is true that the power of sovereignty is increasingly on the retreat and that disciplinary or regulatory disciplinary power is on the advance, how will the power to kill and the function of murder operate in this technology of power, which takes life as both its object and its objective? How can a power such as this kill, if it is true that its basic function is to improve life, to prolong its duration, to improve its chances, to avoid accidents, and to compensate for failings? How, under these conditions, is it possible for a political power to kill, to call for deaths, to demand deaths, to give the order to kill, and to expose not only its enemies but its own citizens to the risk of death? Given that this power's objective is essentially to make live, how can it let die? How can the power of death, the function of death, be exercised in a political system centered upon biopower?

It is, I think, at this point that racism intervenes. I am certainly not saying that racism was invented at this time. It had already been in existence for a very long time. But I think it functioned elsewhere. It is indeed the emergence of this biopower that inscribes it in the mechanisms of the State. It is at this moment that racism is inscribed as the basic mechanism of power, as it is exercised in modern States. As a result, the modern State can scarcely function without becoming involved with racism at some point, within certain limits and subject to certain conditions.

What in fact is racism? It is primarily a way of introducing a break into the domain of life that is under power's control: the break between what must live and what must die. The appearance within the biological continuum of the human race of races, the distinction among races, the hierarchy of races, the fact that certain races are described as good and that others, in contrast, are described as inferior: all this is a way of fragmenting the field of the biological that power controls. It is a way of separating out the groups that exist within a population. It is, in short, a way of establishing a biological type caesura within a population that appears to be a biological domain. This will allow power to treat that population as a mixture of races, or to be more accurate, to treat the species, to subdivide the species it controls, into the subspecies known, precisely, as races. That is the first function of racism: to fragment, to create caesuras within the biological continuum addressed by biopower.

Racism also has a second function. Its role is, if you like, to allow the establishment of a positive relation of this type: "The more you kill, the more deaths you will cause" or "The very fact that you let more die will allow you to live more." I would say that this relation ("If you want to live, you must take lives, you must be able to kill") was not invented by either racism or the modern State. It is the relationship of war: "In order to live, you must destroy your enemies." But racism does make the relationship of war – "If you want to live, the other must die" – function in a way that is completely new and that is quite compatible with the exercise of biopower. On the one hand, racism makes it possible to establish a relationship between my life and the death of the other that is not a military or warlike relationship of confrontation, but a biological-type relationship: "The more inferior species die out, the more abnormal individuals are eliminated, the fewer degenerates there will be in the species as a whole, and the more I – as species rather than individual – can live, the stronger I will be, the more vigorous I will be. I will be able to proliferate." The fact that the other dies does not mean simply that I live in the sense that his death guarantees my safety; the death of the other, the death of the bad race, of the inferior race (or the degenerate, or the abnormal) is something that will make life in general healthier: healthier and purer.

This is not, then, a military, warlike, or political relationship, but a biological relationship. And the reason this mechanism can come into play is that the enemies who have to be done away with are not adversaries in the political sense of the term; they are threats, either external or internal, to the population and for the population. In the biopower system, in other words, killing or the imperative to kill is acceptable only if it results not in a victory over political adversaries, but in the elimination of the biological threat to and the improvement of the species or race. There is a direct connection between the two. In a normalizing society, race or racism is the precondition that makes killing acceptable. When you have a normalizing society, you have a power which is, at least superficially, in the first instance, or in the first line a biopower, and racism is the indispensable precondition that allows someone to be killed, that allows others to be killed. Once the State functions in the biopower mode, racism alone can justify the murderous function of the State.

So you can understand the importance – I almost said the vital importance – of racism to the exercise of such a power: it is the precondition for exercising the right to kill. If the power of normalization wished to exercise the old sovereign right to kill, it must become racist. And if, conversely, a power of sovereignty, or in other words, a power that has the right of life and death, wishes to work with the instruments, mechanisms, and technology of normalization, it too must become racist. When I say "killing," I obviously do not mean simply murder as such, but also every form of indirect murder: the fact of exposing someone to death, increasing the risk of death for some people, or, quite simply, political death, expulsion, rejection, and so on.

I think that we are now in a position to understand a number of things. We can understand, first of all, the link that was quickly – I almost said immediately – established between nineteenth-century biological theory and the discourse of power. Basically, evolutionism, understood in the broad sense – or in other words, not so much Darwin's theory itself as a set, a bundle, of notions (such as: the hierarchy of species that grow from a common evolutionary tree, the struggle for existence among species, the selection that eliminates the less fit) – naturally became within a few years during the nineteenth century not simply a way of transcribing a political discourse into biological terms, and not simply a way of dressing up a political discourse in scientific clothing, but a real way of thinking about the relations between colonization, the necessity for wars, criminality, the phenomena of madness and mental illness, the history of societies with their different classes, and so on. Whenever, in other words, there was a confrontation, a killing or the risk of death, the nineteenth century was quite literally obliged to think about them in the form of evolutionism.

And we can also understand why racism should have developed in modern societies that function in the biopower mode; we can understand why racism broke out at a number of privileged moments, and why they were precisely the moments when the right to take life was imperative. Racism first develops with colonization, or in other words, with colonizing genocide. If you are functioning in the biopower mode, how can you justify the need to kill people, to kill populations, and to kill civilizations? By using the themes of evolutionism, by appealing to a racism.

War. How can one not only wage war on one's adversaries but also expose one's own citizens to war, and let them be killed by the million (and this is precisely what has been going on since the nineteenth century, or since the second half of the nineteenth century), except by activating the theme of racism? From this point onward, war is about two things: it is not simply a matter of destroying a political adversary, but of destroying the enemy race, of destroying that [sort] of biological threat that those people over there represent to our race. In one sense, this is of course no more than a biological extrapolation from the theme of the political enemy. But there is more to it than that.

In the nineteenth century – and this is completely new – war will be seen not only as a way of improving one's own race by eliminating the enemy race (in accordance with the themes of natural selection and the struggle for existence), but also as a way of regenerating one's own race. As more and more of our number die, the race to which we belong will become all the purer.

At the end of the nineteenth century, we have then a new racism modeled on war. It was, I think, required because a biopower that wished to wage war had to articulate the will to destroy the adversary with the risk that it might kill those whose lives it had, by definition, to protect, manage, and multiply. The same could be said of criminality. Once the mechanism of biopower was called upon to make it possible to execute or isolate criminals, criminality was conceptualized in racist terms. The same applies to madness, and the same applies to various abnormalities.

I think that, broadly speaking, racism justifies the death-function in the economy of biopower by appealing to the principle that the death of others makes one biologically stronger insofar as one is a member of a race or a population, insofar as one is an element in a unitary living plurality. You can see that, here, we are far removed from the ordinary racism that takes the traditional form of mutual contempt or hatred between races. We are also far removed from the racism that can be seen as a sort of ideological operation that allows States, or a class, to displace the hostility that is directed toward [them], or which is tormenting the social body, onto a mythical adversary. I think that this is something much deeper than an old tradition, much deeper than a new ideology, that it is something else. The specificity of modern racism, or what gives it its specificity, is not bound up with mentalities, ideologies, or the lies of power. It is bound up with the technique of power, with the technology of power. It is bound up with this, and that takes us as far away as possible from the race war and the intelligibility of history. We are dealing with a mechanism that allows biopower to work. So racism is bound up with the workings of a State that is obliged to use race, the elimination of races and the purification of the race, to exercise its sovereign power. The juxtaposition of – or the way biopower functions through – the old sovereign power of life and death implies the workings, the introduction and activation, of racism. And it is, I think, here that we find the actual roots of racism.

[...]

Notes

1 On the question of disciplinary technology, see *Surveiller et punir*.

2 On all these questions, see *Le pouvoir psychiatrique: Cours au Collège de France, 1973–1974* (Seuil, 2003).

3 Foucault comes back to all these disciplines, especially in *Cours au Collège de France 1977–1978: Sécurité, territoire et population* and *1978–1979: Naissance de la biopolitique: Cours au Collège de France* (Seuil, 2004).

4 Foucault refers here to the theory elaborated in mid-nineteenth-century France by certain alienists and in particular by B.-A. Morel (*Traité de dégénérescences physiques, intellectuelles et morales de l'espèce humaine* [Paris, 1857], *Traités des maladies mentales* [Paris, 1870]); V. Magnan (*Leçons cliniques sur les maladies mentales* [Paris, 1893]); and M. Legrain and V. Magnan (*Les Dégénérés, état mental et syndrômes épisodiques* [Paris, 1895]). This theory of degeneracy, which is based upon the principle that a so-called hereditary taint can be transmitted, was the kernel of medical knowledge about madness and abnormality in the second half of the nineteenth century. It was quickly adopted by forensic medicine, and it had a considerable effect on eugenicist doctrines and practices, and was not without its influence on a whole literature, a whole criminology, and a whole anthropology.

13

"Method" (1976)

Michel Foucault

Hence the objective is to analyze a certain form of knowledge regarding sex, not in terms of repression or law, but in terms of power. But the word *power* is apt to lead to a number of misunderstandings – misunderstandings with respect to its nature, its form, and its unity. By power, I do not mean "Power" as a group of institutions and mechanisms that ensure the subservience of the citizens of a given state. By power, I do not mean, either, a mode of subjugation which, in contrast to violence, has the form of the rule. Finally, I do not have in mind a general system of domination exerted by one group over another, a system whose effects, through successive derivations, pervade the entire social body. The analysis, made in terms of power, must not assume that the sovereignty of the state, the form of the law, or the over-all unity of a domination are given at the outset; rather, these are only the terminal forms power takes. It seems to me that power must be understood in the first instance as the multiplicity of force relations immanent in the sphere in which they operate and which constitute their own organization; as the process which, through ceaseless struggles and confrontations, transforms, strengthens, or reverses them; as the support which these force relations find in one another, thus forming a chain or a system, or on the contrary, the disjunctions and contradictions which isolate them from one

another; and lastly, as the strategies in which they take effect, whose general design or institutional crystallization is embodied in the state apparatus, in the formulation of the law, in the various social hegemonies. Power's condition of possibility, or in any case the viewpoint which permits one to understand its exercise, even in its more "peripheral" effects, and which also makes it possible to use its mechanisms as a grid of intelligibility of the social order, must not be sought in the primary existence of a central point, in a unique source of sovereignty from which secondary and descendent forms would emanate; it is the moving substrate of force relations which, by virtue of their inequality, constantly engender states of power, but the latter are always local and unstable. The omnipresence of power: not because it has the privilege of consolidating everything under its invincible unity, but because it is produced from one moment to the next, at every point, or rather in every relation from one point to another. Power is everywhere; not because it embraces everything, but because it comes from everywhere. And "Power," insofar as it is permanent, repetitious, inert, and self-reproducing, is simply the over-all effect that emerges from all these mobilities, the concatenation that rests on each of them and seeks in turn to arrest their movement. One needs to be nominalistic, no doubt: power is not an institution, and not a structure; neither is it a certain strength we are endowed with; it is the name that one attributes to a complex strategical situation in a particular society.

Should we turn the expression around, then, and say that politics is war pursued by other means? If we still wish to maintain a separation between war and politics, perhaps we should postulate rather that this multiplicity of force relations can be coded – in part but never totally – either in the form of "war," or in the form of "politics"; this would imply two different strategies (but the one always liable to switch into the other) for integrating these unbalanced, heterogeneous, unstable, and tense force relations.

Continuing this line of discussion, we can advance a certain number of propositions:

- Power is not something that is acquired, seized, or shared, something that one holds on to or allows to slip away; power is exercised from innumerable points, in the interplay of nonegalitarian and mobile relations.

- Relations of power are not in a position of exteriority with respect to other types of relationships (economic processes, knowledge relationships, sexual relations), but are immanent in the latter; they are the immediate effects of the divisions, inequalities, and disequilibriums which occur in the latter, and conversely they are the internal conditions of these differentiations; relations of power are not in superstructural positions, with merely a role of prohibition or accompaniment; they have a directly productive role, wherever they come into play.

- Power comes from below; that is, there is no binary and all-encompassing opposition between rulers and ruled at the root of power relations, and serving as a general matrix – no such duality extending from the top down and reacting on more and more limited groups to the very depths of the social body. One must suppose rather that the manifold relationships of force that take shape and come into play in the machinery of production, in families, limited groups, and institutions, are the basis for wide-ranging effects of cleavage that run through the social body as a whole. These then form a general line of force that traverses the local oppositions and links them together; to be sure, they also bring about redistributions, realignments, homogenizations, serial arrangements, and convergences of the force relations. Major dominations are the hegemonic effects that are sustained by all these confrontations.

- Power relations are both intentional and nonsubjective. If in fact they are intelligible, this is not because they are the effect of another instance that

"explains" them, but rather because they are imbued, through and through, with calculation: there is no power that is exercised without a series of aims and objectives. But this does not mean that it results from the choice or decision of an individual subject; let us not look for the headquarters that presides over its rationality; neither the caste which governs, nor the groups which control the state apparatus, nor those who make the most important economic decisions direct the entire network of power that functions in a society (and makes *it* function); the rationality of power is characterized by tactics that are often quite explicit at the restricted level where they are inscribed (the local cynicism of power), tactics which, becoming connected to one another, attracting and propagating one another, but finding their base of support and their condition elsewhere, end by forming comprehensive systems: the logic is perfectly clear, the aims decipherable, and yet it is often the case that no one is there to have invented them, and few who can be said to have formulated them: an implicit characteristic of the great anonymous, almost unspoken strategies which coordinate the loquacious tactics whose "inventors" or decision-makers are often without hypocrisy.

- Where there is power, there is resistance, and yet, or rather consequently, this resistance is never in a position of exteriority in relation to power. Should it be said that one is always "inside" power, there is no "escaping" it, there is no absolute outside where it is concerned, because one is subject to the law in any case? Or that, history being the ruse of reason, power is the ruse of history, always emerging the winner? This would be to misunderstand the strictly relational character of power relationships. Their existence depends on a multiplicity of points of resistance: these play the role of adversary, target, support, or handle in power relations. These points of resistance are present everywhere in the power network. Hence there is no single locus of great Refusal, no soul of revolt, source of all rebellions, or pure law of the revolutionary. Instead there is a plurality of resistances, each of them a special case: resistances that are possible, necessary, improbable; others that are spontaneous, savage, solitary, concerted, rampant, or violent; still others that are quick to compromise, interested, or sacrificial; by definition, they can only exist in the strategic field of power relations. But this does not mean that they are only a reaction or rebound, forming with respect to the basic domination an underside that is in the end always passive, doomed to perpetual defeat. Resistances do not derive from a few heterogeneous principles; but neither are they a lure or a promise that is of necessity betrayed. They are the odd term in relations of power; they are inscribed in the latter as an irreducible opposite. Hence they too are distributed in irregular fashion: the points, knots, or focuses of resistance are spread over time and space at varying densities, at times mobilizing groups or individuals in a definitive way, inflaming certain points of the body, certain moments in life, certain types of behavior. Are there no great radical ruptures, massive binary divisions, then? Occasionally, yes. But more often one is dealing with mobile and transitory points of resistance, producing cleavages in a society that shift about, fracturing unities and effecting regroupings, furrowing across individuals themselves, cutting them up and remolding them, marking off irreducible regions in them, in their bodies and minds. Just as the network of power relations ends by forming a dense web that passes through apparatuses and institutions, without being exactly localized in them, so too the swarm of points of resistance traverses social stratifications and individual unities. And it is doubtless the strategic codification of these points of resistance that makes a revolution possible, somewhat similar to the way in which the state relies on the institutional integration of power relationships.

It is in this sphere of force relations that we must try to analyze the mechanisms of power. In this way we will escape from the system of Law-and-Sovereign which has captivated political thought for such a long time. And if it is true that Machiavelli was among the few – and this no doubt was the scandal of his "cynicism" – who conceived the power of the Prince in terms of force relationships, perhaps we need to go one step further, do without the persona of the Prince, and decipher power mechanisms on the basis of a strategy that is immanent in force relationships.

To return to sex and the discourses of truth that have taken charge of it, the question that we must address, then, is not: Given a specific state structure, how and why is it that power needs to establish a knowledge of sex? Neither is the question: What over-all domination was served by the concern, evidenced since the eighteenth century, to produce true discourses on sex? Nor is it: What law presided over both the regularity of sexual behavior and the conformity of what was said about it? It is rather: In a specific type of discourse on sex, in a specific form of extortion of truth, appearing historically and in specific places (around the child's body, apropos of women's sex, in connection with practices restricting births, and so on), what were the most immediate, the most local power relations at work? How did they make possible these kinds of discourses, and conversely, how were these discourses used to support power relations? How was the action of these power relations modified by their very exercise, entailing a strengthening of some terms and a weakening of others, with effects of resistance and counterinvestments, so that there has never existed one type of stable subjugation, given once and for all? How were these power relations linked to one another according to the logic of a great strategy, which in retrospect takes on the aspect of a unitary and voluntarist politics of sex? In general terms: rather than referring all the infinitesimal violences that are exerted on sex, all the anxious gazes that are directed at it, and all the hiding places whose discovery is made into an impossible task, to the unique form of a great Power, we must immerse the expanding production of discourses on sex in the field of multiple and mobile power relations.

Which leads us to advance, in a preliminary way, four rules to follow. But these are not intended as methodological imperatives; at most they are cautionary prescriptions.

1. Rule of Immanence

One must not suppose that there exists a certain sphere of sexuality that would be the legitimate concern of a free and disinterested scientific inquiry were it not the object of mechanisms of prohibition brought to bear by the economic or ideological requirements of power. If sexuality was constituted as an area of investigation, this was only because relations of power had established it as a possible object; and conversely, if power was able to take it as a target, this was because techniques of knowledge and procedures of discourse were capable of investing it. Between techniques of knowledge and strategies of power, there is no exteriority, even if they have specific roles and are linked together on the basis of their difference. We will start, therefore, from what might be called "local centers" of power-knowledge: for example, the relations that obtain between penitents and confessors, or the faithful and their directors of conscience. Here, guided by the theme of the "flesh" that must be mastered, different forms of discourse – self-examination, questionings, admissions, interpretations, interviews – were the vehicle of a kind of incessant back-and-forth movement of forms of subjugation and schemas of knowledge. Similarly, the body of the child, under surveillance, surrounded in his cradle, his bed, or his room by an entire watch-crew of parents, nurses, servants, educators, and doctors, all attentive to the least manifestations of his sex, has constituted, particularly since the eighteenth century, another "local center" of power-knowledge.

2. Rules of Continual Variations

We must not look for who has the power in the order of sexuality (men, adults, parents, doctors) and who is deprived of it (women, adolescents, children, patients); nor for who has the right to know and who is forced to remain ignorant. We must seek rather the pattern of the modifications which the relationships of force imply by the very nature of their process. The "distributions of power" and the "appropriations of knowledge" never represent only instantaneous slices taken from processes involving, for example, a cumulative reinforcement of the strongest factor, or a reversal of relationship, or again, a simultaneous increase of two terms. Relations of power-knowledge are not static forms of distribution, they are "matrices of transformations." The nineteenth-century grouping made up of the father, the mother, the educator, and the doctor, around the child and his sex, was subjected to constant modifications, continual shifts. One of the more spectacular results of the latter was a strange reversal: whereas to begin with the child's sexuality had been problema-

tized within the relationship established between doctor and parents (in the form of advice, or recommendations to keep the child under observation, or warnings of future dangers), ultimately it was in the relationship of the psychiatrist to the child that the sexuality of adults themselves was called into question.

3. Rule of Double Conditioning

No "local center," no "pattern of transformation" could function if, through a series of sequences, it did not eventually enter into an over-all strategy. And inversely, no strategy could achieve comprehensive effects if did not gain support from precise and tenuous relations serving, not as its point of application or final outcome, but as its prop and anchor point. There is no discontinuity between them, as if one were dealing with two different levels (one microscopic and the other macroscopic); but neither is there homogeneity (as if the one were only the enlarged projection or the miniaturization of the other); rather, one must conceive of the double conditioning of a strategy by the specificity of possible tactics, and of tactics by the strategic envelope that makes them work. Thus the father in the family is not the "representative" of the sovereign or the state; and the latter are not projections of the father on a different scale. The family does not duplicate society, just as society does not imitate the family. But the family organization, precisely to the extent that it was insular and heteromorphous with respect to the other power mechanisms, was used to support the great "maneuvers" employed for the Malthusian control of the birthrate, for the populationist incitements, for the medicalization of sex and the psychiatrization of its nongenital forms.

4. Rule of the Tactical Polyvalence of Discourses

What is said about sex must not be analyzed simply as the surface of projection of these power mechanisms. Indeed, it is in discourse that power and knowledge are joined together. And for this very reason, we must conceive discourse as a series of discontinuous segments whose tactical function is neither uniform nor stable.

To be more precise, we must not imagine a world of discourse divided between accepted discourse and excluded discourse, or between the dominant discourse and the dominated one; but as a multiplicity of discursive elements that can come into play in various strategies. It is this distribution that we must reconstruct, with the things said and those concealed, the enunciations required and those forbidden, that it comprises; with the variants and different effects – according to who is speaking, his position of power, the institutional context in which he happens to be situated – that it implies; and with the shifts and reutilizations of identical formulas for contrary objectives that it also includes. Discourses are not once and for all subservient to power or raised up against it, any more than silences are. We must make allowance for the complex and unstable process whereby discourse can be both an instrument and an effect of power, but also a hindrance, a stumbling-block, a point of resistance and a starting point for an opposing strategy. Discourse transmits and produces power; it reinforces it, but also undermines and exposes it, renders it fragile and makes it possible to thwart it. In like manner, silence and secrecy are a shelter for power, anchoring its prohibitions; but they also loosen its holds and provide for relatively obscure areas of tolerance. Consider for example the history of what was once "the" great sin against nature. The extreme discretion of the texts dealing with sodomy – that utterly confused category – and the nearly universal reticence in talking about it made possible a twofold operation: on the one hand, there was an extreme severity (punishment by fire was meted out well into the eighteenth century, without there being any substantial protest expressed before the middle of the century), and on the other hand, a tolerance that must have been widespread (which one can deduce indirectly from the infrequency of judicial sentences, and which one glimpses more directly through certain statements concerning societies of men that were thought to exist in the army or in the courts). There is no question that the appearance in nineteenth-century psychiatry, jurisprudence, and literature of a whole series of discourses on the species and subspecies of homosexuality, inversion, pederasty, and "psychic hermaphrodism" made possible a strong advance of social controls into this area of "perversity"; but it also made possible the formation of a "reverse" discourse: homosexuality began to speak in its own behalf, to demand that its legitimacy or "naturality" be acknowledged, often in the same vocabulary, using the same categories by which it was medically disqualified. There is not, on the one side, a discourse of power, and opposite it, another discourse that runs counter to it. Discourses are tactical elements or blocks operating in the field of force relations; there can exist different and even contradictory discourses within the same strategy; they can, on the contrary, circulate without changing their form from one strategy to another, opposing strategy. We must not expect the discourses on sex to tell us, above all, what strategy they derive from, or what moral divisions they accompany, or what ideology – dominant or dominated – they represent; rather we must question them on the two levels of their tactical productivity (what reciprocal effects of power and knowledge they ensure) and their strategical integration (what conjunction and what force relationship make their utilization necessary in a given episode of the various confrontations that occur).

In short, it is a question of orienting ourselves to a conception of power which replaces the privilege of the law with the viewpoint of the objective, the privilege of prohibition with the viewpoint of tactical efficacy, the privilege of sovereignty with the analysis of a multiple and mobile field of force relations, wherein far-reaching, but never completely stable, effects of domination are produced. The strategical model, rather than the model based on law. And this, not out of a speculative choice or theoretical preference, but because in fact it is one of the essential traits of Western societies that the force relationships which for a long time had found expression in war, in every form of warfare, gradually became invested in the order of political power.

14

"Postscript on the Societies of Control" (1992)

Gilles Deleuze

1. Historical

Foucault located the *disciplinary societies* in the eighteenth and nineteenth centuries; they reach their height at the outset of the twentieth. They initiate the organization of vast spaces of enclosure. The individual never ceases passing from one closed environment to another, each having its own laws: first the family; then the school ("you are no longer in your family"); then the barracks ("you are no longer at school"); then the factory; from time to time the hospital; possibly the prison, the preeminent instance of the enclosed environment. It's the prison that serves as the analogical model: at the sight of some laborers, the heroine of Rossellini's *Europa '51* could exclaim, "I thought I was seeing convicts."

Foucault has brilliantly analyzed the ideal project of these environments of enclosure, particularly visible within the factory: to concentrate; to distribute in space; to order in time; to compose a productive force within the dimension of space–time whose effect will be greater than the sum of its component forces. But what Foucault recognized as well was the transience of this model: it succeeded that of the *societies of sovereignty*, the goal and functions of which were something quite different (to tax rather than to organize production, to rule on death rather than to administer life); the transition took place over time, and Napoleon seemed to effect the large-scale conversion from one society to the other. But in their turn the disciplines

Gilles Deleuze, "Postscript on the Societies of Control," pp. 3–7, *October* 59 (1992).

underwent a crisis to the benefit of new forces that were gradually instituted and which accelerated after World War II: a disciplinary society was what we already no longer were, what we had ceased to be.

We are in a generalized crisis in relation to all the environments of enclosure – prison, hospital, factory, school, family. The family is an "interior," in crisis like all other interiors – scholarly, professional, etc. The administrations in charge never cease announcing supposedly necessary reforms: to reform schools, to reform industries, hospitals, the armed forces, prisons. But everyone knows that these institutions are finished, whatever the length of their expiration periods. It's only a matter of administering their last rites and of keeping people employed until the installation of the new forces knocking at the door. These are the *societies of control*, which are in the process of replacing disciplinary societies. "Control" is the name Burroughs proposes as a term for the new monster, one that Foucault recognizes as our immediate future. Paul Virilio also is continually analyzing the ultrarapid forms of free-floating control that replaced the old disciplines operating in the time frame of a closed system. There is no need to invoke the extraordinary pharmaceutical productions, the molecular engineering, the genetic manipulations, although these are slated to enter the new process. There is no need to ask which is the toughest regime, for it's within each of them that liberating and enslaving forces confront one another. For example, in the crisis of the hospital as environment of enclosure, neighborhood clinics, hospices, and day care could at first express new freedom, but they could participate as well in mechanisms of control that are equal to the harshest of confinements. There is no need to fear or hope, but only to look for new weapons.

2. Logic

The different internments of spaces of enclosure through which the individual passes are independent variables: each time one is supposed to start from zero, and although a common language for all these places exists, it is *analogical*. One the other hand, the different control mechanisms are inseparable variations, forming a system of variable geometry the language of which is numerical (which doesn't necessarily mean binary). Enclosures are *molds*, distinct castings, but controls are a *modulation*, like a self-deforming cast that will continuously change from one moment to the other, or like a sieve whose mesh will transmute from point to point.

This is obvious in the matter of salaries: the factory was a body that contained its internal forces at the level of equilibrium, the highest possible in terms of production, the lowest possible in terms of wages; but in a society of control, the corporation has replaced the factory, and the corporation is a spirit, a gas. Of course the factory was already familiar with the system of bonuses, but the corporation works more deeply to impose a modulation of each salary, in states of perpetual metastability that operate through challenges, contests, and highly comic group sessions. If the most idiotic television game shows are so successful, it's because they express the corporate situation with great precision. The factory constituted individuals as a single body to the double advantage of the boss who surveyed each element within the mass and the unions who mobilized a mass resistance; but the corporation constantly presents the brashest rivalry as a healthy form of emulation, an excellent motivational force that opposes individuals against one another and runs through each, dividing each within. The modulating principle of "salary according to merit" has not failed to tempt national education itself. Indeed, just as the corporation replaces the factory, *perpetual training* tends to replace the *school*, and continuous control to replace the examination. Which is the surest way of delivering the school over to the corporation.

In the disciplinary societies one was always starting again (from school to the barracks, from the barracks to the factory), while in the societies of control one is never finished with anything – the corporation, the educational system, the armed services being metastable states coexisting in one and the same modulation, like a universal system of deformation. In *The Trial*, Kafka, who had already placed himself at the pivotal point between two types of social formation, described the most fearsome of judicial forms. The *apparent acquittal* of the disciplinary societies (between two incarcerations); and the *limitless postponements* of the societies of control (in continuous variation) are two very different modes of juridicial life, and if our law is hesitant, itself in crisis, it's because we are leaving one in order to enter the other. The disciplinary societies have two poles: the signature that designates the *individual*, and the number or administrative numeration that indicates his or her position within a *mass*. This is because the disciplines never saw any incompatibility between these two, and because at the same time power individualizes and masses together, that is, constitutes those over whom it exercises power into a body and molds the individuality of each member of that body. (Foucault saw the origin of this double charge in the pastoral power of the priest – the flock and each of its animals – but civil power moves in turn and by other means to make itself lay "priest.") In the societies of control, on the other hand, what is important is no longer either a signature or a number, but a code: the code is a *password*, while on the other hand disciplinary societies are regulated by *watchwords* (as much from the point of view of integration as from that of resistance). The numerical language of control is made of codes that mark access to information, or reject it. We no longer find ourselves dealing with the mass/individual pair. Individuals have become "*dividuals*," and masses, samples, data, markets, or "*banks*." Perhaps it is money that expresses the distinction between the two societies best, since discipline always referred back to minted money that locks gold as numerical standard, while control relates to floating rates of exchange, modulated according to a rate established by a set of standard currencies. The old monetary mole is the animal of the space of enclosure but the serpent is that of the societies of control. We have passed from one animal to the other, from the mole to the serpent, in the system under which we live, but also in our manner of living and in our relations with others. The disciplinary man was a discontinuous producer of energy, but the man of control is undulatory, in orbit, in a continuous network. Everywhere *surfing* has already replaced the older *sports*.

Types of machines are easily matched with each type of society – not that machines are determining, but because they express those social forms capable of generating them and using them. The old societies of sovereignty made use of simple machines – levers, pulleys, clocks; but the recent disciplinary societies equipped themselves with machines involving energy, with the passive danger of entropy and the active danger of sabotage; the societies of control operate with machines of a third type, computers, whose passive danger is jamming and whose active one is piracy or the introduction of viruses. This technological evolution must be, even more profoundly, a mutation of capitalism, an already well-known or familiar mutation that can be summed up as follows: nineteenth-century capitalism is a capitalism of concentration, for production and for property. It therefore erects a factory as a space of enclosure, the capitalist being the owner of the means of production but also, progressively, the owner of other spaces conceived through analogy (the worker's familial house, the school). As for markets, they are conquered sometimes by specialization, sometimes by colonization, sometimes by lowering the costs of production. But in the present situation, capitalism is no longer involved in production, which it often relegates to the Third World, even for the complex forms of textiles, metallurgy, or oil production. It's a capitalism of higher-order production. It no longer buys raw materials and no longer sells the finished products: it buys the finished products or assembles parts. What it wants to sell is services but what it wants to buy is stocks. This is no longer a capitalism for production but for the product, which is to say, for being sold or marketed. Thus is essentially dispersive, and the factory has given way to the corporation. The family, the school, the army, the factory are no longer the distinct analogical spaces that converge towards an owner – state or private power – but coded figures – deformable and transformable – of a single corporation that now has only stockholders. Even art has left the spaces of enclosure in order to

enter into the open circuits of the bank. The conquests of the market are made by grabbing control and no longer by disciplinary training, by fixing the exchange rate much more than by lowering costs, by transformation of the product more than by specialization of production. Corruption thereby gains a new power. Marketing has become the center or the "soul" of the corporation. We are taught that corporations have a soul, which is the most terrifying news in the world. The operation of markets is now the instrument of social control and forms the impudent breed of our masters. Control is short-term and of rapid rates of turnover, but also continuous and without limit, while discipline was of long duration, infinite and discontinuous. Man is no longer man enclosed, but man in debt. It is true that capitalism has retained as a constant the extreme poverty of three-quarters of humanity, too poor for debt, too numerous for confinement: control will not only have to deal with erosions of frontiers but with the explosions within shanty towns or ghettos.

3. Program

The conception of a control mechanism, giving the position of any element within an open environment at any given instant (whether animal in a reserve or human in a corporation, as with an electronic collar), is not necessarily one of science fiction. Félix Guattari has imagined a city where one would be able to leave one's apartment, one's street, one's neighborhood, thanks to one's (dividual) electronic card that raises a given barrier; but the card could just as easily be rejected on a given day or between certain hours; what counts is not the barrier but the computer that tracks each person's position – licit or illicit – and effects a universal modulation.

The socio-technological study of the mechanisms of control, grasped at their inception, would have to be categorical and to describe what is already in the process of substitution for the disciplinary sites of enclosure, whose crisis is everywhere proclaimed. It may be that older methods, borrowed from the former societies of sovereignty, will return to the fore, but with the necessary modifications. What counts is that we are at the beginning of something. In the *prison system*: the attempt to find penalties of "substitution," at least for petty crimes, and the use of electronic collars that force the convicted person to stay at home during certain hours. For the *school system*: continuous forms of control, and the effect on the school of perpetual training, the corresponding abandonment of all university research, the introduction of the "corporation" at all levels of schooling. For the *hospital system*: the new medicine "without doctor or patient" that singles out potential sick people and subjects at risk, which in no way attests to individuation – as they say – but substitutes for the individual or numerical body the code of a "dividual" material to be controlled. In the *corporate system*: new ways of handling money, profits, and humans that no longer pass through the old factory form. These are very small examples, but ones that will allow for better understanding of what is meant by the crisis of the institutions, which is to say, the progressive and dispersed installation of a new system of domination. One of the most important questions will concern the ineptitude of the unions: tied to the whole of their history of struggle against the disciplines or within the spaces of enclosure, will they be able to adapt themselves or will they give way to new forms of resistance against the societies of control? Can we already grasp the rough outlines of the coming forms, capable of threatening the joys of marketing? Many young people strangely boast of being "motivated"; they re-request apprenticeships and permanent training. It's up to them to discover what they're being made to serve, just as their elders discovered, not without difficulty, the telos of the disciplines. The coils of a serpent are even more complex that the burrows of a molehill.

15

"Biopolitical Production" (2000)

Michael Hardt and Antonio Negri

The "police" appears as an administration heading the state, together with the judiciary, the army, and the exchequer. True. Yet in fact, it embraces everything else. Turquet says so: "It branches out into all of the people's conditions, everything they do or undertake. Its field comprises the judiciary, finance, and the army." The police includes everything. (Michel Foucault)

From the juridical perspective we have been able to glimpse some of the elements of the ideal genesis of Empire, but from that perspective alone it would be difficult if not impossible to understand how the imperial machine is actually set in motion. Juridical concepts and juridical systems always refer to something other than themselves. Through the evolution and exercise of right, they point toward the material condition that defines their purchase on social reality. Our analysis must now descend to the level of that materiality and investigate there the material transformation of the paradigm of rule. We need to discover the means and forces of the production of social reality along with the subjectivities that animate it.

Biopower in the Society of Control

In many respects, the work of Michel Foucault has prepared the terrain for such an investigation of the

Michael Hardt and Antonio Negri, "Biopolitical Production," pp. 22–34 from *Empire*. Cambridge, MA: Harvard University Press, 2000. Reprinted by permission of the publisher. Copyright © 2000 by the President and Fellows of Harvard College.

material functioning of imperial rule. First of all, Foucault's work allows us to recognize a historical, epochal passage in social forms from *disciplinary society* to the *society of control*. Disciplinary society is that society in which social command is constructed through a diffuse network of *dispositifs* or apparatuses that produce and regulate customs, habits, and productive practices. Putting this society to work and ensuring obedience to its rule and its mechanisms of inclusion and/or exclusion are accomplished through disciplinary institutions (the prison, the factory, the asylum, the hospital, the university, the school, and so forth) that structure the social terrain and present logics adequate to the "reason" of discipline. Disciplinary power rules in effect by structuring the parameters and limits of thought and practice, sanctioning and prescribing normal and/or deviant behaviors. Foucault generally refers to the ancien régime and the classical age of French civilization to illustrate the emergence of disciplinarity, but more generally we could say that the entire first phase of capitalist accumulation (in Europe and elsewhere) was conducted under this paradigm of power. We should understand the society of control, in contrast, as that society (which develops at the far edge of modernity and opens toward the postmodern) in which mechanisms of command become ever more "democratic," ever more immanent to the social field, distributed throughout the brains and bodies of the citizens. The behaviors of social integration and exclusion proper to rule are thus increasingly interiorized within the subjects themselves. Power is now exercised through machines that directly organize the brains (in communication systems, information networks, etc.) and bodies (in welfare systems, monitored activities, etc.) toward a state of autonomous alienation from the sense of life and the desire for creativity. The society of control might thus be characterized by an intensification and generalization of the normalizing apparatuses of disciplinarity that internally animate our common and daily practices, but in contrast to discipline, this control extends well outside the structured sites of social institutions through flexible and fluctuating networks.

Second, Foucault's work allows us to recognize the *biopolitical* nature of the new paradigm of power. Biopower is a form of power that regulates social life from its interior, following it, interpreting it, absorbing it, and rearticulating it. Power can achieve an effective command over the entire life of the population only when it becomes an integral, vital function that every individual embraces and reactivates of his or her own accord. As Foucault says, "Life has now become … an object of power." The highest function of this power is to invest life through and through, and its primary task is to administer life. Biopower thus refers to a situation in which what is directly at stake in power is the production and reproduction of life itself.

These two lines of Foucault's work dovetail with each other in the sense that only the society of control is able to adopt the biopolitical context as its *exclusive* terrain of reference. In the passage from disciplinary society to the society of control, a new paradigm of power is realized which is defined by the technologies that recognize society as the realm of biopower. In disciplinary society the effects of biopolitical technologies were still partial in the sense that disciplining developed according to relatively closed, geometrical, and quantitative logics. Disciplinarity fixed individuals within institutions but did not succeed in consuming them completely in the rhythm of productive practices and productive socialization; it did not reach the point of permeating entirely the consciousnesses and bodies of individuals, the point of treating and

organizing them in the totality of their activities. In disciplinary society, then, the relationship between power and the individual remained a static one: the disciplinary invasion of power corresponded to the resistance of the individual. By contrast, when power becomes entirely biopolitical, the whole social body is comprised by power's machine and developed in its virtuality. This relationship is open, qualitative, and affective. Society, subsumed within a power that reaches down to the ganglia of the social structure and its processes of development, reacts like a single body. Power is thus expressed as a control that extends throughout the depths of the consciousnesses and bodies of the population – and at the same time across the entirety of social relations.

In this passage from disciplinary society to the society of control, then, one could say that the increasingly intense relationship of mutual implication of all social forces that capitalism has pursued throughout its development has now been fully realized. Marx recognized something similar in what he called the passage from the formal subsumption to the real subsumption of labor under capital, and later the Frankfurt School philosophers analyzed a closely related passage of the subsumption of culture (and social relations) under the totalitarian figure of the state, or really within the perverse dialectic of Enlightenment. The passage we are referring to, however, is fundamentally different in that instead of focusing on the unidimensionality of the process described by Marx and reformulated and extended by the Frankfurt School, the Foucauldian passage deals fundamentally with the paradox of plurality and multiplicity – and Deleuze and Guattari develop this perspective even more clearly. The analysis of the real subsumption, when this is understood as investing not only the economic or only the cultural dimension of society but rather the social *bios* itself, and when it is attentive to the modalities of disciplinarity and/or control, disrupts the linear and totalitarian figure of capitalist development. Civil society is absorbed in the state, but the consequence of this is an explosion of the elements that were previously coordinated and mediated in civil society. Resistances are no longer marginal but active in the center of a society that opens up in networks; the individual points are singularized in a thousand plateaus. What Foucault constructed implicitly (and Deleuze and Guattari made explicit) is therefore the paradox of a power that, while it unifies and envelops within itself every element of social life (thus losing its capacity effectively to mediate different social forces), at that very moment reveals a new context, a new milieu of maximum plurality and uncontainable singularization – a milieu of the event.

These conceptions of the society of control and biopower both describe central aspects of the concept of Empire. The concept of Empire is the framework in which the new omniversality of subjects has to be understood, and it is the end to which the new paradigm of power is leading. Here a veritable chasm opens up between the various old theoretical frameworks of international law (in either its contractual and/or UN form) and the new reality of imperial law. All the intermediary elements of the process have in fact fallen aside, so that the legitimacy of the international order can no longer be constructed through mediations but must rather be grasped immediately in all its diversity. We have already acknowledged this fact from the juridical perspective. We saw, in effect, that when the new notion of right emerges in the context of globalization and presents itself as capable of treating the universal, planetary sphere as a single, systemic set, it must assume an immediate prerequisite (acting in a state of exception) and an adequate, plastic, and constitutive technology (the techniques of the police).

Even though the state of exception and police technologies constitute the solid nucleus and the central element of the new imperial right, however, this new regime has nothing to do with the juridical arts of dictatorship or totalitarianism that in other times and with such great fanfare were so thoroughly described by many (in fact too many!) authors. On the contrary, the rule of law continues to play a central role in the context of the contemporary passage: right remains effective and (precisely by means of the state of exception and police techniques) becomes procedure. This is a radical transformation that reveals the unmediated relationship between power and subjectivities, and hence demonstrates both the impossibility of "prior" mediations and the uncontainable temporal variability of the event. Throughout the unbounded global spaces, to the depths of the biopolitical world, and confronting an unforeseeable temporality – these are the determinations on which the

new supranational right must be defined. Here is where the concept of Empire must struggle to establish itself, where it must prove its effectiveness, and hence where the machine must be set in motion.

From this point of view, the biopolitical context of the new paradigm is completely central to our analysis. This is what presents power with an alternative, not only between obedience and disobedience, or between formal political participation and refusal, but also along the entire range of life and death, wealth and poverty, production and social reproduction, and so forth. Given the great difficulties the new notion of right has in representing this dimension of the power of Empire, and given its inability to touch biopower concretely in all its material aspects, imperial right can at best only partially represent the underlying design of the new constitution of world order, and cannot really grasp the motor that sets it in motion. Our analysis must focus its attention rather on the *productive* dimension of biopower.

The Production of Life

The question of production in relation to biopower and the society of control, however, reveals a real weakness of the work of the authors from whom we have borrowed these notions. We should clarify, then, the "vital" or biopolitical dimensions of Foucault's work in relation to the dynamics of production. Foucault argued in several works in the mid-1970s that one cannot understand the passage from the "sovereign" state of the ancien régime to the modern "disciplinary" state without taking into account how the biopolitical context was progressively put at the service of capitalist accumulation: "The control of society over individuals is not conducted only through consciousness or ideology, but also in the body and with the body. For capitalist society biopolitics is what is most important, the biological, the somatic, the corporeal."

One of the central objectives of his research strategy in this period was to go beyond the versions of historical materialism, including several variants of Marxist theory, that considered the problem of power and social reproduction on a superstructural level separate from the real, base level of production. Foucault thus attempted to bring the problem of social reproduction and all the elements of the so-called superstructure back to within the material, fundamental structure and define this terrain not only in economic terms but also in cultural, corporeal, and subjective ones. We can thus understand how Foucault's conception of the social whole was perfected and realized when in a subsequent phase of his work he uncovered the emerging outlines of the society of control as a figure of power active throughout the entire biopolitics of society. It does not seem, however, that Foucault – even when he powerfully grasped the biopolitical horizon of society and defined it as a field of immanence – ever succeeded in pulling his thought away from that structuralist epistemology that guided his research from the beginning. By structuralist epistemology here we mean the reinvention of a functionalist analysis in the realm of the human sciences, a method that effectively sacrifices the dynamic of the system, the creative temporality of its movements, and the ontological substance of cultural and social reproduction. In fact, if at this point we were to ask Foucault who or what drives the system, or rather, who is the "bios," his response would be ineffable, or nothing at all. What Foucault fails to grasp finally are the real dynamics of production in biopolitical society.

By contrast, Deleuze and Guattari present us with a properly poststructuralist understanding of biopower that renews materialist thought and grounds itself solidly in the question of the production of social being. Their work demystifies structuralism and all the philosophical, sociological, and political conceptions that make the fixity of the epistemological frame an ineluctable point of reference. They focus our attention clearly on the ontological substance of social production. Machines produce. The constant functioning of social machines in their various apparatuses and assemblages produces the world along with the subjects and objects that constitute it. Deleuze and Guattari, however, seem to be able to conceive positively only the tendencies toward continuous movement and absolute flows, and thus in their thought, too, the creative elements and the radical ontology of the production of the social remain insubstantial and impotent. Deleuze and Guattari discover the productivity of social reproduction (creative production, production of values, social relations, affects, becomings), but manage to articulate it only superficially and ephemerally, as a chaotic, indeterminate horizon marked by the ungraspable event.

We can better grasp the relationship between social production and biopower in the work of a group of contemporary Italian Marxist authors who recognize the biopolitical dimension in terms of the new nature of productive labor and its living development in society, using terms such as "mass intellectuality," "immaterial labor," and the Marxian concept of "general intellect." These analyses set off from two coordinated research projects. The first consists in the analysis of the recent transformations of productive labor and its tendency to become increasingly immaterial. The central role previously occupied by the labor power of mass factory workers in the production of surplus value is today increasingly filled by intellectual, immaterial, and communicative labor power. It is thus necessary to develop a new political theory of value that can pose the problem of this new capitalist accumulation of value at the center of the mechanism of exploitation (and thus, perhaps, at the center of potential revolt). The second, and consequent, research project developed by this school consists in the analysis of the immediately social and communicative dimension of living labor in contemporary capitalist society, and thus poses insistently the problem of the new figures of subjectivity, in both their exploitation and their revolutionary potential. The immediately social dimension of the exploitation of living immaterial labor immerses labor in all the relational elements that define the social but also at the same time activate the critical elements that develop the potential of insubordination and revolt through the entire set of laboring practices. After a new theory of value, then, a new theory of subjectivity must be formulated that operates primarily through knowledge, communication, and language.

These analyses have thus reestablished the importance of production within the biopolitical process of the social constitution, but they have also in certain respects isolated it – by grasping it in a pure form, refining it on the ideal plane. They have acted as if discovering the new forms of productive forces – immaterial labor, massified intellectual labor, the labor of "general intellect" – were enough to grasp concretely the dynamic and creative relationship between material production and social reproduction. When they reinsert production into the biopolitical context, they present it almost exclusively on the horizon of language and communication. One of the most serious shortcomings has thus been the tendency among these authors to treat the new laboring practices in biopolitical society *only* in their intellectual and incorporeal aspects. The productivity of bodies and the value of affect, however, are absolutely central in this context. We will elaborate the three primary aspects of immaterial labor in the contemporary economy: the communicative labor of industrial production that has newly become linked in informational networks, the interactive labor of symbolic analysis and problem solving, and the labor of the production and manipulation of affects. This third aspect, with its focus on the productivity of the corporeal, the somatic, is an extremely important element in the contemporary networks of biopolitical production. The work of this school and its analysis of general intellect, then, certainly marks a step forward, but its conceptual framework remains too pure, almost angelic. In the final analysis, these new conceptions too only scratch the surface of the productive dynamic of the new theoretical framework of biopower.

Our task, then, is to build on these partially successful attempts to recognize the potential of biopolitical production. Precisely by bringing together coherently the different defining characteristics of the biopolitical context that we have described up to this point, and leading them back to the ontology of production, we will be able to identify the new figure of the collective biopolitical body, which may nonetheless remain as contradictory as it is paradoxical. This body becomes structure not by negating the originary productive force that animates it but by recognizing it; it becomes language (both scientific language and social language) because it is a multitude of singular and determinate bodies that seek relation. It is thus both production and reproduction, structure and superstructure, because it is life in the fullest sense and politics in the proper sense. Our analysis has to descend into the jungle of productive and conflictual determinations that the collective biopolitical body offers us. The context of our analysis thus has to be the very unfolding of life itself, the process of the constitution of the world, of history. The analysis must be proposed not through ideal forms but within the dense complex of experience.

Corporations and Communication

In asking ourselves how the political and sovereign elements of the imperial machine come to be constituted, we find that there is no need to limit our analysis to or even focus it on the established supranational regulatory institutions. The UN organizations, along with the great multi- and transnational finance and trade agencies (the IMF, the World Bank, the GATT, and so forth), all become relevant in the perspective of the supranational juridical constitution only when they are considered within the dynamic of the biopolitical production of world order. The function they had in the old international order, we should emphasize, is not what now gives legitimacy to these organizations. What legitimates them now is rather their newly possible function in the symbology of the imperial order. Outside of the new framework, these institutions are ineffectual. At best, the old institutional framework contributes to the formation and education of the administrative personnel of the imperial machine, the "dressage" of a new imperial élite.

The huge transnational corporations construct the fundamental connective fabric of the biopolitical world in certain important respects. Capital has indeed always been organized with a view toward the entire global sphere, but only in the second half of the twentieth century did multinational and transnational industrial and financial corporations really begin to structure global territories biopolitically. Some claim that these corporations have merely come to occupy the place that was held by the various national colonialist and imperialist systems in earlier phases of capitalist development, from nineteenth-century European imperialism to the Fordist phase of development in the twentieth century. This is in part true, but that place itself has been substantially transformed by the new reality of capitalism. The activities of corporations are no longer defined by the imposition of abstract command and the organization of simple theft and unequal exchange. Rather, they directly structure and articulate territories and populations. They tend to make nation-states merely instruments to record the flows of the commodities, monies, and populations that they set in motion. The transnational corporations directly distribute labor power over various markets, functionally allocate resources, and organize hierarchically the various sectors of world production. The complex apparatus that selects investments and directs financial and monetary maneuvers determines the new geography of the world market, or really the new biopolitical structuring of the world.

The most complete figure of this world is presented from the monetary perspective. From here we can see a horizon of values and a machine of distribution, a mechanism of accumulation and a means of circulation, a power and a language. There is nothing, no "naked life," no external standpoint, that can be posed outside this field permeated by money; nothing escapes money. Production and reproduction are dressed in monetary clothing. In fact, on the global stage, every biopolitical figure appears dressed in monetary garb. "Accumulate, accumulate! This is Moses and the Prophets!"

The great industrial and financial powers thus produce not only commodities but also subjectivities. They produce agentic subjectivities within the biopolitical context: they produce needs, social relations, bodies, and minds – which is to say, they produce producers. In the biopolitical sphere, life is made to work for production and production is made to work for life. It is a great hive in which the queen bee continuously oversees production and reproduction. The deeper the analysis goes, the more it finds at increasing levels of intensity the interlinking assemblages of interactive relationships.

One site where we should locate the biopolitical production of order is in the immaterial nexuses of the production of language, communication, and the symbolic that are developed by the communications industries. The development of communications networks has an organic relationship to the emergence of the new world order – it is, in other words, effect and cause, product and producer. Communication not only expresses but also organizes the movement of globalization. It organizes the movement by multiplying and structuring interconnections through networks. It expresses the movement and controls the sense and direction of the imaginary that runs throughout these communicative connections; in other words, the imaginary is guided and channeled within the communicative machine. What the theories of power of modernity were forced to consider

transcendent, that is, external to productive and social relations, is here formed inside, immanent to the productive and social relations. Mediation is absorbed within the productive machine. The political synthesis of social space is fixed in the space of communication. This is why communications industries have assumed such a central position. They not only organize production on a new scale and impose a new structure adequate to global space, but also make its justification immanent. Power, as it produces, organizes; as it organizes, it speaks and expresses itself as authority. Language, as it communicates, produces commodities but moreover creates subjectivities, puts them in relation, and orders them. The communications industries integrate the imaginary and the symbolic within the biopolitical fabric, not merely putting them at the service of power but actually integrating them into its very functioning.

At this point we can begin to address the question of the *legitimation* of the new world order. Its legitimation is not born of the previously existing international accords nor of the functioning of the first, embryonic supranational organizations, which were themselves created through treaties based on international law. The legitimation of the imperial machine is born at least in part of the communications industries, that is, of the transformation of the new mode of production into a machine. It is a subject that produces its own image of authority. This is a form of legitimation that rests on nothing outside itself and is reproposed ceaselessly by developing its own languages of self-validation.

One further consequence should be treated on the basis of these premises. If communication is one of the hegemonic sectors of production and acts over the entire biopolitical field, then we must consider communication and the biopolitical context coexistent. This takes us well beyond the old terrain as Jürgen Habermas described it, for example. In fact, when Habermas developed the concept of communicative action, demonstrating so powerfully its productive form and the ontological consequences deriving from that, he still relied on a standpoint outside these effects of globalization, a standpoint of life and truth that could oppose the informational colonization of being. The imperial machine, however, demonstrates that this external standpoint no longer exists. On the contrary, communicative production and the construction of imperial legitimation march hand in hand and can no longer be separated. The machine is self-validating, autopoietic – that is, systemic. It constructs social fabrics that evacuate or render ineffective any contradiction; it creates situations in which, before coercively neutralizing difference, seem to absorb it in an insignificant play of self-generating and self-regulating equilibria. As we have argued elsewhere, any juridical theory that addresses the conditions of postmodernity has to take into account this specifically communicative definition of social production. The imperial machine lives by producing a context of equilibria and/or reducing complexities, pretending to put forward a project of universal citizenship and toward this end intensifying the effectiveness of its intervention over every element of the communicative relationship, all the while dissolving identity and history in a completely postmodernist fashion. Contrary to the way many postmodernist accounts would have it, however, the imperial machine, far from eliminating master narratives, actually produces and reproduces them (ideological master narratives in particular) in order to validate and celebrate its own power. In this coincidence of production through language, the linguistic production of reality, and the language of self-validation resides a fundamental key to understanding the effectiveness, validity, and legitimation of imperial right.

Additional Readings

Marx

Giovanni Arrighi. *The Long Twentieth Century: Money, Power, and the Origins of Our Time*. London: Verso, 1994.
Examines the rise of capitalism and the consolidation of social power over the last 700 years through a synthesis of social theory, comparative history, and political economy.

Étienne Balibar. *The Philosophy of Marx*. Translated by Chris Turner. London: Verso, 2007.
A lucid introduction to the philosophical aspects of Marx's work by a leading French Marxist intellectual.

David Harvey. *The Condition of Postmodernity*. Madden, MA: Blackwell, 1990.
An examination of the cultural, social and, above all, economic conditions that both give rise to and are characteristic of the era of postmodernity. Harvey explains the importance of modernity and postmodernity and the ways in which each influences cultures of production.

Fredric Jameson. *Valences of the Dialectic*. New York: Verso, 2009.
A wide-ranging exploration of the dialectic and an excellent example of contemporary Marxist cultural criticism, the book includes an original account of the base–superstructure relationship in the opening chapter.

Raymond Williams. "Base and Superstructure in Marxist Cultural Theory." *New Left Review* 82 (1973): 3–16.
Williams tests the implications of Marx's base–superstructure model for understanding and interpreting culture and considers the ways in which the Marxist tradition might amend the model.

Schmitt

Giorgio Agamben. *Homo Sacer: Sovereign Power and Bare Life*. Translated by Daniel Heller-Roazen. Stanford, CA: Stanford University Press, 1998.
Drawing on Schmitt's notion of the exception, Agamben considers the existence of those individuals who inhabit spaces outside the political and cultural frameworks of the contemporary world.

Gopal Balakrishnan. *The Enemy: An Intellectual Portrait of Carl Schmitt*. London: Verso, 2002.
A comprehensive reconstruction and analysis of Schmitt's previously untranslated major works presented in narrative form.

Ellen Kennedy. *Constitutional Failure: Carl Schmitt in Weimar*. Durham, NC: Duke University Press, 2004.
An examination of Schmitt and his thought within the context of Weimar Germany. Kennedy seeks to demonstrate the centrality of Schmitt's thinking to modern understandings of the constitutional state.

Carl Schmitt. *Political Theology*. Translated by George Schwab. Chicago: University of Chicago Press, 2005.
The wider work from which "Definition of Sovereignty" was drawn, in which Schmitt addresses the role of the sovereign in more detail and considers the manner in which the political may be considered akin to the theological.

Fanon

Nigel Gibson. *Fanon, the Postcolonial Imagination.* Cambridge: Blackwell, 2003.
An introduction to the ideas, legacy, and person of Fanon. Gibson's book calls for a re-evaluation of Fanon as a key critic of modernity and a leading political figure of the twentieth century.

Lewis Gordon. "Fanon's Tragic Revolutionary Violence." In *Fanon: A Critical Reader*, edited by Lewis Gordon, T. Denean Sharpley-Whiting, and Renee T. White. Malden, MA: Blackwell, 2000, 297–308.
In this essay, Gordon considers the key roles of freedom, violence, and tragedy in Fanon's thinking through the lens of Classical Greece and European philosophers such as Nietzsche and Schopenhauer.

David Macey. *Frantz Fanon: A Biography.* New York: Picador, 2002.
Macey's biography seeks to place Fanon's radical critique and the anger that inspired it within the emotional and political context of his life; in doing so, he argues for a multiplicity of Fanons, beyond the simple figure of the violence-encouraging revolutionary.

John Edgar Wideman. *Fanon.* New York: Houghton, 2008.
A novel based on the life of Fanon. The story is told through three interlinked narratives dealing with fragmented episodes of Fanon's life, the story of a man trying to write a screenplay about Fanon, and a semibiographical tale about the author's own continued fascination with Fanon.

Foucault

Michael Dillon and Andrew Neal, eds. *Foucault on Politics, Security and War.* London: Palgrave, 2008.
A series of essays which investigate the way in which Foucault's notion of biopolitics implies that society is grounded in "race war," while examining and explaining key terms such as biopower, bios, and nomos.

Michel Foucault. *The Birth of Biopolitics.* Translated by Graham Burchell. New York: Macmillan, 2008.

The most recent volume published of Foucault's late lectures, which deals with the role of liberal democracy as a form of biopolitics and engages with contemporary economic theory and practice.

Michel Foucault. *Power.* New York: New Press, 2000.
The third volume of Foucault's miscellaneous writings which collects his work on the nature of power and the way it is exercised.

Beatrice Han. *Foucault's Critical Project: Between Transcendental and Historical.* Translated by Edward Pile. Stanford, CA: Stanford University Press, 2002.
Reconsiders Foucault's work in light of the tension between the transcendental and historical which emerges in his thinking. In the process, Han also examines the influence of Kant, Nietzsche, and Heidegger on Foucault.

Jeffrey T. Nealon. *Foucault beyond Foucault: Power and Its Intensifications since 1984.* Stanford, CA: Stanford University Press, 2008.
Nealon argues for the continued importance of Foucault's notion of power, especially as developed in his middle and latter works, while offering a sense of how to adapt Foucault's notions to account for shifting manifestations of power.

Eric Peras. *Foucault 2.0: Beyond Power and Knowledge.* New York: Other Press, 2006.
Situates Foucault within his original intellectual context in order to argue for a dramatic new revision of his work and legacy.

Deleuze

William Bogard. "Welcome to the Society of Control." In *New Politics of Surveillance and Visibility*, edited by Kevin D. Haggerty and Richard V. Ericson. Toronto: University of Toronto Press, 2006, 55–78.
Bogard examines how the proliferation of surveillance technologies could be considered a particular realization of Deleuze's notion of the "Society of Control."

Ian Buchanan and Nicholas Thoburn, eds. *Deleuze and Politics.* Edinburgh: Edinburgh University Press, 2008.

Includes essays from Manuel DeLanda, Jason Read, Eugene Holland and others, which explore the politics of Deleuze's ideas from varying perspectives.

Peter Hallward. *Out of This World: Deleuze and the Philosophy of Creation*. London: Verso, 2006.
Offers a controversial rereading of Deleuze which attempts to resituate him as a philosopher of the spiritual, rather than the material world.

Adrian Parr. *The Deleuze Dictionary*. New York: Columbia University Press, 2005.
An accessible introduction to the work of Deleuze through an encyclopedic format that defines the major terms used in Deleuze's philosophy, and an exploration of his influences and legacy.

Gregory J. Seigworth. "Cultural Studies and Gilles Deleuze." In *New Cultural Studies: Adventures in Theory*, edited by Gary Hall and Clare Birchall. Athens, GA: University of Georgia Press, 2006, 107–27.
This essay considers the role that Deleuze could play in a new Cultural Studies that brings together the two historical strains of structuralism and culturalism.

Hardt and Negri

Nicholas Brown and Imre Szeman. "The Global Coliseum: On Empire." *Cultural Studies* 16.2 (2002): 177–92.
An interview with Hardt and Negri which introduces, summarizes, and clarifies the major theoretical points of *Empire*, and links the argument therein to the wider discussion of globalization.

Paul A. Passavant and Jodi Dean, eds. *Empire's New Clothes: Reading Hardt and Negri*. New York: Routledge, 2004.
A collection of essays by major thinkers such as Slavoj Žižek and Ernesto Laclau which engage with a number of arguments and controversies that arise out of *Empire* and seek to mark the book's innovations and limitations.

Steven Wright. *Storming Heaven: Class Composition and Struggle in Italian Autonomia*. London: Pluto Press, 2002.

A survey of Autonomous Marxist theory as it developed in Italy, from which *Empire* draws its inspiration.

Slavoj Žižek. "Have Michael Hardt and Antonio Negri Rewritten the Communist Manifesto for the Twenty-First Century?" *Rethinking Marxism* 3/4.13 (2001): 190–8.
Eclectic critic Slavoj Žižek assesses *Empire* as an attempt to rethink the system of capitalism in the twenty-first century, which leads him to a sustained consideration of the continued relevance of Leninist political theory.

General

Jean Baudrillard. *Simulacra and Simulation*. Translated by Shelia Glaser. Ann Arbor, MI: University of Michigan Press, 1994.
A series of essays, most notably "The Precession of Simulacra," in which Baudrillard makes the case for his eclectic and iconoclastic theory of contemporary media and society based around the collapse of the real and simulation into the "hyperreal."

Malcolm Bull. "Vectors of the Biopolitical." *New Left Review* 45 (2007): 7–25.
This essay brings together many of the thinkers in this chapter to consider the ways in which Foucault, Schmitt, and Hardt and Negri, among others, contribute to a successful engagement with contemporary regimes of the political.

Jean Comaroff. "Beyond Bare Life: AIDS, (Bio)Politics, and the Neoliberal Order." *Public Culture* 19.1 (2007): 197–219.
Comaroff considers the effect of power in the modern world system through an analysis of the global effort to fight HIV and AIDS, AIDS activism, and associated medical technology as a site of biopolitics.

Michael Denning. *Culture in the Age of Three Worlds*. New York: Verso, 2003.
An examination of the central role of culture in the politics of the twentieth century, especially in the political drama of modernization, colonialism, and globalization.

Achille Mbembe. "Necropolitics." *Public Culture* 15.1 (2003): 11–40.
Drawing on Foucault's notion of biopower, Mbembe argues that sovereignty of the modern state has become caught up in the power over life and the power to put to death.

James C. Scott. *Weapons of the Weak: Everyday Forms of Peasant Resistance.* New Haven, CT: Yale University Press, 1987.
A study of the ideological and material efforts by peasants in Southeast Asia to resist oppression by way of evasion and rebellion.

Part 3

Ideology

Introduction

Ideology is almost uniformly misconceived as bludgeoning doctrine implemented by technocrats or common sense embraced by miscreants, when it is better understood as an impetus to act in accord with social reproduction, of whose overall processes one necessarily has but a partial understanding. Its history stretches back to pre-Enlightenment times, when eighteenth-century ideologues claimed to unfold the laws of human consciousness. Their long-term goal was to prevent popular use of superstition for political gain and replace such practices with public, scientific projects in which reason would prevail. The concept's use has since changed across disparate contexts. In accounting for its lineage, unitary definitions of ideology tend to address only partial details of its complex use and abuse. Nonetheless, it would be a mistake to leave it scattered in the plural – as in a collection of so many *ideologies* – or to address it only in the form of a remedial simplification. One way to contend with ideology's unruliness is to describe the *primary* way it is employed at present and to explain how it came to be used in this way.

Many thinkers characterize ideology as the ideational impetus of our actions and practices. Related words such as "worldview" or "outlook" describe how we envision and negotiate the social and political sphere, but their speculative or inferential qualities keep us from connecting them to our immediate conduct and behavior. Ideology, on the other hand, represents an imperative to *act*. Thus the genealogy of the concept given in this section traces out changes in our ideas about how these imperatives become habitual or unconscious. We often forget how we think or repress ideology's power over us; thinking is bound to bodily and institutional conditions in ways that do not follow any one causal order or narrative. Theories of ideology track the complex interaction of scales and processes which reproduce dominant institutions of power and structures of meaning, and play a constitutive role in their consolidation into the contours of lived reality.

Contemporary interpretations of ideology assess the historical developments which had led to its modern form. Since the early nineteenth century, when the Industrial Revolution in Western Europe cleaved ever-deeper social divisions, the concept has gained increasing critical traction. Ideology offered a way of understanding the antagonistic relations within and between classes, borne amid the apparently "normal" alienation of everyday life. Laborers and their families had little real relations with bourgeois owners and administrators who wandered the same streets; their labor made the life of bourgeoisie possible, a fact which should have generated unrelenting social tension and disharmony given the economic and social disparities between the two groups. Cultural theorists have examined the dynamics of cultural life to better understand how it allowed these groups to coexist despite these inequalities. They have explored what *mediates* the disparity in the character and quality of work, the length and healthiness of lifespan, and the degree of political and economic self-representation in and between the classes.

Religious belief once provided convincing narratives and symbols to alleviate the daily violations produced by social inequality. Masses were lay followers of their faith, with potential social strife quelled by promises of a better life from the pulpit and in scripture. At the same time, more educated groups embraced religious myths because they provided a comprehensive moral narrative which helped to maintain the social and economic status quo. Residues of socially potent religious thought linger today within theories of ideology. For instance, the church is one of Louis Althusser's "ideological state apparatuses." Althusser likens ideological conduct to the bodily compliance exhibited in religious observance and ritual. Religion is also an example of a social imaginary which palliates actually existing social conditions. While related in some ways to religion, especially in terms of the way it shapes beliefs and bodies, ideology has a distinct place in everyday life because it invites behavior and mediates action without necessary reference to an overall cosmology, narrative of an afterlife, or concerted moral project.

Modern theories of ideology range from narrow conceptions of "false consciousness" to blanket notions of "social determination." In the former, ideology is described as a subject's dogmatic or distorted thought conditioned by both political doctrine and economic necessity. Ideology is imagined as a subjective error or an obstacle to knowledge impeding a truthful understanding of the world. According to this logic, the impetus of critique is to right the subject's opinion and make one increasingly conscious of the truth. In the latter case, ideology explains why and how large groups think and act in a patterned or similar way despite the apparent freedom of individuals to do whatever they want. Critique in this situation seeks to guard consciousness from waves of social and cultural conformity. These notions of ideology remain with us today, writ shorthand in editorials and espoused by experts in various media. Narrow and broad definitions of ideology, however, distance us from the primary problem ideological theorists initially sought to locate. That is, how is one's thinking and disposition *anticipated by* and *integrated within* daily economic, social, and political processes that are fundamentally beyond our ability to perceive them directly?

The pertinence of modern ideological analysis lies not just in its ability to show how thoughts and actions are indirectly mediated. Although ideological critique does not *ensure* we are more conscious of the truth or act independently, it has substantial analytic power to specify the fixity and seeming "innocence" of acculturative influences. More than simply hoping to offer a corrective to cultural controls, the theorists in this section explore and challenge the causes of ideology. As Slavoj Žižek explains, "[Ideology] seems to pop up precisely when we attempt to avoid it, while it fails to appear where one would clearly expect it to dwell."[1] Precisely because they hope to understand the deepest and most powerful sites of social shaping, the places and spaces of ideology are more difficult to locate than in the political valences of newspaper op-ed pieces, government press releases, or cable news channels.

Ideological analysis and critique engages the ways we think *beyond* an empirical order of immediate touch and observation. Contrary to the idea that inside one's skull resides a discrete consciousness shaped exclusively by one's familial upbringing and genetic code, ideological theory brings larger forces to bear on the imaginaries which guide our thought. It demonstrates that the creation of ideas is a far more complex affair than person-to-person mimicry or familial interaction. Ideological theory turns its questioning attention to the cultural sphere beyond biology, habit, and home. For instance, a useful question about ideology is whether it is possible to understand how the Western notion of "progress" or the category of reason affects how we think and act day to day. Long-established processes from far afield have shaped the values and vocabularies by which we think, but our capacity to interpret precisely *how* is far from apparent at the level of the everyday. Might it be possible to imagine accurately this expanse and how it shapes one's values, practices, and actions? While each probes the precise nature of ideology, the essays in this section preclude snap judgments on the topic of how we act, think, and imagine, and under what conditions we do so.

Culture might often seem to be an unalienable part of everyday life. This quality is often a reason to conceive of its processes as proximate, timely, and the source of "agency." But it is clear that things are not nearly as straightforward as this. Against easy formulations, ideology provides the subject with a partial detail to substitute for the whole. As the basis of our actions, this partial knowledge is inevitable (we cannot "know" the whole of what comprises culture) and the *consequences* of this limitation are what ideological critique reckons with.

For example, following the lineage of the thinkers in this section, Žižek reminds us that "an ideology is thus not necessarily 'false': as to its positive content, it can be 'true,' quite accurate, since what really matters is not the asserted content as such but the way this content is related to the subjective position implied by its own process of enunciation."[2] Aside from the falsities of what one might think by the influence of ideology, one needs to proceed with the understanding that illusions are, in part, "truthful" insofar as they are required both for a coherent knowledge of the field of culture and by the operations of social life more generally. To give an example: even if opportunities for social mobility (the possibility of moving from lower classes to higher ones) in virtually every society are far more constrained than one's subjective experience might suggest, it is a social illusion – repeatedly endlessly in "rags to riches" narratives – which helps to maintain order in a class-divided society, and which provides individuals with a source of social hope and possibility.

This section presents theories of ideology written since and including Karl Marx and Friedrich Engels's composition of *The German Ideology* in 1845. Famous for describing ideology as a "camera obscura" or an inversion of real social conditions, Marx and Engels use the term to critique supposedly independent forms of thought and the way political power is legitimized and consolidated over time, especially in the formation of state power. Political legitimacy is ensured, they say, with the production of a *form* of thought which engulfs and appropriates others as its own to build a social consensus:

> each new class which puts itself in the place of one ruling before it, is compelled, merely in order to carry through its aim, to represent its interests as the common interest of all the members of society, that is, expressed in ideal form: it has to give its ideas the form of universality, and represent them as the only rational, universally valid ones.[3]

Ideology is at once a thought process and sociopolitical mode of identification. This quality accounts for difficulties one may have in understanding where it comes from and how it is perpetuated. Dissemination of Marx and Engels's ideas throughout Europe redefined the terms by which the politics of coexistence, capitalist or otherwise, was thought and lived. Strictly speaking, culture was a minor component of Marx's original theory of ideology. Nevertheless, Marx and Engels critiqued the ideological characteristics of metaphysics, morality, and religion to show how they sublimate social relations and mystify subjects into believing their thought is independent from the social circumstances in which they live.

Contemporaries Antonio Gramsci and Georg Lukács likely crossed paths in Vienna sometime around 1924. Both were renowned for their extensive and influential reformulations of Marx and Engels's critique of ideology. Ardent in their political ideals and catalysts of left political movements against the capitalist state in Europe, ideology became their fulcrum for retooling possibilities for collective action. Ideology is described by Lukács and Gramsci not only as a part of culture in need of negation but also as the basis by which social transformation will likely occur. For Lukács, the concept of ideology elucidates class conflict and, more specifically, the clashing interests between modern bourgeois and proletarian groups. The landmark concept of Lukács's work – "reification" – extends Marx's primarily market-based problematic of commodification from processes of ground rent, market circulation, and accumulation to the broader cultural sphere. Lukács reinterprets capital as having more complex effects than merely exploitation. He describes reification in an expansive way: "Its basis is that a relation between people takes on a character of a thing and thus acquires a 'phantom objectivity,' an autonomy that seems so strictly rational and all-embracing as to conceal every trace of its fundamental nature: the relation between people."[4] Social formations and their products appear natural, their contingencies and antagonisms effaced or made non-existent in the commodity's genesis. The ideology accompanying class divisions – i.e., its de facto legitimacy – is countervailed by the consciousness of the proletariat, those who produce the "qualitatively determined unity of the product." Gramsci's adjacent concept of hegemony describes the manner in which the consent of subjugated groups is garnered and maintained. Whereas ideologies (and social control more generally) might be imposed without consent, hegemony is both an indirect form of rule *and* the possibility of a struggle for political power by means other than force of arms. Gramsci thus differentiates "war of position" and "war of maneuver" within hegemony. The former describes the cultural battle conducted within the spheres of media and education which might lead to the overthrow of capitalism, bolstered by overwhelming popular support. The concepts developed by Lukács and Gramsci remain essential for understanding the modern vicissitudes of ideological forms and their sociopolitical ramifications.

Louis Althusser's contribution to ideological theory is twofold. First, he associates ideology with a distinct temporal process which produces "concrete subjects."[5] He is explicitly adverse to theories of consciousness and therefore tries to explain ideology according to how we act out its prescriptions. The subject itself does not precede or merely acquire an ideological opinion – rather, ideological apparatuses precede, "recruit," and "constitute" the subject by the way s/he practices or performs her/his social functions. Althusser presents us with a situational account of ideological formation in which the subject's affective, spontaneous behavior is implicated. Second, subjects are made and *remade* within particular institutions and in their observance of specific forms of authority. The reproduction of social life is the hallmark of ideological interpellation, but the failure of the process is also essential to its continuity. Observance of authority is described by Althusser as an instance in which the subject is "hailed" or made to identify with the terms of identity set by religious institutions, families, the militia, and schools. Identification with state apparatuses is never strictly determinative or unilateral, since although one is *invited* to hear the call of authority one is nevertheless not told what to think; it is this gap that underwrites those ideas of "free will" that are in fact essential to the operations of ideology.

As with many politically charged ideas, disagreement over and reinscription of ideology has produced a complex history of the concept. In addition to the divisions and polemics of theorizing ideology are contributions by other writers who argue that it no longer exists, or that the concept no longer has critical use. Many modern cultural theorists disavow ideology and describe it as anachronistic. For example, ideological theories were supplanted at one time by notions of antagonistic social formations bound together by discursive forms of culture. Stuart Hall's succinct piece examines how ideological critique is changing with the advent of discourse theory. Whatever the result of this trend – connected, perhaps, to the end of the Cold War or to the utopian promise of information technology – it has led to a cultural condition described as "post-ideological." Žižek's essay here describes the persistence of ideology and assails assumptions to the contrary. Central to his argument is that forms of social conditioning and ways of thinking organized by those in power and the institutions of the status quo have as much clout today as they ever have. Cultures of previous epochs and their subjects throughout the nineteenth and early twentieth centuries are described as controlled by the necessary forces of industry and states. Those narratives of progress which might suggest that crude forms of social control are over and done with conceal the way ideology maintains its social force, infusing our relations with one another at every level, from the most intimate and personal to those occurring on a global scale.

Notes

1 Slavoj Žižek, "The Specter of Ideology," in *Mapping Ideology*, ed. Slavoj Žižek (London: Verso, 1998), 4. Reproduced in this volume.
2 Ibid., 8.
3 Karl Marx and Friedrich Engels, *The German Ideology*, ed. C. J. Arthur (London: Lawrence & Wishart, 1974), 65–6. Reproduced in this volume.
4 Georg Lukács, *History and Class Consciousness*, trans. Rodney Livingstone (Cambridge, MA: MIT Press, 1971), 85. Reproduced in this volume.
5 Louis Althusser, "Ideology and Ideological State Apparatuses," in *On Ideology* (London: Verso, 2008), 174. Reproduced in this volume.

16

"The German Ideology" (1845)

Karl Marx and Friedrich Engels

A. Ideology in General, German Ideology in Particular

German criticism has, right up to its latest efforts, never quitted the realm of philosophy. Far from examining its general philosophic premises, the whole body of its inquiries has actually sprung from the soil of a definite philosophical system, that of Hegel. Not only in their answers but in their very questions there was a mystification. This dependence on Hegel is the reason why not one of these modern critics has even attempted a comprehensive criticism of the Hegelian system, however much each professes to have advanced beyond Hegel. Their polemics against Hegel and against one another are confined to this – each extracts one side of the Hegelian system and turns this against the whole system as well as against the sides extracted by the others. To begin with they extracted pure unfalsified Hegelian categories such as "substance" and "self-consciousness," later they desecrated these categories with more secular names such as "species," "the Unique," "Man," etc.

The entire body of German philosophical criticism from Strauss to Stirner is confined to criticism of *religious* conceptions. The critics started from real religion and actual theology. What religious consciousness and a religious conception really meant was determined variously as they went along. Their advance consisted in subsuming the allegedly dominant metaphysical,

Karl Marx and Friedrich Engels. "The German Ideology," pp. 148–60, 172–5 from *The Marx–Engels Reader*, 2nd edn, ed. Robert C. Tucker. New York: W. W. Norton, 1978.

political, juridical, moral and other conceptions under the class of religious or theological conceptions; and similarly in pronouncing political, juridical, moral consciousness as religious or theological, and the political, juridical, moral man – "*man*" in the last resort – as religious. The dominance of religion was taken for granted. Gradually every dominant relationship was pronounced a religious relationship and transformed into a cult, a cult of law, a cult of the State, etc. On all sides it was only a question of dogmas and belief in dogmas. The world was sanctified to an ever-increasing extent till at last our venerable Saint Max was able to canonise it *en bloc* and thus dispose of it once for all.

The Old Hegelians had *comprehended* everything as soon as it was reduced to an Hegelian logical category. The Young Hegelians *criticised* everything by attributing to it religious conceptions or by pronouncing it a theological matter. The Young Hegelians are in agreement with the Old Hegelians in their belief in the rule of religion, of concepts, of a universal principle in the existing world. Only, the one party attacks this dominion as usurpation, while the other extols it as legitimate.

Since the Young Hegelians consider conceptions, thoughts, ideas, in fact all the products of consciousness, to which they attribute an independent existence, as the real chains of men (just as the Old Hegelians declared them the true bonds of human society) it is evident that the Young Hegelians have to fight only against these illusions of the consciousness. Since, according to their fantasy, the relationships of men, all their doings, their chains and their limitations are products of their consciousness, the Young Hegelians logically put to men the moral postulate of exchanging their present consciousness for human, critical or egoistic consciousness, and thus of removing their limitations. This demand to change consciousness amounts to a demand to interpret reality in another way, i.e., to recognise it by means of another interpretation. The Young-Hegelian ideologists, in spite of their allegedly "world-shattering" statements, are the staunchest conservatives. The most recent of them have found the correct expression for their activity when they declare they are only fighting against "*phrases*." They forget, however, that to these phrases they themselves are only opposing other phrases, and that they are in no way combating the real existing world when they are merely combating the phrases of this world. The only results which this philosophic criticism could achieve were a few (and at that thoroughly one-sided) elucidations of Christianity from the point of view of religious history; all the rest of their assertions are only further embellishments of their claim to have furnished, in these unimportant elucidations, discoveries of universal importance.

It has not occurred to any one of these philosophers to inquire into the connection of German philosophy with German reality, the relation of their criticism to their own material surroundings.

The premises from which we begin are not arbitrary ones, not dogmas, but real premises from which abstraction can only be made in the imagination. They are the real individuals, their activity and the material conditions under which they live, both those which they find already existing and those produced by their activity. These premises can thus be verified in a purely empirical way.

The first premise of all human history is, of course, the existence of living human individuals. Thus the first fact to be established is the physical organisation of these individuals and their consequent relation to the rest of nature. Of course, we cannot here go either into the actual physical nature of man, or into the natural conditions in which man finds himself – geological, orohydrographical, climatic and so on. The writing of history must always set out from these natural bases and their modification in the course of history through the action of men.

Men can be distinguished from animals by consciousness, by religion or anything else you like. They themselves begin to distinguish themselves from animals as soon as they begin to *produce* their means of subsistence, a step which is conditioned by their physical organisation. By producing their means of subsistence men are indirectly producing their actual material life.

The way in which men produce their means of subsistence depends first of all on the nature of the actual means of subsistence they find in existence and have to reproduce. This mode of production must not be considered simply as being the reproduction of the physical existence of the individuals. Rather it is a definite form of activity of these individuals, a definite form of expressing their life, a definite *mode of life* on their part. As individuals express their life, so they are. What they are, therefore, coincides with their production, both with *what* they produce and with *how* they produce. The nature of individuals thus depends on the material conditions determining their production.

This production only makes its appearance with the *increase of population*. In its turn this presupposes the *intercourse* [*Verkehr*] of individuals with one another. The form of this intercourse is again determined by production.

The relations of different nations among themselves depend upon the extent to which each has developed its productive forces, the division of labour and internal intercourse. This statement is generally recognised. But not only the relation of one nation to others, but also the whole internal structure of the nation itself depends on the stage of development reached by its production and its internal and external intercourse. How far the productive forces of a nation are developed is shown most manifestly by the degree to which the division of labour has been carried. Each new productive force, insofar as it is not merely a quantitative extension of productive forces already known (for instance the bringing into cultivation of fresh land), causes a further development of the division of labour.

The division of labour inside a nation leads at first to the separation of industrial and commercial from agricultural labour, and hence to the separation of *town* and *country* and to the conflict of their interests.

Its further development leads to the separation of commercial from industrial labour. At the same time through the division of labour inside these various branches there develop various divisions among the individuals co-operating in definite kinds of labour. The relative position of these individual groups is determined by the methods employed in agriculture, industry and commerce (patriarchalism, slavery, estates, classes). These same conditions are to be seen (given a more developed intercourse) in the relations of different nations to one another.

The various stages of development in the division of labour are just so many different forms of ownership, i.e., the existing stage in the division of labour determines also the relations of individuals to one another with reference to the material, instrument, and product of labour.

The first form of ownership is tribal [*Stammeigentum*] ownership. It corresponds to the undeveloped stage of production, at which a people lives by hunting and fishing, by the rearing of beasts or, in the highest stage, agriculture. In the latter case it presupposes a great mass of uncultivated stretches of land. The division of labour is at this stage still very elementary and is confined to a further extension of the natural division of labour existing in the family. The social structure is, therefore, limited to an extension of the family; patriarchal family chieftains, below them the members of the tribe, finally slaves. The slavery latent in the family only develops gradually with the increase of population, the growth of wants, and with the extension of external relations, both of war and of barter.

The second form is the ancient communal and State ownership which proceeds especially from the union of several tribes into a *city* by agreement or by conquest, and which is still accompanied by slavery. Beside communal ownership we already find movable, and later also immovable, private property developing, but as an abnormal form subordinate to communal ownership. The citizens hold power over their labouring slaves only in their community, and on this account alone, therefore, they are bound to the form of communal ownership. It is the communal private property which compels the active citizens to remain in this spontaneously derived form of association over against their slaves. For this reason the whole structure of society based on this communal ownership, and with it the power of the people, decays in the same measure as, in particular, immovable private property evolves. The division of labour is already more developed. We already find the antagonism of town and country; later the antagonism between those states which represent town interests and those which represent country interests, and inside the towns themselves the antagonism between industry and maritime commerce. The class relation between citizens and slaves is now completely developed.

This whole interpretation of history appears to be contradicted by the fact of conquest. Up till now violence, war, pillage, murder and robbery, etc., have been accepted as the driving force of history. Here we must limit ourselves to the chief points and take, therefore, only the most striking example – the destruction of an old civilisation by a barbarous people and the resulting formation of an entirely new organisation of society. (Rome and the barbarians; feudalism and Gaul; the Byzantine Empire and the Turks.) With the conquering barbarian people war itself is still, as indicated above, a regular form of intercourse, which is the more eagerly exploited as the increase in population together with the traditional and, for it, the only possible, crude mode of production gives rise to the need for new means of production. In Italy, on the other hand, the concentration of landed property (caused not only by buying-up and indebtedness but also by inheritance, since loose living being rife and marriage rare, the old families gradually died out and their possessions fell into the hands of a few) and its conversion into grazing-land (caused not only by the usual economic forces still operative today but by the importation of plundered and tribute corn and the resultant lack of demand for Italian corn) brought about the almost total disappearance of the free population. The very slaves died out again and again, and had constantly to be replaced by new ones. Slavery remained the basis of the whole productive system. The plebeians, midway between freemen and slaves, never succeeded in becoming more than a proletarian rabble. Rome indeed never became more than a city; its connection with the provinces was almost exclusively political and could, therefore, easily be broken again by political events.

With the development of private property, we find here for the first time the same conditions which we shall find again, only on a more extensive scale, with modern private property. On the one hand, the concentration of private property, which began very early in Rome (as the Licinian agrarian law proves) and proceeded very rapidly from the time of the civil wars and especially under the Emperors; on the other hand, coupled with this, the transformation of the plebeian small peasantry into a proletariat, which, however, owing to its intermediate position between propertied citizens and slaves, never achieved an independent development.

The third form of ownership is feudal or estate property. If antiquity started out from the town and its little territory, the Middle Ages started out from the *country*. This different starting-point was determined by the sparseness of the population at that time, which was scattered over a large area and which received no large increase from the conquerors. In contrast to Greece and Rome, feudal development at the outset, therefore, extends over a much wider territory, prepared by the Roman conquests and the spread of agriculture at first associated with them. The last centuries of the declining Roman Empire and its conquest by the barbarians destroyed a number of productive forces; agriculture had declined, industry had decayed for want of a market, trade had died out or been violently suspended, the rural and urban population had decreased. From these conditions and the mode of organisation of the conquest determined by them, feudal property developed under the influence of the Germanic military constitution. Like tribal and communal ownership, it is based again on a community; but the directly producing class standing over against it is not, as in the case of the ancient community, the slaves, but the enserfed small peasantry. As soon as feudalism is fully developed, there also arises antagonism to the towns. The hierarchical structure of landownership, and the armed bodies of retainers associated with it, gave the nobility power over the serfs. This feudal organisation was, just as much as the ancient communal ownership, an association against a subjected producing class; but the form of association and the relation to the direct producers were different because of the different conditions of production.

This feudal system of landownership had its counterpart in the *towns* in the shape of corporative property, the feudal organisation of trades. Here property consisted chiefly in the labour of each individual person. The necessity for association against the organised robber nobility, the need for communal covered markets in an age when the industrialist was at the same time a merchant, the growing competition of the escaped serfs swarming into the rising towns, the feudal structure of the whole country: these combined to bring about the *guilds*. The gradually accumulated small capital of individual craftsmen and their stable numbers, as against the growing population, evolved the relation of journeyman and apprentice, which brought into being in the towns a hierarchy similar to that in the country.

Thus the chief form of property during the feudal epoch consisted on the one hand of landed property with serf labour chained to it, and on the other of the labour of the individual with small capital commanding the labour of journeymen. The organisation of both was determined by the restricted conditions of production – the small-scale and primitive cultivation of the land, and the craft type of industry. There was little division of labour in the heyday of feudalism. Each country bore in itself the antithesis of town and country; the division into estates was certainly strongly marked; but apart from the differentiation of princes, nobility, clergy and peasants in the country, and masters, journeymen, apprentices and soon also the rabble of casual labourers in the towns, no division of importance took place. In agriculture it was rendered difficult by the strip-system, beside which the cottage industry of the peasants themselves emerged. In industry there was no division of labour at all in the individual trades themselves, and very little between them. The separation of industry and commerce was found already in existence in older towns; in the newer it only developed later, when the towns entered into mutual relations.

The grouping of larger territories into feudal kingdoms was a necessity for the landed nobility as for the towns. The organisation of the ruling class, the nobility, had, therefore, everywhere a monarch at its head.

The fact is, therefore, that definite individuals who are productively active in a definite way enter into these definite social and political relations. Empirical observation must in each separate instance bring out empirically, and without any mystification and speculation, the connection of the social and political structure with production. The social structure and the State are continually evolving out of the life process of definite individuals, but of individuals, not as they may appear in their own or other people's imagination, but as they *really* are; i.e., as they operate, produce materially, and hence as they work under definite material limits, presuppositions and conditions independent of their will.

The production of ideas, of conceptions, of consciousness, is at first directly interwoven with the material activity and the material intercourse of men, the language of real life. Conceiving, thinking, the mental intercourse of men, appear at this stage as the direct efflux of their material behaviour. The same applies to mental production as expressed in the language of politics, laws, morality, religion, metaphysics, etc., of a people. Men are the producers of their conceptions, ideas, etc. – real, active men, as they are conditioned by a definite development of their productive forces and of the intercourse corresponding to these, up to its furthest forms. Consciousness can never be anything else than conscious existence, and the existence of men is their actual life-process. If in all ideology men and their circumstances appear upside-down as in a *camera obscura*, this phenomenon arises just as much from their historical life-process as the inversion of objects on the retina does from their physical life-process.

In direct contrast to German philosophy which descends from heaven to earth, here we ascend from earth to heaven. That is to say, we do not set out from what men say, imagine, conceive, nor from men as narrated, thought of, imagined, conceived, in order to arrive at men in the flesh. We set out from real, active men, and on the basis of their real life-process we demonstrate the development of the ideological reflexes and echoes of this life-process. The phantoms formed in the human brain are also, necessarily, sublimates of their material life-process, which is empirically verifiable and bound to material premises. Morality, religion, metaphysics, all the rest of ideology and their corresponding forms of consciousness, thus no longer retain the semblance of independence. They have no history, no development; but men, developing their material production and their material intercourse, alter, along with this their real existence, their thinking and the products of their thinking. Life is not determined by consciousness, but consciousness by

life. In the first method of approach the starting-point is consciousness taken as the living individual; in the second method, which conforms to real life, it is the real living individuals themselves, and consciousness is considered solely as *their* consciousness.

This method of approach is not devoid of premises. It starts out from the real premises and does not abandon them for a moment. Its premises are men, not in any fantastic isolation and rigidity, but in their actual, empirically perceptible process of development under definite conditions. As soon as this active life-process is described, history ceases to be a collection of dead facts as it is with the empiricists (themselves still abstract), or an imagined activity of imagined subjects, as with the idealists.

Where speculation ends – in real life – there real, positive science begins: the representation of the practical activity, of the practical process of development of men. Empty talk about consciousness ceases, and real knowledge has to take its place. When reality is depicted, philosophy as an independent branch of knowledge loses its medium of existence. At the best its place can only be taken by a summing-up of the most general results, abstractions which arise from the observation of the historical development of men. Viewed apart from real history, these abstractions have in themselves no value whatsoever. They can only serve to facilitate the arrangement of historical material, to indicate the sequence of its separate strata. But they by no means afford a recipe or schema, as does philosophy, for neatly trimming the epochs of history. On the contrary, our difficulties begin only when we set about the observation and the arrangement – the real depiction – of our historical material, whether of a past epoch or of the present. The removal of these difficulties is governed by premises which it is quite impossible to state here, but which only the study of the actual life-process and the activity of the individuals of each epoch will make evident. We shall select here some of these abstractions, which we use in contradistinction to the ideologists, and shall illustrate them by historical examples.

1. History

Since we are dealing with the Germans, who are devoid of premises, we must begin by stating the first premise of all human existence and, therefore, of all history, the premise, namely, that men must be in a position to live in order to be able to "make history."[1] But life involves before everything else eating and drinking, a habitation, clothing and many other things. The first historical act is thus the production of the means to satisfy these needs, the production of material life itself. And indeed this is an historical act, a fundamental condition of all history, which today, as thousands of years ago, must daily and hourly be fulfilled merely in order to sustain human life. Even when the sensuous world is reduced to a minimum, to a stick as with Saint Bruno, it presupposes the action of producing the stick. Therefore in any interpretation of history one has first of all to observe this fundamental fact in all its significance and all its implications and to accord it its due importance. It is well known that the Germans have never done this, and they have never, therefore, had an *earthly* basis for history and consequently never a historian. The French and the English, even if they have conceived the relation of this fact with so-called history only in an extremely one-sided fashion, particularly as long as they remained in the toils of political ideology, have nevertheless made the first attempts to give the writing of history a materialistic basis by being the first to write histories of civil society, of commerce and industry.

The second point is that the satisfaction of the first need (the action of satisfying, and the instrument of satisfaction which has been acquired) leads to new needs; and this production of new needs is the first historical act. Here we recognise immediately the spiritual ancestry of the great historical wisdom of the Germans who, when they run out of positive material and when they can serve up neither theological nor political nor literary rubbish, assert that this is not history at all, but the "prehistoric era." They do not, however, enlighten us as to how we proceed from this nonsensical "prehistory" to history proper; although, on the other hand, in their historical speculation they seize upon this "prehistory" with especial eagerness because they imagine themselves safe there from interference on the part of "crude facts," and, at the same time, because there they can give full rein to their speculative impulse and set up and knock down hypotheses by the thousand.

The third circumstance which, from the very outset, enters into historical development, is that men, who daily remake their own life, begin to make other men, to propagate their kind: the relation between man and woman, parents and children, the *family*. The family, which to begin with is the only social relationship, becomes later, when increased needs create new social relations and the increased population new needs, a subordinate one (except in Germany), and must then be treated and analysed according to the existing empirical data, not according to "the concept of the family," as is the custom in Germany.[2] These three aspects of social activity are not of course to be taken as three different stages, but just as three aspects or, to make it clear to the Germans, three "moments," which have existed simultaneously since the dawn of history and the first men, and which still assert themselves in history today.

The production of life, both of one's own in labour and of fresh life in procreation, now appears as a double relationship: on the one hand as a natural, on the other as a social relationship. By social we understand the co-operation of several individuals, no matter under what conditions, in what manner and to what end. It follows from this that a certain mode of production, or industrial stage, is always combined with a certain mode of co-operation, or social stage, and this mode of co-operation is itself a "productive force." Further, that the multitude of productive forces accessible to men determines the nature of society, hence, that the "history of humanity" must always be studied and treated in relation to the history of industry and exchange. But it is also clear how in Germany it is impossible to write this sort of history, because the Germans lack not only the necessary power of comprehension and the material but also the "evidence of their senses," for across the Rhine you cannot have any experience of these things since history has stopped happening. Thus it is quite obvious from the start that there exists a materialistic connection of men with one another, which is determined by their needs and their mode of production, and which is as old as men themselves. This connection is ever taking on new forms, and thus presents a "history" independently of the existence of any political or religious nonsense which would especially hold men together.

Only now, after having considered four moments, four aspects of the primary historical relationships, do we find that man also possesses "consciousness";[3] but, even so, not inherent, not "pure" consciousness. From the start the "spirit" is afflicted with the curse of being "burdened" with matter, which here makes its appearance in the form of agitated layers of air, sounds, in short, of language. Language is as old as consciousness, language *is* practical consciousness that exists also for other men, and for that reason alone it really exists for me personally as well; language, like consciousness, only arises from the need, the necessity, of intercourse with other men. Where there exists a relationship, it exists for me: the animal does not enter into "*relations*" with anything, it does not enter into any relation at all. For the animal, its relation to others does not exist as a relation. Consciousness is, therefore, from the very beginning a social product, and remains so as long as men exist at all. Consciousness is at first, of course, merely consciousness concerning the *immediate* sensuous environment and consciousness of the limited connection with other persons and things outside the individual who is growing self-conscious. At the same time it is consciousness of nature, which first appears to men as a completely alien, all-powerful and unassailable force, with which men's relations are purely animal and by which they are overawed like beasts; it is thus a purely animal consciousness of nature (natural religion).

We see here immediately: this natural religion or this particular relation of men to nature is determined by the form of society and vice versa. Here, as everywhere, the identity of nature and man appears in such a way that the restricted relation of men to nature determines their restricted relation to one another, and their restricted relation to one another determines men's restricted relation to nature, just because nature is as yet hardly modified historically; and, on the other hand, man's consciousness of the necessity of associating with the individuals around him is the beginning of the consciousness that he is living in society at all. This beginning is as animal as social life itself at this stage. It is mere herd-consciousness, and at this point man is only distinguished from sheep by the fact that with him consciousness takes the place of instinct or that his instinct is a conscious one. This sheep-like or tribal consciousness receives its further development and extension through increased productivity, the increase of needs, and, what is fundamental to both of these, the increase of population. With these there develops the division of labour, which was originally nothing but the division of labour in the sexual act, then that division of labour which develops spontaneously or "naturally" by virtue of natural predisposition (e.g., physical strength), needs, accidents, etc., etc. Division of labour only becomes truly such from the moment when a division of material and mental labour appears.[4] From this moment onwards consciousness *can* really flatter itself that it is something other than consciousness of existing practice, that it *really* represents something without representing something real; from now on consciousness is in a position to emancipate itself from the world and to proceed to the formation of "pure" theory, theology, philosophy, ethics, etc. But even if this theory, theology, philosophy, ethics, etc., comes into contradiction with the existing relations, this can only occur because existing social relations have come into contradiction with existing forces of production; this, moreover, can also occur in a particular national sphere of relations through the appearance of the contradiction, not within the national orbit, but between this national consciousness and the practice of other nations,[5] i.e., between the national and the general consciousness of a nation (as we see it now in Germany).

Moreover, it is quite immaterial what consciousness starts to do on its own: out of all such muck we get only the one inference that these three moments, the forces of production, the state of society, and consciousness, can and must come into contradiction with one another, because the *division of labour* implies the possibility, nay the fact that intellectual and material activity – enjoyment and labour, production and consumption – devolve on different individuals, and that the only possibility of their not coming into contradiction lies in the negation in its turn of the division of labour. It is self-evident, moreover, that "spectres," "bonds," "the higher being," "concept," "scruple," are merely the idealistic, spiritual expression, the conception apparently of the isolated individual, the image of very empirical fetters and limitations, within which the mode of production of life and the form of intercourse coupled with it move.

With the division of labour, in which all these contradictions are implicit, and which in its turn is based on the natural division of labour in the family and the separation of society into individual families opposed to one another, is given simultaneously the *distribution,* and indeed the *unequal* distribution, both quantitative and qualitative, of labour and its products, hence property: the nucleus, the first form, of which lies in the family, where wife and children are the slaves of the husband. This latent slavery in the family, though still very crude, is the first property, but even at this early stage it corresponds perfectly to the definition of modern economists who call it the power of disposing of the labour-power of others. Division of labour and private property are, moreover, identical expressions: in the one the same thing is affirmed with reference to activity as is affirmed in the other with reference to the product of the activity.

Further, the division of labour implies the contradiction between the interest of the separate individual or the individual family and the communal interest of all individuals who have intercourse with one another. And indeed, this communal interest does not exist merely in the imagination, as the "general interest," but first of all in reality, as the mutual interdependence of the individuals among whom the labour is divided. And finally, the division of labour offers us the first example of how, as long as man remains in natural society, that is, as long as a cleavage exists between the particular and the common interest, as long, therefore, as activity is not voluntarily, but naturally, divided, man's own deed becomes an alien power opposed to him, which enslaves him instead of being controlled by him. For as soon as the distribution of labour comes into being, each man has a particular, exclusive sphere of activity, which is forced upon him and from which he cannot escape. He is a hunter, a fisherman, a shepherd, or a critical critic, and must remain so if he does not want to lose his means of livelihood; while in communist society, where nobody has one exclusive sphere of activity but each can become accomplished in any branch he wishes, society regulates the general production and thus makes it possible for me to do one thing today and another tomorrow, to hunt in the morning, fish in the afternoon, rear cattle in the evening, criticise after dinner, just as I have a mind, without ever becoming hunter, fisherman, shepherd

or critic. This fixation of social activity, this consolidation of what we ourselves produce into an objective power above us, growing out of our control, thwarting our expectations, bringing to naught our calculations, is one of the chief factors in historical development up till now.

[…]

History is nothing but the succession of the separate generations, each of which exploits the materials, the capital funds, the productive forces handed down to it by all preceding generations, and thus, on the one hand, continues the traditional activity in completely changed circumstances and, on the other, modifies the old circumstances with a completely changed activity. This can be speculatively distorted so that later history is made the goal of earlier history, e.g., the goal ascribed to the discovery of America is to further the eruption of the French Revolution. Thereby history receives its own special aims and becomes "a person ranking with other persons" (to wit: "Self-Consciousness, Criticism, the Unique," etc.), while what is designated with the words "destiny," "goal," "germ," or "ideal" of earlier history is nothing more than an abstraction formed from later history, from the active influence which earlier history exercises on later history.

The further the separate spheres, which act on one another, extend in the course of this development, the more the original isolation of the separate nationalities is destroyed by the developed mode of production and intercourse and the division of labour between various nations naturally brought forth by these, the more history becomes world history. Thus, for instance, if in England a machine is invented, which deprives countless workers of bread in India and China, and overturns the whole form of existence of these empires, this invention becomes a world-historical fact. Or again, take the case of sugar and coffee which have proved their world-historical importance in the nineteenth century by the fact that the lack of these products, occasioned by the Napoleonic Continental System, caused the Germans to rise against Napoleon, and thus became the real basis of the glorious Wars of Liberation of 1813. From this it follows that this transformation of history into world history is not indeed a mere abstract act on the part of the "self-consciousness," the world spirit, or of any other metaphysical spectre, but a quite material, empirically verifiable act, an act the proof of which every individual furnishes as he comes and goes, eats, drinks and clothes himself.

The ideas of the ruling class are in every epoch the ruling ideas: i.e., the class which is the ruling *material* force of society, is at the same time its ruling *intellectual* force. The class which has the means of material production at its disposal, has control at the same time over the means of mental production, so that thereby, generally speaking, the ideas of those who lack the means of mental production are subject to it. The ruling ideas are nothing more than the ideal expression of the dominant material relationships, the dominant material relationships grasped as ideas; hence of the relationships which make the one class the ruling one, therefore, the ideas of its dominance. The individuals composing the ruling class possess among other things consciousness, and therefore think. Insofar, therefore, as they rule as a class and determine the extent and compass of an epoch, it is self-evident that they do this in its whole range, hence among other things rule also as thinkers, as producers of ideas, and regulate the production and distribution of the ideas of their age: thus their ideas are the ruling ideas of the epoch. For instance, in an age and in a country where royal power, aristocracy and bourgeoisie are contending for mastery and where, therefore, mastery is shared, the doctrine of the separation of powers proves to be the dominant idea and is expressed as an "eternal law."

The division of labour, which we have already seen above as one of the chief forces of history up till now, manifests itself also in the ruling class as the division of mental and material labour, so that inside this class one part appears as the thinkers of the class (its active, conceptive ideologists, who make the perfecting of the illusion of the class about itself their chief source of livelihood), while the others' attitude to these ideas and illusions is more passive and receptive, because they are in reality the active members of this class and have less time to make up illusions and ideas about themselves. Within this class this cleavage can even develop into a certain opposition and hostility between the two parts, which, however, in the case of a practical collision, in which the class itself is endangered, automatically comes to nothing, in which case there also vanishes the semblance that the ruling ideas were not the ideas of the ruling class and had a power

distinct from the power of this class. The existence of revolutionary ideas in a particular period presupposes the existence of a revolutionary class; about the premises for the latter sufficient has already been said above.

If now in considering the course of history we detach the ideas of the ruling class from the ruling class itself and attribute to them an independent existence, if we confine ourselves to saying that these or those ideas were dominant at a given time, without bothering ourselves about the conditions of production and the producers of these ideas, if we thus ignore the individuals and world conditions which are the source of the ideas, we can say, for instance, that during the time that the aristocracy was dominant, the concepts honour, loyalty, etc., were dominant, during the dominance of the bourgeoisie the concepts freedom, equality, etc. The ruling class itself on the whole imagines this to be so. This conception of history, which is common to all historians, particularly since the eighteenth century, will necessarily come up against the phenomenon that increasingly abstract ideas hold sway, i.e., ideas which increasingly take on the form of universality. For each new class which puts itself in the place of one ruling before it, is compelled, merely in order to carry through its aim, to represent its interest as the common interest of all the members of society, that is, expressed in ideal form: it has to give its ideas the form of universality, and represent them as the only rational, universally valid ones. The class making a revolution appears from the very start, if only because it is opposed to a *class*, not as a class but as the representative of the whole of society; it appears as the whole mass of society confronting the one ruling class.[6] It can do this because, to start with, its interest really is more connected with the common interest of all other non-ruling classes, because under the pressure of hitherto existing conditions its interest has not yet been able to develop as the particular interest of a particular class. Its victory, therefore, benefits also many individuals of the other classes which are not winning a dominant position, but only insofar as it now puts these individuals in a position to raise themselves into the ruling class. When the French bourgeoisie overthrew the power of the aristocracy, it thereby made it possible for many proletarians to raise themselves above the proletariat, but only insofar as they became bourgeois. Every new class, therefore, achieves its hegemony only on a broader basis than that of the class ruling previously, whereas the opposition of the non-ruling class against the new ruling class later develops all the more sharply and profoundly. Both these things determine the fact that the struggle to be waged against this new ruling class, in its turn, aims at a more decided and radical negation of the previous conditions of society than could all previous classes which sought to rule.

This whole semblance, that the rule of a certain class is only the rule of certain ideas, comes to a natural end, of course, as soon as class rule in general ceases to be the form in which society is organised, that is to say, as soon as it is no longer necessary to represent a particular interest as general or the "general interest" as ruling.

Once the ruling ideas have been separated from the ruling individuals and, above all, from the relationships which result from a given stage of the mode of production, and in this way the conclusion has been reached that history is always under the sway of ideas, it is very easy to abstract from these various ideas "*the* idea," the notion, etc., as the dominant force in history, and thus to understand all these separate ideas and concepts as "forms of self-determination" on the part of *the* concept developing in history. It follows then naturally, too, that all the relationships of men can be derived from the concept of man, man as conceived, the essence of man, *Man*. This has been done by the speculative philosophers. Hegel himself confesses at the end of the *Geschichtsphilosophie* that he "has considered the progress of the *concept* only" and has represented in history the "true *theodicy*." Now one can go back again to the producers of the "concept," to the theorists, ideologists and philosophers, and one comes then to the conclusion that the philosophers, the thinkers as such, have at all times been dominant in history: a conclusion, as we see, already expressed by Hegel. The whole trick of proving the hegemony of the spirit in history (hierarchy Stirner calls it) is thus confined to the following three efforts.

No. 1. One must separate the ideas of those ruling for empirical reasons, under empirical conditions and as empirical individuals, from these actual rulers, and thus recognise the rule of ideas or illusions in history.

No. 2. One must bring an order into this rule of ideas, prove a mystical connection among the successive ruling ideas, which is managed by understanding them as "acts of self-determination on the part of the concept" (this is possible because by virtue of their empirical basis these ideas are really connected with one another and because, conceived as *mere* ideas, they become self-distinctions, distinctions made by thought).

No. 3. To remove the mystical appearance of this "self-determining concept" it is changed into a person – "Self-Consciousness" – or, to appear thoroughly materialistic, into a series of persons, who represent the "concept" in history, into the "thinkers," the "philosophers," the ideologists, who again are understood as the manufacturers of history, as the "council of guardians," as the rulers.[7] Thus the whole body of materialistic elements has been removed from history and now full rein can be given to the speculative steed.

Whilst in ordinary life every shopkeeper is very well able to distinguish between what somebody professes to be and what he really is, our historians have not yet won even this trivial insight. They take every epoch at its word and believe that everything it says and imagines about itself is true.

This historical method which reigned in Germany and especially the reason why, must be understood from its connection with the illusion of ideologists in general, e.g., the illusions of the jurists, politicians (of the practical statesmen among them, too), from the dogmatic dreamings and distortions of these fellows; this is explained perfectly easily from their practical position in life, their job, and the division of labour.

Notes

1 Marginal note by Marx: "*Hegel*. Geological, hydrographical, etc., conditions. Human bodies. Needs, labour."
2 The building of houses. With savages each family has as a matter of course its own cave or hut like the separate family tent of the nomads. This separate domestic economy is made only the more necessary by the further development of private property. With the agricultural peoples a communal domestic economy is just as impossible as a communal cultivation of the soil. A great advance was the building of towns. In all previous periods, however, the abolition of individual economy, which is

inseparable from the abolition of private property, was impossible for the simple reason that the material conditions governing it were not present. The setting-up of a communal domestic economy presupposes the development of machinery, of the use of natural forces and of many other productive forces – e.g., of water-supplies, of gas-lighting, steam-heating, etc., the removal [of the antagonism] of town and country. Without these conditions a communal economy would not in itself form a new productive force; lacking any material basis and resting on a purely theoretical foundation, it would be a mere freak and would end in nothing more than a monastic economy. – What was possible can be seen in the towns brought about by condensation and the erection of communal buildings for various definite purposes (prisons, barracks, etc.). That the abolition of individual economy is inseparable from the abolition of the family is self-evident. [*Marx*]

3   Marginal note by Marx: "Men have history because they must *produce* their life, and because they must produce it moreover in a *certain* way: this is determined by their physical organisation; their consciousness is determined in just the same way."

4   Marginal note by Marx: "The first form of ideologists, *priests*, is concurrent."

5   Marginal note by Marx: "*Religion*. The Germans and *ideology* as such."

6   Marginal note by Marx: "Universality corresponds to (1) the class versus the estate, (2) the competition, world-wide intercourse, etc., (3) the great numerical strength of the ruling class, (4) the illusion of the *common* interests (in the beginning this illusion is true), (5) the delusion of the ideologists and the division of labour."

7   Marginal note by Marx: "Man = the 'rational human spirit.'"

17

"Reification and the Consciousness of the Proletariat" (1923)

Georg Lukács

To be radical is to go to the root of the matter. For man, however, the root is man himself. (Marx: *Critique of Hegel's Philosophy of Right.*)

It is no accident that Marx should have begun with an analysis of commodities when, in the two great works of his mature period, he set out to portray capitalist society in its totality and to lay bare its fundamental nature. For at this stage in the history of mankind there is no problem that does not ultimately lead back to that question and there is no solution that could not be found in the solution to the riddle of commodity-structure. Of course the problem can only be discussed with this degree of generality if it achieves the depth and breadth to be found in Marx's own analyses. That is to say, the problem of commodities must not be considered in isolation or even regarded as the central problem in economics, but as the central, structural problem of capitalist society in all its aspects. Only in this case can the structure of commodity-relations be made to yield a model of all the objective forms of bourgeois society together with all the subjective forms corresponding to them.

Georg Lukács, "Reification and the Consciousness of the Proletariat," pp. 83–110 from *History and Class Consciousness: Studies in Marxist Dialectics*, trans. Rodney Livingstone. Cambridge, MA: MIT Press, 1971. Copyright © 1971, Massachusetts Institute of Technology, by permission of the MIT Press.

I The Phenomenon of Reification

1

The essence of commodity-structure has often been pointed out. Its basis is that a relation between people takes on the character of a thing and thus acquires a 'phantom objectivity', an autonomy that seems so strictly rational and all-embracing as to conceal every trace of its fundamental nature: the relation between people. It is beyond the scope of this essay to discuss the central importance of this problem for economics itself. Nor shall we consider its implications for the economic doctrines of the vulgar Marxists which follow from their abandonment of this starting-point.

Our intention here is to *base* ourselves on Marx's economic analyses and to proceed from there to a discussion of the problems growing out of the fetish character of commodities, both as an objective form and also as a subjective stance corresponding to it. Only by understanding this can we obtain a clear insight into the ideological problems of capitalism and its downfall.

Before tackling the problem itself we must be quite clear in our minds that commodity fetishism is a *specific* problem of our age, the age of modern capitalism. Commodity exchange and the corresponding subjective and objective commodity relations existed, as we know, when society was still very primitive. What is at issue *here*, however, is the question: how far is commodity exchange together with its structural consequences able to influence the *total* outer and inner life of society? Thus the extent to which such exchange is the dominant form of metabolic change in a society cannot simply be treated in quantitative terms – as would harmonise with the modern modes of thought already eroded by the reifying effects of the dominant commodity form. The distinction between a society where this form is dominant, permeating every expression of life, and a society where it only makes an episodic appearance is essentially one of quality. For depending on which is the case, all the subjective and objective phenomena in the societies concerned are objectified in qualitatively different ways.

Marx lays great stress on the essentially episodic appearance of the commodity form in primitive societies: "Direct barter, the original natural form of exchange, represents rather the beginning of the transformation of use values into commodities, than that of commodities into money. Exchange value has as yet no form of its own, but is still directly bound up with use-value. This is manifested in two ways. Production, in its entire organisation, aims at the creation of use-values and not of exchange values and it is only when their supply exceeds the measure of consumption that use-values cease to be use-values, and become means of exchange, i.e. commodities. At the same time, they become commodities only within the limits of being direct use-values distributed at opposite poles, so that the commodities to be exchanged by their possessors must be use-values to both – each commodity to its non-possessor. As a matter of fact, the exchange of commodities originates not within the primitive communities, but where they end, on their borders at the few points where they come in contact with other communities. That is where barter begins, and from here it strikes back into the interior of the community, decomposing it."[1] We note that the observation about the disintegrating effect of a commodity exchange directed in upon itself clearly shows the qualitative change engendered by the dominance of commodities.

However, even when commodities have this impact on the internal structure of a society, this does not suffice to make them constitutive of that society. To achieve that it would be necessary – as we emphasized above – for the commodity structure to penetrate society in all its aspects and to remould it in its own image. It is not enough merely to establish an external link with independent processes concerned with the production of exchange values. The qualitative difference between the commodity as one form among many regulating the metabolism of human society and the commodity as the universal structuring principle has effects over and above the fact that the commodity relation as an isolated phenomenon exerts a negative influence at best on the structure and organisation of society. The distinction also has repercussions upon the nature and validity of the category itself. Where the commodity is universal it manifests itself differently from the commodity as a particular, isolated, non-dominant phenomenon.

The fact that the boundaries lack sharp definition must not be allowed to blur the qualitative nature of the decisive distinction. The situation where commodity exchange is not dominant has been defined by Marx as follows: "The quantitative ratio in which products are exchanged is at first quite arbitrary. They assume the form of commodities inasmuch as they are exchangeables, i.e. expressions of one and the same third. Continued exchange and more regular reproduction for exchange reduces this arbitrariness more and more. But at first not for the producer and consumer, but for their go-between, the merchant, who compares money-prices and pockets the difference. It is through his own movements that he establishes equivalence. Merchant's capital is originally merely the intervening movement between extremes which it does not control and between premises which it does not create."[2]

And *this* development of the commodity to the point where it becomes the dominant form in society did not take place until the advent of modern capitalism. Hence it is not to be wondered at that the personal nature of economic relations was still understood clearly on occasion at the start of capitalist development, but that as the process advanced and forms became more complex and less direct, it became increasingly difficult and rare to find anyone penetrating the veil of reification. Marx sees the matter in this way: "In preceding forms of society this economic mystification arose principally with respect to money and interest-bearing capital. In the nature of things it is excluded, in the first place, where production for the use-value, for immediate personal requirements, predominates; and secondly, where slavery or serfdom form the broad foundation of social production, as in antiquity and during the Middle Ages. Here, the domination of the producers by the conditions of production is concealed by the relations of dominion and servitude which appear and are evident as the direct motive power of the process of production."[3]

The commodity can only be understood in its undistorted essence when it becomes the universal category of society as a whole. Only in this context does the reification produced by commodity relations assume decisive importance both for the objective evolution of society and for the stance adopted by men towards it. Only then does the commodity become crucial for the subjugation of men's consciousness to the forms in which this reification finds expression and for their attempts to comprehend the process or to rebel against its disastrous effects and liberate themselves from servitude to the 'second nature' so created.

Marx describes the basic phenomenon of reification as follows: "A commodity is therefore a mysterious thing, simply because in it the social character of men's labour appears to them as an objective character stamped upon the product of that labour; because the relation of the producers to the sum total of their own labour is presented to them as a social relation, existing not between themselves, but between the products of their labour. This is the reason why the products of labour become commodities, social things whose qualities are at the same time perceptible and imperceptible by the senses. ... It is only a definite social relation between men that assumes, in their eyes, the fantastic form of a relation between things."[4]

What is of central importance here is that because of this situation a man's own activity, his own labour becomes something objective and independent of him, something that controls him by virtue of an autonomy alien to man. There is both an objective and a subjective side to this phenomenon. *Objectively* a world of objects and relations between things springs into being (the world of commodities and their movements on the market). The laws governing these objects are indeed gradually discovered by man, but even so they confront him as invisible forces that generate their own power. The individual can use his knowledge of these laws to his own advantage, but he is not able to modify the process by his own activity. *Subjectively* – where the market economy has been fully developed – a man's activity becomes estranged from himself, it turns into a commodity which, subject to the non-human objectivity of the natural laws of society, must go its own way independently of man just like any consumer article. "What is characteristic of the capitalist age," says Marx, "is that in the eyes of the labourer himself labour-power assumes the form of a commodity belonging to him. On the other hand it is only at this moment that the commodity form of the products of labour becomes general."[5]

Thus the universality of the commodity form is responsible both objectively and subjectively for the abstraction of the human labour incorporated in commodities. (On the other hand, this universality becomes historically possible because this process of abstraction has been completed.) *Objectively*, in so far as the commodity form facilitates the equal exchange of qualitatively different objects, it can only exist if that formal equality is in fact recognised – at any rate in *this* relation, which indeed confers upon them their commodity nature. *Subjectively*, this formal equality of human labour in the abstract is not only the common factor to which the various commodities are reduced; it also becomes the real principle governing the actual production of commodities.

Clearly, it cannot be our aim here to describe even in outline the growth of the modern process of labour, of the isolated, 'free' labourer and of the division of labour. Here we need only establish that labour, abstract, equal, comparable labour, measurable with increasing precision according to the time socially necessary for its accomplishment, the labour of the capitalist division of labour existing both as the presupposition and the product of capitalist production, is born only in the course of the development of the capitalist system. Only then does it become a category of society influencing decisively the objective form of things and people in the society thus emerging, their relation to nature and the possible relations of men to each other.[6]

If we follow the path taken by labour in its development from the handicraft via co-operation and manufacture to machine industry we can see a continuous trend towards greater rationalisation, the progressive elimination of the qualitative, human and individual attributes of the worker. On the one hand, the process of labour is progressively broken down into abstract, rational, specialised operations so that the worker loses contact with the finished product and his work is reduced to the mechanical repetition of a specialised set of actions. On the other hand, the period of time necessary for work to be accomplished (which forms the basis of rational calculation) is converted, as mechanisation and rationalisation are intensified, from a merely empirical average figure to an objectively calculable work-stint that confronts the worker as a fixed and established reality. With the modern 'psychological' analysis of the work-process (in Taylorism) this rational mechanisation extends right into the worker's 'soul': even his psychological attributes are separated from his total personality and placed in opposition to it so as to facilitate their integration into specialised rational systems and their reduction to statistically viable concepts.[7]

We are concerned above all with the *principle* at work here: the principle of rationalisation based on what is and *can be calculated*. The chief changes undergone by the subject and object of the economic process are as follows: (1) in the first place, the mathematical analysis of work-processes denotes a break with the organic, irrational and qualitatively determined unity of the product. Rationalisation in the sense of being able to predict with ever greater precision all the results to be achieved is only to be acquired by the exact breakdown of every complex into its elements and by the study of the special laws governing production. Accordingly it must declare war on the organic manufacture of whole products based on the *traditional amalgam of empirical experiences of work*: rationalisation is unthinkable without specialisation.[8]

The finished article ceases to be the object of the work-process. The latter turns into the objective synthesis of rationalised special systems whose unity is determined by pure calculation and which must therefore seem to be arbitrarily connected with each other. This destroys the organic necessity with which inter-related special operations are unified in the end-product. The unity of a product as a *commodity* no longer coincides with its unity as a use-value: as society becomes more radically capitalistic the increasing technical autonomy of the special operations involved in production is expressed also, as an economic autonomy, as the growing relativisation of the commodity character of a product at the various stages of production.[9] It is thus possible to separate forcibly the production of a use-value in time and space. This goes hand in hand with the union in time and space of special operations that are related to a set of heterogeneous use-values.

(2) In the second place, this fragmentation of the object of production necessarily entails the fragmentation of its subject. In consequence of the rationalisation of the work-process the human qualities and idiosyncrasies of the worker appear increasingly as *mere sources of error* when contrasted with these abstract special laws functioning according to rational predictions. Neither objectively nor in his relation to his work does man appear as the authentic master of the process; on the contrary, he is a mechanical part incorporated into a mechanical system. He finds it already pre-existing and self-sufficient, it functions independently of him and he has to conform to its laws whether he likes it or not.[10] As labour is progressively rationalised and mechanised his lack of will is reinforced by the way in which his activity becomes less and less active and more and more *contemplative*.[11] The contemplative stance adopted towards a process mechanically conforming to fixed laws and enacted independently of man's consciousness and impervious to human intervention, i.e. a perfectly closed system, must likewise transform the basic categories of man's immediate attitude to the world: it reduces space and time to a common denominator and degrades time to the dimension of space.

Marx puts it thus: "Through the subordination of man to the machine the situation arises in which men are effaced by their labour; in which the pendulum of the clock has become as accurate a measure of the relative activity of two workers as it is of the speed of two locomotives. Therefore, we should not say that one man's hour is worth another man's hour, but rather that one man during an hour is worth just as much as another man during an hour. Time is everything, man is nothing; he is at the most the incarnation of time.

Quality no longer matters. Quantity alone decides everything: hour for hour, day for day. ...."[12]

Thus time sheds its qualitative, variable, flowing nature; it freezes into an exactly delimited, quantifiable continuum filled with quantifiable 'things' (the reified, mechanically objectified 'performance' of the worker, wholly separated from his total human personality): in short, it becomes space.[13] In this environment where time is transformed into abstract, exactly measurable, physical space, an environment at once the cause and effect of the scientifically and mechanically fragmented and specialised production of the object of labour, the subjects of labour must likewise be rationally fragmented. On the one hand, the objectification of their labour-power into something opposed to their total personality (a process already accomplished with the sale of that labour-power as a commodity) is now made into the permanent ineluctable reality of their daily life. Here, too, the personality can do no more than look on helplessly while its own existence is reduced to an isolated particle and fed into an alien system. On the other hand, the mechanical disintegration of the process of production into its components also destroys those bonds that had bound individuals to a community in the days when production was still 'organic'. In this respect, too, mechanisation makes of them isolated abstract atoms whose work no longer brings them together directly and organically; it becomes mediated to an increasing extent exclusively by the abstract laws of the mechanism which imprisons them.

The internal organisation of a factory could not possibly have such an effect – even within the factory itself – were it not for the fact that it contained in concentrated form the whole structure of capitalist society. Oppression and an exploitation that knows no bounds and scorns every human dignity were known even to pre-capitalist ages. So too was mass production with mechanical, standardised labour, as we can see, for instance, with canal construction in Egypt and Asia Minor and the mines in Rome.[14] But mass projects of this type could never be *rationally mechanised*; they remained isolated phenomena within a community that organised its production on a different ('natural') basis and which therefore lived a different life. The slaves subjected to this exploitation, therefore, stood outside what was thought of as 'human' society and even the greatest and noblest thinkers of the time were unable to consider their fate as that of human beings.

As the commodity becomes universally dominant, this situation changes radically and qualitatively. The fate of the worker becomes the fate of society as a whole; indeed, this fate must become universal as otherwise industrialisation could not develop in this direction. For it depends on the emergence of the 'free' worker who is freely able to take his labour-power to market and offer it for sale as a commodity 'belonging' to him, a thing that he 'possesses'.

While this process is still incomplete the methods used to extract surplus labour are, it is true, more obviously brutal than in the later, more highly developed phase, but the process of reification of work and hence also of the consciousness of the worker is much less advanced. Reification requires that a society should learn to satisfy all its needs in terms of commodity exchange. The separation of the producer from his means of production, the dissolution and destruction of all 'natural' production units, etc., and all the social and economic conditions necessary for the emergence of modern capitalism tend to replace 'natural' relations which exhibit human relations more plainly by rationally reified relations. "The social relations between individuals in the performance of their labour," Marx observes with reference to pre-capitalist societies, "appear at all events as their own personal relations, and are not disguised under the shape of social relations between the products of labour."[15]

But this implies that the principle of rational mechanisation and calculability must embrace every aspect of life. Consumer articles no longer appear as the products of an organic process within a community (as for example in a village community). They now appear, on the one hand, as abstract members of a species identical by definition with its other members and, on the other hand, as isolated objects the possession or non-possession of which depends on rational calculations. Only when the whole life of society is thus fragmented into the isolated acts of commodity exchange can the 'free' worker come into being; at the same time his fate becomes the typical fate of the whole society.

Of course, this isolation and fragmentation is only apparent. The movement of commodities on the market, the birth of their value, in a word, the real framework of every rational calculation is not merely subject to strict laws but also presupposes the strict ordering of all that happens. The atomisation of the individual is, then, only the reflex in consciousness of the fact that the 'natural laws' of capitalist production have been extended to cover every manifestation of life in society; that – for the first time in history – the whole of society is subjected, or tends to be subjected, to a unified economic process, and that the fate of every member of society is determined by unified laws. (By contrast, the organic unities of pre-capitalist societies organised their metabolism largely in independence of each other.)

However, if this atomisation is only an illusion it is a necessary one. That is to say, the immediate, practical as well as intellectual confrontation of the individual with society, the immediate production and reproduction of life – in which for the individual the commodity structure of all 'things' and their obedience to 'natural laws' is found to exist already in a finished form, as something immutably given – could only take place in the form of rational and isolated acts of exchange between isolated commodity owners. As emphasised above, the worker, too, must present himself as the 'owner' of his labour-power, as if it were a commodity. His specific situation is defined by the fact that his labour-power is his only possession. His fate is typical of society as a whole in that this self-objectification, this transformation of a human function into a commodity reveals in all its starkness the dehumanised and dehumanising function of the commodity relation.

2

This rational objectification conceals above all the immediate – qualitative and material – character of things as things. When use-values appear universally as commodities they acquire a new objectivity, a new substantiality which they did not possess in an age of episodic exchange and which destroys their original and authentic substantiality. As Marx observes: "Private property *alienates* not only the individuality of men, but also of things. The ground and the earth have nothing to do with ground-rent, machines have nothing to do with profit. For the landowner ground and

earth mean nothing but ground-rent; he lets his land to tenants and receives the rent – a quality which the ground can lose without losing any of its inherent qualities such as its fertility; it is a quality whose magnitude and indeed existence depends on social relations that are created and abolished without any intervention by the landowner. Likewise with the machine."[16]

Thus even the individual object which man confronts directly, either as producer or consumer, is distorted in its objectivity by its commodity character. If that can happen then it is evident that this process will be intensified in proportion as the relations which man establishes with objects as objects of the life process are mediated in the course of his social activity. It is obviously not possible here to give an analysis of the whole economic structure of capitalism. It must suffice to point out that modern capitalism does not content itself with transforming the relations of production in accordance with its own needs. It also integrates into its own system those forms of primitive capitalism that led an isolated existence in pre-capitalist times, divorced from production; it converts them into members of the henceforth unified process of radical capitalism. (Cf. merchant capital, the role of money as a hoard or as finance capital, etc.)

These forms of capital are objectively subordinated, it is true, to the real life-process of capitalism, the extraction of surplus value in the course of production. They are, therefore, only to be explained in terms of the nature of industrial capitalism itself. But in the minds of people in bourgeois society they constitute the pure, authentic, unadulterated forms of capital. In them the relations between men that lie hidden in the immediate commodity relation, as well as the relations between men and the objects that should really gratify their needs, have faded to the point where they can be neither recognised nor even perceived.

For that very reason the reified mind has come to regard them as the true representatives of his societal existence. The commodity character of the commodity, the abstract, quantitative mode of calculability shows itself here in its purest form: the reified mind necessarily sees it as the form in which its own authentic immediacy becomes manifest and – as reified consciousness – does not even attempt to transcend it. On the contrary, it is concerned to make it permanent by 'scientifically deepening' the laws at work. Just as the capitalist system continuously produces and reproduces itself economically on higher and higher levels, the structure of reification progressively sinks more deeply, more fatefully and more definitively into the consciousness of man. Marx often describes this potentiation of reification in incisive fashion. One example must suffice here: "In interest-bearing capital, therefore, this automatic fetish, self-expanding value, money generating money, is brought out in its pure state and in this form it no longer bears the birth-marks of its origin. The social relation is consummated in the relation of a thing, of money, to itself. Instead of the actual transformation of money into capital, we see here only form without content. ... It becomes a property of money to generate value and yield interest, much as it is an attribute of pear trees to bear pears. And the money-lender sells his money as just such an interest-bearing thing. But that is not all. The actually functioning capital, as we have seen, presents itself in such a light that it seems to yield interest not as functioning capital, but as capital in itself, as money-capital. This, too, becomes distorted. While interest is only a portion of the profit, i.e. of the surplus value, which the functioning capitalist squeezes out of the labourer, it appears now, on the contrary, as though interest were the typical product of capital, the primary matter, and profit, in the shape of profit of enterprise, were a mere accessory and by-product of the process of reproduction. Thus we get a fetish form of capital, and the conception of fetish capital. In M-M' we have the meaningless form of capital, the perversion and objectification of production relations in their highest degree, the interest-bearing form, the simple form of capital, in which it antecedes its own process of reproduction. It is the capacity of money, or of a commodity, to expand its own value independently of reproduction – which is a mystification of capital in its most flagrant form. For vulgar political economy, which seeks to represent capital as an independent source of value, of value creation, this form is naturally a veritable find, a form in which the source of profit is no longer discernible, and in which the result of the capitalist process of production – divorced from the process – acquires an independent existence."[17]

Just as the economic theory of capitalism remains stuck fast in its self-created immediacy, the same thing

happens to bourgeois attempts to comprehend the ideological phenomenon of reification. Even thinkers who have no desire to deny or obscure its existence and who are more or less clear in their own minds about its humanly destructive consequences remain on the surface and make no attempt to advance beyond its objectively most derivative forms, the forms furthest from the real life-process of capitalism, i.e. the most external and vacuous forms, to the basic phenomenon of reification itself.

Indeed, they divorce these empty manifestations from their real capitalist foundation and make them independent and permanent by regarding them as the timeless model of human relations in general. (This can be seen most clearly in Simmel's book, *The Philosophy of Money*, a very interesting and perceptive work in matters of detail.) They offer no more than a description of this "enchanted, perverted, topsy-turvy world, in which Monsieur Le Capital and Madame La Terre do their ghost-walking as social characters and at the same time as mere things."[18] But they do not go further than a description and their 'deepening' of the problem runs in circles around the eternal manifestations of reification.

The divorce of the phenomena of reification from their economic bases and from the vantage point from which alone they can be understood, is facilitated by the fact that the [capitalist] process of transformation must embrace every manifestation of the life of society if the preconditions for the complete self-realisation of capitalist production are to be fulfilled.

Thus capitalism has created a form for the state and a system of law corresponding to its needs and harmonising with its own structure. The structural similarity is so great that no truly perceptive historian of modern capitalism could fail to notice it. Max Weber, for instance, gives this description of the basic lines of this development: "Both are, rather, quite similar in their fundamental nature. Viewed sociologically, a 'business-concern' is the modern state; the same holds good for a factory: and this, precisely, is what is specific to it historically. And, likewise, the power relations in a business are also of the same kind. The relative independence of the artisan (or cottage craftsman), of the landowning peasant, the owner of a benefice, the knight and vassal was based on the fact that he himself owned the tools, supplies, financial resources or weapons with the aid of which he fulfilled his economic, political or military function and from which he lived while this duty was being discharged. Similarly, the hierarchie dependence of the worker, the clerk, the technical assistant, the assistant in an academic institute *and* the civil servant and soldier has a comparable basis: namely that the tools, supplies and financial resources essential both for the business-concern and for economic survival are in the hands, in the one case, of the entrepreneur and, in the other case, of the political master."[19]

He rounds off this account – very pertinently – with an analysis of the cause and the social implications of this phenomenon: "The modern capitalist concern is based inwardly above all on *calculation*. It requires for its survival a system of justice and an administration whose workings can be *rationally calculated*, at least in principle, according to fixed general laws, just as the probable performance of *a machine* can be calculated. It is as little able to tolerate the dispensing of justice according to the judge's sense of fair play *in individual cases* or any other irrational means or principles of administering the law … as it is able to endure a patriarchal administration that obeys the dictates of its own caprice, or sense of mercy and, for the rest, proceeds in accordance with an inviolable and sacrosanct, but irrational tradition. … What is specific to modern capitalism as distinct from the age-old capitalist forms of acquisition is that the strictly rational *organisation of work* on the basis of *rational technology* did not come into being *anywhere* within such irrationally constituted political systems nor could it have done so. For these modern businesses with their fixed capital and their exact calculations are much too sensitive to legal and administrative irrationalities. They could only come into being in the bureaucratic state with its rational laws where … the judge is more or less an automatic statute-dispensing machine in which you insert the files together with the necessary costs and dues at the top, whereupon he will eject the judgment together with the more or less cogent reasons for it at the bottom: that is to say, where the judge's behaviour is on the whole *predictable*."

The process we see here is closely related both in its motivation and in its effects to the economic process outlined above. Here, too, there is a breach with the empirical and irrational methods of administration

and dispensing justice based on traditions tailored, subjectively, to the requirements of men in action, and, objectively, to those of the concrete matter in hand. There arises a rational systematisation of all statutes regulating life, which represents, or at least tends towards a closed system applicable to all possible and imaginable cases. Whether this system is arrived at in a purely logical manner, as an exercise in pure legal dogma or interpretation of the law, or whether the judge is given the task of filling the 'gaps' left in the laws, is immaterial for our attempt to understand the *structure* of modern legal reality. In either case the legal system is formally capable of being generalised so as to relate to every possible situation in life and it is susceptible to prediction and calculation. Even Roman Law, which comes closest to these developments while remaining, in modern terms, within the framework of pre-capitalist legal patterns, does not in this respect go beyond the empirical, the concrete and the traditional. The purely systematic categories which were necessary before a judicial system could become universally applicable arose only in modern times.[20]

It requires no further explanation to realise that the need to systematise and to abandon empiricism, tradition and material dependence was the need for exact calculation.[21] However, this same need requires that the legal system should confront the individual events of social existence as something permanently established and exactly defined, i.e. as a rigid system. Of course, this produces an uninterrupted series of conflicts between the unceasingly revolutionary forces of the capitalist economy and the rigid legal system. But this only results in new codifications; and despite these the new system is forced to preserve the fixed, change-resistant structure of the old system.

This is the source of the – apparently – paradoxical situation whereby the 'law' of primitive societies, which has scarcely altered in hundreds or sometimes even thousands of years, can be flexible and irrational in character, renewing itself with every new legal decision, while modern law, caught up in the continuous turmoil of change, should appear rigid, static and fixed. But the paradox dissolves when we realise that it arises only because the same situation has been regarded from two different points of view: on the one hand, from that of the historian (who stands 'outside' the actual process) and, on the other, from that of

paper idea: "In praise of madness: The law and spontaneity.

someone who experiences the effects of the social order in question upon his consciousness.

With the aid of this insight we can see clearly how the antagonism between the traditional and empirical craftsmanship and the scientific and rational factory is repeated in another sphere of activity. At every single stage of its development, the ceaselessly revolutionary techniques of modern production turn a rigid and immobile face towards the individual producer. Whereas the objectively relatively stable, traditional craft production preserves in the minds of its individual practitioners the appearance of something flexible, something constantly renewing itself, something produced by the producers.

In the process we witness, illuminatingly, how here, too, the *contemplative* nature of man under capitalism makes its appearance. For the essence of rational calculation is based ultimately upon the recognition and the inclusion in one's calculations of the inevitable chain of cause and effect in certain events – independently of individual 'caprice'. In consequence, man's activity does not go beyond the correct calculation of the possible outcome of the sequence of events (the 'laws' of which he finds 'ready-made'), and beyond the adroit evasion of disruptive 'accidents' by means of protective devices and preventive measures (which are based in their turn on the recognition and application of similar laws). Very often it will confine itself to working out the probable effects of such 'laws' without making the attempt to intervene in the process by bringing other 'laws' to bear. (As in insurance schemes, etc.)

The more closely we scrutinise this situation and the better we are able to close our minds to the bourgeois legends of the 'creativity' of the exponents of the capitalist age, the more obvious it becomes that we are witnessing in all behaviour of this sort the structural analogue to the behaviour of the worker *vis-à-vis* the machine he serves and observes, and whose functions he controls while he contemplates it. The 'creative' element can be seen to depend at best on whether these 'laws' are applied in a – relatively – independent way or in a wholly subservient one. That is to say, it depends on the degree to which the contemplative stance is repudiated. The distinction between a worker faced with a particular machine, the entrepreneur faced with a given type of mechanical development, the technologist faced

with the state of science and the profitability of its application to technology, is purely quantitative; it does not directly entail *any qualitative difference in the structure of consciousness.*

Only in this context can the problem of modern bureaucracy be properly understood. Bureaucracy implies the adjustment of one's way of life, mode of work and hence of consciousness, to the general socio-economic premises of the capitalist economy, similar to that which we have observed in the case of the worker in particular business concerns. The formal standardisation of justice, the state, the civil service, etc., signifies objectively and factually a comparable reduction of all social functions to their elements, a comparable search for the rational formal laws of these carefully segregated partial systems. Subjectively, the divorce between work and the individual capacities and needs of the worker produces comparable effects upon consciousness. This results in an inhuman, standardised division of labour analogous to that which we have found in industry on the technological and mechanical plane.[22]

It is not only a question of the completely mechanical, 'mindless' work of the lower echelons of the bureaucracy which bears such an extraordinarily close resemblance to operating a machine and which indeed often surpasses it in sterility and uniformity. It is also a question, on the one hand, of the way in which objectively all issues are subjected to an increasingly *formal* and standardised treatment and in which there is an ever-increasing remoteness from the qualitative and material essence of the 'things' to which bureaucratic activity pertains. On the other hand, there is an even more monstrous intensification of the one-sided specialisation which represents such a violation of man's humanity. Marx's comment on factory work that "the individual, himself divided, is transformed into the automatic mechanism of a partial labour" and is thus "crippled to the point of abnormality" is relevant here too. And it becomes all the more clear, the more elevated, advanced and 'intellectual' is the attainment exacted by the division of labour.

The split between the worker's labour-power and his personality, its metamorphosis into a thing, an object that he sells on the market is repeated here too. But with the difference that not every mental faculty is suppressed by mechanisation; only one faculty (or complex of faculties) is detached from the whole personality and placed in opposition to it, becoming a thing, a commodity. But the basic phenomenon remains the same even though both the means by which society instills such abilities and their material and 'moral' exchange value are fundamentally different from labour-power (not forgetting, of course, the many connecting links and nuances).

The specific type of bureaucratic 'conscientiousness' and impartiality, the individual bureaucrat's inevitable total subjection to a system of relations between the things to which he is exposed, the idea that it is precisely his 'honour' and his 'sense of responsibility' that exact this total submission,[23] all this points to the fact that the division of labour which in the case of Taylorism invaded the psyche, here invades the realm of ethics. Far from weakening the reified structure of consciousness, this actually strengthens it. For as long as the fate of the worker still appears to be an individual fate (as in the case of the slave in antiquity), the life of the ruling classes is still free to assume quite different forms. Not until the rise of capitalism was a unified economic structure, and hence a – formally – unified structure of consciousness that embraced the whole society, brought into being. This unity expressed itself in the fact that the problems of consciousness arising from wage-labour were repeated in the ruling class in a refined and spiritualised, but, for that very reason, more intensified form. The specialised 'virtuoso', the vendor of his objectified and reified faculties does not just become the [passive] observer of society; he also lapses into a contemplative attitude *vis-à-vis* the workings of his own objectified and reified faculties. (It is not possible here even to outline the way in which modern administration and law assume the characteristics of the factory as we noted above rather than those of the handicrafts.) This phenomenon can be seen at its most grotesque in journalism. Here it is precisely subjectivity itself, knowledge, temperament and powers of expression that are reduced to an abstract mechanism functioning autonomously and divorced both from the personality of their 'owner' and from the material and concrete nature of the subject matter in hand. The journalist's 'lack of convictions', the prostitution of his experiences and beliefs is comprehensible only as the apogee of capitalist reification.[24]

The transformation of the commodity relation into a thing of 'ghostly objectivity' cannot therefore content itself with the reduction of all objects for the gratification of human needs to commodities. It stamps its imprint upon the whole consciousness of man; his qualities and abilities are no longer an organic part of his personality, they are things which he can 'own' or 'dispose of' like the various objects of the external world. And there is no natural form in which human relations can be cast, no way in which man can bring his physical and psychic 'qualities' into play without their being subjected increasingly to this reifying process. We need only think of marriage, and without troubling to point to the developments of the nineteenth century we can remind ourselves of the way in which Kant, for example, described the situation with the naïvely cynical frankness peculiar to great thinkers.

"Sexual community", he says, "is the reciprocal use made by one person of the sexual organs and faculties of another ... marriage ... is the union of two people of different sexes with a view to the mutual possession of each other's sexual attributes for the duration of their lives."[25]

This rationalisation of the world appears to be complete, it seems to penetrate the very depths of man's physical and psychic nature. It is limited, however, by its own formalism. That is to say, the rationalisation of isolated aspects of life results in the creation of – formal – laws. All these things do join together into what seems to the superficial observer to constitute a unified system of general 'laws'. But the disregard of the concrete aspects of the subject matter of these laws, upon which disregard their authority as laws is based, makes itself felt in the incoherence of the system in fact. This incoherence becomes particularly egregious in periods of crisis. At such times we can see how the immediate continuity between two partial systems is disrupted and their independence from and adventitious connection with each other is suddenly forced into the consciousness of everyone. It is for this reason that Engels is able to define the 'natural laws' of capitalist society as the laws of chance.[26]

On closer examination the structure of a crisis is seen to be no more than a heightening of the degree and intensity of the daily life of bourgeois society. In its unthinking, mundane reality *that* life seems firmly held together by 'natural laws'; yet it can experience a sudden dislocation because the bonds uniting its various elements and partial systems are a chance affair even at their most normal. So that the pretence that society is regulated by 'eternal, iron' laws which branch off into the different special laws applying to particular areas is finally revealed for what it is: a pretence. The true structure of society appears rather in the independent, rationalised and formal partial laws whose links with each other are of necessity purely formal (i.e. their formal interdependence can be formally systematised), while as far as concrete realities are concerned they can only establish fortuitous connections.

On closer inspection this kind of connection can be discovered even in purely economic phenomena. Thus Marx points out – and the cases referred to here are intended only as an indication of the methodological factors involved, not as a substantive treatment of the problems themselves – that "the conditions of direct exploitation [of the labourer], and those of realising surplus-value, are not identical. They diverge not only in place and time, but also logically."[27] Thus there exists "an accidental rather than a necessary connection between the total amount of social labour applied to a social article" and "the volume whereby society seeks to satisfy the want gratified by the article in question."[28] These are no more than random instances. It is evident that the whole structure of capitalist production rests on the interaction between a necessity subject to strict laws in all isolated phenomena and the relative irrationality of the total process. "Division of labour within the workshop implies the undisputed authority of the capitalist over men, who are but parts of a mechanism that belongs to him. The division of labour within society brings into contact independent commodity-producers who acknowledge no other authority than that of competition, of the coercion exerted by the pressure of their mutual interests."[29]

The capitalist process of rationalisation based on private economic calculation requires that every manifestation of life shall exhibit this very interaction between details which are subject to laws and a totality ruled by chance. It presupposes a society so structured. It produces and reproduces this structure in so far as it takes possession of society. This has its foundation already in the nature of speculative calculation, i.e. the

economic practice of commodity owners at the stage where the exchange of commodities has become universal. Competition between the different owners of commodities would not be feasible if there were an exact, rational, systematic mode of functioning for the whole of society to correspond to the rationality of isolated phenomena. If a rational calculation is to be possible the commodity owner must be in possession of the laws regulating every detail of his production. The chances of exploitation, the laws of the 'market' must likewise be rational in the sense that they must be calculable according to the laws of probability. But they must not be governed by a law in the sense in which 'laws' govern individual phenomena; they must not under any circumstances be rationally organised through and through. This does not mean, of course, that there can be no 'law' governing the whole. But such a 'law' would have to be the 'unconscious' product of the activity of the different commodity owners acting independently of one another, i.e. a law of mutually interacting 'coincidences' rather than one of truly rational organisation. Furthermore, such a law must not merely impose itself despite the wishes of individuals, it may *not even be fully and adequately knowable*. For the complete knowledge of the whole would vouchsafe the knower a monopoly that would amount to the virtual abolition of the capitalist economy.

This irrationality, this – highly problematic – 'systematisation' of the whole which diverges *qualitatively and in principle* from the laws regulating the parts, is more than just a postulate, a presupposition essential to the workings of a capitalist economy. It is at the same time the product of the capitalist division of labour. It has already been pointed out that the division of labour disrupts every organically unified process of work and life and breaks it down into its components. This enables the artificially isolated partial functions to be performed in the most rational manner by 'specialists' who are specially adapted mentally and physically for the purpose. This has the effect of making these partial functions autonomous and so they tend to develop through their own momentum and in accordance with their own special laws independently of the other partial functions of society (or that part of the society to which they belong).

As the division of labour becomes more pronounced and more rational, this tendency naturally increases in proportion. For the more highly developed it is, the more powerful become the claims to status and the professional interests of the 'specialists' who are the living embodiments of such tendencies. And this centrifugal movement is not confined to aspects of a particular sector. It is even more in evidence when we consider the great spheres of activity created by the division of labour. Engels describes this process with regard to the relation between economics and laws: "Similarly with law. As soon as the new division of labour which creates *professional lawyers* becomes necessary, another new and independent sphere is opened up which, for all its essential dependence on production and trade, still has also a special capacity for reacting upon these spheres. In a modern state, law must not only correspond to the general economic condition and be its expression, but must also be an *internally coherent expression* which does not, owing to inner contradictions, reduce itself to nought. And in order to achieve this, the faithful reflection of economic conditions suffers increasingly. ...."[30] It is hardly necessary to supplement this with examples of the inbreeding and the interdepartmental conflicts of the civil service (consider the independence of the military apparatus from the civil administration), or of the academic faculties, etc.

3

The specialisation of skills leads to the destruction of every image of the whole. And as, despite this, the need to grasp the whole – at least cognitively – cannot die out, we find that science, which is likewise based on specialisation and thus caught up in the same immediacy, is criticised for having torn the real world into shreds and having lost its vision of the whole. In reply to allegations that "the various factors are not treated as a whole" Marx retorts that this criticism is levelled "as though it were the text-books that impress this separation upon life and not life upon the text-books".[31] Even though this criticism deserves refutation in its naïve form it becomes comprehensible when we look for a moment from the outside, i.e. from a vantage point other than that of a reified consciousness, at the activity of modern science which is both sociologically and methodologically necessary and for that reason 'comprehensible'. Such a look will

reveal (without constituting a 'criticism') that the more intricate a modern science becomes and the better it understands itself methodologically, the more resolutely it will turn its back on the ontological problems of its own sphere of influence and eliminate them from the realm where it has achieved some insight. The more highly developed it becomes and the more scientific, the more it will become a formally closed system of partial laws. It will then find that the world lying beyond its confines, and in particular the material base which it is its task to understand, *its own concrete underlying reality* lies, methodologically and in principle, *beyond its grasp*.

Marx acutely summed up this situation with reference to economics when he declared that "use-value as such lies outside the sphere of investigation of political economy".[32] It would be a mistake to suppose that certain analytical devices – such as we find in the 'Theory of Marginal Utility' – might show the way out of this impasse. It is possible to set aside objective laws governing the production and movement of commodities which regulate the market and 'subjective' modes of behaviour on it and to make the attempt to start from 'subjective' behaviour on the market. But this simply shifts the question from the main issue to more and more derivative and reified stages without negating the formalism of the method and the elimination from the outset of the concrete material underlying it. The formal act of exchange which constitutes the basic fact for the theory of marginal utility likewise suppresses use-value as use-value and establishes a relation of concrete equality between concretely unequal and indeed incomparable objects. It is this that creates the impasse.

Thus the subject of the exchange is just as abstract, formal and reified as its object. The limits of this abstract and formal method are revealed in the fact that its chosen goal is an abstract system of 'laws' that focuses on the theory of marginal utility just as much as classical economics had done. But the formal abstraction of these 'laws' transform economics into a closed partial system. And this in turn is unable to penetrate its own material substratum, nor can it advance from there to an understanding of society in its entirety and so it is compelled to view that substratum as an immutable, eternal 'datum'. Science is thereby debarred from comprehending the development and the demise, the social character of its own material base, no less than the range of possible attitudes towards it and the nature of its own formal system.

Here, once again, we can clearly observe the close interaction between a class and the scientific method that arises from the attempt to conceptualise the social character of that class together with its laws and needs. It has often been pointed out – in these pages and elsewhere – that the problem that forms the ultimate barrier to the economic thought of the bourgeoisie is the crisis. If we now – in the full awareness of our own one-sidedness – consider this question from a purely methodological point of view, we see that it is the very success with which the economy is totally rationalised and transformed into an abstract and mathematically orientated system of formal 'laws' that creates the methodological barrier to understanding the phenomenon of crisis. In moments of crisis the qualitative existence of the 'things' that lead their lives beyond the purview of economics as misunderstood and neglected things-in-themselves, as use-values, suddenly becomes the decisive factor. (Suddenly, that is, for reified, rational thought.) Or rather: these 'laws' fail to function and the reified mind is unable to perceive a pattern in this 'chaos'.

This failure is characteristic not merely of classical economics (which regarded crises as 'passing', 'accidental' disturbances), but of bourgeois economics in toto. The incomprehensibility and irrationality of crises is indeed a consequence of the class situation and interests of the bourgeoisie but it follows equally from their approach to economics. (There is no need to spell out the fact that for us these are both merely aspects of the same dialectical unity.) This consequence follows with such inevitability that Tugan-Baranovsky, for example, attempts in his theory to draw the necessary conclusions from a century of crises by excluding consumption from economics entirely and founding a 'pure' economics based only on production. The source of crises (whose existence cannot be denied) is then found to lie in incongruities between the various elements of production, i.e. in purely quantitative factors. Hilferding puts his finger on the fallacy underlying all such explanations: "They operate only with economic concepts such as capital, profit, accumulation, etc., and believe that they possess the solution to the problem when they have discovered the quantitative

relations on the basis of which either simple and expanded reproduction is possible, or else there are disturbances. They overlook the fact that there are qualitative conditions attached to these quantitative relations, that it is not merely a question of units of value which can easily be compared with each other but also use-values of a definite kind which must fulfil a definite function in production and consumption. Further, they are oblivious of the fact that in the analysis of the process of reproduction more is involved than just aspects of capital in general, so that it is not enough to say that an excess or a deficit of industrial capital can be 'balanced' by an appropriate amount of money-capital. Nor is it a matter of fixed or circulating capital, but rather of machines, raw materials, labour-power of a quite definite (technically defined) sort, if disruptions are to be avoided."[33]

Marx has often demonstrated convincingly how inadequate the 'laws' of bourgeois economics are to the task of explaining the true movement of economic activity in toto. He has made it clear that this limitation lies in the – methodologically inevitable – failure to comprehend use-value and real consumption. "Within certain limits, the process of reproduction may take place on the same or on an increased scale even when the commodities expelled from it have not really entered individual or productive consumption. The consumption of commodities is not included in the cycle of the capital from which they originated. For instance, as soon as the yarn is sold the cycle of the capital-value represented by the yarn may begin anew, regardless of what may next become of the sold yarn. So long as the product is sold, everything is taking its regular course from the standpoint of the capitalist producer. The cycle of the capital-value he is identified with is not interrupted. And if this process is expanded – which includes increased productive consumption of the means of production – this reproduction of capital may be accompanied by increased individual consumption (hence demand) on the part of the labourers, since this process is initiated and effected by productive consumption. Thus the production of surplus-value, and with it the individual consumption of the capitalist, may increase, the entire process of reproduction may be in a flourishing condition, and yet a large part of the commodities may have entered into consumption only in appearance, while in reality they may still remain unsold in the hands of dealers, may in fact still be lying in the market."[34]

It must be emphasised that this inability to penetrate to the real material substratum of science is not the fault of individuals. It is rather something that becomes all the more apparent the more science has advanced and the more consistently it functions – from the point of view of its own premises. It is therefore no accident, as Rosa Luxemburg has convincingly shown,[35] that the great, if also often primitive, faulty and inexact synoptic view of economic life to be found in Quesnay's "Tableau Economique", disappears progressively as the – formal – process of conceptualisation becomes increasingly exact in the course of its development from Adam Smith to Ricardo. For Ricardo the process of the total reproduction of capital (where this problem cannot be avoided) is no longer a central issue.

In jurisprudence this situation emerges with even greater clarity and simplicity – because there is a more conscious reification at work. If only because the question of whether the qualitative content can be understood by means of a rational, calculating approach is no longer seen in terms of a rivalry between two principles within the same sphere (as was the case with use-value and exchange value in economics), but rather, right from the start, as a question of form versus content. The conflict revolving around natural law, and the whole revolutionary period of the bourgeoisie was based on the assumption that the formal equality and universality of the law (and hence its rationality) was able at the same time to determine its content. This was expressed in the assault on the varied and picturesque medley of privileges dating back to the Middle Ages and also in the attack on the Divine Right of Kings. The revolutionary bourgeois class refused to admit that a legal relationship had a *valid* foundation merely because it existed *in fact*. "Burn your laws and make new ones!" Voltaire counselled; "Whence can new laws be obtained? From Reason!"[36]

The war waged against the revolutionary bourgeoisie, say, at the time of the French Revolution, was dominated to such an extent by this idea that it was inevitable that the natural law of the bourgeoisie could only be opposed by yet another natural law

(see Burke and also Stahl). Only after the bourgeoisie had gained at least a partial victory did a 'critical' and a 'historical' view begin to emerge in both camps. Its essence can be summarised as the belief that the content of law is something purely factual and hence not to be comprehended by the formal categories of jurisprudence. Of the tenets of natural law the only one to survive was the idea of the unbroken continuity of the formal system of law; significantly, Bergbohm uses an image borrowed from physics, that of a 'juridical vacuum', to describe everything not regulated by law.[37]

Nevertheless, the cohesion of these laws is purely formal: *what* they express, "the content of legal institutions is never of a legal character, but always political and economic".[38] With this the primitive, cynically sceptical campaign against natural law that was launched by the 'Kantian' Hugo at the end of the eighteenth century, acquired 'scientific' status. Hugo established the juridical basis of slavery, among other things, by arguing that it "had been the law of the land for thousands of years and was acknowledged by millions of cultivated people".[39] In this naïvely cynical frankness the pattern which is to become increasingly characteristic of law in bourgeois society stands clearly revealed. When Jellinek describes the contents of law as metajuristic, when 'critical' jurists locate the study of the contents of law in history, sociology and politics what they are doing is, in the last analysis, just what Hugo had demanded: they are systematically abandoning the attempt to ground law in reason and to give it a rational content; law is henceforth to be regarded as a formal calculus with the aid of which the legal consequences of particular actions (*rebus sic stantibus*) can be determined as exactly as possible.

However, this view transforms the process by which law comes into being and passes away into something as incomprehensible to the jurist as crises had been to the political economist. With regard to the origins of law the perceptive 'critical' jurist Kelsen observes: "It is the great *mystery* of law and of the state that is consummated with the enactment of laws and for this reason it may be permissible to employ inadequate images in elucidating its nature."[40] Or in other words: "It is symptomatic of the nature of law that a norm may be legitimate even if its origins are iniquitous. That is another way of saying that the legitimate origin of a law cannot be written into the concept of law as one of its conditions."[41] This epistemological clarification could also be a factual one and could thereby lead to an advance in knowledge. To achieve this, however, the other disciplines into which the problem of the origins of law had been diverted would really have to propose a genuine solution to it. But also it would be essential really to penetrate the nature of a legal system which serves purely as a means of calculating the effects of actions and of rationally imposing modes of action relevant to a particular class. In that event the real, material substratum of the law would at one stroke become visible and comprehensible. But neither condition can be fulfilled. The law maintains its close relationship with the 'eternal values'. This gives birth, in the shape of a philosophy of law to an impoverished and formalistic re-edition of natural law (Stammler). Meanwhile, the real basis for the development of law, a change in the power relations between the classes, becomes hazy and vanishes into the sciences that study it, sciences which – in conformity with the modes of thought current in bourgeois society – generate the same problems of transcending their material substratum as we have seen in jurisprudence and economics.

The manner in which this transcendence is conceived shows how vain was the hope that a comprehensive discipline, like philosophy, might yet achieve that overall knowledge which the particular sciences have so conspicuously renounced by turning away from the material substratum of their conceptual apparatus. Such a synthesis would only be possible if philosophy were able to change its approach radically and concentrate on the concrete material totality of what can and should be known. Only then would it be able to break through the barriers erected by a formalism that has degenerated into a state of complete fragmentation. But this would presuppose an awareness of the causes, the genesis and the necessity of this formalism; moreover, it would not be enough to unite the special sciences mechanically: they would have to be transformed inwardly by an inwardly synthesising philosophical method. It is evident that the philosophy of bourgeois society is incapable of this. Not that the desire for synthesis is absent; nor can it be maintained that the best people have welcomed with open arms a mechanical existence hostile to life and a

scientific formalism alien to it. *But a radical change in outlook is not feasible on the soil of bourgeois society.* Philosophy can attempt to assemble the whole of knowledge encyclopaedically (see Wundt). Or it may radically question the value of formal knowledge for a 'living life' (see irrationalist philosophies from Hamann to Bergson). But these episodic trends lie to one side of the main philosophical tradition. The latter acknowledges as given and necessary the results and achievements of the special sciences and assigns to philosophy the task of exhibiting and justifying the grounds for regarding as valid the concepts so constructed.

Thus philosophy stands in the same relation to the special sciences as they do with respect to empirical reality. The formalistic conceptualisation of the special sciences become for philosophy an immutably given substratum and this signals the final and despairing renunciation of every attempt to cast light on the reification that lies at the root of this formalism. The reified world appears henceforth quite definitively – and in philosophy, under the spotlight of 'criticism' it is potentiated still further – as the only possible world, the only conceptually accessible, comprehensible world vouchsafed to us humans. Whether this gives rise to ecstasy, resignation or despair, whether we search for a path leading to 'life' via irrational mystical experience, this will do absolutely nothing to modify the situation as it is in fact.

By confining itself to the study of the 'possible conditions' of the validity of the forms in which its underlying existence is manifested, modern bourgeois thought bars its own way to a clear view of the problems bearing on the birth and death of these forms, and on their real essence and substratum. Its perspicacity finds itself increasingly in the situation of that legendary 'critic' in India who was confronted with the ancient story according to which the world rests upon an elephant. He unleashed the 'critical' question: upon what does the elephant rest? On receiving the answer that the elephant stands on a tortoise 'criticism' declared itself satisfied. It is obvious that even if he had continued to press apparently 'critical' questions, he could only have elicited a third miraculous animal. He would not have been able to discover the solution to the real question.

[...]

Notes

1 *A Contribution to the Critique of Political Economy*, trans. N. I. Stone (New York and London, 1904), p. 53.

2 *Capital* III (3 vols) (Moscow: Foreign Language Publishing House, 1961, 1962), p. 324.

3 *Capital* III, p. 810.

4 *Capital* I, p. 72. On this antagonism cf. the purely economic distinction between the exchange of goods in terms of their value and the exchange in terms of their cost of production. *Capital* III, p. 174.

5 *Capital* I, p. 170.

6 Cf. *Capital* I, pp. 322, 345.

7 This whole process is described systematically and historically in *Capital* I. The facts themselves can also be found in the writings of bourgeois economists like Bucher, Sombart, A. Weber and Gottl among others – although for the most part they are not seen in connection with the problem of reification.

8 *Capital* I, p. 384.

9 Ibid., p. 355 (note).

10 That this should appear so is fully justified from the point of view of the *individual* consciousness. As far as class is concerned we would point out that this subjugation is the product of a lengthy struggle which enters upon a new stage with the organisation of the proletariat into a class – but on a higher plane and with different weapons.

11 *Capital* I, pp. 374–6, 423–4, 460, etc. It goes without saying that this 'contemplation' can be more demanding and demoralizing than 'active' labour. But we cannot discuss this further here.

12 *The Poverty of Philosophy* (Moscow: Foreign Language Publishing House, n. d.), pp. 58–9.

13 *Capital* I, p. 344.

14 Cf. Gottl: *Wirtschaft und Technik*, Grundriss der Sozialökonomik II, pp. 234 et seq.

15 *Capital* I, p. 77.

16 This refers above all to capitalist private property. *Der heilige Max. Dokumente des Sozialismus* III, p. 363. Marx goes on to make a number of very fine observations about the effects of reification upon language. A philological study from the standpoint of historical materialism could profitably begin here.

17 *Capital* III, pp. 384–5.

18 Ibid., p. 809.

19 *Gesammelte politische Schriften,* Munich, 1921, pp. 140–2. Weber's reference to the development of English law has no bearing on our problem. On the gradual ascendancy of the principle of economic calculation, see also A. Weber, *Standort der Industrien*, especially p. 216.

20 Max Weber, *Wirtschaft und Gesellschaft*, p. 491.

21 Ibid., p. 129.

22 If we do not emphasise the class character of the state in *this* context, this is because our aim is to understand reification as a *general* phenomenon constitutive of the *whole* of bourgeois society. But for this the question of class would have to begin with the machine.

23 Cf. Max Weber, *Politische Schriften,* p. 154.

24 Cf. the essay by A. Fogarasi in *Kommunismus*, Jg. II, No. 25/26.

25 *Die Metaphysik der Sitten*, Pt. I, § 24.

26 *The Origin of the Family*, in *Selected Works* (S.W.) (2 vols), II, (London: Lawrence and Wishart, 1950), p. 293.

27 *Capital* III, p. 239.

28 Ibid., p. 183.

29 *Capital* I, p. 356.

30 Letter to Conrad Schmidt in S.W. II, pp. 447–8.

31 *A Contribution to the Critique of Political Economy*, p. 276.

32 Ibid., p. 21.

33 *Finanzkapital*, 2nd edn, pp. 378–9.

34 *Capital* II, pp. 75–6.

35 *Die Akkumulation des Kapitals*, 1st edn, pp. 78–9. It would be a fascinating task to work out the links between this process and the development of the great rationalist systems.

36 Quoted by Bergbohm, *Jurisprudenz und Rechtsphilosphie*, p. 170.

37 Ibid., p. 375.

38 Preuss, *Zur Methode der juristischen Begriffsbildung*. In Schmollers Jahrbuch, 1900, p. 370.

39 *Lehrbuch des Naturrechts*, Berlin, 1799, § 141. Marx's polemic against Hugo (Nachlass I, pp. 268 et seq.) is still on Hegelian lines.

40 *Hauptprobleme der Staatsrechtslehre*, p. 411.

41 F. Somlo, *Juristiche Grundlehre*, p. 117.

18

"Hegemony" (1929)

Antonio Gramsci

The Intellectuals

The formation of the intellectuals

Are intellectuals an autonomous and independent social group, or does every social group have its own particular specialised category of intellectuals? The problem is a complex one, because of the variety of forms assumed to date by the real historical process of formation of the different categories of intellectuals.

The most important of these forms are two:

1. Every social group, coming into existence on the original terrain of an essential function in the world of economic production, creates together with itself, organically, one or more strata[1] of intellectuals which give it homogeneity and an awareness of its own function not only in the economic but also in the social and political fields. The capitalist entrepreneur creates alongside himself the industrial technician, the specialist in political economy, the organisers of a new culture, of a new legal system, etc. It should be noted that the entrepreneur himself represents a higher level of social elaboration, already characterised by a certain directive [*dirigente*] and technical (i.e. intellectual) capacity: he must have a certain technical

capacity, not only in the limited sphere of his activity and initiative but in other spheres as well, at least in those which are closest to economic production. He must be an organiser of masses of men; he must be an organiser of the "confidence" of investors in his business, of the customers for his product, etc.

If not all entrepreneurs, at least an *élite* amongst them must have the capacity to be an organiser of society in general, including all its complex organism of services, right up to the state organism, because of the need to create the conditions most favourable to the expansion of their own class; or at the least they must possess the capacity to choose the deputies (specialised employees) to whom to entrust this activity of organising the general system of relationships external to the business itself. It can be observed that the "organic" intellectuals which every new class creates alongside itself and elaborates in the course of its development, are for the most part "specialisations" of partial aspects of the primitive activity of the new social type which the new class has brought into prominence.[2]

Even feudal lords were possessors of a particular technical capacity, military capacity, and it is precisely from the moment at which the aristocracy loses its monopoly of technico-military capacity that the crisis of feudalism begins. But the formation of intellectuals in the feudal world and in the preceding classical world is a question to be examined separately: this formation and elaboration follows ways and means which must be studied concretely. Thus it is to be noted that the mass of the peasantry, although it performs an essential function in the world of production,

Antonio Gramsci, "Hegemony," pp. 5–17, 106–20 from *Selections from the Prison Notebooks of Antonio Gramsci*, ed. and trans. Quintin Hoare and Geoffrey Nowell Smith. New York: International Publishers, 1971. Reprinted by permission of International Publishers.

does not elaborate its own "organic" intellectuals, nor does it "assimilate" any stratum of "traditional" intellectuals, although it is from the peasantry that other social groups draw many of their intellectuals and a high proportion of traditional intellectuals are of peasant origin.[3]

2. However, every "essential" social group which emerges into history out of the preceding economic structure, and as an expression of a development of this structure, has found (at least in all of history up to the present) categories of intellectuals already in existence and which seemed indeed to represent an historical continuity uninterrupted even by the most complicated and radical changes in political and social forms.

The most typical of these categories of intellectuals is that of the ecclesiastics, who for a long time (for a whole phase of history, which is partly characterised by this very monopoly) held a monopoly of a number of important services: religious ideology, that is the philosophy and science of the age, together with schools, education, morality, justice, charity, good works, etc. The category of ecclesiastics can be considered the category of intellectuals organically bound to the landed aristocracy. It had equal status juridically with the aristocracy, with which it shared the exercise of feudal ownership of land, and the use of state privileges connected with property.[4] But the monopoly held by the ecclesiastics in the superstructural field[5] was not exercised without a struggle or without limitations, and hence there took place the birth, in various forms (to be gone into and studied concretely), of other categories, favoured and enabled to expand by the growing strength of the central power of the monarch, right up to absolutism. Thus we find the formation of the *noblesse de robe*, with its own privileges, a stratum of administrators, etc., scholars and scientists, theorists, non-ecclesiastical philosophers, etc.

Since these various categories of traditional intellectuals experience through an "*esprit de corps*" their uninterrupted historical continuity and their special qualification, they thus put themselves forward as autonomous and independent of the dominant social group. This self-assessment is not without consequences in the ideological and political field, consequences of wide-ranging import. The whole of idealist philosophy can easily be connected with this position assumed by the social complex of intellectuals

and can be defined as the expression of that social utopia by which the intellectuals think of themselves as "independent", autonomous, endowed with a character of their own, etc.

One should note however that if the Pope and the leading hierarchy of the Church consider themselves more linked to Christ and to the apostles than they are to senators Agnelli and Benni,[6] the same does not hold for Gentile and Croce, for example: Croce in particular feels himself closely linked to Aristotle and Plato, but he does not conceal, on the other hand, his links with senators Agnelli and Benni, and it is precisely here that one can discern the most significant character of Croce's philosophy.

What are the "maximum" limits of acceptance of the term "intellectual"? Can one find a unitary criterion to characterise equally all the diverse and disparate activities of intellectuals and to distinguish these at the same time and in an essential way from the activities of other social groupings? The most widespread error of method seems to me that of having looked for this criterion of distinction in the intrinsic nature of intellectual activities, rather than in the ensemble of the system of relations in which these activities (and therefore the intellectual groups who personify them) have their place within the general complex of social relations. Indeed the worker or proletarian, for example, is not specifically characterised by his manual or instrumental work, but by performing this work in specific conditions and in specific social relations (apart from the consideration that purely physical labour does not exist and that even Taylor's phrase of "trained gorilla"[7] is a metaphor to indicate a limit in a certain direction: in any physical work, even the most degraded and mechanical, there exists a minimum of technical qualification, that is, a minimum of creative intellectual activity). And we have already observed that the entrepreneur, by virtue of his very function, must have to some degree a certain number of qualifications of an intellectual nature although his part in society is determined not by these, but by the general social relations which specifically characterise the position of the entrepreneur within industry.

All men are intellectuals, one could therefore say: but not all men have in society the function of intellectuals.[8]

When one distinguishes between intellectuals and non-intellectuals, one is referring in reality only to the immediate social function of the professional category of the intellectuals, that is, one has in mind the direction in which their specific professional activity is weighted, whether towards intellectual elaboration or towards muscular-nervous effort. This means that, although one can speak of intellectuals, one cannot speak of non-intellectuals, because non-intellectuals do not exist. But even the relationship between efforts of intellectual-cerebral elaboration and muscular-nervous effort is not always the same, so that there are varying degrees of specific intellectual activity. There is no human activity from which every form of intellectual participation can be excluded: *homo faber* cannot be separated from *homo sapiens*.[9] Each man, finally, outside his professional activity, carries on some form of intellectual activity, that is, he is a "philosopher", an artist, a man of taste, he participates in a particular conception of the world, has a conscious line of moral conduct, and therefore contributes to sustain a conception of the world or to modify it, that is, to bring into being new modes of thought.

The problem of creating a new stratum of intellectuals consists therefore in the critical elaboration of the intellectual activity that exists in everyone at a certain degree of development, modifying its relationship with the muscular-nervous effort towards a new equilibrium, and ensuring that the muscular-nervous effort itself, in so far as it is an element of a general practical activity, which is perpetually innovating the physical and social world, becomes the foundation of a new and integral conception of the world. The traditional and vulgarised type of the intellectual is given by the man of letters, the philosopher, the artist. Therefore journalists, who claim to be men of letters, philosophers, artists, also regard themselves as the "true" intellectuals. In the modern world, technical education, closely bound to industrial labour even at the most primitive and unqualified level, must form the basis of the new type of intellectual.

On this basis the weekly *Ordine Nuovo*[10] worked to develop certain forms of new intellectualism and to determine its new concepts, and this was not the least of the reasons for its success, since such a conception corresponded to latent aspirations and conformed to the development of the real forms of life. The mode of being of the new intellectual can no longer consist in eloquence, which is an exterior and momentary mover of feelings and passions, but in active participation in practical life, as constructor, organiser, "permanent persuader" and not just a simple orator (but superior at the same time to the abstract mathematical spirit); from technique-as-work one proceeds to technique-as-science and to the humanistic conception of history, without which one remains "specialised" and does not become "directive"[11] (specialised and political).

Thus there are historically formed specialised categories for the exercise of the intellectual function. They are formed in connection with all social groups, but especially in connection with the more important, and they undergo more extensive and complex elaboration in connection with the dominant social group. One of the most important characteristics of any group that is developing towards dominance is its struggle to assimilate and to conquer "ideologically" the traditional intellectuals, but this assimilation and conquest is made quicker and more efficacious the more the group in question succeeds in simultaneously elaborating its own organic intellectuals.

The enormous development of activity and organisation of education in the broad sense in the societies that emerged from the medieval world is an index of the importance assumed in the modern world by intellectual functions and categories. Parallel with the attempt to deepen and to broaden the "intellectuality" of each individual, there has also been an attempt to multiply and narrow the various specialisations. This can be seen from educational institutions at all levels, up to and including the organisms that exist to promote so-called "high culture" in all fields of science and technology.

School is the instrument through which intellectuals of various levels are elaborated. The complexity of the intellectual function in different states can be measured objectively by the number and gradation of specialised schools: the more extensive the "area" covered by education and the more numerous the "vertical" "levels" of schooling, the more complex is the cultural world, the civilisation, of a particular state. A point of comparison can be found in the sphere of industrial technology: the industrialisation of a country can be measured by how well equipped it is in the production of machines with which to produce machines, and in the manufacture of ever more accurate instruments for making both machines and further instruments for making machines, etc. The country which is best equipped in the construction of instruments for experimental scientific laboratories and in the construction of instruments with which to test the first instruments, can be regarded as the most complex in the technical-industrial field, with the highest level of civilisation, etc. The same applies to the preparation of intellectuals and to the schools dedicated to this preparation; schools and institutes of high culture can be assimilated to each other. In this field also, quantity cannot be separated from quality. To the most refined technical-cultural specialisation there cannot but correspond the maximum possible diffusion of primary education and the maximum care taken to expand the middle grades numerically as much as possible. Naturally this need to provide the widest base possible for the selection and elaboration of the top intellectual qualifications – i.e. to give a democratic structure to high culture and top-level technology – is not without its disadvantages: it creates the possibility of vast crises of unemployment for the middle intellectual strata, and in all modern societies this actually takes place.

It is worth noting that the elaboration of intellectual strata in concrete reality does not take place on the terrain of abstract democracy but in accordance with very concrete traditional historical processes. Strata have grown up which traditionally "produce" intellectuals and these strata coincide with those which have specialised in "saving", i.e. the petty and middle landed bourgeoisie and certain strata of the petty and middle urban bourgeoisie. The varying distribution of different types of school (classical and professional)[12] over the "economic" territory and the varying aspirations of different categories within these strata determine, or give form to, the production of various branches of intellectual specialisation. Thus in Italy the rural bourgeoisie produces in particular state functionaries and professional people, whereas the urban bourgeoisie produces technicians for industry. Consequently it is largely northern Italy which produces technicians and the South which produces functionaries and professional men.

The relationship between the intellectuals and the world of production is not as direct as it is with the fundamental social groups but is, in varying degrees, "mediated" by the whole fabric of society and by the complex of superstructures, of which the intellectuals are, precisely, the "functionaries". It should be possible both to measure the "organic quality" [*organicità*] of the various intellectual strata and their degree of connection with a fundamental social group, and to establish a gradation of their functions and of the superstructures from the bottom to the top (from the structural base upwards). What we can do, for the moment, is to fix two major superstructural "levels": the one that can be called "civil society", that is the ensemble of organisms commonly called "private", and that of "political society" or "the State". These two levels correspond on the one hand to the function of "hegemony" which the dominant group exercises throughout society and on the other hand to that of "direct domination" or command exercised through the State and "juridical" government. The functions in question are precisely organisational and connective. The intellectuals are the dominant group's "deputies" exercising the subaltern functions of social hegemony and political government. These comprise:

1. The "spontaneous" consent given by the great masses of the population to the general direction imposed on social life by the dominant fundamental group; this consent is "historically" caused by the prestige (and consequent confidence) which the dominant group enjoys because of its position and function in the world of production.
2. The apparatus of state coercive power which "legally" enforces discipline on those groups who do not "consent" either actively or passively. This apparatus is, however, constituted for the whole of society in anticipation of moments of crisis of command and direction when spontaneous consent has failed.

This way of posing the problem has as a result a considerable extension of the concept of intellectual, but it is the only way which enables one to reach a concrete approximation of reality. It also clashes with preconceptions of caste. The function of organising social hegemony and state domination certainly gives rise to a particular division of labour and therefore to a whole hierarchy of qualifications in some of which there is no apparent attribution of directive or organisational functions. For example, in the apparatus of social and state direction there exist a whole series of jobs of a manual and instrumental character (non-executive work, agents rather than officials or functionaries).[13] It is obvious that such a distinction has to be made just as it is obvious that other distinctions have to be made as well. Indeed, intellectual activity must also be distinguished in terms of its intrinsic characteristics, according to levels which in moments of extreme opposition represent a real qualitative difference – at the highest level would be the creators of the various sciences, philosophy, art, etc., at the lowest the most humble "administrators" and divulgators of pre-existing, traditional, accumulated intellectual wealth.[14]

In the modern world the category of intellectuals, understood in this sense, has undergone an unprecedented expansion. The democratic-bureaucratic system has given rise to a great mass of functions which are not all justified by the social necessities of production, though they are justified by the political necessities of the dominant fundamental group. Hence Loria's[15] conception of the unproductive "worker" (but unproductive in relation to whom and to what mode of production?), a conception which could in part be justified if one takes account of the fact that these masses exploit their position to take for themselves a large cut out of the national income. Mass formation has standardised individuals both psychologically and in terms of individual qualification and has produced the same phenomena as with other standardised masses: competition which makes necessary organisations for the defence of professions, unemployment, over-production in the schools, emigration, etc.

The different position of urban and rural-type intellectuals

Intellectuals of the urban type have grown up along with industry and are linked to its fortunes. Their function can be compared to that of subaltern officers in the army. They have no autonomous initiative in elaborating plans for construction. Their job is to articulate the relationship between the entrepreneur and the instrumental mass and to carry out the immediate execution of the production plan decided by the industrial general staff, controlling the elementary stages of work. On the whole the average urban intellectuals are very standardised, while the top urban intellectuals are more and more identified with the industrial general staff itself.

Intellectuals of the rural type are for the most part "traditional", that is they are linked to the social mass of country people and the town (particularly small-town) petite bourgeoisie, not as yet elaborated and set in motion by the capitalist system. This type of intellectual brings into contact the peasant masses with the local and state administration (lawyers, notaries, etc.). Because of this activity they have an important politico-social function, since professional mediation is difficult to separate from political. Furthermore: in the countryside the intellectual (priest, lawyer, notary, teacher, doctor, etc.), has on the whole a higher or at least a different living standard from that of the average peasant and consequently represents a social model for the peasant to look to in his aspiration to escape from or improve his condition. The peasant always thinks that at least one of his sons could become an intellectual (especially a priest), thus becoming a gentleman and raising the social level of the family by facilitating its economic life through the connections which he is bound to acquire with the rest of the gentry. The peasant's attitude towards the intellectual is double and appears contradictory. He respects the social position of the intellectuals and in general that of state employees, but sometimes affects contempt for it, which means that his admiration is mingled with instinctive elements of envy and impassioned anger. One can understand nothing of the collective life of the peasantry and of the germs and ferments of development which exist within it, if one does not take into consideration and examine concretely and in depth this effective subordination to the intellectuals. Every organic development of the peasant masses, up to a certain point, is linked to and depends on movements among the intellectuals.

With the urban intellectuals it is another matter. Factory technicians do not exercise any political function over the instrumental masses, or at least this is a phase that has been superseded. Sometimes, rather, the contrary takes place, and the instrumental masses, at least in the person of their own organic intellectuals, exercise a political influence on the technicians.

The central point of the question remains the distinction between intellectuals as an organic category of every fundamental social group and intellectuals as a traditional category. From this distinction there flow a whole series of problems and possible questions for historical research.

The most interesting problem is that which, when studied from this point of view, relates to the modern political party, its real origins, its developments and the forms which it takes. What is the character of the political party in relation to the problem of the intellectuals? Some distinctions must be made:

1. The political party for some social groups is nothing other than their specific way of elaborating their own category of organic intellectuals directly in the political and philosophical field and not just in the field of productive technique. These intellectuals are formed in this way and cannot indeed be formed in any other way, given the general character and the conditions of formation, life and development of the social group.[16]

2. The political party, for all groups, is precisely the mechanism which carries out in civil society the same function as the State carries out, more synthetically and over a larger scale, in political society. In other words it is responsible for welding together the organic intellectuals of a given group – the dominant one – and the traditional intellectuals.[17] The party carries out this function in strict dependence on its basic function, which is that of elaborating its own component parts – those elements of a social group which has been born and developed as an "economic" group – and of turning them into qualified political intellectuals, leaders [dirigenti] and organisers of all the activities and functions inherent in the organic development of an integral society, both civil and political. Indeed it can be said that within its field the political party accomplishes its function more completely and organically than the State does within its admittedly far larger field. An intellectual who joins the political party of a particular social group is merged with the organic intellectuals of the group itself, and is linked tightly with the group. This takes place through participation in the life of the State only to a limited degree and often not at all. Indeed it happens that many intellectuals think that they *are* the State, a belief which, given the magnitude of the category, occasionally has important consequences and leads to unpleasant complications for the fundamental economic group which *really* is the State.

That all members of a political party should be regarded as intellectuals is an affirmation that can easily lend itself to mockery and caricature. But if one thinks about it nothing could be more exact. There are of course distinctions of level to be made. A party might have a greater or lesser proportion of members in the higher grades or in the lower, but this is not the point. What matters is the function, which is directive and organisational, i.e. educative, i.e. intellectual. A tradesman does not join a political party in order to do business, nor an industrialist in order to produce more at lower cost, nor a peasant to learn new methods of cultivation, even if some aspects of these demands of the tradesman, the industrialist or the peasant can find satisfaction in the party.[18]

For these purposes, within limits, there exists the professional association, in which the economic-corporate activity of the tradesman, industrialist or peasant is most suitably promoted. In the political party the elements of an economic social group get beyond that moment of their historical development and become agents of more general activities of a national and international character. This function of a political party should emerge even more clearly from a concrete historical analysis of how both organic and traditional categories of intellectuals have developed in the context of different national histories and in that of the development of the various major social groups within each nation, particularly those groups whose economic activity has been largely instrumental.

The formation of traditional intellectuals is the most interesting problem historically. It is undoubtedly connected with slavery in the classical world and with the position of freed men of Greek or Oriental origin in the social organisation of the Roman Empire.

Note. The change in the condition of the social position of the intellectuals in Rome between Republican and Imperial times (a change from an aristocratic-corporate to a democratic-bureaucratic régime) is due to Caesar, who granted citizenship to doctors and to masters of liberal arts so that they would be more willing to live in Rome and so that others should be persuaded to come there. ("*Omnesque medicinam Romae professos et liberalium artium doctores, quo libentius et ispi urbem incolerent et coeteri appeterent civitate donavit.*" Suetonius, *Life of Caesar*, XLII.) Caesar therefore proposed: 1. to establish in Rome those intellectuals who were already there, thus creating a permanent category of intellectuals, since without their permanent residence there no cultural organisation could be created; and 2. to attract to Rome the best intellectuals from all over the Roman Empire, thus promoting centralisation on a massive scale. In this way there came into being the category of "imperial" intellectuals in Rome which was to be continued by the Catholic clergy and to leave so many traces in the history of Italian intellectuals, such as their characteristic "cosmopolitanism", up to the eighteenth century.

This not only social but national and racial separation between large masses of intellectuals and the dominant class of the Roman Empire is repeated after the fall of the Empire in the division between Germanic warriors and intellectuals of romanised origin, successors of the category of freedmen. Interweaved with this phenomenon are the birth and development of Catholicism and of the ecclesiastical organisation which for many centuries absorbs the major part of intellectual activities and exercises a monopoly of cultural direction with penal sanctions against anyone who attempted to oppose or even evade the monopoly. [...]

[...]

The concept of passive revolution

The concept of "passive revolution" must be rigorously derived from the two fundamental principles of political science: 1. that no social formation disappears as long as the productive forces which have developed within it still find room for further forward movement; 2. that a society does not set itself tasks for whose solution the necessary conditions have not already been incubated, etc.[19] It goes without saying that these principles must first be developed critically in all their implications, and purged of every residue of mechanicism and fatalism. They must therefore be referred back to the description of the three fundamental moments into which a "situation" or an equilibrium of

forces can be distinguished, with the greatest possible stress on the second moment (equilibrium of political forces), and especially on the third moment (politico-military equilibrium).

It may be observed that Pisacane, in his *Essays*, is concerned precisely with this third moment: unlike Mazzini, he understands all the importance of the presence in Italy of a war-hardened Austrian army, always ready to intervene at any point on the peninsula, and with moreover behind it all the military strength of the Habsburg Empire – an ever-ready matrix of new armies of reinforcement. Another historical element to be recalled is the development of Christianity in the bosom of the Roman Empire. Also the current phenomenon of Gandhism in India, and Tolstoy's theory of non-resistance to evil, both of which have so much in common with the first phase of Christianity (before the Edict of Milan).[20] Gandhism and Tolstoyism are naïve theorisations of the "passive revolution" with religious overtones. Certain so-called "liquidationist"[21] movements and the reactions they provoked should also be recalled, in connection with the tempo and form of certain situations (especially of the third moment). The point of departure for the study will be Vincenzo Cuoco's work on the subject; but it is obvious that Cuoco's phrase for the Neapolitan revolution of 1799 can be no more than a cue, since the concept has been completely modified and enriched.

Can the concept of "passive revolution", in the sense attributed by Vincenzo Cuoco to the first period of the Italian Risorgimento, be related to the concept of "war of position" in contrast to war of manœuvre? In other words, did these concepts have a meaning after the French Revolution, and can the twin figures of Proudhon and Gioberti be explained in terms of the panic created by the Terror of 1793, as Sorellism can be in terms of the panic following the Paris massacres of 1871? In other words, does there exist an absolute identity between war of position and passive revolution? Or at least does there exist, or can there be conceived, an entire historical period in which the two concepts must be considered identical – until the point at which the war of position once again becomes a war of manœuvre?

The "restorations" need to be judged "dynamically", as a "ruse of providence" in Vico's sense.[22]

One problem is the following: in the struggle Cavour–Mazzini, in which Cavour is the exponent of the passive revolution/war of position and Mazzini of popular initiative/war of manœuvre, are not both of them indispensable to precisely the same extent? Yet it has to be taken into account that, whereas Cavour was aware of his role (at least up to a certain point) in as much as he understood the role of Mazzini, the latter does not seem to have been aware either of his own or of Cavour's. If, on the contrary, Mazzini had possessed such awareness – in other words, if he had been a realistic politician and not a visionary apostle (i.e. if he had not been Mazzini) – then the equilibrium which resulted from the convergence of the two men's activities would have been different, would have been more favourable to Mazzinianism. In other words, the Italian State would have been constituted on a less retrograde and more modern basis. And since similar situations almost always arise in every historical development, one should see if it is not possible to draw from this some general principle of political science and art. One may apply to the concept of passive revolution (documenting it from the Italian Risorgimento) the interpretative criterion of molecular changes which in fact progressively modify the pre-existing composition of forces, and hence become the matrix of new changes. Thus, in the Italian Risorgimento, it has been seen how the composition of the moderate forces was progressively modified by the passing over to Cavourism (after 1848) of ever new elements of the Action Party, so that on the one hand neo-Guelphism was liquidated, and on the other the Mazzinian movement was impoverished (Garibaldi's oscillations, etc. also belong to this process). This element is therefore the initial phase of the phenomenon which is later called "transformism", and whose importance as a form of historical development has not as yet, it seems, been adequately emphasised.

Pursue further the notion that, while Cavour was aware of his role in as much as he was critically aware of that of Mazzini, the latter, as a consequence of his scanty or non-existent awareness of Cavour's role, had in fact little awareness of his own either. Hence his vacillations (for example at Milan in the period following the Five Days,[23] and on other occasions) and his ill-timed initiatives – which therefore became factors only benefiting the policies of Piedmont. This is an exemplification of the theoretical problem, posed in the *Poverty of Philosophy*, of how the dialectic must be understood.[24] Neither Proudhon nor Mazzini understood the necessity for each member of a dialectical opposition to seek to be itself totally and throw into the struggle all the political and moral "resources" it possesses, since only in that way can it achieve a genuine dialectical "transcendence" of its opponent. The retort will be made that this was not understood by Gioberti or the theoreticians of the passive revolution or "revolution/restoration"[25] either, but in fact their case is a different one. Their theoretical "incomprehension" expressed in practice the necessity for the "thesis" to achieve its full development, up to the point where it would even succeed in incorporating a part of the antithesis itself – in order, that is, not to allow itself to be "transcended" in the dialectical opposition. The thesis alone in fact develops to the full its potential for struggle, up to the point where it absorbs even the so-called representatives of the antithesis: it is precisely in this that the passive revolution or revolution/restoration consists. The problem of the political struggle's transition from a "war of manœuvre" to a "war of position" certainly needs to be considered at this juncture. In Europe this transition took place after 1848, and was not understood by Mazzini and his followers, as it was on the contrary by certain others: the same transition took place after 1871, etc. At the time, the question was hard to understand for men like Mazzini, in view of the fact that military wars had not yet furnished the model – and indeed military theory was developing in the direction of war of movement. One will have to see whether there are any relevant allusions in Pisacane, who was the military theoretician of Mazzinianism.

However, the main reason for studying Pisacane is that he was the only one who tried to give the Action Party a substantive and not merely formal content – as an antithesis transcending traditional positions. Nor can it be said that, for such an historical outcome to be achieved, a popular armed insurrection was an imperative necessity – as Mazzini believed to the point of obsession (i.e. not realistically, but with the fervour of a missionary). The popular intervention which was not possible in the concentrated and instantaneous form of an insurrection, did not take place even in the "diffused" and capillary form of indirect pressure – though the latter would have been possible, and perhaps was in fact the indispensable premiss for the former. The concentrated or instantaneous form was rendered impossible by the military technique of the time – but only partially so; in other words the impossibility existed in so far as that concentrated and instantaneous form was not preceded by long ideological and political preparation, organically devised in advance to reawaken popular passions and enable them to be concentrated and brought simultaneously to detonation point.

After 1848, only the Moderates made a critique of the methods which had led up to the débâcle. (Indeed the entire Moderate movement renewed itself: neo-Guelphism was liquidated, new men occupied the top positions of leadership.) No self-criticism, by contrast, on the part of the Mazzinians – or rather only a self-criticism by liquidation, in the sense that many elements abandoned Mazzini and came to form the left wing of the Piedmontese party. The only "orthodox" attempt – i.e. from within – was Pisacane's essays; but these never became the platform for a new organic policy, notwithstanding the fact that Mazzini himself recognised that Pisacane had a "strategic conception" of the Italian national revolution.

Other aspects of the relation "passive revolution/war of position" in the Italian Risorgimento can be studied too. The most important of these are, on the one hand what can be called the "personnel" aspect, and on the other that of the "revolutionary levy". The "personnel" aspect can precisely be compared to what occurred in the World War, in the relationship on the one hand between career officers and those called up from the reserves, and on the other between conscripts and volunteers/commandos. The career officers corresponded in the Risorgimento to the regular, organic, traditional, etc. political parties, which at the moment of action (1848) revealed themselves inept or almost so, and which in 1848–9 were overtaken by the popular-Mazzinian-democratic tidal wave. This tidal wave was chaotic, formless, "extempore" so to speak, but it nonetheless, under an improvised leadership (or nearly so – at any rate not one formed beforehand as was the case with the Moderate party), obtained successes which were indubitably greater than those obtained by the Moderates: the Roman Republic and Venice showed a very notable strength of resistance.[26]

In the period after 1848 the relation between the two forces – the regular and the "charismatic" – became organised around Cavour and Garibaldi and produced the greatest results (although these results were later confiscated by Cavour).

This "personnel" aspect is related to that of the "levy". It should be observed that the technical difficulty on which Mazzini's initiatives always came to grief was precisely that of the "revolutionary levy". It would be interesting, from this point of view, to study Ramorino's attempt to invade Savoy, together with the attempts of the Bandiera brothers, Pisacane, etc.,[27] and to compare them with the situation which faced Mazzini in 1848 at Milan and in 1849 in Rome – situations which he did not have the capacity to organise.[28] These attempts of a few individuals could not fail to be nipped in the bud; it would have been a miracle indeed if the reactionary forces, concentrated and able to operate freely (i.e. unopposed by any broad movement of the population), had not crushed initiatives of the Ramorino, Pisacane, Bandiera type – even if these had been better prepared than in fact they were. In the second period (1859–60), the "revolutionary levy" (which is what Garibaldi's Thousand in fact was) was made possible firstly by the fact that Garibaldi grafted himself on to the Piedmontese national forces, and secondly by the fact that the English fleet effectively protected the Marsala landing and the capture of Palermo, and neutralised the Bourbon fleet. In Milan after the Five Days and in republican Rome, Mazzini had opportunities to set up recruitment centres for an organic levy, but he had no intention of doing so. This was the source of his conflict with Garibaldi in Rome, and the reason for his ineffectiveness in Milan compared with Cattaneo and the Milanese democratic group.[29]

In any case, although the course of events in the Risorgimento revealed the enormous importance of the "demagogic" mass movement, with its leaders thrown up by chance, improvised, etc., it was nevertheless in actual fact taken over by the traditional organic forces – in other words, by the parties of long standing, with rationally-formed leaders, etc. And identical results occurred in all similar political events. (Examples of this are the preponderance of the Orleanists over the radical-democratic popular forces in France in 1830; and, ultimately, the French

Is he presenting a circular model of revolutionary history with no substantive change in ruling class?

Revolution of 1789 too – in which Napoleon represents in the last analysis the triumph of the organic bourgeois forces over the Jacobin petit-bourgeois forces.) Similarly in the World War the victory of the old career officers over the reservists, etc. In any case, the absence among the radical-popular forces of any awareness of the role of the other side prevented them from being fully aware of their own role either; hence from weighing in the final balance of forces in proportion to their effective power of intervention; and hence from determining a more advanced result, on more progressive and modern lines.

Still in connection with the concept of "passive revolution" or "revolution/restoration" in the Italian Risorgimento, it should be noted that it is necessary to pose with great precision the problem which in certain historiographical tendencies is called that of the relations between the objective conditions and the subjective conditions of an historical event. It seems obvious that the so-called subjective conditions can never be missing when the objective conditions exist, in as much as the distinction involved is simply one of a didactic character. Consequently it is on the size and concentration of subjective forces that discussion can bear, and hence on the dialectical relation between conflicting subjective forces.

It is necessary to avoid posing the problem in "intellectualistic" rather than historico-political terms. Naturally it is not disputed that intellectual "clairvoyance" of the terms of the struggle is indispensable. But this clairvoyance is a political value only in as much as it becomes disseminated passion, and in as much as it is the premiss for a strong will. In many recent works on the Risorgimento, it has been "revealed" that there existed individuals who saw everything clearly (recall Piero Gobetti's emphasis on Ornato's[30] significance). But these "revelations" are self-destroying, precisely because they are revelations; they demonstrate that what was involved was nothing more than personal reflections which today represent a form of "hindsight". In fact, they never effected a juncture with actual reality, never became a general and operative national-popular consciousness. Out of the Action Party and the Moderates, which represented the real "subjective forces" of the Risorgimento? Without a shadow of doubt it was the Moderates, precisely because they were also aware of the role of the Action

Party: thanks to this awareness, their "subjectivity" was of a superior and more decisive quality. In Victor Emmanuel's crude, sergeant-major's expression "we've got the Action Party in our pocket" there is more historico-political sense than in all Mazzini.

First epilogue

The thesis of the "passive revolution" as an interpretation of the Risorgimento period, and of every epoch characterised by complex historical upheavals. Utility and dangers of this thesis. Danger of historical defeatism, i.e. of indifferentism, since the whole way of posing the question may induce a belief in some kind of fatalism, etc. Yet the conception remains a dialectical one – in other words, presupposes, indeed postulates as necessary, a vigorous antithesis which can present intransigently all its potentialities for development. Hence theory of the "passive revolution" not as a programme, as it was for the Italian liberals of the Risorgimento, but as a criterion of interpretation, in the absence of other active elements to a dominant extent. (Hence struggle against the political morphinism which exudes from Croce and from his historicism.) (It would seem that the theory of the passive revolution is a necessary critical corollary to the Introduction to the *Critique of Political Economy*.) Revision of certain sectarian ideas on the theory of the party, theories which precisely represent a form of fatalism of a "divine right" type. Development of the concepts of mass party and small élite party, and mediation between the two. (Theoretical and practical mediation: is it theoretically possible for there to exist a group, relatively small but still of significant size, let us say several thousand strong, that is socially and ideologically homogeneous, without its very existence demonstrating a widespread state of affairs and corresponding state of mind which only mechanical, external and hence transitory causes prevent from being expressed?)

Material for a critical essay on Croce's two histories, of Italy and of Europe[31]

Historical relationship between the modern French state created by the Revolution and the other modern states of continental Europe. The comparison is vitally important – provided that it is not made on the basis of abstract sociological schemas. It should be based on the study of four elements: 1 revolutionary explosion in France with radical and violent transformation of social and political relations; 2 European opposition to the French Revolution and to any extension of it along class lines; 3. war between France, under the Republic and Napoleon, and the rest of Europe – initially, in order to avoid being stifled at birth, and subsequently with the aim of establishing a permanent French hegemony tending towards the creation of a universal empire; 4 national revolts against French hegemony, and birth of the modern European states by successive small waves of reform rather than by revolutionary explosions like the original French one. The "successive waves" were made up of a combination of social struggles, interventions from above of the enlightened monarchy type, and national wars – with the two latter phenomena predominating. The period of the "Restoration" is the richest in developments of this kind; restoration becomes the first policy whereby social struggles find sufficiently elastic frameworks to allow the bourgeoisie to gain power without dramatic upheavals, without the French machinery of terror. The old feudal classes are demoted from their dominant position to a "governing" one, but are not eliminated, nor is there any attempt to liquidate them as an organic whole; instead of a class they become a "caste" with specific cultural and psychological characteristics, but no longer with predominant economic functions. Can this "model" for the creation of the modern states be repeated in other conditions? Can this be excluded absolutely, or could we say that at least partially there can be similar developments in the form of the appearance of planned economies? Can it be excluded for all states, or only for the large ones? The question is of the highest importance, because the France-Europe model has created a mentality which is no less significant for being "ashamed of itself" or for being an "instrument of government". An important question related to the foregoing is that of the function which the intellectuals thought they fulfilled in this long, submerged process of political and social fragmentation of the restoration. Classical German philosophy was the philosophy of this period, and animated the liberal national movements from 1848 to 1870. Here too is the place to recall the

Hegelian parallel (carried over into the philosophy of praxis) between French practice and German speculation. In reality the parallel can be extended: what is practice for the fundamental class becomes "rationality" and speculation for its intellectuals (it is on the basis of these historical relations that all modern philosophical idealism is to be explained).

The conception of the State according to the productive function of the social classes cannot be applied mechanically to the interpretation of Italian and European history from the French Revolution throughout the nineteenth century. Although it is certain that for the fundamental productive classes (capitalist bourgeoisie and modern proletariat) the State is only conceivable as the concrete form of a specific economic world, of a specific system of production, this does not mean that the relationship of means to end can be easily determined or takes the form of a simple schema, apparent at first sight. It is true that conquest of power and achievement of a new productive world are inseparable, and that propaganda for one of them is also propaganda for the other, and that in reality it is solely in this coincidence that the unity of the dominant class – at once economic and political – resides.

But the complex problem arises of the relation of internal forces in the country in question, of the relation of international forces, of the country's geopolitical position. In reality, the drive towards revolutionary renewal may be initiated by the pressing needs of a given country, in given circumstances, and you get the revolutionary explosion in France, victorious internationally as well. But the drive for renewal may be caused by the combination of progressive forces which in themselves are scanty and inadequate (though with immense potential, since they represent their country's future) with an international situation favourable to their expansion and victory. Raffaele Ciasca's book on "The Origins of the National Programme", while it proved that there existed in Italy the same pressing problems as existed in *ancien régime* France, and a social force which interpreted and represented these problems precisely in the French sense, also proved that these forces were weak and the problems remained at the level of "petty politics".[32] In any case, one can see how, when the impetus of progress is not tightly linked to a vast local economic development which is artificially limited and repressed, but is instead the reflection of international develop-ments which transmit their ideological currents to the periphery – currents born on the basis of the productive development of the more advanced countries – then the group which is the bearer of the new ideas is not the economic group but the intellectual stratum, and the conception of the State advocated by them changes aspect; it is conceived of as something in itself, as a rational absolute. The problem can be formulated as follows: since the State is the concrete form of a productive world and since the intellectuals are the social element from which the governing personnel is drawn, the intellectual who is not firmly anchored to a strong economic group will tend to present the State as an absolute; in this way the function of the intellectuals is itself conceived of as absolute and preeminent, and their historical existence and dignity are abstractly rationalised. This motive is fundamental for an historical understanding of modern philosophical idealism, and is connected with the mode of formation of the modern States of continental Europe as "reaction – national transcendence" of the French Revolution (a motive which is essential for understanding the concepts of "passive revolution" and "revolution/restoration", and for grasping the importance of the Hegelian comparison between the principles of Jacobinism and classical German philosophy). The observation can be made that certain traditional criteria for historical and cultural evaluation of the Risorgimento period must be modified, and in some cases inverted: 1. the Italian currents which are "branded" for their French rationalism and abstract illuminism are perhaps those which in fact most closely adhere to Italian reality, in so far as in reality they conceive of the State as the concrete form of an Italian economic development in progress; a similar content requires a similar political form; 2. the real "Jacobins" (in the pejorative sense which the term has taken on for certain historiographical currents) are the currents which appear most indigenous in that they seem to develop an Italian tradition.[33] But in reality this current is "Italian" only because culture for many centuries was the only Italian "national" manifestation; this is simply a verbal illusion. Where was the basis for this Italian culture? It was not in Italy; this "Italian" culture is the continuation of the mediaeval cosmopolitanism linked to the tradition of the Empire and the Church. Universal concepts with "geographical" seats in Italy. The Italian intellectuals were functionally a cosmopolitan cultural concentration; they absorbed and developed theoretically the reflections of the most solid and indigenous contemporary Italian life. This function can be seen in Machiavelli too, though Machiavelli attempted to turn it to national ends (without success and without any appreciable result). *The Prince*, in fact, was a development of Spanish, French and English experience during the travail of national unification – which in Italy did not command sufficient forces, or even arouse much interest. Since the representatives of the traditional current really wish to apply to Italy intellectual and rational schemas, worked out in Italy it is true, but on the basis of anachronistic experiences rather than immediate national needs, it is they who are the Jacobins in the pejorative sense ….

The history of Europe seen as "passive revolution"

Is it possible to write a history of Europe in the nineteenth century without an organic treatment of the French Revolution and the Napoleonic Wars? And is it possible to write a history of Italy in modern times without the struggles of the Risorgimento? In both cases Croce, for extrinsic and tendentious reasons, excludes the moment of struggle in which the structure is formed and modified, and placidly takes as history the moment of cultural or ethical-political expansion. Does the conception of the "passive revolution" have a "present" significance? Are we in a period of "restoration-revolution" to be permanently consolidated, to be organised ideologically, to be exalted lyrically? Does Italy have the same relation *vis-à-vis* the USSR that the Germany (and Europe) of Kant and Hegel had *vis-à-vis* the France of Robespierre and Napoleon?

Paradigms of ethical-political history. The *History of Europe in the Nineteenth Century* seems to be the work of ethical-political history destined to become the paradigm of Crocean historiography offered to European culture. However, his other studies must be taken into account too: *History of the Kingdom of Naples*; *History of Italy from 1871 to 1915*; *The Neapolitan Revolution of 1799*; and *History of the*

Baroque Era in Italy. The most tendentious and revealing, however, are the *History of Europe* and the *History of Italy*. With respect to these two works, the questions at once arise: is it possible to write (conceive of) a history of Europe in the nineteenth century without an organic treatment of the French Revolution and the Napoleonic Wars? And is it possible to write a history of Italy in modern times without a treatment of the struggles of the Risorgimento? In other words: is it fortuitous, or is it for a tendentious motive, that Croce begins his narratives from 1815 and 1871? I.e. that he excludes the moment of struggle; the moment in which the conflicting forces are formed, are assembled and take up their positions; the moment in which one ethical-political system dissolves and another is formed by fire and by steel; the moment in which one system of social relations disintegrates and falls and another arises and asserts itself? Is it fortuitous or not that he placidly takes as history the moment of cultural or ethical-political expansion? One can say, therefore, that the book on the *History of Europe* is nothing but a fragment of history, the "passive" aspect of the great revolution which started in France in 1789 and which spilled over into the rest of Europe with the republican and Napoleonic armies – giving the old régimes a powerful shove, and resulting not in their immediate collapse as in France but in the "reformist" corrosion of them which lasted up to 1870.

The problem arises of whether this Crocean construction, in its tendentious nature, does not have a contemporary and immediate reference. Whether it does not aim to create an ideological movement corresponding to that of the period with which Croce is dealing, i.e. the period of restoration-revolution, in which the demands which in France found a Jacobin-Napoleonic expression were satisfied by small doses, legally, in a reformist manner – in such a way that it was possible to preserve the political and economic position of the old feudal classes, to avoid agrarian reform, and, especially, to avoid the popular masses going through a period of political experience such as occurred in France in the years of Jacobinism, in 1831, and in 1848. But, in present conditions, is it not precisely the fascist movement which in fact corresponds to the movement of moderate and conservative liberalism in the last century?

Perhaps it is not without significance that, in the first years of its development, fascism claimed a continuity with the tradition of the old "historic" Right. It might be one of the numerous paradoxical aspects of history (a ruse of nature, to put it in Vico's language) that Croce, with his own particular preoccupations, should in effect have contributed to a reinforcement of fascism – furnishing it indirectly with an intellectual justification, after having contributed to purging it of various secondary characteristics, of a superficially romantic type but nevertheless irritating to his classical serenity modelled on Goethe. The ideological hypothesis could be presented in the following terms: that there is a passive revolution involved in the fact that – through the legislative intervention of the State, and by means of the corporative organisation – relatively far-reaching modifications are being introduced into the country's economic structure in order to accentuate the "plan of production" element; in other words, that socialisation and co-operation in the sphere of production are being increased, without however touching (or at least not going beyond the regulation and control of) individual and group appropriation of profit. In the concrete framework of Italian social relations, this could be the only solution whereby to develop the productive forces of industry under the direction of the traditional ruling classes, in competition with the more advanced industrial formations of countries which monopolise raw materials and have accumulated massive capital sums.

Whether or not such a schema could be put into practice, and to what extent, is only of relative importance. What is important from the political and ideological point of view is that it is capable of creating – and indeed does create – a period of expectation and hope, especially in certain Italian social groups such as the great mass of urban and rural petit bourgeois. It thus reinforces the hegemonic system and the forces of military and civil coercion at the disposal of the traditional ruling classes.

This ideology thus serves as an element of a "war of position" in the international economic field (free competition and free exchange here corresponding to the war of movement), just as "passive revolution" does in the political field. In Europe from 1789 to 1870 there was a (political) war of movement in the French Revolution and a long war of position from

1815 to 1870. In the present epoch, the war of movement took place politically from March 1917 to March 1921; this was followed by a war of position whose representative – both practical (for Italy) and ideological (for Europe) – is fascism.

Notes

1 The Italian word here is "*ceti*" which does not carry quite the same connotations as "strata", but which we have been forced to translate in that way for lack of alternatives. It should be noted that Gramsci tends, for reasons of censorship, to avoid using the word class in contexts where its Marxist overtones would be apparent, preferring (as for example in this sentence) the more neutral "social group". The word "group", however, is not always a euphemism for "class", and to avoid ambiguity Gramsci uses the phrase "fundamental social group" when he wishes to emphasise the fact that he is referring to one or other of the major social classes (bourgeoisie, proletariat) defined in strict Marxist terms by its position in the fundamental relations of production. Class groupings which do not have this fundamental role are often described as "castes" (aristocracy, etc.). The word "category", on the other hand, which also occurs on this page, Gramsci tends to use in the standard Italian sense of members of a trade or profession, though also more generally. Throughout this edition we have rendered Gramsci's usage as literally as possible.

2 Mosca's *Elementi di Scienza Politica* (new expanded edition, 1923) are worth looking at in this connection. Mosca's so-called "political class"★ is nothing other than the intellectual category of the dominant social group. Mosca's concept of "political class" can be connected with Pareto's concept of the *élite*, which is another attempt to interpret the historical phenomenon of the intellectuals and their function in the life of the state and of society. Mosca's book is an enormous hotch-potch, of a sociological and positivistic character, plus the tendentiousness of immediate politics which makes it less indigestible and livelier from a literary point of view.

  ★ Usually translated in English as "ruling class", which is also the title of the English version of Mosca's *Elementi* (G. Mosca, *The Ruling Class*, New York, 1939). Gaetano Mosca (1858–1941) was, together with Pareto and Michels, one of the major early Italian exponents of the theory of political *élites*. Although sympathetic to fascism, Mosca was basically a conservative, who saw the *élite* in rather more static terms than did some of his fellows.

3 Notably in Southern Italy. See below, "The Different Position of Urban and Rural-type Intellectuals". Gramsci's general argument, here as elsewhere in the *Quaderni*, is that the person of peasant origin who becomes an "intellectual" (priest, lawyer, etc.) generally thereby ceases to be organically linked to his class of origin. One of the essential differences between, say, the Catholic Church and the revolutionary party of the working class lies in the fact that, ideally, the proletariat should be able to generate its own "organic" intellectuals within the class and who remain intellectuals *of* their class.

4 For one category of these intellectuals, possibly the most important after the ecclesiastical for its prestige and the social function it performed in primitive societies, the category of *medical men* in the wide sense, that is all those who "struggle" or seem to struggle against death and disease, compare the *Storia della medicina* of Arturo Castiglioni. Note that there has been a connection between religion and medicine, and in certain areas there still is: hospitals in the hands of religious orders for certain organisational functions, apart from the fact that wherever the doctor appears, so does the priest (exorcism, various forms of assistance, etc.). Many great religious figures were and are conceived of as great "healers": the idea of miracles, up to the resurrection of the dead. Even in the case of kings the belief long survived that they could heal with the laying on of hands, etc.

5 From this has come the general sense of "intellectual" or "specialist" of the word "*chierico*" (clerk, cleric) in many languages of romance origin or heavily influenced, through church Latin, by the romance languages, together with its correlative "*laico*" (lay, layman) in the sense of profane, non-specialist.

6 Heads of FIAT and Montecatini (Chemicals) respectively.

7 For Frederick Taylor and his notion of the manual worker as a "trained gorilla", see Gramsci's essay *Americanism and Fordism*.

8 Thus, because it can happen that everyone at some time fries a couple of eggs or sews up a tear in a jacket, we do not necessarily say that everyone is a cook or a tailor.

9 I.e. Man the maker (or tool-bearer) and Man the thinker.

10 The *Ordine Nuovo*, the magazine edited by Gramsci during his days as a militant in Turin, ran as a "weekly review of Socialist culture" in 1919 and 1920.

11 "*Dirigente*." This extremely condensed and elliptical sentence contains a number of key Gramscian ideas: on the possibility of proletarian cultural hegemony through domination of the work process, on the distinction

between organic intellectuals of the working class and traditional intellectuals from outside, on the unity of theory and practice as a basic Marxist postulate, etc.

12 The Italian school system above compulsory level is based on a division between academic ("classical" and "scientific") education and vocational training for professional purposes. Technical and, at the academic level, "scientific" colleges tend to be concentrated in the Northern industrial areas.

13 "*Funzionari*": in Italian usage the word is applied to the middle and higher echelons of the bureaucracy. Conversely "administrators" ("*amministratori*") is used here (end of paragraph) to mean people who merely "administer" the decisions of others. The phrase "non-executive work" is a translation of "[*impiego*] *di ordine e non di concetto*" which refers to distinctions within clerical work.

14 Here again military organisation offers a model of complex gradations between subaltern officers, senior officers and general staff, not to mention the NCOs, whose importance is greater than is generally admitted. It is worth observing that all these parts feel a solidarity and indeed that it is the lower strata that display the most blatant *esprit de corps*, from which they derive a certain "conceit" ("*boria*") which is apt to lay them open to jokes and witticisms.

15 The notion of the "unproductive labourer" is not in fact an invention of Loria's but has its origins in Marx's definitions of productive and unproductive labour in *Capital*, which Loria, in his characteristic way, both vulgarised and claimed as his own discovery.

16 Within productive technique those strata are formed which can be said to correspond to NCOs in the army, that is to say, for the town, skilled and specialised workers and, for the country (in a more complex fashion) share-cropping and tenant farmers – since in general terms these types of farmer correspond more or less to the type of the artisan, who is the skilled worker of a mediaeval economy.

17 Although this passage is ostensibly concerned with the sociology of political parties in general, Gramsci is clearly particularly interested here in the theory of the revolutionary party and the role within it of the intellectuals.

18 Common opinion tends to oppose this, maintaining that the tradesman, industrialist or peasant who engages in "politicking" loses rather than gains, and is the worst type of all – which is debatable.

19 These principles, here quoted from memory by Gramsci, are taken from Marx's Preface to *The Critique of Political Economy*: "No social order ever perishes before all the productive forces for which there is room in it have developed; and new, higher relations of production never appear before the material conditions of their existence have matured in the womb of the old society itself. Therefore mankind always sets itself only such tasks as it can solve …"

20 The Edict whereby Constantine, in AD 313, recognised Christianity as the official religion of the Empire.

21 This could be a reference to the liquidationist tendency in the Russian Social-Democratic Party during 1908 and in the following years, condemned at the Fifth Party Congress in December 1908 and the subject of numerous attacks by Lenin who identified its essence as the desire for the Party to abandon illegal activity. However, it seems likely that the reference is to more recent events within the PCI. Between 1922 and 1924, the main reason for Gramsci's continued support for Bordiga was his fear of the "liquidationism" of Tasca and the Right, i.e. their readiness to accept an interpretation of the United Front policy (an interpretation which was incidentally also that of the Comintern) which would lead to fusion with the PSI and the effective "liquidation" of the PCI as formed at Livorno. See, for example, exchange of letters between Gramsci and Piero Sraffa, in *Ordine Nuovo*, April 1924. From 1925 on, the Right was incorporated into the leadership, and after Gramsci's arrest the party was in effect led by Togliatti and Tasca together. After the Comintern's left turn in 1929, Tasca – who was close to Bukharin, Humbert-Droz, etc. – was accused like them of "liquidationism", in the "right" period of 1927–8. Gramsci as always is concerned to establish a dialectical position, rejecting both the "liquidationists" who make passive revolution into a programme and abandon the revolutionary perspective, and also those who react against this by a mechanical, and voluntarist, advocacy of frontal attack when this can only lead to defeat. In fact he is faithful to his interpretation of the "dual perspective" of the Fifth World Congress, against both the "right" period of 1927–8 and the "left" period which followed it.

22 The actual phrase is not Vico's – it is perhaps an echo of Hegel's "ruse of reason" – but the idea is. Vico's theory of divine providence held that men themselves constructed a world according to a divine plan of which they were not aware. "For out of the passions of men each bent on his private advantage, for the sake of which they would live like wild beasts in the wilderness, it [providence] has made the civil institutions by which they may live in human society." Vico, *The New Science*, Cornell, 1968, p. 62.

23 The insurrection in May 1848 against the Austrians.

24 See especially chapter II.

25 The political literature produced on 1848 by Marxist scholars will have to be looked at, but there does not appear to be much to hope for in this direction. What happened in Italy, for instance, was only studied with the help of Bolton King's books, etc. Bolton King (1860–1937) was an English historian, author of *Life of Mazzini* (1902), *A History of Italian Unity* (1899; Italian translation 1909–10); *Fascism in Italy* (1931).

26 The Roman Republic under Garibaldi, and Venice under Manin, held out for several months against the Austrians in 1849 – despite the demoralisation following the defeat of the Piedmontese at Novara.

27 Ramorino tried to invade Savoy in 1834; the Bandiera brothers landed in Calabria in 1844; Pisacane committed suicide after the failure of his landing at Sapri in 1857.

28 In 1848, after the successful "Five Days" insurrection in Milan and the Austrian withdrawal to their "quadrilateral" of fortified towns, Mazzini arrived in Milan and founded *Italia del Popolo*. With this organ, he attempted to combat the notion of a fusion of Piedmont and Lombardy, in favour of his own aim of a united, republican Italy. He failed to gain popular support for his views. In 1849 Mazzini headed the Roman Republic. His policy of entrusting the city's defences to the regular army rather than attempting to mobilise the entire population was symbolised by his appointment of Rosselli, a regular army general, rather than Garibaldi to command the defence forces.

29 Carlo Cattaneo (1801–69), sometimes called the first Italian positivist, edited the influential *Il Politecnico*. During the Five Days of Milan (see previous note) he headed the Council of War; at this time he was favourable to the policy of the Piedmontese monarchy. However, he came to oppose the latter fiercely, feeling that the Italian bourgeois revolution was being sacrificed to Piedmontese ambitions. In 1867 he became a deputy in the Italian parliament, but refused to take the oath of loyalty to the throne of Savoy.

30 Luigi Ornato (1787–1842), an obscure Piedmontese thinker, left no published work except a vulgarisation of Marcus Aurelius but enjoyed a high reputation, e.g. with Gioberti. Gobetti saluted him in the Manifesto for the first number of *La Rivoluzione Liberale* as the "philosopher of the risings of 1821", etc.

31 I.e. *Storia d'Italia dal 1871 al 1915*, and *Storia d'Europa nel secolo decimonono*.

32 Ciasca's book had been reviewed by Mondolfo in an article on interpretations of the Risorgimento written in 1917, which Gramsci had republished in part in *Il Grid del Popolo*, 16 May 1918. The social force referred to is clearly the PSI and the socialist forces in general.

33 These currents are, on the surface of it, the republicans, Mazzinians, etc. (influenced by the ideas of the French Revolution) on the one hand, and the Moderates on the other. However, it is hard not to read into this an indirect comment on the contemporary socialist/communist Left and nationalist/fascist Right respectively.

19

"Ideology and Ideological State Apparatuses (Notes towards an Investigation)" (1970)

Louis Althusser

Reproduction of the means of production

Everyone (including the bourgeois economists whose work is national accounting, or the modern 'macro-economic' 'theoreticians') now recognizes, because Marx compellingly proved it in *Capital* Volume Two, that no production is possible which does not allow for the reproduction of the material conditions of production: the reproduction of the means of production.

The average economist, who is no different in this than the average capitalist, knows that each year it is essential to foresee what is needed to replace what has been used up or worn out in production: raw material, fixed installations (buildings), instruments of production (machines), etc. I say the average economist = the average capitalist, for they both express the point of view of the firm, regarding it as sufficient simply to give a commentary on the terms of the firm's financial accounting practice.

But thanks to the genius of Quesnay who first posed this 'glaring' problem, and to the genius of Marx who resolved it, we know that the reproduction of the material conditions of production cannot be thought at the level of the firm, because it does not exist at that

Louis Althusser, "Ideology and Ideological State Apparatuses (Notes towards an Investigation)," pp. 128–36, 141–50, 154–76, 180–6 from *Lenin and Philosophy and Other Essays*, trans. Ben Brewster. New York: Monthly Review Press, 1971. Reprinted by permission of Monthly Review Press.

level in its real conditions. What happens at the level of the firm is an effect, which only gives an idea of the necessity of reproduction, but absolutely fails to allow its conditions and mechanisms to be thought.

A moment's reflection is enough to be convinced of this: Mr X, a capitalist who produces woollen yarn in his spinning-mill, has to 'reproduce' his raw material, his machines, etc. But *he* does not produce them for his own production – other capitalists do: an Australian sheep-farmer, Mr Y, a heavy engineer producing machine-tools, Mr Z, etc., etc. And Mr Y and Mr Z, in order to produce those products which are the condition of the reproduction of Mr X's conditions of production, also have to reproduce the conditions of their own production, and so on to infinity – the whole in proportions such that, on the national and even the world market, the demand for means of production (for reproduction) can be satisfied by the supply.

In order to think this mechanism, which leads to a kind of 'endless chain', it is necessary to follow Marx's 'global' procedure, and to study in particular the relations of the circulation of capital between Department I (production of means of production) and Department II (production of means of consumption), and the realization of surplus-value, in *Capital*, Volumes Two and Three.

We shall not go into the analysis of this question. It is enough to have mentioned the existence of the necessity of the reproduction of the material conditions of production.

Reproduction of labour power

However, the reader will not have failed to note one thing. We have discussed the reproduction of the means of production – but not the reproduction of the productive forces. We have therefore ignored the reproduction of what distinguishes the productive forces from the means of production, i.e. the reproduction of labour power.

From the observation of what takes place in the firm, in particular from the examination of the financial accounting practice which predicts amortization and investment, we have been able to obtain an approximate idea of the existence of the material process of reproduction, but we are now entering a domain in which the observation of what happens in the firm is, if not totally blind, at least almost entirely so, and for good reason: the reproduction of labour power takes place essentially outside the firm.

How is the reproduction of labour power ensured?

It is ensured by giving labour power the material means with which to reproduce itself: by wages. Wages feature in the accounting of each enterprise, but as 'wage capital',[1] not at all as a condition of the material reproduction of labour power.

However, that is in fact how it 'works', since wages represents only that part of the value produced by the expenditure of labour power which is indispensable for its reproduction: sc. indispensable to the reconstitution of the labour power of the wage-earner (the wherewithal to pay for housing, food and clothing, in short to enable the wage-earner to present himself again at the factory gate the next day – and every further day God grants him); and we should add: indispensable for raising and educating the children in whom the proletarian reproduces himself (in n models where n = 0, 1, 2, etc....) as labour power.

Remember that this quantity of value (wages) necessary for the reproduction of labour power is determined not by the needs of a 'biological' Guaranteed Minimum Wage (*Salaire Minimum Interprofessionnel Garanti*) alone, but by the needs of a historical minimum (Marx noted that English workers need beer while French proletarians need wine) – i.e. a historically variable minimum.

I should also like to point out that this minimum is doubly historical in that it is not defined by the historical needs of the working class 'recognized' by the capitalist class, but by the historical needs imposed by the proletarian class struggle (a double class struggle: against the lengthening of the working day and against the reduction of wages).

However, it is not enough to ensure for labour power the material conditions of its reproduction if it is to be reproduced as labour power. I have said that the available labour power must be 'competent', i.e. suitable to be set to work in the complex system of the process of production. The development of the productive forces and the type of unity historically constitutive of the productive forces at a given moment produce the result that the labour power has to be (diversely) skilled and therefore reproduced as such. Diversely: according to the requirements of the socio-technical division of labour, its different 'jobs' and 'posts'.

How is this reproduction of the (diversified) skills of labour power provided for in a capitalist regime? Here, unlike social formations characterized by slavery or serfdom, this reproduction of the skills of labour power tends (this is a tendential law) decreasingly to be provided for 'on the spot' (apprenticeship within production itself), but is achieved more and more outside production: by the capitalist education system, and by other instances and institutions.

What do children learn at school? They go varying distances in their studies, but at any rate they learn to read, to write and to add – i.e. a number of techniques, and a number of other things as well, including elements (which may be rudimentary or on the contrary thoroughgoing) of 'scientific' or 'literary culture', which are directly useful in the different jobs in production (one instruction for manual workers, another for technicians, a third for engineers, a final one for higher management, etc.). Thus they learn 'know-how'.

But besides these techniques and knowledges, and in learning them, children at school also learn the 'rules' of good behaviour, i.e. the attitude that should be observed by every agent in the division of labour, according to the job he is 'destined' for: rules of morality, civic and professional conscience, which actually means rules of respect for the socio-technical division of labour and ultimately the rules of the order established by class domination. They also learn to 'speak proper French', to 'handle' the workers correctly, i.e. actually (for the future capitalists and their servants) to 'order them about' properly, i.e. (ideally) to 'speak to them' in the right way, etc.

To put this more scientifically, I shall say that the reproduction of labour power requires not only a reproduction of its skills, but also, at the same time, a reproduction of its submission to the rules of the established order, i.e. a reproduction of submission to the ruling ideology for the workers, and a reproduction of the ability to manipulate the ruling ideology correctly for the agents of exploitation and repression, so that they, too, will provide for the domination of the ruling class 'in words'.

In other words, the school (but also other State institutions like the Church, or other apparatuses like the Army) teaches 'know-how', but in forms which ensure *subjection to the ruling ideology* or the mastery of its 'practice'. All the agents of production, exploitation and repression, not to speak of the 'professionals of ideology' (Marx), must in one way or another be 'steeped' in this ideology in order to perform their tasks 'conscientiously' – the tasks of the exploited (the proletarians), of the exploiters (the capitalists), of the exploiters' auxiliaries (the managers), or of the high priests of the ruling ideology (its 'functionaries'), etc.

The reproduction of labour power thus reveals as its *sine qua non* not only the reproduction of its 'skills' but also the reproduction of its subjection to the ruling ideology or of the 'practice' of that ideology, with the proviso that it is not enough to say 'not only but also', for it is clear that *it is in the forms and under the forms of ideological subjection that provision is made for the reproduction of the skills of labour power.*

But this is to recognize the effective presence of a new reality: *ideology.*

Here I shall make two comments.

The first is to round off my analysis of reproduction.

I have just given a rapid survey of the forms of the reproduction of the productive forces, i.e. of the means of production on the one hand, and of labour power on the other.

But I have not yet approached the question of the *reproduction of the relations of production.* This is a *crucial question* for the Marxist theory of the mode of production. To let it pass would be a theoretical omission – worse, a serious political error.

I shall therefore discuss it. But in order to obtain the means to discuss it, I shall have to make another long detour.

The second comment is that in order to make this detour, I am obliged to re-raise my old question: what is a society?

Infrastructure and Superstructure

On a number of occasions[2] I have insisted on the revolutionary character of the Marxist conception of the 'social whole' insofar as it is distinct from the Hegelian 'totality'. I said (and this thesis only repeats famous propositions of historical materialism) that Marx conceived the structure of every society as constituted by 'levels' or 'instances' articulated by a specific determination: the *infrastructure*, or economic base (the 'unity' of the productive forces and the relations of production) and the *superstructure*, which itself contains two 'levels' or 'instances': the politico-legal (law and the State) and ideology (the different ideologies, religious, ethical, legal, political, etc.).

Besides its theoretico-didactic interest (it reveals the difference between Marx and Hegel), this representation has the following crucial theoretical advantage: it makes it possible to inscribe in the theoretical apparatus of its essential concepts what I have called their *respective indices of effectivity.* What does this mean?

It is easy to see that this representation of the structure of every society as an edifice containing a base (infrastructure) on which are erected the two 'floors' of the superstructure, is a metaphor, to be quite precise, a spatial metaphor: the metaphor of a topography (*topique*).[3] Like every metaphor, this metaphor suggests something, makes something visible. What? Precisely this: that the upper floors could not 'stay up' (in the air) alone, if they did not rest precisely on their base.

Thus the object of the metaphor of the edifice is to represent above all the 'determination in the last instance' by the economic base. The effect of this spatial metaphor is to endow the base with an index of effectivity known by the famous terms: the determination in the last instance of what happens in the upper 'floors' (of the superstructure) by what happens in the economic base.

Given this index of effectivity 'in the last instance', the 'floors' of the superstructure are clearly endowed with different indices of effectivity. What kind of indices?

It is possible to say that the floors of the superstructure are not determinant in the last instance, but that they are determined by the effectivity of the base; that if they are determinant in their own (as yet undefined) ways, this is true only insofar as they are determined by the base.

Their index of effectivity (or determination), as determined by the determination in the last instance of the base, is thought by the Marxist tradition in two ways: (1) there is a 'relative autonomy' of the superstructure with respect to the base; (2) there is a 'reciprocal action' of the superstructure on the base.

We can therefore say that the great theoretical advantage of the Marxist topography, i.e. of the spatial metaphor of the edifice (base and superstructure) is simultaneously that it reveals that questions of determination (or of index of effectivity) are crucial; that it reveals that it is the base which in the last instance determines the whole edifice; and that, as a consequence, it obliges us to pose the theoretical problem of the types of 'derivatory' effectivity peculiar to the superstructure, i.e. it obliges us to think what the Marxist tradition calls conjointly the relative autonomy of the superstructure and the reciprocal action of the superstructure on the base.

The greatest disadvantage of this representation of the structure of every society by the spatial metaphor of an edifice, is obviously the fact that it is metaphorical: i.e. it remains *descriptive*.

It now seems to me that it is possible and desirable to represent things differently. NB, I do not mean by this that I want to reject the classical metaphor, for that metaphor itself requires that we go beyond it. And I am not going beyond it in order to reject it as outworn. I simply want to attempt to think what it gives us in the form of a description.

I believe that it is possible and necessary to think what characterizes the essential of the existence and nature of the superstructure *on the basis of reproduction*. Once one takes the point of view of reproduction, many of the questions whose existence was indicated by the spatial metaphor of the edifice, but to which it could not give a conceptual answer, are immediately illuminated.

My basic thesis is that it is not possible to pose these questions (and therefore to answer them) *except from the point of view of reproduction*.

[...]

The state ideological apparatuses

Thus, what has to be added to the 'Marxist theory' of the State is something else.

Here we must advance cautiously in a terrain which, in fact, the Marxist classics entered long before us, but without having systematized in theoretical form the decisive advances implied by their experiences and procedures. Their experiences and procedures were indeed restricted in the main to the terrain of political practice.

In fact, i.e. in their political practice, the Marxist classics treated the State as a more complex reality than the definition of it given in the 'Marxist theory of the State', even when it has been supplemented as I have just suggested. They recognized this complexity in their practice, but they did not express it in a corresponding theory.[4]

I should like to attempt a very schematic outline of this corresponding theory. To that end, I propose the following thesis.

In order to advance the theory of the State it is indispensable to take into account not only the distinction between *State power* and *State apparatus*, but also another reality which is clearly on the side of the (repressive) State apparatus, but must not be confused with it. I shall call this reality by its concept: *the ideological State apparatuses*.

What are the ideological State apparatuses (ISAs)?

They must not be confused with the (repressive) State apparatus. Remember that in Marxist theory, the State Apparatus (SA) contains: the Government, the Administration, the Army, the Police, the Courts, the Prisons, etc., which constitute what I shall in future call the Repressive State Apparatus. Repressive suggests that the State Apparatus in question 'functions by violence' – at least ultimately (since repression, e.g. administrative repression, may take non-physical forms).

I shall call Ideological State Apparatuses a certain number of realities which present themselves to the immediate observer in the form of distinct and specialized institutions. I propose an empirical list of these which will obviously have to be examined in

What do the relation between order and critique and emancipation?

[via Butler]

detail, tested, corrected and reorganized. With all the reservations implied by this requirement, we can for the moment regard the following institutions as Ideological State Apparatuses (the order in which I have listed them has no particular significance):

- the religious ISA (the system of the different Churches),
- the educational ISA (the system of the different public and private 'Schools'),
- the family ISA,[5]
- the legal ISA,[6]
- the political ISA (the political system, including the different Parties),
- the trade-union ISA,
- the communications ISA (press, radio and television, etc.),
- the cultural ISA (Literature, the Arts, sports, etc.).

I have said that the ISAs must not be confused with the (Repressive) State Apparatus. What constitutes the difference?

As a first moment, it is clear that while there is *one* (Repressive) State Apparatus, there is a *plurality* of Ideological State Apparatuses. Even presupposing that it exists, the unity that constitutes this plurality of ISAs as a body is not immediately visible.

As a second moment, it is clear that whereas the – unified – (Repressive) State Apparatus belongs entirely to the *public* domain, much the larger part of the Ideological State Apparatuses (in their apparent dispersion) are part, on the contrary, of the *private* domain. Churches, Parties, Trade Unions, families, some schools, most newspapers, cultural ventures, etc., etc., are private.

We can ignore the first observation for the moment. But someone is bound to question the second, asking me by what right I regard as Ideological *State* Apparatuses, institutions which for the most part do not possess public status, but are quite simply *private* institutions. As a conscious Marxist, Gramsci already forestalled this objection in one sentence. The distinction between the public and the private is a distinction internal to bourgeois law, and valid in the (subordinate) domains in which bourgeois law exercises its 'authority'. The domain of the State escapes it because the latter is 'above the law': the State, which is the State *of* the ruling class, is neither public nor private; on the contrary, it is the precondition for any distinction between public and private. The same thing can be said from the starting-point of our State Ideological Apparatuses. It is unimportant whether the institutions in which they are realized are 'public' or 'private'. What matters is how they function. Private institutions can perfectly well 'function' as Ideological State Apparatuses. A reasonably thorough analysis of any one of the ISAs proves it.

But now for what is essential. What distinguishes the ISAs from the (Repressive) State Apparatus is the following basic difference: the Repressive State Apparatus functions 'by violence', whereas the Ideological State Apparatuses *function 'by ideology'*.

I can clarify matters by correcting this distinction. I shall say rather that every State Apparatus, whether Repressive or Ideological, 'functions' both by violence and by ideology, but with one very important distinction which makes it imperative not to confuse the Ideological State Apparatuses with the (Repressive) State Apparatus.

This is the fact that the (Repressive) State Apparatus functions massively and predominantly *by repression* (including physical repression), while functioning secondarily by ideology. (There is no such thing as a purely repressive apparatus.) For example, the Army and the Police also function by ideology both to ensure their own cohesion and reproduction, and in the 'values' they propound externally.

In the same way, but inversely, it is essential to say that for their part the Ideological State Apparatuses function massively and predominantly *by ideology*, but they also function secondarily by repression, even if ultimately, but only ultimately, this is very attenuated and concealed, even symbolic. (There is no such thing as a purely ideological apparatus.) Thus Schools and Churches use suitable methods of punishment, expulsion, selection, etc., to 'discipline' not only their shepherds, but also their flocks. The same is true of the Family.... The same is true of the cultural IS Apparatus (censorship, among other things), etc.

Is it necessary to add that this determination of the double 'functioning' (predominantly, secondarily) by repression and by ideology, according to whether it is a matter of the (Repressive) State Apparatus or the Ideological State Apparatuses, makes it clear that very subtle explicit or tacit combinations may be woven from the interplay of the (Repressive) State Apparatus and the Ideological State Apparatuses? Everyday life provides us with innumerable examples of this, but they must be studied in detail if we are to go further than this mere observation.

Nevertheless, this remark leads us towards an understanding of what constitutes the unity of the apparently disparate body of the ISAs. If the ISAs 'function' massively and predominantly by ideology, what unifies their diversity is precisely this functioning, insofar as the ideology by which they function is always in fact unified, despite its diversity and its contradictions, *beneath the ruling ideology*, which is the ideology of 'the ruling class'. Given the fact that the 'ruling class' in principle holds State power (openly or more often by means of alliances between classes or class fractions), and therefore has at its disposal the (Repressive) State Apparatus, we can accept the fact that this same ruling class is active in the Ideological State Apparatuses insofar as it is ultimately the ruling ideology which is realized in the Ideological State Apparatuses, precisely in its contradictions. Of course, it is a quite different thing to act by laws and decrees in the (Repressive) State Apparatus and to 'act' through the intermediary of the ruling ideology in the Ideological State Apparatuses. We must go into the details of this difference – but it cannot mask the reality of a profound identity. To my knowledge, *no class can hold State power over a long period without at the same time exercising its hegemony over and in the State Ideological Apparatuses*. I only need one example and proof of this: Lenin's anguished concern to revolutionize the educational Ideological State Apparatus (among others), simply to make it possible for the Soviet proletariat, who had seized State power, to secure the future of the dictatorship of the proletariat and the transition to socialism.[7]

This last comment puts us in a position to understand that the Ideological State Apparatuses may be not only the *stake*, but also the *site* of class struggle, and often of bitter forms of class struggle. The class (or class alliance) in power cannot lay down the law in the ISAs as easily as it can in the (repressive) State apparatus, not only because the former ruling classes are able to retain strong positions there for a long time, but also because the resistance of the exploited classes is able to find means and occasions to express itself there, either by the utilization of their contradictions, or by conquering combat positions in them in struggle.[8]

Let me run through my comments.

If the thesis I have proposed is well-founded, it leads me back to the classical Marxist theory of the State, while making it more precise in one point. I argue that it is necessary to distinguish between State power (and its possession by…) on the one hand, and the State Apparatus on the other. But I add that the State Apparatus contains two bodies: the body of institutions which represent the Repressive State Apparatus on the one hand, and the body of institutions which represent the body of Ideological State Apparatuses on the other.

But if this is the case, the following question is bound to be asked, even in the very summary state of my suggestions: what exactly is the extent of the role of the Ideological State Apparatuses? What is their importance based on? In other words: to what does the 'function' of these Ideological State Apparatuses, which do not function by repression but by ideology, correspond?

On the Reproduction of the Relations of Production

I can now answer the central question which I have left in suspense for many long pages: *how is the reproduction of the relations of production secured?*

In the topographical language (Infrastructure, Superstructure), I can say: for the most part,[9] it is secured by the legal-political and ideological superstructure.

But as I have argued that it is essential to go beyond this still descriptive language, I shall say: for the most part, it is secured by the exercise of State power in the State Apparatuses, on the one hand the (Repressive) State Apparatus, on the other the Ideological State Apparatuses.

What I have just said must also be taken into account, and it can be assembled in the form of the following three features:

1. All the State Apparatuses function both by repression and by ideology, with the difference that the (Repressive) State Apparatus functions massively and predominantly by repression, whereas the Ideological State Apparatuses function massively and predominantly by ideology.

2. Whereas the (Repressive) State Apparatus constitutes an organized whole whose different parts are

centralized beneath a commanding unity, that of the politics of class struggle applied by the political representatives of the ruling classes in possession of State power, the Ideological State Apparatuses are multiple, distinct, 'relatively autonomous' and capable of providing an objective field to contradictions which express, in forms which may be limited or extreme, the effects of the clashes between the capitalist class struggle and the proletarian class struggle, as well as their subordinate forms.

3. Whereas the unity of the (Repressive) State Apparatus is secured by its unified and centralized organization under the leadership of the representatives of the classes in power executing the politics of the class struggle of the classes in power, the unity of the different Ideological State Apparatuses is secured, usually in contradictory forms, by the ruling ideology, the ideology of the ruling class.

Taking these features into account, it is possible to represent the reproduction of the relations of production[10] in the following way, according to a kind of 'division of labour'.

The role of the repressive State apparatus, insofar as it is a repressive apparatus, consists essentially in securing by force (physical or otherwise) the political conditions of the reproduction of relations of production which are in the last resort *relations of exploitation*. Not only does the State apparatus contribute generously to its own reproduction (the capitalist State contains political dynasties, military dynasties, etc.), but also and above all, the State apparatus secures by repression (from the most brutal physical force, via mere administrative commands and interdictions, to open and tacit censorship) the political conditions for the action of the Ideological State Apparatuses.

In fact, it is the latter which largely secure the reproduction specifically of the relations of production, behind a 'shield' provided by the repressive State apparatus. It is here that the role of the ruling ideology is heavily concentrated, the ideology of the ruling class, which holds State power. It is the intermediation of the ruling ideology that ensures a (sometimes teeth-gritting) 'harmony' between the repressive State apparatus and the Ideological State Apparatuses, and between the different State Ideological Apparatuses.

[...]

Why is the educational apparatus in fact the dominant ideological State apparatus in capitalist social formations, and how does it function?

For the moment it must suffice to say:

1. All ideological State apparatuses, whatever they are, contribute to the same result: the reproduction of the relations of production, i.e. of capitalist relations of exploitation.

2. Each of them contributes towards this single result in the way proper to it. The political apparatus by subjecting individuals to the political State ideology, the 'indirect' (parliamentary) or 'direct' (plebiscitary or fascist) 'democratic' ideology. The communications apparatus by cramming every 'citizen' with daily doses of nationalism, chauvinism, liberalism, moralism, etc, by means of the press, the radio and television. The same goes for the cultural apparatus (the role of sport in chauvinism is of the first importance), etc. The religious apparatus by recalling in sermons and the other great ceremonies of Birth, Marriage and Death, that man is only ashes, unless he loves his neighbour to the extent of turning the other cheek to whoever strikes first. The family apparatus ... but there is no need to go on.

3. This concert is dominated by a single score, occasionally disturbed by contradictions (those of the remnants of former ruling classes, those of the proletarians and their organizations): the score of the Ideology of the current ruling class which integrates into its music the great themes of the Humanism of the Great Forefathers, who produced the Greek Miracle even before Christianity, and afterwards the Glory of Rome, the Eternal City, and the themes of Interest, particular and general, etc. nationalism, moralism and economism.

4. Nevertheless, in this concert, one ideological State apparatus certainly has the dominant role, although hardly anyone lends an ear to its music: it is so silent! This is the School.

It takes children from every class at infant-school age, and then for years, the years in which the child is most 'vulnerable', squeezed between the family State apparatus and the educational State apparatus, it drums into them, whether it uses new or old methods, a certain amount of 'know-how' wrapped in the ruling ideology (French, arithmetic, natural history, the sciences, literature) or simply the ruling ideology in its pure state (ethics, civic instruction, philosophy). Somewhere around the age of sixteen, a huge mass of children are ejected 'into production': these are the workers or small peasants. Another portion of scholastically adapted youth carries on: and, for better or worse, it goes somewhat further, until it falls by the wayside and fills the posts of small and middle technicians, white-collar workers, small and middle executives, petty bourgeois of all kinds. A last portion reaches the summit, either to fall into intellectual semi-employment, or to provide, as well as the 'intellectuals of the collective labourer', the agents of exploitation (capitalists, managers), the agents of repression (soldiers, policemen, politicians, administrators, etc.) and the professional ideologists (priests of all sorts, most of whom are convinced 'laymen').

Each mass ejected *en route* is practically provided with the ideology which suits the role it has to fulfil in class society: the role of the exploited (with a 'highly-developed' 'professional', 'ethical', 'civic', 'national' and a-political consciousness); the role of the agent of exploitation (ability to give the workers orders and speak to them: 'human relations'), of the agent of repression (ability to give orders and enforce obedience 'without discussion', or ability to manipulate the demagogy of a political leader's rhetoric), or of the professional ideologist (ability to treat consciousnesses with the respect, i.e. with the contempt, blackmail, and demagogy they deserve, adapted to the accents of Morality, of Virtue, of 'Transcendence', of the Nation, of France's World Role, etc.).

Of course, many of these contrasting Virtues (modesty, resignation, submissiveness on the one hand, cynicism, contempt, arrogance, confidence, self-importance, even smooth talk and cunning on the other) are also taught in the Family, in the Church, in the Army, in Good Books, in films and even in the football stadium. But no other ideological State apparatus has the obligatory (and not least, free) audience of the totality of the children in the capitalist social formation, eight hours a day for five or six days out of seven.

But it is by an apprenticeship in a variety of know-how wrapped up in the massive inculcation of the ideology of the ruling class that the *relations of production* in a capitalist social formation, i.e. the relations of exploited to exploiters and exploiters to exploited, are largely reproduced. The mechanisms which produce this vital result for the capitalist regime are naturally covered up and concealed by a universally reigning ideology of the School, universally reigning because it is one of the essential forms of the ruling bourgeois

ideology: an ideology which represents the School as a neutral environment purged of ideology (because it is … lay), where teachers respectful of the 'conscience' and 'freedom' of the children who are entrusted to them (in complete confidence) by their 'parents' (who are free, too, i.e. the owners of their children) open up for them the path to the freedom, morality and responsibility of adults by their own example, by knowledge, literature and their 'liberating' virtues.

I ask the pardon of those teachers who, in dreadful conditions, attempt to turn the few weapons they can find in the history and learning they 'teach' against the ideology, the system and the practices in which they are trapped. They are a kind of hero. But they are rare and how many (the majority) do not even begin to suspect the 'work' the system (which is bigger than they are and crushes them) forces them to do, or worse, put all their heart and ingenuity into performing it with the most advanced awareness (the famous new methods!). So little do they suspect it that their own devotion contributes to the maintenance and nourishment of this ideological representation of the School, which makes the School today as 'natural', indispensable-useful and even beneficial for our contemporaries as the Church was 'natural', indispensable and generous for our ancestors a few centuries ago.

In fact, the Church has been replaced today *in its role as the dominant Ideological State Apparatus* by the School. It is coupled with the Family just as the Church was once coupled with the Family. We can now claim that the unprecedentedly deep crisis which is now shaking the education system of so many States across the globe, often in conjunction with a crisis (already proclaimed in the *Communist Manifesto*) shaking the family system, takes on a political meaning, given that the School (and the School-Family couple) constitutes the dominant Ideological State Apparatus, the Apparatus playing a determinant part in the reproduction of the relations of production of a mode of production threatened in its existence by the world class struggle.

On Ideology

When I put forward the concept of an Ideological State Apparatus, when I said that the ISAs 'function by ideology', I invoked a reality which needs a little discussion: ideology.

It is well known that the expression 'ideology' was invented by Cabanis, Destutt de Tracy and their friends, who assigned to it as an object the (genetic) theory of ideas. When Marx took up the term fifty years later, he gave it a quite different meaning, even in his Early Works. Here, ideology is the system of the ideas and representations which dominate the mind of a man or a social group. The ideologico-political struggle conducted by Marx as early as his articles in the *Rheinische Zeitung* inevitably and quickly brought him face to face with this reality and forced him to take his earliest intuitions further.

However, here we come upon a rather astonishing paradox. Everything seems to lead Marx to formulate a theory of ideology. In fact, *The German Ideology* does offer us, after the *1844 Manuscripts*, an explicit theory of ideology, but ... it is not Marxist (we shall see why in a moment). As for *Capital*, although it does contain many hints towards a theory of ideologies (most visibly, the ideology of the vulgar economists), it does not contain that theory itself, which depends for the most part on a theory of ideology in general.

I should like to venture a first and very schematic outline of such a theory. The theses I am about to put forward are certainly not off the cuff, but they cannot be sustained and tested, i.e. confirmed or rejected, except by much thorough study and analysis.

Ideology has no history

One word first of all to expound the reason in principle which seems to me to found, or at least to justify, the project of a theory of ideology *in general*, and not a theory of particular ideology*ies*, which, whatever their form (religious, ethical, legal, political), always express *class positions*.

It is quite obvious that it is necessary to proceed towards a theory of ideolog*ies* in the two respects I have just suggested. It will then be clear that a theory of ideolog*ies* depends in the last resort on the history of social formations, and thus of the modes of production combined in social formations, and of the class struggles which develop in them. In this sense it is clear that there can be no question of a theory of ideolog*ies in general*, since ideolog*ies* (defined in the double respect suggested above: regional and class) have a history, whose determination in the last instance

is clearly situated outside ideologies alone, although it involves them.

On the contrary, if I am able to put forward the project of a theory of ideology *in general*, and if this theory really is one of the elements on which theories of ideolog*ies* depend, that entails an apparently paradoxical proposition which I shall express in the following terms: *ideology has no history*.

As we know, this formulation appears in so many words in a passage from *The German Ideology*. Marx utters it with respect to metaphysics, which, he says, has no more history than ethics (meaning also the other forms of ideology).

In *The German Ideology*, this formulation appears in a plainly positivist context. Ideology is conceived as a pure illusion, a pure dream, i.e. as nothingness. All its reality is external to it. Ideology is thus thought as an imaginary construction whose status is exactly like the theoretical status of the dream among writers before Freud. For these writers, the dream was the purely imaginary, i.e. null, result of 'day's residues', presented in an arbitrary arrangement and order, sometimes even 'inverted', in other words, in 'disorder'. For them, the dream was the imaginary, it was empty, null and arbitrarily 'stuck together' (*bricolé*), once the eyes had closed, from the residues of the only full and positive reality, the reality of the day. This is exactly the status of philosophy and ideology (since in this book philosophy is ideology *par excellence*) in *The German Ideology*.

Ideology, then, is for Marx an imaginary assemblage (*bricolage*), a pure dream, empty and vain, constituted by the 'day's residues' from the only full and positive reality, that of the concrete history of concrete material individuals materially producing their existence. It is on this basis that ideology has no history in *The German Ideology*, since its history is outside it, where the only existing history is, the history of concrete individuals, etc. In *The German Ideology*, the thesis that ideology has no history is therefore a purely negative thesis, since it means both:

1. ideology is nothing insofar as it is a pure dream (manufactured by who knows what power: if not by the alienation of the division of labour, but that, too, is a *negative* determination);

2. ideology has no history, which emphatically does not mean that there is no history in it (on the

contrary, for it is merely the pale, empty and inverted reflection of real history) but that it has no history *of its own*.

Now, while the thesis I wish to defend formally speaking adopts the terms of *The German Ideology* ('ideology has no history'), it is radically different from the positivist and historicist thesis of *The German Ideology*.

For on the one hand, I think it is possible to hold that ideolog*ies have a history of their own* (although it is determined in the last instance by the class struggle); and on the other, I think it is possible to hold that ideology *in general has no history*, not in a negative sense (its history is external to it), but in an absolutely positive sense.

This sense is a positive one if it is true that the peculiarity of ideology is that it is endowed with a structure and a functioning such as to make it a non-historical reality, i.e. an *omni-historical* reality, in the sense in which that structure and functioning are immutable, present in the same form throughout what we can call history, in the sense in which the *Communist Manifesto* defines history as the history of class struggles, i.e. the history of class societies.

To give a theoretical reference-point here, I might say that, to return to our example of the dream, in its Freudian conception this time, our proposition: ideology has no history, can and must (and in a way which has absolutely nothing arbitrary about it, but, quite the reverse, is theoretically necessary, for there is an organic link between the two propositions) be related directly to Freud's proposition that the *unconscious is eternal*, i.e. that it has no history.

If eternal means, not transcendent to all (temporal) history, but omnipresent, trans-historical and therefore immutable in form throughout the extent of history, I shall adopt Freud's expression word for word, and write *ideology is eternal*, exactly like the unconscious. And I add that I find this comparison theoretically justified by the fact that the eternity of the unconscious is not unrelated to the eternity of ideology in general.

That is why I believe I am justified, hypothetically at least, in proposing a theory of ideology *in general*, in the sense that Freud presented a theory of the unconscious *in general*.

To simplify the phrase, it is convenient, taking into account what has been said about ideologies, to use the plain term ideology to designate ideology in general, which I have just said has no history, or, what comes to the same thing, is eternal, i.e. omnipresent in its immutable form throughout history (= the history of social formations containing social classes). For the moment I shall restrict myself to 'class societies' and their history.

Ideology is a 'representation' of the imaginary relationship of individuals to their real conditions of existence

In order to approach my central thesis on the structure and functioning of ideology, I shall first present two theses, one negative, the other positive. The first concerns the object which is 'represented' in the imaginary form of ideology, the second concerns the materiality of ideology.

THESIS I: Ideology represents the imaginary relationship of individuals to their real conditions of existence.

We commonly call religious ideology, ethical ideology, legal ideology, political ideology, etc., so many 'world outlooks'. Of course, assuming that we do not live one of these ideologies as the truth (e.g. 'believe' in God, Duty, Justice, etc. ...), we admit that the ideology we are discussing from a critical point of view, examining it as the ethnologist examines the myths of a 'primitive society', that these 'world outlooks' are largely imaginary, i.e. do not 'correspond to reality'.

However, while admitting that they do not correspond to reality, i.e. that they constitute an illusion, we admit that they do make allusion to reality, and that they need only be 'interpreted' to discover the reality of the world behind their imaginary representation of that world (ideology = *illusion/allusion*).

There are different types of interpretation, the most famous of which are the *mechanistic* type, current in the eighteenth century (God is the imaginary representation of the real King), and the '*hermeneutic*' interpretation, inaugurated by the earliest Church Fathers, and revived by Feuerbach and the theologico-philosophical school which descends from him, e.g. the theologian Barth (to Feuerbach, for example, God is the essence of real Man). The essential point is that on condition that we interpret the imaginary transposition (and inversion) of ideology we arrive at the conclusion that in ideology 'men represent their real conditions of existence to themselves in an imaginary form'.

Unfortunately, this interpretation leaves one small problem unsettled: why do men 'need' this imaginary transposition of their real conditions of existence in order to 'represent to themselves' their real conditions of existence?

The first answer (that of the eighteenth century) proposes a simple solution: Priests or Despots are responsible. They 'forged' the Beautiful Lies so that, in the belief that they were obeying God, men would in fact obey the Priests and Despots, who are usually in alliance in their imposture, the Priests acting in the interests of the Despots or *vice versa*, according to the political positions of the 'theoreticians' concerned. There is therefore a cause for the imaginary transposition of the real conditions of existence: that cause is the existence of a small number of cynical men who base their domination and exploitation of the 'people' on a falsified representation of the world which they have imagined in order to enslave other minds by dominating their imaginations.

The second answer (that of Feuerbach, taken over word for word by Marx in his Early Works) is more 'profound', i.e. just as false. It, too, seeks and finds a cause for the imaginary transposition and distortion of men's real conditions of existence, in short, for the alienation in the imaginary of the representation of men's conditions of existence. This cause is no longer Priests or Despots, nor their active imagination and the passive imagination of their victims. This cause is the material alienation which reigns in the conditions of existence of men themselves. This is how, in *The Jewish Question* and elsewhere, Marx defends the Feuerbachian idea that men make themselves an alienated (= imaginary) representation of their conditions of existence because these conditions of existence are themselves alienating (in the *1844 Manuscripts*: because these conditions are dominated by the essence of alienated society – '*alienated labour*').

All these interpretations thus take literally the thesis which they presuppose, and on which they depend, i.e. that what is reflected in the imaginary representation of the world found in an ideology is the conditions of existence of men, i.e. their real world.

Now I can return to a thesis which I have already advanced: it is not their real conditions of existence, their real world, that 'men' 'represent to themselves' in ideology, but above all it is their relation to those conditions of existence which is represented to them there. It is this relation which is at the centre of every ideological, i.e. imaginary, representation of the real world. It is this relation that contains the 'cause' which has to explain the imaginary distortion of the ideological representation of the real world. Or rather, to leave aside the language of causality it is necessary to advance the thesis that it is the *imaginary nature of this relation* which underlies all the imaginary distortion that we can observe (if we do not live in its truth) in all ideology.

To speak in a Marxist language, if it is true that the representation of the real conditions of existence of the individuals occupying the posts of agents of production, exploitation, repression, ideologization and scientific practice, does in the last analysis arise from the relations of production, and from relations deriving from the relations of production, we can say the following: all ideology represents in its necessarily imaginary distortion not the existing relations of production (and the other relations that derive from them), but above all the (imaginary) relationship of individuals to the relations of production and the relations that derive from them. What is represented in ideology is therefore not the system of the real relations which govern the existence of individuals, but the imaginary relation of those individuals to the real relations in which they live.

If this is the case, the question of the 'cause' of the imaginary distortion of the real relations in ideology disappears and must be replaced by a different question: why is the representation given to individuals of their (individual) relation to the social relations which govern their conditions of existence and their collective and individual life necessarily an imaginary relation? And what is the nature of this imaginariness? Posed in this way, the question explodes the solution by a 'clique',[11] by a group of individuals (Priests or Despots) who are the authors of the great ideological mystification, just as it explodes the solution by the alienated character of the real world. We shall see why later in my exposition. For the moment I shall go no further.

THESIS II: Ideology has a material existence.

I have already touched on this thesis by saying that the 'ideas' or 'representations', etc., which seem to make up ideology do not have an ideal (*idéale* or *idéelle*) or spiritual existence, but a material existence. I even suggested that the ideal (*idéale*, *idéelle*) and spiritual existence of 'ideas' arises exclusively in an ideology of the 'idea' and of ideology, and let me add, in an ideology of what seems to have 'founded' this conception since the emergence of the sciences, i.e. what the practicians of the sciences represent to themselves in their spontaneous ideology as 'ideas', true or false. Of course, presented in affirmative form, this thesis is unproven. I simply ask that the reader be favourably disposed towards it, say, in the name of materialism. A long series of arguments would be necessary to prove it.

This hypothetical thesis of the not spiritual but material existence of 'ideas' or other 'representations' is indeed necessary if we are to advance in our analysis of the nature of ideology. Or rather, it is merely useful to us in order the better to reveal what every at all serious analysis of any ideology will immediately and empirically show to every observer, however critical.

While discussing the ideological State apparatuses and their practices, I said that each of them was the realization of an ideology (the unity of these different regional ideologies – religious, ethical, legal, political, aesthetic, etc. – being assured by their subjection to the ruling ideology). I now return to this thesis: an ideology always exists in an apparatus, and its practice, or practices. This existence is material.

Of course, the material existence of the ideology in an apparatus and its practices does not have the same modality as the material existence of a paving-stone or a rifle. But, at the risk of being taken for a Neo-Aristotelian (NB Marx had a very high regard for Aristotle), I shall say that 'matter is discussed in many senses', or rather that it exists in different modalities, all rooted in the last instance in 'physical' matter.

Having said this, let me move straight on and see what happens to the 'individuals' who live in ideology, i.e. in a determinate (religious, ethical, etc.) representation of the world whose imaginary distortion depends on their imaginary relation to their conditions of existence, in other words, in the last instance, to the relations of production and to class relations (ideology = an imaginary relation to real relations). I shall say that this imaginary relation is itself endowed with a material existence.

Now I observe the following.

An individual believes in God, or Duty, or Justice, etc. This belief derives (for everyone, i.e. for all those who live in an ideological representation of ideology, which reduces ideology to ideas endowed by definition with a spiritual existence) from the ideas of the individual concerned, i.e. from him as a subject with a consciousness which contains the ideas of his belief. In this way, i.e. by means of the absolutely ideological 'conceptual' device (*dispositif*) thus set up (a subject endowed with a consciousness in which he freely forms or freely recognizes ideas in which he believes), the (material) attitude of the subject concerned naturally follows.

The individual in question behaves in such and such a way, adopts such and such a practical attitude, and, what is more, participates in certain regular practices which are those of the ideological apparatus on which 'depend' the ideas which he has in all consciousness freely chosen as a subject. If he believes in God, he goes to Church to attend Mass, kneels, prays, confesses, does penance (once it was material in the ordinary sense of the term) and naturally repents and so on. If he believes in Duty, he will have the corresponding attitudes, inscribed in ritual practices 'according to the correct principles'. If he believes in Justice, he will submit unconditionally to the rules of the Law, and may even protest when they are violated, sign petitions, take part in a demonstration, etc.

Throughout this schema we observe that the ideological representation of ideology is itself forced to recognize that every 'subject' endowed with a 'consciousness' and believing in the 'ideas' that his 'consciousness' inspires in him and freely accepts, must '*act* according to his ideas', must therefore inscribe his own ideas as a free subject in the actions of his material practice. If he does not do so, 'that is wicked'.

Indeed, if he does not do what he ought to do as a function of what he believes, it is because he does something else, which, still as a function of the same idealist scheme, implies that he has other ideas in his head as well as those he proclaims, and that he acts according to these other ideas, as a man who is either 'inconsistent' ('no one is willingly evil') or cynical, or perverse.

In every case, the ideology of ideology thus recognizes, despite its imaginary distortion, that the 'ideas' of a human subject exist in his actions, or ought to exist in his actions, and if that is not the case, it lends him other ideas corresponding to the actions (however perverse) that he does perform. This ideology talks of actions: I shall talk of actions inserted into *practices. And* I shall point out that these practices are governed by the *rituals* in which these practices are inscribed, within the *material existence of an ideological apparatus*, be it only a small part of that apparatus: a small mass in a small church, a funeral, a minor match at a sports' club, a school day, a political party meeting, etc.

Besides, we are indebted to Pascal's defensive 'dialectic' for the wonderful formula which will enable us to invert the order of the notional schema of ideology. Pascal says more or less: 'Kneel down, move your lips in prayer, and you will believe.' He thus scandalously inverts the order of things, bringing, like Christ, not peace but strife, and in addition something hardly Christian (for woe to him who brings scandal into the world!) – scandal itself. A fortunate scandal which makes him stick with Jansenist defiance to a language that directly names the reality.

I will be allowed to leave Pascal to the arguments of his ideological struggle with the religious ideological State apparatus of his day. And I shall be expected to use a more directly Marxist vocabulary, if that is possible, for we are advancing in still poorly explored domains.

I shall therefore say that, where only a single subject (such and such an individual) is concerned, the existence of the ideas of his belief is material in that *his ideas are his material actions inserted into material practices governed by material rituals which are themselves defined by the material ideological apparatus from which derive the ideas of that subject*. Naturally, the four inscriptions of the adjective 'material' in my proposition must be affected by different modalities: the materialities of a displacement for going to mass, of kneeling down, of the gesture of the sign of the cross, or of the *mea culpa*, of a sentence, of a prayer, of an act of contrition, of a penitence, of a gaze, of a hand-shake, of an external verbal discourse or an 'internal' verbal discourse (consciousness), are not one and the same materiality. I shall leave on one side the problem of a theory of the differences between the modalities of materiality.

It remains that in this inverted presentation of things, we are not dealing with an 'inversion' at all, since it is clear that certain notions have purely and simply disappeared from our presentation, whereas others on the contrary survive, and new terms appear.

Disappeared: the term *ideas.*
Survive: the terms *subject, consciousness, belief, actions.*
Appear: the terms *practices, rituals, ideological apparatus.*

It is therefore not an inversion or overturning (except in the sense in which one might say a government or a glass is overturned), but a reshuffle (of a non-ministerial type), a rather strange reshuffle, since we obtain the following result.

Ideas have disappeared as such (insofar as they are endowed with an ideal or spiritual existence), to the precise extent that it has emerged that their existence is inscribed in the actions of practices governed by rituals defined in the last instance by an ideological apparatus. It therefore appears that the subject acts insofar as he is acted by the following system (set out in the order of its real determination): ideology existing in a material ideological apparatus, prescribing material practices governed by a material ritual, which practices exist in the material actions of a subject acting in all consciousness according to his belief.

But this very presentation reveals that we have retained the following notions: subject, consciousness, belief, actions. From this series I shall immediately extract the decisive central term on which everything else depends: the notion of the *subject.*

And I shall immediately set down two conjoint theses:

1. there is no practice except by and in an ideology;
2. there is no ideology except by the subject and for subjects.

I can now come to my central thesis.

Ideology interpellates individuals as subjects

This thesis is simply a matter of making my last proposition explicit: there is no ideology except by the subject and for subjects. Meaning, there is no ideology except for concrete subjects, and this destination for ideology is only made possible by the subject: meaning, *by the category of the subject* and its functioning.

By this I mean that, even if it only appears under this name (the subject) with the rise of bourgeois ideology, above all with the rise of legal ideology,[12] the category of the subject (which may function under other names: e.g., as the soul in Plato, as God, etc.) is the constitutive category of all ideology, whatever its determination (regional or class) and whatever its historical date – since ideology has no history.

I say: the category of the subject is constitutive of all ideology, but at the same time and immediately I add that *the category of the subject is only constitutive of all ideology insofar as all ideology has the function (which defines it) of 'constituting' concrete individuals as subjects*. In the interaction of this double constitution exists the functioning of all ideology, ideology being nothing but its functioning in the material forms of existence of that functioning.

In order to grasp what follows, it is essential to realize that both he who is writing these lines and the reader who reads them are themselves subjects, and therefore ideological subjects (a tautological proposition), i.e. that the author and the reader of these lines both live 'spontaneously' or 'naturally' in ideology in the sense in which I have said that 'man is an ideological animal by nature'.

That the author, insofar as he writes the lines of a discourse which claims to be scientific, is completely absent as a 'subject' from 'his' scientific discourse (for all scientific discourse is by definition a subject-less discourse, there is no 'Subject of science' except in an ideology of science) is a different question which I shall leave on one side for the moment.

As St Paul admirably put it, it is in the 'Logos', meaning in ideology, that we 'live, move and have our being'. It follows that, for you and for me, the category of the subject is a primary 'obviousness' (obviousnesses are always primary): it is clear that you and I are subjects (free, ethical, etc....). Like all obviousnesses, including those that make a word 'name a thing' or 'have a meaning' (therefore including the obviousness of the 'transparency' of language), the 'obviousness' that you and I are subjects – and that that does not cause any problems – is an ideological effect, the elementary ideological effect.[13] It is indeed a peculiarity of ideology that it imposes (without appearing to do so, since these are 'obviousnesses') obviousnesses as obviousnesses, which we cannot *fail to recognize* and before which we have the inevitable and natural reaction of crying out (aloud or in the 'still, small voice of conscience'): 'That's obvious! That's right! That's true!'

At work in this reaction is the ideological *recognition* function which is one of the two functions of ideology as such (its inverse being the function of *misrecognition* – *méconnaissance*).

To take a highly 'concrete' example, we all have friends who, when they knock on our door and we ask, through the door, the question 'Who's there?', answer (since 'it's obvious') 'It's me'. And we recognize that 'it is him', or 'her'. We open the door, and 'it's true, it really was she who was there'. To take another example, when we recognize somebody of our (previous) acquaintance ((re)-connaissance) in the street, we show him that we have recognized him (and have recognized that he has recognized us) by saying to him 'Hello, my friend', and shaking his hand (a material ritual practice of ideological recognition in everyday life – in France, at least; elsewhere, there are other rituals).

In this preliminary remark and these concrete illustrations, I only wish to point out that you and I are *always already* subjects, and as such constantly practice the rituals of ideological recognition, which guarantee for us that we are indeed concrete, individual, distinguishable and (naturally) irreplaceable subjects. The writing I am currently executing and the reading you are currently[14] performing are also in this respect rituals of ideological recognition, including the 'obviousness' with which the 'truth' or 'error' of my reflections may impose itself on you.

But to recognize that we are subjects and that we function in the practical rituals of the most elementary everyday life (the hand-shake, the fact of calling you by your name, the fact of knowing, even if I do not know what it is, that you 'have' a name of your own, which means that you are recognized as a unique subject, etc.) – this recognition only gives us the 'consciousness' of our incessant (eternal) practice of ideological recognition – its consciousness, i.e. its *recognition* – but in no sense does it give us the (scientific) *knowledge* of the mechanism of this recognition. Now it is this knowledge that we have to reach, if you will, while speaking in ideology, and from within ideology we have to outline a discourse which tries to break with ideology, in order to dare to be the beginning of a scientific (i.e. subjectless) discourse on ideology.

Thus in order to represent why the category of the 'subject' is constitutive of ideology, which only exists by constituting concrete subjects as subjects, I shall employ a special mode of exposition: 'concrete' enough to be recognized, but abstract enough to be thinkable and thought, giving rise to a knowledge.

As a first formulation I shall say: *all ideology hails or interpellates concrete individuals as concrete subjects*, by the functioning of the category of the subject.

This is a proposition which entails that we distinguish for the moment between concrete individuals on the one hand and concrete subjects on the other, although at this level concrete subjects only exist insofar as they are supported by a concrete individual.

I shall then suggest that ideology 'acts' or 'functions' in such a way that it 'recruits' subjects among the individuals (it recruits them all), or 'transforms' the individuals into subjects (it transforms them all) by that very precise operation which I have called *interpellation* or hailing, and which can be imagined along the lines of the most commonplace everyday police (or other) hailing: 'Hey, you there!'[15]

Assuming that the theoretical scene I have imagined takes place in the street, the hailed individual will turn round. By this mere one-hundred-and-eighty-degree physical conversion, he becomes a *subject*. What? Because he has recognized that the hail was 'really' addressed to him, and that 'it was *really him* who was hailed' (and not someone else). Experience shows that the practical telecommunication of hailings is such that they hardly ever miss their man: verbal call or whistle, the one hailed always recognizes that it is really him who is being hailed. And yet it is a strange phenomenon, and one which cannot be explained solely by 'guilt feelings', despite the large numbers who 'have something on their consciences'.

Naturally for the convenience and clarity of my little theoretical theatre I have had to present things in the form of a sequence, with a before and an after, and thus in the form of a temporal succession. There are individuals walking along. Somewhere (usually behind them) the hail rings out: 'Hey, you there!' One individual (nine times out of ten it is the right one) turns round, believing/suspecting/knowing that it is for him, i.e. recognizing that 'it really is he' who is meant by the hailing. But in reality these things happen without any succession. The existence of ideology and the hailing or interpellation of individuals as subjects are one and the same thing.

I might add: what thus seems to take place outside ideology (to be precise, in the street), in reality takes place in ideology. What really takes place in ideology seems therefore to take place outside it. That is why those who are in ideology believe themselves by definition outside ideology: one of the effects of ideology is the practical *denegation* of the ideological character of ideology by ideology: ideology never says, 'I am ideological'. It is necessary to be outside ideology, i.e. in scientific knowledge, to be able to say: I am in ideology (a quite exceptional case) or (the general case): I was in ideology. As is well known, the accusation of being in ideology only applies to others, never to oneself (unless one is really a Spinozist or a Marxist, which, in this matter, is to be exactly the same thing). Which amounts to saying that ideology *has no outside* (for itself), but at the same time *that it is nothing but outside* (for science and reality).

Spinoza explained this completely two centuries before Marx, who practised it but without explaining it in detail. But let us leave this point, although it is heavy with consequences, consequences which are not just theoretical, but also directly political, since, for example, the whole theory of criticism and self-criticism, the golden rule of the Marxist-Leninist practice of the class struggle, depends on it.

Thus ideology hails or interpellates individuals as subjects. As ideology is eternal, I must now suppress the temporal form in which I have presented the functioning of ideology, and say: ideology has always-already interpellated individuals as subjects, which amounts to making it clear that individuals are always-already interpellated by ideology as subjects, which necessarily leads us to one last proposition: *individuals are always-already subjects*. Hence individuals are 'abstract' with respect to the subjects which they always-already are. This proposition might seem paradoxical.

That an individual is always-already a subject, even before he is born, is nevertheless the plain reality, accessible to everyone and not a paradox at all. Freud shows that individuals are always 'abstract' with respect to the subjects they always-already are, simply by noting the ideological ritual that surrounds the expectation of a 'birth', that 'happy event'. Everyone knows how much and in what way an unborn child is expected. Which amounts to saying, very prosaically, if we agree to drop the 'sentiments', i.e. the forms of family ideology (paternal/maternal/conjugal/fraternal) in which the unborn child is expected: it is certain in advance that it will bear its Father's Name, and will therefore have an identity and be irreplaceable. Before its birth, the child is therefore always-already a subject, appointed as a subject in and by the specific familial ideological configuration in which it is 'expected' once it has been conceived. I hardly need add that this familial ideological configuration is, in its uniqueness, highly structured, and that it is in this implacable and more or less 'pathological' (presupposing that any meaning can be assigned to that term) structure that the former subject-to-be will have to 'find' 'its' place, i.e. 'become' the sexual subject (boy or girl) which it already is in advance. It is clear that this ideological constraint and pre-appointment, and all the rituals of rearing and then education in the family, have some relationship with what Freud studied in the forms of the pre-genital and genital 'stages' of sexuality, i.e. in the 'grip' of what Freud registered by its effects as being the unconscious. But let us leave this point, too, on one side.

[...]

Let us decipher into theoretical language this wonderful necessity for the duplication of *the Subject into subjects* and of *the Subject itself into a subject-Subject*.

We observe that the structure of all ideology, interpellating individuals as subjects in the name of a Unique and Absolute Subject is *speculary*, i.e. a mirror-structure, and *doubly* speculary: this mirror duplication is constitutive of ideology and ensures its functioning. Which means that all ideology is *centred*, that the Absolute Subject occupies the unique place of the Centre, and interpellates around it the infinity of individuals into subjects in a double mirror-connexion such that it *subjects* the subjects to the Subject, while giving them in the Subject in which each subject can contemplate its own image (present and future) the *guarantee* that this really concerns them and Him, and that since everything takes place in the Family (the Holy Family: the Family is in essence Holy), 'God will *recognize* his own in it', i.e. those who have recognized God, and have recognized themselves in Him, will be saved.

Let me summarize what we have discovered about ideology in general.

The duplicate mirror-structure of ideology ensures simultaneously:

1. the interpellation of 'individuals' as subjects;
2. their subjection to the Subject;
3. the mutual recognition of subjects and Subject, the subjects' recognition of each other, and finally the subject's recognition of himself;[16]
4. the absolute guarantee that everything really is so, and that on condition that the subjects recognize what they are and behave accordingly, everything will be all right: Amen – '*So be it*'.

Result: caught in this quadruple system of interpellation as subjects, of subjection to the Subject, of universal recognition and of absolute guarantee, the subjects 'work', they 'work by themselves' in the vast majority of cases, with the exception of the 'bad subjects' who on occasion provoke the intervention of one of the detachments of the (repressive) State apparatus. But the vast majority of (good) subjects work all right 'all by themselves', i.e. by ideology (whose concrete forms are realized in the Ideological State Apparatuses). They are inserted into practices governed by the rituals of the ISAs. They 'recognize' the existing state of affairs (*das Bestehende*), that 'it really is true that it is so and not otherwise', and that they must be obedient to God, to their conscience, to the priest, to de Gaulle, to the boss, to the engineer, that thou shalt 'love thy neighbour as thyself', etc. Their concrete, material behaviour is simply the inscription in life of the admirable words of the prayer: '*Amen – So be it*'.

Yes, the subjects 'work by themselves'. The whole mystery of this effect lies in the first two moments of the quadruple system I have just discussed, or, if you prefer, in the ambiguity of the term *subject*. In the ordinary use of the term, subject in fact means: (1) a free subjectivity, a centre of initiatives, author of and responsible for its actions; (2) a subjected being, who submits to a higher authority, and is therefore stripped of all freedom except that of freely accepting his submission. This last note gives us the meaning of this ambiguity, which is merely a reflection of the effect which produces it: the individual *is interpellated as a (free) subject in order that he shall submit freely to the commandments of the Subject, i.e. in order that he shall (freely) accept his subjection*, i.e. in order that he shall make the gestures and actions of his subjection 'all by himself'. *There are no subjects except by and for their subjection.* That is why they 'work all by themselves'.

'*So be it!* …' This phrase which registers the effect to be obtained proves that it is not 'naturally' so ('naturally': outside the prayer, i.e. outside the ideological intervention). This phrase proves that it *has* to be so if things are to be what they must be, and let us let the words slip: if the reproduction of the relations of production is to be assured, even in the processes of production and circulation, every day, in the 'consciousness', i.e. in the attitudes of the individual-subjects occupying the posts which the socio-technical division of labour assigns to them in production, exploitation, repression, ideologization, scientific practice, etc. Indeed, what is really in question in this mechanism of the mirror recognition of the Subject and of the individuals interpellated as subjects, and of the guarantee given by the Subject to the subjects if they freely accept their subjection to the Subject's 'commandments'? The reality in question in this mechanism, the reality which is necessarily *ignored* (*méconnue*) in the very forms of recognition (ideology = misrecognition/ignorance) is indeed, in the last resort, the reproduction of the relations of production and of the relations deriving from them.

January–April 1969

P.S. If these few schematic theses allow me to illuminate certain aspects of the functioning of the Superstructure and its mode of intervention in the Infrastructure, they are obviously *abstract* and necessarily leave several important problems unanswered, which should be mentioned:

1. The problem of the *total process* of the realization of the reproduction of the relations of production.

As an element of this process, the ISAs *contribute* to this reproduction. But the point of view of their contribution alone is still an abstract one.

It is only within the processes of production and circulation that this reproduction is *realized*. It is realized by the mechanisms of those processes, in which the training of the workers is 'completed', their posts assigned them, etc. It is in the internal mechanisms of these processes that the effect of the different ideologies is felt (above all the effect of legal-ethical ideology).

But this point of view is still an abstract one. For in a class society the relations of production are relations of exploitation, and therefore relations between antagonistic classes. The reproduction of the relations of production, the ultimate aim of the ruling class, cannot therefore be a merely technical operation training and distributing individuals for the different posts in the 'technical division' of labour. In fact there is no 'technical division' of labour except in the ideology of the ruling class: every 'technical' division, every 'technical' organization of labour is the form and mask of a *social* (= class) division and organization of labour. The reproduction of the relations of production can therefore only be a class undertaking. It is realized through a class struggle which counterposes the ruling class and the exploited class.

The *total process* of the realization of the reproduction of the relations of production is therefore still abstract, insofar as it has not adopted the point of view of this class struggle. To adopt the point of view of reproduction is therefore, in the last instance, to adopt the point of view of the class struggle.

2. The problem of the class nature of the ideolog*ies* existing in a social formation.

The 'mechanism' of ideology *in general* is one thing. We have seen that it can be reduced to a few principles expressed in a few words (as 'poor' as those which, according to Marx, define production *in general*, or in Freud, define *the* unconscious *in general*). If there is any truth in it, this mechanism must be *abstract* with respect to every real ideological formation.

I have suggested that the ideologies were *realized* in institutions, in their rituals and their practices, in the ISAs. We have seen that on this basis they contribute to that form of class struggle, vital for the ruling class, the reproduction of the relations of production. But the point of view itself, however real, is still an abstract one.

In fact, the State and its Apparatuses only have meaning from the point of view of the class struggle, as an apparatus of class struggle ensuring class oppression and guaranteeing the conditions of exploitation and its reproduction. But there is no class struggle without antagonistic classes. Whoever says class struggle of the ruling class says resistance, revolt and class struggle of the ruled class.

That is why the ISAs are not the realization of ideology *in general*, nor even the conflict-free realization of the ideology of the ruling class. The ideology of the ruling class does not become the ruling ideology by the grace of God, nor even by virtue of the seizure of State power alone. It is by the installation of the ISAs in which this ideology is realized and realizes itself that it becomes the ruling ideology. But this installation is not achieved all by itself; on the contrary, it is the stake in a very bitter and continuous class struggle: first against the former ruling classes and their positions in the old and new ISAs, then against the exploited class.

But this point of view of the class struggle in the ISAs is still an abstract one. In fact, the class struggle in the ISAs is indeed an aspect of the class struggle, sometimes an important and symptomatic one: e.g. the anti-religious struggle in the eighteenth century, or the 'crisis' of the educational ISA in every capitalist country today. But the class struggles in the ISAs is only one aspect of a class struggle which goes beyond the ISAs. The ideology that a class in power makes the ruling ideology in its ISAs is indeed 'realized' in those ISAs, but it goes beyond them, for it comes from elsewhere. Similarly, the ideology that a ruled class manages to defend in and against such ISAs goes beyond them, for it comes from elsewhere.

It is only from the point of view of the classes, i.e. of the class struggle, that it is possible to explain the ideologies existing in a social formation. Not only is it from this starting-point that it is possible to explain the realization of the ruling ideology in the ISAs and of the forms of class struggle for which the ISAs are the seat and the stake. But it is also and above all from this starting-point that it is possible to understand the provenance of the ideologies which are realized in the ISAs and confront one another there. For if it is true that the ISAs represent the *form* in which the ideology of the ruling class must *necessarily* be realized, and the form in which the ideology of the ruled class must *necessarily* be measured and confronted, ideologies are not 'born' in the ISAs but from the social classes at grips in the class struggle: from their conditions of existence, their practices, their experience of the struggle, etc.

April 1970

Notes

1 Marx gave it its scientific concept: *variable capital*.
2 In *For Marx* and *Reading Capital*, 1965 (English editions 1969 and 1970 respectively).
3 *Topography* from the Greek *topos*: place. A topography represents in a definite space the respective *sites* occupied

by several realities: thus the economic is *at the bottom* (the base), the superstructure *above it*.

4 To my knowledge, Gramsci is the only one who went any distance in the road I am taking. He had the 'remarkable' idea that the State could not be reduced to the (Repressive) State Apparatus, but included, as he put it, a certain number of institutions from '*civil society*': the Church, the Schools, the trade unions, etc. Unfortunately, Gramsci did not systematize his institutions, which remained in the state of acute but fragmentary notes (cf. Gramsci, *Selections from the Prison Notebooks* (International Publishers, 1971), pp. 12, 259, 260–3; see also the letter to Tatiana Schucht, 7 September 1931, in *Lettre del Carcere* (Einaudi, 1968), p. 479.
5 The family obviously has other 'functions' than that of an ISA. It intervenes in the reproduction of labour power. In different modes of production it is the unit of production and/or the unit of consumption.
6 The 'Law' belongs both to the (Repressive) State Apparatus and to the system of the ISAs.
7 In a pathetic text written in 1937, Krupskaya relates the history of Lenin's desperate efforts and what she regards as his failure.
8 What I have said in these few brief words about the class struggle in the ISAs is obviously far from exhausting the question of the class struggle.

To approach this question, two principles must be borne in mind:

The first principle was formulated by Marx in the Preface to *A Contribution to the Critique of Political Economy*: 'In considering such transformations [a social revolution] a distinction should always be made between the material transformation of the economic conditions of production, which can be determined with the precision of natural science, and the legal, political, religious, aesthetic or philosophic – in short, ideological forms in which men become conscious of this conflict and fight it out.' The class struggle is thus expressed and exercised in ideological forms, thus also in the ideological forms of the ISAs. But the class struggle *extends far beyond* these forms, and it is because it extends beyond them that the struggle of the exploited classes may also be exercised in the forms of the ISAs, and thus turn the weapon of ideology against the classes in power.

This by virtue of the *second principle*: the class struggle extends beyond the ISAs because it is rooted elsewhere than in ideology, in the Infrastructure, in the relations of production, which are relations of exploitation and constitute the base for class relations.

9 For the most part. For the relations of production are first reproduced by the materiality of the processes of

production and circulation. But it should not be forgotten that ideological relations are immediately present in these same processes.

10 *For that part* of reproduction to which the Repressive State Apparatus and the Ideological State Apparatus *contribute.*

11 I use this very modern term deliberately. For even in Communist circles, unfortunately, it is a commonplace to 'explain' some political deviation (left or right opportunism) by the action of a 'clique'.

12 Which borrowed the legal category of 'subject in law' to make an ideological notion: man is by nature a subject.

13 Linguists and those who appeal to linguistics for various purposes often run up against difficulties which arise because they ignore the action of the ideological effects in all discourses – including even scientific discourses.

14 NB: this double 'currently' is one more proof of the fact that ideology is 'eternal', since these two 'currentlys' are separated by an indefinite interval; I am writing these lines on 6 April 1969, you may read them at any subsequent time.

15 Hailing as an everyday practice subject to a precise ritual takes a quite 'special' form in the policeman's practice of 'hailing' which concerns the hailing of 'suspects'.

16 Hegel is (unknowingly) an admirable 'theoretician' of ideology insofar as he is a 'theoretician' of Universal Recognition who unfortunately ends up in the ideology of Absolute Knowledge. Feuerbach is an astonishing 'theoretician' of the mirror connexion, who unfortunately ends up in the ideology of the Human Essence. To find the material with which to construct a theory of the guarantee, we must turn to Spinoza.

20

"Recent Developments in Theories of Language and Ideology: A Critical Note" (1980)

Stuart Hall

In recent years the two journals *Screen* and *Screen Education* (sponsored by the Society for Education in Film and Television) have provided the base for the development of a set of challenging hypotheses about the relationship between language, ideology and 'the subject'. Though principally relating to film texts and practices, this theory has far-reaching implications for the analysis of all signifying practices, as well as for the debates on the problem of language/ideology and representation. This body of work (hereinafter, for convenience, 'screen theory') draws extensively on recent French theoretical writing in a number of different fields: film theory (early semiotics, the work of Christian Metz, the debates between the journals *Cahiers du Cinéma* and *Cinétique*), the theory of ideology (Althusser), the psychoanalytic writings of the Lacan group, and recent theories of language and discourse (Julia Kristeva, the 'Tel Quel' group, Foucault). It has also been strongly influenced by the critique of 'realism', defined as the dominant filmic practice in the cinema: this critique originates in Brecht's work and the Brecht–Lukács debate and, to some extent, in the Russian formalists. It has recently much developed in both the theory and the practice of *avant-garde* cinema. 'Screen theory' has reworked and

Stuart Hall, "Recent Developments in Theories of Language and Ideology: A Critical Note," pp. 149–53 from *Culture, Media, Language*. London: Hutchinson, 1980. Reproduced by permission of Taylor & Francis Books UK.

expanded these theories through a series of wide-ranging articles. The problematic which they have been elaborating now constitutes the dominant point of departure in film studies and in the debates around the relation of discourse and ideology.

'Screen theory' originates in the break which the structural linguistics of Saussure first made with earlier theories of language and which was developed into a general paradigm for the study of signifying systems by Lévi-Strauss and the early Barthes. This is the point of departure for early semiotics. But the real theoretical distinctiveness of 'screen theory' arises from the further break between what, for convenience, may be called semiotics 1 and semiotics 2. Crudely, the argument is that semiotics 1 was correct in its attempts to identify signification as a practice for the *production* of meaning, as against earlier theories which assumed that 'reality' was somehow transparently reflected in language. It also advanced the field considerably by dethroning the position of the integral Cartesian subject – the authorial 'I', assumed to be both the source and the guarantor of the 'truth' of any enunciative statement – in favour of an analysis pitched at the level of the relations between elements and the rules governing their combination in signifying systems themselves (Saussure's *Langue*). However, 'screen theory' argues that, in itself, this break with empiricist theories of language is inadequate, since (in Lévi-Strauss's 'myth', Barthes's 'codes' and Althusser's theories of ideology) the whole question of 'the subject' is left as an empty space. The Cartesian subject has been displaced: but what replaces it has not been adequately theorized.

In semiotics 2 this gap is filled by drawing extensively on the psychoanalytic writings of Lacan. Three converging lines of argument sustain this attempt to deploy Lacan to rectify the inadequacies of semiotics 1. First, Lévi-Strauss made much of the 'entry into culture' as the founding moment of signification and symbolic representation, but he located this outside 'the subject', in the cultural and social system itself. Lacan's work retains the structure of Lévi-Strauss's explanation but now locates this as the entry into the 'symbolic' – the moment when 'the subject' enters into/is constituted in language, the network of signifiers. In Lacan the moment of the 'symbolic' is given a psychoanalytic interpretation, based on a re-reading of Freud and linked with the unconscious processes and stages through which the unformed infant becomes a 'subject', as these are outlined in Freud's work. This, however, is no longer the integral and homogeneous 'subject' of Descartes, since it is constituted by unconscious processes; it is not the unitary individual but a set of contradictory 'positions', fixed by those processes in a certain relation to knowledge and language.

Second, these propositions were substantially reinforced by Althusser's later writing on ideology, especially where (in the 'Ideological State Apparatuses' essay) he argues that all ideologies 'work' by and through the constitution of the subject and then gives to the process by which ideological discourses constitute and 'hail' subjects the term 'interpellation' – a concept which has an ambiguous provenance in Lacan.

The third element is harder to pin down exactly, but it arises from the fact that in Lacan's reading Freud's theory of the formation of 'the subject' is a highly linguistic one, and the processes of that formation are especially linked with visual analogues (for example, the 'mirror phase', narcissism, voyeurism, Lacan's work on the 'look' and the 'gaze', the castration complex as a 'scenario of vision', founded on the presence/absence and the 'recognition'/denial through which it is resolved and so on). These have made it especially easy and tenable to forge a connection between the 'primary' psychoanalytic processes through which subjects-as-such are constituted and

the related processes of representation and identification in visual discourses and texts (especially those of the cinema). Metz's article 'The imaginary signifier'[1] is a *locus classicus* of this move from semiotics 1 to a Lacanian psychoanalytic framework, and its republication in *Screen* marked the passage of that journal from the earlier debates on 'realism' to a full-blown Lacanian position.[2] It ought to be said that 'screen theory' is far more than an attempt to supplement existing theories of language, representation and ideology by developing the neglected area of 'the subject'. In effect, all preceding theories have been substantively reworked and/or displaced by the deployment of Lacan's propositions. The premises of historical materialism, for example, which attempt to relate ideologies to political and economic practices, to their functioning and effectivity in specific social formations and in specific historical conjunctures, have been translated on to the terrain of 'the subject'. We would argue that this is accomplished through a series of reductions: the unconscious process through which 'the subject' is constituted is also – it is proposed – the process which constitutes 'the subject' *in language*. It is also the same as that which constitutes 'the subject' for ideology. First a series of homologies, then a series of identities give these apparently distinct (if related) levels a single and common source and foundation. The 'politics' of ideological struggle thus becomes exclusively a problem of and around 'subjectivity' in the Lacanian sense.

'Screen theory' is therefore a very ambitious theoretical construct indeed – for it aims to account for how biological individuals become social subjects, *and* for how those subjects are fixed in positions of knowledge in relation to language and representation, *and* for how they are interpellated in specific ideological discourses. This theory is then lopped back to the earlier concerns with 'realism'. Most filmic texts are held to operate within the conventions and practices of 'realism': they are said to be governed by the rules of *the* classic realist text (in the singular). The classic realist text sets the viewers in a position of transparent and unproblematic knowledge in relation to their representations of 'the real', which they actually produce but which they appear only (naturally) to reflect. They therefore depend on an empiricist relation to knowledge. But – so the argument runs – this is because the rules and conventions of the classic realist text recapitulate and replay the basic positions of 'the subject', already fixed by unconscious processes in the early stages of its formation.

This theory gives texts a central place. Texts do not express a meaning (which resides elsewhere) or 'reflect reality': they produce a representation of 'the real' which the viewer is positioned to take as a mirror reflection of the real world: this is the 'productivity of the text', discussed more fully below. However, this 'productivity' no longer depends in any way on the ideological effectivity of the representations produced, nor on the ideological problematics within which the discourse is operating, nor on the social, political or historical practices with which it is articulated. Its 'productivity' is defined exclusively in terms of the capacity of the text to set the viewer 'in place' in a position of unproblematic identification/knowledge. And that, in turn, is founded on the process of the formation of the subject. Within this framework, then, the functioning of language, the practices of representation and the operations of ideology are all explained by reference to Lacanian psychoanalytic theory. It follows that all ideological struggle must take place, also, at the level of 'the subject' (since this is where the relation of 'the subject' to ideology is constituted and is the mechanism through which ideology functions) and is confined to disrupting the forms of the discourse which recapitulate those primary positions.

This ambitious theory, with its aim to resolve a host of problems unsatisfactorily dealt with in classical Marxist theory, has been forcefully advanced and expounded with considerable sophistication. Nevertheless, it is open to a number of criticisms which have not so far been adequately met. These may be briefly summarized as follows.

1. The theory is substantiated by, first, establishing a series of homologies – 'ideology is structured like a language', 'the unconscious is structured like a language' and so on – which are then declared to be not just 'like' each other but actually 'the same': constituted in the same moment by the same unconscious mechanisms. This movement from homology to identity is a dubious procedure and has not so far been adequately defended.

2. These processes are all declared to be 'the same'. But *one* of them is given exclusive explanatory power over all the others. It is the psychoanalytic process by which 'the subject' is constituted in the 'symbolic' which explains how language/representation function (in any/every other instance). Specific discourses or representations appear to require no other conditions of existence or further premises to be explained and have no other determinate effectivity. But this form of psychoanalytic reductionism seems to 'resolve' the problems of semiotics 1 simply by inverting them. What in Saussure was explained by practices wholly exclusive *of* 'the subject' is now – by a simple inversion – explained exclusively *at* the level of 'the subject'. Except in a largely ritual sense, any substantive reference to social formation has been made to disappear. This gives 'the subject' an all-inclusive place and Lacanian psychoanalysis an exclusive, privileged, explanatory claim.

3. This relates to the 'in-general' form of the argument. The mechanisms which Freud and Lacan identify are, of course, universal. All 'subjects' in all societies at all times are unconsciously constituted in this way. The formation of 'the subject' in this sense is transhistorical and trans-social. It is a theory of the universal 'contradictory' subject – different from 'the subject' of classical philosophy in being intersected by contradiction and unconsciously constituted, but similar to it in the transcendental/universal form in which it is predicated. It is, of course, difficult, if not impossible, to square this universal form of argument with the premises of historical materialism, which requires us always to attend to the pertinent differences – Marx's *differentia specificae*, which *differentiate* one modality of individualism from another – which historicizes the different forms of subjectivity and which needs a reference to specific modes of production, to definite societies at historically specific moments and conjunctures. The two kinds of theory are conceptually incompatible in the form of their argument. This has not prevented 'screen theory' from claiming that its theory of 'the subject' is a 'materialistic' one and satisfactorily resolves the problems posed by historical materialism.

4. Further, suppose that we were to accept the validity of Lacan's theory of the constitution of the

subject, as well as the 'screen theory' argument that we cannot have an adequate theory of language/ideology without taking the functioning of 'the subject' into account. It does not follow that a theory of how the 'subject-in-general' is formed offers, *in itself*, without further determinations, an adequate explanation of how historically specific subjects, already 'positioned' in language-in-general, function in relation to particular discourses or historically specific ideologies in definite social formations. The theory of 'the subject' as advanced by 'screen theory' *may be* a necessary part, but *it is not yet a sufficient explanation of* particular discourses or specific ideologies and their functioning. The practices of language, discourse and ideologies may have other determinations, only some of which can be fixed at the level of 'the subject'. Thus other premises, relating to further conditions of existence and having determinate effects, would have to be introduced in order to move the explanation – as historical materialism requires – from the level of the 'in-general' (compare 'production-in-general' – what Marx described as 'a chaotic abstraction') to the more concrete, historically determinate level (that is, specific modes of production under determinate conditions). 'Screen theory' seems here to have fallen prey to the temptation to treat the most abstract/universal level of abstraction as the most pertinent – indeed, the only 'truly theoretical' – level of explanation.

In its present, all-embracing form 'screen theory' refuses to countenance any propositions about discourse or ideology which are not reducible to, and explicable by, the Lacanian theory of 'the subject'. Thus it claims to explain how 'the subject' is positioned in relation to patriarchal ideology-in-general. But it cannot explain the pertinent differences between different patriarchal ideologies in different social formations at different times. Even less can it explain how patriarchal ideologies may be broken, interrupted or contravened: since, according to the theory, 'the subject' cannot help but enter the 'symbolic' under the patriarchal sign, for it is this which, in imposing the 'Law of Culture' (the 'Law of the Symbolic'), establishes the rule of difference on which language itself is founded. 'The subject' is then, by definition, always already inside patriarchal language/ideology. Thus all ideology is, by definition,

the dominant ideology – the *doxa*. This reproduces all the problems earlier identified in the 'functionalism' of Althusser's 'Ideological State Apparatuses' essay; only now the 'functionalism' of the dominant ideology appears to be given, not at the level of social formation, but at the level of 'the subject'.

5. It is, therefore, conceptually impossible to construct, from this position, an adequate concept of 'struggle' in ideology, since (for example) struggle against patriarchal ideology would be a struggle against the very repressive conditions in which language as such is itself constituted. No alternative model has been proposed as to how 'the subject' might be positioned in language without also being positioned in patriarchal ideology. 'Screen theory' has attempted to deal with this problem by advancing the strategy of 'deconstruction' (for example, deconstructing the practices and positionings of classical realism). But although deconstruction may provide a significant strategy of resistance, especially for the unmasking and interruption of dominant discourses, it certainly does not identify the conditions for the production of alternative languages and discourses. What it appears to do is to establish a simple alternation between being 'in language' (and therefore, inescapably, in ideology) or 'against language'. But a non-patriarchal language cannot be conceptualized in terms of a revolution against language *as such*: this is a contradiction in terms. One effect of this, however, has been that a rather simple and unproblematic identity has been forged between the practices of struggle in ideology and the practices of the *avant-garde*. Julia Kristeva has taken this implied premise to its logical conclusion in her theory of the revolution in language. But this has not proved an adequate resolution of the problem, which arises because the argument has collapsed a theory of the functioning of specific ideologies into a theory of the conditions for language as such.

6. We have taken patriarchal ideologies as our example in the foregoing criticism because 'screen theory' has advanced particularly strong claims in this area (in contrast to classical Marxism), has been deeply influential for feminist theory and film practice – and yet seems to encounter particular difficulties precisely on

this ground. For in Lacan the differences and distinctions which make language and representation possible (a condition of the 'symbolic') are rooted in the marking of sexual difference – the latter providing the paradigm for, as well as the supporting structure of, the former. But the key mechanism which sustains this passage into the 'symbolic' is the resolution of the castration complex. However, this is a highly phallocentric theory, and its effect appears to be to consign women, not just in this culture but forever – and as a condition of having access to representation at all – to a negative entry into language, which is already and always marked by patriarchal dominance. If the 'Law of Culture' is, by definition and always, the 'Law of the Father', and this is the condition of language and the 'symbolic', then it is difficult to see why patriarchy is not – psychoanalytically rather than biologically – a woman's necessary and irreversible destiny.

These debates are by no means yet resolved: they have been vigorously and often contentiously pursued: and they continue to define a central terrain of theorization and argument in this area of work. Consequently, in 1977–8 the Media Group spent the year making itself familiar with this difficult body of work and with the bodies of theory on which it is based. It attempted to identify the central thesis and premises of the 'screen theory' problematic, as well as demystifying a little the forbiddingly arcane language and abstract formulations in which a great deal of the transcriptions from French theory have been cast. It attempted to develop a serious critique of 'screen theory', at the same time revaluing its own premises and practices in the light of that work. This critique is due to be published in its longer form. What follows is an extract from that longer argument, referring specifically to the question of how to think the relations between texts, subjects and readers/viewers. It develops a particular critique of 'screen theory' positions on this theme (similar points have begun to be formulated recently in the pages of *Screen* itself) and begins to advance alternative propositions, which, however, significantly modify earlier arguments as a result of the encounter.

Notes

1 *Screen*, vol. 16, no. 2 (Summer 1975).
2 See the Editorial Statement and the 'Presentation' of 'The imaginery signifier' in *Screen*, ibid.

21

"The Spectre of Ideology" (1989)

Slavoj Žižek

the implicit call is from the beginning is to recognify ideology.

I Critique of Ideology, Today?

By way of a simple reflection on how the horizon of historical imagination is subjected to change, we find ourselves *in medias res*, compelled to accept the unrelenting pertinence of the notion of ideology. Up to a decade or two ago, the system production-nature (man's productive-exploitative relationship with nature and its resources) was perceived as a constant, whereas everybody was busy imagining different forms of the social organization of production and commerce (Fascism or Communism as alternatives to liberal capitalism); today, as Fredric Jameson perspicaciously remarked, nobody seriously considers possible alternatives to capitalism any longer, whereas popular imagination is persecuted by the visions of the forthcoming 'breakdown of nature', of the stoppage of all life on earth – it seems easier to imagine the 'end of the world' than a far more modest change in the mode of production, as if liberal capitalism is the 'real' that will somehow survive even under conditions of a global ecological catastrophe. ... One can thus categorically assert the existence of ideology *qua* generative matrix that regulates the relationship between visible and non-visible, between imaginable and non-imaginable, as well as the changes in this relationship.

This matrix can be easily discerned in the dialectics of 'old' and 'new', when an event that announces a wholly new dimension or epoch is (mis)perceived as

the continuation of or return to the past, or – the opposite case – when an event that is entirely inscribed in the logic of the existing order is (mis)perceived as a radical rupture. The supreme example of the latter, of course, is provided by those critics of Marxism who (mis)perceive our late-capitalist society as a new social formation no longer dominated by the dynamics of capitalism as it was described by Marx. In order to avoid this worn-out example, however, let us turn to the domain of sexuality. One of today's commonplaces is that so-called 'virtual' or 'cyber' sex presents a radical break with the past, since in it, actual sexual contact with a 'real other' is losing ground against masturbatory enjoyment, whose sole support is a virtual other – phone-sex, pornography, up to computerized 'virtual sex'. ... The Lacanian answer to this is that first we have to expose the myth of 'real sex' allegedly possible 'before' the arrival of virtual sex: Lacan's thesis that 'there is no sexual relationship' means precisely that the structure of the 'real' sexual act (of the act with a flesh-and-blood partner) is already inherently phantasmic – the 'real' body of the other serves only as a support for our phantasmic projections. In other words, 'virtual sex' in which a glove simulates the stimuli of what we see on the screen, and so on, is not a monstrous distortion of real sex, it simply renders manifest its underlying phantasmic structure.

An exemplary case of the opposite misperception is provided by the reaction of Western liberal intellectuals to the emergence of new states in the process of the disintegration of real Socialism in Eastern Europe: they (mis)perceived this emergence as a return to the

Slavoj Žižek, "The Spectre of Ideology," pp. 1–25 from *Mapping Ideology*. London: Verso, 1994. Reprinted by permission of Verso.

nineteenth-century tradition of the nation-state, whereas what we are actually dealing with is the exact opposite: the 'withering-away' of the traditional nation-state based upon the notion of the abstract citizen identified with the constitutional legal order. In order to characterize this new state of things, Étienne Balibar recently referred to the old Marxian phrase *Es gibt keinen Staat in Europa* – there no longer exists a proper state in Europe. The old spectre of Leviathan parasitizing on the *Lebenswelt* of society, totalizing it from above, is more and more eroded from both sides. On the one hand, there are the new emerging ethnic communities – although some of them are formally constituted as sovereign states, they are no longer states in the proper modern-age European sense, since they did not cut the umbilical cord between state and ethnic community. (Paradigmatic here is the case of Russia, in which local mafias already function as a kind of parallel power structure.) On the other hand, there are the multiple transnational links, from multinational capital to mafia cartels and inter-state political communities (European Union).

There are two reasons for this limitation of state sovereignty, each of which is in itself compelling enough to justify it: the transnational character of ecological crisis and of nuclear threat. This eroding of state authority from both sides is mirrored in the fact that today the basic political antagonism is that between the universalist 'cosmopolitical' liberal democracy (standing for the force corroding the state from above) and the new 'organic' populism-communitarianism (standing for the force corroding the state from below). And – as Balibar pointed out yet again[1] – this antagonism is to be conceived neither as an external opposition nor as the complementary relationship of the two poles in which one pole balances the excess of its opposite (in the sense that, when we have too much universalism, a little bit of ethnic roots gives people the feeling of belonging, and thus stabilizes the situation), but in a genuinely Hegelian sense – each pole of the antagonism is inherent to its opposite, so that we stumble upon it at the very moment when we endeavour to grasp the opposite pole for itself, to posit it 'as such'.

Because of this inherent character of the two poles, one should avoid the liberal-democratic trap of concentrating exclusively on the horrifying facts and even more horrifying potentials of what is going on today in Russia and some other ex-Communist countries: the new hegemonic ideology of 'Eurasism' preaching the organic link between community and the state as an antidote to the corrosive influence of the 'Jewish' principle of market and social atomism, orthodox national imperialism as an antidote to Western individualism, and so on. In order to combat these new forms of organicist populism effectively one must, as it were, turn the critical gaze back upon oneself and submit to critical scrutiny liberal-democratic universalism itself – what opens up the space for the organicist populism is the weak point, the 'falsity', of this very universalism.

These same examples of the actuality of the notion of ideology, however, also render clear the reasons why today one hastens to renounce the notion of ideology: does not the critique of ideology involve a privileged place, somehow exempted from the turmoils of social life, which enables some subject-agent to perceive the very hidden mechanism that regulates social visibility and non-visibility? Is not the claim that we can accede to this place the most obvious case of ideology? Consequently, with reference to today's state of epistemological reflection, is not the notion of ideology self-defeating? So why should we cling to a notion with such obviously outdated epistemological implications (the relationship of 'representation' between thought and reality, etc.)? Is not its utterly ambiguous and elusive character in itself a sufficient reason to abandon it? 'Ideology' can designate anything from a contemplative attitude that misrecognizes its dependence on social reality to an action-orientated set of beliefs, from the indispensable medium in which individuals live out their relations to a social structure to false ideas which legitimate a dominant political power. It seems to pop up precisely when we attempt to avoid it, while it fails to appear where one would clearly expect it to dwell.

When some procedure is denounced as 'ideological *par excellence*', one can be sure that its inversion is no less ideological. For example, among the procedures generally acknowledged as 'ideological' is definitely the eternalization of some historically limited condition, the act of discerning some higher Necessity in a contingent occurrence (from the grounding of male domination in the 'nature of things' to interpreting AIDS as a punishment for the sinful life of modern man; or, at a more intimate level, when we encounter our 'true love', it seems as if this is what we have been waiting for all our life, as if, in some mysterious way, all our previous life has led to this encounter ...): the senseless contingency of the real is thus 'internalized', symbolized, provided with Meaning. Is not ideology, however, also the opposite procedure of failing to notice the necessity, of misperceiving it as an insignificant contingency (from the psychoanalytic cure, in which one of the main forms of the analysand's resistance is his insistence that his symptomatic slip of tongue was a mere lapse without any signification, up to the domain of economics, in which the ideological procedure *par excellence* is to reduce the crisis to an external, ultimately contingent occurrence, thus failing to take note of the inherent logic of the system that begets the crisis)? In this precise sense, ideology is the exact opposite of internalization of the external contingency: it resides in externalization of the result of an inner necessity, and the task of the critique of ideology here is precisely to discern the hidden necessity in what appears as a mere contingency.

The most recent case of a similar inversion was provided by the way Western media reported on the Bosnian war. The first thing that strikes the eye is the contrast to the reporting on the 1991 Gulf War, where we had the standard ideological personification:

> Instead of providing information on social, political or religious trends and antagonisms in Iraq, the media ultimately reduced the conflict to a quarrel with Saddam Hussein, Evil Personified, the outlaw who excluded himself from the civilized international community. Even more than the destruction of Iraq's military forces, the true aim was presented as psychological, as the humiliation of Saddam who was to 'lose face'. In the case of the Bosnian war, however, notwithstanding isolated cases of the demonization of the Serbian president Milosevic, the predominant attitude reflects that of a quasi-anthropological observer. The media outdo one another in giving us lessons on the ethnic and religious background of the conflict: traumas hundreds of years old are being replayed and acted out, so that, in order to understand the roots of the conflict, one has to know not only the history of Yugoslavia, but the entire history

of the Balkans from medieval times. ... In the Bosnian conflict, it is therefore not possible simply to take sides, one can only patiently try to grasp the background of this savage spectacle, alien to our civilized system of values. ... Yet this opposite procedure involves an ideological mystification even more cunning than the demonization of Saddam Hussein.[2]

In what, precisely, consists this ideological mystification? To put it somewhat crudely, the evocation of the 'complexity of circumstances' serves to deliver us from the responsibility to act. The comfortable attitude of a distant observer, the evocation of the allegedly intricate context of religious and ethnic struggles in Balkan countries, is here to enable the West to shed its responsibility towards the Balkans – that is, to avoid the bitter truth that, far from presenting the case of an eccentric ethnic conflict, the Bosnian war is a direct result of the West's failure to grasp the political dynamic of the disintegration of Yugoslavia, of the West's silent support of 'ethnic cleansing'.

In the domain of theory, we encounter a homologous reversal apropos of the 'deconstructionist' problematization of the notion of the subject's guilt and personal responsibility. The notion of a subject morally and criminally fully 'responsible' for his acts clearly serves the ideological need to conceal the intricate, always-already operative texture of historico-discursive presuppositions that not only provide the context for the subject's act but also define in advance the coordinates of its meaning: the system can function only if the cause of its malfunction can be located in the responsible subject's 'guilt'. One of the commonplaces of the leftist criticism of law is that the attribution of personal responsibility and guilt relieves us of the task of probing into the concrete circumstances of the act in question. Suffice it to recall the moral-majority practice of attributing a moral qualification to the higher crime rate among African Americans ('criminal dispositions', 'moral insensitivity', etc.): this attribution precludes any analysis of the concrete ideological, political and economic conditions of African Americans.

Is not this logic of 'putting the blame on the circumstances' however, taken to its extremes, self-defeating in so far as it necessarily leads to the unforgettable – and no less ideological – cynicism of

Brecht's famous lines from his *Threepenny Opera*: 'Wir wären gut anstatt so roh, doch die Verhältnisse, sie sind nicht so!' ('We would be good instead of being so rude, if only the circumstances were not of this kind')? In other words, are we, the speaking subjects, not always-already *engaged* in recounting the circumstances that predetermine the space of our activity?

A more concrete example of the same undecidable ambiguity is provided by the standard 'progressive' criticism of psychoanalysis. The reproach here is that the psychoanalytic explanation of misery and psychic suffering through unconscious libidinal complexes, or even via a direct reference to the 'death drive', renders the true causes of destructiveness invisible. This critique of psychoanalysis found its ultimate theoretical expression in the rehabilitation of the idea that the ultimate cause of psychic trauma is real childhood sexual abuse: by introducing the notion of the phantasmic origin of trauma, Freud allegedly betrayed the truth of his own discovery.[3] Instead of the concrete analysis of external, actual social conditions – the patriarchal family, its role in the totality of the reproduction of the capitalist system, and so on – we are thus given the story of unresolved libidinal deadlocks; instead of the analysis of social conditions that lead to war, we are given the 'death drive'; instead of the change of social relations, a solution is sought in the inner psychic change, in the 'maturation' that should qualify us to accept social reality as it is. In this perspective, the very striving for social change is denounced as an expression of the unresolved Oedipus complex. … Is not this notion of a rebel who, by way of his 'irrational' resistance to social authority, acts out his unresolved psychic tensions ideology at its purest? However, as Jacqueline Rose demonstrated,[4] such an externalization of the cause into 'social conditions' is no less false, in so far as it enables the subject to avoid confronting the real of his or her desire. By means of this externalization of the Cause, the subject is no longer *engaged* in what is happening to him; he entertains towards the trauma a simple external relationship: far from stirring up the unacknowledged kernel of his desire, the traumatic event disturbs his balance from outside.[5]

The paradox in all these cases is that *the stepping out of (what we experience as) ideology is the very form of our*

enslavement to it. The opposite example of non-ideology which possesses all the standard features of ideology is provided by the role of *Neues Forum* in ex-East Germany. An inherently *tragic* ethical dimension pertains to its fate: it presents a point at which an ideology 'takes itself literally' and ceases to function as an 'objectively cynical' (Marx) legitimization of existing power relations. *Neues Forum* consisted of groups of passionate intellectuals who 'took socialism seriously' and were prepared to risk everything in order to destroy the compromised system and replace it with the Utopian 'third way' beyond capitalism and 'really existing' socialism. Their sincere belief and insistence that they were not working for the restoration of Western capitalism, of course, proved to be nothing but an insubstantial illusion; we could say, however, that precisely as such (as a thorough illusion without substance) it was *stricto sensu non-ideological*: it did not 'reflect', in an inverted-ideological form, any actual relations of power.

The theoretical lesson to be drawn from this is that the concept of ideology must be disengaged from the 'representationalist' problematic: *ideology has nothing to do with 'illusion'*, with a mistaken, distorted representation of its social content. To put it succinctly: a political standpoint can be quite accurate ('true') as to its objective content, yet thoroughly ideological; and, vice versa, the idea that a political standpoint gives of its social content can prove totally wrong, yet there is absolutely nothing 'ideological' about it. With regard to the 'factual truth', the position of *Neues Forum* – taking the disintegration of the Communist regime as the opening-up of a way to invent some new form of social space that would reach beyond the confines of capitalism – was doubtless illusory. Opposing *Neues Forum* were forces who put all their bets on the quickest possible annexation to West Germany – that is to say, of their country's inclusion in the world capitalist system; for them, the people around *Neues Forum* were nothing but a bunch of heroic daydreamers. This position proved accurate – *yet it was none the less thoroughly ideological*. Why? The conformist adoption of the West German model implied an ideological belief in the unproblematic, non-antagonistic functioning of the late-capitalist 'social state', whereas the first stance, although illusory as to its factual content (its 'enunciated'), attested, by means of its 'scandalous' and exorbitant position of enunciation, to an awareness of the antagonism that pertains to late capitalism. This is one way to conceive of the Lacanian thesis according to which truth has the structure of a fiction: in those confused months of the passage of 'really existing socialism' into capitalism, *the fiction of a 'third way' was the only point at which social antagonism was not obliterated.* Herein lies one of the tasks of the 'postmodern' critique of ideology: to designate the elements within an existing social order which – in the guise of 'fiction', that is, of 'Utopian' narratives of possible but failed alternative histories – point towards the system's antagonistic character, and thus 'estrange' us to the self-evidence of its established identity.

II Ideology: the Spectral Analysis of a Concept

In all these *ad hoc* analyses, however, we have already *practicized* the critique of ideology, while our initial question concerned the *concept* of ideology presupposed in this practice. Up till now, we have been guided by a 'spontaneous' pre-comprehension which, although it led us to contradictory results, is not to be underestimated, but rather explicated. For example, we somehow implicitly seem to know what is 'no longer' ideology: as long as the Frankfurt School accepted the critique of political economy as its base, it remained within the co-ordinates of the critique of ideology, whereas the notion of 'instrumental reason' no longer appertains to the horizon of the critique of ideology – 'instrumental reason' designates an attitude that is not simply functional with regard to social domination but, rather, serves as the very foundation of the relationship of domination.[6] An ideology is thus not necessarily 'false': as to its positive content, it can be 'true', quite accurate, since what really matters is not the asserted content as such but *the way this content is related to the subjective position implied by its own process of enunciation.* We are within ideological space proper the moment this content – 'true' or 'false' (if true, so much the better for the ideological effect) – is functional with regard to some relation of social domination ('power', 'exploitation') in an inherently non-transparent way: *the very logic of legitimizing the relation*

of domination must remain concealed if it is to be effective. In other words, the starting point of the critique of ideology has to be full acknowledgement of the fact that it is easily possible to *lie in the guise of truth.* When, for example, some Western power intervenes in a Third World country on account of violations of human rights, it may well be 'true' that in this country the most elementary human rights were not respected, and that the Western intervention will effectively improve the human rights record, yet such a legitimization none the less remains 'ideological' in so far as it fails to mention the true motives of the intervention (economic interests, etc.). The outstanding mode of this 'lying in the guise of truth' today is cynicism: with a disarming frankness one 'admits everything', yet this full acknowledgement of our power interests does not in any way prevent us from pursuing these interests – the formula of cynicism is no longer the classic Marxian 'they do not know it, but they are doing it'; it is 'they know very well what they are doing, yet they are doing it'.

How, then, are we to explicate this implicit pre-comprehension of ours? How are we to pass from *doxa* to truth? The first approach that offers itself is, of course, the Hegelian historical–dialectical transposition of the problem into its own solution: instead of directly evaluating the adequacy or 'truth' of different notions of ideology, one should *read this very multitude of the determinations of ideology as the index of different concrete historical situations* – that is, one should consider what Althusser in his self-critical phase, referred to as the 'topicality of the thought', the way a thought is inscribed into its object; or, as Derrida would have put it, the way the frame itself is part of the framed content.

When, for example, Leninism–Stalinism suddenly adopted the term 'proletarian ideology' in the late 1920s in order to designate not the 'distortion' of proletarian consciousness under the pressure of bourgeois ideology but the very 'subjective' driving force of proletarian revolutionary activity, this shift in the notion of ideology was strictly correlative to the reinterpretation of Marxism itself as an impartial 'objective science', as a science that does not in itself involve the proletarian subjective position: Marxism first, from a neutral distance of metalanguage, ascertains the objective tendency of history towards Communism; then it elaborates the 'proletarian ideology' in order to induce the working class to fulfil its historical mission. A further example of such a shift is the already mentioned passage of Western Marxism from Critique of Political Economy to Critique of Instrumental Reason: from Lukács's *History and Class Consciousness* and the early Frankfurt School, where ideological distortion is derived from the 'commodity form', to the notion of Instrumental Reason which is no longer grounded in a concrete social reality but is, rather, conceived as a kind of anthropological, even quasi-transcendental, primordial constant that enables us to explain the social reality of domination and exploitation. This passage is embedded in the transition from the post-World War I universe, in which hope in the revolutionary outcome of the crisis of capitalism was still alive, into the double trauma of the late 1930s and 1940s: the 'regression' of capitalist societies into Fascism and the 'totalitarian' turn of the Communist movement.[7]

However, such an approach, although it is adequate at its own level, can easily ensnare us in historicist relativism that suspends the inherent cognitive value of the term 'ideology' and makes it into a mere expression of social circumstances. For that reason, it seems preferable to begin with a different, synchronous approach. Apropos of religion (which, for Marx, was ideology *par excellence*), Hegel distinguished three moments: *doctrine*, *belief*, and *ritual*; one is thus tempted to dispose the multitude of notions associated with the term 'ideology' around these three axes: ideology as a complex of ideas (theories, convictions, beliefs, argumentative procedures); ideology in its externality, that is, the materiality of ideology, Ideological State Apparatuses; and finally, the most elusive domain, the 'spontaneous' ideology at work at the heart of social 'reality' itself (it is highly questionable if the term 'ideology' is at all appropriate to designate this domain – here it is exemplary that, apropos of commodity fetishism, Marx never used the term 'ideology'[8]). Let us recall the case of liberalism: liberalism is a doctrine (developed from Locke to Hayek) materialized in rituals and apparatuses (free press, elections, market, etc.) and active in the 'spontaneous' (self-) experience of subjects as 'free individuals'. The order of contributions [...] follows this line that, *grosso modo*, fits the Hegelian triad of In-itself – For-itself – In-and-For-itself.[9]

This logico-narrative reconstruction of the notion of ideology will be centred on the repeated occurrence of the already mentioned reversal of non-ideology into ideology – that is, of the sudden awareness of how the very gesture of stepping out of ideology pulls us back into it.

1. So, to begin with, we have ideology 'in-itself': the immanent notion of ideology as a doctrine, a composite of ideas, beliefs, concepts, and so on, destined to convince us of its 'truth', yet actually serving some unavowed particular power interest. The mode of the critique of ideology that corresponds to this notion is that of *symptomal reading*: the aim of the critique is to discern the unavowed bias of the official text via its ruptures, blanks and slips – to discern in 'equality and freedom' the equality and freedom of the partners in the market exchange which, of course, privileges the owner of the means of production, and so on. Habermas, perhaps the last great representative of this tradition, measures the distortion and/or falsity of an ideological edifice with the standard of non-coercive rational argumentation, a kind of 'regulative ideal' that, according to him, inheres in the symbolic order as such. Ideology is a systematically distorted communication: a text in which, under the influence of unavowed social interests (of domination, etc.) a gap separates its 'official', public meaning from its actual intention – that is to say, in which we are dealing with an unreflected tension between the explicit enunciated content of the text and its pragmatic presuppositions.[10]

Today, however, probably the most prestigious tendency in the critique of ideology, one that grew out of discourse analysis, inverts this relationship: what the tradition of Enlightenment dismisses as a mere disturbance of 'normal' communication turns out to be its positive condition. The concrete intersubjective space of symbolic communication is always structured by various (unconscious) textual devices that cannot be reduced to secondary rhetoric. What we are dealing with here is not a complementary move to the traditional Enlightenment or Habermasian approach but its inherent reversal: what Habermas perceives as the step out of ideology is denounced here as ideology *par excellence*. In the Enlightenment tradition, 'ideology' stands for the blurred ('false') notion of reality caused by various 'pathological' interests (fear of death and of natural forces, power interests, etc.); for discourse analysis, the very notion of an access to reality unbiased by any discursive devices or conjunctions with power is ideological. The 'zero level' of ideology consists in (mis)perceiving a discursive formation as an extra-discursive fact.

Already in the 1950s, in *Mythologies*, Roland Barthes proposed the notion of ideology as the 'naturalization' of the symbolic order – that is, as the perception that reifies the results of discursive procedures into properties of the 'thing itself'. Paul de Man's notion of the 'resistance to (deconstructionist) theory' runs along the same lines: 'deconstruction' met with such resistance because it 'denaturalizes' the enunciated content by bringing to the light of day the discursive procedures that engender evidence of Sense. Arguably the most elaborate version of this approach is Oswald Ducrot's theory of argumentation[11]; although it does not employ the term 'ideology', its ideologico-critical potential is tremendous. Ducrot's basic notion is that one cannot draw a clear line of separation between descriptive and argumentative levels of language: there is no neutral descriptive content; every description (designation) is already a moment of some argumentative scheme; descriptive predicates themselves are ultimately reified-naturalized argumentative gestures. This argumentative thrust relies on *topoi*, on the 'commonplaces' that operate only as naturalized, only in so far as we apply them in an automatic, 'unconscious' way – a successful argumentation presupposes the invisibility of the mechanisms that regulate its efficiency.

One should also mention here Michel Pêcheux, who gave a strict linguistic turn to Althusser's theory of interpellation. His work is centred on the discursive mechanisms that generate the 'evidence' of Sense. That is to say, one of the fundamental stratagems of ideology is the reference to some self-evidence – 'Look, you can see for yourself how things are!' ('Let the facts speak for themselves' is perhaps the arch-statement of ideology – the point being, precisely, that facts *never* 'speak for themselves' but are always *made to speak* by a network of discursive devices. Suffice it to recall the notorious anti-abortion film *The Silent Scream* – we 'see' a foetus which 'defends itself', which 'cries', and so on, yet what we 'don't see' in this very act of seeing is that we 'see' all this against the background of a discursively pre-constructed space. Discourse analysis is perhaps at its strongest in answering this precise question: when a racist Englishman says 'There are too many Pakistanis on our streets!', *how – from what place – does he 'see' this* – that is, how is his symbolic space structured so that he can perceive the fact of a Pakistani strolling along a London street as a disturbing surplus? That is to say, here one must bear in mind Lacan's motto that *nothing is lacking in the real*: every perception of a lack or a surplus ('not enough of this', 'too much of that') always involves a *symbolic* universe.[12]

Last but not least, mention should be made here of Ernesto Laclau and his path-breaking approach to Fascism and populism[13] whose main theoretical result is that meaning does not inhere in elements of an ideology as such – these elements, rather, function as 'free-floating signifiers' whose meaning is fixed by the mode of their hegemonic articulation. Ecology, for example, is never 'ecology as such', it is always enchained in a specific series of equivalences: it can be conservative (advocating the return to balanced rural communities and traditional ways of life), etatist (only a strong state regulation can save us from the impending catastrophe), socialist (the ultimate cause of ecological problems resides in the capitalist profit-orientated exploitation of natural resources), liberal-capitalist (one should include the damage to the environment in the price of the product, and thus leave the market to regulate the ecological balance), feminist (the exploitation of nature follows from the male attitude of domination), anarchic self-managerial (humanity can survive only if it reorganizes itself into small self-reliant communities that live in balance with nature), and so on. The point, of course, is that none of these enchainments is in itself 'true', inscribed in the very nature of the ecological problematic which discourse will succeed in 'appropriating' ecology depends on the fight for discursive hegemony, whose outcome is not guaranteed by any underlying necessity or 'natural alliance'. The other inevitable consequence of such a notion of hegemonic articulation is that etatist, conservative, socialist, and so on, inscription of ecology does not designate a secondary connotation that supplements its primary 'literal' meaning: as Derrida would have put it, this supplement retroactively (re)defines the very nature of 'literal' identity – a conservative enchainment, for example, throws a specific light on the ecological problematic itself ('due to his false arrogance, man forsook his roots in the natural order', etc.).

2. What follows is the step from 'in-itself' to 'for-itself', to ideology in its otherness-externalization: the moment epitomized by the Althusserian notion of Ideological State Apparatuses (ISA) that designate the material existence of ideology in ideological practices, rituals and institutions.[14] Religious belief, for example, is not merely or even primarily an inner conviction, but the Church as an institution and its rituals (prayer, baptism, confirmation, confession …) which, far from being a mere secondary externalization of the inner belief, stand for *the very mechanisms that generate it*. When Althusser repeats, after Pascal: 'Act as if you believe, pray, kneel down, and you shall believe, faith will arrive by itself', he delineates an intricate reflective mechanism of retroactive 'autopoetic' foundation that far exceeds the reductionist assertion of the dependence of inner belief on external behaviour. That is to say, the implicit logic of his argument is: kneel down and *you shall believe that you knelt down because of your belief* – that is, your following the ritual is an expression/effect of your inner belief; in short, the 'external' ritual performatively generates its own ideological foundation.[15]

What we encounter here again is the 'regression' into ideology at the very point where we apparently step out of it. In this respect, the relationship between Althusser and Foucault is of special interest. The Foucauldian counterparts to Ideological State Apparatuses are the disciplinary procedures that operate at the level of 'micro-power' and designate the point at which *power inscribes itself into the body directly, bypassing ideology* – for that precise reason, Foucault never uses the term 'ideology' apropos of these mechanisms of micro-power. This abandoning of the problematic of ideology entails a fatal weakness of Foucault's theory. Foucault never tires of repeating how power constitutes itself 'from below', how it does not emanate from some unique summit: this very semblance of a Summit (the Monarch or some other embodiment of Sovereignty) emerges as the secondary effect of the plurality of micro-practices, of the

complex network of their interrelations. However, when he is compelled to display the concrete mechanism of this emergence, Foucault resorts to the extremely suspect rhetoric of complexity, evoking the intricate network of lateral links, left and right, up and down … a clear case of patching up, since one can never arrive at Power this way – the abyss that separates micro-procedures from the spectre of Power remains unbridgeable. Althusser's advantage over Foucault seems evident: Althusser proceeds in exactly the opposite direction – from the very outset, he conceives these micro-procedures as parts of the ISA; that is to say, as mechanisms which, in order to be operative, to 'seize' the individual, always-already presuppose the massive presence of the state, the transferential relationship of the individual towards state power, or – in Althusser's terms – towards the ideological big Other in whom the interpellation originates.

This Althusserian shift of emphasis from ideology 'in-itself' to its material existence in the ISA proved its fecundity in a new approach to Fascism; Wolfgang Fritz Haug's criticism of Adorno is exemplary here. Adorno refuses to treat Fascism as an ideology in the proper sense of the term, that is, as 'rational legitimization of the existing order'. So-called 'Fascist ideology' no longer possesses the coherence of a rational construct that calls for conceptual analysis and ideologico-critical refutation; that is to say, it no longer functions as a 'lie necessarily experienced as truth' (the sign of recognition of a true ideology). 'Fascist ideology' is not taken seriously even by its promoters; its status is purely instrumental, and ultimately relies on external coercion.[16] In his response to Adorno, however, Haug[17] triumphantly demonstrates how this capitulation to the primacy of the doctrine, far from implying the 'end of ideology', asserts the founding gesture of the ideological as such: the call to unconditional subordination and to 'irrational' sacrifice. What liberal criticism (mis)perceives as Fascism's weakness is the very resort of its strength: within the Fascist horizon, the very demand for rational argumentation that should provide grounds for our acceptance of authority is denounced in advance as an index of the liberal degeneration of the true spirit of ethical sacrifice – as Haug puts it, in browsing through Mussolini's texts, one cannot avoid the uncanny feeling that Mussolini had read Althusser! The direct denunciation of the

Fascist notion of the 'community-of-the-people [*Volksgemeinschaft*]' as a deceptive lure that conceals the reality of domination and exploitation fails to take note of the crucial fact that this *Volksgemeinschaft* was materialized in a series of rituals and practices (not only mass gatherings and parades but also large-scale campaigns to help the hungry, organized sports and cultural activities for the workers, etc.) which performatively produced the effect of *Volksgemeinschaft*.[18]

3. In the next step of our reconstruction, this externalization is, as it were, 'reflected into itself': what takes place is the disintegration, self-limitation and self-dispersal of the notion of ideology. Ideology is no longer conceived as a homogeneous mechanism that guarantees social reproduction, as the 'cement' of society; it turns into a Wittgensteinian 'family' of vaguely connected and heterogeneous procedures whose reach is strictly localized. Along these lines, the critiques of the so-called Dominant Ideology Thesis (DIT) endeavour to demonstrate that an ideology either exerts an influence that is crucial, but constrained to some narrow social stratum, or its role in social reproduction is marginal. At the beginnings of capitalism, for example, the role of the Protestant ethic of hard work as an end-in-itself, and so on, was limited to the stratum of emerging capitalists, whereas workers and peasants, as well as the upper classes, continued to obey other, more traditional ethical attitudes, so that one can in no way attribute to the Protestant ethic the role of the 'cement' of the entire social edifice. Today, in late capitalism, when the expansion of the new mass media in principle, at least, enables ideology effectively to penetrate every pore of the social body, the weight of ideology as such is diminished: individuals do not act as they do primarily on account of their beliefs or ideological convictions – that is to say, the system, for the most part, bypasses ideology in its reproduction and relies on economic coercion, legal and state regulations, and so on.[19]

Here, however, things get blurred again, since the moment we take a closer look at these allegedly extra-ideological mechanisms that regulate social reproduction, we find ourselves knee-deep in the already mentioned obscure domain in which reality is indistinguishable from ideology. What we encounter

here, therefore, is the third reversal of non-ideology into ideology: all of a sudden we become aware of a For-itself of ideology at work in the very In-itself of extra-ideological actuality. First, the mechanisms of economic coercion and legal regulation always 'materialize' some propositions or beliefs that are inherently ideological (the criminal law, for example, involves a belief in the personal responsibility of the individual or the conviction that crimes are a product of social circumstances). Secondly, the form of consciousness that fits late-capitalist 'post-ideological' society – the cynical, 'sober' attitude that advocates liberal 'openness' in the matter of 'opinions' (everybody is free to believe whatever she or he wants; this concerns only his or her privacy), disregards pathetic ideological phrases and follows only utilitarian and/or hedonistic motivations – *stricto sensu* remains an ideological attitude: it involves a series of ideological presuppositions (on the relationship between 'values' and 'real life', on personal freedom, etc.) that are necessary for the reproduction of existing social relations.

What thereby comes into sight is a third continent of ideological phenomena: neither ideology *qua* explicit doctrine, articulated convictions on the nature of man, society and the universe, nor ideology in its material existence (institutions, rituals and practices that give body to it), but the elusive network of implicit, quasi-'spontaneous' presuppositions and attitudes that form an irreducible moment of the reproduction of 'non-ideological' (economic, legal, political, sexual …) practices.[20] The Marxian notion of 'commodity fetishism' is exemplary here: it designates not a (bourgeois) theory of political economy but a series of presuppositions that determine the structure of the very 'real' economic practice of market exchange – in theory, a capitalist clings to utilitarian nominalism, yet in his own practice (of exchange, etc.) he follows 'theological whimsies' and acts as a speculative idealist….[21] For that reason, a direct reference to extra-ideological coercion (of the market, for example) is an ideological gesture *par excellence*: the market and (mass) media are dialectically interconnected;[22] we live in a 'society of the spectacle' (Guy Debord) in which the media structure our perception of reality in advance and render reality indistinguishable from the 'aestheticized' image of it.

III The Spectre and the Real of Antagonism

Is our final outcome, therefore, the inherent impossibility of isolating a reality whose consistency is not maintained by ideological mechanisms, a reality that does not disintegrate the moment we subtract from it its ideological component? Therein resides one of the main reasons for progressive abandonment of the notion of ideology: this notion somehow grows 'too strong', it begins to embrace everything, inclusive of the very neutral extra-ideological ground supposed to provide the standard by means of which one can measure ideological distortion. That is to say, is not the ultimate result of discourse analysis that the order of discourse as such is inherently 'ideological'?

Let us suppose that at some political meeting or academic conference, we are expected to pronounce some profound thoughts on the sad plight of the homeless in our big cities, yet we have absolutely no idea of their actual problems – the way to save face is to produce the effect of depth by means of a purely formal inversion: 'Today, one hears and reads a lot about the plight of the homeless in our cities, about their hardship and distress. Perhaps, however, this distress, deplorable as it may be, is ultimately just a sign of some far deeper distress – of the fact that modern man no longer has a proper dwelling, that he is more and more a stranger in his own world. Even if we constructed enough new buildings to house all homeless people, the true distress would perhaps be even greater. The essence of homelessness is the homelessness of the essence itself; it resides in the fact that, in our world thrown out of joint by the frenetic search for empty pleasures, there is no home, no proper dwelling, for the truly essential dimension of man.'

This formal matrix can be applied to an infinite multitude of themes – say, distance and proximity: 'Today, modern media can bring events from the farthest part of our earth, even from nearby planets, close to us in a split second. Does not this very all-pervasive proximity, however, remove us from the authentic dimension of human existence? Is not the essence of man more distant from us than ever today?' Or the recurrent motif of danger: 'Today, one hears and reads a lot about how the very survival of the human race is threatened by the prospect of ecological catastrophe (the disappearing ozone layer, the greenhouse effect, etc.). The true danger, however, lies elsewhere: what is ultimately threatened is the very essence of man. As we endeavour to prevent the impending ecological catastrophe with newer and newer technological solutions ('environment-friendly' aerosols, unleaded petrol, etc.), we are in fact simply adding fuel to the flames, and thus aggravating the threat to the spiritual essence of man, which cannot be reduced to a technological animal.'

The purely formal operation which, in all these cases, brings about the effect of depth is perhaps ideology at its purest, its elementary cell, whose link to the Lacanian concept of the Master-Signifier is not difficult to discern: the chain of 'ordinary' signifiers registers some positive knowledge about homelessness, whereas the Master-Signifier stands for 'the truly essential dimension' about which we need not make any positive claim (for that reason, Lacan designates the Master-Signifier the 'signifier without signified'). This formal matrix bears witness in an exemplary way to the self-defeating power of a formal discourse analysis of ideology: its weakness resides in its very strength, since it is ultimately compelled to locate ideology in the gap between the 'ordinary' signifying chain and the excessive Master-Signifier that is part of the symbolic order as such.

Here, however, one should be careful to avoid the last trap that makes us slide into ideology under the guise of stepping out of it. That is to say, when we denounce as ideological the very attempt to draw a clear line of demarcation between ideology and actual reality, this inevitably seems to impose the conclusion that the only non-ideological position is to renounce the very notion of extra-ideological reality and accept that all we are dealing with are symbolic fictions, the plurality of discursive universes, never 'reality' – such a quick, slick 'postmodern' solution, however, is ideology par excellence. It all hinges on our persisting in this impossible position: although no clear line of demarcation separates ideology from reality, although ideology is already at work in everything we experience as 'reality', we must none the less maintain the tension that keeps the *critique* of ideology alive. Perhaps, following Kant, we could designate this impasse the 'antinomy of critico-ideological reason': ideology is not all; it is possible to assume a place that enables us to maintain a distance from it, *but this place from which one can denounce ideology must remain empty, it cannot be occupied by any positively determined reality* – the moment we yield to this temptation, we are back in ideology.

How are we to specify this empty place? Perhaps we should take as a starting point the thread that runs through our entire logico-narrative reconstruction of the notion of ideology: it is as if, at every stage, the same opposition, the same *undecidable* alternative Inside/Outside, repeats itself under a different exponent. First, there is the split within ideology 'in-itself': on the one hand, ideology stands for the distortion of rational argumentation and insight due to the weight of the 'pathological' external interests of power, exploitation, and so on; on the other, ideology resides in the very notion of a thought not permeated by some non-transparent power strategy, of an argument that does not rely upon some non-transparent rhetorical devices. ... Next, this very externality splits into an 'inner externality' (the symbolic order, i.e. the decentred discursive mechanisms that generate Meaning) and an 'external externality' (the ISA and social rituals and practices that materialize ideology) – *the externality misrecognized by ideology is the externality of the 'text' itself as well as the externality of 'extra-textual' social reality.* Finally, this 'extra-textual' social reality itself is split into the institutional Exterior that dominates and regulates the life of individuals 'from above' (ISA), and ideology that is not imposed by the ISA but emerges 'spontaneously', 'from below', out of the extra-institutional activity of individuals (commodity fetishism) – to give it names, Althusser versus Lukács. This opposition between ISA and commodity fetishism – between the *materiality that always-already pertains to ideology as such* (material, effective apparatuses which give body to ideology) and *ideology that always-already pertains to materiality as such* (to the social actuality of production) – is ultimately the opposition between State and Market, between the external superior agency that organizes society 'from above' and society's 'spontaneous' self-organization.

This opposition, whose first philosophical manifestation is provided by the couple of Plato and Aristotle, finds its last expression in the guise of the two modes of cynical ideology: 'consumerist', post-Protestant, late-capitalist cynicism, and the cynicism that pertained to the late 'real Socialism'. Although, in both cases, the system functions only on condition that subjects maintain a cynical distance and do not 'take seriously' the 'official' values, the difference is remarkable; it turns upside down the doxa according to which late capitalism, as a (formally) 'free' society, relies on argumentative persuasion and free consent, 'manipulated' and fabricated as it may be; whereas Socialism resorted to the raw force of 'totalitarian' coercion. It is as if in late capitalism 'words do not count', no longer oblige: they increasingly seem to lose their performative power; whatever one says is drowned in the general indifference; the emperor is naked and the media trumpet forth this fact, yet nobody seems really to mind – that is, people continue to act as if the emperor is not naked....

Perhaps the key feature of the symbolic economy of the late 'real Socialism' was, on the contrary, the almost paranoiac *belief in the power of the World* – the state and the ruling party reacted with utmost nervousness and panic at the slightest public criticism, as if some vague critical hints in an essay in an academic philosophical journal, possessed the potential capacity to trigger the explosion of the entire socialist system. Incidentally, this feature renders 'real Socialism' almost sympathetic to our retrospective nostalgic view, since it bears witness to the legacy of the Enlightenment (the belief in the social efficacy of rational argumentation) that survived in it. This, perhaps, was why it was possible to undermine 'real Socialism' by means of peaceful civil society movements that operated at the level of the Word – belief in the power of the Word was the system's Achilles heel.[23]

The matrix of all these repetitions, perhaps, is the opposition between ideology as the universe of 'spontaneous' experience [*vécu*] whose grip we can break only by means of an effort of scientific reflection, and ideology as a radically non-spontaneous machine that distorts the authenticity of our life-experience from outside. That is to say, what we should always bear in mind is that, for Marx, the primordial mythological consciousness of the pre-class society out of which later ideologies grew (true to the heritage of German classicism, Marx saw the paradigm of this primordial social consciousness in Greek mythology) *is not yet ideology proper*, although (or, rather, precisely because) it is immediately *vécu*, and although it is obviously 'wrong', 'illusory' (it involves the divinization of the forces of nature, etc.); ideology proper emerges only with the division of labour and the class split, only when the 'wrong' ideas lose their 'immediate' character and are 'elaborated' by intellectuals in order to serve (to legitimize) the existing relations of domination – in short, only when the division into Master and Servant is conjugated with the division of labour itself into intellectual and physical labour. For that precise reason, Marx refused to categorize commodity fetishism as ideology: for him, ideology was always of the state and, as Engels put it, state itself is the first ideological force. In clear contrast, Althusser conceives ideology as an immediately experienced relationship to the universe – as such, it is eternal; when, following his self-critical turn, he introduces the concept of ISA, he returns in a way to Marx: ideology does not grow out of 'life itself', it comes into existence only in so far as society is regulated by state. (More precisely, the paradox and theoretical interest of Althusser resides in his conjugation of the two lines: in its very character of immediately experienced relationship to the universe, ideology is always-already regulated by the externality of State and its Ideological Apparatuses.)

This tension between 'spontaneity' and organized imposition introduces a kind of reflective distance into the very heart of the notion of ideology: ideology is always, by definition, 'ideology of ideology'. Suffice it to recall the disintegration of real Socialism: Socialism was perceived as the rule of 'ideological' oppression and indoctrination, whereas the passage into democracy-capitalism was experienced as deliverance from the constraints of ideology – however, was not this very experience of 'deliverance' in the course of which political parties and the market economy were perceived as 'non-ideological', as the 'natural state of things', ideological *par excellence?* Our point is that this feature is *universal*: there is no ideology that does not assert itself by means of delimiting itself from another 'mere ideology'. An individual subjected to ideology can never say for himself 'I am in ideology', he always requires *another* corpus of doxa in order to distinguish his own 'true' position from it.

The first example here is provided by none other than Plato: philosophical *epistēmē* versus the confused doxa of the crowd. What about Marx? Although he may appear to fall into this trap (is not the entire

German Ideology based on the opposition of ideological chimera and the study of 'actual life'?), things get complicated in his mature critique of political economy. That is to say, why, precisely, does Marx choose the term *fetishism* in order to designate the 'theological whimsy' of the universe of commodities? What one should bear in mind here is that 'fetishism' is a *religious* term for (previous) 'false' idolatry as opposed to (present) true belief: for the Jews, the fetish is the Golden Calf; for a partisan of pure spirituality, fetishism designates 'primitive' superstition, the fear of ghosts and other spectral apparitions, and so on. And the point of Marx is that the commodity universe provides the necessary fetishistic supplement to the 'official' spirituality: it may well be that the 'official' ideology of our society is Christian spirituality, but its actual foundation is none the less the idolatry of the Golden Calf, money.

In short, Marx's point is that there is no spirit without spirits-ghosts, no 'pure' spirituality without the obscene spectre of 'spiritualized matter'.[25] The first to accomplish this step 'from spirit to spirits' in the guise of the critique of pure spiritual idealism, of its lifeless 'negative' nihilism, was F. W. J. Schelling, the crucial, unjustly neglected philosopher of German Idealism. In the dialogue *Clara* (1810), he drove a wedge into the simple complementary mirror-relationship between Inside and Outside, between Spirit and Body, between the ideal and the real element that together form the living totality of the Organism, by calling attention to the double surplus that 'sticks out'. On the one hand, there is the *spiritual element of corporeality*: the presence, in matter itself, of a non-material but physical element, of a subtle corpse, relatively independent of time and space, which provides the material base of our free will (animal magnetism, etc.); on the other hand, there is the *corporeal element of spirituality*: the materializations of the spirit in a kind of pseudo-stuff, in substanceless apparitions (ghosts, living dead). It is clear how these two surpluses render the logic of commodity fetishism and of the ISA: commodity fetishism involves the uncanny 'spiritualization' of the commodity-body, whereas the ISA materialize the spiritual, substanceless big Other of ideology.

In his recent book on Marx, Jacques Derrida brought into play the term 'spectre' in order to indicate this elusive pseudo-materiality that subverts the classic ontological oppositions of reality and illusion, and so on.[26] And perhaps it is here that we should look for the last resort of ideology, for the pre-ideological kernel, the formal matrix, on which are grafted various ideological formations: in the fact that there is no reality without the spectre, that the circle of reality can be closed only by means of an uncanny spectral supplement. Why, then, is there no reality without the spectre? Lacan provides a precise answer to this question: (what we experience as) reality is not the 'thing itself', it is always-already symbolized, constituted, structured by symbolic mechanisms – and the problem resides in the fact that symbolization ultimately always fails, that it never succeeds in fully 'covering' the real, that it always involves some unsettled, unredeemed symbolic debt. *This real (the part of reality that remains non-symbolized) returns in the guise of spectral apparitions.* Consequently, 'spectre' is not to be confused with 'symbolic fiction', with the fact that reality itself has the structure of a fiction in that it is symbolically (or, as some sociologists put it, 'socially') constructed; the notions of spectre and (symbolic) fiction are co-dependent in their very incompatibility (they are 'complementary' in the quantum-mechanical sense). To put it simply, reality is never directly 'itself', it presents itself only via its incomplete-failed symbolization, and spectral apparitions emerge in this very gap that forever separates reality from the real, and on account of which reality has the character of a (symbolic) fiction: the spectre gives body to that which escapes (the symbolically structured) reality.[27]

The pre-ideological 'kernel' of ideology thus consists of the *spectral apparition that fills up the hole of the real*. This is what all the attempts to draw a clear line of separation between 'true' reality and illusion (or to ground illusion in reality) fail to take into account: if (what we experience as) 'reality' is to emerge, something has to be foreclosed from it – that is to say, 'reality', like truth, is, by definition, never 'whole'. *What the spectre conceals is not reality but its 'primordially repressed', the irrepresentable X on whose 'repression' reality itself is founded*. It may seem that we have thereby lost our way in speculative murky waters that have nothing whatsoever to do with concrete social struggles – is not the supreme example of such 'reality', however, provided by the Marxist concept of *class struggle*? The

consequent thinking-out of this concept compels us to admit that there is no class struggle 'in reality': 'class struggle' designates the very antagonism that prevents the objective (social) reality from constituting itself as a self-enclosed whole.[28]

True, according to the Marxist tradition, class struggle is the 'totalizing' principle of society; this, however, does not mean that it is a kind of ultimate guarantee authorizing us to grasp society as a rational totality ('the ultimate meaning of every social phenomenon is determined by its position within the class struggle'): the ultimate paradox of the notion of 'class struggle' is that society is 'held together' by the very antagonism, splitting, that forever prevents its closure in a harmonious, transparent, rational Whole–by the very impediment that undermines every rational totalization. Although 'class struggle' is nowhere directly given as a positive entity, it none the less functions, *in its very absence*, as the point of reference enabling us to locate every social phenomenon – not by relating it to class struggle as its ultimate meaning ('transcendental signified') but by conceiving it as (an)other attempt to conceal and 'patch up' the rift of class antagonism, to efface its traces. What we have here is the structural-dialectical paradox of *an effect that exists only in order to efface the causes of its existence*, an effect that in a way resists its own cause.

In other words, class struggle is 'real' in the strict Lacanian sense: a 'hitch', an impediment which gives rise to ever-new symbolizations by means of which one endeavours to integrate and domesticate it (the corporatist translation-displacement of class struggle into the organic articulation of the 'members' of the 'social body', for example), but which simultaneously condemns these endeavours to ultimate failure. Class struggle is none other than the name for the unfathomable limit that cannot be objectivized, located within the social totality, since it is itself that limit which prevents us from conceiving society as a closed totality. Or – to put it in yet another way – 'class struggle' designates the point with regard to which 'there is no metalanguage': in so far as every position within social totality is ultimately overdetermined by class struggle, no neutral place is excluded from the dynamics of class struggle from which it would be possible to locate class struggle within the social totality.

This paradoxical status of class struggle can be articulated by means of the crucial Hegelian distinction between Substance and Subject. At the level of Substance, class struggle is conditional on the 'objective' social process; it functions as the secondary indication of some more fundamental discord in this process, a discord regulated by positive mechanisms independent of class struggle ('class struggle breaks out when the relations of production are no longer in accordance with the development of the productive forces').[29] We pass to the level of Subject when we acknowledge that class struggle does not pop up at the end, as the effect of an objective process, but is always-already at work in the very heart of the objective process itself (capitalists develop means of production in order to lower the relative and absolute value of the labour force; the value of the labour force itself is not objectively given but results from the class struggle, etc.). In short, it is not possible to isolate any 'objective' social process or mechanism whose innermost logic does not involve the 'subjective' dynamics of class struggle; or – to put it differently – *the very 'peace', the absence of struggle, is already a form of struggle*, the (temporal) victory of one of the sides in the struggle. In so far as the very invisibility of class struggle ('class peace') is already an effect of class struggle – that is, of the hegemony exerted by one side in the struggle – one is tempted to compare the status of class struggle to that of the Hitchcockian McGuffin: 'What is class struggle? – The antagonistic process that constitutes classes and determines their relationship. – But in our society there is no struggle between the classes! – You see how it functions!'[30]

This notion of class struggle *qua* antagonism enables us to contrast the real of antagonism with the complementary polarity of opposites: perhaps the reduction of antagonism to polarity is one of the elementary ideological operations. Suffice it to recall the standard New Age procedure of presupposing a kind of natural balance of cosmic opposites (reason–emotions, active–passive, intellect–intuition, consciousness–unconscious, *yin–yang*, etc.), and then of conceiving our age as the age that laid too much stress upon one of the two poles, upon the 'male principle' of activity – reason – the solution, of course, lies in re-establishing the equilibrium of the two principles....

The 'progressive' tradition also bears witness to numerous attempts to conceive (sexual, class) antagonism as the coexistence of two opposed positive entities: from a certain kind of 'dogmatic' Marxism that posits 'their' bourgeois science and 'our' proletarian science side by side, to a certain kind of feminism that posits masculine discourse and feminine discourse or 'writing' side by side. Far from being 'too extreme', these attempts are, on the contrary, not extreme enough: they presuppose as their position of enunciation a third neutral medium within which the two poles coexist; that is to say, they back down on the consequences of the fact that there is no point of convergence, no neutral ground shared by the two antagonistic sexual or class positions.[31] As far as science is concerned: science, of course, is not neutral in the sense of objective knowledge not affected by class struggle and at the disposal of all classes, yet for that very reason it is *one*; there are not two sciences, and class struggle is precisely the struggle for this one science, for who will appropriate it. It is the same with 'discourse': there are not two discourses, 'masculine' and 'feminine'; there is *one* discourse split from within by the sexual antagonism – that is to say, providing the 'terrain' on which the battle for hegemony takes place.

What is at stake here could also be formulated as the problem of the status of 'and' as a category. In Althusser 'and' functions as a precise theoretical category: when an 'and' appears in the title of some of his essays, this little word unmistakably signals the confrontation of some general ideological notion (or, more precisely, of a neutral, ambiguous notion that oscillates between its ideological actuality and its scientific potentiality) with its specification which tells us how we are to concretize this notion so that it begins to function as non-ideological, as a strict theoretical concept. 'And' thus *splits up* the ambiguous starting unity, introduces into it the difference between ideology and science.

Suffice it to mention two examples. 'Ideology *and* Ideological State Apparatuses': ISA designate the concrete network of the material conditions of existence of an ideological edifice – that is, that which ideology itself has to misrecognize in its 'normal' functioning. 'Contradiction *and* Overdetermination': in so far as the concept of overdetermination designates the undecidable complex totality *qua* the mode of existence of contradiction, it enables us to discard the idealist-teleological burden that usually weighs upon the notion of contradiction (the teleological necessity that guarantees in advance the 'sublation' of the contradiction in a higher unity).[32] Perhaps the first exemplary case of such an 'and' is Marx's famous 'freedom, equality, *and Bentham*' from *Capital*: the supplementary 'Bentham' stands for the social circumstances that provide the concrete content of the pathetic phrases on freedom and equality – commodity exchange, market bargaining, utilitarian egotism. ... And do we not encounter a homologous conjunction in Heidegger's *Being and Time*? 'Being' designates the fundamental theme of philosophy in its abstract universality, whereas 'time' stands for the concrete horizon of the sense of being.

'And' is thus, in a sense, *tautological*: it conjoins the same content in its two modalities – first in its ideological evidence, then in the extra-ideological conditions of its existence. For that reason, no third term is needed here to designate the medium itself in which the two terms, conjoined by means of the 'and', encounter each other: this third term is already the second term itself that stands for the network (the 'medium') of the concrete existence of an ideological universality. In contrast to this dialectico-materialist 'and', the idealist-ideological 'and' functions precisely as this third term, as the common medium of the polarity or plurality of elements. Therein resides the gap that forever separates Freud from Jung in their respective notions of libido: Jung conceives of libido as a kind of neutral energy with its concrete forms (sexual, creative, destructive libido) as its different 'metamorphoses', whereas Freud insists that libido in its concrete existence is irreducibly *sexual* – all other forms of libido are forms of 'ideological' misrecognition of this sexual content. And is not the same operation to be repeated apropos of 'man *and* woman'? Ideology compels us to assume 'humanity' as the neutral medium within which 'man' and 'woman' are posited as the two complementary poles – against this ideological evidence, one could maintain that 'woman' stands for the aspect of concrete existence and 'man' for the empty-ambiguous universality. The paradox (of a profoundly Hegelian nature) is that 'woman' – that is, the moment of specific difference – functions

as the encompassing ground that accounts for the emergence of the universality of man.

This interpretation of social antagonism (class struggle) as Real, not as (part of) objective social reality, also enables us to counter the worn-out line of argumentation according to which one has to abandon the notion of ideology, since the gesture of distinguishing 'mere ideology' from 'reality' implies the epistemologically untenable 'God's view', that is, access to objective reality as it 'truly is'. The question of the suitability of the term 'class struggle' to designate today's dominant form of antagonism is secondary here, it concerns concrete social analysis; what matters is that the very constitution of social reality involves the 'primordial repression' of an antagonism, so that the ultimate support of the critique of ideology – the extra-ideological point of reference that authorizes us to denounce the content of our immediate experience as 'ideological' – is not 'reality' but the 'repressed' real of antagonism.

[...]

Notes

1   See Étienne Balibar, 'Racism as Universalism', in *Masses, Classes, Ideas* (New York: Routledge, 1994), pp. 198–9.

2   Renata Salecl, *The Spoils of Freedom* (London: Routledge, 1994), p. 13.

3   See Jeffrey Masson, *The Assault on Truth: Freud's Suppression of the Seduction Theory* (New York: Farrar, Straus & Giroux, 1984).

4   Jacqueline Rose, 'Where Does the Misery Come From?', in Richard Feldstein and Judith Roof, eds, *Feminism and Psychoanalysis* (Ithaca, NY and London: Cornell University Press, 1989), pp. 23–39.

5   The very title of Rose's article – 'Where Does the Misery Come From?' – is indicative here: one of the functions of ideology is precisely to explain the 'origins of Evil', to 'objectivize'-externalize its cause, and thus to discharge us of responsibility for it.

6   For that reason, the 'epochal horizons of pre-understanding' (the big theme of hermeneutics) cannot be designated as ideology.

7   For a concise account of the theoretical consequences of this double trauma, see Theodor W. Adorno, 'Messages in a Bottle'. As for the way Adorno's critique of identitarian thought announces post-structuralist 'deconstructionism', see Peter Dews, 'Adorno, Post-Structuralism and the Critique of Identity'.

8   In his *La philosophie de Marx* (Paris: La Découverte 1993), Étienne Balibar drew attention to the enigma of the complete disappearance of the notion of ideology in Marx's texts after 1850. In *The German Ideology*, the (omnipresent) notion of ideology is conceived as the chimera that supplements social production and reproduction – the conceptual opposition that serves as its background is the one between the 'actual life-process' and its distorted reflection in the heads of ideologues. Things get complicated, however, the moment Marx engages in the 'critique of political economy': what he encounters here in the guise of 'commodity fetishism' is no longer an 'illusion' that 'reflects' reality but an uncanny chimera at work in the very heart of the actual process of social production.

The same enigmatic eclipse may be detected in many a post-Marxist author: Ernesto Laclau, for example, after the almost inflationary use of the concept of ideology in his *Politics and Ideology* (London: Verso, 1977), totally renounces it in *Hegemony and Socialist Strategy* (co-authored with Chantal Mouffe, London: Verso, 1985).

9   To avoid a fatal misunderstanding, one must insist that this line of succession is not to be read as a hierarchical progress, as a 'sublation' or 'suppression' of the preceding mode. When, for example, we approach ideology in the guise of Ideological State Apparatuses, this in no way entails the obsolescence or irrelevance of the level of argumentation. Today, when official ideology is increasingly indifferent towards its own consistency, an analysis of its inherent and constitutive inconsistencies is crucial if we are to pierce the actual mode of its functioning.

10 For an exemplary presentation of the Habermasian position, see Seyla Benhabib, 'The Critique of Instrumental Reason'.

11 See Oswald Ducrot, *Le dire et le dit* (Paris: Éditions de Minuit, 1986).

12 See Michel Pêcheux, 'The Mechanism of Ideological (Mis)recognition'. One should bear in mind here that the key source of the critique of ideological evidences in the discourse analysis is Jacques Lacan's 'The Mirror-phase as Formative of the Function of the I', the text that introduced the concept of recognition [*reconnaissance*] as misrecognition [*méconnaissance*].

13 See Laclau, *Politics and Ideology*.

14 See Louis Althusser, 'Ideology and Ideological State Apparatuses'.

15 Herein resides the interconnection between the ritual that pertains to 'Ideological State Apparatuses' and the act of interpellation: when I believe that I knelt down because of my belief, I simultaneously 'recognize' myself in the call of the Other God who dictated that I kneel down. ... This point was developed by Isolde Charim in her intervention 'Dressur und Verneinung' at the colloquium *Der Althusser-Effekt*, Vienna, 17–20 March 1994.

16 See Theodor W. Adorno, 'Beitrag zur Ideologienlehre', in *Gesammelte Schriften: Ideologie* (Frankfurt: Suhrkamp, 1972).

17 See Wolfgang Fritz Haug, 'Annäherung an die faschistische Modalität des Ideologischen', in *Faschismus und Ideologie* 1, Argument-Sonderband 60, Berlin: Argument Verlag, 1980.

18 Discourse analysis and the Althusserian reconceptualization of ideology also opened up a new approach in feminist studies. Its two representative cases are Michèle Barrett's post-Marxist discourse analysis (see her 'Ideology, Politics, Hegemony: From Gramsci to Laclau and Mouffe') and Richard Rorty's pragmatist deconstructionism (see his 'Feminism, Ideology and Deconstruction: A Pragmatist View').

19 See Nicholas Abercrombie, Stephen Hill and Bryan Turner, 'Determinacy and Indeterminacy in the Theory of Ideology'; and Göran Therborn's critical response, 'The New Questions of Subjectivity'. For a general overview of the historical development of the concept of ideology that led to this self-dispersal, see Terry Eagleton, 'Ideology and its Vicissitudes in Western Marxism'.

20 For an approach to this 'implicit' ideology, see Pierre Bourdieu and Terry Eagleton, 'Doxa and Common Life'.

21 For the notion of ideology that structures (social) reality, see Slavoj Žižek, 'How Did Marx Invent the Symptom?'.

22 See Fredric Jameson, 'Postmodernism and the Market'.

23 Cynicism as a postmodern attitude is superbly exemplified by one of the key features of Robert Altman's film *Nashville*: the enigmatic status of its songs. Altman, of course, entertains a critical distance from the universe of country music that epitomizes the *bêtise* of everyday American ideology; one entirely misses the point, however, if one perceives the songs performed in the film as a mocking imitation of 'true' country music – these songs are to be taken quite 'seriously'; one simply has to enjoy them. Perhaps the ultimate enigma of postmodernism resides in this coexistence of the two inconsistent attitudes, misperceived by the usual leftist criticism of young intellectuals who, although theoretically aware of the capitalist machinery

of *Kulturindustrie*, unproblematically enjoy the products of rock industry.

24 Note the case of Kieslowski: his films shot in the damp, oppressive atmosphere of late Socialism (*Decalogue*) practise an almost unheard-of critique of ('official' as well as 'dissident') ideology; whereas the moment he left Poland for the 'freedom' of France, we witness the massive intrusion of ideology (see the New Age obscurantism of *La double vie de Véronique*).

25 Within the domain of the law, this opposition between *Geist* and the obscene *Geisterwelt* assumes the form of the opposition between the explicit public written Law and its superego obverse – that is, the set of unwritten-unacknowledged rules that guarantee the cohesion of a community. (As to this opposition, see Chapter 3 of Slavoj Žižek, *The Metastases of Enjoyment*, London: Verso, 1994.) Suffice it to recall the mysteriously obscene institution of fraternities – sororities in the American campuses, these half-clandestine communities with their secret rules of initiation where the pleasures of sex, drinking, and so on, and the spirit of authority go hand in hand; or the image of the English public school in Lindsay Anderson's *If...* the terror imposed by the elder students upon the younger, who are submitted to the humiliating rituals of power and sexual abuse. Professors can thus play the role of good-humoured liberals, amusing students with jokes, entering the classroom on a bicycle, and so on – the true support of power lies elsewhere, in the elder students whose acts bear witness to an indiscernible mixture of Order and its Transgression, of sexual enjoyment and the 'repressive' exercise of power. In other words, what we find here is a transgression that serves as the ultimate support of Order, an indulgence in illicit sexuality that directly grounds 'repression'.

26 See Jacques Derrida, *Spectres de Marx* (Paris: Galilée, 1993).

27 This gap that separates the real from reality is what opens up the space for *performative* in its opposition to constative. That is to say, without the surplus of the real over reality that emerges in the guise of a spectre, symbolization would merely designate, point towards, some positive content in reality. In its most radical dimension, performative is the attempt to conjure the real, to gentrify the spectre that is the Other: 'spectre' is originally the Other as such, another subject in the abyss of his or her freedom. Lacan's classic example: by saying 'You are my wife!', I thereby oblige–constrain the Other; I endeavour to entrap her abyss into a symbolic obligation.

28 This notion of antagonism comes, of course, from Laclau and Mouffe, *Hegemony and Socialist Strategy*.

29 What gets lost in the notion of social classes *qua* positive entities that get enmeshed in struggle only from time to time is the genuinely dialectical paradox of the relationship between the universal and the particular: although the whole of history hitherto is the history of class struggle (as Marx claims at the beginning of Chapter 1 of *The Communist Manifesto*), there exists (one is almost tempted to write it: ex-sists) *stricto sensu* only one class, the bourgeoisie, the capitalist class. Prior to capitalism, classes were not yet 'for themselves', not yet 'posited as such'; they did not properly exist but 'insisted' as the underlying structuring principle that found its expression in the guise of states, castes, moments of the organic social edifice, of society's 'corporate body', whereas the proletariat *stricto sensu* is no longer a class but a class that coincides with its opposite, a non-class – the historical tendency to negate class division is inscribed into its very class position.

30 For this Hitchcockian analogy I am indebted to Isolde Charim and Robert Pfaller.

31 In the case of sexual difference, the theological name for this third asexual position is 'angel'; for that reason, the question of the *sex of angels* is absolutely crucial for a materialist analysis.

32 This point was developed by Robert Pfaller in his intervention 'Zum Althusserianischen Nominalismus' at the colloquium *Der Althusser-Effekt*.

Additional Readings

Marx and Engels

Étienne Balibar. *Masses, Classes, Ideas*. London: Routledge, 1994.
A collection of essays in which a leading exponent of French Marxist philosophy considers a number of issues such as racism, religion, and civil rights as they emerge in the Marxist tradition.

Jacques Derrida. *Spectres of Marx*. New York: Routledge, 1994.
Derrida's deconstructive take on Marxism which reads Marx's work in light of the role of ghosts, specters, and spirits within his writing.

Frankfurt Institute for Social Research. *Aspects of Sociology*. Translated by John Viertel. Boston: Beacon Press, 1972. See esp. chapter 12, "Ideology."
A sociological introduction to the key ideas of the Frankfurt School, a research institute which has played a key role in the development of contemporary Marxist cultural criticism.

Henri Lefebvre. *The Sociology of Marx*. Translated by Norbert Guterman. New York: Columbia University Press, 1982.
A classic work which asks whether Marx has contemporary significance or is of greater interest as a historical figure. A concise introduction to the sociological aspects of Marx's thought.

Martin Seliger. *The Marxist Conception of Ideology*. Cambridge: Cambridge University Press, 1977.

A comprehensive and systematic account of the way in which the category of ideology is defined and applied in the work of Marx and Engels and their immediate followers.

Lukács

Eva Corredor. *Lukács After Communism: Interviews with Contemporary Intellectuals*. Durham, NC. Duke University Press, 1997.
A series of interviews with leading intellectuals, such as Fredric Jameson and Terry Eagleton, regarding Lukács's legacy and relevance in a world after the fall of communism.

Georg Lukács. *A Defence of History and Class Consciousness*. London: Verso, 2002.
In this extended essay, Lukács offers a defense of his earlier book, *History and Class Consciousness* (from which the essay in this book was excerpted), against the criticisms leveled against it, not least by Joseph Stalin. In the process, Lukács clarifies several key points of his earlier argument.

Galin Tihanov. *The Master and the Slave: Lukács, Bakhtin and the Ideas of the Time*. New York: Oxford University Press, 2000.
A study in comparative history that seeks to understand Lukács's thought in the context of his major contemporary, Mikhail Bakhtin, and the broad intellectual context of Russia and the Soviet Union in the first half of the twentieth century. Tihanov argues that

the two intellectuals' careers followed similar trajectories and that their work is mutually illuminating.

Gramsci

Carl Boggs. *The Two Revolutions: Gramsci and the Dilemmas of Western Marxism*. London: South End Press, 1984.
An examination of the development of Gramsci's thought that attempts to situate his intellectual legacy within the framework of the major thinkers and strains of Marxist theory.

Ernesto Laclau and Chantal Mouffe. *Hegemony and Socialist Strategy: Towards a Radical Democratic Politics*. Translated by Winston Moore and Paul Cammack. London: Verso, 1985.
A hugely influential work that attempts to think through how Gramsci's concept of hegemony can be put into practice to help create a more democratic, more just form of contemporary politics.

Andrew Ross. *No Respect: Intellectuals and Popular Culture*. New York: Routledge, 1989.
A historical critique of modern American popular culture that is heavily influenced by Gramsci's notions of hegemony and the role of the public intellectual.

Althusser

Judith Butler. "'Conscience Doth Make Subjects of Us All': Althusser's Subjection." In *The Psychic Life of Power*, pp. 106–31. Stanford, CA: Stanford University Press, 1997.
Within a wider work that addresses the formation of the subject through the operation of power, Judith Butler focuses on the relevance of Althusser's work to such a project.

Warren Montag. *Louis Althusser*. London: Palgrave Macmillan, 2003.
A brief, but comprehensive, overview of Althusser's work in light of his autobiography and the wide range of posthumous publications available since the 1990s.

Richard Wolff. "Ideological State Apparatuses, Consumerism, and U.S. Capitalism: Lessons for the Left." *Rethinking Marxism* 172.2 (2005): 223–36.
Wolff's essay puts Althusser's notion of the Ideological State Apparatus to work to help understand consumerism and its role in helping sustain the apparent inequalities of US capitalism.

Hall

Paul Gilroy, Lawrence Grossberg, and Angel McRobbie, eds. *Without Guarantees: In Honour of Stuart Hall*. New York: Verso, 2000.
Notable scholars pay homage to the work of Hall in essays which expand and engage with – but also question – his work as it relates to a wide range of issues in modern media and culture.

Stuart Hall. "Encoding/Decoding." In *Culture, Media, Language: Working Papers in Cultural Studies, 1972–79*, pp. 128–38. Edited by Stuart Hall, Dorothy Hobson, Andrew Lowe, and Paul Willis. London: Hutchinson, 1980.
A seminal essay in which Hall outlines a powerful model of semiotics which accounts for how different audiences can take up and respond to texts in a variety of contradictory ways at different moments.

Žižek

Adrian Johnson. *Žižek's Ontology: A Transcendental Materialist Theory of Subjectivity*. Chicago: Northwestern University Press, 2008.
A sophisticated book-length attempt to get at the heart of Žižek's philosophical project and how he makes sense of the vexed notion of subjectivity.

Robert Pfaller. "Where Is Your Hamster? The Concept of Ideology in Žižek's Cultural Theory." In *Traversing the Fantasy*, pp. 105–22. Edited by Geoff Boucher, Jason Glynos, and Matthew Sharpe. Aldershot, UK: Ashgate, 2005.
An introductory attempt to explicate Žižek's theory of ideology with respect to notions of truth, illusions, postmodernism, and psychoanalysis.

Matthew Sharpe. *Slavoj Žižek*. Aldershot, UK: Ashgate, 2004.

Sharpe presents an accessible overview of Žižek's work which attempts to unite the philosopher's writings in the context of a wider singular project.

Slavoj Žižek. *The Sublime Object of Ideology*. New York: Verso, 1989.

Žižek explores the political significance of fantasies of control as they emerge in popular cultural texts such as *Rear Window*, *Alien*, and the operas of Richard Wagner in order to consider the conflict between agency and ideology in a post-communist world.

Slavoj Žižek, ed. *Mapping Ideology*. New York: Verso, 1994.

A volume of essays edited by Žižek which brings together seminal essays on ideology by the leading cultural thinkers of the twentieth century, including Adorno and Althusser, as well as contemporary interpretations of their work.

General

Zygmunt Bauman. "Ideology in the Postmodern World." In *In Search of Politics*, pp. 109–31. Stanford, CA: Stanford University Press, 1999.

Bauman traces the etymology and history of the term "ideology" in order to provide a sense of the different meanings and social functions it has played.

Guy Debord. *The Society of the Spectacle*. Translated by Donald Nicholson-Smith. Boston: Zone Books, 1995.

An iconoclastic work in which radical French philosopher Guy Debord offers cryptic and critical aphorisms regarding the political role of culture, thought, and capitalism in the contemporary moment.

Terry Eagleton. *Ideology: An Introduction*. London: Verso, 1991.

An accessible introduction to the notion of ideology which attempts to unravel the confusion surrounding the idea. Eagleton traces and explains the manifestation of "ideology" in the works of Lukács, Adorno, Bourdieu, and in post-structuralism, among others.

Thomas Kuhn. *The Structure of Scientific Revolutions*. Chicago: University of Chicago Press, 1996.

A classic text in which Kuhn argues that science does not escape from ideology, but is instead fundamentally bound up with culture. In this schema, scientific revolutions are understood as profound sea changes in ideology rather than as examples of progress.

Cary Nelson and Lawrence Grossberg, eds. *Marxism and the Interpretation of Culture*. Chicago: University of Illinois Press, 1988.

An extensive series of essays which offer a survey of the field of Marxist Cultural Criticism at the end of the 1980s. Still relevant, the collection contains a number of works pertaining to the study of ideology.

Michael Pollan. *In Defense of Food: An Eater's Manifesto*. New York: Penguin, 2008.

An incisive case study of the emergence of "nutritionism," the ideological underpinning of contemporary US American food science and its effects in popular culture.

Gayil Talshir, Mathew Humphrey, and Michael Freeden, eds. *Taking Ideology Seriously: 21st Century Reconfigurations*. London: Routledge, 2006.

Constructed around a challenge to the contemporary notion of a "post-ideological world," this volume of essays brings theories of ideology up to date by looking at issues such as globalization.

Part 4

Space and Scale

Introduction

The archive of writing and research which addresses landscape paintings, maps, and travelogues gives us only a fraction of the details needed to understand the spatial characteristics of culture. The interrelation of space and culture is indeed found in geographic studies and debates, though evidence also shows that culture configures the material world itself, in (to name disparate examples) policed national borders, highway underpasses replete with graffiti, virtual spaces generated by fiber optics and electricity grids, and the assumption shared by almost everyone that one "belongs" to a specific locale (from the idea of home to that of nation). As a way to outline how these phenomena relate to one another, this section offers writings that exemplify, modify, and interrogate the way one studies the impact of culture on our ideas of space *and* the spatiality of culture itself.

The relation of space and time has a lengthy and complicated theoretical history. Critical theories of space differ from philosophical or scientific articulations because the term is used to examine social and political *processes* rather than epistemological or ontological truths. The reduction of the idea of space to its conceptual essence, as *res extensa*, is a noteworthy analytic tool, but it becomes much less informative when one accounts for large-scale spaces beyond our sensory capacity. Without the certitude of spatial immediacy, many theorists pursue this "beyond" not with the subject as the measure, but by positing space against temporal causality. For instance, Doreen Massey reminds us that spatial theorists reject "a notion of society as a kind of 3-D (and indeed more usually 2-D) slice which moves through time."[1] Among the most commonly accepted narratives of social life, the category of time is easily accepted as a mode of causation – the predictable minute-by-minute move from past to future – while spatial categories have often been ignored or described as merely the setting of events. This way of thinking fosters a rather staid understanding of history: dual trajectories of linear time (for societies) and biographies (for individuals) are our presumed coordinates for understanding social phenomena. *Where* all of this takes place and how the built environment shapes collective life is the primary problem explored by the writings in this section.

By probing the multiple ways in which ideas of space are created, spatial theories of culture keep us from falling into amorphous and spurious descriptions of collectivities. Perhaps the greatest and most pervasive of these is the grand concept of "civilization," especially when it is imagined in the plural as opposed to naming that moment when we emerged from caves and started collecting taxes (i.e., Western civilization, Chinese civilization, and so on). Samuel Huntington's book *The Clash of Civilizations*, for instance, not only ignores the economic rationale which guides contemporary conflict, but relies uncritically on one of the most mystifying concepts describing social life.[2] "Civilization," a concept easily appealed to as a supposedly obvious and meaningful descriptor of a fixed segment of a cultural space that can be marked off on a map of world, operates as a forceful myth in the way it presumes historical progress and the social cohesion of particular cultures while masking the forces which actually bind people together. Power, ideology, politics, subjectivity – all become mystified in Huntington's account since culture is not contextualized within the realms whereby ordinary material needs are produced and consumed.

To give more specificity to spatial concepts such as civilization, theorists have turned to the work of Karl Marx for his contextualization of the dominant organizing logic of scales, both local and global. In keeping with this lineage of thought, Doreen Massey cites the urban theorist Henri Lefebvre, who recalibrates philosophical notions of time and space to replace the idea of civilization with that of a broader spatial system: capitalism. Capitalist production as the underlying condition of social relations (and not just one force among many) offers us a way of understanding where we are with respect to resources, producers, and consumers, and to those who organize and legitimate the enterprise of the collective itself. Lefebvre argues that space is a primary element of capital's genesis and everyday reproduction:

> The space of capitalist accumulation thus gradually came to life, and began to be fitted out. This process of animation is admiringly referred to as history, and its motor sought in all kinds of factors: dynastic interests, ideologies, the ambitions of the mighty, the formation of nation states, demographic pressures, and so on. This is the road to a ceaseless analyzing of, and searching for, dates and chains of events. Inasmuch as space is the locus of all such chronologies, might it not constitute a principle of explanation at least as acceptable as any other?[3]

Space and context are not simply the benign provenance of capital's spread and intensification. Increased private accumulation is predicated on the ability of capital to commodify realms either protected from economic pressures or remote and unexplored. If for Lefebvre the incessant events restructuring cities bear the traces of capital's spatial contradictions, how do theorists in this section analyze other types of space for signs of the way they are shaped and also shape cultural life?

In a fashion similar to Lefebvre, David Harvey and Michel de Certeau argue that value is primarily produced and appropriated in the subject's bodily relation to its surroundings, urban or otherwise. Each of these theorists addresses how a subject's body is spatially contingent in its own distinct way. Harvey draws directly from Marx's critique of the political economy to focus on the laboring subject, whereas de Certeau stages the relation of the subject and space within the "signifying practices"[4] which form the basis for recreating dominant cultural norms and practices. In both cases, the body is described as a locus of cultural production, generative of material goods and value but also conditioned by these reified structures. Against theorists who uphold "the body" as either liberating or confining (once again trying to use a single standard measure for all social experience), Harvey describes the body as "internally contradictory" and caught up within a process which shapes the forces which reproduce capital. He explains that many theorists before him have "construed [workers's bodies] as passive entities occupying particular performative economic roles … shaped by the external forces of capital circulation and accumulation." However, Harvey reminds us that "it is precisely this analysis that informs [Marx's] other accounts of how transformative processes of human resistance, desire for reform, rebellion, and revolution can and do occur."[5] Harvey attunes us to the ways value is abstracted from bodies and their labor, and he reminds us of the specifically geographical locus of embodiment, which is both generative of and regulated through its productive capacities.

Urban space is often perceived as if it were "an optical artifact." When surveying a map or peering down upon a grid of streets from atop a skyscraper, a city is framed and imagined to be an autonomous mass of buildings and infrastructure. Michel de Certeau proposes that a more acute knowledge of cities may be created at street level through "pedestrian speech acts." When walking down a street one has the ability to test and remake urban norms and boundaries. Such a practice passes largely unacknowledged in daily life, especially when cities are viewed abstractly or at a distance. Echoing Charles Baudelaire and Walter Benjamin's figure of the *flâneur*, de Certeau uses a semiotic vocabulary to reveal the potentially transformative relation a city's inhabitants may have with one another as they wander its streets.[6] Contemporaries of de Certeau, Michel Foucault, and Pierre Bourdieu mapped prisons and households with an eye to the way subjects are controlled and normalized.

However, for de Certeau the sociability of streets offers inherent potential as a "place of transformation and appropriations" which no force of control can disable or prevent.

The tactics de Certeau outlines resonate with the realm of subcultures that Dick Hebdige observed and described in 1970s England. Urban settings have a longstanding association with anonymity, deviance, and subterfuge. They bring people into anonymous contact with one another at a perplexing and often alienating pace and scale. Collective opposition to dominant forms of culture – generated either within cities themselves or from outlying rural cultures – imbued with class-based politics, popular critiques of moral conformity, and generational antagonism have at times produced enclaves defiant to accepted social roles. For Hebdige, subcultures are not an inherent characteristic of urban life but rather a distinct milieu defined by *style* – "teddy boys," punks, skinheads, and so on – carved out of contingent socioeconomic circumstances. Appearing on the surface as ephemeral playfulness or as merely an affront to accepted tastes, subcultures arrange "an imaginary set of relations" negotiated as a preferred way of life counter to or with an affinity for depictions of identity in mass communications. Against the notion that the social life of subcultures develops in deviant isolation from status quo institutions (such as the state or the nuclear family), Hebdige's essay shows how these internally vexed groups are composed through mediating forces which shape their place in the larger contexts of the city and nation.

The modes of power which shape cities have changed to a remarkable degree since the modern construction of London, Paris, New York, and Tokyo. In the 1970s a handful of global and non-democratic financial institutions began a reconfiguration of the very infrastructure of the most densely populated spaces. Mike Davis's essay on contemporary urbanization in the context of the global political economy unfolds with an acute reading of a 2003 UN-Habitat document, *The Challenge of Slums: Global Report on Human Settlements*. An alarming panoramic description of hundreds of urban spaces across six continents, Davis gives us a litany of details that describe the disproportionate impact of globalization – the effects of structural adjustment programs in particular – on the daily lives of slum dwellers worldwide. He writes that "the 1980s' crisis inverted the relative structural positions of the formal and informal sectors: promoting informal survivalism as the new primary mode of livelihood in a majority of Third World cities."[7] Earlier generations of migrants flocked to cities with the promise of improved lives. Davis and others in this section show that such decisions are often made without available alternatives and evidence suggests that no coherent plan exists to alleviate the survivalism of slums. Just as the Great Depression flooded New York and Chicago with workers because local farm life was quickly extinguished (which meant that they also couldn't return when the city turned up no prospects for work), the infusion of staggering numbers of people into Cairo, Guangzhou, Lagos, Mumbai, or São Paulo creates an imperiled existence catalyzed by the financial restructuring of agribusiness and the daily challenge of subsistence living. Davis characterizes the present conjuncture as "surplus humanity": millions of people abandoned to their own fate without recourse to the welfare institutions some cities once ensured.

Meeting the basic needs of proliferating populations is indeed a problem with no other horizon than the global. The rampant privatization brought about by transnational corporations may yet return the preponderance of power to nations. Despite the repeated suggestion that their era has come to an end, nations remain a key part of our global system, jealously guarding the reins of sovereign power even in the face of new international political organizations and agreements. Their continued prominence as an important form of spatial organization is due both to their scale and to the ongoing power of national culture. Though often enormous and traversing numerous time zones, even physically large nations are nevertheless still able to shape their diverse populations into a people. The process by which populations of nations develop an affinity for one another across spatial expanses (Canadians from Vancouver to St. John's, Russians from St. Petersburg to Vladivostok) has played a major role in ways we think about how culture establishes space and vice versa. In *Imagined Communities* (1983), Benedict Anderson describes how the advent of print capitalism, in the forms of daily newspapers and serialized novels, helped to solidify a bond between people who share no daily interaction. Nationhood relies on a form of cultural, "imagined" mediation which shapes its citizens to believe they have a common identity and are ruled by the same sovereign power. Whereas other models of national culture take this equation of space and culture as the product of economic necessity or supposed primordial belonging or blood lineage, Anderson's theory identifies the importance of the narrative material of the imagination in drawing groups of people spread across great distances into a social and political form that, though contingent, has become difficult to conceive otherwise. We seem fated to be national subjects and to participate in the sometimes fatal games of realpolitik which play people off one against the another.

On a scale larger than the nation, globalization has created "fertile grounds" for "deterritorialization," which Arjun Appadurai characterizes as "one of the central forces of the modern world because it brings labouring populations into the lower class sectors and spaces of relatively wealthy societies, while sometimes creating exaggerated and intensified senses of criticism or attachment to politics in the home state."[8] Regarding the present imaginary of culture as a vestige of prior paradigms such as national and urban culture, Appadurai insists we are enmeshed in five "scapes" which configure equivalencies and modes of identification across the planet: ethnoscapes, financescapes, ideoscapes, mediascapes, and technoscapes. Analyses in cultural geography are often content with descriptions of national and regional boundaries, but Appadurai seeks to recast collective boundaries and alter the coordinates by which space and scale are imagined. "The individual actor," he writes, "is the last locus of this perspectival set of landscapes, for these landscapes are eventually navigated by agents who both experience and constitute larger formations, in part from their own sense of what these landscapes offer."[9] Appadurai and Anderson place the challenge of contending with the social logic of daily life within our collective imaginative capacities. Whereas figures such as Huntington obscure how space and scale play primary roles in shaping culture, the writers in this section provide us with tools to better comprehend the realms in which culture is organized (bodies, milieus, cities, nations, etc.) and to create the potential for new, less divisive and exclusionary spaces in the future.

Notes

1   Doreen Massey, "Politics and Space/Time," *New Left Review* I.196 (November–December 1992), 65–84. Reproduced in this volume.
2   See Samuel P. Huntington, *The Clash of Civilizations and the Remaking of World Order* (New York: Simon & Schuster, 1996). Huntington divides the world into a number of civilization zones, determined by similarities in histories, religion, and worldviews. These include Western civilization (North America, Western Europe, Australia), Latin America, Orthodox (largely made up of the former Soviet countries), Buddhist, Sinic (China and much of Asia), Hindu, Muslim, Sub-Saharan, and Japan.
3   Henri Lefebvre, *The Production of Space*, trans. Donald Nicholson-Smith (Oxford: Blackwell, 1991), 275.
4   Michel de Certeau, "Walking in the City," in *The Practice of Everyday Life* (Berkeley: University of California Press, 2002), 104. Reproduced in this volume.
5   David Harvey, "The Body as Accumulation Strategy," in *Spaces of Hope* (Berkeley: University of California Press, 2000), 102. Reproduced in this volume.
6   Walter Benjamin, *The Arcades Project*, trans. Howard Eiland et al. (Cambridge, MA: Belknap Press, 2002) and *The Writer of Modern Life: Essays on Charles Baudelaire*, trans. Harry Zohn et al. (Cambridge, MA: Belknap Press, 2006).
7   Mike Davis, "Planet of Slums," *New Left Review* 26 (March–April 2004), 24. Reproduced in this volume.
8   Arjun Appadurai, "Disjuncture and Difference in the Global Cultural Economy," in *Modernity at Large* (Minneapolis: University of Minnesota Press, 2000), 37–8. Reproduced in this volume.
9   Ibid., 33.

22

"The Function of Subculture" (1979)

Dick Hebdige

The subcultures introduced in the previous sections [of Hebdige's book] have till now been described as a series of mediated responses to the presence in Britain of a sizeable black community. As we have seen, the proximity of the two positions – white working-class youth and Negro – invites identification and even when this identity is repressed or openly resisted, black cultural forms (e.g. music) continue to exercise a major determining influence over the development of each subcultural style. It is now time to explore the relationship between these spectacular subcultures and those other groups (parents, teachers, police, 'respectable' youth, etc.) and cultures (adult working-class and middle-class cultures) against which they are ostensibly defined. Most writers still tend to attribute an inordinate significance to the opposition between young and old, child and parent, citing the rites of passage which, even in the most primitive societies, are used to mark the transition from childhood to maturity.[1] What is missing from these accounts is any idea of historical specificity, any explanation of why these particular forms should occur at this particular time.

[...]

The persistence of class as a meaningful category within youth culture was not, however, generally acknowledged until fairly recently and, as we shall see, the seemingly spontaneous eruption of spectacular youth styles has encouraged some writers to talk of

youth as the new class – to see in youth a community of undifferentiated Teenage Consumers. It was not until the 1960s, when Peter Willmott (1969) and David Downes (1966) published separate pieces of research into the lives of working-class adolescents,[2] that the myth of a classless youth culture was seriously challenged. This challenge is best understood in the context of the larger debate about the function of subculture which has, for many years, preoccupied those sociologists who specialize in deviancy theory. It would seem appropriate to include here a brief survey of some of the approaches to youth and subculture put forward in the course of that debate.

The study of subculture in Britain grew out of a tradition of urban ethnography which can be traced back at least as far as the nineteenth century: to the work of Henry Mayhew and Thomas Archer,[3] and to the novels of Charles Dickens and Arthur Morrison.[4] However, a more 'scientific' approach to subculture complete with its own methodology (participant observation) did not emerge until the 1920s when a group of sociologists and criminologists in Chicago began collecting evidence on juvenile street gangs and deviant groups (professional criminals, bootleggers, etc.). In 1927, Frederick Thrasher produced a survey of over 1000 street gangs, and later William Foote Whyte described at length in *Street Corner Society* the rituals, routines and occasional exploits of one particular gang.

Participant observation continues to produce some of the most interesting and evocative accounts of subculture, but the method also suffers from a number of significant flaws. In particular, the absence

Dick Hebdige, "The Function of Subculture," pp. 73, 75–89 from *Subculture: The Meaning of Style*. London: Routledge, 1991. Reproduced by permission of Taylor & Francis Books UK.

of any analytical or explanatory framework has guaranteed such work a marginal status in the predominantly positivist tradition of mainstream sociology.[5] More crucially, such an absence has ensured that while accounts based upon a participant observation approach provide a wealth of descriptive detail, the significance of class and power relations is consistently neglected or at least underestimated. In such accounts, the subculture tends to be presented as an independent organism functioning outside the larger social, political and economic contexts. As a result, the picture of subculture is often incomplete. For all the Chandleresque qualities of the prose; for all the authenticity and close detail which participant observation made possible, it soon became apparent that the method needed to be supplemented by other more analytical procedures.

During the 1950s, Albert Cohen and Walter Miller sought to supply the missing theoretical perspective by tracing the continuities and breaks between dominant and subordinate value systems. Cohen stressed the compensatory function of the juvenile gang: working-class adolescents who underachieved at school joined gangs in their leisure time in order to develop alternative sources of self-esteem. In the gang, the core values of the straight world – sobriety, ambition, conformity, etc. – were replaced by their opposites: hedonism, defiance of authority and the quest for 'kicks' (Cohen, 1955). Miller, too, concentrated on the value system of the juvenile gang, but he underlined the similarities between gang and parent culture, arguing that many of the values of the deviant group merely reiterated in a distorted or heightened form the 'focal concerns' of the adult working-class population (Miller, 1958). In 1961, Matza and Sykes used the notion of subterranean values to explain the existence of legitimate as well as delinquent youth cultures. Like Miller, the writers recognized that potentially subversive goals and aims were present in systems which were otherwise regarded as perfectly respectable. They found embedded in youth culture those subterranean values (the search for risk, excitement, etc.) which served to underpin rather than undermine the day-time ethos of production (postponement of gratification, routine, etc.) (Matza and Sykes, 1961; Matza, 1964).[6]

Subsequently, these theories were tested in the course of British field work. In the 1960s, Peter Willmott published his research into the range of cultural options open to working-class boys in the East End of London. Contrary to the breezy assertions of writers like Mark Abrams (1959),[7] Willmott concluded that the idea of a completely classless youth culture was premature and meaningless. He observed instead that the leisure styles available to youth were inflected through the contradictions and divisions intrinsic to a class society. It was left to Phil Cohen to explore in detail the ways in which class-specific experience was encoded in leisure styles which after all had largely originated in London's East End. Cohen was also interested in the links between youth and parent cultures, and interpreted the various youth styles as sectional adaptations to changes which had disrupted the *whole* East End community. He defined subculture as a '… compromise solution between two contradictory needs: the need to create and express autonomy and difference from parents … and the need to maintain the parental identifications' (Cohen, 1972). In this analysis, the mod, ted and skinhead styles were interpreted as attempts to mediate between experience and tradition, the familiar and the novel. And for Cohen, the 'latent function' of subculture was to '… express and resolve, albeit magically, the contradictions which remain hidden or unresolved in the parent culture' (Cohen, 1972). The mods, for instance

> … attempted to realise, but in an imaginary relation, the condition of existence of the socially mobile white-collar worker … [while] … their argot and ritual forms … [continued to stress] … many of the traditional values of the parent culture. (Cohen, 1972)

Here at last was a reading which took into account the full interplay of ideological, economic and cultural factors which bear upon subculture. By grounding his theory in ethnographic detail, Cohen was able to insert class into his analysis at a far more sophisticated level than had previously been possible. Rather than presenting class as an abstract set of external determinations, he showed it working out in practice as a material force, dressed up, as it were, in experience and exhibited in style. The raw material of history could be seen refracted, held and 'handled' in the line of a mod's jacket, in the soles on a teddy boy's shoes. Anxieties concerning class and sexuality, the tensions between conformity and deviance, family and school, work and leisure, were all frozen there in a form which was at once visible and opaque, and Cohen provided a way of reconstructing that history; of penetrating the skin of style and drawing out its hidden meanings.

Cohen's work still furnishes the most adequate model available for a reading of subcultural style. However, in order to underline the importance and meaning of class, he had been forced to lay perhaps too much emphasis on the links between the youth and adult working-class cultures. There are equally significant differences between the two forms which must also be acknowledged. As we have seen, a generational consciousness *did* emerge amongst the young in the post-war period, and even where experience was shared between parents and children this experience was likely to be differently interpreted, expressed and handled by the two groups. Thus, while obviously there are points where parent and adolescent 'solutions' converge and even overlap, when dealing with the spectacular subculture we should not grant these an absolute ascendancy. And we should be careful when attempting to tie back subcultural style to its generative context not to overstress the fit between respectable working-class culture and the altogether more marginal forms with which we are concerned here.

For example, the skinheads undoubtedly reasserted those values associated with the traditional working-class community, but they did so *in the face of* the widespread renunciation of those values in the parent culture – *at a time when* such an affirmation of the classic concerns of working-class life was considered inappropriate. Similarly, the mods were negotiating changes and contradictions which were simultaneously affecting the parent culture but they were doing so in the terms of their own relatively autonomous problematic – by inventing an 'elsewhere' (the weekend, the West End) which was defined *against* the familiar locales of the home, the pub, the working-man's club, the neighbourhood.

If we emphasize integration and coherence at the expense of dissonance and discontinuity, we are in danger of denying the very manner in which the subcultural form is made to crystallize, objectify and communicate group experience. We should be hard pressed to find in the punk subculture, for instance, any symbolic attempts to 'retrieve some of the socially cohesive elements destroyed in the parent culture' (Cohen, 1972) beyond the simple fact of cohesion itself: the expression of a highly structured, visible, tightly bounded group identity. Rather, the punks seemed to be parodying the alienation and emptiness which have caused sociologists so much concern,[8] realizing in a deliberate and wilful fashion the direst predictions of the most scathing social critics, and celebrating in mock-heroic terms the death of the community and the collapse of traditional forms of meaning.

We can, therefore, only grant a qualified acceptance to Cohen's theory of subcultural style. Later, I shall be attempting to re-think the relationship between parent and youth cultures by looking more closely at the whole process of signification in subculture. At this stage, however, we should not allow these objections to detract from the overall importance of Cohen's contribution. It is no exaggeration to say that the idea of style as a coded response to changes affecting the entire community has literally transformed the study of spectacular youth culture. Much of the research extracted in *Resistance Through Rituals* (Hall et al., 1976) was premised upon the basic assumption that style could be read in this way. Using Gramsci's concept of hegemony, the authors interpreted the succession of youth cultural styles as symbolic forms of resistance; as spectacular symptoms of a wider and more generally submerged dissent which characterized the whole post-war period. This reading of style opens up a number of issues which demand examination, and the approach to subculture adopted in *Resistance Through Rituals* provides the basis for much of what follows. We begin with the notion of specificity.

Specificity: Two Types of Teddy Boy

If we take as our starting point the definition of culture used in *Resistance Through Rituals* – culture is '… that level at which social groups develop distinct patterns of life and give *expressive form* to their social and material … experience' (Hall et al., 1976) we can see that each subculture represents a different handling of the 'raw material of social … existence' (Hall et al., 1976). But what exactly is this 'raw material'? We learn from Marx that 'Men make their own history, but they do not make it just as they please, they do not make it under circumstances chosen by themselves, but under circumstances directly encountered, given and transmitted from the past' (Marx, 1951). In effect, the material (i.e. social relations) which is continually being transformed into culture (and hence subculture) can never be completely 'raw'. It is always mediated: inflected by the historical context in which it is encountered; posited upon a specific ideological field which gives it a particular life and particular meanings. Unless one is prepared to use some essentialist paradigm of the working class as the inexorable bearers of an absolute trans-historical Truth,[9] then one should not expect the subcultural response to be either unfailingly correct about real relations under capitalism, or even *necessarily* in touch, in any immediate sense, with its material position in the capitalist system. Spectacular subcultures express what is by definition an imaginary set of relations. The raw material out of which they are constructed is both real and ideological. It is mediated to the individual members of a subculture through a variety of channels: school, the family, work, the media, etc. Moreover, this material is subject to historical change. Each subcultural 'instance' represents a 'solution' to a specific set of circumstances, to particular problems and contradictions. For example, the mod and teddy boy 'solutions' were produced in response to different conjunctures which positioned them differently in relation to existing cultural formations (immigrant cultures, the parent culture, other subcultures, the dominant culture). We can see this more clearly if we concentrate on one example.

There were two major moments in the history of the teddy boy subculture (the 1950s and the 1970s). But, whilst they maintained the same antagonistic relation to the black immigrant community as their counterparts of the 1950s, the latter-day teds were differently positioned in relation to the parent culture and other youth cultures.

The early 1950s and late 1970s share certain obvious features: the vocabularies of 'austerity' and 'crisis', though not identical, are similar, and more importantly, anxieties about the effects of black immigration on employment, housing and the 'quality of life' were prominent in both periods. However, the differences are far more crucial. The presence in the latter period

of an alternative, predominantly working-class youth culture (i.e. the punks), many of whose members actively championed certain aspects of West Indian life, serve clearly to distinguish the two moments. The early teds had marked a new departure. They had represented, in the words of George Melly (1972), 'the dark van of pop culture' and though small in number, they had been almost universally vilified by press and parents alike as symptomatic of Britain's impending decline. On the other hand, the very concept of 'revival' in the 1970s gave the teddy boys an air of legitimacy. After all, in a society which seemed to generate a bewildering number of fads and fashions, the teddy boys were a virtual institution: an authentic, albeit dubious part of the British heritage.

The youths who took part in this revival were thus guaranteed in certain quarters at least a limited acceptability. They could be regarded with tolerance, even muted affection, by those working-class adults who, whether original teds or straights, nostalgically inclined towards the 1950s and, possessed of patchy memories, harked back to a more settled and straightforward past. The revival recalled a time which seemed surprizingly remote, and by comparison secure; almost idyllic in its stolid puritanism, its sense of values, its conviction that the future could be better. Freed from time and context, these latter-day teds could be allowed to float as innocent pretenders on the wave of 1970s nostalgia situated somewhere between the Fonz of television's *Happy Days* and a recycled Ovaltine ad. Paradoxically then, the subculture which had originally furnished such dramatic signs of change could be made to provide a kind of continuity in its revived form.

In broader terms, the two teddy boy solutions were responses to specific historical conditions, formulated in completely different ideological atmospheres. There was no possibility in the late 1970s of enlisting working-class support around the cheery imperatives of reconstruction: 'grin and bear it', 'wait and see', etc. The widespread disillusionment amongst working-class people with the Labour Party and Parliamentary politics in general, the decline of the Welfare State, the faltering economy, the continuing scarcity of jobs and adequate housing, the loss of community, the failure of consumerism to satisfy real needs, and the perennial round of industrial disputes, shutdowns and picket line clashes, all served to create a sense of diminishing returns which stood in stark contrast to the embattled optimism of the earlier period. Assisted no doubt by the ideological constructions retrospectively placed upon the Second World War (the fostering around 1973 as a response to protracted industrial disputes, the oil crisis, the three day week, etc. of a patriotic war-time spirit in search of an enemy; the replacement of the concretization 'German' for the concept 'fascist') these developments further combined with the visibility of the black communities to make racism a far more respectable and credible solution to the problems of working-class life.

In addition, the teddy boys' dress and demeanour carried rather different connotations in the 1970s. Of course the 'theft' of an upper-class style which had originally made the whole teddy boy style possible had long been forgotten, and in the process the precise nature of the transformation had been irrevocably lost. What is more the strutting manner and sexual aggressiveness had different meanings in the two periods. The narcissism of the early teds and the carnal gymnastics of jiving had been pitted against what Melly (1972) describes as a 'grey colourless world where good boys played ping pong'. The second generation teds' obstinate fidelity to the traditional 'bad-guy' stereotypes appeared by contrast obvious and reactionary. To the sound of records long since deleted, in clothes which qualified as virtual museum pieces, these latter-day teds resurrected a set of sexual mores (gallantry, courtship,) and a swaggering machismo – that 'quaint' combination of chauvinism, brylcreem and sudden violence – which was already enshrined in the parent culture as *the* model of masculine behaviour: a model untouched by the febrile excesses of the post-war 'permissive society'.

All these factors drew the teddy boy subculture in its second incarnation *closer* to the parent culture and helped to define it against other existing youth cultural options (punks, Northern soul enthusiasts, heavy metal rockers,[10] football fans, mainstream pop, 'respectable', etc.) For these reasons, wearing a drape coat in 1978 did not mean the same things in the same way as it had done in 1956, despite the fact that the two sets of teddy boys worshipped identical heroes (Elvis, Eddie Cochrane, James Dean), cultivated the same

quiffs and occupied approximately the same class position. The twin concepts of *conjuncture* and *specificity* (each subculture representing a distinctive 'moment' – a particular response to a particular set of circumstances) are therefore indispensable to a study of subcultural style.

The Sources of Style

We have seen how the experience encoded in subcultures is shaped in a variety of locales (work, home, school, etc.). Each of these locales imposes its own unique structure, its own rules and meanings, its own hierarchy of values. Though these structures articulate together, they do so syntactically. They are bound together as much through difference (home v. school, school v. work, home v. work, private v. public, etc.) as through similarity. To use Althusser's admittedly cumbersome terms, they constitute different levels of the same social formation. And though they are, as Althusser takes pains to point out, 'relatively autonomous', these structures remain, in capitalist societies, articulated around the 'general contradiction' between Capital and Labour (see particularly Althusser, 1971). The complex interplay between the different levels of the social formation is reproduced in the experience of both dominant and subordinate groups, and this experience, in turn, becomes the 'raw material' which finds expressive form in culture and subculture. Now, the media play a crucial role in defining our experience for us. They provide us with the most available categories for classifying out the social world. It is primarily through the press, television, film, etc. that experience is organized, interpreted, and made to *cohere in contradiction* as it were. It should hardly surprise us then, to discover that much of what finds itself encoded in subculture has already been subjected to a certain amount of prior handling by the media.

Thus, in post-war Britain, the loaded content of subcultural style is likely to be as much a function of what Stuart Hall has called the 'ideological effect'[11] of the media as a reaction to experienced changes in the institutional framework of working-class life. As Hall has argued, the media have 'progressively colonised the cultural and ideological sphere':

As social groups and classes live, if not in their productive then in their 'social' relations, increasingly fragmented and sectionally differentiated lives, the mass media are more and more responsible (a) for providing the basis on which groups and classes construct an image of the lives, meanings, practices and values of *other* groups and classes; (b) for providing the images, representations and ideas around which the social totality composed of all these separate and fragmented pieces can be coherently grasped. (Hall, 1977)

So a credible image of social cohesion can only be maintained through the appropriation and redefinition of cultures of resistance (e.g. working-class youth cultures) in terms of that image. In this way, the media not only provide groups with substantive images of other groups, they also relay back to working-class people a 'picture' of their own lives which is 'contained' or 'framed' by the ideological discourses which surround and situate it.

Clearly, subcultures are not privileged forms; they do not stand outside the reflexive circuitry of production and reproduction which links together, at least on a symbolic level, the separate and fragmented pieces of the social totality. Subcultures are, at least in part, representations of these representations, and elements taken from the 'picture' of working-class life (and of the social whole in general) are bound to find some echo in the signifying practices of the various subcultures. There is no reason to suppose that subcultures spontaneously affirm only those *blocked* 'readings' excluded from the airwaves and the newspapers (consciousness of subordinate status, a conflict model of society, etc.). They also articulate, to a greater or lesser extent, some of the *preferred* meanings and interpretations, those favoured by and transmitted through the authorized channels of mass communication. The typical members of a working-class youth culture in part contest and in part agree with the dominant definitions of who and what they are, and there is a substantial amount of shared ideological ground not only between them and the adult working-class culture (with its muted tradition of resistance) but also between them and the dominant culture (at least in its more 'democratic', accessible forms).

For example, the elaboration of upward and downward options open to working-class youth does not necessarily indicate any significant difference in the relative status of the jobs available to the average mod of 1964 and the skinhead of 1968 (though a census might indeed reveal such a difference). Still less does it reflect *directly* the fact that job opportunities open to working-class youth in general actually diminished during the intervening period. Rather the different styles and the ideologies which structure and determine them represent negotiated responses to a contradictory mythology of class. In this mythology, 'the withering away of class' is paradoxically countered by an undiluted 'classfulness', a romantic conception of the traditional whole way of (working-class) life revived twice weekly on television programmes like *Coronation Street*. The mods and skinheads, then, in their different ways, were 'handling' this mythology as much as the exigencies of their material condition. They were learning to live within or without that amorphous body of images and typifications made available in the mass media in which class is alternately overlooked and overstated, denied and reduced to caricature.

In the same way, the punks were not only directly *responding* to increasing joblessness, changing moral standards, the rediscovery of poverty, the Depression, etc., they were *dramatizing* what had come to be called 'Britain's decline' by constructing a language which was, in contrast to the prevailing rhetoric of the Rock Establishment, unmistakably relevant and down to earth (hence the swearing, the references to 'fat hippies', the rags, the lumpen poses). The punks appropriated the rhetoric of crisis which had filled the airwaves and the editorials throughout the period and translated it into tangible (and visible) terms. In the gloomy, apocalyptic ambience of the late 1970s – with massive unemployment, with the ominous violence of the Notting Hill Carnival, Grunwick, Lewisham and Ladywood – it was fitting that the punks should present themselves as 'degenerates'; as signs of the highly publicized decay which perfectly represented the atrophied condition of Great Britain. The various stylistic ensembles adopted by the punks were undoubtedly expressive of genuine aggression, frustration and anxiety. But these statements, no matter how strangely constructed, were cast in a language which was generally available – a language which was current. This accounts, first, for the appropriateness of the punk metaphor for both the members of the sub-culture and its opponents and, second, for the success of the punk subculture as spectacle: its ability to symptomatize a whole cluster of contemporary problems. It explains the subculture's ability to attract new members and to produce the requisite outraged responses from the parents, teachers and employers towards whom the moral panic was directed and from the 'moral entrepreneurs' – the local councillors, the pundits and MPs – who were responsible for conducting the 'crusade' against it. In order to communicate disorder, the appropriate language must first be selected, even if it is to be subverted. For punk to be dismissed as chaos, it had first to 'make sense' as noise.

We can now begin to understand how the Bowie cult came to be articulated around questions of gender rather than class, and to confront those critics who relate the legitimate concerns of 'authentic' working-class culture exclusively to the sphere of production. The Bowie-ites were certainly not grappling in any *direct* way with the familiar set of problems encountered on the shop floor and in the classroom: problems which revolve around relations with authority (rebellion v. deference, upward v. downward options, etc.). None the less, they were attempting to negotiate a meaningful intermediate space somewhere between the parent culture and the dominant ideology: a space where an alternative identity could be discovered and expressed. To this extent they were engaged in that distinctive quest for a measure of autonomy which characterizes all youth sub- (and counter) cultures. In sharp contrast to their skinhead predecessors, the Bowie-ites were confronting the more obvious chauvinisms (sexual, class, territorial) and seeking, with greater or lesser enthusiasm, to avoid, subvert or overthrow them. They were simultaneously (1) challenging the traditional working-class puritanism so firmly embedded in the parent culture, (2) resisting the way in which this puritanism was being made to signify the working class in the media and (3) adapting images, styles and ideologies made available elsewhere on television and in films (e.g. the nostalgia cult of the early 1970s), in magazines and newspapers (high fashion, the emergence of feminism in its commodity form, e.g. *Cosmopolitan*) in order to construct an alternative identity which communicated a perceived

difference: an Otherness. They were, in short, challenging at a symbolic level the 'inevitability', the 'naturalness' of class and gender stereotypes.

Notes

1 American sociologists and psychologists have tended to lay the stress on adolescence as a period of individualism and transition marked by ritual conflict:

> Although the concepts of 'childish' and 'adult' differ from one culture to another, every culture requires *some* change in the child's habitual ways of thinking, feeling and acting – a change which involves psychic dislocation and therefore constitutes a 'problem' for the individual and their culture. (Kenniston, 1969)

A comparative approach can be illuminating, but it can also serve to obscure important historical and cultural differences. What one can say about youth in general is strictly limited.

2 Both Downes' study of corner-boy culture in Stepney and Poplar, and Willmott's survey of adolescent options in Bethnal Green gave the lie to the myth of the classless teenager. Downes saw the 'delinquent solution' as a way for working class youth to achieve the ends of 'teenage culture' without having legitimate access to the means. Willmott stressed the local character of East End youth culture: leisure time and money were still spent on the 'manor' rather than in the newly opened boutiques and discotheques of London's West End.

3 Mayhew et al. (1851) and Archer (1865) were among the first to attempt a detailed description of the criminal underworld in London's East End 'rookeries'.

4 Charles Dickens, *Oliver Twist* (1896); Arthur Morrison, *A Child of the Jago* (1896), *The Hole in the Wall* (1902). Dickens needs no recommendation. However, the novels of Arthur Morrison are perhaps less familiar. Based on his own childhood experiences in the notorious Jago 'rookery', they provide a fascinating if depressing account of life in a mid-nineteenth-century slum.

5 See Roberts (1976) for a thorough account of the development of PO [participant observation]. Work and the problems it raises: 'PO has never become a complete alternative to positivism in sociology. … Instead, it has formed a sort of sociological "subculture" enclave within the mainstream'. See also Jock Young (1970), for an analysis of the contradictions inherent in the sociology of deviance.

6　In *Delinquency and Drift* Matza gives his original thesis a slightly different tilt by describing how adolescent boys 'drift' into deviance. The pursuit of subterranean goals and values draws them into deviance and this is further reinforced by the labelling process.

7　Abrams was involved in market research rather than sociology and was interested specifically in opening up a youth market based on the American model. He saw age rather than class as the single most important source of difference in an affluent post-war society: 'Under conditions of general prosperity the social study of society in class terms is less and less illuminating. And its place is taken by differences related to age.'

8　Listen for example to Jonathan Richman's 'Road-runner' ('I'm in love with the Modern World'). All the hymns to plastic were no doubt heavily tinged with irony.

9　This seems to be the position which Ros Coward (1977) is attacking in 'Class, Culture and the Social Formation':

> This position is one which posits a direct relation in which Marxist theory is put at the service of socialist tendencies which pre-exist any elaboration. In this way, it reduces the pressing and difficult problem of articulation between the theoretical and the political, and the possibility of the mutual determination between these instances

Coward goes on:

> The Work on sub-cultures … relies on a conception of history as the progressive unfolding of some inner principle (in this case economic contradiction) … it confuses consciousness and political and ideological representation and relies ultimately on a 'belief' that the working-class are the bearers of solution to conflict, that they somehow represent total mastery, the whole person which will be expressed in socialism.

Arguing from a Lacanian position, Coward presses for a displacement away from the study of culture (which she sees as an 'idealist' construct) to an analysis of the constitution of the individual subject in language. (For the reply to this article see *Screen*, vol. 18, no. 3 (Autumn 1978).)

10　Heavy metal is, as the name suggests, a heavily amplified, basic form of rock which relies on the constant repetition of standard guitar riffs. Afficionados can be distinguished by their long hair, denim and 'idiot' dancing (again, the name says it all). Heavy metal has fans amongst the student population, but it also has a large working-class following. It seems to represent a curious blend of hippy aesthetics and football terrace machismo.

11　Stuart Hall (1977) and also John Fiske and John Hartley (1978). The role the media play in shaping and maintaining consent is crucial. Hall argues that 'The media serve, in societies like ours, ceaselessly to perform the critical ideological work of "classifying out the world" within the "discourse of the dominant ideologies".' This is done by the continual drawing and redrawing of the line between 'preferred' and 'excluded' readings, the meaningful and the meaningless, the normal and the deviant. In passing, Hall also defines and makes connections between 'culture', 'ideology' and 'signification'. Obviously a footnote cannot do justice to an argument of such scope and density, and I can only recommend that readers look for themselves.

References

Abrams, M. (1959) *The Teenage Consumer*. London Press Exchange.

Althusser, L. (1971) *Lenin and Philosophy and Other Essays*. New Left Books.

Archer, T. (1865) *The Pauper, the Thief and the Convict*.

Cohen, A. (1955) *Delinquent Boys: The Culture of the Gang*. Free Press.

Cohen, P. (1972) 'Sub-cultural Conflict and Working Class Community', *W.P.C.S.* 2, University of Birmingham.

Coward, R. (1977) 'Class, "Culture" and the Social Formation', *Screen* 18 (1).

Downes, D. (1966) *The Delinquent Solution*. Routledge & Kegan Paul.

Fiske, J. and Hartley, J. (1978) *Reading Television*. Methuen.

Hall, S. (1977) 'Culture, the Media and the "Ideological Effect"', in J. Curran et al. (eds), *Mass Communication and Society*. Arnold.

Hall, S., Clarke, J., Jefferson, T. and Roberts, B. (eds) (1976) *Resistance Through Rituals*. Hutchinson.

Kenniston, K. (1969) 'Alienation and the Decline of Utopia', in D. Burrows and F. Lapides (eds), *Alienation: A Casebook*. Crowell.

Marx, K. (1951) 'The Eighteenth Brumaire', in *Marx and Engels Selected Works*, vol. 1. Lawrence and Wishart.

Matza, D. (1964) *Delinquency and Drift*. Wiley.

Matza, D. and Sykes, G. (1961) 'Juvenile Delinquency and Subterranean Values', *American Sociological Review* 26.

Mayhew, H. et al. (1851) *London Labour and the London Poor.*

Melly, G. (1972) *Revolt into Style.* Penguin.

Miller, W. (1958) 'Lower-class Culture as a Generating Milieu of Gang Delinquency', *Journal of Social Issues* 15.

Roberts, B. (1976) 'Naturalistic Research into Subcultures and Deviance', in S. Hall et al. (eds), *Resistance Through Rituals.* Hutchinson.

Thrasher, F. M. (1927) *The Gang.* University of Chicago Press.

Whyte, W. F. (1955) *Street Corner Society.* University of Chicago Press.

Willmott, P. (1969) *Adolescent Boys in East London.* Penguin.

Young, J. (1970) 'The Zoo-Keepers of Deviance', *Catalyst* 5.

23

"Walking in the City" (1980)

Michel de Certeau

Seeing Manhattan from the 110th floor of the World Trade Center. Beneath the haze stirred up by the winds, the urban island, a sea in the middle of the sea, lifts up the skyscrapers over Wall Street, sinks down at Greenwich, then rises again to the crests of Midtown, quietly passes over Central Park and finally undulates off into the distance beyond Harlem. A wave of verticals. Its agitation is momentarily arrested by vision. The gigantic mass is immobilized before the eyes. It is transformed into a texturology in which extremes coincide – extremes of ambition and degradation, brutal oppositions of races and styles, contrasts between yesterday's buildings, already transformed into trash cans, and today's urban irruptions that block out its space. Unlike Rome, New York has never learned the art of growing old by playing on all its pasts. Its present invents itself, from hour to hour, in the act of throwing away its previous accomplishments and challenging the future. A city composed of paroxysmal places in monumental reliefs. The spectator can read in it a universe that is constantly exploding. In it are inscribed the architectural figures of the *coincidatio oppositorum* formerly drawn in miniatures and mystical textures. On this stage of concrete, steel and glass, cut out between two oceans (the Atlantic and the American) by a frigid body of water, the tallest let-

Michel de Certeau, "Walking in the City," pp. 91–105 from *The Practice of Everyday Life*, trans. Steven Rendall. Berkeley: University of California Press, 1984. Copyright © 1984 by University of California Press. Reproduced by permission of University of California Press.

ters in the world compose a gigantic rhetoric of excess in both expenditure and production.[1]

Voyeurs or Walkers

To what erotics of knowledge does the ecstasy of reading such a cosmos belong? Having taken a voluptuous pleasure in it, I wonder what is the source of this pleasure of "seeing the whole," of looking down on, totalizing the most immoderate of human texts.

To be lifted to the summit of the World Trade Center is to be lifted out of the city's grasp. One's body is no longer clasped by the streets that turn and return it according to an anonymous law; nor is it possessed, whether as player or played, by the rumble of so many differences and by the nervousness of New York traffic. When one goes up there, he leaves behind the mass that carries off and mixes up in itself any identity of authors or spectators. An Icarus flying above these waters, he can ignore the devices of Daedalus in mobile and endless labyrinths far below. His elevation transfigures him into a voyeur. It puts him at a distance. It transforms the bewitching world by which one was "possessed" into a text that lies before one's eyes. It allows one to read it, to be a solar Eye, looking down like a god. The exaltation of a scopic and gnostic drive: the fiction of knowledge is related to this lust to be a viewpoint and nothing more.

Must one finally fall back into the dark space where crowds move back and forth, crowds that, though visible from on high, are themselves unable to see down below? An Icarian fall. On the 110th floor, a poster, sphinx-like, addresses an enigmatic message to the pedestrian who is for an instant transformed into a visionary: *It's hard to be down when you're up.*

The desire to see the city preceded the means of satisfying it. Medieval or Renaissance painters represented the city as seen in a perspective that no eye had yet enjoyed.[2] This fiction already made the medieval spectator into a celestial eye. It created gods. Have things changed since technical procedures have organized an "all-seeing power"?[3] The totalizing eye imagined by the painters of earlier times lives on in our achievements. The same scopic drive haunts users of architectural productions by materializing today the utopia that yesterday was only painted. The 1370 foot high tower that serves as a prow for Manhattan continues to construct the fiction that creates readers, makes the complexity of the city readable, and immobilizes its opaque mobility in a transparent text.

Is the immense texturology spread out before one's eyes anything more than a representation, an optical artifact? It is the analogue of the facsimile produced, through a projection that is a way of keeping aloof, by the space planner urbanist, city planner or cartographer. The panorama-city is a "theoretical" (that is, visual) simulacrum, in short a picture, whose condition of possibility is an oblivion and a misunderstanding of practices. The voyeur-god created by this fiction, who, like Schreber's God, knows only cadavers,[4] must disentangle himself from the murky intertwining daily behaviors and make himself alien to them.

The ordinary practitioners of the city live "down below," below the thresholds at which visibility begins. They walk – an elementary form of this experience of the city; they are walkers, *Wandersmänner*, whose bodies follow the thicks and thins of an urban "text" they write without being able to read it. These practitioners make use of spaces that cannot be seen; their knowledge of them is as blind as that of lovers in each other's arms. The paths that correspond in this intertwining, unrecognized poems in which each body is an element signed by many others, elude legibility. It is as though the practices organizing a bustling city were characterized by their blindness.[5] The networks of these moving, intersecting writings compose a manifold story that has neither author nor spectator, shaped out of fragments of trajectories and alterations of spaces: in relation to representations, it remains daily and indefinitely other.

Escaping the imaginary totalizations produced by the eye, the everyday has a certain strangeness that does not surface, or whose surface is only its upper limit, outlining itself against the visible. Within this ensemble, I shall try to locate the practices that are foreign to the "geometrical" or "geographical" space of visual, panoptic, or theoretical constructions. These practices of space refer to a specific form of *operations* ("ways of operating"), to "another spatiality"[6] (an "anthropological," poetic and mythic experience of space), and to an *opaque and blind* mobility characteristic of the bustling city. A *migrational*, or metaphorical, city thus slips into the clear text of the planned and readable city.

1. From the Concept of the City to Urban Practices

The World Trade Center is only the most monumental figure of Western urban development. The atopia-utopia of optical knowledge has long had the ambition of surmounting and articulating the contradictions arising from urban agglomeration. It is a question of managing a growth of human agglomeration or accumulation. "The city is a huge monastery," said Erasmus. Perspective vision and prospective vision constitute the twofold projection of an opaque past and an uncertain future onto a surface that can be dealt with. They inaugurate (in the sixteenth century?) the transformation of the urban *fact* into the *concept* of a city. Long before the concept itself gives rise to a particular figure of history, it assumes that this fact can be dealt with as a unity determined by an urbanistic *ratio*. Linking the city to the concept never makes them identical, but it plays on their progressive symbiosis: to plan a city is both to *think the very plurality* of the real and to make that way of thinking the plural *effective*; it is to know how to articulate it and be able to do it.

An operational concept?

The "city" founded by utopian and urbanistic discourse[7] is defined by the possibility of a threefold operation:

1. The production of its *own* space (*un espace propre*): rational organization must thus repress all the

physical, mental and political pollutions that would compromise it.

2. The substitution of a nowhen, or of a synchronic system, for the indeterminable and stubborn resistances offered by traditions; univocal scientific strategies, made possible by the flattening out of all the data in a plane projection, must replace the tactics of users who take advantage of "opportunities" and who, through these trap-events, these lapses in visibility, reproduce the opacities of history everywhere.

3. Finally, the creation of a *universal* and anonymous *subject* which is the city itself: it gradually becomes possible to attribute to it, as to its political model, Hobbes' State, all the functions and predicates that were previously scattered and assigned to many different real subjects – groups, associations, or individuals. "The city," like a proper name, thus provides a way of conceiving and constructing space on the basis of a finite number of stable, isolatable, and interconnected properties. *city as definite article.*

Administration is combined with a process of elimination in this place organized by "speculative" and classificatory operations.[8] On the one hand, there is a differentiation and redistribution of the parts and functions of the city, as a result of inversions, displacements, accumulations, etc.; on the other there is a rejection of everything that is not capable of being dealt with in this way and so constitutes the "waste products" of a functionalist administration (abnormality, deviance, illness, death, etc.). To be sure, progress allows an increasing number of these waste products to be reintroduced into administrative circuits and transforms even deficiencies (in health, security, etc.) into ways of making the networks of order denser. But in reality, it repeatedly produces effects contrary to those at which it aims: the profit system generates a loss which, in the multiple forms of wretchedness and poverty outside the system and of waste inside it, constantly turns production into "expenditure." Moreover, the rationalization of the city leads to its mythification in strategic discourses, which are calculations based on the hypothesis or the necessity of its destruction in order to arrive at a final decision.[9] Finally, the functionalist organization, by privileging progress (i.e., time), causes the condition of its own possibility – space itself – to be forgotten; space thus becomes the

blind spot in a scientific and political technology. This is the way in which the Concept-city functions; a place of transformations and appropriations, the object of various kinds of interference but also a subject that is constantly enriched by new attributes, it is simultaneously the machinery and the hero of modernity.

Today, whatever the avatars of this concept may have been, we have to acknowledge that if in discourse the city serves as a totalizing and almost mythical landmark for socioeconomic and political strategies, urban life increasingly permits the re-emergence of the element that the urbanistic project excluded. The language of power is in itself "urbanizing," but the city is left prey to contradictory movements that counterbalance and combine themselves outside the reach of panoptic power. The city becomes the dominant theme in political legends, but it is no longer a field of programmed and regulated operations. Beneath the discourses that ideologize the city, the ruses and combinations of powers that have no readable identity proliferate; without points where one can take hold of them, without rational transparency, they are impossible to administer.

The return of practices

The Concept-city is decaying. Does that mean that the illness afflicting both the rationality that founded it and its professionals afflicts the urban populations as well? Perhaps cities are deteriorating along with the procedures that organized them. But we must be careful here. The ministers of knowledge have always assumed that the whole universe was threatened by the very changes that affected their ideologies and their positions. They transmute the misfortune of their theories into theories of misfortune. When they transform their bewilderment into "catastrophes," when they seek to enclose the people in the "panic" of their discourses, are they once more necessarily right?

Rather than remaining within the field of a discourse that upholds its privilege by inverting its content (speaking of catastrophe and no longer of progress) one can try another path: one can analyze the microbe-like, singular and plural practices which an urbanistic system was supposed to administer or suppress, but which have outlived its decay; one can follow the swarming

everyday life?

activity of these procedures that, far from being regulated or eliminated by panoptic administration, have reinforced themselves in a proliferating illegitimacy, developed and insinuated themselves into the networks of surveillance, and combined in accord with unreadable but stable tactics to the point of constituting everyday regulations and surreptitious creativities that are merely concealed by the frantic mechanisms and discourses of the observational organization.

This pathway could be inscribed as a consequence, but also as the reciprocal, of Foucault's analysis of the structures of power. He moved it in the direction of mechanisms and technical procedures, "minor instrumentalities" capable, merely by their organization of "details," of transforming a human multiplicity into a "disciplinary" society and of managing, differentiating, classifying, and hierarchizing all deviances concerning apprenticeship, health, justice, the army, or work.[10] "These often miniscule ruses of discipline," these "minor but flawless" mechanisms, draw their efficacy from a relationship between procedures and the space that they redistribute in order to make an "operator" out of it. But what spatial practices correspond, in the area where discipline is manipulated, to these apparatuses that produce a disciplinary space? In the present conjuncture, which is marked by a contradiction between the collective mode of administration and an individual mode of reappropriation, this question is no less important, if one admits that spatial practices in fact secretly structure the determining conditions of social life. I would like to follow out a few of these multiform, resistance, tricky and stubborn procedures that elude discipline without being outside the field in which it is exercised, and which should lead us to a theory of everyday practices, of lived space, of the disquieting familiarity of the city.

Is this akin to the motor of biopolitics?

2. The Chorus of Idle Footsteps

The goddess can be recognized by her step. (Virgil, *Aeneid,* I, 405)

Their story begins on ground level, with footsteps. They are myriad, but do not compose a series. They cannot be counted because each unit has a qualitative character: a style of tactile apprehension and kinesthetic

appropriation. Their swarming mass is an innumerable collection of singularities. Their intertwined paths give their shape to spaces. They weave places together. In that respect, pedestrian movements form one of these "real systems whose existence in fact makes up the city."[11] They are not localized; it is rather they that spatialize. They are no more inserted within a container than those Chinese characters speakers sketch out on their hands with their fingertips.

It is true that the operations of walking on can be traced on city maps in such a way as to transcribe their paths (here well-trodden, there very faint) and their trajectories (going this way and not that). But these thick or thin curves only refer, like words, to the absence of what has passed by. Surveys of routes miss what was: the act itself of passing by. The operation of walking, wandering, or "window shopping," that is, the activity of passers-by, is transformed into points that draw a totalizing and reversible line on the map. They allow us to grasp only a relic set in the nowhen of a surface of projection. Itself visible, it has the effect of making invisible the operation that made it possible. These fixations constitute procedures for forgetting. The trace left behind is substituted for the practice. It exhibits the (voracious) property that the geographical system has of being able to transform action into legibility, but in doing so it causes a way of being in the world to be forgotten.

irony of De's project

Pedestrian speech acts

A comparison with the speech act will allow us to go further[12] and not limit ourselves to the critique of graphic representations alone, looking from the shores of legibility toward an inaccessible beyond. The act of walking is to the urban system what the speech act is to language or to the statements uttered.[13] At the most elementary level, it has a triple "enunciative" function: it is a process of *appropriation* of the topographical system on the part of the pedestrian (just as the speaker appropriates and takes on the language); it is a spatial acting-out of the place (just as the speech act is an acoustic acting-out of language); and it implies *relations* among differentiated positions, that is, among pragmatic "contracts" in the form of movements (just as verbal enunciation is an "allocution," "posits another opposite" the speaker and puts contracts between interlocutors into action).[14] It thus seems possible to give a preliminary definition of walking as a space of enunciation.

We could moreover extend this problematic to the relations between the act of writing and the written text, and even transpose it to the relationships between the "hand" (the touch and the tale of the paintbrush [*le et la geste du pinceau*]) and the finished painting (forms, colors, etc.). At first isolated in the area of verbal communication, the speech act turns out to find only one of its applications there, and its linguistic modality is merely the first determination of a much more general distinction between the *forms used* in a system and the *ways of using* this system (i.e., *rules*), that is, between two "different worlds," since "the same things" are considered from two opposite formal viewpoints.

Considered from this angle, the pedestrian speech act has three characteristics which distinguish it at the outset from the spatial system: the present, the discrete, the "phatic."

First, if it is true that a spatial order organizes an ensemble of possibilities (e.g., by a place in which one can move) and interdictions (e.g., by a wall that prevents one from going further), then the walker actualizes some of these possibilities. In that way, he makes them exist as well as emerge. But he also moves them about and he invents others, since the crossing, drifting away, or improvisation of walking privilege, transform or abandon spatial elements. Thus Charlie Chaplin multiplies the possibilities of his cane: he does other things with the same thing and he goes beyond the limits that the determinants of the object set on its utilization. In the same way, the walker transforms each spatial signifier into something else. And if on the one hand he actualizes only a few of the possibilities fixed by the constructed order (he goes only here and not there), on the other he increases the number of possibilities (for example, by creating shortcuts and detours) and prohibitions (for example, he forbids himself to take paths generally considered accessible or even obligatory). He thus makes a selection. "The user of a city picks out certain fragments of the statement in order to actualize them in secret."[15]

He thus creates a discreteness, whether by making choices among the signifiers of the spatial "language" or by displacing them through the use he makes of them. He condemns certain places to inertia or disappearance and composes with others spatial "turns of phrase" that are "rare," "accidental" or illegitimate. But that already leads into a rhetoric of walking.

In the framework of enunciation, the walker constitutes, in relation to his position, both a near and a far, a *here* and a *there*. To the fact that the adverbs *here* and *there* are the indicators of the locutionary seat in verbal communication[16] – a coincidence that reinforces the parallelism between linguistic and pedestrian enunciation – we must add that this location (*here–there*) (necessarily implied by walking and indicative of a present appropriation of space by an "I") also has the function of introducing an other in relation to this "I" and of thus establishing a conjunctive and disjunctive articulation of places. I would stress particularly the "phatic" aspect, by which I mean the function, isolated by Malinowski and Jakobson, of terms that initiate, maintain, or interrupt contact, such as "hello," "well, well," etc.[17] Walking, which alternately follows a path and has followers, creates a mobile organicity in the environment, a sequence of phatic *topoi*. And if it is true that the phatic function, which is an effort to ensure communication, is already characteristic of the language of talking birds, just as it constitutes the "first verbal function acquired by children," it is not surprising that it also gambols, goes on all fours, dances, and walks about, with a light or heavy step, like a series of "hellos" in an echoing labyrinth, anterior or parallel to informative speech.

The modalities of pedestrian enunciation which a plane representation on a map brings out could be analyzed. They include the kinds of relationship this enunciation entertains with particular paths (or "statements") by according them a truth value ("alethic" modalities of the necessary, the impossible, the possible, or the contingent), an epistemological value ("epistemic" modalities of the certain, the excluded, the plausible, or the questionable) or finally an ethical or legal value ("deontic" modalities of the obligatory, the forbidden, the permitted, or the optional).[18] Walking affirms, suspects, tries out, transgresses, respects, etc., the trajectories it "speaks." All the modalities sing a part in this chorus, changing from step to step, stepping in through proportions, sequences, and intensities which vary according to the time, the path taken and the walker. These enunciatory operations are of an unlimited diversity. They therefore cannot be reduced to their graphic trail.

Walking rhetorics

The walking of passers-by offers a series of turns (*tours*) and detours that can be compared to "turns of phrase" or "stylistic figures." There is a rhetoric of walking. The art of "turning" phrases finds an equivalent in an art of composing a path (*tourner un parcours*). Like ordinary language,[19] this art implies and combines styles and uses. *Style* specifies "a linguistic structure that manifests on the symbolic level … an individual's fundamental way of being in the world,"[20] it connotes a singular. Use defines the social phenomenon through which a system of communication manifests itself in actual fact; it refers to a norm. Style and use both have to do with a "way of operating" (of speaking, walking, etc.), but style involves a peculiar processing of the symbolic, while use refers to elements of a code. They intersect to form a style of use, a way of being and a way of operating.[21]

In introducing the notion of a "residing rhetoric" ("*rhétorique habitante*"), the fertile pathway opened up by A. Médam[22] and systematized by S. Ostrowetsky[23] and J.-F. Augoyard,[24] we assume that the "tropes" catalogued by rhetoric furnish models and hypotheses for the analysis of ways of appropriating places. Two postulates seem to me to underlie the validity of this application: (1) it is assumed that practices of space also correspond to manipulations of the basic elements of a constructed order; (2) it is assumed that they are, like the tropes in rhetoric, deviations relative to a sort of "literal meaning" defined by the urbanistic system. There would thus be a homology between verbal figures and the figures of walking (a stylized selection among the latter is already found in the figures of dancing) insofar as both consist in "treatments" or operations bearing on isolatable units,[25] and in "ambiguous dispositions" that divert and displace meaning in the direction of equivocalness[26] in the way a tremulous image confuses and multiplies the photographed object. In these two modes, the analogy can be accepted. I would add that the geometrical space of urbanists and architects seems to have the status of the "proper meaning" constructed by grammarians and linguists in order to have a normal and normative level to which they can compare the drifting of "figurative" language. In reality, this faceless "proper" meaning (*ce "propre" sans figure*) cannot be found in current use, whether verbal or pedestrian; it is merely the fiction produced by a use that is also particular, the metalinguistic use of science that distinguishes itself by that very distinction.[27]

The long poem of walking manipulates spatial organizations, no matter how panoptic they may be: it is neither foreign to them (it can take place only within them) nor in conformity with them (it does not receive its identity from them). It creates shadows and ambiguities within them. It inserts its multitudinous references and citations into them (social models, cultural mores, personal factors). Within them it is itself the effect of successive encounters and occasions that constantly alter it and make it the other's blazon: in other words, it is like a peddler, carrying something surprising, transverse or attractive compared with the usual choice. These diverse aspects provide the basis of a rhetoric. They can even be said to define it.

By analyzing this "modern art of everyday expression" as it appears in accounts of spatial practices,[28] J.-F. Augoyard discerns in it two especially fundamental stylistic figures: synecdoche and asyndeton. The predominance of these two figures seems to me to indicate, in relation to two complementary poles, a formal structure of these practices. *Synecdoche* consists in "using a word in a sense which is part of another meaning of the same word."[29] In essence, it names a part instead of the whole which includes it. Thus "sail" is taken for "ship" in the expression "a fleet of fifty sails"; in the same way, a brick shelter or a hill is taken for the park in the narration of a trajectory. *Asyndeton* is the suppression of linking words such as conjunctions and adverbs, either within a sentence or between sentences. In the same way, in walking it selects and fragments the space traversed; it skips over links and whole parts that it omits. From this point of view, every walk constantly leaps, or skips like a child, hopping on one foot. It practices the ellipsis of conjunctive *loci*.

In reality, these two pedestrian figures are related. Synecdoche expands a spatial element in order to make it play the role of a "more" (a totality) and take its place (the bicycle or the piece of furniture in a store window stands for a whole street or neighborhood).

Asyndeton, by elision, creates a "less," opens gaps in the spatial continuum, and retains only selected parts of it that amount almost to relics. Synecdoche replaces totalities by fragments (a *less* in the place of a *more*); asyndeton disconnects them by eliminating the conjunctive or the consecutive (nothing in place of something). Synecdoche makes more dense: it amplifies the detail and miniaturizes the whole. Asyndeton cuts out: it undoes continuity and undercuts its plausibility. A space treated in this way and shaped by practices is transformed into enlarged singularities and separate islands.[30] Through these swellings, shrinkings, and fragmentations, that is, through these rhetorical operations a spatial phrasing of an analogical (composed of juxtaposed citations) and elliptical (made of gaps, lapses, and allusions) type is created. For the technological system of a coherent and totalizing space that is "linked" and simultaneous, the figures of pedestrian rhetoric substitute trajectories that have a mythical structure, at least if one understands by "myth" a discourse relative to the place/nowhere (or origin) of concrete existence, a story jerry-built out of elements taken from common sayings, an allusive and fragmentary story whose gaps mesh with the social practices it symbolizes.

Figures are the acts of this stylistic metamorphosis of space. Or rather, as Rilke puts it, they are moving "trees of gestures." They move even the rigid and contrived territories of the medico-pedagogical institute in which retarded children find a place to play and dance their "spatial stories."[31] These "trees of gestures" are in movement everywhere. Their forests walk through the streets. They transform the scene, but they cannot be fixed in a certain place by images. If in spite of that an illustration were required, we could mention the fleeting images, yellowish-green and metallic blue calligraphies that howl without raising their voices and emblazon themselves on the subterranean passages of the city, "embroideries" composed of letters and numbers, perfect gestures of violence painted with a pistol, Shivas made of written characters, dancing graphics whose fleeting apparitions are accompanied by the rumble of subway trains: New York graffiti.

If it is true that *forests of gestures* are manifest in the streets, their movement cannot be captured in a picture, nor can the meaning of their movements be

circumscribed in a text. Their rhetorical transplantation carries away and displaces the analytical, coherent proper meanings of urbanism; it constitutes a "wandering of the semantic"[32] produced by masses that make some parts of the city disappear and exaggerate others, distorting it, fragmenting it, and diverting it from its immobile order.

3. Myths: What "Makes Things Go"

The figures of these movements (synecdoches, ellipses, etc.) characterize both a "symbolic order of the unconscious" and "certain typical processes of subjectivity manifested in discourse."[33] The similarity between "discourse"[34] and dreams[35] has to do with their use of the same "stylistic procedures"; it therefore includes pedestrian practices as well. The "ancient catalog of tropes" that from Freud to Benveniste has furnished an appropriate inventory for the rhetoric of the first two registers of expression is equally valid for the third. If there is a parallelism, it is not only because enunciation is dominant in these three areas, but also because its discursive (verbalized, dreamed, or walked) development is organized as a relation between the *place* from which it proceeds (an origin) and the nowhere it produces (a way of "going by").

From this point of view, after having compared pedestrian processes to linguistic formations, we can bring them back down in the direction of oneiric figuration, or at least discover on that other side what, in a spatial practice, is inseparable from the dreamed place. To walk is to lack a place. It is the indefinite process of being absent and in search of a proper. The moving about that the city multiplies and concentrates makes the city itself an immense social experience of lacking a place – an experience that is, to be sure, broken up into countless tiny deportations (displacements and walks), compensated for by the relationships and intersections of these exoduses that intertwine and create an urban fabric, and placed under the sign of what ought to be, ultimately, the place but is only a name, the City. The identity furnished by this place is all the more symbolic (named) because, in spite of the inequality of its citizens' positions and profits, there is only a pullulation of passers-by, a network of residences temporarily appropriated by pedestrian traffic, a shuffling among pretenses of the proper, a universe of rented spaces haunted by a nowhere or by dreamed-of places.

Names and symbols

An indication of the relationship that spatial practices entertain with that absence is furnished precisely by their manipulations of and with "proper" names. The relationships between the direction of a walk (*le sens de la marche*) and the meaning of words (*le sens des mots*) situate two sorts of apparently contrary movements, one extrovert (to walk is to go outside), the other introvert (a mobility under the stability of the signifier). Walking is in fact determined by semantic tropisms; it is attracted and repelled by nominations whose meaning is not clear, whereas the city, for its part, is transformed for many people into a "desert" in which the meaningless, indeed the terrifying, no longer takes the form of shadows but becomes, as in Genet's plays, an implacable light that produces this urban text without obscurities, which is created by a technocratic power everywhere and which puts the city-dweller under control (under the control of what? No one knows): "The city keeps us under its gaze, which one cannot bear without feeling dizzy," says a resident of Rouen.[36] In the spaces brutally lit by an alien reason, proper names carve out pockets of hidden and familiar meanings. They "make sense"; in other words, they are the impetus of movements, like vocations and calls that turn or divert an itinerary by giving it a meaning (or a direction) (*sens*) that was previously unforeseen. These names create a nowhere in places; they change them into passages.

A friend who lives in the city of Sèvres drifts, when he is in Paris, toward the rue des Saints-*Pères* and the rue de *Sèvres*, even though he is going to see his mother in another part of town: these names articulate a sentence that his steps compose without his knowing it. Numbered streets and street numbers (112th St., or 9 rue Saint-Charles) orient the magnetic field of trajectories just as they can haunt dreams. Another friend unconsciously represses the streets which have names and, by this fact, transmit her — orders or identities in the same way as summonses and classifications; she goes instead along paths that have

no name or signature. But her walking is thus still controlled negatively by proper names.

What is it then that they spell out? Disposed in constellations that hierarchize and semantically order the surface of the city, operating chronological arrangements and historical justifications, these words (*Borrègo, Botzaris, Bougainville…*) slowly lose, like worn coins, the value engraved on them, but their ability to signify outlives its first definition. *Saints-Pères, Corentin Celton, Red Square …* these names make themselves available to the diverse meanings given them by passers-by; they detach themselves from the places they were supposed to define and serve as imaginary meeting-points on itineraries which, as metaphors, they determine for reasons that are foreign to their original value but may be recognized or not by passers-by. A strange toponymy that is detached from actual places and flies high over the city like a foggy geography of "meanings" held in suspension, directing the physical deambulations below: *Place de l'Étoile, Concorde, Poissonnière …* These constellations of names provide traffic patterns: they are stars directing itineraries. "The Place de la Concorde does not exist," Malaparte said, "it is an idea."[37] It is much more than an "idea." A whole series of comparisons would be necessary to account for the magical powers proper names enjoy. They seem to be carried as emblems by the travellers they direct and simultaneously decorate.

Linking acts and footsteps, opening meanings and directions, these words operate in the name of an emptying-out and wearing-away of their primary role. They become liberated spaces that can be occupied. A rich indetermination gives them, by means of a semantic rarefaction, the function of articulating a second, poetic geography on top of the geography of the literal, forbidden or permitted meaning. They insinuate other routes into the functionalist and historical order of movement. Walking follows them: "I fill this great empty space with a beautiful name."[38] People are put in motion by the remaining relics of meaning, and sometimes by their waste products, the inverted remainders of great ambitions.[39] Things that amount to nothing, or almost nothing, symbolize and orient walkers' steps: names that have ceased precisely to be "proper."

In these symbolizing kernels three distinct (but connected) functions of the relations between spatial and signifying practices are indicated (and perhaps founded): the *believable*, the *memorable*, and the *primitive*. They designate what "authorizes" (or makes possible or credible) spatial appropriations, what is repeated in them (or is recalled in them) from a silent and withdrawn memory, and what is structured in them and continues to be signed by an in-fantile (*infans*) origin. These three symbolic mechanisms organize the topoi of a discourse on/of the city (legend, memory, and dream) in a way that also eludes urbanistic systematicity. They can already be recognized in the functions of proper names: they make habitable or believable the place that they clothe with a word (by emptying themselves of their classifying power, they acquire that of "permitting" something else); they recall or suggest phantoms (the dead who are supposed to have disappeared) that still move about, concealed in gestures and in bodies in motion; and, by naming, that is, by imposing an injunction proceeding from the other (a story) and by altering functionalist identity by detaching themselves from it, they create in the place itself that erosion or nowhere that the law of the other carves out within it.

[...]

Notes

1 See Alain Médam's admirable "New York City," *Les Temps modernes*, August–September 1976, pp. 15–33; and the same author's *New York Terminal* (Paris: Galilée, 1977).

2 See H. Lavedan, *Les Représentations des villes dans l'art du Moyen Age* (Paris: Van Oest, 1942); R. Wittkower, *Architectural Principles in the Age of Humanism* (New York: Norton, 1962); L. Marin, *Utopiques: Jeux d'espaces* (Paris: Minuit, 1973); etc.

3 M. Foucault, "L'Oeil du pouvoir," in J. Bentham, *Le Panoptique* (Paris: Belfond, 1977), p. 16.

4 D. P. Schreber, *Mémoires d'un névropathe* (Paris: Seuil, 1975), pp. 41, 60, etc.

5 Descartes, in his *Regulae*, had already made the blind man the guarantor of the knowledge of things and places against the illusions and deceptions of vision.

6 M. Merleau-Ponty, *Phénoménologie de la perception* (Paris: Gallimard Tel, 1976), pp. 332–3.

7 See F. Choay, "Figures d'un discours inconnu," *Critique*, April 1973, 293–317.

8 Urbanistic techniques, which classify things spatially, can be related to the tradition of the "art of memory": see Frances A. Yates, *The Art of Memory* (London: Routledge and Kegan Paul, 1966). The ability to produce a spatial organization of knowledge (with "places" assigned to each type of "figure" or "function") develops its procedures on the basis of this "art." It determines utopias and can be recognized even in Bentham's *Panopticon*. Such a form remains stable in spite of the diversity of its contents (past, future, present) and its projects (conserving or creating) relative to changes in the status of knowledge.

9 See André Glucksmann, "Le Totalitarisme en effet," *Traverses*, no. 9, 1977, 34–40.

10 M. Foucault. *Surveiller et punir* (Paris: Gallimard, 1975); *Discipline and Punish*, trans. A. Sheridan (New York: Pantheon, 1977).

11 Ch. Alexander, "La Cité semi-treillis, mais non arbre." *Architecture, Mouvement, Continuité*, 1967.

12 See R. Barthes's remarks in *Architecture d'aujourd'hui*, no. 153, December 1970–January 1971, 11–13: "We speak our city ... merely by inhabiting it. walking through it, looking at it." Cf. C. Soucy, *L'Image du centre dans quatre romans contemporains* (Paris: CSU, 1971), pp. 6–15.

13 See the numerous studies devoted to the subject since J. Searle's "What is a Speech Act?" in *Philosophy in America*, ed. Max Black (London: Allen & Unwin; Ithaca, NY: Cornell University Press, 1965), pp. 221–39.

14 E. Benveniste, *Problèmes de linguistique générale* (Paris: Gallimard, 1974), pp. 11, 79–88, etc.

15 R. Barthes, quoted in C. Souey, *L'Image du centre*, p. 10.

16 "*Here* and *now* delimit the spatial and temporal instance coextensive and contemporary with the present instance of discourse containing I": E. Benveniste, *Problèmes de linguistique générale* (Paris: Gallimard, 1966), 1, p. 253.

17 R. Jakobson, *Essais de linguistique générale* (Paris: Seuil Points, 1970), p. 217.

18 On modalities, see H. Parret, *La Pragmatique des modalités* (Urbino: Centro di Semiotica, 1975); A. R. White, *Modal Thinking* (Ithaca, NY: Cornell University Press, 1975).

19 See Paul Lemaire's analyses, *Les Signes sauvages. Une Philosophie du langage ordinaire* (Ottawa: Université d'Ottawa et Université Saint-Paul, 1981), in particular the introduction.

20 A. J. Greimas, "Linguistique statistique et linguistique structurale," *Le Français moderne*, October 1962, 245.

21 In a neighboring field, rhetoric and poetics in the gestural language of mute people, I am grateful to E. S. Klima of the University of California, San Diego and U. Bellugi, "Poetry and Song in a Language without

Sound," an unpublished paper; see also Klima, "The Linguistic Symbol with and without Sound," in *The Role of Speech in Language*, ed. J. Kavanagh and J. E. Cuttings (Cambridge, Mass.: MIT, 1975).

22 *Conscience de la ville* (Paris: Anthropos, 1977).

23 See Ostrowetsky, "Logiques du lieu," in *Sémiotique de l'espace* (Paris: Denoël-Gonthier Médiations, 1979), pp. 155–73.

24 *Pas à pas. Essai sur le cheminement quotidien en milieu urbain* (Paris: Seuil, 1979).

25 In his analysis of culinary practices, P. Bourdieu regards as decisive not the ingredients but the way in which they are prepared and used: "Le Sens pratique," *Actes de la recherche en sciences sociales*, February 1976, 77.

26 J. Sumpf. *Introduction à la stylistique du français* (Paris: Larousse, 1971), p. 87.

27 On the "theory of the proper," see J. Derrida, *Marges de la philosophie* (Paris: Minuit, 1972), pp. 247–324; *Margins of Philosophy*, trans. A. Bass (Chicago: University of Chicago Press, 1982).

28 Augoyard, *Pas à pas*.

29 T. Todorov, "Synecdoques," *Communications*, no. 16 (1970), 30. See also P. Fontanier, *Les Figures du discours* (Paris: Flammarion, 1968), pp. 87–97; J. Dubois et al., *Rhétorique générale* (Paris: Larousse, 1970), pp. 102–12.

30 On this space that practices organize into "islands," see P. Bourdieu, *Esquisse d'une théorie de la pratique* (Genève: Droz, 1972), p. 215, etc.; "Le Sens pratique," 51–2.

31 See Anne Baldassari and Michel Joubert, *Pratiques relationnelles des enfants à l'espace et institution* (Paris: CRECELE-CORDES, 1976); and by the same authors, "Ce qui se trame," *Parallèles*, no. 1, June 1976.

32 Derrida, *Marges*, 287, on metaphor.

33 Benveniste, *Problèmes*, 1, 86–7.

34 For Benveniste, "discourse is language considered as assumed by the person who is speaking and in the condition of intersubjectivity" (ibid., 266).

35 See for example S. Freud, *The Interpretation of Dreams*, trans. J. Strachey (New York: Basic Books, 1955), Chapter VI, § 1–4, on condensation and displacement, "processes of figuration" that are proper to "dreamwork."

36 Ph. Dard, F. Desbons et al., *La Ville, symbolique en souffrance* (Paris: CEP, 1975), p. 200.

37 See also, for example, the epigraph in Patrick Modiano, *Place de l'Étoile* (Paris: Gallimard, 1968).

38 Joachim du Bellay, *Regrets*, 189.

39 For example, *Sarcelles*, the name of a great urbanistic ambition (near Paris), has taken on a symbolic value for the inhabitants of the town by becoming in the eyes of France as a whole the example of a total failure. This extreme avatar provides its citizens with the "prestige" of an exceptional identity.

24

"Imagined Communities" (1983)

Benedict Anderson

Apprehensions of Time

It would be short-sighted to think of the imagined communities of nations as simply growing out of and replacing religious communities and dynastic realms. Beneath the decline of sacred communities, languages and lineages, a fundamental change was taking place in modes of apprehending the world, which, more than anything else, made it possible to 'think' the nation.

To get a feeling for this change, one can profitably turn to the visual representations of the sacred communities, such as the reliefs and stained-glass windows of mediaeval churches, or the paintings of early Italian and Flemish masters. A characteristic feature of such representations is something misleadingly analogous to 'modern dress'. The shepherds who have followed the star to the manger where Christ is born bear the features of Burgundian peasants. The Virgin Mary is figured as a Tuscan merchant's daughter. In many paintings the commissioning patron, in full burgher or noble costume, appears kneeling in adoration alongside the shepherds. What seems incongruous today obviously appeared wholly natural to the eyes of mediaeval worshippers. We are faced with a world in which the figuring of imagined reality was overwhelmingly visual and aural.

Benedict Anderson, *Imagined Communities: Reflections on the Origin and Spread of Nationalism*, pp. 22–36. London: Verso, 1991. Reprinted by permission of Verso.

Christendom assumed its universal form through a myriad of specificities and particularities: this relief, that window, this sermon, that tale, this morality play, that relic. While the trans-European Latin-reading clerisy was one essential element in the structuring of the Christian imagination, the mediation of its conceptions to the illiterate masses, by visual and aural creations, always personal and particular, was no less vital. The humble parish priest, whose forebears and frailties everyone who heard his celebrations knew, was still the direct intermediary between his parishioners and the divine. This juxtaposition of the cosmic-universal and the mundane-particular meant that however vast Christendom might be, and was sensed to be, it manifested itself *variously* to particular Swabian or Andalusian communities as replications of themselves. Figuring the Virgin Mary with 'Semitic' features or 'first-century' costumes in the restoring spirit of the modern museum was unimaginable because the mediaeval Christian mind had no conception of history as an endless chain of cause and effect or of radical separations between past and present.[1] Bloch observes that people thought they must be near the end of time, in the sense that Christ's second coming could occur at any moment: St. Paul had said that 'the day of the Lord cometh like a thief in the night.' It was thus natural for the great twelfth-century chronicler Bishop Otto of Freising to refer repeatedly to 'we who have been placed at the end of time.' Bloch concludes that as soon as mediaeval men 'gave themselves up to meditation, nothing was farther from their thoughts than the prospect of a long future for a young and vigorous human race.'[2]

Auerbach gives an unforgettable sketch of this form of consciousness:

> If an occurrence like the sacrifice of Isaac is interpreted as prefiguring the sacrifice of Christ, so that in the former the latter is as it were announced and promised and the latter 'fulfills' … the former, then a connection is established between two events which are linked neither temporally nor causally – a connection which it is impossible to establish by reason in the horizontal dimension … It can be established only if both occurrences are vertically linked to Divine Providence, which alone is able to devise such a plan of history and supply the key to its understanding … the here and now is no longer a mere link in an earthly chain of events, it is *simultaneously* something which has always been, and will be fulfilled in the future; and strictly, in the eyes of God, it is something eternal, something omnitemporal, something already consummated in the realm of fragmentary earthly event.[3]

He rightly stresses that such an idea of *simultaneity* is wholly alien to our own. It views time as something close to what Benjamin calls Messianic time, a simultaneity of past and future in an instantaneous present.[4] In such a view of things, the word 'meanwhile' cannot be of real significance.

Our own conception of simultaneity has been a long time in the making, and its emergence is certainly connected, in ways that have yet to be well studied, with the development of the secular sciences. But it is a conception of such fundamental importance that, without taking it fully into account, we will find it difficult to probe the obscure genesis of nationalism. What has come to take the place of the mediaeval conception of simultaneity-along-time is, to borrow again from Benjamin, an idea of 'homogeneous, empty time,' in which simultaneity is, as it were, transverse, cross-time, marked not by prefiguring and fulfilment, but by temporal coincidence, and measured by clock and calendar.[5]

Why this transformation should be so important for the birth of the imagined community of the nation can best be seen if we consider the basic structure of two forms of imagining which first flowered in Europe in the eighteenth century: the novel and the newspaper.[6] For these forms provided the technical means for 're-presenting' the *kind* of imagined community that is the nation.

Consider first the structure of the old-fashioned novel, a structure typical not only of the masterpieces of Balzac but also of any contemporary dollar-dreadful. It is clearly a device for the presentation of simultaneity in 'homogeneous, empty time,' or a complex gloss upon the word 'meanwhile'. Take, for illustrative purposes, a segment of a simple novel-plot, in which a man (A) has a wife (B) and a mistress (C), who in turn has a lover (D). We might imagine a sort of time-chart for this segment as follows:

Time:	I	II	III
Events:	A quarrels with B	A telephones C	D gets drunk in a bar
	C and D make love	B shops	A dines at home with B
		D plays pool	
			C has an ominous dream

Notice that during this sequence A and D never meet, indeed may not even be aware of each other's existence if C has played her cards right.[7] What then actually links A to D? Two complementary conceptions: First, that they are embedded in 'societies' (Wessex, Lübeck, Los Angeles). These societies are sociological entities of such firm and stable reality that their members (A and D) can even be described as passing each other on the street, without ever becoming acquainted, and still be connected.[8] Second, that A and D are embedded in the minds of the omniscient readers. Only they, like God, watch A telephoning C, B shopping, and D playing pool all *at once*. That all these acts are performed at the same clocked, calendrical time, but by actors who may be largely unaware of one another, shows the novelty of this imagined world conjured up by the author in his readers' minds.[9]

The idea of a sociological organism moving calendrically through homogeneous, empty time is a precise analogue of the idea of the nation, which also is conceived as a solid community moving steadily down (or up) history.[10] An American will never meet, or even know the names of more than a handful of his 240,000-odd fellow-Americans. He has no idea of what they are up to at any one time. But he has complete confidence in their steady, anonymous, simultaneous activity.

The perspective I am suggesting will perhaps seem less abstract if we turn to inspect briefly four fictions from different cultures and different epochs, all but one of which, nonetheless, are inextricably bound to nationalist movements. In 1887, the 'Father of Filipino Nationalism', José Rizal, wrote the novel *Noli Me Tangere*, which today is regarded as the greatest achievement of modern Filipino literature. It was also almost the first novel written by an 'Indio.'[11] Here is how it marvellously begins:

> Towards the end of October, Don Santiago de los Santos, popularly known as Capitan Tiago, was giving a dinner party. Although, contrary to his usual practice, he had announced it only that afternoon, it was already the subject of every conversation in Binondo, in other quarters of the city, and even in [the walled inner city of] Intramuros. In those days Capitan Tiago had the reputation of a lavish host. It was known that his house, like his country, closed its doors to nothing, except to commerce and to any new or daring idea.
>
> So the news coursed like an electric shock through the community of parasites, spongers, and gatecrashers whom God, in His infinite goodness, created, and so tenderly multiplies in Manila. Some hunted polish for their boots, others looked for collar-buttons and cravats. But one and all were preoccupied with the problem of how to greet their host with the familiarity required to create the appearance of longstanding friendship, or, if need be, to excuse themselves for not having arrived earlier.
>
> The dinner was being given at a house on Anloague Street. Since we do not recall the street number, we shall describe it in such a way that it may still be recognized – that is, if earthquakes have not yet destroyed it. We do not believe that its owner will have had it torn down, since such work is usually left to God or to Nature, which, besides, holds many contracts with our Government.[12]

Extensive comment is surely unnecessary. It should suffice to note that right from the start the image (wholly new to Filipino writing) of a dinner-party being discussed by hundreds of unnamed people, who do not know each other, in quite different parts of Manila, in a particular month of a particular decade, immediately conjures up the imagined community. And in the phrase 'a house on Anloague Street' which 'we shall describe in such a way that it may still be recognized,' the would-be recognizers are we-Filipino-readers. The casual progression of this house from the 'interior' time of the novel to the 'exterior' time of the [Manila] reader's everyday life gives a hypnotic confirmation of the solidity of a single community, embracing characters, author and readers, moving onward through calendrical time.[13] Notice too the tone. While Rizal has not the faintest idea of his readers' individual identities, he writes to them with an ironical intimacy, as though their relationships with each other are not in the smallest degree problematic.[14]

Nothing gives one a more Foucauldian sense of abrupt discontinuities of consciousness than to compare *Noli* with the most celebrated previous literary work by an 'Indio', Francisco Balagtas (Baltazar)'s *Pinagdaanang Buhay ni Florante at ni Laura sa Cahariang Albania* [The Story of Florante and Laura in the Kingdom of Albania], the first printed edition of which dates from 1861, though it may have been composed as early as 1838.[15] For although Balagtas was still alive when Rizal was born, the world of his masterpiece is in every basic respect foreign to that of *Noli*. Its setting – a fabulous mediaeval Albania – is utterly removed in time and space from the Binondo of the 1880s. Its heroes – Florante, a Christian Albanian nobleman, and his bosom-friend Aladin, a Muslim ('Moro') Persian aristocrat – remind us of the Philippines only by the Christian-Moro linkage. Where Rizal deliberately sprinkles his Spanish prose with Tagalog words for 'realistic', satirical, or nationalist effect, Balagtas unselfconsciously mixes Spanish phrases into his Tagalog quatrains simply to heighten the grandeur and sonority of his diction. *Noli* was meant to be read, while *Florante at Laura* was to be sung aloud. Most striking of all is Balagtas's handling of time. As Lumbera notes, 'the unravelling of the plot does not follow a chronological order. The story begins *in medias res*, so that the complete story comes to us through a series of speeches that serve as flashbacks.'[16] Almost half of the 399 quatrains are accounts of Florante's childhood, student years in Athens, and subsequent military exploits, given by the hero in conversation with Aladin.[17] The 'spoken flashback' was for Balagtas the only alternative to a straightforward single-file narrative. If we learn of Florante's and Aladin's 'simultaneous' pasts, they are connected by their conversing voices, not by the structure of the epic. How distant this technique is from that of the novel: 'In that same spring, while Florante was still studying in Athens, Aladin was expelled from his sovereign's court ...' In effect, it never occurs to Balagtas to 'situate' his protagonists in 'society,' or to discuss them with his audience. Nor, aside from the mellifluous flow of Tagalog polysyllables, is there much 'Filipino' about his text.[18]

In 1816, seventy years before the writing of *Noli*, José Joaquín Fernandez de Lizardi wrote a novel called *El Periquillo Sarniento* [The Itching Parrot], evidently the first Latin American work in this genre. In the words of one critic, this text is 'a ferocious indictment of Spanish administration in Mexico: ignorance, superstition and corruption are seen to be its most notable characteristics.'[19] The essential form of this 'nationalist' novel is indicated by the following description of its content:

> From the first, [the hero, the Itching Parrot] is exposed to bad influences – ignorant maids inculcate superstitions, his mother indulges his whims, his teachers either have no vocation or no ability to discipline him. And though his father is an intelligent man who wants his son to practise a useful trade rather than swell the ranks of lawyers and parasites, it is Periquillo's over-fond mother who wins the day, sends her son to university and thus ensures that he will learn only superstitious nonsense ... Periquillo remains incorrigibly ignorant despite many encounters with good and wise people. He is unwilling to work or take anything seriously and becomes successively a priest, a gambler, a thief, apprentice to an apothecary, a doctor, clerk in a provincial town ... These episodes *permit the author to describe hospitals, prisons, remote villages, monasteries*, while at the same time driving home one major point – that Spanish government and the education system encourage parasitism and laziness ... Periquillo's adventures several times take him among Indians and Negroes ...[20]

Here again we see the 'national imagination' at work in the movement of a solitary hero through a sociological landscape of a fixity that fuses the world inside the novel with the world outside. This picaresque *tour d'horison* – hospitals, prisons, remote villages, monasteries, Indians, Negroes – is nonetheless not a *tour du monde*. The horizon is clearly bounded: it is that of colonial Mexico. Nothing assures us of this sociological solidity more than the succession of plurals. For they conjure up a social space full of *comparable* prisons, none in itself of any unique importance, but all representative (in their simultaneous, separate existence) of the oppressiveness of *this* colony.[21] (Contrast prisons in the Bible. They are never imagined as *typical* of this or that society. Each, like the one where Salome was bewitched by John the Baptist, is magically alone.)

Finally, to remove the possibility that, since Rizal and Lizardi both wrote in Spanish, the frameworks we have been studying are somehow 'European', here is the opening of *Semarang Hitam* [Black Semarang], a tale by the ill-fated young Indonesian communist-nationalist Mas Marco Kartodikromo,[22] published serially in 1924:[23]

> It was 7 o'clock, Saturday evening; young people in Semarang never stayed at home on Saturday night. On this night however nobody was about. Because the heavy day-long rain had made the roads wet and very slippery, all had stayed at home.
>
> For the workers in shops and offices Saturday morning was a time of anticipation – anticipating their leisure and the fun of walking around the city in the evening, but on this night they were to be disappointed – because of lethargy caused by the bad weather and the sticky roads in the kampungs. The main roads usually crammed with all sorts of traffic, the footpaths usually teeming with people, all were deserted. Now and then the crack of a horse-cab's whip could be heard spurring a horse on its way – or the clip-clop of horses' hooves pulling carriages along.
>
> Semarang was deserted. The light from the rows of gas lamps shone straight down on the shining asphalt road. Occasionally the clear light from the gas lamps was dimmed as the wind blew from the east....
>
> A young man was seated on a long rattan lounge reading a newspaper. He was totally engrossed. His occasional anger and at other times smiles were a sure sign of his deep interest in the story. He turned the pages of the newspaper, thinking that perhaps he could find something that would stop him feeling so miserable. All of a sudden he came upon an article entitled:
>
> PROSPERITY
> A destitute vagrant became ill
> and died on the side of the road from exposure.
>
> The young man was moved by this brief report. He could just imagine the suffering of the poor soul as he lay dying on the side of the road ... One moment he felt

an explosive anger well up inside. Another moment he felt pity. Yet another moment his anger was directed at the social system which gave rise to such poverty, while making a small group of people wealthy.

Here, as in *El Periquillo Sarniento*, we are in a world of plurals: shops, offices, carriages, kampungs, and gas lamps. As in the case of *Noli*, we-the-Indonesian-readers are plunged immediately into calendrical time and a familiar landscape; some of us may well have walked those 'sticky' Semarang roads. Once again, a solitary hero is juxtaposed to a socioscape described in careful, *general* detail. But there is also something new: a hero who is never named, but who is frequently referred to as '*our* young man'. Precisely the clumsiness and literary naivety of the text confirm the unselfconscious 'sincerity' of this pronominal adjective. Neither Marco nor his readers have any doubts about the reference. If in the jocular-sophisticated fiction of eighteenth- and nineteenth-century Europe the trope 'our hero' merely underlines an authorial play with a(ny) reader, Marco's 'our young man,' not least in its novelty, *means* a young man who belongs to the collective body of readers of *Indonesian*, and thus, implicitly, an embryonic Indonesian 'imagined community.' Notice that Marco feels no need to specify this community by name: it is already there. (Even if polylingual Dutch colonial censors could join his readership, they are excluded from this 'ourness,' as can be seen from the fact that the young man's anger is directed at 'the,' not 'our,' social system.)

Finally, the imagined community is confirmed by the doubleness of our reading about our young man reading. He does not find the corpse of the destitute vagrant by the side of a sticky Semarang road, but imagines it from the print in a newspaper.[24] Nor does he care the slightest who the dead vagrant individually was: he thinks of the representative body, not the personal life.

It is fitting that in *Semarang Hitam* a newspaper appears embedded in fiction, for, if we now turn to the newspaper as cultural product, we will be struck by its profound fictiveness. What is the essential literary convention of the newspaper? If we were to look at a sample front page of, say, *The New York Times*, we might find there stories about Soviet dissidents, famine in Mali, a gruesome murder, a coup in Iraq, the

discovery of a rare fossil in Zimbabwe, and a speech by Mitterrand. Why are these events so juxtaposed? What connects them to each other? Not sheer caprice. Yet obviously most of them happen independently, without the actors being aware of each other or of what the others are up to. The arbitrariness of their inclusion and juxtaposition (a later edition will substitute a baseball triumph for Mitterrand) shows that the linkage between them is imagined.

This imagined linkage derives from two obliquely related sources. The first is simply calendrical coincidence. The date at the top of the newspaper, the single most important emblem on it, provides the essential connection – the steady onward clocking of homogeneous, empty time.[25] Within that time, 'the world' ambles sturdily ahead. The sign for this: if Mali disappears from the pages of *The New York Times* after two days of famine reportage, for months on end, readers do not for a moment imagine that Mali has disappeared or that famine has wiped out all its citizens. The novelistic format of the newspaper assures them that somewhere out there the 'character' Mali moves along quietly, awaiting its next reappearance in the plot.

The second source of imagined linkage lies in the relationship between the newspaper, as a form of book, and the market. It has been estimated that in the 40-odd years between the publication of the Gutenberg Bible and the close of the fifteenth century, more than 20,000,000 printed volumes were produced in Europe.[26] Between 1500 and 1600, the number manufactured had reached between 150,000,000 and 200,000,000.[27] 'From early on … the printing shops looked more like modern workshops than the monastic workrooms of the Middle Ages. In 1455, Fust and Schoeffer were already running a business geared to standardised production, and twenty years later large printing concerns were operating everywhere in all [sic] Europe.'[28] In a rather special sense, the book was the first modern-style mass-produced industrial commodity.[29] The sense I have in mind can be shown if we compare the book to other early industrial products, such as textiles, bricks, or sugar. For these commodities are *measured* in mathematical amounts (pounds or loads or pieces). A pound of sugar is simply a quantity, a convenient load, not an object in itself. The book, however – and here it prefigures the durables of our time – is a distinct, self-contained object, exactly reproduced on a large scale.[30] One pound of sugar flows into the next; each book has its own eremitic self-sufficiency. (Small wonder that libraries, personal collections of mass-produced commodities, were already a familiar sight, in urban centres like Paris, by the sixteenth century.)[31]

In this perspective, the newspaper is merely an 'extreme form' of the book, a book sold on a colossal scale, but of ephemeral popularity. Might we say: one-day best-sellers?[32] The obsolescence of the newspaper on the morrow of its printing – curious that one of the earlier mass-produced commodities should so prefigure the inbuilt obsolescence of modern durables – nonetheless, for just this reason, creates this extraordinary mass ceremony: the almost precisely simultaneous consumption ('imagining') of the newspaper-as-fiction. We know that particular morning and evening editions will overwhelmingly be consumed between this hour and that, only on this day, not that. (Contrast sugar, the use of which proceeds in an unclocked, continuous flow; it may go bad, but it does not go out of date.) The significance of this mass ceremony – Hegel observed that newspapers serve modern man as a substitute for morning prayers – is paradoxical. It is performed in silent privacy, in the lair of the skull.[33] Yet each communicant is well aware that the ceremony he performs is being replicated simultaneously by thousands (or millions) of others of whose existence he is confident, yet of whose identity he has not the slightest notion. Furthermore, this ceremony is incessantly repeated at daily or half-daily intervals throughout the calendar. What more vivid figure for the secular, historically clocked, imagined community can be envisioned?[34] At the same time, the newspaper reader, observing exact replicas of his own paper being consumed by his subway, barbershop, or residential neighbours, is continually reassured that the imagined world is visibly rooted in everyday life. As with *Noli Me Tangere*, fiction seeps quietly and continuously into reality, creating that remarkable confidence of community in anonymity which is the hallmark of modern nations.

Before proceeding to a discussion of the specific origins of nationalism, it may be useful to recapitulate the main propositions put forward thus far. Essentially, I have been arguing that the very possibility of imagining the nation only arose historically when, and where, three fundamental cultural conceptions, all of great antiquity, lost their axiomatic grip on men's minds. The first of these was the idea that a particular script-language offered privileged access to ontological truth, precisely because it was an inseparable part of that truth. It was this idea that called into being the great transcontinental sodalities of Christendom, the Islamic Ummah, and the rest. Second was the belief that society was naturally organized around and under high centres – monarchs who were persons apart from other human beings and who ruled by some form of cosmological (divine) dispensation. Human loyalties were necessarily hierarchical and centripetal because the ruler, like the sacred script, was a node of access to being and inherent in it. Third was a conception of temporality in which cosmology and history were indistinguishable, the origins of the world and of men essentially identical. Combined, these ideas rooted human lives firmly in the very nature of things, giving certain meaning to the everyday fatalities of existence (above all death, loss, and servitude) and offering, in various ways, redemption from them.

The slow, uneven decline of these interlinked certainties, first in Western Europe, later elsewhere, under the impact of economic change, 'discoveries' (social and scientific), and the development of increasingly rapid communications, drove a harsh wedge between cosmology and history. No surprise then that the search was on, so to speak, for a new way of linking fraternity, power and time meaningfully together. Nothing perhaps more precipitated this search, nor made it more fruitful, than print-capitalism, which made it possible for rapidly growing numbers of people to think about themselves, and to relate themselves to others, in profoundly new ways.

Notes

1 For us, the idea of 'modern dress,' a metaphorical equiv-alencing of past with present, is a backhanded recogni-tion of their fatal separation.

2 Bloch, *Feudal Society*, I, pp. 84–6.

3 Auerbach, *Mimesis*, p. 64. Emphasis added. Compare St. Augustine's description of the Old Testament as 'the shadow of [i.e cast backwards by] the future.' Cited in Bloch, *Feudal Society*, I, p. 90.

4   Walter Benjamin, *Illuminations*, p. 265.

5   Ibid., p. 263. So deep-lying is this new idea that one could argue that every essential modern conception is based on a conception of 'meanwhile'.

6   While the *Princesse de Clèves* had already appeared in 1678, the era of Richardson, Defoe and Fielding is the early eighteenth century. The origins of the modern newspaper lie in the Dutch gazettes of the late seventeenth century; but the newspaper only became a general category of printed matter after 1700. Febvre and Martin, *The Coming of the Book*, p. 197.

7   Indeed, the plot's grip may *depend* at Times I, II, and III on A, B, C and D not knowing what the others are up to.

8   This polyphony decisively marks off the modern novel even from so brilliant a forerunner as Petronius's *Satyricon*. Its narrative proceeds single file. If Encolpius bewails his young lover's faithlessness, we are not simultaneously shown Gito in bed with Ascyltus.

9   In this context it is rewarding to compare any historical novel with documents or narratives from the period fictionalized.

10 Nothing better shows the immersion of the novel in homogeneous, empty time than the absence of those prefatory genealogies, often ascending to the origin of man, which are so characteristic a feature of ancient chronicles, legends, and holy books.

11 Rizal wrote this novel in the colonial language (Spanish), which was then the lingua franca of the ethnically diverse Eurasian and native elites. Alongside the novel appeared also for the first time a 'nationalist' press, not only in Spanish but in such 'ethnic' languages as Tagalog and Ilocano. See Leopoldo Y. Yabes, 'The Modern Literature of the Philippines,' pp. 287–302, in Pierre-Bernard Lafont and Denys Lombard (eds), *Littératures Contemporaines de l'Asie du Sud-Est*.

12 José Rizal, *Noli Me Tangere* (Manila: Instituto Nacional de Historia, 1978), p. 1. My translation. At the time of the original publication of *Imagined Communities*, I had no command of Spanish, and was thus unwittingly led to rely on the instructively corrupt translation of Leon Maria Guerrero.

13 Notice, for example, Rizal's subtle shift, in the same sentence, from the past tense of 'created' (*crió*) to the all-of-us-together present tense of 'multiplies' (*multiplica*).

14 The obverse side of the readers' anonymous obscurity was/is the author's immediate celebrity. As we shall see, this obscurity/celebrity has everything to do with the spread of print-capitalism. As early as 1593 energetic Dominicans had published in Manila the *Doctrina*

Christiana. But for centuries thereafter print remained under tight ecclesiastical control. Liberalization only began in the 1860s. See Bienvenido L. Lumbera, *Tagalog Poetry 1570–1898, Tradition and Influences in its Development*, pp. 35, 93.

15 Ibid., p. 115.

16 Ibid., p. 120.

17 The technique is similar to that of Homer, so ably discussed by Auerbach, *Mimesis*, ch. 1 ('Odysseus' Scar').

18 'Paalam Albaniang pinamamayanan
ng casama, t, lupit, bangis caliluhan,
acong tangulan mo, i, cusa mang pinatay
sa iyo, i, malaqui ang panghihinayang.'
'Farewell, Albania, kingdom now
of evil, cruelty, brutishness and deceit!
I, your defender, whom you now murder
Nevertheless lament the fate that has befallen you.'
This famous stanza has sometimes been interpreted as a veiled statement of Filipino patriotism, but Lumbera convincingly shows such an interpretation to be an anachronistic gloss. *Tagalog Poetry*, p. 125. The translation is Lumbera's. I have slightly altered his Tagalog text to conform to a 1973 edition of the poem based on the 1861 imprint.

19 Jean Franco, *An Introduction to Spanish-American Literature*, p. 34.

20 Ibid., pp. 35–6. Emphasis added.

21 This movement of a solitary hero through an adamantine social landscape is typical of many early (anti-) colonial novels.

22 After a brief, meteoric career as a radical journalist, Marco was interned by the Dutch colonial authorities in Boven Digul, one of the world's earliest concentration camps, deep in the interior swamps of western New Guinea. There he died in 1932, after six years confinement. Henri Chambert-Loir, 'Mas Marco Kartodikromo (c. 1890–1932) ou L'Education Politique,' p. 208, in *Littératures contemporaines de l'Asie du Sud-Est*. A brilliant recent full-length account of Marco's career can be found in Takashi Shiraishi, *An Age in Motion: Popular Radicalism in Java, 1912–1926*, chapters 2–5 and 8.

23 As translated by Paul Tickell in his *Three Early Indonesian Short Stories by Mas Marco Kartodikromo (c. 1890–1932)*, p. 7. Emphasis added.

24 In 1924, a close friend and political ally of Marco published a novel titled *Rasa Merdika* [Feeling Free/The Feel of Freedom]. Of the hero of this novel (which he wrongly attributes to Marco) Chambert-Loir writes that 'he has no idea of the meaning of the word "socialism"': nonetheless he feels a profound malaise in the

face of the social organization that surrounds him and he feels the need to enlarge his horizons by two methods: *travel and reading.*' ('Mas Marco', p. 208. Emphasis added.) The Itching Parrot has moved to Java and the twentieth century.

25 Reading a newspaper is like reading a novel whose author has abandoned any thought of a coherent plot.

26 Febvre and Martin, *The Coming of the Book*, p. 186. This amounted to no less than 35,000 editions produced in no fewer than 236 towns. As early as 1480, presses existed in more than 110 towns, of which 50 were in today's Italy, 30 in Germany, 9 in France, 8 each in Holland and Spain, 5 each in Belgium and Switzerland, 4 in England, 2 in Bohemia, and 1 in Poland. 'From that date it may be said of Europe that the printed book was in universal use' (p. 182).

27 Ibid., p. 262. The authors comment that by the sixteenth century books were readily available to anyone who could read.

28 The great Antwerp publishing house of Plantin controlled, early in the sixteenth century, 24 presses with more than 100 workers in each shop. Ibid., p. 125.

29 This is one point solidly made amidst the vagaries of Marshall McLuhan's *Gutenberg Galaxy* (p. 125). One might add that if the book market was dwarfed by the markets in other commodities, its strategic role in the dissemination of ideas nonetheless made it of central importance to the development of modern Europe.

30 The principle here is more important than the scale. Until the nineteenth century, editions were still relatively small. Even Luther's Bible, an extraordinary best-seller, had only a 4,000-copy first edition. The unusually large first edition of Diderot's *Encyclopédie* numbered no more than 4,250. The average eighteenth-century run was less than 2,000. Febvre and Martin, *The Coming of the Book*, pp. 218–20. At the same time, the book was always distinguishable from other durables by its inherently limited market. Anyone with money can buy Czech cars; only Czech-readers will buy Czech-language books. The importance of this distinction will be considered below.

31 Furthermore, as early as the late fifteenth century the Venetian publisher Aldus had pioneered the portable 'pocket edition.'

32 As the case of *Semarang Hitam* shows, the two kinds of best-sellers used to be more closely linked than they are today. Dickens too serialized his popular novels in popular newspapers.

33 'Printed materials encouraged silent adherence to causes whose advocates could not be located in any one parish and who addressed an invisible public from afar.' Elizabeth L. Eisenstein, 'Some Conjectures about the Impact of Printing on Western Society and Thought,' *Journal of Modern History* 40: 1 (March 1968), p. 42.

34 Writing of the relationship between the material anarchy of middle-class society and an abstract political state-order, Nairn observes that 'the representative mechanism converted real class inequality into the abstract egalitarianism of citizens, individual egotisms into an impersonal collective will, what would otherwise be chaos into a new state legitimacy.' *The Break-up of Britain*, p. 24. No doubt. But the representative mechanism (elections?) is a rare and moveable feast. The generation of the impersonal will is, I think, better sought in the diurnal regularities of the imagining life.

25

"Disjuncture and Difference in the Global Cultural Economy" (1990)

Arjun Appadurai

It takes only the merest acquaintance with the facts of the modern world to note that it is now an interactive system in a sense that is strikingly new. Historians and sociologists, especially those concerned with translocal processes (Hodgson 1974) and the world systems associated with capitalism (Abu-Lughod 1989; Braudel 1981–4; Curtin 1984; Wallerstein 1974; Wolf 1982), have long been aware that the world has been a congeries of large-scale interactions for many centuries. Yet today's world involves interactions of a new order and intensity. Cultural transactions between social groups in the past have generally been restricted, sometimes by the facts of geography and ecology, and at other times by active resistance to interactions with the Other (as in China for much of its history and in Japan before the Meiji Restoration). Where there have been sustained cultural transactions across large parts of the globe, they have usually involved the long-distance journey of commodities (and of the merchants most concerned with them) and of travelers and explorers of every type (Helms 1988; Schafer 1963). The two main forces for sustained cultural interaction before this century have been warfare (and the large-scale political systems sometimes generated by it) and religions of conversion, which have sometimes, as in the case of Islam, taken warfare as one of the legitimate instruments of their expansion. Thus, between travelers and merchants, pilgrims and conquerors, the world has seen much

Arjun Appadurai, "Disjuncture and Difference in the Global Cultural Economy," pp. 27–47 from *Modernity at Large: Cultural Dimensions of Globalization*. Minneapolis: University of Minnesota Press, 1996.

long-distance (and long-term) cultural traffic. This much seems self-evident.

But few will deny that given the problems of time, distance, and limited technologies for the command of resources across vast spaces, cultural dealings between socially and spatially separated groups have, until the past few centuries, been bridged at great cost and sustained over time only with great effort. The forces of cultural gravity seemed always to pull away from the formation of large-scale ecumenes, whether religious, commercial, or political, toward smaller-scale accretions of intimacy and interest.

Sometime in the past few centuries, the nature of this gravitational field seems to have changed. Partly because of the spirit of the expansion of Western maritime interests after 1500, and partly because of the relatively autonomous developments of large and aggressive social formations in the Americas (such as the Aztecs and the Incas), in Eurasia (such as the Mongols and their descendants, the Mughals and Ottomans), in island South-east Asia (such as the Buginese), and in the kingdoms of precolonial Africa (such as Dahomey), an overlapping set of ecumenes began to emerge, in which congeries of money, commerce, conquest, and migration began to create durable cross-societal bonds. This process was accelerated by the technology transfers and innovations of the late eighteenth and nineteenth centuries (e.g., Bayly 1989), which created complex colonial orders centered on European capitals and spread throughout the non-European world. This intricate and overlapping set of Eurocolonial worlds (first Spanish and Portuguese, later principally English, French, and

Dutch) set the basis for a permanent traffic in ideas of peoplehood and selfhood, which created the imagined communities (Anderson 1983) of recent nationalisms throughout the world.

With what Benedict Anderson has called "print capitalism," a new power was unleashed in the world, the power of mass literacy and its attendant large-scale production of projects of ethnic affinity that were remarkably free of the need for face-to-face communication or even of indirect communication between persons and groups. The act of reading things together set the stage for movements based on a paradox – the paradox of constructed primordialism. There is, of course, a great deal else that is involved in the story of colonialism and its dialectically generated nationalisms (Chatterjee 1986), but the issue of constructed ethnicities is surely a crucial strand in this tale.

But the revolution of print capitalism and the cultural affinities and dialogues unleashed by it were only modest precursors to the world we live in now. For in the past century, there has been a technological explosion, largely in the domain of transportation and information, that makes the interactions of a print-dominated world seem as hard-won and as easily erased as the print revolution made earlier forms of cultural traffic appear. For with the advent of the steamship, the automobile, the airplane, the camera, the computer, and the telephone, we have entered into an altogether new condition of neighborliness, even with those most distant from ourselves. Marshall McLuhan, among others, sought to theorize about this world as a "global village," but theories such as McLuhan's appear to have overestimated the communitarian implications of the new media order (McLuhan and Powers 1989). We are now aware that with media, each time we are tempted to speak of the global village, we must be reminded that media create communities with "no sense of place" (Meyrowitz 1985). The world we live in now seems rhizomic (Deleuze and Guattari 1987), even schizophrenic, calling for theories of rootlessness, alienation, and psychological distance between individuals and groups on the one hand, and fantasies (or nightmares) of electronic propinquity on the other. Here, we are close to the central problematic of cultural processes in today's world.

Thus, the curiosity that recently drove Pico Iyer to Asia (1988) is in some ways the product of a confusion between some ineffable McDonaldization of the world and the much subtler play of indigenous trajectories of desire and fear with global flows of people and things. Indeed, Iyer's own impressions are testimony to the fact that, if *a* global cultural system is emerging, it is filled with ironies and resistances, sometimes camouflaged as passivity and a bottomless appetite in the Asian world for things Western.

Iyer's own account of the uncanny Philippine affinity for American popular music is rich testimony to the global culture of the hyperreal, for somehow Philippine renditions of American popular songs are both more widespread in the Philippines, and more disturbingly faithful to their originals, than they are in the United States today. An entire nation seems to have learned to mimic Kenny Rogers and the Lennon sisters, like a vast Asian Motown chorus. But *Americanization* is certainly a pallid term to apply to such a situation, for not only are there more Filipinos singing perfect renditions of some American songs (often from the American past) than there are Americans doing so, there is also, of course, the fact that the rest of their lives is not in complete synchrony with the referential world that first gave birth to these songs.

In a further globalizing twist on what Fredric Jameson has recently called "nostalgia for the present" (1989), these Filipinos look back to a world they have never lost. This is one of the central ironies of the politics of global cultural flows, especially in the arena of entertainment and leisure. It plays havoc with the hegemony of Eurochronology. American nostalgia feeds on Filipino desire represented as a hypercompetent reproduction. Here, we have nostalgia without memory. The paradox, of course, has its explanations, and they are historical; unpacked, they lay bare the story of the American missionization and political rape of the Philippines, one result of which has been the creation of a nation of make-believe Americans, who tolerated for so long a leading lady who played the piano while the slums of Manila expanded and decayed. Perhaps the most radical postmodernists would argue that this is hardly surprising because in the peculiar chronicities of late capitalism, pastiche and nostalgia are central modes of image production and reception. Americans themselves are hardly in the present anymore as they stumble into the mega-technologies of the twenty-first century garbed in the film-noir scenarios of sixties' chills, fifties'

"Disjuncture and Difference in the Global Cultural Economy"

diners, forties' clothing, thirties' houses, twenties' dances, and so on ad infinitum.

As far as the United States is concerned, one might suggest that the issue is no longer one of nostalgia but of a social *imaginaire* built largely around reruns. Jameson was bold to link the politics of nostalgia to the postmodern commodity sensibility, and surely he was right (1983). The drug wars in Colombia recapitulate the tropical sweat of Vietnam, with Ollie North and his succession of masks – Jimmy Stewart concealing John Wayne concealing Spiro Agnew and all of them transmogrifying into Sylvester Stallone, who wins in Afghanistan – thus simultaneously fulfilling the secret American envy of Soviet imperialism and the rerun (this time with a happy ending) of the Vietnam War. The Rolling Stones, approaching their fifties, gyrate before eighteen-year-olds who do not appear to need the machinery of nostalgia to be sold on their parents' heroes. Paul McCartney is selling the Beatles to a new audience by hitching his oblique nostalgia to their desire for the new that smacks of the old. *Dragnet* is back in nineties' drag, and so is *Adam-12*, not to speak of *Batman* and *Mission Impossible*, all dressed up technologically but remarkably faithful to the atmospherics of their originals.

The past is now not a land to return to in a simple politics of memory. It has become a synchronic warehouse of cultural scenarios, a kind of temporal central casting, to which recourse can be taken as appropriate, depending on the movie to be made, the scene to be enacted, the hostages to be rescued. All this is par for the course, if you follow Jean Baudrillard or Jean-François Lyotard into a world of signs wholly unmoored from their social signifiers (all the world's a Disneyland). But I would like to suggest that the apparent increasing substitutability of whole periods and postures for one another, in the cultural styles of advanced capitalism, is tied to larger global forces, which have done much to show Americans that the past is usually another country. If your present is their future (as in much modernization theory and in many self-satisfied tourist fantasies), and their future is your past (as in the case of the Filipino virtuosos of American popular music), then your own past can be made to appear as simply a normalized modality of your present. Thus, although some anthropologists may continue to relegate their Others to temporal

spaces that they do not themselves occupy (Fabian 1983), postindustrial cultural productions have entered a postnostalgic phase.

The crucial point, however, is that the United States is no longer the puppeteer of a world system of images but is only one node of a complex transnational construction of imaginary landscapes. The world we live in today is characterized by a new role for the imagination in social life. To grasp this new role, we need to bring together the old idea of images, especially mechanically produced images (in the Frankfurt School sense); the idea of the imagined community (in Anderson's sense); and the French idea of the imaginary (*imaginaire*) as a constructed landscape of collective aspirations, which is no more and no less real than the collective representations of Émile Durkheim, now mediated through the complex prism of modern media.

The image, the imagined, the imaginary – these are all terms that direct us to something critical and new in global cultural processes: *the imagination as a social practice*. No longer mere fantasy (opium for the masses whose real work is elsewhere), no longer simple escape (from a world defined principally by more concrete purposes and structures), no longer elite pastime (thus not relevant to the lives of ordinary people), and no longer mere contemplation (irrelevant for new forms of desire and subjectivity), the imagination has become an organized field of social practices, a form of work (in the sense of both labor and culturally organized practice), and a form of negotiation between sites of agency (individuals) and globally defined fields of possibility. This unleashing of the imagination links the play of pastiche (in some settings) to the terror and coercion of states and their competitors. The imagination is now central to all forms of agency, is itself a social fact, and is the key component of the new global order. But to make this claim meaningful, we must address some other issues.

Homogenization and Heterogenization

The central problem of today's global interactions is the tension between cultural homogenization and cultural heterogenization. A vast array of empirical facts

could be brought to bear on the side of the homogenization argument, and much of it has come from the left end of the spectrum of media studies (Hamelink 1983; Mattelart 1983; Schiller 1976), and some from other perspectives (Gans 1985; Iyer 1988). Most often, the homogenization argument subspeciates into either an argument about Americanization or an argument about commoditization, and very often the two arguments are closely linked. What these arguments fail to consider is that at least as rapidly as forces from various metropolises are brought into new societies they tend to become indigenized in one or another way: this is true of music and housing styles as much as it is true of science and terrorism, spectacles and constitutions. The dynamics of such indigenization have just begun to be explored systemically (Barber 1987; Feld 1988; Hannerz 1987, 1989; Ivy 1988; Nicoll 1989; Yoshimoto 1989), and much more needs to be done. But it is worth noticing that for the people of Irian Jaya, Indonesianization may be more worrisome than Americanization, as Japanization may be for Koreans, Indianization for Sri Lankans, Vietnamization for the Cambodians, and Russianization for the people of Soviet Armenia and the Baltic republics. Such a list of alternative fears to Americanization could be greatly expanded, but it is not a shapeless inventory: for polities of smaller scale, there is always a fear of cultural absorption by polities of larger scale, especially those that are nearby. One man's imagined community is another man's political prison.

This scalar dynamic, which has widespread global manifestations, is also tied to the relationship between nations and states, to which I shall return later. For the moment let us note that the simplification of these many forces (and fears) of homogenization can also be exploited by nation-states in relation to their own minorities, by posing global commoditization (or capitalism, or some other such external enemy) as more real than the threat of its own hegemonic strategies.

The new global cultural economy has to be seen as a complex, overlapping, disjunctive order that cannot any longer be understood in terms of existing center-periphery models (even those that might account for multiple centers and peripheries). Nor is it susceptible to simple models of push and pull (in terms of migration theory), or of surpluses and deficits (as in traditional models of balance of trade), or of consumers

and producers (as in most neo-Marxist theories of development). Even the most complex and flexible theories of global development that have come out of the Marxist tradition (Amin 1980; Mandel 1978; Wallerstein 1974; Wolf 1982) are inadequately quirky and have failed to come to terms with what Scott Lash and John Urry have called disorganized capitalism (1987). The complexity of the current global economy has to do with certain fundamental disjunctures between economy, culture, and politics that we have only begun to theorize.[1]

I propose that an elementary framework for exploring such disjunctures is to look at the relationship among five dimensions of global cultural flows that can be termed (a) *ethnoscapes*, (b) *mediascapes*, (c) *technoscapes*, (d) *financescapes*, and (e) *ideoscapes*. The suffix *-scape* allows us to point to the fluid, irregular shapes of these landscapes, shapes that characterize international capital as deeply as they do international clothing styles. These terms with the common suffix *-scape* also indicate that these are not objectively given relations that look the same from every angle of vision but, rather, that they are deeply perspectival constructs, inflected by the historical, linguistic, and political situatedness of different sorts of actors: nation-states, multinationals, diasporic communities, as well as subnational groupings and movements (whether religious, political, or economic), and even intimate face-to-face groups, such as villages, neighborhoods, and families. Indeed, the individual actor is the last locus of this perspectival set of landscapes, for these landscapes are eventually navigated by agents who both experience and constitute larger formations, in part from their own sense of what these landscapes offer.

These landscapes thus are the building blocks of what (extending Benedict Anderson) I would like to call *imagined worlds*, that is, the multiple worlds that are constituted by the historically situated imaginations of persons and groups spread around the globe. An important fact of the world we live in today is that many persons on the globe live in such imagined worlds (and not just in imagined communities) and thus are able to contest and sometimes even subvert the imagined worlds of the official mind and of the entrepreneurial mentality that surround them.

By *ethnoscape*, I mean the landscape of persons who constitute the shifting world in which we live: tourists, immigrants, refugees, exiles, guest workers, and other moving groups and individuals constitute an essential feature of the world and appear to affect the politics of (and between) nations to a hitherto unprecedented degree. This is not to say that there are no relatively stable communities and networks of kinship, friendship, work, and leisure, as well as of birth, residence, and other filial forms. But it is to say that the warp of these stabilities is everywhere shot through with the woof of human motion, as more persons and groups deal with the realities of having to move or the fantasies of wanting to move. What is more, both these realities and fantasies now function on larger scales, as men and women from villages in India think not just of moving to Poona or Madras but of moving to Dubai and Houston, and refugees from Sri Lanka find themselves in South India as well as in Switzerland; just as the Hmong are driven to London as well as to Philadelphia. And as international capital shifts its needs, as production and technology generate different needs, as nation-states shift their policies on refugee populations, these moving groups can never afford to let their imaginations rest too long, even if they wish to.

By *technoscape*, I mean the global configuration, also ever fluid, of technology and the fact that technology, both high and low, both mechanical and informational, now moves at high speeds across various kinds of previously impervious boundaries. Many countries now are the roots of multinational enterprise: a huge steel complex in Libya may involve interests from India, China, Russia, and Japan, providing different components of new technological configurations. The odd distribution of technologies, and thus the peculiarities of these technoscapes, are increasingly driven not by any obvious economies of scale, of political control, or of market rationality but by increasingly complex relationships among money flows, political possibilities, and the availability of both un- and highly skilled labor. So, while India exports waiters and chauffeurs to Dubai and Sharjah, it also exports software engineers to the United States – indentured briefly to Tata-Burroughs or the World Bank, then laundered through the State Department to become wealthy resident aliens, who are in turn objects of seductive messages to invest their money and know-how in federal and state projects in India.

The global economy can still be described in terms of traditional indicators (as the World Bank continues to do) and studied in terms of traditional comparisons (as in Project Link at the University of Pennsylvania), but the complicated technoscapes (and the shifting ethnoscapes) that underlie these indicators and comparisons are further out of the reach of the queen of social sciences than ever before. How is one to make a meaningful comparison of wages in Japan and the United States or of real-estate costs in New York and Tokyo, without taking sophisticated account of the very complex fiscal and investment flows that link the two economies through a global grid of currency speculation and capital transfer?

Thus it is useful to speak as well of *financescapes*, as the disposition of global capital is now a more mysterious, rapid, and difficult landscape to follow than ever before, as currency markets, national stock exchanges, and commodity speculations move megamonies through national turnstiles at blinding speed, with vast, absolute implications for small differences in percentage points and time units. But the critical point is that the global relationship among ethnoscapes, technoscapes, and financescapes is deeply disjunctive and profoundly unpredictable because each of these landscapes is subject to its own constraints and incentives (some political, some informational, and some technoenvironmental), at the same time as each acts as a constraint and a parameter for movements in the others. Thus, even an elementary model of global political economy must take into account the deeply disjunctive relationships among human movement, technological flow, and financial transfers.

Further refracting these disjunctures (which hardly form a simple, mechanical global infrastructure in any case) are what I call *mediascapes* and *ideoscapes*, which are closely related landscapes of images. *Mediascapes* refer both to the distribution of the electronic capabilities to produce and disseminate information (newspapers, magazines, television stations, and film-production studios), which are now available to a growing number of private and public interests throughout the world, and to the images of the world created by these media. These images involve many complicated inflections, depending on their mode (documentary or entertainment), their hardware (electronic or preelectronic), their audiences (local, national, or transnational), and the interests of those who own and control them. What is most important about these mediascapes is that they provide (especially in their television, film, and cassette forms) large and complex repertoires of images, narratives, and ethnoscapes to viewers throughout the world, in which the world of commodities and the world of news and politics are profoundly mixed. What this means is that many audiences around the world experience the media themselves as a complicated and interconnected repertoire of print, celluloid, electronic screens, and billboards. The lines between the realistic and the fictional landscapes they see are blurred, so that the farther away these audiences are from the direct experiences of metropolitan life, the more likely they are to construct imagined worlds that are chimerical, aesthetic, even fantastic objects, particularly if assessed by the criteria of some other perspective, some other imagined world.

Mediascapes, whether produced by private or state interests, tend to be image-centered, narrative-based accounts of strips of reality, and what they offer to those who experience and transform them is a series of elements (such as characters, plots, and textual forms) out of which scripts can be formed of imagined lives, their own as well as those of others living in other places. These scripts can and do get disaggregated into complex sets of metaphors by which people live (Lakoff and Johnson 1980) as they help to constitute narratives of the Other and protonarratives of possible lives, fantasies that could become prolegomena to the desire for acquisition and movement.

Ideoscapes are also concatenations of images, but they are often directly political and frequently have to do with the ideologies of states and the counterideologies of movements explicitly oriented to capturing state power or a piece of it. These ideoscapes are composed of elements of the Enlightenment worldview, which consists of a chain of ideas, terms, and images, including *freedom, welfare, rights, sovereignty, representation,* and the master term *democracy.* The master narrative of the Enlightenment (and its many variants in Britain, France, and the United States) was constructed with a certain internal logic and presupposed a certain relationship between reading, representation, and the public sphere. (For the dynamics of this process in the early history of the United States, see Warner 1990.)

But the diaspora of these terms and images across the world, especially since the nineteenth century, has loosened the internal coherence that held them together in a Euro-American master narrative and provided instead a loosely structured synopticon of politics, in which different nation-states, as part of their evolution, have organized their political cultures around different keywords (e.g., Williams 1976).

As a result of the differential diaspora of these keywords, the political narratives that govern communication between elites and followers in different parts of the world involve problems of both a semantic and pragmatic nature: semantic to the extent that words (and their lexical equivalents) require careful translation from context to context in their global movements, and pragmatic to the extent that the use of these words by political actors and their audiences may be subject to very different sets of contextual conventions that mediate their translation into public politics. Such conventions are not only matters of the nature of political rhetoric: for example, what does the aging Chinese leadership mean when it refers to the dangers of hooliganism? What does the South Korean leadership mean when it speaks of discipline as the key to democratic industrial growth?

These conventions also involve the far more subtle question of what sets of communicative genres are valued in what way (newspapers versus cinema, for example) and what sorts of pragmatic genre conventions govern the collective readings of different kinds of text. So, while an Indian audience may be attentive to the resonances of a political speech in terms of some keywords and phrases reminiscent of Hindi cinema, a Korean audience may respond to the subtle codings of Buddhist or neo-Confucian rhetoric encoded in a political document. The very relationship of reading to hearing and seeing may vary in important ways that determine the morphology of these different ideoscapes as they shape themselves in different national and transnational contexts. This globally variable synaesthesia has hardly even been noted, but it demands urgent analysis. Thus *democracy* has clearly become a master term, with powerful echoes from Haiti and Poland to the former Soviet Union and China, but it sits at the center of a variety of ideoscapes, composed of distinctive pragmatic configurations of rough translations of other central terms from the vocabulary of the Enlightenment. This creates ever new terminological kaleidoscopes, as states (and the groups that seek to capture them) seek to pacify populations whose own ethnoscapes are in motion and whose mediascapes may create severe problems for the ideoscapes with which they are presented. The fluidity of ideoscapes is complicated in particular by the growing diasporas (both voluntary and involuntary) of intellectuals who continuously inject new meaning-streams into the discourse of democracy in different parts of the world.

This extended terminological discussion of the five terms I have coined sets the basis for a tentative formulation about the conditions under which current global flows occur: they occur in and through the growing disjunctures among ethnoscapes, technoscapes, financescapes, mediascapes, and ideoscapes. This formulation, the core of my model of global cultural flow, needs some explanation. First, people, machinery, money, images, and ideas now follow increasingly nonisomorphic paths, of course, at all periods in human history, there have been some disjunctures in the flows of these things, but the sheer speed, scale, and volume of each of these flows are now so great that the disjunctures have become central to the politics of global culture. The Japanese are notoriously hospitable to ideas and are stereotyped as inclined to export (all) and import (some) goods, but they are also notoriously closed to immigration, like the Swiss, the Swedes, and the Saudis. Yet the Swiss and the Saudis accept populations of guest workers, thus creating labor diasporas of Turks, Italians, and other circum-Mediterranean groups. Some such guest-worker groups maintain continuous contact with their home nations, like the Turks, but others, like high-level South Asian migrants, tend to desire lives in their new homes, raising anew the problem of reproduction in a deterritorialized context.

Deterritorialization, in general, is one of the central forces of the modern world because it brings laboring populations into the lower-class sectors and spaces of relatively wealthy societies, while sometimes creating exaggerated and intensified senses of criticism or attachment to politics in the home state. Deterritorialization, whether of Hindus, Sikhs, Palestinians, or Ukrainians, is now at the core of a variety of global fundamentalisms, including Islamic and Hindu fundamentalism. In the Hindu case, for example, it is clear that the overseas movement of Indians has been exploited by a variety of interests both within and outside India to create a complicated network of finances and religious identifications, by which the problem of cultural reproduction for Hindus abroad has become tied to the politics of Hindu fundamentalism at home.

At the same time, deterritorialization creates new markets for film companies, art impresarios, and travel agencies, which thrive on the need of the deterritorialized population for contact with its homeland. Naturally, these invented homelands, which constitute the mediascapes of deterritorialized groups, can often become sufficiently fantastic and one-sided that they provide the material for new ideoscapes in which ethnic conflicts can begin to erupt. The creation of Khalistan, an invented homeland of the deterritorialized Sikh population of England, Canada, and the United States, is one example of the bloody potential in such mediascapes as they interact with the internal colonialisms of the nation-state (e.g., Hechter 1975). The West Bank, Namibia, and Eritrea are other theaters for the enactment of the bloody negotiation between existing nation-states and various deterritorialized groupings.

It is in the fertile ground of deterritorialization, in which money, commodities, and persons are involved in ceaselessly chasing each other around the world, that the mediascapes and ideoscapes of the modern world find their fractured and fragmented counterpart. For the ideas and images produced by mass media often are only partial guides to the goods and experiences that deterritorialized populations transfer to one another. In Mira Nair's brilliant film *India Cabaret*, we see the multiple loops of this fractured deterritorialization as young women, barely competent in Bombay's metropolitan glitz, come to seek their fortunes as cabaret dancers and prostitutes in Bombay, entertaining men in clubs with dance formats derived wholly from the prurient dance sequences of Hindi films. These scenes in turn cater to ideas about Western and foreign women and their looseness, while they provide tawdry career alibis for these women. Some of these women come from Kerala, where cabaret clubs and the pornographic film industry have blossomed, partly in response to the purses and tastes of Keralites returned from the Middle East, where their diasporic lives away from women distort their very sense of what the relations between men and women might be. These tragedies of displacement could certainly be replayed in a more detailed analysis of the relations between the Japanese and German sex tours to Thailand and the tragedies of the sex trade in Bangkok, and in other similar loops that tie together fantasies about the Other, the conveniences and seductions of travel, the economics of global trade, and the brutal mobility fantasies that dominate gender politics in many parts of Asia and the world at large.

While far more could be said about the cultural politics of deterritorialization and the larger sociology of displacement that it expresses, it is appropriate at this juncture to bring in the role of the nation-state in the disjunctive global economy of culture today. The relationship between states and nations is everywhere an embattled one. It is possible to say that in many societies the nation and the state have become one another's projects. That is, while nations (or more properly groups with ideas about nationhood) seek to capture or co-opt states and state power, states simultaneously seek to capture and monopolize ideas about nationhood (Baruah 1986; Chatterjee 1986; Nandy 1989). In general, separatist transnational movements, including those that have included terror in their methods, exemplify nations in search of states. Sikhs, Tamil Sri Lankans, Basques, Moros, Quebecois – each of these represents imagined communities that seek to create states of their own or carve pieces out of existing states. States, on the other hand, are everywhere seeking to monopolize the moral resources of community, either by flatly claiming perfect coevality between nation and state, or by systematically museumizing and representing all the groups within them in a variety of heritage politics that seems remarkably uniform throughout the world (Handler 1988; Herzfeld 1982; McQueen 1988).

Here, national and international mediascapes are exploited by nation-states to pacify separatists or even the potential fissiparousness of all ideas of difference. Typically, contemporary nation-states do this by exercising taxonomic control over difference, by creating various kinds of international spectacle to domesticate difference, and by seducing small groups with the fantasy of self-display on some sort of global or cosmopolitan stage. One important new feature of global cultural politics, tied to the disjunctive relationships among the various landscapes discussed earlier, is that state and nation are at each other's throats, and the hyphen that links them is now less an icon of conjuncture than an index of disjuncture. This disjunctive relationship between nation and state has two levels: at the level of any given nation-state, it means that there is a battle of the imagination, with state and nation seeking to cannibalize one another. Here is the seedbed of brutal separatisms – majoritarianisms that seem to have appeared from nowhere and microidentities that have become political projects within the nation-state. At another level, this disjunctive relationship is deeply entangled with the global disjunctures discussed throughout this chapter: ideas of nationhood appear to be steadily increasing in scale and regularly crossing existing state boundaries, sometimes, as with the Kurds, because previous identities stretched across vast national spaces or, as with the Tamils in Sri Lanka, the dormant threads of a transnational diaspora have been activated to ignite the micropolitics of a nation-state.

In discussing the cultural politics that have subverted the hyphen that links the nation to the state, it is especially important not to forget the mooring of such politics in the irregularities that now characterize disorganized capital (Kothari 1989; Lash and Urry 1987). Because labor, finance, and technology are now so widely separated, the volatilities that underlie movements for nationhood (as large as transnational Islam on the one hand, or as small as the movement of the Gurkhas for a separate state in Northeast India) grind against the vulnerabilities that characterize the relationships between states. States find themselves pressed to stay open by the forces of media, technology, and travel that have fueled consumerism throughout the world and have increased the craving, even in the non-Western world, for new commodities and spectacles. On the other hand, these very cravings can become caught up in new ethnoscapes, mediascapes, and, eventually, ideoscapes, such as democracy in China, that the state cannot tolerate as threats to its own control over ideas of nationhood and peoplehood. States throughout the world are under siege, especially where contests over the ideoscapes of democracy are fierce and fundamental, and where there are radical disjunctures between ideoscapes and technoscapes (as in the case of very small countries that lack contemporary technologies of production and information); or between ideoscapes and finance-scapes (as in countries such as Mexico or Brazil, where international lending influences national politics to a very large degree); or between ideoscapes and ethno-scapes (as in Beirut, where diasporic, local, and trans-local filiations are suicidally at battle); or between ideoscapes and mediascapes (as in many countries in the Middle East and Asia) where the lifestyles represented on both national and international TV and cinema completely overwhelm and undermine the rhetoric of national politics. In the Indian case, the myth of the law-breaking hero has emerged to mediate this naked struggle between the pieties and realities of Indian politics, which has grown increasingly brutalized and corrupt (Vachani 1989).

The transnational movement of the martial arts, particularly through Asia, as mediated by the Hollywood and Hong Kong film industries (Zarilli 1995) is a rich illustration of the ways in which long-standing martial arts traditions, reformulated to meet the fantasies of contemporary (sometimes lumpen) youth populations, create new cultures of masculinity and violence, which are in turn the fuel for increased violence in national and international politics. Such violence is in turn the spur to an increasingly rapid and amoral arms trade that penetrates the entire world. The worldwide spread of the AK-47 and the Uzi, in films, in corporate and state security, in terror, and in police and military activity, is a reminder that apparently simple technical uniformities often conceal an increasingly complex set of loops, linking images of violence to aspirations for community in some imagined world.

Returning then to the ethnoscapes with which I began, the central paradox of ethnic politics in today's world is that primordia (whether of language or skin color or neighborhood or kinship) have become globalized. That is, sentiments, whose greatest force is in their ability to ignite intimacy into a political state and turn locality into a staging ground for identity, have become spread over vast and irregular spaces as groups move yet stay linked to one another through sophisticated media capabilities. This is not to deny that such primordia are often the product of invented traditions (Hobsbawm and Ranger 1983) or retrospective affiliations, but to emphasize that because

of the disjunctive and unstable interplay of commerce, media, national policies, and consumer fantasies, ethnicity, once a genie contained in the bottle of some sort of locality (however large), has now become a global force, forever slipping in and through the cracks between states and borders.

But the relationship between the cultural and economic levels of this new set of global disjunctures is not a simple one-way street in which the terms of global cultural politics are set wholly by, or confined wholly within, the vicissitudes of international flows of technology, labor, and finance, demanding only a modest modification of existing neo-Marxist models of uneven development and state formation. There is a deeper change, itself driven by the disjunctures among all the landscapes I have discussed and constituted by their continuously fluid and uncertain interplay, that concerns the relationship between production and consumption in today's global economy. Here, I begin with Marx's famous (and often mined) view of the fetishism of the commodity and suggest that this fetishism has been replaced in the world at large (now seeing the world as one large, interactive system, composed of many complex subsystems) by two mutually supportive descendants, the first of which I call production fetishism and the second, the fetishism of the consumer.

By *production fetishism* I mean an illusion created by contemporary transnational production loci that masks translocal capital, transnational earning flows, global management, and often faraway workers (engaged in various kinds of high-tech putting-out operations) in the idiom and spectacle of local (sometimes even worker) control, national productivity, and territorial sovereignty. To the extent that various kinds of free-trade zones have become the models for production at large, especially of high-tech commodities, production has itself become a fetish, obscuring not social relations as such but the relations of production, which are increasingly transnational. The locality (both in the sense of the local factory or site of production and in the extended sense of the nation-state) becomes a fetish that disguises the globally dispersed forces that actually drive the production process. This generates alienation (in Marx's sense) twice intensified, for its social sense is now compounded by a complicated spatial dynamic that is increasingly global.

As for the *fetishism of the consumer*, I mean to indicate here that the consumer has been transformed through commodity flows (and the mediascapes, especially of advertising, that accompany them) into a sign, both in Baudrillard's sense of a simulacrum that only asymptotically approaches the form of a real social agent, and in the sense of a mask for the real seat of agency, which is not the consumer but the producer and the many forces that constitute production. Global advertising is the key technology for the worldwide dissemination of a plethora of creative and culturally well-chosen ideas of consumer agency. These images of agency are increasingly distortions of a world of merchandising so subtle that the consumer is consistently helped to believe that he or she is an actor, where in fact he or she is at best a chooser.

The globalization of culture is not the same as its homogenization, but globalization involves the use of a variety of instruments of homogenization (armaments, advertising techniques, language hegemonies, and clothing styles) that are absorbed into local political and cultural economies, only to be repatriated as heterogeneous dialogues of national sovereignty, free enterprise, and fundamentalism in which the state plays an increasingly delicate role: too much openness to global flows, and the nation-state is threatened by revolt, as in the China syndrome; too little, and the state exits the international stage, as Burma, Albania, and North Korea in various ways have done. In general, the state has become the arbitrageur of this *repatriation of difference* (in the form of goods, signs, slogans, and styles). But this repatriation or export of the designs and commodities of difference continuously exacerbates the internal politics of majoritarianism and homogenization, which is most frequently played out in debates over heritage.

Thus the central feature of global culture today is the politics of the mutual effort of sameness and difference to cannibalize one another and thereby proclaim their successful hijacking of the twin Enlightenment ideas of the triumphantly universal and the resiliently particular. This mutual cannibalization shows its ugly face in riots, refugee flows, state-sponsored torture, and ethnocide (with or without state support). Its brighter side is in the expansion of many individual horizons of hope and fantasy, in the global spread of oral rehydration therapy and other low-tech instruments of well-

being, in the susceptibility even of South Africa to the force of global opinion, in the inability of the Polish state to repress its own working classes, and in the growth of a wide range of progressive, transnational alliances. Examples of both sorts could be multiplied. The critical point is that both sides of the coin of global cultural process today are products of the infinitely varied mutual contest of sameness and difference on a stage characterized by radical disjunctures between different sorts of global flows and the uncertain landscapes created in and through these disjunctures.

The Work of Reproduction in an Age of Mechanical Art

I have inverted the key terms of the title of Walter Benjamin's famous essay (1969) to return this rather high-flying discussion to a more manageable level. There is a classic human problem that will not disappear however much global cultural processes might change their dynamics, and this is the problem today typically discussed under the rubric of reproduction (and traditionally referred to in terms of the transmission of culture). In either case, the question is, how do small groups, especially families, the classical loci of socialization, deal with these new global realities as they seek to reproduce themselves and, in so doing, by accident reproduce cultural forms themselves? In traditional anthropological terms, this could be phrased as the problem of enculturation in a period of rapid culture change. So the problem is hardly novel. But it does take on some novel dimensions under the global conditions discussed so far in this chapter.

First, the sort of transgenerational stability of knowledge that was presupposed in most theories of enculturation (or, in slightly broader terms, of socialization) can no longer be assumed. As families move to new locations, or as children move before older generations, or as grown sons and daughters return from time spent in strange parts of the world, family relationships can become volatile; new commodity patterns are negotiated, debts and obligations are recalibrated, and rumors and fantasies about the new setting are maneuvered into existing repertoires of knowledge and practice. Often, global labor diasporas involve immense strains on marriages in general and on women in particular, as marriages become the meeting points of historical patterns of socialization and new ideas of proper behavior. Generations easily divide, as ideas about property, propriety, and collective obligation wither under the siege of distance and time. Most important, the work of cultural reproduction in new settings is profoundly complicated by the politics of representing a family as normal (particularly for the young) to neighbors and peers in the new locale. All this is, of course, not new to the cultural study of immigration.

What is new is that this is a world in which both points of departure and points of arrival are in cultural flux, and thus the search for steady points of reference, as critical life choices are made, can be very difficult. It is in this atmosphere that the invention of tradition (and of ethnicity, kinship, and other identity markers) can become slippery, as the search for certainties is regularly frustrated by the fluidities of transnational communication. As group pasts become increasingly parts of museums, exhibits, and collections, both in national and transnational spectacles, culture becomes less what Pierre Bourdieu would have called a habitus (a tacit realm of reproducible practices and dispositions) and more an arena for conscious choice, justification, and representation, the latter often to multiple and spatially dislocated audiences.

The task of cultural reproduction, even in its most intimate arenas, such as husband–wife and parent–child relations, becomes both politicized and exposed to the traumas of deterritorialization as family members pool and negotiate their mutual understandings and aspirations in sometimes fractured spatial arrangements. At larger levels, such as community, neighborhood, and territory, this politicization is often the emotional fuel for more explicitly violent politics of identity, just as these larger politics sometimes penetrate and ignite domestic politics. When, for example, two offspring in a household split with their father on a key matter of political identification in a transnational setting, preexisting localized norms carry little force. Thus a son who has joined the Hezbollah group in Lebanon may no longer get along with parents or siblings who are affiliated with Amal or some other branch of Shi'i ethnic political identity in Lebanon. Women in particular bear the brunt of this sort of friction, for they become pawns in the heritage politics

of the household and are often subject to the abuse and violence of men who are themselves torn about the relation between heritage and opportunity in shifting spatial and political formations.

The pains of cultural reproduction in a disjunctive global world are, of course, not eased by the effects of mechanical art (or mass media), for these media afford powerful resources for counternodes of identity that youth can project against parental wishes or desires. At larger levels of organization, there can be many forms of cultural politics within displaced populations (whether of refugees or of voluntary immigrants), all of which are inflected in important ways by media (and the mediascapes and ideoscapes they offer). A central link between the fragilities of cultural reproduction and the role of the mass media in today's world is the politics of gender and violence. As fantasies of gendered violence dominate the B-grade film industries that blanket the world, they both reflect and refine gendered violence at home and in the streets, as young men (in particular) are swayed by the macho politics of self-assertion in contexts where they are frequently denied real agency, and women are forced to enter the labor force in new ways on the one hand, and continue the maintenance of familial heritage on the other. Thus the honor of women becomes not just an armature of stable (if inhuman) systems of cultural reproduction but a new arena for the formation of sexual identity and family politics, as men and women face new pressures at work and new fantasies of leisure.

Because both work and leisure have lost none of their gendered qualities in this new global order but have acquired ever subtler fetishized representations, the honor of women becomes increasingly a surrogate for the identity of embattled communities of males, while their women in reality have to negotiate increasingly harsh conditions of work at home and in the nondomestic workplace. In short, deterritorialized communities and displaced populations, however much they may enjoy the fruits of new kinds of earning and new dispositions of capital and technology, have to play out the desires and fantasies of these new ethnoscapes, while striving to reproduce the family-as-microcosm of culture. As the shapes of cultures grow less bounded and tacit, more fluid and politicized, the work of cultural reproduction becomes a daily hazard. Far more could, and should, be said about the work of reproduction in an age of mechanical art: the preceding discussion is meant to indicate the contours of the problems that a new, globally informed theory of cultural reproduction will have to face.

Shape and Process in Global Cultural Formations

The deliberations of the arguments that I have made so far constitute the bare bones of an approach to a general theory of global cultural processes. Focusing on disjunctures, I have employed a set of terms (*ethnoscape, financescape, technoscape, mediascape,* and *ideoscape*) to stress different streams or flows along which cultural material may be seen to be moving across national boundaries. I have also sought to exemplify the ways in which these various flows (or landscapes, from the stabilizing perspectives of any given imagined world) are in fundamental disjuncture with respect to one another. What further steps can we take toward a general theory of global cultural processes based on these proposals?

The first is to note that our very models of cultural shape will have to alter, as configurations of people, place, and heritage lose all semblance of isomorphism. Recent work in anthropology has done much to free us of the shackles of highly localized, boundary-oriented, holistic, primordialist images of cultural form and substance (Hannerz 1989; Marcus and Fischer 1986; Thornton 1988). But not very much has been put in their place, except somewhat larger if less mechanical versions of these images, as in Eric Wolf's work on the relationship of Europe to the rest of the world (1982). What I would like to propose is that we begin to think of the configuration of cultural forms in today's world as fundamentally fractal, that is, as possessing no Euclidean boundaries, structures, or regularities. Second, I would suggest that these cultural forms, which we should strive to represent as fully fractal, are also overlapping in ways that have been discussed only in pure mathematics (in set theory, for example) and in biology (in the language of polythetic classifications). Thus we need to combine a fractal metaphor for the shape of cultures (in the plural) with a polythetic account of their overlaps and resemblances. Without this latter step, we shall remain mired in comparative work that relies on the clear separation of the entities to be compared before serious comparison can begin. How are we to compare fractally shaped cultural forms that are also polythetically overlapping in their coverage of terrestrial space?

Finally, in order for the theory of global cultural interactions predicated on disjunctive flows to have any force greater than that of a mechanical metaphor, it will have to move into something like a human version of the theory that some scientists are calling chaos theory. That is, we will need to ask not how these complex, overlapping, fractal shapes constitute a simple, stable (even if large-scale) system, but to ask what its dynamics are: Why do ethnic riots occur when and where they do? Why do states wither at greater rates in some places and times than in others? Why do some countries flout conventions of international debt repayment with so much less apparent worry than others? How are international arms flows driving ethnic battles and genocides? Why are some states exiting the global stage while others are clamoring to get in? Why do key events occur at a certain point in a certain place rather than in others? These are, of course, the great traditional questions of causality, contingency, and prediction in the human sciences, but in a world of disjunctive global flows, it is perhaps important to start asking them in a way that relies on images of flow and uncertainty, hence *chaos*, rather than on older images of order, stability, and systematicness. Otherwise, we will have gone far toward a theory of global cultural systems but thrown out process in the bargain. And that would make these notes part of a journey toward the kind of illusion of order that we can no longer afford to impose on a world that is so transparently volatile.

Whatever the directions in which we can push these macrometaphors (fractals, polythetic classifications, and chaos), we need to ask one other old-fashioned question out of the Marxist paradigm: is there some pregiven order to the relative determining force of these global flows? Because I have postulated the dynamics of global cultural systems as driven by the relationships among flows of persons, technologies, finance, information, and ideology, can we speak of some structural-causal order linking these flows by analogy to the role of the economic order in one version of the Marxist paradigm? Can we speak of some of these flows as being, for a priori structural or historical reasons, always prior to and formative of other flows? My own hypothesis, which can only be tentative at this point, is that the relationship of these various flows to one another as they constellate into particular events and social forms will be radically context-dependent. Thus, while labor flows and their loops with financial flows between Kerala and the Middle East may account for the shape of media flows and ideoscapes in Kerala, the reverse may be true of Silicon Valley in California, where intense specialization in a single technological sector (computers) and particular flows of capital may well profoundly determine the shape that ethnoscapes, ideoscapes, and mediascapes may take.

This does not mean that the causal-historical relationship among these various flows is random or meaninglessly contingent but that our current theories of cultural chaos are insufficiently developed to be even parsimonious models at this point, much less to be predictive theories, the golden fleeces of one kind of social science. What I have sought to provide in this chapter is a reasonably economical technical vocabulary and a rudimentary model of disjunctive flows, from which something like a decent global analysis might emerge. Without some such analysis, it will be difficult to construct what John Hinkson calls a "social theory of postmodernity" that is adequately global (1990, 84).

Note

1   One major exception is Fredric Jameson, whose work on the relationship between postmodernism and late capitalism has in many ways inspired this essay. The debate between Jameson and Aijaz Ahmad in *Social Text*, however, shows that the creation of a globalizing Marxist narrative in cultural matters is difficult territory indeed (Jameson 1986; Ahmad 1987). My own effort in this context is to begin a restructuring of the Marxist narrative (by stressing lags and disjunctures) that many Marxists might find abhorrent. Such a restructuring has to avoid the dangers of obliterating difference within the Third World, eliding the social referent (as some French postmodernists seem inclined to do), and retaining the narrative authority of the Marxist tradition, in favor of greater attention to global fragmentation, uncertainty, and difference.

Bibliography

Abu-Lughod, L. (1989) *Before European Hegemony: The World System A.D. 1250–1350*. New York: Oxford University Press.

Ahmad, A. (1987) Jameson's Rhetoric of Otherness and the "National Allegory," *Social Text* 17: 3–25.

Amin, S. (1980) *Class and Nation: Historically and in the Current Crisis*. New York and London: Monthly Review Press.

Anderson, B. (1983) *Imagined Communities: Reflections on the Origin and Spread of Nationalism*. London: Verso.

Barber, K. (1987) Popular Arts in Africa, *African Studies Review* 30 (3, September): 1–78.

Baruah, S. (1986) Immigration, Ethnic Conflict and Political Turmoil, Assam 1979–1985, *Asian Survey* 26 (11, November): 1184–1206.

Bayly, C. A. (1989) *Imperial Meridian: The British Empire and the World, 1780–1830*. London and New York: Longman.

Benjamin, W. ([1936] 1969) The Work of Art in the Age of Mechanical Reproduction. In H. Arendt (Ed.) *Illuminations*. H. Zohn (Trans.) New York: Schocken Books.

Braudel, F. (1981–1984) *Civilization and Capitalism, 15th–18th Century* (3 vols). London: Collins.

Chatterjee, P. (1986) *Nationalist Thought and the Colonial World: A Derivative Discourse?* London: Zed Books.

Curtin, P. (1984) *Cross-Cultural Trade in World History*. Cambridge: Cambridge University Press.

Deleuze, G., and F. Guattari (1987) *A Thousand Plateaus: Capitalism and Schizophrema*. B. Massumi (Trans.) Minneapolis: University of Minnesota Press.

Fabian, J. (1983) *Time and the Other: How Anthropology Makes Its Object*. New York: Columbia University Press.

Feld, S. (1988) Notes on World Beat, *Public Culture* 1 (1): 31–7.

Gans, E. (1985) *The End of a Culture: Toward a Generative Anthropology*. Berkeley: University of California Press.

Hamelink, C. (1983) *Cultural Autonomy in Global Communications*. New York: Longman.

Handler, R. (1988) *Nationalism and the Politics of Culture in Quebec*. Madison: University of Wisconsin Press.

Hannerz, U. (1987) The World in Creolization, *Africa* 57 (4): 546–59.

Hannerz, U. (1989) Notes on the Global Ecumene, *Public Culture* 1 (2, Spring): 66–75.

Hechter, M. (1975) *Internal Colonialism: The Celtic Fringe in British National Development, 1936–1966*. Berkeley: University of California Press.

Helms, M. W. (1988) *Ulysses' Sail: An Ethnographic Odyssey of Power, Knowledge, and Geographical Distance*. Princeton, NJ: Princeton University Press.

Herzfeld, M. (1982) *Ours Once More: Folklore, Ideology and the Making of Modern Greece*. Austin: University of Texas Press.

Hinkson, J. (1990) Postmodernism and Structural Change, *Public Culture* 2 (2, Spring): 82–101.

Hobsbawm, E., and T. Ranger (Eds.) (1983) *The Innovation of Tradition*. New York: Columbia University Press.

Hodgson, M. (1974) *The Venture of Islam, Conscience and History in a World Civilization* (3 vols). Chicago: University of Chicago Press.

Ivy, M. (1988) Tradition and Difference in the Japanese Mass Media, *Public Culture* 1 (1): 21–9.

Iyer, P. (1988) *Video Night in Kathmandu*. New York: Knopf.

Jameson, F. (1983) Postmodernism and Consumer Society. In H. Foster (Ed.) *The Anti-Aesthetic: Essays on Postmodern Culture*. Port Townsend, Wash.: Bay Press, 111–25.

Jameson, F. (1986) Third World Literature in the Era of Multi-National Capitalism, *Social Text* 15 (Fall): 65–88.

Jameson, F. (1989) Nostalgia for the Present, *South Atlantic Quarterly* 88 (2, Spring): 517–37.

Kothari, R. (1989) *State against Democracy: In Search of Humane Governance*. New York: New Horizons.

Lakoff, G., and M. Johnson (1980) *Metaphors We Live By*. Chicago and London: University of Chicago Press.

Lash, S., and J. Urry (1987) *The End of Organized Capitalism*. Madison: University of Wisconsin Press.

Mandel, E. (1978) *Late Capitalism*. London: Verso.

Marcus, G., and M. Fischer (1986) *Anthropology as Cultural Critique: An Experimental Moment in the Human Sciences*. Chicago: University of Chicago Press.

Mattelart, A. (1983) *Transnationals and the Third World: The Struggle for Culture*. South Hadley, Mass.: Bergin and Garvey.

McLuhan M., and B. R. Powers. (1989) *The Global Village: Transformations in World, Life and Media in the 21st Century*. New York: Oxford University Press.

McQueen, H. (1988) The Australian Stamp: Image, Design and Ideology, *Arena* 84 (Spring): 78–96.

Meyrowitz, J. (1985) *No Sense of Place: The Impact of Electronic Media on Social Behavior*. New York: Oxford University Press.

Nandy, A. (1989) The Political Culture of the Indian State, *Daedalus* 118 (4): 1–26.

Nicoll, F. (1989) My Trip to Alice, *Criticism, Heresy and Interpretation* 3: 21–32.

Schafer, E. (1963) *Golden Peaches of Samarkand: A Study of T'ang Exotics*. Berkeley: University of California Press.

Schiller, H. (1976) *Communication and Cultural Domination*. White Plains, NY: International Arts and Sciences.

Thornton, R. (1988) The Rhetoric of Ethnographic Holism, *Cultural Anthropology* 3 (3, August): 285–303.

Vachani, L. (1989) Narrative, Pleasure and Ideology in the Hindi Film: An Analysis of the Outsider Formula. M. A. Thesis, Annenberg School of Communication University of Pennsylvania.

Wallerstein, I. (1974) *The Modern World System* (2 vols). New York and London: Academic Press.

Warner, M. (1990) *The Letters of the Republic Publication and the Public Sphere in Eighteenth-Century America*. Cambridge, Mass.: Harvard University Press.

Williams, R. (1976) *Keywords*. New York: Oxford University Press.

Wolf, E. (1982) *Europe and the People without History*. Berkeley: University of California Press.

Yoshimoto, M. (1989) The Postmodern and Mass Images in Japan, *Public Culture* 1 (2): 8–25.

Zarilli, P. (1995) Repositioning the Body: An Indian Martial Art and Its Pan-Asian Publics. In C. A. Breckenridge (ed.) *Consuming Modernity: Public Culture in a South Asian World*. Minneapolis: University of Minnesota Press.

26

"Politics and Space/Time" (1992)

Doreen Massey

competing defs of space *abs*

'Space' is very much on the agenda these days. On the one hand, from a wide variety of sources come proclamations of the significance of the spatial in these times: 'It is space not time that hides consequences from us' (Berger); 'The difference that space makes' (Sayer); 'That new spatiality implicit in the postmodern' (Jameson); 'It is space rather than time which is the distinctively significant dimension of contemporary capitalism' (Urry); and 'All the social sciences must make room for an increasingly geographical conception of mankind' (Braudel). Even Foucault is now increasingly cited for his occasional reflections on the importance of the spatial. His 1967 Berlin lectures contain the unequivocal: 'The anxiety of our era has to do fundamentally with space, no doubt a great deal more than with time.' In other contexts the importance of the spatial, and of associated concepts, is more metaphorical. In debates around identity the terminology of space, location, positionality and place figures prominently. Homi Bhabha, in discussions of cultural identity, argues for a notion of a 'third space'. Jameson, faced with what he sees as the global confusions of postmodern times, 'the disorientation of saturated space', calls for an exercise in 'cognitive mapping'. And Laclau, in his own very different reflections on the 'new revolution of our time', uses the terms 'temporal' and 'spatial' as the major differentiators between ways of conceptualizing systems of social relations.

[...]

Doreen Massey, "Politics and Space/Time," pp. 65–76, 79–84 from *New Left Review* 196 (1992) (abridged from original version). Reprinted by permission of New Left Review.

In part this concern about what the term 'space' is intended to mean arises simply from the multiplicity of definitions adopted. Many authors rely heavily on the terms 'space'/'spatial', and each assumes that their meaning is clear and uncontested. Yet in fact the meaning that different authors assume (and therefore – in the case of metaphorical usage – the import of the metaphor) varies greatly. Buried in these unacknowledged disagreements is a debate that never surfaces; and it never surfaces because everyone assumes we already know what these terms mean. Henri Lefebvre, in the opening pages of his book *The Production of Space*, commented on just this phenomenon: the fact that authors who in so many ways excel in logical rigour will fail to define a term which functions crucially in their argument: 'Conspicuous by its absence from supposedly epistemological studies is ... the idea ... of space – the fact that "space" is mentioned on every page notwithstanding.'[1] At least there ought to be a debate about the meaning of this much-used term.

Nonetheless, had this been all that was at issue I would probably not have been exercised to write an article about it. But the problem runs more deeply than this. For among the many and conflicting definitions of space that are current in the literature there are some – and very powerful ones – which deprive it of politics and of the possibility of politics: they effectively depoliticize the realm of the spatial. By no means all authors relegate space in this way. Many, drawing on terms such as 'centre'/'periphery'/'margin', and so forth, and examining the 'politics of location' for instance, think of spatiality in a highly active and politically enabling manner. But for others space is the sphere of the lack of politics.

Precisely because the use of spatial terminology is so frequently unexamined, this latter use of the term is not always immediately evident. This dawned fully on me when I read a statement by Ernesto Laclau in his *New Reflections on the Revolution of Our Time*. 'Politics and space,' he writes on page 68, 'are antinomic terms. Politics only exist insofar as the spatial eludes us.'[2] For someone who, as a geographer, has for years been arguing, along with many others, for a dynamic and politically progressive way of conceptualizing the spatial, this was clearly provocative!

Because my own inquiries were initially stimulated by Laclau's book, and because unearthing the implicit definitions at work implies a detailed reading (which restricts the number of authors who can be considered) this discussion takes *New Reflections* as a starting point, and considers it in most detail. But, as will become clear, the implicit definition used by Laclau, and which depoliticizes space, is shared by many other authors. In its simpler forms it operates, for instance, in the debate over the nature of structuralism, and is an implicit reference point in many texts. It is, moreover, in certain of its fundamental aspects shared by authors, such as Fredric Jameson, who in other ways are making arguments very different from those of Laclau.

To summarize it rather crudely, Laclau's view of space is that it is the realm of stasis. There is, in the realm of the spatial, no true temporality and thus no possibility of politics. It is on this view, and on a critique of it, that much of my initial discussion concentrates. But in other parts of the debate about the nature of the current era, and in particular in relation to 'postmodernity', the realm of the spatial is given entirely different associations from those ascribed to it by Laclau. Thus Jameson, who sees postmodern times as being particularly characterized by the importance of spatiality, interprets it in terms of an unnerving multiplicity: space is chaotic depthlessness.[3] This is the opposite of Laclau's characterization, yet for Jameson it is – once again – a formulation which deprives the spatial of any meaningful politics.

A caveat must be entered from the start. This discussion will be addressing only one aspect of the complex realm that goes by the name of the spatial.

Lefebvre, among others, insisted on the importance of considering not only what might be called 'the geometry' of space but also its lived practices and the symbolic meaning and significance of particular spaces and spatializations. Without disagreeing with that, the concentration here will nonetheless be on the view of space as what I shall provisionally call 'a dimension'. The argument is that different ways of conceptualizing this aspect of 'the spatial' themselves provide very different bases (or in some cases no basis at all) for the politicization of space. Clearly, anyway, the issue of the conceptualization of space is of more than technical interest; it is one of the axes along which we experience and conceptualize the world.

Space and Time

An examination of the literature reveals, as might be expected, a variety of uses and meanings of the term 'space', but there is one characteristic of these meanings that is particularly strong and widespread. This is the view of space which, in one way or another, defines it as stasis, and as utterly opposed to time. Laclau, for whom the contrast between what he labels temporal and what he calls spatial is key to his whole argument, uses a highly complex version of this definition. For him, notions of time and space are related to contrasting methods of understanding social systems. In his *New Reflections on the Revolution of Our Time*, Laclau posits that 'any repetition that is governed by a structural law of successions is space' (p. 41) and 'spatiality means coexistence within a structure that establishes the positive nature of all its terms' (p. 69). Here, then, any postulated causal structure which is complete and self-determining is labelled 'spatial'. This does not mean that such a 'spatial' structure cannot change – it may do – but the essential characteristic is that all the causes of any change which may take place are internal to the structure itself. On this view, in the realm of the spatial there can be no surprises (provided we are analytically well-equipped). In contrast to the closed and self-determining systems of the spatial, Time (or temporality) for Laclau takes the form of dislocation, a dynamic which disrupts the predefined terms of any system of causality. The spatial, because it lacks dislocation, is devoid of the possibility of politics.

This is an importantly different distinction between time and space from that which simply contrasts change with an utter lack of movement. In Laclau's version, there can be movement and change within a so-called spatial system; what there cannot be is real dynamism in the sense of a change in the terms of 'the system' itself (which can therefore never be a simply coherent closed system). A distinction is postulated, in other words, between different types of what would normally be called time. On the one hand, there is the time internal to a closed system, where things may change yet without really changing. On the other hand, there is genuine dynamism, Grand Historical Time. In the former is included cyclical time, the times of reproduction, the way in which a peasantry represents to itself (says Laclau, p. 42) the unfolding of the cycle of the seasons, the turning of the earth. To some extent, too, there is 'embedded time', the time in which our daily lives are set.[4] These times, says Laclau, this kind of 'time' is space.

Laclau's argument here is that what we are inevitably faced with in the world are 'temporal' (by which he means dislocated) structures: dislocation is intrinsic and it is this – this essential openness – which creates the possibility of politics. Any attempt to represent the world 'spatially', including even the world of physical space, is an attempt to ignore that dislocation. Space therefore, in his terminology, is representation, is any (ideological) attempt at closure: 'Society, then, is unrepresentable: any representation – *and thus any space* – is an attempt to constitute society, not to state what it is' (p. 82, my emphasis). Pure spatiality, in these terms, cannot exist: 'The ultimate failure of all hegemonisation [in Laclau's term, spatialization], then, means that the real – including physical space – is in the ultimate instance temporal' (p. 42); or again: 'the mythical nature of any space' (p. 68). This does not mean that the spatial is unimportant. This is not the point at issue, nor is it Laclau's intent. For the 'spatial' as the ideological/mythical is seen by him as itself part of the social and as constitutive of it: 'And insofar as the social is impossible without some fixation of meaning, without the discourse of closure, the ideological must be seen as constitutive of the social' (p. 92).[5] The issue here is not the relative priority of the temporal and the spatial, but their definition. For it is through this logic, and its association of ideas with time

temporality and spatiality, that Laclau arrives at the depoliticization of space. 'Let us begin,' writes Laclau, 'by identifying three dimensions of the relationship of dislocation that are crucial to our analysis. The *first* is that dislocation is the very form of temporality. And temporality must be conceived as the exact opposite of space. The "spatialization" of an event consists of eliminating its temporality' (p. 41; my emphasis).

The second and third dimensions of the relationship of dislocation (see above) take the logic further: 'The *second* dimension is that dislocation [which, remember, is the antithesis of the spatial] is the very form of possibility', and 'The *third* dimension is that dislocation is the very form of freedom. Freedom is the absence of determination' (pp. 42, 43; my emphases). This leaves the realm of the spatial looking like unpromising territory for politics. It is lacking in dislocation, the very form of possibility (the form of temporality), which is also 'the very form of freedom'. Within the spatial there is only determination, and hence no possibility of freedom or of politics.

Laclau's characterization of the spatial is, however, a relatively sophisticated version of a much more general conception of space and time (or spatiality and temporality). It is a conceptualization in which the two are opposed to each other, and in which time is the one that matters and of which History (capital H) is made. Time Marches On but space is a kind of stasis, where nothing really happens. There are a number of ways in which, it seems to me, this manner of characterizing space and the realm of the spatial is questionable. Three of them, chosen precisely because of their contrasts, because of the distinct light they each throw on the problems of this view of space, will be examined here. The first draws on the debates that have taken place in 'radical geography' over the last two decades and more; the second examines the issue from the point of view of a concern with gender; and the third examines the view from physics.

Radical Geography

In the 1970s the discipline of geography experienced the kinds of developments described by Anderson in 'A Culture in Contraflow'[6] for other social sciences. The previously hegemonic positivist 'spatial science'

was increasingly challenged by a new generation of Marxist geographers. The argument turned intellectually on how 'the relation between space and society' should be conceptualized. To caricature the debate, the spatial scientists had posited an autonomous sphere of the spatial in which 'spatial relations' and 'spatial processes' produced spatial distributions. The geography of industry, for instance, would be interpreted as simply the result of 'geographical location factors'. Countering this, the Marxist critique was that all these so-called spatial relations and spatial processes were actually social relations taking a particular geographical form. The geography of industry, we argued, could therefore not be explained without a prior understanding of the economy and of wider social and political processes. The aphorism of the seventies was 'space is a social construct'. That is to say – though the point was perhaps not made clearly enough at the time – space is constituted through social relations and material social practices.

But this, too, was soon to seem an inadequate characterization of the social/spatial relation. For, while it is surely correct to argue that space is socially constructed, the one-sidedness of that formulation implied that geographical forms and distributions were simply outcomes, the end point of social explanation. Geographers would thus be the cartographers of the social sciences, mapping the outcomes of processes which could only be explained in other disciplines – sociology, economics, and so forth. What geographers mapped – the spatial form of the social – was interesting enough, but it was simply an end product: it had no material effect. Quite apart from any demeaning disciplinary implications, this was plainly not the case. The events taking place all around us in the 1980s – the massive spatial restructuring both intranationally and internationationally as an integral part of social and economic changes – made it plain that, in one way or another, 'geography matters'. And so, to the aphorism of the 1970s – that space is socially constructed – was added in the 1980s the other side of the coin: that the social is spatially constructed too, and that makes a difference. In other words, and in its broadest formulation, society is necessarily constructed spatially, and that fact – the spatial organization of society – makes a difference to how it works.

But if spatial organization makes a difference to how society works and how it changes, then far from being the realm of stasis, space and the spatial are also implicated (*contra* Laclau) in the production of history – and thus, potentially, in politics. This was not an entirely new thought. Henri Lefebvre, writing in 1974, was beginning to argue a very similar position: 'The space of capitalist accumulation thus gradually came to life, and began to be fitted out. This process of animation is admiringly referred to as history, and its motor sought in all kinds of factors: dynastic interests, ideologies, the ambitions of the mighty, the formation of nation states, demographic pressures, and so on. This is the road to a ceaseless analysing of, and searching for, dates and chains of events. Inasmuch as space is the locus of all such chronologies, might it not constitute a principle of explanation at least as acceptable as any other?'[7]

This broad position – that the social and the spatial are inseparable and that the spatial form of the social has causal effectivity – is now accepted increasingly widely, especially in geography and sociology,[8] though there are still those who would disagree, and beyond certain groups even the fact of a debate over the issue seems to have remained unrecognized (Anderson, for example, does not pick it up in his survey).[9] For those familiar with the debate, and who saw in it an essential step towards the politicization of the spatial, formulations of space as a static resultant without any effect – whether the simplistic versions or the more complex definitions such as Laclau's – seem to be very much a retrograde step. However, in retrospect, even the debates within radical geography have still fully to take on board the implications of our own arguments for the way in which space might be conceptualized.

Issues of Gender

For there are also other reservations, from completely different sources, that can be levelled against this view of space and that go beyond the debate which has so far taken place within radical geography. Some of these reservations revolve around issues of gender.

First of all, this manner of conceptualizing space and time takes the form of a dichotomous dualism. It is neither a simple statement of difference (A, B, ...)

nor a dualism constructed through an analysis of the interrelations between the objects being defined (capital:labour). It is a dichotomy specified in terms of a presence and an absence; a dualism which takes the classic form of A/not-A. As was noted earlier, one of Laclau's formulations of a definition is: 'temporality must be conceived as the exact opposite of space' (p. 41). Now, apart from any reservations which may be raised in the particular case of space and time (and which we shall come to later), the mode of thinking that relies on irreconcilable dichotomies of this sort has in general recently come in for widespread criticism. All the strings of these kinds of opposition with which we are so accustomed to work (mind–body; nature–culture; Reason–emotion; and so forth) have been argued to be at heart problematical and a hindrance to either understanding or changing the world. Much of this critique has come from feminists.[10]

The argument is two-fold. First, and less importantly here, it is argued that this way of approaching conceptualization is, in Western societies and more generally in societies where child-rearing is performed overwhelmingly by members of one sex (women), more typical of males than of females. This is an argument which generally draws on object-relations-theory approaches to identity-formation. Second, however, and of more immediate significance for the argument being constructed here, it has been contended that this kind of dichotomous thinking, together with a whole range of the sets of dualisms that take this form (we shall look at some of these in more detail below) are related to the construction of the radical distinction between genders in our society, to the characteristics assigned to each of them, and to the power relations maintained between them. Thus, Nancy Jay, in an article entitled 'Gender and Dichotomy', examines the social conditions and consequences of the use of logical dichotomy.[11] She argues not only that logical dichotomy and radical gender distinctions are associated but also, more widely, that such a mode of constructing difference works to the advantage of certain (dominant) social groups, 'that almost any ideology based on A/not-A dichotomy is effective in resisting change. Those whose understanding of society is ruled by such ideology find it very hard to conceive of the possibility of alternative forms of social order (third possibilities). Within such

thinking, the only alternative to the *one* order is disorder' (p. 54). Genevieve Lloyd, too, in a sweeping history of 'male' and 'female' in Western philosophy, entitled *The Man of Reason*, argues that such dichotomous conceptualization, and – what we shall come to later – the prioritization of one term in the dualism over the other, is not only central to much of the formulation of concepts with which Western philosophy has worked but that it is dependent upon, and is instrumental in the conceptualization of, among other things, a particular form of radical distinction between female and male genders.[12] Jay argues that 'Hidden, taken for granted, A/not-A distinctions are dangerous, and because of their peculiar affinity with gender distinctions, it seems important for feminist theory to be systematic in recognizing them' (p. 47). The argument here is that the definition of 'space' and 'time' under scrutiny here is precisely of this form, and on that basis alone warrants further critical investigation.

But there is also a further point. For within this kind of conceptualization, only one of the terms (A) is defined positively. The other term (not-A) is conceived only in relation to A, and as lacking in A. A fairly thorough reading of some of the recent literature that uses the terminology of space and time, and that employs this form of conceptualization, leaves no doubt that it is Time which is conceived of as in the position of 'A', and space which is 'not-A'. Over and over again, time is defined by such things as change, movement, history, dynamism; while space, rather lamely by comparison, is simply the absence of these things. This has two aspects. First, this kind of definition means that it is time, and the characteristics associated with time, that are the primary constituents of both space and time; time is the nodal point, the privileged signifier. And second, this kind of definition means that space is defined by absence, by lack. This is clear in the simple (and often implicit) definitions (time equals change/movement, space equals the lack of these things), but it can also be argued to be the case with more complex definitions such as those put forward by Laclau. For although in a formal sense it is the spatial which in Laclau's formulation is complete and the temporal which marks the lack (the absence of representation, the impossibility of closure), in the whole tone of the argument it is in fact space that is associated with negativity and absence. Thus: 'Temporality must be conceived as the exact opposite of space. The "spatialization" of an event consists of eliminating its temporality' (p. 41).

Now, of course, in current Western culture, or in certain of its dominant theories, woman too is defined in terms of lack. Nor, as we shall see, is it entirely a matter of coincidence that space and the feminine are frequently defined in terms of dichotomies in which each of them is most commonly defined as not-A. There is a whole set of dualisms whose terms are commonly aligned with time and space. With Time are aligned History, Progress, Civilization, Science, Politics and Reason, portentous things with gravitas and capital letters. With space on the other hand are aligned the other poles of these concepts: stasis, ('simple') reproduction, nostalgia, emotion, aesthetics, the body. All these dualisms, in the way that they are used, suffer from the criticisms made above of dichotomies of this form: the problem of mutual exclusivity and of the consequent impoverishment of both of their terms. Other dualisms could be added which also map on to that between time and space. Jameson, for instance, as do a whole line of authors before him, clearly relates the pairing to that between transcendence and immanence, with the former connotationally associated with the temporal and immanence with the spatial. Indeed, in this and in spite of their other differences, Jameson and Laclau are very similar. Laclau's distinction between the closed, cyclical time of simple reproduction (spatial) and dislocated, changing history (temporal), even if the latter has no inevitability in its progressive movement, is precisely that. Jameson who bemoans what he characterizes as the tendency towards immanence and the flight from transcendence of the contemporary period, writes of 'a world peculiarly without transcendence and without perspective …, and indeed without plot in any traditional sense, since all choices would be equidistant and on the same level' (*Postmodernism*, p. 269), and this is a world where, he believes, a sense of the temporal is being lost and the realm of the spatial is taking over.

Now, as has been pointed out many times, these dualisms which so easily map on to each other also map on to the constructed dichotomy between female and male. From Rousseau's seeing woman as a potential source of disorder, as needing to be tamed by Reason, to Freud's famous pronouncement that

woman is the enemy of civilization, to the many subsequent critics and analysts of such statements of the 'obviousness' of dualisms, of their interrelation one with another, and of their connotations of male and female, such literature is now considerable.[13] And space, in this system of interconnected dualisms, is coded female. '"Transcendence", in its origins, is a transcendence *of* the feminine', writes Lloyd (*The Man of Reason*, p. 101), for instance. Moreover, even where the transcodings between dualisms have an element of inconsistency, this rule still applies. Thus where time is dynamism, dislocation and History, and space is stasis, space is coded female and denigrated. But where space is chaos (which you would think was quite different from stasis; more indeed like dislocation), then time is Order … and space is *still* coded female, only in this context interpreted as threatening.

[…]

It is important to be clear about what is being said of this relationship between space/time and gender. It is not being argued that this way of characterizing space is somehow essentially male; there is no essentialism of feminine/masculine here. Rather, the argument is that the dichotomous characterization of space and time, along with a whole range of other dualisms that have been briefly referred to, and with their connotative interrelations, may both reflect and be part of the constitution of, among other things, the masculinity and femininity of the sexist society in which we live. Nor is it being argued that space should simply be reprioritized to share an equal status with, or stand instead of, time. The latter point is important because there have been a number of contributions to the debate recently which have argued that, especially in modernist (including Marxist) accounts, it is time which has been considered the more important. Ed Soja, particularly in his book *Postmodern Geographies*, has made an extended and persuasive case to this effect (although see the critique by Gregory).[14] The story told earlier of Marxism within geography – supposedly the spatial discipline – is indicative of the same tendency. In a completely different context, Terry Eagleton has written in his introduction to Kristin Ross's *The Construction of Social Space* that 'Ross is surely right to claim that this idea [the concept of space] has proved of far less glamorous appeal to radical theorists than the apparently more dynamic, exhilarating notions of narrative and history.'[15]

It is interesting to speculate on the degree to which this de-prioritization might itself have been part and parcel of the system of gender connotations. Ross herself writes: "The difficulty is also one of vocabulary, for while words like "historical" and "political" convey a dynamic of intentionality, vitality, and human motivation, "spatial", on the other hand, connotes stasis, neutrality, and passivity' (p. 8), and in her analysis of Rimbaud's poetry and of the nature of its relation to the Paris Commune she does her best to counter that essentially negative view of spatiality. (Jameson, of course, is arguing pretty much the same point about the past prioritization of time, but his mission is precisely the opposite of Ross's and Soja's; it is to hang on to that prioritization.)

The point here, however, is not to argue for an upgrading of the status of space within the terms of the old dualism (a project which is arguably inherently difficult anyway, given the terms of that dualism), but to argue that what must be overcome is the very formulation of space/time in terms of this kind of dichotomy. The same point has frequently been made by feminists in relation to other dualisms, most particularly perhaps – because of the debate over the writings of Simone de Beauvoir – the dualism of transcendence and immanence. When de Beauvoir wrote 'Man's design is not to repeat himself in time: it is to take control of the instant and mould the future. It is male activity that in creating values has made of existence itself a value; this activity has prevailed over the confused forces of life; it has subdued Nature and Woman',[16] she was making precisely that discrimination between cyclicity and 'real change' which is not only central to the classic distinction between immanence and transcendence but is also part of the way in which Laclau distinguishes between what he calls the spatial and the temporal. De Beauvoir's argument was that women should grasp the transcendent. A later generation of feminists has argued that the problem is the nature of the distinction itself. The position here is both that the two dualisms (immanence/transcendence and space/time) are related and that the argument about the former dualism could and should be extended to the latter. The next line of critique, the view from physics, provides some further hints about the directions which that reformulation might take.

[…]

An Alternative View of Space

A first requirement of developing an alternative view of space is that we should try to get away from a notion of society as a kind of 3-D (and indeed more usually 2-D) slice which moves through time. Such a view is often, even usually, implicit rather than explicit, but it is remarkably pervasive. It shows up in the way people phrase things, in the analogies they use. Thus, just briefly to cite two of the authors who have been referred to earlier, Foucault writes 'We are at a moment, I believe, when our experience of the world is less that of a long life developing through time than that of a network that connects points and intersects with its own skein',[17] and Jameson contrasts 'historiographic deep space or perspectival temporality' with a (spatial) set of connections which 'lights up like a nodal circuit in a slot machine'.[18] The aim here is not to disagree in total with these formulations, but to indicate what they imply. What they both point to is a contrast between temporal movement on the one hand, and on the other a notion of space as instantaneous connections between things at one moment. For Jameson, the latter type of (inadequate) history-telling has replaced the former. And if this is true then it is indeed inadequate. But while the contrast – the shift in balance – to which both authors are drawing attention is a valid one, in the end the notion of space as *only* systems of simultaneous relations, the flashing of a pinball machine, is inadequate. For, of course, the temporal movement is also spatial; the moving elements have spatial relations to each other. And the 'spatial' interconnections which flash across can only be constituted temporally as well. Instead of linear process counterposed to flat surface (which anyway reduces space from three to two dimensions), it is necessary to insist on the irrefutable four-dimensionality (indeed, n-dimensionality) of things. Space is not static, nor time spaceless. Of course spatiality and temporality are different from each other, but neither can be conceptualized as the absence of the other. The full implications of this will be elaborated below, but for the moment the point is to try to think in terms of all the dimensions of space-time. It is a lot more difficult than at first it might seem.

s-t
continuum

Second, we need to conceptualize space as constructed out of interrelations, as the simultaneous coexistence of social interrelations and interactions at all spatial scales, from the most local level to the most global. Earlier it was reported how, in human geography, the recognition that the spatial is socially constituted was followed by the perhaps even more powerful (in the sense of the breadth of its implications) recognition that the social is necessarily spatially constituted too. Both points (though perhaps in reverse order) need to be grasped at this moment. On the one hand, all social (and indeed physical) phenomena/activities/relations have a spatial form and a relative spatial location. The relations which bind communities, whether they be 'local' societies or worldwide organizations; the relations within an industrial corporation; the debt relations between the South and the North; the relations which result in the current popularity in European cities of music from Mali. The spatial spread of social relations can be intimately local or expansively global, or anything in between. Their spatial extent and form also changes over time (and there is considerable debate about what is happening to the spatial form of social relations at the moment). But, whichever way it is, there is no getting away from the fact that the social is inexorably also spatial.

The proposition here is that this fact be used to define the spatial. Thus, the spatial is socially constituted. 'Space' is created out of the vast intricacies, the incredible complexities, of the interlocking and the non-interlocking, and the networks of relations at every scale from local to global. What makes a particular view of these social relations specifically spatial is their simultaneity. It is a simultaneity, also, which has extension and configuration. But simultaneity is absolutely not stasis. Seeing space as a moment in the intersection of configured social relations (rather than as an absolute dimension) means that it cannot be seen as static. There is no choice between flow (time) and a flat surface of instantaneous relations (space). Space is not a 'flat' surface in that sense because the social relations which create it are themselves dynamic by their very nature. It is a question of a manner of thinking. It is not the 'slice through time' which should be the dominant thought but the simultaneous coexistence of social relations that cannot be conceptualized as other than dynamic. Moreover, and again

as a result of the fact that it is conceptualized as created out of social relations, space is by its very nature full of power and symbolism, a complex web of relations of domination and subordination, of solidarity and cooperation. This aspect of space has been referred to elsewhere as a kind of 'power-geometry'.[19]

Third, this in turn means that the spatial has *both* an element of order *and* an element of chaos (or maybe it is the case that we should question that dichotomy also). It cannot be defined on one side or the other of the mutually exclusive dichotomies discussed earlier. Space has order in two senses. First, it has order because all spatial locations of phenomena are caused; they can in principle be explained. Second, it has order because there are indeed spatial systems, in the sense of sets of social phenomena in which spatial arrangement (that is, mutual relative positioning rather than 'absolute' location) itself is part of the constitution of the system. The spatial organization of a communications network, or of a supermarket chain with its warehousing and distribution points and retail outlets, would both be examples of this, as would the activity space of a multinational company. There is an integral spatial coherence here, which constitutes the geographical distributions and the geographical form of the social relations. The spatial form was socially 'planned', in itself directly socially caused, that way. But there is also an element of 'chaos' which is intrinsic to the spatial. For although the location of each (or a set) of a number of phenomena may be directly caused (we know why X is here and Y is there), the spatial positioning of one in relation to the other (X's location in relation to Y) may not be directly caused. Such relative locations are produced out of the independent operation of separate determinations. They are in that sense 'unintended consequences'. Thus, the chaos of the spatial results from die happenstance juxtapositions, the accidental separations, the often paradoxical nature of the spatial arrangements that result from the operation of all these causalities. Both Mike Davis and Ed Soja, for instance, point to the paradoxical mixtures, the unexpected land-uses side by side, within Los Angeles. Thus, the relation between social relations and spatiality may vary between that of a fairly coherent system (where social and spatial form are mutually determinant) and that where the particular spatial form is not directly socially caused at all.

This has a number of significant implications. To begin with, it takes further the debate with Ernesto Laclau. For in this conceptualization space is essentially disrupted. It is, indeed, 'dislocated' and necessarily so. The simultaneity of space as defined here in no way implies the internally coherent closed system of causality which is dubbed spatial' in his *New Reflections*. There is no way that 'spatiality' in this sense 'means coexistence within a structure that establishes the positive nature of all its terms' (p. 69). The spatial, in fact, precisely *cannot* be so. And this means, in turn, that the spatial too is open to politics.

But, further, neither does this view of space accord with that of Fredric Jameson, which, at first sight, might seem to be the opposite of Laclau's. In Jameson's view the spatial does indeed, as we have seen, have a lot to do with the chaotic. While for Laclau spatial discourses are the attempt to represent (to pin down the essentially unmappable), for Jameson the spatial is precisely unrepresentable − which is why he calls for an exercise in 'mapping' (though he acknowledges the procedure will be far more complex than cartography as we have known it so far). In this sense, Laclau and Jameson, both of whom use the terms 'space'/'spatiality', and so on, with great frequency, and for both of whom the concepts perform an important function in their overall schemas, have diametrically opposed interpretations of what the terms actually mean. Yet for both of them their concepts of spatiality work against politics. While for Laclau it is the essential orderliness of the spatial (as he defines it) that means the death of history and politics, for Jameson it is the chaos (precisely, the dislocation) of (his definition of) the spatial that apparently causes him to panic, and to call for a map.

So this difference between the two authors does not imply that, since the view of the spatial proposed here is in disagreement with that of Laclau, it concords with that of Jameson. Jameson's view is in fact equally problematical for politics, although in a different way. Jameson labels as 'space' what he sees as unrepresentable (thus the 'crisis of representation' and the 'increasing spatialization' are to him inextricably associated elements of postmodern society). In this, he perhaps unknowingly recalls an old debate within geography that goes by the name of 'the problem of geographical description'.[20] Thus, thirty years ago H. C. Darby, an eminent figure in the geography of his day, ruminated

that 'A series of geographical facts is much more difficult to present than a sequence of historical facts. Events follow one another in time in an inherently dramatic fashion that makes juxtaposition in time easier to convey through the written word than juxtaposition in space. Geographical description is inevitably more difficult to achieve successfully than is historical narrative.'[21] Such a view, however, depends on the notion that the difficulty of geographical description (as opposed to temporal storytelling) arises in part because in space you can go off in any direction and in part because in space things which are next to each other are not necessarily connected. However, not only does this reduce space to unrepresentable chaos, it is also extremely problematical in what it implies for the notion of *time*. And this would seem on occasions to be the case for Jameson too. For, while space is posed as the unrepresentable, time is thereby, at least implicitly and at those moments, *counterposed* as the comforting security of a story it is possible to tell. This of course clearly reflects a notion of the difference between time and space in which time has a coherence and logic to its telling, while space does not. It is the view of time which Jameson might, according to some of his writings, like to see restored: time/History in the form of the Grand Narrative.[22]

However, this is also a view of temporality, as sequential coherence, that has come in for much questioning. The historical in fact can pose similar problems of representation to the geographical. *Moreover*, and ironically, it is precisely this view of history that Laclau would term spatial: '... with inexorable logic it then follows that there can be no dislocation possible in this process. If everything that happens can be explained *internally* to this world, nothing can be a mere event (which entails a radical temporality, as we have seen) and everything acquires an absolute intelligibility within the grandiose scheme of a pure spatiality. This is the Hegelian–Marxist moment' (*New Reflections*, p. 75). *Further still*, what is crucially wrong with both these views is that they are simply opposing space and time. For both Laclau and Jameson, time and space are causal closure/representability on the one hand and unrepresentability on the other. They simply differ as to which is which! What unites them, and what I argue should be questioned, is the very counterposition in this way of space and time. It is a counterposition which makes it difficult to think the social in terms of the real multiplicities of space-time. This is an argument that is being made forcefully in debates over cultural identity. '[E]thnic identity and difference are socially produced in the here and now, not archeologically salvaged from the disappearing past';[23] and Homi Bhabha enquires 'Can I just clarify that what to me is problematic about the understanding of the "fundamentalist" position in the Rushdie case is that it is *represented* as archaic, almost medieval. It may sound very strange to us, it may sound absolutely absurd to some people, but the point is that the demands over *The Satanic Verses* are being made *now*, out of a particular political state that is functioning very much in our time.'[24] Those who focus on what they see as the terrifying simultaneity of today would presumably find such a view of the world problematical, and would long for such 'ethnic identities' and 'fundamentalisms' to be (re)placed in the past so that one story of progression between differences, rather than an account of the production of a number of different differences at one moment in time, could be told. That this cannot be done is the real meaning of the contrast between thinking in terms of three dimensions plus one, and recognizing fully the inextricability of the four dimensions together. What used to be thought of as 'the problem of geographical description' is actually the more general difficulty of dealing with a world which is 4-D.

But all this leads to a fourth characteristic of an alternative view of space, as part of space-time. For precisely that element of the chaotic, or dislocated, which is intrinsic to the spatial has effects on the social phenomena that constitute it. Spatial form as 'outcome' (the happenstance juxtapositions and so forth) has emergent powers which can have effects on subsequent events. Spatial form can alter the future course of the very histories that have produced it. In relation to Laclau, what this means, ironically, is that one of the sources of the dislocation, on the existence of which he (in my view correctly) insists, is precisely the spatial. The spatial (in my terms) is precisely one of the sources of the temporal (in his terms). In relation to Jameson, the (at least partial) chaos of the spatial (which he recognizes) is precisely one of the reasons why the temporal is not, and cannot be, so tidy and monolithic a tale as he might wish. One way of

thinking about all this is to say that the spatial is integral to the production of history, and thus to the possibility of politics, just as the temporal is to geography. Another way is to insist on the inseparability of time and space, on their joint constitution through the interrelations between phenomena; on the necessity of thinking in terms of space-time.

Notes

1 H. Lefebvre, *The Production of Space* (Oxford, 1991), p. 3.
2 E. Laclau, *New Reflections on the Revolution of Our Time* (London, 1990). Thanks to Ernesto Laclau for many long discussions during the writing of this article.
3 F. Jameson, *Postmodernism, or, the Cultural Logic of Late Capitalism* (London, 1991).
4 See, for instance, the discussion in M. Rustin, 'Place and Time in Socialist Theory', *Radical Philosophy* no. 47 (1987), pp. 30–6.
5 And in this sense, of course, it could be said that Laclau's space is 'political' because any representation is political. But this is the case only in the sense that *different* spaces, different 'cognitive mappings', to borrow Jameson's terminology, can express different political stances. It still leaves each space – and thus the concept of space – as characterized by closure and immobility, as containing no sense of the open, creative possibilities for political action/effectivity. Space is the realm of the discourse of closure, of the fixation of meaning.
6 P. Anderson, 'A Culture in Contraflow', *New Left Review* 180 (March–April 1990), pp. 41–78 and *New Left Review* 182 (July–August 1990), pp. 85–137.
7 Lefebvre, p. 275.
8 See, for instance, D. Massey, *Spatial Divisions of Labour: Social Structures and the Geography of Production* (Basingstoke, 1984); D. Gregory, and J. Urry, eds., *Social Relations and Spatial Structures* (Basingstoke, 1985); and E. Soja, *Postmodern Geographies: The Reassertion of Space in Critical Social Theory* (London, 1989).
9 It should be noted that the argument that 'the spatial' is particularly important in the current era is a different one from that being made here. The argument about the nature of postmodernity is an empirical one about the characteristics of these times. The argument developed within geography was an in-principle position concerning the nature of explanation, and the role of the spatial within this.
10 See, for instance, J. Flax, 'Political Philosophy and the Patriarchal Unconscious: A Psychoanalytic Perspective

on Epistemology and Metaphysics', in S. Harding and M. B. Hintikka, eds., *Discovering Reality: Feminist Perspectives on Epistemology, Metaphysics, Methodology, and Philosophy of Science* (Dordrecht, 1983), pp. 245–81; and in the same volume, the 'Introduction' by Harding and Hintikka (pp. ix–xix), and L. Lange, 'Woman is Not a Rational Animal: On Aristotle's Biology of Reproduction', pp. 1–15; also J. Flax, 'Postmodernism and Gender Relations in Feminist Theory', in L. J. Nicholson, ed., *Feminism/Postmodernism* (London, 1990), pp. 39–62, and N. Hartsock, 'Foucault on Power: A Theory for Women?' in the same volume, pp. 157–75.

11 N. Jay, 'Gender and Dichotomy', *Feminist Studies* vol. 7, no. 1 (Spring, 1981), pp. 38–56.

12 G. Lloyd, *The Man of Reason: 'Male' and 'Female' in Western Philosophy* (London, 1984).

13 See, for instance, D. Dinnerstein, *The Rocking of the Cradle and the Ruling of the World* (London, 1987); M. le Doeuff, *Hipparchia's Choice: An Essay Concerning Women, Philosophy, Etc.* (Oxford, 1991); and Lloyd.

14 Soja; and D. Gregory, 'Chinatown, Part Three? Soja and the Missing Spaces of Social Theory', *Strategies*, no. 3 (1990).

15 K. Ross, *The Emergence of Social Space: Rimbaud and the Paris Commune* (Basingstoke, 1988); Eagleton's *Foreword*, p. xii.

16 S. de Beauvoir, *The Second Sex* (1949), trans. H. M. Parshley (Harmondsworth, 1972), p. 97.

17 M. Foucault, 'Of Other Spaces', *Diacritics* (Spring 1986), p. 22.

18 Jameson, p. 374.

19 D. Massey, 'Power–Geometry and a Progressive Sense of Place', in J. Bird et al., eds., *Mapping the Futures* (London: Routledge, 1993).

20 H. C. Darby, 'The Problem of Geographical Description', *Transactions of the Institute of British Geographers*, vol. 30 (1962), pp. 1–14.

21 Ibid., p. 2.

22 I am hesitant here in interpreting Jameson because, inevitably, his position has developed over the course of his work. I am sure that he would not in fact see narrative as unproblematic. Yet the counterposition of it to his concept of spatiality, and the way in which he formulates that concept, does lead, in those parts of his argument, to that impression being given.

23 M. P. Smith, 'Postmodernism, Urban Ethnography, and the New Social Space of Ethnic Identity', forthcoming in *Theory and Society*.

24 In 'Interview with Homi Bhabha' in J. Rutherford, ed., *Identity: Community, Culture, Difference* (London, 1990), p. 215. At this point, as at a number of others, the argument links up with the discussion by Peter Osborne in his 'Modernity is a Qualitative, Not a Chronological, Category', *New Left Review* 192 (March–April 1992), pp. 65–84.

27

"The Body as an Accumulation Strategy" (2000)

David Harvey

[I]t is crystal clear to me that the body is an accumulation strategy in the deepest sense. (Donna Haraway, *Society and Space,* 1995, 510)

Capital circulates, as it were, through the body of the laborer as variable capital and thereby turns the laborer into a mere appendage of the circulation of capital itself. (David Harvey, *The Limits to Capital,* 1982, 157)

In fact the two processes − the accumulation of men and the accumulation of capital − cannot be separated. (Michel Foucault, *Discipline and Punish,* 1975 [1995], 221)

Why focus on these citations? In part the answer rests on the extraordinary efflorescence of interest in 'the body' as a grounding for all sorts of theoretical enquiries over the last two decades or so. But why this efflorescence? The short answer is that a contemporary loss of confidence in previously established categories has provoked a return to the body as the irreducible basis for understanding (cf. Lowe, 1995, 14). But viewing the body as the irreducible locus for the determination of all values, meanings, and significations is not new. It was fundamental to many strains of pre-Socratic philosophy and the idea that 'man' or 'the body' is 'the measure of all things' has had a long and interesting history. For the ancient Greeks, for example,

'measure' went far beyond the idea of comparison with some external standard. It was regarded as 'a form of insight into the essence of everything' perceived through the senses and the mind. Such insight into inner meanings and proportionalities was considered fundamental in achieving a clear perception of the overall realities of the world and, hence, fundamental to living a harmonious and well-ordered life. Our modern views, as Bohm (1983) points out, have lost this subtlety and become relatively gross and mechanical, although some of our terminology (e.g. the notion of 'measure' in music and art) indicates a broader meaning.

The resurrection of interest in the body in contemporary debates does provide, then, a welcome opportunity to reassess the bases (epistemological and ontological) of all forms of enquiry. Feminists and queer theorists have pioneered the way as they have sought to unravel issues of gender and sexuality in theory and political practices. And the question of how measure lost its connexion to bodily well-being has come back into focus as an epistemological problem of some significance (Poovey, 1998). The thesis I want to pursue here is that the *manner* of this return to 'the body as the measure of all things' is crucial to determining how values and meanings are to be constructed and understood. I want in particular to return to a broader relational meaning of the body as 'the measure of all things' and propose a more dialectical way of understanding the body that can better connect discourses on the body with that other discursive shift that has placed 'globalization' at the center of debate.

1 Bodily Processes

I begin with two fundamental propositions. The first, drawn from writers as diverse as Marx (1964 edition), Elias (1978), Gramsci (1971 edition), Bourdieu (1984), Stafford (1991), Lefebvre (1991), Haraway (1991), Butler (1993), Grosz (1994), and Martin (1994), is that the body is an unfinished project, historically and geographically malleable in certain ways. It is not, of course, infinitely or even easily malleable and certain of its inherent ('natural' or biologically inherited) qualities cannot be erased. But the body continues to evolve and change in ways that reflect both an internal transformative dynamics (often the focus of psychoanalytic work) and the effect of external processes (most often invoked in social constructionist approaches).

The second proposition, broadly consistent with (if not implicitly contained in) the first, is that the body is not a closed and sealed entity, but a relational 'thing' that is created, bounded, sustained, and ultimately dissolved in a spatiotemporal flux of multiple processes. This entails a relational–dialectical view in which the body (construed as a thing-like entity) internalizes the effects of the processes that create, support, sustain, and dissolve it. The body which we inhabit and which is for us the irreducible measure of all things is not itself irreducible. This makes the body problematic, particularly as 'the measure of all things.'

The body is internally contradictory by virtue of the multiple socio-ecological processes that converge upon it. For example, the metabolic processes that

sustain a body entail exchanges with its environment. If the processes change, then the body either transforms and adapts or ceases to exist. Similarly the mix of performative activities available to the body in a given place and time are not independent of the technological, physical, social, and economic environment in which that body has its being. And the representational practices that operate in society likewise shape the body (and in the forms of dress and postures propose all manner of additional symbolic meanings). This means that any challenges to a dominant system of representation of the body (e.g. those mounted by feminists and queer theorists in recent years) become direct challenges to bodily practices. The net effect is to say that different processes (physical and social) 'produce' (both materially and representationally) radically different kinds of bodies. Class, racial, gender, and all manner of other distinctions are marked upon the human body by virtue of the different socio-ecological processes that do their work upon that body.

To put the matter this way is not to view the body as a passive product of external processes. What is remarkable about living entities is the way they capture diffuse energy or information flows and assemble them into complex but well-ordered forms. Creating order out of chaos is, as Prigogyne and Stengers (1984) point out, a vital property of biological systems. As a 'desiring machine' capable of creating order not only within itself but also in its environs, the human body is active and transformative in relation to the processes that produce, sustain, and dissolve it. Thus, bodily persons endowed with semiotic capacities and moral will make their bodies foundational elements in what we have long called 'the body politic.'

To conceptualize the body (the individual and the self) as porous in relation to the environment frames 'self-other' relations (including the relation to 'nature') in a particular way. If, for example, we understand the body to internalize all there is (a strong doctrine of internal relations of the sort I have outlined elsewhere – see Harvey, 1996, Chapter 2) then the reverse proposition also holds. If the self internalizes all things then the self can be 'the measure of all things.' This idea goes back to Protagoras and the Greeks. It allows the individual to be viewed as some kind of decentered center of the cosmos, or, as Munn (1985, 14, 17), in her insightful analysis of social practices on the Melanesian island of Gawa, prefers to put it, 'bodily spacetime serves as a condensed sign of the wider spacetime of which it is a part.' It is only if the body is viewed as being open and porous to the world that it can meaningfully be considered in this way. It is not how the body is seen in the dominant Western tradition. Strathern (1988, 135) underlines the problem:

> The socialized, internally controlled Western person must emerge as a *microcosm of the domesticating process* by which natural resources are put to cultural use ... The only internal relation here is the way a person's parts 'belong' to him or herself. Other relationships bear in from outside. A person's attributes are thus modified by external pressure, as are the attributes of things, but they remain intrinsic to his or her identity.

But in the Melanesian case:

> [The] person is a living commemoration of the actions which produced it ... persons are the objectified form of relationships, and it is not survival of the self that is at issue but the survival or termination of relations. Eating does not necessarily imply nurture; it is not an intrinsically beneficiary act, as it is taken to be in the Western commodity view that regards the self as thereby perpetuating its own existence. Rather, eating exposes the Melanesian person to all the hazards of the relationships of which he/she is composed ... Growth in social terms is not a reflex of nourishment; rather, in being a proper receptacle for nourishment, the nourished person bears witness to the effectiveness of a relationship with the mother, father, sister's husband or whoever is doing the feeding ... Consumption is not a simple matter of self-replacement, then, but the recognition and monitoring of relationships ... The self as individual subject exists ... in his or her capacity to transform relations. (Strathern, 1988, 302)

This relational conception of the body, of self, individual, and, consequently, of political identity is captured in the Western tradition only in dialectical modes of argumentation. Traces of it can also be found in the contemporary work of deep ecologists (cf. Naess and Rothenberg, 1989) and the view is now widespread in literary and feminist theory. It constitutes a rejection of the world view traditionally ascribed to Descartes, Newton, and Locke, which grounds the ideal of the 'civilized' and 'individualized' body (construed as an entity in absolute space and time and as a site of inalienable and bounded property rights) in much of Western thought.

It then follows that the manner of production of spacetime is inextricably connected with the production of the body. 'With the advent of Cartesian logic,' Lefebvre (1991, 1) complains, 'space had entered the realm of the absolute ... space came to dominate, by containing them, all senses and all bodies.' Lefebvre and Foucault (particularly in *Discipline and Punish*) here make common cause: the liberation of the senses and the human body from the absolutism of that produced world of Newtonian/Cartesian space and time becomes central to their emancipatory strategies. And that means challenging the mechanistic and absolute view by means of which the body is contained and disciplined. But by what bodily practices was this Cartesian/Newtonian conception of spacetime produced? And how can such conceptions be subverted?

We here encounter a peculiar conundrum. On the one hand, to return to the human body as the fount of all experience (including that of space and time) is presently regarded as a means (now increasingly privileged) to challenge the whole network of abstractions (scientific, social, political-economic) through which social relations, power relations, institutions, and material practices get defined, represented, and regulated. But on the other hand, no human body is outside of social processes of determination. To return to it is, therefore, to instantiate the social processes being purportedly rebelled against. If, for example, workers are transformed, as Marx suggests in *Capital*, into appendages of capital in both the work place and the consumption sphere (or, as Foucault prefers it, bodies are made over into *docile bodies* by the rise of a powerful disciplinary apparatus, from the eighteenth century onwards) then how can their bodies be a measure, sign, or receiver of anything outside of the circulation of capital or of the various mechanisms that discipline them? Or, to take a more contemporary version of the same argument, if we are all now *cyborgs* (as Haraway in her celebrated manifesto on the topic suggests), then how can we measure anything outside of that deadly embrace of the machine as extension of our own body and body as extension of the machine?

So while return to the body as the site of a more authentic (epistemological and ontological) grounding of the theoretical abstractions that have for too long ruled purely as abstractions may be justified, that return cannot in and of itself guarantee anything except the production of a narcissistic self-referentiality. Haraway (1991, 190) sees the difficulty. 'Objectivity,' she declares, 'turns out to be about particular and specific embodiment and definitely not about the false vision promising transcendence of all limits and responsibility.' So whose body is it that is to be the measure of all things? Exactly how and what is it in a position to measure? These are deep questions to which we will perforce return again and again. We cannot begin to answer them, however, without some prior understanding of how bodies are socially produced.

2 The Theory of the Bodily Subject in Marx

Let us suppose that Marx's categories are not dismissed as 'thoroughly destabilised.' I do not defend that supposition, though I note that from the *Economic and Philosophical Manuscripts* onwards Marx (1964 edition, 143) grounded his ontological and epistemological arguments on real sensual bodily interaction with the world:

> *Sense-perception* must be the basis of all science. Only when it proceeds from sense-perception in the two-fold form of *sensuous* consciousness and of *sensuous* need – that is, only when science proceeds from nature – is it *true* science.

Marx also elaborated a philosophy of internal relations and of dialectics consistent with the relational conception of the body outlined above (particularly by Strathern). The contemporary rush to return to the body as the irreducible basis of all argument is, therefore, a rush to return to the point where Marx, among many others, began.

While he does not tell us everything we might want to know, Marx does propose a theory of the production of the bodily subject under capitalism. Since we all live within the world of capital circulation and accumulation this has to be a part of any argument about the nature of the contemporary body. To evade it (on the specious grounds that Marx's categories are destabilized or, worse still, outmoded and unfashionable) is to evade a vital aspect of how the body must be problematized. And while Marx's theorizing in *Capital* is often read (incorrectly, as I shall hope to show) as a pessimistic account of how bodies, construed as passive entities occupying particular performative economic roles, are shaped by the external forces of capital circulation and accumulation, it is precisely this analysis that informs his other accounts of how transformative processes of human resistance, desire for reform, rebellion, and revolution can and do occur.

A preparatory step is to broaden somewhat the conventional Marxian definition of 'class' (or, more exactly, of 'class relation') under capitalism to mean *positionality in relation to capital circulation and accumulation*. Marx often fixed this relation in terms of property rights over the means of production (including, in the laborer's case, property rights to his or her own body), but I want to argue that this definition is too narrow to capture the content even of Marx's own analyses (Marx, recall, avoided any formal sociological definitions of class throughout his works). Armed with such a definition of 'positionality with respect to capital circulation and accumulation' we can better articulate the internal contradictions of multiple positionalities within which human beings operate. The laborer as person is a worker, consumer, saver, lover, and bearer of culture, and can even be an occasional employer and landed proprietor, whereas the laborer as an economic role – the category Marx analyses in *Capital* – is singular.

Consider, now, one distinctive systemic concept that Marx proposed. *Variable capital* refers to the sale/purchase and use of labor power as a commodity. But as Marx's analysis proceeds it becomes evident that there is a distinct circulation process to variable capital itself. The laborer (a person) sells labor power (a commodity) to the capitalist to use in the labor process in return for a money wage which permits the laborer to purchase capitalist-produced commodities in order to live in order to return to work ... Marx's distinction between the laborer (*qua* person, body, will) and labor power (that which is extracted from the body of the laborer as a commodity) immediately provides an opening for radical critique. Laborers are necessarily alienated because their creative capacities are appropriated as the commodity labor power by capitalists. But we can broaden the question: what effect does the circulation of variable capital (the extraction of labor power and surplus value) have on the bodies (persons and subjectivities) of those through whom it circulates? The answer initially breaks down into a consideration of what happens at different moments of productive consumption, exchange, and individual consumption.

Productive consumption

Productive consumption of the commodity labor power in the labor process under the control of the capitalist requires, *inter alia*, the mobilization of 'animal spirits,' sexual drives, affective feelings, and creative powers of labor to a given purpose defined by capital. It means: harnessing basic human powers of cooperation/collaboration; the skilling, deskilling, and reskilling of the powers of labor in accord with technological requirements; acculturation to routinization of tasks; enclosure within strict spatiotemporal rhythms of regulated (and sometimes spatially confined) activities; frequent subordinations of bodily rhythms and desires 'as an appendage of the machine;' socialization into long hours of concentrated labor at variable but often increasing intensity; development of divisions of labor of different qualities (depending upon the heterogeneity or homogeneity of tasks, the organization of detailed versus social divisions of labor); responsiveness to hierarchy and submission to authority structures within the work place; separations between mental and manual operations and powers; and, last but not least, the production of variability, fluidity, and flexibility of labor powers able to respond to those rapid revolutions in production processes so typical of capitalist development.

I supply this list (drawn from Marx's *Capital*) mainly to demonstrate how the exigencies of capitalist production push the limits of the working body – its capacities and possibilities – in a variety of different and often fundamentally contradictory directions. On the one hand capital requires educated and flexible laborers, but on the other hand it refuses the idea that laborers should think for themselves. While education of the laborer appears important it cannot be the kind of education that permits free thinking. Capital

requires certain kinds of skills but abhors any kind of monopolizable skill. While a 'trained gorilla' may suffice for some tasks, for others creative, responsible workers are called for. While subservience and respect for authority (sometimes amounting to abject submission) is paramount, the creative passions, spontaneous responses, and animal spirits necessary to the 'form-giving fire' of the labor process must also be liberated and mobilized. Healthy bodies may be needed but deformities, pathologies, sickness are often produced. Marx highlights such contradictions:

> [L]arge scale industry, by its very nature, necessitates variation of labour, fluidity of functions, and mobility of the worker in all directions. But on the other hand, in its capitalist form it reproduces the old division of labour with ossified particularities. We have seen how this absolute contradiction does away with all repose, all fixity and all security as far as the worker's life situation is concerned … But if, at present, variation of labour imposes itself after the manner of an overpowering natural law, and with the blindly destructive action of a natural law that meets with obstacles everywhere, large scale industry, through its very catastrophes, makes the recognition of variation of labour and hence of the fitness of the worker for the maximum number of different kinds of labour into a question of life and death. (Marx, 1976 edition, 617)

Marx sees these contradictions being worked out historically and dialectically (largely though not solely through the use of coercive force and active struggle). But part of what the creative history of capitalism has been about is discovering new ways (and potentialities) in which the human body can be put to use as the bearer of the capacity to labor. Marx observes (1976 edition, 617), for example, that 'technology discovered the few grand fundamental forms of motion which, despite all the diversity of the instruments used, apply necessarily to every productive action of the human body.' Older capacities of the human body are reinvented, new capacities revealed. The development of capitalist production entails a radical transformation in what the working body is about. The unfinished project of the human body is pushed in a particular set of contradictory directions. And a whole host of sciences for engineering and exploring the limits of the human body as a productive machine, as a fluid organism, has been established to explore these possibilities. Gramsci (1971 edition), among others, thus emphasizes again and again how capitalism is precisely about the production of a new kind of laboring body.

While such contradictions may be internalized within the labor force as a whole, this does not necessarily mean that they are internalized within the body of each laborer. Indeed, it is the main thrust of Marx's own presentation that the 'collective body' of the labor force is broken down into hierarchies of skill, of authority, of mental and manual functions, etc. in such a way to render the category of variable capital internally heterogeneous. And this heterogeneity is unstable. The perpetual shifting that occurs within the capitalist mode of production ensures that requirements, definitions of skill, systems of authority, divisions of labor, etc. are never stabilized for long. So while the collective laborer will be fragmented and segmented, the definitions of and relations between the segments will be unstable and the movements of individual laborers within and between segments correspondingly complex. It is not hard to see that in the face of these contradictions and multiple instabilities, capitalism will require some sort of disciplinary apparatus of surveillance, punishment and ideological control that Marx frequently alludes to and which Foucault elaborates upon in ways that I find broadly complementary rather than antagonistic to Marx's project. But the instability never goes away (as witnessed by the whole historical geography of skilling, deskilling, reskilling, etc.). While the instability is disconcerting, sometimes destructive, and always difficult to cope with, it provides multiple opportunities for subversion and opposition on the part of the laborers.

But whose body is inserted into the circulation of variable capital and with what effects? Marx does not provide any systematic answer to that question in part because this was not the primary object of his theoretical enquiry (he largely dealt with economic roles rather than with persons). Who exactly gets inserted where is a detailed historical-geographical question that defies any simple theoretical answer. Marx is plainly aware that bodies are differentiated and marked by different physical productive capacities and qualities according to history, geography, culture, and tradition. He is also aware that signs of race, ethnicity, age,

and gender are used as external measures of what a certain kind of laborer is capable of or permitted to do. The incorporation of women and children into the circulation of variable capital in nineteenth-century Britain occurred for certain distinctive reasons that Marx is at pains to elaborate upon. This in turn provoked distinctive effects, one of which was to turn the struggle over the length of the working day and the regulation of factory employment into a distinctive struggle to protect women and children from the impacts of capitalism's 'werewolf hunger' for surplus value. The employment of women and children as wage laborers, furthermore, not only provided 'a new foundation for the division of labor' (Marx, 1976, 615), it also posed (and continues to pose) a fundamental challenge to many traditional conceptions of the family and of gender roles:

> However terrible and disgusting the dissolution of the old family ties within the capitalist system may appear, large scale industry, by assigning an important part in socially organized processes of production, outside the sphere of the domestic economy, to women, young persons and children of both sexes, does nevertheless create a new economic foundation for a higher form of the family and of relations between the sexes ... It is also obvious that the fact that the collective working group is composed of individuals of both sexes and all ages must under the appropriate conditions turn into a source of humane development, although in its spontaneously developed, brutal, capitalist form, the system works in the opposite direction, and becomes a pestiferous source of corruption and slavery, since here the worker exists for the process of production, and not the process of production for the worker.

In remarks on slavery, colonialism, and immigrants (e.g. the Irish into Britain), Marx makes clear that constructions of race and ethnicity are likewise implicated in the circulation process of variable capital. Insofar as gender, race, and ethnicity are all understood as social constructions rather than as essentialist categories, so the effect of their insertion into the circulation of variable capital (including positioning within the internal heterogeneity of collective labor and, hence, within the division of labor and the class system) has to be seen as a powerful force reconstructing them in distinctively capitalist ways.

There are a number of corollaries. Firstly, the productiveness of a person gets reduced to the ability to produce surplus value. To be a productive worker, Marx (1976, 644) ironically notes, 'is therefore not a piece of luck but a misfortune;' the only value that the laborer can have is not determined in terms of work done and useful social effect but through 'a specifically social relation of production … which stamps the worker as capital's direct means of valorization.' The gap between what the laborer as person might desire and what is demanded of the commodity labor power extracted from his or her body is the nexus of alienation. And while workers as persons may value themselves in a variety of ways depending upon how they understand their productivity, usefulness and value to others, the more restricted social valuation given by their capacity to produce surplus value for capital necessarily remains central to their lives (as even highly educated middle-level managers find out when they, too, are laid off). Exactly what that value is, however, depends on conditions external to the labor process, hinging, therefore, upon the question of exchange.

Secondly, lack of productivity, sickness (or of any kind of pathology) gets defined within this circulation process as inability to go to work, inability to perform adequately within the circulation of variable capital (to produce surplus value) or to abide by its disciplinary rules (the institutional effects elaborated on by Rothman [1971] and Foucault [1995] in the construction of asylums and prisons are already strongly registered in Marx's chapters on 'The Working Day' and the 'So-Called Primitive Accumulation'). Those who cannot (for physical, psychic, or social reasons) continue to function as variable capital, furthermore, fall either into the 'hospital' of the industrial reserve army (sickness is defined under capitalism broadly as inability to work) or else into that undisciplined inferno of the lumpenproletariat (read 'underclass') for whom Marx regrettably had so little sympathy. The circulation of variable capital, being so central to how capitalism operates as a social system, defines roles of employed 'insiders' and unemployed 'outsiders' (often victimized and stigmatized) that have ramifications for society as a whole. This brings us back to the moment of 'exchange.'

Exchange of variable capital

The commodity which the laborer (*qua* person) exchanges with the capitalist is labor power, the capacity to engage in concrete labor. The basic condition of the contract is supposedly that the capitalist has the right to whatever the laborer produces, has the right to direct the work, determine the labor process, and have free use of the capacity to labor during the hours and at the rate of remuneration stipulated in the contract. The rights of capital are frequently contested and it is interesting to see on what grounds. While capitalists may have full rights to the commodity labor power, they do not have legal rights over the person of the laborer (that would be slavery). Marx insists again and again that this is a fundamental principle of wage labor under capitalism.

The laborer as person should have full rights over his or her own body and should always enter the labor market under conditions of freedom of contract even if, as Marx (1976, 272–3) notes, a worker is 'free in the double sense that as a free individual he can dispose of his labour-power as his own commodity, and that, on the other hand, he has no other commodity for sale, i.e. he is rid of them, he is free of all the objects needed for the realization of his labour power.' But the distinction between laborer as person and labor power has further implications. The capitalist has not the formal right to put the body of the person at risk, for example, and working practices that do so are open to challenge. This principle carries over even into the realm of the cultural and bodily capital (as Bourdieu defines them): hence much of the resistance to de-skilling, redefinitions of skill, etc. Of course, these legalities are continually violated under capitalism and situations frequently do arise in which the body and person of the laborer is taken over under conditions akin to slavery. But Marx's point is that preservation of the integrity and fullness of the laboring person and body within the circulation process of variable capital is the fulcrum upon which contestation and class struggle both within and without the labor process occurs. Even bourgeois legality (as incorporated in the Factory Acts then and in, say, Occupational Safety and Health regulations now) has to concede the difference between the right to the commodity labor power and the non-right to the person who is bearer of that commodity.

This struggle carries over into the determination of the value of variable capital itself, because here the 'neediness' of the body of the laborer forms the datum upon which conditions of contract depend. In *Capital*, Marx, for purposes of analysis, presumes that in a given place and time such needs are fixed and known (only in this way can he get a clear fix upon how capital is produced through surplus value extraction). But Marx well understood that these conditions are never fixed but depend on physical circumstances (e.g. climate), cultural and social conditions, the long history of class struggle over what is a liveable wage for the laborer, as well as upon a moral conception as to what is or is not tolerable in a civilized society. Consider how Marx (1976, 341) presents the matter in his chapter on 'The Working Day':

> During part of the day the vital force must rest, sleep; during another part the man has to satisfy physical needs, to feed, wash and clothe himself. Besides these purely physical limitations, the extension of the working day encounters moral obstacles. The worker needs time in which to satisfy his intellectual and social requirements, and the extent and number of those requirements is conditioned by the general level of civilization. The length of the working day therefore fluctuates within boundaries that are physical and social.

Marx's primary point of critique of capitalism is that it so frequently violates, disfigures, subdues, maims, and destroys the integrity of the laboring body (even in ways that can be dangerous to the further accumulation of capital). It is, furthermore, in terms of the potentialities and possibilities of that laboring body (its 'species being' as Marx [1964 edition] called it in his early work) that the search for an alternative mode of production is initially cast.

But surplus value depends upon the difference between what labor gets (the value of labor power) and what labor creates (the value of the commodity produced). The use value of the commodity labor power to the capitalist is that it can engage in concrete labor in such a way as to embed a given amount of abstract labor in the commodity produced. For the capitalist it is abstract labor that counts and the value of labor power and the concrete practices of the laborer are disciplined and regulated within the circulation of variable capital by the 'laws of value' which take abstract labor as their datum.

Abstract labor – value – is measured through exchange of commodities over space and time and ultimately on the world market. Value is a distinctive spatiotemporal construction depending upon the development of a whole array of spatiotemporal practices (including the territorialization of the earth's surface through property rights and state formation and the development of geographical networks and systems of exchange for money and all commodities, including that of labor power itself). The value of labor power to the capitalist is itself contingent upon the realization of values across a world of socially constructed spatiotemporal political-economic practices. This limits the value that the laborer can acquire in a particular place both in production and in the market. Furthermore, the conditions of exchange of labor power are limited in labor markets both by systematic biases (gender and racial disparities in remuneration for comparative work are well documented) and by mobilization of an industrial reserve army (either *in situ* or through the migratory movements of both capital and labor searching for 'better' contractual conditions).

It is exactly at this point that the connection between what we now refer to as 'globalization' and the body becomes explicit. But how should this be thought about? Marx depicts the circulation of variable capital as a 'commodity for commodity' exchange: the worker exchanges the use value of labor power for the use value of the commodities that can be bought for the money wage. Exchanges of this sort are usually highly localized and place-specific. The worker must take his or her body to work each day (even under conditions of telecommuting). But labor power is inserted as a commodity into a Money–Commodity–Money circulation process which easily escapes the spatiotemporal restraints of local labor markets and which makes for capital accumulation on the world stage. Accumulation accelerates turnover time (it shortens working periods, circulation times, etc.) while simultaneously annihilating space through time while preserving certain territorialities (of the factory and the nation state) as domains of surveillance and social control. Spatiotemporality defined at one scale (that of 'globalization' and all its associated meanings) intersects with bodies that function at a much more localized scale.

Translation across spatiotemporal scales is here accomplished by the intersection of two qualitatively different circulation processes, one of which is defined through the long historical geography of capital accumulation while the other depends upon the production and reproduction of the laboring body in a far more restricted space. This leads to some serious disjunctions, of the sort that Hareven (1982) identifies in her analysis of *Family Time and Industrial Time*. But as Hareven goes on to show, these two spatiotemporal systems, though qualitatively different from each other, have to be made 'cogredient' or 'compossible' (see Harvey, 1996, for a fuller explication of these terms) with each other. Thus do links between the 'local' and the 'global' become established. Different bodily qualities and modes of valuation (including the degree of respect for the bodily integrity and dignity of the laborer) achieved in different places are brought into a spatially competitive environment through the circulation of capital. Uneven geographical development of the bodily practices and sensibilities of those who sell their labor power becomes one of the defining features of class struggle as waged by both capital and labor.

Put in more direct contemporary terms, the creation of unemployment through down-sizing, the redefinitions of skills and remunerations for skills, the intensification of labor processes and of autocratic systems of surveillance, the increasing despotism of orchestrated detailed divisions of labor, the insertion of immigrants (or, what amounts to the same thing, the migration of capital to alternative labor sources), and the coerced competitive struggle between different bodily practices and modes of valuation achieved under different historical and cultural conditions, all contribute to the uneven geographical valuation of laborers as persons. The manifest effects upon the bodies of laborers who live lives embedded in the circulation of variable capital is powerful indeed. Sweatshops in New York mimic similar establishments in Guatemala and subject the workers incorporated therein to a totalizing and violently repressive regime of body disciplines. The construction of specific spatiotemporal relations through the circulation of capital likewise constructs a connection between the designer shirts we wear upon our backs, the Nike shoes we sport, and the oriental carpets upon which we walk, and the grossly exploited labor of tens of thousands of women and children in Central America, Indonesia, and Pakistan (just to name a few of the points of production of such commodities).

The moment of consumption

The laborer does not only lie in the path of variable capital as producer and exchanger. He/she also lies in that circulation process as consumer and reproducer of self (both individually and socially). Once possessed of money the laborer is endowed with all the autonomy that attaches to any market practice:

> It is the worker himself who converts the money into whatever use-values he desires; it is he who buys commodities as he wishes and, as the *owner of money*, as the buyer of goods, he stands in precisely the same relationship to the sellers of goods as any other buyer. Of course, the conditions of his existence – and the limited amount of money he can earn – compel him to make his purchases from a fairly restricted selection of goods. But some variation is possible as we can see from the fact that newspapers, for example, form part of the essential purchases of the urban English worker. He can save and hoard a little. Or else he can squander his money on drink. Even so, he acts as a free agent; he must pay his own way; he is responsible to himself for the way he spends his wages.   (Marx, 1976, 1033)

This is an example of Marx's tacit appeal to 'positionality in relationship to capital accumulation' as a practical definition of class relations. As the focus shifts so does the meaning of class positionality. The laborer has limited freedom to choose not only a personal lifestyle but also, through the collective exercise of demand preferences, he/she can express his/her desires (individually and collectively) and thereby influence the capitalist choice of what to produce. Elaboration on that idea permits us to see, as we look at the circulation of variable capital as a whole, that what is true for the individual laborer is rather more limited when looked at from the standpoint of the collectivity:

> The capitalist class is constantly giving to the working class drafts, in the form of money, on a portion of the product produced by the latter and appropriated by the former. The workers give these drafts back just as constantly to the capitalists, and thereby withdraw from the

latter their allotted share of their own product ... The individual consumption of the worker, whether it occurs inside or outside the workshop, inside or outside the labour process, remains an aspect of the production and reproduction of capital ... From the standpoint of society, then, the working class, even when it stands outside the direct labour process, is just as much an appendage of capital as the lifeless instruments of labour are. (Marx, 1976, 713, 719)

Deeper consideration of what amounts to a 'company store' relation between capital and labor is instructive. The disposable income of the laborers forms an important mass of effective demand for capitalist output (this is the relation that Marx explores at great length in Volume 2 of *Capital*). Accumulation for accumulation's sake points towards either an increasing mass of laborers to whom necessities can be sold or a changing standard of living of the laborers (it usually means both). The production of new needs, the opening up of entirely new product lines that define different lifestyles and consumer habits, is introduced as an important means of crisis avoidance and crisis resolution. We can then see more clearly how it is that variable capital has to be construed as a circulation process (rather than as a single causal arrow) for it is through the payment of wages that the disposable income to buy the product of the capitalists is partially assured.

But all of this presumes 'rational consumption' on the part of the laborer – rational, that is, from the standpoint of capital accumulation (Marx, 1978 edition, 591). The organization, mobilization, and channeling of human desires, the active political engagement with tactics of persuasion, surveillance, and coercion, become part of the consumptuary apparatus of capitalism, in turn producing all manner of pressures on the body as a site of and a performative agent for 'rational consumption' for further accumulation (cf. Henry Ford's obsession with training social workers to monitor the budgets of his workers).

But the terms of 'rational consumption' are by no means fixed, in part because of the inevitable destabilizing effects of perpetual revolutions in capitalist technologies and products (revolutions which affect the household economy as well as the factory), but also because, given the discretionary element in the worker's use of disposable income, there is as much potential for social struggle over lifestyle and associated bodily

practices as there is in the realm of production itself. Struggles over the social wage – over, for example, the extent, direction, and distributional effects of state expenditures – have become critical in establishing the baseline of what might be meant by a proper standard of living in a 'civilized' country. Struggles over the relation between 'housework' and 'labor in the market' and the gender allocation of tasks within domestic settings also enter into the picture (cf. Marx's 1976 edition, 518, commentary on how the importance of domestic labor gets 'concealed by official political economy' and the revived debate in the 1970s on the role of housework in relation to the circulation of variable capital).

This moment in the circulation of variable capital, though not totally absent in Marx's account, is not strongly emphasized. With the United States (and, presumably, much of the advanced capitalist world) in mind, Lowe (1995, 67) now argues that:

Lifestyle is the social relations of consumption in late capitalism, as distinct from class as the social relations of production. The visual construction and presentation of self in terms of consumption relations has by now over shadowed the class relations of production in the workplace ... [Consumption] is itself dynamically developed by the design and production of changing product characteristics, the juxtaposition of image and sign in lifestyle and format, and the segmentation of consumer markets.

This suggests a double contradiction within the advanced capitalist world (and a nascent contradiction within developing countries). First, by submitting unquestioningly and without significant struggle to the dictates of capital in production (or by channeling struggle solely to the end of increasing disposable income), workers may open for themselves wider terrains of differentiating choice (social or individual) with respect to lifestyle, structures of feeling, household organization, reproductive activities, expressions of desire, pursuit of pleasures, etc. within the moment of consumption. This does not automatically deliver greater happiness and satisfaction. As Marx (1965 edition, 33) notes:

[A]lthough the pleasures of the labourer have increased, the social gratification which they afford has fallen in comparison with the increased pleasures of the capitalist. Our wants and pleasures have their origin in society; we therefore measure them in relation to society; we do not measure them in relation to the objects which serve for their gratification. Since they are of a social nature, they are of a relative nature.

Conversely, by locking workers into certain conceptions of lifestyle, consumer habits, and desire, capitalists can more easily secure compliance within the labor process while capturing distinctive and proliferating market niches for their sales.

Struggles arise between how workers individually or collectively exercise their consumer and lifestyle choices and how capitalist forces try to capture and guide those choices towards rational consumption for sustained accumulation. Marx does not scrutinize such conflicts but no particular difficulty attaches to integrating them into his framework. Plainly, the process is marked by extraordinary heterogeneity at the same time as it is fraught with instability. For example, whole communities of lifestyle (such as those shaped by working classes in industrial settings or by distinctive cultural traditions) may be created within the circulation of variable capital only ultimately to be dissolved (even in the face of considerable resistance) by the same processes that led to their initial formation. The recent history of deindustrialization is full of examples of this.

A wide range of bodily practices and cultural choices with respect to consumption can in principle be embedded in the circulation of variable capital. The range depends, of course, upon the amount of discretionary income in the laborer's possession (and, plainly, the billion or so workers living on less than a dollar a day cannot exercise anywhere near the amount of influence as well-paid workers in the advanced capitalist countries). Variable capital does not determine the specific nature of consumer choices or even of consumer culture, though it certainly works to powerful effect. This means that production must internalize powerful effects of heterogeneous cultural traditions and consumer choices, whether registered collectively through political action (to establish a 'social wage' through welfare programs) or individually through personal consumption choices. It is in this sense that it is meaningful to speak of the moments

of production and consumption as a matter of internal relations, the one with the other.

[…]

Bibliography

Bohm, D. 1983, *Wholeness and the Implicate Order*, London.

Bourdieu, P. 1984, *Distinction: A Social Critique of the Judgement of Taste*, London.

Butler, J. 1993, *Bodies That Matter: On the Discursive Limits of 'Sex'*, New York.

Elias, N. 1978, *The Civilising Process: The History of Manners*, Oxford.

Foucault, M. 1995 edition, *Discipline and Punish: The Birth of the Prison*, New York, XI–XIV.

Gramsci, A. 1971 edition, *Selections from the Prison Notebooks*, London.

Grosz, E. 1994, 'Bodies-cities,' in Colomina, B. (ed.), *Sexuality and Space*, Princeton, pp. 241–53.

Haraway, D. 1991, *Simians, Cyborgs, and Women: The Reinvention of Nature*, London.

Haraway, D. 1995, 'Nature, politics, and possibilities: a debate and discussion with David Harvey and Donna Haraway,' *Society and Space*, 13, 507–27.

Hareven, T. 1982, *Family Time and Industrial Time*, London.

Harvey, D. 1982, *The Limits to Capital*, Oxford.

Harvey, D. 1996, *Justice, Nature and the Geography of Difference*, Oxford.

Lefebvre, H. 1991, *The Production of Space*, Oxford.

Lowe, D. 1995, *The Body in Late-capitalist USA*, Durham, NC.

Martin, E. 1994, *Flexible Bodies*, Boston.

Marx K. 1964 edition, *The Economic and Philosophic Manuscripts of 1844*, New York.

Marx, K. 1965 edition, *Wages, Price and Profit*, Peking.

Marx, K. 1976 edition, *Capital*, Vol. 1, New York.

Marx, K. 1978 edition, *Capital*, Vol. 2, New York.

Munn, N. 1985, *The Fame of Gawa*, Cambridge.

Naess, A., and Rothenberg, D. 1989, *Ecology, Community and Lifestyle*, Cambridge.

Poovey, M. 1998, *A History of the Modern Fact*, Chicago.

Prigoyne, I., and Stengers, I. 1984, *Order out of Chaos: Man's New Dialogue with Nature*, New York.

Rothman, D. 1971, *The Discovery of the Asylum*, Boston.

Stafford, B. 1991, *Body Criticism: Imaging the Unseen in Enlightenment Art and Medicine*, Cambridge, Mass.

Strathern, M. 1988, *The Gender of the Gift*, Berkeley.

28

"Planet of Slums: Urban Involution and the Informal Proletariat" (2004)

Mike Davis

Sometime in the next year, a woman will give birth in the Lagos slum of Ajegunle, a young man will flee his village in west Java for the bright lights of Jakarta, or a farmer will move his impoverished family into one of Lima's innumerable *pueblos jovenes*. The exact event is unimportant and it will pass entirely unnoticed. Nonetheless it will constitute a watershed in human history. For the first time the urban population of the earth will outnumber the rural. Indeed, given the imprecisions of Third World censuses, this epochal transition may already have occurred.

The earth has urbanized even faster than originally predicted by the Club of Rome in its notoriously Malthusian 1972 report, *Limits of Growth*. In 1950 there were 86 cities in the world with a population over one million; today there are 400, and by 2015, there will be at least 550.[1] Cities, indeed, have absorbed nearly two-thirds of the global population explosion since 1950 and are currently growing by a million babies and migrants each week.[2] The present urban population (3.2 billion) is larger than the total population of the world in 1960. The global countryside, meanwhile, has reached its maximum population (3.2 billion) and will begin to shrink after 2020. As a result, cities will account for *all* future world population growth, which is expected to peak at about 10 billion in 2050.[3]

Mike Davis, "Planet of Slums: Urban Involution and the Informal Proletariat," pp. 5–30 from *New Left Review* 26 (2004) (abridged from original version). Reprinted by permission of New Left Review.

1. The Urban Climacteric

Where are the heroes, the colonisers, the victims of the Metropolis? (Brecht, *Diary* entry, 1921)

Ninety-five per cent of this final buildout of humanity will occur in the urban areas of developing countries, whose population will double to nearly 4 billion over the next generation.[4] (Indeed, the combined urban population of China, India and Brazil already roughly equals that of Europe plus North America.) The most celebrated result will be the burgeoning of new megacities with populations in excess of 8 million, and, even more spectacularly, hypercities with more than 20 million inhabitants (the estimated urban population of the world at the time of the French Revolution).[5] In 1995 only Tokyo had incontestably reached that threshold. By 2025, according to the *Far Eastern Economic Review*, Asia alone could have ten or eleven conurbations that large, including Jakarta (24.9 million), Dhaka (25 million) and Karachi (26.5 million). Shanghai, whose growth was frozen for decades by Maoist policies of deliberate under-urbanization, could have as many as 27 million residents in its huge estuarial metro-region.[6] Mumbai (Bombay) meanwhile is projected to attain a population of 33 million, although no one knows whether such gigantic concentrations of poverty are biologically or ecologically sustainable.[7]

But if megacities are the brightest stars in the urban firmament, three-quarters of the burden of population growth will be borne by faintly visible second-tier cities and smaller urban areas: places where, as UN researchers emphasize, 'there is little or no planning to accommodate these people or provide them with services.'[8] In China (officially 43 per cent urban in 1997), the number of official cities has soared from 193 to 640 since 1978. But the great metropolises, despite extraordinary growth, have actually declined in relative share of urban population. It is, rather, the small cities and recently 'citized' towns that have absorbed the majority of the rural labour-power made redundant by post-1979 market reforms.[9] In Africa, likewise, the supernova-like growth of a few giant cities like Lagos (from 300,000 in 1950 to 10 million today) has been matched by the transformation of several dozen small towns and oases like Ouagadougou, Nouakchott, Douala, Antananarivo and Bamako into cities larger than San Francisco or Manchester. In Latin America, where primary cities long monopolized growth, secondary cities like Tijuana, Curitiba, Temuco, Salvador and Belém are now booming, 'with the fastest growth of all occurring in cities with between 100,000 and 500,000 inhabitants.'[10]

Moreover, as Gregory Guldin has urged, urbanization must be conceptualized as structural transformation along, and intensified interaction between, every point of an urban–rural continuum. In his case-study of southern China, the countryside is urbanizing *in situ* as well as generating epochal migrations. 'Villages become more like market and *xiang* towns, and county towns and small cities become more like large cities.' The result in China and much of Southeast Asia is a hermaphroditic landscape, a partially urbanized countryside that Guldin and others argue may be 'a significant new path of human settlement and development … a form neither rural nor urban but a blending of the two wherein a dense web of transactions ties large urban cores to their surrounding regions.'[11] In Indonesia, where a similar process of rural/urban hybridization is far advanced in Jabotabek (the greater Jakarta region), researchers call these novel land-use patterns *desokotas* and debate whether they are transitional landscapes or a dramatic new species of urbanism.[12]

Urbanists also speculate about the processes weaving together Third World cities into extraordinary new networks, corridors and hierarchies. For example, the Pearl River (Hong Kong–Guangzhou) and the Yangtze River (Shanghai) deltas, along with the Beijing–Tianjin corridor, are rapidly developing into urban-industrial megalopolises comparable to Tokyo–Osaka, the lower Rhine, or New York–Philadelphia. But this may only be the first stage in the emergence of an even larger structure: 'a continuous urban corridor stretching from Japan/North Korea to West Java.'[13] Shanghai, almost certainly, will then join Tokyo, New York and London as one of the 'world cities' controlling the global web of capital and information flows. The price of this new urban order will be increasing inequality within and between cities of different sizes and specializations. Guldin, for example, cites intriguing Chinese discussions over whether the ancient income-and-development chasm between city and countryside is now being replaced by an equally fundamental gap between small cities and the coastal giants.[14]

2. Back to Dickens

I saw innumerable hosts, foredoomed to darkness, dirt, pestilence, obscenity, misery and early death. (Dickens, 'A December Vision', 1850)

The dynamics of Third World urbanization both recapitulate and confound the precedents of nineteenth and early twentieth-century Europe and North America. In China the greatest industrial revolution in history is the Archimedean lever shifting a population the size of Europe's from rural villages to smog-choked sky-climbing cities. As a result, 'China [will] cease to be the predominantly rural country it has been for millennia.'[15] Indeed, the great oculus of the Shanghai World Financial Centre may soon look out upon a vast urban world little imagined by Mao or, for that matter, Le Corbusier. But in most of the developing world, city growth lacks China's powerful manufacturing-export engine as well as its vast inflow of foreign capital (currently equal to half of total foreign investment in the developing world).

Urbanization elsewhere, as a result, has been radically decoupled from industrialization, even from development *per se*. Some would argue that this is an expression of an inexorable trend: the inherent tendency of silicon capitalism to delink the growth of production from that of employment. But in sub-Saharan Africa, Latin America, the Middle East and parts of Asia, urbanization-without-growth is more obviously the legacy of a global political conjuncture – the debt crisis of the late 1970s and subsequent IMF-led restructuring of Third World economies in the 1980s – than an iron law of advancing technology. Third World urbanization, moreover, continued its breakneck pace (3.8 per cent per annum from 1960–93) through the locust years of the 1980s and early 1990s in spite of falling real wages, soaring prices and skyrocketing urban unemployment.[16]

This 'perverse' urban boom contradicted orthodox economic models which predicted that the negative feedback of urban recession should slow or even reverse migration from the countryside. The African case was particularly paradoxical. How could cities in Côte d'Ivoire, Tanzania, Gabon and elsewhere – whose economies were contracting by 2 to 5 per cent per year – still sustain population growth of 5 to 8 per cent per annum?[17] Part of the secret, of course, was that IMF- (and now WTO-) enforced policies of agricultural deregulation and 'de-peasantization' were accelerating the exodus of surplus rural labour to urban slums even as cities ceased to be job machines. Urban population growth in spite of stagnant or negative urban economic growth is the extreme face of what some researchers have labelled 'over-urbanization'.[18] It is just one of the several unexpected tracks down which a neoliberal world order has shunted millennial urbanization.

Classical social theory from Marx to Weber, of course, believed that the great cities of the future would follow in the industrializing footsteps of Manchester, Berlin and Chicago. Indeed, Los Angeles, São Paulo, Pusan and, today, Ciudad Juárez, Bangalore and Guangzhou, have roughly approximated this classical trajectory. But most cities of the South are more like Victorian Dublin which, as Emmet Larkin has emphasized, was unique amongst 'all the slumdoms produced in the western world in the nineteenth century … [because] its slums were not a product of the industrial revolution. Dublin, in fact, suffered more from the problems of de-industrialization than industrialization between 1800 and 1850.'[19]

Likewise Kinshasa, Khartoum, Dar es Salaam, Dhaka and Lima grow prodigiously despite ruined import-substitution industries, shrunken public sectors and downwardly mobile middle classes. The global forces 'pushing' people from the countryside – mechanization in Java and India, food imports in Mexico, Haiti and Kenya, civil war and drought throughout Africa, and everywhere the consolidation of small into large holdings and the competition of industrial-scale agribusiness – seem to sustain urbanization even when the 'pull' of the city is drastically weakened by debt and depression.[20] At the same time, rapid urban growth in the context of structural adjustment, currency devaluation and state retrenchment has been an inevitable recipe for the mass production of slums.[21] Much of the urban world, as a result, is rushing backwards to the age of Dickens.

The astonishing prevalence of slums is the chief theme of the historic and sombre report published last October by the United Nations' Human Settlements Programme (UN-Habitat).[22] *The Challenge of the Slums* (henceforth: *Slums*) is the first truly global audit of urban poverty. It adroitly integrates diverse urban case-studies from Abidjan to Sydney with global household data that for the first time includes China and the ex-Soviet Bloc. (The UN authors acknowledge a particular debt to Branko Milanovic, the World Bank economist who has pioneered the use of microsurveys as a powerful lens to study growing global inequality. In one of his papers, Milanovic explains: 'for the first time in human history, researchers have reasonably accurate data on the distribution of income or welfare [expenditures or consumption] amongst more than 90 per cent of the world population.')[23]

Slums is also unusual in its intellectual honesty. One of the researchers associated with the report told me that 'the "Washington Consensus" types (World Bank, IMF, etc.) have always insisted on defining the problem of global slums not as a result of globalization and inequality but rather as a result of "bad governance".' The new report, however, breaks with traditional UN circumspection and self-censorship to squarely indict neoliberalism, especially the IMF's structural adjustment programmes.[24] 'The primary direction of both national and international interventions during the last twenty years has actually increased urban poverty and slums, increased exclusion and inequality, and weakened urban elites in their efforts to use cities as engines of growth.'[25]

Slums, to be sure, neglects (or saves for later UN-Habitat reports) some of the most important land-use issues arising from super-urbanization and informal settlement, including sprawl, environmental degradation, and urban hazards. It also fails to shed much light on the processes expelling labour from the countryside or to incorporate a large and rapidly growing literature on the gender dimensions of urban poverty and informal employment. But these cavils aside, *Slums* remains an invaluable exposé that amplifies urgent research findings with the institutional authority of the United Nations. If the reports of the Intergovernmental Panel on Climate Change represent an unprecedented scientific consensus on the dangers of global warming, then *Slums* sounds an equally authoritative warning about the global catastrophe of urban poverty. (A third report someday may explore the ominous terrain of their interaction.)[26] And, for the purposes of this review, it provides an excellent framework for reconnoitering contemporary debates on urbanization, the informal economy, human solidarity and historical agency.

3. The Urbanization of Poverty

The mountain of trash seemed to stretch very far, then gradually without perceptible demarcation or boundary it became something else. But what? A jumbled and pathless collection of structures. Cardboard cartons, plywood and rotting boards, the rusting and glassless shells of cars, had been thrown together to form habitation. (Michael Thelwell, *The Harder They Come*, 1980)

The first published definition of 'slum' reportedly occurs in Vaux's 1812 *Vocabulary of the Flash Language*, where it is synonymous with 'racket' or 'criminal trade'.[27] By the cholera years of the 1830s and 1840s, however, the poor were living in slums rather than practising them. A generation later, slums had been identified in America and India, and were generally recognized as an international phenomenon. The 'classic slum' was a notoriously parochial and picturesquely local place, but reformers generally agreed with Charles Booth that all slums were characterized by an amalgam

of dilapidated housing, overcrowding, poverty and vice. For nineteenth-century Liberals, of course, the moral dimension was decisive and the slum was first and above all envisioned as a place where a social 'residuum' rots in immoral and often riotous splendour. *Slums*' authors discard Victorian calumnies, but otherwise preserve the classical definition: overcrowding, poor or informal housing, inadequate access to safe water and sanitation, and insecurity of tenure.[28]

This multi-dimensional definition is actually a very conservative gauge of what qualifies as a slum: many readers will be surprised by the UN's counter-experiential finding that only 19.6 per cent of urban Mexicans live in slums. Yet, even with this restrictive definition, *Slums* estimates that there were at least 921 million slum-dwellers in 2001: nearly equal to the population of the world when the young Engels first ventured onto the mean streets of Manchester. Indeed, neoliberal capitalism has multiplied Dickens's notorious slum of Tom-All-Alone in *Bleak House* by exponential powers. Residents of slums constitute a staggering 78.2 per cent of the urban population of the least developed countries and fully a third of the global urban population.[29] Extrapolating from the age structures of most Third World cities, at least half of the slum population is under the age of 20.[30]

The world's highest percentages of slum-dwellers are in Ethiopia (an astonishing 99.4 per cent of the urban population), Chad (also 99.4 per cent), Afghanistan (98.5 percent) and Nepal (92 per cent).[31] The poorest urban populations, however, are probably in Maputo and Kinshasa where (according to other sources) two-thirds of residents earn less than the cost of their minimum required daily nutrition.[32] In Delhi, planners complain bitterly about 'slums within slums' as squatters take over the small open spaces of the peripheral resettlement colonies into which the old urban poor were brutally removed in the mid-1970s.[33] In Cairo and Phnom Penh, recent urban arrivals squat or rent space on rooftops: creating slum cities in the air.

Slum populations are often deliberately and sometimes massively undercounted. In the late 1980s, for example, Bangkok had an 'official' poverty rate of only 5 per cent, yet surveys found nearly a quarter of the population (1.16 million) living in slums and squatter camps.[34] The UN, likewise, recently discovered that it was unintentionally undercounting urban poverty in

Africa by large margins. Slum-dwellers in Angola, for example, are probably twice as numerous as it originally believed. Likewise it underestimated the number of poor urbanites in Liberia: not surprising, since Monrovia tripled its population in a single year (1989–90) as panic-stricken country people fled from a brutal civil war.[35]

There may be more than quarter of a million slums on earth. The five great metropolises of South Asia (Karachi, Mumbai, Delhi, Kolkata and Dhaka) alone contain about 15,000 distinct slum communities with a total population of more than 20 million. An even larger slum population crowds the urbanizing littoral of West Africa, while other huge conurbations of poverty sprawl across Anatolia and the Ethiopian highlands; hug the base of the Andes and the Himalayas; explode outward from the skyscraper cores of Mexico, Jo-burg, Manila and São Paulo; and, of course, line the banks of the rivers Amazon, Niger, Congo, Nile, Tigris, Ganges, Irrawaddy and Mekong. The building blocks of this slum planet, paradoxically, are both utterly interchangeable and spontaneously unique: including the *bustees* of Kolkata, the *chawls* and *zopadpattis* of Mumbai, the *katchi abadis* of Karachi, the *kampungs* of Jakarta, the *iskwaters* of Manila, the *shammasas* of Khartoum, the *umjondolos* of Durban, the *intramurios* of Rabat, the *bidonvilles* of Abidjan, the *baladis* of Cairo, the *gecekondus* of Ankara, the *conventillos* of Quito, the *favelas* of Brazil, the *villas miseria* of Buenos Aires and the *colonias populares* of Mexico City. They are the gritty antipodes to the generic fantasy-scapes and residential themeparks – Philip K. Dick's bourgeois 'Offworlds' – in which the global middle classes increasingly prefer to cloister themselves.

Whereas the classic slum was a decaying inner city, the new slums are more typically located on the edge of urban spatial explosions. The horizontal growth of cities like Mexico, Lagos or Jakarta, of course, has been extraordinary, and 'slum sprawl' is as much of a problem in the developing world as suburban sprawl in the rich countries. The developed area of Lagos, for instance, doubled in a single decade, between 1985 and 1994.[36] The Governor of Lagos State told reporters last year that 'about two thirds of the state's total land mass of 3,577 square kilometres could be classified as shanties or slums'.[37] Indeed, writes a UN correspondent,

much of the city is a mystery … unlit highways run past canyons of smouldering garbage before giving way to dirt streets weaving through 200 slums, their sewers running with raw waste … No one even knows for sure the size of the population – officially it is 6 million, but most experts estimate it at 10 million – let alone the number of murders each year [or] the rate of HIV infection.[38]

Lagos, moreover, is simply the biggest node in the shanty-town corridor of 70 million people that stretches from Abidjan to Ibadan: probably the biggest continuous footprint of urban poverty on earth.[39]

Slum ecology, of course, revolves around the supply of settlement space. Winter King, in a recent study published in the *Harvard Law Review*, claims that 85 per cent of the urban residents of the developing world 'occupy property illegally'.[40] Indeterminacy of land titles and/or lax state ownership, in the last instance, are the cracks through which a vast humanity has poured into the cities. The modes of slum settlement vary across a huge spectrum, from highly disciplined land invasions in Mexico City and Lima to intricately organized (but often illegal) rental markets on the outskirts of Beijing, Karachi and Nairobi. Even in cities like Karachi, where the urban periphery is formally owned by the government, 'vast profits from land speculation … continue to accrue to the private sector at the expense of low-income households'.[41] Indeed national and local political machines usually acquiesce in informal settlement (and illegal private speculation) as long as they can control the political complexion of the slums and extract a regular flow of bribes or rents. Without formal land titles or home ownership, slum-dwellers are forced into quasi-feudal dependencies upon local officials and party bigshots. Disloyalty can mean eviction or even the razing of an entire district.

The provision of lifeline infrastructures, meanwhile, lags far behind the pace of urbanization, and peri-urban slum areas often have no formal utilities or sanitation provision whatsoever.[42] Poor areas of Latin American cities in general have better utilities than South Asia which, in turn, usually have minimum urban services, like water and electricity, that many African slums lack. As in early Victorian London, the contamination of water by human and animal waste remains the cause of the chronic diarrhoeal diseases that kill at least two million urban babies and small children each year.[43] An estimated 57 per cent of urban Africans lack access to basic sanitation and in cities like Nairobi the poor must rely on 'flying toilets' (defecation into a plastic bag).[44] In Mumbai, meanwhile, the sanitation problem is defined by ratios of one toilet seat per 500 inhabitants in the poorer districts. Only 11 per cent of poor neighbourhoods in Manila and 18 per cent in Dhaka have formal means to dispose of sewage.[45] Quite apart from the incidence of the HIV/AIDS plague, the UN considers that two out of five African slum-dwellers live in a poverty that is literally 'life-threatening'.[46]

The urban poor, meanwhile, are everywhere forced to settle on hazardous and otherwise unbuildable terrains – over-steep hillslopes, river banks and floodplains. Likewise they squat in the deadly shadows of refineries, chemical factories, toxic dumps, or in the margins of railroads and highways. Poverty, as a result, has 'constructed' an urban disaster problem of unprecedented frequency and scope, as typified by chronic flooding in Manila, Dhaka and Rio, pipeline conflagrations in Mexico City and Cubatão (Brazil), the Bhopal catastrophe in India, a munitions plant explosion in Lagos, and deadly mudslides in Caracas, La Paz and Tegucigalpa.[47] The disenfranchised communities of the urban poor, in addition, are vulnerable to sudden outbursts of state violence like the infamous 1990 bulldozing of the Maroko beach slum in Lagos ('an eyesore for the neighbouring community of Victoria Island, a fortress for the rich') or the 1995 demolition in freezing weather of the huge squatter town of Zhejiangcun on the edge of Beijing.[48]

But slums, however deadly and insecure, have a brilliant future. The countryside will for a short period still contain the majority of the world's poor, but that doubtful title will pass to urban slums by 2035.[49] At least half of the coming Third World urban population explosion will be credited to the account of informal communities. Two billion slum dwellers by 2030 or 2040 is a monstrous, almost incomprehensible prospect, but urban poverty overlaps and exceeds the slums *per se*. Indeed, *Slums* underlines that in some cities the majority of the poor actually live outside the slum *stricto sensu*.[50] UN 'Urban Observatory' researchers warn, moreover, that by 2020 'urban poverty in the world could reach 45 to 50 per cent of the total population living in cities'.[51]

4. Urban Poverty's 'Big Bang'

After their mysterious laughter, they quickly changed the topic to other things. How were people back home surviving SAP? (Fidelis Balogun, *Adjusted Lives*, 1995)

The evolution of the new urban poverty has been a non-linear historical process. The slow accretion of shanty towns to the shell of the city is punctuated by storms of poverty and sudden explosions of slum-building. In his collection of stories, *Adjusted Lives*, the Nigerian writer Fidelis Balogun describes the coming of the IMF-mandated Structural Adjustment Programme (SAP) in the mid-1980s as the equivalent of a great natural catastrophe, destroying forever the old soul of Lagos and 're-enslaving' urban Nigerians.

> The weird logic of this economic programme seemed to be that to restore life to the dying economy, every juice had first to be SAPped out of the under-privileged majority of the citizens. The middle class rapidly disappeared, and the garbage heaps of the increasingly rich few became the food table of the multiplied population of abjectly poor. The brain drain to the oil-rich Arab countries and to the Western world became a flood.[52]

Balogun's complaint about 'privatizing in full steam and getting more hungry by the day', or his enumeration of SAP's malevolent consequences, would be instantly familiar to survivors, not only of the other 30 African SAPs, but also to hundreds of millions of Asians and Latin Americans. The 1980s, when the IMF and World Bank used the leverage of debt to restructure the economies of most of the Third World, are the years when slums became an implacable future, not just for poor rural migrants, but also for millions of traditional urbanites, displaced or immiserated by the violence of 'adjustment'.

As *Slums* emphasizes, SAPs were 'deliberately anti-urban in nature' and designed to reverse any 'urban bias' that previously existed in welfare policies, fiscal structure or government investment.[53] Everywhere the IMF – acting as bailiff for the big banks and backed by the Reagan and Bush administrations – offered poor countries the same poisoned chalice of devaluation, privatization, removal of import controls and food subsidies, enforced cost-recovery in health and education, and ruthless downsizing of the public sector. (An infamous 1985 telegram from Treasury Secretary George Shultz to overseas USAID officials commanded: 'in most cases, public sector firms should be privatized'.)[54] At the same time, SAPs devastated rural smallholders by eliminating subsidies and pushing them out, 'sink or swim', into global commodity markets dominated by First World agribusiness.[55]

As Ha-Joon Chang points out, SAPs hypocritically 'kicked away the ladder' (i.e., protectionist tariffs and subsidies) that the OECD nations historically employed in their own climb from agriculture to urban high-value goods and services.[56] *Slums* makes the same point when it argues that the 'main single cause of increases in poverty and inequality during the 1980s and 1990s was the retreat of the state'. In addition to the direct SAP-enforced reductions in public-sector spending and ownership, the UN authors stress the more subtle diminution of state capacity that has resulted from 'subsidiarity': the devolution of powers to lower echelons of government and, especially, NGOs, linked directly to major international aid agencies.

> The whole, apparently decentralized structure is foreign to the notion of national representative government that has served the developed world well, while it is very amenable to the operations of a global hegemony. The dominant international perspective [i.e., Washington's] becomes the de facto paradigm for development, so that the whole world rapidly becomes unified in the broad direction of what is supported by donors and international organizations.[57]

Urban Africa and Latin America were the hardest hit by the artificial depression engineered by the IMF and the White House. Indeed, in many countries, the economic impact of SAPs during the 1980s, in tandem with protracted drought, rising oil prices, soaring interest rates and falling commodity prices, was more severe and long-lasting than the Great Depression.

The balance-sheet of structural adjustment in Africa, reviewed by Carole Rakodi, includes capital flight, collapse of manufactures, marginal or negative increase in export incomes, drastic cutbacks in urban public services, soaring prices and a steep decline in real wages.[58] In Kinshasa ('an aberration or rather a sign of things to come?') *assainissement* wiped out the civil servant middle class and produced an 'unbelievable decline in real wages' that, in turn, sponsored a nightmarish rise in crime and predatory gangs.[59] In Dar es Salaam, public service expenditure per person fell 10 per cent per year during the 1980s: a virtual demolition of the local state.[60] In Khartoum, liberalization and structural adjustment, according to local researchers, manufactured 1.1 million 'new poor': 'mostly drawn from the salaried groups or public sector employees'.[61] In Abidjan, one of the few tropical African cities with an important manufacturing sector and modern urban services, submission to the SAP regime punctually led to deindustrialization, the collapse of construction, and a rapid deterioration in public transit and sanitation.[62] In Balogun's Nigeria extreme poverty, increasingly urbanized in Lagos, Ibadan and other cities, metastasized from 28 per cent in 1980 to 66 per cent in 1996. 'GNP per capita, at about $260 today,' the World Bank reports, 'is below the level at independence 40 years ago and below the $370 level attained in 1985.'[63]

In Latin America, SAPs (often implemented by military dictatorships) destabilized rural economies while savaging urban employment and housing. In 1970, Guevarist 'foco' theories of rural insurgency still conformed to a continental reality where the poverty of the countryside (75 million poor) overshadowed that of the cities (44 million poor). By the end of the 1980s, however, the vast majority of the poor (115 million in 1990) were living in urban *colonias* and *villas miseria* rather than farms or villages (80 million).[64]

Urban inequality, meanwhile, exploded. In Santiago, the Pinochet dictatorship bulldozed shanty towns and evicted formerly radical squatters: forcing poor families to become *allegados*, doubled or even tripled-up in the same rented dwelling. In Buenos Aires, the richest decile's share of income increased from 10 times that of the poorest in 1984 to 23 times in 1989.[65] In Lima, where the value of the minimum wage fell by 83 per cent during the IMF recession, the percentage of households living below the poverty threshold increased from 17 percent in 1985 to 44 per cent in 1990.[66] In Rio de Janeiro, inequality as measured in classical Gini coefficients soared from 0.58 in 1981 to 0.67 in 1989.[67] Indeed, throughout Latin America, the 1980s deepened the canyons and elevated the peaks of the world's most extreme social topography. (According to a 2003 World Bank report, Gini coefficients are 10 points higher in Latin America than Asia; 17.5 points higher than the OECD, and 20.4 points higher than Eastern Europe.)[68]

Throughout the Third World, the economic shocks of the 1980s forced individuals to regroup around the pooled resources of households and, especially, the survival skills and desperate ingenuity of women. In China and the industrializing cities of Southeast Asia, millions of young women indentured themselves to assembly lines and factory squalor. In Africa and most of Latin America (Mexico's northern border cities excepted), this option did not exist. Instead, deindustrialization and the decimation of male formal-sector jobs compelled women to improvise new livelihoods as piece workers, liquor sellers, street vendors, cleaners, washers, ragpickers, nannies and prostitutes. In Latin America, where urban women's labour-force participation had always been lower than in other continents, the surge of women into tertiary informal activities during the 1980s was especially dramatic.[69] In Africa, where the icons of the informal sector are women running shebeens or hawking produce, Christian Rogerson reminds us that most informal women are not actually self-employed or economically independent, but work for someone else.[70] (These ubiquitous and vicious networks of micro-exploitation, of the poor exploiting the very poor, are usually glossed over in accounts of the informal sector.)

Urban poverty was also massively feminized in the ex-Comecon countries after capitalist 'liberation' in 1989. In the early 1990s extreme poverty in the former 'transitional countries' (as the UN calls them) soared from 14 million to 168 million: a mass pauperization almost without precedent in history.[71] If, on a global balance-sheet, this economic catastrophe was partially offset by the much-praised success of China in raising incomes in its coastal cities, China's market 'miracle' was purchased by 'an enormous increase in wage inequality among urban workers ... during the period 1988 to 1999.' Women and minorities were especially disadvantaged.[72]

In theory, of course, the 1990s should have righted the wrongs of the 1980s and allowed Third World cities to regain lost ground and bridge the chasms of inequality created by SAPs. The pain of adjustment should have been followed by the analgesic of globalization. Indeed the 1990s, as *Slums* wryly notes, were the first decade in which global urban development took place within almost utopian parameters of neoclassical market freedom.

> During the 1990s, trade continued to expand at an almost unprecedented rate, no-go areas opened up and military expenditures decreased. ... All the basic inputs to production became cheaper, as interest rates fell rapidly along with the price of basic commodities. Capital flows were increasingly unfettered by national controls and could move rapidly to the most productive areas. Under what were almost perfect economic conditions according to the dominant neoliberal economic doctrine, one might have imagined that the decade would have been one of unrivalled prosperity and social justice.[73]

In the event, however, urban poverty continued its relentless accumulation and 'the gap between poor and rich countries increased, just as it had done for the previous 20 years and, in most countries, income inequality increased or, at best, stabilized.' Global inequality, as measured by World Bank economists, reached an incredible Gini coefficient level of 0.67 by the end of the century. This was mathematically equivalent to a situation where the poorest two-thirds of the world receive zero income; and the top third, everything.[74]

5. A Surplus Humanity?

We shove our way about next to City, holding on to it by its thousand survival cracks ... (Patrick Chamoiseau, *Texaco* (1997))

The brutal tectonics of neoliberal globalization since 1978 are analogous to the catastrophic processes that shaped a 'third world' in the first place, during the era of late Victorian imperialism (1870–1900). In the latter case, the forcible incorporation into the world market of the great subsistence peasantries of Asia and Africa entailed the famine deaths of millions and the uprooting of tens of millions more from traditional tenures. The end result, in Latin America as well, was rural 'semi-proletarianization': the creation of a huge global class of immiserated semi-peasants and farm labourers lacking existential security of subsistence.[75] (As a result, the twentieth century became an age, not of urban revolutions as classical Marxism had imagined, but of epochal rural uprisings and peasant-based wars of national liberation.) Structural adjustment, it would appear, has recently worked an equally fundamental reshaping of human futures. As the authors of *Slums* conclude: 'instead of being a focus for growth and prosperity, the cities have become a dumping ground for a surplus population working in unskilled, unprotected and low-wage informal service industries and trade.' 'The rise of [this] informal sector,' they declare bluntly, 'is … a direct result of liberalization.'[76]

Indeed, the global informal working class (overlapping but non-identical with the slum population) is almost one billion strong: making it the fastest growing, and most unprecedented, social class on earth. Since anthropologist Keith Hart, working in Accra, first broached the concept of an 'informal sector' in 1973, a huge literature (mostly failing to distinguish micro-accumulation from sub-subsistence) has wrestled with the formidable theoretical and empirical problems involved in studying the survival strategies of the urban poor.[77] There is a base consensus, however, that the 1980s' crisis inverted the relative structural positions of the formal and informal sectors: promoting informal survivalism as the new primary mode of livelihood in a majority of Third World cities.

Alejandro Portes and Kelly Hoffman have recently evaluated the overall impact of SAPs and liberalization upon Latin American urban class structures since the 1970s. Congruent with UN conclusions, they find that both state employees and the formal proletariat have declined in every country of the region since the 1970s. In contrast, the informal sector of the economy, along with general social inequality, has dramatically expanded. Unlike some researchers, they make a crucial distinction between an informal petty bourgeoisie ('the sum of owners of microenterprises, employing less than five workers, plus own-account professionals and technicians') and the informal proletariat ('the sum of own-account workers minus professionals and technicians, domestic servants, and paid and unpaid workers in microentreprises'). They demonstrate that this former stratum, the 'microentrepreneurs' so beloved in North American business schools, are often displaced public-sector professionals or laid-off skilled workers. Since the 1980s, they have grown from about 5 to 10 per cent of the economically active urban population: a trend reflecting 'the forced entrepreneurialism foisted on former salaried employees by the decline of formal sector employment.'[78]

Overall, according to *Slums*, informal workers are about two-fifths of the economically active population of the developing world.[79] According to researchers at the Inter-American Development Bank, the informal economy currently employs 57 per cent of the Latin American workforce and supplies four out of five new 'jobs'.[80] Other sources claim that more than half of urban Indonesians and 65 per cent of residents of Dhaka subsist in the informal sector.[81] *Slums* likewise cites research finding that informal economic activity accounts for 33 to 40 per cent of urban employment in Asia, 60 to 75 per cent in Central America and 60 per cent in Africa.[82] Indeed, in sub-Saharan cities 'formal job' creation has virtually ceased to exist. An ILO study of Zimbabwe's urban labour markets under 'stagflationary' structural adjustment in the early 1990s found that the formal sector was creating only 10,000 jobs per year in face of an urban workforce increasing by more than 300,000 per annum.[83] *Slums* similarly estimates that fully 90 per cent of urban Africa's new jobs over the next decade will somehow come from the informal sector.[84]

The pundits of bootstrap capitalism, like the irrepressible Hernando de Soto, may see this enormous population of marginalized labourers, redundant civil servants and ex-peasants as actually a frenzied beehive of ambitious entrepreneurs yearning for formal property rights and unregulated competitive space, but it makes more obvious sense to consider most informal workers as the 'active' unemployed, who have no choice but to subsist by some means or starve.[85] The world's estimated 100 million street kids are not likely – apologies to Señor de Soto – to start issuing IPOs or selling chewing-gum futures.[86] Nor will most of China's 70 million 'floating workers', living furtively on the urban periphery, eventually capitalize themselves as small subcontractors or integrate into the formal urban working class. And the informal working class – everywhere subject to micro- and macro-exploitation – is almost universally deprived of protection by labour laws and standards.

Moreover, as Alain Dubresson argues in the case of Abidjan, 'the dynamism of crafts and small-scale trade depends largely on demand from the wage sector'. He warns against the 'illusion' cultivated by the ILO and World Bank that 'the informal sector can efficiently replace the formal sector and promote an accumulation process sufficient for a city with more than 2.5 million inhabitants'.[87] His warning is echoed by Christian Rogerson who, distinguishing (à la Portes and Hoffman) 'survivalist' from 'growth' micro-enterprises, writes of the former: 'generally speaking, the incomes generated from these enterprises, the majority of which tend to be run by women, usually fall short of even a minimum living standard and involve little capital investment, virtually no skills training, and only constrained opportunities for expansion into a viable business'. With even formal-sector urban wages in Africa so low that economists can't figure out how workers survive (the so-called 'wage puzzle'), the informal tertiary sector has become an arena of extreme Darwinian competition amongst the poor. Rogerson cites the examples of Zimbabwe and South Africa where female-controlled informal niches like shebeens and *spazas* are now drastically overcrowded and plagued by collapsing profitability.[88]

The real macroeconomic trend of informal labour, in other words, is the reproduction of absolute poverty. But if the informal proletariat is not the pettiest of petty bourgeoisies, neither is it a 'labour reserve army' or a 'lumpen proletariat' in any obsolete nineteenth-century sense. Part of it, to be sure, is a stealth workforce for the formal economy and numerous studies have exposed how the subcontracting networks of WalMart and other mega-companies extend deep into the misery of the *colonias* and *chawls*. But at the end of the day, a majority of urban slum-dwellers are truly and radically homeless in the contemporary international economy.

Slums, of course, originate in the global country-side where, as Deborah Bryceson reminds us, unequal competition with large-scale agro-industry is tearing traditional rural society 'apart at the seams'.[89] As rural areas lose their 'storage capacity', slums take their place, and urban 'involution' replaces rural involution as a sink for surplus labour which can only keep pace with subsistence by ever more heroic feats of self-exploitation and the further competitive subdivision of already densely filled survival niches.[90] 'Modernization', 'Development' and, now, the unfettered 'Market' have had their day. The labour-power of a billion people has been expelled from the world system, and who can imagine any plausible scenario, under neoliberal auspices, that would reintegrate them as productive workers or mass consumers?

6. Marx and the Holy Ghost

[The Lord says:] The time will come when the poor man will say that he has nothing to eat and work will be shut down … That is going to cause the poor man to go to these places and break in to get food. This will cause the rich man to come out with his gun to make war with the labouring man. … blood will be in the streets like an outpouring rain from heaven. (A prophecy from the 1906 'Azusa Street Awakening')

The late capitalist triage of humanity, then, has already taken place. The global growth of a vast informal proletariat, moreover, is a wholly original structural development unforeseen by either classical Marxism or modernization pundits. *Slums* indeed challenges social theory to grasp the novelty of a true global residuum lacking the strategic economic power of socialized labor, but massively concentrated in a shanty-town world encircling the fortified enclaves of the urban rich.

Tendencies toward urban involution, of course, existed during the nineteenth century. The European industrial revolutions were incapable of absorbing the entire supply of displaced rural labour, especially after continental agriculture was exposed to the devastating competition of the North American prairies from the 1870s. But mass immigration to the settler societies of the Americas and Oceania, as well as Siberia, provided a dynamic safety-valve that prevented the rise of mega-Dublins as well as the spread of the kind of underclass anarchism that had taken root in the most immiserated parts of Southern Europe. Today surplus labour, by contrast, faces unprecedented barriers – a literal 'great wall' of high-tech border enforcement – blocking large-scale migration to the rich countries. Likewise, controversial population resettlement programmes in 'frontier' regions like Amazonia, Tibet, Kalimantan and Irian Jaya produce environmental devastation and ethnic conflict without substantially reducing urban poverty in Brazil, China and Indonesia.

Thus only the slum remains as a fully franchised solution to the problem of warehousing the twenty-first century's surplus humanity. But aren't the great slums, as a terrified Victorian bourgeoisie once imagined, volcanoes waiting to erupt? Or does ruthless Darwinian competition, as increasing numbers of poor people compete for the same informal scraps, ensure self-consuming communal violence as yet the highest form of urban involution? To what extent does an informal proletariat possess that most potent of Marxist talismans: 'historical agency'? Can disincorporated labour be reincorporated in a global emancipatory project? Or is the sociology of protest in the immiserated megacity a regression to the pre-industrial urban mob, episodically explosive during consumption crises, but otherwise easily managed by clientelism, populist spectacle and appeals to ethnic unity? Or is some new, unexpected historical subject, à la Hardt and Negri, slouching toward the supercity?

In truth, the current literature on poverty and urban protest offers few answers to such large-scale questions. Some researchers, for example, would question whether the ethnically diverse slum poor or economically heterogeneous informal workers even constitute a meaningful 'class in itself', much less a potentially activist 'class for itself'. Surely, the informal proletariat bears 'radical chains' in the Marxist sense of having little or no vested interest in the preservation of the existing mode of production. But because uprooted rural migrants and informal workers have been largely dispossessed of fungible labour-power, or reduced to domestic service in the houses of the rich, they have little access to the culture of collective labour or large-scale class struggle. Their social stage, necessarily, must be the slum street or marketplace, not the factory or international assembly line.

Struggles of informal workers, as John Walton emphasizes in a recent review of research on social movements in poor cities, have tended, above all, to be episodic and discontinuous. They are also usually focused on immediate consumption issues: land invasions in search of affordable housing and riots against rising food or utility prices. In the past, at least, 'urban problems in developing societies have been more typically mediated by patron–client relations than by popular activism.'[91] Since the debt crisis of the 1980s, neopopulist leaders in Latin America have had dramatic success in exploiting the desperate desire of the urban poor for more stable, predictable structures of daily life. Although Walton doesn't make the point explicitly, the urban informal sector has been ideologically promiscuous in its endorsement of populist saviours: in Peru rallying to Fujimori, but in Venezuela embracing Chávez.[92] In Africa and South Asia, on the other hand, urban clientelism too often equates with the dominance of ethno-religious bigots and their nightmare ambitions of ethnic cleansing. Notorious examples include the anti-Muslim militias of the Oodua People's Congress in Lagos and the semi-fascist Shiv Sena movement in Bombay.[93]

Will such 'eighteenth-century' sociologies of protest persist into the middle twenty-first century? The past is probably a poor guide to the future. History is not uniformitarian. The new urban world is evolving with extraordinary speed and often in unpredictable directions. Everywhere the continuous accumulation of poverty undermines existential security and poses even more extraordinary challenges to the economic ingenuity of the poor. Perhaps there is a tipping point at which the pollution, congestion, greed and violence of everyday urban life finally overwhelm the ad hoc civilities and survival networks of the slum. Certainly in the old rural world there were thresholds, often calibrated by famine, that passed directly to social eruption. But no one yet knows the social temperature at which the new cities of poverty spontaneously combust.

[…]

Notes

1 UN Population Division, *World Urbanization Prospects, the 2001 Revision* (New York, 2002).

2 Population Information Program, *Population Reports: Meeting the Urban Challenge*, vol. xxx, no. 4 (Fall 2002), p. 1.

3 Wolfgang Lutz, Warren Sandeson and Sergei Scherbov, 'Doubling of World Population Unlikely', *Nature* 387

(19 June 1997), pp. 803–4. However the populations of sub-Saharan Africa will triple and India, double.

4   Global Urban Observatory, *Slums of the World: The Face of Urban Poverty in the New Millennium?* (New York, 2003), p. 10.

5   Although the velocity of global urbanization is not in doubt, the growth rates of specific cities may brake abruptly as they encounter the frictions of size and congestion. A famous instance of such a 'polarization reversal' is Mexico City: widely predicted to achieve a population of 25 million during the 1990s (the current population is probably about 18 or 19 million). See Yue-man Yeung, 'Geography in an Age of Mega-cities', *International Social Sciences Journal* 151 (1997), p. 93.

6   For a perspective, see Yue-man Yeung, 'Viewpoint: Integration of the Pearl River Delta', *International Development Planning Review*, vol. 25, no. 3 (2003).

7   Far Eastern Economic Review, *Asia 1998 Yearbook*, p. 63.

8   UN-Habitat, *The Challenge of the Slums: Global Report on Human Settlements 2003* (London, 2003), p. 3.

9   Gregory Guldin, *What's a Peasant to Do? Village Becoming Town in Southern China* (Boulder, CO, 2001), p. 13.

10 Miguel Villa and Jorge Rodriguez, 'Demographic Trends in Latin America's Metropolises, 1950–1990', in Alan Gilbert, ed., *The Mega-City in Latin America* (Tokyo, 1996), pp. 33–4.

11 Guldin, *Peasant*, pp. 14, 17. See also Jing Neng Li, 'Structural and Spatial Economic Changes and Their Effects on Recent Urbanization in China', in Gavin Jones and Pravin Visaria, eds, *Urbanization in Large Developing Countries* (Oxford, 1997), p. 44.

12 See T. McGee, 'The Emergence of Desakota Regions in Asia: Expanding a Hypothesis', in Northon Ginsburg, Bruce Koppell and T. McGee, eds, *The Extended Metropolis: Settlement Transition in Asia* (Honolulu, 1991).

13 Yue-man Yeung and Fu-chen Lo, 'Global Restructuring and Emerging Urban Corridors in Pacific Asia', in Lo and Yeung, eds, *Emerging World Cities in Pacific Asia* (Tokyo, 1996), p. 41.

14 Guldin, *Peasant*, p. 13.

15 Wang Mengkui, advisor to the State Council, quoted in the *Financial Times*, 26 November 2003. Since the market reforms of the late 1970s it is estimated that almost 300 million Chinese have moved from rural areas to cities. Another 250 or 300 million are expected to follow in coming decades. (*Financial Times*, 16 December 2003.)

16 Josef Gugler, 'Introduction – II. Rural–Urban Migration', in Gugler, ed., *Cities in the Developing World: Issues, Theory and Policy* (Oxford, 1997), p. 43. For a contrarian view that disputes generally accepted World Bank and UN data on continuing high rates of urbanization during the 1980s, see Deborah Potts, 'Urban Lives: Adopting New Strategies and Adapting Rural Links', in Carole Rakodi, ed., *The Urban Challenge in Africa: Growth and Management of Its Large Cities* (Tokyo, 1997), pp. 463–73.

17 David Simon, 'Urbanization, Globalization and Economic Crisis in Africa', in Rakodi, *Urban Challenge*, p. 95.

18 See Josef Gugler, 'Overurbanization Reconsidered', in Gugler, *Cities in the Developing World*, pp. 114–23. By contrast, the former command economies of the Soviet Union and Maoist China restricted in-migration to cities and thus tended toward 'under-urbanization'.

19 Foreword to Jacinta Prunty, *Dublin Slums 1800–1925: A Study in Urban Geography* (Dublin 1998), p. ix.

20 'Thus, it appears that for low income countries, a significant fall in urban incomes may not necessarily produce in the short term a decline in rural–urban migration.' Nigel Harris, 'Urbanization, Economic Development and Policy in Developing Countries', *Habitat International*, vol. 14, no. 4 (1990), pp. 21–2.

21 On Third World urbanization and the global debt crisis, see York Bradshaw and Rita Noonan, 'Urbanization, Economic Growth, and Women's Labour-Force Participation', in Gugler, *Cities in the Developing World*, pp. 9 10.

22 *Slums*: for publication details, see footnote 8.

23 Branko Milanovic, *True World Income Distribution 1988 and 1993*, World Bank, New York, 1999. Milanovic and his colleague Schlomo Yitzhaki are the first to calculate world income distribution based on the household survey data from individual countries.

24 UNICEF, to be fair, has criticized the IMF for years, pointing out that 'hundreds of thousands of the developing world's children have given their lives to pay their countries' debts'. See *The State of the World's Children* (Oxford, 1989), p. 30.

25 *Slums*, p. 6.

26 Such a study, one supposes, would survey, at one end, urban hazards and infrastructural breakdown and, at the other, the impact of climate change on agriculture and migration.

27 Prunty, *Dublin Slums*, p. 2.

28 *Slums*, p. 12.

29 *Slums*, pp. 2–3.

30 See A. Oberai, *Population Growth, Employment and Poverty in Third World Mega-Cities*, (New York, 1993), p. 28. In 1980 the 0–19 cohort of big OECD cities was from 19 to 28 per cent of the population; of Third World mega-cities, 40 to 53 per cent.

31 *Slums of the World*, pp. 33–4.

32 Simon, 'Urbanization in Africa', p. 103; and Jean-Luc Piermay, 'Kinshasa: A Reprieved Mega-city?', in Rakodi, *Urban Challenge*, p. 236.

33 Sabir Ali, 'Squatters: Slums within Slums', in Prodipto Roy and Shangon Das Gupta, eds, *Urbanization and Slums*, (Delhi, 1995), pp. 55–9.

34 Jonathan Rigg, *Southeast Asia: A Region in Transition* (London, 1991), p. 143.

35 *Slums of the World*, p. 34

36 Salah El-Shakhs, 'Toward Appropriate Urban Development Policy in Emerging Mega-cities in Africa', in Rakodi, *Urban Challenge*, p. 516.

37 *Daily Times of Nigeria*, 20 October 2003. Lagos has grown more explosively than any large Third World city except for Dhaka. In 1950 it had only 300,000 inhabitants but then grew almost 10 per cent per annum until 1980, when it slowed to about 6% – still a very rapid rate – during the years of structural readjustment.

38 Amy Otchet, 'Lagos: the Survival of the Determined' *UNESCO Courier*, June 1999.

39 *Slums*, p. 50.

40 Winter King, 'Illegal Settlements and the Impact of Titling Programmes,' *Harvard Law Review*, vol. 44, no. 2 (September 2003) p. 471.

41 United Nations, *Karachi*, Population Growth and Policies in Megacities series (New York, 1988), p. 19.

42 The absence of infrastructure, however, does create innumerable niches for informal workers: selling water, carting nightsoil, recycling trash, delivering propane and so on.

43 World Resources Institute, *World Resources: 1996–97* (Oxford, 1996), p. 21.

44 *Slums of the World*, p. 25.

45 *Slums*, p. 99.

46 *Slums of the World*, p. 12.

47 For an exemplary case-study, see Greg Bankoff, 'Constructing Vulnerability: The Historical, Natural and Social Generation of Flooding in Metropolitan Manila', *Disasters*, vol. 27, no. 3 (2003), pp. 224–38.

48 Otchet, 'Lagos'; and Li Zhang, *Strangers in the City: Reconfigurations of Space, Power and Social Networks within China's Floating Population* (Stanford, 2001); Alan Gilbert, *The Latin American City*, (New York, 1998), p. 16.

49 Martin Ravallion, *On the Urbanization of Poverty*, World Bank paper, 2001.

50 *Slums*, p. 28.

51 *Slums of the World*, p. 12.

52 Fidelis Odun Balogun, *Adjusted Lives: Stories of Structural Adjustment* (Trenton, NJ, 1995), p. 80.

53 *The Challenge of Slums*, p. 30. 'Urban bias' theorists, like Michael Lipton who invented the term in 1977, argue that agriculture tends to be undercapitalized in developing countries, and cities relatively 'overurbanized', because fiscal and financial policies favour urban elites and distort investment flows. At the limit, cities are vampires of the countryside. See Lipton, *Why Poor People Stay Poor: A Study of Urban Bias in World Development* (Cambridge, 1977).

54 Quoted in Tony Killick, 'Twenty-five Years in Development: the Rise and Impending Decline of Market Solutions', *Development Policy Review*, vol. 4 (1986), p. 101.

55 Deborah Bryceson, 'Disappearing Peasantries? Rural Labour Redundancy in the Neoliberal Era and Beyond', in Bryceson, Cristóbal Kay and Jos Mooij, eds, *Disappearing Peasantries? Rural Labour in Africa, Asia and Latin America* (London, 2000), pp. 304–5.

56 Ha-Joon Chang, 'Kicking Away the Ladder: Infant Industry Promotion in Historical Perspective', *Oxford Development Studies*, vol. 31, no. 1 (2003), p. 21. 'Per capita income in developing countries grew at 3 per cent per annum between 1960 and 1980, but at only about 1.5 per cent between 1980 and 2000 … Neoliberal economists are therefore faced with a paradox here. The developing countries grew much faster when they used 'bad' policies during 1960–80 than when they used 'good' (or least 'better') policies during the following two decades.' (p. 28).

57 *Slums*, p. 48.

58 Carole Rakodi, 'Global Forces, Urban Change, and Urban Management in Africa', in Rakodi, *Urban Challenge*, pp. 50, 60–1.

59 Piermay, 'Kinshasa', p. 235–6; 'Megacities', *Time*, 11 January 1993, p. 26.

60 Michael Mattingly, 'The Role of the Government of Urban Areas in the Creation of Urban Poverty', in Sue Jones and Nici Nelson, eds, *Urban Poverty in Africa*, (London, 1999), p. 21.

61 Adil Ahmad and Ata El-Batthani, 'Poverty in Khartoum', *Environment and Urbanization*, vol. 7, no. 2 (October 1995), p. 205.

62 Alain Dubresson, 'Abidjan', in Rakodi, *Urban Challenge*, pp. 261–3.

63 World Bank, *Nigeria: Country Brief*, September 2003.

64 UN, *World Urbanization Prospects*, p. 12.

65 Luis Ainstein, 'Buenos Aires: a Case of Deepening Social Polarization', in Gilbert, *Mega-City in Latin America*, p. 139.

66 Gustavo Riofrio, 'Lima: Mega-city and Mega-Problem', in Gilbert, *Mega-City in Latin America*, p. 159; and Gilbert, *Latin American City*, p. 73.

67 Hamilton Tolosa, 'Rio de Janeiro: Urban Expansion and Structural Change', in Gilbert, *Mega-City in Latin America*, p. 211.

68 World Bank, *Inequality in Latin America and the Caribbean* (New York, 2003).

69 Orlandina de Oliveira and Bryan Roberts, 'The Many Roles of the Informal Sector in Development', in Cathy Rakowski, ed., *Contrapunto: the Informal Sector Debate in Latin America* (Albany, 1994), pp. 64–8.

70 Christian Rogerson, 'Globalization or Informalization? African Urban Economies in the 1990s', in Rakodi, *Urban Challenge*, p. 348.

71 *Slums*, p. 2.

72 Albert Park et al., 'The Growth of Wage Inequality in Urban China, 1988 to 1999', World Bank working paper, February 2003, p. 27 (quote); and John Knight and Linda Song, 'Increasing Urban Wage Inequality in China', *Economics of Transition*, vol. 11, no. 4 (2003) p. 616 (discrimination).

73 *Slums*, p. 34.

74 Shaohua Chen and Martin Ravallion, *How Did the World's Poorest Fare in the 1990s?*, World Bank paper, 2000.

75 See my *Late Victorian Holocausts: El Niño Famines and the Making of the Third World* (London, 2001), especially pp. 206–9.

76 *Slums*, pp. 40, 46.

77 Keith Hart, 'Informal Income Opportunities and Urban Employment in Ghana', *Journal of Modern African Studies*, 11 (1973), pp. 61–89.

78 Alejandro Portes and Kelly Hoffman, 'Latin American Class Structures: Their Composition and Change during the Neoliberal Era', *Latin American Research Review*, vol. 38, no. 1 (2003), p. 55.

79 *Slums*, p. 60.

80 Cited in the *Economist*, 21 March 1998, p. 37.

81 Dennis Rondinelli and John Kasarda, 'Job Creation Needs in Third World Cities', in Kasarda and Allan Parnell, eds, *Third World Cities: Problems, Policies and Prospects* (Newbury Park, CA, 1993), pp. 106–7.

82 *Slums*, p. 103.

83 Guy Mhone, 'The Impact of Structural Adjustment on the Urban Informal Sector in Zimbabwe', *Issues in Development* discussion paper no. 2, International Labour Office, Geneva (n.d.), p. 19.

84 *Slums*, p. 104.

85 Orlandina de Oliveira and Bryan Roberts rightly emphasize that the bottom strata of the urban labour-force should be identified 'not simply by occupational titles or whether the job was formal or informal, but by the household strategy for obtaining an income'. The mass of the urban poor can only exist by 'income pooling, sharing housing, food and other resources' either with kin or *landsmen*. ('Urban Development and Social Inequality in Latin America', in Gugler, *Cities in the Developing World*, p. 290.)

86 Statistic on street kids: *Natural History*, July 1997, p. 4.

87 Dubresson, 'Abidjan', p. 263.

88 Rogerson, 'Globalization or informalization?', pp. 347–51.

89 Bryceson, 'Disappearing Peasantries', pp. 307–8.

90 In Clifford Geertz's original, inimitable definition, 'involution' is 'an overdriving of an established form in such a way that it becomes rigid through an inward over-elaboration of detail'. (*Agricultural Involution: Social Development and Economic Change in Two Indonesian Towns*, Chicago 1963, p. 82.) More prosaically, 'involution', agricultural or urban, can be described as spiraling labour self-exploitation (other factors fixed) which continues, despite rapidly diminishing returns, as long as any return or increment is produced.

91 John Walton, 'Urban Conflict and Social Movements in Poor Countries: Theory and Evidence of Collective Action', paper to 'Cities in Transition Conference', Humboldt University, Berlin, July 1987.

92 Kurt Weyland, 'Neopopulism and Neoliberalism in Latin America: How Much Affinity?', *Third World Quarterly*, vol. 24, no. 6 (2003), pp. 1095–115.

93 For a fascinating if frightening account of Shiv Sena's ascendancy in Bombay at the expense of older Communist and trade-union politics, see Thomas Hansen, *Wages of Violence: Naming and Identity in Postcolonial Bombay* (Princeton, 2001). See also Veena Das, ed., *Mirrors of Violence: Communities, Riots and Survivors in South Asia* (New York, 1990).

Additional Readings

Hebdige

Andy Bennett and Keith Kahn-Harris, eds. *After Subculture: Critical Studies in Contemporary Youth Culture.* London: Palgrave Macmillan, 2004.
A series of essays in which scholars attempt to build upon and go beyond Hebdige's notion of subculture to better understand the application of the term to contemporary youth culture.

David Hesmondhalgh. "Subcultures, Scenes or Tribes? None of the Above." *Journal of Youth Studies* 8.1 (2005): 21–40.
A challenge to the notion of subcultures and its recent replacements, "tribes" and "scenes," which addresses the problems raised by these terms and the possibilities of new ways of conceptualizing youth, particularly in relation to popular music.

de Certeau

Ian Buchanan. "Unknotting Place and Space." In *Michel de Certeau: Cultural Theorist*, pp. 108–25. London: Sage, 2000.
A critical introduction to de Certeau's notion of spatiality with a particular focus on the importance of naming and storytelling.

Catherine Driscoll. "The Moving Ground: Locating Everyday Life." *The South Atlantic Quarterly* 100.2 (2001): 381–98.
In this essay, Driscoll emphasizes the critical role of everyday life in de Certeau's work and attempts to

understand exactly what the theorist means by this ambiguous and contentious term.

Ben Highmore. *Michel de Certeau: Analysing Culture.* London: Continuum, 2006.
An account of de Certeau's thought which argues for his position as a major theorist of cultural studies. Highmore provides an introduction to de Certeau's work and its potential application in a number of disparate disciplines.

Anderson

Michael Billig. *Banal Nationalism.* London: Sage, 1999.
Billig expands upon Anderson's formulation of the imagined community by exploring the ways in which nationalism is evoked and unconsciously reproduced in everyday, unthinking activities.

Jonathan Culler and Pheng Cheah, eds. *Grounds of Comparison: Around the Work of Benedict Anderson.* New York: Routledge, 2002.
A collection of essays addressing the application of the major themes of Anderson's work on nationalism in different contexts and as they apply to different cultural forms and media.

Mark Hamilton. "New Imaginings: The Legacy of Benedict Anderson and Alternative Engagements of Nationalism." *Studies in Ethnicity and Nationalism* 6.3 (2006): 73–89.
An overview of Anderson's work on nationalism which seeks to re-inject his insights into contemporary

discussions on the topic, review his impact and significance, and speak to major debates that emerged from his work.

Appadurai

Ackbar Abbas, John Nguyet Erni, and Wimal Dissanayake, eds. *Internationalising Cultural Studies*. London: Blackwell, 2005.
A collection of essays which emphasize the international nature of cultural studies and the diverse fields of interest which interact and inflect one other in the complex network of globalization.

Setha M. Low and Denise Lawrence-Zúñiga, eds. *The Anthropology of Space and Place: Locating Culture*. London: Blackwell, 2003.
Essays questioning and reappraising the role of space in distinct international contexts, from transnational Tokyo to the Australian Aboriginal landscape.

Terhi Rantanen. "A Man Behind Scapes: An Interview with Arjun Appadurai." *Global Media and Communication* 2.1 (2006): 7–19.
An interview in which Appadurai explains how he has altered and updated his thinking since the publication of the original "-scapes" articles, and the ways in which he thinks it is still relevant to the study of globalization.

Massey

Henri Lefebvre. *The Production of Space*. Translated by Donald Nicholson-Smith. London: Blackwell, 2000.
In this classic work, Lefebvre attempts to bridge the gap between how space is theorized and how it is experienced through attention to a wide range of everyday modes, including literature, architecture, and economics.

Doreen Massey. *For Space*. London: Sage, 2005.
A recent theoretical and philosophical manifesto calling for a reimagination of space as a means to alter our understanding of cities, globalization, and ourselves.

Doreen Massey. *Space, Place and Gender*. Minneapolis: University of Minnesota Press, 1994.

In this volume, Massey traces the development of our ways of thinking about space and place and how the assumptions caught up in these conceptions inflect our thinking regarding gender.

Edward Soja. *Postmodern Geographies: The Reassertion of Space in Critical Social Theory*. New York: Verso, 1989.
In this critique of historicism and the privileging of time over space, Soja argues for the importance of geographical materialism, the relationship between Marxism and geography, and an understanding of "third space" or the luminal area between material infrastructure and our imaginaries of its workings.

Harvey

Noel Castree and Derek Gregory, eds. *David Harvey: A Critical Reader*. London: Wiley-Blackwell, 2006.
A critical interrogation of the work of Harvey in his roles as both geographer and Marxist. These essays seek to address the whole range of Harvey's contribution to the study of space and its relation to modern capitalism and postmodernism.

David Harvey. *Spaces of Capital: Towards a Critical Geography*. New York: Routledge, 2001.
A collection of Harvey's most notable essays, this volume provides a comprehensive introduction and insight into Harvey's theories of geography and their relation to social relations and the philosophical history of the West.

David Harvey. *Paris: Capital of Modernity*. New York: Routledge, 2003.
A case study of Paris in which Harvey demonstrates the strength of his theoretical method through an insightful analysis of the social, economic, artistic, and political mythologies and histories of one of the key sites of urban modernity.

Davis

Mike Davis. *City of Quartz*. New York: Verso, 1990.
Davis's case study of Los Angeles, which analyses the history and current state of the city as a site of social, economic, and cultural forces. Davis argues that the

Space and Scale

city's urban development points toward a heightened sense of racial and class-based conflict and repression.

UN-Habitat. *The Challenge of Slums: Global Report on Human Settlements 2003*. London: UN-Habitat, 2003.
The UN report from which Davis's essay draws much of its material. A statistical and social evaluation of the global growth of slums.

General

Susan Buck-Morss. *The Dialectics of Seeing: Walter Benjamin and the Arcades Project*. Cambridge, MA: MIT Press, 1989.
An insightful analysis of the thought of Walter Benjamin as it relates to the urban milieu of nineteenth-century Paris and the normalization of petit bourgeois luxury.

Richard T. LeGates and Fredric Stout, eds. *The City Reader*, 4th edition. New York: Routledge, 2007.
A wide-ranging collection of historical and contemporary essays which deal with the idea of the city in all its many aspects. Each piece is situated within the wider context of urban studies and its particular relevance to continuing debates explained.

Lucy Lippard. *The Lure of the Local: Senses of Place in a Multicentered Society*. New York: New Press, 1997.
A study of the ways in which we experience space and place from an esteemed art writer. This volume argues that Americans are losing their sense of distinctive place with the advent of mass-produced strip malls, which obliterate traces of an older, more idiosyncratic landscape.

Andy Merrifield. *Metromarxism: A Marxist Tale of the City*. New York: Routledge, 2002.
An account of the relationship between Marxism and the city from the 1850s to the present. It highlights the symbiotic nature of this relationship through readable analyses of leading Marxist thinkers, from Marx to Harvey, Guy Debord, and Manuel Castells.

Raymond Williams. *The Country and the City*. London: The Hogarth Press, 1973.
A classic in which Williams makes a sustained attempt to read English literature in relation to its social background and geographical context. He maps shifting English attitudes toward the urban–rural relationship and shows how this plays out in the terrain of culture.

Part 5

Temporality

Introduction

Time has been a concerted object of philosophical investigation since at least the late seventeenth century, when Isaac Newton's *Principia* (1687) raised the question of its ontological status in terms that have shaped modern science ever since. For Newton, time was a feature of reality itself – the grand stage (along with space) on which all entities are placed and in which events occur. This view of time as an objective and defining characteristic of the universe, ticking by with the steady and impersonal pulse of the second hand, has remained the dominant way in which we understand it. Yet even at the level of ontology, time has proven to be less stable than we might want it to be. Immanuel Kant introduced the possibility of time being an a priori scheme that we impose on the world: time as it appears to humans is due to their particular cognitive apparatus rather than to the apprehension of something fixed outside of us (which is to say: time might be different for animals or angels). Albert Einstein's special theory of relativity further complicated our everyday perception of time as an objective category, by introducing the idea of the absolute character of the speed of light instead of time and showing us the way in which the position of the observer determines the time of events.

Temporality plays a significant role in cultural theory less in terms of such questions about the fundamental character of time, but rather with respect to our understanding of time in relation to the dynamics of human life activity. The present comes about only through a past that has disappeared from view; the activity of the present is oriented toward the production of a future that has not yet come to be. How and why we live out our presents depends on the ways in which we understand the other two dimensions of social time that are not with us. It is with the "how and why" of this aspect of temporality that time is explored in cultural theory. Even if time were an ontological absolute, social time would be in many respects pure accident. History is not a narrative shaped by time, but rather one shaped around changing ideas about temporality – its flow, movement, and direction – which immediately betray our preconceptions and assumptions about the broader forces that give shape and form to culture and society, and our sense of social time itself. As with the past, so too with our sense of the future that lies just over the horizon. Cultural theories which deal with time are interested in understanding the uses to which narratives of temporality have been put and their implications for how we imagine who and what we are and might yet become.

Perhaps the most powerful of these narratives – the one within whose grip we still find ourselves – understands social time in relation to ideas of progress – political, economic, intellectual, but perhaps especially, technological. This deep-seated cultural belief, which has taken various names (Enlightenment, modernity), views time as the arena of human development and advancement, as the medium through which one marks the passage from barbarism to civilization, from cave dwellers to travelers to the moon. The replacement of monarchies by parliamentary democracies or republican systems, the increase in the size of the middle classes in the West from the beginning of the twentieth century to the 1970s, the junking of the Walkman as a result of the rise of the iPod – all of these individual trajectories form part of a larger story about the passage of time with which we are immediately familiar. G. W. F. Hegel is the thinker who is most often seen as having introduced temporality into philosophical thought through his description of the process by which various systems (the mind as well as ethics, politics, and even Nature) develop into their purest expression through a necessary series of intermediary stages leading toward a final conclusion. But Immanuel Kant has an equally important role in the constitution of a link between time and development. In his reading of Kant's "What Is Enlightenment?" (1784), Michel Foucault argues that it is in this text that we witness the first expression of a form of philosophical reflection on the present that will come to define the characteristic "attitude of modernity." "Enlightenment" for Kant describes a process through which humanity moves from a state of immaturity to maturity, actualizing through its individual and collective activity qualities that are only latent, yet to be fully expressed, at the moment he is writing. Foucault finds three novel temporal modes in Kant's text that will come to shape thinking about time in the centuries that follow: the present is seen as an era distinct from others; it is seen as an era that can be examined in "an attempt to decipher in it the heralding signs of a forthcoming event"; and it can be "analyzed as a point of transition toward the dawning of a new world."[1] The process by which humanity "grows up" places individual and collective liberty and the use of human Reason within the flow of time, with the future bringing ever-greater freedom and the past offering examples against which to measure the distance already traveled.

If philosophy is the name for the mode of thought which tries to articulate and produce Enlightenment through Reason, part of what might be said to constitute "theory" is the concerted attack on the unacknowledged presumptions and blind spots of this understanding of social and political time. From a variety of perspectives and with differing motivations, twentieth-century thought has repeatedly drawn attention to the ideologies governing dominant understandings of temporality. For Max Horkheimer and Theodor Adorno, for example, "Enlightenment, understood in the widest sense as the advance of thought, has always aimed at liberating human beings from fear and installing them as masters. Yet the wholly enlightened earth is radiant with triumphant calamity."[3] The liberty that is supposed to be increasing throughout time occurs (if it does at all) only in conjunction with the ever-greater horrors of war, slavery, racism, sexism, and all other manner of social strife. Only a deep faith in human maturity makes it possible to view the world wars, Rwanda, or Abu Ghraib as anomalies rather than as representative elements of a history that is difficult to characterize as progressing in any simple way. Adorno remarks in *Negative Dialectics* (1966) that "no universal history leads from savagery to humanitarianism, but there is one leading from the slingshot to the megaton bomb."[4] Such critical attitudes toward time are repeated in the challenge made within postcolonial theory to the ideologies of growth and development that have continued to sustain differences between the center and periphery, the First World and the Third. Inequalities in power and the distribution of wealth have long been justified by an understanding of development which positions some parts of the world in the present and places others in the past. "Modernization" is a process not just of improving technology and social systems, but of moving into the shared time of the "now" of modern life, which is why "development" is sometimes described as a process by which poorer countries will "catch up" with wealthier ones.

This section includes critical approaches to temporality which have had an impact not just on how we think about history, the present, and the future, but also on how we conceptualize culture in relation to time. Fernand Braudel suggests that "it is not so much time which is the creation of our own minds, as the way in which we break it up."[5] The essays in this section explore the dominant ways in which time has been broken up, present alternative modes of organizing time, and assess and argue about the politics and significance of time for culture. Each of the selections contributes in its own specific way to reframing our ideas about temporality. However, three main themes cut across these pieces and capture the primary ways in which time has been addressed in cultural theory.

First, theory has sought to expose the principles that have organized historical knowledge, in an effort to challenge the gaps and limits within existing historical narratives and to offer new tools for breaking up and organizing time. How we tell stories about time – what we decide to include and exclude, what count as significant enough events in the production of social life to be part of the record, and what form evidence of forces and causes takes – is the product of ideas about knowledge and temporality we hold in the present. As Hayden White points out in *Metahistory*, "there does, in fact, appear to be an irreducible ideological component in every historical account of reality … the very claim to have discerned some kind of formal coherence in the historical record brings with it theories of the nature of the historical world and of historical knowledge itself which have ideological implications for attempts to understand 'the present,' however this 'present' is defined."[6] The imperious scientificity of Standard Time and the hegemony of liberal historiography have meant that ideologies not just of historical content but of its temporal form need to be questioned repeatedly. The great *Annales* historian Braudel challenges histories built up around discrete "events" and stresses the need to pay attention to the *longue durée*, to slow-moving expanses of history produced by geographic limits or the persistence of economic systems whose force and impact are too often absent from accounts of historical development. Michel Foucault points to the multiple ways in which history's interest in origins – the unfolding growth of time from a point in the past to a mature present – has rendered accounts of human time into something like "the evolution of a species" or a map of "the destiny of a people."[7] In contrast, the practice of "genealogy" which he outlines pays attention to "haphazard conflicts" and "profusion of entangled events" in the past; it seeks to "identify the accidents, the minute deviations – or conversely, the complete reversals – the errors, the false appraisals, and the faulty calculations that gave birth to those things that continue to exist and have value for us."[8] Each of the other selections makes a similar break with standard historical narratives in order to offer up new insights into the forces that have shaped and defined the culture and politics of the present.

One of most significant ideological uses of history was in the project of colonialism. Ranajit Guha is one of a number of scholars (Edward Said being perhaps the most well known) who have drawn attention to the role played by historical narratives in justifying the colonial mission to both colonizers and colonized. Guha outlines the manner in which the history of India was invented by the British in a way that showcased the "triumphs and glories of the colonizers and their instruments, the colonial state … to best advantage."[9] In the context of the history of Britain and of the abstract universalism of a capitalism moving toward a global presence, a familiar difference is played out that is at once temporal and racial: rulers and ruled, white and black, prosperous Westerners and poor Others, higher and lower levels of civilizational attainment. The work of postcolonial critics on the impact and implications of such histories forms a second main theme addressed in cultural theory with respect to temporality. In addition to illustrating how such histories have legitimated economic and racial injustice, Guha's essay and that of Roberto Schwarz show that the framework of underdevelopment also produces a lingering feeling of cultural and social belatedness with long-term consequences for how politics is performed in the colonies. The idea that different parts of the world exist in different times – some more advanced in terms of the development to which the whole world is supposedly moving – may be a fiction, but a fiction with real effects. Schwarz describes the cultural consequences of development narratives, which repeat at the level of ideas the sense that the present is inevitably elsewhere. The attempt to break out of the feeling of intellectual and cultural inauthenticity and imitation takes two forms: either a rejection of the colonial heritage in order to place one's nation in the march of progress which defines the present, or a preservation of this very legacy against a too-simple imitation of the culture and ideas of developed countries (primarily the United States). Schwarz's investigation of the cultural implications of the time of development in Brazil reveals the class character of anxieties about national-cultural belatedness, with intriguing implications for how we might think about the return of these same worries about cultural imperialism in the era of globalization.[10]

The essays by Fredric Jameson, Jean-François Lyotard, and Raymond Williams offer a final example of recent theoretical approaches to temporality. Jameson has argued elsewhere that, "if we do not achieve some general sense of a cultural dominant, then we fall back into a view of present history as sheer heterogeneity, random difference, a coexistence of a host of distinct forces whose effectivity is undecidable."[11] Cultural analysis demands not just an identification of a cultural dominant against which it might be possible to identify what Williams describes as "residual" and "emergent" elements – aspects of the cultural present whose formative logic is other than that which characterizes dominant formations – but the identification of distinct temporal periods that allow us to mark off significant shifts and changes. Williams offers a reminder of the complex internal dynamics that take place in any given epoch, which Jameson's essay shows us how to peel back and reveal the relationship of the various levels that make up a period of time. For Jameson, a "period" names a shared "objective situation, to which a whole range of varied responses and creative innovations are possible, but always within that situation's structural limits."[12] Any attempt to identify a slice of time as having a distinct character in relation to others before and after it – whether this takes the form of decades or much larger temporal blocks (antiquity, feudalism, the Enlightenment, modernity) – requires an account of cultural similarity and difference in relation to some causal force (or set of forces). One of the places in which such temporal distinctions have been played out in great detail is in the attempt to capture the difference between modernism and postmodernism. The final chapter of Lyotard's influential book on postmodernism oscillates between "post" as a temporal marker and a formal or aesthetic one. Against this idealist account of cultural change, Jameson and Williams insist on the need to consider the time of culture in relation to the material "conditions of possibility" that produce the coordinates within which social life is carried out at any given time in history; both offer us concepts by which we can shake up the apparent fixity and solidity of the time of our lives.

Notes

1. Michel Foucault, "What Is Enlightenment ?" in *The Foucault Reader*, ed. Paul Rabinow (New York: Pantheon Books, 1984), 32–50.
2. For a different perspective on the relation of "theory" to "philosophy," see Fredric Jameson, "Periodizing the 60s," in *The Ideologies of Theory, Essays 1971–1986* (Minneapolis: University of Minnesota Press, 1988), 193. Reproduced in this volume.
3. Max Horkheimer and Theodor W. Adorno, *Dialectic of Enlightenment: Philosophical Fragments*, ed. Gunzelin Schmid Noerr, trans. Edmund Jephcott (Stanford, CA: Stanford University Press, 2002), 1.
4. Theodor W. Adorno, *Negative Dialectics*, trans. E. B. Ashton (New York: Continuum, 1992), 320.
5. Fernand Braudel, "History and the Social Sciences: The *Longue Durée*," in *On History*, trans. Sarah Matthews (Chicago: The University of Chicago Press, 1980), 48. Reproduced in this volume.
6. Hayden White, *Metahistory* (Baltimore: Johns Hopkins University Press, 1983), 21–2.
7. Michel Foucault, "Nietzsche, Genealogy, History," in *Language, Counter-Memory, Practice: Selected Essays and Interviews*, ed. Donald F. Bouchard (Ithaca, NY: Cornell University Press, 1977), 81.
8. Ibid., 88, 89, and 81 respectively. Reproduced in this volume.
9. Ranajit Guha, *Dominance without Hegemony: History and Power in Colonial India* (Cambridge, MA: Harvard University Press, 1997), 2–3. Reproduced in this volume.
10. In contrast to the decades immediately preceding it, the "time" of globalization is characterized not by zones of more or advanced spaces, but by an isochronism which declares that global time is now uniform – not because divisions in wealth and power have altered significantly, but because of communications technologies, air travel, and the elimination of the ideological challenge posed by the socialist world. This is surely how we should read Francis Fukuyama's infamous declaration of the "end of history" which emerges after the Cold War and inaugurates globalization. Twenty years later, the political consequences of a prolonged period of a unipolar power has resulted in an admission by Robert Kagan that the "abiding belief in the inevitability of human progress, the belief that history moves in only one direction" was wrong. History is back. See Francis Fukuyama, *The End of History and the Last Man* (New York: The Free Press, 1992) and Robert Kagan, *The Return of History and the End of Dreams* (New York: Knopf, 2008).

    For a discussion of globalization as isochronism, see Imre Szeman, "Belated or Isochronic?: Canadian Writing, Time and Globalization," *Essays on Canadian Writing* 71 (2000), 145–53.
11. Fredric Jameson, *Postmodernism; or, the Cultural Logic of Late Capitalism* (Durham, NC: Duke University Press, 1991), 6.
12. Fredric Jameson, "Periodizing the 60s," in *The Ideologies of Theory, Essays 1971–1986* (Volume 2) (Minneapolis: University of Minnesota Press, 1988), 179. Reproduced in this volume.

29

"Nietzsche, Genealogy, History" (1977)

Michel Foucault

1. Genealogy is gray, meticulous, and patiently documentary. It operates on a field of entangled and confused parchments, on documents that have been scratched over and recopied many times.

On this basis, it is obvious that Paul Ree[1] was wrong to follow the English tendency in describing the history of morality in terms of a linear development – in reducing its entire history and genesis to an exclusive concern for utility. He assumed that words had kept their meaning, that desires still pointed in a single direction, and that ideas retained their logic; and he ignored the fact that the world of speech and desires has known invasions, struggles, plundering, disguises, ploys. From these elements, however, genealogy retrieves an indispensable restraint: it must record the singularity of events outside of any monotonous finality; it must seek them in the most unpromising places, in what we tend to feel is without history – in sentiments, love, conscience, instincts; it must be sensitive to their recurrence, not in order to trace the gradual curve of their evolution, but to isolate the different scenes where they engaged in different roles. Finally, genealogy must define even those instances when they are absent, the moment when they remained unrealized (Plato, at Syracuse, did not become Mohammed).

Genealogy, consequently, requires patience and a knowledge of details, and it depends on a vast accumulation of source material. Its "cyclopean monuments"[2] are constructed from "discreet and apparently insignificant truths and according to a rigorous method"; they cannot be the product of "large and well-meaning errors."[3] In short, genealogy demands relentless erudition. Genealogy does not oppose itself to history as the lofty and profound gaze of the philosopher might compare to the molelike perspective of the scholar; on the contrary, it rejects the metahistorical deployment of ideal significations and indefinite teleologies. It opposes itself to the search for "origins."

2. In Nietzsche, we find two uses of the word *Ursprung*. The first is unstressed, and it is found alternately with other terms such as *Entstehung, Herkunft, Abkunft, Geburt*. In *The Genealogy of Morals*, for example, *Entstehung* or *Ursprung* serves equally well to denote the origin of duty or guilty conscience;[4] and in the discussion of logic and knowledge in *The Gay Science*, their origin is indiscriminately referred to as *Ursprung, Entstehung*, or *Herkunft*.[5]

The other use of the word is stressed. On occasion, Nietzsche places the term in opposition to another: in the first paragraph of *Human, All Too Human* the miraculous origin (*Wunderursprung*) sought by metaphysics is set against the analyses of historical philosophy, which poses questions *über Herkunft und Anfang*. *Ursprung* is also used in an ironic and deceptive manner. In what, for instance, do we find the original basis (*Ursprung*) of morality, a foundation sought after since Plato? "In detestable, narrow-minded conclusions. *Pudenda origo*."[6] Or in a related context, where should we seek the origin of religion (*Ursprung*), which Schopenhauer located in a particular metaphysical

Michel Foucault, "Nietzsche, Genealogy, History," pp. 76–100 from *The Foucault Reader*, trans. Paul Rabinow. New York: Pantheon, 1984.

Temporality

sentiment of the hereafter? It belongs, very simply, to an invention (*Erfindung*), a sleight-of-hand, an artifice (*Kunststück*), a secret formula, in the rituals of black magic, in the work of the *Schwarzkünstler*.[7]

One of the most significant texts with respect to the use of all these terms and to the variations in the use of *Ursprung* is the preface to the *Genealogy*. At the beginning of the text, its objective is defined as an examination of the origin of moral preconceptions and the term used is *Herkunft*. Then, Nietzsche proceeds by retracing his personal involvement with this question: he recalls the period when he "calligraphied" philosophy, when he questioned if God must be held responsible for the origin of evil. He now finds this question amusing and properly characterizes it as a search for *Ursprung* (he will shortly use the same term to summarize Paul Ree's activity).[8] Further on, he evokes the analyses that are characteristically Nietzschean and that begin with *Human, All Too Human*. Here, he speaks of *Herkunfthypothesen*. This use of the word *Herkunft* cannot be arbitrary, since it serves to designate a number of texts, beginning with *Human, All Too Human*, which deal with the origin of morality, asceticism, justice, and punishment. And yet the word used in all these works had been *Ursprung*.[9] It would seem that at this point in the *Genealogy* Nietzsche wished to validate an opposition between *Herkunft* and *Ursprung* that did not exist ten years earlier. But immediately following the use of the two terms in a specific sense, Nietzsche reverts, in the final paragraphs of the preface, to a usage that is neutral and equivalent.[10]

Why does Nietzsche challenge the pursuit of the origin (*Ursprung*), at least on those occasions when he is truly a genealogist? First, because it is an attempt to capture the exact essence of things, their purest possibilities, and their carefully protected identities; because this search assumes the existence of immobile forms that precede the external world of accident and succession. This search is directed to "that which was already there," the image of a primordial truth fully adequate to its nature, and it necessitates the removal of every mask to ultimately disclose an original identity. However, if the genealogist refuses to extend his faith in metaphysics, if he listens to history, he finds that there is "something altogether different" behind things: not a timeless and essential secret, but the secret that they have no essence or that their essence was

fabricated in a piecemeal fashion from alien forms. Examining the history of reason, he learns that it was born in an altogether "reasonable" fashion – from chance;[11] devotion to truth and the precision of scientific methods arose from the passion of scholars, their reciprocal hatred, their fanatical and unending discussions, and their spirit of competition – the personal conflicts that slowly forged the weapons of reason.[12] Further, genealogical analysis shows that the concept of liberty is an "invention of the ruling classes"[13] and not fundamental to man's nature or at the root of his attachment to being and truth. What is found at the historical beginning of things is not the inviolable identity of their origin; it is the dissension of other things. It is disparity.[14] *disparity at the origin of each of origin.*

History also teaches how to laugh at the solemnities of the origin. The lofty origin is no more than "a metaphysical extension which arises from the belief that things are most precious and essential at the moment of birth."[15] We tend to think that this is the moment of their greatest perfection, when they emerged dazzling from the hands of a creator or in the shadowless light of a first morning. The origin always precedes the Fall. It comes before the body, before the world and time; it is associated with the gods, and its story is always sung as a theogony. But historical beginnings are lowly: not in the sense of modest or discreet like the steps of a dove, but derisive and ironic, capable of undoing every infatuation. "We wished to awaken the feeling of man's sovereignty by showing his divine birth: this path is now forbidden, since a monkey stands at the entrance."[16] Man originated with a grimace over his future development; and Zarathustra himself is plagued by a monkey who jumps along behind him, pulling on his coattails.

The final postulate of the origin is linked to the first two in being the site of truth. From the vantage point of an absolute distance, free from the restraints of positive knowledge, the origin makes possible a field of knowledge whose function is to recover it, but always in a false recognition due to the excesses of its own speech. The origin lies at a place of inevitable loss, the point where the truth of things corresponded to a truthful discourse, the site of a fleeting articulation that discourse has obscured and finally lost. It is a new cruelty of history that compels a reversal of this relationship and the abandonment of "adolescent" quests: behind the always recent, avaricious, and measured truth, it posits the ancient proliferation of errors. It is now impossible to believe that "in the rending of the veil, truth remains truthful; we have lived long enough not to be taken in."[17] Truth is undoubtedly the sort of error that cannot be refuted because it was hardened into an unalterable form in the long baking process of history.[18] Moreover, the very question of truth, the right it appropriates to refute error and oppose itself to appearance, the manner in which it developed (initially made available to the wise, then withdrawn by men of piety to an unattainable world where it was given the double role of consolation and imperative, finally rejected as a useless notion, superfluous and contradicted on all sides) – does this not form a history, the history of an error we call truth? Truth, and its original reign, has had a history within history from which we are barely emerging "in the time of the shortest shadow," when light no longer seems to flow from the depths of the sky or to arise from the first moments of the day.[19]

A genealogy of values, morality, asceticism, and knowledge will never confuse itself with a quest for their "origins," will never neglect as inaccessible the vicissitudes of history. On the contrary, it will cultivate the details and accidents that accompany every beginning; it will be scrupulously attentive to their petty malice; it will await their emergence, once unmasked, as the face of the other. Wherever it is made to go, it will not be reticent – in "excavating the depths," in allowing time for these elements to escape from a labyrinth where no truth had ever detained them. The genealogist needs history to dispel the chimeras of the origin, somewhat in the manner of the pious philosopher who needs a doctor to exorcise the shadow of his soul. He must be able to recognize the events of history, its jolts, its surprises, its unsteady victories and unpalatable defeats – the basis of all beginnings, atavisms, and heredities. Similarly, he must be able to diagnose the illnesses of the body, its conditions of weakness and strength, its breakdowns and resistances, to be in a position to judge philosophical discourse. History is the concrete body of a development, with its moments of intensity, its lapses, its extended periods of feverish agitation, its fainting spells; and only a metaphysician would seek its soul in the distant ideality of the origin.

3.   *Entstehung* and *Herkunft* are more exact than *Ursprung* in recording the true objective of genealogy; and, while they are ordinarily translated as "origin," we must attempt to reestablish their proper use.

Herkunft is the equivalent of stock or *descent;* it is the ancient affiliation to a group, sustained by the bonds of blood, tradition, or social class. The analysis of *Herkunft* often involves a consideration of race or social type.[20] But the traits it attempts to identify are not the exclusive generic characteristics of an individual, a sentiment, or an idea, which permit us to qualify them as "Greek" or "English"; rather, it seeks the subtle, singular, and subindividual marks that might possibly intersect in them to form a network that is difficult to unravel. Far from being a category of resemblance, this origin allows the sorting out of different traits: the Germans imagined that they had finally accounted for their complexity by saying they possessed a double soul; they were fooled by a simple computation, or rather, they were simply trying to master the racial disorder from which they had formed themselves.[21] Where the soul pretends unification or the self fabricates a coherent identity, the genealogist sets out to study the beginning – numberless beginnings, whose faint traces and hints of color are readily seen by a historical eye. The analysis of descent permits the dissociation of the self, its recognition and displacement as an empty synthesis, in liberating a profusion of lost events.

An examination of descent also permits the discovery, under the unique aspect of a trait or a concept, of the myriad events through which – thanks to which, against which – they were formed. Genealogy does not pretend to go back in time to restore an unbroken continuity that operates beyond the dispersion of forgotten things; its duty is not to demonstrate that the past actively exists in the present, that it continues secretly to animate the present, having imposed a predetermined form on all its vicissitudes. Genealogy does not resemble the evolution of a species and does not map the destiny of a people. On the contrary, to follow the complex course of descent is to maintain passing events in their proper dispersion; it is to identify the accidents, the minute deviations – or conversely, the complete reversals – the errors, the false appraisals, and the faulty calculations that gave birth to those things that continue to exist and have value for us; it is to discover that truth or being does not lie at the root of what we know

narrative of latency

and what we are, but the exteriority of accidents.[22] This is undoubtedly why every origin of morality from the moment it stops being pious – and *Herkunft* can never be – has value as a critique.[23]

Deriving from such a source is a dangerous legacy. In numerous instances, Nietzsche associates the terms *Herkunft* and *Erbschaft*. Nevertheless, we should not be deceived into thinking that this heritage is an acquisition, a possession that grows and solidifies; rather, it is an unstable assemblage of faults, fissures, and heterogeneous layers that threaten the fragile inheritor from within or from underneath: "injustice or instability in the minds of certain men, their disorder and lack of decorum, are the final consequences of their ancestors' numberless logical inaccuracies, hasty conclusions, and superficiality."[24] The search for descent is not the erecting of foundations: on the contrary, it disturbs what was previously considered immobile; it fragments what was thought unified; it shows the heterogeneity of what was imagined consistent with itself. What convictions and, far more decisively, what knowledge can resist it? If a genealogical analysis of a scholar were made – of one who collects facts and carefully accounts for them – his *Herkunft* would quickly divulge the official papers of the scribe and the pleadings of the lawyer – their father[25] – in their apparently disinterested attention, in the "pure" devotion to objectivity.

Finally, descent attaches itself to the body.[26] It inscribes itself in the nervous system, in temperament, in the digestive apparatus; it appears in faulty respiration, in improper diets, in the debilitated and prostrate bodies of those whose ancestors committed errors. Fathers have only to mistake effects for causes, believe in the reality of an "afterlife," or maintain the value of eternal truths, and the bodies of their children will suffer. Cowardice and hypocrisy, for their part, are the simple offshoots of error: not in a Socratic sense, not that evil is the result of a mistake, not because of a turning away from an original truth, but because the body maintains, in life as in death, through its strength or weakness, the sanction of every truth and error, as it sustains, in an inverse manner, the origin – descent. Why did men invent the contemplative life? Why give a supreme value to this form of existence? Why maintain the absolute truth of those fictions which sustain it? "During barbarous ages … if the strength of an individual declined, if he felt himself tired or sick, melancholy or satiated and, as a consequence, without desire or appetite for a short time, he became relatively a better man, that is, less dangerous. His pessimistic ideas only take form as words or reflections. In this frame of mind, he either became a thinker and prophet or used his imagination to feed his superstitions."[27] The body – and everything that touches it: diet, climate, and soil – is the domain of the *Herkunft*. The body manifests the stigmata of past experience and also gives rise to desires, failings, and errors. These elements may join in a body where they achieve a sudden expression, but as often, their encounter is an engagement in which they efface each other, where the body becomes the pretext of their insurmountable conflict.

The body is the inscribed surface of events (traced by language and dissolved by ideas), the locus of a dissociated self (adopting the illusion of a substantial unity), and a volume in perpetual disintegration. Genealogy, as an analysis of descent, is thus situated within the articulation of the body and history. Its task is to expose a body totally imprinted by history and the process of history's destruction of the body.

4. *Entstehung* designates *emergence*, the moment of arising. It stands as the principle and the singular law of an apparition. As it is wrong to search for descent in an uninterrupted continuity, we should avoid thinking of emergence as the final term of a historical development; the eye was not always intended for contemplation, and punishment has had other purposes than setting an example. These developments may appear as a culmination, but they are merely the current episodes in a series of subjugations: the eye initially responded to the requirements of hunting and warfare; and punishment has been subjected, throughout its history, to a variety of needs – revenge, excluding an aggressor, compensating a victim, creating fear. In placing present needs at the origin, the metaphysician would convince us of an obscure purpose that seeks its realization at the moment it arises. Genealogy, however, seeks to reestablish the various systems of subjection: not the anticipatory power of meaning, but the hazardous play of dominations. Emergence is always produced through a particular stage of forces. The analysis of the *Entstehung* must

delineate this interaction, the struggle these forces wage against each other or against adverse circumstances, and the attempt to avoid degeneration and regain strength by dividing these forces against themselves. It is in this sense that the emergence of a species (animal or human) and its solidification are secured "in an extended battle against conditions which are essentially and constantly unfavorable." In fact, "the species must realize itself as a species, as something – characterized by the durability, uniformity, and simplicity of its form – which can prevail in the perpetual struggle against outsiders or the uprising of those it oppresses from within." On the other hand, individual differences emerge at another stage of the relationship of forces, when the species has become victorious and when it is no longer threatened from outside. In this condition, we find a struggle "of egoisms turned against each other, each bursting forth in a splintering of forces and a general striving for the sun and for the light."[28] There are also times when force contends against itself, and not only in the intoxication of an abundance, which allows it to divide itself, but at the moment when it weakens. Force reacts against its growing lassitude and gains strength; it imposes limits, inflicts torments and mortifications; it masks these actions as a higher morality and, in exchange, regains its strength. In this manner, the ascetic ideal was born, "in the instinct of a decadent life which … struggles for its own existence."[29] This also describes the movement in which the Reformation arose, precisely where the church was least corrupt;[30] German Catholicism, in the sixteenth century, retained enough strength to turn against itself, to mortify its own body and history, and to spiritualize itself into a pure religion of conscience.

Emergence is thus the entry of forces; it is their eruption, the leap from the wings to center stage, each in its youthful strength. What Nietzsche calls the *Entstehungsherd*[31] of the concept of goodness is not specifically the energy of the strong or the reaction of the weak, but precisely this scene where they are displayed superimposed or face-to-face. It is nothing but the space that divides them, the void through which they exchange their threatening gestures and speeches. As descent qualifies the strength or weakness of an instinct and its inscription on a body, emergence designates a place of confrontation, but not as a closed

field offering the spectacle of a struggle among equals. Rather, as Nietzsche demonstrates in his analysis of good and evil, it is a "non-place," a pure distance, which indicates that the adversaries do not belong to a common space. Consequently, no one is responsible for an emergence; no one can glory in it, since it always occurs in the interstice.

In a sense, only a single drama is ever staged in this "non-place," the endlessly repeated play of dominations. The domination of certain men over others leads to the differentiation of values;[32] class domination generates the idea of liberty;[33] and the forceful appropriation of things necessary to survival and the imposition of a duration not intrinsic to them account for the origin of logic.[34] This relationship of domination is no more a "relationship" than the place where it occurs is a place; and, precisely for this reason, it is fixed, throughout its history, in rituals, in meticulous procedures that impose rights and obligations. It establishes marks of its power and engraves memories on things and even within bodies. It makes itself accountable for debts and gives rise to the universe of rules, which is by no means designed to temper violence, but rather to satisfy it. Following traditional beliefs, it would be false to think that total war exhausts itself in its own contradictions and ends by renouncing violence and submitting to civil laws. On the contrary, the law is a calculated and relentless pleasure, delight in the promised blood, which permits the perpetual instigation of new dominations and the staging of meticulously repeated scenes of violence. The desire for peace, the serenity of compromise, and the tacit acceptance of the law, far from representing a major moral conversion or a utilitarian calculation that gave rise to the law, are but its result and, in point of fact, its perversion: "guilt, conscience, and duty had their threshold of emergence in the right to secure obligations; and their inception, like that of any major event on earth, was saturated in blood."[35] Humanity does not gradually progress from combat to combat until it arrives at universal reciprocity, where the rule of law finally replaces warfare; humanity installs each of its violences in a system of rules and thus proceeds from domination to domination.

The nature of these rules allows violence to be inflicted on violence and the resurgence of new forces that are sufficiently strong to dominate those in power.

"Nietzsche, Genealogy, History"

law + blood

Cf. Sorel, Benjamin, and Schmitt.

Rules are empty in themselves, violent and unfinalized; they are impersonal and can be bent to any purpose. The successes of history belong to those who are capable of seizing these rules, to replace those who had used them, to disguise themselves so as to pervert them, invert their meaning, and redirect them against those who had initially imposed them; controlling this complex mechanism, they will make it function so as to overcome the rulers through their own rules.

The isolation of different points of emergence does not conform to the successive configurations of an identical meaning; rather, they result from substitutions, displacements, disguised conquests, and systematic reversals. If interpretation were the slow exposure of the meaning hidden in an origin, then only metaphysics could interpret the development of humanity. But if interpretation is the violent or surreptitious appropriation of a system of rules, which in itself has no essential meaning, in order to impose a direction, to bend it to a new will, to force its participation in a different game, and to subject it to secondary rules, then the development of humanity is a series of interpretations. The role of genealogy is to record its history: the history of morals, ideals, and metaphysical concepts, the history of the concept of liberty or of the ascetic life; as they stand for the emergence of different interpretations, they must be made to appear as events on the stage of historical process.

5. How can we define the relationship between genealogy, seen as the examination of *Herkunft* and *Entstehung*, and history in the traditional sense? We could, of course, examine Nietzsche's celebrated apostrophes against history, but we will put these aside for the moment and consider those instances when he conceives of genealogy as *wirkliche Historie*, or its more frequent characterization as historical "spirit" or "sense."[36] In fact, Nietzsche's criticism, beginning with the second of the *Untimely Meditations*, always questioned the form of history that reintroduces (and always assumes) a suprahistorical perspective: a history whose function is to compose the finally reduced diversity of time into a totality fully closed upon itself; a history that always encourages subjective recognitions and attributes a form of reconciliation to all the displacements of the past; a history whose perspective on all that precedes it implies the end of time, a completed

development. The historian's history finds its support outside of time and pretends to base its judgments on an apocalyptic objectivity. This is only possible, however, because of its belief in eternal truth, the immortality of the soul, and the nature of consciousness as always identical to itself. Once the historical sense is mastered by a suprahistorical perspective, metaphysics can bend it to its own purpose, and, by aligning it to the demands of objective science, it can impose its own "Egyptianism." On the other hand, the historical sense can evade metaphysics and become a privileged instrument of genealogy if it refuses the certainty of absolutes. Given this, it corresponds to the acuity of a glance that distinguishes, separates, and disperses; that is capable of liberating divergence and marginal elements – the kind of dissociating view that is capable of decomposing itself, capable of shattering the unity of man's being through which it was thought that he could extend his sovereignty to the events of his past.

Historical meaning becomes a dimension of *wirkliche Historie* to the extent that it places within a process of development everything considered immortal in man. We believe that feelings are immutable, but every sentiment, particularly the noblest and most disinterested, has a history. We believe in the dull constancy of instinctual life and imagine that it continues to exert its force indiscriminately in the present as it did in the past. But a knowledge of history easily disintegrates this unity, depicts its wavering course, locates its moments of strength and weakness, and defines its oscillating reign. It easily seizes the slow elaboration of instincts and those movements where, in turning upon themselves, they relentlessly set about their self-destruction.[37] We believe, in any event, that the body obeys the exclusive laws of physiology and that it escapes the influence of history, but this too is false. The body is molded by a great many distinct regimes; it is broken down by the rhythms of work, rest, and holidays; it is poisoned by food or values, through eating habits or moral laws; it constructs resistances.[38] "Effective" history differs from traditional history in being without constants. Nothing in man – not even his body – is sufficiently stable to serve as the basis for self-recognition or for understanding other men. The traditional devices for constructing a comprehensive view of history and for retracing the past as a patient and continuous development must be systematically dismantled. Necessarily, we must dismiss those tendencies that encourage the consoling play of recognitions. Knowledge, even under the banner of history, does not depend on "rediscovery," and it emphatically excludes the "rediscovery of ourselves." History becomes "effective" to the degree that it introduces discontinuity into our very being – as it divides our emotions, dramatizes our instincts, multiplies our body and sets it against itself. "Effective" history deprives the self of the reassuring stability of life and nature, and it will not permit itself to be transported by a voiceless obstinacy toward a millennial ending. It will uproot its traditional foundations and relentlessly disrupt its pretended continuity. This is because knowledge is not made for understanding; it is made for cutting.

From these observations, we can grasp the particular traits of historical meaning as Nietzsche understood it – the sense which opposes *wirkliche Historie* to traditional history. The former transposes the relationship ordinarily established between the eruption of an event and necessary continuity. An entire historical tradition (theological or rationalistic) aims at dissolving the singular event into an ideal continuity – as a teleological movement or a natural process. "Effective" history, however, deals with events in terms of their most unique characteristics, their most acute manifestations. An event, consequently, is not a decision, a treaty, a reign, or a battle, but the reversal of a relationship of forces, the usurpation of power, the appropriation of a vocabulary turned against those who had once used it, a feeble domination that poisons itself as it grows lax, the entry of a masked "other." The forces operating in history are not controlled by destiny or regulative mechanisms, but respond to haphazard conflicts.[39] They do not manifest the successive forms of a primordial intention and their attraction is not that of a conclusion, for they always appear through the singular randomness of events. The inverse of the Christian world, spun entirely by a divine spider, and different from the world of the Greeks, divided between the realm of will and the great cosmic folly, the world of effective history knows only one kingdom, without providence or final cause, where there is only "the iron hand of necessity shaking the dicebox of chance."[40] Chance is not simply the drawing of lots, but raising the stakes in every attempt to master chance through the will to power, and giving rise to

the risk of an even greater chance.[41] The world we know is not this ultimately simple configuration where events are reduced to accentuate their essential traits, their final meaning, or their initial and final value. On the contrary, it is a profusion of entangled events. If it appears as a "marvelous motley, profound and totally meaningful," this is because it began and continues its secret existence through a "host of errors and phantasms."[42] We want historians to confirm our belief that the present rests upon profound intentions and immutable necessities. But the true historical sense confirms our existence among countless lost events, without a landmark or a point of reference.

Effective history can also invert the relationship that traditional history, in its dependence on metaphysics, establishes between proximity and distance. The latter is given to a contemplation of distances and heights: the noblest periods, the highest forms, the most abstract ideas, the purest individualities. It accomplishes this by getting as near as possible, placing itself at the foot of its mountain peaks, at the risk of adopting the famous perspective of frogs. Effective history, on the other hand, shortens its vision to those things nearest to it – the body, the nervous system, nutrition, digestion, and energies; it unearths the periods of decadence, and if it chances upon lofty epochs, it is with the suspicion – not vindictive but joyous – of finding a barbarous and shameful confusion. It has no fear of looking down, so long as it is understood that it looks from above and descends to seize the various perspectives, to disclose dispersions and differences, to leave things undisturbed in their own dimensions and intensity. It reverses the surreptitious practice of historians, their pretension to examine things furthest from themselves, the groveling manner in which they approach this promising distance (like the metaphysicians who proclaim the existence of an afterlife, situated at a distance from this world, as a promise of their reward). Effective history studies what is closest, but in an abrupt dispossession, so as to seize it at a distance (an approach similar to that of a doctor who looks closely, who plunges to make a diagnosis and to state its difference). Historical sense has more in common with medicine than philosophy; and it should not surprise us that Nietzsche occasionally employs the phrase "historically and physiologically,"[43] since among the philosopher's idiosyncrasies is a complete *dramatizes the micro decisions of wirkliche Historie (brings in issues of ethics as decision)*

Cf. White

denial of the body. This includes, as well, "the absence of historical sense, a hatred for the idea of development, Egyptianism," the obstinate "placing of conclusions at the beginning," of "making last things first."[44] History has a more important task than to be a handmaiden to philosophy, to recount the necessary birth of truth and values; it should become a differential knowledge of energies and failings, heights and degenerations, poisons and antidotes. Its task is to become a curative science.[45]

The final trait of effective history is its affirmation of knowledge as perspective. Historians take unusual pains to erase the elements in their work which reveal their grounding in a particular time and place, their preferences in a controversy – the unavoidable obstacles of their passion. Nietzsche's version of historical sense is explicit in its perspective and acknowledges its system of injustice. Its perception is slanted, being a deliberate appraisal, affirmation, or negation; it reaches the lingering and poisonous traces in order to prescribe the best antidote. It is not given to a discreet effacement before the objects it observes and does not submit itself to their processes; nor does it seek laws, since it gives equal weight to its own sight and to its objects. Through this historical sense, knowledge is allowed to create its own genealogy in the act of cognition; and *wirkliche Historie* composes a genealogy of history as the vertical projection of its position.

6. In this context, Nietzsche links historical sense to the historian's history. They share a beginning that is similarly impure and confused, share the same sign in which the symptoms of sickness can be recognized as well as the seed of an exquisite flower.[46] They arose simultaneously to follow their separate ways, but our task is to trace their common genealogy.

The descent (*Herkunft*) of the historian is unequivocal: he is of humble birth. A characteristic of history is to be without choice: it encourages thorough understanding and excludes qualitative judgments – a sensitivity to all things without distinction, a comprehensive view excluding differences. Nothing must escape it and, more importantly, nothing must be excluded. Historians argue that this proves their tact and discretion. After all, what right have they to impose their tastes and preferences when they seek to determine what actually occurred in the past? Their mistake is to

exhibit a total lack of taste, the kind of crudeness that becomes smug in the presence of the loftiest elements and finds satisfaction in reducing them to size. The historian is insensitive to the most disgusting things; or rather, he especially enjoys those things that should be repugnant to him. His apparent serenity follows from his concerted avoidance of the exceptional and his reduction of all things to the lowest common denominator. Nothing is allowed to stand above him; and underlying his desire for total knowledge is his search for the secrets that belittle everything: "base curiosity." What is the source of history? It comes from the plebs. To whom is it addressed? To the plebs. And its discourse strongly resembles the demagogue's refrain: "No one is greater than you and anyone who presumes to get the better of you – you who are good – is evil." The historian, who functions as his double, can be heard to echo: "No past is greater than your present, and, through my meticulous erudition, I will rid you of your infatuations and transform the grandeur of history into pettiness, evil, and misfortune." The historian's ancestry goes back to Socrates.

This demagoguery, of course, must be masked. It must hide its singular malice under the cloak of universals. As the demagogue is obliged to invoke truth, laws of essences, and eternal necessity, the historian must invoke objectivity, the accuracy of facts, and the permanence of the past. The demagogue denies the body to secure the sovereignty of a timeless idea, and the historian effaces his proper individuality so that others may enter the stage and reclaim their own speech. He is divided against himself: forced to silence his preferences and overcome his distaste, to blur his own perspective and replace it with the fiction of a universal geometry, to mimic death in order to enter the kingdom of the dead, to adopt a faceless anonymity. In this world where he has conquered his individual will, he becomes a guide to the inevitable law of a superior will. Having curbed the demands of his individual will in his knowledge, he will disclose the form of an eternal will in his object of study. The objectivity of historians inverts the relationships of will and knowledge and it is, in the same stroke, a necessary belief in providence, in final causes and teleology – the beliefs that place the historian in the family of ascetics. "I can't stand these lustful eunuchs of history, all the seductions of an

anti-asceticism.

ascetic ideal; I can't stand these blanched tombs producing life or those tired and indifferent beings who dress up in the part of wisdom and adopt an objective point of view."[47]

The *Entstehung* of history is found in nineteenth-century Europe: the land of interminglings and bastardy, the period of the "man-of-mixture." We have become barbarians with respect to those rare moments of high civilization: cities in ruin and enigmatic monuments are spread out before us; we stop before gaping walls; we ask what gods inhabited these empty temples. Great epochs lacked this curiosity, lacked our excessive deference; they ignored their predecessors: the classical period ignored Shakespeare. The decadence of Europe presents an immense spectacle (while stronger periods refrained from such exhibitions), and the nature of this scene is to represent a theater; lacking monuments of our own making, which properly belong to us, we live among crowded scenes. But there is more. Europeans no longer know themselves; they ignore their mixed ancestries and seek a proper role. They lack individuality. We can begin to understand the spontaneous historical bent of the nineteenth century: the anemia of its forces and those mixtures that effaced all its individual traits produced the same results as the mortifications of asceticism; its inability to create, its absence of artistic works, and its need to rely on past achievements forced it to adopt the base curiosity of plebs.

If this fully represents the genealogy of history, how could it become, in its own right, a genealogical analysis? Why did it not continue as a form of demogogic or religious knowledge? How could it change roles on the same stage? Only by being seized, dominated, and turned against its birth. And it is this movement which properly describes the specific nature of the *Entstehung*: it is not the unavoidable conclusion of a long preparation, but a scene where forces are risked in the chance of confrontations, where they emerge triumphant, where they can also be confiscated. The locus of emergence for metaphysics was surely Athenian demogoguery, the vulgar spite of Socrates and his belief in immortality, and Plato could have seized this Socratic philosophy to turn it against itself. Undoubtedly, he was often tempted to do so, but his defeat lies in its consecration. The problem was similar in the nineteenth century: to avoid doing for the popular asceticism of historians what Plato did for Socrates. This historical trait should not be founded on a philosophy of history, but dismantled, beginning with the things it produced; it is necessary to master history so as to turn it to genealogical uses, that is, strictly anti-Platonic purposes. Only then will the historical sense free itself from the demands of a suprahistorical history.

7. The historical sense gives rise to three uses that oppose and correspond to the three Platonic modalities of history. The first is parodic, directed against reality, and opposes the theme of history as reminiscence or recognition; the second is dissociative, directed against identity, and opposes history given as continuity or representative of a tradition; the third is sacrificial, directed against truth, and opposes history as knowledge. They imply a use of history that severs its connection to memory, its metaphysical and anthropological model, and constructs a counter-memory – a transformation of history into a totally different form of time.

First, the parodic and farcical use. The historian offers this confused and anonymous European, who no longer knows himself or what name he should adopt, the possibility of alternative identities, more individualized and substantial than his own. But the man with historical sense will see that this substitution is simply a disguise. Historians supplied the Revolution with Roman prototypes, romanticism with knight's armor, and the Wagnerian era was given the sword of a German hero – ephemeral props that point to our own unreality. No one kept them from venerating these religions, from going to Bayreuth to commemorate a new afterlife; they were free, as well, to be transformed into street vendors of empty identities. The new historian, the genealogist, will know what to make of this masquerade. He will not be too serious to enjoy it; on the contrary, he will push the masquerade to its limit and prepare the great carnival of time where masks are constantly reappearing. No longer the identification of our faint individuality with the solid identities of the past, but our "unrealization" through the excessive choice of identities – Frederick of Hohenstaufen, Caesar, Jesus, Dionysus, and possibly Zarathustra. Taking up these masks, revitalizing the buffoonery of history, we adopt an identity

Cf. founding every ~~historical consciousness~~. [handwritten marginal note]

whose unreality surpasses that of God, who started the charade. "Perhaps, we can discover a realm where originality is again possible as parodists of history and buffoons of God."[48] In this, we recognize the parodic double of what the second of the *Untimely Meditations* called "monumental history": a history given to reestablishing the high points of historical development and their maintenance in a perpetual presence, given to the recovery of works, actions, and creations through the monogram of their personal essence. But in 1874, Nietzsche accused this history, one totally devoted to veneration, of barring access to the actual intensities and creations of life. The parody of his last texts serves to emphasize that "monumental history" is itself a parody. Genealogy is history in the form of a concerted carnival.

The second use of history is the systematic dissociation of identity. This is necessary because this rather weak identity, which we attempt to support and to unify under a mask, is in itself only a parody: it is plural; countless spirits dispute its possession; numerous systems intersect and compete. The study of history makes one "happy, unlike the metaphysicians, to possess in oneself not an immortal soul but many mortal ones."[49] And in each of these souls, history will not discover a forgotten identity, eager to be reborn, but a complex system of distinct and multiple elements, unable to be mastered by the powers of synthesis: "it is a sign of superior culture to maintain, in a fully conscious way, certain phases of its evolution which lesser men pass through without thought. The initial result is that we can understand those who resemble us as completely determined systems and as representative of diverse cultures, that is to say, as necessary and capable of modification. And in return, we are able to separate the phases of our own evolution and consider them individually."[50] The purpose of history, guided by genealogy, is not to discover the roots of our identity, but to commit itself to its dissipation. It does not seek to define our unique threshold of emergence, the homeland to which metaphysicians promise a return; it seeks to make visible all of those discontinuities that cross us. "Antiquarian history," according to the *Untimely Meditations*, pursues opposite goals. It seeks the continuities of soil, language, and urban life in which our present is rooted, and, "by cultivating in a delicate manner that which existed for all time, it tries

to conserve for posterity the conditions under which we were born."[51] This type of history was objected to in the *Meditations* because it tended to block creativity in support of the laws of fidelity. Somewhat later – and already in *Human, All Too Human* – Nietzsche reconsiders the task of the antiquarian, but with an altogether different emphasis. If genealogy in its own right gives rise to questions concerning our native land, native language, or the laws that govern us, its intention is to reveal the heterogeneous systems which, masked by the self, inhibit the formation of any form of identity.

The third use of history is the sacrifice of the subject of knowledge. In appearance, or rather, according to the mask it bears, historical consciousness is neutral, devoid of passions, and committed solely to truth. But if it examines itself and if, more generally, it interrogates the various forms of scientific consciousness in its history, it finds that all these forms and transformations are aspects of the will to knowledge: instinct, passion, the inquisitor's devotion, cruel subtlety, and malice. It discovers the violence of a position that sides against those who are happy in their ignorance, against the effective illusions by which humanity protects itself, a position that encourages the dangers of research and delights in disturbing discoveries.[52] The historical analysis of this rancorous will to knowledge[53] reveals that all knowledge rests upon injustice (that there is no right, not even in the act of knowing, to truth or a foundation for truth) and that the instinct for knowledge is malicious (something murderous, opposed to the happiness of mankind). Even in the greatly expanded form it assumes today, the will to knowledge does not achieve a universal truth; man is not given an exact and serene mastery of nature. On the contrary, it ceaselessly multiplies the risks, creates dangers in every area; it breaks down illusory defenses; it dissolves the unity of the subject; it releases those elements of itself that are devoted to its subversion and destruction. Knowledge does not slowly detach itself from its empirical roots, the initial needs from which it arose, to become pure speculation subject only to the demands of reason; its development is not tied to the constitution and affirmation of a free subject; rather, it creates a progressive enslavement to its instinctive violence. Where religions once demanded the sacrifice of bodies, knowledge now calls for experimentation on ourselves,[54] calls us to the sacrifice of the subject of knowledge. "The desire for knowledge has been transformed among us into a passion which fears no sacrifice, which fears nothing but its own extinction. It may be that mankind will eventually perish from this passion for knowledge. If not through passion, then through weakness. We must be prepared to state our choice: do we wish humanity to end in fire and light or to end on the sands?"[55] We should now replace the two great problems of nineteenth-century philosophy, passed on by Fichte and Hegel (the reciprocal basis of truth and liberty and the possibility of absolute knowledge), with the theme that "to perish through absolute knowledge may well form a part of the basis of being."[56] This does not mean, in terms of a critical procedure, that the will to truth is limited by the intrinsic finitude of cognition, but that it loses all sense of limitations and all claim to truth in its unavoidable sacrifice of the subject of knowledge. "It may be that there remains one prodigious idea which might be made to prevail over every other aspiration, which might overcome the most victorious: the idea of humanity sacrificing itself. It seems indisputable that if this new constellation appeared on the horizon, only the desire for truth, with its enormous prerogatives, could direct and sustain such a sacrifice. For to knowledge, no sacrifice is too great. Of course, this problem has never been posed."[57]

The *Untimely Meditations* discussed the critical use of history: its just treatment of the past, its decisive cutting of the roots, its rejection of traditional attitudes of reverence, its liberation of man by presenting him with other origins than those in which he prefers to see himself. Nietzsche, however, reproached critical history for detaching us from every real source and for sacrificing the very movement of life to the exclusive concern for truth. Somewhat later, as we have seen, Nietzsche reconsiders this line of thought he had at first refused, but directs it to altogether different ends. It is no longer a question of judging the past in the name of a truth that only we can possess in the present, but of risking the destruction of the subject who seeks knowledge in the endless deployment of the will to knowledge.

In a sense, genealogy returns to the three modalities of history that Nietzsche recognized in 1874. It returns to them in spite of the objections that Nietzsche raised in the name of the affirmative and creative powers of life. But they are metamorphosed: the veneration of monuments becomes parody; the respect for ancient continuities becomes systematic dissociation; the critique of the injustices of the past by a truth held by men in the present becomes the destruction of the man who maintains knowledge by the injustice proper to the will to knowledge.

Notes

1   *Ed.*: See F. W. Nietzsche's Preface to *On the Genealogy of Morals* (1887), in *Basic Writings of Nietzsche*, ed. and trans. Walter Kaufmann (New York: Modern Library, 1968), sec. 4, 7.

2   F. W. Nietzsche, *The Gay Science* (1882), trans. Walter Kaufmann (New York: Random House, 1974), no. 7.

3   F. W. Nietzsche, *Human, All Too Human* (1878; New York: Gordon Press, 1974), no. 3.

4   Nietzsche, *Genealogy*, II, sec. 6, 8.

5   Nietzsche, *Gay Science*, nos. 110, 111, 300.

6   F. W. Nietzsche, *The Dawn of Day* (1881; New York: Gordon Press, 1974), no. 102. (*Ed.*: *Pudenda origo* is "shameful origin.").

7   Nietzsche, *Gay Science*, nos. 151, 353; also *Dawn*, no. 62; *Genealogy*, I, sec. 14; F. W. Nietzsche, "The Four Great Errors," in *Twilight of the Idols* (1888) in *The Portable Nietzsche*, ed. and trans. Walter Kaufmann (New York: Viking Press, 1954), sec. 7. (*Ed.*: *Schwarzkünstler* is a black magician.)

8   Paul Ree's text was entitled *Ursprung der Moralischen Empfindungen*.

9   In *Human, All Too Human*, aphorism 92 was entitled *Ursprung der Gerechtigkeit*.

10   In the main body of the *Genealogy*, *Ursprung* and *Herkunft* are used interchangeably in numerous instances (I, sec. 2; II, sec. 8, 11, 12, 16, 17).

11   Nietzsche, *Dawn*, no. 123.

12   Nietzsche, *Human, All Too Human*, no. 34.

13   F. W. Nietzsche, *The Wanderer and His Shadow* (1880), in *Complete Works* (New York: Gordon Press, 1974), no. 9.

14   *Ed.*: A wide range of key terms, found in Foucault's *The Archaeology of Knowledge*, are related to this theme of "disparity": the concepts of series, discontinuity, division, and difference. If the *same* is found in the realm and movement of the dialectics, the *disparate* presents itself as an "event" in the world of chance.

15   Nietzsche, *Wanderer*, no. 3.

16   Nietzsche, *Dawn*, no. 49.

17 F. W. Nietzsche, *Nietzsche contra Wagner* (1888), in *Portable Nietzsche*.

18 Nietzsche, *Gay Science*, nos. 110, 265.

19 Nietzsche, "How the True World Finally Became a Fable," *Twilight of Idols*.

20 For example, on race, see Nietzsche's *Gay Science*, no. 135; *Beyond Good and Evil* (1886), in *Basic Writings*, nos. 200, 242, 244; *Genealogy*, I, sec. 5; on social type see *Gay Science*, nos. 348–9; *Beyond Good and Evil*, no. 260.

21 Nietzsche, *Beyond Good and Evil*, no. 244.

22 Nietzsche, *Genealogy*, III, sec. 17. The *abkunft* of feelings of depression.

23 Nietzsche, "'Reason' in Philosophy," *Twilight of Idols*.

24 Nietzsche, *Dawn*, no. 247.

25 Nietzsche, *Gay Science*, nos. 348–9.

26 Ibid.

27 Nietzsche, *Dawn*, no. 42.

28 Nietzsche, *Beyond Good and Evil*, no. 262.

29 Nietzsche, *Genealogy*, III, no. 13.

30 Nietzsche, *Gay Science*, no. 148. It is also to an anemia of the will that one must attribute the *Entstehung* of Buddhism and Christianity.

31 Nietzsche, *Genealogy*, I, sec. 2.

32 Nietzsche, *Beyond Good and Evil*, no. 260; see also *Genealogy*, II, sec. 12.

33 Nietzsche, *Wanderer*, no. 9.

34 Nietzsche, *Gay Science*, no. 111.

35 Nietzsche, *Genealogy*, II, no. 6.

36 Nietzsche, *Genealogy*, Preface, sec. 7, and I, sec. 2; *Beyond Good and Evil*, no. 224.

37 Nietzsche, *Gay Science*, no. 7.

38 Ibid.

39 Nietzsche, *Genealogy*, II, sec. 12.

40 Nietzsche, *Dawn*, no. 130.

41 Nietzsche, *Genealogy*, II, sec. 12.

42 Nietzsche, *Human, All Too Human*, no. 16.

43 Nietzsche, *Twilight of Idols*, no. 44.

44 Nietzsche, "'Reason' in Philosophy," *Twilight of Idols*, nos. 1, 4.

45 Nietzsche, *Wanderer*, no. 188. (*Ed.*: This conception underlies the task of Foucault's *Madness and Civilization* and *The Birth of the Clinic* even though it is not found as a conscious formulation until *The Archaeology of Knowledge*.)

46 Nietzsche, *Gay Science*, no. 337.

47 Nietzsche, *Genealogy*, III, sec. 26.

48 Nietzsche, *Beyond Good and Evil*, no. 223.

49 Nietzsche, *Wanderer* (Opinions and Mixed Statements), no. 17.

50 Nietzsche, *Human, All Too Human*, no. 274.

51 F. W. Nietzsche, *Untimely Meditations* (1873–4), in *Complete Works*, II, no. 3.

52 Cf. Nietzsche's *Dawn*, nos. 429, 432; *Gay Science*, no. 333; *Beyond Good and Evil*, nos. 229–30.

53 *Ed.*: The French phrase *vouloir-savoir* means both the will to knowledge and knowledge as revenge.

54 Nietzsche, *Dawn*, no. 501.

55 Ibid.

56 Nietzsche, *Beyond Good and Evil*, no. 39.

57 Nietzsche, *Dawn*, no. 45.

30

"Dominant, Residual, and Emergent" (1977)

Raymond Williams

The complexity of a culture is to be found not only in its variable processes and their social definitions – traditions, institutions, and formations – but also in the dynamic interrelations, at every point in the process, of historically varied and variable elements. In what I have called 'epochal' analysis, a cultural process is seized as a cultural system, with determinate dominant features: feudal culture or bourgeois culture or a transition from one to the other. This emphasis on dominant and definitive lineaments and features is important and often, in practice, effective. But it then often happens that its methodology is preserved for the very different function of historical analysis, in which a sense of movement within what is ordinarily abstracted as a system is crucially necessary, especially if it is to connect with the future as well as with the past. In authentic historical analysis it is necessary at every point to recognize the complex interrelations between movements and tendencies both within and beyond a specific and effective dominance. It is necessary to examine how these relate to the whole cultural process rather than only to the selected and abstracted dominant system. Thus 'bourgeois culture' is a significant generalizing description and hypothesis, expressed within epochal analysis by fundamental comparisons with 'feudal culture' or 'socialist culture'. However, as a description of cultural process, over four or five centuries and in scores of different societies, it requires immediate historical and internally comparative differentiation. Moreover, even if this is acknowledged or practically carried out, the 'epochal' definition can exert its pressure as a static type against which all real cultural process is measured, either to show 'stages' or 'variations' of the type (which is still historical analysis) or, at its worst, to select supporting and exclude 'marginal' or 'incidental' or 'secondary' evidence.

Such errors are avoidable if, while retaining the epochal hypothesis, we can find terms which recognize not only 'stages' and 'variations' but the internal dynamic relations of any actual process. We have certainly still to speak of the 'dominant' and the 'effective', and in these senses of the hegemonic. But we find that we have also to speak, and indeed with further differentiation of each, of the 'residual' and the 'emergent', which in any real process, and at any moment in the process, are significant both in themselves and in what they reveal of the characteristics of the 'dominant'.

By 'residual' I mean something different from the 'archaic', though in practice these are often very difficult to distinguish. Any culture includes available elements of its past, but their place in the contemporary cultural process is profoundly variable. I would call the 'archaic' that which is wholly recognized as an element of the past, to be observed, to be examined, or even on occasion to be consciously 'revived', in a deliberately specializing way. What I mean by the 'residual' is very different. The residual, by definition, has been effectively formed in the past, but it is still active in the cultural process, not only and often not at all as an element of the past, but as an effective

Raymond Williams, "Dominant, Residual, and Emergent," pp. 121–7 from *Marxism and Literature*. Oxford: Oxford University Press, 1977.

element of the present. Thus certain experiences, meanings, and values which cannot be expressed or substantially verified in terms of the dominant culture, are nevertheless lived and practised on the basis of the residue – cultural as well as social – of some previous social and cultural institution or formation. It is crucial to distinguish this aspect of the residual, which may have an alternative or even oppositional relation to the dominant culture, from that active manifestation of the residual (this being its distinction from the archaic) which has been wholly or largely incorporated into the dominant culture. In three characteristic cases in contemporary English culture this distinction can become a precise term of analysis. Thus organized religion is predominantly residual, but within this there is a significant difference between some practically alternative and oppositional meanings and values (absolute brotherhood, service to others without reward) and a larger body of incorporated meanings and values (official morality, or the social order of which the other-worldly is a separated neutralizing or ratifying component). Again, the idea of rural community is predominantly residual, but is in some limited respects alternative or oppositional to urban industrial capitalism, though for the most part it is incorporated, as idealization or fantasy, or as an exotic – residential or escape – leisure function of the dominant order itself. Again, in monarchy, there is virtually nothing that is actively residual (alternative or oppositional), but, with a heavy and deliberate additional use of the archaic, a residual function has been wholly incorporated as a specific political and cultural function – marking the limits as well as the methods – of a form of capitalist democracy.

A residual cultural element is usually at some distance from the effective dominant culture, but some part of it, some version of it – and especially if the residue is from some major area of the past – will in most cases have had to be incorporated if the effective dominant culture is to make sense in these areas. Moreover, at certain points the dominant culture cannot allow too much residual experience and practice outside itself, at least without risk. It is in the incorporation of the actively residual – by reinterpretation, dilution, projection, discriminating inclusion and exclusion – that the work of the selective tradition is especially evident. This is very notable in the case of

versions of 'the literary tradition', passing through selective versions of the character of literature to connecting and incorporated definitions of what literature now is and should be. This is one among several crucial areas, since it is in some alternative or even oppositional versions of what literature is (has been) and what literary experience (and in one common derivation, other significant experience) is and must be, that, against the pressures of incorporation, actively residual meanings and values are sustained.

By 'emergent' I mean, first, that new meanings and values, new practices, new relationships and kinds of relationship are continually being created. But it is exceptionally difficult to distinguish between those which are really elements of some new phase of the dominant culture (and in this sense 'species-specific') and those which are substantially alternative or oppositional to it: emergent in the strict sense, rather than merely novel. Since we are always considering relations within a cultural process, definitions of the emergent, as of the residual, can be made only in relation to a full sense of the dominant. Yet the social location of the residual is always easier to understand, since a large part of it (though not all) relates to earlier social formations and phases of the cultural process, in which certain real meanings and values were generated. In the subsequent default of a particular phase of a dominant culture there is then a reaching back to those meanings and values which were created in actual societies and actual situations in the past, and which still seem to have significance because they represent areas of human experience, aspiration, and achievement which the dominant culture neglects, undervalues, opposes, represses, or even cannot recognize.

The case of the emergent is radically different. It is true that in the structure of any actual society, and especially in its class structure, there is always a social basis for elements of the cultural process that are alternative or oppositional to the dominant elements. One kind of basis has been valuably described in the central body of Marxist theory: the formation of a new class, the coming to consciousness of a new class, and within this, in actual process, the (often uneven) emergence of elements of a new cultural formation. Thus the emergence of the working class as a class was immediately evident (for example, in nineteenth-century England) in the cultural process. But there was extreme unevenness of contribution in different parts of the process. The making of new social values and institutions far outpaced the making of strictly cultural institutions, while specific cultural contributions, though significant, were less vigorous and autonomous than either general or institutional innovation. A new class is always a source of emergent cultural practice, but while it is still, as a class, relatively subordinate, this is always likely to be uneven and is certain to be incomplete. For new practice is not, of course, an isolated process. To the degree that it emerges, and especially to the degree that it is oppositional rather than alternative, the process of attempted incorporation significantly begins. This can be seen, in the same period in England, in the emergence and then the effective incorporation of a radical popular press. It can be seen in the emergence and incorporation of working-class writing, where the fundamental problem of emergence is clearly revealed, since the basis of incorporation, in such cases, is the effective predominance of received literary forms – an incorporation, so to say, which already conditions and limits the emergence. But the development is always uneven. Straight incorporation is most directly attempted against the visibly alternative and oppositional class elements: trade unions, working-class political parties, working-class life styles (as incorporated into 'popular' journalism, advertising, and commercial entertainment). The process of emergence, in such conditions, is then a constantly repeated, an always renewable, move beyond a phase of practical incorporation: usually made much more difficult by the fact that much incorporation looks like recognition, acknowledgement, and thus a form of *acceptance*. In this complex process there is indeed regular confusion between the locally residual (as a form of resistance to incorporation) and the generally emergent.

Cultural emergence in relation to the emergence and growing strength of a class is then always of major importance, and always complex. But we have also to see that it is not the only kind of emergence. This recognition is very difficult, theoretically, though the practical evidence is abundant. What has really to be said, as a way of defining important elements of both the residual and the emergent, and as a way of understanding the character of the dominant, is that *no mode of production and therefore no dominant social order and therefore no dominant culture ever in reality includes or exhausts all human practice, human energy, and human intention*. This is not merely a negative proposition, allowing us to account for significant things which happen outside or against the dominant mode. On the contrary it is a fact about the modes of domination, that they select from and consequently exclude the full range of human practice. What they exclude may often be seen as the personal or the private, or as the natural or even the metaphysical. Indeed it is usually in one or other of these terms that the excluded area is expressed, since what the dominant has effectively seized is indeed the ruling definition of the social.

It is this seizure that has especially to be resisted. For there is always, though in varying degrees, practical consciousness, in specific relationships, specific skills, specific perceptions, that is unquestionably social and that a specifically dominant social order neglects, excludes, represses, or simply fails to recognize. A distinctive and comparative feature of any dominant social order is how far it reaches into the whole range of practices and experiences in an attempt at incorporation. There can be areas of experience it is willing to ignore or dispense with: to assign as private or to specialize as aesthetic or to generalize as natural. Moreover, as a social order changes, in terms of its own developing needs, these relations are variable. Thus in advanced capitalism, because of changes in the social character of labour, in the social character of communications, and in the social character of decision-making, the dominant culture reaches much further than ever before in capitalist society into hitherto 'reserved' or 'resigned' areas of experience and practice and meaning. The area of effective penetration of the dominant order into the whole social and cultural process is thus now significantly greater. This in turn makes the problem of emergence especially acute, and narrows the gap between alternative and oppositional elements. The alternative, especially in areas that impinge on significant areas of the dominant, is often seen as oppositional and, by pressure, often converted into it. Yet even here there can be spheres of practice and meaning which, almost by definition from its own limited character, or in its profound deformation, the dominant culture is unable in any real terms to recognize. Elements of emergence may indeed be incorporated, but just as often the incorporated forms are merely facsimiles of the genuinely emergent cultural practice. Any significant emergence, beyond or against a dominant mode, is very difficult under these conditions; in itself and in its repeated confusion with the facsimiles and novelties of the incorporated phase. Yet, in our own period as in others, the fact of emergent cultural practice is still undeniable, and together with the fact of actively residual practice is a necessary complication of the would-be dominant culture.

This complex process can still in part be described in class terms. But there is always other social being and consciousness which is neglected and excluded: alternative perceptions of others, in immediate relationships; new perceptions and practices of the material world. In practice these are different in quality from the developing and articulated interests of a rising class. The relations between these two sources of the emergent – the class and the excluded social (human) area – are by no means necessarily contradictory. At times they can be very close and on the relations between them much in political practice depends. But culturally and as a matter of theory the areas can be seen as distinct.

What matters, finally, in understanding emergent culture, as distinct from both the dominant and the residual, is that it is never only a matter of immediate practice; indeed it depends crucially on finding new forms or adaptations of form. Again and again what we have to observe is in effect a *pre-emergence*, active and pressing but not yet fully articulated, rather than the evident emergence which could be more confidently named. It is to understand more closely this condition of pre-emergence, as well as the more evident forms of the emergent, the residual, and the dominant, that we need to explore the concept of structures of feeling.

31

"Answering the Question: What Is Postmodernism?"* (1979)

Jean-François Lyotard

A Demand

This is a period of slackening – I refer to the color of the times. From every direction we are being urged to put an end to experimentation, in the arts and elsewhere. I have read an art historian who extols realism and is militant for the advent of a new subjectivity. I have read an art critic who packages and sells "Transavantgardism" in the marketplace of painting. I have read that under the name of postmodernism, architects are getting rid of the Bauhaus project, throwing out the baby of experimentation with the bathwater of functionalism. I have read that a new philosopher is discovering what he drolly calls Judaeo-Christianism, and intends by it to put an end to the impiety which we are supposed to have spread. I have read in a French weekly that some are displeased with *Mille Plateaux* [by Deleuze and Guattari] because they expect, especially when reading a work of philosophy, to be gratified with a little sense. I have read from the pen of a reputable historian that writers and thinkers of the 1960 and 1970 avant-gardes spread a reign of terror in the use of language, and that the conditions for a fruitful exchange must be restored by imposing on the intellectuals a common way of speaking, that of the historians. I have been reading a young philosopher of language who complains that Continental thinking, under the challenge of speaking machines, has surrendered to the machines the concern for reality, that it has substituted for the referential paradigm that of "adlinguisticity" (one speaks about speech, writes about writing, intertextuality), and who thinks that the time has now come to restore a solid anchorage of language in the referent. I have read a talented theatrologist for whom postmodernism, with its games and fantasies, carries very little weight in front of political authority, especially when a worried public opinion encourages authority to a politics of totalitarian surveillance in the face of nuclear warfare threats.

I have read a thinker of repute who defends modernity against those he calls the neoconservatives. Under the banner of postmodernism, the latter would like, he believes, to get rid of the uncompleted project of modernism, that of the Enlightenment. Even the last advocates of *Aufklärung*, such as Popper or Adorno, were only able, according to him, to defend the project in a few particular spheres of life – that of politics for the author of *The Open Society*, and that of art for the author of *Ästhetische Theorie*. Jürgen Habermas (everyone had recognized him) thinks that if modernity has failed, it is in allowing the totality of life to be splintered into independent specialties which are left to the narrow competence of experts, while the concrete individual experiences "desublimated meaning" and "destructured form," not as a liberation but in the mode of that immense *ennui* which Baudelaire described over a century ago.

Following a prescription of Albrecht Wellmer, Habermas considers that the remedy for this splintering of culture and its separation from life can only come

Jean-François Lyotard, "Answering the Question: What Is Postmodernism?," pp. 71–82 from *The Postmodern Condition: A Report on Knowledge*. Minneapolis: University of Minnesota Press, 1984.

* Translated by Régis Durand.

from "changing the status of aesthetic experience when it is no longer primarily expressed in judgments of taste," but when it is "used to explore a living historical situation," that is, when "it is put in relation with problems of existence." For this experience then "becomes a part of a language game which is no longer that of aesthetic criticism"; it takes part "in cognitive processes and normative expectations"; "it alters the manner in which those different moments *refer* to one another." What Habermas requires from the arts and the experiences they provide is, in short, to bridge the gap between cognitive, ethical, and political discourses, thus opening the way to a unity of experience.

My question is to determine what sort of unity Habermas has in mind. Is the aim of the project of modernity the constitution of sociocultural unity within which all the elements of daily life and of thought would take their places as in an organic whole? Or does the passage that has to be charted between heterogeneous language games – those of cognition, of ethics, of politics – belong to a different order from that? And if so, would it be capable of effecting a real synthesis between them?

The first hypothesis, of a Hegelian inspiration, does not challenge the notion of a dialectically totalizing *experience*; the second is closer to the spirit of Kant's *Critique of Judgment*; but must be submitted, like the *Critique*, to that severe reexamination which postmodernity imposes on the thought of the Enlightenment, on the idea of a unitary end of history and of a subject. It is this critique which not only Wittgenstein and Adorno have initiated, but also a few other thinkers (French or other) who do not have the honor to be read by Professor Habermas – which at least saves them from getting a poor grade for their neoconservatism.

Realism

The demands I began by citing are not all equivalent. They can even be contradictory. Some are made in the name of postmodernism, others in order to combat it. It is not necessarily the same thing to formulate a demand for some referent (and objective reality), for some sense (and credible transcendence), for an addressee (and audience), or an addressor (and subjective expressiveness) or for some communicational

consensus (and a general code of exchanges, such as the genre of historical discourse). But in the diverse invitations to suspend artistic experimentation, there is an identical call for order, a desire for unity, for identity, for security, or popularity (in the sense of *Öffentlichkeit*, of "finding a public"). Artists and writers must be brought back into the bosom of the community, or at least, if the latter is considered to be ill, they must be assigned the task of healing it.

There is an irrefutable sign of this common disposition: it is that for all those writers nothing is more urgent than to liquidate the heritage of the avant-gardes. Such is the case, in particular, of the so-called transavantgardism. The answers given by Achille Bonito Oliva to the questions asked by Bernard Lamarche-Vadel and Michel Enric leave no room for doubt about this. By putting the avant-gardes through a mixing process, the artist and critic feel more confident that they can suppress them than by launching a frontal attack. For they can pass off the most cynical eclecticism as a way of going beyond the fragmentary character of the preceding experiments; whereas if they openly turned their backs on them, they would run the risk of appearing ridiculously neoacademic. The *Salons* and the *Académies*, at the time when the bourgeoisie was establishing itself in history, were able to function as purgation and to grant awards for good plastic and literary conduct under the cover of realism. But capitalism inherently possesses the power to derealize familiar objects, social roles, and institutions to such a degree that the so-called realistic representations can no longer evoke reality except as nostalgia or mockery, as an occasion for suffering rather than for satisfaction. Classicism seems to be ruled out in a world in which reality is so destabilized that it offers no occasion for experience but one for ratings and experimentation.

This theme is familiar to all readers of Walter Benjamin. But it is necessary to assess its exact reach. Photography did not appear as a challenge to painting from the outside, any more than industrial cinema did to narrative literature. The former was only putting the final touch to the program of ordering the visible elaborated by the quattrocento; while the latter was the last step in rounding off diachronies as organic wholes, which had been the ideal of the great novels of education since the eighteenth century. That the mechanical and the industrial should appear as substitutes for hand or craft was not in itself a disaster – except if one believes that art is in its essence the expression of an individuality of genius assisted by an elite craftsmanship.

The challenge lay essentially in that photographic and cinematographic processes can accomplish better, faster, and with a circulation a hundred thousand times larger than narrative or pictorial realism, the task which academicism had assigned to realism: to preserve various consciousnesses from doubt. Industrial photography and cinema will be superior to painting and the novel whenever the objective is to stabilize the referent, to arrange it according to a point of view which endows it with a recognizable meaning, to reproduce the syntax and vocabulary which enable the addressee to decipher images and sequences quickly, and so to arrive easily at the consciousness of his own identity as well as the approval which he thereby receives from others – since such structures of images and sequences constitute a communication code among all of them. This is the way the effects of reality, or if one prefers, the fantasies of realism, multiply.

If they too do not wish to become supporters (of minor importance at that) of what exists, the painter and novelist must refuse to lend themselves to such therapeutic uses. They must question the rules of the art of painting or of narrative as they have learned and received them from their predecessors. Soon those rules must appear to them as a means to deceive, to seduce, and to reassure, which makes it impossible for them to be "true." Under the common name of painting and literature, an unprecedented split is taking place. Those who refuse to reexamine the rules of art pursue successful careers in mass conformism by communicating, by means of the "correct rules," the endemic desire for reality with objects and situations capable of gratifying it. Pornography is the use of photography and film to such an end. It is becoming a general model for the visual or narrative arts which have not met the challenge of the mass media.

As for the artists and writers who question the rules of plastic and narrative arts and possibly share their suspicions by circulating their work, they are destined to have little credibility in the eyes of those concerned with "reality" and "identity"; they have no guarantee of an audience. Thus it is possible to ascribe the dialectics of the avant-gardes to the challenge posed by the realisms of industry and mass communication to painting and the narrative arts. Duchamp's "ready made" does nothing but actively and parodistically signify this constant process of dispossession of the craft of painting or even of being an artist. As Thierry de Duve penetratingly observes, the modern aesthetic question is not "What is beautiful?" but "What can be said to be art (and literature)?"

Realism, whose only definition is that it intends to avoid the question of reality implicated in that of art, always stands somewhere between academicism and kitsch. When power assumes the name of a party, realism and its neoclassical complement triumph over the experimental avant-garde by slandering and banning it – that is, provided the "correct" images, the "correct" narratives, the "correct" forms which the party requests, selects, and propagates can find a public to desire them as the appropriate remedy for the anxiety and depression that public experiences. The demand for reality – that is, for unity, simplicity, communicability, etc. – did not have the same intensity nor the same continuity in German society between the two world wars and in Russian society after the Revolution: this provides a basis for a distinction between Nazi and Stalinist realism.

What is clear, however, is that when it is launched by the political apparatus, the attack on artistic experimentation is specifically reactionary: aesthetic judgment would only be required to decide whether such or such work is in conformity with the established rules of the beautiful. Instead of the work of art having to investigate what makes it an art object and whether it will be able to find an audience, political academicism possesses and imposes a priori criteria of the beautiful, which designate some works and a public at a stroke and forever. The use of categories in aesthetic judgment would thus be of the same nature as in cognitive judgment. To speak like Kant, both would be determining judgments: the expression is "well formed" first in the understanding, then the only cases retained in experience are those which can be subsumed under this expression.

When power is that of capital and not that of a party, the "transavantgardist" or "postmodern" (in Jencks's sense) solution proves to be better adapted than the antimodern solution. Eclecticism is the degree zero of contemporary general culture: one listens to reggae, watches a western, eats McDonald's food for lunch and local cuisine for dinner, wears Paris perfume in Tokyo and "retro" clothes in Hong Kong; knowledge is a matter for TV games. It is easy to find a public for eclectic works. By becoming kitsch, art panders to the confusion which reigns in the "taste" of the patrons. Artists, gallery owners, critics, and public wallow together in the "anything goes," and the epoch is one of slackening. But this realism of the "anything goes" is in fact that of money; in the absence of aesthetic criteria, it remains possible and useful to assess the value of works of art according to the profits they yield. Such realism accommodates all tendencies, just as capital accommodates all "needs," providing that the tendencies and needs have purchasing power. As for taste, there is no need to be delicate when one speculates or entertains oneself.

Artistic and literary research is doubly threatened, once by the "cultural policy" and once by the art and book market. What is advised, sometimes through one channel, sometimes through the other, is to offer works which, first, are relative to subjects which exist in the eyes of the public they address, and second, works so made ("well made") that the public will recognize what they are about, will understand what is signified, will be able to give or refuse its approval knowlingly, and if possible, even to derive from such work a certain amount of comfort.

The interpretation which has just been given of the contact between the industrial and mechanical arts, and literature and the fine arts is correct in its outline, but it remains narrowly sociologizing and historicizing – in other words, one-sided. Stepping over Benjamin's and Adorno's reticences, it must be recalled that science and industry are no more free of the suspicion which concerns reality than are art and writing. To believe otherwise would be to entertain an excessively humanistic notion of the mephistophelian functionalism of sciences and technologies. There is no denying the dominant existence today of technoscience, that is, the massive subordination of cognitive statements to the finality of the best possible performance, which is the technological criterion. But the mechanical and the industrial, especially when they enter fields traditionally reserved for artists, are carrying with them much more than power effects. The objects and the thoughts which originate in scientific knowledge and the capitalist economy convey with them one of the rules which supports their possibility: the rule that there is no reality unless testified by a consensus between partners over a certain knowledge and certain commitments.

This rule is of no little consequence. It is the imprint left on the politics of the scientist and the trustee of capital by a kind of flight of reality out of the metaphysical, religious, and political certainties that the mind believed it held. This withdrawal is absolutely necessary to the emergence of science and capitalism. No industry is possible without a suspicion of the Aristotelian theory of motion, no industry without a refutation of corporatism, of mercantilism, and of physiocracy. Modernity, in whatever age it appears, cannot exist without a shattering of belief and without discovery of the "lack of reality" of reality, together with the invention of other realities.

What does this "lack of reality" signify if one tries to free it from a narrowly historicized interpretation? The phrase is of course akin to what Nietzsche calls nihilism. But I see a much earlier modulation of Nietzschean perspectivism in the Kantian theme of the sublime. I think in particular that it is in the aesthetic of the sublime that modern art (including literature) finds its impetus and the logic of avant-gardes finds its axioms.

The sublime sentiment, which is also the sentiment of the sublime, is, according to Kant, a strong and equivocal emotion: it carries with it both pleasure and pain. Better still, in it pleasure derives from pain. Within the tradition of the subject, which comes from Augustine and Descartes and which Kant does not radically challenge, this contradiction, which some would call neurosis or masochism, develops as a conflict between the faculties of a subject, the faculty to conceive of something and the faculty to "present" something. Knowledge exists if, first, the statement is intelligible, and second, if "cases" can be derived from the experience which "corresponds" to it. Beauty exists if a certain "case" (the work of art), given first by the sensibility without any conceptual determination, the sentiment of pleasure independent of any interest the work may elicit, appeals to the principle of a universal consensus (which may never be attained).

Taste, therefore, testifies that between the capacity to conceive and the capacity to present an object corresponding to the concept, an undetermined agreement, without rules, giving rise to a judgment which Kant calls reflective, may be experienced as pleasure. The sublime is a different sentiment. It takes place, on the contrary, when the imagination fails to present an object which might, if only in principle, come to match a concept. We have the Idea of the world (the totality of what is), but we do not have the capacity to show an example of it. We have the Idea of the simple (that which cannot be broken down, decomposed), but we cannot illustrate it with a sensible object which would be a "case" of it. We can conceive the infinitely great, the infinitely powerful, but every presentation of an object destined to "make visible" this absolute greatness or power appears to us painfully inadequate. Those are Ideas of which no presentation is possible. Therefore, they impart no knowledge about reality (experience); they also prevent the free union of the faculties which gives rise to the sentiment of the beautiful; and they prevent the formation and the stabilization of taste. They can be said to be unpresentable.

I shall call modern the art which devotes its "little technical expertise" (son "petit technique"), as Diderot used to say, to present the fact that the unpresentable exists. To make visible that there is something which can be conceived and which can neither be seen nor made visible: this is what is at stake in modern painting. But how to make visible that there is something which cannot be seen? Kant himself shows the way when he names "formlessness, the absence of form," as a possible index to the unpresentable. He also says of the empty "abstraction" which the imagination experiences when in search for a presentation of the infinite (another unpresentable): this abstraction itself is like a presentation of the infinite, its "negative presentation." He cites the commandment, "Thou shalt not make graven images" (Exodus), as the most sublime passage in the Bible in that it forbids all presentation of the Absolute. Little needs to be added to those observations to outline an aesthetic of sublime paintings. As painting, it will of course "present" something though negatively; it will therefore avoid figuration or representation. It will be "white" like one of Malevitch's squares; it will enable us to see only by making it impossible to see; it will please only by causing pain. One recognizes in those instructions the axioms of avant-gardes in painting, inasmuch as they devote

themselves to making an allusion to the unpresentable by means of visible presentations. The systems in the name of which, or with which, this task has been able to support or to justify itself deserve the greatest attention; but they can originate only in the vocation of the sublime in order to legitimize it, that is, to conceal it. They remain inexplicable without the incommensurability of reality to concept which is implied in the Kantian philosophy of the sublime.

It is not my intention to analyze here in detail the manner in which the various avant-gardes have, so to speak, humbled and disqualified reality by examining the pictorial techniques which are so many devices to make us believe in it. Local tone, drawing, the mixing of colors, linear perspective, the nature of the support and that of the instrument, the treatment, the display, the museum: the avant-gardes are perpetually flushing out artifices of presentation which make it possible to subordinate thought to the gaze and to turn it away from the unpresentable. If Habermas, like Marcuse, understands this task of derealization as an aspect of the (repressive) "desublimation" which characterizes the avant-garde, it is because he confuses the Kantian sublime with Freudian sublimation, and because aesthetics has remained for him that of the beautiful.

The Postmodern

What, then, is the postmodern? What place does it or does it not occupy in the vertiginous work of the questions hurled at the rules of image and narration? It is undoubtedly a part of the modern. All that has been received, if only yesterday (modo, modo, Petronius used to say), must be suspected. What space does Cézanne challenge? The Impressionists'. What object do Picasso and Braque attack? Cézanne's. What presupposition does Duchamp break with in 1912? That which says one must make a painting, be it cubist. And Buren questions that other presupposition which he believes had survived untouched by the work of Duchamp: the place of presentation of the work. In an amazing acceleration, the generations precipitate themselves. A work can become modern only if it is first postmodern. Postmodernism thus understood is not modernism at its end but in the nascent state, and this state is constant.

Yet I would like not to remain with this slightly mechanistic meaning of the word. If it is true that modernity takes place in the withdrawal of the real and according to the sublime relation between the presentable and the conceivable, it is possible, within this relation, to distinguish two modes (to use the musician's language). The emphasis can be placed on the powerlessness of the faculty of presentation, on the nostalgia for presence felt by the human subject, on the obscure and futile will which inhabits him in spite of everything. The emphasis can be placed, rather, on the power of the faculty to conceive, on its "inhumanity" so to speak (it was the quality Apollinaire demanded of modern artists), since it is not the business of our understanding whether or not human sensibility or imagination can match what it conceives. The emphasis can also be placed on the increase of being and the jubilation which result from the invention of new rules of the game, be it pictorial, artistic, or any other. What I have in mind will become clear if we dispose very schematically a few names on the chessboard of the history of avant-gardes: on the side of melancholia, the German Expressionists, and on the side of *novatio*, Braque and Picasso, on the former Malevitch and on the latter Lissitsky, on the one Chirico and on the other Duchamp. The nuance which distinguishes these two modes may be infinitesimal; they often coexist in the same piece, are almost indistinguishable; and yet they testify to a difference (*un différend*) on which the fate of thought depends and will depend for a long time, between regret and assay.

The work of Proust and that of Joyce both allude to something which does not allow itself to be made present. Allusion, to which Paolo Fabbri recently called my attention, is perhaps a form of expression indispensable to the works which belong to an aesthetic of the sublime. In Proust, what is being eluded as the price to pay for this allusion is the identity of consciousness, a victim to the excess of time (*au trop de temps*). But in Joyce, it is the identity of writing which is the victim of an excess of the book (*au trop de livre*) or of literature.

Proust calls forth the unpresentable by means of a language unaltered in its syntax and vocabulary and of a writing which in many of its operators still belongs to the genre of novelistic narration. The literary institution, as Proust inherits it from Balzac and Flaubert, is admittedly subverted in that the hero is no longer a character but the inner consciousness of time, and in that the diegetic diachrony, already damaged by Flaubert, is here put in question because of the narrative voice. Nevertheless, the unity of the book, the odyssey of that consciousness, even if it is deferred from chapter to chapter, is not seriously challenged: the identity of the writing with itself throughout the labyrinth of the interminable narration is enough to connote such unity, which has been compared to that of *The Phenomenology of Mind*.

Joyce allows the unpresentable to become perceptible in his writing itself, in the signifier. The whole range of available narrative and even stylistic operators is put into play without concern for the unity of the whole, and new operators are tried. The grammar and vocabulary of literary language are no longer accepted as given; rather, they appear as academic forms, as rituals originating in piety (as Nietzsche said) which prevent the unpresentable from being put forward.

Here, then, lies the difference: modern aesthetics is an aesthetic of the sublime, though a nostalgic one. It allows the unpresentable to be put forward only as the missing contents; but the form, because of its recognizable consistency, continues to offer to the reader or viewer matter for solace and pleasure. Yet these sentiments do not constitute the real sublime sentiment, which is in an intrinsic combination of pleasure and pain: the pleasure that reason should exceed all presentation, the pain that imagination or sensibility should not be equal to the concept.

The postmodern would be that which, in the modern, puts forward the unpresentable in presentation itself; that which denies itself the solace of good forms, the consensus of a taste which would make it possible to share collectively the nostalgia for the unattainable; that which searches for new presentations, not in order to enjoy them but in order to impart a stronger sense of the unpresentable. A postmodern artist or writer is in the position of a philosopher: the text he writes, the work he produces are not in principle governed by preestablished rules, and they cannot be judged according to a determining judgment, by applying familiar categories to the text or to the work. Those rules and categories are what the work of art itself is looking for. The artist and the writer, then, are working without rules in order to formulate the rules of what *will have been done*. Hence the fact that work and text have the characters of an *event*; hence also, they always come too late for their author, or, what amounts to the same thing, their being put into work, their realization (*mise en oeuvre*) always begin too soon. *Post modern* would have to be understood according to the paradox of the future (*post*) anterior (*modo*).

It seems to me that the essay (Montaigne) is post-modern, while the fragment (*The Athaeneum*) is modern.

Finally, it must be clear that it is our business not to supply reality but to invent allusions to the conceivable which cannot be presented. And it is not to be expected that this task will effect the last reconciliation between language games (which, under the name of faculties, Kant knew to be separated by a chasm), and that only the transcendental illusion (that of Hegel) can hope to totalize them into a real unity. But Kant also knew that the price to pay for such an illusion is terror. The nineteenth and twentieth centuries have given us as much terror as we can take. We have paid a high enough price for the nostalgia of the whole and the one, for the reconciliation of the concept and the sensible, of the transparent and the communicable experience. Under the general demand for slackening and for appeasement, we can hear the mutterings of the desire for a return of terror, for the realization of the fantasy to seize reality. The answer is: Let us wage a war on totality; let us be witnesses to the unpresentable; let us activate the differences and save the honor of the name.

32

"History and the Social Sciences: The *Longue Durée*" (1980) (written in 1958)

Fernand Braudel

There is a general crisis in the human sciences: they are all overwhelmed by their own progress, if only because of the accumulation of new knowledge and the need to work together in a way which is yet to be properly organized. Directly or indirectly, willingly or unwillingly, none of them can remain unaffected by the progress of the more active among them. But they remain in the grip of an insidious and retrograde humanism no longer capable of providing them with a valid framework for their studies. With varying degrees of clear-sightedness, all the sciences are preoccupied with their own position in the whole monstrous agglomeration of past and present researches, researches whose necessary convergence can now clearly be seen.

Will the human sciences solve these difficulties by an extra effort at definition or by an increase in ill temper? They certainly seem to think so, for (at the risk of going over some very well trodden ground and of raising a few red herrings), today they are engaged more busily than ever in defining their aims, their methods, and their superiorities. You can see them vying with each other, skirmishing along the frontiers separating them, or not separating them, or barely separating them from their neighbors. For each of them, in fact, persists in a dream of staying in, or returning to, its home. A few isolated scholars have managed to bring things together: Claude Lévi-Strauss[1] has pushed "structural" anthropology toward the procedures of linguistics, the horizons of "unconscious" history, and the youthful imperialism of "qualitative" mathematics. He leans toward a science which would unite, under the title of communications science, anthropology, political economy, linguistics … But is there in fact anyone who is prepared to cross the frontiers like this, and to realign things in this way? Given half a chance, geography would even like to split off from history!

But we must not be unfair. These squabbles and denials have a certain significance. The wish to affirm one's own existence in the face of others is necessarily the basis for new knowledge: to deny someone is already to know him. Moreover, without explicitly wishing it, the social sciences force themselves on each other, each trying to capture society as a whole, in its "totality." Each science encroaches on its neighbors, all the while believing it is staying in its own domain. Economics finds sociology closing in on it, history – perhaps the least structured of all the human sciences – is open to all the lessons learned by its many neighbors, and is then at pains to reflect them back again. So, despite all the reluctance, opposition, and blissful ignorance, the beginnings of a "common market" are being sketched out. This would be well worth a trial during the coming years, even if each science might later be better off readopting, for a while, some more strictly personal approach.

But the crucial thing now is to get together in the first place. In the United States this coming together has taken the form of collective research on the cultures of different areas of the modern world, "area studies" being, above all, the study by a team of social

Fernand Braudel, "History and the Social Sciences: The *Longue Durée*," pp. 25–31, 32–8, 47–54 from *On History*. Chicago: University of Chicago Press, 1980. Reprinted by permission of the publisher the University of Chicago Press.

scientists of those political Leviathans of our time: China, India, Russia, Latin America, the United States. Understanding them is a question of life and death! But at the same time as sharing techniques and knowledge, it is essential that each of the participants should not remain buried in his private research, as deaf and blind as before to what the others are saying, writing, or thinking! Equally, it is essential that this gathering of the social sciences should make no omissions, that they should all be there, that the older ones should not be neglected in favor of the younger ones that seem to promise so much, even if they do not always deliver it. For instance, the position allotted to geography in these American exercises is almost nil, and that allowed to history extremely meager. Not to mention the sort of history it is!

The other social sciences are fairly ill informed as to the crisis which our discipline has gone through in the past twenty or thirty years, and they tend to misunderstand not only the work of historians, but also that aspect of social reality for which history has always been a faithful servant, if not always a good salesman: social time, the multifarious, contradictory times of the life of men, which not only make up the past, but also the social life of the present. Yet history, or rather the dialectic of duration as it arises in the exercise of our profession, from our repeated observations, is important in the coming debate among all the human sciences. For nothing is more important, nothing comes closer to the crux of social reality than this living, intimate, infinitely repeated opposition between the instant of time and that time which flows only slowly. Whether it is a question of the past or of the present, a clear awareness of this plurality of social time is indispensable to the communal methodology of the human sciences.

So I propose to deal at length with history, and with time in history. Less for the sake of present readers of this journal, who are already specialists in our field, than for that of those who work in the neighboring human sciences: economists, ethnographers, ethnologists (or anthropologists), sociologists, psychologists, linguists, demographers, geographers, even social mathematicians or statisticians − all neighbors of ours whose experiments and whose researches we have been following for these many years because it seemed to us (and seems so still) that we would thus see history

itself in a new light. And perhaps we in our turn have something to offer them. From the recent experiments and efforts of history, an increasingly clear idea has emerged − whether consciously or not, whether excepted or not − of the multiplicity of time, and of the exceptional value of the long time span. It is this last idea which even more than history itself − history of a hundred aspects − should engage the attention and interest of our neighbors, the social sciences.

History and Time Spans

All historical work is concerned with breaking down time past, choosing among its chronological realities according to more or less conscious preferences and exclusions. Traditional history, with its concern for the short time span, for the individual and the event, has long accustomed us to the headlong, dramatic, breathless rush of its narrative.

The new economic and social history puts cyclical movement in the forefront of its research and is committed to that time span: it has been captivated by the mirage and the reality of the cyclical rise and fall of prices. So today, side by side with traditional narrative history, there is an account of conjunctures which lays open large sections of the past, ten, twenty, fifty years at a stretch ready for examination.

Far beyond this second account we find a history capable of traversing even greater distances, a history to be measured in centuries this time: the history of the long, even of the very long time span, of the *longue durée*. This is a phrase which I have become accustomed to for good or ill, in order to distinguish the opposite of what François Simiand, not long after Paul Lacombe, christened "*l'histoire événementielle*," the history of events. The phrases matter little; what matters is the fact that our discussion will move between these two poles of time, the instant and the *longue durée*.

Not that these words are absolutely reliable. Take the word *event*: for myself I would limit it, and imprison it within the short time span: an event is explosive, a "*nouvelle sonnante*" ("a matter of moment") as they said in the sixteenth century. Its delusive smoke fills the minds of its contemporaries, but it does not last, and its flame can scarcely ever be discerned.

Doubtless philosophers would tell us that to treat the word thus is to empty it of a great part of its meaning. An event can if necessary take on a whole range of meanings and associations. It can occasionally bear witness to very profound movements, and by making play, factitiously or not, with those "causes" and "effects" so dear to the hearts of the historians of yore, it can appropriate a time far greater than its own time span. Infinitely extensible, it becomes wedded, either freely or not, to a whole chain of events, of underlying realities which are then, it seems, impossible to separate. It was by adding things together like this that Benedetto Croce could claim that within any event all history, all of man is embodied, to be rediscovered at will. Though this, of course, is on condition of adding to that fragment whatever it did not at first sight appear to contain, which in turn entails knowing what is appropriate – or not appropriate – to add. It is the clever and perilous process which some of Jean-Paul Sartre's recent thinking seems to propose.[2]

So, to put things more clearly, let us say that instead of a history of events, we would speak of a short time span, proportionate to individuals, to daily life, to our illusions, to our hasty awareness – above all the time of the chronicle and the journalist. Now, it is worth noting that side by side with great and, so to speak, historic events, the chronicle or the daily paper offers us all the mediocre accidents of ordinary life: a fire, a railway crash, the price of wheat, a crime, a theatrical production, a flood. It is clear, then, that there is a short time span which plays a part in all forms of life, economic, social, literary, institutional, religious, even geographical (a gust of wind, a storm), just as much as political.

At first sight, the past seems to consist in just this mass of diverse facts, some of which catch the eye, and some of which are dim and repeat themselves indefinitely. The very facts, that is, which go to make up the daily booty of microsociology or of sociometry (there is microhistory too). But this mass does not make up all of reality, all the depth of history on which scientific thought is free to work. Social science has almost what amounts to a horror of the event. And not without some justification, for the short time span is the most capricious, and the most delusive of all.

Thus there is among some of us, as historians, a lively distrust of traditional history, the history of events – a label which tends to become confused, rather inexactly, with political history. Political history is not necessarily bound to events, nor is it forced to be. Yet except for the factitious panoramas almost without substance in time which break up its narrative,[3] except for the overviews inserted for the sake of variety, on the whole the history of the past hundred years, almost always political history centered on the drama of "great events," has worked on and in the short time span. Perhaps that was the price which had to be paid for the progress made during this same period in the scientific mastery of particular tools and rigorous methods. The momentous discovery of the document led historians to believe that documentary authenticity was the repository of the whole truth. "All we need to do," Louis Halphen wrote only yesterday,[4] is allow ourselves to be borne along by the documents, one after another, just as they offer themselves to us, in order to see the chain of facts and events reconstitute themselves almost automatically before our eyes." Toward the end of the nineteenth century, this ideal of history "in the raw," led to a new style of chronicle, which in its desire for exactitude followed the history of events step by step as it emerged from ambassadorial letters or parliamentary debates. The historians of the eighteenth and early nineteenth centuries had been attentive to the perspectives of the *longue durée* in a way in which, afterwards, only a few great spirits – Michelet, Ranke, Jacob Burckhardt, Fustel – were able to recapture. If one accepts that this going beyond the short span has been the most precious, because the most rare, of historiographical achievements during the past hundred years, then one understands the preeminent role of the history of institutions, of religions, of civilizations, and (thanks to archeology with its need for vast chronological expanses) the ground-breaking role of the studies devoted to classical antiquities. It was only yesterday that they proved the saviors of our profession.

The recent break with the traditional forms of nineteenth-century history has not meant a complete break with the short time span. It has worked, as we know, in favor of economic and social history, and against the interests of political history. This has entailed upheavals and an undeniable renewal, and also, inevitably, changes in method, the shifting of centers of interest with the advent of a quantitative history that has certainly not exhausted all it has to offer.

But above all, there has been an alteration in traditional historical time. A day, a year once seemed useful gauges. Time, after all, was made up of an accumulation of days. But a price curve, a demographic progression, the movement of wages, the variations in interest rates, the study (as yet more dreamed of than achieved) of productivity, a rigorous analysis of money supply all demand much wider terms of reference.

A new kind of historical narrative has appeared, that of the conjuncture, of the cycle, and even of the "intercycle," covering a decade, a quarter of a century and, at the outside, the half-century of Kondratiev's classic cycle. For instance, if we disregard any brief and superficial fluctuations, prices in Europe went up between 1791 and 1817, and went down between 1817 and 1852. This unhurried double movement of increase and decrease represents an entire intercycle measured by the time of Europe, and more or less by that of the whole world. Of course these chronological periods have no absolute value. François Perroux[5] would offer us other, perhaps more valid, dividing lines, measured with other barometers, those of economic growth, income, or the gross national product. But what do all these current debates matter! What is quite clear is that the historian can make use of a new notion of time, a time raised to the level of explication, and that history can attempt to explain itself by dividing itself at new points of reference in response to these curves and to the very way they breathe.

Thus Ernest Labrousse and his students, after their manifesto at the last Rome Historical Congress (1955), set up a vast inquiry into social history in quantitative terms. I do not think I am misrepresenting their intention when I say that this inquiry must necessarily lead to the determination of social conjunctures (and even of structures) that may not share the same rate of progress, fast or slow, as the economic conjuncture. Besides, these two distinguished gentlemen – the economic conjuncture and the social conjuncture, – must not make us lose sight of other actors, though their progress will be difficult if not impossible to track, for lack of a precise way of measuring it. Science, technology, political institutions, conceptual changes, civilizations (to fall back on that useful word) all have their own rhythms of life and growth, and the new history

of conjuctures will be complete only when it has made up a whole orchestra of them all.

In all logic, this orchestration of conjunctures, by transcending itself, should have led us straight to the *longue durée*. But for a thousand reasons this transcendence has not been the rule, and a return to the short term is being accomplished even now before our very eyes. Perhaps this is because it seems more necessary (or more urgent) to knit together "cyclical" history and short-term traditional history than to go forward, toward the unknown. In military terms, it has been a question of consolidating newly secured positions. Ernest Labrousse's first great book, published in 1933, was thus a study of the general movement of prices in France during the eighteenth century,[6] a movement lasting a good hundred years. In 1943, in the most important work of history to have appeared in France in twenty-five years, this very same Ernest Labrousse succumbed to this need to return to a less cumbersome measure of time when he pinpointed the depression of 1774 to 1791 as being one of the most compelling sources, one of the prime launching pads of the French Revolution. He was still employing a demi-intercycle, a large measure. In his address to the International Congress in Paris in 1948, *Comment naissent les révolutions?* ("How are revolutions born?"), he attempted this time to link a new-style pathetic fallacy (short-term economic) to a very old style pathetic fallacy (political, the "revolutionary days"). And behold us back up to our ears in the short time span. Of course, this is a perfectly fair and justifiable procedure, but how very revealing! The historian is naturally only too willing to act as theatrical producer. How could he be expected to renounce the drama of the short time span, and all the best tricks of a very old trade?

Over and above cycles and intercycles, there is what the economists without always having studied it call the secular tendency. But so far only a few economists have proved interested in it, and their deliberations on structural crises, based only on the recent past, as far back as 1929, or 1870 at the very most,[7] not having had to withstand the test of historical verification, are more in the nature of sketches and hypotheses. They offer nonetheless a useful introduction to the history of the *longue durée*. They provide a first key.

The second and far more useful key consists in the word *structure*. For good or ill, this word dominates the problems of the *longue durée*. By *structure*, observers of social questions mean an organization, a coherent and fairly fixed series of relationships between realities and social masses. For us historians, a structure is of course a construct, an architecture, but over and above that it is a reality which time uses and abuses over long periods. Some structures, because of their long life, become stable elements for an infinite number of generations: they get in the way of history, hinder its flow, and in hindering it shape it. Others wear themselves out more quickly. But all of them provide both support and hindrance. As hindrances they stand as limits ("envelopes," in the mathematical sense) beyond which man and his experiences cannot go. Just think of the difficulties of breaking out of certain geographical frameworks, certain biological realities, certain limits of productivity, even particular spiritual constraints: mental frameworks too can form prisons of the *longue durée*.

The example which comes most readily to mind is once again that of the geographical constraint. For centuries, man has been a prisoner of climate, of vegetation, of the animal population, of a particular agriculture, of a whole slowly established balance from which he cannot escape without the risk of everything's being upset. Look at the position held by the movement of flocks in the lives of mountain people, the permanence of certain sectors of maritime life, rooted in the favorable conditions wrought by particular coastal configurations, look at the way the sites of cities endure, the persistence of routes and trade, and all the amazing fixity of the geographical setting of civilizations.

[…]

In a seeming paradox, the main problem lies in discerning the *longue durée* in the sphere in which historical research has just achieved its most notable successes: that is, the economic sphere. All the cycles and intercycles and structural crises tend to mask the regularities, the permanence of particular systems that some have gone so far as to call civilizations[8] – that is to say, all the old habits of thinking and acting, the set patterns which do not break down easily and which, however illogical, are a long time dying.

But let us base our argument on an example, and one which can be swiftly analyzed. Close at hand, within the European sphere, there is an economic system which can be set down in a few lines: it preserved its position pretty well intact from the fourteenth to the eighteenth century or, to be quite sure of our ground, until about 1750. For whole centuries, economic activity was dependent on demographically fragile populations, as was demonstrated by the great decline in population from 1350 to 1450, and of course from 1630 to 1730.[9] For whole centuries, all movement was dominated by the primacy of water and ships, any inland location being an obstacle and a source of inferiority. The great European points of growth, except for a few exceptions which go only to prove the rule (such as the fairs in Champagne which were already on the decline at the beginning of the period, and the Leipzig fairs in the eighteenth century), were situated along the coastal fringes. As for other characteristics of this system, one might cite the primacy of merchants; the prominent role of precious metals, gold, silver, even copper, whose endless vicissitudes would only be damped down, if then, by the decisive development of credit at the end of the sixteenth century; the repeated sharp difficulties caused by seasonal agricultural crises; let us say the fragility of the very basis of economic life; and finally the at first sight utterly disproportionate role accorded to one or two external trade routes: the trade with the Levant from the twelfth to the sixteenth century and the colonial trade in the eighteenth century.

These are what I would define, or rather suggest in my turn following many others, as being the major characteristics of mercantile capitalism in Western Europe, a stage which lasted over the *longue durée*. Despite all the obvious changes which run through them, these four or five centuries of economic life had a certain coherence, right up to the upheavals of the eighteenth century and the industrial revolution from which we have yet to emerge. These shared characteristics persisted despite the fact that all around them, amid other continuities, a thousand reversals and ruptures totally altered the face of the world.

Among the different kinds of historical time, the *longue durée* often seems a troublesome character, full of complications, and all too frequently lacking in any sort of organization. To give it a place in the heart of our profession would entail more than a routine expansion of our studies and our curiosities. Nor would it be a question of making a simple choice in its favor. For the historian, accepting the *longue durée* entails a readiness to change his style, his attitudes, a whole reversal in his thinking, a whole new way of conceiving of social affairs. It means becoming used to a slower tempo, which sometimes almost borders on the motionless. At that stage, though not at any other – this is a point to which I will return – it is proper to free oneself from the demanding time scheme of history, to get out of it and return later with a fresh view, burdened with other anxieties and other questions. In any case, it is in relation to these expanses of slow-moving history that the whole of history is to be rethought, as if on the basis of an infrastructure. All the stages, all the thousands of stages, all the thousand explosions of historical time can be understood on the basis of these depths, this semistillness. Everything gravitates around it.

I make no claim to have defined the historian's profession in the preceding lines – merely one conception of that profession. After the storms we have been through during recent years, happy not to say naïf the man who could believe that we have hit upon true principles, clear limits, the Right School. In fact, all the social sciences find their tasks shifting all the time, both because of their own developments and because of the active development of them all as a body. History is no exception. There is no rest in view, the time for disciples has not yet come. It is a long way from Charles-Victor Langlois and Charles Seignobos to Marc Bloch. But since Marc Bloch, the wheel has not stopped turning. For me, history is the total of all possible histories – an assemblage of professions and points of view, from yesterday, today, and tomorrow.

The only error, in my view, would be to choose one of these histories to the exclusion of all others. That was, and always will be, the cardinal error of historicizing. It will not be easy, we know, to convince all historians of the truth of this. Still less, to convince all the social sciences, with their burning desire to get us back to history as we used to know it yesterday. It will take us a good deal of time and trouble to accommodate all these changes and innovations beneath the old

heading of history. And yet a new historical "science" has been born, and goes on questioning and transforming itself. It revealed itself as early as 1900, with the *Revue de synthèse historique*, and with *Annales* which started to come out in 1929. The historian felt the desire to concentrate his attention on *all* the human sciences. It is this which has given our profession its strange frontiers, and its strange preoccupations. So it must not be imagined that the same barriers and differences exist between the historian and the social scientist as existed yesterday. All the human sciences, history included, are affected by one another. They speak the same language, or could if they wanted to.

Whether you take 1558 or this year of grace 1958, the problem for anyone tackling the world scene is to define a hierarchy of forces, of currents, of particular movements, and then tackle them as an entire constellation. At each moment of this research, one has to distinguish between long-lasting movements and short bursts, the latter detected from the moment they originate, the former over the course of a distant time. The world of 1558, which appeared so gloomy in France, was not born at the beginning of that charmless year. The same with our own troubled year of 1958. Each "current event" brings together movements of different origins, of a different rhythm: today's time dates from yesterday, the day before yesterday, and all former times.

The Quarrel with the Short Time Span

These truths are of course banal. Nonetheless, the social sciences seem little tempted by such remembrance of things past. Not that one can draw up any firm accusation against them and declare them to be consistently guilty of not accepting history or duration as dimensions necessary to their studies. The "diachronic" examination which reintroduces history is never absent from their theoretical deliberations.

Despite this sort of distant acknowledgment, though, it must be admitted that the social sciences, by taste, by deep-seated instinct, perhaps by training, have a constant tendency to evade historical explanation. They evade it in two almost contradictory ways: by concentrating over-much on the "current event" in social studies, thanks to a brand of empirical sociology which, disdainful of all history, confines itself to the facts of the short term and investigations into "real life"; by transcending time altogether and conjuring up a mathematical formulation of more or less timeless structures under the name of "communications science." This last and newest way is clearly the only one which can be of any substantial interest to us. But there are enough devotees of the current event to justify examining both aspects of the question.

We have already stated our mistrust of a history occupied solely with events. To be fair, though, if there is a sin in being overconcerned with events, then history, though the most obvious culprit, is not the only guilty one. All the social sciences have shared in this error. Economists, demographers, geographers are all balanced (and badly balanced) between the demands of yesterday and of today. In order to be right they would need to maintain a constant balance – easy enough, and indeed obligatory, for the demographer, and almost a matter of course for geographers (particularly ours, reared in the Vidalian school) – but rare for economists, held fast to the most short lived of current events, hardly looking back beyond 1945 or forecasting further in advance than a few months, or at most a few years. I would maintain that all economic thinking is trapped by these temporal restrictions. It is up to historians, so economists say, to go back further than 1945, in search of old economies. Economists thus voluntarily rob themselves of a marvelous field of observation, although without denying its value. They have fallen into the habit of putting themselves at the disposal of current events and of governments.

The position of ethnographers and ethnologists is neither so clear nor so alarming. Some of them have taken great pains to underline the impossibility (but intellectuals are always fascinated by the impossible) and the uselessness of applying history within their profession. Such an authoritarian denial of history would hardly have served Malinowski and his disciples. Indeed, how could anthropology possibly not have an interest in history? History and anthropology both spring from the same impulse, as Claude Lévi-Strauss[10] delights in saying. There is no society, however primitive, which does not bear the "scars of events," nor any society in which history has sunk completely without trace. This is something there is no need to complain about or to insist on further.

On the other hand, where sociology is concerned, our quarrel along the frontiers of the short term must necessarily be a rather bitter one. Sociological investigations into the contemporary scene seem to run in a thousand different directions, from sociology to psychology to economics, and to proliferate among us as they do abroad. They are, in their own way, a bet on the irreplaceable value of the present moment, with its "volcanic" heat, its abundant wealth. What good would be served by turning back toward historical time: impoverished, simplified, devastated by silence, reconstructed – above all, let us say it again, *reconstructed*. Is it really as dead, as reconstructed, as they would have us believe, though? Doubtless a historian can only too easily isolate the crucial factor from some past age. To put it in Henri Pirenne's words, he can distinguish without difficulty the "important events," which means "those which bore consequences." An obvious and dangerous over-simplification. But what would the explorer of the present-day not give to have this perspective (or this sort of ability to go forward in time), making it possible to unmask and simplify our present life, in all its confusion – hardly comprehensible now because so overburdened with trivial acts and portents? Claude Lévi-Strauss claims that one hour's talk with a contemporary of Plato's would tell him more than all our classical treatises on the coherence or incoherence of ancient Greek civilization.[11] I quite agree. But this is because for years he has heard a hundred Greek voices rescued from silence. The historian has prepared his way. One hour in modern Greece would tell him nothing, or hardly anything, about contemporary Greek coherence or incoherence.

Even more to the point, the researcher occupied with the present can make out the "fine" lines of a structure only by himself engaging in *reconstruction*, putting forward theories and explanations, not getting embroiled in reality as it appears, but truncating it, transcending it. Such maneuvers allow him to get away from the given situation the better to control it, but they are all acts of reconstruction. I would seriously question whether sociological photography of the present time is any more "true" than the historical portrayal of the past, more particularly the more it tries to get any further away from the *reconstructed*.

Philippe Ariès[12] has emphasized the importance of the unfamiliar, of surprise in historical explanation: you are in the sixteenth century, and you stumble upon some peculiarity, something which seems peculiar to you as a man of the twentieth century. Why this difference? That is the question which one then has to set about answering. But I would claim that such surprise, such unfamiliarity, such distancing – these great highways to knowledge – are no less necessary to an understanding of all that surrounds us and which we are so close to that we cannot see clearly. Live in London for a year and you will not know much about England. But by contrast, in light of what has surprised you, you will suddenly have come to understand some of the most deep-seated and characteristic aspects of France, things which you did not know before because you knew them too well. With regard to the present, the past too is a way of distancing yourself.

In this way historians and social scientists could go on forever batting the ball back and forth between dead documents and all-too-living evidence, the distant past and the too-close present. But I do not believe that this is a crucial problem. Past and present illuminate each other reciprocally. And in exclusively observing the narrow confines of the present, the attention will irresistibly be drawn toward whatever moves quickly, burns with a true or a false flame, or has just changed, or makes a noise, or is easy to see. There is a whole web of events, as wearisome as any in the historical sciences, which lies in wait for the observer in a hurry, the ethnographer dwelling for three months with some Polynesian tribe, the industrial sociologist delivering all the clichés of his latest investigation, or who truly believes that he can thoroughly pin down some social mechanism with cunningly phrased questionnaires and combinations of punched cards. Social questions are more cunning game than that.

In fact, what possible interest can we take, we the human sciences, in the movements of a young girl between her home in the sixteenth arrondissement, her music teacher, and the Ecole des Sciences-Po, discussed in a sound and wide-ranging study of the Paris area?[13] They make up a fine-looking map. But if she had studied agronomy or gone in for water-skiing, the whole pattern of her triangular journeys would have been altered. It is nice to see on a map the distribution of all domiciles belonging to employees in a large concern. But if I do not have an earlier map, if the lapse of time between the two maps is not sufficient to allow the tracing of a genuine movement, then precisely where is the problem without which any inquiry is simply a waste of effort? Any interest in inquiries for inquiry's sake is limited to the collection of data at best. But even then these data will not all be *ipso facto* useful for future work. We must beware of art for art's sake.

In the same way I would question whether any study of a town, no matter which, could be the object of a sociological inquiry in the way that Auxerre[14] was, or Vienne in the Dauphiné,[15] without being set in its historical context. Any town, as an extended social entity with all its crises, dislocations, breakdowns, and necessary calculations, must be seen in relation to the whole complex of districts surrounding it, as well as in relation to those archipelagos of neighboring towns which Richard Häpke, the historian, was one of the first to discuss. Similarly, it must also be considered in relation to the movement, more or less distant in time, sometimes extremely distant, which directs this whole complex. It cannot be of no interest, it must rather surely be crucial to note down particular urban/rural exchanges, particular industrial or mercantile competition, to know whether you are dealing with a movement in the full flush of its youth, or at the end of its run, with the beginnings of a resurgence or a monotonous repetition.

One last remark: Lucien Febvre, during the last ten years of his life, is said to have repeated: "History, science of the past, science of the present." Is not history, the dialectic of time spans, in its own way an explanation of society in all its reality? and thus of contemporary society? And here its role would be to caution us against the event: do not think only of the short time span, do not believe that only the actors which make the most noise are the most authentic – there are other, quieter ones too. As if anybody did not know that already!

[…]

Time for the Historian, Time for the Sociologist

And here I am, after an incursion into the timeless realms of social mathematics, back at the question of time and time spans. And incorrigible historian that I am, I stand amazed yet again that sociologists have managed to avoid it. But the thing is that their time is not ours: it is a great deal less imperious and

time in itself

less concrete and is never central to their problems and their thoughts.

In truth, the historian can never get away from the question of time in history: time sticks to his thinking like soil to a gardener's spade. He may well dream of getting away from it, of course. Spurred on by the anguish of 1940, Gaston Roupnel[16] wrote words on this subject that will make any true historian suffer. Similar is the classic remark made by Paul Lacombe who was also a historian of the grand school: "Time is nothing in itself, objectively, it is only an idea we have."[17] But do these remarks really provide a way out? I myself, during a rather gloomy captivity, struggled a good deal to get away from a chronicle of those difficult years (1940–5). Rejecting events and the time in which events take place was a way of placing oneself to one side, sheltered, so as to get some sort of perspective, to be able to evaluate them better, and not wholly to believe in them. To go from the short time span, to one less short, and then to the long view (which, if it exists, must surely be the wise man's time span); and having got there, to think about everything afresh and to reconstruct everything around one: a historian could hardly not be tempted by such a prospect.

But these successive flights cannot put the historian definitively beyond the bounds of the world's time, beyond historical time, so imperious because it is irreversible, and because it flows at the very rhythm of the earth's rotation. In fact, these different time spans which we can discern are all interdependent: it is not so much time which is the creation of our own minds, as the way in which we break it up. These fragments are reunited at the end of all our labors. The *longue durée*, the conjuncture, the event all fit into each other neatly and without difficulty, for they are all measured on the same scale. Equally, to be able to achieve an imaginative understanding of one of these time spans is to be able to understand them all. The philosopher, taken up with the subjective aspect of things, interior to any notion of time, never senses this weight of historical time, of a concrete, universal time, such as the time of conjuncture that Ernest Labrousse[18] depicts at the beginning of his book like a traveler who is constantly the same and who travels the world imposing the same set of values, no matter the country in which he has disembarked, nor what the social order with which it is invested.

For the historian everything begins and ends with time, a mathematical, godlike time, a notion easily mocked, time external to men, "exogenous," as economists would say, pushing men, forcing them, and painting their own individual times the same color: it is, indeed, the imperious time of the world.

Sociologists, of course, will not entertain this oversimplified notion. They are much closer to the *dialectique de la durée* as put forward by Gaston Bachelard.[19] Social time is but one dimension of the social reality under consideration. It is within this reality just as it is within a given individual, one sign of particularity among others. The sociologist is in no way hampered by this accommodating sort of time, which can be cut, frozen, set in motion entirely at will. Historical time, I must repeat, lends itself less easily to the supple double action of synchrony and diachrony: it cannot envisage life as a mechanism that can be stopped at leisure in order to reveal a frozen image.

This is a more profound rift than is at first apparent: sociologists' time cannot be ours. The fundamental structure of our profession revolts against it. Our time, like economists' time, is one of measure. When a sociologist tells us that a structure breaks down only in order to build itself up afresh, we are happy to accept an explanation which historical observation would confirm anyway. But we would wish to know the precise time span of these movements, whether positive or negative, situated along the usual axis. An economic cycle, the ebb and flow of material life, can be measured. A structural social crisis should be equally possible to locate in time, and through it. We should be able to place it exactly, both in itself and even more in relation to the movement of associated structures. What is profoundly interesting to the historian is the way these movements cross one another, and how they interact, and how they break up: all things which can be recorded only in relation to the uniform time of historians, which can stand as a general measure of all these phenomena, and not in relation to the multiform time of social reality, which can stand only as the individual measure of each of these phenomena separately.

Rightly or wrongly, the historian cannot but formulate such opposed ideas, even when entering into the welcoming, almost brotherly realm of Georges Gurvitch's sociology. Did not a philosopher[20] define him recently as the one "who is driving sociology back into the arms of history"? But even with him, the historian can recognize neither his time spans nor his temporalities. The great social edifice (should one say *model?*) erected by Georges Gurvitch is organized according to five basic architectural aspects:[21] the deeper levels; the level of sociability; the level of social groups; the level of global societies; and the level of time. This final bit of scaffolding, temporalities, the newest and the most recently built, is as if superimposed on the whole.

Georges Gurvitch's temporalities are various. He distinguishes a whole series of them: the time of the *longue durée* and slow motion, time the deceiver and time the surpriser, time with an irregular beat, cyclic time running in place, time running slow, time alternating between running slow and fast, time running fast, explosive time.[22] How could a historian believe in all this? Given such a range of colors, he could never reconstitute a single, white light – and that is something he cannot do without. The historian quickly becomes aware, too, that this chameleon-like time barely adds any extra touch, any spot of color to the categories which had been established earlier. In the city that our friend has built, time, the last to arrive, cohabits quite naturally with all the other categories. It fits itself to the dimensions of their homes and their demands, according to the "levels," sociabilities, groups, and global societies. It is a different way of rewriting the same equations without actually changing them. Each social reality secretes its own peculiar time, or time scale, like common snails. But what do we historians get out of all this? The vast edifice of this ideal city remains static. History is nowhere to be seen. The world's time, historical time is there, but imprisoned, like Aeolus in his goat's skin. It is not history which sociologists, fundamentally and quite unconsciously, bear a grudge against, but historical time – which is a reality that retains its violence no matter how one tries to bring it to order and to break it down. It is a constraint from which the historian is never free, while sociologists on the other hand almost always seem to manage to avoid it, by concentrating either on the instant, which is always present as if suspended somewhere above time, or else on repeated phenomena which do not belong to any age. So they escape the two contradictory movements of the mind, con-fining them within either the narrowest limits of the event or the most extended *longue durée*. Is such an evasion justifiable? That is the crux of the debate between historians and sociologists, and even between historians of differing persuasions.

I do not know whether this rather excessively cut and dried article, relying overmuch, as historians have a tendency to do, on the use of examples, will meet with the agreement of sociologists and of our other neighbors. I rather doubt it. Anyway, it is never a good thing, when writing a conclusion, simply to repeat some insistently recurrent leitmotif. Should history by its very nature be called upon to pay special attention to the span of time and to *all* the movements of which it may be made up, the *longue durée* appears to us, within this array, as the most useful line to take toward a way of observing and thinking common to all the social sciences. Is it too much to ask our neighbors that, at some stage in their reasoning, they might locate their findings and their research along this axis?

For historians, not all of whom would share my views, it would be a case of reversing engines. Their preference goes instinctively toward the short term. It is an attitude aided and abetted by the sacrosanct university courses. Jean-Paul Sartre[23] strengthens their point of view, when he protests against that which is both oversimplified and too ponderous in Marxism in the name of the biographical, of the teeming reality of events. You have not said everything when you have "situated" Flaubert as bourgeois, or Tintoretto as petty bourgeois. I entirely agree. But in every case a study of the concrete situation – whether Flaubert, Valéry, or the foreign policies of the Gironde – ends up by bringing Sartre back to its deep-seated structural context. His research moves from the surface to the depths, and so links up with my own preoccupations. It would link up even better if the hourglass could be turned over both ways – from event to structure, and then from structure and model back to the event.

Marxism is peopled with models. Sartre would rebel against the rigidity, the schematic nature, the insufficiency of the model, in the name of the particular and the individual. I would rebel with him (with certain slight differences in emphasis) not against the model, though, but against the use which has been made of it, the use which it has been felt proper to make. Marx's *call for a new Morgan Longue Durée.*

genius, the secret of his long sway, lies in the fact that he was the first to construct true social models, on the basis of a historical *longue durée*. These models have been frozen in all their simplicity by being given the status of laws, of a preordained and automatic explanation, valid in all places and to any society. Whereas if they were put back within the ever-changing stream of time, they would constantly reappear, but with changes of emphasis, sometimes overshadowed, sometimes thrown into relief by the presence of other structures which would themselves be susceptible to definition by other rules and thus by other models. In this way, the creative potential of the most powerful social analysis of the last century has been stymied. It cannot regain its youth and vigor except in the *longue durée*. Should I add that contemporary Marxism appears to me to be the very image of the danger lying in wait for any social science wholly taken up with the model in its pure state, with models for models' sake?

What I would like to emphasize in conclusion is that the *longue durée* is but one possibility of a common language arising from a confrontation among the social sciences. There are others. I have indicated, adequately, the experiments being made by the new social mathematics. The new mathematics draws me, but the old mathematics, whose triumph is obvious in economics – perhaps the most advanced of the human sciences – does not deserve to be dismissed with a cynical aside. Huge calculations await us in this classic field, but there are squads of calculators and of calculating machines ready too, being rendered daily yet more perfect. I am a great believer in the usefulness of long sequences of statistics, and in the necessity of taking calculations and research further and further back in time. The whole of the eighteenth century in Europe is riddled with our workings, but they crop up even in the seventeenth, and even more in the sixteenth century. Statistics going back an unbelievably long way reveal the depths of the Chinese past to us through their universal language.[24] No doubt statistics simplify the better to come to grips with their subject. But all science is a movement from the complex to the simple.

And yet, let us not forget one last language, one last family of models, in fact: the necessary reduction of any social reality to the place in which it occurs. Let us call it either geography or ecology, without dwelling too long on these differences in terminology. Geography too

often conceives of itself as a world on its own, and that is a pity. It has need of a Vidal de la Blache who would consider not time and place this time, but place and social reality. If that happened, geographical research would put the problems of all the human sciences first on its agenda. For sociologists, not that they would always admit it to themselves, the word ecology is a way of not saying geography, and by the same token of dodging all the problems posed by place and revealed by place to careful observation. Spatial models are the charts upon which social reality is projected, and through which it may become at least partially clear; they are truly models for all the different movements of time (and especially for the *longue durée*), and for all the categories of social life. But, amazingly, social science chooses to ignore them. I have often thought that one of the French superiorities in the social sciences was precisely that school of geography founded by Vidal de la Blache, the betrayal of whose thought and teachings is an inconsolable loss. All the social sciences must make room "for an increasingly geographical conception of mankind."[25] This is what Vidal de la Blache was asking for as early as 1903.

On the practical level – for this article does have a practical aim – I would hope that the social sciences, at least provisionally, would suspend their constant border disputes over what is or is not a social science, what is or is not a structure … Rather let them try to trace those lines across our research which if they exist would serve to orient some kind of collective research, and make possible the first stages of some sort of coming together. I would personally call such lines mathematization, a concentration on place, the *longue durée* … But I would be very interested to know what other specialists would suggest. For it goes without saying that this article has not been placed under the rubric *Débats et Combats*[26] by pure chance. It claims to pose, but not resolve, the obvious problems to which, unhappily, each one of us, when he ventures outside his own specialty, finds himself exposed. These pages are a call to discussion.

Notes

1   Claude Lévi-Strauss, *Structural Anthropology*, trans. Claire Jacobson and Brooke Grundfest Schoepf (London: Allen Lane, The Penguin Press, 1968), 1:300 and passim.

✳ (social antagonism is the necessary lense through which to produce images of the longue durée.)

2   Jean-Paul Sartre, "Questions de méthode," *Les Temps Modernes* nos. 139 and 140 (1957).

3   "Europe in 1500," "The World in 1880," "Germany on the Eve of the Reformation," and so on.

4   Louis Halphen, *Introduction à l'histoire* (Paris: P.U.F., 1946), p. 50.

5   See his *Théorie générale du progrès économique*, Cahiers de l'I.S.E.A., 1957.

6   *Esquisse du mouvement des prix et des revenus en France au XVIIIᵉ siècle*, 2 vols. (Paris: Dalloz, 1933).

7   Considered in René Clémens, *Prolégomènes d'une théorie de la structure économique* (Paris: Domat-Montchrestien, 1952); see also Johann Akerman, "Cycle et structure," *Revue économique*, no. 1 (1952).

8   René Courtin, *La Civilisation économique du Brésil* (Paris: Librairie de Médicis, 1941).

9   As far as France is concerned. In Spain, the demographic decline was visible from the end of the sixteenth century.

10 Claude Lévi-Strauss, *Structural Anthropology*, p. 23.

11 "Diogéne couché," *Les Temps Modernes*, no. 195, p. 17.

12 *Les Temps de l'histoire* (Paris: Plon, 1954), especially p. 298 et seq.

13 P. Chombart de Lauwe, *Paris et l'agglomération parisienne* (Paris: P.U.F., 1952), 1: 106.

14 Suzanne Frère and Charles Bettelheim, *Une Ville française moyenne: Auxerre en 1950*, Cahiers de Sciences Politiques, no. 17 (Paris: Armand Colin, 1951).

15 Pierre Clément and Nelly Xydias, *Vienne su-le-Rhône: Sociologie d'une cité française*, Cahiers des Sciences Politiques, no. 71 (Paris: Armand Colin, 1955).

16 *Histoire et destin* (Paris: Bernard Grasset, 1943), p. 169 and passim.

17 *Revue de synthèse historique* (1900), p. 32.

18 Ernest Labrousse, *La Crise économique française à la veille de la Révolution française* (Paris: P. U. F., 1944), Introduction.

19 *Dialectique de la durée*, 2d edn (Paris: P. U. F., 1950).

20 Gilles Granger, *Événement et structure dans les sciences de l'homme*, Cahiers de l'Institut de Science Économique Appliquée, Série M., no. 1, pp. 41–2.

21 See my doubtless too polemical article "Georges Gurvitch et la discontinuité du social," *Annales E.S.C.* 3 (1953): 347–61.

22 Cf. Georges Gurvitch, *Déterminismes sociaux et liberté humaine* (Paris: P. U. F., 1955), pp. 38–40 and passim.

23 Ibid. See also Jean-Paul Sartre, "Fragment d'un livre à paraître sur le Tintoret," *Les Temps Modernes* (November 1957).

24 Otto Berkelbach, Van der Sprenkel, "Population Statistics of Ming China," B.S.O.A.S., 1953; Marianne Rieger, "Zur Finanz- und Agrargeschichte der Ming Dynastie, 1368–1643," *Sinica*, 1932.

25 P. Vidal de la Blache, *Revue de synthèse historique* (1903), p. 239.

26 Well-known rubric of *Annales E.S.C.*

33

"Periodizing the 60s" (1984)

Fredric Jameson

Nostalgic commemoration of the glories of the 60s and abject public confession of the decade's many failures and missed opportunities are two errors that cannot be avoided by some middle path that threads its way in between. The following sketch starts from the position that History is Necessity, that the 60s had to happen the way it did, and that its opportunities and failures were inextricably intertwined, marked by the objective constraints and openings of a determinate historical situation, of which I thus wish to offer a tentative and provisional model.

To speak of the "situation" of the 60s, however, is necessarily to think in terms of historical periods and to work with models of historical periodization, which are at the present moment theoretically unfashionable, to say the least. Leave aside the existential fact that the veterans of the decade, who have seen so many things change dramatically from year to year think more historically than their predecessors; the classification by generations has become as meaningful for us as it was for the Russians of the late nineteenth century, who sorted character types out with reference to specific decades. And intellectuals of a certain age now find it normal to justify their current positions by way of a historical narrative ("then the limits of Althusserianism began to be evident," etc.). Now, this is not the place for a theoretical justification of periodization in the writing of history, but to those who think that cultural periodization implies some

massive kinship and homogeneity or identity within a given period, it may quickly be replied that it is surely only against a certain conception of what is historically dominant or hegemonic that the full value of the exceptional – what Raymond Williams calls the "residual" or "emergent" – can be assessed. Here, in any case, the "period" in question is understood not as some omnipresent and uniform shared style or way of thinking and acting, but rather as the sharing of an objective situation, to which a whole range of varied responses and creative innovations is then possible, but always within that situation's structural limits.

Yet a whole range of rather different theoretical objections will also bear on the selectiveness of such a historical narrative: if the critique of periodization questions the possibilities of diachrony, these involve the problems of synchrony and in particular of the relationship to be established between the various "levels" of historical change singled out for attention. Indeed, the present narrative will claim to say something meaningful about the 60s by way of brief sketches of but four of those levels: the history of philosophy, revolutionary political theory and practice, cultural production, and economic cycles (and this in a context limited essentially to the United States, France, and the Third World). Such selectiveness seems not merely to give equal historical weight to base and superstructure indifferently, but also to raise the specter of a practice of homologies – the kind of analogical parallelism in which the poetic production of Wallace Stevens is somehow "the same" as the political practice of Che Guevara – which have been thought abusive at least as far back as Spengler.

Fredric Jameson, "Periodizing the 60s," pp. 178–86, 194–208 from *The Ideologies of Theory: Essays 1971–1986*. Minneapolis: University of Minnesota Press, 1988.

There is of course no reason why specialized and elite phenomena, such as the writing of poetry, cannot reveal historical trends and tendencies as vividly as "real life" – or perhaps even more visibly, in their isolation and semi-autonomy which approximates a laboratory situation. In any case, there is a fundamental difference between the present narrative and those of an older organic history that sought "expressive" unification through analogies and homologies between widely distinct levels of social life. Where the latter proposed identities between the forms on such various levels, what will be argued here is a series of significant homologies between the *breaks* in those forms and their development. What is at stake, then, is not some proposition about the organic unity of the 60s on all its levels, but rather a hypothesis about the rhythm and dynamics of the fundamental situation in which those very different levels develop according to their own internal laws.

At that point, what looked like a weakness in this historical or narrative procedure turns out to be an unexpected strength, particularly in allowing for some sort of "verification" of the separate strands of the narrative. One sometimes believes – especially in the area of culture and cultural histories and critiques – that an infinite number of narrative interpretations of history are possible, limited only by the ingenuity of the practitioners whose claim to originality depends on the novelty of the new theory of history they bring to market. It is more reassuring, then, to find the regularities hypothetically proposed for one field of activity (e.g., the cognitive, or the aesthetic, or the revolutionary) dramatically and surprisingly "confirmed" by the reappearance of just such regularities in a widely different and seemingly unrelated field, as will be the case with the economic in the present context.

At any rate, it will already have become clear that nothing like a history of the 60s in the traditional, narrative sense will be offered here. But historical representation is just as surely in crisis as its distant cousin, the linear novel, and for much the same reasons. The most intelligent "solution" to such a crisis does not consist in abandoning historiography altogether, as an impossible aim and an ideological category all at once, but rather – as in the modernist aesthetic itself – in reorganizing its traditional procedures on a different level. Althusser's proposal seems the wisest in this situation: as old-fashioned narrative or "realistic" historiography became problematical, the historian should reformulate her vocation – not any longer to produce some vivid representation of History "as it really happened," but rather to produce the *concept* of history. Such will at least be the gamble of the following pages.

"Periodizing the 60s"

1. Third World Beginnings

[handwritten marginalia: not to produce history but to conceptualize history]

It does not seem particularly controversial to mark the beginnings of what will come to be called the 60s in the Third World with the great movement of decolonization in British and French Africa. It can be argued that the most characteristic expressions of a properly First World 60s are all later than this, whether they are understood in countercultural terms – drugs and rock – or in the political terms of a student New Left and a mass antiwar movement. Indeed, politically, a First World 60s owed much to Third-Worldism in terms of politicocultural models, as in a symbolic Maoism, and, moreover, found its mission in resistance to wars aimed precisely at stemming the new revolutionary forces in the Third World. Belden Fields has indeed suggested that the two First World nations in which the most powerful student mass movements emerged – the United States and France – became privileged political spaces precisely *because* these were two countries involved in colonial wars, although the French New Left appears after the resolution of the Algerian conflict. The one significant exception to all this is in many ways the most important First World political movement of all – the new black politics and the civil rights movement, which must be dated, not from the Supreme Court decision of 1954, but rather from the first sit-ins in Greensboro, North Carolina, in February of 1960. Yet it might be argued that this was also a movement of decolonization, and in any case the constant exchange and mutual influences between the American black movements and the various African and Caribbean ones are continuous and incalculable throughout this period.

The independence of Ghana (1957), the agony of the Congo (Lumumba was murdered in January 1961), the independence of France's sub-Saharan colonies following the Gaullist referendum of 1959, finally the Algerian Revolution (which might plausibly mark our schema here with its internal high point, the Battle of Algiers, in January–March 1957, as with its diplomatic resolution in 1962) – all of these signal the convulsive birth of what will come in time to be known as the 60s:

> Not so very long ago, the earth numbered two thousand million inhabitants: five hundred million *men* and one thousand five hundred million *natives*. The former had the Word; the others merely had use of it.[1]

The 60s was, then, the period when all these "natives" became human beings, and this internally as well as externally: those inner colonized of the First World – "minorities," marginals, and women – fully as much as its external subjects and official "natives." The process can and has been described in a number of ways, each one of which implies a certain "vision of History" and a certain uniquely thematized reading of the 60s proper: it can be seen as a decisive and global chapter in Croce's conception of history as the history of human freedom; as a more classically Hegelian process of the coming to self-consciousness of subject peoples; as some post-Lukácsean or more Marcusean, New Left conception of the emergence of new "subjects of history" of a nonclass type (blacks, students, Third World peoples); or as some poststructuralist, Foucaultean notion (significantly anticipated by Sartre in the passage just quoted) of the conquest of the right to speak in a new collective voice, never before heard on the world stage – and of the concomitant dismissal of the intermediaries (liberals, First World intellectuals) who had hitherto claimed to talk in your name; not forgetting the more properly political rhetoric of self-determination or independence, or the more psychological and cultural rhetoric of new collective "identities."

It is, however, important to situate the emergence of these new collective "identities" or "subjects of history" in the historical situation which made that emergence possible, and in particular to relate the emergence of these new social and political categories (the colonized, race, marginality, gender, and the like) to something like a crisis in the more universal category that had hitherto seemed to subsume all the varieties of social resistance, namely the classical conception of social class. This is to be understood, however, not in some intellectual but rather in an institutional sense; it would be idealistic to suppose the deficiencies in the abstract idea of social class, and in particular in the Marxian conception of class struggle, can have been responsible for the emergence of what seem to be new nonclass forces. What can be noted, rather, is a crisis in the institutions through which a real class politics had however imperfectly been able to express itself. In this respect, the merge of the AFL and the CIO in 1955 can be seen as a fundamental "condition of possibility" for the unleashing of the new social and political dynamics of the 60s: that merger, a triumph of McCarthyism, secured the expulsion of the Communists from the American labor movement, consolidated the new antipolitical "social contract" between American business and the American labor unions, and created a situation in which the privileges of a white male labor force take precedence over the demands of black and women workers and other minorities. These last have therefore no place in the classical institutions of an older working-class politics. They will thus be "liberated" from social class, in the charged and ambivalent sense that Marxism gives to that word (in the context of enclosure, for instance): they are separated from the older institutions and thus "released" to find new modes of social and political expression.

The virtual disappearance of the American Communist Party as a small but significant political force in American society in 1956 suggests another dimension to this general situation: the crisis of the American party is "overdetermined" by its repression under McCarthyism and by the "revolution" in the Soviet bloc unleashed by Khrushchev's de-Stalinization campaign, which will have analogous but distinct and specific equivalents for the European Communist parties. In France, in particular, after the brief moment of a Communist "humanism," developed essentially by philosophers in the eastern countries, and with the fall of Khrushchev himself and the definitive failure of his various experiments in 1964, an unparalleled situation emerges in which, virtually for the first time since the Congress of Tours in 1919, it becomes possible for radical intellectuals to conceive of revolutionary work outside and independent of the French

Communist Party. (The older attitudes – "we know all about it, we don't like it much, but nothing is to be done politically without the CP" – are classically expressed in Sartre's own political journalism, in particular in *Les Communists et la paix*.) Now Trotskyism gets a new lease on life, and the new Maoist forms, followed by a whole explosion of extraparliamentary formations of all ideological complexions, the so-called groupuscules, offer the promise of a new kind of politics equally "liberated" from the traditional class categories.

Two further key events need to be noted here before we go on. For many of us, indeed, the crucial detonator – a new Year I, the palpable demonstration that revolution was not merely a historical concept and a museum piece but real and achievable – was furnished by a people whose imperialist subjugation had developed among North Americans a sympathy and a sense of fraternity we could never have for other Third World peoples in their struggle, except in an abstract and intellectual way. Yet by January 1, 1959, the Cuban Revolution remained symbolically ambiguous. It could be read as a Third World revolution of a type different from either the classical Leninist one or the Maoist experience, for it had a revolutionary strategy entirely its own, the *foco* theory, which we will discuss later. This great event also announces the impending 60s as a period of unexpected political innovation rather than as the confirmation of older social and conceptual schemes.

Meanwhile, personal testimony seems to make it clear that for many white American students – in particular for many of those later active in the New Left – the assassination of President Kennedy played a significant role in delegitimizing the state itself and in discrediting the parliamentary process, seeming to mark the decisive end of the well-known passing of the torch to a younger generation of leadership, as well as the dramatic defeat of some new spirit of public or civic idealism. As for the reality of the appearance, it does not much matter that, in hindsight, such a view of the Kennedy presidency may be wholly erroneous, considering his conservatism and anticommunism, the gruesome gamble of the "missle crisis," and his responsibility for the American engagement in Vietnam itself. More significant, the legacy of the Kennedy regime to the development of a 60s politics may well have been

the rhetoric of youth and of the "generation gap" which he exploited, but which outlived him and dialectically offered itself as an expressive form through which the political discontent of American students and young people could articulate itself.

Such were some of the preconditions or "conditions of possibility" – both in traditional working-class political institutions and in the arena of the legitimation of state power – for the "new" social forces of the 60s to develop as they did. Returning to these new forces, there is a way in which their ultimate fate marks the close of the 60s as well: the end of "Third-Worldism" in the US and Europe largely predates the Chinese Thermidor, and coincides with the awareness of increasing institutional corruption in many of the newly independent states of Africa and the almost complete militarization of the Latin American regimes after the Chilean coup of 1973 (the later revolutionary triumphs in the former Portuguese colonies are henceforth felt to be "Marxist" rather than "Third-Worldist," whereas Vietnam vanishes from American consciousness as completely after the ultimate American withdrawal as did Algeria from French consciousness after the Evian accords of 1963). In the First World of the late 60s, there is certainly a return to a more internal politics, as the antiwar movement in the United States and May 1968 in France testify. Yet the American movement remains organically linked to its Third World "occasion" in the Vietnam War itself, as well as to the Maoist inspiration of the Progressive Labor-type groups which emerge from SDS, such that the movement as a whole will lose its momentum as the war winds down and the draft ceases. In France, the "common program" of the left (1972) – in which the current Socialist government finds its origins – marks a new turn toward Gramscian models and a new kind of "Eurocommunist" spirit which owes very little to Third World antecedents of any kind. Finally, the black movement in the US enters into a crisis at much the same time, as its dominant ideology – cultural nationalism, an ideology profoundly linked to Third World models – is exhausted. The women's movement also owed something to this kind of Third World inspiration, but it too, in the period 1972–4, will know an increasing articulation into relatively distinct ideological positions ("Bourgeois" feminism, lesbian separatism, socialist feminism).

For reasons enumerated above, and others, it seems plausible to mark the end of the 60s around 1972–4; the problem of this general "break" will be returned to at the end of this sketch. For the moment we must complete our characterization of the overall dynamic of Third World history during this period, particularly if it is granted that this dynamic or "narrative line" entertains some privileged relationship of influence on the unfolding of a First World 60s (through direct intervention – wars of national liberation – or through the prestige of exotic political models – most obviously, the Maoist one – or finally, owing to some global dynamic which both worlds share and respond to in relatively distinct ways).

This is, of course, the moment to observe that the "liberation" of new forces in the Third World is as ambiguous as this term frequently tends to be (freedom as separation from older systems); to put it more sharply, it is the moment to recall the obvious, that decolonization historically went hand in hand with neocolonialism, and that the graceful, grudging, or violent end of an old-fashioned imperialism certainly meant the end of one kind of domination but evidently also the invention and construction of a new kind – symbolically, something like the replacement of the British Empire by the International Monetary Fund. This is, incidentally, why the currently fashionable rhetoric of power and domination (Foucault is the most influential of these rhetoricians, but the basic displacement from the economic to the political is already made by Max Weber) is ultimately unsatisfactory; it is of course politically important to "contest" the various forms of power and domination, but the latter cannot be understood unless their functional relationships to economic exploitation are articulated – that is, until the political is once again subsumed beneath the economic. (On the other hand – particularly in the historicizing perspective of the present essay – it will obviously be a significant historical and social *symptom* that, in the mid-60s, people felt it necessary to express their sense of the situation and their projected praxis in a reified political language of power, domination, authority and antiauthoritarianism, and so forth: here, Second and Third World developments – with their conceptions of a "primacy of the political" under socialism – offer an interesting and curious cross-lighting.) Meanwhile, something

similar can be said of the conceptions of collective identity and in particular of the poststructuralist slogan of the conquest of speech, of the right to speak in your own voice, for yourself; but to articulate new demands, in your own voice, is not necessarily to satisfy them, and to speak is not necessarily to achieve a Hegelian recognition from the Other (or at least then only in the more somber and baleful sense that the Other now has to take you into consideration in a new way and to invent new methods for dealing with that new presence you have achieved). In hindsight, the "materialist kernel" of this characteristic rhetoric or ideological vision of the 60s may be found in a more fundamental reflection on the nature of cultural revolution itself (now independent of its local and now historical Chinese manifestation).

The paradoxical, or dialectical, combination of decolonization and neocolonialism can perhaps best be grasped in economic terms by a reflection on the nature of another process whose beginning coincides with the general beginnings we have suggested for this period as a whole. This is a process generally described in the neutral but obviously ideological language of a technological "revolution" in agriculture: the so-called Green Revolution, with its new applications of chemical procedures to fertilization, its intensified strategies of mechanization, and its predictable celebration of progress and wonder-working technology, supposedly destined to free the world from hunger (the Green Revolution, incidentally, finds its Second World equivalent in Khrushchev's disastrous "virgin lands" experiment). But these are far from neutral achievements; nor is their export – essentially pioneered by the Kennedys – a benevolent and altruistic activity. In the nineteenth and early twentieth centuries, capitalist penetration of the Third World did not necessarily mean a capitalist transformation of the latter's traditional modes of production. Rather, they were for the most part left intact, "merely" exploited by a more political and military structure. The very enclave nature of these older agricultural modes – in combination with the violence of the occupier and that other violence, the introduction of money – established a sort of tributary relation that was beneficial to the imperialist metropolis for a considerable period. The Green Revolution carries this penetration and expansion of the "logic of capital" into a new stage.

The older village structure and precapitalist forms of agriculture are now systematically destroyed, to be replaced by an industrial agriculture whose effects are fully as disastrous as, and analogous to, the moment of enclosure in the emergence of capital in what was to become the First World. The "organic" social relations of village societies are now shattered, an enormous landless preproletariat "produced," which migrates to the urban areas (as the tremendous growth of Mexico City can testify), while new, more proletarian, wage-working forms of agricultural labor replaced the older collective or traditional kinds. Such ambiguous "liberation" needs to be described with all the dialectical ambivalence with which Marx and Engels celebrate the dynamism of capital itself in the *Manifesto* or the historical progress achieved by the British occupation of India.

The conception of the Third World 60s as a moment when all over the world chains and shackles of a classical imperialist kind were thrown off in a stirring wave of "wars of national liberation" is an altogether mythical simplification. Such resistance is generated as much by the new penetration of the Green Revolution as it is by the ultimate impatience with the older imperialist structures, the latter itself overdetermined by the historical spectacle of the supremacy of another former Third World entity, namely Japan, in its sweeping initial victories over the old imperial powers in World War II. Eric Wolf's indispensable *Peasant Wars of the Twentieth Century* (1969) underscores the relationship between possibilities of resistance, the development of a revolutionary ethos, and a certain constitutive distance from the more absolutely demoralizing social and economic logic of capital.

The final ambiguity with which we leave this topic is the following: the 60s, often imagined as a period when capital and First World power are in retreat all over the globe, can just as easily be conceptualized as a period when capital is in full dynamic and innovative expansion, equipped with a whole armature of fresh production techniques and new "means of production." It now remains to be seen whether this ambiguity, and the far greater specificity of the agricultural developments in the Third World, have any equivalent in the dynamics with which the 60s unfold in the advanced countries themselves.

[…]

5. The Adventures of the Sign

Postmodernism is one significant framework in which to describe what happened to culture in the 60s, but a full discussion of this hotly contested concept is not possible here. Such a discussion would want to cover, among other things, the following features: that well-known poststructuralist theme, the "death" of the subject (including the creative subject, the *auteur* or the "genius"); the nature and function of a *culture of the simulacrum* (an idea developed out of Plato by Deleuze and Baudrillard to convey some specificity of a reproducible object world, not of copies or reproductions marked as such, but of a proliferation of trompe-l'oeil copies *without originals*); the relation of this last to media culture of the "society of the spectacle" (Debord), under two heads: (1) the peculiar new status of the image, the "material" or what might better be called the "literal," signifier: a materiality or literality from which the older sensory richness of the medium has been abstracted (just as on the other side of the dialectical relationship, the old individuality of the subject and his/her "brushstrokes" have equally been effaced); and (2) the emergence, in the work's temporality, of an aesthetic of *textuality* or what is often described as schizophrenic time; the eclipse, finally, of all depth, especially *historicity* itself, with the subsequent appearance of pastiche and nostalgia art (what the French call *la mode rétro*), and including the supersession of the accompanying models of depth-interpretation in philosophy (the various forms of hermeneutics, as well as the Freudian conception of "repression," of manifest and latent levels).

What is generally objected to in characterizations of this kind is the empirical observation that all these features can be abundantly located in this or that variety of high modernism; indeed, one of the difficulties in specifying postmodernism lies in its symbiotic or parasitical relationship to the latter. In effect, with the canonization of a hitherto scandalous, ugly, disonant, amoral, antisocial, bohemian high modernism offensive to the middle classes, its promotion to the very figure of high culture generally, and perhaps most important, its enshrinement in the academic institution, postmodernism emerges as a way of making creative space for artists now oppressed by those

inversion – 60s as *un-potentiality*

henceforth hegemonic modernist categories of irony, complexity, ambiguity, dense temporality, and particularly, aesthetic and utopian monumentality. In some analogous way, it will be said, high modernism itself won its autonomy from the preceding hegemonic realism (the symbolic language or mode of representation of classical or market capitalism). But there is a difference in that realism itself underwent a significant mutation: it became *naturalism* and at once generated the representation forms of mass culture (the narrative apparatus of the contemporary best seller is an invention of naturalism and one of the most stunningly successful of French cultural exports). High modernism and mass culture then develop in dialectical opposition and interrelationship with one another. It is precisely the waning of their opposition, and some new conflation of the forms of high and mass culture, that characterizes postmodernism itself.

The historical specificity of postmodernism must therefore finally be argued in terms of the social functionality of culture itself. As stated above, high modernism, whatever its overt political content, was oppositional and marginal within a middle-class Victorian or philistine or gilded age culture. Although postmodernism is equally offensive in all the respects enumerated (think of punk rock or pornography), it is no longer at all "oppositional" in that sense; indeed, it constitutes the very dominant or hegemonic aesthetic of consumer society itself and significantly serves the latter's commodity production as a virtual laboratory of new forms and fashions. The argument for a conception of postmodernism as a periodizing category is thus based on the presupposition that, even if *all* the formal features enumerated above were already present in the older high modernism, the very significance of those features changes when they become a cultural *dominant*, with a precise socioeconomic functionality.

At this point it may be well to shift the terms (or the "code") of our description to the seemingly more traditional one of a cultural "sphere," a conception developed by Herbert Marcuse in what is to my mind his single most important text, the great essay "The Affirmative Character of Culture" (1937). (It should be added that the conception of a "public sphere" generally is a very contemporary one in Germany in the works of Habermas and Negt and Kluge, where such a system of categories stands in interesting contrast to the code of "levels" or "instances" in French poststructuralism.) Marcuse there rehearses the paradoxical dialectic of the classical (German) aesthetic, which projects as play and "purposefulness without purpose" a Utopian realm of beauty and culture beyond the fallen empirical world of money and business activity, thereby winning a powerful critical and negative value through its capacity to condemn, by its own very existence, the totality of *what* is, at the same time forfeiting all ability to social or political intervention in what is, by virtue of its constitutive disjunction or autonomy from society and history.

The account therefore begins to concide in a suggestive way with the problematic of autonomous or semi-autonomous levels […]. To historicize Marcuse's dialectic, however, would demand that we take into account the possibility that in our time this very autonomy of the cultural sphere (or level or instance) may be in the process of modification; and that we develop the means to furnish a description of the process whereby such modification might take place, as well as of the prior process whereby culture became "autonomous" or "semi-autonomous" in the first place.

This requires recourse to yet another (unrelated) analytic code, one more generally familiar to us today, since it involves the now classical structural concept of the *sign*, with its two components, the signifier (the material vehicle or image – sound or printed word) and the signified (the mental image, meaning, or "conceptual" content), and a third component – the external object of the sign, its reference or "referent" – henceforth expelled from the unity and yet haunting it as a ghostly residual aftereffect (illusion or ideology). The scientific value of this conception of the sign will be bracketed here since we are concerned, on the one hand, to historicize it, to interpret it as a conceptual symptom of developments in the period, and, on the other, to "set it in motion," to see whether changes in its inner structure can offer some adequate small-scale emblem or electrocardiogram of changes and permutation in the cultural sphere generally throughout this period.

Such changes are already suggested by the fate of the "referent" in the "conditions of possibility" of the new structural concept of the sign (a significant ambiguity must be noted, however: theorists of the sign notoriously glide from a conception of reference as designating a "real" object outside the unity of signi-fier and signified to a position in which the signified itself – or meaning, or the idea or the concept of a thing – becomes somehow identified with the refer-ent and stigmatized along with it; we will return to this below). Saussure, at the dawn of the semiotic rev-olution, liked to describe the relationship of signifier to signified as that of the two sides, the recto and verso, of a sheet of paper. In what is then a logical sequel, and a text that naturally enough becomes equally canonical, Borges will push "representation" to the point of imagining a map so rigorous and ref-erential that it becomes coterminous with its object. The stage is then set for the structuralist emblem par excellence, the Moebius Strip, which succeeds in peeling itself off its referent altogether and thus achieves a free-floating closure in the void, a kind of absolute self-referentiality and autocirculatory from which all remaining traces of reference, or of any externality, have triumphantly been effaced.

To be even more eclectic about it, I will suggest that this process, seemingly internal to the sign itself, requires a supplementary explanatory code, that of the more universal process of reification and fragmenta-tion at one with the logic of capital itself. Nonetheless, taken on its own terms, the inner convulsions of the sign is a useful initial figure of the process of transfor-mation of culture generally, which must in some first moment (that described by Marcuse) separate itself from the "referent" the existing social and historical world itself, only in a subsequent stage of the 60s, in what is here termed "postmodernism," to develop further into some new and heightened, free-floating, self-referential "autonomy."

The problem now turns around this very term, "autonomy," with its paradoxical Althusserian modifi-cation, the concept of "semi-autonomy." The paradox is that the sign, as an "autonomous" unity in its own right as a realm divorced from the referent, can pre-serve that initial autonomy, and the unity and coher-ence demanded by it, only at the price of keeping a phantom of reference alive, as the ghostly reminder of its own outside or exterior, since this allows it closure, self-definition, and an essential boundary line. Marcuse's own tormented dialectic expresses this dra-matically in the curious oscillation whereby his autonomous realm of beauty and culture returns upon some "real world" to judge and negate it, at the same time separating itself so radically from that real world as to become a place of mere illusion and impotent "ideals," the "infinite," and so on.

The first moment in the adventures of the sign is perplexing enough as to demand more concrete, if schematic, illustration in the most characteristic cul-tural productions themselves. It might well be dem-onstrated in the classical French *nouveau roman* (in particular the novels of Robbe-Grillet himself), which established its new language in the early 1960s, using systematic variations of narrative segments to "under-mine" representation, yet in some sense confirming this last by teasing and stimulating an appetite for it.

Because an American illustration seems more appro-priate, however, something similar may be seen in con-nection with the final and canonical form of high modernism in American poetry, namely the work of Wallace Stevens, which becomes, in the years following the poet's death in 1956, institutionalized in the univer-sity as a purer and more quintessential fulfillment of poetic language than the still impure (read: ideological and political) works of an Eliot or a Pound, and can therefore be numbered among the literary "events" of the early 60s. As Frank Lentricchia has shown, in *After the New Criticism*,[2] the serviceability of Stevens' poetic pro-duction for this normative and hegemonic role depends in large measure on the increasing conflation, in that work, of poetic practice and poetic theory:

> This endlessly elaborating poem
> Displays the theory of poetry
> As the life of poetry …

"Stevens" is therefore a locus and fulfillment of aes-thetics and aesthetic theory fully as much as the latter's exemplar and privileged exegetical object; the theory or aesthetic ideology in question is very much an affir-mation of the "autonomy" of the cultural sphere in the sense developed above, a valorization of the supreme power of the poetic imagination over the "reality" it produces. Stevens' work, therefore, offers an extraordi-nary laboratory situation in which to observe the autonomization of culture as a process: a detailed examination of his development (something for which we have no space here) would show how some initial "set toward" or "attention to" a kind of poetic *pensée sauvage,* the operation of great preconscious *stereotypes,* opens up a vast inner world in which little by little the images of things and their "ideas" begin to be substituted for the things themselves. Yet what distinguishes this experience in Stevens is the sense of a vast systematicity in all this, the operation of a whole set of cosmic oppositions far too complex to be reduced to the schemata of "structuralist" binary oppositions, yet akin to those in spirit, and somehow pregiven in the Symbolic Order of the mind, discoverable to the passive exploration of the "poetic imagination," that is, of some heightened and impersonal power of free association in the realm of "objective spirit" or "objective culture." The examination would further show the strategic limitation of this process to landscape, the reduction of the ideas and images of things to the names for things, and finally to those irreducibles that are place names, among which the exotic has a privileged function (Key West, Oklahoma, Yucatan, Java). Here the poetic "totality" begins to trace a ghostly mimesis or *analogon* of the totality of the imperialist world system itself, with Third World materials in a similarly strategic, marginal, yet essential place (much as Adorno showed how Schoenberg's twelve-tone system unconsciously produced a formal imitation of the "total system" of capital). This very unconscious replication of the "real" totality of the world system in the mind is then what allows culture to separate itself as a closed and self-sufficient "system" in its own right: reduplication, and at the same time, floating above the real. It is an impulse shared by most of the great high modernisms, as has been shown most dramatically in the recent critiques of architectural modernism, in particular of the international style, whose great monumental objects constitute themselves, by protecting a protopolitical and utopian spirit of transformation *against* a fallen city fabric all around them and, as Venturi has demonstrated, end up necessarily displaying and speaking of themselves alone. Now, this also accounts for what must puzzle any serious reader of Stevens' verse, namely the extraordinary combination of verbal richness and experimental hollowness or impoverishment in it (the latter being attributable as well to the impersonality of the poetic imagination in Stevens, and to the essentially contemplative and epistemological stance of the subject in it, over and against the static object world of his landscapes).

The essential point here, however, is that this characteristic movement of the high modernist impulse needs to justify itself by way of an ideology, an ideological supplement which can generally be described as that of "existentialism" (the supreme fiction, the meaninglessness of a contingent object world unredeemed by the imagination, etc.). This is the most uninteresting and banal dimension of Stevens' work, yet it betrays along with other existentialisms (e.g., Sartre's tree root in *Nausea*) that fatal seam or link that must be retained in order for the contingent, the "outside world," the meaningless referent, to be just present enough dramatically to be overcome within the language. Nowhere is this ultimate point so clearly deduced, over and over again, as in Stevens, in the eye of the blackbird, the angels, or the Sun itself – that last residual vanishing point of reference as distant as a dwarf star upon the horizon, yet which cannot disappear altogether without the whole vocation of poetry and the poetic imagination being called back into question. Stevens thus exemplifies for us the fundamental paradox of the "autonomy" of the cultural sphere: the sign can become autonomous only by remaining semi-autonomous, and the realm of culture can absolutize itself over against the real world only at the price of retaining a final tenuous sense of that exterior or external world of which it is the replication and the imaginary double.

All of this can also be demonstrated by showing what happens when, in a second moment, the perfectly logical conclusion is drawn that the referent is itself a myth and does not exist, a second moment hitherto described as postmodernism. Its trajectory can be seen as a movement from the older *Nouveau roman* to that of Sollers or of properly "schizophrenic" writing, or from the primacy of Stevens to that of John Ashbery. This new moment is a radical break (which can be localized around 1967 for reasons to be given later), but it is important to grasp it as dialectical, that is, as a passage from quantity to quality in which the *same* force, reaching a certain threshold of excess, in its prolongation now produces qualitatively distinct effects and seems to generate a whole new system.

That force has been described as reification, but we can now also begin to make some connections with another figural language used earlier: in a first moment, reification "liberated" the sign from its referent, but

Analogy ? culture parallels language as a mundane, pervasive, and disorienting system.

this is not a force to be released with impunity. Now, in a second moment, it continues its work of dissolution, penetrating the interior of the sign itself and liberating the signifier from the signified, or from meaning proper. This play, no longer of a realm of signs, but of pure or literal signifiers freed from the ballast of their signifieds, their former meanings, now generates a new kind of textuality in all the arts (and in philosophy as well, as we have seen above) and begins to project the mirage of some ultimate language of pure signifiers which is also frequently associated with schizophrenic discourse. (Indeed, the Lacanian theory of schizophrenia – a language disorder in which syntactical time breaks down and leaves a succession of empty signifiers, absolute moments of a perpetual present, behind itself – has offered one of the more influential explanations and ideological justifications for postmodernist textual practice.)

Such an account would have to be demonstrated in some detail by way of a concrete analysis of the postmodernist experience in all the arts today; but the present argument can be concluded by drawing the consequences of this second moment – the aculture of the signifier or of the simulacrum – for the whole problematic of some "autonomy" of the cultural sphere which has concerned us here. For that autonomous realm is not itself spared by the intensified process by which the classical sign is dissolved; if its autonomy depended paradoxically on its possibility of remaining "semi-autonomous" (in an Althusserian sense) and of preserving the last tenuous link with some ultimate referent (or, in Althusserian language, of preserving the ultimate unity of a properly "structural totality"), then evidently in the new cultural moment culture will have ceased to be autonomous, and the realm of an autonomous play of signs becomes impossible, when that ultimate final referent to which the balloon of the mind was moored is now definitively cut. The break-up of the sign in mid-air determines a fall back into a now absolutely fragmented and anarchic social reality; the broken pieces of language (the pure signifiers) now fall again into the world, as so many more pieces of material junk among all the other rusting and superannuated apparatuses and buildings that litter the commodity landscape and that strew the "collage city," the "delirious New York" of a postmodernist late capitalism in full crisis.

Cf. this figuration to Scholem's version of Kabbalistic sparks or embers.

But, returning to a Marcusean terminology, all of this can also be said in a different way: with the eclipse of culture as an autonomous space or sphere, culture itself falls into the world, and the result is not its disappearance but its prodigious expansion, to the point where culture becomes coterminous with social life in general; now all the levels become "acculturated," and in the society of the spectacle, the image, or the simulacrum, everything has at length become cultural, from the superstructures down into the mechanisms of the infrastructure itself. If this development then places acutely on the agenda the neo-Gramscian problem of a new cultural politics today – in a social system in which the very status of both culture and politics have been profoundly, functionally, and structurally modified – it also renders problematic any further discussion of what used to be called "culture" proper, whose artifacts have become the random experiences of daily life itself.

6. In the Sierra Maestra

The preceding section will, however, have been little more than a lengthy excursion into a very specialized (or "elite") area, unless it can be shown that the dynamic therein visible, with something of the artificial simplification of the laboratory situation, finds striking analogies or homologies in very different and distant areas of social practice. It is precisely this replication of a common diachronic rhythm or "genetic code" which we will not observe in the very different realities of revolutionary practice and theory in the course of the 60s in the Third World.

From the beginning, the Cuban experience affirmed itself as an original one, as a new revolutionary model, to be radically distinguished from more traditional forms of revolutionary practice. *Foco* theory, indeed, as it was associated with Che Guevara and theorized in Regis Debray's influential handbook, *Revolution in the Revolution?* (1967), asserted itself (as the title of the book suggests) both against a more traditional Leninist conception of party practice and against the experience of the Chinese revolution in its first essential stage of the conquest of power (what will later come to be designated as "Maoism," China's own very different "revolution in the revolution," or

Great Proletarian Cultural Revolution, will not become visible to the outside world until the moment when the fate of the Cuban strategy has been sealed).

A reading of Debray's text shows that *foco* strategy, the strategy of the mobile guerrilla base or revolutionary *foyer*, is conceived as yet a third term, as something distinct from *either* the traditional model of class struggle (an essentially *urban* proletariat rising against a bourgeoisie or ruling class) *or* the Chinese experience of a mass peasant movement in the countryside (and also has little in common with a Fanonian struggle for recognition between Colonizer and Colonized). The *foco*, or guerrilla operation, is conceptualized as being neither "in" nor "of" either country or city; geographically, of course, it is positioned in the countryside, yet that location is not the permanently "liberated territory" of the Yenan region, well beyond the reach of the enemy forces of Chiang Kai-shek or of the Japanese occupier. It is not indeed located in the cultivated area of the peasant fields at all, but rather in that third or nonplace which is the wilderness of the Sierra Maestra, neither country nor city, but rather a whole new element in which the guerrilla band moves in perpetual displacement.

This peculiarity of the way in which the spatial coordinates of the Cuban strategy is conceived has, then, immediate consequences for the way in which the class elements of the revolutionary movement are theorized. Neither city nor country; by the same token, paradoxically, the guerrillas themselves are grasped as being neither workers nor peasants (still less, intellectuals), but rather something entirely new, for which the prerevolutionary class society has no categories: new revolutionary subjects, forged in the guerrilla struggle indifferently out of the social material of peasants, city workers, or intellectuals, yet now largely transcending those class categories (just as this moment of Cuban theory will claim largely to transcend the older revolutionary ideologies predicted on class catagories, whether those of Trotskyist workerism, Maoist populism and peasant consciousness, or of Leninist vanguard intellectualism).

What becomes clear in a text like Debray's is that the guerrilla *foco* – so mobile as to be beyond geography in the static sense – is in and of itself a *figure* for the transformed, revolutionary society to come. Its revolutionary militants are not simply "soldiers" to whose

specialized role and function one would then have to "add" supplementary roles in the revolutionary division of labor, such as political commissars and the political vanguard party itself, both explicitly rejected here. Rather, in them is abolished all such prerevolutionary divisions and categories. This conception of a newly emergent revolutionary "space" – situated outside the "real" political, social, and geographical world of country and city, and of the historical social classes, yet at one and the same time a figure or small-scale image and prefiguration of the revolutionary transformation of that real world – may be designated as a properly Utopian space, a Hegelian "inverted world," an autonomous revolutionary sphere, in which the fallen real world over against it is itself set right and transformed into a new socialist society.

For all practical purposes, this powerful model is exhausted, even before Che's own tragic death in Bolivia in 1967, with the failure of the guerrilla movements in Peru and Venezuela in 1966; not uncoincidentally, that failure will be accompanied by something like a disinvestment of revolutionary libido and fascination on the part of a First World Left, the return (with some leavening of the newer Maoism) to its own current situation, in the American antiwar movement and May 1968. In Latin America, however, the radical strategy that effectively replaces *foco* theory is that of the so-called urban guerrilla movement, pioneered in Uruguay by the Tupamaros; it will have become clear that this break-up of the utopian space of the older guerrilla *foco*, the fall of politics back into the world in the form of a very different style of political practice indeed – one that seeks to dramatize features of state power, rather than, as in traditional revolutionary movements, to build toward some ultimate encounter with it – will be interpreted here as something of a structural equivalent to the final stage of the sign as characterized above.

Several qualifications must be made, however. For one thing, it is clear that this new form of political activity will be endowed, by association, with something of the tragic prestige of the Palestinian liberation movement, which comes into being in its contemporary form as a result of the Israeli seizure of the West Bank and the Gaza Strip in 1967, and which will thereafter become one of the dominant worldwide symbols of revolutionary praxis in the late 60s. Equally clearly, however, the struggle of this desperate and victimized people cannot be made to bear responsibility for the excesses of this kind of strategy elsewhere in the world, whose universal results (whether in Latin America, or with Cointelpro in the United States, or, belatedly, in West Germany and Italy) have been to legitimize an intensification of the repressive apparatus of state power.

This objective coincidence between a misguided assessment of the social and political situation on the part of Left militants (for the most part students and intellectuals eager to force a revolutionary conjuncture by voluntaristic acts) and a willing exploitation by the state of precisely those provocations suggests that what is often loosely called "terrorism" must be the object of complex and properly dialectical analysis. However rightly a responsible Left chooses to dissociate itself from such strategy (and the Marxian opposition to terrorism is an old and established tradition that goes back to the nineteenth century) it is important to remember that "terrorism," as a "concept," is also an ideologeme of the Right and must therefore be refused in that form. Along with the disaster films of the late 60s and early 70s, mass culture itself makes clear that "terrorism" – the image of the "terrorist" – is one of the privileged forms in which an ahistorical society imagines radical social change; meanwhile, an inspection of the content of the modern thriller or adventure story also makes it clear that the "otherness" of so-called terrorism has begun to replace older images of criminal "insanity" as an unexamined and seemingly "natural" motivation in the construction of plots – yet another sign of the ideological nature of this particular pseudoconcept. Understood in this way, "terrorism" is a collective obsession, a symptomatic fantasy of the American political unconscious, which demands decoding and analysis in its own right.

As for the thing itself, for all practical purposes it comes to an end with the Chilean coup in 1973 and the fall of virtually all the Latin American countries to various forms of military dictatorship. The belated reemergence of this kind of political activity in West Germany and in Italy must surely at least in part be attributed to the fascist past of these two countries, to their failure to liquidate that past after the war, and to a violent moral revulsion against it on the part of a segment of the youth and intellectuals who grew up in the 60s.

7. Return of the "Ultimately Determining Instance"

The two "breaks" that have emerged in the preceding section – one in the general area around 1967, the other in the immediate neighborhood of 1973 – will not serve as the framework for a more general hypothesis about the periodization of the 60s in general. Beginning with the second of these, a whole series of other, seemingly unrelated events in the general area of 1972–4 suggests that this moment is not merely a decisive one on the relatively specialized level of Third World or Latin American radical politics, but signals the definitive end of what is called the 60s in a far more global way. In the First World, for example, the end of the draft and the withdrawal of American forces from Vietnam (in 1973) spell the end of the mass politics of the antiwar movement (the crisis of the New Left itself – which can be largely dated from the break-up of SDS in 1969 – would seem related to the other break mentioned, to which we will return below), while the signing of the Common Program between the Communist party and the new Socialist party in France (as well as the wider currency of slogans associated with "Eurocommunism" at this time) would seem to mark a strategic turn away from the kinds of political activities associated with May 1968 and its sequels. This is also the movement when as a result of the Yom Kippur war, the oil weapon emerges and administers a different kind of shock to the economies, the political strategies, and the daily life habits of the advanced countries. Concomitantly, on the more general cultural and ideological level, the intellectuals associated with the establishment itself (particularly in the United States) begin to recover from the fright and defensive posture that was theirs during the decade now ending, and again find their voices in a series of attacks on 60s culture and 60s politics, which, as was noted at the beginning, are not even yet at an end. One of the more influential documents was Lionel Trilling's *Sincerity and Authenticity* (1972), an Arnoldian call to reverse the tide of 60s' countercultural "barbarism." (This will, of course, be followed by the equally influential diagnosis of some 60s concept of "authenticity" in terms of a "culture of narcissism.") Meanwhile, in July 1973, some rather different "intellectuals," representing various concrete forms of political and economic power, will begin to rethink the failure in Vietnam in terms of a new global strategy for American and First World interests; their establishment of the Trilateral Commission will at least symbolically be a significant marker in the recovery of momentum by what must be called "the ruling classes." The emergence of a widely accepted new popular concept and term at this same time, the notion of the "multinational corporation," is also another symptom, signifying, as the authors of *Global Reach* have suggested, the moment when private business finds itself obliged to emerge in public as a visible "subject of history" and a visible actor on the world stage – think of the role of ITT in Chile – when the American government, having been badly burned by the failure of the Vietnam intervention, is generally reluctant to undertake further ventures of this kind.

For all these reasons it seems appropriate to mark the definitive end of the "60s" in the general area of 1972–4. But we have omitted until now the decisive element in any argument for a periodization or "punctuation" of this kind, and this new kind of material will direct our attention to a "level" or "instance" which has hitherto significantly been absent from the present discussion, namely the economic itself. For 1973–4 is the moment of the onset of a worldwide economic crisis, whose dynamic is still with us today, and which put a decisive full stop to the economic expansion and prosperity characteristic of the postwar period generally and of the 60s in particular. When we add to this another key economic marker – the recession in West Germany in 1966 and that in the other advanced countries, in particular in the United States a year or so later – we may well thereby find ourselves in a better position more formally to conceptualize the sense of a secondary break around 1967–8 which has begun to surface on the philosophical, cultural, and political levels as they were analyzed or "narrated" above.

Such confirmation by the economic "level" itself of periodizing reading derived from other, sample levels or instances of social life during the 60s will now perhaps put us in a better position to answer the two theoretical issues raised at the beginning of this essay. The first had to do with the validity of Marxist analysis for a period whose active political categories no

longer seemed to be those of social class, and in which in a more general way traditional forms of Marxist theory and practice seemed to have entered a "crisis." The second involved the problem of some "unified field theory" in terms of which such seemingly distant realities as Third World peasant movements and First World mass culture (or indeed, more abstractly, intellectual or superstructural levels like philosophy and culture generally, and those of mass resistance and political practice) might conceptually be related in some coherent way.

A pathbreaking synthesis of Ernest Mandel, in his book *Late Capitalism*,[3] will suggest a hypothetical answer to both these questions at once. The book presents, among other things, an elaborate system of business cycles under capitalism, whose most familiar unit, the seven-to-ten-year alternation of boom, overproduction, recession, and economic recovery, adequately enough accounts for the midpoint break in the 60s suggested above.

Mandel's account of the worldwide crisis of 1974, however, draws on a far more controversial conception of vaster cycles of some thirty- to fifty-year periods each – cycles which are then obviously much more difficult to perceive experientially or "phenomenologically" insofar as they transcend the rhythms and limits of the biological life of individuals. These "Kondratiev waves" (named after the Soviet economist who hypothesized them) have, according to Mandel, been renewed four times since the eighteenth century, and are characterized by quantum leaps in the technology of production, which enable decisive increases in the rate of profit generally, until at length the advantages of the new production processes have been explored and exhausted and the cycle therewith comes to an end. The latest of these Kondratiev cycles is that marked by computer technology, nuclear energy, and the mechanization of agriculture (particularly in foodstuffs and also primary materials), which Mandel dates from 1940 in North America and the postwar period in the other imperialist countries; what is decisive in the present context is his notion that, with the worldwide recession of 1973–4, the dynamics of this latest "long wave" are spent.

The hypothesis is attractive, however, not only because of its abstract usefulness in confirming our periodization schemes, but also because of the actual analysis of this latest wave of capitalist expansion, and of the properly Marxian version he gives of a whole range of developments that have generally been thought to demonstrate the end of the "classical" capitalism theorized by Marx and to require this or that post-Marxist theory of social mutation (as in theories of consumer society, postindustrial society, and the like).

We have already described the way in which neocolonialism is characterized by the radically new technology (the so-called Green Revolution in agriculture: new machinery, new farming methods, and new types of chemical fertilizer and genetic experiments with hybrid plants and the like), with which capitalism transforms its relationship to its colonies from an old-fashioned imperialist control to market penetration, destroying the older village communities and creating a whole new wage-labor pool and lumpenproletariat. The militancy of the new social forces is at one and the same time a result of the "liberation" of peasants from the older self-sustaining village communities, and a movement of self-defense, generally originating in the stabler yet more isolated areas of a given Third World country, against what is rightly perceived as a far more thoroughgoing form of penetration and colonization than the older colonial armies.

It is now in terms of this process of "mechanization" that Mandel will make the link between the neocolonialist transformation of the Third World during the 60s and the emergence of that seemingly very different thing in the First World, variously termed consumer society, postindustrial society, media society, and the like:

> Far from representing a postindustrial society, late capitalism ... constitutes *generalized universal industrialization* for the first time in history. Mechanization, standardization, overspecialization and parcellization of labor, which in the past determined only the realm of commodity production in actual industry, now penetrate into all sectors of social life. It is characteristic of late capitalism that agriculture is step by step becoming just as industrialized as industry, the sphere of circulation [e.g., credit cards and the like] just as much as the sphere of production, and recreation just as much as the organization of work. (p. 387)

With this last, Mandel touches on what he elsewhere calls the mechanization of the superstructure, or, in other words, the penetration of culture itself by what the Frankfurt School called the culture industry, and of which the growth of the media is only a part. We may thus generalize his description as follows: late capitalism in general (and the 60s in particular) constitute a process in which the last surviving internal and external zones of precapitalism – the last vestiges of non-commodified or traditional space within and outside the advanced world – are now ultimately penetrated and colonized in their turn. Late capitalism can therefore be described as the moment when the last vestiges of Nature which survived on into classical capitalism are at length eliminated: namely the Third World and the unconscious. The 60s will then have been the momentous transformational period when this systemic restructuring takes place on a global scale.

With such an account, our "unified field theory" of the 60s is given: the discovery of a single process at work in First and Third Worlds, in global economy, and in consciousness and culture, a properly *dialectical* process, in which "liberation" and domination are inextricably combined. We may now therefore proceed to a final characterization of the period as a whole.

The simplest yet most universal formulation surely remains the widely shared feeling that in the 60s, for a time, everything was possible; that this period, in other words, was a moment of a universal liberation, a global unbinding of energies. Mao Zedong's figure for this process is in this respect most revealing: "Our nation," he cried, "is like an atom. ... When this atom's nucleus is smashed, the thermal energy released will have really tremendous power!"[4] The image evokes the emergence of a genuine mass democracy from the breakup of the older feudal and village structures, and from the therapeutic dissolution of the habits of those structures in cultural revolutions. Yet the effects of fission, the release of molecular energies, the unbinding of "material signifiers," can be a properly terrifying spectacle; and we now know that Mao Zedong himself drew back from the ultimate consequences of the process he had set in motion, when, at the supreme moment of the Cultural Revolution, that of the founding of the Shanghai Commune, he called a halt to the dissolution of the party apparatus and effectively reversed the direction of this collective experiment as a whole (with consequences only too obvious at the present time). In the West, also, the great explosions of the 60s have led, in the worldwide economic crisis, to powerful restorations of the social order and a renewal of the repressive power of the various state apparatuses.

Yet the forces these must now confront, contain, and control are new ones, on which the older methods do not necessarily work. We have described the 60s as a moment when the enlargement of capitalism on a global scale simultaneously produced an immense freeing or unbinding of social energies, a prodigious release of untheorized new forces: the ethnic forces of black and "minority," or Third World, movements everywhere, regionalisms, the development of new and militant bearers of "surplus consciousness" in the student and women's movements, as well as in a host of struggles of other kinds. Such newly released forces do not only not seem to compute in the dichotomous class model of traditional Marxism; they also seem to offer a realm of freedom and voluntarist possibility beyond the classical constraints of the economic infrastructure. Yet this sense of freedom and possibility – which is for the course of the 60s a momentarily objective reality, as well as (from the hindsight of the 80s) a historical illusion – can perhaps best be explained in terms of the superstructural movement and play enabled by the transition from one infrastructural or systemic stage of capitalism to another. The 60s were in that sense an immense and inflationary issuing of superstructural credit; a universal abandonment of the referential gold standard; an extraordinary printing up of ever more devalued signifiers. With the end of the 60s, with the world economic crisis, all the old infrastructural bills then slowly come due once more; and

the 80s will be characterized by an effort, on a world scale, to proletarianize all those unbound social forces that gave the 60s their energy, by an extension of class struggle, in other words, into the farthest reaches of the globe as well as the most minute configurations of local institutions (such as the university system). The unifying force here is the new vocation of a henceforth global capitalism, which may also be expected to unify the unequal, fragmented, or local resistances to the process. And this is finally also the solution to the so-called crisis of Marxism and to the widely noted inapplicability of its forms of class analysis to the new social realities with which the 60s confronted us: "traditional" Marxism, if "untrue" during this period of a proliferation of new subjects of history, must necessarily become true again when the dreary realities of exploitation, extraction of surplus value, proletarianization, and the resistance to it in the form of class struggle, all slowly reassert themselves on a new and expanded world scale, as they seem currently in the process of doing.

Notes

1 J. P. Sartre, "Preface" to Frantz Fanon, *The Wretched of the Earth*, trans. Constance Farrington (New York, 1965).
2 Frank Lentricchia, *After the New Criticism* (Chicago, 1980), esp. pp. 31–5.
3 Ernest Mandel, *Late Capitalism* (London, 1978).
4 Mao Zedong, *Chairman Mao Talks to the People*, ed. S. Schram (New York, 1974), pp. 92–3.

34

"Brazilian Culture: Nationalism by Elimination" (1992)

Roberto Schwarz

We Brazilians and other Latin Americans constantly experience the artificial, inauthentic and imitative nature of our cultural life. An essential element in our critical thought since independence, it has been variously interpreted from romantic, naturalist, modernist, right-wing, left-wing, cosmopolitan and nationalist points of view, so we may suppose that the problem is enduring and deeply rooted. Before attempting another explanation, let us assume that this malaise is a fact. Its everyday manifestations range from the inoffensive to the horrifying. Examples of inappropriateness include Father Christmas sporting an eskimo outfit in a tropical climate and, for traditionalists, the electric guitar in the land of samba. Representatives of the 1964 dictatorship often used to say that Brazil was not ready for democracy, that it would be out place here. In the nineteenth century people spoke of the gulf between the empire's liberal façade, copied from the British parliamentary system, and the actual reality of the system of labour, which was slavery. In his 'Lundu do Escritor Dificil' Mário de Andrade[1] ridiculed his fellow countrymen whose knowledge spanned only foreign matters. Recently, when the São Paulo state government extended its human rights policy to the prisons, there were demonstrations of popular discontent at the idea that such guarantees should be introduced inside prisons when so many people did not enjoy them outside. In this perspective even human rights seem spurious in Brazil. These examples, taken from unrelated spheres

Roberto Schwarz, "Brazilian Culture: Nationalism by Elimination," pp. 1–18 from *Misplaced Ideas: Essays on Brazilian Culture*. London: Verso, 1992. Reprinted by permission of Verso.

and presupposing incompatible points of view, show how widespread the problem is. They all involve the same sense of contradiction between the real Brazil and the ideological prestige of the countries used as models.[2]

Let us examine the problem from a literary point of view. In twenty years of teaching the subject I have witnessed a transition in literary criticism from impressionism, through positivist historiography, American New Criticism, stylistics, Marxism, phenomenology, structuralism, post-structuralism, and now Reception theories. The list is impressive and demonstrates our university's efforts to overcome provincialism. But it is easy to see that the change from one school of thought to another rarely arises from the exhaustion of a particular project; usually it expresses the high regard that Brazilians feel for the newest doctrine from America or Europe. The disappointing impression created, therefore, is one of change and development with no inner necessity and therefore no value. The thirst for terminological and doctrinal novelty prevails over the labour of extending knowledge and is another illustration of the imitative nature of our cultural life. We shall see that the problem has not been correctly posed, although we may start by accepting its relative validity.

In Brazil intellectual life seems to start from scratch with each generation.[3] The hankering for the advanced countries' latest products nearly always has as its reverse side a lack of interest in the work of the previous generation of Brazilian writers, and results in a lack of intellectual continuity. As Machado de Assis noted in 1879: 'A foreign impetus determines the direction of movement.' What is the meaning of this passing over of the internal impulse, which is in any case much less inevitable than it was then? You do not have to be a traditionalist or believe in an impossible intellectual autarky to recognize the difficulties. There is a lack of conviction, both in the constantly changing theories and in their relationship to the movement of society as a whole. As a result little importance is attached to work itself or to the object of investigation. Outstanding analyses and research on the country's culture are periodically cut short and problems that have been identified and tackled with great difficulty are not developed as they deserve. This bias is negatively confirmed by the stature of such few outstanding writers as Machado de Assis,[4] Mário de Andrade and now Antonio Candido. None of them lacked information or an openness to contemporary trends, but they all knew how to make broad and critical use of their predecessors' work, which they regarded not as dead weight but as a dynamic and unfinished element underlying present-day contradictions.

It is not a question of continuity for the sake of it. We have to identify a set of real, specific problems – with their own historical insertion and duration – which can draw together existing forces and allow fresh advances to be made. With all due respect to the theoreticians we study in our faculties, I believe we would do better to devote ourselves to a critical assessment of the ideas put forward by Silvio Romero,[5] Oswald and Mário de Andrade, Antonio Candido, the concretists and the CPCs.[6] A certain degree of cultural density arises out of alliances or disagreements between scientific disciplines, artistic, social and political groups, without which the idea of breaking away in pursuit of the new becomes meaningless. We should bear in mind that to many Latin Americans Brazil's intellectual life appears to have an enviably organic character, and however incredible it may seem, there may be some relative truth in this view.

Little remains of the conceptions and methods that we have passed under review, since the rhythm of change has not allowed them to attain a mature expression. There is a real problem here, part of that feeling of inappropriateness from which we started out. Nothing seems more reasonable, for those who are aware of the damage, than to steer in the opposite direction and think it is enough to avoid copying metropolitan trends in order to achieve an intellectual life with greater substance. This conclusion is illusory, as we shall see, but has strong intuitive support. For a time it was taken up by both right and left nationalists, in a convergence that boded ill for the left and, through its wide diffusion, contributed to a low intellectual level and a high estimation of ideological crudities.

The search for genuine (i.e. unadulterated) national roots leads us to ask: What would popular culture be like if it were possible to isolate it from commercial interests and particularly from the mass media? What would a national economy be like if there were no admixture? Since 1964 the internationalization of capital, the commodification of social relations, and the presence of the mass media have developed so rapidly that these very questions have come to seem implausible. Yet barely twenty years ago they still excited intellectuals and figured on their agenda. A combative frame of mind still prevailed - for which progress would result from a kind of *reconquista*, or rather from the expulsion of the invaders. Once imperialism had been pushed back, its commercial and industrial forms of culture neutralized, and its allied, anti-national section of the bourgeoisie isolated, the way would be clear for the flowering of national culture, which had been *distorted by these elements as by an alien body*. This correct emphasis on the mechanisms of US domination served to mythologize the Brazilian community as object of patriotic fervour, whereas a class analysis would have made this much more problematic. Here a qualification is necessary: such ideas reached their height in the period of the Goulart government, when extraordinary events, which brought about experimentation and democratic realignments on a large scale, were taking place. The period cannot be reduced to the inconsistencies of its self-image - indicative though they are of the illusion inherent in populist nationalism that the outside world is the source of all evil.

In 1964 the right-wing nationalists branded Marxism as an alien influence, perhaps imagining that fascism was a Brazilian invention. But over and above their differences, the two nationalist tendencies were alike in hoping to find their goal by eliminating anything that was not indigenous. The residue would be the essence of Brazil. The same illusion was popular in the last century, but at that time the new national culture owed more to diversification of the European models than to exclusion of the Portuguese. Opponents of the romantic liberal distortion of Brazilian society did not arrive at the authentic country, since once French and English imports had been rooted out, the colonial order was restored. And that was a Portuguese creation. The paradox of this kind of purism is apparent in the person of Policarpo Quaresma, whose quest for authenticity led him to write in Tupi, a language foreign to him.[7] The same goes for Antonio Callado's *Quarup*, in which the real Brazil is found not in the colonial past – as suggested by Lima Barreto's hero – but in the heart of the interior, far from the Atlantic coast with its overseas contacts. A group of characters mark the centre of the country on a map and go off in search of it. After innumerable adventures they reach their destination, where they find … an ants' nest.

The standard US models that arrived with the new communications networks were regarded by the nationalists as an unwelcome foreign presence. The next generation, however, already breathing naturally in this air, considered nationalism to be archaic and provincial. For the first time, as far as I know, the idea spread that it was a worthless enterprise to defend national characteristics against imperialist uniformity. The culture industry would cure the sickness of Brazilian culture – at least for those who were willing to delude themselves.

In the 1960s nationalism also came under fire from those who thought of themselves as politically and artistically more advanced. Their views are now being taken up in the context of international mass media, only this time without the elements of class struggle and anti-imperialism. In this 'world' environment of uniform mythology, the struggle to establish an 'authentic' culture appears as a relic from the past. Its illusory nature becomes evident, and it seems a provincial phenomenon associated with archaic forms of oppression. The argument is irrefutable, but it must be said that in the new context an emphasis on the international dimension of culture becomes no more than a legitimation of the existing mass media. Just as nationalists used to condemn imperialism and hush up bourgeois oppression, so the anti-nationalists invoke the authoritarianism and backwardness of their opponents, with good reason, while suggesting that the

reign of mass communication is either emancipatory or aesthetically acceptable. A modern, critical position, perhaps, but fundamentally conformist. There is another imaginary reversal of roles: although the 'globalists' operate within the dominant ideology of our time, they defend their positions as if they were being hunted down, or as if they were part of the heroic vanguard, aesthetic or libertarian, of the early twentieth century; they line up with the authorities in the manner of one who is starting a revolution.

In the same order of paradox, we can see that the imposition of foreign ideology and the cultural expropriation of the people are realities which do not cease to exist just because there is mystification in the nationalists' theories about them. Whether they are right or wrong, the nationalists become involved in actual conflicts, imparting to them a certain degree of visibility. The mass media modernists, though right in their criticisms, imagine a universalist world which does not exist. It is a question of choosing between the old and the new error, both upheld in the name of progress. The sight of the Avenida Paulista is a fine illustration of what I mean: ugly mansions, once used by the rich to flaunt their wealth, now seem perversely tolerable at the foot of modern skyscrapers, both for reasons of proportion and because of that poetry which emanates from any historically superseded power.

Recent French philosophy has been another factor in the discrediting of cultural nationalism. Its anti-totalizing tendency, its preference for levels of historicity alien to the national milieu, its dismantling of conventional literary scaffolding such as authorship, 'the work', influence, originality, etc. – all these destroy, or at least discredit, that romantic correspondence between individual heroism, masterly execution and collective redemption which imbues the nationalist schemas with their undeniable knowledge-value and potential for mystification. To attack these coordinates can be exciting and partially convincing, besides appeasing national sensibility in an area where one would least expect this to be possible.

A commonplace idea suggests that the copy is secondary with regard to the original, depends upon it, is worth less, and so on. Such a view attaches a negative sign to the totality of cultural forces in Latin America and is at the root of the intellectual malaise that we are discussing. Now, contemporary French philosophers such as Foucault and Derrida have made it their speciality to show that such hierarchies have no basis. Why should the prior be worth more than the posterior, the model more than the imitation, the central more than the peripheral, the economic infrastructure more than cultural life, and so forth? According to the French philosophers, it is a question of conditioning processes (but are they all of the same order?) – prejudices which do not express the life of the spirit in its real movement but reflect the orientation inherent in the traditional human sciences. In their view, it would be more accurate and unbiased to think in terms of an infinite sequence of transformations, with no beginning or end, no first or last, no worse or better. One can easily appreciate how this would enhance the self-esteem and relieve the anxiety of the underdeveloped world, which is seen as tributary to the central countries. We would pass from being a backward to an advanced part of the world, from a deviation to a paradigm, from inferior to superior lands (although the analysis set out to suppress just such superiority). All this because countries which live in the humiliation of having to imitate are more willing than the metropolitan countries to give up the illusion of an original source, even though the theory originated there and not here. Above all, the problem of mirror-culture would no longer be ours alone, and instead of setting our sights on the Europeanization or Americanization of Latin America we would, in a certain sense, be participating in the Latin Americanization of the central cultures.[8]

It remains to be seen whether this conceptual break with the primacy of origins would enable us to balance out or combat relations of actual subordination. Would the innovations of the advanced world suddenly become dispensable once they had lost the distinction of originality? In order to use them in a free and non-imitative manner, it is not enough simply to divest them of their sacred aura. Contrary to what the above analysis might lead us to believe, the breaking down of cultural dazzlement in the underdeveloped countries does not go to the heart of a problem which is essentially practical in character. Solutions are reproduced from the advanced world in response to cultural, economic and political needs, and the notion of copying, with its psychologistic connotations, throws no light whatsoever on this reality. If theory remains at this level, it will continue to suffer from the same limitations, and

the radicalism of an analysis that passes over efficient causes will become in its turn largely delusive. The inevitability of cultural imitation is bound up with a specific set of historical imperatives over which abstract philosophical critiques can exercise no power. Even here nationalism is the weak part of the argument, and its supersession at the level of philosophy has no purchase on the realities to which it owes its strength. It should be noted that while nationalism has recently been almost absent from serious intellectual debate, it has a growing presence in the administration of culture, where, for better or worse, it is impossible to escape from the national dimension. Now that economic, though not political, space has become international – which is not the same as homogeneous – this return of nationalism by the back door reflects the insuperable paradox of the present day.

In the 1920s Oswald de Andrade's 'anthropophagous' Pau-Brazil programme also tried to give a triumphalist interpretation of our backwardness.[9] The disharmony between bourgeois models and the realities of rural patriarchy is at the very heart of his poetry – the first of these two elements appearing in the role of absurd caprice ('Rui Barbosa[10]: A Top Hat in Senegambia'). Its true novelty lies in the fact that the lack of accord is a source not of distress but of optimism, evidence of the country's innocence and the possibility of an alternative, non-bourgeois historical development. This *sui generis* cult of progress is rounded out with a technological wager: Brazil's innocence (the result of Christianization and *embourgeoisement* barely scraping the surface) plus technology equals utopia; modern material progress will make possible a direct leap from pre-bourgeois society to paradise. Marx himself, in his famous letter of 1881 to Vera Zasulich, came up with a similar hypothesis that the Russian peasant commune would achieve socialism without a capitalist interregnum, thanks to the means made available by progress in the West. Similarly, albeit in a register combining jokes, provocation, philosophy of history and prophecy (as, later, in the films of Glauber Rocha), Anthropophagy set itself the aim of leaping a whole stage.

Returning once more to the idea that Western culture has been inappropriately copied in Brazil, we can see that Oswald's programme introduced a change of tone. Local primitivism would give back a modern sense to tired European culture, liberating it from Christian mortification and capitalist utilitarianism. Brazil's experience would be a differentiated cornerstone, with utopian powers, on the map of contemporary history. (The poems of Mario de Andrade and Raúl Bopp[11] on Amazonian slothfulness contain a similar idea.) Modernism therefore brought about a profound change in values: for the first time the processes under way in Brazil were weighed in the context of the present-day world, as having something to offer in that larger context. Oswald de Andrade advocated cultural irreverence in place of subaltern obfuscation, using the metaphor of 'swallowing up' the alien: a copy, to be sure, but with regenerative effect. Historical distance allows us to see the ingenuousness and jingoism contained in these propositions.

The new vogue for Oswald's manifestoes in the 1960s and particularly the 1970s appeared in the very different context of a military dictatorship which, for all its belief in technological progress and its alliance with big capital both national and international, was less repressive than expected in regard to everyday habits and morality. In the other camp, the attempt to overthrow capitalism through revolutionary war also changed the accepted view of what could be termed 'radical'. This now had no connection with the provincial narrowness of the 1920s, when the Antropófago rebellion assumed a highly libertarian and enlightening role. In the new circumstances technological optimism no longer held water, while the brazen cultural irreverence of Oswald's 'swallowing up' acquired a sense of exasperation close to the mentality of direct action (although often with good artistic results). Oswald's clarity of construction, penetrating vision and sense of discovery all suffered as greater value was attached to his primal, 'de-moralizing' literary practices. One example of this evolution is the guiltlessness of the act of swallowing up. What was then freedom against Catholicism, the bourgeoisie and the glare of Europe has become in the eighties an awkward excuse to handle uncritically those ambiguities of mass culture that stand in need of elucidation. How can one fail to notice that the *Antropófagos* – like the nationalists – take as their subject the abstract Brazilian, with no class specification; or that the analogy with the digestive process throws absolutely no light on the politics and aesthetics of contemporary cultural life?

Since the last century educated Brazilians – the concept is not meant as a compliment but refers to a social category – have had the sense of living among ideas and institutions copied from abroad that do not reflect local reality. It is not sufficient, however, to give up loans in order to think and live more authentically. Besides, one cannot so much as conceive of giving them up. Nor is the problem eliminated by a philosophical deconstruction of the concept of copy. The programmatic innocence of the Antropófagos, which allows them to ignore the malaise, does not prevent it from emerging anew. 'Tupi or not Tupi, that is the question!' Oswald's famous saying, with its contradictory use of the English language, a classical line and a play on words to pursue the search for national identity, itself says a great deal about the nature of the impasse.

The problem may appear simpler in historical perspective. Silvio Romero, despite many absurdities, made a number of excellent remarks on the matter. The following extract is taken from a work on Machado de Assis, written in 1897 to prove that this greatest Brazilian writer produced nothing but a literature of Anglomania, incompetent, unattuned, slavish, etc.

> Meanwhile a kind of absurdity developed … a tiny intellectual elite separated itself off from the mass of the population, and while the majority remained almost entirely uneducated, this elite, being particularly gifted in the art of learning and copying, threw itself into political and literary imitation of everything it found in the Old World. So now we have an exotic literature and politics, which live and procreate in a hothouse that has no relationship to the outside temperature and environment. This is the bad side of our feeble, illusory skill of mestizo southerners, passionate, given to fantasy, capable of imitation but organically unsuited to create, invent or produce things of our own that spring from the immediate or remote depths of our life and history.
>
> In colonial times, a skilful policy of segregation cut us off from foreigners and kept within us a certain sense of cohesion. This is what gave us Basilio, Durào, Gonzaga, Alvarenga Peixoto, Claudio and Silva Alvarenga, who all worked in a milieu of exclusively Portuguese and Brazilian ideas.
>
> With the first emperor and the Regency, the first breach [opened] in our wall of isolation by Dom João VI grew wider, and we began to copy the political and literary romanticism of the French.
>
> We aped the Charter of 1814 and transplanted the fantasies of Benjamin Constant; we mimicked the

parliamentarism and constitutional politics of the author of *Adolphe*, intermingled with the poetry and dreams of the author of *René* and *Atala*.

The people … remained illiterate.

The Second Reign*, whose policy was for fifty years vacillating, uncertain and incompetent, gradually opened all the gates in a chaotic manner lacking any criteria or sense of discrimination. Imitation, mimicking of everything – customs, laws, codes, verse, theatre, novel - was the general rule.

Regular sailings assured direct communication with the old continent and swelled the inflow of imitation and servile copying. …

This is why, in terms of copying, mimickry and pastiches to impress the gringos, no people has a better Constitution on paper…, everything is better … on paper. The reality is appalling.[12]

Silvio Romero's account and analysis are uneven, sometimes incompatible. In some instances it is the argument that is interesting, in others the ideology, so that the modern reader will want to examine them separately. The basic schema is as follows: a tiny elite devotes itself to copying Old World culture, separating itself off from the mass of the population, which remains uneducated. As a result, literature and politics come to occupy an exotic position, and we become incapable of *creating things of our own that spring from the depths of our life and history*. Implicit in this demand is the norm of an organic, reasonably homogeneous national culture with popular roots – a norm that cannot be reduced to a mere illusion of literary history or of romanticism, since in some measure it expresses the conditions of modern citizenship. It is in its opposition to this norm that the Brazilian configuration – Europeanized minority, uneducated majority – constitutes an *absurdity*. On the other hand, in order to make the picture more realistic, we should remember that the organic requirement arose at the same time as the expansion of imperialism and organized science – two tendencies which rendered obsolete the idea of a harmonious and auto-centred national culture.

The original sin, responsible for the severing of connections, was the copy. Its negative effects already

* That of the Emperor Pedro II, which lasted from 1840 to 1889.

made themselves felt in the social fissure between *culture* (unrelated to its surroundings) and *production* (not springing from the depths of our life). However, the disproportion between cause and effects is such that it raises some doubts about the cause itself, and Silvio Romero's own remarks are an invitation to follow a different line of argument from the one he pursues. Let us also note in passing that it is in the nature of an absurdity to be avoidable, and that Romero's argument and invective actually suggest that the elite had an obligation to correct the error that had separated it from the people. His critique was seeking to make the class gulf intolerable for *educated people*, since in a country recently emancipated from slavery the weakness of the popular camp inhibited the emergence of other solutions.

It would seem, then, that the origins of our cultural absurdity are to be found in the imitative talent of mestizo southerners who have few creative capacities. The *petitio principii* is quite transparent: imitativeness is explained by a (racial) tendency to that very imitativeness which is supposed to be explained. (The author's argument, we should note, itself imitated the scientific naturalism then in vogue in Europe.) Today such explanations can hardly be taken seriously, although it is worth examining them as an ideological mechanism and an expression of their times. If the Brazilians' propensity for copying is racial in origin, why should the elite have been alone in indulging it? If everyone had copied, all the effects of 'exoticism' (lack of relation to the environment) and 'absurdity' (separation between elite and people) would have vanished as if by magic, and with them the whole problem. It is not copying in general but *the copying of one class* that constitutes the problem. The explanation must lie not in race but in class.

Silvio Romero goes on to sketch how the vice of imitation developed in Brazil. Absolute zero was in the colonial period, when writers 'worked in a milieu of exclusively Portuguese and Brazilian ideas.' Could it be that the distance between elite and people was smaller in that epoch? Or the fondness for copying less strong? Surely not – and anyway that is not what the text says. The 'cohesion' to which it refers is of a different order, the result of a 'skilful policy of segregation' (!) that separated Brazil from everything non-Portuguese. In other words, the comparison between stages lacks an object: the demand for homogeneity points, in one case, to a social structure remarkable for its inequality, and in the other case to the banning of foreign ideas. Still, if the explanation does not convince us, the observation that it seeks to clarify is accurate enough. Before the nineteenth century, the copying of the European model and the distance between educated people and the mass did not constitute an 'absurdity'. In highly schematic terms, we could say that educated people, in the colonial period, felt solidarity towards the metropolis, Western tradition and their own colleagues, but not towards the local population. To base oneself on a foreign model, in cultural estrangement from the local surroundings, did not appear as a defect – quite the contrary! We should not forget that neo-classical aesthetics was itself universalist and greatly appreciated respect for canonical forms, while the theory of art current at that time set a positive value on imitation. As Antonio Candido acutely observed, the Arcadian poet who placed a nymph in the waters of the Carmo was not lacking in originality; he incorporated Minas Gerais into the traditions of the West and, quite laudably, cultivated those traditions in a remote corner of the earth.[13]

The act of copying, then, did not begin with independence and the opening of the ports*, as Silvio Romero would have it. But it is true that only then did it become the insoluble problem which is still discussed today, and which calls forth such terms as 'mimicry', 'apeing' or 'pastiche'. How did imitation acquire these pejorative connotations?

It is well known that Brazil's gaining of independence did not involve a revolution. Apart from changes in external relations and a reorganization of the top administration, the socio-economic structure created by colonial exploitation remained intact, though now for the benefit of local dominant classes. It was thus inevitable that modern forms of civilization entailing freedom and citizenship, which arrived together with the wave of political emancipation, should have appeared foreign and artificial, 'anti-national', 'borrowed', 'absurd' or however else critics cared to describe

them. The strength of the epithets indicates the acrobatics which the self-esteem of the Brazilian elite was forced into, since it faced the depressing alternative of deprecating the bases of its social pre-eminence in the name of progress, or deprecating progress in the name of its social preeminence. On the one hand, there were the slave trade, the latifundia and clientelism – that is to say, a set of relations with their own rules, consolidated in colonial times and impervious to the universalism of bourgeois civilization; on the other hand, stymied by these relations, but also stymying them, there was the Law before which everyone was equal, the separation between public and private, civil liberties, parliament, romantic patriotism, and so on. The ensuring of the stable coexistence of these two conceptions, in principle so incompatible, was at the centre of ideological and moral preoccupations in Brazil in the nineteenth century. For some, the colonial heritage was a relic to be superseded in the march of progress; for others, it was the real Brazil, to be preserved against absurd imitations. Some wanted to harmonize progress and slave labour, so as not to have to give up either, while still others believed that such a reconciliation already existed, with deleterious moral results. Silvio Romero, for his part, used conservative arguments with a progressive intent, focusing on the 'real' Brazil as the continuation of colonial authoritarianism, but doing so in order to attack its foundations. He scorned as ineffectual the 'illusory' country of laws, lawyers and imported culture: 'No people has a better Constitution on paper …; the reality is appalling.'

Silvio Romero's list of 'imitations', not to be allowed through customs, included fashions, patterns of behaviour, laws, codes, poetry, drama and novels. Judged separately against the social reality of Brazil, these articles were indeed superfluous imports which would serve to obscure the real state of impoverishment and create an illusion of progress. In their combination, however, they entered into the formation and equipping of the new nation-state, as well as laying the ground for the participation of new elites in contemporary culture. This modernizing force – whatever its imitative appearance and its distance from the daily course of things – became more inseparably bound up with the reality of Brazil than the institution of slave labour, which was later replaced by other forms of forced labour equally

* In the wake of his flight to Brazil, to escape Napoleon's invasion of Portugal in 1807–8, in which he was escorted by the British fleet, King João VI opened the ports of the colony for the first time to non-Portuguese (largely British) shipping.

incompatible with the aspiration to enlightenment. As time passed, the ubiquitous stamp of 'inauthenticity' came to be seen as the most authentic part of the national drama, its very mark of identity. Grafted from nineteenth-century Europe on to a colonial social being, the various perfections of civilization began to follow different rules from those operating in the hegemonic countries. This led to a widespread sense of the indigenous pastiche. Only a great figure like Machado de Assis had the impartiality to see a peculiar mode of ideological functioning where other critics could distinguish no more than a lack of consistency. Sérgio Buarque de Holanda remarked: 'The speed at which the "new ideas" spread in the old colony, and the fervour with which they were adopted in many circles on the eve of independence, show quite unequivocally that they had the potential to satisfy an impatient desire for change and that the people were ripe for such change. But it is also clear that the social order expressed in these ideas was far from having an exact equivalent in Brazil, particularly outside the cities. The articulation of society, the basic criteria of economic exploitation and the distribution of privileges were so different here that the "new ideas" could not have the same meaning that was attached to them in parts of Europe or ex-English America.'[14]

When Brazil became an independent state, a permanent collaboration was established between the forms of life characteristic of colonial oppression and the innovations of bourgeois progress. The new stage of capitalism broke up the exclusive relationship with the metropolis, converting local property-owners and administrators into a national ruling class (effectively part of the emergent world bourgeoisie), and yet retained the old forms of labour exploitation which have not been fully modernized up to the present day. In other words, the discrepancy between the 'two Brazils' was not due to an imitative tendency, as Silvio Romero and many others thought; nor did it correspond to a brief period of transition.' It was the lasting result of the creation of a nation-state on the basis of slave labour – which, if the reader will forgive the shorthand, arose in turn out of the English industrial revolution and the consequent crisis of the old colonial system. That is to say, *it arose out of contemporary history*.[15] Thus Brazil's backward deformation belongs to the same order of things as the progress of the advanced countries. Silvio Romero's 'absurdities' – in

reality, the Cyclopean discords of world capitalism – are not a historical deviation. They are linked to the finality of a single process which, in the case of Brazil, requires the continuation of forced or semi-forced labour and a corresponding cultural separation of the poor. With certain modifications, much of it has survived to this day. The panorama now seems to be changing, thanks to the desegregationist impulse of mass consumption and mass communications. These new terms of cultural oppression and expropriation have not yet been much studied.

The thesis of cultural copying thus involves an ideology in the Marxist sense of the term – that is, an illusion supported by appearances. The well-known coexistence of bourgeois principles with those of the ancien régime is here explained in accordance with a plausible and wide-ranging schema, essentially individualist in nature, in which effects and causes are systematically inverted.

For Silvio Romero imitation results in the lack of a common denominator between popular and elite culture, and in the elite's low level of permeation by the national. But why not reverse the argument? Why should the imitative character of our life not stem from forms of inequality so brutal that they lack the minimal reciprocity ('common denominator') without which modern society can only appear artificial and 'imported'? At a time when the idea of the nation had become the norm, the dominant class's *unpatriotic* disregard for the lives it exploited gave it the feeling of being alien. The origins of this situation in colonialism and slavery are immediately apparent.

The defects normally associated with imitation can be explained in the same way. We can agree with its detractors that the copy is at the opposite pole from originality, from national creativity, from independent and well-adapted judgements, and so on. Absolute domination entails that culture expresses nothing of the conditions that gave it life, except for that intrinsic sense of futility on which a number of writers have been able to work artistically. Hence the 'exotic' literature and politics unrelated to the 'immediate or remote depths of our life and history'; hence, too, the lack of 'discrimination' or 'criteria' and, above all, the intense conviction that all is mere paper. In other words, the painfulness of an imitative civilization is produced not by imitation – which is present at any event – but by the social structure of the country. It is this which places culture in an untenable position, contradicting its very concept of itself, and which nevertheless was not as sterile, at that time, as Silvio Romero would have us believe. Nor did the segregated section of society remain unproductive. Its modes of expression would later acquire, for educated intellectuals, the value of a non-bourgeois component of national life, an element serving to fix Brazilian identity (with all the evident ambiguities).

The exposure of cultural transplantation has become the axis of a naive yet widespread critical perspective. Let us conclude by summarizing some of its defects.

1. It suggests that imitation is avoidable, thereby locking the reader into a false problem.

2. It presents as a national characteristic what is actually a malaise of the dominant class, bound up with the difficulty of morally reconciling the advantages of progress with those of slavery or its surrogates.

3. It implies that the elites could conduct themselves in some other way which is tantamount to claiming that the beneficiary of a given situation will put an end to it.

4. The argument obscures the essential point, since it concentrates its fire on the relationship between elite and model whereas the real crux is the exclusion of the poor from the universe of contemporary culture.

5. Its implicit solution is that the dominant class should reform itself and give up imitation. We have argued, on the contrary, that the answer lies in the workers gaining access to the terms of contemporary life, so that they can re-define them through their own initiative. This, indeed, would be in this context a concrete definition of democracy in Brazil.

6. A copy refers to a prior original existing elsewhere, of which it is an inferior reflection. Such deprecation often corresponds to the self-consciousness of Latin American elites, who attach mythical solidity – in the form of regional intellectual specialization – to the economic, technological and political inequalities of the international order. The authentic and the creative are to the imitative what the advanced countries are to the backward. But one cannot solve the problem by going to the opposite extreme. As we have

seen, philosophical objections to the concept of originality tend to regard as non-existent a real problem that it is absurd to dismiss. Cultural history has to be set in the world perspective of the economics and culture of the left, which attempt to explain our 'backwardness' as part of the contemporary history of capital and *its advances*.[16] Seen in terms of the copy, the anachronistic juxtaposition of forms of modern civilization and realities originating in the colonial period is a mode of non-being or even a humiliatingly imperfect realization of a model situated elsewhere. Dialectical criticism, on the other hand, investigates the same anachronism and seeks to draw out a figure of the modern world, set on a course that is either full of promise, grotesque or catastrophic.

7. The idea of the copy that we have been discussing counterposes national and foreign, original and imitative. These are unreal oppositions which do not allow us to see the share of the foreign in the nationally specific, of the imitative in the original and of the original in the imitative. (In a key study, Paulo Emilio Salles Gomes refers to our 'creative lack of competence in copying'.[17]) If I am not mistaken, the theory presupposes three elements – a Brazilian subject, reality of the country, civilization of the advanced nations – such that the third helps the first to forget the second. This schema is also unreal, and it obscures the organized, cumulative nature of the process, the potent strength even of bad tradition, and the power relations, both national and international, that are in play. Whatever its unacceptable aspects – unacceptable for whom? – Brazilian cultural life has elements of dynamism which display both originality and lack of originality. Copying is not a false problem, so long as we treat it pragmatically, from an aesthetic and political point of view freed from the mythical requirement of creation *ex nihilo*.

Notes

1   *Mário de Andrade* (1893–1945), novelist, poet and critic, was the acknowledged leader of the modernist movement in Brazil and bore the brunt of the initial scandal that it caused. The language of his *Macunaima: The Hero without Any Character* (1928) synthesizes idioms and dialects from all the regions of Brazil. [*Trs.*]

2 For a balanced and considered opinion on the subject, see Antonio Candido, 'Literatura e subdesenvolvimento', *Argumento* no. 1, São Paulo, October 1973.

3 This observation was made by Vinicius Dantas.

4 *Joaquim Mario Machado de Assis* (1839–1908) is regarded as the greatest of all Portuguese-language novelists. He wrote nine novels and two hundred short stories, including *Epitaph of a Small Winner* (1880), *Dom Casmurro* (1890) and *Esau and Jacob* (1904), which are considered to be far ahead of their time. [*Trs.*]

5 *Silvio Romero* (1851–1914) wrote the first modern history of Brazilian literature, a work which is still of interest today, despite the scientist language of the period. [*Trs.*]

6 The *Centro Popular de Cultura* (CPC) was established in 1961 at the start of the social ferment that ended with the military coup in 1964. The movement was created under the auspices of the National Union of Students, which wanted to fuse together artistic irreverence, political teaching and the people. It produced surprisingly inventive cinema, theatre and other stage performances. Several of its members became major artistic figures: Glauber Rocha, Joaquim Pedro de Andrade and Ferreira Gullar among others. The convergence of the student and popular movements gave rise to completely new artistic possibilities. [*Note supplied by Ana McMac*].

7 'Policarpo Quaresma is the hero of the novel *Triste fim de Policarpo Quaresma* (1915) (translated as *The Patriot* [London: Peter Owen, 1978], by Afonso Henriques de Lima Barreto [1881–1922]). The hero is a caricature patriot, if a sympathetic character, who gradually becomes disillusioned with the state of Brazil. [*Ed.*]

8 See Silviano Santiago, 'O Entre-lugar do discurso latino-americano', in *Uma literatura nos trópicos*, São Paulo 1978; and Haroldo de Campos, 'Da razão antropofágica: diálogo e diferença na cultura brasileira', *Boletim Bibliográfico Biblioteca Mário de Andrade*, vol 44, January–December 1983.

9 *Oswald de Andrade* introduced European avant-garde ideas into Brazil. He espoused extreme primitivism (anthropophagy) and his *Manifesto da Poesia Pau-Brasil* (1924) and *Manifesto Antropofágo* (1928) are the most daring writings of the 'modern movement' which emerged in 1922, attacking academic values and respectability and seeking poetry written in the Brazilian vernacular. [*Trs.*]

10 Rui Barbosa (1849–1923) was a prominent liberal politician, and regarded as a model of culture, linguistic purity and erudition in the early twentieth century: he achieved an almost mythical status, known as 'The Eagle of the Hague' for his diplomacy at an International Conference there in 1906. In this phrase, obviously, it is the incongruity of such false representatives of high culture in Brazil which is underlined. [*Ed.*]

11 The greatest achievement of Raúl Bopp (b. 1898) was his 'cannibalist' poem 'Cobra Norato' (1921), an exploration of the Amazon jungle. [*Trs.*]

12 Silvio Romero, *Machado de Assis*, Rio de Janeiro 1897, pp. 121–3.

13 Antonio Candido, *Formação da literatura brasileira*, São Paulo 1969, vol. 1, p. 74.

14 Sergio Buarque de Holanda, *Do império à republica*, II, São Paulo 1977, pp. 77–8.

15 Emilia Viotti da Costa, *Do monarquia à república: Momentos decisivos*, São Paulo 1977, Chapter 1; Luis Felipe de Alencastro, 'La traite negrière et l'unité nationale brésilienne', *Revue Française de l'Histoîre de l'Outre-Mer*, vol. 46, 1979; Fernando Novais, 'Passagens para o Novo Mundo', *Novos Estudos Cebrap* 9, July 1984.

16 See Celso Furtado, *A Pre-Revolução Brasileira*, Rio de Janeiro 1962, and Fernando H. Cardoso, *Empresario industrial e desenvolvimento económico no Brasil*, São Paulo 1964.

17 Paulo Emilio Salles Gomes, 'Cinema: trajetória no subdesenvolvimento', *Argumento* no. 1, October 1973.

35

"A Dominance without Hegemony and Its Historiography" (1997)

Ranajit Guha

I. Conditions for a Critique of Historiography

Dominance and its historiographies

There was one Indian battle that Britain never won. It was a battle for appropriation of the Indian past. It began with the East India Company's accession to *Diwani* in 1765. The duties of that office required that its incumbent should know the structure of landed property in Bengal, Bihar, and Orissa well enough to be able to collect the revenues on behalf of the Nawab. But since the intricacies of proprietorship could hardly be understood without a grasp of the relations of power which had accumulated to it over time, the *Diwan* had to undertake the function of the historian as well. Consequently, many of the local histories to be written in English during these early days had the concerns of a hard-pressed but still rather inexperienced bureaucracy branded on them. Meant primarily to help the administration to determine inheritance along the lines of descent within the leading landlord families of a district, these are among the first specimens of elitist bias in British Indian historiography.

Ranajit Guha, "Colonialism in South Asia: A Dominance without Hegemony and Its Historiography," pp. 1–20 from *Dominance without Hegemony: History and Power in Colonial India*. Cambridge, MA: Harvard University Press, 1997. Reprinted by permission of the publisher. Copyright ©1999 by the President and Fellows of Harvard College.

A bias of that order was clearly expressed in the assumption that the local aristocracies were the "natural proprietors" of land in India. Based entirely on contemporary Whig doctrines about law and society in Britain, that assumption was soon to be dressed up as a fact of Indian history and used as an argument in favor of a *zamindari* settlement. The past acquired its depth in these accounts from elaborately constructed genealogies going back to (an often mythical) antiquity in some cases and from (genuine or fabricated) Mughal charters as evidence of proprietary right. This had the effect of conferring a sense of spurious continuity on what was a total rupture brought about by the intervention of a European power in the structure of landed property in South Asia. The illusion of continuity was reinforced further by global histories which drew copiously on medieval chronicles in order to situate the British dominion in a line of conquests that had begun with the Turko-Afghans and within a tradition that allowed the conquerors to extract tribute from the conquered.

These preliminary exercises in colonialist historiography, whether done on a local or a global scale, abetted thus in laying the foundations of the raj. Nothing illustrates this better than the way the Indian past was mobilized by the various contending parties in the debates within the Company's administration during the last three decades of the eighteenth century. The history of the subject population was reconstructed there over and over again as the central question of the relation of property to empire became the subject of controversies between Hastings and Francis in the 1770s, between Grant and Shore in the 1780s, and between Shore and Cornwallis in 1788–92 on the eve of the Permanent Settlement. The outcome of such attempts at appropriation was to provide legal and administrative support for those measures which in the course of time set up British rule in the subcontinent eventually as a rule of property.

This rudimentary historiography was soon followed up by a more mature and sophisticated discourse when the time came for the growing colonial state, already secure in its control of the wealth of the land, to reinforce its apparatus of ideological control as well. All the energies and skills of nineteenth-century British scholarship were harnessed to this project. It investigated, recorded, and wrote up the Indian past in a vast corpus which, worked by many hands during the seventy years between Mill's *History of British India* (1812) and Hunter's *Indian Empire* (1881), came to constitute an entirely new kind of knowledge. A colonialist knowledge, its function was to erect that past as a pedestal on which the triumphs and glories of the colonizers and their instrument, the colonial state, could be displayed to best advantage.

Indian history, assimilated thereby to the history of Great Britain, would henceforth be used as a comprehensive measure of difference between the peoples of these two countries. Politically that difference was spelled out as one between rulers and the ruled; ethnically, between a white *Herrenvolk* and blacks; materially, between a prosperous Western power and its poor Asian subjects; culturally, between higher and lower levels of civilization, between the superior religion of Christianity and indigenous belief systems made up of superstition and barbarism – all adding up to an irreconcilable difference between colonizer and colonized. The Indian past was thus painted red.

However, the appropriation of a past by conquest carries with it the risk of rebounding upon the conquerors. It can end up by sacralizing the past for the subject people and encouraging them to use it in their effort to define and affirm their own identity. This, no doubt, was what happened in the instance under discussion, and the appropriated past came to serve as the sign of the Other not only for the colonizers but, ironically, for the colonized as well. The colonized, in their turn, reconstructed their past for purposes opposed to those of their rulers and made it the ground for marking

out their differences in cultural and political terms. History became thus a game for two to play as the alien colonialist project of appropriation was matched by an indigenous nationalist project of counter-appropriation.

The two have been locked in an indecisive battle ever since. The contradictions of colonialism which have inspired this contest in the first place lingered on at the ideological level even after their resolution, in constitutional terms, by the Transfer of Power. The cultural regime of colonialism clearly outlived the raj in the study of the Indian past, as was obvious from the influence which continued to be exerted on it by the more recent avatars of colonialist historiography. What made it possible, indeed necessary, for that influence to persist was a fundamental agreement between the Indian bourgeoisie and the British whom they replaced as rulers about the nature of colonialism itself – that is, what it was and what constituted its power relations. Both proceeded from the standpoint of liberalism to regard the colonial state as an organic extension of the metropolitan bourgeois state and colonialism as an adaptation, if not quite a replication, of the classical bourgeois culture of the West in English rendering. Generally speaking, that phenomenon was regarded by both as a positive confirmation of the universalizing tendency of capital – a point to which we shall soon return.

The rivalries of the two bourgeoisies and their representations in colonialist and nationalist discourses did little to diminish the importance of this essential agreement. On the contrary, all transactions between the two parties which made up the stuff of elite politics followed from an understanding to abide by a common set of rules based on the British constitutionalist parliamentary model. It was a matter of playing cricket. If a nationalist agitation ran into difficulty, the bureaucracy would gloat that Gandhi was on a poor wicket, and he would, on his part, condemn the administration as "un-British" whenever he felt outraged by the harshness of official violence.

Neither side appears to have realized the absurdity of accusing each other of deviating from norms which were displayed as ideals but prevented in fact from realizing themselves to any significant extent at all in the dominant idioms of political practice. This incomprehension, so symptomatic of the malaise of a liberalism grafted on to colonial conditions, informed historical discourses corresponding to both the points of view and underscored their common failure to discern the anomalies that made colonialism into a figure of paradox.

The paradox consists of the fact that the performance of the elite groups whose careers have provided both these historiographies with their principal themes was widely at variance with their historic competence. Thus there were the metropolitan bourgeoisie who professed and practiced democracy at home, but were quite happy to conduct the government of their Indian empire as an autocracy. Champions of the right of the European nations to self-determination, they denied the same right to their Indian subjects until the very last phase of the raj and granted it without grace only when forced to do so under the impact of the anti-imperialist struggles of the subject population. Their antagonism to feudal values and institutions in their own society made little difference (in spite of the much publicized though rather ineffective campaigns against *sati*, child marriage, and so on) to their vast tolerance of pre-capitalist values and institutions in Indian society.

Their opposite numbers, the indigenous bourgeoisie, spawned and nurtured by colonialism itself, adopted a role that was distinguished by its failure to measure up to the heroism of the European bourgeoisie in its period of ascendancy. Pliant and prone to compromise from their inception, they lived in a state of happy accommodation with imperialism for the greater part of their career as a constituted political force between 1885 and 1947. The destruction of the colonial state was never a part of their project. They abjured and indeed resolutely opposed all forms of armed struggle against the raj, and settled for pressure politics as their main tactical means in bargaining for power. Compromise and accommodation were equally characteristic of their attitude to the semi-feudal values and institutions entrenched in Indian society. The liberalism they professed was never strong enough to exceed the limitations of the half-hearted initiatives for reform which issued from the colonial administration. This mediocre liberalism, a caricature of the vigorous democratic culture of the epoch of the rise of the bourgeoisie in the West, operated throughout the colonial period in a symbiotic relationship with the still active and vigorous forces of the semi-feudal culture of India.

How come that liberal historiography of both kinds fails to take notice of such paradoxes? Why is it that on those rare occasions when it does take notice, it still makes no serious attempt to explain them? Why, on the contrary, is the discrepancy between competence and performance in the record of the metropolitan bourgeoisie trivialized so often by liberal-imperialism and its intellectual representatives merely as an exceptional and aberrant instance of malfunctioning in the administrative apparatus of the raj? Why does liberal-nationalism, in its turn, tend to account for discrepancies of the same order in the record of the indigenous bourgeoisie simply as local difficulties generated by some weak survivals of a pre-capitalist culture and destined to be overcome by the leaders of the nation on their march to progress? How is it that no real effort is ever made by historians on either side to link these paradoxes to any structural fault in the historic project of the bourgeoisie?

Containment of historiography in a dominant culture

None of these questions can be answered without dispelling, first of all, the myth of ideological neutrality which is central to liberal historiography. For it is not possible to write or speak about the past without the use of concepts and presuppositions derived from one's experience and understanding of the present, that is, from those ideas by which the writer or speaker interprets his own times to himself and to others. As Hayden White has observed:

> There does, in fact, appear to be an irreducible ideological component in every historical account of reality … the very claim to have discerned some kind of formal coherence in the historical record brings with it theories of the nature of the historical world and of historical knowledge itself which have ideological implications for attempts to understand "the present," however this "present" is defined. To put it another way, the very claim to have distinguished a past from a present world of social thought and praxis, and to have determined the formal coherence of that past world, *implies* a conception of the form that knowledge of the present world also must take, insofar as it is *continuous* with that past world. Commitment to a particular *form* of knowledge predetermines the *kinds* of generalizations one can make about

the present world, the kinds of knowledge one can have of it, and hence the kinds of projects one can legitimately conceive for changing that present or for maintaining it in its present form indefinitely.

The ideological dimensions of a historical account reflect the ethical element in the historian's assumption of a particular position on the question of the nature of historical knowledge and the implications that can be drawn from the study of past events for the understanding of present ones. By the term "ideology" I mean a set of prescriptions for taking a position in the present world of social praxis and acting upon it (either to change the world or to maintain it in its current state).[1]

To change the world *and* to maintain it in its current state have indeed been the dual functions of liberal historiography performed on behalf of the class for which it speaks. A bourgeois discourse par excellence, it helped the bourgeoisie to change or at least significantly to modify the world according to its class interests in the period of its ascendancy, and since then to consolidate and perpetuate its dominance. As such, this historiography may be said not only to share, but actively to propagate, all the fundamental ideas by which the bourgeoisie represents and explains the world both as it is and as it was. The function of this complicity is, in short, to make liberal historiography speak from within the bourgeois consciousness itself.

To commit a discourse to speak from within a given consciousness is to disarm it insofar as its critical faculty is made inoperative thereby with regard to that particular consciousness. For no criticism can be fully activated unless its object is distanced from its agency. This is why liberal historiography, cramped as it is within the bourgeois consciousness, can never attack it vigorously enough as the object of its criticism. Since the paradoxes characteristic of the political culture of colonialism testify to the failure of the bourgeoisie to acknowledge the structural limitations of bourgeois dominance itself, it is hardly surprising that the liberal historical discourse too should be blind to those paradoxes. This is a necessary, one could say congenital, blindness which this historiography acquires by virtue of its class origin.

However, such blindness is by no means limited to bourgeois discourse alone. The knowledge systems that make up any dominant culture are all contained within the dominant consciousness and have therefore the latter's deficiencies built into their optics. The light of criticism emitted by such systems can, under no circumstances, be strong enough to penetrate and scan some of the strategic areas of that consciousness where dominance stores the spiritual gear it needs to justify and sustain itself.

It is notorious, for instance, that the historic cultures of the European antiquity, those of Greece in the fifth and fourth centuries BC and of Rome during a period of four hundred years until the second century AD were not merely tolerant but positively supportive of slavery. Aristotle justified slavery both in psychological and institutional terms when he observed in *The Politics* "that by nature some are free, others slaves, and that for these it is both right and expedient that they should serve as slaves."[2] Herodotus, the historian, believed, according to Finley, "that – barring the inevitable exceptions – slaves as a class were inferior beings, inferior in their psychology, by their nature."[3] And yet another historian, Xenophon, was the author, we are told, of a plan to set up a state fund of public slaves large enough to provide three of them for every Athenian citizen.[4]

It was thus that a dominant culture spoke up for a dominance based on the exploitation of slaves. There is no critical distance separating the intellectual here from the ruler in his understanding of the basic power relations of a slave society. On the contrary, the knowledge philosophers and historians had of slavery was clearly a component of the same consciousness that made the slave-owner knowledgeable about his slaves. Together, the two knowledges constituted the polar ends of an epistemological system in which, as Anderson has so incisively remarked, an ideal of absolute juridical freedom and that of absolute unfreedom came to form a dyad and provide an "ideological correlate" for the material prosperity generated by a slave mode of production.[5] It is not surprising therefore that the historiography which was itself an instance of this ideological correlate was unable to break away from its moorings in slavery and deal critically with it.

Feudal historiography, too, was identified with the ruling culture and situated snugly within the relations of dominance and subordination specific to feudal society. As a result, the voice of the historian in such a society was often indistinguishable from that of the panegyrist, the courtier, and the apologist speaking for gods, kings, and noblemen. Historical discourse was indeed so completely integrated here in the discourse of power that some fundamental aspects of the authority structure were never questioned even by the most questioning of writers. One such distinguished writer was Kalhaṇa, the author of the *Rājataraṅginī*, the twelfth-century chronicle of Kashmir.

It is generally agreed that Kalhaṇa was outstanding, indeed exceptional, in his critical acumen amongst the historians of the pre-Sultanate period of medieval India. The range of his source material and the sophistication with which he used it have evoked the admiration and to some extent the amazement of modern scholars.[6] His evidence included not only the information he gathered from some of the older chronicles and *purāṇas*, but also a good deal of oral tradition. To these he added, anticipating the historian's craft of later times, a reading of epigraphic and numismatic data. On that basis he proceeded to scrutinize as many as eleven royal chronicles written before his time and challenged effectively the work of the prestigious eleventh-century author Kṣemendra by identifying some gross inaccuracies in his "List of Kings." By such a procedure, he claimed, "all wearisome error has been set at rest."[7]

What is even more important for the present discussion is that he was centuries ahead of his own age in attributing the function of a judge to his ideal historian. "That man of merit alone deserves praise," he wrote, "whose language, like that of a judge, in recounting the events of the past has discarded bias as well as prejudice."[8] This was an exceptionally high standard for a medieval annalist to set for himself. There was nothing in the material and spiritual conditions of twelfth-century Kashmir, a feudal state racked, according to Kosambi, by "a war of extermination" between kings and barons (*ḍāmaras*), to enable historical discourse to speak with judicial impartiality about royalty and aristocracy.[9] For a feudal culture which had no use for genuine social criticism left the historian with no choice other than bias or prejudice in writing about the elite groups – bias in favor of those who offered him patronage and prejudice against those who were opposed to his patrons.

It is all the more remarkable therefore that Kalhaṇa's historiographical practice should have approximated

his ideal to a certain degree. Neither Lalitāditya Muktāpīḍa, a king he admired in many respects, nor Harṣa, his father's patron, was spared his criticism.[10] And even though his impartiality seems to have been strained to the utmost in his account of the reign of Jayasiṃha, the ruling prince, he did not pass over the ruler's misdeeds in silence.[11] The faint praise addressed to the monarch fell appreciably short of the conventional *praśasti*, the panegyric composed by a court poet – and the chronicle was written as a *kāvya* – for his patron as an obligatory feudal due. All this is no mean achievement for a medieval chronicler, and it has led Majumdar to credit Kalhaṇa with "the supreme merit of possessing a critical mind and that spirit of skepticism which is the first virtue of a historian."[12]

But how far does this skepticism go, how deep is the thrust of this critical mind? Judging by what Majumdar himself has to say about Kalhaṇa's "belief in witchcraft and magic feats, occasional explanation of events as due to the influence of fate or wrath of gods rather than to any rational cause, and a general didactic tendency inspired by Hindu views of doctrines of *karma* and transmigration,"[13] it is clear that criticism was confined within the bounds of a feudal consciousness even in this outstanding instance of a historical discourse which had set out so bravely to try "in this narrative of past events to repair by all means where there is error."[14] Since the error was branded on the dominant consciousness itself, historiography, unable to jump out of its skin, was forced to work from within the ruling culture.

The verse with which Kalhaṇa concludes his account of the murderous rule of Mihirakula may be cited here as one of many possible illustrations of such containment. "Thus although [he was] wicked," it reads, "that the king had not been assassinated by the people in an uprising, was because he was protected by the very gods who had urged him to do that act."[15] In an age when *rājabhakti* was a principal component of political philosophy, the historian seems to have relied in equal degrees on his own doubts about the record of the Kashmir rulers and on the experience of frequent baronial revolts to ask why there were no popular uprisings and no regicide.

But the question fails to explode. Its skeptical charge is neutralized by a dominant ideology according to which the destiny of kings and kingdoms is governed not by the will of the people but by that of the gods. It is precisely such critical failure – the failure of criticism to exceed the limits of its conceptual universe – that, in the event, reduces Kalhaṇa with all his questioning into an apologist for the feudal polity of his times. Basham is by no means unduly harsh in his judgement when he observes that "In fact the *Rājataraṅgiṇī* is in part a work of political propaganda, written for the purpose of persuading the ruling classes of Kashmir to put their house in order."[16] The author himself came close to assigning such a role to his *kathā* when, at the very beginning of the chronicle, he defined its function as that of entertaining and instructing his royal readership.[17] A witness to the internecine strife of the elite which was undermining the very foundations of this feudal principality, the historian, with all his skepticism, managed after all to secure a comfortable place for his discourse within the ruling ideology. Or, to phrase it according to the taxonomy of ancient Indian knowledge systems, one could say that Itihasa had become an accomplice here to Arthaśāstra.

Where does historical criticism come from?

All of this goes to show that no discourse can oppose a genuinely uncompromising critique to a ruling culture so long as its ideological parameters are the same as those of that very culture. Where then does criticism come from? From outside the universe of dominance which provides the critique with its object, indeed, from another and historically antagonistic universe, as should be evident even from a cursory look at the criticism that has been addressed to the slave-owning and feudal discourses mentioned above. Consider, for instance, two classic comments on Aristotle's justification of slavery. One of these comes from Montesquieu as he writes in *De l'Esprit des Lois* (1748)[18]: "Aristote veut prouver qu'il y a des esclaves par nature, et ce qu'il dit ne le preuve guère … Mais, comme tous les hommes naissent égaux, il faut dire que l'esclavage est contre la nature" (livre xv, ch. vii). ("Aristotle wants to prove that there are slaves by nature, and what he says scarcely proves it … But as all men are born equal, one must say that slavery is against nature.") A little later in the same work he denounces helotry in almost identical terms: "cette *ilotie* est contre

la nature des choses" (livre xv, ch.x). ("This helotism is contrary to the nature of things.") It is illuminating for our purpose to read this together with Hegel's observations on the same subject in the Second Draft (1830) of his *Lectures on the Philosophy of World History – Introduction: Reason in History*:

> The consciousness of freedom first awoke among the Greeks, and they were accordingly free; but, like the Romans, they only knew that Some and not all men as such, are free. Plato and Aristotle did not know this either; thus the Greeks not only had slaves, on which their life and the continued existence of their esteemable freedom depended, but their very freedom itself was on the one hand only a fortuitous, undeveloped, transient and limited efflorescence, and on the other, a harsh servitude of all that is humane and proper to man.[19]

In these two texts, both eminently representative of the ideology of the bourgeoisie in the period of its ascendancy in Western Europe, the critique of slavery proceeds from ideas which were clearly hostile to concepts and values that made up the slave-owner's attitude to slaves in Classical Antiquity. Written at equidistant points in time from the fall of Bastille, one of them comes before that event to denounce slavery in the name of the natural equality of men, while the other follows in its wake and rejects slavery in the name of an unlimited freedom, a universal liberty. Equality and Liberty – two words which heralded the advent of a new ruling class and a new ruling culture – are hallmarks here of a pure externality. They leave the reader in no doubt that this philosophical criticism stands outside the paradigm of slave-owning ideology and has its feet planted firmly in another paradigm, that of the ideology of "wage slavery."

Feudal historiography too is separated from its critique by a paradigmatic distance. Here again criticism arms itself with two well-known devices taken from the arsenal of bourgeois ideology. One of these is rationalism. Even Majumdar with all his admiration for Kalhaṇa feels obliged to reproach him for his belief in witches and magic, in karma and transmigration, and above all for his tendency to explain events by fate and divine will rather than "any rational cause."[20] Nothing heralds more eloquently the advent of a ruling culture that requires the past to be read as an unfolding of Reason rather than Providence and insists on causality rather than faith as the key to historical understanding. Foil to this abstract rationalism is an equally abstract humanism which serves as a second device to oppose feudal ideas, and Basham finds fault with the Kashmir chronicler for his failure to acknowledge man as the maker of his own history and master of his own destiny. "Nowhere does he explicitly state," says this humanist critic, "that man is wholly incapable of moulding in some measure his own history, but superhuman forces or beings evidently have the biggest part in the destiny of man."[21]

The critique in all these instances has come from liberal ideology – the ideology of the bourgeoisie in dominance – which is, by definition, hostile to and destructive of slave-owning and feudal cultures. It is, without doubt, a critique which speaks from outside the ideological domains of the objects criticized. But that, in turn, raises a question of fundamental importance for our inquiry. Where then, one may ask, does the critique of liberalism itself come from? It comes from an ideology that is antagonistic towards the dominant culture and declares war on it even before the class for which it speaks comes to rule. In rushing thus in advance of the conquest of power by its class, this critique demonstrates, all over again, a historic décalage characteristic of all periods of great social transformation when a young and ascendant class challenges the authority of another that is older and moribund but still dominant. The bourgeoisie itself had dramatized such décalage during the Enlightenment by a relentless critique of the *ancien régime* for decades before the French Revolution and anticipating it in effect. And yet, for all the appearance of being in a hurry and arriving before its time, that critique was true to the real contradictions of the epoch in seizing on the feudal mode of production and its power relations as the object of its criticism.

In much the same way, the critique of the dominant bourgeois culture arises from the real contradictions of capitalism and anticipates its dissolution. This too spans a long period of transition during which the ruling culture comes increasingly under attack from a historic opposition invested with such ideals, values and ways of interpreting the world as constitute a challenge to liberalism. Insofar as this challenge precedes the actual dissolution of the material basis of bourgeois

dominance and the corresponding social and political structures, the critique is by its very nature still rather precocious, incomplete, and generally endowed with all the immaturity of a thing in its formative stage. But it is this very want of maturity that drives the critique audaciously, if not prudently in every instance, to probe those fundamental contradictions of the existing system which prefigure its demise.

The universalizing tendency of capital and its limitations

One of such contradictions which serves as a basis for the critique of a bourgeois culture in dominance relates to the *universalizing tendency of capital*. This tendency derives from the self-expansion of capital. Its function is to create a world market, subjugate all antecedent modes of production, and replace all jural and institutional concomitants of such modes and generally the entire edifice of precapitalist cultures by laws, institutions, values, and other elements of a culture appropriate to bourgeois rule.

"The tendency to create the *world market*," writes Marx in the *Grundrisse*, "is directly given in the concept of capital itself. Every limit appears as a barrier to overcome." For capital to overcome such limits means, "Initially, to subjugate every moment of production itself to exchange and to suspend the production of direct use values not entering into exchange, i.e. precisely to posit production based on capital in place of earlier modes of production, which appear primitive [*naturwüchsig*] from its standpoint."[22] It is thanks to this tendency that capital strives constantly to go beyond the spatial and temporal limits to its "self-realization process [*Selbstverwertungsprozess*]" for

> while capital must on one side strive to tear down every spatial barrier to intercourse, i.e. to exchange, and conquer the whole earth for its market, it strives on the other side to annihilate this space with time, i.e., to reduce to a minimum the time spent in motion from one place to another. The more developed the capital, therefore, the more extensive the market over which it circulates, which forms the spatial orbit of its circulation, the more does it strive simultaneously for an even greater extension of the market and for greater annihilation of space by time.[23]

The radical implications of this tendency for the circulation of capital are matched by its bearing on the production aspect as well. It is indeed "the universalizing tendency of capital, which distinguishes it," says Marx, "from all previous stages of production."[24] Unlike its historic antecedents it is a mode characterized, on one side, by a "universal industriousness" generating surplus labor, "value-creating labour," and on the other by "a system of general exploitation of the natural and human qualities, a system of general utility, utilising science itself just as much as all the physical and mental qualities."[25] What an immense perspective of human development is opened up thereby, what a vista of receding horizons over an endless cultural space. To quote from the *Grundrisse* again:

> Thus capital creates the bourgeois society, and the universal appropriation of nature as well as of the social bond itself by the members of society. Hence the great civilizing influence of capital; its production of a stage of society in comparison to which all earlier ones appear as mere *local developments* of humanity and as *nature idolatry* … In accord with this tendency, capital drives beyond national barriers and prejudices as much as beyond nature worship, as well as all traditional, confined, complacent, encrusted satisfactions of present needs, and reproductions of old ways of life. It is destructive towards all this, and constantly revolutionizes it, tearing down all the barriers which hem in the development of the forces of production, the expansion of needs, the all-sided development of production, and the exploitation and exchange of natural and mental forces.[26]

This eloquent passage, taken in isolation from the great body of its author's critique of capital, would make him indistinguishable from any of the myriad nineteenth-century liberals who saw nothing but the positive side of capital in an age when it was growing from strength to strength and there seemed to be no limit to its expansion and capacity to transform nature and society. One need not have been the founder of scientific socialism to compose such a paean, and some of Marx's writings – certain passages from his well-known articles on India, for instance – have indeed been read in isolation and distorted to the point of reducing his evaluation of the historic possibilities of capital into the adulation of a technomaniac.

Read in its proper context, however, the passage quoted above is to be understood as nothing but the initial movement of a critique developed, point counter-point, in two clear steps. For the argument rounds off emphatically to suggest that it is not about expansion alone, but about an expansion predicated firmly and inevitably on limitations capital can never overcome; not simply about a project powered by the possibility of infinite development, but a project predicated on the certainty of its failure to realize itself. Witness how the paragraph which, in the *Grundrisse*, describes the force of capital's universalizing tendency, is followed up immediately by another where the author states in no uncertain terms the restrictive conditions operating on it.

> But from the fact [he writes] that capital posits every such limit [e.g. "national barriers and prejudices," "nature worship," "traditional, confined, complacent, encrusted satisfactions of present needs," "reproductions of old ways of life," and so on] as a barrier and hence gets *ideally* beyond it, it does not by any means follow that it has *really* overcome it, and, since every such barrier contradicts its character, its production moves in contradictions which are constantly overcome but just as constantly posited. Furthermore, the universality towards which it irresistibly strives encounters barriers in its own nature, which will, at a certain stage of its development, allow it to be recognized as being itself the greatest barrier to this tendency, and hence will drive towards its own suspension.[27]

Nothing could be more explicit and indeed more devastating than this critique of the universalist pretensions of capital. It is a critique which distinguishes itself unmistakably from liberalism by a perspective extended well beyond the rule of capital. The continuity of the latter is a fundamental presupposition in every variety of liberal thought, whereas the text cited above envisages the development of capital's universalist tendency to a stage where it "will drive towards its own suspension." Such prescience is particularly remarkable in view of the fact that it was contemporaneous with an ascendant and optimistic phase in the career of liberalism when, as Russell has observed, it was still secure in the belief that "it represented growing forces which appeared likely to become victorious without great difficulty, and to bring by their victory great benefits to mankind."[28]

Marx did not subscribe to this illusion at all. On the contrary, the discrepancy between the universalizing tendency of capital as an ideal and the frustration of that tendency in reality was, for him, a measure of the contradictions of Western bourgeois societies of his time and the differences which gave each of them its specificity. He used this measure to define and explain the uneven character of material development in the contemporary bourgeois world, as illustrated by the clearly differentiated moments of that development in Germany, France, England, and the United States, considered in an ascending order. He used it also to throw light on many of the anomalies and inconsistencies of bourgeois thought and activity. In each instance he identified and defined its distinctive features in terms of the extent and manner of their inadequacy with regard to the universalist ideal.

Since the universalist claim rested largely on the recent series of historic defeats inflicted by the bourgeoisie on the forces of feudalism entrenched in the *anciens régimes* of continental Europe, Marx designed a litmus test for that claim by an examination of the tolerance for feudalism in the most representative aspect of nineteenth-century bourgeois thought, namely political economy. What emerged from this test, beyond doubt, was that even so typically bourgeois a body of knowledge had not quite transcended the limits of feudal thought. On the contrary, some of its theoretical tensions arose directly from the compromise forced on it by varying degrees of proximity to feudalism in time and space.

Thus Petty, Cantillon, and "in general the writers who are *closer to feudal times*" are distinguished from their successors in one important respect: unlike the latter, they "assume that ground-rent is the normal form of surplus-value, whereas profit to them is still vaguely combined with wages, or at best looks to them like a portion of surplus-value filched by the capitalist from the landlord."[29] Again, the differences between Bastiat and Carey in their attitudes towards the expansionist thrust of British capital, their respective preferences for free trade and protection, and even the dissimilarities of structure and style in their arguments are shown to have been the effect of a spatial difference within the history of Western feudalism: one originated in France, a country with a long record of feudal impediment to the progress of capital, and the

other in the United States, "a country where bourgeois society did not develop on the foundation of the feudal system, but developed rather from itself."[30]

The triumph of the universalist tendency was not obvious in bourgeois practice either. The failure of the Prussian revolution of 1848 to achieve the comprehensive character of the English and French revolutions respectively of 1648 and 1789 inspired a series of brilliant but bitter reflections on this theme from Marx in the *Neue Rheinische Zeitung*. The performance of the nineteenth-century German bourgeoisie is distinguished here from that of their class in seventeenth-century England and eighteenth-century France in terms of their respective records in overcoming the old order. Both in 1648 and 1789, he writes, the victory of the bourgeoisie was, for its time, "*the victory of a new social order,* the victory of bourgeois ownership over feudal ownership, of nationality over provincialism, of competition over the guild, of the division of land over primogeniture, of the rule of the landowner over the domination of the owner by the land, of enlightenment over superstition, of the family over the family name, of industry over heroic idleness, of bourgeois law over medieval privileges."[31] Compared to that, in 1848, "it was not a question of establishing a new society" in Germany. The bourgeoisie there was from the outset "inclined to betray the people and to compromise with the crowned representative of the old society, for it itself already belonged to the old society; it did not represent the interests of a new society against an old one, but renewed interests within an obsolete society."[32]

This tendency to compromise with elements of the old order was, for Marx, "the most striking proof" that the German revolution of 1848 was "merely a parody of the French revolution of 1789." In an attack on the failure of the Prussian government to abolish feudal obligations, he contrasted its vacillation in this respect to the vigor and decisiveness of the French bourgeoisie in their struggle against feudalism in 1789. Thus,

> On August 4, 1789, [he wrote] three weeks after the storming of the Bastille, the French people, in a *single* day, got the better of the feudal obligations.
>
> On July 11, 1848, four months after the March barricades, the feudal obligations got the better of the German people …

The French bourgeoisie of 1789 never left its allies, the peasants, in the lurch. It knew that the abolition of feudalism in the countryside and the creation of a free, landowning peasant class was the basis of its rule.

The German bourgeoisie of 1848 unhesitatingly betrays the peasants, who are its *natural allies,* flesh of its own flesh, and without whom it cannot stand up to the aristocracy.

The perpetuation of feudal rights and their endorsement in the form of the (illusory) commutations – such is the result of the German revolution of 1848.[33]

The relevance of this critique for the study of colonialism can hardly be overestimated. For the representation of the colonial project of the European bourgeoisie as a particularly convincing example of the universalist mission of capital has for long been a matter of routine in academic teaching and research, as witness the importance of the rubric "Expansion of Europe" in the curricula of liberal education. The constant play on this theme in text-books, dissertations and learned journals, its propagation by many of the most powerful pedagogic instruments wherever English serves as the medium of learning, has "normalized" it, in a Kuhnian sense, as an integral part of the paradigm of liberal culture.

The effect of all this has been to generate an illusion about the power of capital and promote its universalist pretensions by liberal discourse, as exemplified, among others, by the liberal–colonialist and liberal–nationalist histories of the raj. These show beyond doubt how historiography has got itself trapped in an abstract universalism thanks to which it is unable to distinguish between the ideal of capital's striving towards self-realization and the reality of its failure to do so. That is why the anomalies and contradictions which give colonialism its specific character in India are not central to either of the dominant modes of writing about British rule. For to construct a problematic based on the recognition of such anomalies, which are after all nothing but an unmistakable evidence of the frustration of the universalizing tendency of capital, would be to challenge the liberal paradigm itself. As a component of that paradigm, historiography can hardly afford to do so.

It is this critical failure which has been primarily responsible for a serious misrepresentation of the power relations of colonialism in historical discourse. The essential point about that misrepresentation is that

dominance under colonial conditions has quite erroneously been endowed with hegemony. This is so because liberal historiography has been led to presume that capital, in its Indian career, succeeded in overcoming the obstacles to its self-expansion and subjugating all precapitalist relations in material and spiritual life well enough to enable the bourgeoisie to speak for all of that society, as it had done on the occasion of its historic triumphs in England in 1648 and France in 1789. Resistance to the rule of capital has been made to dissolve ideally into a hegemonic dominance.

In other words, there is no acknowledgment in either of the dominant modes of historical discourse that in reality the universalist project we have been discussing hurtled itself against an insuperable barrier in colonialism. Hence the attempt, in colonialist writings, to make the rule of British capital in India appear as a rule based on the consent of the subject population – that is, as hegemonic – and correspondingly to construct, in nationalist writings, the dominance of the Indian bourgeoisie as the political effect of a consensus representing all of the will of the people – that is, as hegemonic again.

There is little in this sweet and sanitized image of dominance to expose or explain the harsh realities of politics during the raj. On the contrary, the presumption of hegemony makes for a seriously distorted view of the colonial state and its configuration of power. It is important, therefore, that the critique of historiography should begin by questioning the universalist assumptions of liberal ideology and the attribution of hegemony taken for granted in colonialist and nationalist interpretations of the Indian past. It must begin, in short, by situating itself outside the universe of liberal discourse.

[…]

Notes

1 Hayden White, *Metahistory* (Baltimore: Johns Hopkins University Press, 1983), pp. 21–2.
2 Aristotle, *The Politics* (Harmondsworth: Penguin Books, 1974), p. 34.
3 M. I. Finley, *Ancient Slavery and Modern Ideology* (Harmondsworth: Penguin Books, 1983), p. 119.
4 Perry Anderson, *Passages from Antiquity to Feudalism* (London: New Left Books, 1975), p. 23.

5   Ibid.

6   See, for instance, R. C. Majumdar, "Ideas of History in Sanskrit Literature," and A. L. Basham, "The Kashmir Chronicle" both in C. H. Philips, ed., *Historians of India, Pakistan and Ceylon* (London: Oxford University Press, 1961).

7   *Rājataraṅginī*, translated by Ranjit Sitaram Pandit (New Delhi: Sahitya Akademi, 1968), I:13–15.

8   Ibid., 1:7.

9   D. D. Kosambi, *An Introduction to the Study of Indian History* (Bombay: Popular Prakashan, 1975), 2nd rev. edn., p. 365.

10 Majumdar, "Ideas of History," p. 23; Basham, "Kashmir Chronicle," p. 62.

11 Basham, "Kashmir Chronicle," pp. 62–3.

12 Majumdar, "Ideas of History," p. 21.

13 Ibid., p. 23.

14 *Rājataraṅginī*, I:9–10.

15 Ibid., n. 324.

16 Basham, "Kashmir Chronicle," p. 62.

17 *Rājataraṅginī*, I:9–10. For a discussion of the errors in Bühler's reading of this verse and its correct interpretation, see the translator's note in ibid., pp. 7–9, and Majumdar, "Ideas of History," p. 21.

18 Montesquieu, *De l'Esprit des Lois* (Paris: Garnier, n.d.), I:260; and Montesquieu, *The Spirit of the Laws*, trans. and ed. by A. M. Cobler, B. C. Miller and H. S. Stone (Cambridge: Cambridge University Press, 1989), p. 252.

19 G. W. F. Hegel, *Lectures on the Philosophy of World History. Introduction: Reason in History*, trans. H. B. Nisbet (Cambridge: Cambridge University Press, 1982), p. 54.

20 Majumdar, "Ideas of History," p. 23.

21 Basham, "Kashmir Chronicle," p. 64.

22 Karl Marx, *Grundrisse* (Harmondsworth: Penguin Books, 1973), p. 408.

23 Ibid., p. 539.

24 Ibid., p. 540.

25 Ibid., p. 409.

26 Ibid., pp. 409–10.

27 Ibid., p. 410.

28 Bertrand Russell, *History of Western Philosophy* (London: George Allen & Unwin, 1965), p. 578.

29 Karl Marx, *Capital* (Chicago: Charles H. Kerr, 1909), 3:910. Emphasis added.

30 Marx, *Grundrisse*, p. 884. Much of the section "Bastiat and Carey" on pp. 883–93 of this work is taken up with that question.

31 Karl Marx and Frederick Engels, *Collected Works* (London: Lawrence & Wishart, 1976–94), 8:161.

32 Ibid., p. 162.

33 Marx and Engels, *Collected Works*, 7:294–5.

Additional Readings

Foucault

Phillip Goldstein. "From Archaeology to Genealogy: Michel Foucault and Post-Marxist Histories." In *Post-Marxist Theory: An Introduction*, pp. 37–51. New York: SUNY Press, 2005.
An excellent, lucid introduction to Foucault's historical methodology in light of the intellectual work of post-Marxism.

Carlos Prado. *Starting with Foucault: An Introduction to Genealogy*. Boulder, CO: Westview Press, 1995.
An overview of Foucault's thought, with an emphasis on the concept of genealogy as seen from the perspective of both continental and analytic philosophy.

Rudi Visker. *Michel Foucault: Genealogy as Critique*. Translated by Chris Turner. New York: Verso, 1995.
An interpretation and defense of Foucault's notion of genealogy as an unorthodox method which focuses attention upon critical issues of control and exclusion.

Williams

John Clarke. "Subordinating the Social." *Cultural Studies* 21.6 (2007): 974–87.
Clarke applies Williams's temporal framework of emergent, dominant, and residual cultural modes to analyze the shift from welfare capitalism to neoliberalism.

Gayatri Chakravorty Spivak. *Death of a Discipline*. New York: Columbia University Press, 2003.
From one of the foremost scholars of postcolonial theory and criticism comes a call to deconstruct previous modes of comparative literature and imagine a critical ethic on par with the demands of globalization.

Lyotard

Steven Best and Douglas Kellner. *The Postmodern Adventure*. New York: Guilford Press, 2001.
An accessible and wide-ranging introduction to the changes in politics, art, culture, theory, and identity which mark the shift to the postmodern era.

Jürgen Habermas. "Modernity versus Postmodernity." *New German Critique* 22 (1981): 3–14.
The essay to which Lyotard was in many ways responding. In this key text, Habermas argues that postmodernism reflects a loss of political and cultural direction in the postwar period.

Fredric Jameson. *Postmodernism, or the Cultural Logic of Late Capitalism*. Durham, NC: Duke University Press, 1991.
A now classic text in which Jameson maps the main characteristics of the cultural shift from modernism into postmodernism in a variety of fields and examples, using popular culture, art, ideology, space and architecture, language and economics.

Braudel

Fernand Braudel. *On History*. Translated by Sarah Matthews. Chicago: University of Chicago Press, 1980.
The first collection of Braudel's published in English, this volume provides an overview of his work and his reflections on the intellectual framework of historical studies.

Manuel DeLanda. *A Thousand Years of Non-Linear History*. Cambridge, MA: Zone Books, 2000.
An attempt to update the work of Braudel in light of recent developments in philosophy. DeLanda traces the history of the last thousand years in terms of concrete movements and interactions of energy and matter through populations.

Immanuel Wallerstein. *World-Systems Analysis*. Durham, NC: Duke University Press, 2004.
A seminal example of the school of historical analysis and understanding which grew out of Braudel's work. A concise and comprehensible introduction to the historical method of world systems analysis.

Jameson

Marshall Berman. *All That Is Solid Melts into Air: The Experience of Modernity*. London: Verso, 1983.
In this paradigmatic study, Berman articulates the distinction between modernity, modernism, and modernization in order to provide cultural studies with the critical vocabulary with which to make sense of the legacies of the modern period.

Sean Homer. "Narratives of History, Narratives of Time." In *On Jameson: From Postmodernism to Globalization*, edited by Caren Irr and Ian Buchanan, pp. 71–94. Albany, NY: State University of New York Press, 2005.
An essay that focuses on Jameson's treatment of time and history throughout his *oeuvre*.

Fredric Jameson. "The End of Temporality." *Critical Inquiry* 29 (2003): 695–718.
Jameson reconsiders postmodernity as an era concerned with questions of space over time, a state of affairs which potentially brings about an end to notions of progress or change.

Schwarz

John Gledson. "Introduction" to Roberto Schwarz, *Misplaced Ideas: Essays on Brazilian Culture*, pp. ix–xix. London: Verso, 1992.
Gledson's introduction situates Schwarz and his work within the cultural milieu of Brazil and Latin America, and provides an account of his dialogue with his historical forebears.

Elías José Palti. "The Problem of 'Misplaced Ideas' Revisited: Beyond the 'History of Ideas' in Latin America." *Journal of the History of Ideas* 67.1 (2006): 149–79.
Palti updates and challenges Schwarz's theoretical framework for making sense of the spread of ideas in "peripheral" countries in the context of new developments in the study of the history of ideas.

Mary Louise Pratt. "The Anticolonial Past." *Modern Language Quarterly* 65.3 (2004): 443–56.
Pratt presents an anti-colonial historical model, arising out of the moment of decolonization, with which to account for the spread of Western modernity.

Imre Szeman. "Literature on the Periphery of Capitalism: Brazilian Theory, Canadian Culture." *Ilha do Desterro* (Brazil) 40 (2001): 25–42.
Szeman argues that Schwarz's insights about the nature of cultural nationalism in Brazil is relevant to an understanding of contemporary Canadian culture as well.

Guha

Vinayak Chaturvedi, ed. *Mapping Subaltern Studies and the Postcolonial*. New York: Verso, 2000.
This set of essays functions as a comprehensive introduction to the work produced by subaltern studies: the investigation of history from the perspective of those dominated by colonial practices and processes.

Ranajit Guha. *History at the Limit of World-History*. New York: Columbia University Press, 2002.

A critique of the ways in which Western philosophies of history contribute to the oppressive regimes of imperialism. Guha argues for the need for a new historiography which extends to the everyday life of populations.

Robert Marks. *The Origins of the Modern World: A Global and Ecological Narrative*. New York: Rowman & Littlefield, 2002.
In a highly instructive work, Marks questions the "rise of the West" narrative implicit in globalization discourse and considers the possibility of a non-Eurocentric understanding of world history.

General

Walter Benjamin. "Theses on the Philosophy of History." In *Illuminations: Essays and Reflections*, edited by Hannah Arendt and translated by Harry Zohn, pp. 245–55. New York: Pimilco, 1999.
In this renowned work, Walter Benjamin lays out a series of observations regarding history which range from Marxist dialectics to quasi-mystical visions.

Dipesh Chakrabarty. *Provincializing Europe: Postcolonial Thought and Historical Difference*. Princeton, NJ: Princeton University Press, 2007.
An acclaimed attempt to displace European thought from the histories of non-European spaces and places.

Johannes Fabian. *Time and the Other: How Anthropology Makes Its Object*. New York: Columbia University Press, 1983.
A radical critique of anthropological practice which examines the way the Other is constructed as existing in times other than that of the analyst.

Peter Linebaugh and Marcus Rediker. *The Many-Headed Hydra: The Hidden History of the Revolutionary Atlantic*. Boston: Beacon Press, 2000.
A history of commoners, this volume tells a history of outcast and overlooked groups and their forgotten exertion and jubilance which helped shape the modern, and primarily Atlantic, world.

Paul Virilio. *Speed and Politics*. New York: Semiotext(e), 1977.
Virilio argues that speed is the shaping force of civilization: an argument with radical political ramifications, and an iconoclastic challenge to standard ways of conceptualizing time.

Hayden White. *Tropics of Discourse: Essays in Cultural Criticism*. Baltimore: Johns Hopkins Press, 1986.
A classic series of essays which unpack the role of interpretation and meaning in history, and argue that literature has a much closer relation to history than is normally conceived.

Part 6

Subjectivity

Introduction

Theories of "who we are" form the basis of narratives of every facet of ourselves and others; they shape one's sense of self, explain the behavior and motivations of others, and provide insight into the form taken by all manner of social systems. They also give form to numerous cultural genres: the *Bildungsroman* in writing, the biopic in film, confessional pop ballads, and fractured self-portraits in fine art. Discussions of identity often stall, however, in the limited ruminations of "Who am I?" and "Who are you?" Perhaps the most recurring misunderstanding of identity – one which these common questions point to – is that it is believed to be primordial and located in the body's immediate sense experience. "I" and "you" are treated not as markers of a contradictory swarm of impressions, attributes, dispositions, and histories, but as names for a core principle or fixed ontological characteristic, the "ghost in the machine" or the wizard behind the curtain which manages sensory experience in an individual's unwavering march through time. Identity is said to be this core – the "soul" for the more religious-minded, or perhaps the "mind" investigated in analytic philosophy, a pit in the middle of the fruit of the body which permits the invention of science fiction scenarios in which one can be transposed into another's body or into the body of a machine, and still be oneself (even *Robocop* rediscovers "himself" under the layer of programmed directives he is given). Cultural theory insists on a more complex understanding of identity, which demands that we think of this "I" according to larger social forces and political structures.

In scrutinizing the way language frames how we think about human identity, cultural theorists analyze whether "human" is an appropriate word for naming who we are. "Human" implies a universal model of "human nature" whose unchanging characteristics are thought to be applicable to everyone. Since the presumption of such an essence all too quickly settles ontological questions, making it unnecessary to delineate all of the various shapes in which humans have imagined themselves *as* human over time, theorists prefer the concept "subject" to shift the focus from universal, natural forces to immanent, cultural ones.

David Macey, among many others, values the concept of "subject" because of its versatile linguistic capacity. It denotes passivity, as in "subject to," as well as activity, as in "subject of." As a political-juridical category, it describes a person of relative subordination to a sovereign, as in "the King's subjects." Finally, as a grammatical term the word stands for "the subject of the sentence."[1] The many meanings of this word allow theorists to interpret and engage a range of problems that often overlap and compound one another. For instance, against the deep-seated presence of racism and the sanctioned interdiction of supposed "abnormalities" of all variety (physical, mental, and otherwise), theorists such as Judith Butler, Luce Irigaray, and Paul Gilroy employ variations of the concept of subjectivity as a counterweight to words like "human," "Being," "soul," "individual," "man," or "person," which have had a long history of describing people in a way which has permitted cultural and physical violence under the guise of having identified truths about the human condition.

Some of the most consequential investigations of subjectivity have been produced within feminist criticism. In dialogue with the ideas of Michel Foucault, Luce Irigaray, and Jacques Lacan, and set against strict biological definitions of the body, Judith Butler's influential theory of the subject focuses on its gendered interpellation and performance. Divesting the subject of all innate characteristics, she shows how subjectivity is shaped in contingent conflict with and compulsive reiteration of heterosexual norms. Ritual articulations such as "It's a girl!" when a baby is born draw upon a small number of predetermined cultural identities (invoking the institutions which make them available) to evaluate and identify the qualities of a subject: from the moment of birth one is already interpellated into a gender through a social process which is re-enacted again and again. The ongoing possibility of identifying with one of these fixed identities – "heterosexual female," for example – and the insistence that it be lived out through a consistent set of behaviors and characteristics, necessarily means alternative forms of subjecthood are lost or repressed along the way. Butler's theories of subjectivity have enabled a huge range of inquiries into the constitution of subjectivity and reflections on the politics of culture and the possibilities of being otherwise.

Working with similar insights which feminism has provided for better understanding the social performance of identity, Donna Haraway pushes us to challenge our received ideas about subjectivity. Haraway situates the subject within a post-Cold War context to assess prospects for a feminist politics in which "people are not afraid of their joint kinship with animals and machines, not afraid of partial identities and contradictory standpoints."[2] The "cyborg" of her famous manifesto is located *in medias res* of capitalist technological and scientific processes. For Haraway, claims that the subject is a universal and autonomous being are not only patently wrong, but tend to mystify the unavoidable reliance of subjects on other beings whose presence has usually been deemed incidental or of minor consequence. Provocatively, she argues for a substantial extension of our understanding of subjectivity beyond the limits of the human. Subject formation is for her not exclusively "social" (i.e., limited to human relations), since one engages with machines and animals in addition to other subjects, and in ways that have a significant impact on the types of beings we are. Haraway's call for a cyborg politics presents all subjects with the

task of reconstructing the boundaries, in partial connection with others, in communication with all of our parts. It is not just that science and technology are possible means of great human satisfaction, as well as a matrix of complex dominations. Cyborg imaginary can suggest a way out of the maze of dualisms in which we have explained our bodies and our tools to ourselves.[3]

Feminist theory has consistently and energetically challenged claims about what men and women are "naturally" predisposed to be or to do. The work of Butler, Haraway, and others, demands that we think considerably more about the ways in which subjectivity is produced and organized, about the borders we too quickly draw around the self, and the impact and implications of these definitions on those who cross these borders in search of better understandings of selfhood.

If subjectivity is a concept used to shift issues pertaining to identity away from earlier histories of invidious suppositions (if not outright xenophobia and hatred) and narrow formulations, what then characterizes our current situation? How do the writings in this section invite us to interpret contemporary violations and mystifications of subjectivity? One of the challenges in investigating subjectivity is the realization that theoretical insight doesn't resolve long-held ideas about identity; indeed, the inevitable gap between belief and behavior is part of the phenomenon that "subject" names and "identity" represses. For example, even those who believe that all races and ethnicities are equal are not free from racism. This is not only because of the lingering traces of the fear of blackness sedimented into one's view of things or in the explicit racism of others. Our current social world is partly a product of a racist past which cannot be undone by thought alone. Earlier periods of history continue to deeply influence how we understand who we are individually and together, and indeed what it means to be a "we" to begin with.

For instance, the social and psychical aftermath of colonialism has not simply diminished since the time when the British systematically murdered and "civilized" thousands of people to claim India, or when France colonized Algeria to extend its political and economic domain.[4] Many of today's geopolitical strategies bear a close resemblance to their colonial precedents in the way they label national or ethnic cultures as anachronistic, inferior, and in need of paternalistic intervention. The rhetoric of "development" often employed today – a rhetoric which has returned after being the subject of sustained critique by dependency theories in the 1960s and 1970s – is closely analogous to the colonial incursions of yesteryear.[5] Incessantly invoked as an undifferentiated mass, Africa is portrayed on television and in cinema as a land of helpless children and crazed warlords. However, the socioeconomic problems experienced by countries in Africa are not endemic, but the consequence of economic development through schemes such as the Washington Consensus and the plans of financial institutions such as the International Monetary Fund and the World Trade Organization.[6] Caricatured representations of African identity as primitive and mysterious continue to be used now to reduce a complex global form of injustice to one of innate and thus unalterable identity.[7] In this manner, ethnic identity – which, it has to be said, can constitute an enormous social and political resource against the worst ravages of capitalist exploitation – can nevertheless be used to legitimate the injustices produced by contemporary geopolitical forms of power.

These politically sanctioned programs of oppression eventually left colonized peoples and subsequent postcolonial generations the work of understanding the ramifications of a violent and repressive past. Frantz Fanon's continued relevance resides in the nuanced way he gauged the effects of colonialism on his own present. In *Black Skin, White Masks* (1952) and *Wretched of the Earth* (1961) he narrates the profound difficulties of psychical and social alienation produced by colonialism. While living in France, Fanon realized the unique way in which his identity was denigrated and reduced to the status of "a negro." This bigotry – a vestige of colonial politics – stood in the way of the autonomy he sought and expected to find as a supposedly "free" French citizen. The after-effects of colonialism are described by Fanon in lively and conceptually deft prose which incorporates ideas from psychoanalysis and phenomenology; he characterizes this experience as a form of loss perpetuating an older comportment of colonial submission. Misidentification of Fanon's identity in French society not only estranges him from others but also creates a fissure within his own psychical perception. "I am overdetermined from the outside," he writes. "I am a slave not to the 'idea' others have of me, but to my appearance."[8] Fanon points to the cultural effects of the massive politico-economic reorganization which occurred during and after colonialism, highlighting the complex way in which ideologies, state policies, economics, and social life are all implicated in the creation of the subject-position picked out by the racist gaze.

Prejudicial notions of identity circulate in many different spaces and with varying degrees of intensity. Many arise within prosaic circumstances, such as institutional forms of knowledge that study, render intelligible, and remedy subjects. The fields of medicine, psychiatry, legal and punitive corrections, religion, and education all have double-edged effects on subjectivity. The idea of the healthy body produced in medicine, for instance, seems unobjectionable – the outcome of a clear-eyed, scientific view about best practices for the particular kinds of creatures that we are. But this scientific body, too, is a cultural and social invention, informed by qualitative assumptions about the "normal" or "optimal" body and its life imperatives.[9] Normalization is a process which instructs, animates, and sustains the lives of subject, but which also proscribes many of its actions. In the context of contemporary multicultural societies, Paul Gilroy explores the elusive qualities of national subjectivity generated within diasporic black British solidarity and anti-apartheid movements. Identity is a troubling concept for Gilroy given how it operates in institutions and forms of knowledge that attempt to quell or co-opt opposition to their structures. Nations are no different than other modes of power. He explains that

> the problematic intellectual heritage of Euro-American modernity still determines the manner in which nationality is understood within black political discourse. In particular, it conditions the continuing aspiration to acquire a supposedly authentic, natural and stable identity. This identity is the premise of a thinking "racial" self that is both socialized and unified by its connection with other kindred souls …[10]

The assimilation of subjects within national cultures and by their protocols constitutes one of the most powerful examples of the way in which a cultural invention is used to create and manage a "natural" identity. Nationality and identity are linked formally and legally (e.g., birth certificates and passports), and in indirect ways which can blanket over ethnic, indigenous, and subaltern differences. Through his investigation of musical expression in hip-hop and the Fisk University Jubilee Singers, Gilroy argues that music has power "in developing our struggles by communicating information, organizing consciousness and testing out, deploying or amplifying the forms of subjectivity which are required by political agency."[11] Seen as entertainment for youth and demonized in traditional British circles, opposition to assimilation through song offers a challenge to supremacist ideologies governing the colonial past and present, including those of modern nationalism which insists that everyone in a specific geographical space imagine themselves as a uniform "we."

In addition to potent gender antagonisms and the residual controls instilled within former empires, subjectivity is also a site of the ongoing production of sexual difference. In formulating one of the most compelling recent accounts of the sexual subject in *Epistemology of the Closet*, Eve Sedgwick stages the subject within seven "axioms" for its interpretation. For her, the inevitable blurring of public and private spheres vexes the desires of subjects. Her extended meditation on the category of "queer" – in which disparate sexual acts such as "sodomy" become rooted within a medical typology of sex to stand for "homosexual" identity on the whole – is positioned between universal and minoritizing discourses which do not provide the "truth" of sexuality per se (as most discourses promise). Rather her theorization of queer subjectivity draws from Victorian-era literature and builds on many insights articulated by Michel Foucault in *The History of Sexuality* (1976), to discern "the performative effects of the self-contradictory discursive field of sexuality created by their overlap."[12] Sedgwick pursues the question of "knowing" the sexual subject in these terms, but cautions us not to abstract this knowledge from the prevalent social animus of "homophobic pressure." The looming pressure creates a resentment between opposed groups, as a condition of knowledge alters desires and the ability to articulate or enact them unfettered: "there is a satisfaction in dwelling on the degree to which the power our enemies over us is implicated, not in their command of knowledge, but precisely in their ignorance."[13] In keeping sexual difference apart and yet closely related to gender differences and their history, Sedgwick prevents us from conflating categories and provides an analytic for understanding the "invention" and emergence of "homosexuality" as a category of subjectivity and as performed according to and against the circumstances of social norms.

Philosophical traditions also have a hand in describing subjectivity in spurious ways. For instance, identity and knowledge have intersected in ways that thinkers such as Lacan, Haraway, and Irigaray have found essential to investigate, however divergent their critiques might be from one another. Seminal for Lacan in the discussion of the subject are three sources: René Descartes's *Discourse on Method* (1637), Sigmund Freud's writings on the unconscious, and the linguistic theory of Ferdinand de Saussure. Lacan's primary target, the "Cartesian Subject," is the form of subjectivity purported to have proven our innate sense of self based in sense-certainty. Lacan associates this model of subjectivity with the rise of psychological models of the person which assert that the ego self-consciously orders one's affects, manner of expression, and knowledge of the world. Against self-certainty, he argues that the unconscious is not a realm of drives (as Freud argued), but rather part of the "logic of the signifier." The unconscious prevents us from expressing ourselves clearly and distinctly. "Structured like a language," the unconscious speaks through us symptomatically to provide clues for who we are. The inflection of Freud's pseudo-biological models with Saussure's linguistic ones keeps Lacan's topology of the unconscious from becoming yet another essentialist model of the subject. Lacan's theories have had a lasting impact on cultural theory, especially in work that examines ideology, subject formation, and its concomitant psychical capacities.

Subjectivity belongs to a cluster of histories and ongoing interpretations that when studied in any given detail threatens to overwhelm our concepts and explanatory models; there is always a temptation to retreat to the comfort of the "I" which originates in and claims to know everything about the interiority of the self. Subjectivity is at the heart of being, but of a being constantly shaped by the world in which it lives out its existence. The most powerful theories about subjectivity are those which give us a better understanding of the circuits of social power which shape subjects, yet remain fully aware that this shaping is an ongoing process. The aim of cultural theories of subjectivity is not to finally determine some identity – however complex and variegated – hidden under all the sedimented layers of history, but to see how this history has in fact made us what we are.

Notes

1   David Macey, "Subject" in *Dictionary of Critical Theory* (New York: Penguin, 2001), 369.

2   Donna Haraway, "A Cyborg Manifesto," in *Simians, Cyborgs and Women: The Reinvention of Nature* (New York: Routledge, 1991), 154. Reproduced in this volume.

3   Ibid., 181.

4   On the latter, Gillo Pontecorvo's *The Battle of Algiers* (1965) is a seminal film.

5   For a discussion of these connections, see Samir Amin, *Unequal Development: An Essay on the Social Formations of Peripheral Capitalism* (New York: Monthly Review Press, 1976) and David Harvey, "Notes Towards a Theory of Uneven Geographical Development," in *Spaces of Global Capitalism: Toward a Theory of Uneven Development* (London: Verso, 2006), 69–116.

6   See Samuel Huntington, *The Clash of Civilizations and the Remaking of World Order* (New York: Simon & Schuster, 1996). For a (controversial) view inside the process of contemporary global development, see John Perkins, *Confessions of an Economic Hitman* (New York: Plume, 2005).

7   For a primary theory of colonial knowledge not included in this volume, see Edward Said's *Orientalism* (New York: Vintage, 1979). See also Homi K. Bhabha's *The Location of Culture* (London: Routledge, 1994) and Anne McClintok's *Imperial Leather: Race, Gender and Sexuality in the Colonial Contest* (New York: Routledge, 1995).

8   Frantz Fanon, "The Lived Experience of the Black Man," in *Black Skin, White Masks*, trans. Richard Philcox (New York: Grove Press, 2008), 95. Reproduced in this volume.

9   See Michel Foucault's *The Birth of Biopolitics: Lectures at the College de France, 1978–1979*, trans. Graham Burchell (London: Palgrave Macmillan, 2008); Giorgio Agamben, *Homo Sacer: Sovereign Power and Bare Life*, trans. Daniel Heller-Roazen (Palo Alto, CA: Stanford University Press, 1998); Kaushik Sunder Rajan, *Biocapital: The Constitution of Postgenomic Life* (Durham, NC: Duke University Press, 2006).

10 Paul Gilroy, "It Ain't Where You're From, It's Where You're At: The Dialectics of Diasporic Identification," in *Small Acts: Thoughts on the Politics of Black Cultures* (New York: Serpent's Tail, 1993), 121. Reproduced in this volume.

11 Ibid., 132–3.

12 Eve K. Sedgwick, "Axiomatic," in *Epistemology of the Closet* (Berkeley: University of California Press, 1991), 9. Reproduced in this volume.

13 Ibid., 7.

36

"The Lived Experience
of the Black Man" (1952)

Frantz Fanon

"Dirty nigger!" or simply "Look! A Negro!"

I came into this world anxious to uncover the meaning of things, my soul desirous to be at the origin of the world, and here I am an object among other objects.

Locked in this suffocating reification, I appealed to the Other so that his liberating gaze, gliding over my body suddenly smoothed of rough edges, would give me back the lightness of being I thought I had lost, and taking me out of the world put me back in the world. But just as I get to the other slope I stumble, and the Other fixes me with his gaze, his gestures and attitude, the same way you fix a preparation with a dye. I lose my temper, demand an explanation. … Nothing doing. I explode. Here are the fragments put together by another me.

As long as the black man remains on his home territory, except for petty internal quarrels, he will not have to experience his being for others. There is in fact a "being for other," as described by Hegel, but any ontology is made impossible in a colonized and acculturated society. Apparently, those who have written on the subject have not taken this sufficiently into consideration. In the weltanschauung of a colonized people, there is an impurity or a flaw that prohibits any ontological explanation. Perhaps it could be argued that this is true for any individual, but such an argument would be concealing the basic problem.

Frantz Fanon, "The Lived Experience of the Black Man," pp. 89–114 from *Black Skin, White Masks*, trans. Richard Philcox. New York: Grove Press, 2008. Copyright © 1952 by Éditions du Seuil. English translation copyright © 2008 by Richard Philcox. Used by permission of Grove/Atlantic, Inc.

Ontology does not allow us to understand the being of the black man, since it ignores the lived experience. For not only must the black man be black; he must be black in relation to the white man. Some people will argue that the situation has a double meaning. Not at all. The black man has no ontological resistance in the eyes of the white man. From one day to the next, the Blacks have had to deal with two systems of reference. Their metaphysics, or less pretentiously their customs and the agencies to which they refer, were abolished because they were in contradiction with a new civilization that imposed its own.

In the twentieth century the black man on his home territory is oblivious of the moment when his inferiority is determined by the Other. Naturally, we have had the opportunity to discuss the black problem with friends and, less often, with African-Americans. Together we proclaimed loud and clear the equality of man in the world. In the Antilles there is also that minor tension between the cliques of white Creoles, Mulattoes, and Blacks. But we were content to intellectualize these differences. In fact, there was nothing dramatic about them. And then …

And then we were given the occasion to confront the white gaze. An unusual weight descended on us. The real world robbed us of our share. In the white world, the man of color encounters difficulties in elaborating his body schema. The image of one's body is solely negating. It's an image in the third person. All around the body reigns an atmosphere of certain uncertainty. I know that if I want to smoke, I shall have to stretch out my right arm and grab the pack of cigarettes lying at the other end of the table. As for the matches, they are in the left drawer, and I shall have to move back a little. And I make all these moves, not out of habit, but by implicit knowledge. A slow construction of my self as a body in a spatial and temporal world – such seems to be the schema. It is not imposed on me; it is rather a definitive structuring of my self and the world – definitive because it creates a genuine dialectic between my body and the world.

For some years now, certain laboratories have been researching for a "denegrification" serum. In all seriousness they have been rinsing out their test tubes and adjusting their scales and have begun research on how the wretched black man could whiten himself and thus rid himself of the burden of this bodily curse. Beneath the body schema I had created a historical-racial schema. The data I used were provided not by "remnants of feelings and notions of the tactile, vestibular, kinesthetic, or visual nature"[1] but by the Other, the white man, who had woven me out of a thousand details, anecdotes, and stories. I thought I was being asked to construct a physiological self, to balance space and localize sensations, when all the time they were clamoring for more.

"Look! A Negro!" It was a passing sting. I attempted a smile.

"Look! A Negro!" Absolutely. I was beginning to enjoy myself.

"Look! A Negro!" The circle was gradually getting smaller. I was really enjoying myself.

"*Maman*, look, a Negro; I'm scared!" Scared! Scared! Now they were beginning to be scared of me. I wanted to kill myself laughing, but laughter had become out of the question.

I couldn't take it any longer, for I already knew there were legends, stories, history, and especially the *historicity* that Jaspers had taught me. As a result, the body schema, attacked in several places, collapsed, giving way to an epidermal racial schema. In the train, it was a question of being aware of my body, no longer in the third person but in triple. In the train, instead of one seat, they left me two or three. I was no longer enjoying myself. I was unable to discover the feverish coordinates of the world. I existed in triple: I was taking up room. I approached the Other … and the Other, evasive, hostile, but not opaque, transparent and absent, vanished. Nausea.

I was responsible not only for my body but also for my race and my ancestors. I cast an objective gaze over myself, discovered my blackness, my ethnic features; deafened by cannibalism, backwardness, fetishism, racial stigmas, slave traders, and above all, yes, above all, the grinning *Y a bon Banania*.

Disoriented, incapable of confronting the Other, the white man, who had no scruples about imprisoning me, I transported myself on that particular day far, very far, from my self, and gave myself up as an object. What did this mean to me? Peeling, stripping my skin, causing a hemorrhage that left congealed black blood all over my body. Yet this reconsideration of myself, this thematization, was not my idea. I wanted quite simply to be a man among men. I would have liked to enter our world young and sleek, a world we could build together.

I refused, however, any affective tetanization. I wanted to be a man, and nothing but a man. There were some who wanted to equate me with my ancestors, enslaved and lynched: I decided that I would accept this. I considered this internal kinship from the universal level of the intellect – I was the grandson of slaves the same way President Lebrun was the grandson of peasants who had been exploited and worked to the bone.

The alert was soon over, in fact.

In the United States, Blacks are segregated. In South America, they are whipped in the streets and black strikers are gunned down. In West Africa, the black man is a beast of burden. And just beside me there is this student colleague of mine from Algeria who tells me, "As long as the Arab is treated like a man, like one of us, there will be no viable answer."

"You see, my dear fellow, color prejudice is totally foreign to me." "But do come in, old chap, you won't find any color prejudice here." "Quite so, the Black is just as much a man as we are." "It's not because he's black that he's less intelligent than we are." "I had a Senegalese colleague in the regiment, very smart guy."

Where do I fit in? Or, if you like, where should I stick myself?

"Martinican, a native from one of our 'old' colonies."

Where should I hide?

"Look, a Negro! *Maman*, a Negro!"

"Ssh! You'll make him angry. Don't pay attention to him, monsieur, he doesn't realize you're just as civilized as we are."

My body was returned to me spread-eagled, disjointed, redone, draped in mourning on this white winter's day. The Negro is an animal, the Negro is bad, the Negro is wicked, the Negro is ugly; look, a Negro; the Negro is trembling, the Negro is trembling because he's cold, the small boy is trembling because he's afraid of the Negro, the Negro is trembling with cold, the cold that chills the bones, the lovely little boy is trembling because he thinks the Negro is trembling with rage, the little white boy runs to his mother's arms: "*Maman*, the Negro's going to eat me."

The white man is all around me; up above the sky is tearing at its navel; the earth crunches under my feet and sings white, white. All this whiteness burns me to a cinder.

I sit down next to the fire and discover my livery for the first time. It is in fact ugly. I won't go on because who can tell me what beauty is?

Where should I put myself from now on? I can feel that familiar rush of blood surge up from the numerous dispersions of my being. I am about to lose my temper. The fire had died a long time ago, and once again the Negro is trembling.

"Look how handsome that Negro is."

"The handsome Negro says, 'Fuck you,' madame."

Her face colored with shame. At last I was freed from my rumination. I realized two things at once: I had identified the enemy and created a scandal. Overjoyed. We could now have some fun.

The battlefield had been drawn up; I could enter the lists.

I don't believe it! Whereas I was prepared to forget, to forgive, and to love, my message was flung back at me like a slap in the face. The white world, the only decent one, was preventing me from participating. It demanded that a man behave like a man. It demanded of me that I behave like a black man – or at least like a Negro. I hailed the world, and the world amputated my enthusiasm. I was expected to stay in line and make myself scarce.

I'll show them! They can't say I didn't warn them. Slavery? No longer a subject of discussion, just a bad memory. My so-called inferiority? A hoax that it would be better to laugh about. I was prepared to forget everything, provided the world integrated me. My incisors were ready to go into action. I could feel them, sharp. And then …

I don't believe it! Whereas I had every reason to vent my hatred and loathing, they were rejecting me? Whereas I was the one they should have begged and implored, I was denied the slightest recognition? I made up my mind, since it was impossible to rid myself of an *innate complex*, to assert myself as a BLACK MAN. Since the Other was reluctant to recognize me, there was only one answer: to make myself known.

In *Anti-Semite and Jew* Sartre writes: "They [the Jews] have allowed themselves to be poisoned by the stereotype that others have of them, and they live in fear that their acts will correspond to this stereotype.… We may say that their conduct is perpetually overdetermined from the inside" (p. 95).

The Jewishness of the Jew, however, can go unnoticed. He is not integrally what he is. We can but hope and wait. His acts and behavior are the determining factor. He is a white man, and apart from some debatable features, he can pass undetected. He belongs to the race that has never practiced cannibalism. What a strange idea, to eat one's father! Serves them right; they shouldn't be black. Of course the Jews have been tormented – what am I saying? They have been hunted, exterminated, and cremated, but these are just minor episodes in the family history. The Jew is not liked as soon as he has been detected. But with me things take on a *new* face. I'm not given a second chance. I am overdetermined from the outside. I am a slave not to the "idea" others have of me, but to my appearance.

I arrive slowly in the world; sudden emergences are no longer my habit. I crawl along. The white gaze, the only valid one, is already dissecting me. I am *fixed*. Once their microtomes are sharpened, the Whites objectively cut sections of my reality. I have been betrayed. I sense, I see in this white gaze that it's the arrival not of a new man, but of a new type of man, a new species. A Negro, in fact!

I slip into corners, my long antenna encountering the various axioms on the surface of things: the Negro's clothes smell of Negro; the Negro has white teeth; the Negro has big feet; the Negro has a broad chest. I slip into corners; I keep silent; all I want is to be anonymous, to be forgotten. Look, I'll agree to everything, on condition I go unnoticed!

"Hey, I'd like you to meet my black friend … Aimé Césaire, a black *agrégé* from the Sorbonne … Marian

Anderson, the greatest black singer ... Dr. Cobb, who discovered white blood cells, is black ... Hey, say hello to my friend from Martinique (be careful, he's very touchy)."

Shame. Shame and self-contempt. Nausea. When they like me, they tell me my color has nothing to do with it. When they hate me, they add that it's not because of my color. Either way, I am a prisoner of the vicious circle.

I turn away from these prophets of doom and cling to my brothers, Negroes like myself. To my horror, they reject me. They are almost white. And then they'll probably marry a white woman and have slightly brown children. Who knows, gradually, perhaps ...

I was dreaming.

"You must understand that I am one of Lyon's biggest fans of black people."

The proof was there, implacable. My blackness was there, dense and undeniable. And it tormented me, pursued me, made me uneasy, and exasperated me.

Negroes are savages, morons, and illiterates. But I knew personally that in my case these assertions were wrong. There was this myth of the Negro that had to be destroyed at all costs. We were no longer living in an age when people marveled at a black priest. We had doctors, teachers, and statesmen. OK, but there was always something unusual about them. "We have a Senegalese history teacher. He's very intelligent. ... Our physician's black. He's very gentle."

Here was the Negro teacher, the Negro physician; as for me, I was becoming a nervous wreck, shaking at the slightest alert. I knew for instance that if the physician made one false move, it was over for him and for all those who came after him. What, in fact, could one expect from a Negro physician? As long as everything was going smoothly, he was praised to the heavens; but watch out – there was no room whatsoever for any mistake. The black physician will never know how close he is to being discredited. I repeat, I was walled in: neither my refined manners nor my literary knowledge nor my understanding of the quantum theory could find favor.

I insisted on, I demanded an explanation. Speaking softly, as if addressing a child, they explained to me that some people have adopted a certain opinion, but, they added, "We can only hope it will soon disappear." And what was that? Color prejudice.

It [color prejudice] is nothing more than the unreasoning hatred of one race for another, the contempt of the stronger and richer peoples for those whom they consider inferior to themselves and the bitter resentment of those who are kept in subjection and are so frequently insulted. As colour is the most obvious outward manifestation of race it has been made the criterion by which men are judged, irrespective of their social or educational attainments. The light-skinned races have come to despise all those of a darker colour, and the dark-skinned peoples will no longer accept without protest the inferior position to which they have been relegated.[2]

I was not mistaken. It was hatred; I was hated, detested, and despised, not by my next-door neighbor or a close cousin, but by an entire race. I was up against something irrational. The psychoanalysts say that there is nothing more traumatizing for a young child than contact with the rational. I personally would say that for a man armed solely with reason, there is nothing more neurotic than contact with the irrational.

I felt the knife blades sharpening within me. I made up my mind to defend myself. Like all good tacticians I wanted to rationalize the world and show the white man he was mistaken.

In the Jew, Jean-Paul Sartre says, there is

a sort of impassioned imperialism of reason: for he wishes not only to convince others that he is right; his goal is to persuade them that there is an absolute and unconditioned value to rationalism. He feels himself to be a missionary of the universal; against the universality of the Catholic religion, from which he is excluded, he asserts the "catholicity" of the rational, an instrument by which to attain to the truth and establish a spiritual bond among men.[3]

And, the author adds, though there may be Jews who have made intuition the basic category of their philosophy, their intuition

has no resemblance to the Pascalian subtlety of spirit, and it is this latter – based on a thousand imperceptible perceptions – which to the Jew seems his worst enemy. As for Bergson, his philosophy offers the curious appearance of an anti-intellectualist doctrine constructed entirely by the most rational and most critical of intelligences. It is through argument that he establishes the existence of pure duration, of philosophic intuition; and that very intuition which discovers duration or life, is itself universal, since anyone may practice it, and it leads toward the universal, since its objects can be named and conceived.[4]

I set about enthusiastically making a checklist and researching my surroundings. As times changed, we have seen how the Catholic religion justified, then condemned slavery and discrimination. But by reducing everything to the notion of human dignity, it had gutted prejudice. Scientists reluctantly admitted that the Negro was a human being; in vivo and in vitro the Negro was identical to the white man: same morphology, same histology. Reason was assured of victory on every level. I reintegrated the brotherhood of man. But I was soon disillusioned.

Victory was playing cat and mouse; it was thumbing its nose at me. As the saying goes: now you see me, now you don't. Everyone was in agreement with the notion: the Negro is a human being – i.e., his heart's on his left side, added those who were not too convinced. But on certain questions the white man remained uncompromising. Under no condition did he want any intimacy between the races, for we know "crossings between widely different races can lower the physical and mental level. … Until we have a more definite knowledge of the effect of race-crossings we shall certainly do best to avoid crossings between widely different races."[5]

As for me, I would know full well how to react. And in one sense, if I had to define myself I would say I am in expectation; I am investigating my surroundings; I am interpreting everything on the basis of my findings. I have become a sensor.

At the start of my history that others have fabricated for me, the pedestal of cannibalism was given pride of place so that I wouldn't forget. They inscribed on my chromosomes certain genes of various thickness representing cannibalism. Next to the *sex linked*, they discovered the *racial linked*.[6] Science should be ashamed of itself!

But I can understand this "psychological mechanism," for everyone knows that it is not just psychological. Two centuries ago, I was lost to humanity; I was a slave forever. And then along came a group of men and declared that enough was enough. My tenacity did the rest; I was rescued from the civilizing deluge. I moved forward.

Too late. Everything had been predicted, discovered, proved, and exploited. My shaky hands grasped at nothing; the resources had been exhausted. Too late! But there again I want to know why.

Ever since someone complained that he had arrived too late and everything had already been said, there seems to be nostalgia for the past. Could it be that paradise lost described by Otto Rank? How many of those, apparently focused on the womb of the world, have devoted their lives to the intellection of the Delphic oracle or have endeavored to rediscover the voyages of Ulysses! The pan-spiritualists, seeking to prove the existence of a soul in animals, argue as follows: a dog lies down on its master's grave and starves to death. It was left to Janet to demonstrate that said dog, unlike man, was quite simply incapable of eliminating the past. We speak of the glory that was Greece, says Artaud; but, he adds, if people today can no longer understand the *Choephoroi* by Aeschylus, it's Aeschylus who is at fault. It's in the name of tradition that the anti-Semites base their "point of view." It's in the name of tradition, the long, historical past and the blood ties with Pascal and Descartes, that the Jews are told: you will never belong here. Recently, one of these good French folks declared on a train where I was sitting: "May the truly French values live on and the race will be safeguarded! At the present time we need a national union. No more internal strife! A united front against the foreigners [and turning to me] whoever they may be."

It should be said in his defense that he stank of cheap red wine. If he could, he would have told me that as a freed slave my blood was incapable of being inflamed by the names of Villon or Taine.

Disgraceful!

The Jew and I: not satisfied with racializing myself, by a happy stroke of fate, I was turning more human. I was drawing closer to the Jew, my brother in misfortune.

Disgraceful!

At first glance it might seem strange that the attitude of the anti-Semite can be equated with that of the negrophobe. It was my philosophy teacher from the Antilles who reminded me one day: "When you hear someone insulting the Jews, pay attention; he is talking about you." And I believed at the time he was universally right, meaning that I was responsible in my body and soul for the fate reserved for my brother. Since then,

I have understood that what he meant quite simply was that the anti-Semite is inevitably a negrophobe.

"You have come too late, much too late. There will always be a world – a white world – between you and us: that impossibility on either side to obliterate the past once and for all." Understandably, confronted with this affective ankylosis of the white man, I finally made up my mind to shout my blackness. Gradually, putting out pseudopodia in all directions, I secreted a race. And this race staggered under the weight of one basic element. *Rhythm!* Listen to Senghor, our bard:

> It is the most sensory and least material of things. It is the vital element par excellence. It is the essential condition and the hallmark of Art, as breathing is to life; breathing that accelerates or slows, becomes regular or spasmodic according to the tension of the individual and the degree and nature of his emotion. Such is rhythm primordial in its purity; such it is in the masterpieces of Negro art, especially sculpture. The composition of a theme of sculptural form in opposition to a sister theme, like breathing in to breathing out, is repeated over and over again. Rhythm is not symmetry that produces monotony but is alive and free. … That is how the tyranny of rhythm affects what is least intellectual in us, allowing us to penetrate the spirituality of the object; and that lack of constraint which is ours is itself rhythmic.[7]

Have I read it correctly? I give it an even closer reading. On the other side of the white world there lies a magical black culture. Negro sculpture! I began to blush with pride. Was this our salvation?

I had rationalized the world, and the world had rejected me in the name of color prejudice. Since there was no way we could agree on the basis of reason, I resorted to irrationality. It was up to the white man to be more irrational than I. For the sake of the cause, I had adopted the process of regression, but the fact remained that it was an unfamiliar weapon; here I am at home; I am made of the irrational; I wade in the irrational. Irrational up to my neck. And now let my voice ring out:

> Those who have invented neither gunpowder nor compass
> Those who have never known how to subdue either steam or electricity
> Those who have explored neither the seas nor the sky

> But those who know all the nooks and crannies of the country of suffering
> Those whose voyages have been uprootings
> Those who have become flexible to kneeling
> Those who were domesticated and christianized
> Those who were inoculated with bastardization …

Yes, all those are my brothers – a "bitter brotherhood" grabs us alike. After having stated the minor premise, I hail something else overboard:

> But those without whom the earth would not be the earth
> Gibbosity all the more beneficial as the earth more and more
> Abandons the earth
> Silo where is stored and ripens what is earthiest about the earth
> My negritude is not a stone, its deafness hurled against the clamor of day
> My negritude is not an opaque spot of dead water over the dead eye of the earth
> My negritude is neither a tower nor a cathedral
> It reaches deep down into the red flesh of the soil
> It reaches deep into the blazing flesh of the sky
> It pierces opaque prostration with its straight patience.[8]

Eia! The drums jabber out the cosmic message. Only the black man is capable of conveying it, of deciphering its meaning and impact. Astride the world, my heels digging into its flanks, I rub the neck of the world like the high priest rubbing between the eyes of his sacrificial victim.

> Those who open themselves up, enraptured, to the essence of all things
> Ignorant of surfaces but enraptured by the movement of all things
> Indifferent to subduing but playing the game of the world
> Truly the eldest sons of the world
> Porous to all the breaths of the world
> Brotherly zone of all the breaths of the world
> Undrained bed of all the waters of the world
> Spark of the sacred fire of the world
> Flesh of the flesh of the world palpitating with the very movement of the world![9]

Blood! Blood! … Birth! Vertigo of tomorrow! Three-quarters foundering in the stupefaction of daylight, I feel myself flushed with blood. The arteries of the world, shaken, pulled up and uprooted, have turned toward me and enriched me. "Blood! Blood! All our blood moved by the male heart of the sun."[10]

Sacrifice served as an intermediary between creation and me – it wasn't the origins I rediscovered, but the Origin. Nevertheless, beware of rhythm, the Mother Earth bond, and that mystic, carnal marriage between man and the cosmos.

In *La vie sexuelle en Afrique noire*, a book with a wealth of observations, De Pédrals implies that in Africa, whatever the field, there is always a certain magical social structure. And, he adds, "all these elements can be found on a greater scale in secret societies. Insofar as the circumcised adolescents of either sex are bound under pain of death not to divulge to the uninitiated what they have undergone, and insofar as the initiation into a secret society always calls for acts of *sacred love*, there are grounds for considering circumcision and excision and their rites as constituting minor secret societies."[11]

I am walking on hot coals. Sheets of water threaten my soul on fire. These rites make me think twice. Black magic! Orgies, Sabbaths, pagan ceremonies, gris–gris. Coitus is an occasion to invoke the family gods. It is a sacred act, pure and absolute, bringing invisible forces into action. What is one to think of all these manifestations, of all these initiations, and of all these workings? From every direction I am assaulted by the obscenity of the dances and propositions. Close by, a song rings out:

> Our hearts once burned hot
> Now they are cold
> All we think of is Love
> On our return to the village
> When we meet a huge phallus
> Oh! Then we shall make love
> For our sex will be dry and clean.[12]

The ground, up till now a bridled steed, begins to rock with laughter. Are these nymphomaniacs virgins? Black magic, primitive mentality, animism and animal eroticism – all this surges toward me. All this typifies people who have not kept pace with the evolution of humanity. Or, if you prefer, they constitute third-rate humanity. Having reached this point, I was long reluctant to commit myself. Then even the stars became aggressive. I had to choose. What am I saying? I had no choice.

Yes, we niggers are backward, naive, and free. For us the body is not in opposition to what you call the soul. We are in the world. And long live the bond between Man and the Earth! Moreover, our writers have helped me to convince you that your white civilization lacks a wealth of subtleness and sensitivity. Listen:

Emotive sensitivity. *Emotion is Negro as reason is Greek.*[13] Water wrinkled by every breeze? Soul exposed beaten by the winds whose fruit often drops before maturity? Yes, in one sense, the black man today is richer *in gifts than in works*.[14] But the tree thrusts its roots into the earth. The river runs deep, churning precious specks of gold. And the African-American poet, Langston Hughes, sings:

> I have known rivers
> Ancient dark rivers
> My soul has grown deep
> Like the deep rivers.

The very nature of the black man's emotion and sensitivity, moreover, explains his attitude confronted with objects perceived with such an essential violence. It's a need for uninhibitedness, an active attitude of communion, indeed identification, provided the action, I was about to say the personality of the object, is powerful. Rhythmic attitude: remember the word.[15]

So here we have the Negro rehabilitated, "standing at the helm," governing the world with his intuition, rediscovered, reappropriated, in demand, accepted; and it's not a Negro, oh, no, but the Negro, alerting the prolific antennae of the world, standing in the spotlight of the world, spraying the world with his poetical power, "porous to every breath in the world." I embrace the world! I am the world! The white man has never understood this magical substitution. The white man wants the world; he wants it for himself. He discovers he is the predestined master of the world. He enslaves it. His relationship with the world is one of appropriation. But there are values that can be served only with my sauce. As a magician I stole from the white man a "certain world," lost to him and his kind. When that happened the white man must have felt an aftershock he was unable to identify, being unused to such reactions. The reason was that above the objective world of plantations and banana and rubber trees, I had subtly established the real world.

The essence of the world was my property. Between the world and me there was a relation of coexistence. I had rediscovered the primordial One. My "speaking hands" tore at the hysterical throat of the world. The white man had the uncomfortable feeling that I was slipping away and taking something with me. He searched my pockets, probed the least delineated of my convolutions. There was nothing new. Obviously I must have a secret. They interrogated me; turning away with an air of mystery, I murmured:

Tokowaly, uncle, do you remember the nights gone by
When my head weighed heavy on the back of your
    patience or
Holding my hand your hand led me by shadows and
    signs
The fields are flowers of glowworms, stars hang on the
    grass and the trees
Silence is everywhere
Only the scents of the bush hum, swarms of reddish
    bees that drown the crickets' shrill sounds,
And muffled drums, the distant breathing of the night,
You Tokowaly, you listen to what cannot be heard, and
    you explain to me what the ancestors are saying in
    the sea-like serenity of the constellations,
The familiar bull, the scorpion, the leopard, the
    elephant and the fish,
And the milky brilliance of the Spirits in the shell of
    celestial infinity,
But here comes the complicity of the goddess Moon
    and the veils of the shadows fall,
Night of Africa, my black night, mystical and bright,
    black and shining.[16]

So here I was poet of the world. The white man had discovered poetry that had nothing poetic about it. The soul of the white man was corrupted, and as a friend who taught in the United States told me: "The Blacks represent a kind of insurance for humanity in the eyes of the Whites. When the Whites feel they have become too mechanized, they turn to the Coloreds and request a little human sustenance." At last I had been recognized; I was no longer a nonentity.

I was soon to become disillusioned. Momentarily taken aback, the white man explained to me that genetically I represented a phase. "Your distinctive qualities have been exhausted by us. We have had our back-to-nature mystics such as you will never have. Take a closer look at our history and you'll understand how far this

fusion has gone." I then had the feeling things were repeating themselves. My originality had been snatched from me. I wept for a long time, and then I began to live again. But I was haunted by a series of corrosive stereotypes: the Negro's sui generis smell … the Negro's sui generis good nature … the Negro's sui generis naïveté.

I tried to escape without being seen, but the Whites fell on me and hamstrung me on the left leg. I gauged the limits of my essence; as you can guess, it was fairly meager. It was here I made my most remarkable discovery, which in actual fact was a rediscovery.

In a frenzy I excavated black antiquity. What I discovered left me speechless. In his book on the abolition of slavery Schoelcher presented us with some compelling arguments. Since then, Frobenius, Westermann, and Delafosse, all white men, have voiced their agreement: Segu, Djenné, cities with over 100,000 inhabitants; accounts of learned black men (doctors of theology who traveled to Mecca to discuss the Koran). Once this had been dug up, displayed, and exposed to the elements, it allowed me to regain a valid historic category. The white man was wrong, I was not a primitive or a subhuman; I belonged to a race that had already been working silver and gold 2,000 years ago. And then there was something else, something the white man could not understand. Listen:

What sort of people were these, then, who had been torn away from their families, their country, and their gods with a savagery unparalleled in history?

Gentle people, polite, considerate, unquestionably superior to those who tortured them, that pack of adventurers who smashed, raped, and insulted Africa the better to loot her.

They knew how to erect houses, administer empires, build cities, cultivate the land, smelt iron ore, weave cotton, and forge steel.

Their religion had a beauty of its own, based on mysterious contacts with the city's founder. Their customs were agreeable, built on solidarity, goodwill, and respect for age.

No coercion, but mutual aid, the joy of living, and freely consented discipline.

Order – strength – poetry and liberty.

From the untroubled private citizen to the almost mythical leader there was an unbroken chain of understanding and trust. No science? Yes of course there was, but they had magnificent myths to protect them from fear where the keenest of observations and the boldest of imagination harmonized and fused. No art? They had their magnificent sculpture where human emotion exploded so violently that it set in motion, according to the haunting laws of rhythm, the elements invoked to capture and redistribute the most secret forces of the universe.[17]

Monuments in the very heart of Africa? Schools? Hospitals? Not a single bourgeois in the twentieth century, no Durand, no Smith or Brown even suspects that such things existed in Africa before the Europeans came. ...

But Schoelcher signals their presence as recorded by Caillé, Mollien, and the Cander brothers. And although he mentions nowhere that when the Portuguese landed on the shores of the Congo in 1498, they discovered a rich and flourishing state and that the elders at the court of Ambasse were dressed in silks and brocade, at least he knows that Africa raised itself to a legal notion of state, and midway through this century of imperialism he hints that after all European civilization is but one among many – and not the most merciful.[18]

I put the white man back in his place; emboldened, I jostled him and hurled in his face: accommodate me as I am; I'm not accommodating anyone. I snickered to my heart's delight. The white man was visibly growling. His reaction was a long time coming. I had won. I was overjoyed.

"Lay aside your history, your research into the past, and try to get in step with our rhythm. In a society such as ours, industrialized to the extreme, dominated by science, there is no longer room for your sensitivity. You have to be tough to be able to live. It is no longer enough to play ball with the world; you have to master it with integrals and atoms. Of course, they will tell me, from time to time when we are tired of all that concrete, we will turn to you as our children, our naive, ingenuous, and spontaneous children. We will turn to you as the childhood of the world. You are so authentic in your life, so playful. Let us forget for a few moments our formal, polite civilization and bend down over those heads, those adorable expressive faces. In a sense, you reconcile us with ourselves."

So they were countering my irrationality with rationality, my rationality with the "true rationality." I couldn't hope to win. I tested my heredity. I did a complete checkup of my sickness. I wanted to be typically black – that was out of the question. I wanted to be white – that was a joke. And when I tried to claim my negritude intellectually as a concept, they snatched it away from me. They proved to me that my reasoning was nothing but a phase in the dialectic:

> But there is something more serious. The Negro, as we have said, creates an anti-racist racism. He does not at all wish to dominate the world; he wishes the abolition of racial privileges wherever they are found; he affirms his solidarity with the oppressed of all colors. At a blow the subjective, existential, ethnic notion of *Negritude* "passes," as Hegel would say, into the objective, positive, exact notion of the *proletariat*. "For Césaire," says Senghor, "the 'White' symbolizes capital as the Negro, labor. ... Among the black men of his race, it is the struggle of the world proletariat which he sings."
>
> This is easier to say than work out. And without doubt it is not by hazard that the most ardent of apostles of Negritude are at the same time militant Marxists.
>
> But nevertheless the notion of race does not intersect with the notion of class: the one is concrete and particular, the other is universal and abstract; one resorts to that which Jaspers names comprehension and the other to intellection; the first is the product of a psycho-biological syncretism and the other is a methodical construction emerging from experience. In fact, Negritude appears as the weak stage of a dialectical progression: the theoretical and practical affirmation of white supremacy is the thesis; the position of Negritude as antithetical value is the moment of negativity. But this negative moment is not sufficient in itself and the Blacks who employ it well know it; they know that it serves to pave the way for the synthesis or the realization of the human society without race. Thus Negritude is dedicated to its own destruction, it is transition and not result, a means and not the ultimate goal.[19]

When I read this page, I felt they had robbed me of my last chance. I told my friends: "The generation of young black poets has just been dealt a fatal blow." We had appealed to a friend of the colored peoples, and this friend had found nothing better to do than demonstrate the relativity of their action. For once this friend, this born Hegelian, had forgotten that consciousness needs to get lost in the night of the absolute, the only condition for attaining self-consciousness. To counter rationalism he recalled the negative side, but he forgot that this negativity draws its value from a virtually substantial absoluity. Consciousness committed to experience knows nothing, has to know nothing, of the essence and determination of its being.

Black Orpheus marks a date in the intellectualization of black *existence*. And Sartre's mistake was not only to seek the source of the spring, but in a certain way to drain the spring dry.

Will the source of Poetry silence itself? Or indeed will the great black river, despite all, color the sea into which it flows? No matter; to each epoch its poetry, for each epoch the circumstances of history elect a nation, a race, a class, to seize again the torch, by creating situations which can express or surpass themselves only through Poetry. At times the poetic élan coincides with the revolutionary élan and at times they diverge. Let us salute today the historic chance which will permit the Blacks to "raise the great Negro shout with a force that will shake the foundations of the world" (Césaire).[20]

And there you have it; I did not create a meaning for myself; the meaning was already there, waiting. It is not as the wretched nigger, it is not with my nigger's teeth, it is not as the hungry nigger that I fashion a torch to set the world alight; the torch was already there, waiting for this historic chance.

In terms of consciousness, black consciousness claims to be an absolute density, full of itself, a stage pre-existent to any opening, to any abolition of the self by desire. In his essay Jean-Paul Sartre has destroyed black impulsiveness. He should have opposed the unforeseeable to historical destiny. I needed to lose myself totally in negritude. Perhaps one day, deep in this wretched romanticism …

In any case *I needed* not to know. This struggle, this descent once more, should be seen as a completed aspect. There is nothing more disagreeable than to hear: "You'll change, my boy; I was like that too when I was young. … You'll see, you'll get over it."

The dialectic that introduces necessity as a support for my freedom expels me from myself. It shatters my impulsive position. Still regarding consciousness, black consciousness is immanent in itself. I am not a potentiality of something; I am fully what I am. I do not have to look for the universal. There's no room for probability inside me. My black consciousness does not claim to be a loss. It *is*. It merges with itself.

[…]

Notes

1   Jean Lhermitte, *L'image de notre corps* (Éditions de la Nouvelle Revue Critique), p. 17.
2   Sir Alan Burns, *Colour Prejudice* (Allen and Unwin, London, 1948), p. 16.
3   *Anti-Semite and Jew*, pp. 112–13.
4   Ibid., p. 115.
5   Jon Alfred Mjoen, "Harmonic and Disharmonic Race-Crossings," Second International Congress of Eugenics (1921), *Eugenics in Race and State*, vol. 2, p. 60, quoted in Burns, op. cit., p. 120.
6   Translator's note: In English in the original.
7   Senghor, "Ce que l'homme noir apporte," *L'Homme de couleur*, pp. 309–10.
8   Césaire, *Notebook of a Return to My Native Land*, trans. Rosello and Pritchard, pp. 110–14.
9   Ibid., p. 115.
10 Ibid.
11 De Pédrals, *La vie sexuelle en Afrique noire* (Payot), p. 83.
12 A. M. Vergiat, *Les rites secrets des primitifs de l'Oubangui* (Payot, Paris, 1951), p. 113.
13 My italics.
14 My italics.
15 Senghor, op. cit., p. 205.
16 Senghor, *Chants d'ombre* (Éditions du Seuil, 1945).
17 Aimé Césaire, Introduction to Victor Schoelcher, *Esclavage et colonisation*, p. 7.
18 Ibid., p. 8.
19 Jean-Paul Sartre, *Orphée Noir*, preface to *Anthologie de la nouvelle poésie nègre et malgache*, translated by S. W. Allen as *Black Orpheus* (Présence Africaine, Paris, 1976), pp. 59–60.
20 Ibid., p. 65.

37

"The Instance of the Letter in the Unconscious, or Reason since Freud" (1957) *from 2nd stage of Lacan*.

Jacques Lacan

"Of Children Who Are Wrapped in Swaddling Bands"
O cities of the sea, I behold in you your citizens, women as well as men,
tightly bound with stout bonds around their arms and legs by folk who will
have no understanding of [y]our speech; and you will only be able to give
vent to your griefs and sense of loss of liberty by making tearful complaints,
and sighs, and lamentation one to another; for those who bind you will
not have understanding of your speech nor will you understand them.[1]
(Leonardo Da Vinci)

I. The Meaning of the Letter

My title conveys the fact that, beyond this speech, it is the whole structure of language that psychoanalytic experience discovers in the unconscious. This is to alert prejudiced minds from the outset that the idea that the unconscious is merely the seat of the instincts may have to be reconsidered.

But how are we to take the letter here? Quite simply, literally [*à la lettre*].

By "letter" I designate the material medium [*support*] that concrete discourse borrows from language.

This simple definition assumes that language is not to be confused with the various psychical and somatic functions that serve it in the speaking subject.

Jacques Lacan, "The Instance of the Letter in the Unconscious, or Reason since Freud," pp. 413–28, 429–41 from *Écrits*, trans. Bruce Fink. New York: Norton, 2006.

The primary reason for this is that language, with its structure, exists prior to each subject's entry into it at a certain moment in his mental development.

Let us note that, although the deficits of aphasia are caused by purely anatomical lesions in the cerebral systems that provide the mental center for these functions, they prove, on the whole, to be distributed between the two aspects of the signifying effect of what I am calling here "the letter" in the creation of signification.[2] This point will become clearer in what follows.

And the subject, while he may appear to be the slave of language, is still more the slave of a discourse in the universal movement of which his place is already inscribed at his birth, if only in the form of his proper name.

Reference to the experience of the community as the substance of this discourse resolves nothing. For this experience takes on its essential dimension in the tradition established by this discourse. This tradition, long before the drama of history is inscribed in it, grounds the elementary structures of culture. And these very structures display an ordering of exchanges which, even if unconscious, is inconceivable apart from the permutations authorized by language.

With the result that the ethnographic duality of nature and culture is giving way to a ternary conception of the human condition – nature, society, and culture – the last term of which may well be reduced to language, that is, to what essentially distinguishes human society from natural societies.

But I shall neither take sides here nor take this as a point of departure, leaving to their own obscurity the original relations between the signifier and labor. To settle accounts with the general function *of praxis* in the genesis of history by way of a quip, I will confine myself to mentioning that the very society that wished to restore the hierarchy responsible for the relations between production and ideological superstructures to its rightful political place, alongside the privilege of the producers, has nevertheless failed to give birth to an Esperanto whose relations to socialist reality [*réel*] would have ruled out from the start any possibility of literary formalism.[3]

For my part, I will put my faith in only those premises whose value has already been proven, in that they have allowed language to attain the status in experience of a scientific object.

This is what permits linguistics[4] to present itself in the pilot position in this domain, around which a reclassification of the sciences is signaling, as is usually the case, a revolution in knowledge; only the necessities of communication have made me term this domain [...] "the sciences of man" – despite the confusion that may hide behind it.

To pinpoint the emergence of the discipline of linguistics, I will say that, as in the case of every science in the modern sense, it consists in the constitutive moment of an algorithm that grounds it. This algorithm is the following:

[handwritten: or original algorithm of Linguistics as science.]

$$\frac{S}{s}$$

It is read as follows: signifier over signified, "over" corresponding to the bar separating the two levels.

The sign written in this way should be attributed to Ferdinand de Saussure, although it is not reduced to this exact form in any of the numerous schemas in which it appears in the printed version of the various lectures from the three courses he gave in 1906–7, 1908–9, and 1910–11, which a group of his devoted disciples collected under the title, *Cours de linguistique générale* – a publication of prime importance for the transmission of a teaching worthy of the name, that is, that one can stop only on its own movement.

This is why it is legitimate for us to credit him for the formalization $\frac{S}{s}$, which characterizes the modern stage of linguistics, despite the diversity between schools of linguistics.

The major theme of this science is thus based, in effect, on the primordial position of the signifier and the signified as distinct orders initially separated by a barrier resisting signification.

This is what makes possible an exact study of the connections characteristic of the signifier, and of the magnitude of their function in generating the signified.

For this primordial distinction goes well beyond the debate over the arbitrariness of the sign, such as it has been elaborated since the reflections of Antiquity, and even beyond the impasse, already sensed at that time, which opposed the one-to-one correspondence between word and thing, even in the act of naming – despite the appearances suggested by the role imputed to the index finger pointing to an object as an infant learns its mother tongue, or in the use of so-called concrete academic methods in the study of foreign languages [*langues*].

We can take things no further along this path than to demonstrate that no signification can be sustained except by reference to another signification.[5] This ultimately leads us to the remark that there is no existing language [*langue*] whose ability to cover the field of the signified can be called into question, one of the effects of its existence as a language [*langue*] being that it fulfills all needs there. Were we to try to grasp the constitution of the object in language, we could but note that this constitution is found only at the level of the concept – which is very different from any nominative – and that the *thing* [*chose*], when quite obviously reduced to the noun, splits into the double, divergent ray of

Subjectivity

the cause in which the thing has taken shelter in French, and of the nothing [*rien*] to which the thing has abandoned its Latin dress (*rem*).

These considerations, as existent as they may be to philosophers, divert us from the locus whence language questions us about its very nature. And we will fail to sustain this question as long as we have not jettisoned the illusion that the signifier serves [*répond à*] the function of representing the signified, or better, that the signifier has to justify [*répondre de*] its existence in terms of any signification whatsoever.

For even if it is reduced to this latter formulation, the heresy is the same – the heresy that leads logical positivism in search of the "meaning of meaning," as its objective is called in the language [*langue*] in which its devotees snort. It can be seen here how this sort of analysis can reduce the text the most highly charged with meaning to insignificant trifles. Only mathematical algorithms resist this process; they are considered to be devoid of meaning, as they should be.[6]

The fact remains that if we were able to subtract solely the notion of the parallelism of its upper and lower terms from the algorithm $\frac{S}{s}$, each term only being taken globally, it would remain the enigmatic sign of a total mystery. Which, of course, is not the case.

In order to grasp its function, I will begin by reproducing the faulty illustration by which its usage is classically introduced:

TREE

We can see here how it lends itself to the kind of direction indicated above as erroneous.

In my lecture, I replaced this illustration with another, which can be considered more correct only because it exaggerates in the incongruous dimension psychoanalysts have not yet altogether given up, because of their justified sense that their conformism derives its value from it alone. Here is the other illustration:

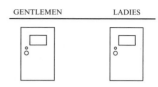

GENTLEMEN   LADIES

Here we see that, without greatly extending the scope of the signifier involved in the experiment – that is, by simply doubling the nominal type through the mere juxtaposition of two terms whose complementary meanings would seem to have to reinforce each other – surprise is produced by the precipitation of an unexpected meaning: the image of two twin doors that symbolize, with the private stall offered Western man for the satisfaction of his natural needs when away from home, the imperative he seems to share with the vast majority of primitive communities that subjects his public life to the laws of urinary segregation.

The point is not merely to silence the nominalist debate with a low blow, but to show how the signifier in fact enters the signified – namely, in a form which, since it is not immaterial, raises the question of its place in reality. For in having to move closer to the little enamel plaques that bear it, the squinting gaze of a near-sighted person might be justified in wondering whether it is indeed here that we must see the signifier, whose signified would in this case be paid its last respects by the solemn procession in two lines from the upper nave.

But no contrived example can be as telling as what is encountered in the lived experience of truth. Thus I have no reason to be unhappy I invented the above, since it awoke in the person the most worthy of my trust a childhood memory which, having come serendipitously to my attention, is best placed here.

A train arrives at a station. A little boy and a little girl, brother and sister, are seated across from each other in a compartment next to the outside window that provides a view of the station platform buildings going by as the train comes to a stop. "Look," says the brother, "we're at Ladies!" "Imbecile!" replies his sister, "Don't you see we're at Gentlemen."

Aside from the fact that the rails in this story materialize the bar in the Saussurian algorithm in a form designed to suggest that its resistance may be other than dialectical, one would have to be half-blind to be confused as to the respective places of the signifier and the signified here, and not to follow from what radiant center the signifier reflects its light into the darkness of incomplete significations.

For the signifier will raise Dissension that is merely animal in kind, and destined to the natural fog of forgetfulness, to the immeasurable power of ideological warfare, which is merciless to families and a torment to the gods. To these children, Gentlemen and Ladies will henceforth be two homelands toward which each of their souls will take flight on divergent wings, and regarding which it will be all the more impossible for them to reach an agreement since, being in fact the same homeland, neither can give ground regarding the one's unsurpassed excellence without detracting from the other's glory.

Let us stop there. It sounds like the history of France. Which it is more humane to recall here, and rightly so, than that of England, destined to flip from the Large to the Small End of Dean Swift's egg.

It remains to be grasped up what steps and down what corridor the S of the signifier, visible here in the plurals [hommes and dames] by which it focuses its welcome beyond the train window, must pass to impress its curves upon the ducts by which – like hot air and cold air – indignation and scorn hiss on this side.

One thing is certain: this access must not, in any case, carry any signification with it if the algorithm, $\frac{S}{s}$, with its bar is appropriate to it. For insofar as the algorithm itself is but a pure function of the signifier, it can reveal only a signifying structure in this transfer.

Now the structure of the signifier is, as is commonly said of language, that it is articulated.

This means that its units – no matter where one begins in tracing out their reciprocal encroachments and expanding inclusions – are subject to the twofold condition of being reduced to ultimate differential elements and of combining the latter according to the laws of a closed order.

These elements, the decisive discovery of linguistics, are *phonemes*; we must not look for any *phonetic* constancy in the modulatory variability to which this term applies, but rather for the synchronic system of differential couplings that are necessary to discern vocables in a given language [*langue*]. This allows us to see that an essential element in speech itself was predestined to flow into moveable type which, in Didots or Garamonds squeezing into lower-cases, renders validly present what I call the "letter" – namely, the essentially localized structure of the signifier.

The second property of the signifier, that of combining according to the laws of a closed order, affirms the necessity of the topological substratum, of which the term I ordinarily use, "signifying chain," gives an approximate idea: links by which a necklace firmly hooks onto a link of another necklace made of links.

Such are the structural conditions that define the order of the signifier's constitutive encroachments up to the unit immediately above the sentence as grammar, and the order of the signifier's constitutive inclusions up to the verbal locution as the lexicon.

In the limits within which these two approaches to understanding linguistic usage are confined, it is easy to see that only signifier-to-signifier correlations provide the standard for any and every search for signification; this is indicated by the notion of "usage" of a taxeme or semanteme, which refers to contexts just one degree above that of the units in question.

But it is not because grammatical and lexical approaches are exhausted at a certain point that we must think that signification rules unreservedly beyond it. That would be a mistake.

For the signifier, by its very nature, always anticipates meaning by deploying its dimension in some sense before it. As is seen at the level of the sentence when the latter is interrupted before the significant term: "I'll never…," "The fact remains…," "Still perhaps …" Such sentences nevertheless make sense, and that sense is all the more oppressive in that it is content to make us wait for it.[7]

But the phenomenon is no different, which – making her appear, with the sole postponement of a "but," as comely as the Shulamite, as honest as a virtuous maiden – adorns and readies the Negress for the wedding and the poor woman for the auction block.

Whence we can say that it is in the chain of the signifier that meaning *insists*, but that none of the chain's elements *consists* in the signification it can provide at that very moment.

The notion of an incessant sliding of the signified under the signifier thus comes to the fore – which Ferdinand de Saussure illustrates with an image resembling the wavy lines of the upper and lower Waters in miniatures from manuscripts of Genesis. It is a twofold flood in which the landmarks – fine streaks of rain traced by vertical dotted lines that supposedly delimit corresponding segments – seem insubstantial.

All our experience runs counter to this, which made me speak at one point in my seminar on the psychoses of the "button ties" [*points de capiton*] required by this schema to account for the dominance of the letter in the dramatic transformation that dialogue can effect in the subject.[8]

But while the linearity that Saussure considers to be constitutive of the chain of discourse – in accordance with its emission by a single voice and with the horizontal axis along which it is situated in our writing – is in fact necessary, it is not sufficient. It applies to the chain of discourse only in the direction in which it is oriented in time, even being taken up therein as a signifying factor in all languages [*langues*] in which the time of "Peter hits Paul" is reversed when the terms are inverted.

But it suffices to listen to poetry, which Saussure was certainly in the habit of doing,[9] for a polyphony to be heard and for it to become clear that all discourse is aligned along the several staves of a musical score.

Indeed, there is no signifying chain that does not sustain – as if attached to the punctuation of each of its units – all attested contexts that are, so to speak, "vertically" linked to that point.

Thus, if we take up the word *arbre* (tree) again, this time not in its nominal isolation, but at the endpoint of one of these punctuations, we see that it is not simply because the word *barre* (bar) is its anagram that it crosses the bar of the Saussurian algorithm.

For broken down into the double specter of its vowels and consonants, it calls up – with the robur-oak [*robre*] and the plane tree [*platane*] – the significations of strength and majesty that it takes on in our flora. Tapping all the symbolic contexts in which it is used in the Hebrew of the Bible, it erects on a barren hill the shadow of the cross. Next it reduces to a capital Y, the sign of dichotomy – which, without the illustration that historiates armorials, would owe nothing to the tree, however genealogical it claims to be. Circulatory tree, arbor vitae of the cerebellum, lead tree or silver amalgam [*arbre de Diane*], crystals precipitated into a tree that conducts lightning, is it your countenance that traces our destiny for us in the fire-scorched tortoiseshell, or your flash that brings forth from an infinite night that slow change in being in the Ἐν Πάντα of language:

No! says the Tree, it says No! in the scintillating
Of its superb head

verses that I consider to be as legitimately heard in the harmonics of the tree as their reverse:

Which the storm treats universally
As it does a blade of grass.

For this modern verse is organized according to the same law of the parallelism of the signifier, whose concert governs both primitive Slavic epic poetry and the most refined Chinese poetry.

This can be seen in the common mode of beings [*l'étant*] from which the tree and the blade of grass are chosen, so that the signs of contradiction – saying "No!" and "treat as" – can come into being here, and so that, through the categorical contrast between the particularity of "superb" and the "universally" of its reduction, the indiscernible scintillating of the eternal instant may be accomplished in the condensation of *tête* (head) and *tempête* (storm).

But all this signifier can only operate, it may be objected, if it is present in the subject. I answer this objection by assuming that he has shifted to the level of the signified.

For what is important is not whether the subject know more or less about it. (If GENTLEMEN and LADIES were written in a language [*langue*] with which the little boy and girl were unfamiliar, their quarrel would simply be more exclusively a quarrel over words, but it would be no less ready to take on signification for all that.)

What this structure of the signifying chain discloses is the possibility I have – precisely insofar as I share its language [*langue*] with other subjects, that is, insofar as this language [*langue*] exists – to use it to signify *something altogether different* from what it says. This is a function of speech that is more worthy of being pointed out than that of disguising the subject's thought (which is usually indefinable) – namely, the function of indicating the place of this subject in the search for truth.

I need but plant my tree in a locution, *grimper à l'arbre*, or even project onto it the derisive light that a descriptive context gives the word, *arborer*, to not let myself be imprisoned in some sort of *communiqué* of the facts, however official it may be, and if I know the truth, convey it, despite all the censors, *between-the-lines* using nothing but the signifier that can be constituted by my acrobatics through the branches of the tree. These acrobatics may be provocative to the point of burlesque or perceptible only to the trained eye, depending on whether I wish to be understood by the many or the few.

The properly signifying function thus depicted in language has a name. We learned this name in our childhood grammar book on the last page, where the shade of Quintilian, relegated to some phantom chapter to convey final considerations on style, seemed suddenly to hasten its voice due to the threat of being cut off.

It is among the figures of style, or tropes – from which the verb "to find" [*trouver*] comes to us – that this name is, in fact, found. This name is *metonymy*.

I shall refer only to the example of it given there: "thirty sails." For the worry I felt, over the fact that the word "ship" [*bâteau*] that was hiding therein seemed to split its presence there in two by having been able to borrow its figurative sense from the very rehashing of this example, veiled [*voilait*] not so much those illustrious sails [*voiles*] as the definition they were supposed to illustrate.

The part taken for the whole – I said to myself, if the thing is supposed to be based on reality [*réel*] – leaves us with hardly any idea what we are to conclude about the size of the fleet these thirty sails are nevertheless supposed to gauge: for a ship to have but one sail is very rare indeed.

This shows that the connection between ship and sail is nowhere other than in the signifier, and that metonymy is based on the *word-to-word* nature of this connection.[10]

I shall designate as metonymy the first aspect of the actual field the signifier constitutes, so that meaning may assume a place there.

The other aspect is *metaphor*. Let me illustrate it immediately; Quillet's dictionary seemed appropriate to me to provide a sample that would not be suspected of being deliberately selected, and I didn't pursue the farce any farther than Victor Hugo's well-known verse, "His sheaf was neither miserly nor hateful …," with which I presented metaphor, when the time came for it, in my seminar on the psychoses.

Let us say that modern poetry and the Surrealist school led us to take a major step forward here by showing that any conjunction of two signifiers could just as easily constitute a metaphor, if an additional condition – that of the greatest disparity of the images signified – weren't required for the production of the poetic spark, in other words, for metaphoric creation to occur.

Of course, this radical position is based on the so-called "automatic writing" experiment, which would not have been attempted without the assurance its pioneers drew from Freud's discovery. But it remains marked by confusion because the doctrine behind it is false.

Metaphor's creative spark does not spring forth from the juxtaposition of two images, that is, of two equally actualized signifiers. It flashes between two signifiers, one of which has replaced the other by taking the other's place in the signifying chain, the occulted signifier remaining present by virtue of its (metonymic) connection to the rest of the chain.

One word for another: this is the formula for metaphor, and if you are a poet you will make it into a game and produce a continuous stream, nay, a dazzling weave of metaphors. You will, moreover, obtain the intoxicating effect of Jean Tardieu's dialogue that goes by this title, due solely to the demonstration it provides of the radical superfluousness of all signification to a perfectly convincing representation of bourgeois comedy.

In Hugo's verse, it is obvious that not the slightest light emanates from the assertion that a sheaf is neither miserly nor hateful, because it is clear that the sheaf has no more the merit than the demerit of these attributes, since miserliness and hatred, along with the sheaf, are properties of Booz, who exercises them when he uses the sheaf as he sees fit, without making his feelings known to it.

If "his sheaf" refers back to Booz, as is clearly the case nevertheless, it is because it replaces him in the signifying chain – at the very place that awaited him, because it had been raised up a step by the clearing away of miserliness and hatred. But the sheaf has thus cleared this place of Booz, ejected as he now is into the outer darkness where miserliness and hatred harbor him in the hollow of their negation.

But once *his* sheaf has thus usurped his place, Booz cannot go back to it, the slender thread of the little "his" that attaches him to it being an additional obstacle thereto, because it binds this return with a title of ownership that would detain him in the heart of miserliness and hatred. His asserted generosity is thus reduced to *less than nothing* by the munificence of the sheaf which, being drawn from nature, knows neither our reserve nor our rejections, and even in its accumulation remains prodigal by our standards.

But if, in this profusion, the giver disappears with the gift, it is only to reemerge in what surrounds the figure of speech in which he was annihilated. For it is the radiance of fecundity – which announces the surprise the poem celebrates, namely, the promise of acceding to paternity that the old man receives in a sacred context.

Thus it is between a man's proper name qua signifier and the signifier that metaphorically abolishes it that the poetic spark is produced, and it is all the more effective here in bringing about the signification of paternity in that it reproduces the mythical event through which Freud reconstructed the path along which the mystery of paternity advances in the unconscious of every man.

The structure of modern metaphor is no different. Hence the jaculation, "Love is a pebble laughing in the sun," recreates love in a dimension that I have said strikes me as tenable, as opposed to its ever imminent slippage into the mirage of some narcissistic altruism.

We see that metaphor is situated at the precise point at which meaning is produced in nonmeaning – that is, at the passage which, as Freud discovered, when crossed in the opposite direction, gives rise to the word that is "the word" ["*le mot*"] par excellence in French, the word that has no other patronage there than the signifier *esprit*[11] – and at which it becomes palpable that, in deriding the signifier, man defies his very destiny.

But to return to metonymy now, what does man find in it, if it must be more than the power to skirt the obstacles of social censure? Doesn't this form, which gives oppressed truth its field, manifest a certain servitude that is inherent in its presentation?

It's worth taking the time to read a book in which Leo Strauss, from the land that has traditionally offered asylum to those who have chosen freedom, reflects on the relations between the art of writing and persecution.[12] By honing in on the sort of connaturality that ties this art to this condition, he allows us to glimpse something that imposes its form here, in the effect of truth on desire.

But haven't we been feeling for a while now that, in following the paths of the letter to reach the Freudian truth, we are getting hot, its flames spreading all around us?

Of course, as it is said, the letter kills while the spirit gives life. I don't disagree, having had to pay homage somewhere here to a noble victim of the error of seeking in the letter, but I also ask how the spirit could live without the letter. The spirit's pretensions would nevertheless remain indisputable if the letter hadn't proven that it produces all its truth effects in man without the spirit having to intervene at all.

This revelation came to Freud, and he called his discovery the unconscious.

II. The Letter in the Unconscious

In Freud's complete works, one out of three pages presents us with philological references, one out of two pages with logical inferences, and everywhere we see a dialectical apprehension of experience, linguistic analysis becoming still more prevalent the more directly the unconscious is involved.

Thus what is at stake on every page in *The Interpretation of Dreams* is what I call the letter of discourse, in its texture, uses, and immanence in the matter in question. For this book inaugurates both Freud's work and his royal road to the unconscious. And we are informed of this by Freud, whose confession in letters to Fliess that have since been made public, when he launches this book toward us in the early days of this century,[13] merely confirms what he continued to proclaim to the end: that the whole of his discovery lies in this no-holds-barred expression of his message.

The first clause, articulated already in the introductory chapter because its exposition cannot be postponed, is that the dream is a rebus. And Freud stipulates that it must be understood quite literally [*à la lettre*], as I said earlier. This is related to the instance in the dream of the same "literating" (in other words, phonemic) structure in which the signifier is articulated and analyzed in discourse. Like the unnatural figures of the boat on the roof, or the man with a comma for a head, which are expressly mentioned by Freud, dream images are to be taken up only on the basis of their value as signifiers, that is, only insofar as they allow us to spell out the "proverb" presented by the oneiric rebus. The linguistic structure that enables us to read dreams is at the crux of the "signifierness of dreams," at the crux of the *Traumdeutung*.

Freud shows us in every possible way that the image's value as a signifier has nothing to do with its signification, giving as an example Egyptian hieroglyphics in which it would be ridiculous to deduce from the frequency in a text of a vulture (which is an aleph) or a chick (which is a vau) indicating a form of the verb "to be" and plurals, that the text has anything whatsoever to do with these ornithological specimens. Freud takes his bearings from certain uses of the signifier in this writing that are effaced in ours, such as the use of determinatives, where a categorical figure is added as an exponent to the literal figuration of a verbal term; but this is only to bring us back to the fact that we are dealing with writing where even the supposed "ideogram" is a letter.

But psychoanalysts who have no training in linguistics don't need the current confusion regarding the term "ideogram" to believe in a symbolism deriving from natural analogy, or even from instinct's coaptational image. This is so true that, apart from the French school, which attends to this, it is with a statement like "reading coffee grounds is not the same as reading hieroglyphics" that I must recall to its own principles a technique whose pathways cannot be justified unless they aim at the unconscious.

It must be said that this is admitted only reluctantly, and that the mental vice denounced above enjoys such favor that the contemporary psychoanalyst can be expected to say that he decodes before resolving to take the journey with Freud (turn at the statue of Champollion, says the guide) that is necessary for him to understand that he deciphers – the latter differing in that a cryptogram only takes on its full dimensions when it is in a lost language [*langue*].

Taking this journey simply amounts to going further in the *Traumdeutung*.

Entstellung, translated as "transposition" – which Freud shows to be the general precondition for the functioning of the dream – is what I designated earlier, with Saussure, as the sliding of the signified under the signifier, which is always happening (unconsciously, let us note) in discourse.

But the two aspects of the signifier's impact on the signified are also found here:

Verdichtung, "condensation," is the superimposed structure of signifiers in which metaphor finds its field; its name, condensing in itself the word *Dichtung*, shows the mechanism's connaturality with poetry, to the extent that it envelops poetry's own properly traditional function.

Verschiebung or "displacement" – this transfer of signification that metonymy displays is closer to the German term; it is presented, right from its first appearance in Freud's work, as the unconscious' best means by which to foil censorship.

What distinguishes these two mechanisms, which play a privileged role in the dream-work, *Traumarbeit*, from their homologous function in discourse? Nothing, except a condition imposed upon the signifying material, called *Rücksicht auf Darstellbarkeit*, which must be translated as "consideration of the means of staging" (the translation by "role of the possibility of representation" being overly approximate here). But this condition constitutes a limitation operating within the system of writing, rather than dissolving the system into a figurative semiology in which it would intersect the phenomena of natural expression. This would probably allow us to shed light on problems with certain types of pictography, which we are not justified in regarding as evolutionary stages simply because they were abandoned in writing as imperfect. Let us say, then, that dreams are like the parlor game in which each person, in turn, is supposed to get the spectators to guess some well-known saying or variant of it solely by silent gestures. The fact that dreams have speech at their disposal makes no difference since, for the unconscious, speech is but one staging element among others. It is precisely when games and dreams alike run up against the lack of taxemic material by which to represent logical relationships such as causality, contradiction, hypothesis, and so on that they prove they have to do with writing, not mime. The subtle procedures dreams end up using to represent these logical connections – in a much less artificial way than games usually employ – are taken up specifically in Freud's work, where it is once again confirmed that the dream-work proceeds in accordance with the laws of the signifier.

The rest of the dream revision is termed "second-ary" by Freud, taking on its value from what is at stake: they are fantasies or daydreams, *Tagtraum*, to use the term Freud prefers to use to situate them in their wish-fulfilling function (*Wunscherfüllung*). Given that these fantasies may remain unconscious, their distinctive feature is clearly their signification. Now, Freud tells us that their role in dreams is either to serve as signifying elements for the statement of the unconscious thought (*Traumgedanke*), or to be used in the secondary revision that occurs – that is, in a function not to be distinguished, he says, from our waking thought (*von unserem wachen Denken nicht zu unterscheiden*). No better idea of this function's effects can be given than by comparing it to patches of colorwash which, when applied here and there on a stencil, can make stick figures – which are rather unprepossessing in themselves – in a rebus or hieroglyphics look more like a painting of people.

I apologize for seeming to spell out Freud's text myself; it is not merely to show how much is to be gained by not lopping off parts of it. It is to be able to situate what has happened in psychoanalysis in terms of its earliest reference points, which are fundamental and have never been revoked.

Right from the outset, people failed to recognize the constitutive role of the signifier in the status Freud immediately assigned to the unconscious in the most precise and explicit ways.

The reason for this was twofold, the least perceived being, naturally, that this formalization was not sufficient by itself to bring people to recognize the instance of the signifier, because when the *Traumdeutung* was published it was way ahead of the formalizations of linguistics for which one could no doubt show that it paved the way by the sheer weight of its truth.

The second reason is merely the flip side of the first, for if psychoanalysts were fascinated exclusively by the significations highlighted in the unconscious, it was because these significations derived their most secret attraction from the dialectic that seemed to be immanent in them.

I demonstrated to those who attend my seminar that the apparent changes of direction or rather changes in tack along the way – that Freud, in his primary concern to ensure the survival of his discovery along with the basic revisions it imposed upon

our knowledge, felt it necessary to apply to his doctrine – were due to the need to counteract the ever-accelerating effects of this partiality.

For, I repeat, given the situation he found himself in, where he had nothing corresponding to the object of his discovery that was at the same level of scientific maturity, he at least never failed to maintain this object at the level of its ontological dignity.

The rest was the work of the gods and took such a course that analysis today finds its bearings in the imaginary forms I have just shown to be sketched out through inverse printing on the text they mutilate. It is to them that the analyst's aim now adapts, confusing them, in the interpretation of dreams, with the visionary liberation of the hieroglyphic aviary, and seeking more generally to verify the exhaustion of the analysis in a sort of "scanning"[14] of these forms wherever they appear – with the idea that they bear witness both to the exhaustion of the regressions and to the remodeling of "the object-relation" that is supposed to typify the subject.[15]

The technique that is based on such positions can give rise to many varied effects, which are quite difficult to criticize behind their therapeutic aegis. But an internal critique can emerge from the flagrant discordance between the mode of operation by which the technique legitimates itself – namely, the fundamental rule of psychoanalysis, all the instruments of which, starting with "free association," derive their justification from its inventor's conception of the unconscious – and the complete ignorance reigning there of this very conception of the unconscious. The most trenchant supporters of this technique let themselves off the hook here with a mere flourish: the fundamental rule must, they say, be observed all the more religiously since it is only the fruit of a lucky accident. In other words, Freud never really knew what he was doing.

A return to Freud's texts shows, on the contrary, the absolute coherence between his technique and his discovery, and this coherence allows us to situate his procedures at their proper level.

This is why any rectification of psychoanalysis requires a return to the truth of that discovery, which is impossible to obscure in its original moment.

For in the analysis of dreams, Freud intends to give us nothing other than the laws of the unconscious in their broadest extension. One of the reasons why dreams were the most propitious here is, Freud tells us, that they reveal these laws no less in normal subjects than in neurotics.

In neither, however, does the efficacy of the unconscious cease upon awakening. Psychoanalytic experience consists in nothing other than establishing that the unconscious leaves none of our actions outside its field. The presence of the unconscious in the psychological order – in other words, in the individual's relational functions – nevertheless deserves to be more precisely defined. It is not coextensive with that order, for we know that, while unconscious motivation manifests itself just as much in conscious psychical effects as in unconscious ones, conversely it is elementary to note that a large number of psychical effects that are legitimately designated as unconscious, in the sense of excluding the characteristic of consciousness, nevertheless bear no relation whatsoever, by their nature, to the unconscious in the Freudian sense. It is thus only due to an incorrect use of the term that "psychical" and "unconscious" in this sense are confused, and that people thus term psychical what is actually an effect of the unconscious on the soma, for example.

[…]

Is the place that I occupy as subject of the signifier concentric or eccentric in relation to the place I occupy as subject of the signified? That is the question.

The point is not to know whether I speak of myself in a way that conforms to what I am, but rather to know whether, when I speak of myself, I am the same as the self of whom I speak. And there is no reason not to bring in the term "thought" here. For Freud uses the term to designate the elements at stake in the unconscious, that is, in the signifying mechanisms I just pointed to there.

It is nonetheless true that the philosophical *cogito* is at the center of the mirage that renders modern man so sure of being himself in his uncertainties about himself, and even in the distrust he has long since learned to exercise regarding the pitfalls of pride.

Now if, turning the weapon of metonymy against the nostalgia that it serves, I stop myself from seeking any meaning beyond tautology, and if, in the name of "war is war" and "a penny's a penny," I resolve to be only what I am, how can I escape here from the obvious fact that I am in this very act?

And how – in going to the other, metaphoric, pole of the signifying quest, and dedicating myself to becoming what I am, to coming into being – can I doubt that, even if I were to lose myself there, I am there?

Now it is on these very points, where the obvious is subverted by the empirical, that the trick of the Freudian conversion lies.

This signifying game of metonymy and metaphor – up to and including its active tip [*pointe*] that "cotter-pins" my desire to a refusal of the signifier or to a lack of being, and links my fate to the question of my destiny – this game is played, in its inexorable subtlety, until the match is over, where I am not because I cannot situate myself there.

That is, it wasn't going very far to say the words with which I momentarily dumbfounded my audience: I am thinking where I am not, therefore I am where I am not thinking. These words render palpable to an attentive ear with what elusive ambiguity the ring of meaning flees from our grasp along the verbal string.

What we must say is: I am not, where I am the plaything of my thought; I think about what I am where I do not think I am thinking.

This two-sided mystery can be seen to intersect the fact that truth is evoked only in that dimension of ruse whereby all "realism" in creation derives its virtue from metonymy, as well as this other fact that access to meaning is granted only to the double elbow of metaphor, when we hold in our hand their one and only key: namely, the fact that the S and *s* of the Saussurian algorithm are not in the same plane, and man was deluding himself in believing he was situated in their common axis, which is nowhere.

At least until Freud made this discovery. For if what Freud discovered isn't precisely that, it is nothing.

The contents of the unconscious, in their deceptive ambiguity, supply us no reality in the subject more consistent than the immediate; it is from truth that they derive their virtue in the dimension of being: *Kern unseres Wesen* is Freud's own expression.

Metaphor's two-stage mechanism is the very mechanism by which symptoms, in the analytic sense, are determined. Between the enigmatic signifier of sexual trauma and the term it comes to replace in a current signifying chain, a spark flies that fixes in a symptom – a metaphor in which flesh or function is taken as a signifying element – the signification, that is inaccessible to the conscious subject, by which the symptom may be dissolved.

And the enigmas that desire – with its frenzy mimicking the gulf of the infinite and the secret collusion whereby it envelops the pleasure of knowing and of dominating in jouissance – poses for any sort of "natural philosophy" are based on no other derangement of instinct than the fact that it is caught in the rails of metonymy, eternally extending toward the *desire for something else*. Hence its "perverse" fixation at the very point of suspension of the signifying chain at which the screen-memory is immobilized and the fascinating image of the fetish becomes frozen.

There is no other way to conceive of the indestructibility of unconscious desire – given that there is no need which, when its satiation is prohibited, does not wither, in extreme cases through the very wasting away of the organism itself. It is in a kind of memory, comparable to what goes by that name in our modern thinking machines (which are based on an electronic realization of signifying composition), that the chain is found which *insists* by reproducing itself in the transference, and which is the chain of a dead desire.

It is the truth of what this desire has been in his history that the subject cries out through his symptom, as Christ said that stones themselves would have cried out, had the children of Israel not lent them their voices.

And this is also why psychoanalysis alone allows us to differentiate in memory the function of remembering. The latter, rooted in the signifier, resolves the Platonic aporias of reminiscence through the ascendancy of history in man.

One need but read *Three Essays on the Theory of Sexuality* – which is covered over for the masses by so many pseudo-biological glosses – to note that Freud has all accession to the object derive from a dialectic of return.

Having thus begun with Holderlin's νόστος, Freud arrives less than twenty years later at Kierkegaard's repetition; that is, his thought, in submitting at the outset to the humble but inflexible consequences of the talking cure alone, was never able to let go of the living servitudes that, starting from the royal principle of the Logos, led him to rethink the deadly Empedoclean antinomies.

And how, if not on the "other scene" Freud speaks of as the locus of the dream, are we to understand his recourse as a man of science to a *Deus ex machina* that is less derisory in that here it is revealed to the spectator that the machine directs the director himself? How can we fathom the fact that a scientist of the nineteenth century valued more highly than all his other works his *Totem and Taboo* – with its obscene, ferocious figure of the primordial father, who is inexhaustibly redeemed in the eternal blinding of Oedipus – before which contemporary ethnologists bow as before the development of an authentic myth, unless we realize that he had to bow to a force of evidence that went beyond his prejudices?

Similarly, the imperious proliferation of particular symbolic creations – such as what are called the sexual theories of children – which account for even the smallest details of the neurotic's compulsions, answer to the same necessities as do myths.

This is why, to bring you to the precise point of the commentary on Freud's work I am developing in my seminar, little Hans, left in the lurch at the age of five by the failings of his symbolic entourage, and faced with the suddenly actualized enigma to him of his sex and his existence, develops – under the direction of Freud and his father, who is Freud's disciple – all the possible permutations of a limited number of signifiers in the form of a myth, around the signifying crystal of his phobia.

We see here that, even at the individual level, man can find a solution to the impossible by exhausting all possible forms of the impossibilities that are encountered when the solution is put into the form of a signifying equation. This is a striking demonstration that illuminates the labyrinth of a case study which thus far has been used only as a scrap heap. It also makes us grasp that the nature of neurosis is revealed in the fact that a symptom's development is coextensive with its elimination in the treatment: whether phobic, hysterical, or obsessive, neurosis is a question that being raises for the subject "from where he was before the subject came into the world" (this subordinate clause is the very expression Freud uses in explaining the Oedipus complex to little Hans).

At stake here is the being that appears in a split second in the emptiness of the verb "to be" and, as I said, this being raises its question for the subject. What does that mean? It does not raise it *before* the subject, since the subject cannot come to the place where being raises it, but being raises it *in* the subject's *place* – in other words, being raises the question in that place *with* the subject, just as one raises a problem *with* a pen and as antiquity's man thought *with* his soul.

Freud brought the ego into his doctrine in this way, defining it by the resistances that are specific to it.[16] I have tried to get people to understand that these resistances are imaginary in nature, like the coaptational lures that ethology shows us in display or combat in animal behavior, these lures being reduced in man to the narcissistic relation introduced by Freud and elaborated by me in "The Mirror Stage." While Freud – by situating in this ego the synthesis of the perceptual functions in which the sensorimotor selections are integrated – seems to agree with the tradition that delegates to the ego the task of answering for reality, this reality is simply all the more included in the suspension of the ego.

For this ego, distinguished first for the imaginary inertias it concentrates against the message of the unconscious, operates only by covering over the displacement the subject is with a resistance that is essential to discourse as such.

This is why an exhaustion of the defense mechanisms, as palpable as Fenichel renders it in his *Problems of Psychoanalytic Technique* because he is a practitioner (whereas his whole theoretical reduction of the neuroses and psychoses to genetic anomalies in libidinal development is pure platitude), turns out to be the other side of unconscious mechanisms, without Fenichel accounting for or even realizing it. Periphrasis, hyperbaton, ellipsis, suspension, anticipation, retraction, negation, digression, and irony, these are the figures of style (Quintilian's *figurae sententiarum*), just as catachresis, litotes, antonomasia, and hypotyposis are the tropes, whose names strike me as the most appropriate ones with which to label these mechanisms. Can one see here mere manners of speaking, when it is the figures themselves that are at work in the rhetoric of the discourse the analysand actually utters?

By obstinately characterizing resistance as having an emotional permanence, thereby making it foreign

to discourse, contemporary psychoanalysts simply show that they have succumbed to one of the fundamental truths Freud rediscovered through psychoanalysis. Which is that we cannot confine ourselves to giving a new truth its rightful place, for the point is to take up our place in it. The truth requires us to go out of our way. We cannot do so by simply getting used to it. We get used to reality [*réel*]. The truth we repress.

Now it is especially necessary to the scholar, the sage, and even the quack, to be the only one who knows. The idea that deep within the simplest of souls – and, what's more, in the sickest – there is something ready to blossom is one thing. But that there may be someone who seems to know as much as them about what we ought to make of it ... come to our rescue yon categories of primitive, pre-logical, and archaic thought – nay, of magical thought, so convenient to attribute to others! It is not fitting that these country bumpkins should keep us breathless by posing enigmas to us that prove overly clever.

To interpret the unconscious as Freud did, one would have to be, as he was, an encyclopedia of the arts and muses, as well as an assiduous reader of the *Fliegende Blätter*. And the task would become no easier were we to put ourselves at the mercy of a thread spun of allusions and quotations, puns and equivocations. Must we make a career out of "antidoted fanfreluches"?

Indeed, we must resolve to do so. The unconscious is neither the primordial nor the instinctual, and what it knows of the elemental is no more than the elements of the signifier.

The three books that one might call canonical with regard to the unconscious – the *Traumdeutung*, The *Psychopathology of Everyday Life*, and *Jokes (Witz) and Their Relation to the Unconscious* – are but a web of examples whose development is inscribed in formulas for connection and substitution (though multiplied tenfold by their particular complexity, diagrams of them sometimes being provided by Freud outside the main body of the text), which are the formulas I give for the signifier in its *transference* function. For in the *Traumdeutung* it is in terms of such a function that the term *Übertragung*, or transference, which later gave its name to the mainspring of the intersubjective link between analysand and analyst, is introduced.

Such diagrams are not solely constitutive in neurosis of each of the symptoms, but they alone allow us to encompass the thematic of its course and resolution – as the major case histories provided by Freud demonstrate admirably.

To fall back on a more limited fact, but one that is more manageable as it provides a final seal with which to close these remarks, I will cite the 1927 article on fetishism and the case Freud reports there of a patient for whom sexual satisfaction required a certain shine on the nose (*Glanz auf der Nase*).[17] The analysis showed that he owed it to the fact that his early English-speaking years had displaced the burning curiosity that attached him to his mother's phallus – that is, to that eminent want-to-be, whose privileged signifier Freud revealed – into a "glance at the nose," rather than a "shine on the nose" in the forgotten language [*langue*] of his childhood.

It was the abyss, open to the thought that a thought might make itself heard in the abyss, that gave rise to resistance to psychoanalysis from the outset – not the emphasis on man's sexuality, as is commonly said. The latter is the object that has clearly predominated in literature throughout the ages. And the evolution of psychoanalysis has succeeded by a comical stroke of magic in turning it into a moral instance, the cradle and waiting area of oblativity and attraction. The soul's Platonic steed, now blessed and enlightened, goes straight to heaven.

The intolerable scandal when Freudian sexuality was not yet holy was that it was so "intellectual." It was in this respect that it showed itself to be the worthy stooge of all those terrorists whose plots were going to ruin society.

At a time when psychoanalysts are busy refashioning a right-thinking psychoanalysis, whose crowning achievement is the sociological poem of the "autonomous ego," I would like to say, to those who are listening to me, how they can recognize bad psychoanalysts: by the word they use to deprecate all research on technique and theory that furthers the Freudian experience in its authentic direction. That word is "intellectualization" – execrable to all those who, living in fear of putting themselves to the test by drinking the wine of truth, spit on men's bread, even though their spittle can never again have any effect but that of leavening.

III. The Letter, Being, and the Other

Is what thinks in my place, then, another ego? Does Freud's discovery represent the confirmation, at the level of psychological experience, of Manichaeism?[18]

There can, in fact, be no confusion on this point: what Freud's research introduced us to was not some more or less curious cases of dual personality. Even at the heroic era I have been describing – when, like animals in the age of fairy tales, sexuality spoke – the diabolical atmosphere that such an orientation might have given rise to never materialized.[19]

The goal Freud's discovery proposes to man was defined by Freud at the height of his thought in these moving terms: *Wo Es war, soll Ich werden*. Where it was, I must come into being.

This goal is one of reintegration and harmony, I might even say of reconciliation [*Versöhnung*].

But if we ignore the self's radical eccentricity with respect to itself that man is faced with – in other words, the very truth Freud discovered – we will renege on both the order and pathways of psychoanalytic mediation; we will make of it the compromise operation that it has, in effect, become – precisely what both the spirit and letter of Freud's work most repudiate. For, since he constantly points out that compromise is behind all the miseries his analysis assuages, we can say that resorting to compromise, whether explicit or implicit, disorients all psychoanalytic action and plunges it into darkness.

But neither does it suffice to rub shoulders with the moralistic tartufferies of our time or to be forever spouting forth about the "total personality" in order to have said anything articulate about the possibility of mediation.

The radical heteronomy that Freud's discovery shows gaping within man can no longer be covered over without whatever tries to hide it being fundamentally dishonest.

Which other is this, then, to whom I am more attached than to myself [*moi*], since, at the most assented to heart of my identity to myself, he pulls the strings?

His presence can only be understood in an alterity raised to the second power, which already situates him in a mediating position in relation to my own splitting from myself, as if from a semblable.

If I have said that the unconscious is the Other's discourse (with a capital O), it is in order to indicate the beyond in which the recognition of desire is tied to the desire for recognition.

In other words, this other is the Other that even my lie invokes as a guarantor of the truth in which my lie subsists.

Here we see that the dimension of truth emerges with the appearance of language.

Prior to this point, we have to admit the existence – in the psychological relation, which can be precisely isolated in the observation of animal behavior – of subjects, not because of some projective mirage, it being the psychologist's vacuous watchword to hack this phantom to pieces, but because of the manifested presence of intersubjectivity. In the animal hidden in his lookout, in the well-laid trap, in the straggler ruse by which a runaway separated from the flock throws a raptor off the scent, something more emerges than in the fascinating erection of display or combat. Yet there is nothing here that transcends the function of a lure in the service of a need, or that affirms a presence in that beyond-the-veil where the whole of Nature can be questioned about its design.

For the question to even arise (and we know that it arose for Freud in *Beyond the Pleasure Principle*), there must be language.

For I can lure my adversary with a movement that runs counter to my battle plan, and yet this movement has its deceptive effect only insofar as I actually make it for my adversary.

But in the proposals by which I initiate peace negotiations with him, what my negotiations propose is situated in a third locus which is neither my speech nor my interlocutor.

This locus is nothing but the locus of signifying convention, as is seen in the comedy of the distressed complaint of the Jew to his pal: "Why are you telling me you are going to Cracow so I'll believe you are going to Lemberg, when you really are going to Cracow?"

Of course the aforementioned flock-movement can be understood in the conventional register of a game's strategy, where it is on the basis of a rule that I deceive my adversary; but here my success is assessed as connoting betrayal – that is, it is assessed in the relationship to the Other who is the guarantor of Good Faith.

Here the problems are of an order whose heteronomy is simply ignored if it is reduced to some "awareness of others," or whatever people choose to call it. For the "existence of the other" having, not long ago, reached the ears of Midas, the psychoanalyst, through the partition that separates him from the phenomenologists' confabs, the news is now being whispered through the reeds: "Midas, King Midas, is the other of his patient. He himself said so."

What sort of breakthrough is that? The other – which other?

Which other was the young André Gide aiming at when he defied the landlady, in whose care his mother had placed him, to treat him as a responsible being by unlocking right in front of her – with a key that was fake only insofar as it opened all locks of the same kind – the lock that she herself considered to be the worthy signifier of her educational intentions? Was it she who would later intervene and to whom the child would laughingly say: "Do you really think a lousy padlock can ensure my obedience?" But by simply remaining out of sight and waiting until that evening before lecturing the kid, after giving him a suitably cold reception upon his return home, it was not simply a female other whose angry face she showed him, but another André Gide, one who was no longer really sure, either then or even later when he thought back on it, what he had wanted to do – who had been changed right down to his very truth by the doubt cast on his good faith.

Perhaps it would be worth dwelling on this realm of confusion – which is simply that in which the whole human *opera buffa* is played out – to understand the pathways by which analysis proceeds, not only to restore order here but also to instate the conditions for the possibility of its restoration.

Kern unseres Wesen, "the core of our being" – it is not so much that Freud commands us to target this, as so many others before him have done with the futile adage "Know thyself," as that he asks us to reconsider the pathways that lead to it.

Or, rather, the "this" which he proposes we attain is not a this which can be the object of knowledge, but a this – doesn't he say as much? – which constitutes my being and to which, as he teaches us, I bear witness as much and more in my whims, aberrations, phobias, and fetishes, than in my more or less civilized personage.

Madness, you are no longer the object of the ambiguous praise with which the sage furnished the impregnable burrow of his fear. And if he is, after all, not so badly ensconced there, it is because the supreme agent at work since time immemorial, digging its tunnels and maze, is reason itself, the same Logos he serves.

Then how do you explain the fact that a scholar like Erasmus, with so little talent for the "commitments" that solicited him in his age, as in any other, could hold such an eminent place in the revolution brought about by a Reformation in which man has as much of a stake in each man as in all men?

It is by touching, however lightly, on man's relation to the signifier – in this case, by changing the procedures of exegesis – that one changes the course of his history by modifying the moorings of his being.

It is precisely in this respect that anyone capable of glimpsing the changes we have lived through in our own lives can see that Freudianism, however misunderstood it has been and however nebulous its consequences have been, constitutes an intangible but radical revolution. There is no need to go seeking witnesses to the fact:[20] everything that concerns not just the human sciences, but the destiny of man, politics, metaphysics, literature, the arts, advertising, propaganda – and thus, no doubt, economics – has been affected by it.

But is this anything more than the dissonant effects of an immense truth where Freud has traced a pure path? It must be said here that a technique that takes advantage of the psychological categorization alone of its object is not following this path, as is the case of contemporary psychoanalysis apart from a return to the Freudian discovery.

Thus the vulgarity of the concepts by which its practice shows its mettle, the embroidery of Freudery [fofreudisme] which is now mere decoration, and what must be called the discredit in which it prospers, together bear witness to the fundamental repudiation of that discovery.

Through his discovery, Freud brought the border between object and being that seemed to mark the limits of science within its ambit.

This is the symptom of and prelude to a reexamination of man's situation in the midst of beings [dans l'étant], as all the postulates of knowledge have heretofore assumed it to be – but please don't be content to classify the fact that I am saying so as a case of Heideggerianism, even prefixed by a "neo-" that adds nothing to the trashy style by which it is common to spare oneself any reflection with the quip, "Separate that out for me from its mental jetsam."

When I speak of Heidegger, or rather when I translate him, I strive to preserve the sovereign signifierness of the speech he proffers.

If I speak of the letter and being, if I distinguish the other from the Other, it is because Freud suggests them to me as the terms to which resistance and transference effects refer – effects against which I have had to wage unequal battle in the twenty years that I have been engaged in the practice that we all, repeating after Freud, call impossible: that of psychoanalysis. It is also because I must help others avoid losing their way there.

It is to prevent the field they have inherited from falling fallow, and to that end to convey that if the symptom is a metaphor, it is not a metaphor to say so, any more than it is to say that man's desire is a metonymy. For the symptom *is* a metaphor, whether one likes to admit it or not, just as desire *is* a metonymy, even if man scoffs at the idea.

Thus, if I am to rouse you to indignation over the fact that, after so many centuries of religious hypocrisy and philosophical posturing, no one has yet validly articulated what links metaphor to the question of being and metonymy to its lack, something of the object of this indignation must still be there – something that, as both instigator and victim, corresponds to it: namely, the man of humanism and the irremediably contested debt he has incurred against his intentions.

Notes

1   *Codice Atlantico*, 145. r. a., trans. Louise Servicen (Paris: Gallimard), vol. II, p. 400.
2   This point – so useful in overturning the concept of "psychological function," which obscures everything related to the matter – becomes clear as day in the purely linguistic analysis of the two major forms of aphasia

classified by one of the leaders of modern linguistics, Roman Jakobson. See the most accessible of his works (coauthored by Morris Halle), *Fundamentals of Language* ('s Gravenhage and New York: Mouton, 1956), part II, chapters 1 to 4; see too the collection of translations into French of his works that we owe to Nicolas Ruwet, *Essais de linguistique générale* (Paris: Minuit, 1963).

3 Recall that discussion about the need for a new language in communist society really did take place, and that Stalin, much to the relief of those who lent credence to his philosophy, put an end to it as follows: language is not a superstructure.

4 By "linguistics" I mean the study of existing languages [*langues*] as regards their structure and the laws they reveal; this does not include the theory of abstract codes (incorrectly placed under the heading of communication theory), so-called information theory (originating in physics), or any more or less hypothetically generalized semiology.

5 Cf. St. Augustine's *De Magistro*; I analyzed the chapter "De significatione locutionis" in my seminar on June 23, 1954.

6 Thus I. A. Richards, author of a book about procedures appropriate for reaching this objective, shows us their application in another book. He selects for his purposes a page from Meng Tzu (Mencius, to the Jesuits) and calls the piece *Mencius on the Mind*, given its object. The guarantees provided of the purity of the experiment are nothing compared to the luxury of the approaches employed. And the man of letters, an expert on the traditional Canon that contains the text, is met right on the spot in Peking where our demonstration-model wringer has been transported, regardless of the cost.

But we will be no less transported, though less expensively, upon witnessing the transformation of a bronze, which gives off bell-tones at the slightest contact with thought, into a rag with which to wipe clean the slate of the most depressing British psychologism. And not, alas, without quickly dentifying it with the author's own brain – all that remains of his object or of him after he has exhausted the meaning [*sens*] of the one and the common sense of the other.

7 It is in this respect that verbal hallucination, when it takes this form, sometimes opens a door that communicates with the Freudian structure of psychosis – a door which was hitherto missed since it went unnoticed (see my Seminar from 1955–6).

8 I did so on June 6, 1956, taking as an example the first scene of *Athaliah*, incited, I confess, by an allusion – made in passing by a highbrow critic in *The New Statesman and Nation* – to the "supreme bitchery" of Racine's heroines, designed to dissuade us from making reference to Shakespeare's savage tragedies, which has become compulsory in analytic circles where such references serve to whitewash the vulgarity of Philistinism.

9 (Added in 1966:) The publication by Jean Starobinski, in *Le Mercure de France* (February 1964), of the notes left by Saussure on anagrams and their hypogrammatical use, from the Saturnine verses to the writings of Cicero, provide the corroboration I didn't have at the time.

10 I pay homage here to what this formulation owes to Roman Jakobson, that is, to his written work, in which a psychoanalyst can always find something to structure his own experience, and which renders superfluous the "personal communications" that I could tout as much as anyone else.

Indeed, one can recognize in such oblique forms of allegiance the style of that immortal couple, Rosencrantz and Guildenstern, who are a set that cannot be broken up, not even by the imperfection of their destiny, for it lasts by the same method as Jeannot's knife, and for the very reason for which Goethe praised Shakespeare for presenting the character in their doublet: all by themselves they are the whole *Gesellschaft*, Society in a nutshell (*Wilhelm Meisters Lehrjahre*, Vol. 5, ed. Trunz [Hamburg: Christian Wegner Verlag], p. 299) – I mean the International Psychoanalytical Association.

(We should extract the whole passage from Goethe: Dieses leise Auftreten, dieses Schmiegen und Biegen, dies Jasagen, Streicheln und Schmeicheln, dieses Behendigkeit, dies Schwänzein, diese Allheit und Leerheit, diese rechtliche Schurkerei, diese Unfähigleit, wie kann sie durch einen Menschen ausgedruckt werden? Es sollten ihrer wenigstens ein Dutzend sein, wenn man sie haben könnte; denn sie bloss in Gesellschaft etwas, sie sind die Gesellschaft.)

Let us be grateful, in this context, to the author of "Some Remarks on the Role of Speech in Psycho-Analytic Technique" (*IJP* XXXVII, 6 [1956]: 467) for taking the trouble to point out that his remarks are "based on" work by him that dates back to 1952. This no doubt explains why he has assimilated nothing of the work published since then, but which he is nevertheless aware of since he cites me as its publisher (*sic*. I know what "editor" means).

11 *Esprit* is clearly the equivalent of the German *Witz* with which Freud marked the aim of his third fundamental book on the unconscious. The far greater difficulty of finding an equivalent in English is instructive: "wit," weighed down by a discussion running from Davenant and Hobbes to Pope and Addison, left its essential

virtues to "humor," which is something else. The only other choice is "pun," but its meaning is too narrow.

12 Leo Strauss, *Persecution and the Art of Writing* (Glencoe, Illinois: The Free Press, 1957).

13 See the correspondence, in particular, letters 107 and 119 selected by its editors.

14 This is the procedure by which a study ensures results through a mechanical exploration of the entire extent of its object's field.

15 (Added in 1966:) By referring only to the development of the organism, the typology neglects the structure in which the subject is caught up in fantasy, the drive, and sublimation, respectively. I am currently developing the theory of this structure.

16 (Added in December 1968:) This and the next paragraph were rewritten solely to achieve greater clarity of expression.

17 "Fetischismus," *GW* XIV, 311.

18 One of my colleagues went as far as this thought in wondering if the id (*Es*) of Freud's last doctrine wasn't in fact the "bad ego." (Added in 1966:) You see the kind of people I had to work with.

19 Note, nevertheless, the tone with which people spoke in that period of the impish pranks of the unconscious: *Der Zufall und die Koboldstreiche des Unbewussten* ("Chance and the Impish Pranks of the Unconscious"), one of Silberer's titles, which would be absolutely anachronistic in the present context of soul-managers.

20 I'll highlight the most recent in what flowed quite smoothly from François Mauriac's pen, in the *Figaro littéraire* on May 25, by way of an apology for refusing "to tell us his life story." If one can no longer undertake to do this with the old enthusiasm, the reason, he tells us, is that, "for half a century, Freud, whatever we may think of him," has left his mark there. And after briefly yielding to the received idea that it would be to submit to the "history of our body," Mauriac quickly returns to what his writer's sensibility could not help but let slip out: our discourse, in endeavoring to be complete, would publish the deepest confessions of the souls of all our loved ones.

38

"This Sex Which Is Not One" (1977)

Luce Irigaray

Female sexuality has always been conceptualized on the basis of masculine parameters. Thus the opposition between "masculine" clitoral activity and "feminine" vaginal passivity, an opposition which Freud – and many others – saw as stages, or alternatives, in the development of a sexually "normal" woman, seems rather too clearly required by the practice of male sexuality. For the clitoris is conceived as a little penis pleasant to masturbate so long as castration anxiety does not exist (for the boy child), and the vagina is valued for the "lodging" it offers the male organ when the forbidden hand has to find a replacement for pleasure-giving.

In these terms, woman's erogenous zones never amount to anything but a clitoris-sex that is not comparable to the noble phallic organ, or a hole-envelope that serves to sheathe and massage the penis in intercourse: a non-sex, or a masculine organ turned back upon itself, self-embracing.

About woman and her pleasure, this view of the sexual relation has nothing to say. Her lot is that of "lack," "atrophy" (of the sexual organ), and "penis envy," the penis being the only sexual organ of recognized value. Thus she attempts by every means available to appropriate that organ for herself: through her somewhat servile love of the father-husband capable of giving her one, through her desire for a child-penis, preferably a boy, through access to the cultural values still reserved by right to males alone and therefore always masculine, and so on. Woman lives her own desire only as the expectation that she may at last come to possess an equivalent of the male organ.

Yet all this appears quite foreign to her own pleasure, unless it remains within the dominant phallic economy. Thus, for example, woman's autoeroticism is very different from man's. In order to touch himself, man needs an instrument: his hand, a woman's body, language … And this self-caressing requires at least a minimum of activity. As for woman, she touches herself in and of herself without any need for mediation, and before there is any way to distinguish activity from passivity. Woman "touches herself" all the time, and moreover no one can forbid her to do so, for her genitals are formed of two lips in continuous contact. Thus, within herself, she is already two – but not divisible into one(s) – that caress each other.

This autoeroticism is disrupted by a violent break-in: the brutal separation of the two lips by a violating penis, an intrusion that distracts and deflects the woman from this "self-caressing" she needs if she is not to incur the disappearance of her own pleasure in sexual relations. If the vagina is to serve *also*, but *not only*, to take over for the little boy's hand in order to assure an articulation between autoeroticism and heteroeroticism in intercourse (the encounter with the totally other always signifying death), how, in the classic representation of sexuality, can the perpetuation of autoeroticism for woman be managed? Will woman not be left with the impossible alternative between a defensive virginity, fiercely turned in upon itself, and a body open to penetration that no longer knows, in this "hole" that constitutes its sex, the pleasure of its own touch? The more or less exclusive – and highly anxious – attention paid to erection in Western sexuality proves to what extent the imaginary that governs it is foreign to the feminine. For the most part, this sexuality offers nothing but imperatives dictated by male rivalry: the "strongest" being the one who has the best "hard-on," the longest, the biggest, the stiffest penis, or even the one who "pees the farthest" (as in little boys' contests). Or else one finds imperatives dictated by the enactment of sadomasochistic fantasies, these in turn governed by man's relation to his mother: the desire to force entry, to penetrate, to appropriate for himself the mystery of this womb where he has been conceived, the secret of his begetting, of his "origin." Desire/need, also to make blood flow again in order to revive a very old relationship – intrauterine, to be sure, but also pre-historic – to the maternal.

Woman, in this sexual imaginary, is only a more or less obliging prop for the enactment of man's fantasies. That she may find pleasure there in that role, by proxy, is possible, even certain. But such pleasure is above all a masochistic prostitution of her body to a desire that is not her own, and it leaves her in a familiar state of dependency upon man. Not knowing what she wants, ready for anything, even asking for more, so long as he will "take" her as his "object" when he seeks his own pleasure. Thus she will not say what she herself wants; moreover, she does not know, or no longer knows, what she wants. As Freud admits, the beginnings of the sexual life of a girl child are so "obscure," so "faded with time," that one would have to dig down very deep indeed to discover beneath the traces of this civilization, of this history, the vestiges of a more archaic civilization that might give some clue to woman's sexuality. That extremely ancient civilization would undoubtedly have a different alphabet, a different language … Woman's desire would not be expected to speak the same language as man's; woman's desire has doubtless been submerged by the logic that has dominated the West since the time of the Greeks.

Within this logic, the predominance of the visual, and of the discrimination and individualization of form, is particularly foreign to female eroticism. Woman takes pleasure more from touching than from looking, and her entry into a dominant scopic economy signifies, again, her consignment to passivity: she is to be the beautiful object of contemplation. While her body finds itself thus eroticized, and called to a double movement of exhibition and of chaste retreat in order to stimulate the drives of the "subject," her sexual organ represents *the horror of nothing to see.* A defect in this systematics of representation and desire. A "hole" in its scoptophilic lens. It is already evident in Greek statuary that this nothing-to-see has to be excluded, rejected, from such a scene of representation. Woman's genitals are simply absent, masked, sewn back up inside their "crack."

This organ which has nothing to show for itself also lacks a form of its own. And if woman takes pleasure precisely from this incompleteness of form which allows her organ to touch itself over and over again, indefinitely, by itself, that pleasure is denied by a civilization that privileges phallomorphism. The value granted to the only definable form excludes the one that is in play in female autoeroticism. The *one* of form, of the individual, of the (male) sexual organ, of the proper name, of the proper meaning … supplants, while separating and dividing, that contact of *at least two* (lips) which keeps woman in touch with herself, but without any possibility of distinguishing what is touching from what is touched.

Whence the mystery that woman represents in a culture claiming to count everything, to number everything by units, to inventory everything as individualities. *She is neither one nor two.* Rigorously speaking, she cannot be identified either as one person, or as two. She resists all adequate definition. Further, she has no "proper" name. And her sexual organ, which is not *one* organ, is counted as *none.* The negative, the underside, the reverse of the only visible and morphologically designatable organ (even if the passage from erection to detumescence does pose some problems): the penis.

But the "thickness" of that "form," the layering of its volume, its expansions and contractions and even the spacing of the moments in which it produces itself as form – all this the feminine keeps secret. Without knowing it. And if woman is asked to sustain, to revive, man's desire, the request neglects to spell out what it implies as to the value of her own desire. A desire of which she is not aware, moreover, at least not explicitly. But one whose force and continuity are capable of nurturing repeatedly and at length all the masquerades of "feminity" that are expected of her.

It is true that she still has the child, in relation to whom her appetite for touch, for contact, has free rein, unless it is already lost, alienated by the taboo against touching of a highly obsessive civilization. Otherwise her pleasure will find, in the child, compensations for and diversions from the frustrations that she too often encounters in sexual relations per se. Thus maternity fills the gaps in a repressed female sexuality. Perhaps man and woman no longer caress each other except through that mediation between them that the child – preferably a boy – represents? Man, identified with his son, rediscovers the pleasure of maternal fondling; woman touches herself again by caressing that part of her body: her baby-penis-clitoris.

What this entails for the amorous trio is well known. But the Oedipal interdiction seems to be a somewhat categorical and factitious law – although it does provide the means for perpetuating the authoritarian discourse of fathers – when it is promulgated in a culture in which sexual relations are impracticable because man's desire and woman's are strangers to each other. And in which the two desires have to try to meet through indirect means, whether the archaic one of a sense-relation to the mother's body, or the present one of active or passive extension of the law of the father. These are regressive emotional behaviors, exchanges of words too detached from the sexual arena not to constitute an exile with respect to it: "mother" and "father" dominate the interactions of the couple, but as social roles. The division of labor prevents them from making love. They produce or reproduce. Without quite knowing how to use their leisure. Such little as they have, such little indeed as they wish to have. For what are they to do with leisure? What substitute for amorous resource are they to invent? Still …

Perhaps it is time to return to that repressed entity, the female imaginary. So woman does not have a sex organ? She has at least two of them, but they are not identifiable as ones. Indeed, she has many more. Her sexuality, always at least double, goes even further: it is *plural*. Is this the way culture is seeking to characterize itself now? Is this the way texts write themselves/are written now? Without quite knowing what censorship they are evading? Indeed, woman's pleasure does not have to choose between clitoral activity and vaginal passivity, for example. The pleasure of the vaginal caress does not have to be substituted for that of the clitoral caress. They each contribute, irreplaceably, to woman's pleasure. Among other caresses … Fondling the breasts, touching the vulva, spreading the lips, stroking the posterior wall of the vagina, brushing against the mouth of the uterus, and so on. To evoke only a few of the most specifically female pleasures. Pleasures which are somewhat misunderstood in sexual difference as it is imagined – or not imagined, the other sex being only the indispensable complement to the only sex.

But *woman has sex organs more or less everywhere*. She finds pleasure almost anywhere. Even if we refrain from invoking the hystericization of her entire body, the geography of her pleasure is far more diversified, more multiple in its differences, more complex, more subtle, than is commonly imagined – in an imaginary rather too narrowly focused on sameness.

"She" is indefinitely other in herself. This is doubtless why she is said to be whimsical, incomprehensible, agitated, capricious … not to mention her language, in which "she" sets off in all directions leaving "him" unable to discern the coherence of any meaning. Hers are contradictory words, somewhat mad from the standpoint of reason, inaudible for whoever listens to them with ready-made grids, with a fully elaborated code in hand. For in what she says, too, at least when she dares, woman is constantly touching herself. She steps ever so slightly aside from herself with a murmur, an exclamation, a whisper, a sentence left unfinished … When she returns, it is to set off again from elsewhere. From another point of pleasure, or of pain. One would have to listen with another ear, as if hearing *an "other meaning" always in the process of weaving itself, of embracing itself with words, but also of getting rid of words in order not to become fixed, congealed in them.* For if "she" says something, it is not, it is already no longer, identical with what she means. What she says is never identical with anything, moreover; rather, it is contiguous. *It touches (upon).* And when it strays too far from that proximity, she breaks off and starts over at "zero": her body-sex.

It is useless, then, to trap women in the exact definition of what they mean, to make them repeat (themselves) so that it will be clear; they are already elsewhere in that discursive machinery where you expected to surprise them. They have returned within themselves. Which must not be understood in the same way as within yourself. They do not have the interiority that you have, the one you perhaps suppose they have. Within themselves means *within the intimacy of that silent, multiple, diffuse touch.* And if you ask them insistently what they are thinking about, they can only reply: Nothing. Everything.

Thus what they desire is precisely nothing, and at the same time everything. Always something more and something else besides that *one* – sexual organ, for example – that you give them, attribute to them. Their desire is often interpreted, and feared, as a sort of insatiable hunger, a voracity that will swallow you whole. Whereas it really involves a different economy more than anything else, one that upsets the linearity of a project, undermines the goal-object of a desire, diffuses the polarization toward a single pleasure, disconcerts fidelity to a single discourse …

Must this multiplicity of female desire and female language be understood as shards, scattered remnants of a violated sexuality? A sexuality denied? The question has no simple answer. The rejection, the exclusion of a female imaginary certainly puts woman in the position of experiencing herself only fragmentarily, in the little-structured margins of a dominant ideology, as waste, or excess, what is left of a mirror invested by the (masculine) "subject" to reflect himself, to copy himself. Moreover, the role of "femininity" is prescribed by this masculine specula(riza)tion and corresponds scarcely at all to woman's desire, which may be recovered only in secret, in hiding, with anxiety and guilt.

But if the female imaginary were to deploy itself, if it could bring itself into play otherwise than as scraps, uncollected debris, would it represent itself, even so, in the form of *one* universe? Would it even be volume instead of surface? No. Not unless it were understood, yet again, as a privileging of the maternal over the feminine. Of a phallic maternal, at that. Closed in upon the jealous possession of its valued product. Rivaling man in his esteem for productive excess. In such a race for power, woman loses the uniqueness of her pleasure. By closing herself off as volume, she renounces the pleasure that she gets from the *non-suture of her lips:* she is undoubtedly a mother, but a virgin mother; the role was assigned to her by mythologies long ago. Granting her a certain social power to the extent that she is reduced, with her own complicity, to sexual impotence.

(Re-)discovering herself, for a woman, thus could only signify the possibility of sacrificing no one of her pleasures to another, of identifying herself with none of them in particular, *of never being simply one.* A sort of expanding universe to which no limits could be fixed and which would not be incoherence nonetheless – nor that polymorphous perversion of the child in which the erogenous zones would lie waiting to be regrouped under the primacy of the phallus.

Woman always remains several, but she is kept from dispersion because the other is already within her and is autoerotically familiar to her. Which is not to say that she appropriates the other for herself, that she reduces it to her own property. Ownership and property are doubtless quite foreign to the feminine. At least sexually. But not *nearness.* Nearness so pronounced that it makes all discrimination of identity, and thus all forms of property, impossible. Woman derives pleasure from what is *so near that she cannot have it, nor have herself.* She herself enters into a ceaseless exchange of herself with the other without any possibility of identifying either. This puts into question all prevailing economies: their calculations are irremediably stymied by woman's pleasure, as it increases indefinitely from its passage in and through the other.

However, in order for woman to reach the place where she takes pleasure as woman, a long detour by way of the analysis of the various systems of oppression brought to bear upon her is assuredly necessary. And claiming to fall back on the single solution of pleasure risks making her miss the process of going back through a social practice that *her* enjoyment requires.

For woman is traditionally a use-value for man, an exchange value among men; in other words, a commodity. As such, she remains the guardian of material substance, whose price will be established, in terms of the standard of their work and of their need/desire, by "subjects": workers, merchants, consumers. Women are marked phallically by their fathers, husbands, procurers. And this branding determines their value in sexual commerce. Woman is never anything but the locus of a more or less competitive exchange between two men, including the competition for the possession of mother earth.

How can this object of transaction claim a right to pleasure without removing her/itself from established commerce? With respect to other merchandise in the marketplace, how could this commodity maintain a relationship other than one of aggressive jealousy? How could material substance enjoy her/itself without provoking the consumer's anxiety over the disappearance of his nurturing ground? How could that exchange – which can in no way be defined in terms "proper" to woman's desire – appear as anything but a pure mirage, mere foolishness, all too readily obscured by a more sensible discourse and by a system of apparently more tangible values?

A woman's development, however radical it may seek to be, would thus not suffice to liberate woman's desire. And to date no political theory or political practice has resolved, or sufficiently taken into consideration, this historical problem, even though Marxism has proclaimed its importance. But women do not constitute, strictly speaking, a class, and their dispersion among several classes makes their political struggle complex, their demands sometimes contradictory.

There remains, however, the condition of underdevelopment arising from women's submission by and to a culture that oppresses them, uses them, makes of them a medium of exchange, with very little profit to them. Except in the quasi monopolies of masochistic pleasure, the domestic labor force, and reproduction. The powers of slaves? Which are not negligible powers, moreover. For where pleasure is concerned, the master is not necessarily well served. Thus to reverse the relation, especially in the economy of sexuality, does not seem a desirable objective.

But if women are to preserve and expand their autoeroticism, their homosexuality, might not the renunciation of heterosexual pleasure correspond once again to that disconnection from power that is traditionally theirs? Would it not involve a new prison, a new cloister, built of their own accord? For women to undertake tactical strikes, to keep themselves apart from men long enough to learn to defend their desire, especially through speech, to discover the love of other women while sheltered from men's imperious choices that put them in the position of rival commodities, to forge for themselves a social status that compels recognition, to earn their living in order to escape from the condition of prostitute … these are certainly indispensable stages in the escape from their proletarization on the exchange market. But if their aim were simply to reverse the order of things, even supposing this to be possible, history would repeat itself in the long run, would revert to sameness: to phallocratism. It would leave room neither for women's sexuality, nor for women's imaginary, nor for women's language to take (their) place.

39

"A Cyborg Manifesto" (1985)

Donna Haraway

An Ironic Dream of a Common Language for Women in the Integrated Circuit

This chapter is an effort to build an ironic political myth faithful to feminism, socialism, and materialism. Perhaps more faithful as blasphemy is faithful, than as reverent worship and identification. Blasphemy has always seemed to require taking things very seriously. I know no better stance to adopt from within the secular-religious, evangelical traditions of United States politics, including the politics of socialist-feminism. Blasphemy protects one from the moral majority within, while still insisting on the need for community. Blasphemy is not apostasy. Irony is about contradictions that do not resolve into larger wholes, even dialectically, about the tension of holding incompatible things together because both or all are necessary and true. Irony is about humour and serious play. It is also a rhetorical strategy and a political method, one I would like to see more honoured within socialist-feminism. At the centre of my ironic faith, my blasphemy, is the image of the cyborg.

A cyborg is a cybernetic organism, a hybrid of machine and organism, a creature of social reality as well as a creature of fiction. Social reality is lived social relations, our most important political construction, a world-changing fiction. The international women's

Donna Haraway, "A Cyborg Manifesto: Science, Technology, and Socialist-Feminism in the Late Twentieth Century," pp. 149–56, 161–6, 169–77, 178–81 from *Simians, Cyborgs, and Women: The Reinvention of Nature*. New York: Routledge, 1991.

movements have constructed 'women's experience', as well as uncovered or discovered this crucial collective object. This experience is a fiction and fact of the most crucial, political kind. Liberation rests on the construction of the consciousness, the imaginative apprehension, of oppression, and so of possibility. The cyborg is a matter of fiction and lived experience that changes what counts as women's experience in the late twentieth century. This is a struggle over life and death, but the boundary between science fiction and social reality is an optical illusion.

Contemporary science fiction is full of cyborgs – creatures simultaneously animal and machine, who populate worlds ambiguously natural and crafted.

Modern medicine is also full of cyborgs, of couplings between organism and machine, each conceived as coded devices, in an intimacy and with a power that was not generated in the history of sexuality. Cyborg 'sex' restores some of the lovely replicative baroque of ferns and invertebrates (such nice organic prophylactics against heterosexism). Cyborg replication is uncoupled from organic reproduction. Modern production seems like a dream of cyborg colonization work, a dream that makes the nightmare of Taylorism seem idyllic. And modern war is a cyborg orgy, coded by C3I, command-control-communication-intelligence, an $84 billion item in 1984's US defence budget. I am making an argument for the cyborg as a fiction mapping our social and bodily reality and as an imaginative resource suggesting some very fruitful couplings. Michael Foucault's biopolitics is a flaccid premonition of cyborg politics, a very open field.

By the late twentieth century, our time, a mythic time, we are all chimeras, theorized and fabricated hybrids of machine and organism; in short, we are cyborgs. Ths cyborg is our ontology; it gives us our politics. The cyborg is a condensed image of both imagination and material reality, the two joined centres structuring any possibility of historical transformation. In the traditions of 'Western' science and politics – the tradition of racist, male-dominant capitalism; the tradition of progress; the tradition of the appropriation of nature as resource for the productions of culture; the tradition of reproduction of the self from the reflections of the other – the relation between organism and machine has been a border war. The stakes in the border war have been the territories of production, reproduction, and imagination. This chapter is an argument for pleasure in the confusion of boundaries and for responsibility in their construction. It is also an effort to contribute to socialist-feminist culture and theory in a postmodernist, non-naturalist mode and in the utopian tradition of imagining a world without gender, which is perhaps a world without genesis, but maybe also a world without end. The cyborg incarnation is outside salvation history. Nor does it mark time on an oedipal calendar, attempting to heal the terrible cleavages of gender in an oral symbiotic utopia or post-oedipal apocalypse. As Zoe Sofoulis argues in her unpublished manuscript on Jacques Lacan, Melanie Klein, and nuclear culture, Lacklein, the most terrible and perhaps the most promising monsters in cyborg worlds are embodied in non-oedipal narratives with a different logic of repression, which we need to understand for our survival.

The cyborg is a creature in a post-gender world; it has no truck with bisexuality, pre-oedipal symbiosis, unalienated labour, or other seductions to organic wholeness through a final appropriation of all the powers of the parts into a higher unity. In a sense, the cyborg has no origin story in the Western sense – a 'final' irony since the cyborg is also the awful apocalyptic telos of the 'West's' escalating dominations of abstract individuation, an ultimate self united at last from all dependency, a man in space. An origin story in the 'Western', humanist sense depends on the myth of original unity, fullness, bliss and terror, represented by the phallic mother from whom all humans must separate, the task of individual development and of history, the twin potent myths inscribed most powerfully for us in psychoanalysis and Marxism. Hilary Klein has argued that both Marxism and psychoanalysis, in their concepts of labour and of individuation and gender formation, depend on the plot of original unity out of which difference must be produced and enlisted in a drama of escalating domination of woman/nature. The cyborg skips the step of original unity, of identification with nature in the Western sense. This is its illegitimate promise that might lead to subversion of its teleology as star wars.

The cyborg is resolutely committed to partiality, irony, intimacy, and perversity. It is oppositional, utopian, and completely without innocence. No longer structured by the polarity of public and private, the cyborg defines a technological polls based partly on a revolution of social relations in the oikos, the household. Nature and culture are reworked; the one can no longer be the resource for appropriation or incorporation by the other. The relationships for forming wholes from parts, including those of polarity and hierarchical domination, are at issue in the cyborg world. Unlike the hopes of Frankenstein's monster, the cyborg does not expect its father to save it through a restoration of the garden; that is, through the fabrication of a heterosexual mate, through its completion in a finished whole, a city and cosmos. The cyborg does not dream of community on the model of the organic family, this time without the oedipal project. The cyborg would not recognize the Garden of Eden; it is not made of mud and cannot dream of returning to dust. Perhaps that is why I want to see if cyborgs can subvert the apocalypse of returning to nuclear dust in the manic compulsion to name the Enemy. Cyborgs are not reverent: they do not remember the cosmos. They are wary of holism, but needy for connection – they seem to have a natural feel for united front politics, but without the vanguard party. The main trouble with cyborgs, of course, is that they are the illegitimate offspring of militarism and patriarchal capitalism, not to mention state socialism. But illegitimate offspring are often exceedingly unfaithful to their origins. Their fathers, after all, are inessential.

I will return to the science fiction of cyborgs at the end of this chapter, but now I want to signal three crucial boundary breakdowns that make the following political-fictional (political-scientific) analysis possible. By the late twentieth century in United States scientific culture, the boundary between human and animal is thoroughly breached. The last beachheads of uniqueness have been polluted if not turned into amusement parks – language tool use, social behaviour, mental events, nothing really convincingly settles the separation of human and animal. And many people no longer feel the need for such a separation; indeed, many branches of feminist culture affirm the pleasure of connection of human and other living creatures. Movements for animal rights are not irrational denials of human uniqueness; they are a clear-sighted recognition of connection across the discredited breach of nature and culture. Biology and evolutionary theory over the last two centuries have simultaneously produced modern organisms as objects of knowledge and reduced the line between humans and animals to a faint trace re-etched in ideological struggle or professional disputes between life and social science. Within this framework, teaching modern Christian creationism should be fought as a form of child abuse.

Biological-determinist ideology is only one position opened up in scientific culture for arguing the meanings of human animality. There is much room for radical political people to contest the meanings of the breached boundary.[1] The cyborg appears in myth precisely where the boundary between human and animal is transgressed. Far from signalling a walling off of people from other living beings, cyborgs signal disturbingly and pleasurably tight coupling. Bestiality has a new status in this cycle of marriage exchange.

The second leaky distinction is between animal-human (organism) and machine. Pre-cybernetic machines could be haunted; there was always the spectre of the ghost in the machine. This dualism structured the dialogue between materialism and idealism that was settled by a dialectical progeny, called spirit or history, according to taste. But basically machines were not self-moving, self-designing, autonomous. They could not achieve man's dream, only mock it. They were not man, an author to himself, but only a caricature of that masculinist reproductive dream. To think they were otherwise was paranoid. Now we are not so sure. Late twentieth-century machines have made thoroughly ambiguous the difference between natural and artificial, mind and body, self-developing and externally designed, and many other distinctions that used to apply to organisms and machines. Our machines are disturbingly lively, and we ourselves frighteningly inert.

Technological determination is only one ideological space opened up by the reconceptions of machine and organism as coded texts through which we engage in the play of writing and reading the world.[2] 'Textualization' of everything in poststructuralist, postmodernist theory has been damned by Marxists and socialist feminists for its utopian disregard for the lived relations of domination that ground the 'play' of arbitrary reading.[3] It is certainly true that postmodernist strategies, like my cyborg myth, subvert myriad organic wholes (for example, the poem, the primitive culture, the biological organism). In short, the certainty of what counts as nature – a source of insight and promise of innocence – is undermined, probably fatally. The transcendent authorization of interpretation is lost, and with it the ontology grounding 'Western' epistemology. But the alternative is not cynicism or faithlessness, that is, some version of abstract existence, like the accounts of technological determinism destroying 'man' by the 'machine' or 'meaningful political action' by the 'text'. Who cyborgs will be is a radical question; the answers are a matter of survival. Both chimpanzees and artefacts have politics, so why shouldn't we (de Waal, 1982; Winner, 1980)?

The third distinction is a subset of the second: the boundary between physical and non-physical is very imprecise for us. Pop physics books on the consequences of quantum theory and the indeterminacy principle are a kind of popular scientific equivalent to Harlequin romances [the US equivalent of Mills & Boon] as a marker of radical change in American white heterosexuality: they get it wrong, but they are on the right subject. Modern machines are quintessentially microelectronic devices: they are everywhere and they are invisible. Modern machinery is an irreverent upstart god, mocking the Father's ubiquity and spirituality. The silicon chip is a surface for writing; it is etched in molecular scales disturbed only by atomic noise, the ultimate interference for nuclear scores. Writing, power, and technology are old partners in Western stories of the origin of civilization, but miniaturization has changed our experience of mechanism. Miniaturization has turned out to be about power; small is not so much beautiful as pre-eminently dangerous, as in cruise missiles. Contrast the TV sets of the 1950s or the news cameras of the 1970s with the TV wrist bands or hand-sized video cameras now advertised. Our best machines are made of sunshine; they are all light and clean because they are nothing but signals, electromagnetic waves, a section of a spectrum, and these machines are eminently portable, mobile – a matter of immense human pain in Detroit and Singapore. People are nowhere near so fluid, being both material and opaque. Cyborgs are ether, quintessence.

The ubiquity and invisibility of cyborgs is precisely why these sunshine-belt machines are so deadly. They are as hard to see politically as materially. They are about consciousness – or its simulation.[4] They are floating signifiers moving in pickup trucks across Europe, blocked more effectively by the witch-weavings of the displaced and so unnatural Greenham women, who read the cyborg webs of power so very well, than by the militant labour of older masculinist politics, whose natural constituency needs defence jobs. Ultimately the 'hardest' science is about the realm of greatest boundary confusion, the realm of pure number, pure spirit, C3I, cryptography, and the preservation of potent secrets. The new machines are so clean and light. Their engineers are sun-worshippers mediating a new scientific revolution associated with the night dream of post-industrial society. The diseases evoked by these clean machines are 'no more' than the minuscule coding changes of an antigen in the immune system, 'no more' than the experience of stress. The nimble fingers of 'Oriental' women, the old fascination of little Anglo-Saxon Victorian girls with doll's houses, women's enforced attention to the small take on quite new dimensions in this world. There might be a cyborg Alice taking account of these new dimensions. Ironically, it might be the unnatural cyborg women making chips in Asia and spiral dancing in Santa Rita jail whose constructed unities will guide effective oppositional strategies.

So my cyborg myth is about transgressed boundaries, potent fusions, and dangerous possibilities which progressive people might explore as one part of needed political work. One of my premises is that most American socialists and feminists see deepened dualisms of mind and body, animal and machine, idealism and materialism in the social practices, symbolic formulations, and physical artefacts associated with 'high technology' and scientific culture. From *One-Dimensional Man* (Marcuse, 1964) to *The Death of Nature* (Merchant, 1980), the analytic resources developed by progressives have insisted on the necessary domination of technics and recalled us to an imagined organic body to integrate our resistance. Another of my premises is that the need for unity of people trying to resist world-wide intensification of domination has never been more acute. But a slightly perverse shift of perspective might better enable us to contest for meanings, as well as for other forms of power and pleasure in technologically mediated societies.

From one perspective, a cyborg world is about the final imposition of a grid of control on the planet, about the final abstraction embodied in a Star Wars apocalypse waged in the name of defence, about the final appropriation of women's bodies in a masculinist orgy of war (Sofia, 1984). From another perspective, a cyborg world might be about lived social and bodily realities in which people are not afraid of their joint kinship with animals and machines, not afraid of permanently partial identities and contradictory standpoints. The political struggle is to see from both perspectives at once because each reveals both dominations and possibilities unimaginable from the other vantage point. Single vision produces worse illusions than double vision or many-headed monsters. Cyborg unities are monstrous and illegitimate; in our present political circumstances, we could hardly hope for more potent myths for resistance and recoupling. I like to imagine LAG, the Livermore Action Group, as a kind of cyborg society, dedicated to realistically converting the laboratories that most fiercely embody and spew out the tools of technological apocalypse, and committed to building a political form that acutally manages to hold together witches, engineers, elders, perverts, Christians, mothers, and Leninists long enough to disarm the state. Fission Impossible is the name of the affinity group in my town. (Affinity: related not by blood but by choice, the appeal of one chemical nuclear group for another, avidiy.)[5]

Fractured Identities

It has become difficult to name one's feminism by a single adjective – or even to insist in every circumstance upon the noun. Consciousness of exclusion through naming is acute. Identities seem contradictory, partial, and strategic. With the hard-won recognition of their social and historical constitution, gender, race, and class cannot provide the basis for belief in 'essential' unity. There is nothing about being 'female' that naturally binds women. There is not even such a state as 'being' female, itself a highly complex category constructed in contested sexual scientific discourses and other social practices. Gender, race, or class consciousness is an achievement forced on us by the terrible historical experience of the contradictory social realities of patriarchy, colonialism, and capitalism. And who counts as 'us' in my own rhetoric? Which identities are available to ground such a potent political myth called 'us', and what could motivate enlistment in this collectivity? Painful fragmentation among feminists (not to mention among women) along every possible fault line has made the concept of woman elusive, an excuse for the matrix of women's dominations of each other. For me – and for many who share a similar historical location in white, professional middle-class, female, radical, North American, mid-adult bodies – the sources of a crisis in political identity are legion. The recent history for much of the US left and US feminism has been a response to this kind of crisis by endless splitting and searches for a new essential unity. But there has also been a growing recognition of another response through coalition – affinity, not identity.[6]

Chela Sandoval (n.d., 1984), from a consideration of specific historical moments in the formation of the new political voice called women of colour, has theorized a hopeful model of political identity called 'oppositional consciousness', born of the skills for reading webs of power by those refused stable membership in the social categories of race, sex, or class. 'Women of color', a name contested at its origins by those whom it would incorporate, as well as a historical consciousness marking systematic breakdown of all the signs of Man in 'Western' traditions, constructs a kind of postmodernist identity out of otherness, difference, and specificity. This postmodernist identity is fully political, whatever might be said about other possible postmodernisms. Sandoval's oppositional consciousness is about contradictory locations and heterochronic calendars, not about relativisms and pluralisms.

[...]

The Informatics of Domination

In this attempt at an epistemological and political position, I would like to sketch a picture of possible unity, a picture indebted to socialist and feminist principles of design. The frame for my sketch is set by the extent and importance of rearrangements in world-wide social relations tied to science and technology. I argue for a politics rooted in claims about fundamental changes in the nature of class, race, and gender in an emerging system of world order analogous in its novelty and scope to that created by industrial capitalism; we are living through a movement from an organic, industrial society to a polymorphous, information system – from all work to all play, a deadly game. Simultaneously material and ideological, the dichotomies may be expressed in the following chart of transitions from the comfortable old hierarchical dominations to the scary new networks I have called the informatics of domination:

Representation	Simulation
Bourgeois novel, realism	Science fiction, postmodernism
Organism	Biotic component
Depth, integrity	Surface, boundary
Heat	Noise
Biology as clinical practice	Biology as inscription
Physiology	Communications engineering
Small group	Subsystem
Perfection	Optimization
Eugenics	Population control
Decadence, *Magic Mountain*	Obsolescence, *Future Shock*
Hygiene	Stress management
Microbiology, tuberculosis	Immunology, AIDS

Organic division of labour	Ergonomics/cybernetics of labour
Functional specialization	Modular construction
Reproduction	Replication
Organic sex role specialization	Optimal genetic strategies
Biological determinism	Evolutionary inertia, constraints
Community ecology	Ecosystem
Racial chain of being	Neo-imperialism, United Nations humanism
Scientific management in home/factory	Global factory/Electronic cottage
Family/market/factory	Women in the integrated circuit
Family wage	Comparable worth
Public/private	Cyborg citizenship
Nature/culture	Fields of difference
Co-operation	Communications enhancement
Freud	Lacan
Sex	Genetic engineering
Labour	Robotics
Mind	Artificial intelligence
Second World War	Star Wars
White capitalist patriarchy	Informatics of domination

This list suggests several interesting things.[7] First, the objects on the right-hand side cannot be coded as 'natural', a realization that subverts naturalistic coding for the left-hand side as well. We cannot go back ideologically or materially. It's not just that 'god' is dead; so is the 'goddess'. Or both are revivified in the worlds charged with microelectronic and biotechnological politics. In relation to objects like biotic components, one must not think in terms of essential properties, but in terms of design, boundary constraints, rates of flows, systems logics, costs of lowering constraints. Sexual reproduction is one kind of reproductive strategy among many, with costs and benefits as a function of the system environment. Ideologies of sexual reproduction can no longer reasonably call on notions of sex and sex role as organic aspects in natural objects like organisms and families. Such reasoning will be unmasked as irrational, and ironically corporate executives reading *Playboy* and anti-porn radical feminists will make strange bedfellows in jointly unmasking the irrationalism.

Likewise for race, ideologies about human diversity have to be formulated in terms of frequencies of parameters, like blood groups or intelligence scores. It is 'irrational' to invoke concepts like primitive and civilized. For liberals and radicals, the search for integrated social systems gives way to a new practice called 'experimental ethnography' in which an organic object dissipates in attention to the play of writing. At the level of ideology, we see translations of racism and colonialism into languages of development and underdevelopment, rates and constraints of modernization. Any objects or persons can be reasonably thought of in terms of disassembly and reassembly; no 'natural' architectures constrain system design. The financial districts in all the world's cities, as well as the export-processing and free-trade zones, proclaim this elementary fact of 'late capitalism'. The entire universe of objects that can be known scientifically must be formulated as problems in communications engineering (for the managers) or theories of the text (for those who would resist). Both are cyborg semiologies.

One should expect control strategies to concentrate on boundary conditions and interfaces, on rates of flow across boundaries and not on the integrity of natural objects. 'Integrity' or 'sincerity' of the Western self gives way to decision procedures and expert systems. For example, control strategies applied to women's capacities to give birth to new human beings will be developed in the languages of population control and maximization of goal achievement for individual decision-makers. Control strategies will be formulated in terms of rates, costs of constraints, degrees of freedom. Human beings, like any other component or subsystem, must be localized in a system architecture whose basic modes of operation are probabilistic, statistical. No objects, spaces, or bodies are sacred in themselves; any component can be interfaced with any other if the proper standard, the proper code, can be constructed for processing signals in a common language. Exchange in this world transcends the universal translation effected by capitalist markets that Marx analysed so well. The privileged pathology affecting all kinds of components in this universe is stress – communications breakdown (Hogness, 1983). The cyborg is not subject to Foucault's biopolitics; the cyborg simulates politics, a much more potent field of operations.

This kind of analysis of scientific and cultural objects of knowledge which have appeared historically since the Second World War prepares us to notice some important inadequacies in feminist analysis which has proceeded as if the organic, hierarchical dualisms ordering discourse in 'the West' since Aristotle still ruled. They have been cannibalized, or as Zoe Sofia (Sofoulis) might put it, they have been 'techno-digested'. The dichotomies between mind and body, animal and human, organism and machine, public and private, nature and culture, men and women, primitive and civilized are all in question ideologically. The actual situation of women is their integration/exploitation into a world system of production/reproduction and communication called the informatics of domination. The home, workplace, market, public arena, the body itself – all can be dispersed and interfaced in nearly infinite, polymorphous ways, with large consequences for women and others – consequences that themselves are very different for different people and which make potent oppositional international movements difficult to imagine and essential for survival. One important route for reconstructing socialist-feminist politics is through theory and practice addressed to the social relations of science and technology, including crucially the systems of myth and meanings structuring our imaginations. The cyborg is a kind of disassembled and reassembled, postmodern collective and personal self. This is the self feminists must code.

Communications technologies and biotechnologies are the crucial tools recrafting our bodies. These tools embody and enforce new social relations for women world-wide. Technologies and scientific discourses can be partially understood as formalizations, i.e., as frozen moments, of the fluid social interactions constituting them, but they should also be viewed as instruments for enforcing meanings. The boundary is permeable between tool and myth, instrument and concept, historical systems of social relations and historical anatomies of possible bodies, including objects of knowledge. Indeed, myth and tool mutually constitute each other.

Furthermore, communications sciences and modern biologies are constructed by a common move – the translation of the world into a problem of coding, a search for a common language in which all resistance to instrumental control disappears and all heterogeneity can be submitted to disassembly, reassembly, investment, and exchange.

In communications sciences, the translation of the world into a problem in coding can be illustrated by looking at cybernetic (feedback-controlled) systems theories applied to telephone technology, computer design, weapons deployment, or data base construction and maintenance. In each case, solution to the key questions rests on a theory of language and control; the key operation is determining the rates, directions, and probabilities of flow of a quantity called information. The world is subdivided by boundaries differentially permeable to information. Information is just that kind of quantifiable element (unit, basis of unity) which allows universal translation, and so unhindered instrumental power (called effective communication). The biggest threat to such power is interruption of communication. Any system breakdown is a function of stress. The fundamentals of this technology can be condensed into the metaphor C3I, command-control-communication-intelligence, the military's symbol for its operations theory.

In modern biologies, the translation of the world into a problem in coding can be illustrated by molecular genetics, ecology, sociobiological evolutionary theory, and immunobiology. The organism has been translated into problems of genetic coding and read-out. Biotechnology, a writing technology, informs research broadly.[8] In a sense, organisms have ceased to exist as objects of knowledge, giving way to biotic components, i.e., special kinds of information-processing devices. The analogous moves in ecology could be examined by probing the history and utility of the concept of the ecosystem. Immunobiology and associated medical practices are rich exemplars of the privilege of coding and recognition systems as objects of knowledge, as constructions of bodily reality for us. Biology here is a kind of cryptography. Research is necessarily a kind of intelligence activity. Ironies abound. A stressed system goes awry; its communication processes break down; it fails to recognize the difference between self and other. Human babies with baboon hearts evoke national ethical perplexity – for animal rights activists at least as much as for the guardians of human purity. In the US gay men and intravenous drug users are the 'privileged' victims of an awful immune system disease that marks (inscribes on the body) confusion of boundaries and moral pollution (Treichler, 1987).

But these excursions into communications sciences and biology have been at a rarefied level; there is a mundane, largely economic reality to support my claim that these sciences and technologies indicate fundamental transformations in the structure of the world for us. Communications technologies depend on electronics. Modern states, multinational corporations, military power, welfare state apparatuses, satellite systems, political processes, fabrication of our imaginations, labour-control systems, medical constructions of our bodies, commercial pornography, the international division of labour, and religious evangelism depend intimately upon electronics. Microelectronics is the technical basis of simulacra; that is, of copies without originals.

Microelectronics mediates the translations of labour into robotics and word processing, sex into genetic engineering and reproductive technologies, and mind into artificial intelligence and decision procedures. The new biotechnologies concern more than human reproducdon. Biology as a powerful engineering science for redesigning materials and processes has revolutionary implications for industry, perhaps most obvious today in areas of fermentation, agriculture, and energy. Communications sciences and biology are constructions of natural-technical objects of knowledge in which the difference between machine and organism is thoroughly blurred; mind, body, and tool are on very intimate terms. The 'multinational' material organization of the production and reproduction of daily life and the symbolic organization of the production and reproduction of culture and imagination seem equally implicated. The boundary-maintaining images of base and superstructure, public and private, or material and ideal never seemed more feeble.

I have used Rachel Grossman's (1980) image of women in the integrated circuit to name the situation of women in a world so intimately restructured through the social relations of science and technology.[9] I used the odd circumlocution, 'the social relations of science and technology', to indicate that we are not dealing with a technological determinism, but with a historical system depending upon structured relations among people. But the phrase should also indicate that science and technology provide fresh sources of power, that we need fresh sources of analysis and political action (Latour, 1984). Some of the rearrangements of race, sex, and class rooted in high-tech-facilitated social relations can make socialist-feminism more relevant to effective progressive politics.

[…]

Women in the Integrated Circuit

Let me summarize the picture of women's historical locations in advanced industrial societies, as these positions have been restructured partly through the social relations of science and technology. If it was ever possible ideologically to characterize women's lives by the distinction of public and private domains – suggested by images of the division of working-class life into factory and home, of bourgeois life into market and home, and of gender existence into personal and political realms – it is now a totally misleading ideology, even to show how both terms of these dichotomies construct each other in practice and in theory. I prefer a network ideological image, suggesting the profusion of spaces and identities and the permeability of boundaries in the personal body and in the body politic. 'Networking' is both a feminist practice and a multinational corporate strategy – weaving is for oppositional cyborgs.

So let me return to the earlier image of the informatics of domination and trace one vision of women's 'place' in the integrated circuit, touching only a few idealized social locations seen primarily from the point of view of advanced capitalist societies: Home, Market, Paid Work Place, State, School, Clinic-Hospital, and Church. Each of these idealized spaces is logically and practically implied in every other locus, perhaps analogous to a holographic photograph. I want to suggest the impact of the social relations mediated and enforced by the new technologies in order to help formulate needed analysis and practical work. However, there is no 'place' for women in these networks, only geometries of difference and contradiction crucial to women's cyborg identities. If we learn how to read these webs of power and social life, we might learn new couplings, new coalitions. There is no way to read the following list from a standpoint of 'identification', of a unitary self. The issue is dispersion. The task is to survive in the diaspora.

Home: Women-headed households, serial monogamy, flight of men, old women alone, technology of domestic work, paid homework, re-emergence of home sweat-shops, home-based businesses and telecommuting, electronic cottage, urban homelessness, migration, module architecture, reinforced (simulated) nuclear family, intense domestic violence.

Market: Women's continuing consumption work, newly targeted to buy the profusion of new production from the new technologies (especially as the competitive race among industrialized and industrializing nations to avoid dangerous mass unemployment necessitates finding ever bigger new markets for ever less clearly needed commodities); bimodal buying power, coupled with advertising targeting of the numerous affluent groups and neglect of the previous mass markets; growing importance of informal markets in labour and commodities parallel to high-tech, affluent market structures; surveillance systems through electronic funds transfer; intensified market abstraction (commodification) of experience, resulting in ineffective utopian or equivalent cynical theories of community; extreme mobility (abstraction) of marketing/financing systems; inter-penetration of sexual and labour markets; intensified sexualization of abstracted and alienated consumption.

Paid Work Place: Continued intense sexual and racial division of labour, but considerable growth of membership in privileged occupational categories for many white women and people of colour; impact of new technologies on women's work in clerical, service, manufacturing (especially textiles), agriculture, electronics; international restructuring of the working classes; development of new time arrangements to facilitate the homework economy (flex time, part time, over time, no time); homework and out work; increased pressures for two-tiered wage structures; significant numbers of people in cash-dependent populations world-wide with no experience or no further hope of stable employment; most labour 'marginal' or 'feminized'.

State: Continued erosion of the welfare state; decentralizations with increased surveillance and control; citizenship by telematics; imperialism and political power broadly in the form of information rich/information poor differentiation; increased high-tech militarization increasingly opposed by many social groups; reduction of civil service jobs as a result of the growing capital intensification of office work, with implications for occupational mobility for women of colour; growing privatization of material and ideological life and culture; close integration of privatization and militarization, the high-tech forms of bourgeois capitalist personal and public life; invisibility of different social groups to each other, linked to psychological mechanisms of belief in abstract enemies.

School: Deepening coupling of high-tech capital needs and public education at all levels, differentiated by race, class, and gender; managerial classes involved in educational reform and refunding at the cost of remaining progressive educational democratic structures for children and teachers; education for mass ignorance and repression in technocratic and militarized culture; growing anti-science mystery cults in dissenting and radical political movements; continued relative scientific illiteracy among white women and people of colour; growing industrial direction of education (especially higher education) by science-based multinationals (particularly in electronics- and biotechnology-dependent companies); highly educated, numerous elites in a progressively bimodal society.

Clinic-hospital: Intensified machine–body relations; renegotiations of public metaphors which channel personal experience of the body, particularly in relation to reproduction, immune system functions, and 'stress' phenomena; intensification of reproductive politics in response to world historical implications of women's unrealized, potential control of their relation to reproduction; emergence of new, historically specific diseases; struggles over meanings and means of health in environments pervaded by high technology products and processes; continuing feminization of health work; intensified struggle over state responsibility for health; continued ideological role of popular health movements as a major form of American politics.

Church: Electronic fundamentalist 'super-saver' preachers solemnizing the union of electronic capital and automated fetish gods; intensified importance of churches in resisting the militarized state; central struggle over women's meanings and authority in religion;

continued relevance of spirituality, intertwined with sex and health, in political struggle.

The only way to characterize the informatics of domination is as a massive intensification of insecurity and cultural impoverishment, with common failure of subsistence networks for the most vulnerable. Since much of this picture interweaves with the social relations of science and technology, the urgency of a socialist-feminist politics addressed to science and technology is plain. There is much now being done, and the grounds for political work are rich. For example, the efforts to develop forms of collective struggle for women in paid work, like SEIU's District 925 [Service Employees International Union's office workers' organization in the US], should be a high priority for all of us. These efforts are profoundly deaf to technical restructuring of labour processes and reformations of working classes. These efforts also are providing understanding of a more comprehensive kind of labour organization, involving community, sexuality, and family issues never privileged in the largely white male industrial unions.

The structural rearrangements related to the social relations of science and technology evoke strong ambivalence. But it is not necessary to be ultimately depressed by the implications of late twentieth-century women's relation to all aspects of work, culture, production of knowledge, sexuality, and reproduction. For excellent reasons, most Marxisms see domination best and have trouble understanding what can only look like false consciousness and people's complicity in their own domination in late capitalism. It is crucial to remember that what is lost, perhaps especially from women's points of view, is often virulent forms of oppression, nostalgically naturalized in the face of current violation. Ambivalence towards the disrupted unities mediated by high-tech culture requires not sorting consciousness into categories of clear-sighted critique grounding a 'solid political epistemology' versus 'manipulated false consciousness', but subtle understanding of emerging pleasures, experiences, and powers with serious potential for changing the rules of the game.

There are grounds for hope in the emerging bases for new kinds of unity across race, gender, and class, as these elementary units of socialist-feminist analysis themselves suffer protean transformations.

Intensifications of hardship experienced world-wide in connection with the social relations of science and technology are severe. But what people are experiencing is not transparently clear, and we lack sufficiently subtle connections for collectively building effective theories of experience. Present efforts – Marxist, psychoanalytic, feminist, anthropological – to clarify even 'our' experience are rudimentary.

[…]

American radical feminists like Susan Griffin, Audre Lorde, and Adrienne Rich have profoundly affected our political imaginations – and perhaps restricted too much what we allow as a friendly body and political language.[10] They insist on the organic, opposing it to the technological. But their symbolic systems and the related positions of ecofeminism and feminist paganism, replete with organicisms, can only be understood in Sandoval's terms as oppositional ideologies fitting the late twentieth century. They would simply bewilder anyone not preoccupied with the machines and consciousness of late capitalism. In that sense they are part of the cyborg world. But there are also great riches for feminists in explicitly embracing the possibilities inherent in the breakdown of clean distinctions between organism and machine and similar distinctions structuring the Western self. It is the simultaneity of breakdowns that cracks the matrices of domination and opens geometric possibilities. What might be learned from personal and political 'technological' pollution? I look briefly at two overlapping groups of texts for their insight into the construction of a potentially helpful cyborg myth: constructions of women of colour and monstrous selves in feminist science fiction.

Earlier I suggested that 'women of colour' might be understood as a cyborg identity, a potent subjectivity synthesized from fusions of outsider identities and in the complex political-historical layerings of her 'bio-mythography', Zami (Lorde, 1982; King, 1987a, 1987b). There are material and cultural grids mapping this potential, Audre Lorde (1984) captures the tone in the title of her *Sister Outsider*. In my political myth, Sister Outsider is the offshore woman, whom US workers, female and feminized, are supposed to regard as the enemy preventing their solidarity, threatening their security. Onshore, inside the boundary of the United States, Sister Outsider is a potential amidst the races and ethnic identities of women manipulated for division, competition, and exploitation in the same industries. 'Women of colour' are the preferred labour force for the science-based industries, the real women for whom the world-wide sexual market, labour market, and politics of reproduction kaleidoscope into daily life. Young Korean women hired in the sex industry and in electronics assembly are recruited from high schools, educated for the integrated circuit. Literacy, especially in English, distinguishes the 'cheap' female labour so attractive to the multinationals.

Contrary to orientalist stereotypes of the 'oral primitive', literacy is a special mark of women of colour, acquired by US black women as well as men through a history of risking death to learn and to teach reading and writing. Writing has a special significance for all colonized groups. Writing has been crucial to the Western myth of the distinction between oral and written cultures, primitive and civilized mentalities, and more recently to the erosion of that distinction in 'postmodernist' theories attacking the phallogocentrism of the West, with its worship of the monotheistic, phallic, authoritative, and singular work, the unique and perfect name.[11] Contests for the meanings of writing are a major form of contemporary political struggle. Releasing the play of writing is deadly serious. The poetry and stories of US women of colour are repeatedly about writing, about access to the power to signify; but this time that power must be neither phallic nor innocent. Cyborg writing must not be about the Fall, the imagination of a once-upon-a-time wholeness before language, before writing, before Man. Cyborg writing is about the power to survive, not on the basis of original innocence, but on the basis of seizing the tools to mark the world that marked them as other.

The tools are often stories, retold stories, versions that reverse and displace the hierarchical dualisms of naturalized identities. In retelling origin stories, cyborg authors subvert the central myths of origin of Western culture. We have all been colonized by those origin myths, with their longing for fulfilment in apocalypse. The phallogocentric origin stories most crucial for feminist cyborgs are built into the literal technologies – technologies that write the world, biotechnology and microelectronics – that have recently textualized our bodies as code problems on the grid of C3I. Feminist cyborg stories have the task of recoding communication and intelligence to subvert command and control.

Figuratively and literally, language politics pervade the struggles of women of colour; and stories about language have a special power in the rich contemporary writing by US women of colour. For example, retellings of the story of the indigenous woman Malinche, mother of the mestizo 'bastard' race of the new world, master of languages, and mistress of Cortes, carry special meaning for Chicana constructions of identity. Cherríe Moraga (1983) in *Loving in the War Years* explores the themes of identity when one never possessed the original language, never told the original story, never resided in the harmony of legitimate heterosexuality in the garden of culture, and so cannot base identity on a myth or a fall from innocence and right to natural names, mother's or father's.[12] Moraga's writing, her superb literacy, is presented in her poetry as the same kind of violation as Malinche's mastery of the conqueror's language – a violation, an illegitimate production, that allows survival. Moraga's language is not 'whole'; it is self-consciously spliced, a chimera of English and Spanish, both conqueror's languages. But it is this chimeric monster, without claim to an original language before violation, that crafts the erotic, competent, potent identities of women of colour. Sister Outsider hints at the possibility of world survival not because of her innocence, but because of her ability to live on the boundaries, to write without the founding myth of original wholeness, with its inescapable apocalypse of final return to a deathly oneness that Man has imagined to be the innocent and all-powerful Mother, freed at the End from another spiral of appropriation by her son. Writing marks Moraga's body, affirms it as the body of a woman of colour, against the possibility of passing into the unmarked category of the Anglo father or into the orientalist myth of 'original illiteracy' of a mother that never was. Malinche was mother here, not Eve before eating the forbidden fruit. Writing affirms Sister Outsider, not the Woman-before-the-Fall-into-Writing needed by the phallogocentric Family of Man.

Writing is pre-eminently the technology of cyborgs, etched surfaces of the late twentieth century. Cyborg politics is the struggle for language and the struggle against perfect communication, against the one code that translates all meaning perfectly, the central dogma of phallogocentrism. That is why cyborg politics insist on noise and advocate pollution, rejoicing in the illegitimate fusions of animal and machine. These are the couplings which make Man and Woman so problematic, subverting the structure of desire, the force imagined to generate language and gender, and so subverting the structure and modes of reproduction of 'Western' identity, of nature and culture, of mirror and eye, slave and master, body and mind. 'We' did not originally choose to be cyborgs, but choice grounds a liberal politics and epistemology that imagines the reproduction of individuals before the wider replications of 'texts'.

From the perspective of cyborgs, freed of the need to ground politics in 'our' privileged position of the oppression that incorporates all other dominations, the innocence of the merely violated, the ground of those closer to nature, we can see powerful possibilities. Feminisms and Marxisms have run aground on Western epistemological imperatives to construct a revolutionary subject from the perspective of a hierarchy of oppressions and/or a latent position of moral superiority, innocence, and greater closeness to nature. With no available original dream of a common language or original symbiosis promising protection from hostile 'masculine' separation, but written into the play of a text that has no finally privileged reading or salvation history, to recognize 'oneself' as fully implicated in the world, frees us of the need to root politics in identification, vanguard parties, purity, and mothering. Stripped of identity, the bastard race teaches about the power of the margins and the importance of a mother like Malinche. Women of colour have transformed her from the evil mother of masculinist fear into the originally literate mother who teaches survival.

[...]

One consequence is that our sense of connection to our tools is heightened. The trance state experienced by many computer users has become a staple of science-fiction film and cultural jokes. Perhaps paraplegics and other severely handicapped people can (and sometimes do) have the most intense experiences of complex hybridization with other communication devices.[13] Anne McCaffrey's pre-feminist *The Ship Who Sang* (1969) explored the consciousness of a cyborg, hybrid of girl's brain and complex machinery, formed after the birth of a severely handicapped child. Gender, sexuality, embodiment, skill: all were reconstituted in the story. Why should our bodies end at the skin, or include at best other beings encapsulated by skin? From the seventeenth century till now, machines could be animated – given ghostly souls to make them speak or move or to account for their orderly development and mental capacities. Or organisms could be mechanized – reduced to body understood as resource of mind. These machine/organism relationships are obsolete, unnecessary. For us, in imagination and in other practice, machines can be prosthetic devices, intimate components, friendly selves. We don't need organic holism to give impermeable wholeness, the total woman and her feminist variants (mutants?). Let me conclude this point by a very partial reading of the logic of the cyborg monsters of my second group of texts, feminist science fiction.

The cyborgs populating feminist science fiction make very problematic the statuses of man or woman, human, artefact, member of a race, individual entity, or body. Katie King clarifies how pleasure in reading these fictions is not largely based on identification. Students facing Joanna Russ for the first time, students who have learned to take modernist writers like James Joyce or Virginia Woolf without flinching, do not know what to make of *The Adventures of Alyx* or *The Female Man*, where characters refuse the reader's search for innocent wholeness while granting the wish for heroic quests, exuberant eroticism, and serious politics. *The Female Man* is the story of four versions of one genotype, all of whom meet, but even taken together do not make a whole, resolve the dilemmas of violent moral action, or remove the growing scandal of gender. The feminist science fiction of Samuel R. Delany, especially *Tales of Neveyon*, mocks stories of origin by redoing the neolithic revolution, replaying the founding moves of Western civilization to subvert their plausibility. James Tiptree, Jr, an author whose fiction was regarded as particularly manly until her 'true' gender was revealed, tells tales of reproduction based on non-mammalian technologies like alternation of generations of male brood pouches and male nurturing. John Varley constructs a supreme cyborg in his arch-feminist exploration of Gaea, a mad goddess-planet-trickster-old woman-technological device on whose surface an extraordinary array of post-cyborg symbioses are spawned. Octavia Butler writes of an African sorceress pitting her powers of transformation against the genetic manipulations of her rival (*Wild Seed*), of time warps that bring a modern US black woman into slavery where her actions in relation to her white master-ancestor determine the possibility of her own birth (*Kindred*), and of the illegitimate insights into identity and community of an adopted cross-species child who came to know the enemy as self (*Survivor*). In *Dawn* (1987), the first instalment of a series called Xenogenesis, Butler tells the story of Lilith Iyapo, whose personal name recalls Adam's first and repudiated wife and whose family name marks her status as the widow of the son of Nigerian immigrants to the US. A black woman and a mother whose child is dead, Lilith mediates the transformation of humanity through genetic exchange with extra-terrestrial lovers/rescuers/destroyers/genetic engineers, who reform earth's habitats after the nuclear holocaust and coerce surviving humans into intimate fusion with them. It is a novel that interrogates reproductive, linguistic, and nuclear politics in a mythic field structured by late twentieth-century race and gender.

Because it is particularly rich in boundary transgressions, Vonda McIntyre's Superluminal can close this truncated catalogue of promising and dangerous monsters who help redefine the pleasures and politics of embodiment and feminist writing. In a fiction where no character is 'simply' human, human status is highly problematic. Orca, a genetically altered diver, can speak with killer whales and survive deep ocean conditions, but she longs to explore space as a pilot, necessitating bionic implants jeopardizing her kinship with the divers and cetaceans. Transformations are effected by virus vectors carrying a new developmental code, by transplant surgery, by implants of microelectronic devices, by analogue doubles, and other means. Lacnea becomes a pilot by accepting a heart implant and a host of other alterations allowing survival in transit at speeds exceeding that of light. Radu Dracul survives a virus-caused plague in his outerworld planet to find himself with a time sense that changes the boundaries of spatial perception for the whole species. All the characters explore the limits of language; the dream of

communicating experience; and the necessity of limitation, partiality, and intimacy even in this world of protean transformation and connection. Superluminal stands also for the defining contradictions of a cyborg world in another sense; it embodies textually the intersection of feminist theory and colonial discourse in the science fiction I have alluded to in this chapter. This is a conjunction with a long history that many 'First World' feminists have tried to repress, including myself in my readings of Superluminal before being called to account by Zoe Sofoulis, whose different location in the world system's informatics of domination made her acutely alert to the imperialist moment of all science fiction cultures, including women's science fiction. From an Australian feminist sensitivity, Sofoulis remembered more readily McIntyre's role as writer of the adventures of Captain Kirk and Spock in TV's Star Trek series than her rewriting the romance in Superluminal.

Monsters have always defined the limits of community in Western imaginations. The Centaurs and Amazons of ancient Greece established the limits of the centred polls of the Greek male human by their disruption of marriage and boundary pollutions of the warrior with animality and woman. Unseparated twins and hermaphrodites were the confused human material in early modern France who grounded discourse on the natural and supernatural, medical and legal, portents and diseases – all crucial to establishing modern identity.[14] The evolutionary and behavioural sciences of monkeys and apes have marked the multiple boundaries of late twentieth-century industrial identities. Cyborg monsters in feminist science fiction define quite different political possibilities and limits from those proposed by the mundane fiction of Man and Woman.

There are several consequences to taking seriously the imagery of cyborgs as other than our enemies. Our bodies, ourselves; bodies are maps of power and identity. Cyborgs are no exception. A cyborg body is not innocent; it was not born in a garden; it does not seek unitary identity and so generate antagonistic dualisms without end (or until the world ends); it takes irony for granted. One is too few, and two is only one possibility. Intense pleasure in skill, machine skill, ceases to be a sin, but an aspect of embodiment. The machine is not an it to be animated, worshipped, and dominated. The machine is us, our processes, an aspect of our embodiment. We can be responsible for machines; they do not dominate or threaten us. We are responsible for boundaries; we are they. Up till now (once upon a time), female embodiment seemed to be given, organic, necessary; and female embodiment seemed to mean skill in mothering and its metaphoric extensions. Only by being out of place could we take intense pleasure in machines, and then with excuses that this was organic activity after all, appropriate to females. Cyborgs might consider more seriously the partial, fluid, sometimes aspect of sex and sexual embodiment. Gender might not be global identity after all, even if it has profound historical breadth and depth.

The ideologically charged question of what counts as daily activity, as experience, can be approached by exploiting the cyborg image. Feminists have recently claimed that women are given to dailiness, that women more than men somehow sustain daily life, and so have a privileged epistemological position potentially. There is a compelling aspect to this claim, one that makes visible unvalued female activity and names it as the ground of life.

But the ground of life? What about all the ignorance of women, all the exclusions and failures of knowledge and skill? What about men's access to daily competence, to knowing how to build things, to take them apart, to play? What about other embodiments? Cyborg gender is a local possibility taking a global vengeance. Race, gender, and capital require a cyborg theory of wholes and parts. There is no drive in cyborgs to produce total theory, but there is an intimate experience of boundaries, their construction and deconstruction. There is a myth system waiting to become a political language to ground one way of looking at science and technology and challenging the informatics of domination – in order to act potently.

One last image: organisms and organismic, holistic politics depend on metaphors of rebirth and invariably call on the resources of reproductive sex. I would suggest that cyborgs have more to do with regeneration and are suspicious of the reproductive matrix and of most birthing. For salamanders, regeneration after injury, such as the loss of a limb, involves regrowth of structure and restoration of function with the constant possibility of twinning or other odd topographical productions at the site of former injury. The regrown limb can be monstrous, duplicated, potent. We have all been injured, profoundly. We require regeneration, not rebirth, and the possibilities for our reconstitution include the utopian dream of the hope for a monstrous world without gender.

Cyborg imagery can help express two crucial arguments in this essay: first, the production of universal, totalizing theory is a major mistake that misses most of reality, probably always, but certainly now; and second, taking responsibility for the social relations of science and technology means refusing an anti-science metaphysics, a demonology of technology, and so means embracing the skilful task of reconstructing the boundaries of daily life, in partial connection with others, in communication with all of our parts. It is not just that science and technology are possible means of great human satisfaction, as well as a matrix of complex dominations. Cyborg imagery can suggest a way out of the maze of dualisms in which we have explained our bodies and our tools to ourselves. This is a dream not of a common language, but of a powerful infidel heteroglossia. It is an imagination of a feminist speaking in tongues to strike fear into the circuits of the supersavers of the new right. It means both building and destroying machines, identities, categories, relationships, space stories. Though both are bound in the spiral dance, I would rather be a cyborg than a goddess.

Notes

1 Useful references to left and/or feminist radical science movements and theory and to biological/biotechnical issues include: Bleier (1984, 1986), Harding (1986), Fausto-Sterling (1985), Gould (1981), Hubbard et al. (1982), Keller (1985), Lewontin et al. (1984), *Radical Science Journal* (became *Science as Culture* in 1987), 26 Freegrove Road, London N7 9RQ; *Science for the People*, 897 Main St, Cambridge, MA 02139.

2 Starting points for left and/or feminist approaches to technology and politics include: Cowan (1983), Rothschild (1983), Traweek (1988), Young and Levidow (1981, 1985), Weizenbaum (1976), Winner (1977, 1986), Zimmerman (1983), Athanasiou (1987), Cohn (1987a, 1987b), Winograd and Flores (1986), Edwards (1985). *Global Electronics Newsletter*, 867 West Dana St, #204,

Mountain View, CA 94041; *Processed World*, 55 Sutter St, San Francisco, CA 94104; ISIS, Women's International Information and Communication Service, PO Box 50 (Cornavin), 1211 Geneva 2, Switzerland, and Via Santa Maria Dell'Anima 30, 00186 Rome, Italy. Fundamental approaches to modern social studies of science that do not continue the liberal mystification that it all started with Thomas Kuhn, include: Knorr-Cetina (1981), Knorr-Cetina and Mulkay (1983), Latour and Woolgar (1979), Young (1979). The 1984 Directory of the Network for the Ethnographic Study of Science, Technology, and Organizations lists a wide range of people and projects crucial to better radical analysis; available from NESSTO, PO Box 11442, Stanford, CA 94305.

3   A provocative, comprehensive argument about the politics and theories of 'postmodernism' is made by Fredric Jameson (1984), who argues that postmodernism is not an option, a style among others, but a cultural dominant requiring radical reinvention of left politics from within; there is no longer any place from without that gives meaning to the comforting fiction of critical distance. Jameson also makes clear why one cannot be for or against postmodernism, an essentially moralist move. My position is that feminists (and others) need continuous cultural reinvention, postmodernist critique, and historical materialism; only a cyborg would have a chance. The old dominations of white capitalist patriarchy seem nostalgically innocent now: they normalized heterogeneity, into man and woman, white and black, for example. 'Advanced capitalism' and postmodernism release heterogeneity without a norm, and we are flattened, without subjectivity, which requires depth, even unfriendly and drowning depths. It is time to write *The Death of the Clinic*. The clinic's methods required bodies and works; we have texts and surfaces. Our dominations don't work by medicalization and normalization any more; they work by networking, communications redesign, stress management. Normalization gives way to automation, utter redundancy. Michel Foucault's *Birth of the Clinic* (1963), *History of Sexuality* (1976), and *Discipline and Punish* (1975) name a form of power at its moment of implosion. The discourse of biopolitics gives way to technobabble, the language of the spliced substantive; no noun is left whole by the multinationals. These are their names, listed from one issue of *Science*: Tech-Knowledge, Genentech, Allergen, Hybritech, Compupro, Genencor, Syntex, Allelix, Agrigenetics Corp., Syntro, Codon, Repligen, MicroAngelo from Scion Corp., Percom Data, Inter Systems, Cyborg Corp., Statcom Corp., Intertec. If we are imprisoned by language, then escape from that prison-house requires language poets, a kind

of cultural restriction enzyme to cut the code; cyborg heteroglossia is one form of radical cultural politics. For cyborg poetry, see Perloff (1984); Fraser (1984). For feminist modernist/postmodernist 'cyborg' writing, see HOW(ever), 871 Corbett Ave, San Francisco, CA 94131.

4   Baudrillard (1983). Jameson (1984, p. 66) points out that Plato's definition of the simulacrum is the copy for which there is no original, i.e., the world of advanced capitalism, of pure exchange. See *Discourse* 9 (Spring/Summer 1987) for a special issue on technology (cybernetics, ecology, and the postmodern imagination).

5   For ethnographic accounts and political evaluations, see Epstein (forthcoming), Sturgeon (1986). Without explicit irony, adopting the spaceship earth/whole earth logo of the planet photographed from space, set off by the slogan 'Love Your Mother', the May 1987 Mothers and Others Day action at the nuclear weapons testing facility in Nevada none the less took account of the tragic contradictions of views of the earth. Demonstrators applied for official permits to be on the land from officers of the Western Shoshone tribe, whose territory was invaded by the US government when it built the nuclear weapons test ground in the 1950s. Arrested for trespassing, the demonstrators argued that the police and weapons facility personnel, without authorization from the proper officials, were the trespassers. One affinity group at the women's action called themselves the Surrogate Others; and in solidarity with the creatures forced to tunnel in the same ground with the bomb, they enacted a cyborgian emergence from the constructed body of a large, non-heterosexual desert worm.

6   Powerful developments of coalition politics emerge from 'Third World' speakers, speaking from nowhere, the displaced centre of the universe, earth: 'We live on the third planet from the sun' – *Sun Poem* by Jamaican writer, Edward Kamau Braithwaite, review by Mackey (1984). Contributors to Smith (1983) ironically subvert naturalized identities precisely while constructing a place from which to speak called home. See especially Reagon (in Smith, 1983, pp. 356–68). Trinh T. Minh-ha (1986–7).

7   This chart was published in 1985. My previous efforts to understand biology as a cybernetic command-control discourse and organisms as 'natural-technical objects of knowledge' were Haraway (1979, 1983, 1984).

8   For progressive analyses and action on the biotechnology debates: *GeneWatch, a Bulletin of the Committee for Responsible Genetics*, 5 Doane St, 4th Floor, Boston, MA 02109; Genetic Screening Study Group (formerly the Sociobiology Study Group of Science for the People), Cambridge, MA; Wright (1982, 1986); Yoxen (1983).

9   Starting references for 'women in the integrated circuit': D'Onofrio-Flores and Pfafflin (1982), Fernandez-Kelly (1983), Fuentes and Ehrenreich (1983), Grossman (1980), Nash and Fernandez-Kelly (1983), Ong (1987), Science Policy Research Unit (1982).

10 But all these poets are very complex, not least in their treatment of themes of lying and erotic, decentred collective and personal identities. Griffin (1978), Lorde (1984), Rich (1978).

11 Derrida (1976, especially part II); Lévi-Strauss (1961, especially 'The Writing Lesson'); Gates (1985); Kahn and Neumaier (1985); Ong (1982); Kramarae and Treichler (1985).

12 The sharp relation of women of colour to writing as theme and politics can be approached through: Program for 'The Black Woman and the Diaspora: Hidden Connections and Extended Acknowledgments', An International Literary Conference, Michigan State University, October 1985; Evans (1984); Christian (1985); Carby (1987); Fisher (1980); *Frontiers* (1980, 1983); Kingston (1977); Lerner (1973); Giddings (1985); Moraga and Anzaldúa (1981); Morgan (1984). Anglophone European and Euro-American women have also crafted special relations to their writing as a potent sign: Gilbert and Gubar (1979), Russ (1983).

13 James Clifford (1985, 1988) argues persuasively for recognition of continuous cultural reinvention, the stubborn non-disappearance of those 'marked' by Western imperializing practices.

14 DuBois (1982), Daston and Park (n.d.), Park and Daston (1981). The noun *monster* shares its root with the verb *to demonstrate*.

References

Athanasiou, Tom (1987) 'High-tech politics: the case of artificial intelligence', *Socialist Review* 92: 7–35.

Baudrillard, Jean (1983) *Simulations*, P. Foss, P. Patton, P. Beitchman, trans. New York: Semiotext[e].

Bleier, Ruth (1984) *Science and Gender: A Critique of Biology and Its Themes on Women*. New York: Pergamon.

Bleier, Ruth, ed. (1986) *Feminist Approaches to Science*. New York: Pergamon.

Butler, Octavia (1987) *Dawn*. New York: Warner.

Carby, Hazel (1987) *Reconstructing Womanhood: The Emergence of the Afro-American Woman Novelist*. New York: Oxford University Press.

Christian, Barbara (1985) *Black Feminist Criticism: Perspectives on Black Women Writers*. New York: Pergamon.

Clifford, James (1985) 'On ethnographic allegory', in James Clifford and George Marcus, eds *Writing Culture: The Poetics and Politics of Ethnography*. Berkeley: University of California Press.

Clifford, James (1988) *The Predicament of Culture: Twentieth-Century Ethnography, Literature, and Art*. Cambridge, MA: Harvard University Press.

Cohn, Carol (1987a) 'Nuclear language and how we learned to pat the bomb', *Bulletin of Atomic Scientists*, pp. 17–24.

Cohn, Carol (1987b) 'Sex and death in the rational world of defense intellectuals', *Signs* 12(4): 687–718.

Cowan, Ruth Schwartz (1983) *More Work for Mother: The Ironies of Household Technology from the Open Hearth to the Microwave*. New York: Basic.

Daston, Lorraine and Park, Katherine (n.d.) 'Hermaphrodites in Renaissance France', unpublished paper.

de Waal, Frans (1982) *Chimpanzee Politics: Power and Sex among the Apes*. New York: Harper & Row.

Derrida, Jacques (1976) *Of Grammatology*, G.C. Spivak, trans. and introd. Baltimore: Johns Hopkins University Press.

D'Onofrio-Flores, Pamela and Pfafflin, Sheila M., eds (1982) *Scientific-Technological Change and the Role of Women in Development*. Boulder: Westview.

DuBois, Page (1982) *Centaurs and Amazons*. Ann Arbor: University of Michigan Press.

Edwards, Paul (1985) 'Border wars: the science and politics of artificial intelligence', *Radical America* 19(6): 39–52.

Epstein, Barbara (forthcoming) *Political Protest and Cultural Revolution: Nonviolent Direct Action in the Seventies and Eighties*. Berkeley: University of California Press.

Evans, Mari, ed. (1984) *Black Women Writers: A Critical Evaluation*. Garden City, NY: Doubleday/Anchor.

Fausto-Sterling, Anne (1985) *Myths of Gender: Biological Theories about Women and Men*. New York: Basic.

Fernandez-Kelly, Maria Patricia (1983) *For We Are Sold, I and My People*. Albany: State University of New York Press.

Fisher, Dexter, ed. (1980) *The Third Woman: Minority Women Writers of the United States*. Boston: Houghton Mifflin.

Foucault, Michel (1963) *The Birth of the Clinic; An Archaeology of Medical Perception*, A.M. Smith, trans. New York: Vintage, 1975.

Foucault, Michel (1975) *Discipline and Punish: The Birth of the Prison*, Alan Sheridan, trans. New York: Vintage, 1979.

Foucault, Michel (1976) *The History of Sexuality*, Vol. 1: *An Introduction*, Robert Hurley, trans. New York: Pantheon, 1978.

Fraser, Kathleen (1984) *Something. Even Human Voices. In the Foreground, a Lake*. Berkeley, CA: Kelsey St Press.

Gates, Henry Louis (1985) 'Writing "race" and the difference it makes', in '*Race*', *Writing, and Difference*, special issue, *Critical Inquiry* 12(1): 1–20.

Giddings, Paula (1985) *When and Where I Enter: The Impact of Black Women on Race and Sex in America*. Toronto: Bantam.

Gilbert, Sandra M. and Gubar, Susan (1979) *The Madwoman in the Attic: The Woman Writer and the Nineteenth-Century Literary Imagination*. New Haven, CT: Yale University Press.

Gould, Stephen J. (1981) *Mismeasure of Man*. New York: Norton.

Griffin, Susan (1978) *Woman and Nature: The Roaring Inside Her*. New York: Harper & Row.

Grossman, Rachel (1980) 'Women's place in the integrated circuit', *Radical America* 14(1): 29–50.

Haraway, Donna J. (1979) 'The biological enterprise: sex, mind, and profit from human engineering to sociobiology', *Radical History Review* 20: 206–37.

Haraway, Donna J. (1983) 'Signs of dominance: from a physiology to a cybernetics of primate society', *Studies in History of Biology* 6: 129–219.

Haraway, Donna J. (1984) 'Class, race, sex, scientific objects of knowledge: a socialist-feminist perspective on the social construction of productive knowledge and some political consequences', in Violet Haas and Carolyn Perucci eds *Women in Scientific and Engineering Professions*. Ann Arbor: University of Michigan Press, pp. 212–29.

Harding, Sandra (1986) *The Science Question in Feminism*. Ithaca: Cornell University Press.

Hogness, E. Rusten (1983) 'Why stress? A look at the making of stress, 1936–56', unpublished paper available from the author, 4437 Mill Creek Rd, Healdsburg, CA 95448.

Hubbard, Ruth, Henifin, Mary Sue, and Fried, Barbara, eds (1982) *Biological Woman, the Convenient Myth*. Cambridge, MA: Schenkman.

Jameson, Fredric (1984) 'Post-modernism, or the cultural logic of late capitalism', *New Left Review* 146: 53–92.

Kahn, Douglas and Neumaier, Diane, eds (1985) *Cultures in Contention*. Seattle: Real Comet.

Keller, Evelyn Fox (1985) *Reflections on Gender and Science*. New Haven: Yale University Press.

King, Katie (1987a) 'Canons without innocence', University of California at Santa Cruz, PhD thesis.

King, Katie (1987b) *The Passing Dreams of Choice ... Once Before and After: Audre Lorde and the Apparatus of Literary Production*, book prospectus, University of Maryland at College Park.

Kingston, Maxine Hong (1977) *China Men*. New York: Knopf.

Knorr-Cetina, Karin (1981) *The Manufacture of Knowledge*. Oxford: Pergamon.

Knorr-Cetina, Karin and Mulkay, Michael, eds (1983) *Science Observed: Perspectives on the Social Study of Science*. Beverly Hills: Sage.

Kramarae, Cheris and Treichler, Paula (1985) *A Feminist Dictionary*. Boston: Pandora.

Latour, Bruno (1984) *Les microbes, guerre et paix, suivi des irréductions*. Paris: Métailié.

Latour, Bruno and Woolgar, Steve (1979) *Laboratory Life: The Social Construction of Scientific Facts*. Beverly Hills: Sage.

Lerner, Gerda, ed. (1973) *Black Women in White America: A Documentary History*. New York: Vintage.

Lévi-Strauss, Claude (1971) *Tristes Tropiques*, John Russell, trans. New York: Atheneum.

Lewontin, R.C., Rose, Steven, and Kamin, Leon J. (1984) *Not in Our Genes: Biology, Ideology, and Human Nature*. New York: Pantheon.

Lorde, Audre (1982) *Zami, a New Spelling of My Name*. Trumansberg, NY: Crossing, 1983.

Lorde, Audre (1984) *Sister Outsider*. Trumansberg, NY: Crossing.

McCaffrey, Anne (1969) *The Ship Who Sang*. New York: Ballantine.

Mackey, Nathaniel (1984) 'Review', *Sulfur* 2: 200–5.

Marcuse, Herbert (1964) *One-Dimensional Man: Studies in the Ideology of Advanced Industrial Society*. Boston: Beacon.

Merchant, Carolyn (1980) *The Death of Nature: Women, Ecology, and the Scientific Revolution*. New York: Harper & Row.

Moraga, Cherríe (1983) *Loving in the War Years: lo que nunca pasó por sus labios*. Boston: South End.

Moraga, Cherríe and Anzaldúa, Gloria, eds (1981) *This Bridge Called My Back: Writings by Radical Women of Color*. Watertown: Persephone.

Morgan, Robin, ed. (1984) *Sisterhood Is Global*. Garden City, NY: Anchor/Doubleday.

Ong, Aihwa (1987) *Spirits of Resistance and Capitalist Discipline: Factory Workers in Malaysia*. Albany: State University of New York Press.

Ong, Walter (1982) *Orality and Literacy: The Technologizing of the Word*. New York: Methuen.

Park, Katherine and Daston, Lorraine J. (1981) 'Unnatural conceptions: the study of monsters in sixteenth- and seventeenth-century France and England', *Past and Present* 92: 20–54.

Perloff, Marjorie (1984) 'Dirty language and scramble systems', *Sulfur* 11: 178–83.

Rich, Adrienne (1978) *The Dream of a Common Language*. New York: Norton.

Rothschild, Joan, ed. (1983) *Machina ex Dea: Feminist Perspectives on Technology*. New York: Pergamon.

Russ, Joanna (1983) *How to Suppress Women's Writing*. Austin: University of Texas Press.

Sandoval, Chela (1984) 'Dis-illusionment and the poetry of the future: the making of oppositional consciousness',

University of California at Santa Cruz, PhD qualifying essay.

Sandoval, Chela (n.d.) *Yours in Struggle: Women Respond to Racism, a Report on the National Women's Studies Association.* Oakland, CA: Center for Third World Organizing.

Science Policy Research Unit (1982) *Microelectronics and Women's Employment in Britain.* University of Sussex.

Smith, Barbara, ed. (1983) *Home Girls: A Black Feminist Anthology.* New York: Kitchen Table, Women of Color Press.

Sofia, Zoe (also Zoe Sofoulis) (1984) 'Exterminating fetuses: abortion, disarmament, and the sexo-semiotics of extraterrestrialism', *Diacritics* 14(2): 47–59.

Sturgeon, Noel (1986) 'Feminism, anarchism, and non-violent direct action politics', University of California at Santa Cruz, PhD qualifying essay.

Traweek, Sharon (1988) *Beamtimes and Lifetimes: The World of High Energy Physics.* Cambridge, MA: Harvard University Press.

Treichler, Paula (1987) 'AIDS, homophobia, and biomedical discourse: an epidemic of signification', *October* 43: 31–70.

Trinh T. Minh-ha (1986–7) 'Introduction', and 'Difference: "a special third world women issue"', *Discourse: Journal for Theoretical Studies in Media and Culture* 8: 3–38.

Weizenbaum, Joseph (1976) *Computer Power and Human Reason.* San Francisco: Freeman.

Winner, Langdon (1977) *Autonomous Technology: Technics out of Control as a Theme in Political Thought.* Cambridge, MA: MIT Press.

Winner, Langdon (1980) 'Do artifacts have politics?', *Daedalus* 109(1): 121–36.

Winner, Langdon (1986) *The Whale and the Reactor.* Chicago: University of Chicago Press.

Winograd, Terry and Flores, Fernando (1986) *Understanding Computers and Cognition: A New Foundation for Design.* Norwood, NJ: Ablex.

Wright, Susan (1982, July/August) 'Recombinant DNA: the status of hazards and controls', *Environment* 24(6): 12–20, 51–53.

Wright, Susan (1986) 'Recombinant DNA technology and its social transformation, 1972–82', *Osiris*, 2nd series, 2: 303–60.

Young, Robert M. (1979, March) 'Interpreting the production of science', *New Scientist* 29: 1026–8.

Young, Robert M. and Levidow, Les, eds (1981, 1985) *Science, Technology and the Labour Process,* 2 vols. London: CSE and Free Association Books.

Yoxen, Edward (1983) *The Gene Business.* New York: Harper & Row.

Zimmerman, Jan, ed. (1983) *The Technological Woman: Interfacing with Tomorrow.* New York: Praeger.

40

"Subjects of Sex/Gender/Desire" (1990)

Judith Butler

One is not born a woman, but rather becomes one. (Simone de Beauvoir)

Strictly speaking, "women" cannot be said to exist. (Julia Kristeva)

Woman does not have a sex. (Luce Irigaray)

The deployment of sexuality ... established this notion of sex. (Michel Foucault)

The category of sex is the political category that founds society as heterosexual. (Monique Wittig)

I. "Women" as the Subject of Feminism

For the most part, feminist theory has assumed that there is some existing identity, understood through the category of women, who not only initiates feminist interests and goals within discourse, but constitutes the subject for whom political representation is pursued. But *politics* and *representation* are controversial terms. On the one hand, *representation* serves as the operative term within a political process that seeks to extend visibility and legitimacy to women as political subjects; on the other hand, representation is

the normative function of a language which is said either to reveal or to distort what is assumed to be true about the category of women. For feminist theory, the development of a language that fully or adequately represents women has seemed necessary to foster the political visibility of women. This has seemed obviously important considering the pervasive cultural condition in which women's lives were either misrepresented or not represented at all.

Recently, this prevailing conception of the relation between feminist theory and politics has come under challenge from within feminist discourse. The very subject of women is no longer understood in stable or abiding terms. There is a great deal of material that not only questions the viability of "the subject" as the ultimate candidate for representation or, indeed, liberation, but there is very little agreement after all on what it is that constitutes, or ought to constitute, the category of women. The domains of political and linguistic "representation" set out in advance the criterion by which subjects themselves are formed, with the result that representation is extended only to what can be acknowledged as a subject. In other words, the qualifications for being a subject must first be met before representation can be extended.

Foucault points out that juridical systems of power produce the subjects they subsequently come to represent.[1] Juridical notions of power appear to regulate political life in purely negative terms – that is, through the limitation, prohibition, regulation, control, and even "protection" of individuals related to that political structure through the contingent and retractable operation of choice. But the subjects regulated by such structures are, by virtue of being subjected to them, formed, defined, and reproduced in accordance with the requirements of those structures. If this analysis is right, then the juridical formation of language and politics that represents women as "the subject" of feminism is itself a discursive formation and effect of a given version of representational politics. And the feminist subject turns out to be discursively constituted by the very political system that is supposed to facilitate its emancipation. This becomes politically problematic if that system can be shown to produce gendered subjects along a differential axis of domination or to produce subjects who are presumed to be masculine. In such cases, an uncritical appeal to such a system for the emancipation of "women" will be clearly self-defeating.

The question of "the subject" is crucial for politics, and for feminist politics in particular, because juridical subjects are invariably produced through certain exclusionary practices that do not "show" once the juridical structure of politics has been established. In other words, the political construction of the subject proceeds with certain legitimating and exclusionary aims, and these political operations are effectively concealed and naturalized by a political analysis that takes juridical structures as their foundation. Juridical power inevitably "produces" what it claims merely to represent; hence, politics must be concerned with this dual function of power: the juridical and the productive. In effect, the law produces and then conceals the notion of "a subject before the law"[2] in order to invoke that discursive formation as a naturalized foun-

dational premise that subsequently legitimates that law's own regulatory hegemony. It is not enough to inquire into how women might become more fully represented in language and politics. Feminist critique ought also to understand how the category of "women," the subject of feminism, is produced and restrained by the very structures of power through which emancipation is sought.

Indeed, the question of women as the subject of feminism raises the possibility that there may not be a subject who stands "before" the law, awaiting representation in or by the law. Perhaps the subject, as well as the invocation of a temporal "before," is constituted by the law as the fictive foundation of its own claim to legitimacy. The prevailing assumption of the ontological integrity of the subject before the law might be understood as the contemporary trace of the state of nature hypothesis, that foundationalist fable constitutive of the juridical structures of classical liberalism. The performative invocation of a nonhistorical "before" becomes the foundational premise that guarantees a presocial ontology of persons who freely consent to be governed and, thereby, constitute the legitimacy of the social contract.

Apart from the foundationalist fictions that support the notion of the subject, however, there is the political problem that feminism encounters in the assumption that the term women denotes a common identity. Rather than a stable signifier that commands the assent of those whom it purports to describe and represent, women, even in the plural, has become a troublesome term, a site of contest, a cause for anxiety. As Denise Riley's title suggests, Am I That Name? is a question produced by the very possibility of the name's multiple significations.[3] If one "is" a woman, that is surely not all one is; the term fails to be exhaustive, not because a pregendered "person" transcends the specific paraphernalia of its gender, but because gender is not always constituted coherently or consistently in different historical contexts, and because gender intersects with racial, class, ethnic, sexual, and regional modalities of discursively constituted identities. As a result, it becomes impossible to separate out "gender" from the political and cultural intersections in which it is invariably produced and maintained.

Mandine?

The political assumption that there must be a universal basis for feminism, one which must be found in an identity assumed to exist cross-culturally, often accompanies the notion that the oppression of women has some singular form discernible in the universal or hegemonic structure of patriarchy or masculine domination. The notion of a universal patriarchy has been widely criticized in recent years for its failure to account for the workings of gender oppression in the concrete cultural contexts in which it exists. Where those various contexts have been consulted within such theories, it has been to find "examples" or "illustrations" of a universal principle that is assumed from the start. That form of feminist theorizing has come under criticism for its efforts to colonize and appropriate non-Western cultures to support highly Western notions of oppression, but because they tend as well to construct a "Third World" or even an "Orient" in which gender oppression is subtly explained as symptomatic of an essential, non-Western barbarism. The urgency of feminism to establish a universal status for patriarchy in order to strengthen the appearance of feminism's own claims to be representative has occasionally motivated the shortcut to a categorial or fictive universality of the structure of domination, held to produce women's common subjugated experience.

Although the claim of universal patriarchy no longer enjoys the kind of credibility it once did, the notion of a generally shared conception of "women," the corollary to that framework, has been much more difficult to displace. Certainly, there have been plenty of debates: Is there some commonality among "women" that preexists their oppression, or do "women" have a bond by virtue of their oppression alone? Is there a specificity to women's cultures that is independent of their subordination by hegemonic, masculinist cultures? Are the specificity and integrity of women's cultural or linguistic practices always specified against and, hence, within the terms of some more dominant cultural formation? If there is a region of the "specifically feminine," one that is both differentiated from the masculine as such and recognizable in its difference by an unmarked and, hence, presumed universality of "women"? The masculine/feminine binary constitutes not only the exclusive framework in which that specificity can be recognized, but in every other way the "specificity" of the feminine is

once again fully decontextualized and separated off analytically and politically from the constitution of class, race, ethnicity, and other axes of power relations that both constitute "identity" and make the singular notion of identity a misnomer.[4]

My suggestion is that the presumed universality and unity of the subject of feminism is effectively undermined by the constraints of the representational discourse in which it functions. Indeed, the premature insistence on a stable subject of feminism, understood as a seamless category of women, inevitably generates multiple refusals to accept the category. These domains of exclusion reveal the coercive and regulatory consequences of that construction, even when the construction has been elaborated for emancipatory purposes. Indeed, the fragmentation within feminism and the paradoxical opposition to feminism from "women" whom feminism claims to represent suggest the necessary limits of identity politics. The suggestion that feminism can seek wider representation for a subject that it itself constructs has the ironic consequence that feminist goals risk failure by refusing to take account of the constitutive powers of their own representational claims. This problem is not ameliorated through an appeal to the category of women for merely "strategic" purposes, for strategies always have meanings that exceed the purposes for which they are intended. In this case, exclusion itself might qualify as such an unintended yet consequential meaning. By conforming to a requirement of representational politics that feminism articulate a stable subject, feminism thus opens itself to charges of gross misrepresentation.

Obviously, the political task is not to refuse representational politics – as if we could. The juridical structures of language and politics constitute the contemporary field of power; hence, there is no position outside this field, but only a critical genealogy of its own legitimating practices. As such, the critical point of departure is *the historical present*, as Marx put it. And the task is to formulate within this constituted frame a critique of the categories of identity that contemporary juridical structures engender, naturalize, and immobilize.

Perhaps there is an opportunity at this juncture of cultural politics, a period that some would call "postfeminist," to reflect from within a feminist perspective on the injunction to construct a subject of feminism. Within feminist political practice, a radical rethinking of the ontological constructions of identity appears to be necessary in order to formulate a representational politics that might revive feminism on other grounds. On the other hand, it may be time to entertain a radical critique that seeks to free feminist theory from the necessity of having to construct a single or abiding ground which is invariably contested by those identity positions or anti-identity positions that it invariably excludes. Do the exclusionary practices that ground feminist theory in a notion of "women" as subject paradoxically undercut feminist goals to extend its claims to "representation"?[5]

Perhaps the problem is even more serious. Is the construction of the category of women as a coherent and stable subject an unwitting regulation and reification of gender relations? And is not such a reification precisely contrary to feminist aims? To what extent does the category of women achieve stability and coherence only in the context of the heterosexual matrix?[6] If a stable notion of gender no longer proves to be the foundational premise of feminist politics, perhaps a new sort of feminist politics is now desirable to contest the very reifications of gender and identity, one that will take the variable construction of identity as both a methodological and normative prerequisite, if not a political goal.

To trace the political operations that produce and conceal what qualifies as the juridical subject of feminism is precisely the task of *a feminist genealogy* of the category of women. In the course of this effort to question "women" as the subject of feminism, the unproblematic invocation of that category may prove to *preclude* the possibility of feminism as a representational politics. What sense does it make to extend representation to subjects who are constructed through the exclusion of those who fail to conform to unspoken normative requirements of the subject? What relations of domination and exclusion are inadvertently sustained when representation becomes the sole focus of politics? The identity of the feminist subject ought not to be the foundation of feminist politics, if the formation of the subject takes place within a field of power regularly buried through the assertion of that foundation. Perhaps, paradoxically, "representation" will be shown to make sense for feminism only when the subject of "women" is nowhere presumed.

II. The Compulsory Order of Sex/Gender/Desire

Although the unproblematic unity of "women" is often invoked to construct a solidarity of identity, a split is introduced in the feminist subject by the distinction between sex and gender. Originally intended to dispute the biology-is-destiny formulation, the distinction between sex and gender serves the argument that whatever biological intractability sex appears to have, gender is culturally constructed: hence, gender is neither the causal result of sex nor as seemingly fixed as sex. The unity of the subject is thus already potentially contested by the distinction that permits of gender as a multiple interpretation of sex.

If gender is the cultural meanings that the sexed body assumes, then a gender cannot be said to follow from a sex in any one way. Taken to its logical limit, the sex/gender distinction suggests a radical discontinuity between sexed bodies and culturally constructed genders. Assuming for the moment the stability of binary sex, it does not follow that the construction of "men" will accrue exclusively to the bodies of males or that "women" will interpret only female bodies. Further, even if the sexes appear to be unproblematically binary in their morphology and constitution (which will become a question), there is no reason to assume that genders ought also to remain as two.[7] The presumption of a binary gender system implicitly retains the belief in a mimetic relation of gender to sex whereby gender mirrors sex or is otherwise restricted by it. When the constructed status of gender is theorized as radically independent of sex, gender itself becomes a free-floating artifice, with the consequence that *man* and *masculine* might just as easily signify a female body as a male one, and *woman* and *feminine* a male body as easily as a female one.

This radical splitting of the gendered subject poses yet another set of problems. Can we refer to a "given" sex or a "given" gender without first inquiring into how sex and/or gender is given, through what means?

culture makes gender

And what is "sex" anyway? Is it natural, anatomical, chromosomal, or hormonal, and how is a feminist critic to assess the scientific discourses which purport to establish such "facts" for us?[8] Does sex have a history?[9] Does each sex have a different history, or histories? Is there a history of how the duality of sex was established, a genealogy that might expose the binary options as a variable construction? Are the ostensibly natural facts of sex discursively produced by various scientific discourses in the service of other political and social interests? If the immutable character of sex is contested, perhaps this construct called "sex" is as culturally constructed as gender; indeed, perhaps it was always already gender, with the consequence that the distinction between sex and gender turns out to be no distinction at all.[10]

It would make no sense, then, to define gender as the cultural interpretation of sex, if sex itself is a gendered category. Gender ought not to be conceived merely as the cultural inscription of meaning on a pregiven sex (a juridical conception); gender must also designate the very apparatus of production whereby the sexes themselves are established. As a result, gender is not to culture as sex is to nature; gender is also the discursive/cultural means by which "sexed nature" or "a natural sex" is produced and established as "prediscursive," prior to culture, a politically neutral surface *on which* culture acts. [...] At this juncture it is already clear that one way the internal stability and binary frame for sex is effectively secured is by casting the duality of sex in a prediscursive domain. This production of sex as the prediscursive ought to be understood as the effect of the apparatus of cultural construction designated by *gender*. How, then, does gender need to be reformulated to encompass the power relations that produce the effect of a prediscursive sex and so conceal that very operation of discursive production?

III. Gender: The Circular Ruins of Contemporary Debate

Is there "a" gender which persons are said to *have*, or is it an essential attribute that a person is said to *be*, as implied in the question "What gender are you?"

When feminist theorists claim that gender is the cultural interpretation of sex or that gender is culturally constructed, what is the manner or mechanism of this construction? If gender is constructed, could it be constructed differently, or does its constructedness imply some form of social determinism, foreclosing the possibility of agency and transformation? Does "construction" suggest that certain laws generate gender differences along universal axes of sexual difference? How and where does the construction of gender take place? What sense can we make of a construction that cannot assume a human constructor prior to that construction? On some accounts, the notion that gender is constructed suggests a certain determinism of gender meanings inscribed on anatomically differentiated bodies, where those bodies are understood as passive recipients of an inexorable cultural law. When the relevant "culture" that "constructs" gender is understood in terms of such a law or set of laws, then it seems that gender is as determined and fixed as it was under the biology-is-destiny formulation. In such a case, not biology, but culture, becomes destiny.

On the other hand, Simone de Beauvoir suggests in *The Second Sex* that "one is not born a woman, but, rather, becomes one."[11] For Beauvoir, gender is "constructed," but implied in her formulation is an agent, a *cogito*, who somehow takes on or appropriates that gender and could, in principle, take on some other gender. Is gender as variable and volitional as Beauvoir's account seems to suggest? Can "construction" in such a case be reduced to a form of choice? Beauvoir is clear that one "becomes" a woman, but always under a cultural compulsion to become one. And clearly, the compulsion does not come from "sex." There is nothing in her account that guarantees that the "one" who becomes a woman is necessarily female. If "the body is a situation,"[12] as she claims, there is no recourse to a body that has not always already been interpreted by cultural meanings; hence, sex could not qualify as a prediscursive anatomical facticity. Indeed, sex, by definition, will be shown to have been gender all along.[13]

The controversy over the meaning of *construction* appears to founder on the conventional philosophical polarity between free will and determinism. As a consequence, one might reasonably suspect that some common linguistic restriction on thought both forms and limits the terms of the debate. Within those terms, "the body" appears as a passive medium on which cultural meanings are inscribed or as the instrument through which an appropriative and interpretive will determines a cultural meaning for itself. In either case, the body is figured as a mere *instrument* or *medium* for which a set of cultural meanings are only externally related. But "the body" is itself a construction, as are the myriad "bodies" that constitute the domain of gendered subjects. Bodies cannot be said to have a signifiable existence prior to the mark of their gender; the question then emerges: To what extent does the body *come into being* in and through the mark(s) of gender? How do we reconceive the body no longer as a passive medium or instrument awaiting the enlivening capacity of a distinctly immaterial will?[14]

Whether gender or sex is fixed or free is a function of a discourse which, it will be suggested, seeks to set certain limits to analysis or to safeguard certain tenets of humanism as presuppositional to any analysis of gender. The locus of intractability, whether in "sex" or "gender" or in the very meaning of "construction," provides a clue to what cultural possibilities can and cannot become mobilized through any further analysis. The limits of the discursive analysis of gender presuppose and preempt the possibilities of imaginable and realizable gender configurations within culture. This is not to say that any and all gendered possibilities are open, but that the boundaries of analysis suggest the limits of a discursively conditioned experience. These limits are always set within the terms of a hegemonic cultural discourse predicated on binary structures that appear as the language of universal rationality. Constraint is thus built into what that language constitutes as the imaginable domain of gender.

Although social scientists refer to gender as a "factor" or a "dimension" of an analysis, it is also applied to embodied persons as "a mark" of biological, linguistic, and/or cultural difference. In these latter cases, gender can be understood as a signification that an (already) sexually differentiated body assumes, but even then that signification exists only *in relation* to another, opposing signification. Some feminist theorists claim that gender is "a relation," indeed, a set of relations, and not an individual attribute. Others, following

Beauvoir, would argue that only the feminine gender is marked, that the universal person and the masculine gender are conflated, thereby defining women in terms of their sex and extolling men as the bearers of a body-transcendent universal personhood.

In a move that complicates the discussion further, Luce Irigaray argues that women constitute a paradox, if not a contradiction, within the discourse of identity itself. Women are the "sex" which is not "one." Within a language pervasively masculinist, a phallogocentric language, women constitute the *unrepresentable*. In other words, women represent the sex that cannot be thought, a linguistic absence and opacity. Within a language that rests on univocal signification, the female sex constitutes the unconstrainable and undesignatable. In this sense, women are the sex which is not "one," but multiple.[15] In opposition to Beauvoir, for whom women are designated as the Other, Irigaray argues that both the subject and the Other are masculine mainstays of a closed phallogocentric signifying economy that achieves its totalizing goal through the exclusion of the feminine altogether. For Beauvoir, women are the negative of men, the lack against which masculine identity differentiates itself; for Irigaray, that particular dialectic constitutes a system that excludes an entirely different economy of signification. Women are not only represented falsely within the Sartrian frame of signifying-subject and signified-Other, but the falsity of the signification points out the entire structure of representation as inadequate. The sex which is not one, then, provides a point of departure for a criticism of hegemonic Western representation and of the metaphysics of substance that structures the very notion of the subject.

What is the metaphysics of substance, and how does it inform thinking about the categories of sex? In the first instance, humanist conceptions of the subject tend to assume a substantive person who is the bearer of various essential and nonessential attributes. A humanist feminist position might understand gender as an *attribute* of a person who is characterized essentially as a pregendered substance or "core," called the person, denoting a universal capacity for reason, moral deliberation, or language. The universal conception of the person, however, is displaced as a point of departure for a social theory of gender by those historical and anthropological positions that understand gender as a relation among socially constituted subjects in specifiable contexts. This relational or contextual point of view suggests that what the person "is," and, indeed, what gender "is," is always relative to the constructed relations in which it is determined.[16] As a shifting and contextual phenomenon, gender does not denote a substantive being, but a relative point of convergence among culturally and historically specific sets of relations.

Irigaray would maintain, however, that the feminine "sex" is a point of linguistic *absence*, the impossibility of a grammatically denoted substance, and, hence, the point of view that exposes that substance as an abiding and foundational illusion of a masculinist discourse. This absence is not marked as such within the masculine signifying economy – a contention that reverses Beauvoir's argument (and Wittig's) that the female sex is marked, while the male sex is not. For Irigaray, the female sex is not a "lack" or an "Other" that immanently and negatively defines the subject in its masculinity. On the contrary, the female sex eludes the very requirements of representation, for she is neither "Other" nor the "lack," those categories remaining relative to the Sartrian subject, immanent to that phallogocentric scheme. Hence, for Irigaray, the feminine could never be the *mark of a subject*, as Beauvoir would suggest. Further, the feminine could not be theorized in terms of a determinate *relation* between the masculine and the feminine within any given discourse, for discourse is not a relevant notion here. Even in their variety, discourses constitute so many modalities of phallogocentric language. The female sex is thus also *the subject* that is not one. The relation between masculine and feminine cannot be represented in a signifying economy in which the masculine constitutes the closed circle of signifier and signified. Paradoxically enough, Beauvoir prefigured this impossibility in *The Second Sex* when she argued that men could not settle the question of women because they would then be acting as both judge and party to the case.[17]

The distinctions among the above positions are far from discrete; each of them can be understood to problematize the locality and meaning of both the "subject" and "gender" within the context of socially instituted gender asymmetry. The interpretive possibilities of gender are in no sense exhausted by the alternatives suggested above. The problematic circularity of a feminist inquiry into gender is underscored by the presence of positions which, on the one hand, presume that gender is a secondary characteristic of persons and those which, on the other hand, argue that the very notion of the person, positioned within language as a "subject," is a masculinist construction and prerogative which effectively excludes the structural and semantic possibility of a feminine gender. The consequence of such sharp disagreements about the meaning of gender (indeed, whether *gender* is the term to be argued about at all, or whether the discursive construction of *sex* is, indeed, more fundamental, or perhaps *women* or *woman* and/or *men* and *man*) establishes the need for a radical rethinking of the categories of identity within the context of relations of radical gender asymmetry.

For Beauvoir, the "subject" within the existential analytic of misogyny is always already masculine, conflated with the universal, differentiating itself from a feminine "Other" outside the universalizing norms of personhood, hopelessly "particular," embodied, condemned to immanence. Although Beauvoir is often understood to be calling for the right of women, in effect, to become existential subjects and, hence, for inclusion within the terms of an abstract universality, her position also implies a fundamental critique of the very disembodiment of the abstract masculine epistemological subject.[18] That subject is abstract to the extent that it disavows its socially marked embodiment and, further, projects that disavowed and disparaged embodiment on to the feminine sphere, effectively renaming the body as female. This association of the body with the female works along magical relations of reciprocity whereby the female sex becomes restricted to its body, and the male body, fully disavowed, becomes, paradoxically, the incorporeal instrument of an ostensibly radical freedom. Beauvoir's analysis implicitly poses the question: Through what act of negation and disavowal does the masculine pose as a disembodied universality and the feminine get constructed as a disavowed corporeality? The dialectic of master-slave, here fully reformulated within the non-reciprocal terms of gender asymmetry, prefigures what Irigaray will later describe as the masculine signifying economy that includes both the existential subject and its Other.

Beauvoir proposes that the female body ought to be the situation and instrumentality of women's freedom, not a defining and limiting essence.[19] The theory of embodiment informing Beauvoir's analysis is clearly limited by the uncritical reproduction of the Cartesian distinction between freedom and the body. Despite my own previous efforts to argue the contrary, it appears that Beauvoir maintains the mind/body dualism, even as she proposes a synthesis of those terms.[20] The preservation of that very distinction can be read as symptomatic of the very phallogocentrism that Beauvoir underestimates. In the philosophical tradition that begins with Plato and continues through Descartes, Husserl, and Sartre, the ontological distinction between soul (consciousness, mind) and body invariably supports relations of political and psychic subordination and hierarchy. The mind not only subjugates the body, but occasionally entertains the fantasy of fleeing its embodiment altogether. The cultural associations of mind with masculinity and body with femininity are well documented within the field of philosophy and feminism.[21] As a result, any uncritical reproduction of the mind/body distinction ought to be rethought for the implicit gender hierarchy that the distinction has conventionally produced, maintained, and rationalized.

The discursive construction of "the body" and its separation from "freedom" in Beauvoir fails to mark along the axis of gender the very mind-body distinction that is supposed to illuminate the persistence of gender asymmetry. Officially, Beauvoir contends that the female body is marked within masculinist discourse, whereby the masculine body, in its conflation with the universal, remains unmarked. Irigaray clearly suggests that both marker and marked are maintained within a masculinist mode of signification in which the female body is "marked off," as it were, from the domain of the signifiable. In post–Hegelian terms, she is "cancelled," but not preserved. On Irigaray's reading, Beauvoir's claim that woman "is sex" is reversed to mean that she is not the sex she is designated to be, but, rather, the masculine sex *encore* (and *en corps*) parading in the mode of otherness. For Irigaray, that phallogocentric mode of signifying the female sex perpetually reproduces phantasms of its own self-amplifying desire. Instead of a self-limiting linguistic gesture that grants alterity or difference to

women, phallogocentrism offers a name to eclipse the feminine and take its place.

IV. Theorizing the Binary, the Unitary, and Beyond

Beauvoir and Irigaray clearly differ over the fundamental structures by which gender asymmetry is reproduced; Beauvoir turns to the failed reciprocity of an asymmetrical dialectic, while Irigaray suggests that the dialectic itself is the monologic elaboration of a masculinist signifying economy. Although Irigaray clearly broadens the scope of feminist critique by exposing the epistemological, ontological, and logical structures of a masculinist signifying economy, the power of her analysis is undercut precisely by its globalizing reach. Is it possible to identify a monolithic as well as a monologic masculinist economy that traverses the array of cultural and historical contexts in which sexual difference takes place? Is the failure to acknowledge the specific cultural operations of gender oppression itself a kind of epistemological imperialism, one which is not ameliorated by the simple elaboration of cultural differences as "examples" of the selfsame phallogocentrism? The effort to *include* "Other" cultures as variegated amplifications of a global phallogocentrism constitutes an appropriative act that risks a repetition of the self-aggrandizing gesture of phallogocentrism, colonizing under the sign of the same those differences that might otherwise call that totalizing concept into question.[22]

Feminist critique ought to explore the totalizing claims of a masculinist signifying economy, but also remain self-critical with respect to the totalizing gestures of feminism. The effort to identify the enemy as singular in form is a reverse-discourse that uncritically mimics the strategy of the oppressor instead of offering a different set of terms. That the tactic can operate in feminist and antifeminist contexts alike suggests that the colonizing gesture is not primarily or irreducibly masculinist. It can operate to effect other relations of racial, class, and heterosexist subordination, to name but a few. And clearly, listing the varieties of oppression, as I began to do, assumes their discrete, sequential coexistence along a horizontal axis that does not describe their convergences within the social field.

A vertical model is similarly insufficient; oppressions cannot be summarily ranked, causally related, distributed among planes of "originality" and "derivativeness."[23] Indeed, the field of power structured in part by the imperializing gesture of dialectical appropriation exceeds and encompasses the axis of sexual difference, offering a mapping of intersecting differentials which cannot be summarily hierarchized either within the terms of phallogocentrism or any other candidate for the position of "primary condition of oppression." Rather than an exclusive tactic of masculinist signifying economies, dialectical appropriation and suppression of the Other is one tactic among many, deployed centrally but not exclusively in the service of expanding and rationalizing the masculinist domain.

The contemporary feminist debates over essentialism raise the question of the universality of female identity and masculinist oppression in other ways. Universalistic claims are based on a common or shared epistemological standpoint, understood as the articulated consciousness or shared structures of oppression or in the ostensibly transcultural structures of femininity, maternity, sexuality, and/or *écriture feminine*. The opening discussion in this chapter argued that this globalizing gesture has spawned a number of criticisms from women who claim that the category of "women" is normative and exclusionary and is invoked with the unmarked dimensions of class and racial privilege intact. In other words, the insistence upon the coherence and unity of the category of women has effectively refused the multiplicity of cultural, social, and political intersections in which the concrete array of "women" are constructed.

Some efforts have been made to formulate coalitional politics which do not assume in advance what the content of "women" will be. They propose instead a set of dialogic encounters by which variously positioned women articulate separate identities within the framework of an emergent coalition. Clearly, the value of coalitional politics is not to be underestimated, but the very form of coalition, of an emerging and unpredictable assemblage of positions, cannot be figured in advance. Despite the clearly democratizing impulse that motivates coalition building, the coalitional theorist can inadvertently reinsert herself as sovereign of the process by trying to assert an ideal form for coalitional structures *in advance*, one that will effectively guarantee unity as the outcome. Related efforts to determine what is and is not the true shape of a dialogue, what constitutes a subject-position, and, most importantly, when "unity" has been reached, can impede the self-shaping and self-limiting dynamics of coalition.

The insistence in advance on coalitional "unity" as a goal assumes that solidarity, whatever its price, is a prerequisite for political action. But what sort of politics demands that kind of advance purchase on unity? Perhaps a coalition needs to acknowledge its contradictions and take action with those contradictions intact. Perhaps also part of what dialogic understanding entails is the acceptance of divergence, breakage, splinter, and fragmentation as part of the often tortuous process of democratization. The very notion of "dialogue" is culturally specific and historically bound, and while one speaker may feel secure that a conversation is happening, another may be sure it is not. The power relations that condition and limit dialogic possibilities need first to be interrogated. Otherwise, the model of dialogue risks relapsing into a liberal model that assumes that speaking agents occupy equal positions of power and speak with the same presuppositions about what constitutes "agreement" and "unity" and, indeed, that those are the goals to be sought. It would be wrong to assume in advance that there is a category of "women" that simply needs to be filled in with various components of race, class, age, ethnicity, and sexuality in order to become complete. The assumption of its essential incompleteness permits that category to serve as a permanently available site of contested meanings. The definitional incompleteness of the category might then serve as a normative ideal relieved of coercive force.

Is "unity" necessary for effective political action? Is the premature insistence on the goal of unity precisely the cause of an ever more bitter fragmentation among the ranks? Certain forms of acknowledged fragmentation might facilitate coalitional action precisely because the "unity" of the category of women is neither presupposed nor desired. Does "unity" set up an exclusionary norm of solidarity at the level of identity that rules out the possibility of a set of actions which disrupt the very borders of identity concepts, or which seek to accomplish precisely that disruption as an explicit political aim? Without the presupposition or goal of "unity," which is, in either case, always instituted at a conceptual level, provisional unities might emerge in the context of concrete actions that have purposes other than the articulation of identity. Without the compulsory expectation that feminist actions must be instituted from some stable, unified, and agreed-upon identity, those actions might well get a quicker start and seem more congenial to a number of "women" for whom the meaning of the category is permanently moot.

This antifoundationalist approach to coalitional politics assumes neither that "identity" is a premise nor that the shape or meaning of a coalitional assemblage can be known prior to its achievement. Because the articulation of an identity within available cultural terms instates a definition that forecloses in advance the emergence of new identity concepts in and through politically engaged actions, the foundationalist tactic cannot take the transformation or expansion of existing identity concepts as a normative goal. Moreover, when agreed-upon identities or agreed-upon dialogic structures, through which already established identities are communicated, no longer constitute the theme or subject of politics, then identities can come into being and dissolve depending on the concrete practices that constitute them. Certain political practices institute identities on a contingent basis in order to accomplish whatever aims are in view. Coalitional politics requires neither an expanded category of "women" nor an internally multiplicitous self that offers its complexity at once.

Gender is a complexity whose totality is permanently deferred, never fully what it is at any given juncture in time. An open coalition, then, will affirm identities that are alternately instituted and relinquished according to the purposes at hand; it will be an open assemblage that permits of multiple convergences and divergences without obedience to a normative telos of definitional closure.

V. Identity, Sex, and the Metaphysics of Substance

What can be meant by "identity," then, and what grounds the presumption that identities are self-identical, persisting through time as the same, unified and internally coherent? More importantly, how do these assumptions inform the discourses on "gender identity"? It would be wrong to think that the discussion of "identity" ought to proceed prior to a discussion of gender identity for the simple reason that "persons" only become intelligible through becoming gendered in conformity with recognizable standards of gender intelligibility. Sociological discussions have conventionally sought to understand the notion of the person in terms of an agency that claims ontological priority to the various roles and functions through which it assumes social visibility and meaning. Within philosophical discourse itself, the notion of "the person" has received analytic elaboration on the assumption that whatever social context the person is "in" remains somehow externally related to the definitional structure of personhood, be that consciousness, the capacity for language, or moral deliberation. Although that literature is not examined here, one premise of such inquiries is the focus of critical exploration and inversion. Whereas the question of what constitutes "personal identity" within philosophical accounts almost always centers on the question of what internal feature of the person establishes the continuity or self-identity of the person through time, the question here will be: To what extent do *regulatory practices* of gender formation and division constitute identity, the internal coherence of the subject, indeed, the self-identical status of the person? To what extent is "identity" a normative ideal rather than a descriptive feature of experience? And how do the regulatory practices that govern gender also govern culturally intelligible notions of identity? In other words, the "coherence" and "continuity" of "the person" are not logical or analytic features of personhood, but, rather, socially instituted and maintained norms of intelligibility. Inasmuch as "identity" is assured through the stabilizing concepts of sex, gender, and sexuality, the very notion of "the person" is called into question by the cultural emergence of those "incoherent" or "discontinuous" gendered beings who appear to be persons but who fail to conform to the gendered norms of cultural intelligibility by which persons are defined.

"Intelligible" genders are those which in some sense institute and maintain relations of coherence and continuity among sex, gender, sexual practice, and desire. In other words, the spectres of discontinuity and incoherence, themselves thinkable only in relation to existing norms of continuity and coherence, are constantly prohibited and produced by the very laws that seek to establish causal or expressive lines of connection among biological sex, culturally constituted genders, and the "expression" or "effect" of both in the manifestation of sexual desire through sexual practice.

The notion that there might be a "truth" of sex, as Foucault ironically terms it, is produced precisely through the regulatory practices that generate coherent identities through the matrix of coherent gender norms. The heterosexualization of desire requires and institutes the production of discrete and asymmetrical oppositions between "feminine" and "masculine," where these are understood as expressive attributes of "male" and "female." The cultural matrix through which gender identity has become intelligible requires that certain kinds of "identities" cannot "exist" – that is, those in which gender does not follow from sex and those in which the practices of desire do not "follow" from either sex or gender. "Follow" in this context is a political relation of entailment instituted by the cultural laws that establish and regulate the shape and meaning of sexuality. Indeed, precisely because certain kinds of "gender identities" fail to conform to those norms of cultural intelligibility, they appear only as developmental failures or logical impossibilities from within that domain. Their persistence and proliferation, however, provide critical opportunities to expose the limits and regulatory aims of that domain of intelligibility and, hence, to open up within the very terms of that matrix of intelligibility rival and subversive matrices of gender disorder.

[...]

Gender can denote a *unity* of experience, of sex, gender, and desire, only when sex can be understood in some sense to necessitate gender – where gender is a psychic and/or cultural designation of the self – and desire – where desire is heterosexual and therefore differentiates itself through an oppositional relation to that other gender it desires. The internal coherence or unity of either gender, man or woman, thereby requires both a stable and oppositional heterosexuality. That institutional heterosexuality both requires and produces the univocity of each of the gendered terms that constitute the limit of gendered

possibilities within an oppositional, binary gender system. This conception of gender presupposes not only a causal relation among sex, gender, and desire, but suggests as well that desire reflects or expresses gender and that gender reflects or expresses desire. The metaphysical unity of the three is assumed to be truly known and expressed in a differentiating desire for an oppositional gender – that is, in a form of oppositional heterosexuality. Whether as a naturalistic paradigm which establishes a causal continuity among sex, gender, and desire, or as an authentic-expressive paradigm in which some true self is said to be revealed simultaneously or successively in sex, gender, and desire, here "the old dream of symmetry," as Irigaray has called it, is presupposed, reified, and rationalized.

This rough sketch of gender gives us a clue to understanding the political reasons for the substantializing view of gender. The institution of a compulsory and naturalized heterosexuality requires and regulates gender as a binary relation in which the masculine term is differentiated from a feminine term, and this differentiation is accomplished through the practices of heterosexual desire. The act of differentiating the two oppositional moments of the binary results in a consolidation of each term, the respective internal coherence of sex, gender, and desire.

The strategic displacement of that binary relation and the metaphysics of substance on which it relies presuppose that the categories of female and male, woman and man, are similarly produced within the binary frame. Foucault implicitly subscribes to such an explanation. In the closing chapter of the first volume of *The History of Sexuality* and in his brief but significant introduction to *Herculine Barbin, Being the Recently Discovered Journals of a Nineteenth-Century Hermaphrodite*,[24] Foucault suggests that the category of sex, prior to any categorization of sexual difference, is itself constructed through a historically specific mode of *sexuality*. The tactical production of the discrete and binary categorization of sex conceals the strategic aims of that very apparatus of production by postulating "sex" as "a cause" of sexual experience, behavior, and desire. Foucault's genealogical inquiry exposes this ostensible "cause" as "an effect," the production of a given regime of sexuality that seeks to regulate sexual experience by instating the discrete categories of sex as foundational and causal functions within any discursive account of sexuality.

Foucault's introduction to the journals of the hermaphrodite, Herculine Barbin, suggests that the genealogical critique of these reified categories of sex is the inadvertent consequence of sexual practices that cannot be accounted for within the medicolegal discourse of a naturalized heterosexuality. Herculine is not an "identity," but the sexual impossibility of an identity. Although male and female anatomical elements are jointly distributed in and on this body, that is not the true source of scandal. The linguistic conventions that produce intelligible gendered selves find their limit in Herculine precisely because she/he occasions a convergence and disorganization of the rules that govern sex/gender/desire. Herculine deploys and redistributes the terms of a binary system, but that very redistribution disrupts and proliferates those terms outside the binary itself. According to Foucault, Herculine is not categorizable within the gender binary as it stands; the disconcerting convergence of heterosexuality and homosexuality in her/his person are only occasioned, but never caused, by his/her anatomical discontinuity. Foucault's appropriation of Herculine is suspect, but his analysis implies the interesting belief that sexual heterogeneity (paradoxically foreclosed by a naturalized "hetero"-sexuality) implies a critique of the metaphysics of substance as it informs the identitarian categories of sex. Foucault imagines Herculine's experience as "a world of pleasures in which grins hang about without the cat."[25] Smiles, happinesses, pleasures, and desires are figured here as qualities without an abiding substance to which they are said to adhere. As free-floating attributes, they suggest the possibility of a gendered experience that cannot be grasped through the substantializing and hierarchizing grammar of nouns (*res extensa*) and adjectives (attributes, essential and accidental). Through his cursory reading of Herculine, Foucault proposes an ontology of accidental attributes that exposes the postulation of identity as a culturally restricted principle of order and hierarchy, a regulatory fiction.

If it is possible to speak of a "man" with a masculine attribute and to understand that attribute as a happy but accidental feature of that man, then it is also possible to speak of a "man" with a feminine attribute, whatever that is, but still to maintain the integrity of the gender. But once we dispense with the priority of "man" and "woman" as abiding substances, then it is no longer possible to subordinate dissonant gendered features as so many secondary and accidental characteristics of a gender ontology that is fundamentally intact. If the notion of an abiding substance is a fictive construction produced through the compulsory ordering of attributes into coherent gender sequences, then it seems that gender as substance, the viability of *man* and *woman* as nouns, is called into question by the dissonant play of attributes that fail to conform to sequential or causal models of intelligibility.

The appearance of an abiding substance or gendered self, what the psychiatrist Robert Stoller refers to as a "gender core,"[26] is thus produced by the regulation of attributes along culturally established lines of coherence. As a result, the exposure of this fictive production is conditioned by the deregulated play of attributes that resist assimilation into the ready made framework of primary nouns and subordinate adjectives. It is of course always possible to argue that dissonant adjectives work retroactively to redefine the substantive identities they are said to modify and, hence, to expand the substantive categories of gender to include possibilities that they previously excluded. But if these substances are nothing other than the coherences contingently created through the regulation of attributes, it would seem that the ontology of substances itself is not only an artificial effect, but essentially superfluous.

In this sense, *gender* is not a noun, but neither is it a set of free-floating attributes, for we have seen that the substantive effect of gender is performatively produced and compelled by the regulatory practices of gender coherence. Hence, within the inherited discourse of the metaphysics of substance, gender proves to be performative – that is, constituting the identity it is purported to be. In this sense, gender is always a doing, though not a doing by a subject who might be said to preexist the deed. The challenge for rethinking gender categories outside of the metaphysics of substance will have to consider the relevance of Nietzsche's claim in *On the Genealogy of Morals* that "there is no 'being' behind doing, effecting, becoming; 'the doer' is merely a fiction added to the deed – the deed is everything."[27] In an application that Nietzsche himself would not have anticipated or condoned, we might state as a corollary: There is no gender identity behind the expressions of gender; that identity is performatively constituted by the very "expressions" that are said to be its results.

VI. Language, Power, and the Strategies of Displacement

A great deal of feminist theory and literature has nevertheless assumed that there is a "doer" behind the deed. Without an agent, it is argued, there can be no agency and hence no potential to initiate a transformation of relations of domination within society. Wittig's radical feminist theory occupies an ambiguous position within the continuum of theories on the question of the subject. On the one hand, Wittig appears to dispute the metaphysics of substance, but on the other hand, she retains the human subject, the individual, as the metaphysical locus of agency. While Wittig's humanism clearly presupposes that there is a doer behind the deed, her theory nevertheless delineates the performative construction of gender within the material practices of culture, disputing the temporality of those explanations that would confuse "cause" with "result." In a phrase that suggests the intertextual space that links Wittig with Foucault (and reveals the traces of the Marxist notion of reification in both of their theories), she writes:

> A materialist feminist approach shows that what we take for the cause or origin of oppression is in fact only the *mark* imposed by the oppressor; the "myth of woman," plus its material effects and manifestations in the appropriated consciousness and bodies of women. Thus, this mark does not preexist oppression … sex is taken as an "immediate given," a "sensible given," "physical features," belonging to a natural order. But what we believe to be a physical and direct perception is only a sophisticated and mythic construction, an "imaginary formation."[28]

Because this production of "nature" operates in accord with the dictates of compulsory heterosexuality, the emergence of homosexual desire, in her view, transcends the categories of sex: "If desire could liberate itself, it would have nothing to do with the preliminary marking by sexes."[29]

Wittig refers to "sex" as a mark that is somehow applied by an institutionalized heterosexuality, a mark that can be erased or obfuscated through practices that effectively contest that institution. Her view, of course, differs radically from Irigaray's. The latter would understand the "mark" of gender to be part of the hegemonic signifying economy of the masculine that operates through the self-elaborating mechanisms of specularization that have virtually determined the field of ontology within the Western philosophical tradition. For Wittig, language is an instrument or tool that is in no way misogynist in its structures, but only in its applications.[30] For Irigaray, the possibility of another language or signifying economy is the only chance at escaping the "mark" of gender which, for the feminine, is nothing but the phallogocentric erasure of the female sex. Whereas Irigaray seeks to expose the ostensible "binary" relation between the sexes as a masculinist ruse that excludes the feminine altogether, Wittig argues that positions like Irigaray's reconsolidate the binary between masculine and feminine and recirculate a mythic notion of the feminine. Clearly drawing on Beauvoir's critique of the myth of the feminine in *The Second Sex*, Wittig asserts, "there is no 'feminine writing.'"[31]

Wittig is clearly attuned to the power of language to subordinate and exclude women. As a "materialist," however, she considers language to be "another order of materiality,"[32] an institution that can be radically transformed. Language ranks among the concrete and contingent practices and institutions maintained by the choices of individuals and, hence, weakened by the collective actions of choosing individuals. The linguistic fiction of "sex," she argues, is a category produced and circulated by the system of compulsory heterosexuality in an effort to restrict the production of identities along the axis of heterosexual desire. In some of her work, both male and female homosexuality, as well as other positions independent of the heterosexual contract, provide the occasion either for the overthrow or the proliferation of the category of sex. In *The Lesbian Body* and elsewhere, however, Wittig appears to take issue with genitally organized sexuality *per se* and to call for an alternative economy of pleasures which would both contest the construction of female subjectivity marked by women's supposedly distinctive reproductive function.[33] Here the proliferation of pleasures outside the reproductive economy suggests both a specifically feminine form of erotic diffusion, understood as a counterstrategy to the reproductive construction of genitality. In a sense, *The Lesbian Body* can be understood, for Wittig, as an "inverted" reading of Freud's *Three Essays on the Theory of Sexuality,* in which he argues for the developmental superiority of genital sexuality over and against the less restricted and more diffuse infantile sexuality. Only the "invert," the medical classification invoked by Freud for "the homosexual," fails to "achieve" the genital norm. In waging a political critique against genitality, Wittig appears to deploy "inversion" as a critical reading practice, valorising precisely those features of an undeveloped sexuality designated by Freud and effectively inaugurating a "post-genital politics."[34] Indeed, the notion of development can be read only as normalization within the heterosexual matrix. And yet, is this the only reading of Freud possible? And to what extent is Wittig's practice of "inversion" committed to the very model of normalization that she seeks to dismantle? In other words, if the model of a more diffuse and antigenital sexuality serves as the singular, oppositional alternative to the hegemonic structure of sexuality, to what extent is that binary relation fated to reproduce itself endlessly? What possibility exists for the disruption of the oppositional binary itself?

Wittig's oppositional relationship to psychoanalysis produces the unexpected consequence that her theory presumes precisely that psychoanalytic theory of development, now fully "inverted," that she seeks to overcome. Polymorphous perversity, assumed to exist prior to the marking by sex, is valorised as the telos of human sexuality.[35] One possible feminist psychoanalytic response to Wittig might argue that she both undertheorizes and underestimates the meaning and function of *the language* in which "the mark of gender" occurs. She understands that marking practice as contingent, radically variable, and even dispensable. The status of a primary *prohibition* in Lacanian theory operates more forcefully and less contingently than the notion of a *regulatory practice* in Foucault or a materialist account of a system of heterosexist oppression in Wittig.

In Lacan, as in Irigaray's post-Lacanian reformulation of Freud, sexual difference is not a simple binary that retains the metaphysics of substance as its foundation. The masculine "subject" is a fictive construction produced by the law that prohibits incest and forces an infinite displacement of a heterosexualizing desire. The feminine is never a mark of the subject; the feminine could not be an "attribute" of a gender. Rather, the feminine is the signification of lack, signified by the Symbolic, a set of differentiating linguistic rules that effectively create sexual difference. The masculine linguistic position undergoes individuation and heterosexualization required by the founding prohibitions of the Symbolic law, the law of the Father. The incest taboo that bars the son from the mother and thereby instates the kinship relation between them is a law enacted "in the name of the Father." Similarly, the law that refuses the girl's desire for both her mother and father requires that she take up the emblem of maternity and perpetuate the rules of kinship. Both masculine and feminine positions are thus instituted through prohibitive laws that produce culturally intelligible genders, but only through the production of an unconscious sexuality that reemerges in the domain of the imaginary.

The feminist appropriation of sexual difference, whether written in opposition to the phallogocentrism of Lacan (Irigaray) or as a critical reelaboration of Lacan, attempts to theorize the feminine, not as an expression of the metaphysics of substance, but as the unrepresentable absence effected by (masculine) denial that grounds the signifying economy through exclusion. The feminine as the repudiated/excluded within that system constitutes the possibility of a critique and disruption of that hegemonic conceptual scheme. The works of Jacqueline Rose[36] and Jane Gallop[37] underscore in different ways the constructed status of sexual difference, the inherent instability of that construction, and the dual consequentiality of a prohibition that at once institutes a sexual identity and provides for the exposure of that construction's tenuous ground. Although Wittig and other materialist feminists within the French context would argue that sexual difference is an unthinking replication of a reified set of sexed polarities, these criticisms neglect the critical dimension of the unconscious which, as a site of repressed sexuality, reemerges within the discourse of the subject as the very impossibility of its coherence. As Rose points out very clearly, the construction of a coherent sexual identity along the disjunctive axis of the feminine/masculine is bound to fail;[38] the disruptions of this coherence through the inadvertent reemergence of the repressed reveal not only that "identity" is constructed, but that the prohibition that constructs identity is inefficacious (the paternal law ought to be understood not as a deterministic divine will, but as a perpetual bumbler, preparing the ground for the insurrections against him).

The differences between the materialist and Lacanian (and post-Lacanian) positions emerge in a normative quarrel over whether there is a retrievable sexuality either "before" or "outside" the law in the mode of the unconscious or "after" the law as a post-genital sexuality. Paradoxically, the normative trope of polymorphous perversity is understood to characterize both views of alternative sexuality. There is no agreement, however, on the manner of delimiting that "law" or set of "laws." The psychoanalytic critique succeeds in giving an account of the construction of "the subject" – and perhaps also the illusion of substance – within the matrix of normative gender relations. In her existential-materialist mode, Wittig presumes the subject, the person, to have a presocial and pregendered integrity. On the other hand, "the paternal Law" in Lacan, as well as the monologic mastery of phallogocentrism in Irigaray, bear the mark of a monotheistic singularity that is perhaps less unitary and culturally universal than the guiding structuralist assumptions of the account presume.[39]

But the quarrel seems also to turn on the articulation of a temporal trope of a subversive sexuality that flourishes *prior* to the imposition of a law, *after* its overthrow, or during its reign as a constant challenge to its authority. Here it seems wise to reinvoke Foucault who, in claiming that sexuality and power are coextensive, implicitly refutes the postulation of a subversive or emancipatory sexuality which could be free of the law. We can press the argument further by pointing out that "the before" of the law and "the after" are discursively and performatively instituted modes of temporality that are invoked within the terms of a normative framework which asserts that subversion, destabilization, or displacement requires a sexuality that somehow escapes the hegemonic prohibitions on sex. For Foucault, those prohibitions are invariably and inadvertently productive in the sense that "the subject" who is supposed to be founded and produced in and through those prohibitions does not have access

to a sexuality that is in some sense "outside," "before," or "after" power itself. Power, rather than the law, encompasses both the juridical (prohibitive and regulatory) and the productive (inadvertently generative) functions of differential relations. Hence, the sexuality that emerges within the matrix of power relations is not a simple replication or copy of the law itself, a uniform repetition of a masculinist economy of identity. The productions swerve from their original purposes and inadvertently mobilize possibilities of "subjects" that do not merely exceed the bounds of cultural intelligibility, but effectively expand the boundaries of what is, in fact, culturally intelligible.

The feminist norm of a postgenital sexuality became the object of significant criticism from feminist theorists of sexuality, some of whom have sought a specifically feminist and/or lesbian appropriation of Foucault. This utopian notion of a sexuality freed from heterosexual constructs, a sexuality beyond "sex," failed to acknowledge the ways in which power relations continue to construct sexuality for women even within the terms of a "liberated" heterosexuality or lesbianism.[40] The same criticism is waged against the notion of a specifically feminine sexual pleasure that is radically differentiated from phallic sexuality. Irigaray's occasional efforts to derive a specific feminine sexuality from a specific female anatomy have been the focus of anti-essentialist arguments for some time.[41] The return to biology as the ground of a specific feminine sexuality or meaning seems to defeat the feminist premise that biology is not destiny. But whether feminine sexuality is articulated here through a discourse of biology for purely strategic reasons,[42] or whether it is, in fact, a feminist return to biological essentialism, the characterization of female sexuality as radically distinct from a phallic organization of sexuality remains problematic. Women who fail either to recognize that sexuality as their own or understand their sexuality as partially constructed within the terms of the phallic economy are potentially written off within the terms of that theory as "male-identified" or "unenlightened." Indeed, it is often unclear within Irigaray's text whether sexuality is culturally constructed, or whether it is only culturally constructed within the terms of the phallus. In other words, is specifically feminine pleasure "outside" of culture as its prehistory or as its utopian future? If so, of what use is such a notion for negotiating the contemporary struggles of sexuality within the terms of its construction?

The pro-sexuality movement within feminist theory and practice has effectively argued that sexuality is always constructed within the terms of discourse and power, where power is partially understood in terms of heterosexual and phallic cultural conventions. The emergence of a sexuality constructed (not determined) in these terms within lesbian, bisexual, and heterosexual contexts is, therefore, *not* a sign of a masculine identification in some reductive sense. It is not the failed project of criticizing phallogocentrism or heterosexual hegemony, as if a political critique could effectively undo the cultural construction of the feminist critic's sexuality. If sexuality is culturally constructed within existing power relations, then the postulation of a normative sexuality that is "before," "outside," or "beyond" power is a cultural impossibility and a politically impracticable dream, one that postpones the concrete and contemporary task of rethinking subversive possibilities for sexuality and identity within the terms of power itself. This critical task presumes, of course, that to operate within the matrix of power is not the same as to replicate uncritically relations of domination. It offers the possibility of a repetition of the law which is not its consolidation, but its displacement. In the place of a "male-identified" sexuality in which "male" serves as the cause and irreducible meaning of that sexuality, we might develop a notion of sexuality constructed in terms of phallic relations of power that replay and redistribute the possibilities of that phallicism precisely through the subversive operation of "identifications" that are, within the power field of sexuality, inevitable. If "identifications," following Jacqueline Rose, can be exposed as phantasmatic, then it must be possible to enact an identification that displays its phantasmatic structure. If there is no radical repudiation of a culturally constructed sexuality, what is left is the question of how to acknowledge and "do" the construction one is invariably in. Are there forms of repetition that do not constitute a simple imitation, reproduction, and, hence, consolidation of the law (the anachronistic notion of "male identification" that ought to be discarded from a feminist vocabulary)? What possibilities of gender configurations exist among the various emergent and occasionally convergent matrices of cultural intelligibility that govern gendered life?

Within the terms of feminist sexual theory, it is clear that the presence of power dynamics within sexuality is in no sense the same as the simple consolidation or augmentation of a heterosexist or phallogocentric power regime. The "presence" of so-called heterosexual conventions within homosexual contexts as well as the proliferation of specifically gay discourses of sexual difference, as in the case of "butch" and "femme" as historical identities of sexual style, cannot be explained as chimerical representations of originally heterosexual identities. And neither can they be understood as the pernicious insistence of heterosexist constructs within gay sexuality and identity. The repetition of heterosexual constructs within sexual cultures both gay and straight may well be the inevitable site of the denaturalization and mobilization of gender categories. The replication of heterosexual constructs in non-heterosexual frames brings into relief the utterly constructed status of the so-called heterosexual original. Thus, gay is to straight *not* as copy is to original, but, rather, as copy is to copy. The parodic repetition of "the original" reveals the original to be nothing other than a parody of the *idea* of the natural and the original.[43] Even if heterosexist constructs circulate as the available sites of power/discourse from which to do gender at all, the question remains: What possibilities of recirculation exist? Which possibilities of doing gender repeat and displace through hyperbole, dissonance, internal confusion, and proliferation the very constructs by which they are mobilized?

Consider not only that the ambiguities and incoherences within and among heterosexual, homosexual, and bisexual practices are suppressed and redescribed within the reified framework of the disjunctive and asymmetrical binary of masculine/feminine, but that these cultural configurations of gender confusion operate as sites for intervention, exposure, and displacement of these reifications. In other words, the "unity" of gender is the effect of a regulatory practice that seeks to render gender identity uniform through a compulsory heterosexuality. The force of this practice is, through an exclusionary apparatus of production, to restrict the relative meanings of "heterosexuality," "homosexuality," and "bisexuality" as well as the subversive sites of their convergence and resignification. That the power regimes of heterosexism and phallogocentrism seek to augment themselves through a constant repetition of their logic, their metaphysic, and their naturalized ontologies does not imply that repetition itself ought to be stopped – as if it could be. If repetition is bound to persist as the mechanism of the cultural reproduction of identities, then the crucial question emerges: What kind of subversive repetition might call into question the regulatory practice of identity itself?

If there is no recourse to a "person," a "sex," or a "sexuality" that escapes the matrix of power and discursive relations that effectively produce and regulate the intelligibility of those concepts for us, what constitutes the possibility of effective inversion, subversion, or displacement within the terms of a constructed identity? What possibilities exist *by virtue of* the constructed character of sex and gender? Whereas Foucault is ambiguous about the precise character of the "regulatory practices" that produce the category of sex, and Wittig appears to invest the full responsibility of the construction to sexual reproduction and its instrument, compulsory heterosexuality, yet other discourses converge to produce this categorial fiction for reasons not always clear or consistent with one another. The power relations that infuse the biological sciences are not easily reduced, and the medico–legal alliance emerging in nineteenth-century Europe has spawned categorial fictions that could not be anticipated in advance. The very complexity of the discursive map that constructs gender appears to hold out the promise of an inadvertent and generative convergence of these discursive and regulatory structures. If the regulatory fictions of sex and gender are themselves multiply contested sites of meaning, then the very multiplicity of their construction holds out the possibility of a disruption of their univocal posturing.

Clearly this project does not propose to lay out within traditional philosophical terms an *ontology* of gender whereby the meaning of *being* a woman or a man is elucidated within the terms of phenomenology. The presumption here is that the "being" of gender is *an effect,* an object of a genealogical investigation that maps out the political parameters of its construction in the mode of ontology. To claim that gender is constructed is not to assert its illusoriness or artificiality, where those terms are understood to reside within a binary that counterposes the "real" and the "authentic"

as oppositional. As a genealogy of gender ontology, this inquiry seeks to understand the discursive production of the plausibility of that binary relation and to suggest that certain cultural configurations of gender take the place of "the real" and consolidate and augment their hegemony through that felicitous self-naturalization.

If there is something right in Beauvoir's claim that one is not born, but rather *becomes* a woman, it follows that *woman* itself is a term in process, a becoming, a constructing that cannot rightfully be said to originate or to end. As an ongoing discursive practice, it is open to intervention and resignification. Even when gender seems to congeal into the most reified forms the "congealing" is itself an insistent and insidious practice, sustained and regulated by various social means. It is, for Beauvoir, never possible finally to become a woman, as if there were a *telos* that governs the process of acculturation and construction. Gender is the repeated stylization of the body, a set of repeated acts within a highly rigid regulatory frame that congeal over time to produce the appearance of substance, of a natural sort of being. A political genealogy of gender ontologies, if it is successful, will deconstruct the substantive appearance of gender into its constitutive acts and locate and account for those acts within the compulsory frames set by the various forces that police the social appearance of gender. To expose the contingent acts that create the appearance of a naturalistic necessity, a move which has been a part of cultural critique at least since Marx, is a task that now takes on the added burden of showing how the very notion of the subject, intelligible only through its appearance as gendered, admits of possibilities that have been forcibly foreclosed by the various reifications of gender that have constituted its contingent ontologies.

[...]

Notes

1   See Michel Foucault, "Right of Death and Power over Life," in *The History of Sexuality, Volume 1, An Introduction,* trans. Robert Hurley (New York: Vintage, 1980), originally published as *Histoire de la sexualité 1: La volonté de savoir* (Paris: Gallimard, 1978). In that final chapter, Foucault discusses the relation between the juridical and productive law. His notion of the productivity of the law

is clearly derived from Nietzsche, although not identical with Nietzsche's will-to-power. The use of Foucault's notion of productive power is not meant as a simple-minded "application" of Foucault to gender issues.

2 References throughout this work to a subject before the law are extrapolations of Derrida's reading of Kafka's parable "Before the Law," in *Kafka and the Contemporary Critical Performance: Centenary Readings,* ed. Alan Udoff (Bloomington: Indiana University Press, 1987).

3 See Denise Riley, *Am I That Name?: Feminism and the Category of 'Women' in History* (New York: Macmillan, 1988).

4 See Sandra Harding, "The Instability of the Analytical Categories of Feminist Theory," in *Sex and Scientific Inquiry,* eds. Sandra Harding and Jean F. O'Barr (Chicago: University of Chicago Press, 1987), pp. 283–302.

5 I am reminded of the ambiguity inherent in Nancy Cott's title, *The Grounding of Modern Feminism* (New Haven: Yale University Press, 1987). She argues that the early twentieth-century US feminist movement sought to "ground" itself in a program that eventually "grounded" that movement. Her historical thesis implicitly raises the question of whether uncritically accepted foundations operate like the "return of the repressed"; based on exclusionary practices, the stable political identities that found political movements may invariably become threatened by the very instability that the foundationalist move creates.

6 I use the term *heterosexual matrix* throughout the text to designate that grid of cultural intelligibility through which bodies, genders, and desires are naturalized. I am drawing from Monique Wittig's notion of the "heterosexual contract" and, to a lesser extent, on Adrienne Rich's notion of "compulsory heterosexuality" to characterize a hegemonic discursive/epistemic model of gender intelligibility that assumes that for bodies to cohere and make sense there must be a stable sex expressed through a stable gender (masculine expresses male, feminine expresses female) that is oppositionally and hierarchically defined through the compulsory practice of heterosexuality.

7 For an interesting study of the *berdache* and multiple-gender arrangements in Native American cultures, see Walter L. Williams, *The Spirit and the Flesh: Sexual Diversity in American Indian Culture* (Boston: Beacon Press, 1988). See also, Sherry B. Ortner and Harriet Whitehead, eds., *Sexual Meanings: The Cultural Construction of Sexuality* (New York: Cambridge University Press, 1981). For a politically sensitive and provocative analysis of the *berdache,* transsexuals, and the contingency of gender dichotomies, see Suzanne J. Kessler and Wft *Approach* (Chicago: University of Chicago Press, 1978).

8 A great deal of feminist research has been conducted within the fields of biology and the history of science that assess the political interests inherent in the various discriminatory procedures that establish the scientific basis for sex. See Ruth Hubbard and Marian Lowe, eds., *Genes and Gender,* vols. 1 and 2 (New York: Gordian Press, 1978, 1979); the two issues on feminism and science of *Hypatia: A Journal of Feminist Philosophy,* vol. 2, no. 3, Fall 1987, and vol. 3, no. 1, Spring 1988, and especially The Biology and Gender Study Group, "The Importance of Feminist Critique for Contemporary Cell Biology" in this last issue (Spring 1988); Sandra Harding, *The Science Question in Feminism* (Ithaca: Cornell University Press, 1986); Evelyn Fox Keller, *Reflections on Gender and Science* (New Haven: Yale University Press, 1984); Donna Haraway, "In the Beginning was the Word: The Genesis of Biological Theory," *Signs: Journal of Women in Culture and Society,* vol. 6, no. 3, 1981; Donna Haraway, *Primate Visions* (New York: Routledge, 1989); Sandra Harding and Jean F. O'Barr, *Sex and Scientific Inquiry* (Chicago: University of Chicago Press, 1987); Anne Fausto-Sterling, *Myths of Gender: Biological Theories About Women and Men* (New York: Norton, 1979).

9 Clearly Foucault's *History of Sexuality* offers one way to rethink the history of "sex" within a given modern Eurocentric context. For a more detailed consideration, see Thomas Laqueur and Catherine Gallagher, eds., *The Making of the Modern Body: Sexuality and Society in the 19th Century* (Berkeley: University of California Press, 1987), originally published as an issue of *Representations,* no. 14, Spring 1986.

10 See my "Variations on Sex and Gender: Beauvoir, Wittig, Foucault," in *Feminism as Critique,* eds. Seyla Benhabib and Drucilla Cornell (Basil Blackwell, dist. by University of Minnesota Press, 1987).

11 Simone de Beauvoir, *The Second Sex,* trans. E. M. Parshley (New York: Vintage, 1973), p. 301.

12 Ibid., p. 38.

13 See my "Sex and Gender in Beauvoir's *Second Sex*" *Yale French Studies, Simone de Beauvoir: Witness to a Century,* no. 72, Winter 1986.

14 Note the extent to which phenomenological theories such as Sartre's, Merleau-Ponty's, and Beauvoir's tend to use the term *embodiment.* Drawn as it is from theological contexts, the term tends to figure "the" body as a mode of incarnation and, hence, to preserve the external and dualistic relationship between a signifying immateriality and the materiality of the body itself.

15 See Luce Irigaray, *This Sex Which Is Not One*, trans. Catherine Porter with Carolyn Burke (Ithaca: Cornell University Press, 1985), originally published as Ce *sexe qui n'en est pas un* (Paris: Éditions de Minuit, 1977).

16 See Joan Scott, "Gender as a Useful Category of Historical Analysis," in *Gender and the Politics of History* (New York: Columbia University Press, 1988), pp. 28–52, repr. from *American Historical Review*, vol. 91, no. 5, 1986.

17 Beauvoir, *The Second Sex*, p. xxvi.

18 See my "Sex and Gender in Beauvoir's *Second Sex*."

19 The normative ideal of the body as both a "situation" and an "instrumentality" is embraced by both Beauvoir with respect to gender and Frantz Fanon with respect to race. Fanon concludes his analysis of colonization through recourse to the body as an instrument of freedom, where freedom is, in Cartesian fashion, equated with a consciousness capable of doubt: "O my body, make of me always a man who questions!" (Frantz Fanon, *Black Skin, White Masks* [New York: Grove Press, 1967] p. 323, originally published as *Peau noire, masques blancs* [Paris: Éditions de Seuil, 1952]).

20 The radical ontological disjunction in Sartre between consciousness and the body is part of the Cartesian inheritance of his philosophy. Significantly, it is Descartes' distinction that Hegel implicitly interrogates at the outset of the "Master-Slave" section of *The Phenomenology of Spirit*. Beauvoir's analysis of the masculine Subject and the feminine Other is clearly situated in Hegel's dialectic and in the Sartrian reformulation of that dialectic in the section on sadism and masochism in *Being and Nothingness*. Critical of the very possibility of a "synthesis" of consciousness and the body, Sartre effectively returns to the Cartesian problematic that Hegel sought to overcome. Beauvoir insists that the body can be the instrument and situation of freedom and that sex can be the occasion for a gender that is not a reification, but a modality of freedom. At first this appears to be a synthesis of body and consciousness, where consciousness is understood as the condition of freedom. The question that remains, however, is whether this synthesis requires and maintains the ontological distinction between body and mind of which it is composed and, by association, the hierarchy of mind over body and of masculine over feminine.

21 See Elizabeth V. Spelman, "Woman as Body: Ancient and Contemporary Views," *Feminist Studies,* vol. 8, no. 1, Spring 1982.

22 Gayatri Spivak most pointedly elaborates this particular kind of binary explanation as a colonizing act of marginalization. In a critique of the "self-presence of the cognizing supra-historical self," which is characteristic of the epistemic imperialism of the philosophical cogito, she locates politics in the production of knowledge that creates and censors the margins that constitute, through exclusion, the contingent intelligibility of that subject's given knowledge-regime: "I call 'politics as such' the prohibition of marginality that is implicit in the production of any explanation. From that point of view, the choice of particular binary oppositions … is no mere intellectual strategy. It is, in each case, the condition of the possibility for centralization (with appropriate apologies) and, correspondingly, marginalization" (Gayatri Chakravorty Spivak, "Explanation and Culture: Marginalia," in *In Other Worlds: Essays in Cultural Politics* [New York: Routledge, 1987], p. 113).

23 See the argument against "ranking oppressions" in Cherríe Moraga, "La Güera," in *This Bridge Called My Back: Writings of Radical Women of Color*, eds. Gloria Anzaldúa and Cherríe Moraga (New York: Kitchen Table, Women of Color Press, 1982).

24 Michel Foucault, ed., *Herculine Barbin, Being the Recently Discovered Memoirs of a Nineteenth-Century Hermaphrodite*, trans. Richard McDougall (New York: Colophon, 1980), originally published as *Herculine Barbin, dite Alexina B. presenté par Michel Foucault* (Paris: Gallimard, 1978). The French version lacks the introduction supplied by Foucault with the English translation.

25 Foucault, ed., *Herculine Barbin*, p. x.

26 Robert Stoller, *Presentations of Gender* (New Haven: Yale University Press, 1985), pp. 11–14.

27 Friedrich Nietzsche, *On the Genealogy of Morals*, trans. Walter Kaufmann (New York: Vintage, 1969), p. 45.

28 Monique Wittig, "One Is Not Born a Woman," *Feminist Issues*, vol. 1, no. 2, Winter 1981 p. 48. Wittig credits both the notion of the "mark" of gender and the "imaginary formation" of natural groups to Colette Guillaumin whose work on the mark of race provides an analogy for Wittig's analysis of gender in "Race et nature: Système des marques, idée de group naturel et rapport sociaux," *Pluriel*, vol. 11, 1977. The "Myth of Woman" is a chapter of Beauvoir's *The Second Sex*.

29 Monique Wittig, "Paradigm," in *Homosexualities and French Literature: Cultural Contexts/Critical Texts*, eds. Elaine Marks and George Stambolian (Ithaca: Cornell University Press, 1979), p. 114.

30 Clearly, Wittig does not understand syntax to be the linguistic elaboration or reproduction of a kinship system paternally organized. Her refusal of structuralism at this level allows her to understand language as

gender-neutral. Irigaray's *Parler n'est jamais neutre* (Paris: Éditions de Minuit, 1985) criticizes precisely the kind of humanist position, here characteristic of Wittig, that claims the political and gender neutrality of language.

31 Monique Wittig, "The Point of View: Universal or Particular?" *Feminist Issues*, vol. 3, no. 2, Fall 1983, p. 63.

32 Monique Wittig, "The Straight Mind," *Feminist Issues,* vol. 1, no. 1, Summer 1980, p. 108.

33 Monique Wittig, *The Lesbian Body,* trans. Peter Owen (New York: Avon, 1976), originally published as *Le corps lesbien* (Paris: Éditions de Minuit, 1973).

34 I am grateful to Wendy Owen for this phrase.

35 Of course, Freud himself distinguished between "the sexual" and "the genital," providing the very distinction that Wittig uses against him. See, for instance, "The Development of the Sexual Function" in Freud, *Outline of a Theory of Psychoanalysis,* trans. James Strachey (New York: Norton, 1979).

36 Jacqueline Rose, *Sexuality in the Field of Vision* (London: Verso, 1987).

37 Jane Gallop, *Reading Lacan* (Ithaca: Cornell University Press, 1985); *The Daughter's Seduction: Feminism and Psychoanalysis* (Ithaca: Cornell University Press, 1982).

38 "What distinguishes psychoanalysis from sociological accounts of gender (hence for me the fundamental impasse of Nancy Chodorow's work) is that whereas for the latter, the internalisation of norms is assumed roughly to work, the basic premise and indeed starting point of psychoanalysis is that it does not. The unconscious constantly reveals the 'failure' of identity" (Jacqueline Rose, *Sexuality in the Field of Vision,* p. 90).

39 It is, perhaps, no wonder that the singular structuralist notion of "the Law" clearly resonates with the prohibitive law of the Old Testament. The "paternal law" thus comes under a post-structuralist critique through the understandable route of a French reappropriation of Nietzsche. Nietzsche faults the Judeo-Christian "slave-morality" for conceiving the law in both singular and prohibitive terms. The will-to-power, on the other hand, designates both the productive and multiple possibilities of the law, effectively exposing the notion of "the Law" in its singularity as a fictive and repressive notion.

40 See Gayle Rubin, "Thinking Sex: Notes for a Radical Theory of the Politics of Sexuality," in *Pleasure and Danger,* ed. Carole S. Vance (Boston: Routledge and Kegan Paul, 1984), pp. 267–319. Also in *Pleasure and*

Danger, see Carole S. Vance, "Pleasure and Danger: Towards a Politics of Sexuality," pp. 1–28; Alice Echols, "The Taming of the Id: Feminist Sexual Politics, 1968–83," pp. 50–72; Amber Hollibaugh, "Desire for the Future: Radical Hope in Pleasure and Passion," pp. 401–10. See Amber Hollibaugh and Cherríe Moraga, "What We're Rollin Around in Bed with: Sexual Silences in Feminism," and Alice Echols, "The New Feminism of Yin and Yang," in *Powers of Desire: The Politics of Sexuality,* eds. Ann Snitow, Christine Stansell, and Sharon Thompson (London: Virago, 1984); *Heresies,* no. 12, 1981, the "sex issue"; Samois ed., *Coming to Power* (Berkeley: Samois, 1981); Dierdre English, Amber Hollibaugh, and Gayle Rubin, "Talking Sex: A Conversation on Sexuality and Feminism," *Socialist Review,* no. 58, July–August 1981; Barbara T. Kerr and Mirtha N. Quintanales, "The Complexity of Desire: Conversations on Sexuality and Difference," *Conditions,* #8; vol. 3, no. 2, 1982, pp. 52–71.

41 Irigaray's perhaps most controversial claim has been that the structure of the vulva as "two lips touching" constitutes the nonunitary and autoerotic pleasure of women prior to the "separation" of this doubleness through the pleasure-depriving act of penetration by the penis. See Irigaray, *Ce sexe qui n'en est pas un.* Along with Monique Plaza and Christine Delphy, Wittig has argued that Irigaray's valorization of that anatomical specificity is itself an uncritical replication of a reproductive discourse that marks and carves up the female body into artificial "parts" like "vagina," "clitoris," and "vulva." At a lecture at Vassar College, Wittig was asked whether she had a vagina, and she replied that she did not.

42 See a compelling argument for precisely this interpretation by Diana J. Fuss, *Essentially Speaking* (New York: Routledge, 1989).

43 If we were to apply Fredric Jameson's distinction between parody and pastiche, gay identities would be better understood as pastiche. Whereas parody, Jameson argues, sustains some sympathy with the original of which it is a copy, pastiche disputes the possibility of an "original" or, in the case of gender, reveals the "original" as a failed effort to "copy" a phantasmatic ideal that cannot be copied without failure. See Fredric Jameson, "Postmodernism and Consumer Society," in *The Anti-Aesthetic: Essays on Postmodern Culture,* ed. Hal Foster (Port Townsend, WA: Bay Press, 1983).

41

"It Ain't Where You're From, It's Where You're At" (1990)

Paul Gilroy

Music is our witness, and our ally. The beat is the confession which recognizes, changes and conquers time. Then, history becomes a garment we can wear and share, and not a cloak in which to hide; and time becomes a friend.
(James Baldwin)

No nation now but the imagination. (Derek Walcott)

The subject of this paper is culture and resistance and I want to begin by asking you to consider how resistance itself is to be understood. I think that our recent political history, as people in but not necessarily of the modern, Western world, a history which involves processes of political organization that are explicitly transcultural and international in nature, demands that we consider this question very carefully. What is being resisted and by what means? Slavery? Capitalism? Coerced industrialization? Racial terror? Or ethnocentrism and European solipsism? How are the discontinuous, plural histories of diaspora resistance to be *thought*, to be theorized by those who have experienced the consequences of racial domination?

In this paper, I want to look specifically at the positions of the nation-state, and the idea of nationality in accounts of black resistance and black culture, particularly music. Towards the end, I will also use a brief discussion of black music to ask implicit questions about the tendencies towards ethnocentrism and

Paul Gilroy, "It Ain't Where You're From, It's Where You're At," pp. 120–45 from *Small Acts: Thoughts on the Politics of Black Cultures*. London: Serpent's Tail, 1993. Reprinted by permission of the rights holder Paul Gilroy. All rights reserved.

ethnic absolutism of black cultural theory. The problem of weighing the claims of national identity against other contrasting varieties of subjectivity and identification has a special place in the intellectual history of blacks in the West. W. E. B. Du Bois's concept of 'double consciousness'[1] is only the best-known resolution of a familiar problem which points towards the core dynamic of racial oppression as well as the fundamental antinomy of diaspora blacks. How has this doubleness, what Richard Wright calls the 'dreadful objectivity'[2] which flows from being both inside and outside the West, affected the conduct of political movements against racial oppression and towards black autonomy? Can the inescapable pluralities involved in the movements of black peoples, in Africa and in exile, ever be synchronized? How would these struggles be periodized in relation to modernity: the fatal intermediation of capitalism, industrialization and a new conception of political democracy? Does even posing those questions in this way signify nothing except the reluctant intellectual affiliation of diaspora blacks to an approach which attempts a premature totalization of our infinite struggles, an approach which has deep roots within the ambiguous intellectual traditions of the European enlightenment?

In my view, the problematic intellectual heritage of Euro-American modernity still determines the manner in which nationality is understood within black political discourse. In particular, it conditions the continuing aspiration to acquire a supposedly authentic, natural and stable identity. This identity is the premise of a thinking 'racial' self that is both socialized and unified by its connection with other kindred souls encountered usually, though not always, within the fortified frontiers of those discrete ethnic cultures which also happen to coincide with the contours of a sovereign nation-state that guarantees their continuity. Consider for a moment the looseness with which the term 'black nationalism' is used both by its advocates and by sceptics. Why is a more refined political language for dealing with these crucial issues of identity, kinship and affiliation such a long time coming?

This area of difficulty has recently become associated with a second, namely the over-integrated conceptions of culture which mean that black political struggles are construed as somehow automatically *expressive* of the national or ethnic differences with which they are articulated. This over-integrated sense of cultural and ethnic particularity is very popular today and blacks do not monopolize it. It masks the arbitrariness of its own political choices in the morally charged language of ethnic absolutism and this poses significant dangers because it overlooks the development of political ideology and ignores the restless, recombinant qualities of our affirmative political cultures. The critical political project forged in the journey from slave ship to citizenship is in danger of being wrecked by the seemingly insoluble conflict between two distinct but currently symbiotic perspectives which can be loosely identified as the essentialist and the pluralist standpoints.

The antagonistic relationship between these outlooks is especially intense in discussions of black art and cultural criticism. The essentialist view comes in gender-specific forms, but has often been characterized by an archaic pan-Africanism that, in Britain at least, is now politically inert. In the newer garb of Africentricity it has still proved unable to specify precisely where the highly prized but doggedly evasive essence of black artistic sensibility is currently located. This perspective sees the black artist as a potential leader. It is often allied to a realist approach to aesthetics which minimizes the substantive political and philosophical issues involved in the processes of artistic representation. Its absolutist conception of ethnic cultures can be identified by the way in which it registers uncomprehending disappointment with the actual cultural choices and patterns of the mass of black people in this country. It looks for an artistic practice that can disabuse them of the illusions into which they have been seduced by their condition of exile. The community is felt to be on the wrong road and it is the artist's job to give them a new direction, first by recovering and then by donating the racial awareness that the masses seem to lack.

This perspective currently confronts a pluralistic position which affirms blackness as an open signifier and seeks to celebrate complex representations of a black particularity that is *internally* divided: by class, sexuality, gender, age and political consciousness. There is no unitary idea of black community here and the authoritarian tendencies of those who would 'police' black cultural expression in the name of their own particular history or priorities are rightly repudiated. Essentialism is replaced by a libertarian alternative: the saturnalia which attends 'the dissolution of the essential black subject'. Here, the polyphonic qualities of black cultural expression form the main aesthetic consideration and there is often an uneasy but exhilarating fusion of 'modernist' and populist techniques and styles. From this perspective, the cultural achievements of popular black cultural forms like music are a constant source of inspiration and are prized for their implicit warning against the pitfalls of artistic conceit. The difficulty with this second tendency is that, in leaving racial essentialism behind by viewing 'race' itself as a social and cultural construction, it has been insufficiently alive to the lingering power of specifically 'racial' forms of power and subordination. Each outlook attempts to compensate for the obvious weaknesses in the other camp but so far there has been little open and explicit debate between them.

This conflict, initially formulated in debates over black aesthetics and cultural production, is valuable as a preliminary guide to some of the dilemmas faced by cultural and intellectual *historians* of the African diaspora. The problems it raises become acute, particularly for those who seek to comprehend cultural developments and political resistances which have had scant regard for either modern borders or pre-modern frontiers. At its worst, the lazy, casual invocation of cultural insiderism which characterizes the essentialist view is nothing more than a melancholy symptom of the growing cleavages *within* the black communities. There, uneasy spokespeople of the black middle classes – some of them professional cultural commentators, artists, writers, painters and film-makers as well as career politicians – have fabricated a volkish political outlook as an expression of their own contradictory position. Although the 'neo' is never satisfactorily explained, this is often presented as a neo-nationalism. It incorporates meditation on the special needs and desires of the relatively privileged castes within black communities, but its most consistent trademark is the persistent mystification of that group's increasingly problematic relationships with the black poor who, after all, supply them with a dubious entitlement to speak on behalf of black people in general.

The idea of blacks as a 'national' or proto-national group with its own hermetically enclosed culture plays a key role in this mystification and, though seldom overtly named, the misplaced idea of a 'national interest' gets invoked here as a means to silence dissent and censor political debate.

These problems take on a specific aspect in Britain, which still lacks anything that can credibly be called a black bourgeoisie. However, they are not confined to this country and they cannot be overlooked. The idea of nationality and the assumptions of cultural absolutism come together in various other ways.[3] For example, the archaeology of black critical knowledges in which we are engaged, currently involves the construction of canons which seems to be proceeding on an exclusively *national* basis – Afro-American, Anglophone Caribbean and so on. (This is not just my oblique answer to the pressure to produce an equivalent inventory of black English or British cultural forms and expressions.) If it seems indelicate to ask whom the formation of such canons might serve, then the related question of where the impulse to formalize and codify elements of our cultural heritage in this particular pattern comes from may be a better one with which to commence.

The historiography of canon formation raises interesting issues for the intellectual historian in and of itself. But if the way that these issues occur around the question of the canon appears too obscure, similar problems are also evident in recent debates over hip-hop culture, the powerful expressive medium of America's urban black poor. Rap is a hybrid form rooted in the syncretic social relations of the South Bronx where Jamaican sound-system culture, transplanted during the 1970s, put down new roots and in conjunction with specific technological innovations, set in train a process that was to transform black America's sense of itself and a large portion of the popular music industry as well. How does a form which flaunts and glories in its own malleability as well as its transnational character become interpreted as an expression of some authentic Afro-American essence? Why is rap discussed as if it sprang intact from the entrails of the blues?[4] What is it about Afro-America's writing elite which means that they need to claim this diasporic cultural form in such an assertively nationalist way?[5] Hip-hop culture has recently provided the raw material for a bitter contest between black vernacular expression and repressive censorship of artistic work. This has thrown some black commentators into a quandary which they resolve by invoking the rhetoric of cultural insiderism and drawing the distinctive cloak of ethnicity even more tightly around their shoulders. It is striking, for example, that apologists for the woman-hating antics of the 2 Live Crew have been so far unconcerned that the vernacular tradition they desire to affirm has its own record of reflection on the specific ethical obligations and political responsibilities which constitute the unique burden of the black artist. This may have generational, even authoritarian, implications because the 'racial' community is always a source of constraint as well as a source of support and protection for its artists and intellectuals but, leaving the question of misogyny aside for a moment, to collude in the belief that black vernacular is *nothing* more than a playfully parodic cavalcade of Rabelaisian subversion decisively weakens the positions of the artist, the critical commentator[6] and the community as a whole. What is more significant is surely the failure of either academic or journalistic commentary on black popular music in America to develop a reflexive political aesthetics capable of distinguishing the 2 Live Crew and their ilk from their equally 'authentic' but possibly more compelling and certainly more constructive peers.[7] I am not suggesting that the self-conscious racial pedagogy of artists like KRS1, The Poor Righteous Teachers, Lakim Shabazz or The X Clan can be straightforwardly counterposed against the carefully calculated affirmative nihilism of Ice Cube, Above The Law and Compton's Most Wanted. The different styles and political perspectives expressed within the music are linked both by the bonds of a stylized but aggressively masculinist discourse and by formal borrowings from the linguistic innovations of Jamaica's distinct traditions of 'kinetic orality'[8]. The debt to Caribbean forms is more openly acknowledged in the ludic Afrocentrisms of The Jungle Brothers, De La Soul and A Tribe Called Quest, which may represent a third alternative – in its respectful and egalitarian representation of women and in its ambivalent relationship to America. This stimulating and innovative work operates a rather different conception of black authenticity which effectively contrasts the local (black nationalism) with the global (black internationalism) and Americanism with Ethiopianism. It is important to emphasize that all three strands within hip-hop contribute to a folk-cultural constellation where neither the political compass of weary leftism nor the shiny navigational instruments of premature black post-modernism[9] in aesthetics offer very much that is useful.

An additional, and possibly more profound, area of political difficulty comes into view where the voguish language of absolute cultural difference I have described provides an embarrassing link between the practice of blacks who comprehend racial politics through it and the activities of their foresworn opponents – the racist New Right – who approach the complex dynamics of race, nationality and ethnicity through a similar set of precise, culturalist equations.

This unlikely convergence must also be analysed. It too leads rapidly and directly back to the status of nationality and national cultures in a post-modern world where nation-states are being eclipsed by a new economy of power which accords national citizenship a new significance. In seeking to account for it we have to explore how the over-integrated, absolutist

and exclusivist approach to the relationship between 'race', ethnicity and culture places those who claim to be able to resolve the relationship between incommensurable discourses in command of the cultural resources of the group as a whole. They claim this vanguard position by virtue of an ability to translate from one culture to another, mediating decisive class oppositions along the way. At this point it matters little whether the black communities are conceived as entire and self-sustaining nations or proto-national collectivities. Black intellectuals have persistently succumbed to the lure of those romantic conceptions of 'race', 'people' and 'nation' which place themselves, rather than the people they supposedly represent, in charge of the strategies for nation-building, state formation and racial uplift.

This point again underscores the fact that the status of nationality and the precise weight we should attach to the conspicuous differences of language, culture and identity which divide the blacks of the diaspora from each other, let alone from Africans in Africa, are unresolved within the political tradition that promises to bring the disparate peoples of the black Atlantic world together one day. Furthermore, the black intellectuals who have tried to deal with these matters have been highly dependent on European theories of national, cultural and racial identity. Du Bois's 1888 Fisk graduation address on Bismarck provides an interesting example here, particularly as Du Bois also admitted to styling his own moustache on the one that graced the Kaiser's face. In one of his autobiographies, *Dusk of Dawn*, he explored the significance of European history and its nation-states for his developing understanding of what a cohesive national identity for black Americans might involve:

> I was graduated from Fisk in 1888 and took as my subject 'Bismarck'. This choice in itself showed the abyss between my education and the truth in the world. Bismarck was my hero. He made a nation out of a mass of bickering peoples. He had dominated the whole development with his strength until he crowned an emperor at Versailles. This foreshadowed in my mind the kind of thing that American Negroes must do, marching forward with strength and determination under trained leadership ... I was blithely European and imperialist in outlook; democratic as democracy was conceived in America.[10]

This understanding of national development and identity formation had (and still enjoys) a special appeal among the 'bickering peoples' of the modern African diaspora into the Western hemisphere. It has been integral to their responses to racism and directly inspired some of their efforts to construct independent nation-states in Africa. The idea of nationality occupies a central, if shifting, place in the work of Alexander Crummell, Edward Wilmot Blyden, Martin Delany and Frederick Douglass. This important group of Enlightenment men, whose lives and political sensibilities can ironically be defined through the persistent criss-crossing of national boundaries, often seems to share the decidedly Hegelian belief that the combination of Christianity and a nation-state represents the overcoming of all antimonies. The polymath Delany, who sets less store by Christianity than the others and is still routinely cited as the father of black nationalism, expresses this cogently in his 1852 book, which begins significantly by comparing blacks in America to the disenfranchised minority 'nations' of Europe.

> That there have [sic] in all ages, in almost every nation, existed a nation within a nation – a people who although forming a part and parcel of the population, yet were from force of circumstances, known by the peculiar position they occupied, forming in fact, by deprivation of political equality with others, no part, and if any, but a restricted part of the body politics of such nations, is also true ... Such then is the condition of various classes in Europe; yes, nations, for centuries within nations, even without the hope of redemption among those who oppress them. And however unfavourable their condition, there is none more so than that of the coloured people of the United States.[11]

Richard Wright's later repeated warnings that blacks 'can be fascists too'[12] also spring to mind, possibly as a post-modern coda to this distinctly modern line of thought. As I hinted in the brief discussion of hip-hop culture, these problems of nationality, exile and cultural affiliation accentuate the fragmentation and inescapable differentiation of the black subject. The fragmentation to which they refer has recently been compounded further by the questions of gender, sexuality and male domination which have been made unavoidable by the struggles of black women.

I cannot attempt to resolve these tensions here, but the dimension of differentiation to which they refer provides an important frame for what follows and I hope they will not be overlooked in our discussion. As indices of differentiation, they are especially important because the intra-communal antagonisms which appear between the local and immediate dimensions of our struggles and their hemispheric, even global, dynamics can only grow. Black voices from within the overdeveloped countries may be able to resonate in harmony with those produced from Africa or they may, with varying degrees of reluctance, turn away from the global project of black advancement once the symbolic political, if not the material and economic, liberation of southern Africa is completed. The open letter to Kwame Nkrumah which concludes Wright's important and neglected book *Black Power* is a complex piece of writing that seems to me to prefigure some of these alarming possibilities. Delany's 1859 *Report of the Niger Valley Exploring Party* (another text apparently excluded from the emergent official canon of Afro-American letters) is also germane to the dialectics of diasporic identification. Delany, who was a doctor, interestingly describes the sequence of clinical symptoms he experienced as his elation at arrival in Africa gave way to a special and characteristic form of melancholy:

> The first sight and impressions of the coast of Africa are always inspiring, producing the most pleasant emotions. These pleasing sensations continue for several days, more or less until they merge into feelings of almost intense excitement ... a hilarity of feeling almost akin to approaching intoxication ... like the sensation produced by the beverage of champagne wine ... The first symptoms are succeeded by a relaxity of feelings in which there is a disposition to stretch, gape and yawn with fatigue. The second may or may not be succeeded by actual febrile attacks ... but whether or not such symptoms ensue, there is one most remarkable ... A feeling of regret that you left your native country for a strange one; an almost frantic desire to see friends and nativity; a despondency and loss of the hope of ever seeing those you love at home again. These feelings, of course, must be resisted and regarded as a mere morbid affection [sic] of the mind ... When an entire recovery takes place, the love of the country is most ardent and abiding.[13]

The ambivalence of exile conveyed by these remarks has a long history. At this point, it is necessary to appreciate that discomfort at the prospect of fissures and fault lines in the topography of affiliation which made pan-Africanism such a powerful structure of feeling is not *necessarily* eased by references to the diaspora. This powerful idea is frequently wheeled in when we need to appreciate the things that (potentially) connect us to each other rather than to think seriously about our divisions and the means to comprehend and overcome them, if indeed this is possible.

I am making a point about the type of theorizing we need to develop and a point about the practical conduct of our political lives. Both these aspects come together in the question of contemporary South African politics and they have a bearing on how we might begin to consider the struggles inside that country in relation to the tempo of struggles around South African liberation which we conduct in this country and elsewhere. Here too, of course, the issue of popular music as a vehicle for political sensibility which transcends nationality is central and unavoidable.

I want to make all these abstract and difficult points more concrete and accessible by turning to some of the lessons to be learned from considering the musical traditions of blacks in the West. The history and significance of these musics are consistently overlooked by black writers for two reasons: first, because they escape the frameworks of national of ethnocentric analysis, and second, because talking seriously about the politics and aesthetics of black vernacular cultures demands a confrontation with the order of 'intra-racial' differences. These may be to do with class, gender, sexuality or other factors, but they provide severe embarrassment to the rhetoric of racial and cultural homogeneity. As these internal divisions have grown, the price of that embarrassment has been an aching silence.

To break that silence, I want to examine the role of black musical expression in reproducing what Zygmunt Bauman has called a distinctive 'counter culture of modernity'. The shifting relationship of music-making to other modes of black cultural expression requires a much more sustained treatment than I can give it here. However, I want to use a brief consideration of black musical development to move our critical thoughts beyond an understanding of cultural processes which,

as I have already suggested, is currently torn between seeing them as either the expression of an essential, unchanging, sovereign racial self or as the effluent from a constituted subjectivity that emerges contingently from the endless play of racial signification conceived solely in terms of the inappropriate model which *textuality* provides. The vitality and complexity of this musical culture offers a means to get beyond the related oppositions between essentialists and pluralists on the one hand and between tradition, modernity and post-modernity on the other.

Black music's obstinate and consistent commitment to the idea of a better future is a puzzle to which our enforced separation from literacy and the compensatory refinement of musical art supplies less than half an answer. The power of music in developing our struggles by communicating information, organizing consciousness and testing out, deploying or amplifying the forms of subjectivity which are required by political agency – individual and collective, defensive and transformational – demands attention to both the formal attributes of this tradition of expression and its distinctive *moral* basis. The formal qualities of this music are becoming better known,[14] so I shall concentrate here on the moral aspects and in particular on the disjunction between the ethical value of the music and its ethnic significance.

In the simplest possible terms, by posing the world as it is against the world as the racially subordinated would like it to be, this musical culture supplies a great deal of the courage required to go on living in the present. It is both produced by and expressive of that 'transvaluation of all values' precipitated by the history of racial terror in the new world. It contains a theodicy but moves beyond theodicy because the profane dimensions of that racial terror made theodicy impossible.[15]

I have considered its distinctive critique of capitalist social relations elsewhere.[16] Here, because I want to suggest that its critical edge includes but also surpasses anti-capitalism, I want to draw out some of its inner philosophical dynamics and place emphasis on the connection between its normative character and its utopian aspirations. These are interrelated and even inseparable from each other and from the critique of racial capitalism.[17] Comprehending them requires us to link together analysis of the lyrical content and the forms of musical expression as well as the often hidden social relations in which these deeply encoded oppositional practices are created and consumed. The issue of normative content focuses attention on what might be called the politics of fulfilment[18]: the notion that a future society will be able to realize the social and political promise that present society has left unaccomplished. Reflecting the primary semantic position of the Bible, this is primarily a discursive mode of communication. Though by no means literal, it relates mainly to what is said, shouted, screamed or sung. The issue of utopia is more complex not least because it strives continually to move beyond the grasp of the merely linguistic, textual or discursive. It references what, following Seyla Benhabib's suggestive lead, I propose to call the politics of transfiguration. This emphasizes the emergence of qualitatively new desires, social relations and modes of association within the racial community of interpretation and resistance *and* between that group and its erstwhile oppressors. It points specifically to the formation of a community of needs and solidarity which is magically made audible in the music itself and palpable in the social relations of its cultural consumption and reproduction.

The politics of fulfilment practised by the descendants of slaves demands that bourgeois civil society lives up to the promises of its own rhetoric and offers a means whereby demands for justice, rational organization of the productive processes, etc., can be expressed. It is immanent within modernity and is no less a valuable element of modernity's counter-discourse for being so consistently ignored. Created under the nose of the overseer, the utopian desires which fuel the politics of transfiguration must be invoked by other deliberately opaque means. This politics exists on a lower frequency where it is played, danced and acted, as well as sung about, because words, even words stretched by melisma and supplemented or mutated by the screams which still index the conspicuous power of the slave sublime, will never be enough to communicate its unsayable claims to truth. The wilfully damaged signs which betray the utopian politics of transfiguration therefore partially transcend modernity. This is not a counter-discourse but a counter-culture that defiantly constructs its own critical, intellectual and moral genealogy anew in a par-

tially hidden public sphere of its own. The politics of transfiguration therefore reveals the internal problems in the concept of modernity. The bounds of politics are extended precisely because this tradition of expression refuses to accept that the political is a readily separable domain. Its basic desire is to conjure up and enact the new modes of friendship, happiness and solidarity that are consequent on the overcoming of the racial oppression on which modernity and the duality of rational Western progress as excessive barbarity relied. Thus the vernacular arts of the children of slaves give rise to a verdict on the role of art which is strikingly in harmony with Adorno's reflections on the dynamics of European artistic expression in the wake of Auschwitz:

> Art's Utopia, the counterfactual yet-to-come, is draped in black. It goes on being a recollection of the possible with a critical edge against the real; it is a kind of imaginary restitution of that catastrophe, which is world history; it is a freedom which did not pass under the spell of necessity and which may well not come to pass ever at all.[19]

These sibling dimensions of black sensibility, the politics of fulfilment and the politics of transfiguration, are not coextensive. There are significant tensions between them but they are closely associated in the vernacular cultures of the diaspora. They can also be used to reflect the doubleness with which I began and which is often argued to be our constitutive experience in the modern world: in the West but not of it. The politics of fulfilment is content to play occidental rationality at its own game. It necessitates a hermeneutic orientation which can assimilate the semiotic, verbal and textual. The politics of transfiguration strives in pursuit of the sublime, struggling to repeat the unrepeatable, to present the unpresentable. Its rather different hermeneutic focus pushes towards the mimetic, dramatic and performative.

It seems especially significant that the cultural traditions which these musics allow us to map out, do not seek to exclude problems of inequality or to make racial justice an exclusively abstract matter. Their grounded ethics offers, among other things, a continuous commentary on the systematic and pervasive relations of domination that supply its conditions of existence.

Their grounded aesthetics is never separated off into an autonomous realm where familiar political rules cannot be applied and where, as Salman Rushdie puts it, 'the little room of literature' can continue to enjoy its special privileges as a heroic resource for the well-heeled adversaries of liberal capitalism.[20]

I am proposing then, that we re-read and rethink this tradition of cultural expression not simply as a succession of literary tropes and genres, but as a philosophical discourse which refuses the modern, occidental separation of ethics and aesthetics, culture and politics. The traditional teaching of ethics and politics – practical philosophy – came to an end some time ago, even if its death agonies were prolonged. This tradition had maintained the idea that a good life for the individual and the problem of the best social and political order for the collectivity could be discerned by rational means. Although it is seldom acknowledged even now, this tradition lost its exclusive claim to rationality, in part, through the way that slavery became internal to Western civilization and through the obvious complicity which both plantation slavery and colonial regimes revealed between rationality and the practice of racial terror.

Not perceiving its residual condition, blacks in the West eavesdropped on and then took over a fundamental question from that tradition. Their progress from the status of slaves to the status of citizens led them to enquire into what the best possible forms of social and political existence might be. The memory of slavery, actively preserved as a living, intellectual resource in their expressive political culture, helped them to generate a new set of answers to this enquiry. They had to fight – often through the invocation of spirituality – to hold on to the unity of ethics and politics sundered from each other by modernity's insistence that the true, the good and the beautiful had distinct origins and belong to different domains of knowledge. First, slavery itself and then their memory of it induced many of them to query the foundational moves of modern philosophy and social thought whether they came from the natural-rights theorists who sought to distinguish between the spheres of morality and legality, the idealists who wanted to emancipate politics from morals so that it could become a sphere of strategic action, or the political economists of the bourgeoisie who first formulated the separation of economic activity from both ethics and politics. The brutal excess of the slave plantation supplied a set of moral and political responses to each of these attempts.

The history of black music enables us to trace something of the means through which the unity of ethics and politics has been reproduced as a form of folk knowledge. This sub-culture often appears to be the intuitive expression of some racial essence but is in fact an elementary historical acquisition produced from the viscera of an alternative tradition of cultural and political expression which considers the world critically from the point of view of its emancipatory transformation. In the future, it will become a place which is capable of satisfying the (redefined) needs of human beings that will emerge once the violence – epistemic and concrete – of racial typology is at an end. Reason is thus reunited with the happiness and freedom of individuals and the reign of justice within the collectivity.

I have already implied that there is a degree of convergence here with other projects towards a critical theory of society, particularly Marxism. However, where lived crisis and systemic crisis come together, Marxism allocates priority to the latter while the memory of slavery insists on the priority of the former. Their convergence is also undercut by the simple fact that in the critical tradition of blacks in the West, social self-creation through labour is not the core of emancipatory hopes. For the descendants of slaves, work signifies only servitude, misery and subordination. Artistic expression, expanded beyond recognition from the grudging gifts offered by the masters as a token substitute for freedom from bondage, therefore becomes the means towards both individual self-fashioning and communal liberation. Poiesis and poetics begin to coexist in novel forms – autobiographical writing, special and uniquely creative ways of manipulating spoken language and, above all, the music.

Antiphony (call and response) is the principal formal feature of these musical traditions. It reaches out beyond music into other modes of cultural expression, supplying, along with improvisation, montage and dramaturgy, the hermeneutic keys to the full medley of black artistic practices from kinestcs to rhetoric.

The intense and often bitter dialogues, which make the black arts movement move, offer a small reminder that there is a 'democratic' moment enshrined in the practice of antiphony which anticipates new, non-dominating social relationships. Lines between self and other are blurred and special forms of pleasure are created as a result. Ellison's famous observation on the inner dynamics of jazz uses visual art as its central analogy and can be extended beyond the specific context it was written to illuminate:

> There is in this a cruel contradiction implicit in the art form itself. For true jazz is an art of individual assertion within and against the group. Each true jazz moment ... springs from a contest in which the artist challenges all the rest; each solo flight, or improvisation, represents (like the canvasses of a painter) a definition of his identity: as individual, as member of the collectivity and as a link in the chain of tradition. Thus because jazz finds its very life in improvisation upon traditional materials, the jazz man must lose his identity even as he finds it ...[21]

By way of a conclusion, I want to illustrate these arguments further by very briefly bringing forward two concrete historical instances in which the musical traditions of the black Atlantic world acquired a special political valency. These examples are simultaneously both national, in that they had a direct impact on British politics, and diasporic, in that they tell us something fundamental about the limits of that national perspective. They are not, of course, the only examples I could have chosen. They have been selected somewhat at random, although the fact that they span a century will, I hope, be taken as preliminary evidence for the existence of fractal[22] patterns of cultural and political affiliation which will need further elaboration and detailed critical consideration. Both, in rather different ways, reflect the special position of Britain within the black Atlantic world, standing at the apex of the semi-triangular structure which saw commodities and people shipped to and fro across the ocean.

The first relates to the visits by the Fisk University Jubilee Singers[23] to England, Ireland, Wales and Scotland in the early 1870s under the philanthropic patronage of the Earl of Shaftesbury. The Fisk Singers have a profound historical importance because they were the first group to perform spirituals on a public platform, offering this form of black music as mass entertainment.[24] Their success is especially significant amidst the changed cultural and ideological circumstances that attended the 're-making' of the English working class in the era of imperialism.[25] In explicit opposition to minstrelsy, which was becoming an established element in popular culture by this time,[26] the Fisk Singers constructed an aura of seriousness and projected the memory of slavery outwards as the means to make their musical performances intelligible and pleasurable. The choir had taken to the road seven years after the founding of their Alma Mater to raise funds. They produced books to supplement the income from their concert performances and these volumes ran to over 60,000 copies sold between 1877 and the end of the century. Interestingly, these publications included a general historical account of Fisk and its struggles, some unusual autobiographical statements from the members of the ensemble and the music and lyrics of between 104 and 139 songs from their extensive repertoire. In my opinion, this unusual combination of communicative modes and genres is especially important for anyone seeking to locate the origins of the polyphonic montage technique developed by Du Bois in *The Souls of Black Folk*.

The Fisk Singers' text describes Queen Victoria listening to 'John Brown's Body' 'with manifest pleasure', the Prince of Wales requesting 'No More Auction Block for Me' and the choir being waited upon by Mr and Mrs Gladstone after their servants had been dismissed.[27] These images are important, although the choir's performances to enormous working-class audiences in British cities may be more significant for contemporary anti-racism struggling to escape the strictures of its own apparent novelty. It is clear that for their liberal patrons, the music and song of the Fisk Singers offered an opportunity to feel closer to God while the memory of slavery, recovered by their performances, entrenched the feelings of moral rectitude which flowed from the commitment to political reform for which the imagery of elevation from slavery was emblematic long after emancipation. The Fisk Singers' music can be shown to have articulated what Du Bois calls 'the articulate message of the slave to the world' into British culture and society at several distinct and class-specific points. The spirituals enforced the patrician moral concerns of Shaftesbury and Gladstone but also introduced a specific moral sensibility into the lives of the lower orders who, it would appear, began to create Jubilee choirs of their own.[28]

My second example of diasporic cultural innovation is contemporary, although it relates to the song 'I'm So Proud', originally written and performed by the Chicagoan vocal trio The Impressions at the peak of their artistic and commercial success in the mid-1960s. The Impressions' 1960s hits like 'Gypsy Woman', 'Grow Closer together', 'Minstrel and Queen' and 'People Get Ready' were extremely popular among blacks in Britain and in the Caribbean. In Jamaica, the male vocal trio format popularized by the band inaugurated a distinct genre within the vernacular musical form which would eventually be marketed internationally as reggae.[29] The Wailers were only one of many groups that patterned themselves on The Impressions and strove to match the singing of the Americans for harmonic texture, emotional dynamics and black metaphysical grace. A new version of The Impressions' hit 'I'm So Proud' has recently topped the reggae charts in Britain. Re-titled 'Proud of Mandela', it was performed by the toaster Macka B and the Lovers' Rock singer Kofi who had produced her own version of the tune itself, patterned on another soft soul version issued by the American singer Deniece Williams in 1983.

I want to make no special claims for the formal, musical merits of this particular record, but I think that it is exemplary in that it brings Africa, America, Europe and the Caribbean seamlessly together. It was produced in Britain by the children of Caribbean and African settlers from raw materials supplied by black Chicago but filtered through Kingstonian sensibility in order to pay tribute to a black hero whose global significance lies beyond his partial South African citizenship and the impossible national identity which goes with it. The very least that this music and its history can offer us today is an analogy for comprehending the lines of affiliation and association which take the idea of the diaspora beyond its symbolic status as the fragmentary opposite of an imputed racial essence. Foregrounding the role of music allows us to see England, or perhaps London, as an important junction point on the web of black Atlantic political culture: a place where, by virtue of local factors like the informality of racial segregation, the configuration of class relations and the contingency of linguistic

convergences of global phenomena such as anti-colonial and emancipationist political formations are still being sustained, reproduced and amplified.

Notes

I have taken the title of this essay directly from lyrics written and performed by Rakim (W. Griffin). In his recordings with his sometime partner Eric B, Rakim has persistently returned to the problem of diasporic identification and the connected issue of the relationship between local and global components of blackness. His 'I Know You Got Soul' (1987) was received as a classic recording in London's soul underground, and since then he has produced what I regard as the most complex and exciting poetry to emerge from the hip-hop movement. The dread recording which directly inspired the production of this essay is called 'The Ghetto' and is included on the MCA (1990) album 'Let the Rhythm Hit 'Em'. I wish to thank my children for tolerating the repeated playing of this cut at bone-breaking volume, Vron Ware for her insight and bell hooks for the transatlantic dialogue which has helped me to frame this piece of work.

1   W. E. B. Du Bols, *The Souls of Black Folk* (1903) reprinted Bantam, New York, 1989. See also the discussion of this in ch. 4 of my book *Promised Lands*.

2   This phrase is taken from Wright's novel *The Outsider*, Harper and Row, New York, 1965. In his book of essays, *White Man Listen!*, Anchor Books, New York, 1964, he employs the phrase 'dual existence' to map the same terrain.

3   Etienne Balibar and Immanuel Wallerstein, *Race, Nation, Class*, Verso, London, 1991.

4   Nelson George, *The Death of Rhythm and Blues*, Omnibus, London, 1988.

5   I should emphasize that it is the assimilation of these cultural forms to an unthinking notion of nationality which is the object of my critique here. Of course, certain cultural forms become articulated with sets of social and political forces over long periods of time. These forms may be played with and lived with as though they were 'natural' emblems of racial and ethnic particularity. This may even be an essential defensive attribute of the interpretive communities involved. However, the notion of nationality cannot be borrowed as a ready-made means to make sense of the special dynamics of this process.

6   Henry Louis Gates Jr, 'Rap Music: Don't knock it if you're not onto its "lies"', *Herald Tribune*, 20 June 1990.

7   I am prepared to defer to black Americans who argue that it is probably necessary to be both defenders and critics of the 2 Live Crew. However, watching the MTV video of their hit single, 'Banned in the USA', I found it difficult to accept the way in which the powerful visual legacy of the black movement of the 1950s and 1960s had been appropriated and made over so that it became readily and unproblematically continuous with the group's own brand of American patriotism.

8   Cornel West, 'Black Culture and Postmodernism' in B. Kruger and P. Mariani (eds), *Re-Making History*, Dia Foundation, Bay Press, Seattle, 1989.

9   Trey Ellis's famous piece on the new black aesthetic in a recent issue of *Calialoo* exemplifies the perils of this casual, 'anything goes' post-modernism for the black arts movement. It was striking how, for example, profound questions of class antagonism within the black communities were conjured out of sight. Apart from his conflation of forms which are not merely different but actively oppose one another, Ellis does not seriously consider the notion that the NBA might have a very particular and highly class-specific articulation within a small and isolated segment of the black middle class which struggles with its own dependency on the cultural lifeblood of the black poor.

10 *Dusk of Dawn: An Essay Toward an Autobiography of a Race Concept*, Library of America, 1986, p. 577.

11 *The Condition, Elevation, Emigration and Destiny of the Colored People of the United States, Politically Considered*, Philadelphia, 1852.

12 Wright's famous introduction to *Native Son* 'How Bigger was Born' and *The Outsider* include fulsome statements of this warning.

13 *Report of the Niger Valley Exploring Party*, republished as *Search for a Place: Black Separatism and Africa 1860*, University of Michigan Press, Ann Arbor, 1969, p. 64.

14 Anthony Jackson's dazzling exposition of James Jamerson's bass style is, in my view, indicative of the type of detailed critical work which needs to be done on the form and dynamics of black musical creativity. His remarks on Jamerson's use of harmonic and rhythmic ambiguity and selective employment of dissonance were especially helpful. To say that the book from which it is taken has been geared to the needs of the performing musician rather than the cultural historian is to indict the current state of cultural history rather than the work of Jackson and his collaborator, Dr Licks. See 'An Appreciation of the Style' in Dr Licks (ed.) *Standing in the Shadows of Motown*, Hal Leonard, Detroit, 1989.

15 I am thinking here both of Wright's tantalizing discussion of 'The Dozens' in the essay on the 'Literary Tradition of the Negro in the United States' in *White Man Listen!* and also of Levinas's remarks on useless suffering in another context: 'useless and unjustifiable suffering [is] exposed and displayed … without any shadow of consoling theodicy' (see 'Useless Suffering' in R. Bernasconi and D. Wood (eds), *The Provocation of Levinas*, Routledge, London, 1988). Jon Michael Spencer's thoughtful but fervently Christian discussion of what he calls the Theodicy of the Blues is also relevant here. See *The Theology of American Popular Music*, a special issue of *Black Sacred Music*, vol. 3, no. 2, Fall 1989 (Duke University Press). I do not have space to develop my critique of Spencer here.

16 *There Ain't No Black in the Union Jack: The Cultural Politics of Race and Nation*, Hutchinson, London, 1987, ch. 5.

17 Cedric Robinson, *Black Marxism*, Zed Press, London, 1982.

18 This concept and its pairing with the politics of transfiguration have been adapted from Seyla Benhabib's inspiting book *Critique, Norm and Utopia*, Columbia University Press, New York, 1987.

19 *Aesthetic Theory*, Routledge, London, p. 196

20 Salman Rushdie, *Is Nothing Sacred?* The Herbert Read Memorial Lecture 1990, Granta, Cambridge.

21 Ralph Ellison, *Shadow and Act*, Random House, New York, 1964, p. 234. There are in Ellison's remarks the components of a definitive response to the position of Adorno in 'Uber Jazz'; see also Susan Buck Morss, *The Origin of Negative Dialectics*, Free Press, New York pp. 108–10.

22 I am thinking of fractal geometry as an analogy here because it allows for the possibility that a line of infinite length can enclose a finite area. The opposition between totality and infinity is thus recast in a striking image of the scope for agency in restricted conditions.

23 The radical historian Peter Linebaugh has recently discussed the etymology of the word 'jubilee' and some of the political discourses that surround it: 'Jubilating', *Midnight Notes*, Fall 1990. Reviews of the singers' performances in England can be found in *East Anglian Daily Times*, 21 November 1874 and the *Surrey Advertiser*, 5 December 1874.

24 John M. MacKenzie (ed.), *Imperialism and Popular Culture*, Manchester University Press, 1986.

25 Gareth Stedman Jones, 'Working-class Culture and Working-class Politics in London 1870–1900: Notes on the remaking of a working class' in *Languages of Class*, Cambridge University Press, Cambridge, 1983.

26 An 'Eva Gets Well' version of *Uncle Tom's Cabin* was doing excellent business on the London stage in 1878.

See also Robert C. Toll, *Blacking Up: The Minstrel Show in Nineteenth Century America*, Oxford University Press, Oxford, 1974; Barry Anthony, 'Early Nigger Minstrel Acts in Britain', *Music Hall*, vol. 12, April 1980; and Josephine Wright, 'Orpheus Myron McAdoo', *Black Perspective in Music*, vol. 4, no. 3, Fall 1976.

27   These events are described in Gladstone's diaries for 14 and 29 July 1873. Apart from the singers' own text, there is a lengthy discussion of these events in the New York *Independent*, 21 August 1873. See also Ella Sheppard Moore, 'Historical Sketch of The Jubilee Singers', *Fisk University News*, October 1911, p. 42.

28   In his essay on the Fisk Singers in Britain, Doug Seroff cites the example of the East London Jubilee Singers of Hackney Juvenile Mission, a 'ragged school' formed after an inspirational visit by the Fisk Singers to Hackney in June 1873. John Newman, the manager of the Mission, 'felt that such singing from the soul should not be forgotten, and speedily set to work to teach the children of the Mission the songs the Jubilee singers had sung'; see R. Lotz and I. Pegg (eds), *Under the Imperial Carpet: Essays in Black History 1780–1950*, Rabbit Press, Crawley, 1986. Listening recently to my 7-year-old son's primary school singing 'Oh Freedom' in furtherance of the multicultural and anti-racist educational policies of the Borough of Islington was confirmation that slave songs are still being sung in inner London schools in the 1990s.

29   The phenomenon of Jamaican male vocal trios is discussed by Randall Grass, 'Iron Sharpen Iron: The great Jamaican harmony trios' in P. Simon (ed.), *Reggae International*, Thames & Hudson, London, 1983. Key exponents of this particular art would be The Heptones, The Paragons, The Gaylads, The Meditations, The Itals, Carlton and The Shoes, Justice Hines and The Dominoes, Toots and The Maytals, Yabby Yu and The Prophets, The Gladiators, The Melodians, The Ethiopians, The Cables, The Tamlins, The Congoes, The Mighty Diamonds, The Abyssimians, Black Uhuru, Israel Vibration and, of course, The Wailers, whose Neville O'Reilly/Bunny Livingstone/Bunny Wailer does the best Curtis Mayfield impersonation of the lot.

"It Ain't Where You're From, It's Where You're At"

42

"Axiomatic" (1990)

Eve Sedgwick

Epistemology of the Closet [from which this reading is taken] proposes that many of the major nodes of thought and knowledge in twentieth-century Western culture as a whole are structured – indeed, fractured – by a chronic, now endemic crisis of homo/heterosexual definition, indicatively male, dating from the end of the nineteenth century. The book will argue that an understanding of virtually any aspect of modern Western culture must be, not merely incomplete, but damaged in its central substance to the degree that it does not incorporate a critical analysis of modern homo/heterosexual definition; and it will assume that the appropriate place for that critical analysis to begin is from the relatively decentered perspective of modern gay and antihomophobic theory.

The passage of time, the bestowal of thought and necessary political struggle since the turn of the century have only spread and deepened the long crisis of modern sexual definition, dramatizing, often violently, the internal incoherence and mutual contradiction of each of the forms of discursive and institutional "common sense" on this subject inherited from the architects of our present culture. The contradictions I will be discussing are not in the first place those between prohomosexual and antihomosexual people or ideologies, although the book's strongest motivation is indeed the gay-affirmative one. Rather, the contradictions that seem most active are the ones internal to all the important twentieth-century understandings of homo/

heterosexual definition, both heterosexist and anti-homophobic. [...] Briefly, they are two. The first is the contradiction between seeing homo/heterosexual definition on the one hand as an issue of active importance primarily for a small, distinct, relatively fixed homosexual minority (what I refer to as a minoritizing view), and seeing it on the other hand as an issue of continuing, determinative importance in the lives of people across the spectrum of sexualities (what I refer to as a universalizing view). The second is the contradiction between seeing same-sex object choice on the one hand as a matter of liminality or transitivity between genders, and seeing it on the other hand as reflecting an impulse of separatism – though by no means necessarily political separatism – within each gender. The purpose [...] is not to adjudicate between the two poles of either of these contradictions, for, if its argument is right, no epistemological grounding now exists from which to do so. Instead, I am trying to make the strongest possible introductory case for a hypothesis about the centrality of this nominally marginal, conceptually intractable set of definitional issues to the important knowledges and understandings of twentieth-century Western culture as a whole.

The word "homosexual" entered Euro-American discourse during the last third of the nineteenth century – its popularization preceding, as it happens, even that of the word "heterosexual."[1] It seems clear that the sexual behaviors, and even for some people the conscious identities, denoted by the new term "homosexual" and its contemporary variants already had a long, rich history. So, indeed, did a wide range of other sexual behaviors and behavioral clusters.

Eve Kosofsky Sedgwick, "Axiomatic," pp. 1–12, 16–18, 22–6, 27–47, 48–9, 52–3, 59–60 from *Epistemology of the Closet*. Berkeley: University of California Press, 1990.

What *was* new from the turn of the century was the world-mapping by which every given person, just as he or she was necessarily assignable to a male or a female gender, was now considered necessarily assignable as well to a homo- or a hetero-sexuality, a binarized identity that was full of implications, however confusing, for even the ostensibly least sexual aspects of personal existence. It was this new development that left no space in the culture exempt from the potent incoherences of homo/heterosexual definition.

New, institutionalized taxonomic discourses – medical, legal, literary, psychological – centering on homo/heterosexual definition proliferated and crystallized with exceptional rapidity in the decades around the turn of the century, decades in which so many of the other critical nodes of the culture were being, if less suddenly and newly, nonetheless also definitively reshaped. Both the power relations between the genders and the relations of nationalism and imperialism, for instance, were in highly visible crisis. For this reason, and because the structuring of same-sex bonds can't, in any historical situation marked by inequality and contest *between* genders, fail to be a site of intensive regulation that intersects virtually every issue of power and gender,[2] lines can never be drawn to circumscribe within some proper domain of sexuality (whatever that might be) the consequences of a shift in sexual discourse. Furthermore, in accord with Foucault's demonstration, whose results I will take to be axiomatic, that modern Western culture has placed what it calls sexuality in a more and more distinctively privileged relation to our most prized constructs of individual identity, truth, and knowledge, it becomes truer and truer that the language of sexuality not only intersects with but transforms the other languages and relations by which we know.

Accordingly, one characteristic of the readings in this book is to attend to performative aspects of texts, and to what are often blandly called their "reader relations," as sites of definitional creation, violence, and rupture in relation to particular readers, particular institutional circumstances. An assumption underlying the book is that the relations of the closet – the relations of the known and the unknown, the explicit and the inexplicit around homo/heterosexual definition –

have the potential for being peculiarly revealing, in fact, about speech acts more generally. It has felt throughout this work as though the density of their social meaning lends any speech act concerning these issues – and the outlines of that "concern," it turns out, are broad indeed – the exaggerated propulsiveness of wearing flippers in a swimming pool: the force of various rhetorical effects has seemed uniquely difficult to calibrate.

But, in the vicinity of the closet, even what *counts* as a speech act is problematized on a perfectly routine basis. As Foucault says: "there is no binary division to be made between what one says and what one does not say; we must try to determine the different ways of not saying such things. ... There is not one but many silences, and they are an integral part of the strategies that underlie and permeate discourses.[3] "Closetedness" itself is a performance initiated as such by the speech act of a silence – not a particular silence, but a silence that accrues particularity by fits and starts, in relation to the discourse that surrounds and differentially constitutes it. The speech acts that coming out, in turn, can comprise are as strangely specific. And they may have nothing to do with the acquisition of new information. I think of a man and a woman I know, best friends, who for years canvassed freely the emotional complications of each other's erotic lives – the man's eroticism happening to focus exclusively on men. But it was only after one particular conversational moment, fully a decade into this relationship, that it seemed to either of these friends that permission had been given to the woman to refer to the man, in their conversation together, as *a gay man*. Discussing it much later, both agreed they had felt at the time that this one moment had constituted a clear-cut act of coming out, even in the context of years and years beforehand of exchange predicated on the man's *being* gay. What was said to make this difference? Not a version of "I am gay," which could only have been bathetic between them. What constituted coming out for this man, in this situation, was to use about himself the phrase "coming out" – to mention, as if casually, having come out to someone else. (Similarly, a T-shirt that ACT UP sells in New York bearing the text, "I am out, therefore I am," is meant to do for the wearer, not the constative work of reporting that s/he *is* out, but the performative work of coming out in the first place.) And [...] the fact that silence is rendered as pointed and performative as speech, in relations around the closet, depends on and highlights more broadly the fact that ignorance is as potent and as multiple a thing there as is knowledge.

Knowledge, after all, is not itself power, although it is the magnetic field of power. Ignorance and opacity collude or compete with knowledge in mobilizing the flows of energy, desire, goods, meanings, persons. If M. Mitterrand knows English but Mr. Reagan lacks – as he did lack – French, it is the urbane M. Mitterrand who must negotiate in an acquired tongue, the ignorant Mr. Reagan who may dilate in his native one. Or in the interactive speech model by which, as Sally McConnell-Ginet puts it, "the standard ... meaning can be thought of as what is recognizable solely on the basis of interlocutors' mutual knowledge of established practices of interpretation," it is the interlocutor who has or pretends to have the *less* broadly knowledgeable understanding of interpretive practice who will define the terms of the exchange. So, for instance, because "men, with superior extralinguistic resources and privileged discourse positions, are often less likely to treat perspectives different from their own as mutually available for communication," their attitudes are "thus more likely to leave a lasting imprint on the common semantic stock than women's."[4]

Such ignorance effects can be harnessed, licensed, and regulated on a mass scale for striking enforcements – perhaps especially around sexuality, in modern Western culture the most meaning-intensive of human activities. The epistemological asymmetry of the laws that govern rape, for instance, privileges at the same time men and ignorance, inasmuch as it matters not at all what the raped woman perceives or wants just so long as the man raping her can claim not to have noticed (ignorance in which male sexuality receives careful education).[5] And the rape machinery that is organized by this epistemological privilege of unknowing in turn keeps disproportionately under discipline, of course, women's larger ambitions to take more control over the terms of our own circulation.[6] Or, again, in an ingenious and patiently instructive orchestration of ignorance, the US Justice Department ruled in June, 1986, that an employer may freely fire persons with AIDS exactly so long as the employer can claim to be ignorant of the medical fact, *quoted in the ruling,*

that there is no known health danger in the workplace from the disease.[7] Again, it is clear in political context that the effect aimed at – in this case, it is hard to help feeling, aimed at with some care – is the ostentatious declaration, for the private sector, of an organized open season on gay men.[8]

Although the simple, stubborn fact or pretense of ignorance (one meaning, the Capital one, of the word "stonewall") can sometimes be enough to enforce discursive power, a far more complex drama of ignorance and knowledge is the more usual carrier of political struggle. Such a drama was enacted when, only a few days after the Justice Department's private-sector decision, the US Supreme Court correspondingly opened the public-sector bashing season by legitimating state antisodomy laws in *Bowers v. Hardwick.*[9] In a virulent ruling whose language made from beginning to end an insolent display of legal illogic – of what Justice Blackmun in dissent called "the most willful blindness"[10] – a single, apparently incidental word used in Justice White's majority opinion became for many gay or antihomophobic readers a focus around which the inflammatory force of the decision seemed to pullulate with peculiar density.[11] In White's opinion,

> to claim that a right to engage in sodomy is "deeply rooted in this nation's history and tradition" or "implicit in the concept of ordered liberty" is, at best, facetious.[12]

What lends the word "facetious" in this sentence such an unusual power to offend, even in the context of a larger legal offense whose damage will be much more indelible, has to be the economical way it functions here as switchpoint for the cyclonic epistemological undertows that encompass power in general and issues of homosexual desire in particular.

One considers: (1) *prima facie*, nobody could, of course, actually for an instant mistake the intent of the gay advocates as facetious. (2) *Secunda facie*, it is thus the court itself that is pleased to be facetious. Trading on the assertion's very (3) transparent stupidity (not just the contemptuous demonstration that powerful people don't have to be acute or right, but even more, the contemptuous demonstration – this is palpable throughout the majority opinions, but only in this word does it bubble up with active pleasure – of how obtuseness itself arms the powerful against their enemies), the court's joke here (in the wake of the mock-ignorant mock-jocose threat implicit in "at best") is (4) the clownish claim to be able at will to "read" – i.e., project into – the minds of the gay advocates. This being not only (5) a parody of, but (6) more intimately a kind of aggressive jamming technique against, (7) the truth/paranoid fantasy that it is gay people who can read, or project their own desires into, the minds of "straight" people.

Inarguably, there is a satisfaction in dwelling on the degree to which the power of our enemies over us is implicated, not in their command of knowledge, but precisely in their ignorance. The effect is a real one, but it carries dangers with it as well. The chief of these dangers is the scornful, fearful, or patheticizing reification of "ignorance"; it goes with the unexamined Enlightenment assumptions by which the labeling of a particular force as "ignorance" seems to place it unappealably in a demonized space on a never quite explicit ethical schema. (It is also dangerously close in structure to the more palpably sentimental privileging of ignorance as an originary, passive innocence.) The angles of view from which it can look as though a political fight is a fight against ignorance are invigorating and maybe revelatory ones but dangerous places for dwelling. The writings of, among others, Foucault, Derrida, Thomas Kuhn, and Thomas Szasz have given contemporary readers a lot of practice in questioning both the ethical/political disengagement and, beyond that, the ethical/political simplicity of the category of "knowledge," so that a writer who appeals too directly to the redemptive potential of simply upping the cognitive wattage on any question of power seems, now, naive. The corollary problems still adhere to the category of "ignorance," as well, but so do some additional ones: there are psychological operations of shame, denial, projection around "ignorance" that make it an especially galvanizing category for the individual reader, even as they give it a rhetorical potency that it would be hard for writers to forswear and foolhardy for them to embrace.

Rather than sacrifice the notion of "ignorance," then, I would be more interested at this point in trying, as we are getting used to trying with "knowledge," to pluralize and specify it. That is, I would like to be able to make use in sexual-political thinking of the deconstructive understanding that particular insights generate, are lined with, and at the same time are themselves structured by particular opacities. If ignorance is not – as it evidently is not – a single Manichaean, aboriginal maw of darkness from which the heroics of human cognition can occasionally wrestle facts, insights, freedoms, progress, perhaps there exists instead a plethora of *ignorances* and we may begin to ask questions about the labor, erotics, and economics of their human production and distribution. Insofar as ignorance is ignorance *of* a knowledge – a knowledge that may itself, it goes without saying, be seen as either true or false under some other regime of truth – these ignorances, far from being pieces of the originary dark, are produced by and correspond to particular knowledges and circulate as part of particular regimes of truth. We should not assume that their doubletting with knowledges means, however, that they obey identical laws identically or follow the same circulatory paths at the same pace.[13]

Historically, the framing of *Epistemology of the Closet* begins with a puzzle. It is a rather amazing fact that, of the very many dimensions along which the genital activity of one person can be differentiated from that of another (dimensions that include preference for certain acts, certain zones or sensations, certain physical types, a certain frequency, certain symbolic investments, certain relations of age or power, a certain species, a certain number of participants, etc. etc. etc.), precisely one, the gender of object choice, emerged from the turn of the century, and has remained, as *the* dimension denoted by the now ubiquitous category of "sexual orientation." This is not a development that would have been foreseen from the viewpoint of the fin de siècle itself, where a rich stew of male algolagnia, child-love, and autoeroticism, to mention no more of its components, seemed to have as indicative a relation as did homosexuality to the whole, obsessively entertained problematic of sexual "perversion" or, more broadly, "decadence." Foucault, for instance, mentions the hysterical woman and the masturbating child, along with "entomologized" sexological categories such as zoophiles, zooerasts, auto-monosexualists, and gynecomasts, as typifying the new sexual taxonomies, the "*specification of individuals*" that facilitated the modern freighting of sexual definition with epistemological and power relations.[14] True as his notation is, it suggests without beginning to answer the further question: why the category of "the masturbator," to choose only one example, should by now have entirely lost its diacritical potential for specifying a particular kind of person, an identity, at the same time as it continues to be true − becomes increasingly true − that, for a crucial strain of Western discourse, in Foucault's words "the homosexual was now a species."[15] So, as a result, is the heterosexual, and between *these* species the human species has come more and more to be divided. *Epistemology of the Closet* does not have an explanation to offer for this sudden, radical condensation of sexual categories; instead of speculating on its causes, the book explores its unpredictably varied and acute implications and consequences.

At the same time that this process of sexual specification or species-formation was going on, the book will argue, less stable and identity-bound understandings of sexual choice also persisted and developed, often among the same people or interwoven in the same systems of thought. Again, the book will not suggest (nor do I believe there currently exists) any standpoint of thought from which the rival claims of these minoritizing and universalizing understandings of sexual definition could be decisively arbitrated as to their "truth." Instead, the performative effects of the self-contradictory discursive field of force created by their overlap will be my subject. And, of course, it makes every difference that these impactions of homo/heterosexual definition took place in a setting, not of spacious emotional or analytic impartiality, but rather of urgent homophobic pressure to devalue one of the two nominally symmetrical forms of choice.

As several of the formulations above would suggest, one main strand of argument in this book is deconstructive, in a fairly specific sense. The analytic move it makes is to demonstrate that categories presented in a culture as symmetrical binary oppositions − heterosexual/homosexual, in this case − actually subsist in a more unsettled and dynamic tacit relation according to which, first, term B is not symmetrical with but subordinated to term A; but, second, the ontologically valorized term A actually depends for its meaning on the simultaneous subsumption and exclusion of term B; hence, third, the question of priority between the

supposed central and the supposed marginal category of each dyad is irresolvably unstable, an instability caused by the fact that term B is constituted as at once internal and external to term A. Harold Beaver, for instance, in an influential 1981 essay sketched the outlines of such a deconstructive strategy:

> The aim must be to reverse the rhetorical opposition of what is "transparent" or "natural" and what is "derivative" or "contrived" by demonstrating that the qualities predicated of "homosexuality" (as a dependent term) are in fact a condition of "heterosexuality"; that "heterosexuality," far from possessing a privileged status, must itself be treated as a dependent term.[16]

To understand these conceptual relations as irresolvably unstable is not, however, to understand them as inefficacious or innocuous. It is at least premature when Roland Barthes prophesies that "once the paradigm is blurred, utopia begins: meaning and sex become the objects of free play, at the heart of which the (polysemant) forms and the (sensual) practices, liberated from the binary prison, will achieve a state of infinite expansion."[17] To the contrary, a deconstructive understanding of these binarisms makes it possible to identify them as sites that are *peculiarly* densely charged with lasting potentials for powerful manipulation − through precisely the mechanisms of self-contradictory definition or, more succinctly, the double bind. Nor is a deconstructive analysis of such definitional knots, however necessary, at all sufficient to disable them. Quite the opposite: I would suggest that an understanding of their irresolvable instability has been continually available, and has continually lent discursive authority, to antigay as well as to gay cultural forces of this century. Beaver makes an optimistic prediction that "by disqualifying the autonomy of what was deemed spontaneously immanent, the whole sexual system is fundamentally decentred and exposed."[18] But there is reason to believe that the oppressive sexual system of the past hundred years was if anything born and bred (if I may rely on the pith of a fable whose value doesn't, I must hope, stand or fall with its history of racist uses) in the briar patch of the most notorious and repeated decenterings and exposures.

These deconstructive contestations can occur, moreover, only in the context of an entire cultural network of normative definitions, definitions themselves equally unstable but responding to different sets of contiguities and often at a different rate. The master terms of a particular historical moment will be those that are so situated as to entangle most inextricably and at the same time most differentially the filaments of other important definitional nexuses. In arguing that homo/heterosexual definition has been a presiding master term of the past century, one that has the same, primary importance for all modern Western identity and social organization (and not merely for homosexual identity and culture) as do the more traditionally visible cruxes of gender, class, and race, I'll argue that the now chronic modern crisis of homo/heterosexual definition has affected our culture through its ineffaceable marking particularly of the categories secrecy/disclosure, knowledge/ignorance, private/public, masculine/feminine, majority/minority, innocence/initiation, natural/artificial, new/old, discipline/terrorism, canonic/noncanonic, wholeness/decadence, urbane/provincial, domestic/foreign, health/illness, same/different, active/passive, in/out, cognition/paranoia, art/kitsch, utopia/apocalypse, sincerity/sentimentality, and voluntarity/addiction.[19] And rather than embrace an idealist faith in the necessarily, immanently self-corrosive efficacy of the contradictions inherent to these definitional binarisms, I will suggest instead that contests for discursive power can be specified as competitions for the material or rhetorical leverage required to set the terms of, and to profit in some way from, the operations of such an incoherence of definition.

Perhaps I should say something about the project of hypothesizing that certain binarisms that structure meaning in a culture may be "ineffaceably marked" by association with this one particular problematic – ineffaceably even when invisibly. Hypothesizing is easier than proving, but indeed I cannot imagine the protocol by which such hypotheses might be *tested*; they must be deepened and broadened – not the work of one book – and used, rather than proved or disproved by a few examples. The collecting of instances of each binarism that would appear to "common sense" to be unmarked by issues of homo/heterosexual definition, though an inexhaustibly stimulating heuristic, is not, I believe, a good test of such a hypothesis. After all, the particular kinds of skill that might be required to produce the most telling interpretations have hardly

been a valued part of the "common sense" of this epistemologically cloven culture. If a painstaking process of accumulative reading and historical de- and recontextualization does not render these homologies resonant and productive, that is the only test they can directly fail, the only one they need to pass.

[…]

A note on terminology. There is, I believe, no satisfactory rule for choosing between the usages "homosexual" and "gay," outside of a post-Stonewall context where "gay" must be preferable since it is the explicit choice of a large number of the people to whom it refers. Until recently it seemed that "homosexual," though it severely risked anachronism in any application before the late nineteenth century, was still somehow less temporally circumscribed than "gay," perhaps because it sounded more official, not to say diagnostic. That aura of timelessness about the word has, however, faded rapidly – less because of the word's manifest inadequacy to the cognitive and behavioral maps of the centuries *before* its coining, than because the sources of its authority for the century *after* have seemed increasingly tendentious and dated. Thus "homosexual" and "gay" seem more and more to be terms applicable to distinct, nonoverlapping periods in the history of a phenomenon for which there then remains no overarching label. Accordingly I have tried to use each of the terms appropriately in contexts where historical differentiation between the earlier and later parts of the century seemed important. But to designate "the" phenomenon (problematical notion) as it stretches across a larger reach of history, I have used one or the other interchangeably, most often in contrast to the immediately relevant historical usage. (E.g., "gay" in a turn-of-the-century context or "homosexual" in a 1980s context would each be meant to suggest a categorization broad enough to include at least the other period as well.) I have not followed a convention, used by some scholars, of differentiating between "gay" and "homosexual" on the basis of whether a given text or person was perceived as embodying (respectively) gay affirmation or internalized homophobia; an unproblematical ease in distinguishing between these two things is not an assumption of this study. The main additional constraint on the usage of these terms in this book is a preference against employing the noun "gayness," or "gay" itself as a noun. I think what underlies this preference is a sense that the association of same-sex desire with the traditional, exciting meanings of the adjective "gay" is still a powerfully assertive act, perhaps not one to be lightly routinized by grammatical adaptations.

Gender has increasingly become a problem for this area of terminology, and one to which I have, again, no consistent solution. "Homosexual" was a relatively gender-neutral term and I use it as such, though it has always seemed to have at least some male bias – whether because of the pun on Latin *homo* = man latent in its etymological macaronic, or simply because of the greater attention to men in the discourse surrounding it (as in so many others). "Gay" is more complicated since it makes a claim to refer to both genders but is routinely yoked with "lesbian" in actual usage, as if it did not – as increasingly it does not – itself refer to women. As I suggest in Axiom 3, this terminological complication is closely responsive to real ambiguities and struggles of gay/lesbian politics and identities: e.g., there are women-loving women who think of themselves as lesbians but not as gay, and others who think of themselves as gay women but not as lesbians. Since the premises of this study make it impossible to presuppose either the unity or the distinctness of women's and men's changing, and indeed synchronically various, homosexual identities, and since its primary though not exclusive focus is in fact on male identities, I sometimes use "gay and lesbian" but more often simply "gay," the latter in the oddly precise sense of a phenomenon of same-sex desire that is being treated as indicatively but not exclusively male. When I mean to suggest a more fully, equitably two-sexed phenomenon I refer to "gay men and women," or "lesbians and gay men"; when a more exclusive one, to "gay men."

Finally, I feel painfully how different may be a given writer's and reader's senses of how best to articulate an argument that may for both seem a matter of urgency. I have tried to be as clear as I can about the book's moves, motives, and assumptions throughout; but even aside from the intrinsic difficulty of its subject and texts, it seems inevitable that the style of its writing will not conform to everyone's ideal of the pellucid. The fact that – if the book is right – the most significant stakes for the culture are involved in precisely the volatile, fractured, dangerous relations of visibility and articulation around homosexual possibility makes the prospect of its being misread especially fraught; to the predictable egoistic fear of its having no impact or a risible one there is added the dread of its operating destructively.

[...]

Axiom 1: People are different from each other.

It is astonishing how few respectable conceptual tools we have for dealing with this self-evident fact. A tiny number of inconceivably coarse axes of categorization have been painstakingly inscribed in current critical and political thought: gender, race, class, nationality, sexual orientation are pretty much the available distinctions. They, with the associated demonstrations of the mechanisms by which they are constructed and reproduced, are indispensable, and they may indeed override all or some other forms of difference and similarity. But the sister or brother, the best friend, the classmate, the parent, the child, the lover, the ex-: our families, loves, and enmities alike, not to mention the strange relations of our work, play, and activism, prove that even people who share all or most of our own positionings along these crude axes may still be different enough from us, and from each other, to seem like all but different species.

Everybody has learned this, I assume, and probably everybody who survives at all has reasonably rich, unsystematic resources of nonce taxonomy for mapping out the possibilities, dangers, and stimulations of their human social landscape. It is probably people with the experience of oppression or subordination who have most *need* to know it; and I take the precious, devalued arts of gossip, immemorially associated in European thought with servants, with effeminate and gay men, with all women, to have to do not even so much with the transmission of necessary news as with the refinement of necessary skills for making, testing, and using unrationalized and provisional hypotheses about what *kinds of people* there are to be found in one's world.[20] The writing of a Proust or a James would be exemplary here: projects precisely of *nonce* taxonomy, of the making and unmaking and *re*making and redissolution of hundreds of old and new categorical imaginings concerning all the kinds it may take to make up a world.

I don't assume that all gay men or all women are very skilled at the nonce-taxonomic work represented by gossip, but it does make sense to suppose that our distinctive needs are peculiarly disserved by its devaluation. For some people, the sustained, foregrounded pressure of loss in the AIDS years may be making such needs clearer: as one anticipates or tries to deal with the absence of people one loves, it seems absurdly impoverishing to surrender to theoretical trivialization or to "the sentimental" one's descriptive requirements that the piercing bouquet of a given friend's particularity be done some justice. What is more dramatic is that – in spite of every promise to the contrary – every single theoretically or politically interesting project of postwar thought has finally had the effect of delegitimating our space for asking or thinking in detail about the multiple, unstable ways in which people may be like or different from each other. This project is not rendered otiose by any demonstration of how fully people may differ also from themselves. Deconstruction, founded as a very science of *différ(e/a)nce*, has both so fetishized the idea of difference and so vaporized its possible embodiments that its most thoroughgoing practitioners are the last people to whom one would now look for help in thinking about particular differenc*es*. The same thing seems likely to prove true of theorists of postmodernism. Psychoanalytic theory, if only through the almost astrologically lush plurality of its overlapping taxonomies of physical zones, developmental stages, representational mechanisms, and levels of consciousness, seemed to promise to introduce a certain becoming amplitude into discussions of what different people are like – only to turn, in its streamlined trajectory across so many institutional boundaries, into the sveltest of metatheoretical disciplines, sleeked down to such elegant operational entities as *the* mother, *the* father, *the* preoedipal, *the* oedipal, *the* other or Other. Within the less theorized institutional confines of intrapsychoanalytic discourse, meanwhile, a narrowly and severely normative, difference-eradicating ethical program has long sheltered under developmental narratives and a metaphorics of health and pathology.[21] In more familiar ways, Marxist, feminist, postcolonial, and other engagé critical projects have deepened understandings of a few crucial axes of difference, perhaps necessarily at the expense of more ephemeral or less global impulses of differential group-

ing. In each of these inquiries, so much has been gained by the different ways we have learned to deconstruct the category of *the individual* that it is easy for us now to read, say, Proust as the most expert operator of our modern technologies for dismantling taxonomies of the person. For the emergence and persistence of the vitalizing worldly taxonomic energies on which Proust also depends, however, we have no theoretical support to offer. And these defalcations in our indispensable antihumanist discourses have apparently ceded the potentially forceful ground of profound, complex variation to humanist liberal "tolerance" or repressively trivializing celebration at best, to reactionary suppression at worst.[22]

This is among other things a way of saying that there is a large family of things *we know* and need to know about ourselves and each other with which we have, as far as I can see, so far created for ourselves almost no theoretical room to deal. The shifting interfacial resistance of "literature itself" to "theory" may mark, along with its other denotations, the surface tension of this reservoir of unrationalized nonce-taxonomic energies; but, while distinctively representational, these energies are in no sense peculiarly literary.

In the particular area of sexuality, for instance, I assume that most of us know the following things that can differentiate even people of identical gender, race, nationality, class, and "sexual orientation" – each one of which, however, if taken seriously as pure *difference*, retains the unaccounted-for potential to disrupt many forms of the available thinking about sexuality.

- Even identical genital acts mean very different things to different people.
- To some people, the nimbus of "the sexual" seems scarcely to extend beyond the boundaries of discrete genital acts; to others, it enfolds them loosely or floats virtually free of them.
- Sexuality makes up a large share of the self-perceived identity of some people, a small share of others'.
- Some people spend a lot of time thinking about sex, others little.
- Some people like to have a lot of sex, others little or none.
- Many people have their richest mental/emotional involvement with sexual acts that they don't do, or even don't *want* to do.

- For some people, it is important that sex be embedded in contexts resonant with meaning, narrative, and connectedness with other aspects of their life; for other people, it is important that they not be; to others it doesn't occur that they might be.
- For some people, the preference for a certain sexual object, act, role, zone, or scenario is so immemorial and durable that it can only be experienced as innate; for others, it appears to come late or to feel aleatory or discretionary.
- For some people, the possibility of bad sex is aversive enough that their lives are strongly marked by its avoidance; for others, it isn't.
- For some people, sexuality provides a needed space of heightened discovery and cognitive hyperstimulation. For others, sexuality provides a needed space of routinized habituation and cognitive hiatus.
- Some people like spontaneous sexual scenes, others like highly scripted ones, others like spontaneous-sounding ones that are nonetheless totally predictable.
- Some people's sexual orientation is intensely marked by autoerotic pleasures and histories – sometimes more so than by any aspect of alloerotic object choice. For others the autoerotic possibility seems secondary or fragile, if it exists at all.
- Some people, homo-, hetero-, and bisexual, experience their sexuality as deeply embedded in a matrix of gender meanings and gender differentials. Others of each sexuality do not.

The list of individual differences could easily be extended. That many of them could differentiate one from another period of the same person's life as well as one person's totality from another's, or that many of them record differentia that can circulate from one person to another, does not, I believe, lessen their authority to demarcate; they demarcate at more than one site and on more than one scale. The impact of such a list may seem to depend radically on a trust in the self-perception, self-knowledge, or self-report of individuals, in an area that is if anything notoriously resistant to the claims of common sense and introspection: where would the whole, astonishing and metamorphic Western romance tradition (I include psychoanalysis) be if people's sexual desire, of all things, were even momentarily assumed to be transparent to

themselves? Yet I am even more impressed by the leap of presumptuousness necessary to dismiss such a list of differences than by the leap of faith necessary to entertain it. To alienate conclusively, *definitionally*, from anyone on any theoretical ground the authority to describe and name their own sexual desire is a terribly consequential seizure. In this century, in which sexuality has been made expressive of the essence of both identity and knowledge, it may represent the most intimate violence possible. It is also an act replete with the most disempowering mundane institutional effects and potentials. It is, of course, central to the modern history of homophobic oppression.

[...]

Axiom 2: The study of sexuality is not coextensive with the study of gender; correspondingly, antihomophobic inquiry is not coextensive with feminist inquiry. But we can't know in advance how they will be different.

Sex, gender, sexuality: three terms whose usage relations and analytical relations are almost irremediably slippery. The charting of a space between something called "sex" and something called "gender" has been one of the most influential and successful undertakings of feminist thought. For the purposes of that undertaking, "sex" has had the meaning of a certain group of irreducible, biological differentiations between members of the species Homo sapiens who have XX and those who have XY chromosomes. These include (or are ordinarily thought to include) more or less marked dimorphisms of genital formation, hair growth (in populations that have body hair), fat distribution, hormonal function, and reproductive capacity. "Sex" in this sense – what I'll demarcate as "chromosomal sex" – is seen as the relatively minimal raw material on which is then based the social construction of *gender*. Gender, then, is the far more elaborated, more fully and rigidly dichotomized social production and reproduction of male and female identities and behaviors – of male and female *persons* – in a cultural system for which "male/female" functions as a primary and perhaps model binarism affecting the structure and meaning of many, many other binarisms whose apparent connection to chromosomal sex will often be exiguous or nonexistent. Compared to chromosomal sex, which is seen (by these definitions) as tending to be immutable, immanent in the individual, and biologically based, the meaning of gender is seen as culturally mutable and variable, highly relational (in the sense that each of the binarized genders is defined primarily by its relation to the other), and inextricable from a history of power differentials between genders. This feminist charting of what Gayle Rubin refers to as a "sex/gender system,"[23] the system by which chromosomal sex is turned into, and processed as, cultural gender, has tended to minimize the attribution of people's various behaviors and identities to chromosomal sex and to maximize their attribution to socialized gender constructs. The purpose of that strategy has been to gain analytic and critical leverage on the female-disadvantaging social arrangements that prevail at a given time in a given society, by throwing into question their legitimate ideological grounding in biologically based narratives of the "natural."

"Sex" is, however, a term that extends indefinitely beyond chromosomal sex. That its history of usage often overlaps with what might, now, more properly be called "gender" is only one problem. ("I can only love someone of my own sex." Shouldn't "sex" be "gender" in such a sentence? "M. saw that the person who approached was of the opposite sex." Genders – insofar as there are two and they are defined in contradistinction to one another – may be said to be opposite; but in what sense is XX the opposite of XY?) Beyond chromosomes, however, the association of "sex," precisely through the physical body, with reproduction and with genital activity and sensation keeps offering new challenges to the conceptual clarity or even possibility of sex/gender differentiation. There is a powerful argument to be made that a primary (or *the* primary) issue in gender differentiation and gender struggle is the question of who is to have control of women's (biologically) distinctive reproductive capability. Indeed, the intimacy of the association between several of the most signal forms of gender oppression and "the facts" of women's bodies and women's reproductive activity has led some radical feminists to question, more or less explicitly, the usefulness of insisting on a sex/gender distinction. For these reasons, even usages involving the "sex/gender system" within feminist theory are able to use "sex/gender" only to delineate a problematical *space* rather than a crisp distinction. My own loose usage in this book will be to denominate that problematized space of the sex/gender system, the whole package of physical and cultural distinctions between women and men, more simply under the rubric "gender." I do this in order to reduce the likelihood of confusion between "sex" in the sense of "the space of differences between male and female" (what I'll be grouping under "gender") and "sex" in the sense of sexuality.

For meanwhile the whole realm of what modern culture refers to as "sexuality" and *also* calls "sex" – the array of acts, expectations, narratives, pleasures, identity-formations, and knowledges, in both women and men, that tends to cluster most densely around certain genital sensations but is not adequately defined by them – that realm is virtually impossible to situate on a map delimited by the feminist-defined sex/gender distinction. To the degree that it has a center or starting point in certain physical sites, acts, and rhythms associated (however contingently) with procreation or the potential for it, "sexuality" in this sense may seem to be of a piece with "chromosomal sex": biologically necessary to species survival, tending toward the individually immanent, the socially immutable, the given. But to the extent that, as Freud argued and Foucault assumed, the distinctively sexual nature of human sexuality has to do precisely with its excess over or potential difference from the bare choreographies of procreation, "sexuality" might be the very opposite of what we originally referred to as (chromosomal-based) sex: it could occupy, instead, even more than "gender" the polar position of the relational, the social/symbolic, the constructed, the variable, the representational (see Figure 42.1). To note that, according to these different findings, *something* legitimately called sex or sexuality is all over the experiential and conceptual map is to record a problem less resolvable than a necessary choice of analytic paradigms or a determinate slippage of semantic meaning; it is rather, I would say, true to quite a range of contemporary worldviews and intuitions to find that sex/sexuality *does* tend to represent the full spectrum of positions between the most intimate and the most social, the most predetermined and the most aleatory, the most physically rooted and the most symbolically infused, the most innate and the most learned, the most autonomous and the most relational traits of being.

Biological	Cultural
Essential	Constructed
Individually immanent	Relational

Constructivist Feminist Analysis

chromosomal sex ———————————————————— gender
                                                        gender inequality

Radical Feminst Analysis

chromosomal sex
reproductive relations ———————————————— reproductive relations
sexual inequality   sexual inequality

Foucault-influenced Analysis

chromosomal sex ——————— reproduction ——————— sexuality

Figure 42.1   Some mappings of sex, gender, and sexuality

If all this is true of the definitional nexus between sex and sexuality, how much less simple, even, must be that between sexuality and gender. It will be an assumption of this study that there is always at least the potential for an analytic distance between gender and sexuality, even if particular manifestations or features of particular sexualities are among the things that plunge women and men most ineluctably into the discursive, institutional, and bodily enmeshments of gender definition, gender relation, and gender inequality. This, too, has been posed by Gayle Rubin:

> I want to challenge the assumption that feminism is or should be the privileged site of a theory of sexuality. Feminism is the theory of gender oppression.... Gender affects the operation of the sexual system, and the sexual system has had gender-specific manifestations. But although sex and gender are related, they are not the same thing.[24]

This book will hypothesize, with Rubin, that the question of gender and the question of sexuality, inextricable from one another though they are in that each can be expressed only in the terms of the other, are nonetheless not the same question, that in twentieth-century Western culture gender and sexuality represent two analytic axes that may productively be imagined as

being as distinct from one another as, say, gender and class, or class and race. Distinct, that is to say, no more than minimally, but nonetheless usefully.

Under this hypothesis, then, just as one has learned to assume that every issue of racial meaning must be embodied through the specificity of a particular class position – and every issue of class, for instance, through the specificity of a particular gender position – so every issue of gender would necessarily be embodied through the specificity of a particular sexuality, and vice versa; but nonetheless there could be use in keeping the analytic axes distinct.

An objection to this analogy might be that gender is *definitionally* built into determinations of sexuality, in a way that neither of them is definitionally intertwined with, for instance, determinations of class or race. It is certainly true that without a concept of gender there could be, quite simply, no concept of homo- or heterosexuality. But many other dimensions of sexual choice (auto- or alloerotic, within or between generations, species, etc.) have no such distinctive, explicit definitional connection with gender; indeed, some dimensions of sexuality might be tied, not to gender, but *instead* to differences or similarities of race or class. The definitional narrowing-down in this century of sexuality as a whole to a binarized calculus of *homo-* or *hetero*sexuality is a weighty fact but an entirely historical one. To use that fait accompli as a reason for analytically conflating sexuality per se with gender would obscure the degree to which the fact itself requires explanation. It would also, I think, risk obscuring yet again the extreme intimacy with which all these available analytic axes do after all mutually constitute one another: to assume the distinctiveness of the *intimacy* between sexuality and gender might well risk assuming too much about the definitional *separability* of either of them from determinations of, say, class or race.

It may be, as well, that a damaging bias toward heterosocial or heterosexist assumptions inheres unavoidably in the very concept of gender. This bias would be built into any gender-based analytic perspective to the extent that gender definition and gender identity are necessarily relational between genders – to the extent, that is, that in any gender system, female identity or definition is constructed by analogy, supplementarity, or contrast to male, or vice versa. Although many gender-based forms of analysis do involve accounts, sometimes fairly rich ones, of intragender behaviors and relations, the ultimate definitional appeal in any gender-based analysis must necessarily be to the diacritical frontier between different genders. This gives heterosocial and heterosexual relations a conceptual privilege of incalculable consequence. Undeniably, residues, markers, tracks, signs referring to that diacritical frontier between genders are everywhere, as well, internal to and determinative of the experience of each gender and its intragender relations; gender-based analysis can never be dispensed with in even the most purely intragender context. Nevertheless it seems predictable that the analytic bite of a purely gender-based account will grow less incisive and direct as the distance of its subject from a social interface between different genders increases. It is unrealistic to expect a close, textured analysis of same-sex relations through an optic calibrated in the first place to the coarser stigmata of gender difference.[25] The development of an alternative analytic axis – call it sexuality – might well be, therefore, a particularly urgent project for gay/lesbian and antihomophobic inquiry.

It would be a natural corollary to Axiom 2 to hypothesize, then, that gay/lesbian and antihomopho-

bic inquiry still has a lot to learn from asking questions that feminist inquiry has learned to ask – but only so long as we don't demand to receive the same answers in both interlocutions. In a comparison of feminist and gay theory as they currently stand, the newness and consequent relative underdevelopment of gay theory are seen most clearly in two manifestations. First, we are by now very used to asking as feminists what we aren't yet used to asking as antihomophobic readers: how a variety of forms of oppression intertwine systemically with each other; and especially how the person who is disabled through one set of oppressions may *by the same positioning* be enabled through others. For instance, the understated demeanor of educated women in our society tends to mark both their deference to educated men and their expectation of deference from women and men of lower class. Again, a woman's use of a married name makes graphic at the same time her subordination as a woman and her privilege as a presumptive heterosexual. Or, again, the distinctive vulnerability to rape of women of all races has become in this country a powerful tool for the racist enforcement by which white people, including women, are privileged at the expense of Black people of both genders. That one is *either* oppressed *or* an oppressor, or that if one happens to be both, the two are not likely to have much to do with each other, still seems to be a common assumption, however, in at any rate male gay writing and activism,[26] as it hasn't for a long time been in careful feminist work.

Indeed, it was the long, painful realization, *not* that all oppressions are congruent, but that they are *differently* structured and so must intersect in complex embodiments that was the first great heuristic breakthrough of socialist-feminist thought and of the thought of women of color.[27] This realization has as its corollary that the comparison of different axes of oppression is a crucial task, not for any purpose of ranking oppressions, but to the contrary because each oppression is likely to be in a uniquely indicative relation to certain distinctive nodes of cultural organization. The *special* centrality of homophobic oppression in the twentieth century, I will be arguing, has resulted from its inextricability from the question of knowledge and the processes of knowing in modern Western culture at large.

The second and perhaps even greater heuristic leap of feminism has been the recognition that categories of gender and, hence, oppressions of gender can have a structuring force for nodes of thought, for axes of cultural discrimination, whose thematic subject isn't explicitly gendered at all. Through a series of developments structured by the deconstructive understandings and procedures sketched above, we have now learned as feminist readers that dichotomies in a given text of culture as opposed to nature, public as opposed to private, mind as opposed to body, activity as opposed to passivity, etc. etc., are, under particular pressures of culture and history, likely places to look for implicit allegories of the relations of men to women; more, that to fail to analyze such nominally ungendered constructs in gender terms can itself be a gravely tendentious move in the gender politics of reading. This has given us ways to ask the question of gender about texts even where the culturally "marked" gender (female) is not present as either author or thematic.

The dichotomy heterosexual/homosexual, as it has emerged through the last century of Western discourse, would seem to lend itself peculiarly neatly to a set of analytic moves learned from this deconstructive moment in feminist theory. In fact, the dichotomy heterosexual/homosexual fits the deconstructive template much more neatly than male/female itself does, and hence, importantly differently. The most dramatic difference between gender and sexual orientation – that virtually all people are publicly and unalterably assigned to one or the other gender, and from birth – seems if anything to mean that it is, rather, sexual orientation, with its far greater potential for rearrangement, ambiguity, and representational doubleness, that would offer the apter deconstructive object. An essentialism of sexual object-choice is far less easy to maintain, far more visibly incoherent, more visibly stressed and challenged at every point in the culture than any essentialism of gender. This is not an argument for any epistemological or ontological privileging of an axis of sexuality over an axis of gender; but it is a powerful argument for their potential distinctness one from the other.

Even given the imperative of constructing an account of sexuality irreducible to gender, however, it should already be clear that there are certain distortions necessarily built into the relation of gay/lesbian and antihomophobic theory to a larger project of

conceiving a theory of sexuality as a whole. The two can after all scarcely be coextensive. And this is true not because "gay/lesbian and antihomophobic theory" would fail to cover heterosexual as well as same-sex object-choice (any more than "feminist theory" would fail to cover men as well as women), but rather because, as we have noted, sexuality extends along so many dimensions that aren't well described in terms of the gender of object-choice at all. Some of these dimensions are habitually condensed under the rubrics of object-choice, so that certain discriminations of (for instance) *act* or of (for another instance) *erotic localization* come into play, however implicitly and however incoherently, when categories of object-choice are mobilized. One used, for instance, to hear a lot about a high developmental stage called "heterosexual genitality," as though cross-gender object-choice automatically erased desires attaching to mouth, anus, breasts, feet, etc.; a certain anal-erotic salience of male homosexuality is if anything increasingly strong under the glare of heterosexist AIDS-phobia; and several different historical influences have led to the de-genitalization and bodily diffusion of many popular, and indeed many lesbian, understandings of lesbian sexuality. Other dimensions of sexuality, however, distinguish object-choice quite differently (e.g., human/animal, adult/child, singular/plural, autoerotic/alloerotic) or are not even about object choice (e.g., orgasmic/nonorgasmic, noncommercial/commercial, using bodies only/using manufactured objects, in private/in public, spontaneous/scripted).[28] Some of these other dimensions of sexuality have had high diacritical importance in different historical contexts (e.g., human/animal, autoerotic/alloerotic). Others, like adult/child object-choice, visibly do have such importance today, but without being very fully subsumed under the hetero/homosexual binarism. Still others, including a host of them I haven't mentioned or couldn't think of, subsist in this culture as nondiacritical differences, differences that seem to make little difference beyond themselves – except that the hyperintensive structuring of sexuality in our culture sets several of them, for instance, at the exact border between legal and illegal. What I mean at any rate to emphasize is that the implicit condensation of "sexual theory" into "gay/lesbian and antihomophobic theory," which corresponds roughly to our by now unquestioned reading of the phrase "sexual ori-entation" to mean "gender of object-choice," is at the very least damagingly skewed by the specificity of its historical placement.

Axiom 3: There can't be an a priori decision about how far it will make sense to conceptualize lesbian and gay male identities together. Or separately.

Although it was clear from the beginning of this book project that its central focus would be on male sexual definition, the theoretical tools for drawing a circum-ferential boundary around that center have been elu-sive. They have changed perceptibly even during the period of this writing. In particular, the interpretive frameworks within which lesbian writers, readers, and interlocutors are likely to process male-centered reflections on homo/heterosexual issues are in a phase of destabilizing flux and promise.

The lesbian interpretive framework most readily available at the time this project began was the separa-tist-feminist one that emerged from the 1970s. According to that framework, there were essentially no valid grounds of commonality between gay male and lesbian experience and identity; to the contrary, women-loving women and men-loving men must be at precisely opposite ends of the gender spectrum. The assumptions at work here were indeed radical ones: most important, as we'll be discussing further in the next chapter, the stunningly efficacious re-visioning, in female terms, of same-sex desire as being at the very definitional center of each gender, rather than as occupying a cross-gender or liminal position between them. Thus, women who loved women were seen as *more* female, men who loved men as quite possibly more male, than those whose desire crossed bounda-ries of gender. The axis of sexuality, in this view, was not only exactly coextensive with the axis of gender but expressive of its most heightened essence: "Feminism is the theory, lesbianism is the practice." By analogy, male homosexuality could be, and often was, seen as the practice for which male supremacy was the theory.[29] A particular reading of modern gen-der history was, of course, implicit in and in turn pro-pelled by this gender-separatist framework. In accord with, for instance, Adrienne Rich's understanding of many aspects of women's bonds as constituting a

"lesbian continuum," this history, found in its purest form in the work of Lilian Faderman, deemphasized the definitional discontinuities and perturbations between more and less sexualized, more and less pro-hibited, and more and less gender-identity-bound forms of female same-sex bonding.[30] Insofar as lesbian object-choice was viewed as epitomizing a specificity of female experience and resistance, insofar as a sym-metrically opposite understanding of gay male object-choice also obtained, and insofar also as feminism necessarily posited male and female experiences and interests as different and opposed, the implication was that an understanding of male homo/heterosex-ual definition could offer little or no affordance or interest for any lesbian theoretical project. Indeed, the powerful impetus of a gender-polarized feminist ethical schema made it possible for a profoundly anti-homophobic reading of lesbian desire (as a quintessence of the female) to fuel a correspondingly homophobic reading of gay male desire (as a quintessence of the male).

Since the late 1970s, however, there have emerged a variety of challenges to this understanding of how lesbian and gay male desires and identities might be mapped against each other. Each challenge has led to a refreshed sense that lesbians and gay men may share important though contested aspects of one another's histories, cultures, identities, politics, and destinies. These challenges have emerged from the "sex wars" within feminism over pornography and s/m, which seemed to many pro-sex feminists to expose a devastating continuity between a certain, theretofore privileged feminist understanding of a resistant female identity, on the one hand, and on the other the most repressive nineteenth-century bourgeois construc-tions of a sphere of pure femininity. Such challenges emerged as well from the reclamation and relegitima-tion of a courageous history of lesbian trans-gender role-playing and identification.[31] Along with this new historical making-visible of self-defined mannish les-bians came a new salience of the many ways in which male and female homosexual identities had in fact been constructed through and in relation to each other over the last century – by the variously homo-phobic discourses of professional expertise, but also and just as actively by many lesbians and gay men.[32] The irrepressible, relatively class-nonspecific popular culture in which James Dean has been as numinous an icon for lesbians as Garbo or Dietrich has for gay men seems resistant to a purely feminist theorization.[33] It is in these contexts that calls for a theorized axis of sexuality as distinct from gender have developed. And after the anti-s/m, antipornography liberal-feminist move toward labeling and stigmatizing particular sexualities joined its energies with those of the much longer-established conservative sanctions against all forms of sexual "deviance," it remained only for the terrible accident of the HIV epidemic and the terrifyingly genocidal overdeterminations of AIDS discourse to reconstruct a category of the pervert capacious enough to admit homosexuals of any gender. The newly virulent homophobia of the 1980s, directed alike against women and men even though its medical pretext ought, if anything, logically to give a relative exemptive privilege to lesbians,[34] reminds urgently that it is more to friends than to enemies that gay women and gay men are perceptible as distinct groups. Equally, however, the internal perspective of the gay movements shows women and men increasingly, though far from uncontestingly and far from equally, working together on mutually antihomophobic agendas. The contributions of lesbians to current gay and AIDS activism are weighty, not despite, but because of the intervening lessons of feminism. Feminist perspectives on medicine and health-care issues, on civil disobedience, and on the politics of class and race as well as of sexuality have been centrally enabling for the recent waves of AIDS activism. What this activism returns to the lesbians involved in it may include a more richly pluralized range of imaginings of lines of gender and sexual identification.

Thus, it can no longer make sense, if it ever did, simply to assume that a male-centered analysis of homo/heterosexual definition will have no lesbian relevance or interest. At the same time, there are no algorithms for assuming a priori what its lesbian relevance could be or how far its lesbian interest might extend. It seems inevitable to me that the work of defining the circumferential boundaries, vis-à-vis lesbian experience and identity, of any gay male-centered theoretical articulation can be done only from the point of view of an alternative, feminocentric theoretical space, not from the heart of the male-centered project itself.

However interested I am in understanding those boundaries and their important consequences, therefore, the project of this particular book, just as it will not *assume* their geography, is not the one that can trace them. That limitation seems a damaging one chiefly insofar as it echoes and prolongs an already scandalously extended eclipse: the extent to which women's sexual, and specifically homosexual, experience and definition tend to be subsumed by men's during the turn-of-the-century period most focused on in my discussion, and are liable once again to be subsumed *in* such discussion. If one could demarcate the extent of the subsumption precisely, it would be less destructive, but "subsumption" is not a structure that makes precision easy. The problem is obvious even at the level of nomenclature and affects, of course, that of this book no less than any other; I have discussed above the particular choices of usage made here. Corresponding to those choices, the "gay theory" I have been comparing with feminist theory doesn't mean exclusively gay male theory, but for the purpose of this comparison it includes lesbian theory insofar as that (a) isn't simply coextensive with feminist theory (i.e., doesn't subsume sexuality *fully* under gender) and (b) doesn't a priori deny all theoretical continuity between male homosexuality and lesbianism. But, again, the extent, construction, and meaning, and especially the history of any such theoretical continuity – not to mention its consequences for practical politics – must be open to every interrogation. That gay theory, falling under this definition and centering insistently on lesbian experience, can still include strongly feminist thought would be demonstrated by works as different as those of Gayle Rubin, Audre Lorde, Katie King, and Cherríe Moraga.

Axiom 4: The immemorial, seemingly ritualized debates on nature versus nurture take place against a very unstable background of tacit assumptions and fantasies about both nurture and nature.

If there is one compulsory setpiece for the Introduction to any gay-oriented book written in the late 1980s, it must be the meditation on and attempted adjudication of constructivist versus essentialist views of homosexuality. The present study is hardly the first to demur vigorously from such a task, although I can only wish that its demurral might be vigorous enough to make it one of the last to need to do so. My demurral has two grounds. The first, as I have mentioned and will discuss further in later chapters, is that any such adjudication is impossible to the degree that a conceptual deadlock between the two opposing views has by now been built into the very structure of every theoretical tool we have for undertaking it. The second one is already implicit in a terminological choice I have been making: to refer to "minoritizing" versus "universalizing" rather than to essentialist versus constructivist understandings of homosexuality. I prefer the former terminology because it seems to record and respond to the question, "In whose lives is homo/heterosexual definition an issue of continuing centrality and difficulty?" rather than either of the questions that seem to have gotten conflated in the constructivist/essentialist debate: on the one hand what one might call the question of phylogeny, "How fully are the meaning and experience of sexual activity and identity contingent on their mutual structuring with other, historically and culturally variable aspects of a given society?"; and on the other what one might call that of ontogeny, "What is the cause of homo-[or of hetero-] sexuality in the individual?" I am specifically offering minoritizing/universalizing as an *alternative* (though not an equivalent) to essentialist/constructivist, in the sense that I think it can do some of the same analytic work as the latter binarism, and rather more tellingly. I think it may isolate the areas where the questions of ontogeny and phylogeny most consequentially overlap. I also think, as I suggested in Axiom 1, that it is more respectful of the varied proprioception of many authoritative individuals. But I am additionally eager to promote the obsolescence of "essentialist/constructivist" because I am very dubious about the ability of even the most scrupulously gay-affirmative thinkers to divorce these terms, especially as they relate to the question of ontogeny, from the essentially gay-genocidal nexuses of thought through which they have developed. And beyond that: even where we may think we know the conceptual landscape of their history well enough to do the delicate, always dangerous work of prying them loose from their historical backing to attach to them newly enabling meanings, I fear that the special volatility of postmodern bodily and technological relations may

make such an attempt peculiarly liable to tragic misfire. Thus, it would seem to me that gay-affirmative work does well when it aims to minimize its reliance on any particular account of the origin of sexual preference and identity in individuals.

In particular, my fear is that there currently exists no framework in which to ask about the origins or development of individual gay identity that is not already structured by an implicit, trans-individual Western project or fantasy of eradicating that identity. It seems ominously symptomatic that, under the dire homophobic pressures of the last few years, and in the name of Christianity, the subtle constructivist argument that sexual aim is, at least for many people, not a hard-wired biological given but, rather, a social fact deeply embedded in the cultural and linguistic forms of many, many decades is being degraded to the blithe ukase that people are "free at any moment to" (i.e., must immediately) "choose" to adhere to a particular sexual identity (say, at a random hazard, the heterosexual) rather than to its other. (Here we see the disastrously unmarked crossing of phylogenetic with ontogenetic narratives.) To the degree – and it is significantly large – that the gay essentialist/constructivist debate takes its form and premises from, and insistently refers to, a whole history of other nature/nurture or nature/culture debates, it partakes of a tradition of viewing culture as malleable relative to nature: that is, culture, unlike nature, is assumed to be the thing that can be changed; the thing in which "humanity" has, furthermore, a right or even an obligation to intervene. This has certainly been the grounding of, for instance, the feminist formulation of the sex/gender system described above, whose implication is that the more fully gender inequality can be shown to inhere in human culture rather than in biological nature, the more amenable it must be to alteration and reform. I remember the buoyant enthusiasm with which feminist scholars used to greet the finding that one or another brutal form of oppression was not biological but "only" cultural! I have often wondered what the basis was for our optimism about the malleability of culture by any one group or program. At any rate, never so far as I know has there been a sufficiently powerful place from which to argue that such manipulations, however triumphal the ethical imperative behind them, were not a right that belonged to anyone who might have the power to perform them.

The number of persons or institutions by whom the existence of gay people – never mind the existence of *more gay people* – is treated as a precious desideratum, a needed condition of life, is small, even compared to those who may wish for the dignified treatment of any gay people who happen already to exist. Advice on how to make sure your kids turn out gay, not to mention your students, your parishioners, your therapy clients, or your military subordinates, is less ubiquitous than you might think. By contrast, the scope of institutions whose programmatic undertaking is to prevent the development of gay people is unimaginably large. No major institutionalized discourse offers a firm resistance to that undertaking; in the United States, at any rate, most sites of the state, the military, education, law, penal institutions, the church, medicine, mass culture, and the mental health industries enforce it all but unquestioningly, and with little hesitation even at recourse to invasive violence. So for gay and gay-loving people, even though the space of cultural malleability is the only conceivable theatre for our effective politics, every step of this constructivist nature/culture argument holds danger: it is so difficult to intervene in the seemingly natural trajectory that begins by identifying a place of cultural malleability; continues by inventing an ethical or therapeutic mandate for cultural manipulation; and ends in the overarching, hygienic Western fantasy of a world without any more homosexuals in it.

That's one set of dangers, and it is against them, I think, that essentialist understandings of sexual identity accrue a certain gravity. The resistance that seems to be offered by conceptualizing an unalterably *homosexual body*, to the social engineering momentum apparently built into every one of the human sciences of the West, can reassure profoundly. Furthermore, it reaches deeply and, in a sense, protectively into a fraught space of life-or-death struggle that has been more or less abandoned by constructivist gay theory: that is, the experience and identity of gay or proto-gay children. The ability of anyone in the culture to support and honor gay kids may depend on an ability to name them as such, notwithstanding that many gay adults may never have been gay kids and some gay kids may not turn into gay adults. It seems plausible

that a lot of the emotional energy behind essentialist historical work has to do not even in the first place with reclaiming the place and eros of Homeric heroes, Renaissance painters, and medieval gay monks, so much as with the far less permissible, vastly more necessary project of recognizing and validating the creativity and heroism of the effeminate boy or tommish girl of the fifties (or sixties or seventies or eighties) whose sense of constituting precisely a *gap* in the discursive fabric of the given has not been done justice, so far, by constructivist work.

At the same time, however, just as it comes to seem questionable to assume that cultural constructs are peculiarly malleable ones, it is also becoming increasingly problematical to assume that grounding an identity in biology or "essential nature" is a stable way of insulating it from societal interference. If anything, the gestalt of assumptions that undergird nature/nurture debates may be in the process of direct reversal. Increasingly it is the conjecture that a particular trait is genetically or biologically based, *not* that it is "only cultural," that seems to trigger an estrus of manipulative fantasy in the technological institutions of the culture. A relative depressiveness about the efficacy of social engineering techniques, a high mania about biological control: the Cartesian bipolar psychosis that always underlay the nature/nurture debates has switched its polar assignments without surrendering a bit of its hold over the collective life. And in this unstable context, the dependence on a specified *homosexual body* to offer resistance to any gay-eradicating momentum is tremblingly vulnerable. AIDS, though it is used to proffer every single day to the news-consuming public the crystallized vision of a world after the homosexual, could never by itself bring about such a world. What whets these fantasies more dangerously, because more blandly, is the presentation, often in ostensibly or authentically gay-affirmative contexts, of biologically based "explanations" for deviant behavior that are absolutely invariably couched in terms of "excess," "deficiency," or "imbalance" – whether in the hormones, in the genetic material, or, as is currently fashionable, in the fetal endocrine environment. If I had ever, in any medium, seen any researcher or popularizer refer even once to any supposed gay-producing circumstance as the *proper* hormone balance, or the *conducive* endocrine environment, for gay generation, I would be less chilled by the breezes of all this technological confidence. As things are, a medicalized dream of the prevention of gay bodies seems to be the less visible, far more respectable underside of the AIDS-fueled public dream of their extirpation. In this unstable balance of assumptions between nature and culture, at any rate, under the overarching, relatively unchallenged aegis of a culture's desire that gay people *not be*, there is no unthreatened, unthreatening conceptual home for a concept of gay origins. We have all the more reason, then, to keep our understanding of gay origin, of gay cultural and material reproduction, plural, multi-capillaried, argus-eyed, respectful, and endlessly cherished.

Axiom 5: The historical search for a Great Paradigm Shift may obscure the present conditions of sexual identity.

Since 1976, when Michel Foucault, in an act of polemical bravado, offered 1870 as the date of birth of modern homosexuality,[35] the most sophisticated historically oriented work in gay studies has been offering ever more precise datings, ever more nuanced narratives of the development of homosexuality "as we know it today."[36] The great value of this scholarly movement has been to subtract from that "as we know it today" the twin positivist assumptions (1) that there must be some *transhistorical* essence of "homosexuality" available to modern knowledge, and (2) that the history of understandings of same-sex relations has been a history of increasingly direct, true knowledge or comprehension of that essence. To the contrary, the recent historicizing work has assumed (1) that the differences between the homosexuality "we know today" and previous arrangements of same-sex relations may be so profound and so integrally rooted in other cultural differences that there may be no continuous, defining essence of "homosexuality" to *be* known; and (2) that modern "sexuality" and hence modern homosexuality are so intimately entangled with the historically distinctive contexts and structures that now count as *knowledge* that such "knowledge" can scarcely be a transparent window onto a separate realm of sexuality but, rather, itself constitutes that sexuality.

These developments have promised to be exciting and productive in the way that the most important work of history or, for that matter, of anthropology

may be: in radically defamiliarizing and denaturalizing, not only the past and the distant, but the present. One way, however, in which such an analysis is still incomplete – in which, indeed, it seems to me that it has tended inadvertently to *re*familiarize, *re*naturalize, damagingly reify an entity that it could be doing much more to subject to analysis – is in counterposing against the alterity of the past a relatively unified homosexuality that "we" *do* "know today." It seems that the topos of "homosexuality as we know it today," or even, to incorporate more fully the antipositivist finding of the Foucauldian shift, "homosexuality as we *conceive of it* today," has provided a rhetorically necessary fulcrum point for the denaturalizing work on the past done by many historians. But an unfortunate side effect of this move has been implicitly to underwrite the notion that "homosexuality as we conceive of it today" itself comprises a coherent definitional field rather than a space of overlapping, contradictory, and conflictual definitional forces. Unfortunately, this presents more than a problem of oversimplification. To the degree that power relations involving modern homo/heterosexual definition have been structured by the very tacitness of the double-binding force fields of conflicting definition – to the degree that, […] the presumptuous, worldly implication "We Know What That Means" happens to be "the particular lie that animates and perpetuates the mechanism of [modern] homophobic male self-ignorance and violence and manipulability" – to that degree these historical projects, for all their immense care, value, and potential, still risk reinforcing a dangerous consensus of knowingness about the genuinely *un*known, more than vestigially contradictory structurings of contemporary experience.

As an example of this contradiction effect, let me juxtapose two programmatic statements of what seem to be intended as parallel and congruent projects. In the foundational Foucault passage to which I alluded above, the modern category of "homosexuality" that dates from 1870 is said to be

characterized … less by a type of sexual relations than by a certain quality of sexual sensibility, a certain way of inverting the masculine and the feminine in oneself. Homosexuality appeared as one of the forms of sexuality when it was transposed from the practice of sodomy onto a kind of interior androgyny, a hermaphrodism of the soul. The sodomite had been a temporary aberration; the homosexual was now a species.

In Foucault's account, the unidirectional emergence in the late nineteenth century of "the homosexual" as "a species," of homosexuality as a minoritizing identity, is seen as tied to an also unidirectional, and continuing, emergent understanding of homosexuality in terms of gender inversion and gender transitivity. This understanding appears, indeed, according to Foucault, to underlie and constitute the common sense of the homosexuality "we know today." A more recent account by David M. Halperin, on the other hand, explicitly in the spirit and under the influence of Foucault but building, as well, on some intervening research by George Chauncey and others, constructs a rather different narrative – but constructs it, in a sense, *as if it were the same one*:

> Homosexuality and heterosexuality, as we currently understand them, are modern, Western, bourgeois productions. Nothing resembling them can be found in classical antiquity. ... In London and Paris, in the seventeenth and eighteenth centuries, there appear ... social gathering-places for persons of the same sex with the same socially deviant attitudes to sex and gender who wish to socialize and to have sex with one another. ... This phenomenon contributes to the formation of the great nineteenth-century experience of "sexual inversion," or sex-role reversal, in which some forms of sexual deviance are interpreted as, or conflated with, gender deviance. The emergence of homosexuality out of inversion, the formation of a sexual orientation independent of relative degrees of masculinity and femininity, takes place during the latter part of the nineteenth century and comes into its own only in the twentieth. Its highest expression is the "straight-acting and -appearing gay male," a man distinct from other men in absolutely no other respect besides that of his "sexuality."[37]

Halperin offers some discussion of why and how he has been led to differ from Foucault in discussing "inversion" as a stage that in effect preceded "homosexuality." What he does not discuss is that his reading of "homosexuality" as "we currently understand" it – his presumption of the reader's commonsense, present-tense conceptualization of homosexuality, the point from which all the thought experiments of differentiation

must proceed – is virtually the opposite of Foucault's. For Halperin, what is presumed to define modern homosexuality "as we understand" it, in the form of the straight-acting and -appearing gay male, is gender intransitivity; for Foucault, it is, in the form of the feminized man or virilized woman, gender transitivity.

What obscures this difference between two historians, I believe, is the underlying structural congruence of the two histories: each is a unidirectional narrative of supersession. Each one makes an overarching point about the complete conceptual alterity of earlier models of same-sex relations. In each history one model of same-sex relations is superseded by another, which may again be superseded by another. In each case the superseded model then drops out of the frame of analysis. For Halperin, the power and interest of a postinversion notion of "sexual orientation independent of relative degrees of masculinity and femininity" seem to indicate that that notion must necessarily be seen as superseding the inversion model; he then seems to assume that any elements of the inversion model still to be found in contemporary understandings of homosexuality may be viewed as mere historical remnants whose process of withering away, however protracted, merits no analytic attention. The end point of Halperin's narrative differs from that of Foucault, but his proceeding does not: just as Halperin, having discovered an important *intervening* model, assumes that it must be a *supervening* one as well, so Foucault had already assumed that the nineteenth-century intervention of a minoritizing discourse of sexual identity in a previously extant, universalizing discourse of "sodomitic" sexual acts must mean, for all intents and purposes, the eclipse of the latter.

[...]

Axiom 6: The relation of gay studies to debates on the literary canon is, and had best be, tortuous.

Early on in the work on *Epistemology of the Closet*, in trying to settle on a literary text that would provide a first example for the kind of argument I meant the book to enable, I found myself circling around a text of 1891, a narrative that in spite of its relative brevity has proved a durable and potent centerpiece of gay male intertextuality and indeed has provided a durable and potent physical icon for gay male desire. It tells the story of a young Englishman famous for an extreme beauty of face and figure that seems to betray his aristocratic origin – an origin marked, however, also by mystery and class misalliance. If the gorgeous youth gives his name to the book and stamps his bodily image on it, the narrative is nonetheless more properly the story of a male triangle: a second, older man is tortured by a desire for the youth for which he can find no direct mode of expression, and a third man, emblem of suavity and the world, presides over the dispensation of discursive authority as the beautiful youth murders the tortured lover and is himself, in turn, by the novel's end ritually killed.

But maybe, I thought, one such text would offer an insufficient basis for cultural hypothesis. Might I pick two? It isn't yet commonplace to read *Dorian Gray* and *Billy Budd* by one another's light, but that can only be a testimony to the power of accepted English and American literary canons to insulate and deform the reading of politically important texts. In any gay male canon the two contemporaneous experimental works must be yoked together as overarching gateway texts of our modern period, and the conventionally obvious differences between them of style, literary positioning, national origin, class ethos, structure, and thematics must cease to be taken for granted and must instead become newly salient in the context of their startling erotic congruence. The book of the beautiful male English body foregrounded on an international canvas; the book of its inscription and evocation through a trio of male figures – the lovely boy, the tormented desirer, the deft master of the rules of their discourse; the story in which the lover is murdered by the boy and the boy is himself sacrificed; the deftly magisterial recounting that finally frames, preserves, exploits, and desublimates the male bodily image: *Dorian Gray* and *Billy Budd* are both that book.

The year 1891 is a good moment to which to look for a cross-section of the inaugural discourses of modern homo/heterosexuality – in medicine and psychiatry, in language and law, in the crisis of female status, in the career of imperialism. *Billy Budd* and *Dorian Gray* are among the texts that have set the terms for a modern homosexual identity. And in the Euro-American culture of this past century it has been notable that foundational texts of modern gay culture – *A la recherche du temps perdu* and *Death in Venice*, for instance, along with *Dorian Gray* and *Billy*

Budd – have often been the identical texts that mobilized and promulgated the most potent images and categories for (what is now visible as) the canon of homophobic mastery.

Neither *Dorian Gray* nor *Billy Budd* is in the least an obscure text. Both are available in numerous paperback editions, for instance; and, both conveniently short, each differently canonical within a different national narrative, both are taught regularly in academic curricula. As what they are taught, however, and as what canonized, comes so close to disciplining the reading permitted of each that even the contemporaneity of the two texts (*Dorian Gray* was published as a book the year *Billy Budd* was written) may startle. That every major character in the archetypal American "allegory of good and evil" is English; that the archetypal English fin-de-siècle "allegory of art and life" was a sufficiently American event to appear in a Philadelphia publisher's magazine nine months before it became a London book – the canonic regimentation that effaces these international bonds has how much the more scope to efface the intertext and the intersexed. [...]

[...]

What's now in place, in contrast, in most scholarship and most curricula is an even briefer response to questions like these: Don't ask. Or, less laconically: You shouldn't know. The vast preponderance of scholarship and teaching, accordingly, even among liberal academics, does simply neither ask nor know. At the most expansive, there is a series of dismissals of such questions on the grounds that:

1. Passionate language of same-sex attraction was extremely common during whatever period is under discussion – and therefore must have been completely meaningless. Or

2. Same-sex genital relations may have been perfectly common during the period under discussion – but since there was no language about them, *they* must have been completely meaningless. Or

3. Attitudes about homosexuality were intolerant back then, unlike now – so people probably didn't do anything. Or

4. Prohibitions against homosexuality didn't exist back then, unlike now – so if people did anything, it was completely meaningless. Or

5. The word "homosexuality" wasn't coined until 1869 – so everyone before then was heterosexual. (Of course, heterosexuality has always existed.) Or

6. The author under discussion is certified or rumored to have had an attachment to someone of the other sex – so their feelings about people of their own sex must have been completely meaningless. Or (under a perhaps somewhat different rule of admissible evidence)

7. There is no actual proof of homosexuality, such as sperm taken from the body of another man or a nude photograph with another woman – so the author may be assumed to have been ardently and exclusively heterosexual. Or (as a last resort)

8. The author or the author's important attachments may very well have been homosexual – but it would be provincial to let so insignificant a fact make any difference at all to our understanding of any serious project of life, writing, or thought.

These responses reflect, as we have already seen, some real questions of sexual definition and historicity. But they only reflect them and don't reflect *on* them: the family resemblance among this group of extremely common responses comes from their closeness to the core grammar of *Don't ask; You shouldn't know*. It didn't happen; it doesn't make any difference; it didn't mean anything; it doesn't have interpretive consequences. Stop asking just here; stop asking just now; we know in advance the kind of difference that could be made by the invocation of *this* difference; it makes no difference; it doesn't mean. The most openly repressive projects of censorship, such as William Bennett's literally murderous opposition to serious AIDS education in schools on the grounds that it would communicate a tolerance for the lives of homosexuals, are, through this mobilization of the powerful mechanism of the open secret, made perfectly congruent with the smooth, dismissive knowingness of the urbane and the pseudo-urbane.

[…]

Axiom 7: The paths of allo-identification are likely to be strange and recalcitrant. So are the paths of auto-identification.

In the Introduction to *Between Men* I felt constrained to offer a brief account of how I saw the political/theoretical positioning of "a woman and a feminist writing (in part) about male homosexuality";[38] my account was, essentially, that this was an under-theorized conjunction and it was about time someone put her mind to it. Issues of male homosexuality are, obviously, even more integral to the present volume, and the intervening years have taught me more about how important, not to say mandatory, such an accounting must be – as well as how almost prohibitively difficult. I don't speak here of the question of anyone's "right" to think or write about the subjects on which they feel they have a contribution to make: to the degree that rights can be measured at all, I suppose this one can be measured best by what contribution the work does make, and to whom. Beyond the difficulty of wielding a language of rights, however, I find that abstractive formulations like that phrase in the Introduction to *Between Men* always seem to entail a hidden underpinning of the categorical imperative, one that may dangerously obscure the way political commitments and identifications actually work. Realistically, what brings me to this work can hardly be that I am *a* woman, or *a* feminist, but that I am this particular one. The grounds on which a book like this one might be persuasive or compelling to you, in turn, are unlikely to be its appeal to some *bienpensant*, evenly valenced lambency of your disinterested attention. Realistically, it takes deeply rooted, durable, and often somewhat opaque energies to write a book; it can take them, indeed, to read it. It takes them, as well, to make any political commitment that can be worth anything to anyone.

What, then, would make a good answer to implicit questions about someone's strong group-identification across politically charged boundaries, whether of gender, of class, of race, of sexuality, of nation? It could never be a version of "But everyone *should* be able to make this identification." Perhaps everyone should, but everyone does not, and almost no one makes more than a small number of very narrowly channeled ones. (A currently plausible academic ideology, for instance, is that everyone in a position of class privilege *should* group-identify across lines of class; but who hasn't noticed that of the very few US scholars under 50 who have been capable of doing so productively, and over the long haul, most also "happen to have been" red diaper babies?) If the ethical prescription is explanatory at all – and I have doubts about that – it is anything but a full explanation. It often seems to me, to the contrary, that what these implicit questions really ask for is narrative, and of a directly personal sort. When I have experimented with offering such narrative, in relation to this ongoing project, it has been with several aims in mind.[39] I wanted to disarm the categorical imperative that seems to do so much to promote cant and mystification about motives in the world of politically correct academia. I wanted to try opening channels of visibility – toward the speaker, in this case – that might countervail somewhat against the terrible one-directionality of the culture's spectacularizing of gay men, to which it seems almost impossible, in any powerful gay-related project, not also to contribute. I meant, in a sense, to give hostages, though the possible thud of them on the tarmac of some future conflict is not something I can contemplate. I also wanted to offer (though on my own terms) whatever tools I could with which a reader who needed to might begin unknotting certain overdetermined impactions that inevitably structure these arguments. Finally, I have come up with such narrative because I desired and needed to, because its construction has greatly interested me, and what I learned from it has often surprised me.

[...]

Notes

1   On this, see Jonathan Katz, *Gay/Lesbian Almanac: A New Documentary* (New York: Harper & Row, 1983), pp. 147–50; for more discussion, David M. Halperin, *One Hundred Years of Homosexuality* (New York: Routledge, 1989), p. 155n.1 and pp. 158–9n.17.

2   This is an argument of my *Between Men: English Literature and Male Homosocial Desire* (New York: Columbia University Press, 1985).

3   Michel Foucault, *The History of Sexuality*. Volume 1: *An Introduction*, trans. Robert Hurley (New York: Pantheon, 1978), p. 27.

4   Sally McConnell-Ginet, "The Sexual (Re)Production of Meaning: A Discourse-Based Theory," manuscript, pp. 387–8, quoted in Cheris Kramarae and Paula A. Treichler, *A Feminist Dictionary* (Boston: Pandora Press, 1985), p. 264; emphasis added.

5   Catherine A. MacKinnon makes this point more fully in "Feminism, Marxism, Method, and the State: An Agenda for Theory," *Signs* 7, no. 3 (Spring 1982): 515–44.

6   Susan Brownmiller made the most forceful and influential presentation of this case in *Against Our Will: Men, Women, and Rape* (New York: Simon & Schuster, 1975).

7   Robert Pear, "Rights Laws Offer Only Limited Help on AIDS, US Rules," *New York Times*, June 23, 1986. That the ruling was calculated to offer, provoke, and legitimize harm and insult is clear from the language quoted in Pear's article: "A person," the ruling says, for instance, "cannot be regarded as handicapped [and hence subject to federal protection] simply because others shun his company. Otherwise, a host of personal traits, from ill temper to poor personal hygiene, would constitute handicaps."

8   Not that gay men were intended to be the only victims of this ruling. In even the most conscientious discourse concerning AIDS in the United States so far there has been the problem, to which this essay does not pretend to offer any solution, of doing justice at once to the relative (and increasing) heterogeneity of those who actually have AIDS and to the specificity with which AIDS discourse at every level has until very recently focused on male homosexuality. In its worldwide epidemiology, of course, AIDS has no distinctive association with gay men, nor is it likely to for long here either. The acknowledgment/management of this fact was the preoccupation of a strikingly sudden media-wide discursive shift in the winter and early spring of 1987. If the obsessionally homophobic focus of AIDS phobia up to that moment scapegoated gay men by (among other things) subjecting their sexual practice and lifestyles to a glaring and effectually punitive visibility, however, it worked in an opposite way to expunge the claims by expunging the visibility of most of the disease's other victims. So far, here, these victims have been among groups already the most vulnerable – intravenous drug users, sex workers, wives and girlfriends of closeted men – on whom invisibility, or a public subsumption under the incongruous heading of gay men, can have no protective effect. (It has been notable, for instance, that media coverage of prostitutes with AIDS has shown no interest in the health of the women themselves, but only in their potential for infecting men. Again, the campaign to provide drug users with free needles had not until early 1987 received even the exiguous state support given to safer-sex education for gay men.) The damages of homophobia on the one hand, of classism/racism/sexism on the other; of intensive regulatory visibility on the one hand, of discursive erasure on the other: these pairings are not only incommensurable (and why measure them against each other rather than

against the more liberating possibilities they foreclose?) but very hard to interleave with each other conceptually. The effect has been perhaps most dizzying when the incommensurable damages are condensed upon a single person, e.g., a nonwhite gay man. The focus of this book is on the specific damages of homophobia; but to the extent that it is impelled by (a desire to resist) the public pressures of AIDS phobia, I must at least make clear how much that is important even to its own ambitions is nonetheless excluded from its potential for responsiveness.

9   Graphic encapsulation of this event on the front page of the *Times*: at the bottom of the three-column lead story on the ruling, a photo ostensibly about the influx of various navies into a welcoming New York for "the Liberty celebration" shows two worried but extremely good-looking sailors in alluring whites, "asking directions of a police officer" (*New York Times*, July 1, 1986).

10 "The Supreme Court Opinion. Michael J. Bowers, Attorney General of Georgia, Petition v. Michael Hardwick and John and Mary Doe, Respondents," text in *New York Native*, no. 169 (July 14, 1986): 15.

11 The word is quoted, for instance, in isolation, in the sixth sentence of the *Times's* lead article announcing the decision (July 1, 1986). The *Times* editorial decrying the decision (July 2, 1986) remarks on the crudity of this word before outlining the substantive offensiveness of the ruling. The *New York Native* and the gay leaders it quoted also gave the word a lot of play in the immediate aftermath of the ruling (e.g., no. 169 [July 14, 1986]: 8, 11).

12 *New York Native*, no. 169 (July 14, 1986): 13.

13 For an essay that makes these points more fully, see my "Privilege of Unknowing," *Genders*, no. 1 (Spring 1988): 102–24, a reading of Diderot's *La Religieuse*, from which the preceding six paragraphs are taken.

14 Foucault, *History of Sexuality*, pp. 105, 43.

15 Foucault, *History of Sexuality*, p. 43.

16 Harold Beaver, "Homosexual Signs," *Critical Inquiry* 8 (Autumn 1981): 115.

17 *Roland Barthes by Roland Barthes*, trans. Richard Howard (New York: Hill and Wang, 1977), p. 133.

18 Beaver, "Homosexual Signs," pp. 115–16.

19 My casting of all these definitional nodes in the form of binarisms, I should make explicit, has to do not with a mystical faith in the number two but, rather, with the felt need to schematize in some consistent way the treatment of social vectors so exceedingly various. The kind of falsification necessarily performed on each by this reduction cannot, unfortunately, itself be consistent. But the scope of the kind of hypothesis

I want to pose does seem to require a drastic reductiveness, at least in its initial formulations.

20 On this, see Patricia Meyer Spacks, *Gossip* (New York: Alfred A. Knopf, 1985).

21 For a good discussion of this, see Henry Abelove, "Freud, Male Homosexuality, and the Americans," *Dissent* 33 (Winter 1986): 59–69.

22 Gayle Rubin discusses a related problem, that of the foreclosed space for acknowledging "benign sexual variation," in her "Thinking Sex: Notes for a Radical Theory of the Politics of Sexuality," in Carole S. Vance, ed., *Pleasure and Danger: Exploring Female Sexuality* (Boston: Routledge & Kegan Paul, 1984), p. 283.

23 Gayle Rubin, "The Traffic in Women: Notes on the 'Political Economy' of Sex," in Rayna R. Reiter, ed., *Toward an Anthropology of Women* (New York: Monthly Review Press, 1975), pp. 157–210.

24 Rubin, "Thinking Sex," pp. 307–8.

25 For valuable related discussions, see Katie King, "The Situation of Lesbianism as Feminism's Magical Sign: Contests for Meaning and the US Women's Movement, 1968–1972," in *Communication* 9 (1986): 65–91. Special issue, "Feminist Critiques of Popular Culture," ed. Paula A. Treichler and Ellen Wartella, 9: 65–91; and Teresa de Lauretis, "Sexual Indifference and Lesbian Representation," *Theatre Journal* 40 (May 1988): 155–77.

26 Gay male-centered work that uses more complex models to investigate the intersection of different oppressions includes Gay Left Collective, eds., *Homosexuality: Power and Politics* (London: Allison & Busby, 1980); Paul Hoch, *White Hero Black Beast: Racism, Sexism, and the Mask of Masculinity* (London: Pluto, 1979); Guy Hocquenghem, *Homosexual Desire*, trans. Daniella Dangoor (London: Allison & Busby, 1978); Mario Mieli, *Homosexuality and Liberation: Elements of a Gay Critique*, trans. David Fernbach (London: Gay Men's Press, 1980); D. A. Miller, *The Novel and the Police* (Berkeley and Los Angeles: University of California Press, 1988); Michael Moon, "'The Gentle Boy from the Dangerous Classes': Pederasty, Domesticity, and Capitalism in Horatio Alger," *Representations*, no. 19 (Summer 1987): 87–110; Michael Moon, *Disseminating Whitman* (Cambridge: Harvard University Press, 1990); and Jeffrey Weeks, *Sexuality and its Discontents: Meanings, Myths and Modern Sexualities* (London: Longman, 1980).

27 The influential socialist-feminist investigations have included Michèle Barrett, *Women's Oppression Today: Problems in Marxist Feminist Analysis* (London: Verso, 1980); Zillah Eisenstein, ed., *Capitalist Patriarchy and*

the Case for Socialist Feminism (New York: Monthly Review Press, 1979); and Juliet Mitchell, *Women's Estate* (New York: Vintage, 1973). On the intersections of racial with gender and sexual oppressions, see, for example, Elly Bulkin, Barbara Smith, and Minnie Bruce Pratt, *Yours in Struggle: Three Feminist Perspectives on Anti-Semitism and Racism* (New York: Long Haul Press, 1984); Bell Hooks [Gloria Watkins], *Feminist Theory: From Margin to Center* (Boston: South End Press, 1984); Katie King, "Audre Lorde's Lacquered Layerings: The Lesbian Bar as a Site of Literary Production," *Cultural Studies* 2, no. 3 (1988): 321–42; Audre Lorde, *Sister Outsider: Essays and Speeches* (Trumansburg, NY: The Crossing Press, 1984); Cherríe Moraga, *Loving in the War Years: Lo que nunca paso por sus labios* (Boston: South End Press, 1983); Cherríe Moraga and Gloria Anzaldua, eds., *This Bridge Called My Back: Writings by Radical Women of Color* (Watertown: Persephone, 1981; rpt. ed., New York: Kitchen Table: Women of Color Press, 1984); and Barbara Smith, ed., *Home Girls: A Black Feminist Anthology* (New York: Kitchen Table: Women of Color Press, 1983). Good overviews of several of these intersections as they relate to women and in particular to lesbians, can be found in Ann Snitow, Christine Stransell, and Sharon Thompson, eds., *The Powers of Desire: The Politics of Sexuality* (New York: Monthly Review/New Feminist Library, 1983); Vance, *Pleasure and Danger*; and de Lauretis, "Sexual Indifference."

28   This list owes something to Rubin, "Thinking Sex," esp. pp. 281–2.

29   See, among others, Marilyn Frye, *The Politics of Reality: Essays in Feminist Theory* (Trumansburg, NY: The Crossing Press, 1983), and Luce Irigaray, *This Sex Which Is Not One*, trans. Catherine Porter with Carolyn Burke (Ithaca: Cornell University Press, 1985), pp. 170–91.

30   Adrienne Rich, "Compulsory Heterosexuality and Lesbian Existence," in Catharine R. Stimpson and Ethel Spector Person, eds., *Women, Sex, and Sexuality* (Chicago: University of Chicago Press, 1980), pp. 62–91; Lilian Faderman, *Surpassing the Love of Men* (New York: William Morrow, 1982).

31   See, for instance, Esther Newton, "The Mythic Mannish Lesbian: Radclyffe Hall and the New Woman," in Estelle B. Freedman, Barbara C. Gelpi, Susan L. Johnson, and Kathleen M. Weston, eds., *The Lesbian Issue: Essays from SIGNS* (Chicago: University of Chicago Press, 1985), pp. 7–25; Joan Nestle, "Butch – Fem Relationships," pp. 21–4, and Amber Hollibaugh

and Cherríe Moraga, "What We're Rollin' Around in Bed With," pp. 58–62, both in *Heresies* 12, no. 3 (1981); Sue-Ellen Case, "Towards a Butch-Femme Aesthetic," *Discourse: Journal for Theoretical Studies in Media and Culture* 11, no. 1 (Fall–Winter 1988–1989): 55–73; de Lauretis, "Sexual Indifference"; and my "Across Gender, Across Sexuality: Willa Cather and Others," *SAQ* 88, no. 1 (Winter 1989): 53–72.

32   On this see, among others, Judy Grahn, *Another Mother Tongue: Gay Words, Gay Worlds* (Boston: Beacon Press, 1984).

33   On James Dean, see Sue Golding, "James Dean: The Almost-Perfect Lesbian Hermaphrodite," *On Our Backs* (Winter 1988): 18–19, 39–44.

34   This is not, of course, to suggest that lesbians are less likely than persons of any other sexuality to contract HIV infection, when they engage in the (quite common) acts that can transmit the virus, with a person (and there are many, including lesbians) who already carries it. In this particular paradigm-clash between a discourse of sexual *identity* and a discourse of sexual *acts*, the former alternative is uniquely damaging. No one should wish to reinforce the myth that the epidemiology of AIDS is a matter of discrete "risk groups" rather than of particular acts that can call for particular forms of prophylaxis. That myth is dangerous to self-identified or publicly identified gay men and drug users because it scapegoats them, and dangerous to everyone else because it discourages them from protecting themselves and their sex or needle partners. But, for a variety of reasons, the incidence of AIDS among lesbians has indeed been lower than among many other groups.

35   Foucault, *History of Sexuality*, p. 43.

36   See, for instance, Alan Bray, *Homosexuality in Renaissance England* (London: Gay Men's Press, 1982); Katz, *Gay/Lesbian Almanc*; Halperin, *One Hundred Years of Homosexuality*; Jeffrey Weeks, *Sex, Politics, and Society: The Regulation of Sexuality since 1800* (London: Longman, 1981); and George Chauncey, Jr., "From Sexual Inversion to Homosexuality: Medicine and the Changing Conceptualization of Female Deviance," *Salmagundi*, no. 58–9 (Fall 1982–Winter 1983): 114–45.

37   Halperin, *One Hundred Years of Homosexuality*, pp. 8–9.

38   *Between Men*, p. 19.

39   The longest such narrative appears as "A Poem Is Being Written," *Representations*, no. 17 (Winter 1987): 110–43. More fragmentary or oblique ones occur in "Tide and Trust," *Critical Inquiry* 15, no. 4 (Summer 1989): 745–57; and in "Privilege of Unknowing."

Additional Readings

Fanon

Aimé Césaire. *Notebook of a Return to the Native Land.* Translated by Clayton Eshleman. Boston: Wesleyan University Press, 2001.
Immensely influential poem that articulates Césaire's position on negritude.

Frantz Fanon. *Black Skin, Whites Masks.* Translated by Richard Philcox. New York: Grove Press, 2008.
The groundbreaking work from which the chapter in this section is excerpted, in which Fanon investigates the dependency and feelings of inadequacy that assail Black subjects living in a White world.

Achille Mbembe. *On the Postcolony.* Berkeley: University of California Press, 2001.
A series of essays covering a wide range of relevant topics, in particular the manner in which colonialism impinges upon the embodied subjectivity and experience of the colonized.

Max Silverman. *Frantz Fanon's* Black Skin White Masks. Manchester: Manchester University Press, 2005.
A collection of essays discussing, critiquing, and expanding upon Fanon's classic text from a variety of interdisciplinary perspectives.

Lacan

Bruce Fink. *Lacan to the Letter: Reading* Écrits *Closely.* Minneapolis: University of Minnesota Press, 2004.
An introduction and a model example of close reading which seeks to elucidate Lacan's complicated theories through a subtle and attentive return to the source.

Jacques Lacan. *My Teaching.* Translated by David Macey. London: Verso, 2009.
A collection of Lacan's essays for a non-specialized audience which draw on examples from popular culture and everyday life to clarify the key ideas of Lacanian psychoanalysis in a lively manner.

Slavoj Žižek. *How to Read Lacan.* London: Granta, 2006.
A passionate defense of Lacanian thought by the leading contemporary advocate of psychoanalysis, particularly as it applies to culture. An astute introduction to the work of Lacan, full of examples.

Irigaray

Rosalyn Diprose. *The Bodies of Women.* London: Routledge, 1994.
An examination of the ethical ramifications of sexual difference such as those argued for by Irigaray which places sexual difference at the center of all social meaning.

Elizabeth Grosz. *Volatile Bodies: Towards a Corporeal Feminism.* Bloomington, IN: Indiana University Press, 1994.
A seminal work, Grosz's book extends upon Irigaray's project of a female subjectivity embodied

in both the workings of language and the corporeal form.

Alison Stone. *Luce Irigaray and the Philosophy of Sexual Difference*. New York: University of Cambridge Press, 2006.
A defense of Irigaray's thought and its particular mode of essentialism which connects feminist embodiment to the philosophical traditions of Idealism and Romanticism.

Haraway

Mary Flanagan and Austin Booth, eds. *Reload: Rethinking Women + Cyberculture*. Cambridge, MA: MIT Press, 2002.
A collection of theoretical writing and women's cyberfiction which seeks to imagine cyberspace as a site of gender and considers the profound effect that rapid technological change has on culture and society.

Thomas Foster. *The Souls of Cyberfolk*. Minneapolis: University of Minnesota Press, 2005.
An examination of the ways in which cyberpunk and cyborg theory have defined new ways of thinking about technology and its function in society.

Donna Haraway and Thyrza Nichols Goodeve. *How Like a Leaf: An Interview with Donna Haraway*. London: Routledge, 1999.
An interview between Haraway and one of her former students about the many facets of her development as a theorist.

Isabelle Stengers. *Power and Invention: Situating Science*. Minneapolis: University of Minnesota Press, 1997.
An account of the mutual interaction between science and society that seeks to transcend the traditional boundaries of scientific discourse and investigate the possibility of a "women's science."

Butler

Amy Allen. *The Power of Feminist Theory*. Boulder CO: Westview Press, 1999.

This volume both introduces and advocates for modern feminist theory, of which Butler is a leading light. Features a major section on Butler's work, especially as it applies to questions of power.

Michel Foucault. *The History of Sexuality, Vol. I: An Introduction*. Translated by Alan Sheridan. New York: Vintage, 1990.
Foucault's enormously influential critical study of the category of sex and power in Western societies.

Erving Goffman. *The Presentation of the Self in Everyday Life*. London: Penguin Books, 1990.
A seminal work of sociology which lays out an alternative explanation of the notion of performativity and identity.

Moya Lloyd. *Judith Butler: From Norms to Politics*. Cambridge: Polity, 2007.
Simultaneously an introductory exposition and a critical analysis of Butler's work, this volume sets out to explain Butler's major theoretical terms and situate her thought in its intellectual context.

Gilroy

Paul Gilroy. *The Black Atlantic: Modernity and Double Consciousness*. Cambridge, MA: Harvard University Press, 1993.
In this highly influential book, Gilroy details the black Atlantic culture that exists outside of and beyond traditional categories of ethnicity and nationality.

Paul Gilroy. *"There Ain't No Black in the Union Jack": The Cultural Politics of Race and Nation*. Chicago: University of Chicago Press, 1991.
Gilroy's account of the complexity of modern racial politics in England with respect to historical context and the left–right political divide.

Herman Gray. *Cultural Moves: African Americans and the Politics of Representation*. Berkeley: University of California Press, 2005.
A sweeping examination of the varied forms and projects of black popular culture over the last decade, and the role that cultural production has had

in shaping the overarching cultural character of the age.

Sedgwick

Stephen M. Barber and David L. Clark, eds. *Regarding Sedgwick: Essays on Queer Culture and Critical Theory.* New York: Routledge, 2002.
A collection of essays that assesses and expands upon the legacy of Sedgwick's thought with particular emphasis paid to issues of subjectivity and ethics.

Judith Halberstam. *In a Queer Time and Place: Transgender Bodies, Subcultural Lives.* New York: New York University Press, 2005.
A pioneering account transgenderism that seeks to explore the embodied experience of transgender alongside an analysis of transgender culture and the transgender gaze.

Eve K. Sedgwick. *Tendencies.* Durham, NC: Duke University Press, 1993.
A collection of Sedgwick's most notable and influential essays, ranging across poetry, autobiography, polemic, and analysis, and tackling an assortment of esoteric and everyday questions.

General

Eduardo Cadava, ed. *Who Comes After the Subject?* London: Routledge, 1999.
An overview of contemporary French philosophy as it relates to the manner in which the subject appears in a range of intellectual debates and discussions.

Sigmund Freud. *The Freud Reader.* Edited by Peter Gay. London: Norton, 1995.
Perhaps the most comprehensive single-volume collection of Sigmund Freud's writings, spanning his development as a thinker, classical texts in the genesis of the discipline, and psychoanalytic theory as it pertains to culture and its techniques.

G. W. F. Hegel. *The Phenomenology of Spirit.* Translated by A. V. Miller. Oxford: Oxford University Press, 1979.
A classic work in which Hegel articulates his theory of history and philosophy, especially as relates to the realization of consciousness through historical process.

Edward Said. *Orientalism.* New York: Random House, 1994.
A key work in which Said argues that Western knowledge of the East was used to create a repressive system of unequal subjectivities rooted in a distorted distribution of knowledge.

Paul Smith. *Discerning the Subject.* Minneapolis: University of Minnesota Press, 1988.
A wide-ranging but concisely written study of the concept of the subject in the fields of Marxism, film theory, pedagogy, psychoanalysis, feminism, and semiotics.

Glossary of Terms

Aesthetics

The philosophical study of beauty and art extends back to antiquity. Cultural theory tends to follow Immanuel Kant's description of aesthetics as a distinct mode of cognition and perception. The perceiver is described by Kant as "disinterestedly interested" when encountering beauty in order to stress the fact that even if an aesthetic judgment does not employ logic or reason, it is nevertheless universal; that is, not simply a matter of individual opinion or taste: the beautiful is beautiful for everyone. Kant's theory has received widespread critical attention by theorists such as Theodor Adorno, Pierre Bourdieu, and Herbert Marcuse, who have questioned the political and social implications of the supposed universality of the aesthetic.

Affect

A word whose theoretical use spans the seventeenth-century materialist philosophy of Baruch Spinoza, nineteenth-century German psychology, and the contemporary writings of Gilles Deleuze and Eve Sedgwick. In Spinoza's *Ethics* affects are described as multifaceted modes in which bodies (generally defined as "matter" and not exclusively as "human bodies") interact with one another. Often defined narrowly in popular discourse as "emotion" or "excitement," affect is in fact a broader categorization of concepts (i.e., depression, ecstasy, joy, shame) that seeks to understand how bodies interact beyond narrower psychological and physiological criteria.

Alienation

A concept that describes a tendency in which subjects become separate from one another, from determining their own needs, and from the means to bridge these divisions. Alienated consciousness is a confluence of these types of separation within the subject. Not only is alienation a concept used to describe the cultural consequence of exclusion, it is also used to counter their effects and its normalcy. Many theorists see educational institutions and radical political and social movements as ways to reduce or eliminate alienation.

Avant-garde

Pioneering or highly innovative artistic forms, groups, or trends are described as avant-garde because they challenge or overturn established aesthetic norms and institutions. A military term denoting the foremost group in an infantry regiment, it was used initially by Henri St. Simon (1760–1825) to describe elite French social classes of lawyers, scientists, and artists. The word has since been used to trace how formal and social rebellions occur in the art world. For example, Peter Bürger's theory of the avant-garde draws from modern histories of Dada and Surrealism, artistic movements that challenged the norms of the bourgeois art establishment in the first half of the twentieth century.

Biopolitics

This relatively recent concept was developed by Michel Foucault in a series of lectures in 1978. Foucault describes European governments since the eighteenth century as biopolitical because governance and social control became increasingly organized around the management of the social and physical health of populations. In disciplinary societies, governments exercise control through punishment and the threat of death. By comparison, biopolitics seeks to control and order birth rates, hygiene, sanity, and sexual mores, organizing the shape and character of the social body through the management of life. The concept has been reinterpreted by Giorgio Agamben, Antonio Negri, and others, who use Foucault's ideas to examine the historical precedents of the contemporary exercise of biopolitics (e.g., in the writings of Aristotle and Hannah Arendt, the events of the Holocaust, etc.) as well as its future implications on a global scale.

Capital

Karl Marx and cultural theorists following him describe capital as the social relations of production that appear to us in the form of commodities. Economists define capital differently: as an asset that (hopefully) accrues a profit. The difference in definition here follows from the fact that the former trace the entire production process that results in capital (historically and materially) instead of exclusively focusing on the end product. Capital is thus seen as an extensive process involving technology, the extraction of value from bodies and minds, and an entire cultural and social sphere of relations and knowledge related to this process. *Capitalism* is the name for this process, which again differs from the standard economic definition, which views it as a form of economic organization based on profit accumulation, a free market, and the pursuit of individual self-interest that is supposed to result in collective social good.

Class

Class is a general categorization of a group which shares similar experiences, traditions, degrees of wealth, types of employment and education, and access to political participation. Classes have tended to be given names such as bourgeois (upper class), proletarian (working class), or middle class, but these large-scale definitions are often limiting and make it difficult to understand the multiple ways in which group identity in contemporary societies is experienced. Class distinctions have tended to be organized around economic status, but social status is also negotiated culturally through the establishment of ideas of "taste," appropriate modes of dress and behavior, and so on. Class divisions persist today on a global scale and can lead to significant socioeconomic conflicts.

Cognitive Mapping

Fredric Jameson used this concept to explain and counteract the ways in which the experience of alienation makes it

difficult to understand the character of everyday life within the larger scale and history of cultural and economic processes. Drawn from a reading of Kevin Lynch's *Image of the City* (1960), this concept makes explicit spatial dimensions of those spheres of daily life (such as the economic and cultural) which were once separate and today coincide in confusing ways.

Colonialism

An economic, political, and cultural process in which nations or dominant groups invade, reorganize, and assimilate entire regions or countries. Colonialism is distinct from imperialism, which is a form of political control that can be exercised at a distance or indirectly (e.g., US "cultural imperialism" points to the potential impact of US films, television programs, novels, etc., in countries around the world). By contrast, colonialism requires the incursive nation to settle within the colonized space and exert control over its people and resources through physical (e.g., military force) and cultural (e.g., schooling, the establishment of official languages) means.

Commodity and Commodity Fetishism

A commodity is a product or service produced for exchange or use by someone other than their producer. To understand a commodity is to know how it is produced and to realize the manner in which commodities become fetishes, obscuring the reality of their process of production and seeming to be a natural part of social reality. Due in part to this complex process of value-making, Karl Marx and others describe the commodity as having magical or illusory qualities that make it appear to be untouched by the labor process that brings it into being. The process that creates these qualities is called commodity fetishism.

The Commons

Perhaps more typically named "the public sphere" (if not quite the same as it), this concept describes a physical and cultural space free of market controls or the protocols of privatization. Due to the increasing enclosure and commodification of previously public political processes, forms of cultural expression, and spaces for social interaction (ranging from elections to editorial critique, from access to the airwaves to the use of public space), cultural theorists appeal to historical examples of the commons, and generate models and ideas about new commons, in order to show the necessity and viability of genuinely democratic and non-hierarchical social and political structures.

Critique

A term widely used to convey a contention made against ideas, practices, or artifacts; in popular use, to critique something is to denounce or negate it as in some way deficient or problematic. In cultural theory, "critique" names an investigative process by which the origin and conditions of possibility for a given idea or practice are identified and explored in depth, often with the aim of highlighting the social and historical character of widely accepted (and so naturalized) modes of thought and action. The distinction between "immanent critique" and "transcendental critique," made initially by members of the Frankfurt School, has come to be increasingly important in contemporary thought. Immanent critique works from within the concept, object, or practice under investigation, and attempts to develop an understanding based on its premises, assertions, and internal contradictions. By contrast, transcendental critique works from the outside, either basing critique on pre-existing norms and concepts by which it makes its assessment, or hoping through critique to establish foundational (as opposed to historical and contingent) insights and conclusions.

Dialectic

Though it has a lengthy philosophical history as a mode of inquiry based in question and answer, contemporary notions of dialectical thinking emerged in the nineteenth-century German Idealist tradition, especially in the work of G. W. F. Hegel (1770–1831). Dialectics was reconceived as a self-critical method of thinking that attempts to expand one's ability to conceive how thought is mediated by seemingly extraneous factors, such as temporality, space, and the socioeconomic conditions of daily life. While dialectics is often mistakenly imagined as a highly mechanical method, consisting of the establishment of thesis, antithesis, and then synthesis of ideas, it is instead of a mode of thought which interrogates the contradictions within ideas with the aim of generating new ones, which are themselves assessed and interrogated. For Hegel and Marx this movement is a progressive one which characterizes not just the history of ideas, but the movement of history itself.

Diaspora

Literally meaning "to disperse," the concept has been used to describe the forced or voluntary displacement of ethnicities, religions, and other populations from once indigenous geographical spaces. Cultural theorists trace how this displacement affects potential and actual community formation and how new communities cohere in places distant from those where diasporic individuals or communities once dwelt.

Discourse

A broadly used term that conveys the linguistic characteristics of a given cultural phenomenon. Linguist Émile Benveniste (1902–76) defines discourse as any utterance that implicates a speaker and listener. This working definition is used by numerous cultural theorists who explore the production of meaning as a social process rather than as one based in the mind or through predetermined laws of communication. The term was also used by Michel Foucault, for whom "discourse" was the name of distinct areas of knowledge (e.g., historiography, medicine, philosophy, psychiatry, etc.), the practices and rules surrounding them, and the mode by which power works through the exercise of language and control over "truth."

Empiricism

An epistemology based in the acquisition of knowledge through the five senses. The founding theorists of empiricism – John Locke, David Hume, and John Stuart Mill – argued against rationalism and theories of knowledge produced without direct experiential evidence. These thinkers believed all thought derived from impressions acquired from one's interaction with the physical world of objects. Cultural theory has often questioned this theory of knowledge because experience-based epistemologies elide or ignore the historical contingency of many of their suppositions, and underestimate the difficulty of apprehending phenomena in the cultural and social world with the same (supposed) degree of certainty as the physical one.

Enlightenment

An intellectual period spanning the seventeenth and eighteenth centuries, and primarily located in Britain, Germany, and France. Critical of all forms of authority, especially religion and older economic organizational models, the large number of novel philosophical positions associated with the time arose with publication of Denis Diderot's *Encyclopédie* (1750–65). Philosophers in the Enlightenment expressed a faith in reason and saw the production of knowledge as inherently progressive. However, many theorists have since questioned its liberating potential, while still others now view the ideas generated during this time as responsible for some aspects of the contemporary era's technological, ideological, and political destructiveness.

Epistemology

A term which means "the theory of knowledge" and whose inquiries are among the most prominent in philosophical or theoretical inquiry. Many cultural theorists examine the practices and underlying conditions of epistemologies to discover how learning and knowledge are situated within discourses and institutions of expertise, power, and capital.

Ethnicity

A broad social category which describes complex religious, cultural, and national characteristics which generate ideas of belonging to a specific social group often (though not always) located in a defined geographical space. While race is thought to be determined by physiological or genetic traits, ethnicity is usually imagined to be a more flexible type of affiliation; nevertheless, the precise relationship of ethnicity to race remains an issue open to theoretical challenges and debate. Both race and ethnicity have formed the basis of discrimination and stereotyping by majorities against minorities.

Gender

Conceptually distinct from the genetically determined category of "sex," gender names the complex ways in which sexual difference is lived out socially, politically, and culturally. The concept of gender draws attention to the social and historical production of the norms, codes of conduct, "natural" forms of behavior, and defined social roles (e.g., woman as care giver, man as wage earner) that cultures assign to different members of society and seek to naturalize through appeals to their biological origins and necessity. Gender theorists

have made fundamental contributions to our understanding of the ways in which the production and management of difference has limited the range of individual identities and produced significant social and political injustice.

Labor

A purposeful activity common to all forms of human society. Subjects labor in various ways as a key expression of their existence, within a variety of conditions and divisions that are often inherited from previous generations. Political acknowledgment of the significance of all forms of labor has fostered labor movements, unions, and legal frameworks, all of which seek to protect the laborer against sanctioned abuse and exploitation. Feminism has challenged the unofficial status of labor conducted outside of the delineated workplace by women, such as the unpaid work carried out in domestic space.

Nation

Nations are "imagined communities" according to Benedict Anderson, and his influential account suggests that a subject's identity is largely shaped by her nation's culture. Thought nations have come to seem like almost natural divisions of people; they constitute fictions of group belonging which have come over time to connect political and social rights to geography with significant force. A nation is a people whose close affiliation to one another is defined by a shared geography established through a complex conglomerate of state and legal institutions, and traditions and belief structures. Though globalization was thought to have created conditions in which nations and national belonging would come to an end, nations remain one of the primary modes of group identification in the world today.

(Neo-)Liberalism

Liberalism is an ideology that became politically relevant in the seventeenth century. Among its main principles are the rights of the individual and his or her freedoms, a secular constitution and legal framework of authority, and the nation-state as the primary organizational form of power. Neoliberalism adheres to many of the principles of liberalism and attempts to extend its market orthodoxy to spaces and practices once deemed protected from the brute logic of capitalist economics, i.e., education, labor, medicine, morality.

Orientalism

A discipline and theory produced within a range of Western institutions (i.e., diplomatic practices, academic disciplines, art museums, periodicals, narrative forms) which serves to construct pernicious myths about Near and Middle East cultures. Among these myths or fantasies is the image of the oriental as lacking subjectivity and as deviously fanatical. The older stereotypes of the Orient developed in the eighteenth and nineteenth centuries and famously detailed by Edward Said in *Orientalism* (1978) have returned with great force in the general views adopted since 9/11 about the beliefs and practices of Middle Easterners.

Patriarchy

This term literally means "rule of the father" and describes a related set of social norms and institutions – rooted in the hetero-normative family and everyday gender relations – which seeks to ensure male domination. A sustained patriarchy seeks to disempower women and dominate all sociopolitical spheres of authority. Despite decades of sustained criticism, patriarchy continues to play a significant role in the organization of contemporary societies around the world.

Phenomenology

The "study of things shown" is rooted in the work of René Descartes (1596–1650), but it has been reimagined in the writings of Edmund Husserl (1859–1938) and Martin Heidegger (1889–1976). Primary in importance for phenomenology is an understanding of how appearances affect consciousness prior to the attempt to conceptualize objects and events. By bracketing out prior assumptions, this method seeks to grasp things intelligibly rather than to prescribe their qualities from within thought or consciousness.

(Post-)Fordism

A dominant mode of economics that follows the reorganization of Fordist forms of production. Fordism (a term derived from the practices of US industrialist Henry Ford) was characterized by the repetitive labor of the production line, exemplified by the North American automobile industry and its (relatively) high-paid labor force.

In the later part of the twentieth century, in many parts of the world this form of industrial labor has been replaced by new forms of work based on the provision of services (everything from nursing to call-center employees to bond traders) and the reshaping of industrial production around a globally dispersed, more malleable, and cheaper labor force. The cultural and social implications of post-Fordism include less job security, a decrease in unionization and the size of middle classes, greater disparities in wealth around the world, new geographic zones of industrial labor (e.g., the *maquiladoras* in Mexico), the privatization of government services, and the financialization of daily life.

Praxis

Refers to action in which subjects make a conscious plan or calculation. Praxis is differentiated from rudimentary labor, especially when enacted in the framework of politics. The concept has a long theoretical history stretching back to Aristotle, who divided all human endeavors into theoretical and practical work, with praxis signifying an application of a theory. Theorists as diverse as Sir Phillip Sidney, Antonio Gramsci, and Slavoj Žižek examine the category of praxis as a way to think through the ramifications of carrying out a theory or plan of action.

Problematic (problématique)

When used as a noun, this term conveys the way in which Louis Althusser (and his followers) complicate and instigate ways to theorize in the present. Theoretical contradictions and antinomies are two categories of problematic, whose horizon of interpretation is the social totality. Often the aim of cultural theory is to explain how problems have no easy, immediate solutions. Problematics are valued by theorists of culture because many other discourses offer superficial answers to important issues, or use accusation or fault (seen in *ad hominem* political attacks) to evade the difficulty with which larger socioeconomic causes must be explained and understood.

Progress

Progress is an ideology that imagines history as a linear movement of improvement and inherent innovation. As one of the most powerful ideologies of modern societies, "progress" has the tendency to prescribe interpretations of particular events or periods of time, making them seem either a good or difficult step toward a better time; seldom is history seen as somehow regressing or staying the same. The causes of progress are generally linked to developments in technology, politics, economics, or culture. Since the trauma of World War II, and in the context of the globe's ongoing environmental crisis, some social critics have tried to draw attention to the limits and problems of seeing human activity through the lens of ideas of progress.

Queer

A synonym for "gay" or "homosexual," and once used primarily in a pejorative way. Countering use of this word as invective, activists in the 1980s reappropriated the term in the ongoing social and political struggle against discrimination and scapegoating of gays, lesbians, bisexuals, and transgendered individuals and communities. Since its revaluation as a word, queer theory has played an invaluable role in refashioning our understanding of subjectivity and the forms taken by political, social, and cultural activism.

Race

This concept is used to categorize biological, genetic, and physical characteristics in order to "type" cultural or ethnic groups. Although imagined as a scientific, descriptive tool, race has been used to relate biology to supposed social and cultural traits possessed by groups (e.g., intelligence), often with the aim of establishing hierarchies and justifying stereotypes. Race is not a pre-existing category representative of any reality in identity, but rather an indelible myth used to serve social and political purposes. Race has inevitably led to the practices and attitudes of *racism*.

Revolution

A historical event or brief period of time in which an established order is dismantled or overthrown. Revolutions are numerous throughout history, with the Industrial Revolution and the American and French Revolutions being the most well known. The demand for the instant change of longstanding political and social orthodoxies is often the impetus behind revolution, but revolutions are also the unwitting result of developing discontent with daily life or the power of new ideas to garner rapid,

widespread support. "Counter-revolution" signifies the attempt by established powers to thwart, undermine, or oppose revolution.

Simulacrum

This term gained increased importance in the work of Gilles Deleuze and Jean Baudrillard, who describe it as a form of representation with no object or event to which it refers. This is different than an image (or, in empiricism, an idea), which is believed to reflect or be a mimetic representation of reality. Visual representation has the power to mediate the way spectators see reality, and as such simulacra are influential in changing the very way "reality" is conceived.

Spectacle

A term used to describe a concerted and large-scale expression of visual phenomena which threatens to overwhelm the spectator's senses. In cultural theory, a more technical concept of spectacle is associated with the writings and practices of Guy Debord and the Situationists in the 1960s. Writing in a Marxist tradition, Debord understood spectacle as the latest stage in the development of capitalist social relations. In *Society of the Spectacle* (1967), he describes an ever-greater intensification of commodification – now including the production of immaterial commodities such as images – which resulted in ever more disparate and distant social relations. "Separation perfected" became the phrase associated with the spectacle's alienating consequence.

Three Worlds (First World, Second World, Third World)

This geopolitical division was first named by French journalist Alfred Sauvy in 1952. With the onset of the Cold War, an ideological and territorial conflict between the United States and the USSR created cultural and political divisions across the globe. The First World identified the dominant capitalist regimes allied with the United States (such as Great Britain and France), while the Second named the countries allied directly with the USSR (such as Cuba and Yugoslavia). The Third World was associated with former colonies. The non-alignment movement arranged after the Bandung conference in 1955 sought to mobilize Third World countries against the respective hegemonies of the other two worlds. Since the end of the Cold War in 1989 these terms have been used to identify relative levels of economic development and political progress (as viewed from the West).

Totality

A horizon of cultural interpretation and theorization, a totality is a concrete historical period or overall relation of social forces, developments, and changes within which theorists situate their analysis. Different categories can substitute for the word "totality" in cultural theory, including "world history," "global capitalism," and "civilization." Theorists G. W. F. Hegel, Karl Marx, Georg Lukács, Jean-Paul Sartre, and Fredric Jameson see totality as a "vantage point" within which they interpret and engage with the interconnectedness and disjuncture of different realms of daily life: collectives, economic processes, political and ideological institutions, cultural industries, and ideologies, to name a few. Totality as an interpretative imperative prevents a myopic perspective from misidentifying the causes of specific events or topics.

The Unconscious

The unconscious is the name for cognitive processes which occur beneath or behind conscious thought. Among its varied theorizations, Freudian psychoanalysis imagines the unconscious to be the most important dimension of psychical life. The unconscious is said to be a source of the subject's deepest drives, which become "knowable" only when exhibited in symptoms such as dreams and slips of the tongue.

Utopia

Taken literally, utopia means "no place," but the word has been used most commonly to signify an ideal society. Utopias typically take the form of philosophical or literary creations that portray a near future place in which the social problems and quandaries defining a historical period are resolved through significant social change. This genre and the social desire it expresses can be found in nearly all cultural artifacts, from the philosophy of Plato to contemporary science fiction novels and films. Fredric Jameson has suggested that throughout history utopian constructions have flourished when political energies are most greatly stalled.

Virtual

Connotations of this word may cause one to believe it only describes the experience of navigating a human avatar through a programmed space on a computer. While much critical work examines the ramifications of this activity, "virtual" also means that which is highly abstract to the point of being "unreal" and "in principle" meaningful for this reason. Virtual is therefore useful for delineating ontological questions concerning what is real, actual, potential, and possible in any given situation.

Sources

The authors and publisher gratefully acknowledge the permission granted to reproduce the copyright material in this book:

1   Matthew Arnold, "Sweetness and Light," pp. 58, 59–60, 61–4, 65, 66–7, 68–70, 71–2, 78–80 from *Culture and Anarchy and Other Writings*, ed. Stefan Collini. Cambridge: Cambridge University Press, 1993. Reprinted by permission of Cambridge University Press.

2   Thorstein Veblen, "Conspicuous Consumption," pp. 187–98, 199–200, 202–4 from *The Consumer Society Reader*, ed. Juliet Schor and Douglas B. Holt. New York: The New Press, 2000.

3   Herbert Marcuse, "The Affirmative Character of Culture," pp. 88–117, 130–3 from *Negations: Essays in Critical Theory*. London: Free Association Books, 1988. Reprinted by permission of Free Association Books Ltd.

4   Max Horkheimer and Theodor W. Adorno, "The Culture Industry," pp. 120–47 from *Dialectic of Enlightenment*. New York: Herder and Herder, 1972.

5   Raymond Williams, "Culture Is Ordinary," pp. 5–6, 14 from *Resources of Hope: Culture, Democracy, Socialism*, ed. Robin Gable. London: Verso, 1989.

6   Fredric Jameson, "Reification and Utopia in Mass Culture," pp. 130–2, 133–5, 138–48 from *Social Text* 1 (1979).

7   Stuart Hall, "Notes on Deconstructing 'the Popular,'" pp. 227–39 from *People's History and Socialist Theory*, ed. R. Samuel. London: Routledge, 1981. Reproduced by permission of Taylor & Francis Books UK.

8   Pierre Bourdieu, "The Forms of Capital," pp. 46–58 from *Handbook of Theory and Research for the Sociology of Education*, ed. J. Richardson, trans. Richard Nice. New York: Greenwood, 1986. Reproduced by permission of ABC-CLIO, LLC.

9   Karl Marx, "Preface," pp. 19–23 from *A Contribution to the Critique of Political Economy*. New York: International Publishers, 1970. Reprinted by permission of International Publishers.

10   Carl Schmitt, "Definition of Sovereignty," pp. 5–15 from *Political Theology: Four Chapters on the Concept of Sovereignty*, trans. George Schwab. Cambridge, MA: MIT Press, 1986. Copyright © 1986 Massachusetts Institute of Technology, by permission of the MIT Press.

11   Frantz Fanon, "The Trials and Tribulations of National Consciousness," pp. 97–110, 119–22, 140–4 from *The Wretched of the Earth*, trans. Constance Farrington. New York: Grove Press, 1968. Copyright © 1963 by *Préence Africaine*, English translation copyright © 2004 by Richard Philcox. Used by permission of Grove/Atlantic, Inc.

12   Michel Foucault, "17 March 1976," pp. 239–58 from *Society Must Be Defended: Lectures at the Collège de France, 1975–76*. New York: Picador, 2003.

13   Michel Foucault, "Method," pp. 92–102 from *The History of Sexuality, Volume I: An Introduction*, trans. Robert Hurley. New York: Vintage, 1980. Originally published in French as *La Volonté du Savoir*. Reprinted by permission of Georges Borchardt, Inc., for Editions Gallimard. Copyright © Editions Gallimard, 1976. Translation copyright © Random House, Inc., 1978.

14   Gilles Deleuze, "Postscript on the Societies of Control," pp. 3–7, *October* 59 (1992).

15   Michael Hardt and Antonio Negri, "Biopolitical Production," pp. 22–34 from *Empire*. Cambridge, MA: Harvard University Press, 2000. Reprinted by permission of the publisher. Copyright © 2000 by the President and Fellows of Harvard College.

16   Karl Marx and Friedrich Engels. "The German Ideology," pp. 148–60, 172–5 from *The Marx–Engels*

Reader, 2nd edn, ed. Robert C. Tucker. New York: W.W. Norton, 1978. Copyright © 1978, 1972, by W.W. Norton & Company, Inc. Used by permission of W.W. Norton & Company, Inc.

17 Georg Lukács, "Reification and the Consciousness of the Proletariat," pp. 83–110 from History and Class Consciousness: Studies in Marxist Dialectics, trans. Rodney Livingstone. Cambridge, MA: MIT Press, 1971. Copyright © 1971, Massachusetts Institute of Technology, by permission of the MIT Press.

18 Antonio Gramsci, "Hegemony," pp. 5–17, 106–20 from Selections from the Prison Notebooks of Antonio Gramsci, ed. and trans. Quintin Hoare and Geoffrey Nowell Smith. New York: International Publishers, 1971. Reprinted by permission of International Publishers.

19 Louis Althusser, "Ideology and Ideological State Apparatuses (Notes towards an Investigation)," pp. 128–36, 141–50, 154–76, 180–6 from Lenin and Philosophy and Other Essays, trans. Ben Brewster. New York: Monthly Review Press, 1971. Reprinted by permission of Monthly Review Press.

20 Stuart Hall, "Recent Developments in Theories of Language and Ideology: A Critical Note," pp. 149–53 from Culture, Media, Language. London: Hutchinson, 1980. Reproduced by permission of Taylor & Francis Books UK.

21 Slavoj Žižek, "The Spectre of Ideology," pp. 1–25 from Mapping Ideology. London: Verso, 1994. Reprinted by permission of Verso.

22 Dick Hebdige, "The Function of Subculture," pp. 73, 75–89 from Subculture: The Meaning of Style. London: Routledge, 1991. Reproduced by permission of Taylor & Francis Books UK.

23 Michel de Certeau, "Walking in the City," pp. 91–105 from The Practice of Everyday Life, trans. Steven Rendall. Berkeley: University of California Press, 1984. Copyright © 1984 by University of California Press. Reproduced by permission of University of California Press.

24 Benedict Anderson, Imagined Communities: Reflections on the Origin and Spread of Nationalism, pp. 22–36. London: Verso, 1991. Reprinted by permission of Verso.

25 Arjun Appadurai, "Disjuncture and Difference in the Global Cultural Economy," pp. 27–47 from Modernity at Large: Cultural Dimensions of Globalization. Minneapolis: University of Minnesota Press, 1996.

26 Doreen Massey, "Politics and Space/Time," pp. 65–76, 79–84 from New Left Review 196 (1992) (abridged from original version). Reprinted by permission of New Left Review.

27 David Harvey, "The Body as an Accumulation Strategy," pp. 97–113 from Spaces of Hope. Berkeley: University of California Press, 2000. Copyright © 2000 by University of California Press. Reproduced by permission of University of California Press.

28 Mike Davis, "Planet of Slums: Urban Involution and the Informal Proletariat," pp. 5–30 from New Left Review 26 (2004) (abridged from original version). Reprinted by permission of New Left Review.

29 Michel Foucault, "Nietzsche, Genealogy, History," pp. 76–100 from The Foucault Reader, trans. Paul Rabinow. New York: Pantheon, 1984.

30 Raymond Williams, "Dominant, Residual, and Emergent," pp. 121–7 from Marxism and Literature. Oxford: Oxford University Press, 1977. By permission of Oxford University Press.

31 Jean-François Lyotard, "Answering the Question: What Is Postmodernism?," pp. 71–82 from The Postmodern Condition: A Report on Knowledge. Minneapolis: University of Minnesota Press, 1984.

32 Fernand Braudel, "History and the Social Sciences: The Longue Durée," pp. 25–31, 32–8, 47–54 from On History. Chicago: University of Chicago Press, 1980. Reprinted by permission of the publisher the University of Chicago Press.

33 Fredric Jameson, "Periodizing the 60s," pp. 178–86, 194–208 from The Ideologies of Theory: Essays 1971–1986. Minneapolis: University of Minnesota Press, 1988.

34 Roberto Schwarz, "Brazilian Culture: Nationalism by Elimination," pp. 1–18 from Misplaced Ideas. Essays on Brazilian Culture. London: Verso, 1992. Reprinted by permission of Verso.

35 Ranajit Guha, "Colonialism in South Asia: A Dominance without Hegemony and Its Historiography," pp. 1–20 from Dominance without Hegemony: History and Power in Colonial India. Cambridge, MA: Harvard University Press, 1997. Reprinted by permission of the publisher. Copyright © 1999 by the President and Fellows of Harvard College.

36 Frantz Fanon, "The Lived Experience of the Black Man," pp. 89–114 from Black Skin, White Masks, trans. Richard Philcox. New York: Grove Press, 2008. Copyright © 1952 by Éditions du Seuil. English translation copyright © 2008 by Richard Philcox. Used by permission of Grove/Atlantic, Inc.

37 Jacques Lacan, "The Instance of the Letter in the Unconscious, or Reason since Freud," pp. 413–28, 429–41 from Écrits, trans. Bruce Fink. New York: Norton, 2006. By permission of Écrits (New York: Norton, 2006).

Sources

38 Luce Irigaray, "This Sex Which Is Not One," pp. 23–33 from *This Sex Which Is Not One*, trans. Catherine Porter and Carolyn Burke. Ithaca, NY: Cornell University Press, 1985. Translation copyright © 1985 by Cornell University. Used by permission of the publisher, Cornell University Press.

39 Donna Haraway, "A Cyborg Manifesto: Science, Technology, and Socialist-Feminism in the Late Twentieth Century," pp. 149–56, 161–6, 169–77, 178–81 from *Simians, Cyborgs, and Women: The Reinvention of Nature*. New York: Routledge, 1991. Reprinted by permission of Free Association Books Ltd.

40 Judith Butler, "Subjects of Sex/Gender/Desire," pp. 3–24, 30–44 from *Gender Trouble: Feminism and the Subversion of Identity*. New York: Routledge, 2006. Copyright © 2006 by Taylor & Francis Books. Reproduced by permission of Taylor & Francis Group LLC.

41 Paul Gilroy, "It Ain't Where You're From, It's Where You're At," pp. 120–45 from *Small Acts: Thoughts on the Politics of Black Cultures*. London: Serpent's Tail, 1993. Reprinted by permission of the rights holder Paul Gilroy. All rights reserved.

42 Eve Kosofsky Sedgwick, "Axiomatic," pp. 1–12, 16–18, 22–6, 27–47, 48–9, 52–3, 59–60 from *Epistemology of the Closet*. Berkeley: University of California Press, 1990.

Index